Marriages & Families

MAKING CHOICES IN A DIVERSE SOCIETY

Tenth Edition

Mary Ann Lamanna

University of Nebraska, Omaha

Agnes Riedmann

California State University, Stanislaus

THOMSON

Australia • Brazil • Canada • Mexico • Singapore • Spain • United Kingdom • United States

THOMSON

WADSWORTH

Acquisitions Editor: *Chris Caldeira*

Development Editor: *Sherry Symington*

Assistant Editor: *Christina Beliso*

Editorial Assistant: *Tali Beesley*

Technology Project Manager: *Dave Lionetti*

Marketing Manager: *Michelle Williams*

Marketing Assistant: *Ileana Shevlin*

Marketing Communications Manager: *Linda Yip*

Project Manager, *Editorial Production: Cheri Palmer*

Creative Director: *Rob Hugel*

Art Director: *Caryl Gorska*

Print Buyer: *Karen Hunt*

Permissions Editors: *Tim Sisler and Don Schlotman*

Production Service/Compositor: *Lachina Publishing Services*

Text Designer: *Ellen Pettengell*

Photo Researcher: *Sarah Evertson*

Copy Editor: *Carolyn Crabtree*

Illustrator: *Heidi Grosch*

Cover Designer: *Riezebos Holzbaur Design Group, LLC*

Cover Image: © *Nicole S. Young/iStockphoto*

Printed in Cananda

1 2 3 4 5 6 7 11 10 09 08 07

For more information about our products, contact us at:
Thomson Learning Academic Resource Center 1-800-423-0563

For permission to use material from this text or product, submit a request online at **http://www.thomsonrights.com.** Any additional questions about permissions can be submitted by e-mail to **thomsonrights@thomson.com.**

Library of Congress Control Number: 2007940206

Student Edition:
ISBN-13: 978-0-495-39092-3
ISBN-10: 0-495-39092-5

Loose-leaf Edition:
ISBN-13: 978-0-495-50406-1
ISBN-10: 0-495-50406-8

Thomson Higher Education
10 Davis Drive
Belmont, CA 94002-3098
USA

dedication

to our families, especially

Bill, Beth, Angel, Chris, Natalie, Alex, and Livia

Larry, Valerie, Sam, Janice, and Simon

About the Authors

MARY ANN LAMANNA is Professor Emerita of Sociology at the University of Nebraska at Omaha. She received her bachelor's degree Phi Beta Kappa from Washington University (St. Louis) in political science, her master's degree in sociology (minor in psychology) from the University of North Carolina, Chapel Hill, and her doctorate in sociology from the University of Notre Dame.

Research and teaching interests include family, reproduction, and gender and law. She is the author of *Emile Durkheim on the Family* (Sage, 2002) and co-author of a book on Vietnamese refugees. She has articles in law, sociology, and medical humanities journals. Current research concerns the sociology of literature, specifically "novels of terrorism" and a sociological analysis of Marcel Proust's novel *In Search of Lost Time*. Professor Lamanna has two adult children, Larry and Valerie.

AGNES RIEDMANN is Professor of Sociology at California State University, Stanislaus. She attended Clarke College, Dubuque. She received her bachelor's degree from Creighton University and her doctorate from the University of Nebraska. Her professional areas of interest are theory, family, and the sociology of body image. She is author of *Science That Colonizes: A Critique of Fertility Studies in Africa* (Temple University Press, 1993). Current research projects involve various aspects of comparative family sociology as well as gender issues. Dr. Riedmann has two children, Beth and Bill; two granddaughters, Natalie and Livia; and a grandson, Alex.

Brief Contents

Chapter   1 Family Commitments: Making Choices in a Changing Society xxviii

Chapter   2 Exploring the Family 20

Chapter   3 American Families in Social Context 46

Chapter   4 Our Gendered Identities 74

Chapter   5 Loving Ourselves and Others 100

Chapter   6 Our Sexual Selves 120

Chapter   7 Marriage: From Social Institution to Private Relationship 152

Chapter   8 Nonmarital Living Arrangements: Living Alone, Cohabitation, Same-Sex Couples, and Other Options 182

Chapter   9 Choosing a Marriage Partner, and the First Years of Marriage 206

Chapter 10 To Parent or Not to Parent 232

Chapter 11 Raising Children in a Multicultural Society 264

Chapter 12 Work and Family 292

Chapter 13 Communication in Marriage and Families 328

Chapter 14 Power and Violence in Families 350

Chapter 15 Family Stress, Crises, and Resilience 388

Chapter 16 Divorce: Before and After 412

Chapter 17 Remarriage and Stepfamilies 454

Chapter 18 Aging Families 482

Contents

Chapter 1 Family Commitments: Making Choices in a Changing Society xxviii

Defining Family 2

There Is No Typical Family 3

Issues for Thought: Pets as Family? 4

New Definitions of the Family 5

Facts about Families: American Families Today 6

The Freedom and Pressures of Choosing 9

Personal Troubles and Societal Influences 9

Issues for Thought: Which of These Is a Family? 10

Social Influences and Personal Choices 10

Making Choices 10

Choosing by Default 10

Choosing Knowledgeably 11

A Family of Individuals 12

Families as a Place to Belong 13

Familistic (Communal) Values and Individualistic (Self-Fulfillment) Values 13

"Family Decline" or "Family Change"? 14

Facts about Families: Focus on Children 15

Partners as Individuals and Family Members 17

Marriages and Families: Four Themes 18

Chapter 2 Exploring the Family 20

Theoretical Perspectives on the Family 22

The Family Ecology Perspective 22

Issues for Thought: Safety and Risk in the Family Environment 24

The Family Development Perspective 27

The Structure–Functional Perspective 29

The Interactionist Perspective 31

Exchange Theory 33

Family Systems Theory 34

Conflict and Feminist Perspectives 35

The Biosocial Perspective 36

Studying Families 37

The Blinders of Personal Experience 38

Scientific Investigation: Removing Blinders 38

The Ethics of Research on Families 38

Methods of Data Collection 39

Chapter 3 American Families in Social Context 46

Historical Events 48

Age Structure 49

The Economy and Social Class 49

Economic Change and Inequality 49

Facts about Families: Military Families 50

Blue-Collar and White-Collar Families and the Wealthy 53

Race and Ethnicity 54

Conceptualizing Race and Ethnicity 54

Issues for Thought: Studying Families and Ethnicity 57

Racial/Ethnic Diversity in the United States 58

African American Families 58

Latino (Hispanic) Families 60

A Closer Look at Family Diversity: Family Ties and Immigration 62

Asian American Families 64

Pacific Islander Families 65

American Indian (Native American) Families 65

White Families 67

Multicultural Families 68

Religion 70

Chapter 4 Our Gendered Identities 74

Gendered Identities 76

A Closer Look at Family Diversity: Race, Class, and Gender in the Nanny Hunt 76

Gender Expectations and Cultural Messages 77

Issues for Thought: Challenges to Gender Boundaries 78

To What Extent Do Women and Men Follow Cultural Expectations? 80

The Gender Similarities Hypothesis 81

Gender Inequality 81

Male Dominance in Politics 81

Male Dominance in Religion 82

Gender and Health 83

Gender and Education 83

Male Dominance in the Economy 84

Is Anatomy Destiny? 85

Gender and Socialization 86

Theories of Socialization 87

Settings for Socialization 88

Girls versus Boys? 91

Social Change and Gender 92

The Women's Movement 93

Men's Movements 95

Personal and Family Change 96

The Future of Gender 96

Chapter 5 Loving Ourselves and Others 100

Personal Ties in an Impersonal Society 102

What Is Love? 102

Love Is a Deep and Vital Emotion 103

Love Satisfies Legitimate Personal Needs 103

Love Involves Caring and Acceptance 103

Do Men and Women Care Differently? 104

Love and Intimacy: Commitment to Sharing 104

My Family: Couple Discovers Love Twenty-five Years after Teen Marriage 106

Six Love Styles 106

Three Things Love Isn't 109

Martyring 109

Manipulating 109

Limerence 110

Self-Worth as a Prerequisite to Loving 110

Self-Love versus Narcissism 111

Self-Esteem and Personal Relationships 111

Emotional Interdependence 111

As We Make Choices: Learning to Love Yourself More 112

Love as a Discovery 114

The Wheel of Love 114

Keeping Love 115

Chapter 6 Our Sexual Selves 120

Sexual Development and Orientation 122

Children's Sexual Development 122

Sexual Orientation 123

A Closer Look at Family Diversity: Is It Okay to Be Asexual? 124

Theoretical Perspectives on Human Sexuality 125

The Exchange Perspective: Rewards, Costs, and Equality in Sexual Relationships 125

The Interactionist Perspective: Negotiating Cultural Messages 125

Changing Cultural Scripts 126

Early America: Patriarchal Sex 126

The Twentieth Century: The Emergence of Expressive Sexuality 127

The 1960s Sexual Revolution: Sex for Pleasure 127

The 1980s and 1990s: Challenges to Heterosexism 128

The Twenty-first Century: Risk, Caution—and Intimacy 130

Negotiating (Hetero)sexual Expression 130

Four Standards of Nonmarital Sex 131

Issues for Thought: "Hooking Up" and "Friends with Benefits" 132

Extramarital Affairs 132

Sexuality Throughout Marriage 135

How Often? 135

Facts about Families: How Do We Know What We Do?
A Look at Sex Surveys 136

Young Spouses 137

Spouses in Middle Age 138

Older Partners 138

What About Boredom? 138

Sexual Satisfaction in Marriage and Other Partnerships 139

Race/Ethnicity and Sexual Expression 139

Sex as a Pleasure Bond 140

Sexual Pleasure and Self-Esteem 140

Sexual Pleasure and Gender 141

Communication and Cooperation 141

Some Principles for Sexual Sharing 141

Making the Time for Intimacy 142

**Sexual Expression, Family Relations, and HIV/AIDS
and Other Sexually Transmitted Diseases 142**

HIV/AIDS and Heterosexuals 142

HIV/AIDS and Gay Men 143

HIV/AIDS and Family Crises 143

HIV/AIDS and Children 143

Facts about Families: Who Has HIV/AIDS? 144

The Politics of Sex 144

Politics and Research 146

Adolescent Sexuality and Sex Education 146

Sexual Responsibility 148

Chapter 7 Marriage: From Social Institution to Private Relationship 152

Marital Status: The Changing Picture 154

Facts about Families: Marital Status—The Increasing
Proportion of Unmarrieds 156

**The Time-Honored Marriage Premise: Permanence
and Sexual Exclusivity 158**

Expectations of Permanence 158

Expectations of Sexual Exclusivity 158

Issues for Thought: Three Very Different Subcultures
with Norms Contrary to Sexual Exclusivity 159

**From "Yoke Mates" to "Soul Mates"—A Changing
Marriage Premise 160**

Weakened Kinship Authority 160

Finding One's Own Marriage Partner 162

Love—and Marriage 162

My Family: An Asian Indian-American Student's Essay
on Arranged Marriages 163

Deinstitutionalized Marriage 164

Institutional Marriage 164

Companionate Marriage 165

Individualized Marriage 166

**Individualized Marriage and the Pluralistic Family—
Decline or Inevitable Change? 168**

Deinstitutionalized Marriage: Examining the Consequences 168

*Child Outcomes and Marital Status: Does Marriage
Matter? 169*

A Closer Look at Family Diversity: African Americans
and "Jumping the Broom" 172

**Working Toward a Family "Turnaround"—The Policy
Debate 173**

Policies from the Family Decline Perspective 173

Policies from the Family Change Perspective 177

**Happiness and Life Satisfaction: How Does Marriage
Matter? 178**

Chapter 8 Nonmarital Living Arrangements: Living Alone, Cohabitation, Same-Sex Couples, and Other Options 182

**Reasons for the Increasing Proportion
of Unmarrieds 184**

Demographic, Economic, and Technological Changes 184

Cultural Changes 185

The Various Living Arrangements of Nonmarrieds 186

Living Alone 186

Living Alone Together 186

Living with Parents 187

Group or Communal Living 188

Cohabitation and Family Life 189

Cohabitation as an Acceptable Living Arrangement 190

Alternative to Unattached Singlehood and to Marriage 190

A Closer Look at Family Diversity: The Meaning of Cohabitation for Puerto Ricans, Compared to Mexican Americans 191

The Cohabiting Relationship 191

As We Make Choices: Some Things to Know about the Legal Side of Living Together 192

Cohabiting Families and Raising Children 195

Same-Sex Couples and Family Life 196

The Same-Sex Couple's Relationship 196

Facts about Families: Same-Sex Couples and Legal Marriage in the United States 197

Same-Sex Partners and Raising Children 198

The Debate over Legal Marriage for Same-Sex Couples 200

The Unmarried and Life Satisfaction 202

Maintaining Supportive Social Networks 203

Chapter 9   Choosing a Marriage Partner, and the First Years of Marriage 206

Mate Selection and Marital Stability 208

Attachment Theory 209

Age at Marriage and Marital Stability 209

The Intergenerational Transmission of Divorce Risk 210

Minimizing Mate Selection Risk 211

The Marriage Market 211

Arranged and Free-Choice Marriages 211

The Marital Exchange 213

Homogamy: Narrowing the Pool of Eligibles 214

Reasons for Homogamy 215

Examples of Heterogamy—The Statistical Exceptions 216

Heterogamy and Marital Stability 219

Heterogamy and Human Values 220

Developing the Premarital Relationship and Moving Toward Marital Commitment 220

Issues for Thought: Date or Acquaintance Rape 221

Physical Attractiveness and Rapport 222

Defining the Relationship 222

As We Make Choices: Harmonious Needs in Mate Selection 223

Dating Violence—A Serious Sign of Trouble 223

The Possibility of Breaking Up 224

Cohabitation and Marital Quality and Stability 225

As We Make Choices: Some Advice on Breaking Up 226

Marital Satisfaction and Choices Throughout Life 226

Preparation for Marriage 227

The First Years of Marriage 227

Creating Couple Connection 228

Creating Adaptable Marriage Relationships 229

Some Things to Talk About 229

Chapter 10   To Parent or Not to Parent 232

Fertility Trends in the United States 235

Family Size 236

Differential Fertility Rates 236

A Closer Look at Family Diversity: Choosing Large Familes in a Small Family Era 237

Facts about Families: Race/Ethnicity and Differential Fertility Rates 238

The Decision to Parent or Not to Parent 240

Social Pressures to Have Children 240

Is American Society Antinatalist? 240

Motivation for Parenthood 241

Costs of Having Children 242

How Children Affect Marital Happiness 242

Remaining Child-Free 243

Having Children: Options and Circumstances 244

The Timing of Parenthood 244

The One-Child Family 246

Nonmarital Births 247

Stepparents' Decisions about Having Children 250

Multipartnered Fertility 251

Preventing Pregnancy 251

Abortion 252

The Politics of Abortion 253

The Safety of Abortions 253

Involuntary Infertility and Reproductive Technology 254

The Social and Biological Context of Infertility 254

Infertility Services and Reproductive Technology 255

Reproductive Technology: Social and Ethical Issues 256

Reproductive Technology: Making Personal Choices 257

Adoption 257

Facts about Families: "Test-Tube" Babies Grow Up 258

The Adoption Process 259

Adoption of Racial/Ethnic Minority Children 259

Adoption of Older Children and Children with Disabilities 260

International Adoptions 260

Chapter 11 Raising Children in a Multicultural Society 264

Parents in Modern America 266

Issues for Thought: Parent Job Description 267

The Transition to Parenthood 268

Mothers and Fathers: Images and Reality 270

Old and New Images of Parents 270

Mothers and Fathers: What Do They Do? 270

Facts about Families: Fathers as Primary Parents 271

Sharing Parenthood 272

Authoritative Parenting 272

Issues for Thought: Growing Up in a Household Characterized by Conflict 273

As We Make Choices: Communicating with Children— How to Talk So Kids Will Listen and Listen So Kids Will Talk 275

Is Spanking Ever Appropriate? 276

The Resilient Child 277

Social Class and Parenting 277

The Working Poor 278

Middle- and Upper-Middle-Class Parents 279

Racial/Ethnic Diversity and Parenting 280

African American Parents and Children 280

Native American Parents and Children 281

Hispanic Parents and Children 281

Asian American Parents and Children 282

Parents and Multiracial Children 282

Religious Minority Parents and Children 283

Raising Children of Racial/Ethnic Identity in a Racist and Discriminatory Society 283

Grandparents as Parents 285

Foster Parents 285

Parents and Young Adult Children 286

Independent Adults and Their Parents 288

Toward Better Parent-Child Relationships 288

Chapter 12 Work and Family 292

Women in the Labor Force 294

Women's Entry into the Labor Force 294

Women's Market Work 295

The Wage Gap 296

Opting Out, Stay-at-Home Moms, and Neotraditional Families 297

Men's Market Work 299

The Provider Role 300

Why Do Men Leave the Labor Force? 301

Two-Earner Marriages—Work/Family Options 302

Two-Career Marriages 302

Part-Time Employment 303

Shift Work 303

Doing Paid Work at Home 303

A Closer Look at Family Diversity: Diversity and Child Care 304

Leaving the Labor Force and Reentry 305

Unpaid Family Work 306

Caring for Dependent Family Members 306

Housework 306

Juggling Employment and Family Work 310

Work, Family, and Leisure: Attitudes and Time Allocation 310

Facts about Families: Where Does the Time Go? 312

How Are Children Faring? 313

How Are Parents Faring? 315

Social Policy, Work, and Family 316

What Is Needed to Resolve Work–Family Issues? 316

As We Make Choices: Child Care and Children's Outcomes 318

As We Make Choices: Selecting a Child-Care Facility 320

Who Will Provide What Is Needed to Resolve Work–Family Issues? 322

The Two-Earner Marriage and the Relationship 323

Gender Strategies 324

Maintaining Intimacy While Negotiating Provider Roles and the Second Shift 324

Chapter 13 Communication in Marriage and Families 328

Communication and Couple Satisfaction 330

Let Your Partner Know That You're Listening 332

Fact about Families: Six Characteristics of Cohesive Families 332

Show Interest in What Your Partner Is Telling You 333

Have Some Fun Together 333

As We Make Choices: Ten Rules for a Successful Relationship 334

Conflict and Love 334

Denying Conflict: Some Results 335

Supportive Couple Communication and Conflict Management 336

The Four Horsemen of the Apocalypse 336

Issues for Thought: A Look Behind the Scenes at Communication Research 337

What Is Supportive Communication? 338

Gender Differences in Couple Communication 338

Avoiding the Four Horsemen of the Apocalypse 341

Bonding Fights—Ten Guidelines 342

Guideline 1: Level with Each Other 342

Guideline 2: To Avoid Attacks, Use I-Statements When You Can 343

Guideline 3: Avoid Mixed, or Double, Messages 343

Guideline 4: Choose the Time and Place Carefully 344

Guideline 5: Focus Anger Only on Specific Issues 344

Guideline 6: Ask for a Specific Change, but Be Open to Compromise 344

Guideline 7: Be Willing to Change Yourself 344

Guideline 8: Don't Try to Win 344

Guideline 9: Remember to End the Argument 345

Guideline 10: Be Willing to Forgive 345

Toward Better Communication 345

The Myth of Conflict-Free Conflict 347

Chapter 14 Power and Violence in Families 350

What Is Power? 352

What Does Marital Power Involve? 352

Power Bases 352

The Dynamics of Marital Power 353

Classical Perspectives on Marital Power 354

Current Research on Marital Power 356

The Future of Marital Power 360

As We Make Choices: Peer Marriage 362

Power Politics versus No-Power Relationships 363

Power Politics in Marriage 363

Alternatives to Power Politics 363

As We Make Choices: Disengaging from Power Struggles 364

My Family: An Ice-Skating Homemaker in a Me-or-Him Bind 365

The Role That Marriage Counselors Can Play 366

Family Violence 367

Major Sources of Data on Family Violence 367

Intimate Partner Violence 368

Gender Issues in Intimate Partner Violence 371

Abuse among Lesbian, Gay Male, and Bisexual Couples 376

Stopping Relationship Violence 377

Violence Against Children 379

Child-to-Parent Abuse 384

Chapter 15 Family Stress, Crisis, and Resilience 388

Theoretical Perspectives on Family Stress and Crises 390

What Precipitates a Family Crisis? 392

Types of Stressors 392

Issues for Thought: Caring for Patients at Home—A Family Stressor 396

Stressor Overload 397

The Course of a Family Crisis 398

The Period of Disorganization 398

Recovery 399

Family Stress, Crisis, Adjustment, and Adaptation: A Theoretical Model 400

A Closer Look at Family Diversity: Stressor Pile-Up Among Single-Mother Families in Homeless Shelters 400

Stressor Pile-Up 400

Appraising the Situation 402

Crisis-Meeting Resources 403

Meeting Crises Creatively 404

A Positive Outlook 404

Spiritual Values and Support Groups 405

Open, Supportive Communication 405

Adaptability 405

Informal Social Support 406

An Extended Family 406

Community Resources 407

Crisis: Disaster or Opportunity? 407

Issues for Thought: When a Parent Is in Prison 408

Chapter 16 Divorce: Before and After 412

Today's High U.S. Divorce Rate 414

Why Are Couples Divorcing? 416

Economic Factors 416

High Expectations of Marriage 417

Decreased Social, Legal, and Moral Constraints 417

Intergenerational Transmission of Divorce 418

Other Factors Associated with Divorce 418

Thinking about Divorce: Weighing the Alternatives 419

Marital Happiness, Barriers to Divorce, and Alternatives to the Marriage 419

"Would I Be Happier?" 420

Is Divorce a Temporary Crisis or a Permanent Stress? 421

Getting the Divorce 422

The Emotional Divorce 422

The Legal Divorce 423

The Community Divorce 424

The Economic Consequences of Divorce 425

Divorce, Single-Parent Families, and Poverty 425

Husbands, Wives, and Economic Divorce 426

Child Support 427

Divorce and Children 428

The Various Stresses for Children of Divorce 429

My Family: How It Feels When Parents Divorce 430

Custody Issues 434

A Closer Look at Family Diversity: A Noncustodial Mother Tells Her Story 436

Parent Education for Co-Parenting Ex-Spouses 439

His and Her Divorce 440

Her Divorce 440

His Divorce 440

Some Positive Outcomes? 441

Facts about Families: Postdivorce Pathways 442

Adult Children of Divorced Parents and Intergenerational Relationships 443

Should Divorce Be Harder to Get? 444

Is Divorce Necessarily Bad for Children? 445

Is Making Divorce Harder to Get a Realistic Idea? 445

Surviving Divorce 445

Social Policy Support for Children of Divorce 445

The Good Divorce 446

My Family: The Postdivorce Family as a Child-Raising Institution 447

As We Make Choices: Ten Keys to Successful Co-Parenting 448

Chapter 17 Remarriage and Stepfamilies 454

Remarriage: Some Basic Facts 456

Facts about Families: Remarriages and Stepfamilies—
Diversity by Race/Ethnicity and Sexual
Orientation 458

*Remarriage, Stepfamilies, and Children's Living
Arrangements 458*

**Choosing Partners the Next Time: Variations
on a Theme 459**

Remarriage Advantages for Women and Men 460

Homogamy in Remarriage 461

**Spouses' Happiness/Satisfaction and Stability
in Remarriage 461**

Happiness/Satisfaction in Remarriage 461

The Stability of Remarriages 462

*Negative Stereotypes and Remarital Satisfaction
and Stability 462*

My Family: My (Step)Family 463

The Various Types of Remarried and Stepfamilies 464

*Differences Between First Marriages with Children and
Stepfamilies 464*

Stepfamilies and Ambiguous Norms 465

Stepfamily Boundary Ambiguity 465

A Closer Look at Famliy Diversity: Immigrant
Stepfamilies 466

Kin Networks in Stepfamilies 467

Family Law and Stepfamilies 467

Children's Well-Being in Stepfamilies 468

Stepparenting: A Challenge in Remarriage 469

Some Reasons Stepparenting Is Difficult 469

Stepmothers 471

As We Make Choices: Some Stepparenting Tips 472

Stepfathers 473

Having a Mutual Child 475

My Family: From Stepfather to Father—Creating a
Resilient Stepfamily 476

Creating Supportive Stepfamilies 478

Chapter 18 Aging Families 482

Our Aging Population 484

Aging Baby Boomers 484

Longer Life Expectancy 484

*Racial/Ethnic Composition of the Older American
Population 486*

Living Arrangements of Older Americans 487

*Gender Differences in Older Americans' Living
Arrangements 487*

*Racial/Ethnic Differences in Older Americans' Living
Arrangements 487*

Aging in Today's Economy 488

Older Women's Finances 489

Marriage Relationships in Later Life 490

Retirement 491

Later-Life Divorce, Widowhood, and Remarriage 492

Widowhood and Widowerhood 492

**Older Parents, Adult Children,
and Grandchildren 493**

Older Parents and Adult Children 493

Grandparenthood 494

Aging Families and Caregiving 496

As We Make Choices: Community Resources
for Eldercare 497

Adult Children as Eldercare Providers 498

Issues for Thought: Child—and Grandchild—
Caregivers 498

Gender Differences in Providing Eldercare 499

My Family: Looking After—A Son's Memoir 500

The Sandwich Generation 500

Eldercare as a Family Process 501

Elder Abuse and Neglect 502

Racial/Ethnic Diversity and Family Eldercare 503

**The Changing American Family and Eldercare
in the Future 504**

Toward Better Caregiving 505

How to find the Appendices

The following appendices are available in full color on the Tenth Edition's book companion site at **www.thomsonedu.com/sociology/lamanna**. To access the appendices, click on "Appendices" from the left navigation bar. You can also access suggested readings in the same manner.

Appendix A: Human Sexual Anatomy

Appendix B: Human Sexual Response

Appendix C: Sexually Transmitted Diseases

Appendix D: Sexual Dysfunctions and Therapy

Appendix E: Conception, Pregnancy, and Childbirth

Appendix F: Contraceptive Techniques

Appendix G: High-Tech Fertility

Appendix H: Marriage and Close Relationship Counseling

Appendix I: Managing a Famliy Budget

Glossary 511

References 525

Credits 603

Name Index 605

Subject Index 621

Boxes

A CLOSER LOOK AT FAMILY DIVERSITY

Family Ties and Immigration 62

Race, Class, and Gender in the Nanny Hunt 76

Is It Okay to Be Asexual? 124

African Americans and "Jumping the Broom" 172

The Meaning of Cohabitation for Puerto Ricans, Compared to Mexican Americans 191

Choosing Large Families in a Small-Family Era 237

Diversity and Child Care 304

Stressor Pile-Up Among Single-Mother Families in Homeless Shelters 400

A Noncustodial Mother Tells Her Story 436

Immigrant Stepfamilies 466

AS WE MAKE CHOICES

Learning to Love Yourself More 112

Some Things to Know about the Legal Side of Living Together 192

Harmonious Needs in Mate Selection 223

Some Advice on Breaking Up 226

Communicating with Children—How to Talk So Kids Will Listen and Listen So Kids Will Talk 275

Child Care and Children's Outcomes 318

Selecting a Child-Care Facility 320

Ten Rules for a Successful Relationship 334

Peer Marriage 362

Disengaging from Power Struggles 364

Ten Keys to Successful Co-parenting 448

Some Stepparenting Tips 472

Community Resources for Eldercare 497

FACTS ABOUT FAMILIES

American Families Today 6

Focus on Children 15

Military Families 50

How Do We Know What We Do? A Look at Sex Surveys 136

Who Has HIV/AIDS? 144

Marital Status—The Increasing Proportion of Unmarrieds 156

Same-Sex Couples and Legal Marriage in the United States 197

Race/Ethnicity and Differential Fertility Rates 238

"Test-Tube" Babies Grow Up 258

Fathers as Primary Parents 271

Where Does the Time Go? 312

Six Characteristics of Cohesive Families 332

Postdivorce Pathways 442

Remarriages and Stepfamilies—Diversity by Race/Ethnicity and Sexual Orientation 458

ISSUES FOR THOUGHT

Pets as Family? 4

Which of These Is a Family? 10

Safety and Risk in the Family Environment 24

Studying Families and Ethnicity 57

Challenges to Gender Boundaries 78

"Hooking Up" and "Friends with Benefits" 132

Three Very Different Subcultures with Norms Contrary to Sexual Exclusivity 159

Date or Acquaintance Rape 221

Parent Job Description 267

Growing Up in a Household Characterized by Conflict 273

A Look Behind the Scenes at Communication Research 337

Caring for Patients at Home—A Family Stressor 396

When a Parent Is in Prison 408

Child—and Grandchild—Caregivers 498

MY FAMILY

Couple Discovers Love Twenty-five Years After Teen Marriage 106

An Asian Indian–American Student's Essay on Arranged Marriages 163

An Ice-Skating Homemaker in a Me-or-Him Bind 365

How It Feels When Parents Divorce 430

The Postdivorce Family as a Child-Raising Institution 447

My (Step)Family 463

From Stepfather to Father—Creating a Resilient Stepfamily 476

Looking After—A Son's Memoir 500

Preface

As we complete our work on the tenth edition of *Marriages and Families*, we look back over nine earlier editions. Together, these represent thirty years spent observing the contemporary American family. Not only has the family changed during this time, but so has social science's interpretation of it. It is gratifying to be a part of the enterprise of learning about the family and to share that knowledge with students.

Our own perspective on the family has developed and changed during this period. Interested from the beginning in the various ways that gender plays out in families, we have also studied demography and history, and we have paid increasing attention to social structure in our analysis. We take account of increasing racial/ethnic diversity, as well as the fluidity of the concepts of race and ethnicity and a greater societal awareness of their socially constructed nature. At the same time, in recent editions and in response to our reviewers, we have given more attention to the contributions of psychology and to a social psychological understanding of family interaction and its consequences.

We have recognized the growing interest in biosocial perspectives. We have highlighted the family ecology perspective in keeping with the importance of social context and public policy. And we cannot help but be aware of the cultural and political tensions surrounding the family today.

We continue to affirm the power of families in directing the courses of individual lives. Meanwhile, we give considerable attention to policies needed to provide support for today's families: working parents, families in poverty, single-parent families, families of varied racial/ethnic backgrounds, remarried families, same-sex couples, and other nontraditional families—as well as the classic nuclear family with one employed parent (not an easy or common choice today). Virtually all families need social policy support.

At the same time, we note that after thirty years of dramatic change, there is evidence that a degree of stability may have settled on the family. Divorce rates have stabilized and teen birthrates have declined dramatically. Making individual accommodations to work–family strains despite weak institutional support, many couples seem to have adjusted to changing gender roles.

Marriage and family values continue to be important in contemporary American life. Our students come to a marriage and family course because family life is important to them. Our aim now, as it has been from the first edition, is to help students question assumptions and to reconcile conflicting ideas and values as they make choices throughout their lives. We enjoy and benefit from the contact we've had with faculty and students who have used this book. Their enthusiasm and criticism have stimulated many changes in the book's content. To know that a supportive audience is interested in our approach to the study of the family has enabled us to continue our work over a long period.

The Book's Themes

Several themes are interwoven throughout this text: people are influenced by the society around them as they make choices, social conditions change in ways that may impede or support family life, there is an interplay between individual families and the larger society, and individuals make family-related choices throughout adulthood.

Making Choices Throughout Life

The process of creating and maintaining marriages and families requires many personal choices, and people continue to make family-related decisions, even "big" ones, throughout their lives.

Personal Choice and Social Life

Tension frequently exists between the individual and the social environment. Many personal troubles result from societal influences, values, or assumptions; inadequate societal support for family goals; and conflict between family values and individual values. By understanding some of these possible sources of tension and conflict, individuals can perceive their personal troubles more clearly and work constructively toward solutions. They may choose to form or join groups to achieve family goals. They may become involved in the political process to develop state or federal social policy supportive of the family. The accumulated decisions of individuals and families may also shape the social environment.

A Changing Society

In the past, people tended to emphasize the dutiful performance of social roles in marriage and in the family structure. Today, people are more apt to view marriages as committed relationships in which they expect to find companionship, intimacy, and support and often to become parents and share the responsibilities of raising children. This book examines the implications of this shift in perspective. Individualism, economic pressure, time pressures, social diversity, and an awareness of the risk of marital impermanence are features of the social context in which personal decision making takes place today. As fewer social guidelines seem fixed, personal decision making becomes even more challenging.

The Themes Throughout the Life Course

The book's themes are introduced in Chapter 1, and they reappear throughout the text. We developed these themes by looking at the interplay between findings in the social sciences and the experiences of the people around us. Ideas for topics arose from the needs and concerns we perceived. The attitudes, behavior, and relationships of real people have a complexity that we have tried to portray in this book. Interwoven with these themes is the concept of the life course—the idea that adults may change through reevaluation and restructuring throughout their lives. This emphasis on the life course creates a comprehensive picture of marriages and families and encourages us to continue to add topics that are new to marriage and family texts. Meanwhile, this book makes these points:

- People's personal problems and their interaction with the social environment change as they and their marriages and families grow older.

- People reexamine their relationships and their expectations for relationships as they and their marriages and families mature.

- Because marriage and family forms are more flexible today, people may change the style of their marriages and families throughout their lives.

Marriages and Families—Making Choices

Making decisions about one's marriage and family, either knowledgeably or by default, begins in early adulthood and lasts into old age. People choose whether they will adhere to traditional beliefs, values, and attitudes about gender roles or negotiate more flexible roles and relationships. They may rethink their values about sex and become more knowledgeable and comfortable with their sexual choices.

Women and men may choose to remain single, to form heterosexual or same-sex relationships outside of marriage, or to marry. They have the option today of staying single longer before marrying. Single people make choices about their lives ranging from choices about living arrangements to decisions about whether to engage in sex only in marriage or committed relationships, to engage in sex for recreation, or to abstain from sex altogether. Many unmarried individuals live as cohabiting couples (often with children), a more and more common family form.

Once individuals form couple relationships, they have to decide how they are going to structure their lives as committed partners. Will the partners be legally married? Will they become domestic partners? Will theirs be a dual-career union? Will they plan periods in which one partner is employed, interspersed with times in which both are wage earners? Will they have children? Will they use the new reproductive technology to become parents? Will other family members live with them—siblings or parents, for example, or, later, adult children?

Couples will make these decisions not once, but over and over during their lifetimes. Within a committed relationship, partners also choose how they will deal with conflict. Will they try to ignore conflicts and risk the prospect of devitalized relationships? Will they vent their anger in hostile, alienating, or physically violent ways? Or will they practice bonding ways of communicating, disagreeing, and negotiating—ways that emphasize sharing and can deepen intimacy?

How will the partners distribute power in the marriage? Will they work toward a no-power relationship, in which one individual is more concerned with helping and supporting the other than with gaining a power advantage? How will the partners allocate work responsibilities in the home? What value will they place on their sexual lives together? Throughout their experience, family members continually face decisions about how to balance each one's need for individuality with the need for togetherness.

Parents also have choices. In raising their children, they can choose the authoritative parenting style, for example, in which parents define themselves as having more experience than their youngsters and take an active role in responsibly guiding and monitoring their children, while simultaneously striving to develop supportive, mutually cooperative family relationships.

Many spouses face decisions about whether to divorce. They weigh the pros and cons, asking themselves which is the better alternative: living together as they are or separating? Even when a couple decides to divorce, there are choices to make, whether consciously or not: Will they try to cooperate as much as possible or insist on blame and revenge? What living and economic support arrangements will work best for themselves and their children? How will they handle the legal process? The majority of divorced individuals eventually face decisions about remarriage. In the absence of cultural models, they choose how they will define stepfamily relationships.

When families encounter crises—and every family will face *some* crises—members must make additional decisions. Will they view each crisis as a challenge to be met, or will they blame one another? What resources can they use to handle the crisis? Then, too, as more and more Americans live longer, families will "age." As a result, more and more Americans will have not only living grandparents but also great grandparents. And increasingly we will face issues concerning giving—and receiving—family eldercare.

An emphasis on knowledgeable decision making does not mean that individuals can completely control their lives. People can influence but never directly determine how those around them behave or feel about them. Partners cannot control one another's changes over time, and they cannot avoid all accidents, illnesses, unemployment, deaths, or even divorce. Society-wide conditions may create unavoidable crises for individual families. However, families *can* control how they respond to such crises. Their responses will meet their own needs better when they refuse to react automatically and choose instead to act as a consequence of knowledgeable decision making.

Key Features

As marriages and families have evolved over the last three decades, so has this text. Its subtitle, *Making Choices in a Diverse Society*, speaks to the significant changes that have taken place since the first edition of this textbook. With its ongoing thorough updating and inclusion of current research, plus its emphasis on students' being able to make choices in an exceedingly diverse society, this book has become an unparalleled resource for gaining insights into today's marriages and families.

Over the past nine editions, we have had four goals in mind for student readers: first, to help them better understand themselves and their family situations; second, to make students more conscious of the personal decisions that they will make throughout their lives and of the societal influences that affect those decisions; third, to help students better appreciate the variety and diversity among families today; and fourth, to encourage them to recognize the need for structural, social policy support for families. To these ends, this text has become recognized for its accessible writing style, up-to-date research, well-written boxed features, and useful chapter learning aids.

Up-to-Date Research and Statistics

As users have come to expect, we have thoroughly updated the text's research base and statistics, emphasizing cutting-edge research that addresses the diversity of marriages and families, as well as all other topics. In accordance with this approach, users will notice several new tables and figures. Revised tables and figures have been updated with the latest available statistics—data from the U.S. Census Bureau and other governmental agencies, as well as survey and other research data.

Boxed Features

The several themes described earlier are reflected in the boxed features.

Former users will recognize many of these boxes as having appeared in previous editions. Others, maybe some of your favorites, are no longer with us. (For us, decisions about what to cut are often more difficult than those about what to add.) All the boxes in this edition have been thoroughly updated. The sections below describe our five box categories.

AS WE MAKE CHOICES. We highlight the theme of making choices with a group of boxes throughout the text, for example, "Ten Rules for a Successful Relationship," "Selecting a Child-Care Facility," and "Community Resources for Eldercare." These boxes emphasize human agency and are designed to help students through crucial decisions.

A CLOSER LOOK AT FAMILY DIVERSITY. In order to help accomplish our goal of encouraging students to better appreciate the diversity of today's families, we have presented the latest research and statistical information on diverse family forms, lesbian and gay male families, and families of diverse race and ethnicity. We have consciously integrated these materials throughout the textbook, always with an eye toward avoiding stereotypical, simplistic generalizations and, instead, explaining data in sociological and sociohistorical contexts. Besides integrating information on ethnic diversity throughout the text proper, we have a series of boxes titled A CLOSER LOOK AT FAMILY DIVERSITY, for example, "Diversity and Child Care" and "Family Ties and Immigration," among others.

MY FAMILY. Agnes Riedmann talked with individuals in a variety of social categories about their experiences in marriages and families. These interviews comprise some of the MY FAMILY boxes. Other boxes of this type, such as "Looking After—A Son's Memoir," are excerpts from previously published material. Some student essays also appear as MY FAMILY boxes. An example is the one in Chapter 17 titled "My (Step)Family." All the MY FAMILY boxes are designed to balance and complement the chapter's material. We hope that the presentation of these individuals' stories will help students to see their own lives more clearly and will encourage them to discuss and reevaluate their own attitudes and values.

ISSUES FOR THOUGHT. These boxes feature research designed to spark students' critical thinking or discussion or both. As an example, a box in Chapter 3 explores thought-provoking issues related to "Studying Families and Ethnicity." As another example, a box in Chapter 7 explores "Three Very Different Subcultures with Norms Contrary to Sexual Exclusivity." As a final example, a new box in Chapter 18 presents the issue of "Child—and Grandchild—Caregivers."

FACTS ABOUT FAMILIES. These boxes present demographic and other factual information on focused topics such as family members' time use: "Where Does the Time Go?" Two other examples discuss "Fathers as Primary Parents" and "Remarriages and Stepfamilies—Diversity by Race/Ethnicity and Sexual Orientation."

FOCUS ON CHILDREN. A sixth important feature, which is not specifically a box, is called Focus on Children. When you see this icon you are being alerted to important material related to children. We include this focus for two reasons. First, the sociology of the child has become increasingly important as an area of scholarly interest; hence, we want to include focused coverage on children in order to help professors bring more of this material into their courses. Second, the amount of news on children's issues has given rise to concern about the extent to which contemporary America's children are well nurtured. We want to encourage students to examine the condition of children today from a sociological perspective. We hope that, as a consequence, students will be able to make informed decisions now and in the future.

Chapter Learning Aids

We have devised a series of chapter learning aids to help students comprehend and retain the material they read.

- **Chapter Summaries** are presented in bulleted, point-by-point lists of the key material in the chapter.

- **Key Terms** alert students to the key concepts presented in the chapter. A full glossary is provided at the end of the text.

- **Questions for Review and Reflection** have been created by the authors to assist students in reviewing the material. Thought questions encourage students to think critically and to integrate material from other chapters with that presented in the current chapter.

- **Footnotes**, although not overused, are presented when we feel that a point needs to be made but might disrupt the flow of the text itself.

- **Suggested Readings** on the book website give students ideas for further reading on topics and issues presented in the chapter.

Key Changes in This Edition

This edition includes many key changes, some of which are outlined here.

In the tenth edition, we have restructured the chapter outline. "Exploring the Family" is now Chapter 2, carrying forward from Chapter 1 an introduction to the study of the family. "American Families in Social Context" is Chapter 3 and pairs well, we believe, with Chapter 4, "Our Gendered Identities." These two chapters examine how family experience varies by social class, race/ethnicity, religion, and gender.

In addition, Chapters 7, 8, and 9 have been reconceptualized. In this edition, Chapter 7, "Marriage: From Social Institution to Private Relationship" (formerly Chapter 8), describes the changing nature of marriage today and explores issues and public policy initiatives surrounding such change. Chapter 8, "Nonmarital Living Arrangements: Living Alone, Cohabitation, Same-Sex Couples, and Other Options" (formerly Chapter 9), presents reasons for the increasing proportion of unmarrieds and describes the various living arrangements of nonmarrieds. Chapter 9 in this edition is now titled "Choosing a Marriage Partner, and the First Years of Marriage." By combining courtship and the early years of marriage in one chapter, we are better able to emphasize preparation for marriage as well as ways that mate selection impacts marital satisfaction and stability.

As with previous revisions, we have given considerable attention to chapter—and within chapter—organization in order both to streamline the material presented whenever possible and to ensure a good flow of ideas. In this edition we have also worked to consolidate similar material that had previously been addressed in separate chapters.

Meanwhile, we have substantially revised each and every chapter. Every chapter is updated with the latest research throughout. We mention some (but not all!) specific changes here, as well as highlighting some important changes introduced in the previous edition.

Chapter 1, Family Commitments: Making Choices in a Changing Society, continues to present the choices and life course themes of the book, as well as pointing to the significance for the family of larger social forces. The chapter's discussion of the "politics" of the family—that is, conflicting views on the changing family—has been updated to reflect the most current literature. The box FACTS ABOUT FAMILIES: "American Families Today" has been shortened by our creating a separate box for statistical information on children. In Chapter 1, students are asked to reflect on the question "What is a family?" This question is raised in two ISSUES FOR THOUGHT boxes: "Which of These Is a Family?" and "Pets as Family?" In the latter, we ask: *Are* pets family, or not?

Chapter 2, Exploring the Family, has a "Utility of the Perspective" discussion added to each theory section. Sections on family ecology, family development, and biosocial perspectives have been expanded, and a section on conflict theory added. The family ecology section now has more on neighborhood environments and on the question of whether social isolation has increased. We have also added a subsection, "Emerging Adulthood," that signals a new life stage—the long transition from adolescence to a settled adulthood.

Theoretical perspectives are summarized in a chart of key concepts and research applications. In addition, a definition of science and a discussion of the ethics of research have been added to the methods section of this chapter. The box "Safety and Risk in the Family Environment" has been updated in the context of the war on terrorism, the war in Iraq, and Hurricane Katrina. There are recommended websites that offer supplemental materials for parents and children.

Chapter 3, American Families in Social Context, has a new box on military families. A new section, "Conceptualizing Race and Ethnicity," has been added, which emphasizes diversity *within* major racial/ethnic groups and notes the increasingly fluid nature of racial/ethnic categories. The box "Studying Families and Ethnicity" has been moved to this chapter and rewritten with new research examples. Prompted by the Census Bureau's separation of Asian from Hawaiian and Other Pacific Islander categories, a section on Pacific Islander families has been added.

Significant changes in Latino family patterns are reported, and we have also included more on differences among African American families by class. Coverage of immigrant families takes account of the current politics of immigration, pointing especially to how U.S. immigration policy affects binational families.

Although the section "Technology and the Family" no longer appears because much of its content has become general knowledge, recognition of and discussions on technological developments appear throughout the book—for example, maintaining ties between college students and their parents (Chapter 1), social class differences in Internet access (Chapter 3); cyberadultery (Chapter 6), Internet matchmaking (Chapter 9), reproductive technology (Chapter 10), parental surveillance of children (Chapter 11), working at home versus tethered to the office (Chapter 12), and how noncustodial parents keep in touch with children through technology (Chapter 16).

Chapter 4, Our Gendered Identities, has been thematically updated to take into account the fact that the more essentialist perspective of "men" versus "women" has given way to the intersection of gender with race, class, sexuality, and globalization. Older rhetoric reflecting a 1970s perspective has been deleted—without losing the theme of gender inequality. A new box—A CLOSER LOOK AT FAMILY DIVERSITY: "Race, Class, and Gender in the Nanny Hunt"—illustrates *intersectionality*—that is, a race/class/gender framing of gender issues.

Entirely new material on gender differences is presented. A new section on the gender similarities hypothesis includes research supporting the hypothesis that there are actually few differences between males and females in traits and abilities. The section "Is Anatomy Destiny?" has been shortened and included at the end of the gender inequality section. Carried over from the previous edition is the box ISSUES FOR THOUGHT: "Challenges to Gender Boundaries"—a discussion of intersexuality (regarding individuals born with characteristics of both sexes or those who consciously choose to change their sexual and gender identity).

Chapter 4 also includes discussion of gender inequality in major social institutions. This section includes new subsections on "Gender and Health" and "Gender and Education." The section on education addresses the concern about lower rates of college enrollment and graduation for males. A section within the socialization segment looks at the related conflict between advocacy for girls and for boys—is there a "war against boys"? In addition, there is an updated perspective on the Women's and Men's Movements and on the future of gender.

Chapter 5, Loving Ourselves and Others, is updated throughout. In response to reviewers, an addition to this chapter is a section on limerence, which involves discussion of the fact that limerence is not the same thing as love. Another addition is discussion of recent research on biochemistry—that is, hormones, such as oxytocin—and their possible contribution to falling and remaining in love.

Chapter 6, Our Sexual Selves, presents two new boxes: one on asexuality as a legitimate sexual orientation and another on an emergent sexual script, "Hooking Up." Material on extramarital affairs has been moved to this chapter and new data included. The section "Platform and Pulpit" now appears as "The Politics of Sex" and includes discussion of the politicization of research and of sex education.

Chapter 7, Marriage: From Social Institution to Private Relationship (formerly Chapter 8), has been reconceptualized. This chapter first explores the changing picture regarding marriage, noting the increasing proportion of unmarrieds today. Then, after describing the time-honored (originally Western) marriage premise of permanence and sexual exclusivity, the chapter describes how these expectations came about historically as well as ways that they have changed.

This chapter introduces Andrew Cherlin's concept, *deinstitutionalized marriage*, setting marital deinstitutionalization in historical context. We explore the most current research on the consequences of deinstitutionalized marriage for adults and children. With comprehensive discussion of issues surrounding the Healthy Marriage Initiative, this chapter analyzes the public policy debate over the desirability of legal marriage vis-à-vis other family forms. As is the case throughout this textbook, we have paid attention to family diversity. An example is a new box on African American weddings: "African Americans and 'Jumping the Broom.'" Linking the macro/structural perspective with the more personal/micro point of view, we end this chapter with the section, "Happiness and Life Satisfaction: How Does Marriage Matter?"

Chapter 8, Nonmarital Living Arrangements: Living Alone, Cohabitation, Same-Sex Couples, and Other Options (formerly Chapter 9), discusses reasons for the increasing proportion of unmarrieds. These include demographic, economic, technological, and cultural changes. After describing the various living arrangements of nonmarrieds—with a new section on "living alone together"—the chapter presents a largely expanded discussion of cohabitation and family life, including discussion of the cohabiting relationship itself as well as the most recent research on the consequences of raising children in a cohabiting family. This chapter also includes extensive sections on same-sex couples and family life, now consolidated in this chapter, with much material on this topic moved to this chapter from the previous edition's Chapter 8. The chapter ends with an exploration of life satisfaction among unmarrieds.

Chapter 9, Choosing a Marriage Partner, and the First Years of Marriage (formerly Chapter 7), places greater emphasis on the ways in which mate selection impacts marital satisfaction and stability. This chapter also gives more attention to the differences—and similarities—between arranged and free-choice marriages, as well as to ways in which bargaining in today's free-choice marriage market has changed. As in the past, this chapter includes discussion of homogamy as well as increasing marital heterogamy.

Then the chapter turns to an exploration of developing the premarital relationship and moving toward marital commitment, with new sections on defining the relationship as marriage-bound and on engagement. Cohabitation as a courtship practice is fully explored in this chapter, with discussion of the most current research on the impact of cohabitation on marital quality and stability. This chapter also explores preparation for marriage and tasks associated with the first years of marriage, such as creating couple connection and forging an adaptable marriage relationship.

Chapter 10, To Parent or Not To Parent, includes a new section on multipartnered fertility and a new box, "Choosing Large Families in a Small-Family Era." Pertinent material from a box that appeared in previous editions, "Meddling with Nature," has been incorporated in the text section on social and ethical issues in reproductive technology. The box on children born to families through reproductive technology has been retained and updated.

Chapter 11, Raising Children in a Multicultural Society, like all the chapters in this edition, has been thoroughly updated with the most current research. As in recent prior editions, after describing the authoritative parenting style, we note its acceptance by mainstream experts in the parenting field. We then present a critique that questions whether this parenting style is universally appropriate or simply a white, middle-class pattern that may not be so suitable to other social contexts. We also discuss challenges faced by parents who are raising religious- or ethnic-minority children in potentially discriminatory environments.

Indeed, in this edition, we give heightened attention to the difficulties that all parents face in contemporary America. An example is the new box, "PARENT—Job Description." A related example is footnote 2. Again, as with all other chapters in this text, we keep in mind the linkage between structural conditions and personal decisions. For instance, we present the latest research on spanking. Other examples include the box (familiar to former users), "Communicating with Children—How to Talk So Kids Will Listen and Listen So Kids Will Talk" as well as the final section of this chapter, "Toward Better Parent–Child Relationships." Discussion of same-sex parenting has been moved to Chapter 8.

Chapter 12, Work and Family, includes an updated discussion of women's leaving the labor force and reentry—are women "opting out"? There is more on men's labor force patterns, and this frames the discussion of stay-at-home fathers and "househusbands." This chapter also examines the persistence of gender differences in the "second shift" of housework and child care within the context of the wage gap between men and women. Data on work, family, and leisure are updated, and there are new figures on time spent with children, jobs held by women and men, who works in a married couple family, and the priority given to work and family by baby boomers, Generation X, and Generation Y.

Although in many chapters of this text, we incorporate material from important new books, two on the intersection of work and family are worth mentioning here: Bianchi, Robinson, and Milkie, *Changing Rhythms of American Family Life*, and Jacobs and Gerson, *The Time Divide*. We continue to follow the National Institute of Child Health and Human Development study of child care. In the boxes "Selecting a Child-Care Facility" and "Child Care and Children's Outcomes," we present the latest information on child-care decisions as they relate to work and family.

Chapter 13, Communication in Marriages and Families, now places greater emphasis on family cohesion as a function of positive couple communication and offers more on supportive couple communication in general, rather than simply with regard to disagreements or conflict. The opening sections of this chapter discuss the positive results of such practices as letting your partner know that you are listening, showing interest in what your partner is telling you, and having fun together. At the same time, this chapter continues to recognize the negative effects of denying conflict and to discuss ways that couples can engage in supportive communication while experiencing conflict. A new box, "A Look Behind the Scenes at Communication Research," gives further insight into John Gottman and colleagues' research on couple communication.

Chapter 14, Power and Violence in Families, now includes a chart on the bases of power. This chapter now consolidates the classic research on family power, while current research on marital and partner power has been expanded to include issues of household work and money management, as well as decision making per se. A discussion of equality and equity concludes the part of the chapter on marital and partner power.

In the section on family violence, the controversial question of gender symmetry in intimate partner violence continues to be considered. We have added a new section on child-to-parent violence. Sibling violence and child sexual abuse are treated in separate subsec-

tions. The older National Family Violence Survey material has been made more concise, and the section on data sources has been shortened.

Chapter 15, Family Stress, Crises, and Resilience, continues to emphasize and expand discussion of the growing body of research on resilience in relation to family stress and crises. Using updated research and contemporary examples, such as deployment to war as a family stressor, this chapter includes a new box on caring for seriously ill patients at home. As has been the case in previous editions, we end this chapter on a positive, albeit realistic, note with a final section exploring family crisis as disaster or opportunity.

Chapter 16, Divorce: Before and After, has been reorganized. The box on divorce statistics has been deleted, with some of the material put into a footnote. There is less emphasis on the Wallerstein/Hetherington debate (still there, but briefer). We present new research on who initiates the divorce and what difference that makes for divorcing individuals. With reference to the most recent research, we also present a somewhat more positive look at divorce outcomes for men and women. A new box on "Postdivorce Pathways" explores diversity in outcomes. There is also now a subsection on stable unhappy marriages.

There is a new section on what impact multiple family transitions might have on child outcomes. A new box presents us with a noncustodial mother's account of what that role is like.

Chapter 17, Remarriages and Stepfamilies, continues to emphasize and expand upon diversity within stepfamilies. For example, a FACTS ABOUT FAMILIES box explores stepfamily diversity not only by race/ethnicity but also by sexual orientation. Meanwhile, we continue to give greater attention to the "nuclear-family model monopoly," whereby the cultural assumption is that the first-marriage family is the "real" model for family living, with all other family forms viewed as deficient. Within this context, we give greater attention in this edition to all family members' experiences while living in stepfamilies. As well as being completely updated, this chapter now includes expanded discussions of boundary ambiguity in stepfamilies as well as the newest research data on remarrieds' decision to have a mutual child. As with other chapters in this text, we focus on the intersection of the macro with the micro as we include a box on stepparenting tips as well as a final section, "Creating Supportive Stepfamilies."

Chapter 18, Aging Families, has been updated throughout, not only with the latest research but also with recognition of emerging challenges—and opportunities, such as more time for grandparenthood—related to an aging population. This chapter includes the most up-to-date research on gender as related to caregiving, as well as a new box on young children as caregivers. The discussion of elder abuse has been moved to this chapter from Chapter 14.

Appendices. All the appendices, which appear on the book companion website, have been updated. For example, material on sexually transmitted diseases other than AIDS has been expanded in response to reviewers' comments. An updated discussion of birthing looks at the relative merits of the medical and natural childbirth models and the preferences of today's mothers.

Supplements

Supplements for the Instructor

Annotated Instructor's Edition. Written by Kevin Bush, Miami University, the Annotated Instructor's Edition contains helpful ideas for the instructor to integrate into the class lecture. Annotations include Teaching Tips and Film/Video Tips, as well as Clicker/Discussion Tips.

Instructor's Resource Manual with Test Bank. This revised and updated Instructor's Resource Manual contains detailed lecture outlines; chapter summaries; and lecture, activity, and discussion suggestions, as well as film and video resources. It also includes student learning objectives, chapter review sheets, and Internet and InfoTrac® College Edition exercises. A Resource Integration Guide (RIG) is part of this manual, as is a list of additional print, video, and online resources, and concise user guides for ThomsonNOW™, InfoTrac College Edition, WebTutor™, and more. This test bank consists of a variety of questions, including multiple choice, true/false, completion, short answer, and essay questions for each chapter of the text, with answer explanations and page references to the text.

PowerLecture with JoinIn™ and ExamView®. This easy-to-use, one-stop digital library and presentation tool includes the following:

- Preassembled **Microsoft® PowerPoint® lecture slides** with graphics from the text, making it easy for you to assemble, edit, publish, and present custom lectures for your course. Also included are all photos from the text along with video clips.

- The PowerLectures CD-ROM includes polling and quiz questions that can be used with the **JoinIn on TurningPoint®** ("clickers") personal response system. The CD also contains video clips with correlated assessment questions.

- PowerLectures also features **ExamView testing software** that includes all the test items from the printed *Test Bank* in electronic format, enabling you to create customized tests of up to 250 items that can be delivered in print or online.

ABC® News Video Series: Marriage and Family, Volumes 1 & 2. Illustrate the relevance of marriage and family to everyday life with this exclusive series of videos for the Marriage and Family course. Jointly created by Wadsworth and ABC, each video consists of footage originally broadcast on ABC and specifically selected to illustrate important sociological concepts.

Lecture Ideas for Courses on the Family, Volumes 1 & 2. This handy booklet, offered free to adopters, contains numerous suggestions for activities, lecture ideas, or classroom discussions, all contributed by instructors around the country. Contact your local Wadsworth rep to find out how you can access this useful teaching resource.

Supplements for the Student

Study Guide. This Study Guide includes a chapter summary, learning objectives, key terms, key term completion exercises, Internet and InfoTrac College Edition activities, and key theoretical perspectives for each chapter. Practice tests also contain multiple-choice, true/false, short answer, and essay questions, complete with answers and page references at the end of each chapter.

ThomsonNOW™. ThomsonNOW Personalized Study, a diagnostic tool (including a chapter-specific *Pre-test*, *Individualized Study Plan* and *Post-test*), helps students master concepts and prepare for exams by creating a study plan based on the students' performance on the pre-test. Easily assign Personalized Study for the entire term, and, if you want, results will automatically post to your grade book. Order new student texts packaged with the access code to ensure that your students have four months of free access from the moment they purchase the text. Contact your local Wadsworth representative for ordering details.

Media-Based Supplements

InfoTrac College Edition. Available as a free option with newly purchased texts, InfoTrac College Edition gives instructors and students four months of free access to an extensive online database of reliable, full-length articles (not just abstracts) from thousands of scholarly and popular publications going as far back as 1980. Among the journals available 24/7 are *American Journal of Sociology, Social Forces, Social Research,* and *Sociology.* InfoTrac College Edition now also comes with InfoMark™, a tool that allows you to save your search parameters, as well as save links to specific articles. (Available to North American college and university students only; journals are subject to change.)

Audio Study Tools. Your students will enjoy the MP3-ready Audio Lecture Overviews for each chapter and a comprehensive audio glossary of key terms for quick study and review. Whether walking to class, doing laundry, or studying at their desk, students now have the freedom to choose when, where, and how they interact with their audio-based educational media. Contact your Thomson Wadsworth sales rep for more information.

Web Tutor™ on BB/WebCT®. This web-based learning tool takes the sociology course beyond the classroom. Students gain access to a full array of study tools, including chapter outlines, chapter-specific quizzing material, interactive games and maps, and videos. With WebTutor, instructors can provide virtual office hours, post syllabi, track student progress with the quizzing material, and even customize the content to suit their needs.

Companion Website. This text's companion site includes chapter-specific resources for instructors and students. For instructors, the site offers a password-protected instructor's manual, PowerPoint presentation slides, and more. For students, there is a multitude of text-specific study aids, including practice quizzes, web links, flash cards, virtual explorations, and more.

Acknowledgments

This book is a result of a joint effort on our part; neither of us could have conceptualized or written it alone. We want to thank some of the many people who helped us. Looking back on the long life of this book, we acknowledge Steve Rutter for his original vision of the project and his faith in us. We also want to thank Sheryl Fullerton, Serina Beauparlant, and Eve Howard, who saw us through earlier editions as editors and friends.

As has been true of our past editions, the people at Wadsworth Publishing Company have been professionally competent and a pleasure to work with. We are especially grateful to Chris Caldeira, Sociology Editor, who has guided this edition, and Bob Jucha, who was our editor on several previous revisions; to Sherry Symington, Development Editor, who worked with us "hands-on"

throughout several editions, and Tali Beesley, Sociology Editorial Assistant, who managed the manuscript as a practical matter.

Cheri Palmer, Senior Production Project Manager, oversaw the process of moving the book from manuscript to print and was ready to ensure communication among the many people who worked on the book. Christina Beliso, Assistant Editor, had responsibility for the fine array of print supplements that are available with this tenth edition of *Marriages and Families,* and Dave Lionetti, Technology Project Manager, developed the web-based materials. Timothy Sisler, Permissions Editor, and Sarah D'Stair made sure we were accountable to other authors and publishers when we used their work.

Anne Pietromica and Katie Swank of Lachina Publishing Services led a production team whose specialized competence and coordinated efforts have made the book a reality. They were excellent to work with, always available and responsive to our questions, flexible when our other responsibilities or travel made it difficult to keep up with the schedule, and helpful when we needed to make last-minute changes. They managed a complex production process smoothly and effectively to ensure a timely completion of the project and a book whose look and presentation of content are very pleasing to us—and, we hope, to the reader.

The production effort also included Carolyn Crabtree, copyeditor, who did an outstanding job of bringing our draft manuscript into conformity with style guidelines and who was amazing in terms of her ability to notice fine details—inconsistencies or omissions in citations, references, and elements of the manuscript. Sarah Evertson of Image Quest worked with us to find photos that captured the ideas we presented in words. Ellen Pettengell developed the overall design of the book, one we are very pleased with. Heidi Grosch designed the figures, converting numbers into pictures. Martha Ghent proofread the book pages, and Renee Quale compiled the index. Once it is completed, our textbook needs to find the faculty and students who will use it. Michelle Williams, Marketing Manager at Wadsworth, and Linda Yip, Marketing Communications Manager, helped capture the essence of our book in the various marketing materials that present our book to its prospective audience.

Closer to home, Agnes Riedmann wishes to acknowledge her late mother, Ann Langley Czerwinski, Ph.D., who helped her significantly with past editions. Agnes would also like to acknowledge family and friends who have supported her throughout the thirty years that she has worked on this book.

Sam Walker has contributed to each edition of this book through his enthusiasm and encouragement for

Mary Ann Lamanna's work on the project. Larry and Valerie Lamanna and other family members have enlarged their mother's perspective on the family by bringing her into personal contact with other family worlds—those beyond the everyday experience of family life among the social scientists!

At this point, we would also like to acknowledge one another as co-authors. Each of us brings somewhat different strengths to this process. We are not alike—a fact that has continuously made for a better book, in our opinion. At times we have lengthy e-mail conversations back and forth over the inclusion of one phrase. Many times we have disagreed over the course of the past thirty years—over how long to make a section, how much emphasis to give a particular topic, whether a certain citation is the best one to use, occasionally over the tone of an anxious or frustrated e-mail. But we have always agreed on the basic vision and character of this textbook. And we continue to grow in our mutual respect for one another as scholars, writers, and authors.

Reviewers gave us many helpful suggestions for revising the book. Peter Stein's work as a thorough, informed, and supportive reviewer through this and previous editions has been an especially important contribution. Although we have not incorporated all suggestions from reviewers, we have considered them all carefully and used many. The review process makes a substantial, and indeed essential, contribution to each revision of the book.

Tenth Edition Reviewers

Terry Humphrey, Palomar College; Sampson Lee Blair, State University of New York, Buffalo; Lue Turner, University of Kentucky; Stacy Ruth, Jones County Junior College; Shirley Keeton, Fayetteville State University; Robert Bausch, Cameron University; Paula Tripp, Sam Houston State University; Kevin Bush, Miami University; Jane Smith, Concordia University; Peter Stein, William Paterson University.

Ninth Edition Reviewers

Sylvia M. Asay, University of Nebraska—Kearney; Nicole Banton, Seminole Community College; Theodore N. Greenstein, North Carolina State University; Marsha McGee, University of Louisiana–Monroe; Junelyn Peeples, Chaffey Community College; Frances Marx Stehle, Portland State University; Suzan Waller, Rose State College; Toni Zimmerman, Colorado State University.

Of Special Importance

Students and faculty members who tell us of their interest in the book are a special inspiration. To all of the people who gave their time and gave of themselves—interviewees, students, our families and friends—many thanks. We see the fact that this book is going into a tenth edition as a result of a truly interactive process between ourselves and students who share their experiences and insights in our classrooms; reviewers who consistently give us good advice; editors and production experts whose input is invaluable; and our family, friends, and colleagues whose support is invaluable.

Marriages & Families

MAKING CHOICES IN A DIVERSE SOCIETY

Family Commitments: Making Choices in a Changing Society

© Yellow Dog Productions/Getty Images/Stone

Defining Family

There Is No Typical Family

Issues for Thought: Pets as Family?

New Definitions of the Family

Facts About Families: American Families Today

The Freedom and Pressures of Choosing

Personal Troubles and Societal Influences

Issues for Thought: Which of These Is a Family?

Social Influences and Personal Choices

Making Choices

Choosing by Default

Choosing Knowledgeably

A Family of Individuals

Families as a Place to Belong

Familistic (Communal) Values and Individualistic (Self-Fulfillment) Values

"Family Decline" or "Family Change"?

Facts about Families: Focus on Children

Partners as Individuals and Family Members

Marriages and Families: Four Themes

Today's Americans, like those before them, place a high value on the family. Most of us hope to experience ongoing happiness in committed unions and families. A 2004 Monitoring the Future survey of high school seniors reports that 82 percent of girls and 70 percent of boys say that having a good marriage and family life is "extremely important" to them (Whitehead and Popenoe 2006, Figure 14).

Yet we may wonder about the chances of finding family happiness. There continue to be long-term, happy marriages. But some who would like to marry or form a committed relationship have not yet found partners. The high divorce rate has called into question the stability of marriage. Recent books talk about "conjugal succession," perhaps a series of marriages for each person (Paul 2002, p. 251).

We remain hopeful about family commitment and fulfillment. Families are central to society as an institution and to our everyday lives. They undertake the pivotal tasks of raising children and providing intimacy, affection, and companionship to members.

Hoping alone won't make enduring or emotionally satisfying families. Maintaining a family requires both commitment and knowing what you're doing. This theme of knowledge plus dedication is a good part of what this book is about. We will return to it later in this chapter and throughout the text. Right now, though, we need to discuss what a family is.

Defining Family

What is a **family**? In everyday conversation we make assumptions about what families are or should be. Traditionally, both law and social science have specified that the family consists of people related by blood, marriage, or adoption. Some definitions of the family have also specified a common household, economic interdependency, and sexual and reproductive relations (Murdock 1949). The U.S. Census Bureau defines a family as "a group of two or more persons related by blood, marriage, or adoption and residing together in a household" (U.S. Census Bureau 2006c, p. 6).

In their classic work *The Family: From Institution to Companionship* 1953 [1945], Ernest Burgess and Harvey Locke think of the family as a **primary group**—a term coined by early sociologist Charles Cooley (1909) to describe any group in which there is a close, face-to-face relationship.[1] In a primary group, people communicate

---

[1] Another example of a primary group relationship is a close friendship. In contrast to a primary group, a **secondary group** is characterized by more distant, practical, and unemotional relationships as, for example, in a professional organization or business association.

In today's technological society, a primary group is not necessarily a *face-to-face* one. Now, close personal relationships of family and friends are often maintained through e-mail, text messaging, instant messaging, cell phones, and websites, as well as conventional telephone calls.

An indirect indicator of the centrality of the family to American life is the degree to which family themes are used as advertising motifs. In the first photo, a family spashing happily in the ocean fronts an ad for "Hottest Hotels," while the text of the second photo describes the family life of the father and the child pictured in the photo.

© Ryan McVay/Getty Images/Photodisc

A primary group is a small group marked by close, face-to-face relationships. Group members share experiences, express emotions, and, in the ideal case, know they are accepted and valued. In many ways, families, friends, and teams are similar primary groups: Joys are celebrated spontaneously, tempers can flare quickly, and expression is often physical.

with one another as whole human beings. They laugh and cry together, they share experiences, and they quarrel, too, because that's part of being close. Primary groups can give each of us the feeling of being accepted and liked for who we are.

Burgess and Locke's view of family companionship, however, was more limited than current views. It assumed that family interaction occurred primarily in the context of traditional (heterosexual, married-couple, gender-differentiated) social roles, rather than emphasizing spontaneity, individuality, and intimacy. Today's social scientists continue to recognize the family's important responsibility in performing necessary social roles, such as child rearing, economic support, and domestic maintenance. But many social scientists (including us) place more emphasis on companionship and emotional support than did Burgess and Locke. Moreover, today family members are not necessarily bound to each other by legal marriage, by blood, or by adoption but may experience family relationships and commitment in other forms (Struening 2002, p. 15).

Burgess and Locke specified that family members "constitute a household," that is, people residing together. We would expand their definition to include, for example, commuter couples, noncustodial parents, parents with adult children living elsewhere, extended kin such as aunts and uncles, and adult siblings and stepsiblings. In other words, the term *family* can identify relationships beyond partners, parents, and children living in one household.

How expansive can a definition of family be? When asked to list their family members, some of our students include their dogs, cats, or other pets. Are pets family members? "Issues for Thought: Pets as Family?" poses this question.

There Is No Typical Family

Until recently, societal attitudes, religious beliefs, and law converged into a fairly common expectation about what form the American family should take: husband, wife, and children in an independent household—the **nuclear family** model.

Today, only 7 percent of families fit the 1950s nuclear family ideal of married couple and children, with a husband-breadwinner and wife-homemaker (Fields 2004, p. 2; U.S. Bureau of Labor Statistics 2006a, Table 4). Social scientists no longer assume that a family has a male breadwinner and a female homemaker; dual-career families are common, and there are reversed-role families (working wife, househusband). There is a proliferation of different family forms: single-parent families, stepfamilies, cohabiting heterosexual couples, gay and lesbian families, and three-generation families.

Figure 1.1 displays the types of households in which Americans live. The concept of **household** is broader than that of "family" as it includes nonfamilial living arrangements as well. The most common household type today is that of married couples *without* children, where the children have grown up and left or the couple has not yet had children or doesn't plan to. Less than a quarter of households are nuclear families of husband, wife, and children; this compares to 44 percent in 1960 (Casper and Bianchi 2002, p. 8).

About as many households (26.4 percent) are maintained by individuals living alone as by married couples with children. There are also female-headed (7.3 percent) and male-headed (1.7 percent) single-parent households, unmarried couple households (5.1 percent), and

No statistics on pets appear in the "Facts about Families: American Families Today" box later in this chapter. Should there be? Dogs and cats are called "*companion* animals." Are pets family members?

Pets are present in 58 percent of American households. Almost 80 percent of families with children have pets. Most people who own pets think of them as part of the family. A large majority of dog and cat owners refer to themselves as "mommy" or "daddy" with reference to their pets (American Veterinary Medical Association 2002); Block 2002; Edmondson and Galper 1998; Gardyn 2002; Voith 1985). "[A]t least for some urban dwellers, pets are inside the family circle," concludes a recent study of pet owners (S. Cohen 2002). A recent dramatic example of this attachment to pets was the refusal of many pet owners to evacuate from New Orleans during Hurricane Katrina without their pets (A. Parker 2006).

People talk to their pets and believe that they understand. An American Kennel Club study found that both dog owners (79 percent) and nonowners (63 percent) say a person is "not alone" if a dog is there (Umminger and Pompa 2005). Stores carry greeting cards for pets to "send" to their humans on important family occasions ("Pet Lovers . . ." 2002), and almost 6 million pet owners celebrate their dog's birthday (Darlin 2006).

Some pet owners take their animals to day care, spas, psychotherapy, acupuncture, massage, swimming lessons, and photo shoots. They vacation with them at hotels with expensive pet pampering facilities and, of course, give them

gifts, often expensive (Alexander 2003; Gardyn 2002; Gunderson 2006; Howard 2005; Newman 2005). Health care for a pet can involve a $1,200 MRI or kidney dialysis or transplant. So it may not be too surprising that some owners buy pet health insurance and set up trust funds to care for a pet after their death (Darlin 2005; Mott 2005). Some have deposited their pet's DNA for future cloning (Eisenberg 2005).

Pet owners are willing to spend money on pet health care because losing a pet can be very painful. In some states, a bereaved owner may sue for emotional suffering or loss of companionship if a pet is accidentally or intentionally killed by a third party (L. Parker 2005). Even for those who don't claim a disability need for an animal's presence, pets are important "companion animals." A study of children and pets finds that pets perform certain support functions for children, particularly as providers of comfort and esteem and as an audience for secrets (McNicholas and Collis 2004). Pets seem to increase family adaptability and reduce stress. Studies suggest that the presence of pets can help when owners are lonely or depressed, or during a family crisis (Karen Allen 2002).

In the words of one veterinary researcher, "Clearly, dogs are assuming more importance in people's lives" (Gail Golab in Egan 2001, p. 24). Caroline Knapp's *Pack of Two* (1999) points to changes in the family—more people living alone, delayed marriage, cohabitation, and the deferral of parenthood—that have opened a void that pets may fill. In *The New Work of Dogs* (2003), journalist

Jon Katz argues that dogs used to have work responsibilities, tending sheep and the like. Now companion animals have an important new role—that of sustaining the mental health and emotional equilibrium of their owners in an era of work pressures and insecure family lives.

As the tendency to think of pets as family continues and especially as spending on pets grows, some are uneasy about giving so much attention to animals when the needs of society's children are so great. Another, more philosophical, concern involves the "humanization"of pets—acting as if animals were truly human (Masters 2005). It used to be that "'a pet was a pet' and 'there was a very clear boundary as to what you would do'" (veterinarian Robert Gilbert in J. Brody 2001, p. 4). There is also some concern about the pressures placed on pets and the potential for mistreatment that could occur when owners become disappointed that their needs are not met (J. Katz 2003).

For those who worry that pets are replacing people in emotional networks (L. Simon 1984), recent research is reassuring: "[N]ot even the most bonded person believes his or her pet is human. Pets seem to occupy an overlapping but different space from humans in a family" (S. Cohen 2002, p. 633).

Critical Thinking

Do you think of pets as family members? Dogs, cats, or any and all pets? Is it appropriate to broaden the definition of *family* to include other than humans? What changes in the family may have encouraged changes in our attitudes about pets?

other family households containing relatives other than spouses or children (7.5 percent). "Facts about Families: American Families Today" presents additional information about today's families.

The increasing family and household diversity that we see now has led some scholars to argue that "the new

family diversity [is] 'an intrinsic feature . . . rather than a temporary aberration of contemporary family life'" (Stacey 1996, p. 37, quoting Castro Martin and Bumpass 1989, p. 49).

Sociologist Frank Furstenberg's definition of the family captures this diversity: "My definition of 'family'

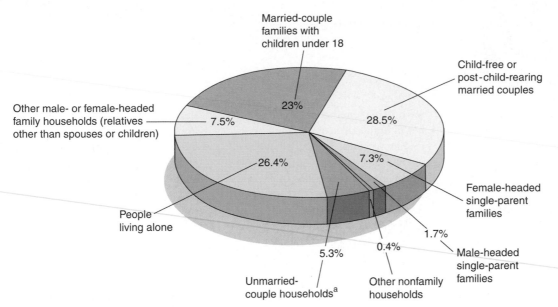

FIGURE 1.1 The many kinds of American households, 2004. A household is a person or a group of people who occupy a dwelling unit. This figure displays both family and nonfamily households.

Source: U.S. Census Bureau 2005a, Table 1101; 2006b, Tables 53, 57.

a. Unmarried-couple households may be composed of two male partners (6.5 percent); two female partners (6.1 percent); or a heterosexual couple (87.4 percent). The Census Bureau classifies unmarried-couple households as "nonfamily households."

© Michael Heron/CORBIS

includes membership related by blood, legal ties, adoption, and informal ties including *fictive* or socially agreed upon kinship" (Furstenberg 2005, p. 810). Laura Dawn's book of stories about people who, in the aftermath of Hurricane Katrina, took in people whom they didn't know, describes "how strangers became family" (Dawn 2006).

New Definitions of the Family

Not only social scientists and legal scholars are rethinking the family. The definitional problem has moved out of the academy and into the wider world. As families have become less traditional, the legal definition of a family has become more flexible. Law, government agencies, and to some extent private bureaucracies such as insurance companies must make decisions about what a family is. If zoning laws, rental practices, employee privileges, and insurance policies cover families, decisions must be made

In a world of demographic, cultural, and political changes, our views of family structure and life cycle have begun to broaden. For example, today there are more single-parent families, gay partners and parents, remarried families, and families in which adult children care for their aging parents. Whatever their form, families can remain a center of love and support.

American Families Today [a, b]

What do U.S. marriages and families look like today? Statistics can't tell the whole story of the family, but they are an important beginning. Later chapters will discuss these family situations in more detail.

The demographic data presented in this box are generalizations that do not take into account differences among various sectors of American society. In Chapter 3 we will explore that social diversity, but for now, let's look at these overall statistics.

Critical Thinking

As you read these facts about families, think about today's American family. What do these statistics tell you about the strengths and weaknesses of the contemporary American family and about family change?

1. *Fewer people are currently married.* Fifty-two percent of the adult population was currently married in 2005, compared to 62 percent as recently as 1990. Twenty-nine percent have never married; 10 percent are divorced, and 6 percent widowed (U.S. Census Bureau 2006b, Table A1; 2006c, Table 50).

2. *People have been postponing marriage in recent years.* In 2005, the median age at first marriage was 25.8 for women, 27.1 for men, compared to 20.8 for women and 23.5 for men in 1970. Marriage remains an almost universal experience; 91 percent of adults have been married or plan to marry (Bergman 2006a; Saad 2006b).

3. *Cohabitation has emerged as a new family form as well as a transitional lifestyle choice.* From 1990 to 2000 there was a 72 percent increase in the number of unmarried-couple households (Simmons and O'Connell 2003). Unmarried-couple families are only 5 percent of households at any one time, but more than 50 percent of first marriages were preceded by cohabitation (Smock and Gupta 2002).

Some cohabiting relationships seem to be alternatives to marriage rather than a transition to marriage or a temporary living arrangement. "Increasing rates of cohabitation have largely offset decreasing rates of marriage" (Bramlett and Mosher 2001, p. 2). More than 40 percent of heterosexual cohabiting couples lived with children under eighteen in 2003. These might be children of the couple or children from a previous marriage or relationship (Fields 2004).

4. *Some cohabitants maintain gay and lesbian domestic partnerships.* Not all cohabiting couples are heterosexual. Almost 600,000 same-sex couple households were reported to the 2000 census (U.S. Census Bureau 2003a, Table 69). Twenty-two percent of male same-sex partner households and 34 percent of female same-sex households include children (Simmons and O'Connell 2003). (Cohabitation is discussed in more detail in Chapter 8.)

5. *The number of people living alone is substantial.* Single-person households now represent over a quarter of American households (Bergman 2006a). Delayed marriage is a contributing factor, as is the comparatively good health and economic situation of older people (enabling unmarried seniors to choose to live independently). Because of the increased number of people living alone and the smaller number of children per family, the average size of a U.S. household dropped from 3.14 people in 1970 to 2.57 in 2005 (U.S. Census Bureau 2006b, Table AVG1).

6. *Many adult children live with their parents.* Of young adults age eighteen to twenty-four, 56 percent of men and 46 percent of women lived with parents in 2003. The others are more apt to cohabit or to live with roommates than to live alone (or with spouses). In the twenty-five to thirty-four age group, 52 percent live with spouses, but 14 percent of men and 7 percent of women live with parents (Fields 2004).

7. *There are other multigenerational households.* Some 3.7 percent of all households are multigenerational—that is, composed of three generations of family members. These are more likely to be found in areas of new immigration; in areas where there are housing shortages or high costs; and in areas where there are high proportions of unwed mothers who live with their families. The most common form of multigenerational household (65 percent) is that of a grandparent providing a home for an adult child and grandchildren. Some 2 percent of multigenerational households contain four generations (Simmons and O'Neill 2001).

8. *Parenthood is increasingly postponed and fertility has declined.* From a high point

of 3.6 children per woman in 1957, the **total fertility rate** dropped to 1.7 in 1976 (Weeks 2002, p. 238). It then rose and has been around two children per woman for a decade and a half (Martin et al. 2005).[c]

Childlessness has increased in recent decades. Almost twice as many women (19 percent) reached their forties in 2004 without becoming mothers as in 1976. Rates of childlessness seem to be leveling off now, though (Dye 2005).

A more common pattern is delayed childbearing. The twenties are still the most fertile ages for women, but a striking shift toward births in older age groups has occurred since 1990. Births to teens are at historic low levels (Hamilton, Ventura, Martin, and Sutton 2006, Figure 1).

9. *The nonmarital birth rate has begun to increase again after a period of stability.* Births to unmarried mothers were 37 percent of all births in 2005 compared to half that in 1980 and 4 percent in 1950. Keep in mind that almost half of nonmarital births occur to cohabiting couples (Cherlin 2005; Deen 2005; Dye 2005; Hamilton et al. 2006; Hamilton, Martin, and Ventura 2006; Martin et al. 2005).

10. *Divorce rates have stabilized, although they remain at high levels.* The divorce rate, which had risen slowly from the mid-nineteenth century onward, doubled from 1965 to the end of the 1970s. Then it began to drop, falling 30 percent between 1980 and 2004 (Cherlin 2005; U.S. Census Bureau 2006c, Tables 72, 117).

The majority of married adults have married only once, and most of those who divorced are currently remarried. Still, between 40 and 50 percent of recent first marriages are likely to end in divorce (Kreider 2005; Kreider and Fields 2002; Whitehead and Popenoe 2006).[d]

11. *Remarriage rates have declined, but remain high.* Three-quarters of divorced women remarry within ten years. Remarriage rates of men are even higher (Bramlett and Mosher 2001).

12. *The population is aging.* The movement of the large baby boom generation into their senior years has implications for family caregiving. This will be a generation of elderly that had smaller families as well as higher divorce rates than in the past, so fewer involved adult children are available to take responsibility. At the same time, this generation of older Americans has lower levels of disability and poverty and higher levels of education, and many are likely to remain independent longer (Bergman 2006c).

13. *A much higher proportion of older men than older women are married.* Seventy-one percent of men 65 and older are married, compared to 41 percent of women in that age group. Older women are more likely to be widowed (44 percent) than are men (14 percent).

Older Americans are most likely of all age groups to be living alone. Only 7 percent of older men and 17 percent of older women lived with relatives (He et al. 2006, Chapter 6; U.S. Census Bureau 2006c, Table 52).

a. The data we present are drawn from U.S. government reports and from surveys. The release of government data typically lags its collection by one or two years or more. Thus data that may appear out of date may be the latest data available. This is especially true of marriage and divorce data because the Census Bureau ceased collecting such data in the early 1990s. The best available data on marriage and divorce come from 1995, 1996, and 2001 surveys of individuals about their marital history (Bramlett and Mosher 2001; Kreider and Fields 2002; Kreider 2005).

Different government agencies may release data on the same topic, but in slightly different formats. Samples and analytic techniques may vary from year to year and from agency to agency. Thus there may be minor differences in the data you see in one table compared to another on the same general topic.

b. The Census Bureau uses the term *household* for any group of people residing together. Not all households are families by the Census Bureau definition—that is, persons related by blood, marriage, or adoption. Talking about *households* presents a picture of how all people in the United States live. Data on *families*, by definition, do not include those living in nonfamily settings.

Figures will be different depending on whether *household* or *family* is the unit of analysis. For example, single-parent family households were 9 percent of all *households* in 2004, but 13 percent of all *families* (U.S. Census Bureau 2006c, Table 53).

c. The *total fertility rate* for a year is a calculation that represents the number of births that women would have over their reproductive lifetimes if all women at each age had babies at the rate current for each age group. *Replacement level* is the average number of births per woman needed to replace the population.

d. It is difficult to be precise about the likelihood of divorce for those currently married or about to marry because of differences among generations, the absence of detailed statistics, differences in risk between first and later marriages, and the uncertainty of future developments. Divorce rates are discussed in more detail in Chapter 16.

One advertisement portrays a happy gay family, making the statement that this is a home like any other. Advertisers have departed from the safe image of the nuclear family to portray nontraditional family forms, as well as family crises such as divorce, as we see in the other photo. The second photo goes so far as to take a rather lighthearted view of divorce. Advertisers say they are trying to accurately reflect their customers, many of whom do not fit into the nuclear-family tableau often seen in commercials" (Bosman 2006; see also Lauro 2000).

Families are charged with the pivotal tasks of raising children and providing members with ongoing intimacy, affection, and companionship. Family members consider their identity to be significantly attached to the group.

about which groups of people can be considered a family. The Sept. 11th Victim Compensation Fund struggled with this issue in allocating compensation to survivors of September 11 victims. New York State law was amended to permit commission discretion in making awards to both heterosexual and gay partners (Gross 2002), while President Bush signed a federal bill extending benefits to domestic partners of firefighters and police officers who lose their lives in the line of duty (M. Allen 2002).

Some employers as well have sought to redefine *family* in applying their benefits policies. A majority of the Fortune 500 companies now offer domestic partner benefits, as do thirteen state governments, and 201 city and county governments (Human Rights Campaign 2006). Federal practices permit low-income unmarried couples to qualify as families and live in public housing. Some states provide some state-level spousal rights to same-sex couples, while the state of Massachusetts now allows same-sex marriage (Human Rights Campaign 2005). Same-sex marriage is discussed further in Chapter 8.

In defining *family* in cases that come before them, judges who depart from a traditional definition have used the criteria of common residence and economic interdependency, along with the more intangible qualities of stability and commitment (*Dunphy v. Gregor* 1994). From this point of view, the definition of family "should not rest on fictitious legal distinctions or genetic history, but instead should find its foundation in the reality of family life.... [It] is the totality of the relationship as evidenced by the dedication, caring and self-sacrifice of the parties which should, in the final analysis, control" (Judge Vito Titone in *Braschi v. Stahl Associates Company* 1989).

We, the authors, have worked to balance in this text an appreciation for flexibility and diversity in family structure and relations—and for freedom of choice—with the increased concern of many social scientists about what they see as diminished marital and child-rearing commitment. We have adopted a definition of the family that combines elements of some definitions discussed here. "A family is any sexually expressive or parent–child or other kin relationship in which people—usually related by ancestry, marriage, or adoption—(1) form an economic unit and care for any young, (2) consider their identity to be significantly attached to the group, and (3) commit to maintaining that group over time." This definition combines some practical and objective criteria with a more social-psychological sense of family identity.

We hope our definition and the others will stimulate your thoughts and discussion about what a family is. Ultimately, there is no one correct answer to the question "What is a family?" To begin to think more about your own definition of "family," you might want to examine "Issues for Thought: Which of These Is a Family?"

To a significant extent, the diversity that we see in families today is a result, over time, of people's making personal choices about family living. We turn now to a discussion of such choices.

The Freedom and Pressures of Choosing

This text is different from others you may have read. It is not intended specifically to prepare you for a particular occupation. Instead, it has three other goals: (1) to help you understand your past and present family situations and anticipate future possibilities; (2) to help you appreciate the variety and diversity among families today; and (3) to make you more conscious of the personal decisions you must make throughout your life and of the societal influences that affect those decisions.

As families have become less rigidly structured, people have made fewer choices "once and for all." Of course, previous decisions do have consequences, and they represent commitments that limit later choices. Nevertheless, many people reexamine their decisions about family—and face new choices—throughout the course of their lives. Thus choice is an important emphasis of this book.

The best way to make decisions about our personal lives is to make them knowledgeably. It helps to know something about all the alternatives; it also helps to know what kinds of social pressures affect our decisions. As we'll see, people are influenced by the beliefs and values of their society. There are **structural constraints**, economic and social forces, that limit personal choices.

In a very real way, we and our personal decisions and attitudes are products of our environment.

But in just as real a way, people can influence society. Individuals create social change by continually offering new insights to their groups. Sometimes social change occurs because of conversation with others. Sometimes it requires forming social organizations and becoming politically involved. Sometimes it involves many people living their lives according to their values even when these differ from more generally accepted group or cultural norms.

We can apply this view to the phenomenon of living together, or cohabitation. Forty years ago, it was widely accepted that unmarried couples who lived together were immoral. But in the seventies, some college students challenged university restrictions on cohabitation, and subsequently many more people than before—students and nonstudents, young and old—chose to live together. As cohabitation rates increased, societal attitudes became more favorable. Over time, cohabitation has become "mainstream" (Smock and Gupta 2002). Many religions and individuals continue to object to cohabitation outside marriage. Still, it is now easier for people to choose this option. We are influenced by the society around us, but we are also free to influence it. And we do that every time we make a choice.

Personal Troubles and Societal Influences

People's private lives are affected by what is happening in the society around them. In his book *The Sociological Imagination* (2000 [1959]), sociologist C. Wright Mills developed the notion that personal troubles are connected to events and patterns in the larger social world. Many times what seem to be personal troubles are shared by others, and these troubles often reflect societal influences. When a family breadwinner cannot find work, for example, the cause may not lie in his or her lack of ambition but rather in the economy's inability to provide a job. The difficulty of juggling work and family is not usually just a personal question of individual time management skills but of society-wide influences—the totality of time required for employment, commuting, and family care in a society that provides limited support for working families.

This text assumes that people need to understand themselves (and their problems) in the context of the larger society. Individuals' choices depend largely on the alternatives that exist in their social environment and on cultural values and attitudes toward those alternatives. Moreover, if people are to shape the kinds of family living they want, they must not limit their attention to their own marriages and families.

A husband and wife and their off-spring.

A single woman and her three young children.

A fifty-two-year-old woman and her adoptive mother.

A man, his daughter, and the daughter's son.

An eighty-four-year-old widow and her dog, Fido.

A man and all of his ancestors back to Adam and Eve.

The 1979 World Champion Pittsburgh Pirates (theme song: "We Are Family").

Three adult sisters living together.

Two lesbians in an intimate relationship and their children from a previous marriage of one woman and a previous relationship of the other woman with a male friend.

Two children, their divorced parents, the current spouses of their divorced parents, and the children from previous marriages of their stepparents.

A child, his stepfather, and the stepfather's wife subsequent to his divorce from the child's mother.

Two adult male cousins living together.

A seventy-seven-year-old man and his lifelong best friend.

A childless husband and wife who live one thousand miles apart.

A widow and her former husband's grandfather's sister's granddaughter.

A divorced man, his girlfriend, and her child.

Both sets of parents of a deceased married couple.

A married couple, one son and his wife, and the latter couple's children, all living together.

Six adults and their twelve young children, all living together in a communal fashion.

Critical Thinking

Identify which groups you consider to be a family. What is it that makes them "family" or "not family"?

Source: From *Family Theories: An Introduction,* by James K. White and David M. Klein, p. 22. Copyright © 2002 by Sage Publications, Inc. Reprinted by Permission.

Making knowledgeable family decisions increasingly means getting involved in national and local political campaigns. One's role as a family member, as much as one's role as a citizen, has come to require participation in public policy decisions so as to create a desirable context for family life and family choices. Although no social policy can guarantee "ideal" families, such policies may contribute to a good foundation for family life.

Social Influences and Personal Choices

Social factors influence people's personal choices in three ways. First, it is always easier to make the common choice. In the 1950s and early 1960s, when people tended to marry earlier than they do now, it was more difficult for women to remain single after graduation and for men to remain unmarried past their mid-twenties. Now, staying single longer is a more comfortable choice.

A second way that social factors can influence personal choices is by expanding people's options. For example, the availability of effective contraceptives makes limiting one's family size, if desired, easier than in the past and enables deferral of marriage with less risk that a sexual relationship will lead to pregnancy. New forms of reproductive technology provide new options for parenthood.

Third, social factors can also limit people's options. As one example, American society has never offered polyg-amy (more than one spouse) as a legal option. Those who would like to form plural marriages risk prosecution (Janofsky 2001). Until the 1967 *Loving v. Virginia* Supreme Court decision, a number of states prohibited racial intermarriage. Presently the possibility of same-sex marriage is being contested in the courts, with only the state of Massachusetts offering it (as we go to press). More broadly, economic changes of the last thirty years, which make well-paid employment more problematic and higher education more essential, have influenced individual choices to delay marriage (Sassler and Gold-scheider 2004).

Making Choices

All people make choices, even when they are not aware of it. Let's look more closely at two forms of decision making—choosing by default and choosing knowledgeably—along with the consequences of each. One effect of taking a course in marriage and the family may be to make you more aware of when choices are available and how a decision may be related to subsequent options and choices.

Choosing by Default

Unconscious decisions are called **choosing by default**. Choices made by default are ones that people make

Extended education, delayed marriage, and high housing costs, among other financial pressures, have made it more common for young adults to continue to live with their parents or to move back home. There is less of a "generation gap" between parents and children today—they seem to enjoy each other's company.

1.2, "The Cycle of Knowledgeable Decision Making," maps this process. You may want to look back at this figure as you go through the course and think about the decisions to be made at various life stages.

Choosing Knowledgeably

Today, society offers many options. People can stay single, cohabit, or marry. They can form communal living groups or family-like ties with others. They can decide to divorce or to stay married. Couples or individuals can have children biologically, with the aid of reproductive technology, or through adoption. They can parent stepchildren or foster children. One important component of **choosing knowledgeably** is recognizing as many options or alternatives as possible. This text is designed in part to help you do that.

A second component in making knowledgeable choices is recognizing the social pressures that may influence personal choices. Some of these pressures are economic, whereas others relate to cultural norms that are often taken for granted. Sometimes people decide that they agree with socially accepted or prescribed behavior. They concur in the teachings of their religion, for example. Other times people decide that they strongly disagree with socially prescribed beliefs, values, and standards. Whether they agree with such standards or not, once people recognize the force of social pressures, they can choose whether or not to act in accordance with them.

An important aspect of making knowledgeable choices is considering the consequences of each alternative rather than just gravitating toward the one that initially seemed most attractive. For example, a couple deciding whether to move so that one partner can be promoted or take a new job may want to list the consequences. In the positive column, one partner may have a higher position and earn more money, and the region to which the couple would move may have a nicer climate. In the negative column, the other partner may have to disrupt his or her career, and both may have to leave relatives. Listing positive and negative consequences of alternatives—either mentally or on paper—helps one see the larger picture and thus make a more knowledgeable decision.

Part of this process requires becoming aware of your values and choosing to act consistently with them. Contradictory sets of values exist in American society. For example, standards regarding nonmarital sex range from

when they are not aware of all the alternatives or when they pursue the proverbial path of least resistance. If you're taking this class, for example, but you're unaware that a class in modern dance (which you would have preferred) is meeting at the same time, you have chosen not to take the class in modern dance. But you have done so by default because you didn't find out about all the alternatives before you registered.

Another kind of decision by default occurs when people pursue a course of action primarily because it seems the easiest thing to do. Sometimes, college students choose their courses or even their majors by default. They try to register only to find that the classes they had planned to take are closed. So they register for something they hadn't planned on, do well enough, and continue in that program of study.

Many decisions concerning marriages and families are also made by default. For example, spouses may focus on career success to the neglect of their relationship simply because this is what society expects of them. Strong day-to-day pressures on the job may erode family time. The goal of spending more time with the family is on the horizon but is never reached because it is not consciously planned for.

Although most of us have made at least some decisions by default, almost everyone can recall having the opposite experience: choosing knowledgeably. Figure

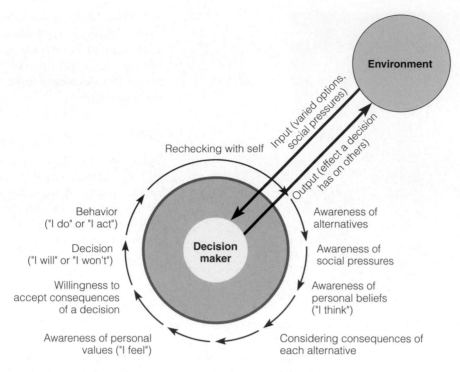

FIGURE 1.2 The cycle of knowledgeable decision making.

Source: Adapted from *Shifting Gears,* by Nena O'Neill and George O'Neill, p. 167, 1974. Copyright © 1974 by Nena O'Neill and George O'Neill. Reprinted by permission of the publisher, M. Evans and Company, New York, NY.

abstinence to sex in committed relationships to sex for recreation only. Contradictory values can cause people to feel ambivalent about what they want for themselves.

Clarifying one's values involves cutting through this ambivalence in order to decide which of several standards, for example, are more strongly valued. It is important to respect the so-called gut factor—the emotional dimension of decision making. Besides rationally considering alternatives, people have subjective (often almost visceral) feelings about what feels right or wrong, good or bad. Respecting one's feelings is an important part of making the right decision. Following one's feelings can mean grounding one's decisions in a religious or spiritual tradition or in one's cultural heritage, for these have a great deal of emotional power and often represent deep commitments.

Another important component of decision making is rechecking. Once a choice is made and a person acts on it, the process is not necessarily complete. As Figure 1.2 suggests, people constantly recheck their decisions throughout the entire decision-making cycle, testing these decisions against their experiences and against any changes in the social environment.

Underlying this discussion is the assumption that individuals cannot have everything. Every time people make an important decision or commitment, they rule out alternatives—for the time being, and perhaps permanently. People cannot simultaneously have the relative freedom of a child-free union and the gratification that often accompanies parenthood.

In some respects, though, people can focus on some goals and values during one part of their lives, then turn their attention to different ones at other times. Four decades ago, we used to think of adults as people who entered adulthood in their early twenties, found work, married, had children, and continued on the same track until the end of the life course. That view has changed. Today we view adulthood as a time with potential for continued personal development, growth, and change.

In a family setting, development and change involve more than one individual. Multiple life courses must be coordinated, and if one member changes, that affects the values and choices of other members of the family. Moreover, life in American families reflects a tension in American culture between family solidarity and individual freedom.

A Family of Individuals

Americans place a high value on the family. Ninety-one percent of Americans report that family relations are extremely important to them (Bogenschneider 2000, p. 1138).

Midlife changes can be both exhilarating and intimidating, as these college students have probably found. Certainly the decision of a middle-aged adult to earn a college degree involves many emotional and practical changes. But by making knowledgeable choices—by weighing alternatives, considering consequences, clarifying values and goals, and continually rechecking—personal decisions and changes can be both positive and dynamic.

Meanwhile, expressing our *individuality* within the context of a *family* requires us to negotiate innumerable day-to-day issues. How much privacy can each person have at home? What things and places in the family dwelling belong just to one particular individual? What family activities should be scheduled, how often, and when? What outside friendships and activities can a family member sustain?

Familistic (Communal) Values and Individualistic (Self-Fulfillment) Values

Familistic values such as family togetherness, stability, and loyalty focus on the family as a whole. They are *communal* values; that is, they emphasize the needs, goals, and identity of the group. Many of us have an image of the ideal family in which members spend considerable time together, enjoying one another's company. For many of us, the family is a major source of stability. We tend to believe that the family is the group most deserving our loyalty. Those of us who marry vow publicly to stay with our partners as long as we live. We expect our partners, parents, children, and even our more distant relatives to remain loyal to the family unit.

But just as family values permeate American society, so do **individualistic (self-fulfillment) values**. These American values encourage people to think in terms of personal happiness and goals and the development of a distinct individual identity. An individualistic orientation gives more weight to the expression of individual preferences and the maximization of individual talents and options.

American society has never had a remarkably strong tradition of *familism*, the virtual sacrifice of individual family members' needs and goals for the sake of the **extended family** (the larger kin group) (Sirjamaki 1948; Lugo Steidel and Contreras 2003). Our national cultural heritage prizes individuality, individual rights, and personal freedom. But on the other hand, an overly individualistic orientation could put stress on family relationships if there is little emphasis on contributing to other family members' happiness or postponing personal satisfactions in order to attain family goals.

Families as a Place to Belong

Whether families are conventional nuclear families or newer in form, they create a place to belong, serving as a repository or archive of family memories and traditions. They provide a setting for the development of identity, both a family identity and an individual self-concept.

Whatever the future course of an individual's adult life, familial experiences and relationships are likely to have a profound influence on identity. Parents, especially, and siblings and other relatives are usually the most influential or significant figures in a young child's life. The responses of those other people channel the development of the child's **self-concept,** an individual's idea about his or her worth and about what sort of person she or he is). A child who is loved comes to think he or she is a valuable and loving person. A child who is given some tasks and encouraged to do things comes to think of him- or herself as competent.

Family identities and traditions emerge through interaction within the family and the creation of rituals—family dinnertime, birthday and holiday celebrations, vacation trips or homes, and hobbies, such as working together in a garden each summer. Family identity typically includes the cultural heritage of the family. All the children in one family may be given Irish or Hispanic names, for example.

"Family Decline" or "Family Change"?

As students interested in the family, you are no doubt aware of the current debate about the state of the family. Family change has become the stuff of talk radio, academic analysis, and political debate. Critics have described it as "family breakdown." "Many argue that family life has been seriously degraded by the movement away from marriage and traditional gender roles. Others view family life as amazingly diverse, resilient, and adaptive to new circumstances" (Bianchi and Casper 2000, p. 3).

The tension between familistic and individualistic values is an issue in current debate on the family. The pull of both **familistic (communal) values** and *individualistic values* creates in society and in ourselves a tension that we must resolve. "It is within the family . . . that the paradox of continuity and change, the problem of balancing individuality and allegiance, is most immediate" (Bengston, Biblarz, and Roberts 2007, p. 323).

Families are composed of individuals, each seeking self-fulfillment and a unique identity, but they also offer a place to learn and express togetherness, stability, and loyalty. Families also perform a special archival function: Events, rituals, and histories are created and preserved, and, in turn, become intrinsic parts of each individual. These sisters are sharing memories recorded in family photos.

Sociologist John Sirjamaki (1948), writing in the optimistic and stable post–World War II era, concluded that the emotional attachment of spouses would ensure family stability. Some contemporary family advocates are not so sure: Scholars and advocates with a **"family decline" perspective** (e.g., Whitehead and Popenoe 2006) point to what they see as a cultural change toward excessive individualism that they characterize as the self-indulgence of the baby boom generation. Barbara Dafoe Whitehead writes: "Beginning in the late 1950's, Americans began to change their ideas about the individual's obligations to family and society. . . . [T]his change was away from an ethic of obligation to others and toward an obligation to self" (1997, p. 4). There is concern that the pursuit of self-realization underlies the increase in divorce and unmarried parenthood and has undermined responsible parenting" (Whitehead and Popenoe 2006).

The debate over the family is grounded in data about family change since 1960: Marriage age rose, and the proportion of the adult population married declined; cohabitation increased; single-mother families increased; and child poverty increased, creating concern about the care and socialization of children as well as the best interests of adults. Combined with increased longevity and lower fertility rates, these changes have meant that a smaller portion of adulthood is spent in marriage and/or child rearing (Brooks 2002; Cherlin 2005; McLanahan, Donahue, and Haskins 2005; Whitehead and Popenoe 2006). Moreover, fewer family households contain children (see "Facts about Families: Focus on Children"). According to the "family decline" perspective, this situation "has reduced the childcenteredness of our nation and contributed to the weakening of the institution of marriage" (Popenoe and Whitehead 2005, p. 23). ("Facts about Families: Focus on Children" provides some statistical indicators of the family setting of today's children).

Not every family expert concurs that the family is in decline: **"family change,"** yes, but not "decline." Historically speaking, family change is seen as normal: "Marriage has been in a constant state of evolution since the

Facts about Families

Focus on Children

Perhaps the greatest concern Americans have about contemporary family change is its impact on children. What do these family data tell us about the family lives of children today?

1. *There are now fewer children (and more elderly).* Children under eighteen composed 25 percent of the U.S. population in 2005, a substantial drop from 1964, when 36 percent of the population were children (U.S. Census Bureau 2007a, Table 4; U.S. Federal Interagency Forum on Child and Family Statistics 2006, p. 4; and see Figure 1.3). Fewer than half of all *married-couple households* contained children in 2005, and only 47 percent of all *family households* (U.S. Census Bureau 2006a). Today—as a consequence of later marriage, lower fertility, and a longer lifespan—a smaller part of Americans' adult lives are spent raising children (Whitehead and Popenoe 2006).

2. *A majority of children live in two-parent households.* "Two married parents are the norm" (R. Bernstein 2003). After an earlier decline, the percentage of children living with two married parents has been essentially stable for the last ten years. In 2005, 67 percent of children under eighteen lived with two married parents.

   Twenty-eight percent of children lived with only one of their parents (23 percent with mother; 5 percent with father), and the other 4 percent did not live with either parent (U.S. Federal Interagency Forum 2006, p. 4).

   Of those not living with any parent, the largest group of children (44 percent) was cared for by grandparents, 33 percent by other relatives, while the rest were in foster care or other nonfamily arrangements (U.S. Federal Interagency Forum 2005, pp. 8–9).

3. *Over the last five years, the proportion of children living in single-parent families has stabilized.* Single-parent households grew rapidly in the first half of the 1990s. Since then the percentage of children in single-parent households has declined slightly. There are four times as many single-mother households as single-father households (U.S. Federal Interagency Forum 2005, p. 8, Figure POP6-A).

   The census category "single-parent family household" obscures the fact that there may be other adults present in that household, such as grandparents. It is also the case that some households defined by the Census Bureau as single-parent households are actually two-parent households. In 18 percent of "single-father" households and 11 percent of "single-mother" households there is a cohabiting partner (U.S. Federal Interagency Forum 2005, p. 9). The Census Bureau assumes that such a partner functions as a second parent (Fields 2003, pp. 4–5).

4. *There is considerable variation in children's living arrangements.* A 2001 study on the living arrangements of children in two-parent households found 88 percent of children living with their biological parents (3 percent unmarried), 6 percent with biological mother and stepfather, 1 percent with biological father and stepmother, 1 percent with adoptive mother and father, 1 percent with adoptive father and biological mother, and smaller numbers with an adoptive mother and biological father or an adoptive parent and a stepparent (Kreider and Fields 2005, Table 1).

   A snapshot taken at one time understates family instability. A child

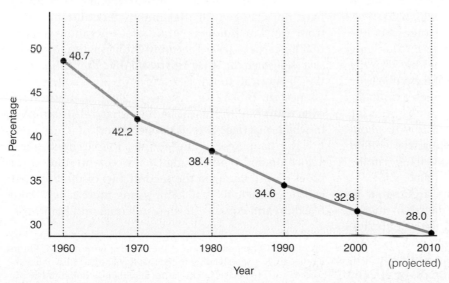

FIGURE 1.3 Percentage of households with a child or children under age 18, 1960–2010, United States.

Source: David Popenoe and Barbara Dafoe Whitehead. 2005. *The State of Our Unions 2005.* Piscataway, NJ: National Marriage Project, Rutgers, p. 23. Copyright © 2005 David Popenoe and Barbara Dafoe Whitehead. All rights reserved. Reprinted by permission.

continues

continued

may live in an intact two-parent family, a single-parent household, with a cohabiting parent, and in a remarried family in sequence (Raley and Wildsmith 2004). More than half of American children are expected to live in a single-parent household at some point in their lives. On average, a child can expect to spend 3 years in a single-parent household, 1.5 years with a cohabiting parent, and 11.5 years with married parents (perhaps including a stepparent (Bumpass and Lu 2000).

5. *Children are more likely to live with a grandparent today than in the recent past.* In 1970, 3 percent of children lived in a household containing a grandparent, but by 2001 that rate had more than doubled, to 9 percent. In about a quarter of the cases, grandparents had sole responsibility for raising the child, but many households containing grandparents are *extended family* households that include other relatives as well (Kreider and Fields 2005, Tables 7, 8, 10).

6. *Most parents are working parents.* Almost two-thirds of children in married-couple households have two working parents. Children in single-parent households are even more likely to be living with employed parents (U.S. Bureau of Labor Statistics 2006a, Table 4).

7. *Children are more likely than the general population or the elderly to be living in poverty.* In 2005, the poverty rate of children stood at 17.6 percent, whereas that of the general adult population was 11.1 percent and that of the elderly 10.1 percent. The child poverty rate is lower now than its peak of 22.3 percent in 1983, but higher than in 1970 (DeNavas-Walt, Proctor, and Lee 2006). We will discuss the economic circumstances of families further in Chapters 3 and 12.

---

dawn of the Stone Age," declares historian Stephanie Coontz (2005a, p. A-17). "Marriage has . . . [now] become more flexible, but also more optional" (Coontz 2005a, p. A-17), with new options of cohabitation or a satisfying and respected single life, "'But although the institution of marriage is undergoing a powerful revolution, there is no marriage crisis'" ("Speaker Says . . ." 2006, p. 5).

For those concerned about family change over the past several decades, there may be some encouraging signs. The divorce rate has declined somewhat over the last twenty-five years. The rate of nonmarital childbearing has leveled off somewhat, and there has been a dramatic decline in teen birth rates. As demographers Suzanne Bianchi and Lynne Casper observe: "Our rhetoric about the dramatically changing family may be a step behind reality. Recent trends suggest a quieting of changes in the family, or at least of the pace of change" (2000, p. 3).

Generally, "family change" scholars argue that in many ways families are better off today than in the past. In the nineteenth or early twentieth centuries, families were more apt to live in extreme poverty. Families were often broken up by illness and death, and children sent to orphanages, foster homes, or already burdened relatives.[2] Single mothers, as well as wives in lower-class, working-class, and immigrant families, were not home with children, but went out to labor in factories, workshops, or domestic service. Nonmarital pregnancy rates were higher in the 1950s than they are today (Coontz 1992; Yorburg 2002). The proportion of children living with father only in 1990 wasn't much different from that of a century ago (Kreider and Fields 2005, p. 12).

Some scholars and policy makers argue further that broad cultural values of individualism and collectivism have not changed all that much. For instance, data from the Longitudinal Study of Generations suggest that an earlier upward trend in individualism may have reversed since the early 1970s and that after this period, the "historical trend is toward greater collectivism" (Bengston, Biblarz, and Roberts 2002, p. 119). Moreover, many Americans would not wish to return to an era in which marriage served property and practical ends, not the happiness of the couple. Researchers Arland Thornton and Linda Young-DeMarco, who studied attitudes toward family in the second part of the twentieth century, conclude that "Americans increasingly value freedom and equality in their personal and family lives

---

[2] A relative (Raymond) of one of the authors, born in 1904, lost his mother at age seven. Relatives urged that Raymond and his siblings be placed in an orphanage, but his father kept them at home and eventually remarried. The father died when Raymond was fifteen. Raymond continued to live with his stepmother, who was a most caring and supportive figure, but she soon died as well. He then lived with a series of older siblings, who pressured him to drop out of high school. Raymond persisted in working to support his continued education and eventually became a physician (Ritter 1990).

while at the same time maintaining their commitment to the ideas of marriage, family, and children" (2001, p. 1031).

Scholars and policy makers with a "family change" perspective do not ignore the difficulties which divorce and nonmarital parenthood present to families and children. But they view the family as "an adaptable institution" (Amato et al. 2003, p. 21) and argue that it makes more sense to provide support to families as they exist today rather than to attempt to turn back the clock to an idealized past. They attribute family change as much to *economic* trends and changes as to *cultural* change.

They point to the structural forces that have affected decisions to marry and created stress on family life: the decline in manufacturing jobs that used to provide solid support for working-class families, the insecurity of even middle class jobs and the inability of income to keep pace with inflation, the related need for more education, and the entry of women into the labor force. These economic trends have shaped marital timing, fertility rates, and the willingness and ability of lower-income individuals especially to enter into a marriage (Cherlin 2005; Edin and Kefalas 2005; McLanahan, Donahue, and Haskins 2005). "Accompanying . . . the economic changes was a broad cultural shift among Americans that eroded norms both of marriage before childbearing and of stable lifelong bonds after marriage" (Cherlin 2005, p. 46).

Moreover, families are struggling with new economic and time pressures that affect their ability to realize their family values. "Family change" scholars "believe that at least part of the increase in divorce, living together, and single parenting has less to do with changing values than with inadequate support for families in the U.S., especially compared to other advanced industrial countries" (Yorburg 2002, p. 33). Many European countries, for example, have family leave policies that enable parents to take time off from work to be with young children and that provide more generous economic support for families in crisis.

This debate about the family is explored further in Chapter 7. As scholars, family advocates, and the public continue "this crucial national conversation among Americans struggling to interpret and make sense of the

George and Gaynel Couran were married in 1916. "That was the girl for me. I got the woman I wanted," said George at the couple's eightieth wedding anniversary. Judging by her expression, Gaynel undoubtedly got the man she wanted. The Courans learned to balance individualism and familism over the course of their marriage.

place of marriage and family in today's society" (Nock 2005, p. 13), we ask: What does this mean at the ground level of married couples (and other partners)?

Partners as Individuals and Family Members

The changing shape of the family has meant that family lives have become less predictable than at the midtwentieth century. The course of family living results in large part from the decisions and choices two adults make, moving in their own ways and at their own paces through their lives. Assuming that partners' respective beliefs, values, and behaviors mesh fairly well at the point of marriage, any change in either spouse is likely to adversely affect the fit.

One consequence of ongoing adult developmental change in two individuals is that the marriage may be at risk. If one or both change considerably over time, they may grow apart instead of together. A challenge for contemporary relationships is to integrate divergent personal change into the relationship while nurturing any children involved.

How can partners make it through such changes and still stay together? Two guidelines may be helpful. The first is for people to take responsibility for their own past choices and decisions rather than blaming previous "mistakes" on their mates. The second is for individuals to be aware that married life is far more complex than the traditional image commonly portrayed.

It helps to recognize that a changing spouse may be difficult to live with for a while. A relationship needs to be flexible enough to allow for each partner's individual changes—to allow family members some degree of freedom.

At the same time, we must remind ourselves of the benefits of family living and the commitment necessary to sustain it. Individual happiness and family commitment are not inevitably in conflict; research shows that a supportive marriage has a significant positive impact on individual well-being (Waite and Gallagher 2000). We will continue to explore the tension between individualistic and familistic values throughout this text.

Marriages and Families: Four Themes

In this chapter we have defined the term *family* and discussed decision making and diversity in the context of family living. We can now state explicitly the four themes of this text.

1. Personal decisions must be made throughout the life course. Decision making is a trade-off; once we choose an option, we discard alternatives. No one can have everything. Thus, the best way to make choices is knowledgeably.

2. People are influenced by the society around them. Cultural beliefs and values influence our attitudes and decisions. Societal or structural conditions can limit or expand our options.

3. We live in a society characterized by considerable change, including increased ethnic, economic, and family diversity; by tension between familistic and individualistic values; by decreased marital and family permanence; and by increased political and policy attention to the needs of children and families. This dynamic situation can make personal decision making more challenging than in the past and more important.

4. Personal decision making feeds into society and changes it. We affect our social environment every time we make a choice. Making family decisions can also mean choosing to become politically involved in order to effect family-related social change. Making

family choices consciously, according to our values, gives our family lives greater integrity.

Summary

- This chapter introduced the subject matter for this course and presented the four themes that this text develops. The chapter began by addressing the challenge of defining the term *family*.

- In "Facts about Families: American Families Today" and "Facts about Families: Focus on Children," we pointed to statistical evidence that we live in a changing society. Family diversity has progressed to the point that there is no typical family form today.

- Marriages and families are composed of separate, unique individuals. Our culture values both families and individuals.

- Families fill the important function of providing members a place to belong and grounding identity development. Finding personal freedom within families is an ongoing, negotiated process.

- Whether we are in an era of "family decline" or "family change" is a matter of debate.

- People make choices, either actively and knowledgeably or by default, that determine the courses of their lives. People must make choices and decisions throughout their life course. Those choices and decisions are limited by social structure and at the same time are causes for change in that structure.

- It is now widely recognized that change and development continue throughout adult life. Because adults change, marriages and families are not static: Every time one individual in a relationship changes, the relationship changes, however subtly. Throughout this text we will discuss some creative ways in which partners can alter their relationship in order to meet their changing needs.

- We continue our examination of the family in Chapter 2, "Exploring the Family," and in Chapter 3, which discusses the social context in which families make choices. Within a socially diverse society such as ours, many individuals are part of a racial/ethnic or religious community or social class that has a distinct family heritage.

Questions for Review and Reflection

1. Without looking to find ours, write your definition of *family*. Now compare yours to ours. How are the two similar? How are they different? Does your definition have some advantages over ours?

2. What important changes in family patterns do you see today? Do you see positive changes, negative changes, or both? What do they mean for families, in your opinion?

3. What are some examples of a personal or family problem that is at least partly a result of problems in the society?

4. Do you want your family life to be similar to or different from that of your parents? In what ways?

5. **Policy Question.** Are there changes in law and social policy that you would like to see put in place to enhance family life?

Key Terms

choosing by default 10
choosing knowledgeably 11
extended family 13
familistic (communal) values 14
family 2
"family change" perspective 14
"family decline" perspective 14
household 3

individualistic (self-fulfillment) values 13
nuclear family 3
primary group 2
secondary group 2
self-concept 13
structural constraints 9
total fertility rate 7

Online Resources

Companion Website for This Book

www.thomsonedu.com/sociology/lamanna

Visit the book companion website, where you will find flash cards, practice quizzes, Internet links, suggested readings, InfoTrac College Edition exercises, and more to help you study.

ThomsonNOW™ for Marriage and Family

Spend time on what you need to master rather than on information you already have learned. Take a pre-test for this chapter, and ThomsonNOW will generate a personalized study plan based on your results. The study plan will identify the topics you need to review and direct you to online resources such as videos, narrated learning modules, and interactive activities to help you master those topics. You can then take a post-test to help you determine the concepts you have mastered and what you will still need to work on. Try it out! Go to **www.thomsonedu.com/login** to sign in with an access code or to purchase access to this product.

Exploring the Family

Theoretical Perspectives on the Family

The Family Ecology Perspective

Issues for Thought: Safety and Risk in the Family Environment

The Family Development Perspective

The Structure–Functional Perspective

The Interactionist Perspective

Exchange Theory

Family Systems Theory

Conflict and Feminist Perspectives

The Biosocial Perspective

Studying Families

The Blinders of Personal Experience

Scientific Investigation: Removing Blinders

The Ethics of Research on Families

Methods of Data Collection

When we begin a course on the family, we are eager to have our questions answered:

- "What's a good family?"
- "How do I make that happen?"
- "Whom should I choose?"
- "What do I need to know to be a good parent?"
- "What's happening to the family today?"

In Chapter 1 we outlined some trends in family life, changes you may be aware of from observing life around you or through the media. What these changes mean—how to interpret them—is not always easy. There are many visions of the family, and what an observer reads into the data depends partly on his or her perspective.

From politicians we hear about family trends with words such as *conservative* or *liberal* attached. But in forming their interpretations, social scientists often use the formal vocabulary of social theory and research methodology to characterize marriage and family patterns.

This chapter invites you to share this way of seeing families. First, we look at some theoretical perspectives that shape our thinking about families. Then we consider the knotty problem of studying a phenomenon as close to our hearts as family life.

Theoretical Perspectives on the Family

Theoretical perspectives are ways of viewing reality. As a tool of analysis they are the equivalent of lenses through which observers view, organize, and then interpret what they see. A theoretical perspective leads researchers to identify those aspects of families that are of interest to them. It suggests explanations for why family patterns and practices are the way they are.

There are a number of different theoretical perspectives on the family. Sometimes, the perspectives complement one another and may appear together in a single piece of research. In other instances, the perspectives seem contradictory, leading scholars and policy makers into a heated debate. This may frustrate students who hope to find the one "correct" answer.

Instead it is useful to think of each theoretical perspective as a point of view on the family. As with a physical object such as a building, when we see a family from different angles, we have a better grasp of what it is than if we look at it from a single, fixed position.

In this chapter, we describe eight theoretical perspectives: (1) family ecology, (2) family development,

(3) structure–functionalism, (4) the interactionist perspective, (5) exchange theory, (6) family systems theory, (7) conflict and feminist perspectives, and (8) biosocial perspectives. We will see that each perspective not only illuminates our understanding in its own way but also has emerged in its own social and historical context. Table 2.1, "Theoretical Perspectives on the Family," presents a summary of these theoretical perspectives.

The Family Ecology Perspective

The **family ecology perspective** explores how a family influences and is influenced by the surrounding environment. We use the family ecology perspective throughout this book when we stress that society does not determine family members' behavior but does present limitations and constraints for families, as well as possibilities and opportunities. Families' lives and choices are affected by economic, educational, religious, and cultural institutions, for example, and by historical circumstances such as the depression, World War II, and the present threat of terrorism.

Every family is embedded in "a set of nested structures, each inside the next, like a set of Russian dolls" (Bronfenbrenner 1979, p. 3). At the foundation is the *natural physical–biological environment*—climate, soil, plants, animals, and so forth. The *human-built environment* develops when nature is altered by human action. As human settlement occurs, for example, roads and houses are built. Agriculture and industrial development affect the natural environment. The *social–cultural environment* is entirely a human creation and consists of cultural values, cultural products like language and law, and social and economic systems. All parts of the model are interrelated and influence one another (Bubolz and Sontag 1993; and see Figure 2.1).

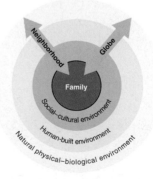

FIGURE 2.1   The family ecology perspective. The family is embedded in natural physical–biological, human-built, and social–cultural environments.

Source: Adapted with permission from "Human Ecology Theory," pp. 419–48 in *Sourcebook of Family Theories and Methods,* ed. by Pauline G. Boss et al. Copyright © 1993, Springer-Verlag.

Table 2.1 Theoretical Perspectives on the Family

Theoretical Perspective	Theme	Key Concepts	Current Research
Family Ecology	The ecological context of the family affects family life and children's outcomes.	Natural physical–biological environment; Human-built environment; Social–cultural environment.	Family policy; Neighborhood effects
Family Development	Families experience predictable changes over time.	Family life cycle; Developmental tasks; "On-time" transitions; Role-sequencing	Emerging adulthood; Timing of employment, marriage and parenthood
Structure–Functional	The family performs essential functions for society.	Social institution; Family structure; Family functions; Extended family; Nuclear family	Cross-cultural and historical comparisons; Critique of contemporary family
Interactionist	The internal dynamics of a group of interacting individuals construct the family.	Interaction; Self-concept; Identity; Meaning; Roles; Role-taking; Internalization; Role-making	Meaning assigned to domestic work
Exchange Theory	The resources that individuals bring to a relationship or family affect formation, continuation, nature, and power dynamics of a relationship.	Resources; Rewards and costs; Family power and decision making; Exchange balance	Family power; Entry and exit from marriage; Family violence
Systems Theory	The family as a whole is more than the sum of its parts.	System; Equilibrium; Boundaries; Family therapy	Family efficacy and crisis management; Family boundaries
Conflict	Social and economic relations are not equally beneficial to the parties; conflict and exploitation characterize relations of inequality.	Inequality; Power; Class	Effect on families of economic inequality in the U.S.; Racial/ethnic and immigration status variations; Effect on families of the changing global economy
Feminist	Gender is central to the analysis of the family; male dominance in society and in the family is oppressive of women.	Male dominance; Power and inequality	Work and family; Family power; Domestic violence; Advocacy of women's issues
Biosocial	Evolution of the human species has put in place certain biological endowments that shape and limit family choices.	Evolutionary heritage; Genes, hormones, and brain processes; Inclusive fitness	Connections between biological markers and family behavior; Evolutionary heritage explanations for gender differences, sexuality and reproduction, and parenting behavior; Development of research methods that can explore the respective influences of "nature" and "nurture"

The ecology of families may be analyzed at various levels, from the neighborhood to the global. Increasing *globalization*, for example, means that job opportunities for American family members are affected by the decisions of multinational corporations. The September 11 terrorist attacks on the United States and the subsequent Afghan and Iraq wars are part of a global conflict that has affected American family life in countless ways.

The family ecology perspective emerged in the latter part of the nineteenth century, a period marked by concern about the welfare and stability of families. After losing ground to other theories, the family ecology model resurfaced in the 1960s with the War on Poverty, a program directed toward the elimination of the high levels of poverty that then existed. The family ecology model continues to be prominent in research and in political discussion and debate (Booth and Crouter 2001; Bubolz and Sontag 1993).

Today's family ecologists stress the interdependence of all the world's families—not only with one another but also with our fragile physical–biological environment. In this vein, the Family Energy Project at Michigan State University has studied families' energy usage (Bubolz and Sontag 1993). Although it is crucial, the interaction of families with the physical–biological environment is beyond the scope of this text. Our interest centers on families in their sociocultural environments.

Family ecology theory tells us to look at the environment surrounding the family. What is that environment like in terms of actual risk and perception of risk? The September 11 terrorist attacks, high-profile kidnappings and school killings, and natural disasters such as Hurricane Katrina certainly inspire worry. However, some social scientists speculate that fear may have outstripped the reality of risk. Historian Peter Stearns argues that Americans have become "anxious parents." Smaller families, which enhance the preciousness and perceived vulnerability of each child; urbanization and its mythic dangers; and increased media portrayal of danger have led to a general "culture of fear" (Glassner 1999) that makes "anxiety about children . . . a central matter in twentieth-century American culture" (Fass 2003a; Stearns 2003).

In his book *The Culture of Fear*, sociologist Barry Glassner demythologizes some common fears. According to Glassner and others, many threats have either declined or have been misrepresented as rising. These include kidnapping by a stranger, teen suicide, day-care abuse of children, teen births, adolescent drug use, in-school violence, and other juvenile violent crime (Glassner 1999; Leinwand 2002; U.S. Federal Interagency

Forum 2006, Indicator BEH3). School crime rates declined between 1992 and 2004 ("Serious Violent Crime at School" 2006). Sexual assaults against youth age twelve to seventeen fell 79 percent from 1993 to 2003 (Crimes Against Children Research Center 2005; Koch 2005). Plus, childhood accidents have been reduced by safety protections, such as car seats and bicycle helmets, that previous generations did not have (Moretti 2002).

What about the reality of risk in high-crime areas? Parents often keep their children inside, away from danger, likely a necessary strategy, but one that is problematic in terms of child development (Fox 2000; Marriott 1995). In fact, parents in high-crime areas often try other means before resorting to this kind of restriction. In one study of parenting in Philadelphia, parents turned to keeping children at home only when communal efforts such as group overtures for more police attention failed (Furstenberg et al. 1999). Parents also employ "neighborhood survival tactics" such as setting rules, evaluating peers, checking in via cell phones and pagers, encouraging children to bring friends home, and involving children in activities to keep them off the street and away from questionable peers (Kurz 2002; Letiecq and Koblinsky 2001, 2004).

It is important to consider that extended deep poverty may pose as great a risk to children's well-being as do street dangers (Elder et al. 1995). In fact, poverty and violence go together, and "children living in poor neighborhoods are disproportionately exposed to high levels of community violence . . . as a routine feature of the child's social ecology" (Fox 2000, p. 166).

In ecological settings with fewer obvious dangers, one must consider what an overly strong parental response to risk communicates to children. If parental surveillance is constant, warnings are frequent, and children are unreasonably restricted to the home, how can they *not* develop a high anxiety about living in the everyday world? On the other hand, the awareness of certain dangers, though often exaggerated, has led to worthwhile programs and parental conversations that inoculate children against being taken advantage of by predators.

Of course, we can never completely shield children from global terrorism, war, local dangers, or natural disasters. Plus, it is appropriate for children to have fears about parents and relatives serving in the military in such dangerous and volatile areas as Afghanistan and Iraq. A *realistic* analysis of risk, collecting

An exploration of the ecological setting of the family may identify important factors in community support for families. The relationship of work to family life, discussed in Chapter 12, is another ecological focus. So is the impact of incarceration on families, as rates of imprisonment increase. (See "When a Parent Is in Prison" in Chapter 15.) Part of the ecology of the family today is the perception of risk in local or global settings. (See "Issues for Thought: Safety and Risk in the Family Environment.")

Other topics of recent interest to family ecologists are *family policy* and the effectiveness of *neighborhoods*.

Family Policy In a narrow sense, **family policy** is all the procedures, regulations, attitudes, and goals of govern-

ment that affect families. More generally, family policy concerns itself with the circumstances in the broader society that affect the family. American families worry about making ends meet: how we will support ourselves, find comfortable housing, educate our children, get affordable health care, finance our old age. Poverty is a real problem for many U.S. families, and research suggests that deep poverty in early childhood affects outcomes for children (Duncan and Brooks-Gunn 2002; Wagmiller et al. 2006). Family ecologists might point out that the United States provides fewer services to families than does any other industrialized nation, while Western Europe offers many examples of a successful partnership between government and families in the interests of family support.

information on strategies appropriate in dangerous neighborhoods—or safer ones (J. Brody 2003b), a plan for talking with children about protection from salient risks, and a "check it out" attitude toward scary media stories would seem to be a good parental approach.

The government disaster preparedness agency, FEMA (Federal Emergency Management Agency), offers a website addressed to children (www.fema.gov/kids) that includes "National Security Emergencies." FEMA has added a new website program called "Ready Kids" (www.ready.gov/kids). The Department of Defense operates a support program for children (Hagan 2005), and the American Academy of Pediatrics has developed a guide for pediatricians (www.aap.org/terrorism/index.html). The National Child Traumatic Stress Network, sponsored by UCLA and Duke University, is another good resource (www.nctsnet.org). Also, child development specialist Judith Myers-Walls has expanded her discussion of "Talking to Children about Terrorism and Armed Conflict" (2002) to include advice on "Children as Victims of Hurricane Katrina" and "Talking with Children When the Talking Gets Tough" (2005a, b, 2007; see References for Myers-Walls' web addresses).

© Syracuse Newspapers/Logan Wallace/The Image Works

Police and civilian defense officials work with schoolchildren to enable them to feel confident that they have a course of action to follow in the event of a family or community emergency. The designation of a meeting point for family members is an important part of emergency planning.

Critical Thinking

What risks to children do you see in family environments with which you are familiar? How should parents communicate with children about risk in high-risk neighborhoods? In low-risk neighborhoods? Have September 11 and Hurricane Katrina changed things?

The ecology perspective encourages researchers and policy makers to investigate what might be done to create environments that improve families' quality of life. In recent years the federal government and the states have developed programs to encourage and support marriage, to encourage father involvement in fragile families, to discourage teen sexual activity, and to move single mothers from welfare to work (discussed in Chapter 7).[1]

[1]Space does not permit a comprehensive review of current and proposed family policies and programs and their effectiveness. The book's companion website provides bibliographic information for review articles on family policy (see Amato 2005; Dion 2005; Duncan and Chase-Lansdale 2004; Offner 2005; Ooms 2005; and Seefeldt and Smock 2004).

Given the social and political diversity of American society, all parents or political actors are unlikely to agree on the best course of action. Not only are Americans not in agreement on the role government should play vis-à-vis families, but they are divided on what "family" means in a policy sense. Some argue that only heterosexual, nuclear families should be encouraged, whereas others believe in supporting a variety of families—single-parent or gay and lesbian families, for example (Bogenschneider 2006; Waite 2001). Indeed, the diversity of family lifestyles in the United States makes it extremely difficult to develop family policies that would satisfy all, or even most, of us.

Then, too, more government help to families would be costly. On the other hand, the estimated costs of *not* having family programs might be higher. Disadvantaged children whose adult lives take a bad turn could eventually cost society more in unemployment compensation and incarceration expenses than would preventive investments in support of these children and their families (Eckholm 2007).

Neighborhood and Community Although family policy is primarily pursued at the national or state level, social scientists have become interested in the local ecology of families: their neighborhoods and relationships within the community (Scanzoni 2001a). Neighborhoods are especially important for the well-being and development of teenagers, who spend much time outside the home (Kurz 2002).

It's been assumed that in the past there were neighborhoods

> where there were many children and parents considered the neighborhood safe enough so that children could be allowed simply to "go out to play." Nowadays most neighborhoods, even in small towns, have many fewer children, also there are fewer neighbors home during the day to keep a watchful eye on children. . . . And parents are almost universally concerned about the safety of their children with strangers who come into the neighborhood. (Maccoby 1998)

Social scientists have examined both inner-city and suburban neighborhoods. Children in poor neighborhoods are at great risk of negative social, educational, economic, and health outcomes (Mather and Rivers 2006). Other neighborhood risk factors for these outcomes as well as violence are high crime rates, low educational attainment by adults, and a higher percentage of female-headed households (Knoester and Haynie 2005; Shumow, Vandell, and Posner 1999).

Glen Elder and his colleagues (Elder et al. 1995) studied low-income inner-city parents. The researchers found less collective support available to African American parents and fewer programs available for their children, even compared to low-income white parents in inner-city settings. "Parents who live in neighborhoods where social cohesion is low and poverty is high must make sizeable investments of personal energy and ingenuity to ensure a protective community for their children" (Elder et al. 1995, p. 782, citing Walker and Furstenberg 1994). Elder and his colleagues noted that those African American parents who successfully involved themselves in the community had a strong sense of efficacy. But the challenge was considerable, because poor mothers typically have more hours of work, less flexibility, more night jobs, and little money for household help compared to professional working mothers, and

so have less time available for active parenting and community involvement (Kurz 2002).

Surprisingly—given the reputation of suburbs as lacking the sense of community of traditional urban neighborhoods—researchers have found some close-knit neighborhoods in suburban areas that perform the thought-to-be-lost function of "bringing up kids together" (Bould 2003). Typically, these are racially homogeneous neighborhoods, with stay-at-home moms who bonded when children were small and who continue to have a level of trust that permits families to monitor and discipline each other's children. Bould ponders the trade-off this seems to require in terms of women's role choices and neighborhood diversity.

Recently concern has arisen about the possible social isolation of Americans at all social levels. Research indicates that the number of people with whom Americans discuss "important matters" has declined, especially among educated middle-class individuals (McPherson and Smith-Lovin 2006). The authors speculate that American involvement in community and neighborhood has declined due to longer working hours, the movement of women into the labor force, commuting patterns, more heterogeneous neighborhoods, and the tendency to rely on technological tools for interpersonal contact. At the same time, Americans are now more likely to have a close confidant of another race, suggesting that interracial bridges among people are increasing (Hulbert 2006).

There are a number of ways to think about neighborhood and community cohesion, and research on this topic has barely begun. One sociologist argues that Americans have simply changed the form of their community engagement, less dependent on the neighborhood and more likely to involve professional associations, volunteer work in advocacy and service organizations, and participation in self-help groups as well as religious organizations (Wuthnow 2002, Chapter 2).

How Useful Is the Family Ecology Perspective? From the preceding examples, we can see that the family ecology perspective sensitizes us to issues that may not be addressed in other theories. It turns our attention to what may be done about social problems that affect the family, whether through neighbors and citizens coming together or through strategies of formal policy development and lobbying for change.

A weakness of the family ecology perspective is that it is so broad and inclusive that virtually nothing is left out. More and more, however, social scientists are exploring family ecology in concrete settings. They are also going beyond the former focus of family ecological theory on poverty and disadvantage to look at the eco-

People in this neighborhood join together in activities of benefit to all. This group is organizing a Neighborhood Watch program.

logical settings of more privileged families. Examining the kinds of economic and social advantages enjoyed by the middle and upper levels of society may provide insight into the conditions that would enable *all* families to succeed. Moreover, there are sometimes elements in an upper-socioeconomic-level environment—excessive achievement pressure or the isolation of children from busy, achievement-oriented parents—that are problematic (Luthar 2003). In any case, pointing to the ecology of family life challenges the notion that family satisfaction and success are due solely to individual effort (S. Marks 2001).

The Family Development Perspective

Whereas family ecology analyzes family and society as interdependent parts of a whole, the **family development perspective** emphasizes the family itself as the unit of analysis. The concept of the **family life cycle** is central here, based on the idea that the family changes in predictable ways over time.

The Family Life Cycle Typical stages of family life are marked by (1) the addition or subtraction of family members (through birth, death, and leaving home), (2) the various stages that the children go through, and (3) changes in the family's connections with other social institutions (retirement from work, for example, or a child's entry into school). These stages of family development are termed the *family life cycle*.[2] Ideally they succeed one another in an orderly progression and have their requisite **developmental tasks**, challenges that must be mastered in one stage for a successful transition to the next. **"On-time" transitions** are thought most likely to be successful for role performance (Hogan and Astone 1986). **Role sequencing**, the order in which major transitions to adult roles take place, is also theorized to be important. The **normative order hypothesis** proposes that the work-marriage-parenthood sequence is best for mental health and happiness (Jackson 2004).

Various versions of the stages of the family life cycle have been offered, but there is some convergence on a six- to eight-stage model (Aldous 1996; Duvall and Miller 1985; Rodgers and White 1993). The family begins with marriage and the establishment of an independent

[2] The term *family life cycle* is misleading in some ways, because the word *cycle* implies circular repetition, while a family's lifetime experience is linear. It proceeds from the formation of the particular family to the end of the family through dissolution or death.

Alternative terms are *family career* (Aldous 1996) or *family life course*, which connects the family to the multidisciplinary study of life course development. We have chosen to retain the original and commonly used term *family life cycle*.

residence for the couple. The *newly established couple* stage comes to an end when the arrival of the first baby thrusts the couple into the *families of preschoolers* stage. Entry of the oldest child into school brings about further changes in family life, as *families of primary school children* need to coordinate schedules with the school and parents are faced with the task of helping their children meet the school's expectations. *Families with adolescents* may be dealing with more complex problems such as sexual activity or drug and alcohol abuse. Children become increasingly expensive during this stage, and anticipated college costs add to parents' financial pressures.

Families in the middle years help their offspring to enter the adult world of employment and begin their own family formation. Later, these parents return to a couple focus with (if they are fortunate!) the time and money to pursue leisure activities. Still later, *aging families* must adjust to retirement and perhaps health crises or debilitating chronic illness. The death of a spouse marks the end of the family life cycle (Aldous 1996).

The family development perspective emerged and prospered from the 1930s through the 1950s—an era in which the taken-for-granted family was nuclear: two monogamous heterosexual parents and their children. Accordingly, the model assumed that family life follows certain conventional patterns: Couples marry, and marriage precedes parenthood; families are nuclear and reside independently from other relatives; all families have children; fathers are employed and mothers are not; parents remain together for a lifetime. Today—and, in fact, in the past as well—many of us do not proceed so predictably along these well-marked paths.

Critics have noted the white, middle-class bias of the family life cycle. Moreover, due to economic, ethnic, and cultural differences, two families in the same life cycle stage may be very different from each other. For these reasons, the family development perspective in its traditional form is less popular now than it once was.

Meanwhile, family development theorists continue to see the model as useful (Mattessich and Hill 1987, p. 445). Despite growing diversity and broader time frames, there is still a sense in our society of a right time to have a child or retire. The family development perspective has been used effectively as a research framework. One interesting, though small, study (twenty families) examined ties to kin and friends over the life cycle by looking at families' photo albums. Families were very closed during the preschool years, reaching out more to friends and kin when the children entered school. Kin ties became especially important later in the family life cycle (Gardner 1990).

Emerging Adulthood A current area of research and theory is the transition to adulthood. This is the period between adolescence and adulthood that precedes the family life cycle as defined earlier. **Emerging adulthood** can be viewed as a stage in individual development that affects entry into the family life cycle per se.

Scholars have become aware of the historical contingency of the family life cycle (Shanahan 2000). In different historical periods and for different generations, "normal" timing of the family life cycle has varied. In the post–World War II era, marriage and parenthood typically occurred at a much younger age than today. "'There used to be a societal expectation that people in their early twenties would have finished their schooling, set up a household, gotten married, and started their careers. . . . But now that's the exception rather than the norm'" (sociologist Frank Furstenberg Jr. in Lewin 2003; and Furstenberg et al. 2004). The transition to adulthood has become elongated and now is completed much later. The primary reason for this change is that it takes longer to earn enough to support a family. A bachelor's degree or beyond is essential for professional and managerial positions. Moreover, wages and job stability are not what they used to be, even for the middle class. For those with less than a college education, the kinds of jobs that used to provide access to a solid standard of family living are not so available or well-paid as they were thirty or forty years earlier. The kinds of government educational and housing programs that enabled the World War II generation to marry young no longer exist. (Changes in the American economy are discussed in detail in Chapter 3.)

Parents are called upon to subsidize young adults' education, housing, and career establishment, rendering independence from parents—a previous marker of adulthood—a much later occurrence. That can also mean a lengthy period of self-development:

> Among the most privileged young adults—those who receive ample support from their parents—this is a time of unparalleled freedom from family responsibilities and an opportunity for self-exploration and development. For the less advantaged, early adulthood is a time of struggle to gain the skills and credentials required for a job that can support the family they wish to start (or perhaps have already started), and a struggle to feel in control of their lives (Furstenberg et al. 2004, p. 34).

Furstenberg and his colleagues conducted interviews with five hundred young adults in various parts of the United States. They found marriage and parenthood no longer the marks of adulthood they used to be. Vast majorities of their respondents did identify some other traditional markers of adult status: completing one's education, achieving financial independence, obtaining full-time work, gaining the ability to support a family, and leaving one's parents' home (Furstenberg et al. 2004, Figure 1).

Other, more psychosocial indicators of adulthood were reported to psychologist Jeffrey Arnett (2004) in his interviews with over three hundred individuals age twenty to twenty-nine. The three criteria for adulthood noted by his respondents were: "accept responsibility for yourself; make independent decisions; and become financially independent" (p. 15). Attainment of these adult qualities was seen to be the outcome of a period of identity exploration, instability (of residence, work, and relationships), self-focus, feeling "in-between," and sensing widening possibilities. Arnett did not characterize "self-focus" as a bad thing, but rather an inevitable feature of a stage in which "there are few ties that entail daily obligations and commitments to others" (p. 13).

The concept of *emerging adulthood* conveys this sense of ongoing change and development, "a time of life when many different directions remain possible, when little about the future has been decided for certain, when the scope of independent exploration of life's possibilities is greater for most people than it will be at any other period of the life course" (Arnett 2000, p. 469). By age thirty, "a new web of commitments and obligations is well established for most people" (Arnett 2004, p. 12).

Researchers (and journalists) who have interviewed parents and adult children note that the "generation gap," which might have made financial dependency and close living annoying to one or both generations, seems to have vanished. According to sociologist Barbara Risman, parents and adolescents or emerging adults today have more in common in lifestyle and values than did baby boomers and their depression/World War II–era parents (in Jayson 2006a).

Ironically, as the arrival at adulthood has been postponed for many and seems to provide a new freedom of choice, new pressures have arisen for the early birds. Having a baby in one's twenties, for example, may be seen as "out of step," a risky life course move (Jong-Fast 2003). This does suggest the utility of the life course perspective. The notion that doing something "on time"—or not—makes a difference suggests that, in fact, there *are* culturally defined family life cycle expectations.

The Utility of the Family Development Perspective The family development perspective has been made more useful by modifications that recognize racial/ethnic and other family variations such as child-free unions, single parenthood, divorce and remarriage, adoption,

gay/lesbian families, and working couples (Allen and Wilcox, 2000; Brodzinsky, Smith, and Brodzinski 1998, Chapter 3; Carter and McGoldrick 1999; K. Downs, Coleman, and Ganong 2000; T. Johnson and Colucci 1999; Rodgers and White 1993; S. Slater 1995).

Family development researchers have shown a willingness to explore assumptions rather than taking them for granted. One such study, of "Early," On-time," and "Late" fathers, found, contrary to expectation, that Late fathers were highly involved in caregiving and very positive about parenthood compared to the On-time or Early fathers (Cooney et al. 1993).

Research on the sequencing of worker, spouse, and parent roles did find the normative order of education, employment, marriage, and parenthood to be generally best for mental health. Yet contrary to that expectation, African Americans whose parenthood preceded marriage were less depressed than those who married before parenthood (P. Jackson 2004).

Defining the family life cycle in terms of children and child-rearing stages, carefully distinguishing those areas of family life that are logically related to these stages, examining diverse settings, and exploring the assumptions of the theory are ways in which family scientists tinker with the family development perspective to match it to the empirical reality of today's families.

The Structure–Functional Perspective

In the **structure–functional perspective**, the family is seen as a **social institution** that performs certain essential functions for society. Institutions are patterned and predictable ways of thinking and behaving—beliefs, values, attitudes, and norms—that are organized around vital aspects of group life and serve essential social functions; that is, they meet the needs of members and enable the society to survive. What those functions are depends on the society and how it is organized. Likewise, **family structure**, or the form of the family, varies according to the society in which it is embedded.

In preindustrial or traditional societies, the family structure was an extended one, involving whole kinship groups. The **extended family** of parents, children, grandparents, and other relatives performed most societal functions, including economic production (the family farm, for example), protection of family members, vocational training, and maintenance of social order.

In industrial or modern societies, the typical family structure is more often the **nuclear family** (husband, wife, children). It has lost many functions formerly performed by the traditional extended family (W. Goode 1963). Economic production now takes place primarily in factories, shops, and corporations, not the home. Police and fire departments, the military, juvenile authorities, and mental health services provide protection and maintain social order. Schools, technical institutes, and universities educate and train the upcoming generation. The extended family does continue to play a supportive role in many cases.

Nevertheless, in contemporary society, the family remains principally accountable for at least three important **family functions**: to raise children responsibly, to provide economic support, and to give emotional security.

Family Function 1: To Raise Children Responsibly If a society is to persist beyond one generation, it is necessary that adults not only bear children but also feed, clothe, and shelter them during their long years of dependency. Furthermore, a society needs new members who are properly trained in the ways of the culture and who will be dependable members of the group. All this requires that children be responsibly raised. Virtually every society places this essential task on the shoulders of families.

A related family function has traditionally been to control its members' sexual activity. Although there are several reasons for the social control of sexual activity, the most important one is to ensure that reproduction takes place under circumstances that guarantee the responsible care and socialization of children. The universally approved locus of reproduction remains the married-couple family. Still, in the United States today, the child-rearing function is often performed by divorced or never-married parents and sometimes by grandparents.

Family Function 2: To Provide Economic Support A second family function involves providing economic support. For much of history, the family was primarily an economic unit rather than an emotional one (Shorter 1975; L. Stone 1980). Although the modern family is no longer a self-sufficient economic unit, virtually every family engages in activities aimed at providing for such practical needs as food, clothing, and shelter.

The extended family—grandparents, aunts, and uncles—is often an important source of security. Extended families meet most needs in a traditional society—economic and material needs and child care, for example—and they have strong bonds. In urban societies, specialized institutions such as factories, schools, and public agencies often meet practical needs. But extended families may also help one another materially in urban society, especially during crises.

© Hill Street Studios/Getty Images/Blend Images

Family economic functions now consist of earning a living outside the home, pooling resources, and making consumption decisions together. In assisting one another economically, family members create some sense of material security. For example, spouses and partners offer each other a kind of unemployment insurance. And family members care for one another in additional practical ways, such as nursing and transportation during illness.

Family Function 3: To Give Emotional Security Although historically the family was a pragmatic institution involving material maintenance, in today's world, the family has grown more important as a source of emotional security (Coontz 2005b). This is not to say that families can solve all our longings for affection, companionship, and intimacy. (Sometimes, in fact, the family situation itself is a source of stress, as we'll discuss in Chapters 14 and 15.) But families and committed intimate relationships typically offer important emotional support to adults and children. Family may mean having a place where you may be yourself, even sometimes your worst self, and still belong.

In today's impersonal world, the family has grown more important as a source of emotional support. Family members cannot fulfill all of one another's emotional needs, but committed family relationships can and do offer important emotional security.

does not take into consideration racial/ethnic or class variation in family structures. Nonetheless, virtually all social scientists assume the one basic premise underlying structure–functionalism: that families are an important social institution performing essential social functions.

The Interactionist Perspective[3]

As the name implies, the **interactionist perspective** focuses on **interaction**, the face-to-face encounters and relationships of individuals who act in awareness of one another. This point of view explores the back-and-forth talk, gestures, and actions that go on in families. Members respond verbally or nonverbally to what other members say and do. These interchanges take on a reality of their own; they construct or create a fam-

The Utility of the Structure–Functional Perspective The structure–functional perspective calls attention to cross-cultural variations in family structure and functions. It points to the essential role the family plays in different societies and how that may change over time.

As it dominated family sociology in the United States during the 1950s, however, the structure–functional perspective emphasized the heterosexual nuclear family as the only "normal" or "functional" family structure. Furthermore, the structure–functional perspective argued the functionality of specialized gender roles: the *instrumental* husband-father, who supports the family economically and wields authority inside and outside the family, and the *expressive* wife-mother-homemaker, whose main function is to enhance emotional relations at home and socialize young children (Parsons and Bales 1955). These views fit nicely into a post–World War II society, characterized by an expanding economy in which a man's wage could support a family. But they no longer match family reality.

The structure–functional perspective has been criticized for giving us an image of smoothly working families characterized by shared values, overlooking gender inequality and power issues, spousal or parent–child conflict, and even family violence. The perspective has been further criticized because it generally fails to recognize that what is functional for one group or category of people may not be so for others. Finally, structure–functionalism

ily. Put another way, something called "family" emerges from the relationships and interactions among family members. Unlike structure–functionalism, which posits a standard family form, the interactionist perspective refuses to identify a standard family structure. The family is not a stock social unit but the creation of its participants as they spontaneously relate to one another.

Originating in the work of Charles Horton Cooley (1902, 1909) and George Herbert Mead (1934), the interactionist perspective was an important theoretical orientation in sociology during the 1920s and 1930s, when family studies was establishing itself as a legitimate social science. The orientation remains a popular and fruitful one.

A major concept in the interactionist perspective is the **self-concept** (the basic feelings people have about themselves, their abilities and characteristics, and their worth) and the related concept of **identity** (a sense of uniqueness and inner sameness). The self is developed initially in a family setting. Parents especially, and siblings and other relatives are the most influential or significant figures in a young child's life, together with

[3] This discussion of the interactionist perspective does not attempt to analyze different traditions in interactionism such as *symbolic interactionism* (Blumer 1969; Cooley 1909; G. H. Mead 1934), *dramaturgical sociology* (Goffman 1959; Lyman and Scott 1975), and a more *structural interactionism* (Gecas 1982; Stryker 2003 [1980]).

"This family is way to functional."

peers. The responses of these other people channel the development of the child's self-concept. Family identity and traditions emerge through interaction, with the growth of relationships and the creation of rituals (Bossard and Boll 1943; Fiese et al. 2002).

A related concept is that of **meaning**—what a given activity or statement conveys symbolically. For example, a man's or woman's domestic work may symbolize love and family caring (Nippert-Eng 1996), or it may be seen as boring and unappreciated, and therefore demeaning. The difference in meaning has a strong effect on spouses' satisfaction with their division of labor.

Selves and interaction have much to do with **roles**, or positions in the social structure that have associated behavior expectations. Even young children connect certain behaviors to the different roles of mother, father, teacher, police officer, and so on, and much of their play consists of imitating these visible roles. **Role-taking**, or playing out the expected behavior associated with a social position, is how children begin to learn behavior appropriate to the roles they may play in adult life. When they later assume specific family or occupational roles, they continue to learn appropriate behavior by observing and interacting with others. Behavior and attitudes associated with roles become **internalized**, or incorporated into the self.

Thinking about families in interactionist terms, researchers investigate questions such as the following: How do two separate individuals interact in a marriage or a committed partnership to fashion a couple identity (P. Berger and Kellner 1970)? How do families define the appropriateness of feelings (Hochschild 1979)? What acts or objects symbolize a family's idea of itself (LaRossa and Reitzes 1993)? What kinds of **role-making** take place in families, as they adapt typical family roles

of husband and wife to their own preferences? Perhaps a husband will do the typical masculine chores at home, while the wife cooks and cleans, but both are heavily involved in child care and both take responsibility for earning the family's living.

Interaction theory is difficult to specify with precision because it implies that each family is different and that behavior does not have a single meaning but can be variously interpreted by the individuals involved. This can be very difficult to get at in research focused on the interior of the family. Often family members are asked about their thoughts and behavior, rather than being observed, although the method of participant observation (discussed later in this chapter), is also used.

The Utility of the Interactionist Perspective An often-voiced criticism of the interactionist perspective is that it makes intuitive sense but is difficult to test empirically. A related criticism is that because it is qualitative and relatively subjective, the research connected with the interactionist perspective lacks rigor.

Enthusiasts of the interactionist perspective have gone a long way to refute these criticisms by using quantitative methods and carefully documenting fieldwork. A longitudinal study of the impact of group membership on self-concept confirmed Cooley's notion that social feedback shapes the self-concept, a process he termed the **looking-glass self** (Yeung and Martin 2003). Fred Davis's *Passage through Crisis* (1991 [1963]), a study of families in which a child contracted polio, remains significant today in its insightful analysis of the impact on family dynamics of a child's health crisis.

Perhaps the most serious criticism of interactionism is that it overestimates the power of individuals to create their own realities, ignoring the extent to which humans inhabit a world not of their own making. However, the intersection between family choices and norms of the wider world may be a focus of interesting research. Sociologist Kristin Park studied the interaction strategies employed by voluntarily childless couples, who have a stigmatized family identity. Some couples employed defensive strategies, making a claim of biological inability to have children. Others aggressively asserted the merits of a child-free lifestyle (Park 2002).

Interactionists have not always been sensitive to cultural variation, instead taking interaction to be the same in all settings. The interactionist perspective needs to be expanded to consider an important question: "How do geography, race/ethnicity, class, gender, age, and time relate to family interaction?" (LaRossa and Reitzes 1993, p. 36). There is in fact a growing interest in how culture shapes interactionist concepts. A study comparing Americans and certain Asian societies found the latter to have a self-concept that was more interdependent, situated in ties to others, than was true of the Americans studied, who had a much more autonomous and independent sense of the self (P. Smith and Bond 1993, pp. 93–99).

Exchange Theory

Exchange theory is the application of an economic perspective to social relationships. Developed around 1960 and flourishing during the 1960s and 1970s, this orientation focuses on how individuals' personal **resources** such as education, income, physical attractiveness, and personality affect their formation of and continuation in relationships. This theory also considers how a person's emotional involvement and dependence on a relationship affects her or his relative power in the relationship.

The basic premise of exchange theory is that people use their resources to bargain and secure advantage in relationships. The exchange of **rewards and costs** among participants shapes power and influence in the family, the household division of labor, and commitment to the relationship (Sabatelli and Shehan 1993). Rewards and costs can be material or nonmaterial: gifts, travel, and entertainment; maintenance of a home; economic support; affection, sex, emotional support, and communication; help in meeting other family members' needs; being considerate of in-laws and friends of the partner, and so on.

Marriages tend to take place between people of equal social status (see Chapter 9). Relationships based on exchanges that are equal or equitable (fair, if not actually

equal) thrive, whereas those in which the **exchange balance** feels consistently one-sided are more likely to dissolve or be unhappy. Decision making within a marriage, as well as decisions to divorce and responses to domestic violence, are affected by the relative resources of the spouses. People without resources or alternatives to a relationship typically defer to the preferences of others and are less likely to leave a relationship (Brehm et al. 2002; Sprecher and Schwartz 1994; Van Yperen and Buunk 1990).

Looking back, one can see the beginnings of this theory in the work of Willard Waller, who identified the **principle of least interest**. The partner with less commitment to the relationship is the one who has more power, including the power to exploit the other. The spouse who is more willing to break up the marriage or to shatter rapport and refuse to be the first to make up can maintain dominance (Waller 1951, pp. 190–92).

Recent longitudinal research on dating couples found the principle of least interest alive and well in the late twentieth century. Partners in a dating relationship did tend to feel they each had different levels of involvement. The less-involved members felt they had more control over the continuation or ending of the relationship. Relationship satisfaction and stability, however, were associated with equal emotional involvement (Sprecher, Schmeeckle, and Felmlee 2006).

Exchange theory must fight the human tendency to see family relationships in more romantic and emotional terms. Yet dating relationships, marriage and other committed partnerships, divorce, and even parent–child relationships show signs of being influenced by the relative assets of the parties. Money is power, and the children of wealthier parents are more likely to share their parents' values, for example (Luster, Rhoades, and Haas 1989). "'Parents with fewer resources may find it difficult to enforce discipline and influence their children's behavior'" (economist Robert Pollak in Belt 2000, p. 22).

The Utility of Exchange Theory As applied to the family, exchange theory is subject to the criticism that it assumes a human nature that is unrealistically rational and even cynical at heart about the role of love and responsibility. Exchange theorists do consider the emotional attachment and commitment that make couples concerned about their *partner's* rewards as well as their own. But they also note that inequality and/or an unfavorable balance of

This extended African American family is celebrating Kwanzaa, created in the 1960s by black militant Ron Karenga based on African traditions. An estimated 10 million black Americans now celebrate Kwanzaa as a ritual of family, roots, and community. The experience of adopting or creating family rituals fits the interactionist perspective on the family.

© Lawrence Migdale

rewards and costs tend to erode positive feelings over the long term (Brehm et al. 2002).

Maybe exchange theory tells us things we don't want to know: about the conscious or unconscious role of power, calculation of resources, and emotional and material dependency in marriage and other family relations. But if we *do* understand the role of exchange in relationships, we can act to make them more equitable.

Family Systems Theory

Family systems theory is an umbrella term for a wide range of specific theories that look at the family as a whole. Originating in natural science, systems theory was applied to the family by psychotherapists and was then adopted by family scholars and practitioners in other disciplines.

A **system** is a combination of elements or components that are interrelated and organized into a whole. Like an organic system (the body, for example) or a mechanical or a cybernetic system (a computer), the parts of a family make a whole that is more than the sum of the parts. A family functions regularly in a certain way; emotional expression and behavior of family members tend to persist. Put another way, systems tend toward **equilibrium**. Like a computer program directing a space vehicle, information about behavior provides feedback to the system, which then adjusts itself. Change in the external environment or in one of the internal parts sets in motion a process to restore equilibrium (Whitchurch and Constantine 1993).

In family dynamics, this tendency toward equilibrium puts pressure on a changing family member to revert to his or her original behavior within the family system. For change to occur, the family system as a whole must change. Indeed, that is the goal of family therapy based on systems theory. The family may see one member as the problem, but if the psychologist draws the whole family into therapy, the family *system* should begin to change. Without therapeutic intervention, the family may replicate problem behaviors over the generations. Similarly, it might be unrealistic for a spouse to attempt to resolve marital difficulties by leaving the family (by divorcing). Family systems theorists would expect that an individual would be likely to re-create a family system similar to the one that she or he left.

Social scientists have moved systems theory away from its therapeutic origins to employ it in a more general analysis of families. They have been especially interested in how family systems handle information, deal with problems, respond to crises, and regulate contact with the outside world. **Family boundaries**, as well as the closeness or distance between family members, are important issues in systems theory (D. Kantor and Lehr 1975). Systems theorists are interested in how families maintain a sense of family identity through rituals and holiday celebrations (Broderick 1993, Chapter 7).

The Utility of Family Systems Theory Criticism of the family systems perspective has often related to its lack of specificity: So the family is a system—then what? In working concretely with families in therapy, however, a family systems approach may be very useful to both therapists and clients. If family members come to understand how their own family system operates, they can use this knowledge to achieve desired goals. Moreover, specific conceptual frameworks have emerged that go beyond the basic idea of a system (e.g., D. Kantor and Lehr 1975).

To look at the family as a system can be a creative perspective for research. Rather than seeing only the influence of parents on children, for example, system theorists are sensitized to the fact that this is not a one-way relationship, and they have explored *Children's Influence on Family Dynamics: The Neglected Side of Family Relationships* (Crouter and Booth 2003).

Researchers have used concepts such as family boundaries as research starting points. For example, **boundary ambiguity** (Boss 1997) is common in stepfamilies: Do children of divorced parents belong to two (or more) families? Are former spouses and their relatives part of the family (S. Stewart 2005a)?

The study of family systems is methodologically complex (O'Brien 2005). Another weakness of systems theory is that it does not take note of social structure. Transactions with a particular family's external world of work, school, religious affiliation, and extended family may be addressed, but the overall structure of economic opportunity, racial/ethnic and gender stratification, and other features of the larger society are not analyzed.

Systems theory tends to diffuse responsibility for conflict by attributing dysfunction to the *system*. This makes it difficult to extend social support to victimized family members while establishing legal accountability for others, as in incest or domestic violence (M. Stewart 1984).

But systems theory often gives family members insight into the effects of their behavior. It may make visible the hidden benefits or costs of certain family patterns. For example, doctors were puzzled by the fact that death rates were higher among kidney dialysis patients with *supportive* families. Family systems theorists attributed the higher rates to the unspoken desire of the patients to lift the burden of care from the close-knit family they loved (D. Reiss, Gonzalez, and Kramer 1986).

Conflict and Feminist Perspectives

We like to think of families as beneficial for all members. For decades, sociologists talked about how traditional family roles were functional for society, ignoring the politics of gender and differentials of power and privilege within the family.

The conflict and feminist perspectives bring latent conflict and inequality into the open. A first way of thinking about the **conflict perspective** is that it is the opposite of structure–functional theory. Not all a family's practices are good; not all family behaviors contribute to family well-being; what is good for one family member is not necessarily good for another. Family interaction can include domestic violence as well as holiday rituals—sometimes both on the same day.

Conflict theory calls attention to power—more specifically, unequal power. It explains behavior patterns such as the unequal division of household labor in terms of the distribution of power between husbands and wives. Because power within the family derives from power outside it, conflict theorists are keenly interested in the political and economic organization of the larger society.

The conflict perspective traces its intellectual roots to Karl Marx, who analyzed class conflict. Applied to the family by Marx's colleague Friedrich Engels (1942 [1884]), the conflict perspective attributed family and marital problems to class inequality in capitalist society.

In the 1960s, a renewed interest in Marxism sparked the application of the conflict perspective to families in a different way. Although Marx and Engels had focused on economic classes, the emerging feminist movement applied conflict theory to the sex/gender system—that is, to relationships and power differentials between men and women in the larger society and in the family.

Although there are many variations within the **feminist perspective**, the central focus is on gender issues. A unifying theme is that male dominance in family and society is oppressive to women. **Patriarchy**, the idea that men dominate women in all societies, is a central concept.

The Utility of Conflict and Feminist Perspectives

The conflict and feminist perspectives examine inequality within the family. Moreover, the feminist perspective brings attention to women and their experiences (Osmond and Thorne 1993). Women's domestic work was largely invisible in social science until feminist theories began to treat household labor as work that has economic value.

The application of feminist perspectives has permitted us to see some things about families that had been overlooked before. Social scientists became aware of wife abuse, marital rape, child abuse, and other forms of domestic violence. These family behaviors had been there all along, but not remarked upon or treated as social problems. Feminists have pointed to the unequal division of labor in the home and asserted the oppressive nature of conventional men's and women's roles for both sexes.

Unlike the perspectives described earlier, which were developed primarily by scholars, feminist theories emerged from political and social movements over the past forty years. As such, the mission of feminist theory is to use knowledge to actively confront and end the oppression of women and related patterns of subordination based on social class, race/ethnicity, age, or sexual orientation. Feminist theorizing has contributed to political action regarding gender and race discrimination in wages; divorce laws that disadvantage women; sexual and physical violence against women and children; and reproductive issues, such as abortion rights and the inclusion of contraception in health insurance. Feminist perspectives promote recognition and support for women's unpaid work; the greater involvement of men in housework and child care; efforts to fund quality day care and paid parental leaves; and transformations in family therapy so that counselors recognize the reality of gender inequality in family life and treat women's concerns with respect (Goldner 1993).

Conflict and feminist perspectives are sometimes difficult to accept for those in privileged statuses. For some social scientists these perspectives are too political, too value-laden, too tied to advocacy to be valid academic approaches. For some scholars, the categories used in feminist analysis are too vague and ahistorical. For example, patriarchy, posited to exist in all societies from primitive to postindustrial, seems to lose its meaning as an analytic category when it minimizes differences between America in the twenty-first century and ancient Rome, where husbands allegedly had life and death power over women.

Feminists advocating change in the sex/gender system and the family are frequently under fire from conservative media, politicians, religious leaders, and academics (e.g., Blankenhorn [1995] and Popenoe [1993; 1996]). Such critics fear that feminism may have taken women's rights too far, resulting in harmful effects on marriage and children.

Feminists maintain that these assertions of a negative impact of feminism on the family are biased. Opponents do not acknowledge, for example, that feminists value women's caregiving in the family. Feminists also argue that there are other explanations for the changes that concern critics. Moreover, from the feminist perspective, championing the traditional nuclear family at the cost of women's equality and well-being is unconscionable. Feminists argue that there is more than one effective way to structure family life (Fox and Murry 2000; Stacey 1993).

The Biosocial Perspective

A **biosocial perspective** on the family, also termed *sociobiology* or *evolutionary psychology*, is characterized by "concepts linking psychosocial factors to physiology, genetics, and evolution" (A. Booth, Carver, and Granger 2000, p. 1018). This perspective argues that human anatomy/physiology, genetics, and hormones affect much of human behavior and, more specifically, many family-related behaviors.

Over the past twenty-five years, the biosocial perspective has emerged as a significant theoretical perspective on the family. Researchers have employed a biosocial perspective to examine such family phenomena as sexual bonding, decisions about whether to have children, parenting behavior, parent–child attachment, gender differences in children and adults, sexual development and behavior, courtship and mate selection, and marital stability and quality (A. Booth, Carver, and Granger 2000).

Much of contemporary human behavior is explained by the biosocial perspective as having evolved in ways that enable survival and continuation of the human species. Successful behavior patterns are encoded in the genes, and this **evolutionary heritage** is transmitted to succeeding generations.[4] In the contemporary version of evolutionary theory, it is the survival of one's *genes,* termed **inclusive fitness** (W. Hamilton 1964), rather than the survival of individual descendants that is important. Protective behavior is thought to be oriented to the survival and reproduction of all close kin who carry those genes, not only direct descendants (Dawkins 1976).

The biosocial perspective presumes that certain human behaviors, because they evolved for the purpose of human survival, are both "natural" and difficult to change. It is asserted, for example, that traditional gender roles evolved from patterns shared with our mammalian ancestors that were useful in early hunter–gatherer societies. Gender differences—males allegedly more aggressive than females, and mothers more likely than fathers to be primarily responsible for child care—are seen as anchored in hereditary biology (Rossi 1984; Udry 1994, 2000).

---

[4] The biosocial perspective has its roots in Charles Darwin's *The Origin of Species* (1859). Darwin proposed that species evolve according to the principle of *survival of the fittest.* Only the strongest, more intelligent, and adaptable members of a species survive to reproduce, a process whereby the entire species is strengthened and prospers over time.

Biosocial explanations are offered for other contemporary family patterns. Research suggests that children are more likely to be abused by non-biologically related parents or caregivers than by biological parents. Non-biological parent figures are less likely to invest money and time in their children's development and future prospects (Case, Lin, and McLanahan 2000). The biosocial perspective explains this by arguing that parents "naturally" protect the carriers of their genetic material (Gelles and Lancaster 1987).

Sociobiologists are careful to point out that biological predisposition does *not* mean that a person's behavior cannot be influenced or changed by social structure. "Nature" (genetics, hormones, and brain function) and "nurture" (culture and social relations) are seen as interacting to produce human attitudes and behavior. As an example, research on testosterone levels in married couples found high levels of the husbands' testosterone to be associated with poorer marital quality when their role overload was high, but with better marital quality when role overload was low. In other words, "testosterone enables positive behavior in some instances and negative behavior in others" (A. Booth, Johnson, and Granger 2005, p. 483).

Psychiatrist Michael Rutter, in his presidential address to the Society for Research in Child Development, noted that "quantitative genetic studies have increasingly . . . found major interplay between genetic and non-genetic [environmental] factors, such that the outcomes cannot sensibly be attributed just to one or the other, because they depend on both" (2002, pp. 1, 2).

Biological theories of human behavior have in the past been used to justify systems of inequality and oppression. As a result, many scholars are concerned

"The title of my science project is 'My Little Brother: Nature or Nurture.'"

about deterministic interpretations of biological influences. Evolutionary perspectives have been the basis for current criticism of nonreproductive partner relationships and the employment of mothers as contrary to nature (Daly and Wilson 2000). And though he acknowledges that there are many successful stepfamilies and adoptions, sociologist David Popenoe (1994) finds these family forms to be unsupported by our evolutionary heritage. He concludes that "we as a society should be doing more to halt the growth of stepfamilies" (p. 21). It is not surprising that biosocial perspectives have been politically and academically controversial.

Still, social science researchers are doing interesting work from a biosocial perspective. Research has connected higher testosterone levels in men to poorer marital functioning, more extramarital sex, more marital separation, and a greater likelihood of divorce (A. Booth and Dabbs 1993). Husbands and wives with similar and low levels of testosterone are found to have better marital adjustment regarding problem solving and social support (Cohan, Booth, and Granger 2003).

The Utility of Biosocial Perspectives on the Family An "explosion" of biosocial research on the family is anticipated in the next decade (A. Booth, Carver, and Granger 2000, p. 1018) as social scientists move past an earlier distaste for biological explanations to explore this new paradigm. Family scholars and those who use their research should be careful to avoid interpretations shaped by ideological bias—whether this is a presumption that biology is destiny or a contrary postulate that biosocial perspectives are inherently invalid.

In this text, we explore and appraise the biosocial perspective when discussing gender (Chapter 4), extramarital sex (Chapter 6), child care (Chapter 12), and children's well-being in stepfamilies (Chapter 17).

Studying Families

Ideally, social scientists employ both theory and research in studying families. Theory and research are closely integrated, ideally at least, with theory directing us to

© Martin Rodgers/Stock Boston

These folks are waiting patiently for medical attention in a neighborhood clinic. How might scholars from different theoretical orientations see this photograph? *Family ecologists* might remark on the quality of the facilities—or speculate about the family's home and neighborhood—and how this affects family health and relations. Scholars from the *family development* perspective would likely note that this woman is in the child-rearing stage of the family life cycle. *Structure–functionalists* would be quick to note the child-raising (and, perhaps, expressive) function(s) that this woman is performing for society. *Interactionists* would be more inclined to explore the mother's body language: What is she saying nonverbally to the child on her lap? What is he saying to her? *Exchange theorists* might speculate about this woman's personal power and resources relative to others in her family. *Family system theorists* might point out that this mother and child are part of a family system: Should one person leave or become seriously and chronically ill, for example, the roles and relationships in the entire family would change and adapt as a result. *Conflict theorists* would compare this crowded and understaffed clinic for the poor with the better equipped and staffed doctors' offices that provide health care to the middle and upper classes—and conflict theorists would demand change. *Feminist theorists* might point out that typically it is mothers, not fathers, who are primarily responsible for their children's health—and ask why. The answer from a *biosocial perspective* would be that women have evolved a stronger nurturing capacity that is hormonally based.

the topics we should study and the concepts and methods we should use to do so.

The great variation in family forms and the variety of social settings for family life mean that few of us can rely on firsthand experience alone in studying the family. Although we "know" about the family because we have lived in one, our **experiential reality**—beliefs we have about the family—may not be accurate. We may also be misled by media images and common sense—what everybody "knows." This **agreement reality**—what members of a society agree is true—may misrepresent the actual experience of families (Babbie 1992, p. 17).

We turn now to consider the difficulties inherent in studying the family and then to a presentation of various methods used by social scientists. Although imperfect, the methods of scientific inquiry bring us a clearer knowledge of the family than does either personal experience or speculation based on media images. Scientific methods represent a form of agreement reality that sets special standards for the acceptance of statements about the family.

The Blinders of Personal Experience

Most people grow up in some form of family and know something about what marriages and families are. Although personal experience provides us with information, it may also act as blinders. We assume that our own family is normal or typical. If you grew up in a large family, for example, in which a grandparent or an aunt or uncle shared your home, you probably assumed (for a short time at least) that everyone had a big family. Perceptions like this are usually outgrown at an early age, but some family styles may be taken for granted or assumed to be universal when they are not. Some families talk and argue loudly, for example, while in other families controversial topics are avoided. The members of your family may spend a lot of time alone, perhaps reading, whereas in other families it may be cause for alarm if a family member—adult or child—is not talking to others around the kitchen table.

Personal experience, then, may make us believe that most people's family lives are similar to our own when often this is not the case. We may be very committed to the view of family life shaped by our experiences and our own choices.

In looking at marriage and family customs around the world, we can easily perceive the error of assuming that all marriage and family practices are like our own. But not only do common American assumptions about family life not hold true in other places, they also frequently don't even describe our own society. Lesbian or gay male families; black, Latino, and Asian families; Jewish, Protestant, Catholic, Latter-Day Saints (Mormon),

Islamic, Buddhist, and nonreligious families; upper-class, middle-class, and lower-class families; urban and rural families—all represent some differences in family lifestyle. However, the tendency to use the most familiar yardstick for measuring things is a strong one, even among social scientists.

Scientific Investigation: Removing Blinders

Seeing beyond our personal experience involves learning what kinds of families other people are experiencing and with what consequences. To do this, we use the scientific method of acquiring knowledge. **Science** can be defined as "a logical system that bases knowledge on . . . systematic observation," *empirical evidence,* facts we verify with our senses (Macionis 2006, p. 15).

The scientific method includes theoretical interpretation of observed data. What explanation best fits the known facts? In turn, theories generate hypotheses or ideas about reality, which are then tested in further research.

Scientific results are cumulative. Over time a particular view of reality will be seen to have more evidence behind it than others. It is well established, for example, that marriage carries many benefits for the individual, the couple, and their children (Waite and Gallagher 2000). It is also well established that the arrival of children is associated with a decline in marital happiness (Twenge, Campbell, and Foster 2003), probably due to the challenges of child rearing and adjustments to the couple's relationship.

This last is a conclusion that is not so pleasing to hear. But part of being a scientist is having *objectivity:* "The ideal of objective inquiry is to let the facts speak for themselves and not be colored by the personal values and biases of the researcher. In reality, of course, total neutrality is impossible for anyone" (Macionis 2006, p. 18). But following standard research practices and submitting the results to review by other scientists is likely in the long run to correct the biases of individual researchers. "We must be dedicated to finding the truth *as it is* rather than as we think it *should be*" (p. 18).

Over time our understanding of family phenomena is likely to change as new research is undertaken and new theoretical perspectives developed.

The Ethics of Research on Families

Exploring the lives of families as social science researchers do carries responsibility with it. To address past abuses, most researchers now must have their research plans reviewed by a special board of experts and community representatives called an **institutional review board (IRB)**. In fact, no federally funded research can proceed without an IRB review, and most institutions require one for all research on human subjects (P. Cohen 2007a).

The IRB scrutinizes each research proposal for adherence to professional ethical standards for the protection of human subjects. These standards include **informed consent** (the research participants must be apprised of the nature of the research and then give their consent); lack of coercion; protection from harm; confidentiality of data and identities; compensation of participants for their time, risk, and expenses; and eventual sharing of research results with participants and other appropriate audiences.

IRBs do not focus on evaluating the research topic or methodology—other than to make sure that the research is scientifically sound enough to merit participation of the human subjects. Also, samples must be selected "equitably." Where feasible, research should be designed to provide medical knowledge about various population subgroups (University of Nebraska 2006). (A Chapter 3 box, "Studying Families and Ethnicity," discusses the issue of racial/ethnic bias in research.)

Methods of Data Collection

In studying the family, we rely on data gathered systematically from many sources through techniques of **scientific investigation**. These techniques—surveys, laboratory observation and experiments, naturalistic observation, case studies, longitudinal studies, and historical and cross-cultural data—will be referred to throughout this text, so we will briefly describe them now.

Surveys Surveys are part of our everyday experience. When conducting scientific surveys, researchers engage in face-to-face or telephone interviews or distribute questionnaires. Questions are often structured so that after a statement (such as "I like to go places with my partner"), the respondent has answers from which to choose. Researchers spend much energy and time wording such *closed-ended* questions so that, as much as possible, all respondents will interpret questions in the same way. It is also important to be attentive to the wording of questions because choice of words can influence responses considerably. Respondents tend to be much more favorable to "assistance to the poor," for example, than to "welfare" (Babbie 2007, p. 251).

Survey questions may also be *open-ended*. For example, the question might be "How do you feel about going places with your partner?" or "Tell me about going places with your partner." Many social scientists believe that open-ended questions are better for finding out what people really feel or believe than are questions that offer only a limited set of responses to choose from.

Once the surveys are completed, survey responses are tallied and analyzed, usually with computerized coding and statistical programs. Next the researcher draws conclusions about respondents' attitudes and behavior. Finally, the researcher must decide to whom the conclusions are applicable. Do the results apply only to those who are in the sample studied or more generally to other people similar to the research participants?

In order that their conclusions may be *generalized* (applied to people other than those directly questioned), survey researchers do their best to ensure that their respondents constitute a *representative sample* of the people they intend to draw conclusions about. Popular magazine surveys, for example, are seldom representative of the total American public. Results from a survey in which all respondents are young, white, middle-class college students cannot be considered representative of Americans in general. So researchers and political pollsters may use *random samples,* in which households or individuals are randomly selected from a comprehensive list (see Babbie 2007). A random sample is considered representative of the population from which it is drawn. A national random sample of approximately 1,500 people may validly represent the U.S. population.

Survey research has certain advantages over other inquiry techniques. The main advantage is uniformity. Also, surveys are a relatively efficient means of gathering large amounts of information. Plus, data sets already collected and archived may be a rich resource for others doing research on the family.

Surveys have disadvantages, too. Because they ask uniform or standardized questions, surveys may miss points that respondents would consider important. Surveys neither tell us about the context in which a question is answered nor guarantee that in a real-life situation a person will act in a manner consistent with the answer given to the interviewer.

Also, respondents have a tendency to say what they think they *should* say. If asked whether or how often physical abuse occurs in the home, for example, those who engage in family violence might be reluctant to say so. Respondents might answer differently depending on the sex, age, race, and lifestyle of the person interviewing them or distributing the written questionnaire. A forty-five-year-old male asked about his experience with sexual dysfunction may be expected to reply differently to a male of twenty than he would to one of sixty—or to a female researcher of any age.

A further disadvantage of surveys is the tendency of respondents to forget the past or to reinterpret what happened in the past. Because of this tendency, social scientists recognize the value of longitudinal studies—studies in which the same group of respondents is surveyed or interviewed intermittently over a period of years.

Laboratory Observation and Experiments Because of the relative ease of conducting surveys, the flexibility of the format, and the availability of samples (even a classroom sample may provide some useful information), surveys have been a primary source of information about family living. Other techniques are also used, however.

In laboratory observation or an experiment, behaviors are carefully monitored or measured under controlled conditions. Families may be asked to discuss a hypothetical case or problem or to play a game while their behavior is observed and recorded. Later those data can be analyzed to assess the family's interaction style and the nature of their relationships. Laboratory methods are useful in measuring physiological changes associated with anger, fear, sexual response, or behavior that is difficult to report verbally.

In an **experiment**, subjects from a pool of similar participants will be randomly assigned to groups (*experimental* and *control groups*) that will be given different experiences (*treatments*). Families whose child is undergoing a bone-marrow transplant may be asked to participate in an experiment to determine how they may best be helped to cope with the situation. One group of families may be assigned to a support group in which the expression of feelings, even negative ones,

is encouraged (Experimental Group 1). Another set of families may be assigned to a group in which the emphasis is on providing information about transplantation and maintaining a positive, cheerful outlook (Experimental Group 2). A third group of families may receive no special intervention (Control Group). If at the conclusion of the experiment the groups differ in attitudes and behavior according to some measures of coping behavior, mental health, and family functioning, then the outcome is presumed to be a result of the experimental treatment. Put another way, because no other differences are presumed to exist among the randomly assigned groups, the results of the experiment provide evidence of the effects of the therapeutic interventions.

A true experiment has these features of random assignment and experimental manipulation of the important variable. **Laboratory observation**, on the other hand, simply means that behavior is *observed* in a laboratory setting, but it does not involve random assignment or experimental manipulation of a variable.

The experiment just described takes place in a field (real-life) setting, but experiments are often conducted in a laboratory setting because researchers have more control over what will happen. They have more chance to plan the activities, measure the results, determine who is involved, and eliminate outside influences.

A research team plans data collection and analysis for a survey of how families spend their time together.

Experiments, whether in real life or a laboratory, have both advantages and disadvantages. One advantage of experiments is that social scientists may observe human behavior directly, rather than depending on what respondents *tell* them. The experimenter may control the experience of the subjects and may ensure, to some extent, the initial similarity of subjects in the two groups. A disadvantage of this research technique is that the behaviors being observed often take place in an artificial situation, and whether an artificial situation is analogous to real life is always debatable. A family asked to solve a hypothetical problem through group discussion may behave differently in a formal laboratory experiment than they would at home around the kitchen table discussing a real problem.

Another limitation of experimental research is that the subject pool is often drawn from college classrooms and therefore is not representative of the general population. Sometimes, "volunteers" must participate in an experiment for class credit; in such cases, the authenticity of results is often in question.

Naturalistic Observation Many aspects of human behavior and interaction don't lend themselves to experiment, so social scientists use another technique in an attempt to overcome artificiality. In **naturalistic observation**, the researcher lives with a family or social group or spends extensive time with family or group members, carefully recording their activities, conversations, gestures, and other aspects of everyday life. The researcher attempts to discern family relationships and communication patterns and to draw implications and conclusions for understanding family behavior in general.

The principal advantage of naturalistic observation is that it allows us to view family behavior as it actually happens in its own natural—as opposed to artificial—setting. The most significant disadvantage of this tool is that findings and conclusions may be highly subjective. That is, what is recorded, analyzed, and assumed to be accurate depends on what one or a few observers think is significant. Another drawback to naturalistic observation is that it requires enormous amounts of time to observe only a few families. And these families may not be representative of family living in general. Perhaps because of these disadvantages, relatively few studies use this technique.

Still, Fred Davis's (1991) observational study of the interaction of families of polio victims, first published in 1963, remains an important piece of observational research that provides useful insights into the dynamics of families in crisis. It may become even more relevant now that medical science has enabled more children to survive serious illness; they and their families will live with crisis and chronic disease for an extended period.

This study is a good example of the *interactionist* theoretical perspective, which is often the framework for naturalistic observation.

Clinicians' Case Studies A fourth way that we get information about families is from **case studies** compiled by clinicians—psychologists, psychiatrists, marriage counselors, and social workers—who counsel people with marital and family problems. As they see individuals, couples, or whole families over a period of time, these counselors become acquainted with communication patterns and other interactions within families. Clinicians offer us knowledge about family behavior and attitudes by describing cases or by telling us about their conclusions based on a series of cases.

The advantages of case studies are the vivid detail and realistic flavor that enable us to experience vicariously the family life of others. The insights of clinicians may be helpful. But case studies also have important weaknesses. There is always a subjective or personal element in the way the clinician views the family. Inevitably, any one person has a limited viewpoint. Clinicians' professional training may lead them to overemphasize or underemphasize certain aspects of family life or to mistake cultural patterns for psychological truths. Psychiatrists, for example, used to assume that the career interests of women were abnormal and caused the development of marital and sexual problems (Chesler 2005).

Another potential bias of case studies is that people who present themselves for counseling may differ in important ways from those who do not. Most obviously, they may have more problems. For example, throughout the 1950s psychiatrists reported that gays in therapy had many emotional difficulties. Subsequent studies of gay males not in therapy concluded that gays were no more likely to have mental health problems than were heterosexuals (American Psychological Association 2007).

Longitudinal Studies **Longitudinal studies** provide long-term information about individuals or groups, as researchers conduct follow-up investigations (usually by means of interviews or questionnaires) for some years after an initial study. Observational or experimental studies could be repeated, but this is rarely done.

A good example of longitudinal research is the ongoing study by Booth, White, and colleagues. In 1980 they interviewed a group of adults who were married at the time, and then reinterviewed them three more times during the 1980s and 1990s. The researchers traced the demographic and relationship patterns affecting marital quality and stability, divorce, and remarriage. In 1992 and 1995, the now-grown children of these marriages were interviewed, and information about their educational and occupational attainment and family status was added to the study (A. Booth Johnson, White, and Edwards 1985; L. White and Keith 1990; Amato and Booth 1997; and many other articles).

A difficulty encountered in longitudinal studies, besides cost, is the frequent loss of subjects due to death, relocation, or their loss of interest. Social change occurring over a long period of time may make it difficult to ascertain what, precisely, has influenced family change. Yet cross-sectional data (one-time comparison of different groups) cannot show change in the same individuals over time.

Historical and Cross-Cultural Data   Analyzing historical records is a research approach that came to attention beginning in the 1960s with some interesting work by social historians in France (Ariès 1962) and England (Laslett 1971). Whether done by historians or other social scientists, historical research continues to be an important method of family research.

Zelizer's (1985) study of insurance documents and other historical materials conveys the changing status of the child from economic to emotional asset. Historical studies of marriage and divorce in the United States give us a picture of the past, which is not always as we thought it was in terms of stability and harmony (Cott 2000; Hartog 2000).

Drawbacks of historical research are the unevenness and unavailability of data. Scholars can use only those data which were preserved and to which they have access. Typically, the upper classes, who had both the leisure and resources to record their activities, are overrepresented. But historical scholars have been very creative. Hanawalt (1986) constructed a rich picture of the medieval family through an examination of death records.

Demographic and economic data and legal records are especially useful for analyses of the family institution. Scholars are on less-solid footing in describing intimate family matters because they must rely on materials such as individuals' diaries, which may not be representative of the period. More recently, however, the use of these personal materials has been defended, and the results have challenged earlier historians' assumptions that premodern family life lacked emotional intimacy (Osment 2001).

Sociologists, especially those who place more emphasis on cross-cultural comparison than we are able to do in this text, continue to look to anthropological fieldwork as well as survey data for information on family life and structure in societies in both developed and developing nations.

The Application of Scientific Techniques   All research tools represent a compromise. Each has its special strengths and weaknesses. However, the strengths of one research tool may make up for the weaknesses of another. To get around the drawbacks of each technique, social scientists may combine two or more tools in their research.

Ideally, a number of scientists examine one topic by several different methods. The scientific conclusions in this text result from many studies and from various and complementary research tools. Despite the drawbacks and occasional blinders, the total body of information available from sociological, psychological, and counseling literature provides a reasonably accurate portrayal of marriage and family life today.

Summary

- Different theoretical perspectives—family ecology, family development, structure–functional, interactionist, exchange, family systems, conflict, feminist, and biosocial—illuminate various features of families and provide a foundation for research.

- The structure–functional perspective draws attention to functions performed by the family. Cross-cultural comparisons show us that assumptions about family structure, family functions, and family ways of courtship, marriage, gender, parenting, and kinship based on our own culture are limited. Family life is quite diverse across cultures.

- How do we know what families are like? We can call upon personal experience for the beginning of an answer to this question. But everyone's personal experience is limited. Scientific investigation—with its ideal of objectivity, cumulative results, and various methodological techniques for gathering empirical data—is designed to provide a more effective and accurate way of gathering knowledge about the family.

- Methodologies of data collection include surveys, laboratory observation and experiments, naturalistic observation, clinicians' case studies, longitudinal studies, and historical and cross-cultural data.

- Researchers need to be guided by professional standards and ethical principles of protection for research participants.

Questions for Review and Reflection

1. Choose one of the theoretical perspectives on the family, and discuss how you might use it to understand something about life in *your* family.

2. Choose a magazine photo, and analyze its content from a structure–functional perspective. (*Hint:* Together the people in the photo may constitute the group under analysis, with each person meeting certain of the group's needs, or functions.) Then analyze the photo from another theoretical perspective. How do your insights differ depending on which theoretical perspective is used?

3. Why is the family a major social institution? Does your family fulfill each of the family functions identified in the text? How?

4. Review the techniques of scientific investigation, and discuss why science is often considered a better way to gain knowledge than is personal experience alone. When might this not be the case?

5. **Policy Question.** What aspect of family life would it be helpful for policy makers to know more about as they make law and design social programs? How might this topic be researched? Is it controversial?

Key Terms

agreement reality 38

biosocial perspective 36

boundary ambiguity 34

case study 41

conflict perspective 35

developmental task 27

emerging adulthood 28

equilibrium 34

evolutionary heritage 36

exchange balance 33

exchange theory 33

experiential reality 38

experiment 40

extended family 29

family boundaries 34

family development perspective 27

family ecology perspective 22

family function 30

family life cycle 27

family policy 24

family structure 29

family systems theory 34

feminist perspective 35

identity 31

inclusive fitness 36

informed consent 39

interaction 31

interactionist perspective 31

internalize 32

institutional review board (IRB) 38

laboratory observation 40

longitudinal study 41

looking-glass self 32

meaning 32

naturalistic observation 41

normative order hypothesis 27

nuclear family 29

"on-time" transition 27

patriarchy 35

principle of least interest 33

resources 33

rewards and costs 33

role 32

role-making 32

role sequencing 27

role-taking 32

science 38

scientific investigation 39

self-concept 31

social institution 29

structure–functional perspective 29

survey 39

system 34

theoretical perspective 22

Online Resources

Companion Website for This Book

www.thomsonedu.com/sociology/lamanna

Visit the book companion website, where you will find flash cards, practice quizzes, Internet links, suggested readings, InfoTrac College Edition exercises, and more to help you study.

ThomsonNOW™ for Marriage and Family

Spend time on what you need to master rather than on information you already have learned. Take a pre-test for this chapter, and ThomsonNOW will generate a personalized study plan based on your results. The study plan will identify the topics you need to review and direct you to online resources such as videos, narrated learning modules, and interactive activities to help you master those topics. You can then take a post-test to help you determine the concepts you have mastered and what you will still need to work on. Try it out! Go to **www .thomsonedu.com/login** to sign in with an access code or to purchase access to this product.

American Families
in Social Context

3

Historical Events

Age Structure

The Economy and Social Class

Economic Change and Inequality

Facts about Families: Military Families

Blue-Collar and White-Collar Families and the Wealthy

Race and Ethnicity

Conceptualizing Race and Ethnicity

Issues for Thought: Studying Families and Ethnicity

Racial/Ethnic Diversity in the United States

African American Families

Latino (Hispanic) Families

A Closer Look at Family Diversity: Family Ties and Immigration

Asian American Families

Pacific Islander Families

American Indian (Native American) Families

White Families

Multicultural Families

Religion

© Myrleen Ferguson Cate / PhotoEdit

Families are families, right? Well, yes and no. Families meet important needs for their members and for society. Family members make commitments to one another and share an identity. Yet Chapter 1 showed us that families are not all alike in form. We also saw in Chapter 1 that social factors influence our personal options and choices. Put another way, individuals and families vary as a result of the social settings in which they exist.

In this chapter, we will explore the social context in which today's families live out their opportunities and choices. We'll examine variations in family life associated with race/ethnicity, immigration, religion, and the events of our nation's recent history. We'll look at how the economy affects families and at the impact of the changing age structure of American society

This chapter focuses on U.S. society, but we need to point out that economic and technological changes affect families in other societies in both the developed and developing worlds. We begin here with a look at how historical events in the United States have affected family life.

Historical Events

Historical events and conditions affect options, choices, and the everyday lives of families. In the early twentieth century,[1] for example, the shift from an agricultural to an industrial economy brought people from farm to city. There was a "great migration" of rural southern African Americans to the urban north.

American family life has been a different experience during the Great Depression, World War II, the optimistic fifties, the tumultuous sixties, the economically constricted seventies and eighties, the time-crunched nineties, and the current era of a globalized economy. In the depression years, couples delayed marriage and parenthood and had fewer children than they wanted (Elder 1974). During World War II, married couples were separated for long periods. Married women were encouraged to get defense jobs and to place their children in day care. Some husbands and fathers were casualties of war. Families in certain nationality groups—Japanese and some Italians—were sent to internment camps and had their property seized even though many were U.S. citizens or long-term residents (Taylor 2002c; Tonelli 2004).

The end of the war was followed by a spurt in the divorce rate, when hastily contracted wartime marriages proved to be mistakes or extended separation led couples to grow apart. World War II was also followed by an uptick in marriages and childbearing. In the 1950s, family life was not overshadowed by national crisis. The aftermath of the war saw an expanding economy and a postwar prosperity based on the production of consumer goods. The GI bill enabled returning soldiers to get a college education, and the less well-educated could get good jobs in automobile and other factories. In those prosperous times, people could afford to get married young and have larger families. Men earned a "family wage" (enough to support a family), and children were cared for by stay-at-home mothers. Divorce rates slowed their long-term increase. The expanding economy and government subsidies for housing and education provided a sound basis for family life (Coontz 1992).

The large baby boom cohort born to these parents (1946–1964) has had a powerful impact on American society, giving us the cultural and sexual revolutions of "the sixties" as they moved from adolescence to young adulthood in the Vietnam War era. They are likely to reshape middle age and aging, as they move into their senior years (Davies and Love 2002; Pew Research Center 2005).

The baby boomers had a relatively secure childhood in both psychological and economic terms. The generation that followed has encountered a more challenging economic and family environment (Bengston, Biblarz, and Roberts 2002). Today, a man is far less likely to earn a family wage. Partly for that reason, more wives seek employment, including mothers of infants and preschool children. Moreover, the feminist movement opened opportunities for women and changed ideas about women's and men's roles in the family and workplace. Educational careers were extended and marriage delayed for both sexes, as young people prepared for a competitive economic environment. (Gender will be discussed in more detail in Chapter 4; work and family, in Chapter 12; and the economy, later in this chapter.)

In the 1960s and 1970s, marriage rates declined and divorce rates increased dramatically—perhaps in response to a declining job market for working-class men, the increased economic independence of women, and the cultural revolution of the sixties, which encouraged more individualistic perspectives. These trends, as well as the sexual revolution, contributed to a dramatic rise in nonmarital births.

The present historical moment is one of adaptation to these rather profound cultural changes and to economic ups and downs much affected by globalization of the economy. Also of significance today is the "war on terror." The September 11, 2001, attacks on the United States created a pervasive sense of insecurity, triggered

---

[1] American families have a rich history prior to the twentieth century. The limited history section of this chapter cannot do justice to American families' experiences in these various historical eras. As supplements, we especially recommend *Domestic Revolutions: A Social History of American Family Life* (Mintz and Kellogg 1988); *Historical Influences on Lives and Aging* (Schaie and Elder 2005); and *Huck's Raft: A History of American Childhood* (Mintz 2004)

new overseas wars, and led to a debate about what changes in our way of life might be necessary.

Of course, the family has faced the necessity of adapting to demographic, social, economic, and political change throughout its history. Families have also coped with internal and external wars. "Facts About Families: Military Families" focuses attention on those families whose lives are structured by war and military service today.

Age Structure

Historical change involves not only specific events but also the basic facts of human life. One of the most dramatic developments of the twentieth century was the increased longevity of our population. Life expectancy in 1900 was forty-seven years, but an American child born in 2004 is expected to live to seventy-eight (Miniño, Heron, and Smith 2006, Table 1).

Aging itself has changed; the years that have been added to our lives have been healthy and active ones (Bergman 2006c). Survival to older ages has meant that men and women over sixty-five are now more likely to be living with spouses than in the past. For those without spouses, maintaining an independent residence has become more feasible economically and in terms of health. The advent of the "war on terror" has brought the elderly new respect, as their experiences living through World War II seem currently relevant (Witchel 2001).

Among the positive consequences of increased longevity are more years invested in education, longer marriages for those who do not divorce, a longer period during which parents and children interact as adults, and a long retirement during which family activities and other interests may be pursued or second careers launched. More of us will have longer relationships with grandparents, and some will know their great-grandparents (Rosenbloom 2006).

At the same time, the increasing numbers of elderly people must be cared for by a smaller group of middle-aged and young adults. Moreover, divorce and remarriage may change family relationships in ways that affect the willingness of adult children to care for their parents (Bergman 2006c). The impact of a growing proportion of elderly will also be felt economically. As the ratio of retired elderly to working-age people grows, so will the problem of funding Social Security and Medicare.

At the other end of the age structure, the declining proportion of children is likely to affect social policy support for families raising children. Fewer children may mean less attention and fewer resources devoted to their needs in a society under pressure to provide care for the elderly: "Adults are less likely to be living with children, . . . neighborhoods are less likely to contain children, and . . . children are less likely to be a consideration in daily life. . . . [T]he need[s] and concerns of children . . . gradually may be receding from our consciousness" (Whitehead and Popenoe 2001, p. 15). Only 20 percent of those eligible to vote have children (Conlin 2003b).

In the foregoing discussion of history and of the age structure of our population, there is an underlying theme: the economy. Economic opportunities, resources, and obligations are an important aspect of the American society in which families are embedded. We turn now to a more detailed discussion of the economic foundation of the contemporary family.

The Economy and Social Class

We tend to think of the United States as a classless society. Yet **life chances**—the opportunities one has for education and work, whether one can afford to marry, the schools that children attend, and a family's health care—all depend on family economic resources. Income and class position may affect access to an important feature of contemporary society: technology. Nine in ten family households with incomes of more than $75,000 have a computer, and eight in ten have Internet access. Comparable figures for family households with incomes of less than $25,000 are 40 percent and 30 percent, respectively (Day, Janus, and Davis 2005).

Class differences in economic resources affect the timing of leaving home, marrying, and assuming caretaking responsibilities:

> An elderly widow with a paid-off house and investments can afford home health care; her children and grandchildren need not organize themselves around her care. In contrast, a family sharing a grandmother's subsidized housing becomes homeless on her death, and the mother, who has already lost many work days because of the grandmother's illness, may be fired while apartment hunting. (Kliman and Madsen 1999, p. 93)

Money may not buy happiness, but it does afford a myriad of options: sufficient and nutritious food, comfortable residences, better health care, keeping in touch with family and friends through the Internet, education at good universities, vacations, household help, and family counseling.

Economic Change and Inequality

Americans overall are better off economically than they were in the 1970s. But incomes have grown little for the middle and working classes in recent years. Although the U.S. economy was good for many Americans during the 1990s, others experienced increased job insecurity,

Military Families

Unless you have a personal connection or history of military service, you probably have not thought about the lives of military families until recently. Now in this time of overseas wars, attention is focused on military personnel and their families.

A Military Family Life

The military can be considered a "total institution" (Goffman 1961). That is, it encompasses all aspects of life—living quarters, associates, schedules, locus of work and social activities, decision-making authority, and, above all, "the sublimation of individual interests to institutional goals [which can extend] to the sacrifice of one's own life" (Lundquist and Smith 2005, p. 1). Segal and Segal (2004) sum it up as the "risk of injury or death . . . separation from family . . . frequent geographic relocation . . . residence in foreign countries . . . long and unpredictable duty hours and shift work . . . pressures to conform . . . [and] the masculine nature of the organization" (pp. 32–33).

Yet one research team argues that the military is a more "family-friendly" setting (at least in peacetime) than the civilian world. To attract an all-volunteer force, a number of benefits and support systems were put in place that include family housing, extensive health insurance, and day-care and school-age activity centers for older children. Other advantages include job security, a sense of community and community support— and even discount shopping.

"Flat Daddies," cardboard cutouts of a parent deployed to Iraq or Afghanistan, serve as symbolic placeholders in the families left behind. Flat Daddies and Flat Mommies may go to school and sports events or be brought to the holiday dinner table to serve as a reminder and emotional focus for the duration of a family member's absence. "Flat Toby" is a real person to his wife and children in the Austin household in Colorado Springs. "'It's nice to see him each day, just to remember that he's still with us. . . . It's one of the best things I've done during this deployment. I really think it's helped us stay connected, to remember that he's still with us'" (Zezima 2006, p. 8A; see also MacQuarrie 2006).

Half of U.S. military service members are married, and almost three-quarters have children. Some couples (12 percent) are dual military. The military, which brings together many men and women of marriageable age, seems to provide an "active marriage market" (McCone and O'Donnell 2006). Six percent of military personnel are single parents (Segal and Segal 2004).

Lundquist and Smith (2005) report that military women have slightly more children than civilian women, attributed by these authors to institutional support for families.[a] Despite the many obvious pressures on military marriages, couples seem to have similar (enlisted personnel) or lower (officers) divorce rates than comparable civilian couples (McCone and O'Donnell 2006).

loss of benefits, longer workdays, and more part-time and temporary work (Teachman, Tedrow, and Crowder 2000). Almost 7 percent of families were classified as "working poor" in 2004 (at least one wage earner, but below poverty-level incomes) (U.S. Bureau of Labor Statistics 2006c).

Programs of assistance for the poor have been cut, and there is increased economic risk and volatility as well as uncertainty about the future of such benefits as pensions and health insurance (Hacker 2006). In the 2006 election exit polls, only 30 percent of Ameri-

Military Families in Wartime

Some effects of war on the family seem obvious—family separation and the risk of death (Alvarez 2006a). Yet as the Iraq war has become more controversial, morale problems have increased for both troops and their families at home. Although the troops have strong popular support, sacrifice seems limited to military personnel and their families (Haberman 2006).

Separation of a military parent from spouse or partner and children is not a new feature of wartime. But the Iraq and Afghanistan wars have seen repeated and lengthy deployments. One newly married couple, for example, has spent a total of two weeks together in the fourteen months of their marriage. There are more dual military couples serving in Iraq and Afghanistan than in past military conflicts (Morris 2007).

A large percentage of armed forces stationed overseas are composed of National Guard and Reserve troops, who have not usually anticipated such extensive separation from family. Many of these troops are older and have well-established civilian careers or businesses that are severely disrupted by military service (Skipp and Ephron 2006).

On the positive side, technological developments such as e-mail, websites, and webcams facilitate communication between soldiers and their families. Sometimes, though, this can lead to tension, as the overseas partner attempts to maintain active control of the household (Skipp and Ephron 2006). On the other hand, some wives say that war is making their men open up emotionally: "'He's changed dramatically since he's been over there. . . . He tells me now that I'm his best friend. He's never said that before'" ("'Hon, I Miss You'" 2003).

Women make up 15 percent of today's military (U.S. Census Bureau 2007b; Segal and Segal 2004). Although they are not assigned to combat per se, support service personnel in Iraq and Afghanistan are as much at risk of injury and death as combat infantry. Some counselors have wondered about the difficulty soldier-mothers may have in returning from the battlefield to the "normal" life of parent and child (Alvarez 2006b; St. George 2006).

There are other problems subsequent to military service in wartime that are more intense for the Iraq war. Because of improved medical care and transportation, more soldiers are surviving with very severe wounds, especially multiple amputations and brain injuries. The soldier who went to war may not return as the same person (Ruane 2006; Zoroya 2006). Initial statistics also suggest that post-traumatic stress disorder is more frequent among military returning from Iraq than in some past wars, attributable to the constant risk of danger from unseen bombs and snipers.

Finally, some families must face the tragedy of losing their loved one. In an era in which cohabitation, divorce, and single parenthood are common, ambiguous or tentative family relationships have led to disputes over remains and burials (Murphy and Marshall 2005) and over insurance and other benefits based on a deceased's military service.

The armed services have made a considerable effort to support families and especially to reach out to the some 600,000 children who have a parent in service. A *Sesame Street* DVD explains deployment and emotions at a child's level (Elfrink 2006). There are programs for at-risk youth, as well as vouchers for getaways and marriage enrichment programs for couples (Ansay, Perkins, and Nelson 2004).

Critical Thinking

Do you know one or more families that have been affected by a family member's serving in Iraq or Afghanistan? How do their experiences illustrate the fact that history and events impact individual and family life?

a. This conclusion is based on a sample of 456 enlisted military personnel from the 1979 National Longitudinal Survey of Youth. Because these data are older and were collected in peacetime, conclusions must be tentative. This sample was chosen despite these limitations because it is the only data year that has fertility data on military women.

cans agreed that the next generation is likely to see an improved situation (Peters and Leonhardt 2006).

Economists are divided as to whether the increasing **globalization** of the economy—more outsourcing of jobs to other countries and the replacement of manufacturing by service jobs—is rendering the economic foundation of the American family more precarious or is opening new opportunities. In a striking example of the transformation of the American economy, Detroit's Big Three car manufacturers now employ half the number

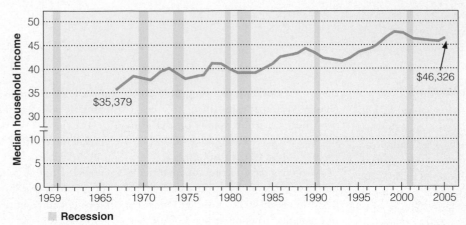

Recession

FIGURE 3.1 Median household income, 1967 to 2005.

Note: Income is adjusted for inflation, presented in 2005 dollars.

Source: DeNavas-Walt, Proctor, and Lee 2006, Figure 1.

of autoworkers they did forty years ago, and soon more will be working for Japanese than for American companies—at half the wage and benefit level (Reich 2006). White-collar jobs, especially those in technological and engineering fields and some financial services, are moving overseas to countries like India and China (A. Bernstein 2004). But other research concludes that "dire predictions of job losses from shifting high technology work to low-wage nations with strong education systems [are] greatly exaggerated" because more complex, higher-end employment will replace the lost jobs (Lohr 2006, p C-11).

Income Regardless of economic change, the overall long-term trend in household income has been upward, though falling back during periods of recession (see Figure 3.1). However, this picture masks a distribution of income in the United States that is highly unequal. In 2005, the top one-fifth of U.S. households received half the nation's total income, while the poorest one-fifth received just 3.4 percent. Over the past thirty years, the inequality gap has grown. The rich have gotten richer, and the poor have gotten poorer. "The income gap is now as extreme as it was in the 1920s, wiping out decades of rising equality," states Princeton economist Paul Krugman (2006a, p. 46).

Even during the recent period of economic growth, the bulk of the gains were realized at higher income levels, while most lost ground or failed to gain. Median income did not rise from 2000 to 2004 after adjusting for inflation. Only in 2005 was there an increase in real incomes for households. Much of this gain had more to do with more jobs (per worker) and more time on the job (and investment income for those possessing such assets) (Greenhouse and Leonhardt 2006; Lyman 2006; Peters and Leonhardt 2006). Median household income is still below what it was in 1998 (DeNavas-Walt, Proctor, and Lee 2006, Table A-1). "[T]he income of

the bottom 60 percent of Americans has barely budged since 1979" (B. Stein 2006, p. Bus-3).

Income varies by race and ethnicity (see Figure 3.2), but all middle to lower groups show moderate gains at best

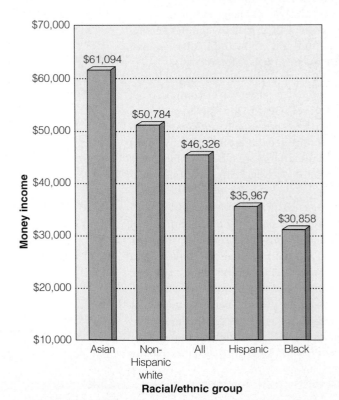

FIGURE 3.2 Median household income by race and Hispanic origin of householder, 2005.

Note: Precisely comparable data are not available for smaller racial/ethnic groups. Three-year median household income (averaged 2003–2005) was $33,627 for American Indians/Alaska Natives and $54,318 for Native Hawaiians and Other Pacific Islanders.

Source: DeNavas-Walt, Proctor, and Lee 2006, Tables 1 and 2.

© Jeff Greenberg/The Image Works

Economic inequality is rising in the United States. Not only lower income sectors, but also the middle class have failed to gain ground.

over the long term. Most of the gain has accrued to those with a college education (Bergman 2006b), but even they have not done well over the last five years, showing gains just a little better than inflation (Leonhardt 2006a, p. 63).

Women have gained more than men since 1970, while men's wages were largely stagnant (DeNavas-Walt, Proctor, and Lee 2006, Figure 3). Still, access to a male wage remains an advantage. Experts debate the extent to which changes in the family—that is, more female-headed, single-parent households—have contributed to poverty levels (see Chapter 7). Incomes do vary by family type. Married-couple households had the highest incomes in 2005—$66,067 compared to $46,756 for male-headed households and $30,650 for female-headed households (DeNavas-Walt, Proctor, and Lee 2006, Table 1). Some scholars point to the increasing tendency for well-educated, high-earning men to marry their female counterparts, while men and women at the lower end of the economic scale marry each other, creating a "real marriage penalty." Families diverge even more in income because of this multiplier effect (Paul 2006; Schwartz and Mare 2005).

Poverty Poverty rates show somewhat the same pattern as income: long-term improvement but increased disadvantage in the short term. Poverty rates fell dramatically in the 1960s and have risen and fallen since then (see Figure 3.3). The poverty rate has risen since 2000 to 12.6 percent in 2005. The child poverty rate is 17.6 percent, higher than child poverty rates in other wealthy industrialized nations. One in six children in the United States is in poverty (DeNavas-Walt, Proctor, and Lee 2006, p. 13 and Table B-2; United Nations Children's Fund 2005).

Poverty rates vary by racial/ethnic group. Non-Hispanic whites had the lowest poverty rate in 2005 (8 percent), followed by Asian Americans (11 percent) and Native Hawaiians and Other Pacific Islanders (12 percent). Native Americans (25 percent), African Americans (25 percent), and Hispanics (22 percent) have higher rates of poverty. Although the poverty *rate* of non-Hispanic whites is low, they compose 44 percent of the *total number of persons in poverty* because they are such a large part of the population (DeNavas-Walt, Proctor, and Lee 2006, pp. 14 and 20 and Table 5).

Blue-Collar and White-Collar Families and the Wealthy

Lifestyles vary by **social class** (which is often measured in terms of education, occupation, and income). In studying social class, social scientists have often compared blue-collar and white-collar workers in terms of their values and lifestyles. Working-class people—blue-collar workers—are employed as mechanics, truckers, machine operators, and factory workers—jobs typically

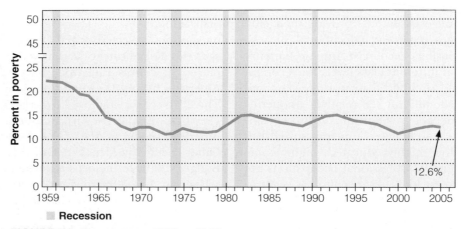

FIGURE 3.3 Poverty rate, 1959 to 2005.

Source: DeNavas-Walt, Proctor, and Lee 2006, Figure 4.

requiring uniforms or durable work clothes. Some jobs, such as police officer, occupy an intermediate position. White-collar workers include professionals, managers, clerical workers, salespeople, and so forth, who have traditionally worn white shirts to work.

To complicate matters, the nature of some blue-collar jobs has changed dramatically with the advent of computerized manufacturing and the technological transformation of health care support work. At the same time, some professions—medicine, for example—have lost ground in terms of income and autonomy. White-collar job security has been eroded by changes in the economy.

Social scientists do not agree on whether blue- and white-collar workers have become increasingly alike in their values and attitudes in recent decades. Certainly, the widespread availability of certain consumer products at relatively low cost—cell phones, other electronics, stylish clothing, plane travel, and even home ownership—blurs the class distinctions that used to be much more obvious. "'You can make a case that the upper half lives as well as the upper 5 percent did 50 years ago'" (Scott and Leonhardt 2005; see also Steinhauer 2005). At the same time that we see rising economic inequality, our cultural class distinctions are less clear (Yabroff 2006).

Blue- and white-collar employees, however, may continue to look at life differently, even at similar income levels. Regarding marriage, for example, working-class couples tend to emphasize values associated with parenthood and job stability and may be more traditional in gender-role ideology. White-collar couples are more inclined to value companionship, self-expression, and communication. Middle-class parents value self-direction and initiative in children, whereas parents in working-class families stress obedience and conformity (Hochschild 1989; Lareau 2003b; Luster, Rhoades, and Haas 1989; Tom Smith 1999, pp. 12–19).

Middle-class parenting strategies include involving children in a myriad of stimulating activities and lessons to enhance their development. Although there is no doubt that middle-class parents provide their children with advantages regarding educational success, health care, and housing, sociologist Annette Lareau's study of parenting at different class levels finds certain advantages accruing to children in working-class and poor families. These children see relatives frequently and have much deeper relationships with cousins and older relatives, as well as less time-pressured lives (Lareau 2003a). More highly educated, high-income parents with managerial/professional occupations are less likely than those at lower socioeconomic levels to have dinner with their child every day during a typical week (Dye and Johnson 2007, Tables D7, D8; Roberts 2007b). The achievement pressures and social isolation more characteristic of affluent suburban families result in some surprisingly high rates of depression and substance abuse among upper-middle- and upper-class preteens and adolescents (Luthar 2003).

Race and Ethnicity

Social class can be as important as race or ethnicity in shaping people's family lives. The attitudes, behaviors, and experiences of middle-class blacks, for example, differ from those of poor African Americans (Billingsley 1992). Lareau's study of child socialization found class to be more significant than race in terms of parental values and interactions with their children (2003b).

Yet, racial/ethnic heritage—the family's place within our culturally diverse society—affects preferences, options, and decisions, not to mention opportunities. Moreover, the growth of immigration in recent decades will increase the impact of ethnicity on family life because new immigrants retain more of their ethnic culture than do those who have been in the United States longer.

Conceptualizing Race and Ethnicity

To begin this discussion, we need to consider what is meant by race and ethnicity.

Race The term **race** implies a biologically distinct group, but scientific thinking rejects the idea that there are separate races clearly distinguished by biological markers. Features such as skin color that Americans use to place someone in a racial group are superficial, genetically speaking. Instead, race is a social construction reflecting how Americans think about different social groups. "'Race is a real cultural, political, and economic concept, but it's not biological,'" says biology professor Alan Templeton ("Genetically, Race Doesn't Exist" 2003, p. 4).

In this text, we use the racial/ethnic categories formally adopted by the U.S. government because we draw on statistics collected by the Census Bureau and other agencies. Racial categorization and how individuals are placed in census categories have varied throughout American history (Lee and Edmonston 2005, pp. 8–9) The 2000 census employed five major racial categories: (1) white, (2) black or African American, (3) Asian, (4) American Indian or Alaska Native, and (5) Hawaiian or Other Pacific Islander (U.S. Office of Management and Budget 1999). In the census, racial identity is based on self-report. In 2000, individuals were permitted to indicate more than one race, but only 2.4 percent did so (Jones and Smith 2001).[2]

This last point highlights one problem with census racial categories: Many people have mixed ancestry.

"White"Americans may have some ancestors who were African American or Native American, while most "African Americans" have white as well as black ancestry and some have Native American or Asian ancestry (Bean et al. 2004; J. Davis 1991).

Ethnicity You'll notice that "Latino" is not listed as a racial category. That's because Hispanic or Latino is considered an **ethnic identity**, not a *race*. **Ethnicity** has no biological connotations, but refers to cultural distinctions often based in language, religion, foodways, and history.

For census purposes, there are two major categories of ethnicity: Hispanic and non-Hispanic.[3] Hispanics may be of any race (U.S. Census Bureau 2003b).[4] In many statistical analyses, Hispanics are separated out from other whites so that *non-Hispanic white* and *Hispanic* become separate categories.

Minority In a final distinction, African Americans, Hispanics, American Indians, Asians, and Hawaiians and Other Pacific Islanders are often grouped into a category termed minority group or minority. This conveys the idea that persons in those groups experience some disadvantage, exclusion, or discrimination in American society as compared to the dominant group: non-Hispanic white Americans.[5]

"Actually, I prefer the term Arctic-American."

The Utility and Use of Racial/Ethnic Category Systems
One can reasonably argue that no category system can truly capture cultural identity. Moreover, the dramatic increase in immigration of Latinos and Asians, groups that are neither black nor white (the traditional racial dividing line), and the growth of intermarriage have made the notion of distinct racial/ethnic categories especially problematic. As racial/ethnic categories become more fluid and as the identity choices of individuals with a mixed heritage vary, racial/ethnic identity may come to be seen as voluntary—"optional" rather than automatic (Bean et al. 2004, p. 23).

A further point is that there is considerable diversity *within* major racial/ethnic groupings. There are Caribbean and African blacks, for example, as well as those descended from slave populations. Within each major racial/ethnic category, there are often significant differences in family patterns, as Figure 3.4 illustrates.

Within-group diversity makes generalizations about racial/ethnic groups somewhat questionable. "Hispanic" or "Latino" categories are "useful for charting broad demographic changes in the United States . . . [but they] conceal variation in the family characteristics of Latino groups [Cubans and Mexicans, for example] whose differences are often greater than the overall differences between Latinos and non-Latinos" (Baca Zinn and Wells 2007, pp. 422, 424). As another example, though blacks have high poverty rates and low incomes generally, in the New York borough of Queens, black median household income in 2005 was greater than that of whites (Roberts 2006).

Moreover, there are areas of social life in which racial/ethnic differences seem minor if they exist at all.

---

[2] The Census Bureau does *not* include Arab as a separate major racial/ethnic category. More than one million Americans identified themselves as of Arab ancestry in the 2000 census (de la Cruz and Brittingham 2003).

[3] The Census Bureau does record more finely differentiated cultural identities of both Hispanics and non-Hispanics using terms such as *ancestry* and *national origin*. Examples of these categories include German, Russian, Mexican, and Salvadoran.

[4] The racial composition of the Latino population is not knowable with certainty. Latino countries of origin typically have more nuanced racial vocabularies than does the United States. Moreover, some Latinos view their ethnic identity as a racial one (AmeriStat Staff 2001; Fears 2003).

In the 2000 census, the racial self-identification of Hispanics' ethnic identity was 48 percent white; 2 percent black; 42 percent "some other race"; 6 percent more than one race; and 2 percent specific other races. Demographers infer from these responses that 90 percent of Hispanics would be classified as "white" (Bean et al. 2004; Kent et al. 2001; Lee and Edmonston 2005, p. 19).

[5] *Minority* in a sociological context does not have its everyday meaning of fewer than 50 percent. Regardless of size, if a group is distinguishable and in some way disadvantaged within a society, it is considered by sociologists a *minority group* (Ferrante 2000).

The term *minority* has become a contested one, viewed by some as demeaning; as ignoring differences among groups and variation in the self-identities of individuals; and as not recognizing the likely future of the United States as a "majority-minority" nation (Gonzalez 2006a; Wilkinson 2000). We will try to avoid using it other than when speaking of numerical differences or in reporting Census Bureau data so labeled.

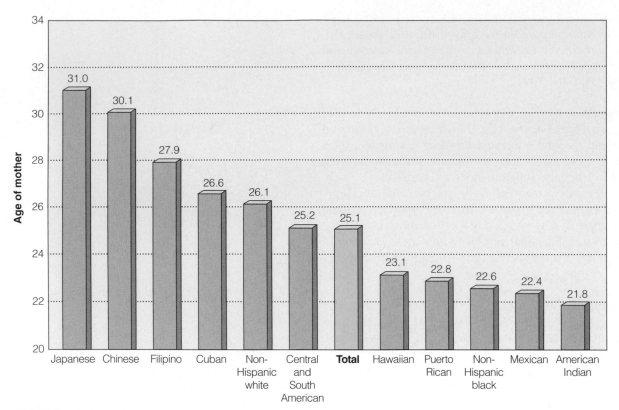

FIGURE 3.4 Mean age of mother at first birth by race and Hispanic origin: United States, 2002.

Note: This graph indicates the average age of mothers at the birth of their first child for a variety of racial/ethnic groups. It illustrates the point that differences in family patterns exist *within* major racial/ethnic groups.

Source: J. Martin et al. 2003, Figure 5.

Little difference in family patterns is apparent between blacks and whites serving in the military, for example (Hickes 2004; Lundquist 2004). In his ethnographic study of fathers who had been high school classmates, anthropologist Nicholas Townsend remarks that

> [i]n my interviews, the racial-ethnic category was not associated with different fundamental values about the place of fatherhood and family in men's lives. . . . I found a remarkable degree of uniformity in men's depictions of the central elements of fatherhood. (2002, p. 20)

As these examples make clear, "the complex multicultural reality of American society means that categories used by government agencies such as the Census Bureau are . . . 'illogical'" (Walker, Spohn, and DeLone 2007, p. 9). So why use them?

First, we use them, qualifiedly, because they do have social meaning in our society. Racial/ethnic stratification still exists in our society. The income of white households is much higher and poverty rates significantly lower than those of African American or Hispanic households. Social policy to ensure equal opportunity requires a base of information about group outcomes.

Second, to learn more about families than mere speculation can tell us, we need to make use of data collected in this format by the government and other researchers. These data can tell us something about the contexts of family life and the impact that social attitudes about "race" and ethnicity have on life chances. "[R]acial statuses, although not representing biological differences, are of sociological interest in their forms, their changes, and their consequences" (American Sociological Association 2002).

Now it's time to use these racial/ethnic categories to explore the features of family life in various social settings. In doing so, we turn to research rather than rely on assumptions about differences—which may be mistaken. Of course, researchers may themselves be influenced by stereotyped assumptions, but they have become much more conscious of such pitfalls in recent decades, as "Issues for Thought: Studying Families and Ethnicity" indicates.

As men and women from diverse racial/ ethnic backgrounds came into the field of family studies, they pointed out how limited and biased our theoretical and research perspectives had been. To begin to understand the question of bias, we might think of theory and research on racial/ethnic family groups as falling into one of three frameworks: cultural equivalent, cultural deviant, and cultural variant (W. Allen 1978).

The **cultural equivalent perspective** emphasizes those features that other racial/ethnic families have in common with mainstream white families. An example would be research finding that middle-class black parents bring up their children much the same as do middle-class white parents (Lareau 2002).

The **cultural deviant perspective** views the qualities that distinguish minority racial/ethnic families from mainstream white middle-class families as negative or pathological. An example would be analysis that laments the high prevalence of female-headed families among blacks compared to non-Hispanic whites or Asians.

For many years, research on African Americans was focused on poor, single-parent households in the inner city while research on Latinos focused on Mexican immigrants' alleged "patriarchal" culture and other barriers to economic advancement and assimilation (Baca Zinn and Wells 2007; S. Hill 2006; Taylor 2007). This approach still exists, and may even have intensified in current media and policy attention to the African American marriage "crisis" (U.S. Administration for Children and Families n.d.) and the "caste" barrier between single-parent and married-couple families (Hymowitz 2006). But following the negative reaction to the earlier, limited portrayal of racial/ethnic family differences, researchers began to report on the strengths of black families, pointing to strong extended-family support, more egalitarian spousal relation-

ships, and class, regional, and rural/urban diversity.

In the *cultural deviant* and *cultural equivalent* approaches, white middle-class families are considered the standard against which "other" families are compared, either favorably or unfavorably—a situation conducive to bias. In the third approach, minority families are studied on their own terms. This **cultural variant perspective** calls for making culturally and contextually relevant interpretations of minority family lives. For example, a substantial proportion of African American single-mother households contain other adults who take part in rearing the children (Taylor 2007). Another study of Hispanic and non-Hispanic white families points to the different ways in which extended families function. Although the Hispanic families provide instrumental help, the white families provide financial help. Both families are close in terms of communication (Sarkisian, Gerena, and Gerstel 2006); the image of white families as lacking an extended-family context is thus challenged.

Cultural variant approaches may lead to "reverse theorizing." Ideas, insights, and concepts developed in the study of families that vary from the majority group are applied to enrich family studies more generally. For example, Annette Lareau (2003a) points to the rich family life of working- and lower-class children, whose parents are less focused on educational and achievement goals and activities so that they have more time to spend with relatives and lead less-stressful lives than seemingly more-privileged middle-class children (Levine 2006).

Research using a comparative approach has shown us that the same family phenomenon may have different outcomes in different racial/ethnic settings. For example, premarital cohabitation is associated with future marital disruption among whites but not among

African Americans or Latinos, where it may function as a marital substitute and so represent more stable unions.

The cultural variant approach can have policy implications. Research on extended-family ties illuminates the great amount of instrumental help that Hispanic extended families provide to their members. This means that workplace policies that presume only nuclear family members need the flexibility to provide family care does not take into account the real lives of Hispanic families (Sarkisian, Gerena, and Gerstel 2006).

Today's research on family and ethnicity tends to be more complex and sophisticated than in the past. Concern about family fragility and individual disorganization is balanced by recognition of diversity and of community and family strengths. Multiple influences on racial/ethnic families are acknowledged: (1) mainstream culture; (2) ethnic settings; and (3) the negative impact of disadvantaged neighborhoods or family circumstances that can produce a "minority culture" (S. Hill 2004). Structural influences—economic opportunity, that is—are seen as a powerful influence on family relations and behavior. The role of "agency," or the initiative of families, is recognized: "What happens on a daily basis in family relations and domestic settings also constructs families. . . . Families should be seen as settings in which people are agents and actors, coping with, adapting to, and changing social structures to meet their needs" (Baca Zinn 2004, p. 426; see also S. Hill 2004).

Critical Thinking

Does your family heritage or your observation of families make you aware of some family patterns that you would see as different from common American assumptions about families? How could these observations be applied to help researchers learn more about families in a variety of family settings?

Racial/Ethnic Diversity in the United States

The United States is an increasingly diverse nation. In 2005, the nation was 66 percent non-Hispanic white; 12.8 percent black; 4.2 percent Asian; 1 percent American Indian/Alaska Native; and less than 1 percent Native Hawaiian and Other Pacific Islander. The Hispanic population has increased dramatically: Hispanics are now 14.4 percent of the population, surpassing blacks as the largest racial/ethnic group after whites.[6] Hispanics account for one-half of current population growth. Their increasing numbers derive from immigration and from fertility rates that are higher than those of blacks or whites (Haub 2006; U.S. Census Bureau 2007a, Table 14).

The child population is even more diverse at a little less than 60 percent non-Hispanic white; 20 percent Hispanic; 15 percent black; 4 percent Asian and Pacific Islander; 1 percent American Indian/Alaska Native; and less than 1 percent Native Hawaiian and Other Pacific Islander. Almost 3 percent of children are reported to be of more than one race (U.S. Census Bureau 2007a, Table 14).

Presently, racial/ethnic minorities compose over one-third of the U.S. population and over 40 percent of the child population. By 2050, non-Hispanic whites are expected to be only half the population (U.S. Census Bureau 2004b and 2007a, Table 14). In five "majority-minority" states, racial/ethnic minorities already compose over half the population (R. Bernstein 2005b). As these trends unfold, they describe a world that younger people find familiar: "'Beginning with Generation X, [for] people in their 20s to early 40s and all the generations that follow, multicultural is normal'" (marketing expert Ann Fishman in El Nasser and Grant 2005, p. 4-A).

African American Families

African Americans are increasingly split into a middle class that has benefited from the opportunities opened by the Civil Rights Movement and a substantial sector that remains disadvantaged. Thirty percent of African American households had incomes of $50,000 or more

The child population of the United States is more racially and ethnically diverse than the adult population and will become even more diverse in the future.

in 2005 (DeNavas-Walt, Proctor, and Lee 2006, Table A-1). Yet a higher proportion of black children than those of other racial/ethnic groups lives in poverty (U.S. Census Bureau 2006c, Table 694). Black women are more than twice as likely as white women to suffer the death of an infant (Mathews and MacDorman 2006, Table A).

Childbearing and child rearing are increasingly divorced from marriage. True of all racial/ethnic groups, this trend is especially pronounced among blacks, with 70 percent of births in 2005 to unmarried mothers (Hamilton, Martin, and Ventura 2006, Table 1). Black divorce rates are higher as well, although the more substantial difference between blacks and whites is that blacks are far more likely to have never married (U.S. Administration for Children and Families n.d.). As a consequence, only 35 percent of African American children are living with married parents, compared to 77 percent of white (non-Hispanic) and 65 percent of Hispanic children (U.S. Federal Interagency Forum 2005, p. 8; and see Chapter 7 for further discussion).

Differences between African Americans and whites in the proportion of two-parent families are not new, but as recently as the 1960s, more than 70 percent of black families were headed by married couples (Billingsley 1968); in 2004, only 46 percent were (U.S. Census Bureau 2006c, Table 62). Experts do not agree on the cause of the decline in marriage and two-parent fami-

---

[6] Percentages may not always add up to 100, due to rounding errors and to the complexities of classifying individuals who indicated more than one race in the census multicategory system.

lies among African Americans. The idea that African Americans value marriage less has been contradicted by research. For example, a Gallup poll taken in 2006 finds 69 percent of blacks agreeing that marriage is "very important" "when a man and woman plan to spend the rest of their lives together as a couple"—*higher than the figure for whites* (Saad 2006c).

Given similar values regarding marriage, some suggest that the primary source of difference in marital patterns is economic. Our economy's shift away from manufacturing has meant the elimination of the relatively well-paying entry-level positions that once sustained black working-class families. Low levels of black male employment and income may preclude marriage or doom it from the start (Taylor 2007; W. J. Wilson 1987).

African American women have traditionally been employed, and they may be less dependent on the earnings of a spouse for economic survival. But the *economic independence* explanation of low marriage rates is not supported by research; it appears that the better their earnings, the more likely black women are to marry (M. B. Tucker 2000). Research also indicates that the availability of welfare is not a significant factor in a black woman's decision to marry (Teachman 2000).

Another possible explanation for the lower marriage rates of African Americans is the **sex ratio**, the number of eligible men available for women seeking marital partners (Taylor 2007). High rates of incarceration, what some black scholars call "the prisonization of black America" (Clayton and Moore 2003, p. 85),[7] as well as poorer health and higher mortality have taken many African American men out of circulation.

Many scholarly and policy analyses of the African American family emphasize the "crisis" of marriage among blacks (U.S. Administration for Children and Families n.d.), and we have reported that here. At the same time, African American scholars rightly complain of "sweeping generalizations" and "pejorative characterizations" (Taylor 2002a, p. 19) that often reflect a research focus on lower-income blacks in the inner city (Taylor 2007; Willie and Reddick 2003).

Recent research gives more attention to middle-class blacks (e.g., Pattillo-McCoy 1999) and gives us more nuanced portraits of those families not organized around a married couple. Sociologist Jennifer Hamer (2001) undertook a qualitative study of eighty-eight lower-income black fathers living away from their children. These fathers view spending time with children, providing emotional support and discipline, and serving as role models and guides as among their most important parental functions, although they also tried to do what they could by way of economic support.

Scholars have noted the strengths of black families (Robert Hill 2003 [1972]; S. A. Hill 2004; Taylor 2007), especially strong kinship bonds. Single-parent families or unmarried individuals are often embedded in extended families and experience family-oriented daily lives. As a family system, African American families are child-focused. Blacks are disposed to accept children regardless of circumstances: "Children are prized" (Crosbie-Burnett and Lewis 1999, p. 457). In a child-focused family system, the extended family and community are involved in caring for children; their survival and well-being do not depend on the parents alone (Uttal 1999, p. 855).

With regard to couple dynamics, we find that married blacks have more egalitarian gender roles than do whites, characterized by role flexibility and power sharing. Other research finds that African American men do more housework and are more supportive of working wives than are other men, but are traditional in other respects. Child socialization is less gender differentiated in African American families (McLoyd et al. 2000; Taylor 2002a).

As we write, the direction of change in the circumstances of African American families is uncertain. Since 1966 there has been a small but steady rise in the percentage of black families headed by married couples ("Married Households" 2003). Yet, poverty and racism continue to create stress on many African American families. Segregation persists in much of everyday life even in the suburban middle-class settings to which many African Americans have moved (El Nasser 2001; Janny Scott 2001). The income of a number of black families has risen, but conditions at the lowest economic levels have not shown improvement, nor have blacks at higher income levels acquired assets that compare with those of non-Hispanic whites (Krivo and Kaufman 2004; Stoll 2004; "Study Says" 2004). Moreover, "[b]lack baby boomers did not close the income gap even though [they came] of age after the civil rights era" (Fears 2004, p. A02). Middle-class blacks have comparatively lower-status jobs and incomes, and some must cope with de facto housing segregation and neighborhoods that often have higher crime rates, poorer schools, and fewer services. Even highly educated, high-income African American families face some problems that represent lingering racism and assumptions based on stereotypes, finding

---

[7] "Racial profiling, mandatory minimum sentences, and especially the disparities in drug laws [which more heavily penalize crimes involving drugs typically used by blacks] have had a dramatic effect on the incarceration rates of young males, especially in urban inner-city neighborhoods" (Clayton and Moore 2003, p. 86). African Americans comprise 13 percent of drug users, but represent 35 percent of drug arrests and 53 percent of drug convictions (Eckholm 2006; "Incarceration and Fewer Jobs" 2003).

it difficult to obtain nannies or other in-the-home child care, for example (Kantor 2006). "The reality . . . is that even the black and white *middle classes* remain separate and unequal" (Pattillo-McCoy 1999, p. 2).

In analyzing the contemporary situation of African Americans, scholars have begun to note and investigate the increasing geographic dispersion, class separation, and gender differences that characterize the post–civil rights era (S. A. Hill 2004). Blacks are ethnically heterogeneous now, as foreign-born blacks (African and Caribbean immigrants) comprise 7.8 percent of the black population, compared to 1.3 percent in 1970 ("Foreign-Born Make Up" 2002). Research on "African American" families needs to include study of those diverse cultural communities (W. Allen, James, and Dana 1998). The extent to which African American families are influenced by mainstream middle-class values, African values, and "minority culture" (their disadvantaged position in the American stratification system; S. A. Hill 2004, pp. 15–16) is a likely focus of future research. The prominence of the extended family and the inclusion of "fictive kin" (unrelated persons given symbolic kinship status) seem to be an African cultural heritage (S. A. Hill 2004; Taylor 2007), as is the value of motherhood and productive work roles for women.

Latino (Hispanic) Families

Although the first Spanish settlements in what is now the United States date to the sixteenth century, many Latinos are recent immigrants from Mexico, Central America, the Caribbean, or South America. A majority of U.S. Latinos were born in this country, but 40 percent were foreign born (Haub 2006).

Latino families may be binational. **Binational families** are those in which some family members are American citizens or legal residents, while others are **undocumented immigrants** (i.e., not legally in the United States and subject to sudden deportation). Issues affecting families of immigrants from various nations are discussed in "A Closer Look at Family Diversity: Family Ties and Immigration." Here we examine Latino family circumstances more generally.

On average, Latino families are less economically advantaged than non-Hispanic white families. Some 28 percent of Latino children are poor compared to 18 percent of all children. Even in married-couple families, almost 20 percent of children are poor due to the relatively low earnings of employed Hispanic parents (DeNavas-Walt, Proctor, and Lee 2006).

Educational levels are relatively low; only 57 percent of Latinos have graduated from high school and 11 per-

cent from college (Ramirez and de la Cruz 2003). This may be partially due to a "Hispanic culture of hard work" that draws Latinos into the labor force early to contribute to family welfare ("Hispanic Nation" 2004). Latino parents, like parents in all racial/ethnic groups, have high educational aspirations for their children (Omaha Public Schools [OPS] Dual Language Research Group 2006; Schneider, Martinez, and Owens 2006). But language difficulties, the initial economic disadvantage of Hispanic youth, and low educational levels of parents are often compounded by poor schools and weak relationships with teachers as well as pressures to help out at home (Schneider, Martinez, and Owens 2006). Dropping out of high school may also depend on neighborhood context. Although Latino youth drop out more than non-Hispanic youth in the inner city, in suburban areas there is no difference (Oropesa and Landale 2004).

Hispanics are most likely to be employed in service-level occupations and to have higher rates of unemployment than the general population (Ramirez and de la Cruz 2003). The second generation is characterized by **segmented assimilation.** Although some are doing quite well in attaining a secure place in the American socio-economic system, many face a substantial likelihood of downward social mobility. Skill levels overall are low, and those educated for the professions may encounter a hostility to people of immigrant heritage that will affect their prospects. Some Hispanics have taken an entrepreneurial route, starting small businesses (Bergman 2006d; Oropesa and Landale 2004; Portes, Fernandez-Kelly, and Haller 2004).[8]

Hispanics tend to marry at young ages—42 percent of women were married by ages twenty to twenty-four (Oropesa and Landale 2004; Wildsmith and Raley 2006). Mexican Americans are more "married" than other disadvantaged groups in the United States, and Cuban and Mexican marriage and marital dissolution rates are similar to those of non-Hispanic whites. Puerto Ricans share a Caribbean tradition of informal marriage, cohabitation that resembles marriage (Rodman 1971; and see Chapter 8, "A Closer Look at Family Diversity: Cohabiting Means Different Things to Different People—The Meaning of Cohabitation for Puerto Ricans, Compared to Mexican Americans").

---

[8] Recent scholars of immigration have challenged the classic assumption that over time immigrants assimilate into American society and culture. Portes and Rumbaut (2000) argue that though this is true of some migrants, it is not true of others. Whether or not immigrants secure a place in the mainstream economy depends on the human capital of the migrants (their education and skills), the match to the labor market, and reception of a particular immigrant group at a particular time by the government (e.g., refugee support programs) and by co-ethnics already present in the United States.

Latinas do not necessarily limit their lives to traditional roles. They enter the labor force and undertake important activities in the community.

Hispanic birth rates are the highest of any racial/ethnic group, but they vary by ethnicity. Mexican American birth rates are among the highest in the United States, while those of Cubans are among the lowest. Interestingly, Central American, Cuban, and Mexican immigrants all have lower **infant mortality rates** than non-Hispanic whites despite higher levels of poverty and lower levels of education and income (Mathews, Menacker, and MacDorman 2003, Table D). One possible explanation, besides extended family support, is that Latinas, especially recent immigrants, are more likely to refrain from smoking, drinking, and drug use (Chung 2006; Pew Hispanic Center 2002).

Almost half of births to Latina women in 2005 were to unmarried women. Puerto Rican women are especially likely to be unmarried at a child's birth, perhaps a consequence of the Caribbean pattern of acceptance of informal marital ties. Mexican American women typically have their first child in marriage, but some suggest that the nonmarital birth pattern may be becoming characteristic of lower-income Mexican American women (Baca Zinn and Pok 2002; Baca Zinn and Wells 2007; Hamilton, Martin, and Ventura 2006; J. Martin et al. 2003; Phillips and Sweeney 2005; Wildsmith and Raley 2006).

At the same time, the assumption that Latinos are conservative on sexual issues is supported by survey results indicating high rates of disapproval of abortion and of opposition to the legalization of homosexual relations and same-sex marriage (Baca Zinn and Pok 2002; Baca Zinn and Wells 2007; McLoyd et al. 2000; Perez 2002; Taylor 2002b). Hispanics, especially Mexican immigrants, are seen to have a "pro-nuptial" family culture that some have hoped would leaven the mainstream American culture of a "retreat from marriage" (Brooks 2006). Alas, calculations by Oropesa and Landale (2004) reveal that even as the United States becomes increasingly Hispanic, there would not be that much of an impact on marital rates and marital stability. Moreover, these authors speculate that it is at least as likely that second and third generations post-immigration would become assimilated enough to join the mainstream retreat from marriage. One must also take into account changes in the home countries toward higher divorce rates and more cohabitation—new immigrants will not necessarily bring a traditional "pro-nuptial" culture with them (Oropesa and Landale 2004).

One researcher detects a "growing ambivalence among some Latinas about marriage in the face of the conflicts generated through increased women's economic power and traditional gender role beliefs" (M. B. Tucker 2000, p. 180). Latina women are starting to have smaller families, "resisting the social pressures that shaped the Hispanic tradition of big families." They increasingly postpone marriage and limit families in favor of working and getting an education to have better economic prospects (Navarro 2004).

Single-mother families are increasing as nonmarital births are rising and "marriage is no longer the exclusive context for reproduction and sexual intimacy among Hispanics" (Oropesa and Landale 2004, p. 916). One interpretation is that single motherhood in the United States requires less dependency on the extended family and single mothers do not experience the shame they might in Mexico. Nevertheless, two-parent families remain the most common form of children's living arrangements. In 2005, 65 percent of Hispanic children were living with married-couple parents. Some single mothers are cohabiting, while almost half of single-parent fathers are (Fields 2003; Hamilton, Martin, and Ventura 2006, Table 1; Oropesa and Landale 2004; U.S. Demographic Internet Staff 2006, Table C-2; Wildsmith and Raley 2006).

Latino families are more likely to be extended and larger than those of non-Hispanic whites (Ramirez and de la Cruz 2003, Figure 6). Both structural factors (economic necessity) and culture seem to shape an

Family Ties and Immigration

There is more racial and ethnic diversity among American families than ever before, and much of this diversity results from immigration. The foreign-born now constitute 12 percent of the U.S. population. Seventeen percent of America's children live in a household headed by a foreign-born parent (Lugaila and Overturf 2004; Martin and Midgley 2006).

The United States admits approximately one million legal immigrants each year. Asia, Latin America, and the Caribbean—not Europe—are now the major sending regions. In addition to legal immigrants, there are approximately 11 million undocumented immigrants (not legal residents) residing in the United States. The vast majority of these are from Mexico, Central America, and the Caribbean, but there are also substantial numbers from such countries as Canada, Poland, and Ireland. Although immigrants were previously concentrated in a few states, now they are much more geographically dispersed. Almost one-third of foreign-born Americans have become naturalized citizens ("Illegal Immigrant Population" 2001; Martin and Midgley 2006).

Why do immigrants choose to come here? For the most part, immigrants leave a poorer country for a richer one in hopes of bettering their family's economic situation. Some immigrants are highly educated professionals who cannot find suitable employment in their home country. Finally, many refugees have arrived here and spread out across the United States to areas that previously had little immigration. Nebraska, for example, is home to clusters of Afghani, Cuban, Hmong, Serbian, Somali, Sudanese, Soviet Jewish, and Vietnamese refugees and to Mexicans and Central Americans who have come to work in the meatpacking plants.

Immigrants may be single individuals or they may be young or middle-aged married adults who migrate with spouses or children or who plan to bring them here. As immigrants establish themselves, they begin to send for relatives, and ethnic kin and community networks develop. In fact, the majority of legal immigrants enter the United States through family sponsorship (Martin and Midgley 2006).

One feature of recent immigration is that immigrants may have transnational identities and families. A **transnational family** is one that maintains significant contact with two countries: the country of origin and the United States. With modern communication and transportation, migrants often maintain close ties with relatives in the home country. They may experience back-and-forth changes of residence, frequent family visits, business dealings, money transfers to family, placement of children with relatives in the other country, and seeking marital partners in the home country.

Many immigrant families are binational families—that is, members of the nuclear family have different legal statuses. One spouse may be a legal resident, the other not. Children born here are automatically citizens, but one or both of their parents may be illegal residents of the United States. An estimated 3.1 million children have had their undocumented parents deported (Preston 2007). Many young adults whose immigrant parents brought them to the United States as children and who are therefore not legal residents and at risk of deportation do not have connections in the country of origin: "My life has been American" (Gonzalez 2006b).

Concern about English-language competency seems largely misplaced. Although 84 percent of immigrants do speak another language at home, most want to learn English; the demand for English language courses exceeds the supply (Santos 2007). Today's immigrants seem to make a quicker transition to English than in the past. It is telling to note that media targeting a Latino audience have begun to realize they need programming in English for their younger audience (Kent and Lalasz 2006; Martin and Midgley 2006; Navarro 2006a; Pew Hispanic Center 2006; U.S. Federal Interagency Forum on Child and Family Statistics 2003).

The foreign-born population is a diverse group, but on average poorer, more likely to be in the workforce, and younger than the general population. Despite higher levels of poverty, foreign-born adults are healthier than U.S.-born adults and have greater longevity (N. Bernstein 2004b; Dey and Lucas 2006).

The immigrant population is diverse educationally; 33 percent have college degrees, more than the U.S. average, but immigrants are also more likely to have less than a high school education. Immigrants' earnings are only 79 percent of the U.S. median, but Asian and Middle Eastern immigrants have higher incomes. Immigrants have shown a high level of entrepreneurship, and many start small businesses.

Many immigrants are in the childbearing years, and one-fourth of current births are to foreign-born women (Martin and Midgley 2006). Children of immigrants are more likely (78 percent) than U.S.-born children to be living in two-parent families (Beavers and D'Amico 2005; Martin and Midgley 2006).

The freedom of American children and youth may create tension between immigrant parents and children (Baca Zinn and Pok 2002). Children of immigrants may make unfavorable comparisons of their stoic and practical parents to the more openly emotional and expressive American families they see (perhaps only on TV). Parents, in turn, fear their children's loss of traditional culture (Pyke 2007).

It may be difficult to supervise children in the new setting. The long hours

Many Immigrants to the United States start small businesses. This immigrant family owns a bakery.

and hard work of immigrant parents give them little time to watch over children. Some parents have been separated from their children, leaving them behind in the care of relatives for long periods, engaging in "transnational motherhood" (Hondagneu-Sotelo and Avila 1997).

Marriages of recent immigrants seem less egalitarian than those of couples of similar background whose families have been in the United States longer. Yet migration is likely to change husband–wife roles even in cultures in which family life is experienced as carrying on tradition and accepting the decisions of family heads. Male heads of household typically lose status when male privilege and authority here is not what it was in the home country, and they may have to take jobs at a much lower status level. Women, who usually enter the labor force after coming to the United States, begin to experience an independence and autonomy that carry over into the

negotiation of new roles and patterns of family life (Hondagneu-Sotelo and Messner 1994; Jo 2002; Kibria 2007).

Immigrants bring many strengths to this country: the "immigrant ethos" of strong family ties and high aspirations, hard work, and achievement. Children in immigrant families spend more time on homework and have higher GPAs than the U.S. average, and they adjust well to school. Immigrants exhibit a strong devotion to family and community, respect for work and education, good health, spirituality, and low crime rates (D. Brooks 2006; Detzner and Xiong 1999; Lewin 2001a, Reardon-Anderson, Capps, and Fix 2002; Waters 1997).

A movement directed toward eventual legalization of undocumented immigrants took shape in 2006, with support from the Bush administration, businesses, and religious, ethnic, and other advocacy groups. They point to the reality of the illegal immigrant population, to the need to stabilize families and prevent exploitation of workers, and to the limited number of visas and the difficulty of the legal process itself (N. Bernstein 2006; Gonzalez 2006b; Navarro 2006b; Preston 2006c). Immigrant advocates also ask whether a large underground population is desirable from a public health and criminal justice perspective.

At the same time, the public in general and many political leaders would like to reduce legal immigration and deport illegal aliens, or at least not give them opportunities for citizenship or legal residence. Polls indicate that a majority of Americans want both legal and illegal immigration reduced (Martin and Midgley 2006). Young people, however, are more open to immigration (Pew Research Center 2007). A bill to modify U.S. immigration policy and provide a path to citizenship for undocumented immigrants failed to pass Congress in 2007 (Steinhauer 2007b).

Immigrant families pay payroll, property, and sales taxes while having very limited access to government benefits; taxes paid outweigh services consumed.[a] The latest research suggests that there is a small uptick to the gross domestic product and a moderation of prices due to lower wages paid to immigrant workers (Martin and Midgley 2006). But costs and benefits are not evenly distributed. Most immigrant family tax dollars go to the federal government, whereas the costs of immigrants' schooling or emergency health care are largely paid by local governments. Whether immigration is a net gain or loss regarding taxes and benefits depends on the age and occupational level of the immigrant. Probably more is spent to aid elderly and less-educated immigrants, while younger, more-educated immigrants will pay more in taxes than they gain in benefits (Martin and Midgley 2003).[b]

Whatever our views on immigration policy, immigrants are generally responsible family members doing what they can to improve their family lives.

Critical Thinking

What are some strengths exhibited by immigrant families? What are some challenges they face?

At the societal level, what benefits does recent increased immigration offer the United States? What challenges does it bring?

a. Illegal immigrants are not entitled to most government services; emergency health care and children's elementary and secondary education are the exceptions. There are also some limitations on benefits for legal residents who are not citizens.

b. Data-based analyses of the impact of immigration on various sectors of American society are too extensive to be presented in this text. Recommended articles summarizing this research include the following: Broder 2006; Krugman 2006b; Lowenstein 2006; Porter 2006a; Postrel 2005; Preston 2006a, 2006b; and Samuelson 2005.

extended family co-residence pattern (Sarkisian, Gerena, and Gerstel 2006).

Gender roles are an area of family change that has been shaped by immigration. In the United States, regardless of cultural ideals about the importance of women's maternal and domestic roles, Latina wives must typically enter the labor force to contribute to the family economy. That can lead to increased autonomy and independence and a stronger voice in family decisions. On average, Mexican immigrant women in this country have less power than men in terms of decision making and the division of household labor, but more power than in Mexico. Salvadoran women, who often have been in the labor force in their home country, nevertheless cite the greater autonomy they experience here in terms of freedom to come and go without the close monitoring of the husband and the ease of obtaining help against an abusive spouse (Baca Zinn and Pok 2002; Baca Zinn and Wells 2007; Hirsch 2003; Hondagneu-Sotelo and Messner 1994; Oropesa and Landale 2004; Zentgraf 2002).

Given class and cultural diversity among Latinos, continued immigration, family change in the home countries, and increasing intermarriage, the future direction of the Latino family is difficult to predict.

Asian American Families[9]

Although their numbers are relatively small, Asian Americans are one of the fastest growing of all racial/ethnic groups (R. Bernstein 2005a). The majority of the Asian American population is foreign born, but this is likely to change over time as Asian immigrants establish families in this country.

Asian Americans are often termed a "model minority" because of their strong educational attainment (the highest proportion of college graduates), high representation in managerial and professional occupations, and family incomes that are the highest of all racial/ethnic groups (Bergman 2006b; DeNavas-Walt, Proctor, and Lee 2006, Table 1; Reeves and Bennett 2004).

But this image has its negative side: "The model-minority stereotype is a persistent social issue that has important implications for Asian-American children" (Lott 2004; see also Vartanian et al. 2003) As Juanita Tamayo Lott, author of a book on Asian Americans, puts it:

> Asian Americans have the dubious distinction of being labeled a "model minority"—based on their stereotype

[9] For the 2000 census, the previous "Asian/Pacific Islander" category was divided into two categories: "Asian" and "Hawaiian Native and Other Pacific Islander."

as overachievers and as models to other racial minority groups. . . . First, expectations of all Asian-American children (and adults) are initially higher than for other population groups. . . . Second, many overachieving Asian-American children feel they are never good enough, as the bar for achievement continues to be raised. Third, Asian-American children who do not fit the model-minority stereotype are treated as underachievers, resulting in low self-esteem and self-worth.

A higher percentage of Asian Americans are married than is true for the general population or non-Hispanic whites. Asian American children are very likely (84 percent) to be living in married-couple families; only 10 percent live in single-mother families and 4 percent in single-father families (U.S. Demographic Internet Staff 2006, Table C-2). Infant mortality rates are low (lower than those of whites) and teen birth rates and nonmarital births are also very low (Hamilton, Martin, and Ventura 2006, Table 1; Mathews and MacDorman 2006, Table A, C)). Asian Americans are most likely of all groups to be caring for older family members (American Association of Retired Persons 2004).

As with all racial/ethnic groups, there is considerable within-category diversity; in fact, more diversity exists in terms of language, religion, and customs than in any other broad racial/ethnic category. The contrast among various Asian ancestry groups is striking. Fifty-five percent of Hmong are under eighteen, while only 12 percent of Japanese are. Sixty-seven percent of Asian Indians and Pakistanis are married, but only 49 percent of Cambodians. South Asians tend to marry at young ages, while Japanese, Korean, and Chinese women delay marriage. Sixty-four percent of Asian Indians are college graduates, but less than 10 percent of Cambodians, Hmong, and Laotians have college degrees. Income and poverty status also vary (Lichter and Qian 2004, Table 1; Reeves and Bennett 2004, Figures 3, 4, and 9).

Discrimination and hostility toward Asians still exist, and Asian Americans are more likely than whites to be poor (DeNavas-Walt, Proctor, and Lee 2006, Table 4). Even advantaged youth may feel marginalized at school and among peers—that is, may not feel they are fully accepted (Purkayastha 2002). At the same time, Asian Americans have high rates of intermarriage and are less residentially segregated than most other racial/ethnic groups (Ishii-Kuntz 2000; S. M. Lee 1998).

Asian American families are more cohesive and less individualistic than are non-Hispanic white families. Scholars explain the survival of extended family commitment among Asian Americans in the United States less by cultural heritage than by the need for family cohesion in the face of economic pressures and discrimination against Asian immigrants (Taylor 2002b). Indo-American families are strongly transnational, maintaining cohesive relations with the home country through visits, business linkages, remittances, and marriage arrangements (Purkayastha 2002).

Ironically, some scholars credit the increased independence of Asian women in the United States to discrimination. To begin with, the image of Asian women as subordinated to men in patriarchal households was not always the reality. In the United States, Asian women entered the labor force because of the low wages of men. The internment of Japanese-American citizens and legal residents during World War II undercut men's patriarchal authority over both women and children. Contemporary Japanese married couples evidence greater equality than in the past, although there is still a gendered division of labor (Takagi 2002). Male dominance may continue to be characteristic of more recent immigrants and some subgroups, but not of Chinese, Japanese, and Koreans (Ishii-Kuntz 2000).

Asian American parents worry about whether their children will become too "Americanized," getting divorced and losing the priority of family (Lott 2004). Youth struggle with being "between two worlds," feeling and wanting to be American, yet seen as "'forever foreigners'" because of their appearance. But with maturity, many return to an affirmation of their Asian cultural identity and its strengths (Mustafa and Chu 2006).

Pacific Islander Families

We don't know much yet about the families of Pacific Islanders, now considered separately from Asians. Major groups are Native Hawaiians, Samoans, and Guamians. Hawaiians, of course, are American citizens by birth, and so are American Samoans, Guamians, and those born in the North Mariana Islands. U.S. residents born in the other Pacific islands may have become naturalized citizens or are not citizens.

The Pacific Islander population is relatively young, so it is not surprising that it has a higher proportion of "never married" individuals than the overall American population. Just over half are married, a figure that closely corresponds to the overall U.S. figure. Pacific Islanders are more likely to reside in family households (32 percent) than the U.S. population generally (21 percent).

Educational attainment is similar to the United States overall at the high school level, but Pacific Islanders have a smaller proportion of college graduates, and there are fewer professionals and more service workers. Median household income is slightly higher ($54,318

for 2003–2005) and poverty slightly lower (2.2 percent) than for the total United States (DeNavas-Walt, Proctor, and Lee 2006, Tables 2 and 5). The infant mortality rate is higher (Mathews et al. 2003).

American Indian (Native American) Families[10]

A unique feature of Native American families is the relationship of tribal societies to the U.S. government. At present there are over 500 federally recognized tribes (Willeto and Goodluck 2004).

In the latter half of the nineteenth century, American Indians were forcibly removed from their original tribal lands to reservations, and some tribes were dissolved. Assimilation policies led to the creation of boarding schools, where young American Indian children were placed for years with little contact with family or tribe. American Indians were encouraged to seek better conditions for their infants by placing them for adoption with white families; many of those adoptions appear in retrospect to have been forced or fraudulent (Fanshel 1972). Given the history of Native American oppression, "it is not surprising . . . that American Indians suffer the highest rates of most social problems in the U.S." (Willeto and Goodluck 2004). Tribes have high rates of teen suicide, school violence, teen pregnancy, and drug and alcohol abuse (Kershaw 2005; Madrigal 2001).

In the 1960s, American Indians successfully advocated for their rights, and a degree of tribal sovereignty was formalized in federal law. The Indian Child Welfare Act of 1978 gave tribes communal responsibility for tribal children. The law favors "placement of tribal children in tribal homes . . . so that they can learn the customs, values, and traditions that make them separate and distinctive cultures in the United States" (Madrigal 2001, pp.1505–6).[11]

Although American Indian households have a median income that is significantly lower than that of whites or

---

[10] Although Alaska Native tribes are included in this category, for convenience and because little research has been done on Alaska Natives, we will refer to "Native Americans" or "American Indians." As to the choice between those terms, both are accepted by substantial numbers of respondents surveyed on this point. Others argue that only the individual tribal names should be used because their cultures are "vastly different" (Gaffney 2006).

[11] In situations where children need to be removed from the home or a biological mother wishes to relinquish a child for adoption, the parent or the state welfare authorities cannot make those arrangements on their own; the tribe must agree and may, in fact, wish to place the child on the reservation rather than in a white adoptive home. Where agreement cannot be reached among the parties, the issue may be referred to tribal or state courts (B. J. Jones 1995).

Asians, one-third of Native American families have incomes of more than $50,000 (DeNavas-Walt, Proctor, and Lee 2006, Table 2; U.S. Census Bureau 2006c, Table 37). Yet the poverty rate is high—25 percent on average for the years 2003–2005 (DeNavas-Walt, Proctor, and Lee 2006, Table 5). The child poverty rate reaches 50 percent in female-headed families (Lugaila and Overturf 2004, Figure 5). Native Americans are one of the poorest racial/ethnic groups in the United States (Snipp 2005). In common with other economically disadvantaged groups, American Indians have high rates of adolescent births and nonmarital births; 62 percent of births are to unmarried women. Overall birthrates, however, are less than the U.S. average (Martin et al. 2006, Tables 2, 4, 18). The American Indian infant mortality rate is higher than the overall U.S. rate (Mathews and MacDorman 2006, Table A).

Still, the American Indian population has seen a tremendous rate of growth in recent censuses, doubling between 1990 and 2000. This surge is ascribed to "ethnic shifting." Individuals who might in the past have hidden their heritage, fearing discrimination, no longer feel they need to. Others, who did not have a clear American Indian identity or heritage have investigated their background, found some Native American ancestry, and so claimed an American Indian identity (Hitt 2005).

American Indians have a higher rate of cohabitation and a lower percentage of married couples than the U.S. average. More than half of married American Indians have spouses who are not Native Americans. Still, Native Americans are more likely to live in family households than the U.S. average (73 percent compared to 68 percent) (Ogunwole 2006; Snipp 2005). American Indian tribes are now beginning to deal with issues of gay lifestyles and same-sex marriage (Duncan 2005; Leland 2006).

In 2000, 29 percent of American Indian and Alaska Native children lived with mother only and 10 percent with father only, while 52 percent lived with two parents. Another 10 percent did not live with either parent (Lugaila and Overturf 2004, Table 2-PHC-T-30). Children and youth often move between households of extended family members, and, given the high rates of alcoholism on the reservation, children may be placed

Many social factors condition people's options and choices. One such factor is an individual's place within our culturally diverse society. These rural Navajo reservation children are learning to weave baskets to sell to tourists. Even within a racial/ethnic group, however, families and individuals may differ in the degree to which they retain their original culture. Many Navajo live in urban settings off the reservation or go back and forth between the reservation and towns or cities.

with foster families, Indian or non-Indian (Lobo 2001). Children often live with grandparents on the reservation when their parents go to the city to find work; jobs are scarce on the reservation (Snipp 2005). Officials of one tribe estimated that only half of the reservation children lived with a parent year round (Kershaw 2005).

Native American culture gives great respect to elders as leaders and mentors. Older women may also be relied upon for care of grandchildren. In return, Native American families take care of the elderly, although they are finding that more difficult to do when so many adults live off the reservation.

Acculturation seems to have lessened the dominant position of men in the family. The increase in female-headed families has been "the most significant role change in recent times," and one that has enhanced female authority and status in the family and the tribe (Yellowbird and Snipp 2002, p. 243). The number of women tribal leaders has doubled in the last twenty-five years, and it seems that one result is greater attention to child welfare, other social services, and education. At the same time, some women tribal leaders believe the resistance they have often encountered is due to their gender (Davey 2006).

How American Indian families live depends on the tribe and on whether they live on or off the reservation. Only one-third live on reservations, which is surprising, given the historic and symbolic importance of the reservation (Ogunwole 2006). City dwellers often return to the reservation on ceremonial occasions; to visit friends and family; as a refuge in times of hardship; and to expose their children to tribal traditions. Both on and off the reservation, Native American adults may move around frequently, as they stay in the homes of family members or friends (Lobo 2001).

Because of their high rates of intermarriage and mobility of residence between the reservation and the city, American Indians have complex racial/cultural identities. Self-identity does not always match tribal registration (Snipp 2002). American Indian identity for all but those living on a reservation has become rather fluid and uncertain. Many American Indians have more ancestors who are white than Indian and so appear white. Further identity confusion results from the fact that non-Indians have taken up certain Indian symbols and practices, leaving "real" American Indians wondering what markers do distinguish them (Hitt 2005).

Dorothy Miller developed a typology to explore the relative influence of Indian and mainstream American culture on urban Indian families. **Miller's typology of urban Native American families** posits a continuum from traditional to bicultural to transitional to marginal families. **Traditional families** retain Indian ways, with minimal influence from the urban settings they live in. **Bicultural families** develop a successful blend of native beliefs and the adaptations necessary to live in urban settings. **Transitional families** have lost Native American culture and are becoming assimilated to the white working class. **Marginal families** have become alienated from both American Indian and mainstream cultures. In her empirical research, Miller found bicultural and marginal families to be most common, as transitional and traditional families move toward the bicultural model (D. Miller 1979, cited in Yellowbird and Snipp 2002, pp. 239–43).

Even on reservations or in Alaskan tribal areas, modern culture has penetrated due to the Internet and television (Kershaw 2004). Some envision that as the cultures of individual tribes fade, eventually a "new urban Pan-Indian tribe" will emerge ("Pow Wow Culture" 2006).

White Families

Non-Hispanic whites continue to be the numerical majority in the United States, comprising 66 percent of the population. Yet, in talking about family cultures, we have tended not to see anything distinctive about white families or to consider them part of a spectrum of racial/ethnic diversity. However, in recent years academics and other scholars have begun to devote conscious attention to whether "white" as a racial category indicates a distinct culture and identity.

White families are largely of European descent and so are sometimes termed **Euro-American families**. There have been many studies of family life in specific European-American settings. Studies of working-class families and rural families are usually based on whites. Much that is written about "the family" or "the American family" is grounded in patterns common among middle-class whites. But the concept of "white families" has not really been considered except for the presentation of government statistical data.

The Demographics of White Families In those terms, the non-Hispanic white family household, compared to those of most other racial/ethnic groups, appears more likely to be headed by a married couple and less likely to include family members beyond the nuclear family. Whites are older than other groups, on average, and have lower fertility rates, so white families are less likely than Hispanic or black families to have children under eighteen living at home. White families have higher incomes than all groups but Asians and lower poverty rates than all other racial/ethnic groups. White women are less likely than black and Hispanic women to bear children as teenagers or to have nonmarital births. In 2005, 76 percent of non-Hispanic white children lived with two parents (DeNavas-Walt, Proctor, and Lee 2006; Fields 2004; Hamilton, Martin, and Ventura 2006, Table 1; Sarkisian, Gerena, and Gerstel 2006; U.S. Census Bureau 2006c, Tables 14, 53, 62, 64; U.S. Demographic Internet Staff 2006, Table C-2).

In terms of family structure and economic resources, white children and families are more advantaged. Yet the ties that provide mutual support and care of younger and older members are not as strong. White respondents reported less caregiving to aging family members; they are also less likely to rely on family members as child-care providers (American Association of Retired Persons 2004; Uttal 1999). Residential separation of whites from most other racial/ethnic groups continues even in suburban settings (Frey 2002).

Whiteness Studies As part of academic interest in whether there is something distinctive about being white, some universities have developed Whiteness Studies programs—analogous to Black Studies or Latino Studies. Scholars and students began to consider what it means to be white.

One theme is "privilege"—the idea that non-Hispanic whites have advantages in our society that

At Arlington National Cemetery, Buddhist monks escort the coffin of an American soldier killed in Iraq. Immigration has contributed to increasing religious diversity in the United States. There has been a Buddhist presence in the United States since at least the nineteenth century, and Buddhist practices have been followed by many Americans of non-Asian backgrounds. But the number of Buddhists more than doubled from 1990 to 2001 as the Asian American population increased through immigration.

go unnoticed by them (McDermott and Samson 2005). Another is that the European ethnic identities claimed by whites are not the equivalent of minority racial/ethnic identities. Unlike blacks, Latinos, Asians, and American Indians, whose opportunities and living conditions may be somewhat determined by their racial/ethnic background, whites' lives are not strongly shaped by their European ethnic heritage. At this point, Euro-Americans have been so assimilated into American society that European ethnic identities are "voluntary" and "symbolic." Individuals can choose to highlight them, or not, depending on the occasion and the pleasure certain cultural practices (holidays, food) may give them (Waters 2007).

In the future, more white Americans may begin to think about identity in racial/ethnic terms, as high levels of immigration and the increasing visibility of Latinos, Asians, and Native Americans as well as African Americans challenge an unconscious assumption that "American" equals "white."

At the same time, there is as much diversity among white families as there is within other broad racial/ethnic groups. To consider "white" the same as middle-class is to ignore the existence of some marginalized identities for whites: regional identities such as "redneck" and "hillbilly," pejorative class identities such as "trailer trash," as well as well-recognized class differences and gay/lesbian identities (McDermott and Samson 2005; Royster 2005).

Whiteness Studies programs and scholars have examined militant and racist "white power" movements, which advocate white superiority and racial separatism, sometimes engaging in violence (Childress and Johnson 2004; McDermott and Samson 2005). Whiteness Studies programs go beyond scholarship to mobilize *antiracist* attitudes and behaviors of students and the public.

Much writing on whiteness to date is theoretical, literary, media analysis, and personal narrative. Performance art and media pieces are modes of expression also characteristic of whiteness studies (K. Talbot 1997). A recent review of the literature on white racial/ethnic identity argues for more empirical social science research on white racial identities in specific and varied settings (McDermott and Samson 2005; Storrs 2002).

Multicultural Families[12]

Golfer Tiger Woods's emergence as a celebrity made interracial and interethnic families visible. Multiracial and multiethnic families are created by marriage

[12] Measuring multiracial identity is difficult. Sample surveys taken before the 2000 census indicated that a straightforward question would not work. A decision was made to allow respondents to check more than one race in the 2000 census. However, only around 2.6 percent of the population did so (Jones 2005; Jones and Smith 2001).

Matt Miller/The World-Herald

Multiracial families are increasingly common in the United States. Multiracial families are formed through interracial marriage or formation of a nonmarital partnership and also by the adoption of children across racial lines.

or establishment of an unmarried-couple household (often followed by the birth of children), and/or by adoption of children who are of a different race than their new parents. Since colonial times there has been racial mixing in the United States in marital and other sexual relationships (J. Davis 1991). Now the former dichotomy of black and white has expanded into a multiplicity of racial/ethnic identities, including multiracial or multiethnic identities and families.

About 7 percent of married-couple households include spouses whose racial/ethnic identities (regarding racial self-identification and Hispanic heritage) differ as reported to the 2000 census. This pattern was even more common in households of unmarried couples. Fifteen percent of opposite-sex partners and male same-sex partners and 13 percent of female partners reported different racial/ethnic identities (Simmons and O'Connell 2003).

However, only a small percentage of individuals claim a multiracial identity. Only 2.6 percent of the population checked more than one race in the 2000 census. The self-identified two-race population is younger than the overall U.S. population; 25 percent are under ten (N. Jones 2005). The proportion of multiracial children in the population is likely to grow with increasing intermarriage and perhaps a greater tendency to acknowledge a mixed racial/ethnic heritage. One estimate is that by the end of the century 37 percent of African Americans, 40 percent of Asians, and two-thirds of Latinos will claim a multiracial identity (G. Rodriguez 2003).

"Claim" is the key word here, and the future depends on how individuals come to see their racial/ethnic identity. How individuals define their multiracial/multiethnic identity when their heritage is mixed varies by age, gender, and the racial/ethnic combination (Jayson 2006b; N. Jones 2005; Rockquemore 2002). Most blacks are well aware that typically they would have a mixed race heritage, but thus far most have maintained a black self-identity. Less than half of parents of multiracial children report them as multiracial (Tafoya, Johnson, and Hill 2004). As immigration brings new racial/ethnic identities to the fore and intermarriage increases, American patterns of racial/ethnic self-identification are likely to become more fluid and to reflect a multicultural heritage (Bean et al. 2004).

As yet, we have had few studies focused on multiracial/multiethnic families in all their complexity. The Census Bureau reports fifty-seven combinations of race and ethnicity, while the studies that exist have varying combinations of race and ethnicity. Research on multiracial/multiethnic families has essentially just begun.

Census data indicate that multiracial couples are more apt to cohabit than same-race couples (Lichter and Qian 2004). But another study reports that multiracial children are no more likely to live in unmarried or unstable families than are single-race children, although this varies with the particular racial/ethnic combination (Goldstein and Harknett 2006). Class indicators—occupation, income, education—also vary considerably by racial/ethnic combination (N. Jones 2005). A study of adolescents based on the National Longitudinal Study of Adolescent Health finds mixed evidence as to the adjustment of multiracial adolescents, but "few negative outcomes" when other factors are controlled (M. Campbell 2002).

Tensions may arise out of cultural differences within families, and issues may need to be worked out before a couple and their children can reap the benefit of their rich cultural mix. However, a *Washington Post* national survey of 540 interracial married or cohabiting couples tells us that families have been accepting, on the whole. African American/white couples have encountered more difficulty in marriage or with parents than have Asian/white or Latino/non-Hispanic white couples (Fears and Dean 2001; "Race and Ethnicity in 2001" 2001). Yet by and large, the *Washington Post* survey indicates that interracial couples are positive about the benefits of diversity. They believe that their children are more advantaged than disadvantaged by their multicultural heritage. (Interracial marriage is discussed in more detail in Chapter 9.)

Religion

Religion was a very important topic of study in the early development of sociology, but interest declined as the twentieth century progressed. "[R]eligion is now back on the map for serious sociological analysis" (S. Gallagher 2002, p. 4). Indeed, religious affiliation and practice is a significant influence on family life, ranging from what holidays are celebrated to the placement of family relations into a moral framework.

Looking at religion over the life course, family scientist Elizabeth Miller (2000) finds that religion offers rituals to mark such important family milestones as birth, coming of age, marriage, and death. Religious affiliation provides families with a sense of community, support in times of crisis, and a set of values that give meaning to life. Membership in religious congregations is associated with age and life cycle; young people who have not been actively religious tend to become so as they marry and have children. At the same time, family disruption—divorce, separation, and remarriage—seems to lead to a renewed sense of religion's importance (Edgell 2006).

The United States is among the most religious of modern industrial nations. Eighty percent of American adults surveyed in 2001 indicated a religious identification (U.S. Census Bureau 2007a, Table 73).[13] The historically dominant religion in the United States has been Protestantism, especially "mainstream" denominations such as Presbyterianism and Methodism. But mainstream Protestantism has been in decline. Presently, about 25 percent of the U.S. population belongs to a mainstream Protestant denomination, while conservative (evangelical) Protestantism is a growing force, now encompassing 25 percent of Americans. Roman Catholics make up 25 percent of the population, while Jews are about 2 percent (Wilcox 2004, Table 1).

The U.S. Muslim population was estimated at around 4,750,000 in 2005 ("How Many Muslims" 2005). With immigration from Asia, Hindus and Buddhists have increased in numbers. The extent of religious diversity in the contemporary United States is illustrated by the fact that a Midwestern city like Omaha, Nebraska, has a Buddhist center, a Hindu temple, and a mosque.

Some other religions have become increasingly visible, notably Native American religion and neo-paganism or Wicca—a nature-based religion drawing on European pre-Christian traditions.

[13] The Census Bureau does not collect data on religion, but publishes survey results in its *Statistical Abstract*. These data are from the American Religious Identification Survey in 2001 over 50,000 households (Kosmin, Mayer, and Keysar 2001) reported in the 2007 Statistical Abstract (U.S. Census Bureau 2007a, Table 73).

Earlier research in the sociology of religion focused on how Catholics and Jews differed from Protestants in their family patterns. The formalities of doctrine have not always had the effect we might assume. Catholics, for example, appear to have shifted from traditional church teachings to modern conceptualizations of family and sexuality, and their views do not differ much from those of the general population on such issues as homosexuality, birth control, and family size (D. Moore 2005a). Almost 70 percent of married Catholics of reproductive age use contraception despite church teaching (Fehring and Schlidt 2001). But studies still find contemporary Catholics to be different from Protestants in their more communal, rather than individualistic, worldview (Greeley 1989).

Today, social scientists find certain other religious groups more interesting to study, notably Latter-day Saints (popularly, but incorrectly, termed *Mormons*) and conservative Christians. Encouragement of large families by the LDS Church is reflected in the distinctively high fertility of the state of Utah (Hamilton, Martin, and Ventura 2006, Table 8,). Latter-day Saints and Evangelical Christians reject homosexuality perhaps more strongly than some others, although younger people are more liberal ("Born Again Adults Remain" 2001). Conservative Protestant Christians and Latter-day Saints, as well as Catholics, are strongly opposed to abortion.

Members are not always in conformity with their church's teachings. But religious influences tend to be powerful enough to produce differences in responses to surveys about attitudes and values in many family-related areas. Religious values and teaching may, in turn, influence views on public policy, as "growing levels of concern with family decline [in the 1980s and 1990s] . . . were disproportionately concentrated among evangelical Protestants" (C. Brooks 2002, p. 207).

The theology of conservative Christian religions endorses traditional gender roles, specifically the concept of "headship," the man as head of the family. But there is a diversity of viewpoints on gender roles *within* the evangelical community (Bartkowski 2001; S. Gallagher 2004). Researchers find a similar diversity among Latter-day Saints women (Beaman 2001). For some, headship is a symbolic value denoting a separation from aspects of American culture thought immoral or threatening. It is not necessarily an everyday reality. A "servant-head" and "mutual submission" interpretation of headship seems to lead to egalitarian decision making in day-to-day family life. "Headship has been reorganized along expressive lines, emptying the concept of virtually all of its authoritativeness" (Wilcox 2004, p. 173).

Evangelical women believe they benefit from the headship concept because they perceive it as provid-

Two volunteers at the American Muslim Women's Association work on a craft project to benefit poorer immigrants and refugees. This organization, with many professional members, also works to reshape the roles of women in Islam. One young woman wears a headscarf; the other does not. Some modern young Muslim women have recently adopted the head scarf to express an intensified identification with Islam in the context of experiences of discrimination or challenge to their religious community.

ing them with love, respect, and security. Conservative Christian men, more than mainstream Protestant men, seem more emotionally expressive with their wives and children, and more committed to their marriages. Conservative Christian husbands also have lower rates of domestic violence than average (Wilcox 2004; S. Gallagher 2003, 2004).

Marital sharing and equality do not seem to extend to household labor. Both men and women see a woman's role as giving priority to the domestic sphere, while husbands do not expect to do many household tasks. Economic need shapes a pragmatic approach to the employment of women, but conservative Christian women are more likely to scale back their work hours and job level upon marriage and/or childbirth (Glass and Nath 2006). With regard to marital stability, "born-again" Christians are far less likely than other Americans to enter cohabiting relationships, but their divorce rates do not differ ("Born Again Adults Less" 2001).

Religion may be associated with child-rearing practices. Conservative Protestants appear more likely than the general population to emphasize obedience and to use physical punishment. At the same time, they seem more emotionally expressive in their child rearing and more likely to praise and hug their children. It also appears that conservative Protestant fathers are more likely than mainstream Protestant or unaffiliated fathers to engage in one-on-one interaction with children in leisure activities, projects, homework help, and just talking. They are more likely than religiously unaffiliated fathers to have dinner with children and to participate in youth activities as coaches or leaders. Catholic fathers follow the same pattern of involvement (Wilcox 1998, 2002).

Those religions such as Islam or Judaism that depart from a Christian tradition have the added burden of raising children in a society that does not support their faith; this could be said of conservative Protestant groups as well. Interfaith marriage provides a similar challenge. Holidays may be difficult because outsiders may expect Muslim or Jewish children to join in Christian celebrations. Some religious groups consider Halloween to be satanic and do not permit their children to celebrate it. Religiously mixed couples may experience tension over how to celebrate the holidays as a family (Haddad and Smith 1996; Horowitz 1999).

Issues other than holiday celebrations may be involved. Conservative Christians may not permit their children to date (Goodstein 2001). Islamic families provide an example of the difficulty of maintaining a religiously appropriate family life in the context of a culture that does not share their beliefs. For Muslims, dating, marital choice, child rearing, employment of women, dress, and marital decision making are all religious issues. As one Muslim mother stated to a researcher:

> I think that integration into the non-Muslim environment has to be done with the sense that we have to preserve our Islamic identity. As long as the activity or whatever the children are doing is not in conflict with Islamic values or ways, it is permissible. But when we see it is going to be something against Islamic values, we try to teach our children that this is not correct to our beliefs and practices. They understand it and they are trying to cope with that. (Haddad and Smith 1996, p. 19)

Muslim families now have the added burden of facing suspicion and hostility in the wake of 9/11, but those experiences have also fostered a stronger identity. Younger Muslims seem more consciously and conservatively religious ("U.S. Muslims" 2004).

For all religions, finding a balance between participating in the larger society and preserving unique values and behaviors and a sense of community is a challenge in a society characterized by religious freedom rather than a religious establishment. Yet that freedom seems to be cherished by virtually all religious groups in the United States.

As we explore various aspects of American families in greater detail throughout the remainder of this text, it may help you to recall that families differ according to social context—religion, race/ethnicity, social class, age structure, and the historical time in which they live. In the next chapter, we examine gender as a major determinant of experiences in the family.

Summary

- Families exist in a social context that affects many aspects of family life.

- Historical events and trends have affected family life over the last century. These include economic and cultural trends, as well as wars and other national crises.

- The age structure affects family patterns and social policy regarding families. The proportion of older Americans in the population is increasing, so we may anticipate growing responsibility for them. The proportion of children in the population is decreasing, leading to questions about the future of society's commitment to children.

- The economy has a strong impact on family life. Americans do not like to acknowledge class differences, but economic resources affect family options. So do differences in values and preferences that characterize blue-collar and white-collar sectors of society.

- Race and ethnicity shape family life because African American, Latino, Asian, American Indian, Pacific Islander, and white families have some differences in structure, resources, and culture. The increasing rate of racial/ethnic intermarriage suggests that more families in the future will be multicultural.

- Immigration has risen to a level that contributes visibly to the diversity of family life.

- Religious traditions and prescriptions shape family life. In studying the family, we are apt to take more notice of religions that maintain distinctive family norms.

Questions for Review and Reflection

1. In the everyday lives of families (yours or those you observe), what economic pressures, opportunities, and choices do you see?

2. Describe one specific social context of family life as presented in the text. Does what you read match what you see in everyday life?

3. Do you see the lives of military families as basically similar to or different from those of other families?

4. What are some significant aspects of the family lives of immigrant families? Do you think immigrant families will change over time?

5. **Policy Question.** Which age group is increasing as a proportion of the U.S. population, children or the elderly? What social changes might occur as a result? What social policies do we need to maintain or develop to care for children and the elderly?

Key Terms

binational family 60
cultural deviant perspective 57
cultural equivalent perspective 57
cultural variant perspective 57
ethnicity, ethnic identity 55
Euro-American families 67
globalization 51
infant mortality rate 61
life chances 49
Miller's typology of urban Native American families:
  bicultural 67

marginal 67
traditional 67
transitional 67
race 54
segmented assimilation 60
sex ratio 59
social class 53
transnational family 62
undocumented immigrant 60

Online Resources

Companion Website for This Book

www.thomsonedu.com/sociology/lamanna

Visit the book companion website, where you will find flash cards, practice quizzes, Internet links, suggested readings, InfoTrac College Edition exercises, and more to help you study.

ThomsonNOW™ for Marriage and Family

Spend time on what you need to master rather than on information you already have learned. Take a pre-test for this chapter, and ThomsonNOW will generate a personalized study plan based on your results. The study plan will identify the topics you need to review and direct you to online resources such as videos, narrated learning modules, and interactive activities to help you master those topics. You can then take a post-test to help you determine the concepts you have mastered and what you will still need to work on. Try it out! Go to **www.thomsonedu.com/login** to sign in with an access code or to purchase access to this product.

Our Gendered Identities

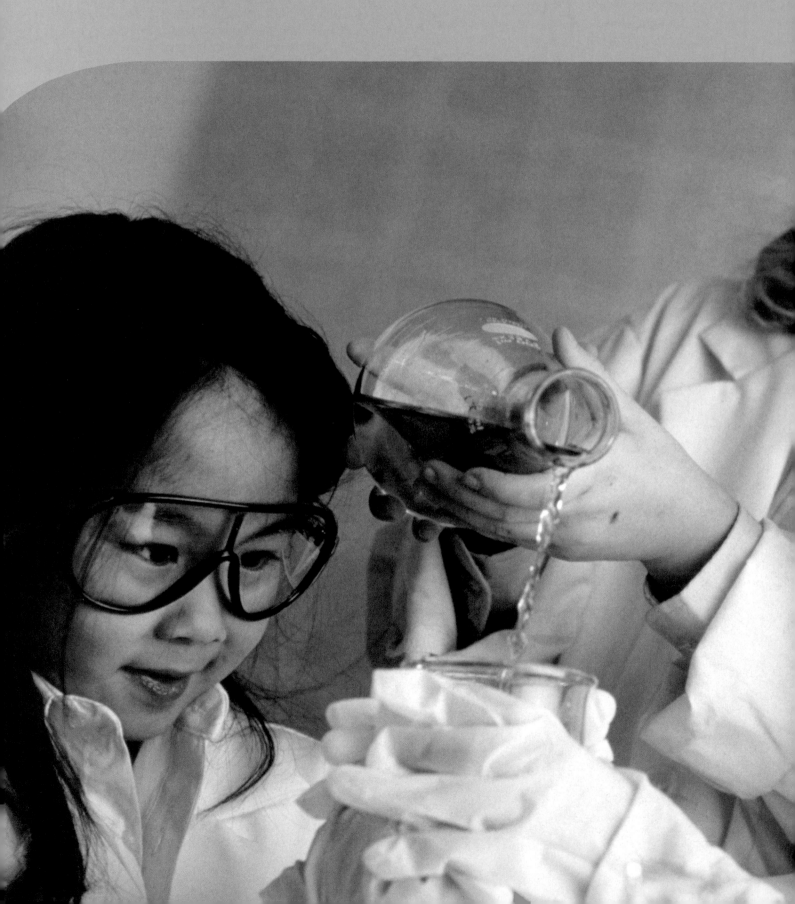

4

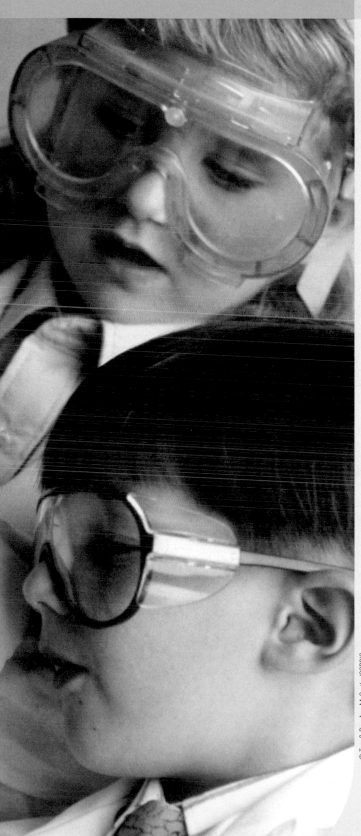

© Tom & Dee Ann McCarthy/CORBIS

A Closer Look at Family Diversity: Race, Class, and Gender in the Nanny Hunt

Gendered Identities

Gender Expectations and Cultural Messages

Issues for Thought: Challenges to Gender Boundaries

To What Extent Do Women and Men Follow Cultural Expectations?

The Gender Similarities Hypothesis

Gender Inequality

Male Dominance in Politics

Male Dominance in Religion

Gender and Health

Gender and Education

Male Dominance in the Economy

Is Anatomy Destiny?

Gender and Socialization

Theories of Socialization

Settings for Socialization

Girls versus Boys?

Social Change and Gender

The Women's Movement

Men's Movements

Personal and Family Change

The Future of Gender

New York Times *reporter Jodi Kantor wrote this column based on her interviews with black professional parents. It seemed to us to illustrate how race, class, and gender can intersect in the everyday lives of individuals.*

Jennifer Freeman sat in a Chicago coffee bar, counting her blessings and considering her problem. She had a husband with an M.B.A. degree, two children and a job offer that would let her dig out the education degree she had stashed away during years of playdates and potty training. But she could not accept the job. After weeks of searching, Ms. Freeman, who is African-American, still could not find a nanny for her son, 5, and daughter, 3.

As more blacks move up the economic ladder, one fixture—some would say necessity—of the upper-middle-class income bracket often eludes them. . . . "We've attained whatever level society says is successful, we're included at work, but when we need the support for our children and we can afford it, why do we get treated this way?" asked Tanisha Jackson, an African-American mother of three in a Washington suburb, who searched on and off for five years before hiring a nanny. "It's a slap in the face."

Numerous black parents successfully employ nannies, and many sitters say they pay no regard to race. But interviews with dozens of nannies and agencies that employ them in Atlanta, Chicago, New York and Houston turned up many nannies—often of African-American or Caribbean descent themselves—who avoid working for families of those backgrounds. Their reasons included accusations of low pay and extra work, fears that employers would look down at them, and suspicion that any neighborhood inhabited by blacks had to be unsafe. [There were also comments that could only be described as racist, including some made by blacks.]

The result is that many black parents do not have the same child care options as their colleagues and neighbors. They must settle for illegal immigrants or non-English speakers instead of more experienced or credentialed nannies, rely on day care, or scale back their professional options to spend more time at home.

"Very rarely will an African-American woman work for an African-American boss" [said one owner of a nanny service]. . . . Many of the African-American nannies who make up 40 percent of her work force fear that people of their own color will be "uppity and demanding," said [this owner], who is white. After interviews, she said, those nannies "will call us and say, 'Why didn't you tell me' the family is black?" In several cities, nanny agencies decline to serve certain geographic areas—not because of redlining, these agencies say, but because the

---

As we think about family life, we need to consider gender issues. Cultural expectations about how boys and girls, men and women should behave and relate to each other are important influences on personal identities, family roles, and life choices. But to what extent have traditional expectations changed?

"Gender influences virtually every aspect of people's lives and relationships." This statement from earlier editions of this textbook is now being challenged by changes that have taken place in our society. Some scholars assert, or at least explore, "the declining significance of gender" (Blau, Brinton, and Grusky 2006).

Others see gender identity and gender inequality as continuing to be enormously important, but point to how our thinking about gender has changed. From an earlier 1970s perspective in which all women were seen to be disadvantaged compared to all men, we now look at gender in its structural linkages to race, class, and sexual orientation, as well as to global interconnections (Andersen and Collins 2007; Baca Zinn, Hondagneu-Sotelo, and Messner 2007). For example, a black woman immigrant from Haiti, a single mother who works as a domestic, has a very different life from her employer, a white woman lawyer, an Ivy League graduate with a professional husband. The husband's life is much different from that of a white male high school dropout who remains single into his forties because he finds himself financially unable to marry (Porter and O'Donnell 2006).

As noted in our analysis of race/ethnicity in Chapter 3, *within-group* differences have become an important theme in the study of gender. The interplay of race, class, and gender can be seen in "A Closer Look at Family Diversity: Race, Class, and Gender in the Nanny Hunt."

Gendered Identities

We are using the term *gender* rather than *sex* for an important reason. The word **sex** is used in reference to male or female anatomy and physiology. We use the term **gender** (or **gender role**) far more broadly—to describe societal attitudes and behaviors expected of and associated with the two sexes (Duck and Wood 2006, p. 170).[1] Another concept, **gender identity**, refers to the degree to which an individual sees herself or himself as feminine or masculine.

[1] The distinction between *sex* and *gender,* first made by sociologist Ann Oakley (1972), is a dominant perspective in social science (Laner 2003). But not all social theorists agree with this conceptualization. Judith Butler (1990) argues that the two are essentially one—gender—and others agree that the biological as well as behavioral aspects of sex are socially constructed (Cresswell 2003).

nannies, who decide which jobs to take, do not want to work there. . . .

Ms. Freeman finally found a friend, another black mother, to watch her children. . . . [Another couple], the Boones[,] now use day care. It is inconvenient, . . . but "there is no way we're doing the whole nanny thing again," said Ms. Boone, who is African-American and Puerto Rican. . . .

Like Ms. Freeman in Chicago and Ms. Jackson in Maryland, the Boones worry that nanny troubles could limit their professional advancement. In earlier generations, Ms. Jackson said, "We were the nannies." Now, blacks "want to have it all," working and raising children. "But to have it all you need help," she said. And that means qualified help. . . .

An exception to the usual stroller parade of black sitters with white children, some white nannies do care for black children—and experience slights

because of it. Margaret Kop, a Polish sitter in Chicago, said that [one of the other nannies made a racist comment about the child in her care]. On the way home, Ms. Kop cried, stung by the insult to the child she loved. . . .

The problem [professional black families have in finding nannies] may be as much about class as race, said Kimberly McClain DaCosta, a Harvard sociologist. For nannies, working for an employer of the same background or skin color "highlights their lower economic status."

[Some black families] have race-based preferences themselves. . . . These parents want their children "socialized into what it's like to be black in a racist society, but they also want their children to be socialized into being middle class. That's hard for one person to do," said [Cameron L. Macdonald, a white sociology professor]. . . . Ms. DaCosta is an African-American parent herself. She

and her husband, who is Caribbean, have successfully employed several nannies for their three children. . . . They preferred a black sitter, who would instantly understand matters like how to do their daughter's hair. Ms. DaCosta and her husband now use au pairs, checking the photos on their applications and announcing their own race at the start of the phone interview. "We don't want any surprises," she said.

Critical Thinking

Give examples of each category—race, class, and gender—and discuss how they intersect in this article.

Source: From Jodi Kantor, "Nanny Hunt Can Be a 'Slap in the Face' for Blacks," *New York Times,* Dec. 26, 2006. Copyright © 2006 by the New York Times Co. Reprinted by permission.

A further complication occurs because a small number of people are born with ambiguous sexual characteristics or do not feel at ease with their sex as recorded at birth. "Issues for Thought: Challenges to Gender Boundaries" addresses variations in biology that affect sex and gender identification.

In this chapter, we will examine various aspects of gender. In doing so, we'll consider personality traits and cultural scripts typically associated with masculinity and femininity. We'll analyze gender inequality in social institutions. We'll discuss the possible influence of biology and examine the socialization process, as we explore whether people are taught to behave as either females or males, are born that way, or simply adapt to the social structures and opportunities they find as they become adults. We'll discuss the lives of adults as they select from options available to them. And we'll examine the social movements that have arisen around gender issues. We'll speculate about what the future may hold in terms of gender equality.

Gender Expectations and Cultural Messages

We live in an ambivalent time regarding gendered attitudes and behavior. On the one hand, it is now taken for granted that women have careers and that most will

work after they become mothers. Examples of women in nontraditional roles abound: women as astronauts, CEOs, and officers and enlisted personnel in the military. On the other hand, the media and research explore the continuing disadvantages faced by women and the uncertainty that many women have about their choices and the ability to realize them.

Men have begun to consider where they stand as well—in relationships, in the family, and at work. Some men have begun to move into traditionally female occupations, and married fathers are doing more at home than they used to (Bianchi, Robinson, and Milkie 2006).

American attitudes have grown more liberal regarding men's and women's roles. Few agree, for example, that "sons in a family should be given more encouragement to go to college than daughters," an expression of **traditional sexism** (Sherman and Spence 1997). Traditional sexism is the belief that women's roles should be confined to the family and that women are not as fit as men for certain tasks or for leadership positions. Such beliefs have declined since the 1970s (Twenge 1997a, 1997b).

But now a more subtle **modern sexism** has replaced traditional sexism. It takes the form of agreement with statements like: "discrimination in the labor force is no longer a problem" and "in order not to appear sexist,

We take for granted that sex is a dichotomy: You are either male or female. Yet somewhere between one percent and four percent of live births are **intersexual**—that is, the children have some anatomical, chromosomal, or hormonal variation from the male or female biology that is considered "normal." "Chromosomes, hormones, the internal sex structures, the gonads and the external genitalia all vary more than most people realize" (Fausto-Sterling 2000, p. 20; Laner 2003; Preves 2003; Sax 2002).

In the 1950s, psychologist John Money and his colleagues at Johns Hopkins University began the study of intersex babies (then termed *hermaphrodites*). In this clinical program, hermaphrodites were assigned a gender identity, and parents were advised to treat them accordingly. The children typically underwent surgery to give them genitals more closely approximating the assigned gender.

Intersexuality emerged as an area of political activism with the formation of the Intersex Society of North America in 1993 (S. Lerner 2003). Members have demonstrated against arbitrary gender assignment and the surgical "correction" of intersexed infants, arguing instead

for the acceptance of gender ambiguity (Preves 2002). Some medical ethicists take the position that "the various forms of intersexuality should be defined as normal" (Lawrence McCullough, quoted in Fausto-Sterling 2000, p. 21).

Although some **transsexuals** (who have been raised as one sex, while emotionally identifying with the other) still wish surgery to conform their bodies to their gender identity, others "are content to inhabit a more ambiguous zone" (p. 22). They may adopt the dress and demeanor of the sex with which they identify, vary their appearance and self-presentation, or adopt a style that is not gender-identified.

The term **transgendered** describes an identity adopted by those who are uncomfortable in the gender of their birth. They may be in transition to a new gender or simply wish to continue to occupy a middle ground. "Some people think it's important to be seen as a specific gender; that's not me," says a Wesleyan college student (in F. Bernstein 2004, p. ST-1). Some universities have established nongendered housing at the request of transgendered students (F. Bernstein 2004). Some bureaucratic

forms now include a "transgender" box as well as those for "male" and "female," suggesting the beginning of societal accommodation to a more complex sex/gender system. In fact, the city of New York now permits individuals to align their birth certificates with a changed sexual identity, whether or not they have had sex change surgery (Cave 2006).

The biological, psychological, and social realities presented by intersexed or transgendered individuals are challenges to the notion that there are clearly demarcated masculine and feminine genders and gender roles. In turn, parents, physicians, mental health professionals, and educators are coping with ethical decisions regarding surgery and socialization for those born with ambiguous sex characteristics or who appear in childhood to have uncertain sexual identities (P. L. Brown 2006; Lerner 2003; Weil 2006).

Critical Thinking

Have transgendered individuals been politically visible in your campus or community? What are your own thoughts as to whether gender is a dichotomy or can be a continuum along which individuals may vary?

---

many men are inclined to overcompensate women" (Campbell, Schellenberg, and Senn 1997; Tougas et al. 1995). Modern sexism denies that gender discrimination persists and includes the belief that women are asking for too much (Swim et al. 1995). Moreover, though work, family, and civic roles have changed and modernized, there is still a sense on the part of the average person that men and women are different in personality and aptitudes (Ridgeway 2006).

You can probably think of some characteristics typically associated with being feminine or masculine. Stereotypically masculine people are often thought to have **agentic** (from the root word *agent*) or **instrumental character traits**—confidence, assertiveness, and ambition—that enable them to accomplish difficult tasks or goals. A relative absence of agency characterizes our expectations of women, who are thought to embody **communal** or **expressive character traits**: warmth, sensitivity, the

ability to express tender feelings, and placing concern about others' welfare above self-interest.

The ways in which men are expected to show agency and women expressiveness are embedded in the culture around us. Let's examine some of our cultural messages about masculinity and femininity.

Masculinities We need to state the obvious: Men are not all alike. Recognizing this, scholars have begun to analyze **masculinities** in the plural, rather than the singular—a recent and subtle change meant to promote our appreciation for the differences among men. Anthropologist David Gilmore (1990), having examined expectations for men cross-culturally, argues that what is common among the world's concepts of masculinity—and what separates these from cultural messages regarding women—is that a man must somehow prove that he is a "real man" whereas a woman is allowed to take gender for granted. So one cul-

More and more women are entering nontraditional occupations such as the military

tural message is that men are expected to distance themselves from anything considered feminine.

Second, a man should be occupationally or financially successful, or at least should be working to support his family—which should include children sired in marriage. A man is also expected to be confident and self-reliant, even tough. "When necessary, a man is expected to stand up for his family . . . to defend his pride, his honor, his name, and that of his family. Men are always responsible for military defense even when women may participate in warfare" (Nock 2001, p. 771; see also David and Brannon 1976). An alternative cultural message emphasizes adventure, sometimes coupled with violence and/or the need to outwit, humiliate, and defeat other men in barroom brawls, contact sports, and war.

Scholars have expanded on this last idea. If a male finds that legitimate avenues to occupational success are blocked to him because of, for example, lack of education or racial/ethnic status, he might "make it" through an alternative route, through physical aggression, rapping, or striking a "cool pose." The latter involves dress and postures manifesting fearlessness and detachment, adapted by some racial/ethnic minority males for emotional survival in a discriminatory and hostile society (Majors and Billson 1992). A corresponding stereotypical white working-class male response to economic dis-

advantage and social change involves a denigrating and hostile critique of blacks, other minorities, and women or the "hypermasculinity [of] shop floors, motorcycle clubs, and urban gangs" (Pyke 1996, p. 531; see also David and Brannon 1976; Fine et al. 1997).

During the 1980s, a new cultural message emerged. According to this message, the "liberated" male or "new man" is emotionally sensitive and expressive, valuing tenderness and equal relationships with women (Messner 1997, pp. 36–38, 41). Yet another transformation of the ideal male image occurred in response to the terrorist attacks of 9/11. We see

the return of manly men. . . . : They are the knights in shining fire helmets. . . . the welders, policemen, and businessmen with can-do attitudes who are unafraid to tackle armed hijackers. . . . Brawny, heroic, manly men . . . stoic, muscle-bound and exuding competence from every pore. (P. L. Brown 2001, p. WK-5)

Cultural messages are complex, for 9/11 also brought us some examples of well-known American men shedding tears in public (N. Wax 2001).

Feminities There are a variety of ways of being a woman, according to cultural messages of **femininities**. The pivotal expectation for a woman requires her to offer emotional support. Traditionally, the ideal woman was physically attractive, not too competitive, a good listener, and adaptable. Considered fortunate if she had a man in her life, she acted as his helpmate, aiding and cheering his accomplishments. In addition to caring for a man, a woman was expected to be a good mother and put her family's and children's needs before her own. The "strong black woman" cultural message combined assertiveness, independence, employment, and child care (Basow 1992, p. 132).

An expectation that has emerged as women entered the workforce and the feminist movement arrived is that of the "professional woman": independent, ambitious, self-confident. This cultural model may combine with the traditional one to form the "superwoman" message, according to which a good wife and/or mother also efficiently attains career success and/or supports her children by herself. An emerging female expectation is the "satisfied single": a woman (either heterosexual or lesbian, usually employed, and perhaps a parent) who is quite happy not to be in a serious relationship with a male.

Gender Expectations and Diversity The view of men as instrumental and women as expressive was based primarily on people's images of white, middle-class heterosexuals. But there are racial/ethnic variations in gender expectations. For example, African American males and females are thought to be more similar to one another in terms of expressiveness and instrumental competence than are non-Hispanic whites (Canary and Emmers-Sommer 1997). Compared to white men, black men are viewed as more emotionally expressive. Compared to white women, black women are viewed as less passive and less dependent.

Latinas and Asian women are stereotyped as being more submissive than non-Hispanic white women. Latino men are stereotyped as extremely patriarchal, following a *machismo* cultural ideal of extreme masculinity and male dominance (Hondagneu-Sotelo 1996; McLoyd et al. 2000). In addition to racial/ethnic components, there are age, class, and sexual orientation differences in gender expectations.

Yet, research indicates that racial/ethnic differences in role expectations and behaviors, particularly for males, are actually not as strong as either stereotypes or sociohistorical perspectives have suggested. The preeminence of the male provider role is a powerful theme in *all* racial/ethnic groups (e.g., Taylor, Tucker, and Mitchell-Kernan 1999). African American families have "flexible family roles," but the male's involvement in child care and other expressive roles does not have the same priority as the provider role, despite the difficulty encountered by African American males in fulfilling this role.

Black men and women express preferences for egalitarian relationships (Kane 2000). African American men are more supportive of employed wives than white men are. Yet, gender ideology among African Americans does differentiate the sexes by the importance of the male provider role. Women are likely to perform more of the household labor than men (though African American men do more than white men) (Blee and Tickamyer 1995; Haynes 2000; Orbuch and Eyster 1997). African American men show up as more conservative than white men in other ways—for example, in a stronger conviction that men and women are essentially different: Men are "manly," and women are "womanly," or soft and feminine (Haynes 2000, p. 834).

Similarly complex gender patterns are observed in Latino families. For example, Mexican American women carry the primary responsibility for housework and child care (Coltrane 1996). But roles have been modified in the migration process and with women's entry into the labor force. Mexican American women do more housework and child care than men, but less than their counterparts in Mexico. And they have more influence over household decisions (Hondagneu-Sotelo and Messner 1999; Hondagneu-Sotelo 1996).

These are but a few examples of the complexity of role expectations and behavior in real-life families.

To What Extent Do Women and Men Follow Cultural Expectations?

It is one thing to recognize cultural images but another to follow them. Consequently, we continue to ask: To what extent do individual men and women, boys and girls, exhibit gender-differentiated behaviors?

In adult life, women seem to have greater connectedness in interpersonal relations and to enter the caregiving professions in greater numbers than men, while men are more socially dominant, physically aggressive, and interested in competitive, achievement-oriented occupations (Beutel and Marini 1995). But there is great individual variation, and the situational context accounts for much of the apparent difference between men and women (Myers 2001, Chapter 5).

Moreover, behavior vis-à-vis the gendered expectations we've discussed generally fits an overlapping pattern (Basow 1992). We can visualize this as two overlapping distribution curves (see Figure 4.1). For example, although the majority of men are taller than the majority of women, the area of overlap in men's and women's heights is considerable, and some men are shorter than some women. It is also true that differences among women or among men (*within-group variation*) are usually greater than the average difference between men and women (*between-group variation*).

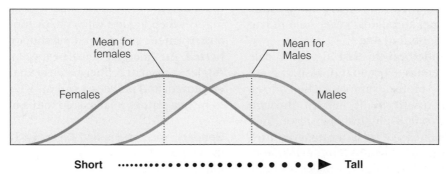

FIGURE 4.1 How females and males differ on one trait, height, conceptualized as overlapping normal distribution curves. Means (averages) may differ by sex, but trait distributions of men and women occupy much common ground.

"It's her first bench-clearing brawl."

Traditional stereotypes of children define males as aggressive and competitive and girls as sensitive and concerned for others. Real behavior is far more varied than these stereotypes and depends very much on the situation.

Although males and females differ little on basic traits and abilities, the opportunities available in the social structure affect the options of men and women and, ultimately, their behaviors as they adapt to those options. The "deceptive differences" (Epstein 1988) we observe or think we observe typically involve men and women assigned to different social roles. A woman secretary, for example, is expected to be compliant and supportive of her male boss's decisions. To observers, she seems to have a gentle and submissive personality, while he is seen to have leadership qualities (Eagly, Wood, and Dickman 2000; Ridgeway and Smith-Lovin 1999).

The Gender Similarities Hypothesis

The preponderance of research on gender differences suggests that in fact they are few. Psychologist Janet Hyde (2005) offers a **gender similarities hypothesis** to replace the usual assumption of gender differences. Media typically present males and females as very different in their cognitive strengths, communication styles, moral reasoning, and personality traits. The gender similarities hypothesis "holds that males and females are similar on most, but not all, psychological variables. . . . That is, men and women, as well as boys and girls, are more alike than they are different" (p. 581). Hyde's conclusion, endorsed by the American Psychological Association, is based on a review of forty-six meta-analyses[2] covering cognitive traits and abilities, verbal and nonverbal communication, social and personality variables such as

aggression and leadership, psychological well-being and self-esteem, motor abilities, and moral reasoning.

Hyde finds virtually no difference on most traits, a few moderate differences, and very few large differences. This conclusion applies even to math and verbal ability, self-esteem, and tendency toward aggression, areas where gender differences were thought to be pronounced. She did find evidence of gender differences (1) in motor performance, especially in throwing distance and speed; (2) in sexuality, especially male's greater incidence of masturbation and acceptance of casual sex; and (3) in physical aggressiveness. She did not find clear differences in relational aggression (see also Crick et al. 1999). Other research that fails to find confirmation of most stereotypical gender differences in emotions and emotional expression supports the gender similarities hypothesis (Simon and Nath 2004).

Hyde goes on to argue that mistaken assumptions about gender differences have serious costs, hurting women's opportunities in the workplace, men's confidence in nontraditional family roles, and both sexes' confidence in their ability to communicate with each other.

Despite the validity of Hyde's gender similarities hypothesis, virtually all societies, including our own, are structured around some degree of gender inequality.

Gender Inequality

Male dominance describes a situation in which the male(s) in a dyad or group assume authority over the female(s). On the societal level, male dominance is the assignment to men of greater control and influence over society's institutions and, usually, greater benefits. "In essentially every society, men are socially dominant. In no known societies do women dominate men" (Myers 2001, p. 182).

In this section we address gender difference and gender inequality in certain major social institutions: politics and government, religion, health, education, and the economy.

Male Dominance in Politics

As of 2003, in the U.S. Congress, there were fourteen women in the Senate and fifty-nine in the House of Representatives (U.S. Census Bureau 2006c, Table 395). In 2007, Democratic congresswoman Nancy Pelosi became Speaker, the highest position in the House of Representatives and second after the vice president in the line of

[2] Meta-analysis is the combination of many pieces of research to evaluate a social science hypothesis, taking into account the strengths of each study's sample and methodology. Hyde's article (2005) provides a detailed technical discussion of this methodology.

Nancy Pelosi attained the powerful political post of Speaker of the House of Representatives in 2007. Here she presides at a press conference together with other House leaders. Although the number of female senators and members of the House of Representatives has increased in recent years and women have had some senior appointments in the executive branch in addition to Pelosi's congressional position, women remain a minority in positions of political power.

succession. A recent *New York Times* article quotes political strategists as saying that "[v]oters have grown more accustomed to women in powerful positions" (Toner 2007).

Beginning with the Clinton administration and continuing under President George W. Bush, women have been more visible in the executive branch of government as well. Condoleeza Rice, an African American woman, has served as national security adviser and secretary of state. Women justices have served on the Supreme Court.

One can see considerable progress, though not parity, when women comprise only 14 percent of Congress and a minority of the cabinet and Supreme Court. Surveys report that 78 percent of the public say they would be willing to vote for a woman for president—but only 51 percent believe their family, friends, and coworkers are willing to do so (Rasmussen Reports 2006).

Male Dominance in Religion

Religion as an institution evidences male dominance as well. Although most U.S. congregations have more female than male participants, men more often hold positions of authority, while women perform secretarial, housekeeping, and low-level administrative chores. Women have entered the pastorate in Protestant Christian churches and have become rabbis in Reform Jewish congregations, but in both cases remain a minority. In mainstream Protestant denominations, women typically do not receive ministerial appointments to large congregations. Women have been prohibited from holding ministerial positions or teaching in seminaries of the Southern Baptist Convention. Women are prohibited from holding Catholic clerical or lay deacon positions.

As with politics, there are some striking exceptions that suggest future change. Women have been elected as bishops and denomination leaders in the African Methodist Episcopal, Anglican, United Methodist, and Presbyterian churches (Banerjee 2006a, 2006b; "Professor Says" 2007; Van Biema 2004; Zelizer 2004).

The effects of personal religious involvement on women's daily lives are complex. On the one hand, the growth of evangelical Protestantism, Islamic fundamentalism, and the Latter-day Saints religion along with the charismatic renewal in the Catholic Church, has fostered a traditional family ideal of male headship and a corresponding rejection of feminist-inspired redefinitions of family roles. On the other hand, actual practice seems more egalitarian than formal doctrine (see Chapter 3). There is a feminist movement among Arab Muslim women who seek to combine their religio-cultural heritage with equal rights for females (J. Tucker 1993).

Gender and Health

When it comes to health, we can no longer speak of male advantage. From birth onward, indeed prior to birth (fetal loss), males have higher death rates. Male infants have higher rates of infant mortality and adverse conditions (Mathews and Hamilton 2005). Nature recognizes this disparity, and in the United States, around 105 boys are born for every 100 girls, with boys outnumbering girls under age eighteen (U.S. Census Bureau 2005b).

Life expectancy for the total population reached 77.8 years in 2004—80.4 years for females and 75.2 years for males, a difference of 5.2 years (Miniño, Heron, and Smith 2006, Table A; Miniño et al. 2007). The gap between males and females peaked in 1979 at almost eight years and has been decreasing since (see Figure 4.2).

Gender difference in longevity has been attributed to greater risk factors for boys and men, including smoking and drinking, accidents, suicide, and murder victimization, as well as some not-well-understood vulnerability to infection and stress. Men also have far fewer doctor visits (i.e., check-ups) than women (Painter 2006; Rabin 2006).

For years, medical researchers paid women little attention. But partly due to the feminist movement, "women's

health has been a national priority" (Rabin 2006). Now men's advocacy groups are calling for increased attention to men's health and greater investment in research on their unique health conditions—funding for breast cancer research, for example, exceeds that for prostate cancer by 40 percent. On the other hand, breast cancer strikes earlier and more lethally. In any case, we can applaud the increasing attention to gender equality in medical research and the gradual convergence in longevity.

Gender and Education

It is presently in dispute as to whether it is women or men who are disadvantaged in higher education. (The relative circumstances of boys and girls in K–12 schooling will be discussed in the *Gender and Socialization* section later in this chapter.)

As Students Women have been the majority of college students since 1979 and now surpass men in the proportion of the total population that are college graduates (Lewin 2006c; Spraggins 2005; "Threats" 2003). In 2003, women earned 57 percent of bachelor's and 59 percent of master's degrees (U.S. Census Bureau 2006c, Table 286), 49 percent of first professional degrees, and 48 percent of doctorates (West and Curtis 2006).

The changing gender balance in higher education—indeed, in high school completion, with 72 percent of girls but only 65 percent of boys graduating high school (Lewin 2006b)—has led to cries of alarm: "leaving men in the dust" (Lewin 2006a, p. A1); "stagnation for men" ("Study: Academic Gains" 2006). Advocates of attention to boys argue that with the advances made by women (attributable to feminism) it is now "boys' turn." Otherwise, "many will needlessly miss out on success in life" ("Big [Lack of] Men" 2005).

In response to the assumption that women "have it made" and men are the disadvantaged category, counterarguments and data have been offered: "The Patriarchy Isn't Falling" (Gandy 2005). First of all, men's college enrollments have *not* declined; they have simply not increased as rapidly as women's (National Center for Educational Statistics 2006). Second, the disadvantage to males depends on age and class. Among traditional-age, upper-income students, *males*—white, black, Hispanic, and Asian—remain a majority of college enrollees (Lewin 2006c), though barely so. Women's master's degrees are primarily in education, nursing, and social work, traditional female areas, and not those leading to the most elite careers. Moreover, sexual harassment continues to be a problem on college campuses (for men as well as women, and for gays and lesbians) (AAUW Educational Foundation 2006; Dziech 2003).

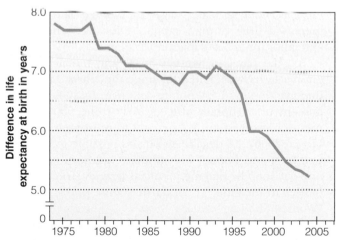

FIGURE 4.2 The difference in life expectancy between males and females, United States, 1975–2004. From a difference of almost eight years in 1979, this gap has been steadily decreasing.

Sources: Hoyert et al. 2006, Figure 3, and Miniño, Heron, and Smith 2006, Table A.

"There is every reason to celebrate the success of women," says a Department of Education official ("Study: Academic Gains" 2006). Nevertheless, some colleges now have what amounts to affirmative action for men, admitting men with weaker records than some women applicants. This amounts, it is argued, to discrimination against qualified women ("Boys' Turn" 2006; Britz 2006). Some education scholars believe that "the new emphasis on young men's problems . . . is misguided in a world where men still dominate the math-science axis, earn more money, and wield more power than women" (Lewin 2006a, p. 18).

The data have made visible two patterns. First, it becomes clear that the college achievement gap is greater among racial/ethnic groups *within* gender categories and especially points to black and Hispanic male disadvantage (Aronson 2003). This has set off an intense debate over whether these trends show a worrisome achievement gap between men and women or whether the concern should be directed toward the educational difficulties of poor boys, black, white, or Hispanic (Lewin 2006a, p. 18).

A second and alarming pattern is the apparent difference between males and females in goals and attitudes toward schooling. Such attitudes have long-run implications for males' educational attainment, placement in the workforce, and ability to maintain a marriage that has a stable financial underpinning. A *USA Today* study found that 84 percent of girls but only 67 percent of boys think it is important to continue beyond high school ("Boys' Academic Slide" 2003). Boys have poorer study habits and less concern about doing well in their studies. Whether the schools themselves have been unwelcoming and unadapted to boys is another thrust of this debate, one we will take up later in the chapter.

As Faculty Women were 39 percent of full-time college and university faculty in the 2005–2006 academic year. With the expansion of women's graduate degree attainment (48 percent of doctorates), one would think that they would have a stronger presence by now. Instead, women are less likely to be full-time faculty; less likely to be in tenure-track positions; less likely to be tenured; and less likely to be full professors (West and Curtis 2006). Disadvantage to women is especially strong at the more elite schools. Sixty-two percent of those hired by Ivy League universities in 2005 were men (Arenson 2005).

Little gain is seen in faculty racial/ethnic diversity. In 2003, 47 percent of college faculty were white males; 36 percent, white females; 6 percent, black; 5 percent, Asian/Pacific Islanders; 4 percent, Hispanic; and less than 1 percent, Native American (National Center for Educational Statistics 2006).

Male Dominance in the Economy

It is on gender inequality in the economy that most attention has been focused. Although the situation is changing, men have been and continue to be dominant economically. In 2006, women who were employed full time earned 81 percent of what men employed full time did (U.S. Bureau of Labor Statistics 2007). When differences in years of experience, hours per year, time out of the labor force, industry, occupation, race, marital status, and job tenure are all taken into account, women's earnings were 80 percent of men's in 2000 (Weinberg 2004).

Younger women earn a larger proportion (88 percent) of what men do (U.S. Bureau of Labor Statistics 2006b). Black (86 percent) and Hispanic (88 percent) female/male comparisons are more favorable to women than are those of non-Hispanic whites (81 percent) or Asians (80 percent). But this is primarily because black and Hispanic men have much lower earnings than do white men (U.S. Bureau of Labor Statistics 2007).

Even in the same occupational categories, women earn less than men. For instance, in 2000, in the highest-paying occupation, that of physician, women made $80,000 while men earned $140,000 on average (Weinberg 2004). The difference is thought to be related to choice of occupational specialty and practice setting.

Overall, the earnings gap between men and women has narrowed in recent decades, as Figure 4.3 indicates. This was true at first primarily among younger women, but now "women's gains in wage parity with comparable men have been prevalent across a wide spectrum" (Blau and Kahn 2006, p. 37). Some proportion of the convergence is due to falling wages for men or their increased time out of the labor force, but by and large the narrowing gap is due to rising wages for women as they have increased their human capital (education and skills) and labor force participation (England 2006).

Yet, the pay gap between male and female college graduates has widened a bit since the 1990s. Men continue to dominate corporate America. In 2005 only 16 percent of corporate officers in Fortune 500 companies were women; only 2 percent were women of color (Joyce 2006). "A decade ago it was possible to imagine that men and women with similar qualifications might one day soon be making identical salaries. Today that is harder to imagine" (Leonhardt 2006b, p. A1; see also "Women Still Lag" 2004).

Chapter 12 explores men's and women's work in more detail. But let us look here at some proposed explanations for gender inequality in the economy. Some argue that jobs more frequently held by males may pay better because they in fact are more difficult, require more training, or have less-favorable working conditions. Assumptions that jobs typically filled by women are less

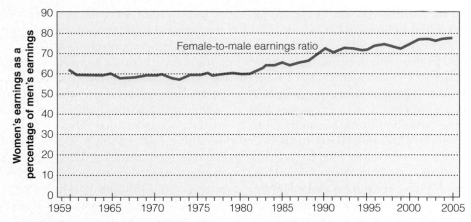

FIGURE 4.3 Female-to-male earnings ratio of full-time, year-round workers fifteen years and older by sex: 1960–2005.
Source: DeNavas-Walt, Proctor, and Lee 2006.

challenging can affect pay scales. Women may themselves buy into gender stereotypes and believe they are less competent to achieve certain jobs or occupational levels. And as women enter the job pool for certain professional jobs (journalism, for example), the field becomes more crowded and wages and salaries are less competitive (Blau, Brinton, and Grusky 2006).

Some point to the different choices women may make, of lower-paying occupations that offer more emotional satisfaction, flexible scheduling, shorter hours, and compatibility with stopping and starting employment around childbearing and children's needs. In economic terms, different "tastes" lead to different jobs, which have greater or lesser rewards. In fact, women are less apt to work full time and to remain in the labor force continually. They may not want to invest in job-specific training or skills that they think will not pay off for them in the long run (Blau, Brinton, and Grusky 2006; Blau and Kahn 2006).

In addition, employers' *assumptions* that women will opt out may affect their careers, and this is where the costs of gender stereotyping come in. Employers may be less likely to select women for advanced training and positions with upward mobility potential (A. Preston 2003 [2000]) even though the women affected may be highly ambitious, with a commitment to continuous employment. This is a subtle form of discrimination that ultimately leads to women advancing and earning less. This, in turn, makes it more likely that a woman's income will be seen as less essential to the family than a man's, and that the family will favor his career in terms of residential mobility, taking time-pressured jobs and promotions, and the like.

But not all of the wage gap is explainable by objective characteristics of men's and women's employment skills histories or women's own choices. It is likely that

discrimination against women as employees continues to some degree. After various factors associated with earnings are taken into account, research finds a varying, but perhaps as much as a 20 percent, differential in earnings that is usually attributed to discrimination, albeit of a nonobvious sort (Blau and Kahn 2006).

We have been discussing gender inequality. The state of affairs can be nicely summed up by Figure 4.3, which illustrates the gains women have made economically *and* the gap that still hasn't closed. Male dominance in the United States today is, of course, more moderate than in our past or compared to contemporary societies that are more traditional or overtly oppressive of women. Still, cross-culturally and historically, it appears that virtually all societies have been characterized by some degree of male dominance.

This leads us to ask whether male dominance might be anchored in biology. To what extent does biology influence patterns of gender roles and behaviors? Put another way, is what Sigmund Freud once proposed true—that "anatomy is destiny"? This question is likely to be answered differently today than it was just a few years ago.

Is Anatomy Destiny?

Biological theories of gender difference were initially offered by ethologists, who study humans as an evolved animal species (e.g., Tiger 1969). Tiger, who primarily studied baboons, found males to be dominant and argued that *Homo sapiens* inherited this condition through natural selection. Newer data on nonhuman primates have challenged these conclusions as socially constructed myths. Primate species vary in their behavior, and within species there is some environmentally shaped variation (Haraway 1989; Wood and Eagly 2002, p. 721). The facts suggest that male and female behavior is not differentiated in a consistent way in the animal species most closely related to humans.

A subsequent biological theory of gendered behavior focused on genes. In this view, in order to continue their genes, individuals act to maximize their reproduction or that of close kin. Different strategies characterize males (who seek to impregnate many females) and females (who seek the best conditions in which to nurture their small number of children) (Dawkins 1976).

Other evolutionary perspectives focus on the hunting–gathering era of early human evolution. Men, because of their greater physical strength and their freedom from reproductive responsibility, were able to hunt. But women, who might be pregnant or breastfeeding, gathered food that was naturally available close to home while they also cared for children. According to these evolutionary theories, circumstances elicited different adaptive strategies and skills from men and women that then became encoded in the genes—greater aggression and spatial skills for men, nurturance and domesticity for women. According to this perspective, these traits remain part of our genetic heritage and are today the foundation of gender differences in personality traits, abilities, and behavior (Maccoby 1998, Chapter 5).

The genetic heritage is expressed through **hormonal processes**.[3] However, the relationship between hormones and behavior goes in both directions: What's happening in one's environment may influence hormone secretion levels. Several small studies have found, for example, that the hormonal levels of new fathers undergo changes parallel to those associated with maternal behavior (lower testosterone and cortisol and detectable levels of estradiol) (Berg and Wynne-Edwards 2001; Storey et al. 2000). Testosterone rises in men in response to an athletic or other competition or in response to insults (Wood and Eagly 2002, pp. 701–2).

Another area of biological research and theorizing on gender differences has to do with brain organization and functioning. *Brain lateralization* refers to the relative dominance and the synchronization of the two hemispheres of the brain. Some scientists have argued that male and female brains differ due to greater amounts

of testosterone secreted by a male fetus. Male fetuses are exposed to relatively large amounts of testosterone at mid-pregnancy, resulting not only in the masculinization of their genitals but also, according to this theory, an organization of brain structure that gives rise to "masculine" behavior and abilities. As a result, different sides of the brain may be dominant in males and females, or males and females may differ in the degree to which the two brain halves work together. These differences are thought to account for differences in verbal and mathematical ability and visual/spatial skills (Blum 1997; Springer and Deutsch 1994).

Overall, brain lateralization studies have produced conflicting—and unconvincing—evidence concerning sex differences in brain organization or a connection to verbal, spatial, or mathematical abilities. Furthermore, gender differences in measured math ability and achievement have declined dramatically, arguing against a biological explanation (Hyde, Fennema, and Lamon, 1990; Kimmel 2000, pp. 30–33; L. Rogers 2001; Wood and Eagly 2002, p. 720).

Many contemporary *biologists* have relinquished deterministic models in their thinking about gender and family. They present an evolutionary theory that acknowledges strong environmental effects on animal behavior. Much current biological theorizing leaves plenty of room for culture (e.g., Emlen 1995; Geary and Flinn 2001).

Attention in *psychology* has turned toward biological underpinnings of universal human qualities, such as the ability to feel emotions and become attached to others (Myers 2001; Pinker 2002). Cognitive psychologists continue to debate the existence and significance of gender differences, however (Harvard University 2005; Kimura 1999, 2002; Pinker 2005; Spelke 2005).

Sociologists who work from a biosocial perspective are finding complex interactions among gender, social roles, and biological indicators rather than categorical gender differences (Alan Booth and colleagues). It is safe to say that there is convergence on the opinion that in gender, as well as other behavior, biology interacts with culture in complex and constantly changing ways that cannot be reduced to biological determinism.

Although adult men and women seem to be converging in social roles and personal qualities, gender differences and separation still seem rather powerful in the younger years. We look now at the various theories and practices related to the socialization of boys and girls.

Gender and Socialization

Psychologist Eleanor Maccoby, earlier associated with a review of research on sex differences that found them few and mostly unimportant (Maccoby and Jacklin

---

[3] **Hormones** are chemical substances secreted into the bloodstream by the endocrine glands; they influence the activities of cells, tissues, and body organs. The primary male sex hormones are androgens. Testosterone, produced in the male testes, is an androgen. Testosterone levels in males peak in adolescence and early adulthood, then slowly decline throughout the rest of a man's life. Females also secrete testosterone and other androgens, but in smaller amounts. The primary female hormones are estrogen and progesterone, secreted by the female ovaries.

Sex hormones influence *sexual dimorphism,* differences between the sexes in body structure and size, muscle development, fat distribution, hair growth, voice quality, and the like. The degree to which hormones produce gender-differentiated behavior is disputed.

1974), has now come to see biology as grounding some *childhood* differences between the sexes, as well as children's tendency to prefer sex-segregated play.

Maccoby sees boys' rough play, earlier separation from adults, poor impulse control, and competition-seeking behavior, and girls' interest in young infants, earlier verbal fluency, and earlier self-regulation as biologically based. She attributes these differences to *prenatal* hormonal priming (see also Hines et al. 2002), noting that hormonal levels *during childhood* do *not* match these observed patterns. Nor do hormonal levels vary much by sex until adolescence. It is worth noting that she sees the biological influence as very specific: *not* marking the existence of generalized sex differences.

That brings us to look at biology and childhood in a different way. In contrast to other species, much of the behavior of humans involves behavior that is learned, not programmed as instincts. There is a lengthy period of dependency on parents or other adults during which this learning takes place (Geary and Flinn 2001). This process, termed **socialization**, is "[a] process by which people develop their human capacities and acquire a unique personality and identity and by which culture is passed from generation to generation" (Ferrante 2000, p. 521).

In this section we look specifically at *gender* socialization, but the socialization processes discussed here are applicable to other aspects of cultural values and behav-

Children learn much about gender roles from their parents, whether they are taught consciously or unconsciously. Parents may model roles and reinforce expectations of appropriate behavior. Children also internalize messages from available cultural influences and materials surrounding them.

ioral expectations as well. First, we examine some theories of socialization, then we look at specific settings for gender socialization, and finally we address some current issues regarding boys and girls.

Theories of Socialization

There are a number of competing theories of gender socialization, each with some supporting evidence (Hines et al. 2002).

Social Learning Theory According to **social learning theory** (Bandura and Walters 1963), children learn gender roles as they are taught by parents, schools, and the media. Children observe and imitate *models* of gender behavior such as parents and/or they are *rewarded (or punished)* by parents and others for gender-appropriate or -inappropriate behavior. Fathers seem to have stronger expectations for gender-appropriate behavior than do mothers. Although this theory makes intuitive sense, researchers have found little association between children's personalities and parents' characteristics (M. Andersen 1988; Losh-Hesselbart 1987).

Self-Identification Theory Some psychologists think that what comes first is not rules about what boys and girls should do but rather the child's awareness of being a boy or a girl. In this **self-identification theory** (also termed *cognitive-developmental theory*), children categorize themselves as male or female, typically by age three. They then identify behaviors in their families, in the media, or elsewhere appropriate to their sex and adopt those behaviors. In effect, children socialize themselves from available cultural materials (Kohlberg 1966).

Gender Schema Theory Similar to self-identification theory, gender schema theory posits that children develop a framework of knowledge (a **gender schema**) about what girls and boys typically do (Bem 1981). Children then use this framework to organize how they interpret new information and think about gender. Once a child has developed a gender schema, the schema influences how she or he processes new information, with gender-consistent information remembered better than gender-inconsistent information. For example, a child with a traditional gender schema might generalize that physicians are men even though the child has sometimes had appointments with female physicians. Overall, gender schema theorists see gender schema as maintaining traditional stereotypes.

Chodorow's Theory of Gender Sociologist Nancy Chodorow (1978) has constructed a theory of gender that combines psychoanalytic ideas about identification of children with parents (*object relations theory*) with an awareness of those parents' social roles in our society. According to **Chodorow's theory**, infants develop a primary identification with the person primarily responsible for their early care. Later, children must learn to differentiate psychologically and emotionally between themselves and their primary caregiver.

Children's primary caregivers are virtually always female. Because a daughter is developing a gender identity similar to her principal caregiver's (her mother), she can readily model her mother's behavior. But a boy cannot model his mother's behavior and also develop a culturally consistent gender identity. He learns instead that he is "not female." He must suppress "feelings of overwhelming love, attachment, and dependence on his mother" (Thurman 1982, p. 35), leaving his gender identity less secure (W. Pollack 1998).

Chodorow attributes differences between adult men and women to this gender divergence in early socialization experience. Boys are disappointed and angry at the necessary—but abrupt and emotionally charged—detachment from their mother. Gradually, however, they come to value their relatively absent fathers as models of agency, independence, and "the superiority of masculine . . . prerogatives" (Thurman 1982, p. 35). Conversely, "relatedness," or expressiveness, is allowed and fostered among girls.

Research does not strongly support Chodorow's theory, and in an era of numerous single-parent families and changing parental roles, it seems less applicable. Nevertheless, Chodorow has been very influential in academic thinking on gender.

Symbolic Interaction Theory In **symbolic interaction theory** (Cooley 1902; 1909; G. H. Mead 1934), children develop self-concepts based on social feedback—the *looking-glass self* (see Chapter 2). Also important is their *role-taking*, as they play out roles in interaction with significant others such as parents and peers. As children grow they take on roles representing wider social networks, and eventually *internalize* norms of the community (termed by Mead *the generalized other*). Although this is a general theory of socialization, you can see how it can be applied to gender. Little girls play "mommy" with their dolls and kitchen sets, while little boys play with cars or hypermasculine action figures. But things are changing, and it is now likely that little girls as well as little boys play "going to work."

All the socialization theories presented here seem plausible, but none has conclusive research support. Self-identification theory, gender schema theory, and Chodorow's theory as well as biologically deterministic theories are especially lacking (Bussey and Bandura 1999). It is also the case that gender socialization is a moving target in a rapidly changing social world.

Settings for Socialization

We'll turn now to some empirical findings regarding gender socialization in concrete and specific settings: the family, play and games among peers, media influences, and the schools. We saw in Chapter 3 that religious groups often specify appropriate gender roles, and they are also a setting for gender socialization.

 Boys and Girls in the Family From the 1970s on, parents have reported treating their sons and daughters similarly.[4] "[T]he specialization of men for dominance and women for subordination that emerged [as a socialization pattern] in patriarchal societies has eroded with the weakening of gender hierarchies in postindustrial societies" (Wood and Eagly 2002, p. 717). Differential socialization still exists, but it is typically not conscious. Instead, it "reflects the fact that the parents themselves accept the general societal roles for men and women," though this is no longer universal (Kimmel 2000, p. 123).

FOCUS ON CHILDREN

Still, encouragement of gender-typed interests and activities continues. A study of 120 babies' and toddlers' rooms found that girls had more dolls, fictional characters, children's furniture, and the color pink; boys had more sports equipment, tools, toy vehicles, and the colors blue, red, and white. Fathers, more than mothers, enforce gender stereotypes, especially for sons; it is more acceptable, for example, for girls to be tomboys (Adams and Coltrane 2004; Bussey and Bandura 1999; Feldman 2003, p. 207; Kimmel 2000, Chapter 6; Pomerleau et al. 1990).

Exploratory behavior is more encouraged in boys than girls (Feldman 2003, p. 207). Toys considered appropriate for boys encourage physical activity and

---

[4] Because most of the classic research presented in this section has focused on middle-class whites, findings may or may not apply to other racial/ethnic or class groups. Racial/ethnic and class variation in child rearing is discussed in Chapter 11.

independent play, whereas "girl toys" elicit closer physical proximity and more talk between child and caregiver (Caldera, Huston, and O'Brien 1989). Even parents who support nonsexist child rearing for their daughters are often concerned if their sons are not aggressive or competitive "enough"—or are "too" sensitive (Pleck 1992). Girls are increasingly allowed or encouraged to develop instrumental attitudes and skills. Meanwhile, boys are still discouraged from, or encounter parental ambivalence about, developing attitudes and skills of tenderness or nurturance (Kindlon and Thompson 1999; Pollack 1998).

Beginning when children are about five and increasing through adolescence, parents allocate household chores—both the number and kinds—to their children differentially, according to the child's sex. With African American children often an exception, Patricia will more likely be assigned cooking and laundry tasks; Paul will find himself painting and mowing (Burns and Homel 1989; McHale et al. 1990). Because girls' chores typically must be done daily, while boys' are sporadic, girls spend more

Toys send messages about gender roles. What does this toy say?

Courtesy Deb Glover and Celeste Wheeler

time doing chores—a fact that "may convey a message about male privilege" (Basow 1992, p. 131). African American girls, however, are raised to be more independent and less passive, while research also indicates that African American boys, as well as girls, are socialized for roles that include employment and child care (Hale-Benson 1986; Staples and Boulin Johnson 1993).

Although relations in the family provide early feedback and help shape a child's developing identity, play and peer groups become important as children try out identities and adult behaviors. In fact, the author of one review of psychological research argues that peers have much more influence on child and adolescent development in general than do parents (J. Harris 1998).

Play and Games The role of **play** is an important concept in the interactionist perspective. In G. H. Mead's theory (1934), play is not idle time, but a significant vehicle through which children develop appropriate concepts of adult roles, as well as images of themselves.

FOCUS ON CHILDREN

Boys and girls tend to play separately and differently (Maccoby 1998). Girls play in one-to-one relationships or in small groups of two and three; their play is relatively cooperative, emphasizes turn taking, requires little competition, and has relatively few rules. In "feminine" games like jump rope or hopscotch, the goal is skill rather than winning (Basow 1992). Boys more often play in fairly large groups, characterized by more fighting and attempts to effect a hierarchical pecking order. Boys also seem to exhibit high spirits and having fun (Maccoby 1998). From preschool through adolescence, children who play according to traditional gender roles are more popular with their peers; this is more true for boys (C. L. Martin 1989).

Especially in elementary schools, many cross-sexual interaction rituals such as playground games are based on and reaffirm boundaries and differences between girls and boys. Sociologist Barrie Thorne (1992), who spent eleven months doing naturalistic observation at two elementary schools, calls these rituals **borderwork**.

Sports play a role, both the informal and organized sports of childhood and the images presented in the media (Messner 2002). Now girls have more organized sports available to them, as well as more media models of women athletes. Girls who take part in sports have greater self-esteem and self-confidence (Andersen and Taylor 2002; Dworkin and Messner 1999).

The Power of Cultural Images Media images often convey gender expectations. Children's programming more often depicts boys than girls in dominant, agentic roles

(B. Carter 1991). On music videos, females are likely to be shown trying to get a man's attention. Some videos broadcast shockingly violent misogynous (hatred of women) messages. In TV commercials, men predominate by about nine to one as the authoritative narrators or voiceovers, even when the products are aimed at women (Craig 1992; Kilbourne 1994). Cultural images in the media indicate to the audience what is "normal."

Socialization in Schools There is considerable evidence that the way girls and boys are treated differently in school is detrimental to both genders (AAUW 1992; Kindlon and Thompson 1999; W. Pollack 1998; Sadker and Sadker 1994;). School organization, classroom teachers, and textbooks all convey the message that boys are more important than girls. At the same time, some critics posit that school expectations are unreasonably difficult for the typical boy to meet.

Teachers' Practices Research shows that teachers pay more attention to males than to females, and males tend to dominate learning environments from nursery school through college (Lips 2004). Researchers who observed more than 100 fourth-, sixth-, and eighth-grade classes over a three-year period found that boys consistently and clearly dominated classrooms. Teachers called on and encouraged boys more often than girls. If a girl gave an incorrect answer, the teacher was likely to call on another student, but if a boy was incor-

rect, the teacher was more likely to encourage him to learn by helping him discover his error and correct it (Sadker and Sadker 1994). Compared to girls, boys are more likely to receive a teacher's attention, to call out in class, to demand help or attention from the teacher, to be seen as model students, or to be praised by teachers. Boys are also more likely to be disciplined harshly by teachers (Gurian 1996; Kindlon and Thompson 1999; Pollack 1998).

In subtle ways, teachers may reinforce the idea that males and females are more different than similar. There are times when boys and girls interact together relatively comfortably—in the school band, for example. But in classrooms, teachers often pit girls and boys against each other in spelling bees or math contests (Thorne 1992).

African American Girls, Latinas, and Asian American Girls in Middle and High School Journalist Peggy Orenstein (1994) spent one year observing pupils and teachers in two California middle schools, one mostly white and middle class and the other predominantly African American and Hispanic and of lower socioeconomic status. Orenstein found that in both schools, girls were subtly encouraged to be quiet and nonassertive whereas boys were rewarded for boisterous and even aggressive behaviors.

However, African American girls were louder and less unassuming than non-Hispanic white girls were when they began school—and some continued along this path. In fact, they called out in the classroom as often as boys did. But Orenstein noted that teachers' reactions differed. The participation, and even antics, of white boys in the classroom was considered inevitable and rewarded with extra attention and instruction, whereas the assertiveness of African American girls was defined as "menacing, something that, for the sake of order in the classroom, must be squelched" (p. 181). Orenstein further found that Latinas, along with Asian American girls, had special difficulty being heard or even noticed. Probably socialized into quiet demeanor at home and often having language difficulties, these girls' scholastic or leadership abilities largely went unseen. In some cases, their classroom teachers did not even know who the girls were when Orenstein mentioned their names.

FOCUS ON CHILDREN

© Cassy Cohen/PhotoEdit

Are boys behaving differently than girls in this photo? How does this fit with the discussion of gender and socialization in school? What does that discussion say about girls in school? Boys in school?

In high school, Latina girls experience cross-pressures when the desire to succeed in school and move on to a career is in tension with the traditional assumption of wife and mother roles at a young age. Twenty-five percent do not finish high school, compared to 12 percent of black and 10 percent of white girls (U.S. Census Bureau 2006c, Table 258). Factors such as poverty and language barriers, as well as the pressure to contribute to the family, affect the educational attainment of both boys and girls. But young Latinas, especially recent immigrants, seem torn between newer models for women as mothers *and* career women and the traditional model of marriage and homemaking (Canedy 2001). Nevertheless, the majority of Latinas and Latinos finish high school.

School Organization In 2004, 74 percent of all public school employees were women, while only a little over half (53 percent) of the principals and assistant principals and officials and administrators (51 percent) were women. Eighty-six percent of elementary teachers were women, and 59 percent of secondary teachers. These numbers represent a change toward greater balance since 1982, when only 21 percent of principals, 24 percent of officials and administrators, and 49 percent of secondary teachers were women (U.S. Census Bureau 2003a, Table 252).

Programs and Outcomes One concern related to schooling has been whether girls are channeled into or themselves avoid the traditionally masculine areas in high school study. We don't really know the answer to this question. A recent review of one thousand research studies (AAUW Educational Foundation 1999) reports that high school boys and girls now take similar numbers of science courses, but boys are more likely to take all three core courses: biology, chemistry, and physics. Girls enroll in Advanced Placement (AP) courses in greater numbers than boys, including AP biology. But fewer girls than boys get high enough scores on AP tests to get college credit. Girls take fewer computer courses, and they cluster in traditional female occupations in career-oriented programs.

Girls versus Boys?

FOCUS ON CHILDREN   Girls have long been the primary focus of attention in examining the possible bias of educational institutions. The previous sections make a good case for such concern, and the 1994 Women's Equal Education Act declares girls an "under-served population." Despite the litany of difficulties girls and women may face in educational settings, the intention is to identify problems that need continued attention. In fact, girls are doing well, on the whole. Women and girls "are on a tear through the educational system. . . . In the past 30 years, nearly every inch of progress . . . has gone to them" (Thor Mortenson of the Dell Institute for the Study of Opportunity in Higher Education, in Conlin 2003a, p. 76).

In recent years, attention has turned to boys. Some writers attack the "myth of girls in crisis" (Sommers 2000a, p. 61). Sommers's critique goes beyond a concern for balance to argue that there is a "war on boys" (2000b). In Sommers's view, boys are actively discriminated against by the educational establishment: "[B]oys are resented, both as the unfairly privileged sex and as obstacles on the path to gender justice" (2000b, p. 60; see also 2000a, p. 23).

Sommers and others have some valid points. They point to the declining male share of college enrollments and note that on a number of indicators, girls do better in school: better grades, higher educational aspirations, greater enrollment in AP and other demanding academic programs. Currently, girls are even more likely to outnumber boys in higher-level math and science courses, student government, honor society, and student newspaper staffs. More boys fall behind grade level and more are suspended, and they are far more likely to be shunted into special education classes or to have their inattentive and restless behavior defined as deviant, and medicated. Indicators of deviant behavior—crime, alcohol, and drugs—show more involvement by boys.

To the argument that boys do better on SAT and other standardized tests, Sommers responds that the pool of girls taking the test is more apt to include disadvantaged and/or marginal students, whereas their male counterparts do not take these exams. Boys have a greater incidence of diagnosis of emotional disorders, learning disorders, attention-deficit disorders, and teen deaths (Conlin 2003a; Goldberg 1998; Sommers 2000a, 2000b). The "gender gap" in current bachelor's degrees is noted. In every racial/ethnic group, women receive more degrees ("A Widening Gulf" 2003).

Other analysts do not necessarily share Sommers's allegations of active discrimination against boys. But they argue that attention to girls' educational needs and the success of men in the work world tended to obscure boys' problems in school. They see a mismatch between typical boy behavior—high levels of physical activity and more challenges to teachers and school rules—and school expectations about sitting still, following rules, and concentrating (Poe 2004). Moreover, a survey by the Public Education Network (Metropolitan Life Insurance Company 1997) found that 31 percent of boys in grades 7–12 felt that teachers do not listen to them, compared to 19 percent of girls.

A recent research study (Meadows, Land, and Lamb 2005) sought to examine and compare the situations of boys and girls. The researchers took note of Sommers's critique regarding boys, as well as the research cited earlier on the disadvantaged situation of girls in schools. They noted Carol Gilligan's influential books (1982; Gilligan, Lyons, and Hanmer 1990), which argue that girls' strengths in relationships and emotional expressions are devalued in an individualistic and competitive American society and that girls become discouraged as they arrive on the threshold of adolescence (see also Pipher 1995).[5]

Essentially, Meadows and her colleagues asked: How goes it with boys and girls? For answers they turned to the status of boys and girls on twenty-eight social indicators of well-being, which are also combined into an index. These indicators measure seven life domains: material well-being, health, safety, productive activity, intimacy, place in the community, and emotional well-being (p. 5). Meadows and her colleagues concluded that "gender differences in well-being, when they do exist, are very slight and that overall both boys and girls in the United States currently enjoy a higher quality of life than they did in 1985" (p. 1).

This study addresses the question of the overall well-being of boys and girls, inspired by assertions of a "war against boys" (Sommers 2000b) and a "girl-poisonous culture" (Pipher 1995) and comes to reassuring conclusions. Regarding *education* specifically, "[T]he results reported here do not support current claims by many feminists that girls are at a disadvantage . . . when it comes to educational attainment. If anything, it is boys who are falling behind, particularly at higher levels of education" (Meadows et al. 2005, p. 44). This points to the question of whether schooling should change in some way.

Sommers proposes single-sex schools; restoration of a competitive, structured, and achievement-oriented environment; and elimination of attempts to get boys to express their emotions (Sommers 2000a, 2000b).

Other approaches to concerns about boys are exactly opposite to the approach of Sommers. Psychiatrist William Pollack's perspective is that "what we call . . . normal boy development . . . not only isn't normal, but it's traumatic and that trauma has major consequences" (quoted in Goldberg 1998, p. A–12; see also Kimmel 2001). To express vulnerability runs the risk of victimization. Boys, particularly racial/ethnic minority youth, face a dilemma in that acting tough to protect themselves is threatening to adults (psychologist Dan Kind-

"We don't believe in pressuring the children. When the time is right, they'll choose the appropriate gender."

lon, cited in Goldberg 1998). One effort suggested by this line of thought is to take measures to decrease bullying (Kimmel 2001). Another is to encourage boys to express their emotions and to redefine the male role to include emotional expression (Kindlon and Thompson 1999).

Other proposals include: (1) accepting a certain level of boys' rowdy play as not deviant, (2) implementing more active learning-by-doing to permit physical movement in classroom settings, and (3) encouraging activities shared by boys and girls and boy–girl dialogues about gender (Kindlon and Thompson 1999). The bottom line may be the observation by Marie C. Wilson, president of the Ms. Foundation for Women: "We'd be so naive to think we could change the lives of girls without boys' lives changing" (quoted in Goldberg 1998, p. A-12). It may be that "girls and boys are on the same side in this issue."

In this section on socialization, we have examined how socialization shapes gender identities and gendered behavior. Socialization continues throughout adulthood as we negotiate and learn new roles—or as those already learned are renegotiated or reinforced. The varied opportunities we encounter as adults influence the adult roles we choose and play out, and the qualities and skills we develop. And those have changed in recent decades, in response to the Women's Movement and the men's movements that followed.

Social Change and Gender

The increasing convergence of men's and women's social roles, though incomplete, reflects a dramatic change from the more gender-differentiated world of

---

[5] Meadows et al. (2005) note that Gilligan's conclusions about gender differences are based on small numbers of interviews with girls (no boys) and on anecdotes and that she has never been willing to make her data available for review by other scholars.

the mid-twentieth century. Such changes are due not only to structural forces (especially economic) that led to women's increased entry into the labor force but also to active change efforts by women and their allies in the Women's Movement. Men's movements followed.

The Women's Movement

The nineteenth century saw a feminist movement develop, but from around 1920 until the mid-1960s there was virtually no activism regarding women's rights and women's roles.[6] Women did make some gains in the 1920s and 1930s in education and occupational level, but these were eroded during the more familistic post–World War II era.

Media glorification of housewife and breadwinner roles made them seem natural despite the reality of increased women's employment. But contradictions between what women were actually doing and the roles prescribed for them became increasingly apparent. Higher levels of education for women left college-educated women with a significant gap between their abilities and the housewife role assigned to them. Employed women chafed at the unequal pay and working conditions in which they labored and began to think that their interest lay in increasing equal opportunity. Betty Friedan's book *The Feminine Mystique* (1963) captured this dissatisfaction and made it a topic of public discussion. Further, the Civil Rights Movement of the 1960s provided a model of activism. In a climate in which social change seemed possible, dissatisfaction with traditional roles precipitated a social movement—the Second Wave of the Women's Movement. This movement challenged heretofore accepted traditional roles and strove to increase gender equality.

In 1961 President Kennedy set up a Presidential Commission on the Status of Women, and some state commissions were established subsequently. The National Organization for Women (NOW) was founded in 1966. Meanwhile, in Congress, the Civil Rights Act of 1964 had been amended by opponents (as a political tactic) to include sex—and it passed! Title VII of the Civil Rights Act gradually began to be enforced. Grassroots feminist groups with a variety of agendas and political postures developed across the country.

NOW had multiple goals—opening educational and occupational opportunities to women, along with establishing support services like child care. As well, NOW recognized the commitment of a majority of women to marriage and motherhood and spoke to the possibility of "real choice" (National Organization for Women 1966). Although supporting traditional heterosexual marriage for those who chose it, the organization came to support the more controversial choice (in those times) of a lesbian lifestyle, as well as reproductive choice, including abortion.

Women vary in their attitudes toward the Women's Movement and in what issues are important to them. Figure 4.4 indicates "top priority" issues that were evident in a survey of women conducted in 2003.

Some women of color and white working-class women may find the Women's Movement irrelevant to the extent that it focuses on psychological oppression or on professional women's opportunities rather than on "the daily struggle to make ends meet that is faced by working class women" (Aronson 2003, p. 907). Black women have always labored in the productive economy under duress or out of financial necessity and did not experience the enforced delicacy of women in the Victorian period. Nor were they ever housewives in large numbers, so the feminist critique of that role may seem irrelevant (Hunter and Sellers 1998).

Chicano/Chicana (Mexican American) activism gave *la familia* a central place as a distinctive cultural value. Latinos of both sexes placed a high value on family solidarity, with individual family members' needs and desires subsumed to the collective good, so that Chicana feminists' critiques of unequal gender relations in *la familia* often met with hostility (Segura and Pesquera 1995).

African American and Latino women consider racial/ethnic as well as gender discrimination in setting their priorities (Arnott and Matthaei 2007). In fact, it is more precise to say their feminist views are characterized by *intersectionality*—structural connections among race, class, and gender (Baca Zinn, Hondagneu-Sotelo, and Messner 2007; Roth 2004).

In some ways, such as their experience with racial/ethnic discrimination and their relatively low wages, Chicanas are more like Mexican American men, who are also subordinated, than they are like non-Hispanic white women. Nevertheless, a Chicana feminism emerged during the 1960s and 1970s. Generally, Chicanas support women's economic issues, such as equal employment and day care, while showing less support for abortion rights than do Anglo women. Latinas formed some grassroots community organizations of their own to offer social services such as job training, community-based alternatives to juvenile incarceration, and bilingual child development centers. The Mexican American Women's National Association (now MANA) was established in 1974 (Segura and Pesquera 1995).

African American women are more critical of gender inequality than are white women (Kane 2000).

---

[6] The "First Wave" of feminism began with a convention on women's rights that produced the Seneca Falls Declaration in 1848. Nineteenth-century women were also active in abolitionist and temperance movements. The First Wave of feminism came to an end when a major goal, voting rights for women, was achieved in 1920 (Rossi 1973).

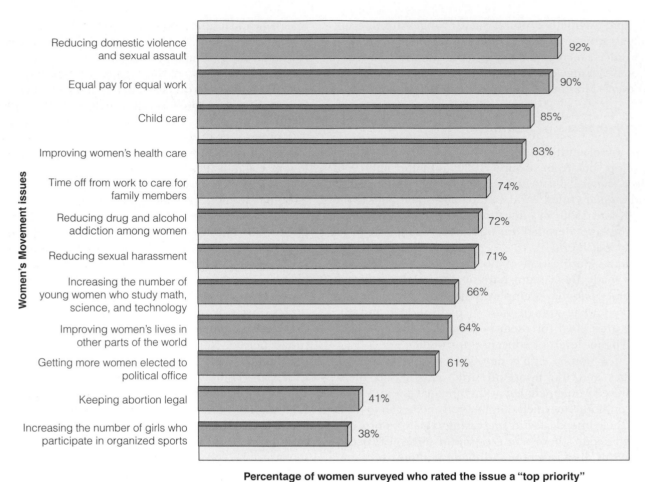

Percentage of women surveyed who rated the issue a "top priority"

FIGURE 4.4 "Top priority" issues for the Women's Movement. More than 3,300 women were asked to indicate which issues they felt the Women's Movement should focus on. The 2003 survey was conducted for the Center for the Advancement of Women by Princeton Survey Research Associates.

Source: Center for the Advancement of Women 2003, p. 11 (www.advancewomen.org).

A National Urban League report states that "a feminist perspective has much to offer Black America" (West 2003). African American women and men are more likely than whites to endorse political organizing for women's issues (Hunter and Sellers 1998). Sixty-eight percent of Latina women (*n* = 354) and 63 percent of African American women (*n* = 352) surveyed in 2001 as part of a national sample of 2,329 "strongly agree" that there is a need for a women's movement today (Center for the Advancement of Women 2003).

There are other variations in attitudes toward the Women's Movement. Some women deplore the rise of feminism and encourage traditional marriage and motherhood as the best path to women's self-fulfillment (Enda 1998; Marshall 1995; Passno 2000). Many feminists would define the movement as one that advances the interests and status of women as mothers and care-givers, as well as workers (Coburn 1999). Surveys in the 1980s indicate that large majorities reject the notion

that the Women's Movement is anti-family (Hall and Rodriguez 2003).

The media often assert that a younger "post-feminist" generation does not support a women's movement. The assumption is that they may have a negative image of feminism or be latently feminist, but believe that women's rights' goals have already been achieved. Sometimes such articles assert that younger women are simply too busy with work and family to have the time to be active.

Differences of opinion among women on issues related to sexuality and reproduction are undoubtedly divisive. Most recent research finds a complex array of definitions of feminism (Aronson 2003; Center for the Advancement of Women 2003), and cultural meanings of *feminism* do seem to vary by age cohort (Peltola, Milkie, and Presser 2004).

Nevertheless, research suggests that "post-feminism" is a myth. Hall and Rodriguez, who did an extensive review of survey data, found an increase in support

Dan Koeck/The New York Times/Redux

Native Americans, members of what were once hunting and gathering and hoe cultures, have a complex heritage that varies by tribe but may include a matrilineal tradition in which women owned (and may still own) houses, tools, and land. Native American women's political power declined with the spread of Europeans into their territories and the subsequent reorganization of Indian life by federal legislation in the 1920s. Recently, Native American women have begun to regain their power. Erma J. Vizenor is chairwoman of the White Earth Nation, the largest tribe in Minnesota. Dr. Vizenor, who holds a doctorate from Harvard, is one of 133 women tribal leaders.

for the Women's Movement from the 1970s and 1980s to the middle or late 1990s (see also Bolzendahl and Myers 2004). Young adults age eighteen to twenty-nine reported more favorable attitudes than older cohorts (Hall and Rodriguez 2003, p. 895; see also Aronson 2003). "One might note that many of the ideologies associated with feminism have become relatively common place and speak to the success of feminism in attaining much broader acceptance of gender equality" (Schnittker, Freese, and Powell 2003, pp. 619–20). Although not all supporters of the Women's Movement self-identify as feminists, a majority (54 percent) "say that being a feminist is an important part of who they are" (Center for the Advancement of Women 2003).

Men's Movements

As the Women's Movement encouraged changes in gender expectations and social roles, some men responded by initiating a men's movement. The first National Conference on Men and Masculinity was held in 1975 and has been held almost annually since. The focus of this men's movement is on changes that men want in their lives and how best to get them. One goal has been to give men a forum—in consciousness-raising groups, in men's studies college courses, and, increasingly, on the Internet—in which to air their feelings about gender and think about their life goals and their relationships with others.

Kimmel (1995) divides today's men's movement into three fairly distinct camps: antifeminists, profeminists, and masculinists. *Antifeminists* believe that the Women's Movement has caused the collapse of the natural order, one that guaranteed male dominance, and they work to reverse this trend. The National Organization for Men (NOM) opposes feminism, which it claims is "designed to denigrate men, exempt women from the draft and to encourage the disintegration of the family" (Siller 1984, quoted in Kimmel 1995, p. 564).

According to Mark Kann, men's self-interest may lead to an antifeminist response even among men who wish women well in an abstract sense:

> I would suggest . . . that men's immediate self-interest rarely coincides with feminist opposition to patriarchy. Consider that men need money and leisure to carry out their experiments in self-fulfillment. Is it not their immediate interest to monopolize the few jobs that promise affluence and autonomy by continuing to deny women equal access to them? . . . Why should they commit themselves to those aspects of feminism that reduce men's social space? It is one thing to try out the joys of parenting, for example, but quite another to assume sacrificial responsibility for the pains of parenting.
> (Kann 1986, p. 32)

Profeminists support feminists in their opposition to patriarchy. They analyze men's problems as stemming from a patriarchal system that privileges white heterosexual men while forcing all males into restrictive gender roles. In 1983, profeminist men formed the National Organization for Changing Men (changed in 1990 to the National Organization for Men Against Sexism, or NOMAS), whose purposes are to transcend gender stereotypes while supporting women's and gays' struggles for respect and equality (Doyle 1989).

The newer *masculinists,* who emerged in the early 1990s, tend not to focus on patriarchy as problematic (although they might agree that it is). Instead, masculinists work to develop a positive image of masculinity, one combining strength with tenderness. Their path to this is through therapy, consciousness-raising groups, and rituals. Through rituals, men are to get in touch with their feelings and heal the buried rage and grief caused by the oppressive nature of corporate culture, the psychological and/or physical absence of their fathers, and men's general isolation due to a learned reluctance to share their feelings (Kimmel 1995). Robert Bly's *Iron John* (1990) is a prominent example of these ideas.

In examining men's movements and their goals, it is important to appreciate that men's social situations vis-à-vis traditional roles are as diverse as women's. The idea of a universal patriarchy and male dominance is challenged by the obvious point that all men are not privileged in the larger society (Connell 2005), whether or not they are so in gender relations. "When race, social class, sexual orientation, physical abilities, and immigrant or national status are taken into account, we can see that in some circumstances 'male privilege' is partly—sometimes substantially—muted" (Baca Zinn, Hondagneu-Sotelo, and Messner 2004, p. 170, citing Kimmel and Messner 1998).

Personal and Family Change

Sometimes, in response to available options, adults reconsider earlier choices regarding gender roles. For example, a small proportion of men choose to be full-time fathers and/or househusbands. Others may effect more subtle changes, such as breaking through previously learned isolating habits to form more intimate friendships and deeper family relationships.

Ironically that very expansion in the range of people's opportunities may lead to mixed feelings and conflicts, both within oneself and between men and women as we confront the "lived messiness" of gender in contemporary life (Heywood and Drake 1997, p. 8). Stay-at-home moms may worry about the family budget and about their options if their marriages fail or if they desire to work when children are older. They may feel others consider them uninteresting or incompetent. Women who are employed may wish they could stay home full time with their families or at least have less-hectic days and more family time. Moreover, a wife's career success and work demands may lead her into renegotiating gender boundaries at home, and that may produce domestic tension.

Modern men may be torn between egalitarian principles and the advantages of male privilege. For one thing, husbands are still expected to succeed as principal family breadwinners. The "new man" is expected to succeed economically *and* to value relationships and emotional openness. Although women want men to be sensitive and emotionally expressive, they also want them to be self-assured and confident. Men often face prejudice when they take jobs traditionally considered women's (Campbell 1991). They may encounter more resistance than women when they try to exercise "family friendly" options in the workplace (Hochschild 1997).

These conflicts are more than psychological. They are in part a consequence of our society's failure to provide support for employed parents in the form of adequate maternity and paternity leave or day care, for example. American families continue to deal individually with problems of pregnancy, recovery from childbirth, and early child care as best they can. Adequate job performance, let alone career achievement, is difficult for women under such conditions regardless of ability. Declining economic opportunities for non-college men, coupled with criticisms of male privilege sparked by the Women's Movement, lead some men to feel unfairly picked on (N. Scott 1992). Perhaps more common is the ambivalence of a man who wants his wife and daughters to have the same opportunities he does and who is willing to pitch in at home—but who envies the freedom from domestic cares and ability to concentrate on work of a man in a more traditional household.

Today's men, like today's women, find it difficult to have it all. If women find it difficult to combine a sustained work career with motherhood, men face a conflict between maintaining their privileges and enjoying supportive relationships. But many "will find that equality and sharing offer compensations to offset their attendant loss of power and privilege" (Gerson 1993, p. 274).

Chapter 12 discusses work and family in more detail, while Chapter 14 addresses family power.

The Future of Gender

"Gender is a ruling idea in people's lives—even where egalitarian ideology is common, as among young, affluent, educated Americans. . . . Despite the extraordinary improvements in women's status over the past two centuries, some aspects of gender have seemed exceptionally resistant to erosion in recent decades," notably child raising and occupational achievement and pay. "[P]eople still think about women and men differently and . . . men still occupy most of the highest positions of political and economic power" (Jackson 2006, pp. 215, 229).

If men and women are seen through a lens of differential competence, if men and women continue to interact with men in situations in which they (men) have greater power and status, assumptions about inherent status differences are supported. Moreover, gender differences may be maintained because of the power of gendered self-concepts. Men and women may have a psychological stake in the maintenance of these differences as important aspects of personal identity (Ridgeway 2006).

Yet sociologist Robert Max Jackson is convinced that the forces of history will sweep gender inequality aside. Two hundred years of change suggest that indeed gen-

Reprinted by permission of Anne Gibbons.

© 1996 Anne Gibbons

der is not embedded so deeply in society that it cannot change. "It is fated to end because essential organizational characteristics and consequences of a modern, industrial, market-oriented, electorally governed society are inherently inconsistent with the conditions needed to sustain gender inequality" (Jackson 2006, p. 241).

Looking at marriage and the family, sociologist Steven Nock expects marriages of "equally dependent spouses" to represent the future toward which American marriage is evolving. By this he means a model in which both spouses are earners as well as family caretakers, and they are dependent on their common earnings as the basis of their family life. In the short run, women's increased earnings have enabled them to leave a marriage of poor emotional quality. Yet, the falling divorce rate suggests that in the long run this will not be the case because

> we are returning to a more traditional form of marriage than we have had in the last century. Marriage was historically based on extensive dependency by both partners. . . . I believe that the recent increases in marital stability reflect the gradual working out of the gender issues first confronted in the 1960s. If so, this implies that young men and women are forming new types of marriages that are based on a new understanding of gender ideals. And if so, the growth of equal dependency that we are likely to see in the next decade bodes well. (Nock 2001, pp. 773–74).

Gendered expectations and behaviors—both as they have and have not changed—underpin many of the topics explored throughout this text. For example, gender is important to discussions of family power, communication, and parental roles, as well as to work and family roles. In future chapters we will explore these topics, keeping in mind gendered expectations and social change.

Summary

- Roles of men and women have changed over time, but living in our society remains a somewhat different experience for women and for men. Gendered cultural messages and social structure influence people's behavior, attitudes, and options. But in many respects, men and women are more alike than different.

- Generally, traditional masculine expectations require that men be confident, self-reliant, and occupationally successful—and engage in "no sissy stuff." During the 1980s, the "liberated male" cultural message emerged, according to which men are expected to value tenderness and equal relationships with women. We have seen the return of respect to the physically tough and protective "manly man."

- Traditional feminine expectations involve a woman's being a man's helpmate and a "good mother." An emergent feminine role is the successful "professional woman." When coupled with the more traditional roles, this results in the "superwoman."

- Individuals vary in the degree to which they follow cultural models for gendered behavior. The extent to which men and women differ from each other and follow these cultural messages can be visualized as two overlapping normal distribution curves.

- Although there are significant changes, male dominance remains evident in politics, in religion, and in the economy.

- There are racial/ethnic and class differences in stereotypes, as well as some differences in actual gender and family patterns. This, and other diversity, has come to be expressed in responses to the women's and men's movements.

- Biology interacts with culture to produce human behavior, and the two influences are not really separable. Sociologists give considerable attention to the socialization process, for which there are several theoretical explanations. Advocates have expressed concern about barriers to the opportunities and achievements of both boys and girls.

- Underlying both socialization and adult behavior are the social structural pressures and constraints that shape men's and women's choices and behaviors. These have changed in recent decades, in part as a consequence of the Women's Movement and subsequent men's movements.

- Turning our attention to the actual lives of adults in contemporary society, we find women and men negotiating gendered expectations and making choices in a context of change at work and in the family. New cultural ideals are far from realization, and efforts to create lives balancing love and work involve conflict and struggle, but promise fulfillment as well.

- Whether gender will continue to be a moderator of economic opportunities and life choices in the future is uncertain, as men's and women's roles and activities converge, but men remain more advantaged. It is likely that gender identity will continue to be important to both men and women.

- Some social scientists predict that the shared economic and family roles emerging in younger marriages will produce more stable marriages.

Questions for Review and Reflection

1. What are some characteristics generally associated with males in our society? What traits are associated with females? How might these affect our expectations about the ways that men and women should behave? Are these images still influential?

2. Do you think men are dominant in major social institutions such as politics, religion, education, and the economy? Or are they no longer dominant? Give evidence to support your opinion.

3. Which theory of gender socialization presented in this chapter seems most applicable to what you see in the real world? Can you give some examples from your own experience of gender socialization?

4. Women and men may renegotiate and change their gendered attitudes and behaviors as they progress through life. What evidence do you see of this in your own life or in others' lives?

5. **Policy Question.** What family law and policy changes of recent years do you think are related to the women's and men's movements? What policies do you think would be needed to promote greater gender equality and/or more satisfying lives for men and women?

Key Terms

agentic (instrumental) character traits 78
borderwork 89
Chodorow's theory of gender socialization 88
communal (expressive) character traits 78
femininities 79
gender 76
gender identity 76
gender role 76
gender schema theory of gender socialization 87
gender similarities hypothesis 81
hormonal processes 86
hormones 86
intersexual 78

male dominance 81
masculinities 78
modern sexism 77
play 89
self-identification theory of gender socialization 87
sex 76
social learning theory of gender socialization 87
socialization 87
symbolic interaction theory of gender socialization 88
traditional sexism 77
transgendered 78
transsexual 78

Online Resources

Companion Website for This Book

www.thomsonedu.com/sociology/lamanna

Visit the book companion website, where you will find flash cards, practice quizzes, Internet links, suggested readings, InfoTrac College Edition exercises, and more to help you study.

ThomsonNOW™ for Marriage and Family

Spend time on what you need to master rather than on information you already have learned. Take a pre-test for this chapter, and ThomsonNOW will generate a personalized study plan based on your results. The study plan will identify the topics you need to review and direct you to online resources such as videos, narrated learning modules, and interactive activities to help you master those topics. You can then take a post-test to help you determine the concepts you have mastered and what you will still need to work on. Try it out! Go to **www.thomsonedu.com/login** to sign in with an access code or to purchase access to this product.

Loving Ourselves
and Others

5

Personal Ties in an Impersonal Society

What Is Love?

Love Is a Deep and Vital Emotion

Love Satisfies Legitimate Personal Needs

Love Involves Caring and Acceptance

Do Men and Women Care Differently?

Love and Intimacy: Commitment to Sharing

My Family: Couple Discovers Love Twenty-five Years after Teen Marriage

Six Love Styles

Three Things Love Isn't

Martyring

Manipulating

Limerence

Self-Worth as a Prerequisite to Loving

Self-Love versus Narcissism

Self-Esteem and Personal Relationships

Emotional Interdependence

As We Make Choices: Learning to Love Yourself More

Love as a Discovery

The Wheel of Love

Keeping Love

More than half of American adults say they believe in "love at first sight," and almost three-quarters believe in "one true love" (Carlson 2001; Robison 2003). We all want to be loved. But when asked what love is, most of us have trouble answering. Love *is* difficult to define; in attempting to do so, we "toy with mystery" (Peck 1978).

In this chapter, we'll discuss the need for loving in today's society and describe one writer's view of some forms that love takes. We'll examine what love is (and isn't). We'll explore the idea that "love implies choice. We do not have to love. We choose to love." We practice, or do, love (Carter 2001). And we can learn to love (Jaksch 2002). We begin by looking at what love means in an impersonal, modern society.

Personal Ties in an Impersonal Society

We say that modern society is impersonal because so much of the time we are encouraged to think and behave in ways that deny our emotional need to be cared for and to care for others (Bellah et al. 1985; Real 2002). An impersonal society exaggerates the rational and economic aspects of human beings and tends to ignore people's need for affection and human contact.[1] For example, we expect people to leave their friends and relatives to move to job-determined new locations because job mobility is an economically efficient way of organizing production and management. Our society places greater value on achievement and consumerism than on the attitudes and behaviors necessary to maintain a long-term loving relationship (Lewis, Amini, and Lannon 2000; Love 2001).

Furthermore, some observers argue that many Americans—especially young people—have grown increasingly cynical, calculating, and distrustful of others over the past three decades (Bulcroft 2000; Dowd and Pallotta 2000). This situation sets up a paradox: Our need for love is heightened while loving becomes more difficult (Alper 2003). Yet most people continue to search for at least one caring person with whom to share their private time. Some find love and nourish it; some don't discover love at all. But we all need love—not only to receive it but also to give it (Gold and Rogers 1995). Physicians and psychologists point out that loving acts,

both given and received, enhance physical health and are essential for emotional survival (Ciaramigoli and Ketcham 2000; Fletcher 2002; Lewis, Amini, and Lannon 2000; Stratton 2003).

What Is Love?

Love exists between parents and children, and between people of the same and opposite sexes. Love may or may not involve sexuality. When it does involve sexuality, "romantic" love can be heterosexual or homosexual. Psychoanalyst Rollo May defines love as "a delight in the presence of the other person and an affirming of his [or her] value and development as much as one's own" (1975, p. 116). Feminist theorist bell hooks defines love as "the will to nurture one's own or another's spiritual growth, revealed through acts of care, respect, knowing, and assuming responsibility" (2000, p. 136). We include these definitions here because we like them and think they complement ours. We define **love** as a deep and vital emotion that satisfies certain needs, combined with a caring for and acceptance of the beloved and resulting in an intimate relationship. We'll discuss each part of this definition.

Love is a deep and vital emotion, combined with a caring for and acceptance of the beloved, and resulting in an intimate relationship. Defined this way, love is increasingly important in an impersonal society such as ours.

[1] This impersonality of modern society has been a principal concern of sociologists (see Durkheim 1933 [1893]; Berger, Berger, and Kellner 1973; Hochschild 2003; Simmel 1950; Weber 1948) since sociology first appeared as a distinct discipline in the Western world, roughly at the time of the Industrial Revolution.

Love Is a Deep and Vital Emotion

An **emotion** is a strong feeling, arising without conscious mental or rational effort, which motivates an individual to behave in certain ways. Anger, reverence, and fear are emotions that evoke certain behaviors. When people feel joy, for instance, they may beam, even "jump for joy." Love is also an emotion that evokes behavior. Loving parents are motivated to see what is wrong when their child begins to cry.

Love Satisfies Legitimate Personal Needs

Human beings need recognition and affection. A second element of love is that it fills this basic need. Giving and receiving love enable people to fulfill their needs for nurturance, creativity, and self-revelation (Lewis, Amini, and Lannon 2000).

It's all very well to state that a person's emotional needs can be fulfilled by love, but what kind of—and how many—needs can we expect to be satisfied? Psychologists stress that being loved cannot fulfill all needs, and they distinguish between legitimate and illegitimate needs.

Legitimate Needs Sometimes called "being needs," **legitimate needs** arise in the present rather than out of deficits accumulated in the past (Crosby 1991, pp. 50–51). Ongoing social and emotional support is certainly a legitimate human need (Strobe and Strobe 1996). People can legitimately expect emotional support and understanding, companionship, and often sexual sharing from their partners. But they should not expect their partners to make them feel lovable or worthwhile. Indeed, achieving a sense of individuality and personal identity is a step that best precedes relationship formation (Vannoy 1991; Cramer 2003). People's legitimate need in loving becomes the desire to share themselves with loved ones to enrich their—and their loved ones'—lives (Maslow 1943).

Illegitimate Needs Sometimes called "deficiency needs," **illegitimate needs** arise from feelings of self-doubt, unworthiness, and inadequacy (Crosby 1991). Often, people who feel deficient count on others to convince them that they are worthwhile (Cramer 2003). "If you are not eternally showing me that you live for me," they seem to say, "then I feel like nothing" (Satir 1972, p. 136). They strive to borrow security from others. To expect others to fill such needs is asking the impossible: No amount of loving will convince a person that she or he is worthwhile or lovable if that person doesn't already believe it. Hence, illegitimate needs for affection are insatiable. However, love does satisfy legitimate needs.

Love Involves Caring and Acceptance

A third element of love is the acceptance of partners for themselves and "not for their ability to change themselves or to meet another's requirements to play a role" (Dahms 1976, p. 100). People are free to be themselves in a loving relationship, to expose their feelings, frailties, and strengths (Armstrong 2003). Related to this acceptance is caring, or empathy—the concern a person has for the partner's growth and the willingness to "affirm [the partner's] potentialities" (May 1975, p. 116; Jaksch 2002). Psychologist Erich Fromm (1956) chastises Americans for their emphasis on wanting to *be loved* rather than on learning to *love*. Many of our ways to be loved or make ourselves lovable, Fromm writes, "are the same as those used to make oneself successful, 'to win friends and influence people.' As a matter of fact, what most people in our culture mean by being lovable is

This chapter focuses on romantic love, or love with a sexual component. However, love also exists, of course, between individuals who are not romantically involved, such as siblings.

essentially a mixture between being popular and having sex appeal" (p. 2). Showing empathy, of course, is something very different (Ciaramigoli and Ketcham 2000).

Rollo May defines empathy, or caring, as a state "composed of the recognition of another; a fellow human being like one's self; of identification of one's self with the pain or joy of the other" (1969, p. 289). Each partner tries to understand and accept how the other perceives situations and people. As an example, if your loved one tells you that he or she dislikes a friend of yours, the accepting response is not "That's impossible!" A more loving response would be, "Tell me why." This doesn't mean that you, too, have to decide to dislike your friend. But even when loved ones do not share or condone specific attitudes and behavior, they accept each other as they are (Dahms 1976, pp. 100–101).

Furthermore, caring and acceptance involve *honoring,* or "conferring distinction" upon, one's beloved:

> Honor is not judgmental. Honor does not involve the belief that your opinions, concerns, and desires are somehow superior to your partner's. Honor does not involve getting your mate to see things your way. . . . Honor is a "lifting up," a holding up of your mate with reverence. (Smalley 2000, p. 10)

Do Men and Women Care Differently?

Research shows that both women and men value psychic as well as sexual intimacy (Fehr and Broughton 2001; Hook et al. 2003; Sprecher and Toro-Morn 2002). Note, however, that desiring or experiencing feelings of intimacy and expressing those desires or feelings are not the same thing. Sociologists have observed that in our society, women verbally express feelings of love more than men do. Research indicates that women today do not believe that they should be more self-sacrificing in relationships (Heiss 1991). However, their socialization has been directed more strongly to attachment than to autonomy. Women have been raised to be more aware of their feelings and how to communicate them. Men may more often be baffled by questions about inner feelings (Real 2002).

Seeking emotional satisfaction in marriage and other romantic relationships has been part of a general contemporary trend toward self-development and the cultivation of emotional intimacy for both sexes. But many men have not been as well prepared as women for these new expectations. Earlier, before the nineteenth century, men's and women's domestic activities involved economic production, not personal intimacy. With the development of separate gender spheres in industrializing societies during the nineteenth century, love and feeling became the domain of women, whereas work was seen to be the appropriate masculine mode. As a result

of this historical legacy, we have come to see men as less well equipped for the emotional relatedness considered essential to the companionate model of marriage that emerged in the twentieth century (Real 2002). (Companionate marriage is discussed in Chapter 7.)

Sociologist Francesca Cancian (1987) has argued that men are equally loving but that in our society, women, not men, are made to feel primarily responsible for love's endurance or success. Furthermore, in our society love is expressed mostly on feminine terms—i.e., verbally—and women are the more verbal sex. Nonverbal expressions of love that men may make, such as doing favors or reducing their partners' burdens, are not credited as love. This situation can result in both partners feeling manipulated and powerless. "The consequences of love would be more positive if love were the responsibility of men as well as women and if love were defined more broadly to include instrumental help as well as emotional expression" (Cancian 1985, p. 262).

Cancian has also argued that a more balanced view of how love is to be expressed—one that includes masculine as well as feminine elements—would find men equally loving and emotionally profound. Less abstractly, a lover could consider the possibility that the partner expresses love differently and accept such differences, or else negotiate change openly. It is possible that as gender roles continue to change, men and women will develop more balanced capacities for autonomy and intimacy, "the very capacities necessary for sustaining the loving relationships on which marriages now depend" (Vannoy 1991, p. 262).

Love and Intimacy: Commitment to Sharing

Love involves **intimacy**—"an interpersonal process that involves the expression and sharing of emotions, communication of personal feelings and information, development of shared affection, support, and feeling closely connected with another person" (Wagner-Raphael, Seal, and Ehrhardt 2001, p. 243), together with the willingness to commit oneself to that person despite the need for some personal sacrifices. We'll look more closely at two elements of this definition: first, the experience of sharing intimacy, and second, the **commitment** involved in intimacy. Then we'll look at the triangular theory of love, which puts it all together.

Psychic and Sexual Intimacy Intimacy involves sharing. This sharing may take place on two often overlapping planes. At one level is **sexual intimacy**. In popular terminology, people who have a sexual relationship are "intimate" with each other. At another level is **psychic intimacy**: people engaging in self-disclosure. That is, they share their thoughts, feelings, goals, and needs (Smalley

2000). This is the sense in which we use the term here. Although sexual intimacy may either result from or lead to psychic intimacy, the two concepts are not synonymous. Strangers and people who like each other may enjoy sexual intimacy. Those who share with and accept each other experience psychic intimacy. They engage in the "work of attention": making the effort to set aside existing preoccupations in order to listen to each other (Peck 1978, p. 120; Armstrong 2003). Research on married couples indicates that partners who are self-disclosing and openly express feelings of love to each other perceive their marriages to be more intimate and score high on measures of marital adjustment (Love 2001). Psychic and/or sexual intimacy enhances feelings of attachment, which in turn strengthens the will to commit (Hein 2000; Peck and Peck 2006).

Commitment In love, committing oneself to another person requires the determination to develop a relationship "where experiences cover many areas of personality; where problems are worked through; where conflict is expected and seen as a normal part of the growth process; and where there is an expectation that

Love involves intimacy, the capacity to share one's inner self with someone else and to commit oneself to that person despite the need for some personal sacrifices. But love—and commitment—aren't meant to be all work. Love needs to feel supportive, at least most of the time, and fun, at least sometimes.

© David Young-Wolf/PhotoEdit

the relationship is basically viable and worthwhile" (Altman and Taylor 1973, pp. 184–87; Armstrong 2003). "My Family: Couple Discovers Love Twenty-five Years after Teen Marriage" illustrates commitment.

Committed lovers have fun together; they also share more tedious times. They express themselves freely and authentically (Smalley 2000). Committed partners do not see problems or disagreements as indications that their relationship is over. They view their relationship as worth keeping, and they work to maintain it in spite of difficulties (Love 2001). Commitment is characterized by this willingness to work through problems and conflicts as opposed to calling it quits when problems arise. In this view, commitment involves consciously investing in the relationship (Etcheverry and Le 2005). Committed partners "regularly, routinely, and predictably attend to each other and their relationship no matter how they feel" (Peck 1978, p. 118).

The Triangular Theory of Love Psychological research expands upon these notions. Psychologist Robert Sternberg (1988a, 1988b, 2006) believes that the qualities most important to a lasting relationship are not so visible in the early stages. In his research on relationships varying in length from one month to thirty-six years, he found three components of love: intimacy, passion, and commitment. According to Sternberg's triangular theory of love, **Intimacy** "refers to close, connected, and bonded feelings in a loving relationship. It includes feelings that create the experience of warmth in a loving relationship . . . [such as] experiencing happiness with the loved one; . . . sharing one's self and one's possessions with the loved one; receiving . . . and giving emotional support to the loved one; [and] having intimate communication with the loved one." **Passion** "refers to the drives that lead to romance, physical attraction, sexual consummation, and the like in a loving relationship."

Commitment—the "decision/commitment component of love"—consists of "two aspects, one short-term and one long-term. The short-term one is the decision that one loves someone. The long-term aspect is the commitment to maintain that love" (Sternberg 1988a, pp. 120–21). **Consummate love** (see Figure 5.1), composed of all three components, is "complete love, . . . a kind of love toward which many of us strive, especially in romantic relationships"

The three components of consummate love develop at different times, as love grows and changes: "Passion is the quickest to develop, and the quickest to fade. . . . Intimacy develops more slowly, and commitment more gradually still" (Sternberg, quoted in Goleman 1985). Passion, or "chemistry," peaks early in the relationship but generally continues at a stable, although fluctuating, level and remains important both to our good health

| **My Family** | Couple Discovers Love Twenty-five Years after Teen Marriage |

Married at ages sixteen and eighteen, respectively, Sharon and Gary were together nearly twenty-five years and had four children before deciding to separate. When they finally got back together after a ten-month separation, they publicly restated their wedding vows in a religious ceremony. Here they talk about what commitment to loving means to them.

Interviewer: How did you two get back together?

Sharon: For me, it was that I had to be connected. I just need someone regular to check in with, to have dinner with, to care where you are and what you are doing.

Gary: For me, it was just love. For a long time I didn't love Sharon after we got married, and then I grew to love her very much. Then when we separated— it was both of our idea to separate—I think once she moved out it was an empty place. I knew that I just needed

her back. I needed to have her there to share my love with her. . . .

Sharon: I think our troubles started when we got married. I was pregnant, our parents didn't approve, and we both thought we were doing the right thing. We tried for years to do the right things, and it wasn't quite right. A lot of things we never talked about and buried, they got deep . . . he told me he didn't love me when we first got married. . . . I got married because I loved him like crazy and I knew I could make it work. I tried really hard. I did all the right things. I thought if we had a child it would tie us together.

Gary: I got married because it was the honorable thing to do. I don't regret being married. I don't regret being married as young as I was. . . . It took a few years, and I ended up loving her.

Interviewer: You got to know Sharon?

Gary: I don't know if I've ever got to know Sharon. Probably the last year I have got to know Sharon more than I had up until then.

Interviewer: Why's that?

Gary: That's because we didn't say nothing. We could argue, and neither one of us would tell why we were mad or what the problem was.

Sharon: We didn't argue that much either.

Gary: No.

Sharon: Just glaring, that kind of stuff. . . . We were young, and I used to cry for his attention. And when I cried, he left. A few of those and you think, "What good is this doing me?" So I quit crying.

Gary: Well, if I had known what else to do, I probably would have done that. Today I give her a hug and try to hold

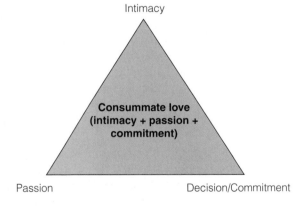

Figure 5.1 The three components of love: triangular theory.
Source: Adapted from "Triangular Love," by Robert J. Sternberg (1988), fig. 6.1, p. 121. In Robert J. Steinberg and Michael L. Barnes (eds.), *The Psychology of Love.* Copyright © 1988 Yale University Press. Adapted by permission.

(Kluger 2004) and to the long-term maintenance of the relationship (Love 2001, Montgomery and Sorell 1997). Intimacy, which includes conveying and understanding each other's needs, listening to and supporting each

other, and sharing common values, becomes increasingly important as time goes on.

In fact, psychologist and marriage counselor Gary Smalley (2000) argues that a couple is typically together for about six years before they feel safe enough to share their deepest relational needs with one another. Commitment is essential; however, commitment without intimacy and some level of passion is hollow. In other words, all these elements of love are important. And because these components not only develop at different rates but also exist in various combinations of intensity, a relationship is always changing, if only subtly (Sternberg 1988b).

Of course, the triangular theory of love is not the only way of looking at love. One interesting typology, developed by social scientist John Alan Lee, looks at the wide variation in love styles.

Six Love Styles

Loving relationships may take many forms or personalities, just as the individuals in a relationship may. John Alan Lee (1973) classified six love styles, initially based her. Back then, you know, laughter was easier.

Sharon: I don't remember if I ever told him what I needed. . . . I don't think so. I just wanted comfort and understanding, I guess. I think I usually cried over something—lack of money or fears.

Gary: We had plenty of all that.

Sharon: I found out with the separation, though; finally, I realized that Gary loved me. The turning point was when Gary made a commitment to help me get into the apartment. It made me look at him differently. It was the commitment; it was obvious that he cared—and not for his own personal thing. He wasn't just saying to get out. He was saying, "I want you to be well." He came to help me do that.

Interviewer: What did he do?

Sharon: Painted, laid carpet, and ripped wallpaper, those things.

Gary: I was doing that because I cared about her. . . .

Sharon: I remember it was a Sunday that I first got into the apartment where I was going to move to. It was pretty awful. I called Gary and said could I have another week, and he came over and brought breakfast. . . .

Interviewer: Why did you guys have a public ceremony when you got back together?

Gary: I think one of the reasons that I wanted it was because there were a lot of our friends who knew what had gone on between us. I just wanted them to be part of our getting back together. . . . It was very touching to me, very emotional. We never had anything like this. We got married by the justice of the peace—very cold. . . . It was just: "Let's get this over with so people can start counting the months." And hoping that the baby would come up a month late or something.

Sharon: This time we invited our whole church and our whole square-dance club and our whole group of people that we both work with. . . . We called our parents and asked for their blessing.

Gary: [At the ceremony,] I felt a lot of love. . . .

Critical Thinking

How does Gary and Sharon's story illustrate the idea of commitment in loving? How does it illustrate Francesca Cancian's (1985) opinion that a more balanced view of love would find men equally loving?

---

on interviews with 120 respondents, half of them male and half female. All were heterosexual, white, and of Canadian or English descent. Lee subsequently applied his typology to an analysis of gay relationships (Lee 1981). Researchers have developed a Love Attitudes Scale (LAS): eighteen to twenty-four specific questions to measure Lee's typology (Hendrick, Hendrick, and Dicke 1998). Although not all subsequent research has found all six dimensions, this typology of love styles has withstood the test of time, has proven to be more than hypothetical (Frey and Hojjat 1998; Lacey et al. 2004), and may even have cross-cultural relevance (Masanori, Daibo, and Kanemasa 2004).

Love styles are distinctive characteristics or personalities that loving or lovelike relationships may take. The word *lovelike* is included in this definition because not all love styles amount to genuine loving as we have defined it. Moreover, people do not necessarily confine themselves to one style or another; they may incorporate different aspects of several styles into their relationships. In any case, these love styles tell us that people may love passionately, quietly, pragmatically, playfully, and self-sacrificingly.

Eros Eros (AIR-ohs) is a Greek word meaning "love"; it forms the root of our word *erotic*. This love style is characterized by intense emotional attachment and powerful sexual feelings or desires. When erotic couples establish sustained relationships, these are characterized by continued active interest in sexual and emotional fulfillment, plus the development of emotional rapport. Romeo and Juliet, who fell in love on first meeting, were erotic lovers, as are an older couple you may know who seem endlessly fascinated by each other. A sample question on the Love Attitudes Scale (LAS) designed to measure eros asks the respondent to agree or disagree with this statement: "My partner and I have the right chemistry between us." Agreement would indicate erotic love (Hendrick, Hendrick, and Dicke 1998).

Storge Storge (STOR-gay) is an affectionate, companionate style of loving. This love style focuses on deepening mutual commitment, respect, friendship over time, and common goals. Sexual intimacy comes about as partners develop increasing understanding of each other. The storgic lover's basic attitude to his or her partner is one of familiarity: "I've known you a long time, seen you in many moods" (Lee 1973, p. 87). In other words, my partner is my friend. Storgic lovers are likely to agree that "I always expect to be friends with the one I love" (Hendrick, Hendrick, and Dicke 1998).

Pragma Pragma (PRAG-mah) is the root word for *pragmatic*. Pragmatic love emphasizes the practical element in human relationships, particularly in marriages.

Pragmatic love involves rational assessment of a potential partner's assets and liabilities. Here, a relationship provides a practical base for both economic and emotional security. Arranged marriages are often examples of pragma. But so is the person who decides very rationally to get married to a suitable partner. These LAS questions measure pragma: "A main consideration in choosing a partner is/was how he/she would reflect on my family" and "I tried to plan my life carefully before choosing a partner" (Hendrick, Hendrick, and Dicke 1998).

Agape is a love style that emphasizes unselfish concern for another's needs. Often called *altruistic love,* agape emphasizes nurturing. This love style exists between partners and also between and among other family members and friends.

Agape Agape (ah-GAH-pay) is a Greek word meaning "love feast." Agape emphasizes unselfish concern for the beloved's needs even when that requires some personal sacrifice. Often called *altruistic love,* agape emphasizes nurturing others with little conscious desire for return other than the intrinsic satisfaction of having loved and cared for someone else. The sexual component of love seems less important in agape. Agapic lovers would likely agree that they "would rather suffer myself than let my partner suffer" and that "I try to always help my partner through difficult times" (Hendrick, Hendrick, and Dicke 1998).

Ludus Ludus (LEWD-us) focuses on love as play or fun. Ludus emphasizes the recreational aspects of sexuality and enjoying many sexual partners rather than searching for one serious relationship. Of course, ludic flirtation and playful sexuality may be part of a more committed relationship based on one of the other love styles. LAS questions designed to measure ludus include the following: "I enjoy playing the game of love with a number of different partners" and "I try to keep my partner a little uncertain about my commitment to him/her" (Hendrick, Hendrick, and Dicke 1998). One small study of 173 men in a private Midwestern university found a positive relationship between ludus and (usually verbal) sexual coercion among college males (Russell and Oswald 2002).

Mania Mania, a Greek word, designates a wild or violent mental disorder, an obsession or craze. Mania rests on strong sexual attraction and emotional intensity, as does eros. However, it differs from eros in that manic partners are extremely jealous and moody, and their need for attention and affection is insatiable. Manic lovers alternate between euphoria and depression. The slightest lack of response from the love partner causes anxiety and resentment. Manic lovers would be likely to say, "When my partner doesn't pay attention to me, I feel sick all over" or "I cannot relax if I feel my partner is with someone else" (Hendrick, Hendrick, and Dicke 1998). Because one of its principal characteristics is extreme jealousy, we may learn of manic love in the news when a relationship ends violently. Of Lee's six love styles, mania least fits our definition of love, described earlier.

These six love styles represent different ways that people may feel about and behave toward each other in lovelike relationships. In real life, a relationship is never entirely one style, and the same relationship may be characterized, at different times, by features of several styles. Lovers may be erotic *and* pragmatic. Loving may assume qualities of quiet understanding and respect, along with playfulness. How do these love styles relate to relationship satisfaction and to the continuity of marriage and other intimate relationships?

© Merritt Vincent/PhotoEdit

Psychologists Marilyn Montgomery and Gwendolyn Sorell (1997) administered the LAS to 250 single college students and married adults of all ages. Among other things, they found that erotic love attitudes existed throughout marriage and were related to high marital satisfaction. Agapic attitudes were also positively associated with relationship satisfaction (Neimark 2003). Interestingly, Montgomery and Sorell found storge to be important only in marriages with children. Ludus did not affect satisfaction with a relationship among singles. However, at least as measured by the LAS (which emphasizes ludic lovers' lack of commitment), ludic attitudes are associated with diminished marital satisfaction. One study found a relationship between ludus and narcissism, discussed later in this chapter (Campbell, Foster, and Finkel 2002). We turn now to an examination of three things love isn't: martyring, manipulating, and limerence.

Three Things Love Isn't

Love is not inordinate self-sacrifice. And, loving is not the continual attempt to get others to feel or do what we want them to—although each of these ideas is frequently mistaken for love. Nor is love all those crazy feelings you get when you can't get someone out of your mind. We'll examine these misconceptions in detail.

Martyring

Love isn't martyring. **Martyring** involves maintaining relationships by consistently ignoring one's own legitimate needs while trying to satisfy virtually all of a partner's needs, even illegitimate ones. Martyring differs from agapic love, described earlier. Agapic love involves giving much attention to the needs of a beloved with joy—and not ignoring one's own legitimate needs at the same time. Periods of self-sacrifice are necessary through difficult times. However, as a premise of the relationship, excessive self-sacrifice or martyring is unworkable. Martyrs may have good intentions, believing that love involves doing unselfishly for others without voicing their own needs in return. Consequently, however, martyrs seldom feel that they receive genuine affection. Martyrs may

- Be reluctant to suggest what they would like (concerning recreation or entertainment, for example), preferring to leave decisions to others.
- Allow others to be constantly late for engagements and never protest directly.
- Work on helping loved ones develop talents and interests while ignoring or neglecting their own.

"Damn it, Ethel, all I'm asking you for is one lousy kidney!"

- Be sensitive to others' feelings and problems while hiding their own disappointments and hurts.

Although it may sound noble, there's a catch to martyring. Believing that they're not receiving much emotional support, martyrs grow angry, although they seldom express their anger directly. (In Chapter 13, we will discuss how unexpressed anger can damage a loving relationship.) Martyrs may think "it is better to be wanted as a victim than to not be wanted at all" (Szasz 1976, p. 62). The reluctance of martyrs to express legitimate needs is damaging to a relationship, for it prevents openness and intimacy.

Martyring has other negative consequences. Social psychologists have been researching the concept of equity, the balance of rewards and costs to the partners in a relationship. In love relationships and marriage, as well as in other relationships, people seem most comfortable when things feel generally fair or equitable—when, over time, partners are reasonably well balanced in terms of what they are giving to and getting from the relationship (Risman and Johnson-Sumerford 1998; Crawford, Feng, and Fischer 2003).

Manipulating

Manipulators follow this maxim: If I can get her [or him] to do what I want done, then I'll be sure she [or he] loves me. **Manipulating** means seeking to control the feelings, attitudes, and behavior of your partner or partners in underhanded ways rather than by directly (not abusively!) stating your case. Manipulating is not the same thing as love. Manipulators may

- Ask others to do things for them that they could do for themselves, and generally expect to be waited on.

- Assume that others will (if they "really" love them) be happy to do whatever the manipulators choose, not only regarding recreation, for example, but also in more important matters.

- Be consistently late for engagements ("if he [or she] will wait patiently for me, he [or she] loves me").

- Want others to help them develop their interests and talents but seldom think of reciprocating.

Aware that they are exploiting others, habitual manipulators may experience guilt and try to relieve this guilt by minimizing their loved one's complaints or finding fault with their partner, sometimes with verbal abuse. "You don't really love me," they may accuse. Manipulating, like martyring, can destroy a relationship.

You may have already noticed that martyring and manipulating complement each other. Martyrs and manipulators are often attracted to each other, forming what family counselor John Crosby (1991) calls **symbiotic relationships**, in which each partner expects the other to provide a sense of meaning or purpose. Often symbiotic relationships are quite stable, although at the same time they can be unhappy—maybe even dangerously violent. Should one symbiotic partner learn to stand on his or her own feet, the relationship is less likely to last. Manipulating and martyring are both sometimes mistaken for love.[2] But they are not love, for one simple reason: Both relationships share a refusal to accept oneself or one's partner realistically. Indeed, both martyrs and manipulators may be trying to rescue or "fix" a loved one.

Limerence

Have you ever been so taken with someone that you couldn't get him or her out of your mind? We're not talking a relationship here. The object of your atten-

tion may hardly know you exist, as they say. You review every second of the last time you saw him or her; you fantasize about how you might actually land this one. If the object of your attention does anything at all that you can define as positive toward you, you're ecstatic. If things don't seem to be going your way, you're near to despair. Psychologist Dorothy Tennov (1999 [1979]) and her graduate students have named this situation **limerence** (LIM-er-ence). They emphasize the following points about limerence: First, limerence is not just "lust" or sexual attraction. It is much more than that. People in limerence fantasize about being with the limerent object in all kinds of situations—not just sexual ones. Second, limerence is pretty normal; many of us have experienced it. And third, limerence is not love. Indeed, limerence is characterized by little, if any, concern for the well-being of the limerent object. Limerence can turn into genuine love, but more often than not, it doesn't.

The next section examines a personal characteristic that many psychologists (although not all) believe to be a prerequisite for loving: self-esteem.

Self-Worth as a Prerequisite to Loving

"I'm more interested," writes Leo Buscaglia, "in who is a loving person. . . . I believe that probably the most important thing is that this loving person is a person who loves him [or her] self" (1982, p. 9). **Self-worth**, or self-esteem,[3] is part of a person's self-concept; it involves feelings that people have about their own value. Psychologist Nathaniel Branden has described self-worth as "the disposition to experience oneself as competent to cope with the basic challenges of life and as worthy of happiness" (1994, p. 21). And what is happiness? Psychologist Martin

---

[2] Students reading this section sometimes ask whether martyring is the same as being co-dependent. The answer is *yes, pretty much*. **Co-dependents** have been defined as "persons who gravitate toward relationships with exploitative or abusive partners around whom they organize their lives and to whom they remain strongly committed despite the absence of any identifiable rewards or personal fulfillment for themselves" (Wright and Wright 1999, p. 528; Simko 2006). A grass-roots concept that originally emerged in self-help groups to describe spouses and children of alcoholics/addicts, co-dependency was typically dismissed as unscientific by professionals. However, the concept has begun to find its way into respected family therapy journals, and researchers have begun to investigate it (Wells, Glickauf-Hughes, and Jones 1999; Wright and Wright 1999; Dear and Roberts, 2002).

[3] The concept of *self-esteem* is controversial among psychologists and others today (Owens 2001). Some "postmodern" philosophers and psychologists argue that there is no such thing as a constant self; hence, there can be no such thing as global self-esteem (Cravens 1997). Other critics see the self-esteem movement, which began in the United States after World War II, as too individualistic and leading to self-absorption, which in turn discourages people from taking any real interest in social or political issues (Bellah et al. 1985). Furthermore, psychologists who study violence have argued that parents' and teachers' efforts to promote self-esteem in children can actually foster its opposite, narcissism, and that narcissism can lead to violent outbursts (Bushman and Baumeister 1998; Fink 2003; Goode 2002). Nevertheless, much research has been done on self-esteem, and the majority of psychologists, especially counseling psychologists, continue to research and find use in the concept (e.g., Campbell, Foster, and Finkel 2002; Jaret, Reitzes, and Shapkina 2005; Marcussen 2006). Having considered the arguments, we continue to explore the concept of self-esteem in this edition.

Seligman argues that authentic happiness does not result simply from having a "pleasant life," characterized by self-centered pleasures or acquiring things like a new car stereo. Instead, we attain authentic happiness by developing our strengths and devoting ourselves to meaningful work or other activities and to family life or some other cause greater than ourselves (Lawson 2004b).

Accordingly, Branden (1994) argues that beliefs and feelings about one's self-worth are a consequence, not simply an uncontrollable condition or a narcissistic focus on self. A sense of self-worth results from real accomplishments, not simply from hearing or telling oneself that one is, for example, "special" (K. Johnson 1998). Because self-worth is a consequence of all the things we do, we can enhance it by working to develop our talents, by affirming or supporting others, and by doing things that contribute to our communities (Katz 1993; Neimark 2003; Satir 1988). Branden (1994) has identified the following six "pillars" or practices that enhance our feelings of self-worth:

1. Being aware of what's going on around us, or living consciously (p. 67)

2. Being a friend to myself, or self-acceptance (p. 94)

3. Being willing to take responsibility for my actions and for attaining my goals, or self-responsibility (p. 185)

4. "Honoring" our wants, needs, and values, and seeking "appropriate forms of their expression in reality," or self-assertiveness (p. 118)

5. Setting realistic goals and working toward their achievement, or living purposefully (p. 130)

6. Practicing behavior that is congruent with my values, or personal integrity (p. 143)

"As We Make Choices: Learning to Love Yourself More" gives suggestions for enhancing self-esteem.

Self-Love versus Narcissism

In discussing feelings of self-worth, or self-esteem, we need to distinguish between well-grounded *self-love* and its opposite, *narcissism*[4] (Slater 2002; Campbell 2005). Self-love enhances a person's capacity to love others. People commonly confuse self-love with conceit—a self-centered, selfish outlook (Katz 1993; Fink 2003). But psychologists point out that self-love and narcissism are

opposites (Swagger 2005). **Narcissism** is characterized by an exaggerated sense of self-importance (Ashmun 2004), together with an overblown concern with one's own self-image and how one *appears* to others—not with one's own or others' *true* feelings. That is, narcissism reflects concern chiefly with oneself, without regard for the well-being of others. Narcissists are often smug, acting as if they are superior. Many psychologists believe that such attitudes and behaviors actually result from *low* self-esteem (Begley 1998; Slater 2002). Whether people genuinely love themselves—as opposed to being narcissistic—affects their personal relationships (Campbell, Foster, and Finkel 2002; Campbell 2005; Foster, Shrira, and Campbell 2006).

Self-Esteem and Personal Relationships

Research indicates that self-esteem does a lot to influence the way people respond to others (Longmore and Demaris 1997; Page, Stevens, and Galvin 1996; Rugel and Martinovich 1997). For instance, psychologist Brad Bushman, who conducted a study of what he called "unjustified and unstable self-esteem" (i.e., narcissism), argued that "narcissists are supersensitive to criticisms or slights because deep down they suspect that their feeling of superiority is built on quicksand" (quoted in Begley 1998; Bushman and Baumeister 1998, p. 227).

People with sufficient self-esteem are likely to be more responsive to praise, whereas those without much self-esteem "are forever on the alert for criticism . . . and remember it long afterward." People sufficient in self-esteem are better at picking up signs of interest from other people and responding to them genuinely, whereas people low in self-esteem often miss such cues and, in general, are "set for rejection" (Walster and Walster 1978, pp. 54–55; Cramer 2003; Murray, Holmes, and Griffin 2000). Then too,

> [w]hen we develop a good sense of ourselves—intimacy with what is within—we are able to express ourselves creatively, bond with others, and risk being genuinely vulnerable. We can have our needs met if only for the simple reason that we know what they are. (Hein 2000, p. 2)

And, finally, the more that people can accept themselves, the more that they can accept others.

Emotional Interdependence

Besides self-esteem, or self-love, a quality necessary for loving is the ability to be emotionally interdependent. Interdependence is different from both dependence and independence. **Dependence** involves reliance on another or others for continual support or assurance, coupled with subordination—being easily influenced

---

[4] The term *narcissism* is derived from an ancient Greek myth. In that story, a young, good-looking man named Narcissus wants to be loved by someone but, instead, falls in love with his own image when he happens to see his reflection in a pond. Enchanted with himself and moving his face closer and closer to his reflection in the water, Narcissus topples into the pool and drowns.

As We Make Choices   Learning to Love Yourself More

We all feel inadequate at times. What can you do with feelings of inadequacy besides worry about them? As one psychologist put it, "You can't just sit and psych yourself into high self-esteem" (Krueger 2003). However, people can work in many ways to improve their sense of self-worth. For example, you may choose to do the following:

- Identify your best personality traits, such as curiosity, humor, or courage. Remember these when you face challenging situations, and try to find ways to manifest them.

- Pursue satisfying and useful occupations that realistically reflect your strengths and interests ("Young children make me nervous, but I'd like to teach, so I'll consider secondary or higher education").

- Use empathy, respect, courtesy, and kindness when interacting with others. In doing so, you affirm not only others but yourself.

- Work to develop the skills and interests you have rather than fret about those you don't.

- Try being more honest about yourself and open with people.

- Make efforts to appreciate the good things you have rather than focus on the more negative things in your life.

Write a "gratitude list" of things that you can be grateful for.

- Avoid excessive daydreaming and fantasy living ("Boy, things would be different if only I were a little taller" or "If only I had not gotten married so young, things would be better").

- Volunteer. Studies show that volunteers tend to live longer and feel better about themselves.

- Expand your world of interest. Take a nonrequired course outside your major just for the fun of it, or develop a new hobby.

- "Keep on keeping on"—even when you are discouraged, realizing that one little step in the right direction is often good enough.

- Be satisfied about being smart *enough,* slender *enough,* or successful *enough* rather than imposing unrealistic standards on yourself. ("Easy does it.")

- Touch and be touched. Give someone a hug or pat on the back; get a massage or shampoo.

- Relax. ("If I feel this way, it means this is a human way to feel, and everybody else has probably felt this way too at one time or another.")

- Forgive somebody. "If physical exercise had a mental equivalent, it would probably be the process of forgiveness. Researchers continue to tally the benefits of burying the hatchet—lower blood pressure and heart rate, less depression, a better immune system and a longer life, among others" (Goodman 2004).

- Decide to be your own good friend, complimenting yourself when you do things well enough and not criticizing yourself too harshly.

- Try to focus less on how you imagine others are appraising you (Jaret, Reitzes, and Shapkina 2005).

- Practice not thinking in "absolutes: 'You always screw up!' 'You will never be a success!'—these are lies. We don't always screw up" (Burney 1995). And we are successful at many things.

Critical Thinking

You may recall from Chapter 2 that the interactionist theoretical perspective assumes that individuals develop identities and self-concepts through social interaction. How do the above suggestions illustrate this point?

Sources: Burney 1995; Goodman 2004; Hamachek 1971, 1992; Jaret, Reitzes, and Shapkina 2005; Lawson 2004b; Neimark 2003; Slater 2002.

---

or controlled by those who are also greatly needed. **Independence**, on the other hand, involves self-reliance and self-sufficiency and may imply that the individual functions in isolation from others. It emphasizes separation from others.

Loving is different from both dependence and independence as we have defined them. Loving is **interdependence**, a relationship in which individuals retain a degree of autonomy and sense of self, yet simultaneously make strong commitments to each other (Carter 2001). Our culture's emphasis on self-reliance as a central virtue ignores the fact that all of us are interdependent.

We rely on parents, spouses or partners, other relatives, and friends far more than our culture encourages us to recognize (Cancian 1985, pp. 261–62).

Regarding interdependence, therapist John Crosby has distinguished between A-frame (dependent), H-frame (independent), and M-frame (interdependent) relationships. **A-frame relationships** are symbolized by the capital letter *A*: Partners have a strong couple identity but little sense of themselves as individuals. Like the long lines in the letter *A*, they lean on each other. The relationship is structured so that "if one lets go, the other falls" (Crosby 1991, p. 55). And that is exactly

Love is a process of discovery, which involves continual exploration, commitment, and sharing.

Getty Images/Digital Vision

what happens when only one partner outgrows his or her dependency in a martyr–manipulator relationship.

H-frame relationships are structured like a capital *H*: Partners stand virtually alone, each self-sufficient and neither influenced much by the other. There is little or no couple identity and little emotionality: "If one lets go, the other hardly feels a thing" (Crosby 1991, p. 55). **M-frame relationships** rest on interdependence: Each partner has an adequate sense of self (unlike in the A-frame relationship), and partners experience loving as a deep emotion (unlike in the H-frame relationship). The relationship involves mutual influence and emo-

tional support. In a recent qualitative study of 108 heterosexual and same-gender couples of various race/ethnicity and religious backgrounds, researchers found that a moderate degree of personal autonomy actually facilitated couple intimacy:

Maintaining interpersonal boundaries in these relationships apparently helped to sustain a sense of psychological intimacy; that is, individuals felt "safe" in revealing their inner thoughts and feelings because they could count on a partner to respect their separateness and to accept, if not understand, them. (Mackey, Diemer, and O'Brien 2000, p. 206)

Emotional Interdependence and Attachment Psychology and counseling psychologists often analyze an individual's relationship in terms of that person's attachment style. This perspective, known as **attachment theory**, holds that during infancy and childhood a young person develops a general style of attaching to others. Once a youngster's attachment style is established, she or he unconsciously applies that style to later, adult relationships.

An individual's primary caretakers (usually parents and most often mother) exhibit a "style" of attachment with the young child. The three basic styles of attachment are **secure**, **insecure/anxious**, and **avoidant**. Children who can trust that a caretaker will be there to attend to their practical and emotional needs develop a secure attachment style. Children who are, or feel, uncared for or abandoned develop either an insecure/anxious or an avoidant attachment style. In adulthood, a secure attachment style involves trust that the relationship will provide necessary and ongoing emotional and social support—legitimate needs, described earlier in this chapter.

An insecure/anxious attachment style entails concern that the beloved will disappear, a situation often characterized as "fear of abandonment." An adult with an avoidant attachment style dodges closeness and genuine intimacy either by evading relationships altogether or demonstrating ambivalence, seeming preoccupied, or otherwise establishing distance in intimate situations (Benoit and Parker 1994; Fletcher 2002; Hazen and Shaver 1994). Individual or relationship therapy may help people change their attachment style (Fuller and Fincham 1997; Furman and Flanagan 1997).

Correlating attachment theory with Crosby's relationship typology, described earlier, a secure attachment style would characterize partners in an emotionally interdependent (Collins and Feeney 2000), or M-frame, relationship. An insecure/anxious attachment style would likely be evidenced in partners engaged in an A-frame (dependent) relationship. An avoidant style would characterize partners in an independent (Murray, Holmes, and Griffin 2000), or H-frame, relationship. We will now discuss how love happens.

Love as a Discovery

Psychologists warn that romantically inclined individuals who insist on waiting for their ideal lover to come around the next corner may wait forever—and miss opportunities to love real people who may already be in their lives. However, even when it is easily found, love needs to be continuously discovered. The words *discover* and find have similar meanings. But to discover involves a process, whereas to find refers to a singular act. Loving is a process of discovery. It is something people must do—and keep doing—rather than just a feeling they come upon (Love 2001; Smalley 2000). In Erich Fromm's words, love is "an activity, not a passive affect; it is a 'standing in,' not a 'falling for'" (1956, p. 22). It's fine to say that love is a process of discovery. But that doesn't answer the question of how love happens. To describe the process of love's development, social scientist Ira Reiss has proposed what he calls the "wheel theory of love."

The Wheel of Love

According to Reiss's theory, there are four stages in the development of love, which he sees as a circular process—a **wheel of love**—capable of continuing indefinitely. The four stages—rapport, self-revelation, mutual dependency, and personality need fulfillment—are shown in Figure 5.2, and they describe the span from attraction to love.

Rapport Feelings of rapport rest on mutual trust and respect. A principal factor that makes people more likely to establish rapport is similarity of values, interests, and background (Gottlieb 2006)—social class, religion, and so forth, as Chapter 9 explores. The outside circle in Figure 5.2 is meant to convey this point. But rapport can also be established between people of different backgrounds, who may perceive one another as an interesting contrast to themselves or see qualities in one another that they admire (Reiss and Lee 1988).

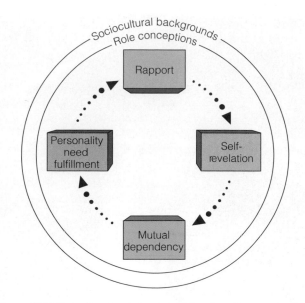

Figure 5.2 Reiss's wheel theory of the development of love.

Source: From *Family Systems in America,* 3rd ed., by I. Reiss © 1980 Wadsworth, a division of Thomson Learning.

Meanwhile, Robert Sternberg (1998; Sternberg, Hojjat, and Barnes 2001), whose triangular theory of love is described earlier in this chapter, has a complementary view on developing rapport. According to Sternberg, people have ideas, or stories, about how a love relationship will be. For example, the travel love plot sees partners beginning an exciting journey together; the garden story views a relationship as needing to be nourished; and the business story always considers the financial implications of the relationship. Individuals with the same love stories are likely to develop rapport, according to Sternberg.

Self-Revelation **Self-revelation**, or **self-disclosure**, involves gradually sharing intimate information about oneself. People have internalized different views about how much self-revelation is proper. The middle circle of Figure 5.2, "Role conceptions," signifies that ideas about social class-, ethnic-, or gender-appropriate behaviors influence how partners self-disclose and respond to one another's self-revelations and other activities.

For most of us, falling in love produces anxiety. We fear that our love won't be returned. Maybe we worry about being exploited or are afraid of becoming too dependent. One way of dealing with these anxieties is, ironically, to let others see us as we really are and to share our motives, beliefs, and feelings (Peck and Peck 2006). As reciprocal self-revelation continues, an intimate relationship may develop while a couple progresses to the third stage in the wheel of love: developing interdependence, or mutual dependency.

Mutual Dependency In this stage of a relationship, the two people desire to spend more time together and thereby develop the kind of interdependence or, in Reiss's terminology, mutual dependency, described in the discussion of M-frame relationships. Partners develop habits that require the presence of both partners. Consequently, they begin to depend on or need each other. For example, watching a good DVD may now seem lonely without the other person because enjoyment has come to depend not only on the movie but on sharing it with the other. Interdependency leads to the fourth stage: a degree of mutual personality need fulfillment.

Personality Need Fulfillment As their relationship develops, two people find that they satisfy a majority of each other's emotional needs. As personality needs are satisfied, greater rapport is developed, which leads to deeper self-revelation, more mutually dependent habits, and still greater need satisfaction. Reiss uses the term *personality need fulfillment* to describe the stage of a relationship in which a stable pattern of emotional exchange and mutual support has developed. The relationship meets both partners' basic human needs, both practical and emotional.

Returning to Reiss's image of this four-stage process as a wheel, then, the wheel turns indefinitely in a lasting, deep relationship. Or the wheel may turn only a few times in a passing romance. Finally, the wheel can reverse itself and turn in the other direction. As Reiss explains, "If one reduced the amount of self-revelation through an argument . . . , that would affect the dependency and need-fulfillment processes, which would in turn weaken the rapport process, which would in turn lower the revelation level even further" (Reiss and Lee, 1988, p. 104).

Keeping Love

The wheel theory suggests that once people fall in love, they may not necessarily stay in love. Relationships may "keep turning," or they may slow down or reverse themselves. Sometimes love's reversal, and eventual breakup, is a good thing: "Perhaps the hardest part of a rela-

tionship is knowing when to salvage things and when not to" (Sternberg 1988a, p. 242).[5] Chapter 9 explores this issue more fully. But here we want to point out that being committed is not always noble, as in cases of relationships characterized by violence or consistent verbal abuse, for example (partner abuse is discussed in Chapter 14). Committed love will require some sacrifices over the course of time. However, as one therapist puts it, "Love should not hurt" (Doble 2006).

That said, keeping a supportive love relationship is not automatic; "you have to *make* it last" (Love 2001, p. viii). How? A good start is to recognize that we may not have an accurate idea of what real love is (Love 2001). For instance, we may have grown up with poor role modeling on the part of our parents (Zimmerman and Thayer 2004). Regardless how our parents behaved, maintaining love involves being aware of the many erroneous cultural myths that delude us about love. Marriage and relationship therapist Patricia Love has identified the following misconceptions that limit our ability to maintain love:

- Misconception 1. Infatuation equals love; chemistry is all that matters.
- Misconception 2. If it isn't perfect, it wasn't meant to be.
- Misconception 3. You can't rekindle passion; once love dies, you can never get it back.

© image100/Alamy

Finding love is a beginning. *Keeping* love involves recognizing the importance of the relationship, engaging in ongoing supportive communication, and making a conscious decision to spend time together. These behaviors result in mutuality, or partners' meeting many of each other's legitimate needs.

---

[5] The media and various websites, some by counseling psychologists, have introduced the concept of the "love addict" to popular culture. According to this perspective, "love addicts" are people who cannot let go even of a harmful relationship, sometimes to the point of violence (Peabody 2002; Schaeffer 1997). Like co-dependence (see footnote 2 in this chapter), the concept of love addiction has roots in twelve-step programs and is used primarily by some psychologists and therapists (Bird 2006).

- Misconception 4. There is one true soul mate for everyone; if you meet the right person, you will live happily ever after.

- Misconception 5. Love conquers all; if a relationship is tough, it means you have the wrong partner.

- Misconception 6. Love is a static state; once you fall in love, you get on a high and stay there forever.

- Misconception 7. Love is a feeling, and you either have it or you don't. (Adapted from Love 2001, Chapter 1)

We will respond to these misconceptions now.

Infatuation Is But a Beginning Many social scientists and others strongly criticize the way that American culture tends to equate love with infatuation, or chemistry. "Every pop-cultural medium portrays the heights of adult intimacy as the moment when two attractive people who don't know a thing about each other tumble into bed and have passionate sex" (Lewis, Amini, and Lannon 2000, p. 207). But infatuation "merely brings the players together" (Lewis, Amini, and Lannon 2000, pp. 206–7). We need to move from infatuation to "the deep connection that is the hallmark and destination of true love" (Love 2001, p. xi).

Love Is Not Perfect and Doesn't Conquer All Nevertheless, "the fact is that love grows in response to getting your needs met" (Love 2001, p. xi). What's the difference? The disparity between these two thoughts lies in the dual ideas of (1) being realistic and (2) having mutuality. Being realistic means that you don't expect your partner to meet *all* your needs *all the time*. Although it's important not to confuse love with martyring, as discussed earlier in this chapter, no one person can meet all of even our legitimate needs (Jaksch 2002). So one aspect of discovering love involves finding ways to get some of our needs met outside the relationship—by extended family, friends, work, or other activities. Another realistic requirement for getting your needs met, of course, is to know what they are and be able and willing to express them.

Mutuality means both partners meet one another's needs. Using the metaphor of a battery, psychologist Gary Smalley (2000) describes this situation as "constantly recharging your mate's 'needs battery'":

> Human beings have internal "needs batteries," and our actions produce either positive or negative "charges" to our mate's battery. Loving attention given to each other's needs undoubtedly has a positive effect, while selfish, draining charges have a negative effect. (p. 8)

When each partner attends to the other, "both thrive" (Lewis, Amini, and Lannon 2000, p. 208).

Love Involves Much More Than a Feeling You Get Lovers don't automatically live happily ever after. What can help to make it happen? First, partners need to recognize the importance of their relationship. Keeping love may demand seeing your relationship as priceless—worth whatever it takes to nurture or strengthen it (Smalley 2000). Second, keeping love requires ongoing, supportive communication, discussed at length in Chapter 13. "Knowing ourselves is one task of adulthood, and communicating that knowledge is the task of forming a relationship" (Hein 2000, p. 3). Third, keeping love entails being kind, not rude, as well as cultivating feelings of joy when connecting with one's mate (Neimark 2003). Of course, listening is important, a skill discussed further in Chapter 13. Fourth, counselors suggest scheduling play into your relationship and planning surprises (Lawson 2004b). Although they needn't cost money, occasionally shared new activities or experiences are a good idea (Aron et al. 2000).

Interestingly, one reason that shared new activities help to keep love going may have to do with brain chemistry (Gottlieb 2006; Slater 2006). Research suggests that two hormones in particular may be related to finding and keeping love. The first, **dopamine**, is a chemical naturally produced in our brains. Although dopamine has many functions, its importance to love is that it acts upon the pleasure center in our brains, giving us powerful feelings of enjoyment and motivating us to do whatever we're doing that is so pleasurable over and over again (Berridge and Robinson 1998). Dopamine helps to explain why we have a second helping of a really tasty dessert, for example. Furthermore, dopamine is associated with new or novel pleasurable experiences and activities. Research shows that when people are newly in love, they tend to have higher brain levels of dopamine (Slater 2006). Dopamine makes you "high on" your partner.

The second hormone relevant here is **oxytocin**, also produced naturally in our brains. Some researchers have nicknamed oxytocin the "love" or "cuddle" hormone (Barker n.d.; Bosse 1999). Like dopamine, oxytocin has several functions (inducing labor and stimulating breast milk production in females, for example). Research in mammals has long demonstrated that oxytocin facilitates more general maternal, nurturing behaviors ("Oxytocin" 1997). In addition, oxytocin seems to be related to human feelings of deep friendship, trust, sexuality, love, bonding, and commitment ("Biology of Social Bonds" 1999; Bosse 1999).

It's important to remember that, although hormones affect feelings and behavior, the reverse is also true: Behaviors can stimulate hormone production. So, no matter how long we've been in a relationship, we're encouraged to do novel, exciting things together in order to produce dopamine, hence strengthening our bond. We're further encouraged to touch, cuddle, massage one another, and have orgasms together in order to produce oxytocin, thereby helping to keep love going (Slater 2006). All this gives a somewhat new slant to the phrase "making love," doesn't it? (Sex as a "pleasure bond" is further discussed in Chapter 6.)

Then too, "[r]elationships live on time. . . . Some couples cannot love because the two simply don't spend enough time in each other's presence to allow it" (Lewis, Amini, and Lannon 2000, p. 205). Spending time together, committing to learning to know each other over time, and committing to self-disclosure involve risks—risks that some social scientists see men and women today as less willing to take (Bulcroft 2000). Recently, social scientists have argued that benevolent, loving relationships require some things that might sound old-fashioned—virtues such as prudence, humility, tolerance, gratitude, justice, charity, and forgiveness (Ciaramigoli and Ketcham 2000; Jeffries 2000; Slater 2002). We can learn to love, even if it's difficult. A first step is knowing what love and loving are. In Chapter 6, we'll discuss sexual expressions of love.

Summary

- Love is a deep and vital emotion resulting from significant need satisfaction, coupled with caring for and acceptance of the beloved, and resulting in an intimate relationship.

- Loving is a caring, responsible, and sharing relationship involving deep feelings, and it is a commitment to intimacy.
- Intimacy involves disclosing one's inner feelings, a process that is always emotionally risky.
- Loving also takes the ability to be emotionally interdependent, an acceptance of oneself as well as a sense of empathy, and a willingness to let down barriers set up for self-preservation.
- In an impersonal society, love provides an important source of fulfillment and intimacy.
- Genuine loving in our competitive society is possible and can be learned.
- Loving is one form of interdependence.
- Love should not be confused with martyring or manipulating.
- Love should not be confused with limerence.
- John Lee lists six love types: eros, or passionate love; storge, or friendship love; pragma, or pragmatic love; agape, or altruistic love; ludus, or love play; and mania, or possessive love.
- A sense of self-worth is important to loving.
- People discover love; they don't simply find it. The term *discovering* implies a process—developing and maintaining a loving relationship require seeing the relationship as valuable, committing to mutual needs satisfaction and self-disclosure, engaging in supportive communication, and spending time together.

Questions for Review and Reflection

1. What kinds of needs can a love relationship satisfy? What needs can never be satisfied by a love relationship?
2. Sternberg offers the triangular theory of love. What are its components? Are they useful concepts in analyzing any love experience(s) you have had?
3. Describe Reiss's wheel theory of love. Compare it to your idea of how love develops.
4. What is the difference between self-love and narcissism? How is each related to a person's capacity to love others?
5. **Policy Question.** Discuss the social-cultural irony involved in the facts that (1) loving is increasingly important for emotional survival; and (2) our popular culture generates myths, or misconceptions, that make it difficult to love authentically.

Key Terms

A-frame relationships 112
agape 108
attachment theory 113
avoidant attachment style 113
co-dependents 110
commitment 104
commitment (Sternberg's theory) 105
consummate love 105
dependence 111
dopamine 116
emotion 103
eros 107
H-frame relationships 113
illegitimate needs 103
independence 112
insecure/anxious attachment style 113
interdependence 112
intimacy 104
intimacy (Sternberg's theory) 105
legitimate needs 103
limerence 110
love 102

love styles 107
ludus 108
mania 108
manipulating 109
martyring 109
M-frame relationships 113
mutuality 116
narcissism 111
oxytocin 116
passion (Sternberg's theory) 105
pragma 108
psychic intimacy 104
secure attachment style 113
self-disclosure 114
self-revelation 114
self-worth 110
sexual intimacy 104
Sternberg's triangular theory of love 105
storge 107
symbiotic relationships 110
wheel of love 114

Online Resources

Companion Website for This Book

www.thomsonedu.com/sociology/lamanna

Visit the book companion website, where you will find flash cards, practice quizzes, Internet links, suggested readings, InfoTrac College Edition exercises, and more to help you study.

ThomsonNOW™ for Marriage and Family

Spend time on what you need to master rather than on information you already have learned. Take a pre-test for this chapter, and ThomsonNOW will generate a personalized study plan based on your results. The study plan will identify the topics you need to review and direct you to online resources such as videos, narrated learning modules, and interactive activities to help you master those topics. You can then take a post-test to help you determine the concepts you have mastered and what you will still need to work on. Try it out! Go to **www .thomsonedu.com/login** to sign in with an access code or to purchase access to this product.

Our Sexual Selves

© Alexandra Michaels/ Getty Images/ Riser

6

Sexual Development and Orientation

Children's Sexual Development

Sexual Orientation

A Closer Look at Family Diversity: Is It Okay to Be Asexual?

Theoretical Perspectives on Human Sexuality

The Exchange Perspective: Rewards, Costs, and Equality in Sexual Relationships

The Interactionist Perspective: Negotiating Cultural Messages

Changing Cultural Scripts

Early America: Patriarchal Sex

The Twentieth Century: The Emergence of Expressive Sexuality

The 1960s Sexual Revolution: Sex for Pleasure

The 1980s and 1990s: Challenges to Heterosexism

The Twenty-first Century: Risk, Caution—and Intimacy

Negotiating (Hetero)sexual Expression

Four Standards of Nonmarital Sex

Issues for Thought: "Hooking Up" and "Friends with Benefits"

Extramarital Affairs

Sexuality Throughout Marriage

How Often?

Facts about Families: How Do We Know What We Do? A Look at Sex Surveys

Young Spouses

Spouses in Middle Age

Older Partners

What About Boredom?

Sexual Satisfaction in Marriage and Other Partnerships

Race/Ethnicity and Sexual Expression

Sex as a Pleasure Bond

Sexual Pleasure and Self-Esteem

Sexual Pleasure and Gender

Communication and Cooperation

Some Principles for Sexual Sharing

Making the Time for Intimacy

Sexual Expression, Family Relations, and HIV/AIDS and Other Sexually Transmitted Diseases

HIV/AIDS and Heterosexuals

HIV/AIDS and Gay Men

HIV/AIDS and Family Crises

HIV/AIDS and Children

Facts about Families: Who Has HIV/AIDS?

The Politics of Sex

Politics and Research

Adolescent Sexuality and Sex Education

Sexual Responsibility

From childhood to old age, people are sexual beings. Sexuality has a lot to do with the way we think about ourselves and how we relate to others. It goes without saying that sex plays a vital role in marriages and other intimate partner relationships.

Despite the pleasure it may give, sexuality may be one of the most baffling aspects of our selves. Finding mutually satisfying ways of expressing sexual feelings can be a challenge.

In this chapter, we will look briefly at children's sexual development. We define sexual orientation and examine the situation of gay men, lesbians, and bisexuals in today's society. We will review the changing cultural meanings of sexuality through our history, as well as the varied sexual standards present in contemporary culture. We will discuss sex as a pleasure bond that requires open, honest, and supportive communication, and then look at the role sex plays throughout marriage.

We will look at some challenges that are associated with sexual expression. What happens when one or both partners has an affair? How has the emergence of HIV/AIDS as a pandemic disease affected sexual relationships and families? Finally, we will examine ways that sexuality, research on sex, and sex education have become political issues in our society.

Before we discuss sexuality in detail, we want to point out our society's tendency to reinforce the differences between women and men and to ignore the common feelings, problems, and joys that make us all human. The truth is, men and women aren't really so different. Many physiological parts of the male and female genital systems are either alike or analogous, and sexual response patterns are similar in men and women (Masters and Johnson 1966).

Space limits our ability to present much detail on the various possibilities of sexual expression, which include kissing, fondling, cuddling, and even holding hands, as well as more overtly sexual activities. We consider that you might have concerns about sexuality that are difficult to address in the limited space of this textbook. We present more detailed information on sexual anatomy, sexual response patterns, sexually transmitted diseases, sexual problems, and contraception in the appendices, as well as information on the physiology of conception and birth and on reproductive technology.[1]

[1] Seven online appendices give information on sexual and reproductive topics: Appendix A: Human Sexual Anatomy, Appendix B: Human Sexual Response, Appendix C: Sexually Transmitted Diseases, Appendix D: Sexual Dysfunctions and Therapy, Appendix E: Conception, Pregnancy, and Childbirth, Appendix F: Contraceptive Techniques, and Appendix G: High-Tech Fertility. These appendices can be accessed at the book website.

Sexual Development and Orientation

Knowledge about children's sexual development and the emergence of sexual orientation is not as extensive as we would like, but there are some things we do know.

Children's Sexual Development

FOCUS ON CHILDREN "Human beings are sexual beings throughout their entire lives" (DeLamater and Friedrich 2002, p. 10). As early as twenty-four hours after birth, male newborns get erections, and infants may touch their genitals. In a study of almost one thousand children in Minneapolis and Los Angeles, pediatric researchers' concern was to establish a baseline of "normative" sexual behavior—that is, to indicate to parents, social workers, and others the normality of children's sexual interest. These researchers found that young children often exhibit overtly sexual behaviors.

Reports by "primary female caregivers," using the Child Behavior Checklist and Child Sexual Behavior Inventory, indicate that between the ages of two and five, a substantial number of children engage in "rhythmic manipulation" of their genitals, which the researchers term a "natural form of sexual expression" (DeLamater and Friedrich 2002, p. 10). Children may also try to look at others who are nude or undressing or try to touch their mother's breasts or genitals. Sixty percent of boys and 44 percent of girls in this age group touched their own sex organs (Friedrich et al. 1998, Tables 3, 4). Children also "play doctor," examining each other's genitals. There were few sex differences overall. Researchers are interested in these physical manifestations of childhood sexual development. But they place this in context, noting that overall sensual experiences from infancy onward shape later sexual expression, while attachment to parents in infancy and childhood provides the emotional security essential to later sexual relationships (DeLamater and Friedrich 2002; Friedrich et al. 1998; Marano 1997).

As Figure 6.1 shows, this early sexual behavior peaks at age five, declining thereafter until sexual attraction first manifests itself around age eleven or twelve. Children are maturing about two years earlier than they were one hundred years ago and much later than in 1500, when the average age of puberty was nineteen in England (Mackay 2000, p. 16; O'Connor 2005; Sanghavi 2006). As the age of puberty has declined, the age at marriage has risen, leaving a more extended period during which sexual activity may occur among adolescents and unmarried adults.

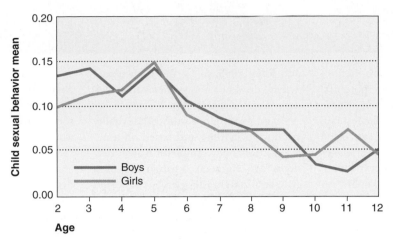

FIGURE 6.1 Mean Child Sexual Behavior Index scores for boys and girls age two through twelve. The graph lines indicate the proportion of the children in the study who have engaged in such sexual behaviors as showing interest in their genitals, touching themselves, trying to look at others who are nude or undressing, or trying to touch their mother's breasts.

Source: Friedrich et al. 1998, Figure 1.

Sexual Orientation

As we develop into sexually expressive individuals, we manifest a sexual orientation. **Sexual orientation** refers to whether an individual is drawn to a partner of the same sex or the opposite sex. **Heterosexuals** are attracted to opposite sex partners and **homosexuals** to same-sex partners.[2] **Bisexuals** are attracted to people of both sexes. A person's sexual orientation does not necessarily predict his or her sexual behavior; abstinence is a behavioral choice, as is sexual expression with partners of the nonpreferred sex. All these terms designate one's choice of sex partner only, not general masculinity or femininity or other aspects of personality.

We tend to think of sexual orientation as a dichotomy: One is either "gay" or "straight." Actually, sexual orientation may be a continuum. Freud, Kinsey, and many present day psychologists and biologists maintain that humans are inherently bisexual; that is, we all have the latent physiological and emotional structures necessary for responding sexually to either sex.

From the interactionist point of view (Chapter 2), the very concepts "bisexual," "heterosexual," and "homo-

sexual" are social inventions. They emerged in the late nineteenth century in scientific and medical literature (Seidman 2003, pp. 46–49, 56–58). Although same-sex sexual relations existed all along, the conceptual categories and the notion of sexual orientation itself were cultural creations. Developing a sexual orientation today may be influenced by the resultant tendency to think in dichotomous terms: individuals may sort themselves into the available categories and behave accordingly. In time, social pressures to view oneself as either straight or gay may inhibit latent bisexuality or inconsistencies (Gagnon and Simon 2005; Rosario et al. 2006). In this light, the recent assertion of **asexuality** as a sexual orientation represents a challenge to the traditional dichotomy. *Asexuality* is described in "A Closer Look at Family Diversity: Is It Okay to Be Asexual?"

The reason some individuals develop a gay sexual orientation has not been definitively established—nor do we yet understand the development of heterosexuality. Among gays, sexual identity through a sense of being different might have been felt in childhood. Sexual attraction to same-sex persons occurs as early as ten for boys and fourteen for girls. Same-sex sexual activity typically begins around age fourteen for males, while women's initial experiences tend to occur around age sixteen. "Coming out"—identifying oneself as gay to others—occurs on average just before or after high school graduation (Savin-Williams 2006).

Individuals vary in this process. A study of 156 lesbian, gay, and bisexual youths recruited from gay organizations and public colleges in New York City found

---

[2] Everyday terms are *straight* (heterosexual), *gay*, and *lesbian*. The term *gay* is synonymous with *homosexual* and refers to males or females. But often *gay* or *gay male* is used in reference to men, while *lesbian* is used to refer to gay women. The Committee on Lesbian and Gay Concerns of the American Psychological Association (1991) prefers the terms *gay male* or *gay man* and *lesbian* to *homosexual* because the committee thinks that the latter term may be associated with negative stereotypes.

Is It Okay to Be Asexual?

A majority of Americans are heterosexual—that is, attracted to potential partners of the opposite sex. Some Americans are **GLBT**: gay male, lesbian, bisexual, or transgendered, attracted to same-sex partners or those of either sex, as the case may be. A newly identified sexual orientation is asexuality. An unknown but probably small number of Americans simply do not experience sexual attraction to others. This is different from *celibacy* or *abstinence*, which is a *decision* not to have sexual relations, at least for a time, but not from a lack of desire.

Asexuals have emotional feelings and may desire intimate relationships with others, just not sexual ones. Some asexuals experience physical arousal or even masturbate, "but feel no desire for partnered sexuality" (Jay 2005).

Little research on asexuals exists; asexuals have been virtually invisible. In fact, by age forty-four, 97 percent of men and 98 percent of women have had sexual intercourse (Mosher, Chandra,

and Jones 2005, p. 1). But such sexual activity does not always mean that feelings of sexual desire exist.

In an exploratory study of asexuality conducted in 1994 and based on a national probability sample of British residents age eighteen through fifty-nine (Bogaert 2004), 1.05 percent reported themselves to be asexual even though 44 percent were or had been married or cohabiting. Women were more likely to report an asexual orientation than men, but age was not related to asexuality. An interesting finding of this study was that there were large differences between sexual and asexual people in education and social class, with asexuals more likely to have less education and lower social origins. Bogaert speculates that asexuality may be related to a less-advantaged social environment. Needless to say, this and other findings of the study need to be tested against further research conducted in other societies with diverse class structures.

The Asexual Visibility and Education Network (AVEN) was founded in 2001 as a networking and information resource (www.asexuality.org). This group would like to see *asexuality* become a recognized sexual orientation so that absence of sexual desire is not treated as dysfunctional but, rather, as a "normal" alternative. Clinicians vary in whether they agree, but as one example, Dr. Irwin Goldstein, director of the Boston University Center for Sexual Medicine, considers that "[l]ack of interest in sex is not necessarily a disorder or even a problem . . . unless it causes distress" (Duenwald 2005, p. 2).

Critical Thinking

Had you been aware of the concept of asexuality before reading about it here?

In your opinion, does our society define asexuality as dysfunctional? Can you think of examples that support your viewpoint? Might asexuality become recognized as a legitimate sexual orientation?

---

that 57 percent consistently identified as gay/lesbian and were more certain and accepting of their same-sex sexuality, involved in gay social activities, and more comfortable with others knowing. Fifteen percent consistently identified as bisexual. But another 18 percent experienced a gradual transition to the establishment of a gay self-identity. Contrary to stereotype, female youth were more likely to have a consistent gay sexual orientation earlier than male youth (Rosario et al. 2006).

Deciding who is to be categorized as **gay**, **lesbian**, or bisexual for research purposes is not easy—How much experience? How exclusively homosexual? With possible concealment of sexual orientation by survey respondents, this precludes any certain calculation of how many gays and lesbians there are in our society. Until fairly recently, it was stated that about 10 percent of adult individuals are gay or lesbian. However, the National Health and Social Life Survey (NHSLS: Laumann et al. 1994) suggests that the proportion of homosexual individuals in the population is probably lower. An analysis of combined NHSLS data and University of

Chicago National Opinion Research Center (NORC) survey data finds that 4.7 percent of men have had some same-sex experience since age eighteen, while 2.5 percent had exclusively same-sex experience over the last year. Of women, 3.5 percent report some adult same-sex experience, while for 1.4 percent, experience has been exclusively same-sex over the last year (Black et al. 2000).

In terms of self-identification, the National Survey of Family Growth, conducted in 2002 and 2003 by the U.S. Centers for Disease Control and Prevention, found that approximately 4.1 percent of each sex in the eighteen to forty-four age range report a gay, lesbian, or bisexual self-identification, while 90 percent identify as heterosexual (Mosher, Chandra, and Jones 2005, pp. 1–3, Table B; Gates 2006).

The existence of a fairly constant proportion of gays in virtually every society—in societies that treat homosexuality harshly as well as those that treat it permissively—suggests a biological imperative (Bell, Weinberg, and Hammersmith 1981), as does the fact that 450 mammal and bird species engage in same-sex sexual activity (Mackay 2000, p. 22).

Based on studies by themselves and colleagues, Bailey, Bobrow, Wolfe, and Mikach (1995) claim "empirical support for partial genetic transmission of both male and female sexual orientation," whereas "no existing theory of parent-to-child environmental transmission has received unambiguous support" (p. 125). Several sociologists agree that the Bailey and colleagues' study of gay men and their sons "provides evidence of a moderate degree of parent-to-child transmission of sexual orientation" (Stacey and Biblarz 2001, p. 171). Yet, a majority of children raised in lesbian families self-identified as heterosexual in adulthood (Golombok and Tasker 1996, p. 8) as did 90 percent of gay men's sons (Bailey et al. 1995). No specific genetic differences between heterosexuals and gays have been conclusively established (Greenberg, Bruess, and Haffner 2002, p. 367). Research on biological influences on sexual orientation continues, with recent Canadian research on the prenatal impact of previous male offspring of a mother (Kaplan 2006) and analysis of brain responses to hormones ("Lesbians' Brains . . ." 2006).

Virtually all the studies of child sexual development attempting to determine the origin of sexual orientation have methodological limitations (L. Rogers 2001; Stacey and Biblarz 2001): "Research and theory on sexual development remain . . . rudimentary" (Stacey and Biblarz, p. 178).

Whether a same-sex sexual orientation finds expression is clearly affected by environment, apart from or in conjunction with any genetic dispositions. A study using data from the General Social Survey and the National Health and Social Life Survey found increases in same-sex partnering between 1998 and 2002, especially for women (A. Butler 2005). Butler points to changes in social norms and in the legal climate, as well as increasing economic opportunities for women, as likely factors shaping this change.

Theoretical Perspectives on Human Sexuality

We saw in Chapter 2 that there are various theoretical perspectives concerning marriage and families. The same is true for human sexuality. We can, for example, look at sexuality using a *structure–functional* perspective. In this case, we see sex as a focus of norms designed to regulate sexuality so that it serves the societal function of responsible reproduction. From a *biosocial perspective*, we consider that humans—like the species from which they evolved—are designed for the purpose of transmit-

ting their genes to the next generation. A woman can generally have only one offspring a year, so she must be more discriminating when choosing a partner. For a man, each new mate offers a real chance for carrying on his genetic material into the future. According to this biosocial perspective, men are inclined toward casual sex with many partners, whereas women are inclined to be selective and monogamous (Dawkins 1976).

Yet, as social scientists, we see the remarkable cross-cultural and historical variation in the meaning and expression of sexuality, as well as the bargaining about sex that goes on between individuals. Two ways of looking at sexual relations more sociologically are *exchange theory* and *interaction theory*, both introduced in Chapter 2.

The Exchange Perspective: Rewards, Costs, and Equality in Sexual Relationships

From a general *exchange theory* perspective, women's sexuality and associated fertility are resources that can be exchanged for economic support, protection, and status in society. But an exchange theory perspective that brings sex closer to our human experience is the **interpersonal exchange model of sexual satisfaction** (Lawrance and Byers 1995).

In the interpersonal exchange model of sexual satisfaction, satisfaction is seen to depend on the *costs* and *rewards* of a sexual relationship, as well as the participant's *comparison level*—what the person expects out of the relationship. Also important is the *comparison level for alternatives*—what other options are available, and how good are they compared to the present relationship? Finally, in this day and age, expectations are likely to include some degree of *equality*.

Research to test this model found that these elements of the relationship did indeed predict sexual satisfaction in married and cohabiting couples (Lawrance and Byers 1995).

The Interactionist Perspective: Negotiating Cultural Messages

The *interactionist* perspective emphasizes the interpersonal negotiation of relationships in the context of sexual scripts: "*That* we are sexual is determined by a biological imperative toward reproduction, but *how* we are sexual—where, when, how often, with whom, and why—has to do with cultural learning, with meaning transmitted in a cultural setting" (Fracher and Kimmel 1992). Cultural messages give us legitimate reasons for having sex, as well as who should take the sexual initiative, how long a sexual encounter should last, how important it is to experience orgasm, what positions are acceptable, and whether it is appropriate to masturbate,

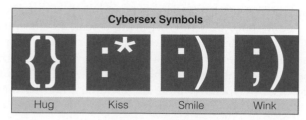

Cybersex Symbols			
Hug	Kiss	Smile	Wink

Cybersex. Is it sex—cyberstyle—or is it abstinence? From an interactionist perspective, we might say that society is still constructing the answer.

among other things. Recently, cultural messages have concerned what sexual interaction or relationships are appropriately conducted over the Internet.

An **interactionist perspective on human sexuality** holds that women and men are influenced by the **sexual scripts** that they learn from their culture (Gagnon and Simon 2005). They then negotiate the particulars of their sexual encounter and developing relationship (A. Stein 1989, p. 7).

Sex partners assign meaning to their sexual activity—that is, sex is symbolic of something, which might be affection, communication, recreation, or play, for example. Whether each gives their sexual relationship the same meaning has a lot to do with satisfaction and outcomes. For example, if one is only playing while the other is expressing deep affection, trouble is likely. A relationship goal for couples becoming committed is to establish a joint meaning for their sexual relationship.

Sex has different cultural meanings in different social settings. In the United States (and elsewhere), messages about sex have changed over time.

Changing Cultural Scripts

From colonial times until the nineteenth century, the purpose of sex in America was defined as reproductive. A new definition of sexuality emerged in the nineteenth century and flourished in the twentieth. Sex became significant for many people as a means of communication and intimacy (D'Emilio and Freedman 1988).

Early America: Patriarchal Sex

In a patriarchal society, descent, succession, and inheritance are traced through the male genetic line, and the socioeconomic system is male dominated. Sex is defined as a physiological activity, valued for its procreative potential. **Patriarchal sexuality** is characterized by many beliefs, values, attitudes, and behaviors developed to protect the male line of descent. Men are to control women's sexuality. Exclusive sexual possession by a man of a woman in monogamous marriage ensures that her children will be legitimately his. Men are thought to be born with an urgent sex drive, whereas women are seen as naturally sexually passive; orgasm is expected for men but not for women. Unmarried men and husbands whose wives do not meet their sexual needs may gratify those needs outside marriage. Sex outside marriage is wrong for women, however.

Morning on the Cape by Leon Kroll.

© "Morning on the Cape," 1935. Leon Kroll. American, 1884-1974. Oil on canvas, 36x58 in. Carnegie Museum of Art, Pittsburgh; Patrons Art Fund, 36.1

© Paul Fusco/ Magnum Photos

Self-disclosure and physical pleasure are key qualities in building sexually intimate relationships. Tenderness is a form of sexual expression valued not just as a prelude to sex but as an end in itself.

Although it has been significantly challenged, the patriarchal sexual script persists to some extent and corresponds to traditional gender expectations. If masculinity is a quality that must be achieved or proven, one arena for doing so is sexual accomplishment or conquest. A 1992 national survey by the National Opinion Research Center (NORC) at the University of Chicago, based on a representative sample of 3,432 Americans age eighteen to fifty-nine, found that men were considerably more likely than women to perform, or "do," sex. For example, more than three times as many men as women reported masturbating at least once a week. Three-quarters of the men reported always reaching orgasm in intercourse, while the fraction for women was nearer to one-quarter. Men are also much more likely to think about sex (54 percent of men and 19 percent of women said they think about it at least once a day) and to have multiple partners. Men are also more excited by the prospect of group sex (Laumann et al. 1994). One might return to a biosocial perspective to explain these differences except that they are less pronounced among the youngest cohort.

The Twentieth Century: The Emergence of Expressive Sexuality

A different sexual message has emerged as the result of societal changes that include the decreasing economic dependence of women and the availability of new methods of birth control. Because of the increasing emphasis on couple intimacy, women's sexual expression is more encouraged than it had been earlier (D'Emilio and Freedman 1988). Expressive sexuality sees sexuality as basic to the humanness of both women and men; there is no one-sided sense of ownership. Orgasm is important for women as well as for men. Sex is not only, or even primarily, for reproduction, but is an important means of enhancing human intimacy. Hence, all forms of sexual activity between consenting adults are acceptable.

The 1960s Sexual Revolution: Sex for Pleasure

Although the view of sex as intimacy continues to predominate, in the 1920s an alternative message began to emerge wherein sex was seen as a legitimate means to individual pleasure, whether or not it was embedded in a serious couple relationship. Probably as a result, the generation of women born in the first decade of the twentieth century showed twice the incidence of nonmarital intercourse[3] as those born earlier (D'Emilio

[3] *Nonmarital* sex refers to sexual activity by people who are not married to each other, whether they have never married or are divorced, widowed, or currently married (although we usually use the term *extramarital sex* for this last situation). *Nonmarital sex* replaces the previously common term *premarital sex*. *Premarital* connotes the anticipation of marriage, reflecting the fact that before the sexual revolution a substantial portion of nonmarital sexual activity took place between people who were formally engaged or informally pledged to marry or who would subsequently marry.

and Freedman 1988). This probably occurred mostly in relationships that anticipated marriage (Zeitz 2003). Further liberalization of attitudes and behaviors characterized the sexual revolution of the 1960s.

What was so revolutionary about the sixties? For one thing, the birth control pill became widely available; as a result, people were freer to have intercourse with more certainty of avoiding pregnancy.[4] At least for heterosexuals, laws regarding sexuality became more liberal. Until the U.S. Supreme Court decision in *Griswold v. Connecticut* (1965) recognized a right of "marital privacy," the sale or provision of contraception was illegal in some states. The idea that sexual and reproductive decision making belonged to the couple, not the state, was extended to single individuals and minors by subsequent decisions (*Eisenstadt v. Baird* 1972; *Carey v. Population Services International* 1977).

Americans' attitudes and behavior regarding sex changed during this period. In 1959 about four-fifths of Americans surveyed said they disapproved of sex outside marriage. In 2006, only 25 percent said it was "always wrong" (T. Smith 1999; Schott 2007). Not only did attitudes become more liberal, but behaviors (particularly women's behaviors) changed as well. The rate of nonmarital sex and the number of partners rose, while age at first intercourse dropped (Wells and Twenge 2005). The trend toward higher rates of nonmarital sex has continued. Now "almost all Americans have sex before marrying" (Finer 2007, p. 73).

Today, sexual activity often begins in the teen years. In 2005, almost half (46.8 percent) of high school students had had sexual experience (47.9 percent of males and 45.7 percent of females), and 33.9 percent are currently sexually active. For the vast majority (85 percent) of teens who had experienced sex, their first experience was with a romantic partner although some 7.5 percent of students were forced to have sex (Eaton et al. 2006; Ryan, Manlove, and Franzetta 2003).

Table 6.1 shows the percentages of sexually experienced teens in each of the major racial/ethnic groups. Black male and female students are the most likely to be sexually experienced and currently sexually active, according to the Youth Risk Behavior Surveillance System, a national high school–based survey conducted by the U.S. Centers for Disease Control and Prevention (Eaton et al. 2006). Not surprisingly, sexual experience increases with age.

Perhaps the most significant change ushered in by the sexual revolution, among heterosexuals at least, has been in marital sex. "Today's married couples have

Table 6.1 Sexual Experience of High School Students by Race/Ethnicity and Gender, 2005

| | PERCENTAGE WHO . . . | | | |
| | "EVER HAD SEXUAL INTERCOURSE" | | "ARE CURRENTLY SEXUALLY ACTIVE" | |
Ethnicity	Males	Females	Males	Females
White	42%	44%	31%	34%
Black	75%	61%	51%	44%
Hispanic	58%	44%	36%	34%

Source: Eaton et al. 2006, Tables 44, 46.

sexual intercourse more often, experience more sexual pleasure, and engage in a greater variety of sexual activities and techniques than people surveyed in the 1950s" (Greenberg, Bruess, and Haffner 2002, p. 437). In the NORC study, 88 percent of married partners said they enjoy great sexual pleasure (Laumann et al. 1994).

The 1980s and 1990s: Challenges to Heterosexism

If the sexual revolution of the 1960s focused on freer attitudes and behaviors among heterosexuals, recent decades have expanded that liberalism to encompass lesbian and gay male sexuality. Until several decades ago, most people thought about sexuality almost exclusively as between men and women. In other words, our thinking was characterized by **heterosexism**—the taken-for-granted system of beliefs, values, and customs that places superior value on heterosexual behavior and that denies or stigmatizes nonheterosexual relations. However, since "Stonewall" (a 1969 police raid on a U.S. gay bar) galvanized the gay community into advocacy, gay males and lesbians have not only become increasingly visible but have also challenged the notion that heterosexuality is the one proper form of sexual expression.

Gay men and lesbians have won legal victories, new tolerance by some religious denominations, greater understanding on the part of some heterosexuals, and sometimes positive action by government. Some states and communities have passed sexual orientation antidiscrimination laws. Corporations also are increasingly likely to enact antidiscrimination policies.

The public's attitudes toward homosexuality, though never as favorable as toward nonmarital sex generally, became more favorable in the 1990s after earlier high rates of disapproval. In the early 1970s, about 70 percent thought homosexual relations were "always wrong." In 1986 the Supreme Court decision in *Bowers v. Hardwick* declined to extend privacy protection to gay male or lesbian relationships, and homosexual conduct remained criminalized in some states. Then in a 2003 case (*Lawrence et al. v. Texas*), the Supreme Court reversed its ear-

---

[4] It is important to note that both sexual liberation and the use of birth control were already in progress. "The pill did not create America's sexual revolution so much as it accelerated it" (Zeitz 2003).

Lesbian and gay male unions and families have become increasingly visible over the past decade. Meanwhile, discrimination and controversy persist.

lier decision, striking down a Texas law criminalizing homosexual acts, thus legalizing same sex sexual relations. At present, 56 percent of those surveyed in a Gallup poll agreed that "homosexual relations should be legal" (Saad 2006a).

Americans are divided over whether gay men and lesbians choose their sexual orientation, a split that shapes attitudes. People who see being gay as a choice are less sympathetic to lesbians or gay men regarding jobs and other rights (Loftus 2001). The American Psychological Association, as well as the U.S. Surgeon General, takes the position that sexual orientation is not a choice and cannot be changed at will (American Psychological Association 2001; U.S. Surgeon General 2001, p. 4).

Americans are more likely to approve of civil rights protections for gays and lesbians than of a gay or lesbian lifestyle, and that approval has continued to strengthen since the 1970s. In 2006, 89 percent of Americans surveyed in a Gallup poll agreed that gays "should have equal job opportunities" (Saad 2006a). The workplace is "becoming friendlier" to gay, lesbian, and bisexual employees, and the vast majority of Forbes 500 companies include sexual orientation in their antidiscrimination policies (Joyce 2005b). Gay employees are increasingly open about their sexual orientation ("The Office Closet Empties Out" 2006).

A recent survey reported that almost two-thirds of gays and lesbians who had "come out" found accep-

tance by their families, and 76 percent of gays, lesbians, and bisexuals say there is more acceptance today (Kaiser Family Foundation 2001). Nevertheless, **homophobia**—viewing homosexuals with fear, dread, aversion, or hatred—is still present in American society. A survey conducted in 2000 found that 74 percent of gays and lesbians reported experiencing prejudice, 32 percent in the form of physical violence (Kaiser Family Foundation 2001).

Comparing Gay Male and Lesbian Sexual Behaviors
Philip Blumstein and Pepper Schwartz (1983), who studied a large national sample of 12,000 volunteers from the Seattle, San Francisco, and Washington, D.C., areas,[5] described lesbian relationships as the "least sexualized" of four kinds of couples: heterosexual cohabiting and married couples, lesbians, and gay men. Lesbians have sex less frequently than gay men, although it may be difficult to make comparisons because lesbians' physical relationship can take the form of hugging, cuddling, and kissing, not only genital contact (Peplau, Fingerhut, and

[5] Although the Blumstein and Schwartz study was published in 1983 and is not a random sample, it "continues to be the most extensive study on the sexuality of gay and lesbian couples to date" (Christopher and Sprecher 2000, p. 1007). These data are still being used by well-respected researchers (e.g., Kurdek 2006). Still, one must keep in mind that these data predate the AIDS epidemic and other societal changes that have an impact on sexuality and sexual expression.

Beals 2004; Frye 1992). Nevertheless, lesbians report greater sexual satisfaction than do heterosexual women: "Their greater tenderness, patience, and knowledge of the female body are said to be the reasons" (Konner 1990, p. 26). Gay male sexuality is more often "body-centered" (Ruefli, Yu, and Barton 1992), while lesbian sexuality is more person-centered.

Gay men are more accepting of nonmonogamous relationships than are lesbians—or heterosexuals (Christopher and Sprecher 2000). They have more transitory sex than lesbians; casual sex among lesbians is relatively rare.

We have discussed differences, but patterns of sexual frequency and satisfaction in gay and lesbian relationships resemble those of heterosexual marriage and cohabitation in some ways. In all couple types studied by Kurdek (1991)—gay, lesbian, heterosexual cohabitants, and married couples—sexual satisfaction within each group was associated with general relationship satisfaction and with sexual frequency. "Despite variability in structure, close dyadic relationships work in similar ways" (Kurdek 2006, p. 509).

The Twenty-first Century: Risk, Caution—and Intimacy

Although pleasure seeking was the icon of sixties sexuality, caution in the face of risk characterizes contemporary times. Disappointment and heartbreak in sexual relations invested with romantic feelings is nothing new. But a generation of young adults that grew up with parental divorce is especially risk averse. Moreover, this generation is the first to come of age *after* the emergence of the AIDS epidemic.

Some heterosexual young adults see AIDS as a threat only for other people. Others do acknowledge the risk, but decide to take their chances. "Most emerging adults . . . say that fear of AIDS has become the framework for their sexual consciousness, deeply affecting their attitudes toward sex and the way they approach sex with potential partners," perhaps asking for a test result or insisting on condom use (Arnett 2004, p. 91). (HIV/AIDS is discussed in more detail later in this chapter.)

Sexually active singles generally have lower rates of activity than do either married or cohabiting partners (Christopher and Sprecher 2000). A number of singles have multiple partners over time; perhaps a third of young adult women had more than one partner during the year prior to one survey, while 45 percent of men did (Laumann et al. 1994).

Today, there is risk in a sexual encounter. Critics of sexual liberation argue that this is especially disadvantageous for women (Shalit 1999). At the same time, a more liberal sexual environment offers the potential

"How about a kiss?"

for expressive sexuality and true sexual intimacy. People now have more knowledge of the principles of building good relationships (whether or not they always succeed in putting them into practice). Now that the possibility of satisfying sexual relationships seems more attainable, how do men and women negotiate those sexual relationships inside and outside of marriage?

Negotiating (Hetero)sexual Expression[6]

Although relationships between the sexes are more equal today than in the past, many—though assuredly not all—women and men today may have internalized divergent sexual scripts, or messages. Today's heterosexuals negotiate sexual relationships in a context in which new expectations of equality and similarity coexist within a heritage of gender-related difference. Men may be somewhat more accepting of recreational sex than women are, while studies continue to show that women are more interested than men in romantic preliminaries (Purnine and Carey 1998).

A research project designed to test the persistence of male dominance in dating assigned men and women to play nontraditional roles in conversations about having sex (women were to initiate a request for sex while men were to respond; Gilbert et al. 1999). The research participants found, for the most part, that they simply couldn't do it! "Some [heterosexual] men were concerned that refusing . . . sexual intimacy [when a woman asked] would mean they were gay or would be perceived as gay" (p. 770). It was difficult to get women—but not men—role players to talk about wanting sex.

[6] The idea that sexual expression is negotiated was developed in regard to heterosexual relationships; this principle may be applied to gay and lesbian relationships.

Still, "the pressure on men to be more sensitive, less predatory, and less macho has been mounting for several decades" (Schwartz and Rutter 1998, p. 48).

For both sexes, "'relational sex'—sex in the context of a relationship—is the preferred model of sex for both men and women" (p. 45, citing Laumann et al. 1994). After the sexual revolution of the 1960s, men did become more interested in communicating intimately through sex, whereas women showed more interest than before in physical pleasure (Pietropinto and Simenauer 1977). Masters and Johnson argue that more-equal gender expectations lead to better sex: "The most effective sex is not something a man does to or for a woman but something a man and a woman do together as equals" (1976, p. 88).

This discussion points again to the fact that cultural messages vary and that sexual relationships are negotiated in a social context. "Since early in the 20th century the bonds between marriage and sexual activity have been unraveling" (T. Smith 2006, p. 26). In the next sections we discuss nonmarital—outside of marriage—sexual activity. After that we will examine sexuality throughout marriage—where most sexual activity takes place—and then look at what is known about racial/ethnic diversity in sexual expression.

Four Standards of Nonmarital Sex

Sociologist Ira Reiss (1976) developed a four-fold classification of societal standards that illustrates the varied cultural messages about nonmarital sex. Reiss's four standards—abstinence, permissiveness with affection, permissiveness without affection, and the double standard—were originally developed to apply to premarital sex among heterosexual couples. However, they have since been applied to the sexual activities of unmarried persons generally. (Later we'll discuss extramarital sex—that is, sexual relations of married persons or cohabitants outside of their committed relationship.)

Abstinence The standard of **abstinence** maintains that regardless of the circumstances, nonmarital intercourse is wrong for both women and men. Many contemporary religious groups, especially the conservative Christian and Islamic communities, encourage abstinence as a moral imperative.

The proportion of teen boys and girls who are sexually active has shown a downward trend in the last few years (Santelli et al. 2000). Generally, teens who do not engage in sexual activity give conservative values or fear of pregnancy, disease, or parents as their reasons (Blinn-Pike 1999). A study of college students suggests that women who refrain from sexual activity do so because of an absence of love, a fear of pregnancy or sexually transmitted diseases (STDs), or a belief system that endorses nonmarital virginity. Men's hesitancy to pursue sexual involvement comes more often from feeling "inadequate or insecure" (Christopher and Sprecher 2000, p. 1009, citing Sprecher and Regan 1996).

There are other reasons for adopting an abstinence standard. Some women have withdrawn from nonmarital sexual relationships entirely, because of or in order to avoid bad experiences. They withdraw from sexual risk, at least for a time, rather than feeling vulnerable in the open sexual climate of the sexual revolution. The feminist movement is cited as empowering women to be abstinent if they wish (Ali and Scelfo 2002).

Advocates of abstinence claim that it is "a new sexual revolution" (G. Laub 2005, p. 103) in a "campus life [that] has become so drenched in sexuality, from the flavored condoms handed out by a resident adviser to the social pressure of the hook-up scene." At Princeton, a pro-abstinence organization, the Anscombe Society, was formed to support abstinence and to provide a setting for exploration and discussion of the abstinence alternative (Peterson 2005b, p. B3). As well, other organizations and books (e.g. Winner 2006) offer intellectually sophisticated and sexually frank discussions of this alternative.

Permissiveness with Affection The standard of **permissiveness with affection** permits nonmarital intercourse for both men and women equally, provided they have a fairly stable, affectionate relationship. This standard may be the most widespread sexual norm among unmarrieds. A Gallup poll taken in 2005 found that 58 percent of Americans find sex between an unmarried man and woman "morally acceptable" (Carroll 2005, p. 177).

In a 1997 national poll by *U.S. News & World Report* magazine, a majority of respondents under the age of forty-five said that adult, nonmarital sex "generally benefits people" in addition to offering sexual pleasure. A majority also felt that having had a few sexual partners makes it easier for a person to choose a sexually compatible spouse (Whitman 1997). The previously mentioned NORC survey concluded that we have sex mainly with people we know and care about. Seventy-one percent of Americans have only one sexual partner in the course of a year (Laumann et al. 1994).

Permissiveness without Affection Sometimes called recreational sex, **permissiveness without affection** allows intercourse for women and men regardless of how much stability or affection is in their relationship. Casual sex—intercourse between partners only briefly acquainted—is permitted.

The increased placement of sex into a relational context would seem to lead to a rejection of this standard. Instead, a *New York Times* article surprised many by describing a pattern among adolescents termed

Two similar new patterns of sexual behavior—"hooking up" and "friends with benefits"—made their appearance at the turn of the twenty-first century. First described in the media (Denizet-Lewis 2004), they are now recognized as contemporary *sexual scripts* whose implications for sexuality and marriage are as yet not well understood. Researchers believe that "hooking up" and "friends with benefits" have been around for awhile, but not talked about enough to have been visible to researchers and others not immersed in youth culture.

One pair of researchers believes that "the demise of the date and the rise of the hookup is a national trend" (England and Thomas 2007, p. 152). Indeed, a growing body of research suggests that, at least among a majority of U.S. students, *dating*—preplanned couple outings—has virtually disappeared as a college or high school script. With

the gradual demise of dating over the past several decades, *getting together* became more common among young men and women, as they congregated in groups for an activity or just to socialize (Libby 1976). Now that same improvised sociability has been extended to "hooking up" or finding a friend "with benefits"—that is, pairing off from the group for a sexual encounter.

The definitions of "hooking up" and "friends with benefits" are somewhat ambiguous. For instance, "hooking up" may simply mean spending additional time together with minimal sexual contact. The majority of participants in one study reported that "nothing" was the most common outcome of a hookup (Bogle 2004, p. 213). In fact, hooking up can mean anything from kissing and hugging to manual genital stimulation to oral sex or sexual intercourse (England and Thomas 2007).

Nevertheless, the basic idea in hooking up and friends with benefits is that a sexual encounter means nothing more than just that—sexual activity. In fact, hooking up can occur with no prior acquaintance between the parties and no further contact afterward. *Friends with benefits* is described as sex that takes place with friends, but with neither pretensions of nor expectations for romantic love or commitment. At least that is the initial premise.

These sexual scripts may have emerged because many of today's young adults—delaying marriage, spending long years in education and career development, and concerned about the fragility of committed relationships—still want to have sex. They want some sense of connection that can be limited to the physical or to friendship without risking romantic disappointment and emotional loss. When hooking up

---

"**friends with benefits**" (Denizet-Lewis 2004). Teens may "**hook up**" casually for sexual encounters with friends and acquaintances, completely outside a romantic relationship context. In fact, that seems partly the point. Teens or young adults who feel themselves to be unready for romance and commitment explore their sexuality in what is intended to be an emotionally neutral context. Of course, it doesn't always work out that way.

Sexual activity does not necessarily mean intercourse; oral sex is quite common. "Issues for Thought: 'Hooking Up' and 'Friends with Benefits'" discusses this new sexual script.

The Double Standard According to the **double standard**, women's sexual behavior must be more conservative than men's. In its original form, the double standard meant that women should not have sex before or outside marriage, whereas men could. More recently, the double standard has required that women be in love to have sex, or at least have fewer partners than men have. Now it appears that there are even different expectations for males and females in "hooking up."

An exploratory study of this phenomenon among undergraduates at two Eastern colleges found some informal rules: Women should be less aggressive,

should not hang around fraternity houses, and should have fewer partners than men. It was quite difficult for these college women to maintain reputation and self-esteem while engaging in hooking up—"the only game in town" (Bogle 2004, p. 99). Men have greater sexual freedom and greater power in these relationships. Bogle concludes: "[T]here is one crucial commonality . . . [of *hooking up* and dating, its predecessor sexual script]. . . . [*Men*] *have a greater share of power in both eras*" (p. 229).

In our society generally, men and women may have different expectations, with men exposed to cultural conditioning that encourages them to separate sex from intimacy, while among women, sexual expression more often symbolizes connection with a partner and communicates intimacy. One observer also argues that gender differences in permissiveness may reflect differences in social power and vulnerability, prompting a woman's strategy of self-protection through adherence to conventional cultural expectations (Howard 1988).

Extramarital Affairs

Up to this point we've been examining scripts for sex among unmarried. Now we will look at a different form of sex outside marriage—extramarital affairs.

or finding friends with benefits occurs among high school students, similar reasons may be in place. As one or both sex partners anticipate leaving for college, they may want to keep their options open (Edwards 2006). "As they see it, if they're not going to marry for another ten years, why not focus on other things (friendships, school, work, sports)? . . . And if they're not hurting anyone and not getting anyone pregnant, where is the harm in a little casual fun?" (Denizet-Lewis 2004).

What does this development mean for young lives and future marriage prospects? Reactions of social scientists range from alarm at the disappearance of a courtship path to marriage (Glenn and Marquardt 2001) to the thought that hooking up is simply the new way to begin a relationship that may become serious despite its initial intent (England and Thomas 2007). By carefully outlin-ing the positives and negatives of both dating and hooking up, one observer reminds us that dating also has drawbacks as a relationship development process (Bogle 2004).

Meanwhile, some observers note that men continue to have greater relation-ship power in hook-up settings, as indeed they did in the dating era. Now that there are more women than men on most college campuses, male power is reinforced inasmuch as competition among heterosexual women for the fewer available men is heightened. Perhaps partly as a result, one research team found an "orgasm gap," with men getting more sexual pleasure than they are giving in hook-up encounters (England and Thomas 2007, p. 157; Bogle 2004).

There is a surprising amount of research on hooking up for such a newly recognized phenomenon (Bogle 2004; Edwards 2006; England and Thomas 2007; Glenn and Marquardt 2001; Hughes, Morrison, and Asada 2005; Lambert, Kahn, and Apple 2003; Manning, Giordano, and Longmore 2006). Maybe academics, shut up in their offices analyzing data, find vicarious enjoyment in the topic. More seriously, though, due to researchers' interest, we should in time learn more about how the gap between "hooking up" and "married with children" is to be bridged.

Critical Thinking

What do you think about the advisability of hooking up or having friends with benefits? How might a researcher from the interactionist perspective investigate the way that couples bridge the gap between "hooking up" and "married with children"?

Marriage typically involves promises of sexual exclusivity—that spouses will have sexual relations only with each other. In this era of expressive sexuality, "people still feel that the self-disclosure involved in sexuality symbolizes the love relationship and therefore sexuality should not be shared with extramarital partners" (Reiss 1986, pp. 56–57).

Although "adultery is universal" (Mackay 2000, p. 36), the proscription against extramarital sex is stronger in the United States than in many other parts of the world. Over 90 percent of Americans consider extramarital affairs "morally unacceptable" (Mason and Crabtree 2004). Cohabiting couples also generally expect each other to be sexually faithful (94 percent, compared to 99 percent of married couples). However, the rate of sexual infidelity is higher among cohabitors than among marrieds (Treas and Giesen 2000). Some researchers distin-guish among emotional infidelity, sexual infidelity, and combined emotional and sexual infidelity. The latter is most disapproved and emotional (without sexual) infi-delity least disapproved (Blow and Hartnett 2005).

Statistics on extramarital affairs are based on what people report: Some spouses hesitate to admit an affair; others boast about affairs that didn't really happen. Nevertheless, an important U.S. national survey on sexuality undertaken in the 1990s indicated that one-quarter of all husbands and 15 percent of wives ages eighteen through fifty-nine reported having had at least one affair during the marriage (Laumann et al. 1994). Although these rates are lower than those found in ear-lier research, "nonetheless, these percentages translate into a significant number of Americans who have experi-enced sex with someone other than their spouse at least once" (Christopher and Sprecher 2000, p. 1006). This same study reports that only 4 percent of spouses had an outside opposite-sex partner in the twelve months prior to data collection (Laumann et al. 1994; Treas and Giesen 2000). Interestingly, the first statistical study of sexual behavior undertaken by economists (based on General Social Survey data for 1988–2000) reports (in economic jargon) that for all Americans "the happi-ness maximizing number of sexual partners . . . is *one*" (Blanchflower and Oswald 2004, p. 13).

Another survey conducted in 2002 by the Centers for Disease Control and Prevention found that 92 percent of married men and 93 percent of married women had sexual contact with only one opposite-sex partner (the spouse) during the past year. This compares to 80 per-cent of male and female cohabitants whose sexual rela-tions were limited to their cohabiting partner.

"Hey look, this goes any further, I should probably tell you we're married."

Of married men, 3.4 percent reported a lifetime experience of affairs with other men; 5.3 percent of cohabiting men reported such experience. Comparatively, of married women, 7.2 percent reported some sexual experience with other women, and 10.8 percent of cohabiting women did so. (The higher rates for women are probably due to the much looser definition of "sexual experience" for women; Mosher, Chandra, and Jones 2005, Tables 1, 2, 8.)

Risk Factors Sociologists Judith Treas and Deirdre Giesen (2000) developed a conceptual model of risk factors for extramarital sex. They tested this model with data from the 1992 National Health and Social Life Survey, a national probability sample, which included 2,870 married or cohabiting individuals ages eighteen through fifty-nine.[7]

Treas and Giesen found entering an extramarital affair to be a rational decision. Affairs are generally *not* spontaneous, the result of too much alcohol, for example, nor are they the consequence of overwhelming romantic passion. Rather, "[p]eople contemplating sexual infidelity described considered decisions" (Treas and Giesen 2000, p. 49).

It is not surprising that individuals who have a stronger sex interest—they think about sex every day—and who have more permissive sexual values and more past

---

[7] This study draws on the National Health and Social Life Survey data set (Laumann et al. 1994), but analyzes only data from married and cohabiting respondents.

sex partners—are more likely than others to engage in extramarital affairs. Of those who believe extramarital affairs are "not at all wrong," 76 percent have had an affair, compared to 10 percent of those who think affairs are "always wrong" (Treas and Giesen 2000). Lower satisfaction with a marital or cohabiting relationship is another unsurprising risk factor. Relationship dissatisfaction is a motive more important to women. Sexual dissatisfaction and declines in frequency are also associated with affairs, especially for men (Blow and Hartnett 2005).

Opportunity plays a role. Couples who lead separate lives and who have jobs requiring travel are more likely to have extramarital affairs (Treas and Giesen 2000). Workplace opportunity per se was not a significant factor for lifetime rates of extramarital affairs, but it was associated with having an affair in the last twelve months. The researchers speculate that if an opportunity came along at a low point in the marriage, it might be taken advantage of.

The 1990s saw the emergence of a new brand of marital infidelity—adultery on the net, or **cyberadultery**. The Internet has created new opportunities for individuals to develop secret relationships. The emotional connection may lead to a meeting—and then perhaps to a sexual relationship. At the same time, the Internet makes it more likely that a spouse or employer will be able to find out about an affair (Cooper 2002; 2004; Crooks and Baur 2005, p. 415). Such a discovery often triggers a couple's move into therapy.

Historically, societies have depended on community pressures to control disapproved sexual activity of any sort. Treas and Giesen found that shared social networks of family and friends, as well as church attendance, seemed to operate as social controls discouraging affairs.

Union duration of marriage or cohabitation, which can be a measure of both *investment* in the relationship and *habituation*, showed a positive relationship with likelihood of extramarital sex during the union. This provides some support for the **habituation hypothesis**—that is, that familiarity reduces the reward power of a sexual encounter with a spouse or partner compared to a new relationship (Liu 2000). At the same time, union duration is also a simple measure of exposure to the risk of an extramarital affair (Treas and Giesen 2000).

Previous researchers have found gender differences evident in the analyis of patterns of extramarital sex (C. Harris 2003a), with more husbands than wives having had an affair sometime during their marriage (Laumann et al. 1994). If a wife has an affair, she is more likely to do so because she feels emotionally distanced by her husband. Men who have affairs are far more likely to do so for the sexual excitement and variety they hope to find. Moreover, "men feel more betrayed by their wives having sex with someone else; women feel more betrayed by their husbands being emotionally involved with someone else" (S. Glass 1998, p. 35; Blow and Hartnett 2005; Christopher and Sprecher 2000). The Treas and Giesen (2000) analysis, however, suggests that when other risk factors are controlled, gender differences are reduced or eliminated.

Effects of Extramarital Affairs The secrecy required by an affair erodes the connection between the spouses. When discovered, the betrayal may spark jealousy—or it may create a crisis that motivates a search for the resolution of marital problems (Crooks and Baur 2005, p. 415).

Extramarital sex *can* have positive effects such as encouraging closer relationships, paying greater attention to couple communication, and placing a higher value on the family (Olson et al. 2002). But only a small percentage of couples see an improved relationship (Blow and Hartnett 2005). Not only has trust been eroded and feelings been hurt, but the uninvolved spouse may also have been exposed to various sexually transmitted diseases—not a rare occurrence (Crooks and Baur 2005). For many spouses, concern about AIDS heightens anger and turmoil over affairs (T. Smith 2006). The uninvolved spouse may feel exploited financially as well, because what were thought to be joint funds have been unilaterally spent on dinners, gifts, hotel rooms, or weekends away.

Research is mixed as to whether infidelity "causes" divorce. That seems to depend on the previous level of marital satisfaction, the motives attributed to the unfaithful spouse, attitudes toward infidelity in general, and the efforts of both spouses to work things out (Blow and Hartnett 2005). In one study, fewer than one-quarter of couples ended up divorcing (Schneider, Irons, and Corley 1999).

Recovering from an Extramarital Affair Given that affairs do occur, people will have much to think about if they discover that their spouse has had (or is having) one. The uninvolved mate will need to consider how important the affair is relative to the marital relationship as a whole. Can she or he regain trust? In some cases, the answer is no; trust never gets reestablished, and the heightened suspicion gets incorporated into other problems the couple might have (Levine 1998).

Whether trust can be reestablished depends on several factors. One is how much trust there is in the first place. One researcher (Hansen 1985) has suggested that for this reason, new relationships may be especially vulnerable to breaking up after an affair. But many couples do recover from an affair, although "it's hard to

do without a therapist" (S. Glass 1998, p. 44). Therapists suggest that doing so requires that the offending spouse

- apologize sincerely and without defending her or his behavior
- allow and hear the verbally vented anger and rage of the offended partner (but not permit physical abuse)
- allow for trust to rebuild gradually and to realize that this may take a long time—up to two years or more
- do things to help the offended partner to regain trust—keep agreements, for example, and call if he or she is running late

Meanwhile, the offended spouse needs to decide whether she or he is committed to the marriage and, if so, needs to be willing to let go of resentments as much as is possible. Finally, the couple should consider marriage counseling (described in Appendix H). According to Shirley Glass, "The affair creates a loss of innocence and some scar tissue. I tell couples things will never be the same. But the relationship may be stronger" (1998, p. 44).

Sexuality Throughout Marriage

It might surprise you that various aspects of nonmarital sex are more likely to be studied than are those within marriage and that sexual activities of teens receive more research attention than those of adults (L. Davis 2006). "More is known about sexuality in marriage at this time than has ever been true in the past. But we still have only a limited view of how sexuality is integrated into the normal flow of married life" (Christopher and Sprecher 2000, p. 1013).

Research in recent years has been much better methodologically, but has tended to focus on sexual frequency: How often do married couples have sex, and what factors affect this frequency? Before we get to the answers, we need to say something about how the information is gathered. "Facts About Families: How Do We Know What We Do? A Look at Sex Surveys" discusses the history and progress of research on sexuality.

How Often?

Social scientists are interested in sexual frequency because they like to examine trends over time and to relate these to other aspects of intimate relationships. For the rest of us, "How often?" is typically a question motivated by curiosity about our own sexual behavior compared to that of others. Either way, what do we know?

How Do We Know What We Do? A Look at Sex Surveys

How do we know what Americans do sexually? Chapter 2 points out that a *Playboy* magazine survey about sex would yield results different from one in *Family Circle* magazine. In serious social science, researchers strive for *representative samples* that reflect, or represent, all the people about whom they want to know something.

Pioneering Research

The pioneer surveys on sex in the United States were the Kinsey reports on male and female sexuality (Kinsey, Pomeroy, and Martin 1948, 1953). Kinsey used volunteers; he believed that a statistically representative survey of sexual behavior would be impossible because many of the randomly selected respondents would refuse to answer or would lie.

Recent Surveys

More recent scientific studies on sexual behavior have used random samples. In 1992, the National Opinion Research Center (NORC) at the University of Chicago conducted interviews with a representative sample of 3,432 Americans, age eighteen to fifty-nine—the National Health and Social Life Survey (Laumann et al. 1994). Eighty percent agreed to be interviewed—an impressively high response rate.

Respondents were questioned in ninety-minute face-to-face interviews. To provide some anonymity for the more sensitive part of the interview—questions about oral and anal sex, for example—specific sexual behavior questions were asked by means of a questionnaire. The respondent wrote answers and sealed them in an unlabeled envelope.

Findings of the National Health and Social Life Survey may be generalized to the U.S. population under age sixty with a high degree of confidence. Indeed, the results have been welcomed as the first-ever truly scientific nationwide survey of sex in the United States. But because the NORC sample included only people under sixty, it cannot tell us anything about the sexual activities of older Americans.

Another study of sex among marrieds (Call, Sprecher, and Schwartz 1995) sought to compensate for the NORC study's deficiencies by using another national data set, the National Survey of Families and Households (NSFH). In 1987–88 the NSFH staff, affiliated with the University of Wisconsin, did in-person interviews with a representative national sample of 13,000 respondents age eighteen and over (Sweet, Bumpass, and Call 1988), and the survey was repeated in 1992–94. Considered very reliable, the NSFH data are used as a basis for analysis regarding many topics discussed in this text. Some analyses have combined the National Survey of Families and Households and NORC data (Black et al. 2000).

A more recent survey, the National Survey of Family Growth, was conducted in 2002 and early 2003 by the U.S. Centers for Disease Control and Prevention. This survey also had an almost 80 percent response rate. It consists of in-person, in-home interviews with 12,571 people—4,928 men and 7,642 women. Measures of sexual behavior were collected by means of computer-assisted self-interviewing. This survey was limited to those fifteen through forty-four years of age, with different analyses involving various age combinations within this range (Mosher, Chandra, and Jones 2005).

NORC (the National Opinion Research Center of the University of Chicago) continues to conduct a biennial General Social Survey that includes questions about sexual behavior. It publishes extensive reports on sexual behavior (e.g., T. Smith 2006) as well as providing current data on attitudes of the general public toward sexual activity.

Conclusions based on survey research on sensitive matters such as sexuality must always be qualified by an awareness of their limitations—the possibility that respondents have minimized or exaggerated their sexual activity or that people willing to answer a survey on sex are not representative of the public. Nevertheless, with data from these national sample surveys, we have far more reliable information than ever before.

Married couples have sex more often than single individuals, though less often than cohabiting couples (Christopher and Sprecher 2000; T. Smith 2006). In the NORC survey, the average frequency of sex for sexually active, married respondents under age sixty was seven times a month. About 40 percent of marrieds said they had intercourse at least twice a week (Laumann et al. 1994). Of course, these figures are averages: "People

don't have sex every week; they have good weeks and bad weeks" (Pepper Schwartz, quoted in Adler 1993).

So does the ratio of good to bad weeks change over the course of a marriage? Yes: You have fewer good weeks (sorry).

Fewer Good Weeks To examine sexual frequency throughout marriage, Call, Sprecher, and Schwartz

(1995) looked at the responses of 6,785 marrieds with a spouse in the household (and 678 respondents who were cohabiting) in the NSFH data set described earlier. Like researchers before them and since (T. Smith 2006), they found that sexual activity is highest among young marrieds. About 96 percent of spouses under age twenty-five reported having had sex at least once during the previous month. The proportion of sexually active spouses gradually diminished until about age fifty, when sharp declines were evident. Among those fifty to fifty-four years old, 83 percent said they had sex within the previous month; for those between sixty-five and sixty-nine, the figure was 57 percent; 27 percent of respondents over age seventy-four reported having had sex within the previous month.

Figure 6.2 shows the mean (average) frequency of sexual intercourse during the month prior to the interview by age and marital status. When examining Figure 6.2, note that the researchers report separate means for all the marrieds in the sample and then for the sexually active spouses only. The figure also shows frequency rates for cohabitors. The average number of times that married people under age twenty-five had sex is about twelve a month. That number drops to about eight times a month at ages thirty through thirty-four, then to about six times monthly at about age fifty. After that, frequency of inter-

course drops more sharply; spouses over age seventy-four average having sex less than once each month.

It used to be that describing sexuality over the course of a marriage would be nearly the same as discussing sex as people grow older. Today this is not the case. Many couples are remarried, so that at age forty-five, or even seventy, a person may be newly married. Nonetheless, we may logically assume that young spouses are in the early years of marriage.

Young Spouses

Young spouses have sexual intercourse more frequently than do older mates. Young married partners, as a rule, have fewer distractions and worries. The high frequency of intercourse in this age group may also reflect a self-fulfilling prophecy: These couples may have sex more often partly because society expects them to.

After the first few years, sexual frequency declines (T. Smith 2006). Why so? The sexual intensity of the honeymoon period subsides, and "from then on almost everything—children, jobs, commuting, housework, financial worries—that happens to a couple conspires to reduce the degree of sexual interaction while almost nothing leads to increasing it" (Greenblatt 1983, p. 294). Indeed, later research does indicate that pregnancy, the

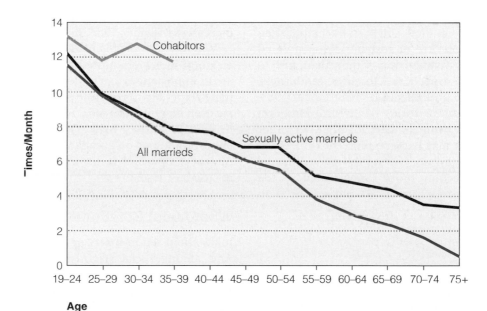

FIGURE 6.2 Frequency of sex last month by age and marital status. The line for "sexually active marrieds" represents the frequency of sex for those married respondents who supplied a figure or whose spouse did. The "all marrieds" line includes in the average the frequency of sex (zero) for those married persons who indicated that they are not sexually active. There were not enough cohabitants over age thirty-five in the sample to calculate sex frequency for older cohabitants.

Source: From Call, Sprecher, and Schwartz 1995, p. 646.

presence of small children, and a less than certain birth control method are factors that reduce sexual activity in young marriages. Employment, however, does not, as those couples who wish to be more sexually active seem to manage their time effectively for that purpose (Call, Sprecher, and Schwartz 1995).

Researchers have begun to wonder how sexual relations in early marriage might differ between couples who have established a sexual relationship before marriage and those who did not (Sprecher 2002), but there has been little examination of the transition from premarital to marital sex.

Spouses in Middle Age

On average, as people get older they have sex less often. Physical aging is not the only explanation for the decline of sexual activity over time, although it appears to be the most important one. Marital satisfaction was the second-largest predictor of sexual frequency.

Sexual satisfaction, marital satisfaction, and sexual frequency are interrelated throughout marriage (Byers 2005; Call, Sprecher, and Schwartz 1995; Crooks and Baur 2005; Sprecher and Schwartz 1994; T. Smith 2006). But "even among couples who rate their marriages as very happy and among those who say they are still 'in love,' frequency of intercourse declines with age" (T. Smith 2006, p. 13).

Despite the declining frequency of sexual intercourse, respondents in one small study emphasized the continuing importance of sexuality. They pointed to the total marital relationship rather than just to intercourse—to such aspects as "closeness, tenderness, love, companionship and affection" (Greenblatt 1983, p. 298)—as well as other forms of physical closeness such as cuddling or lying in bed together. In other words, with time, sex may become more broadly based in the couple's relationship. During this period, sexual relating may also become more sophisticated, as the partners become more experienced and secure (Purnine and Carey 1998).

Older Partners

In our society, images of sex tend to be associated with youth, beauty, and romance; to many young people, sex seems out of place in the lives of older adults. Not too many years ago, public opinion was virtually uniform in seeing sex as unlikely—even inappropriate—for older people. With Masters and Johnson's work in the 1970s indicating that many older people are sexually active, public opinion began to swing the other way. Then, in the 1980s, researchers began to caution against the romanticized notion that biological aging could be abolished (Cole 1983, pp. 35, 39). Of course, physical changes associated with aging do affect sexuality (Christopher and Sprecher 2000, p. 1002).

A majority (56 percent) of those individuals forty-five and older in a nationally representative sample surveyed by the American Association of Retired Persons agreed that a satisfying sexual relationship is important to one's quality of life. But they rated family and friends, health, being in good spirits, financial security, spiritual well-being, and a good relationship with a partner as more important than a fulfilling sexual connection (Jacoby 2005).

Men and women in their late forties both placed an equal and high priority on sex, but by age sixty a gender gap became evident. Sixty-two percent of men but only 27 percent of women gave sex a high priority (DeLamater and Sill 2005).

Some older partners shift from intercourse to petting as a preferred sexual activity. On the other hand, sexual intercourse does not necessarily cease with age. Among the sexually active, 90 percent said they found their mates "very attractive physically" (Greeley 1991). You can see in Figure 6.2 that, for older respondents, among whom the proportion of sexually inactive couples is large, the mean average frequency seriously understates what is happening in sexually active marriages; sexually active spouses over age seventy-four have sex about four times a month. Indeed, retirement "creates the possibility for more erotic spontaneity, because leisure time increases" (Allgeier 1983, p. 146).

When health problems do not interfere, both women's and men's emotional and psychological outlooks are as important as age in determining sexual functioning. Factors such as monotony, lack of an understanding partner, mental or physical fatigue, and overindulgence in food or alcohol may all have a profound negative effect on a person's capacity for sexual expression. Another important factor is regular sexual activity—as in "use it or lose it."

What About Boredom?

Jokes about sex in marriage are often about boredom. And among social scientists, one explanation often offered for the decline in marital sexual frequency is **habituation**—the decreased interest in sex that results from the increased accessibility of a sexual partner and the predictability in sexual behavior with that partner over time. Decreases due to habituation seem to occur early in the marriage; sexual frequency declines sharply after about the first year of marriage no matter how old (or young) the partners are. The reason for "this rather quick loss of intensity of interest and performance" appears to have two components: "a reduction in the

"Owen, look—the good sex fairy."

novelty of the physical pleasure provided by sex with a particular partner and a reduction in the perceived need to maintain high levels of sexual behavior" (Call, Sprecher, and Schwartz 1995, p. 649).

Given that the decline in marital frequency occurs most sharply early in marriage and only gradually after that, these researchers reasoned that "it is difficult to determine . . . whether habituation to sex actually occurs" throughout the marriage (Call, Sprecher, and Schwartz 1995, p. 647). Comparisons of first-married and remarried couples can shed some light on this.

Remarried respondents reported somewhat higher rates of sex frequency compared to people in first marriages who were the same age, and this was particularly true for those under age forty. Because people who remarry do renew the novelty of marital sex with a new partner, this finding is evidence for the habituation hypothesis (Call, Sprecher, and Schwartz 1995).

Sexual Satisfaction in Marriage and Other Partnerships

All this discussion of the frequency of intercourse may tempt us to forget that committed partners' sexuality is essentially about intimacy and self-disclosure. In other words, sex between partners—heterosexual partners and gay and lesbian partners as well—both gives pleasure and reinforces their relationship. A recent study found that those who "reported both the greatest emotional satisfaction and the greatest physical pleasure in their intimate relationships were those who were partnered in a monogamous relationship" (Hendrick 2000, p. 4). Another study comparing cohabiting, married, and single individuals found that cohabiting and mar-

ried individuals had the highest—and equal—levels of physical pleasure, with emotional satisfaction with sex greatest among married people (Waite and Joyner 2001).

Despite declining sexual frequency, sexual satisfaction remains high in marriages over the life course (of course, the less satisfied may have opted for divorce); 88 percent report that they are "extremely" or "very physically pleased" (Laumann et al. 1994; see also Christopher and Sprecher 2000, p. 1003). General satisfaction with sexual relationships was also characteristic of gay and lesbian couples.

Race/Ethnicity and Sexual Expression

Much research has been done on youth of varying racial/ethnic background. Table 6.1 reports differences in the sexual experience of high school students. Among adults, most work has been done on African American sexuality. The problem in discussing racial/ethnic variation in sexual expression is that it is difficult to find a research base for drawing conclusions about African American sexual expression that is not heavily influenced by myths, stereotypes, unrepresentative samples, and a focus on youth and social problems or that is simply insufficient (Bowser 1999; Staples 1999a, pp. 40–41). A recent edition of a text on black families does not contain index entries for sex, reproduction, same-sex, or similar concepts (Willie and Reddick 2003). Even less information exists about sexual expression among racial/ethnic groups other than whites. Research is still needed on "sexual development and behavior patterns across the life cycle, for diversified cultural groups in diversified geographic regions" (Belcastro 1985, p. 56). That said, let us present some data that do exist and be cautious about drawing generalized conclusions.

Looking at *individual* sexual behavior of men and women age fifteen through forty-four, the 2002 National Survey of Family Growth provides some bare bones information on racial/ethnic differences. Black men are more likely (22 percent) to have had three or more partners in the twelve months prior to the survey, compared to Hispanic (14 percent) or white men (8 percent). Black women are also more likely to have had multiple partners (11 percent) than are Hispanic (6 percent) or white women (6 percent). Comparisons between white males and females and their black and Hispanic counterparts about experience with oral and anal sex vary with the particular item. Overall, whites are more likely to have had "unconventional sex" (Mosher, Chandra, and Jones 2005, Tables 1, 2, p. 12).

At least one sex researcher (Belcastro 1985) has argued that African Americans and non-Hispanic whites are more similar than dissimilar in at least some aspects of their sexual behavior. Recent research on *married couples* finds that frequency of sex does not vary significantly with race, social class, or religion (Christopher and Sprecher 2000).

Gay/lesbian sexuality, like heterosexual behavior, has been explored among African Americans mostly in the context of problems (e.g., AIDS) and at the lower end of the social scale. An exception is found in the analysis of the 2000 census data on black same-sex households, which make up 14 percent of all such households. Black same-sex households tend to be less well off economically than other same-sex households. They are more likely to be raising children (Dang and Frazer 2004).

Social scientists writing about gay black male sexuality believe it is not as visible as among whites because blacks may find white gay subcultures alien, and they may tend to be integrated into heterosexual communities and extended families that strongly disapprove of homosexuality. As part of that social integration, black gay men may be more likely to be bisexual than exclusively homosexual and less likely to assert a gay identity even when engaged primarily in same-sex relations (Cochran and Mays 1999). This pattern of engaging in sex with other men while maintaining a straight masculine identity has been labeled "the down low" (Denizet-Lewis 2003).

Black lesbians are relatively invisible due to their smaller numbers and integration into extended family relationships. The black lesbians in a qualitative study of 530 lesbians and 66 bisexual women were well-educated, middle-class women in their thirties, who first became conscious of their attraction to women at around age fourteen, with first same-sex sexual experience at age nineteen. Their adult relationships have been generally satisfying and close (Mays and Cochran 1999).

Now let us turn to a more general discussion of sexual expression as conceptualized by sex researchers William Masters and Virginia Johnson, who initiated contemporary sex therapy.

Sex as a Pleasure Bond

The convergence of sexual satisfaction with general satisfaction serves to support Masters and Johnson's view of sex as a **pleasure bond** (1976), by which partners commit themselves to expressing their sexual feelings with each other.

In sharing sexual pleasure, partners realize that sex is something partners do with each other, not to or for each other. Each partner participates actively, as

© The Newark Museum / Art Resource, NY

an equal in the sexual union. Further, each partner assumes **sexual responsibility**—that is, responsibility for his or her own sexual response. When this happens, the stage is set for conscious, mutual cooperation. Partners feel freer to express themselves sexually.

Such expression requires a high degree of self-esteem, the willingness to transcend gendered expectations, and the ability to create and maintain an atmosphere of mutual cooperation. We'll look at each of these elements in turn.

Sexual Pleasure and Self-Esteem

Research shows a correlation between sexual satisfaction and self-esteem (Wiederman and Hurst 1998; Larson et al. 1998). High self-esteem is important to pleasurable sex in several ways. First, self-esteem allows a person the freedom to receive pleasure. People with low self-esteem tend to become uncomfortable when offered a favor, a present, or praise. This problem is heightened when the gift is sexual pleasure. People with low self-esteem may turn off their erotic feelings because unconsciously they feel they don't deserve them.

Second, self-esteem allows individuals to acknowledge and accept their own tastes and preferences. This is vital in sexual relationships because there is a great deal of individuality in sexual expression.

Third, self-esteem provides us the freedom to search for new pleasures. As we've seen, some individuals let their sexual relationship grow stale because they do not accept or appreciate their own sexuality and their need to experiment and explore with their partner.

Fourth, high self-esteem lets each of us ask our partner to help satisfy our preferences. Finally, high self-esteem allows us to engage in **pleasuring**: spontaneously doing what feels good at the moment and letting orgasm happen (or not), rather than working to produce it. Masters and Johnson point out that trying too hard may cause sexual problems. They use the term **spectatoring** to describe the practice of emotionally removing oneself from a sexual encounter in order to watch and judge one's productivity, and they state that this practice can be self-inhibiting.

Sexual Pleasure and Gender

Another important element in making sex a pleasure bond is the ability to transcend gender stereotypes. For instance, a man may reject tender sexual advances and activities because he believes he has to be emotionally unfeeling or be the initiator of sexual activity.

Likewise, women may have trouble in receiving or asking for pleasure because they feel uncomfortable or guilty about being assertive. Many women have been culturally conditioned to put their partner's needs first, so heterosexual women may proceed to intercourse before they are sufficiently aroused to reach climax. Then they are less likely to enjoy sex, which can detract from the experience for both partners.

Sex can be more effective as a pleasure bond when the partners appreciate any real gender differences that may exist and transcend restrictive gender stereotypes. To do this, partners must be equal and must communicate in bonding rather than alienating ways (see Chapter 13).

Communication and Cooperation

A third element in sharing sex as a pleasure bond is communication and cooperation. Partners may use conjugal sex as an arena for power struggles, or they may cooperate to enrich their sexual relationship and to nurture each other's sexual self-concept. To create a cooperative sexual atmosphere, partners must be willing to clearly communicate their own sexual needs and to hear and respond to their partner's needs and preferences as well.

When conflicts arise—and they do in any honest sexual relationship—they need to be constructively negotiated. For example, one partner may desire to have sex more frequently than the other does. The couple might agree that the partner who wants sex more often should stop pressing, and the other partner promises to consider what external pressures such as workload might be lessening his or her sexual feelings.

Other couples might have conflicts over whether to engage in oral or anal sex. It is important to communicate about such strong differences. Sometimes, a couple can work out a compromise; in other cases, compromise may be difficult or impossible. Therapists generally agree that no one should be urged to do something that he or she finds abhorrent.

Open communication is important not only in resolving conflicts but also in sharing anxieties or doubts. Sex is a topic that is especially difficult for many people to talk about, yet misunderstanding about sex may cause stress in a relationship. Good sex is not something that just happens when two people are in love. Forming a good sexual relationship is a process that necessarily involves partners in open verbal and nonverbal communication. To have satisfying sex, both partners need to tell each other what pleases them.

Some Principles for Sexual Sharing

Some important principles may be distilled from the previous discussion to serve as guidelines for establishing and maintaining a nurturing, cooperative atmosphere.

Partners should avoid passing judgment on each other's sexual fantasies, needs, desires, or requests. Labeling a partner or communicating nonverbally that something is disgusting or wrong may lower a person's sexual self-esteem and destroy the trust in a relationship. Nor should partners presume to know what the other is thinking or feeling, or what would be good for the other sexually. In a cooperative relationship, each partner accepts the other as the final authority on his or her own feelings, tastes, and preferences.

Another principle is what Masters and Johnson (1976) call the "principle of mutuality." Mutuality implies that "all sexual messages between two people, whether conveyed by words or actions, by tone of voice or touch of fingertips, be exchanged in the spirit of having a common cause." Mutuality means "two people united in an effort to discover what is best for both" (p. 53).

An attitude of mutuality is important because it fills each partner's need to feel secure, to know that any sexual difficulties, failures, or misgivings will not be used against him or her: "Together they succeed or together they fail in the sexual encounter, sharing the responsibility for failure, whether it is reflected in his performance or hers" (pp. 57, 89).

A final principle of sexual sharing is to maintain a **holistic view of sex**—that is, to see sex as an extension of the whole relationship rather than as a purely physical exchange, a separate aspect of marriage. One woman described it this way: "I don't quite understand these references to the sex side of life. It is life. My husband and I are first of all a man and a woman—sexual creatures all through" (quoted in Cuber and Harroff 1965, p. 136).

Deepening the commitment to sharing and cooperation may make sex a growing and continuing pleasure bond. This does not mean that a couple will regularly have great sex by some external standard. It means that each partner chooses to try—and keep on trying—to make sex satisfying for both.

Making the Time for Intimacy

Just as it is important for families to arrange their schedules so that they may spend time together, it's also important for couples to plan time to be alone and intimate (Masters, Johnson, and Kolodny 1994). Planning time for intimacy involves making conscious choices. Boredom with sex after many years in a marriage may be at least partly the consequence of a decision by default.

Therapists suggest that couples might create romantic settings at home or spend a night in a hotel. They can open themselves to new experiences, such as describing their sexual fantasies to each other, reading sex manuals together, or renting an erotic movie. Partners may choose to set aside at least one night a week for themselves alone, without work, movies, television, the DVD player, the computer, another couple's company, or the children. They do not have to have intercourse during these times: They should do only what they feel like doing. But scheduling time alone together does mean mutually agreeing to exclude other preoccupations and devote full attention to each other.

This suggestion may be easier for parents with young children who are put to bed fairly early. A common complaint from parents of older children is that the children stay up later and by the time they are teenagers, the parents no longer have any private evening time together. One woman's solution to this problem:

> Our house shuts down at 9:30 now. That doesn't mean we say "It's your bedtime, kids. You're tired and you need your sleep." It means we say, "Your dad (or your mom) and I need some time alone." The children go to their rooms at 9:30. Help with homework, lunch money, decisions about what they'll wear tomorrow—all those things get taken care of by 9:30 or they don't get taken care of. (Monestero 1990.)

The important thing, these therapists stress, is that partners don't lose touch with either their sexuality or their ability to share it with each other.

We have been talking about human sexual expression as a pleasure bond. It is terribly unfortunate that sexuality can also be associated with disease and death. Indeed, the fact that it is so difficult to make a transition to the next topic points to the multifaceted, even contradictory, nature of contemporary human sexual expression.

Sexual Expression, Family Relations, and HIV/AIDS and Other Sexually Transmitted Diseases

HIV/AIDS has now been known for almost thirty years. The HIV, or "human immunodeficiency virus," which produces AIDS, has existed longer than that, but it was only in 1981 that AIDS was recognized as the cause of a rapidly increasing number of deaths.

An HIV infection eventually progresses to full-blown AIDS. AIDS stands for "acquired immune deficiency syndrome"; it is a viral disease that destroys the immune system. With a lowered resistance to disease, a person with AIDS becomes vulnerable to infections and other diseases that other people easily fight off. "Facts About Families: Who Has HIV/AIDS?" presents some details on the demographics and transmission modes of HIV/AIDS.

Because of its lethal character—over 500,000 deaths in the United States through 2005 (U.S. Centers for Disease Control and Prevention 2006b)—we give most attention in this chapter to HIV/AIDS. But other **sexually transmitted diseases (STDs)**[8] also have the power to significantly affect lives and relationships; around 19 million new cases arise each year (U.S. Centers for Disease Control and Prevention 2006c). These STDs can have powerful effects on health and reproduction; needless to say, they have an impact on sexual relationships. Appendix C describes various STDs and presents information on transmission modes, prevention, and treatment.

A theme of this text is that sociocultural conditions affect people's choices. We examine here the impact of HIV/AIDS as a societal phenomenon that has changed the consequences of decisions about sexual activity.

HIV/AIDS and Heterosexuals

Some heterosexual adults have responded to the threat of AIDS with changed behavior. Sexually active singles may now want to have a longer period of acquaintance

---

[8] The term *sexually transmitted infections (STIs)* is also used and is equivalent to *sexually transmitted diseases (STDs)*.

before initiating sexual contact, hoping to experience greater attraction, security, or commitment before deciding that sex is worth it. Heterosexuals report increased use of condoms and fewer partners than in the past (T. Smith 2006). They may insist on a recent blood test verification of HIV status or, more often, condom use. "Even for many [young adults] . . . who have been on the conservative side in their behavior, AIDS is part of their consciousness. . . . They realize that even if they have been careful in their sexual behavior, their partners may not have been, and that puts them at risk" (Arnett 2004, p. 91).

Some opt for periods of celibacy. At the same time, women, teens, and older Americans, especially, may not perceive their risk. Given the increasing heterosexual transmission of HIV/AIDS, "women should embrace a philosophy of always protecting themselves from HIV" ("Third of New HIV Cases" 2004). Perhaps 20 percent of gay men marry at least once (K. Butler 2006b; J. Gross 2006d). Consequently, some heterosexual women may be regularly exposed to the virus if their husbands are sexually active with men.

HIV/AIDS and Gay Men

Many gay men modified their sexual behavior in the 1980s. Multiple, frequent, and anonymous sexual contacts had been common elements of lifestyle and sexual ideology for many gays (Blumstein and Schwartz 1983). But attitudes and behavior changed enough, at least among men in their thirties and over, to have dramatically reduced the incidence of new cases among gay males for a time.

The decline of deaths thanks to new medications has meant that for many, AIDS has become a chronic disease rather than a death sentence; life expectancy is now twenty-four years post-diagnosis ("Life Expectancy" 2006). As the mood in the gay community has lightened, some gay men have returned to unprotected sex with many and anonymous partners, and we have seen a surge of HIV infections among younger gay men (Altman 2005). Gay activists and public health professionals have expressed concern that drug ads with pictures of relatively hearty gay men convey a misleading message about the difficulties of living with AIDS, a message that may reduce caution and prevention (Fierstein 2003; M. Gross 2006).

HIV/AIDS and Family Crises

Some families will face crises and loss because of AIDS. Telling one's family members that one has HIV/AIDS is a crisis in itself. Due to shame about the disease, some relatives grieve amid a shroud of secrecy, thereby isolating themselves. In addition, HIV/AIDS victims and their families and friends are living with the burden of personal care for friends, lovers, or family members with AIDS.

Some married heterosexuals have lost partners to the disease or are helping infected partners fight health battles. AIDS contracted from a blood transfusion means a prolonged medical battle for the partner, and perhaps children who may be infected; this is less common since blood screening began in 1985. At least that is a tragedy that may be shared. AIDS resulting from drug use frequently occurs in transient relationships, but in marital settings it often indicates a family that has many problems. In cases in which a partner (more often the husband) develops AIDS from sex outside the relationship, the marriage may end. As more senior citizens develop AIDS, grandparents may fear that they will be stigmatized by their grown children and isolated from their grandchildren (Stock 1997).

The burdens of AIDS are not all emotional, nor do they involve only physical care of victims; some are financial. New drug therapies cost thousands of dollars a year. AIDS patients may be unable to work and thus lose health insurance as well as income. (Some government programs now exist to assist with costs.)

HIV/AIDS and Children

Most children with AIDS contracted it from their mothers during pregnancy, at birth, or through breast milk. This form of AIDS transmission has declined dramatically due to voluntary prenatal HIV testing of pregnant women and the subsequent administration of prenatal drug therapies.

Women who have tested positive for HIV/AIDS are not always willing to give up the prospect of motherhood; some are deciding to have children after diagnosis now that the risk of transmission may be drastically reduced by medication (Villarosa 2001). Men with HIV are beginning to hope for parenthood also, with a procedure called "sperm washing" designed to minimize transmission to a female partner (Kolata 2002a).

Children with AIDS have a unique array of treatment requirements and are often in the hospital. Some were abandoned by their parents to hospital care. Others are raised by grandparents or foster parents. A new set of problems has arisen as AIDS babies enter their teens. Clinical professionals report behavioral, emotional, and cognitive problems among some of the AIDS babies who have survived to adolescence. Public health workers are starting to take note of the teens' needs for services (Villarosa 2002b; Dee 2005).

Who Has HIV/AIDS?[a]

Over one million people are living with HIV or full-blown AIDS: 44 percent black, 35 percent white, 19 percent Hispanic, and 1 percent each Asian/Pacific Islander and Native American/Alaska Native. The cumulative total of AIDS cases reported through 2005 is almost a million, with around 40,000 new cases diagnosed each year. There have been over a half million deaths since AIDs was first identified in 1981 (Altman 2005; U.S. Centers for Disease Control and Prevention 2006b, p. 8, Tables 3, 7, 8).

On the positive side, infections are being caught in the early stages, and new treatments have enabled longer lives for those with the virus.[b] On the other hand, the increase in infections suggests a growing sense of complacency among groups at risk of contracting the disease. Estimates are that one-quarter of those with HIV have not been tested and are unaware of their condition (Altman 2005). "Because more effective treatments are available, there seems to be a perception, particularly in the gay community, that HIV is a manageable disease. . . . I think the disease just doesn't have the fear that it once carried" (Dr. Robert Johnson, director of the CDC's HIV and AIDS Prevention Division in O'Connor 2003, p. 28). Also, information efforts do not seem to be reaching minorities.

Age and HIV/AIDS

HIV/AIDS has most affected young and middle-aged adults. As of 2005, around

More AIDS infections are caught in the early stages now, thanks to the wide distribution of information about AIDS prevention and testing.

70 percent of AIDS cases were diagnosed in people in the twenty-five through forty-four age range. The proportion of HIV/AIDS cases among teenagers is small, under 1 percent (U.S. Centers for Disease Control and Prevention 2006b, Table 3), but keep in mind that individuals who are older at diagnosis may have been infected as adolescents. Expanded testing and treatment of HIV-infected pregnant women have lowered the rate of new cases of prenatal transmission to fewer than 1 percent of births to infected women (Villarosa 2001). There were only fifty-eight new cases of AIDS in children

in 2005 (U.S. Centers for Disease Control and Prevention 2006b, Table 3).

We seldom think of AIDS as affecting older individuals, but around 5 percent of cases are found among those age fifty-five through sixty-four. Only 1 percent of AIDS cases are reported for individuals age sixty-five and older, but that is over 14,000 cases among senior citizens (U.S. Centers for Disease Control and Prevention 2006b, Table 3). Currently, there are efforts to create programs to educate older Americans about risks and precautions concerning HIV/AIDS (Villarosa 2003).

HIV/AIDS and other sexually transmitted diseases are more than a medical or a family problem—they are conditions imbued with social meanings and consequences. Politics enters into decisions about policy related to HIV/AIDS—and policy regarding sexuality in general.

The Politics of Sex

One of the most striking changes over the past several decades has been the emergence of sexual and reproductive issues as political controversies. Religious and

Gender and HIV/AIDS

Men accounted for 74 percent of AIDS cases diagnosed in 2005 among adolescents and adults. The dominant source of AIDS among males is having sex with other men (61 percent), with intravenous drug use and heterosexual contacts also significant causes of infection. Cumulatively, 72 percent of AIDS cases among women arose from heterosexual contact and 26 percent from intravenous drug use (U.S. Centers for Disease Control and Prevention 2006b, Table 3).[c]

Race/Ethnicity and HIV/AIDS

Racial and ethnic minorities have been disproportionately affected by HIV/AIDS. As Figure 6.3 indicates, rates of AIDS cases diagnosed in 2005 were highest among non-Hispanic blacks,

with the rate for Hispanics moderately high. American Indians/Alaska Natives, whites, and Asians and Pacific Islanders have the lowest rates of AIDS. In each racial/ethnic category, men have higher rates than women (U.S. Centers for Disease Control and Prevention 2006b, Tables 5a, 5b).

Critical Thinking

Pick one of the above demographic categories—for example, teen women. What ideas can you think of for an HIV/AIDS prevention program for this group? You may want to consult Appendix C, "Sexually Transmitted Diseases," on the website.

a. The term HIV/AIDS is used in general references to this sexually transmitted disease. When speaking about numbers of cases, HIV (the virus that causes AIDS) and AIDS (the active disease)

are often distinguished. Most of those who become infected with the HIV virus will progress to full-blown AIDS.

The incidence (number of new cases) and prevalence (current cases) of HIV infection are only estimates, as there is no population-wide screening program. Many people who may be HIV-positive are not tested, and test results are not always reported consistently. Consequently, most of the data in these sections on the social distribution of HIV/AIDS are based on AIDS cases, as those are more definite in diagnosis and reported more accurately.

b. Initially, many cases of AIDS arose through infection from blood transfusions, but this mode of transmission declined after 1985, when donated blood began to be rigorously screened for HIV. Blood transfusion accounted for less than 1 percent of cases in 2005 (U.S. Centers for Disease Control and Prevention 2006b, Table 6).

c. Infection from woman-to-woman sexual contact is rare (U.S. Centers for Disease Control and Prevention 2007).

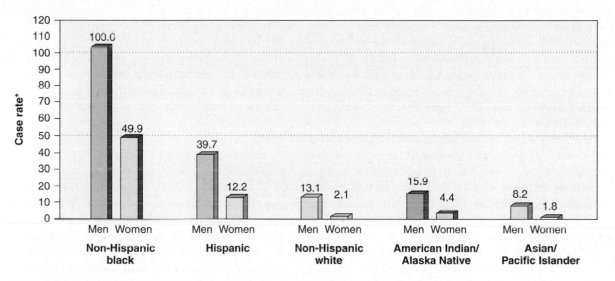

FIGURE 6.3 Estimated rates of AIDS cases reported among adults and adolescents by race/ethnicity, 2005.

* Number of cases per 100,000 in respective racial/ethnic and gender group.

Source: U.S. Centers for Disease Control and Prevention 2006b, Table 5a.

political conservatives and secular and religious individuals and organizations with a more liberal set of values—more open to nonmarital sexuality, for example—confront each other. Adding to the political mix, public health professionals approach policy from a research-based and pragmatic perspective, seeking the

most effective means to achieve sexual and reproductive health goals.

Controversies over AIDS—and over how to educate youth about AIDS and about sex in general—illustrate the conflict between a morally neutral and pragmatic public health policy and a religious fundamentalist moral approach. Other sexuality issues engendering political conflict include abortion and contraception.

Political controversy has influenced both research and education about sexuality in the United States over the last few decades.

Politics and Research

At first, the emergence of AIDS seemed to legitimate sex research and lead to the funding of research on sexual behavior because of the implications for controlling the AIDS epidemic (Christopher and Sprecher 2000). The need for more comprehensive and current data on sexual behavior twice led to efforts to mount federally funded national sample surveys to be conducted by teams of well-respected social scientists. The studies were initially funded, but then Congress canceled a pilot study on the grounds that a sex survey would be too controversial. NORC conducted a much smaller, though national, sample survey without federal funds through the support of grants from private agencies.

A planned survey of 24,000 teens in grades seven to eleven was also canceled ("U.S. Scraps" 1991). Ironically, comparisons with other countries suggest that our society's tendency to deny sexuality at the same time we encourage it sends mixed messages that, among other negative consequences, probably help account for the unusually high rates of teen pregnancy and abortion in the United States (Risman and Schwartz 2002). The climate for the scientific study of sexuality remains hostile enough that "only the brave study sex" (Carey 2004).

The politicization of research has taken other forms. Some reports of research that do not support the government position on an issue have been removed from government websites or changed after initial posting (Lewontin 2004; Simoncelli 2005). For example, a review of many studies which concluded that abortion does *not* cause breast cancer (contradicting the position of the Right to Life Movement) was removed from the National Cancer Institute website. Research on sex education which found that providing information about contraception to teens does *not* increase their sexual activity was removed from the U.S. Centers for Disease Control and Prevention website. The CDC fact sheet on condoms was changed to de-emphasize the protective value of condoms vis-à-vis HIV infection.

Adolescent Sexuality and Sex Education

In the 1980s, then surgeon general C. Everett Koop, himself a fundamentalist Christian and political conservative, was moved by public health concerns to propose explicit education about AIDS to children as young as nine, including the topics of homosexuality, genital intercourse, and condoms (Koop n.d.). A later surgeon general encountered a hostile reception when he released a report calling for a more comprehensive program of sex education than federal policy supported (U.S. Surgeon General 2001; "White House Distances" 2001).

Adolescent Sexual Activity Indeed, adolescents are sexually active; 47 percent of high school students responding to the 2005 Youth Risk Behavior Surveillance (Eaton et al. 2006) have had sexual intercourse. What may surprise you is that teen sex has declined since 1991; in that year, 54 percent of high school youth had had intercourse. Studies suggest that males have changed more than females; a slim majority of high school males (47.9 percent) were virgins in 2005 (Eaton et al. 2006; Risman and Schwartz 2002). The downward trend in adolescent sexual activity (and births) predates the emphasis on "abstinence-only" sex education programs (Dailard 2003; "Improvements" 2006).

Experts attribute the decline to comprehensive sex education and to fear of sexual disease. Some have argued that socio-sexual values have simply become more conservative generally, but that possibility has not been adequately researched (N. Bernstein 2004a; Risman and Schwartz 2002; Santelli et al. 2007). Data from the National Survey of Family Growth (1995 and 2002 waves) indicate that 86 percent of the decline in pregnancy risk is due to improved contraception (regular use, better methods), while only 14 percent is due to delayed sex (Santelli, Lindberg, Finer, and Singh 2007).

Sociologist Frank Furstenberg, who has long researched teen sex, reproduction, and parenthood, as well as the transition to adulthood, believes that young people have observed how difficult it is in today's economy to establish a satisfying life if parenthood comes too early. He thinks that teenagers "getting the picture" might be a key element, as they strive to delay sex and prevent pregnancy to avoid the difficult lives they have seen around them (in N. Bernstein 2004a).

The decline in teen sexual activity has slowed in the twenty-first century, virtually "flat-lining" since 2001 except for declines in current sexual activity of black youth (Brenner et al. 2006; Feijoo 2004; "Improvements" 2006). Moreover, in assessing the decline of teen sexual activity, it is important to note that a lot depends on one's definition of sexual activity. Yes, sexual intercourse is less frequent among adolescents than in the past. It is also true that teens exhibit surprisingly high rates of oral sex: 55 percent of males ages fifteen through nineteen and 54 percent of females engage in oral sex (Mosher, Chandra, and Jones 2005, Tables

Percentage of parents of high school students who say sex education should cover . . .

Topic	Percentage
HIV/AIDS	99%
How to talk with parents about sex and relationship issues*	98
The basics of how babies are made, pregnancy, and birth	97
Waiting to have sexual intercourse until older	96
How to get tested for HIV and other STDs	96
How to deal with the emotional issues and consequences of being sexually active*	96
Waiting to have sexual intercourse until married*	94
How to talk with a girlfriend or boyfriend about "how far to go sexually"*	94
Birth control and methods of preventing pregnancy	93
How to use and where to get contraceptives	85
Abortion*	83
How to put on a condom*	79
That teens can obtain birth control pills . . . without permission from a parent*	73
Homosexuality and sexual orientation*	73

FIGURE 6.4 What parents want sex education to teach their children.

* Questions marked with an asterisk were asked of only half the sample.

Source: Survey of 1,001 parents of children in seventh to twelfth grade sponsored by National Public Radio (NPR)/Kaiser Family Foundation/Kennedy School of Government (2004). The survey was conducted in September/October 2003. The high school parent subsample = 450.

of sexual conduct. "Abstinence-only" programs may mention contraception, if at all, only to cite allegedly high failure rates. Programs are urged to convey to students that nonmarital sex for people *of any age* is likely to have harmful physical and psychological effects (J. Brody 2004; Dailard 2002).

Surveys of parents indicate that they prefer that an "abstinence-plus" sex education program be presented in the schools, one that would include contraception and AIDS prevention as well as promotion of abstinence. As Figure 6.4 indicates, more than 80 percent of parents support teaching about birth control, and 73 percent want sex education to cover sexual orientation (National Pubic Radio [NPR]/Kaiser Family Foundation/Kennedy School of Government 2004). Yet a substantial and growing number of school sex education programs are "abstinence only" as government funding is limited to such programs (Lindberg, Santelli, and Singh 2006).

Research indicates that comprehensive sex education programs (that include contraception) do not lead to any earlier commencement of sexual activity; in fact, research indicates that comprehensive sex education delays the start of sexual activity. "Encouraging abstinence and urging better use of contraception are compatible goals" (Kirby 2001, p. 18). There is as yet no evidence that "abstinence-only" programs are effective in delaying sex or preventing pregnancy ("The Abstinence-Only Delusion" 2007; Begley 2007; J. Brody 2004; "Conclusions Are Reported" 2007; Kirby, Laris, and Rolleri 2006).

Although abstinence-only education has yet to be proven effective in delaying sex, early research found that virginity pledges taken in certain circumstances seemed to delay adolescent sexual activity (Bearman and Brückner 2001). More recent research found that though virginity pledges do delay the initiation of sexual activity, once these teens become sexually active they do so without precautions and have higher rates of pregnancy and STDs than other teens (Altman 2004).

Those results compare adolescents who are still minors. A study based on the National Longitudinal

3, 4). Many adolescents do not consider oral sex to be "sex" so they can still consider themselves virgins. They also seem to be attracted to oral sex because it does not present a risk of pregnancy (true) or of sexually transmitted disease (not true).

Sex Education Current controversy centers on whether sex education should be "abstinence only" or "abstinence plus" (also termed "comprehensive"). Since 1996, the federal government has taken the official position that abstention from sexual relations unless in a monogamous marriage is the only protection against sexually transmitted disease and pregnancy—and that abstinence is the only morally and rationally appropriate principle

Study of Adolescent Health, which compared young adults (nineteen through twenty-five) who had made a virginity pledge and those who had not, found that contraceptive use did not differ at this later point. Moreover, there seem to be persistent differences in sexual activity in the two groups, with pledgers having lower rates. However, both groups had high rates of intercourse (89.7 percent and 75 percent, respectively) and other sexual activity. In other words, "by the time they become young adults, some 81 percent of pledgers have engaged in some type of sexual activity" (Rector and Johnson 2005, p. 13).

Sex education needs to take into account the teen propensity to engage in oral sex and to consider it risk-free despite high rates of STDs among youth (Halpern-Felsher et al. 2005). Moreover, the first experience for a small proportion of teens—7 percent—is forced sex (Eaton et al. 2006). Some others' experiences are ambiguous as to wantedness (Houts 2005).

Sex education programs may emphasize peer pressure, troubled families and neighborhoods, or hormonal processes and rarely consider the broad array of teen motivations for sexual activity. It seems that both adolescent males and females seek sex because they expect it to meet needs for intimacy, sexual pleasure, and social status (Ott et al. 2006). These issues need to be taken into account in sex education programs. Long-time sex education researcher Douglas Kirby and his colleagues have identified some programs that seem effective in discouraging early sexual activity and sexual risks (Kirby, Laris, and Rolleri 2006).

Sexual Responsibility

People today are making decisions about sex in a climate characterized by political conflict over sexual issues. Premarital and other nonmarital sex, homosexuality, abortion, and contraception represent political issues as well as personal choices. Public and private communication must rise to new levels. The AIDS epidemic has brought the importance of sexual responsibility to our attention in a dramatic way.

Making knowledgeable choices is a must. Because there are various standards today concerning sex, each individual must determine what sexual standard he or she values, which is not always easy. Today's adults may be exposed to several different standards throughout the course of their lives. Even when people feel they have clear values, applications to particular situations may be difficult. People who believe in the standard of sexual permissiveness with affection, for example, must

Intimacy and sexuality require communication—physical as well as verbal—from both partners. Sexuality has become more expressive and less patriarchal in the United States, and each generation finds itself reevaluating sexual assumptions, behaviors, and standards.

determine when a particular relationship is affectionate enough.

Making these choices and feeling comfortable with them requires recognizing and respecting your own values, instead of just being influenced by others when in a sexual situation. Anxiety may accompany the choice to develop a sexual relationship, and there is considerable potential for misunderstanding between partners. This section addresses some principles of sexual responsibility that may serve as guidelines for sexual decision making.

One obvious responsibility concerns the possibility of pregnancy. Partners should plan responsibly whether, when, and how they will conceive children and then use effective birth control methods accordingly.

A second responsibility concerns the possibility of contracting sexually transmitted diseases (STDs) or transmitting them to someone else. Individuals should be aware of the facts concerning HIV/AIDS and other STDs. They need to assume responsibility for protecting themselves and their partners. They need to know how to recognize the symptoms of an STD and what to do if they get one (see Appendix C).

A third responsibility concerns communicating with partners or potential sexual partners. In one study, 35 percent of men reported lying to a partner in order to have sex with her, and 60 percent of women thought they had been lied to. Such lies involved overstating love and caring, denying other simultaneous relationships, and reporting fewer sex partners than was true (Goleman 1988). Emotional harm from misrepresentation may be more serious than rejection due to a genuine change of heart.

People should be honest with partners about their motives for wanting to have sexual relations with them. As we've seen in this chapter, sex may mean many different things to different people. A sexual encounter may mean love and intimacy to one partner and be a source of achievement or relaxation to the other. Honesty lessens the potential for misunderstanding and hurt between partners. People should treat each other as people rather than things—as people with needs and feelings.

A fourth responsibility is to oneself. In expressing sexuality today, each of us must make decisions according to our own values. A person may choose to follow values held on the basis of religious commitment or put forth by ethicists or by psychologists or counselors. People's values change over the course of their lives, and what's right at one time may not appear so later. Despite the confusion caused both by internal changes as our personalities develop and by the social changes going on around us, it is important for individuals to make thoughtful decisions about sexual relationships.

Sex has an enormous potential for good in bringing pleasure and intensifying couple intimacy. Having cautioned about risk and responsibility, let's close with the voice of one of sociology's founders, writing in the late nineteenth century: "[T]he sex act . . . produces . . . the most intimate communion that can exist between two conscious beings" (Emile Durkheim in "L'Education sexuelle" 1911).

Summary

- Social attitudes and values play an important role in the forms of sexual expression that people find comfortable and enjoyable.

- Despite decades of conjecture and research, it is still unclear just how sexual orientation develops and whether it is genetic or socially shaped. Recent decades have witnessed increased acceptance of gay, lesbian, bisexual, and transgender (GLBT) individuals, though some disapproval, discrimination, and hostility remain.

- Whatever one's sexual orientation, sexual expression is negotiated amid cultural messages about what is sexually permissible or desirable. In the United States, these cultural messages have moved from patriarchal sex, based on male dominance and on reproduction as its principal purpose, to a message that encourages sexual expressiveness in myriad ways for both genders equally.

- Four standards of nonmarital sex are: abstinence, permissiveness with affection, permissiveness without affection, and the double standard—the latter diminished since the 1960s, but still alive. Extramarital sex is not approved, but it does occur and represents a challenge to marital trust.

- Marital sex changes throughout the life course. Young spouses have sex more often than do older mates. Although the frequency of sexual intercourse declines over time and the length of a marriage, some 27 percent of married people over age seventy-four are sexually active.

- Making sex a pleasure bond, whether a couple is married or not, involves cooperation in a nurturing, caring relationship. To fully cooperate sexually, partners need to develop high self-esteem, to break free from restrictive gendered stereotypes, and to communicate openly.

- HIV/AIDS has had an impact on relationships, marriages, and families.

- Sexuality, sexual expression, and sex education are public issues at present, and different segments of American society have divergent views.

- Whatever the philosophical or religious grounding of one's perspective on sexuality, there are certain guidelines for personal sexual responsibility that we should all heed.

Questions for Review and Reflection

1. Give some examples to illustrate changes in sexual behavior and social attitudes about sex. What might change in the future?

2. Do you think that sex is changing from "his and hers" to "theirs"? What do you see as some difficulties in making this transition?

3. Discuss the principles for sexual sharing suggested in this chapter. Are there any you would add or sub-

tract? What about the premises of sexual responsibility? Do you agree with the list?

4. How do you think HIV/AIDS affects sex and sex relationships—or does it?

5. **Policy Question.** What role, if any, should government play regarding sex education, research and information on sex, and sexual regulation?

Key Terms

abstinence 131
asexual 124
asexuality 123
bisexual 123
cyberadultery 134
double standard 132
expressive sexuality 127
friends with benefits 132
gay 124
GLBT 124
habituation 138
habituation hypothesis 134
heterosexism 128
heterosexual 123
HIV/AIDS 142
holistic view of sex 141
homophobia 129

homosexual 123
hooking up 132
interactionist perspective on human sexuality 126
interpersonal exchange model of sexual satisfaction 125
lesbian 124
patriarchal sexuality 126
permissiveness with affection 131
permissiveness without affection 131
pleasure bond 140
pleasuring 141
sexual orientation 123
sexual responsibility 140
sexual script 126
sexually transmitted diseases (STDs) 142
spectatoring 141

Online Resources

Companion Website for This Book

www.thomsonedu.com/sociology/lamanna

Visit the book companion website, where you will find flash cards, practice quizzes, Internet links, suggested readings, InfoTrac College Edition exercises, and more to help you study.

ThomsonNOW™ for Marriage and Family

Spend time on what you need to master rather than on information you already have learned. Take a pre-test for this chapter, and ThomsonNOW will generate a personalized study plan based on your results. The study plan will identify the topics you need to review and direct you to online resources such as videos, narrated learning modules, and interactive activities to help you master those topics. You can then take a post-test to help you determine the concepts you have mastered and what you will still need to work on. Try it out! Go to **www.thomsonedu.com/login** to sign in with an access code or to purchase access to this product.

Marriage: From Social Institution to Private Relationship

© Royalty-Free/Digital Vision/PictureQuest

Marital Status: The Changing Picture

Facts about Families: Marital Status—The Increasing Proportion of Unmarrieds

The Time-Honored Marriage Premise: Permanence and Sexual Exclusivity

Expectations of Permanence

Expectations of Sexual Exclusivity

Issues for Thought: Three Very Different Subcultures with Norms Contrary to Sexual Exclusivity

From "Yoke Mates" to "Soul Mates"— A Changing Marriage Premise

Weakened Kinship Authority

Finding One's Own Marriage Partner

Love—and Marriage

My Family: An Asian Indian–American Student's Essay on Arranged Marriages

Deinstitutionalized Marriage

Institutional Marriage

Companionate Marriage

Individualized Marriage

Individualized Marriage and the Pluralistic Family—*Decline* or Inevitable *Change?*

Deinstitutionalized Marriage—Examining the Consequences

Focus on Children: Child Outcomes and Marital Status. Does Marriage Matter?

A Closer Look at Family Diversity: African Americans and "Jumping the Broom"

Working Toward a Family "Turnaround"— The Policy Debate

Policies from the Family Decline Perspective

Policies from the Family Change Perspective

Happiness and Life Satisfaction: How Does Marriage Matter?

About 90 percent of American adults today are, have been, or will be married for at least part of their lives (Bergman 2006a). Consistently surveys show married people to be happier and healthier than unmarrieds. Nevertheless, according to a 2006 Gallup poll, fewer than two-thirds of American adults under age fifty think that it's very important for a committed couple to marry—even when they plan to spend the rest of their lives together (Saad 2006b). That's a major change from fifty or sixty years ago when, for the vast majority of committed (heterosexual) partners, marriage seemed the only option. However, although the situation is much less clear-cut than two or three decades ago, for now marriage remains the most socially acceptable—and stable—gateway to family life.

In this chapter and the one that follows we explore marriage as a changing institution, along with alternatives to marriage. This chapter describes what distinguishes marriage from other relationships, then examines the changing nature of marriage. Chapter 8 explores alternatives to marriage. Chapter 9 looks at married couples' relationships.

Here we'll see that getting married announces a personal life-course decision to one's relatives, to the community, and, yes, to the state. Despite wide variations, marriages today have an important element in common: the commitment that partners make publicly—to each other and to the institution of marriage itself (Cherlin 2004; Goode 2007 [1982]). Put another way, getting married—as opposed to "living together," for example—is not only a private relationship but also a publicly proclaimed commitment. We'll further explore research on the benefits of marriage for adults and children, and examine government initiatives to strengthen marriage. We begin by looking at marital status in the United States today.

Marital Status: The Changing Picture

Do you have friends who are "living together"? Do you know a cohabiting couple who is raising children? Maybe you know someone who says that she or he is "happily divorced." Do you know married couples who don't have children, either because they're putting it off or they don't want children at all? If you're in your twenties or thirties, you may have trouble believing that not long ago these situations were far from ordinary. However, marriage is different now than it was in the days of our parents and grandparents. Figure 7.1 shows

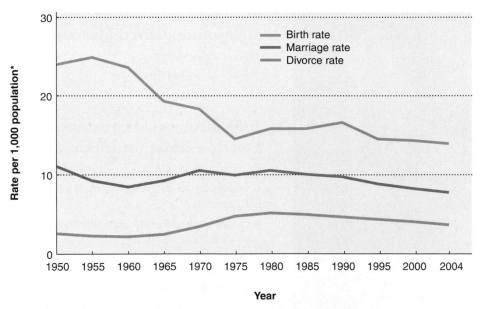

Figure 7.1 U.S. Marriage, Divorce, and Birth Rates, 1950 to 2004.
Sources: U.S. Census Bureau 2007a, Table 72; Hamilton et al. 2005; Munson and Sutton 2006.

the marriage, divorce, and birth rates in the United States from 1950 to 2004. As you can see from that figure:

1. The marriage rate has generally declined—from 11.1 marriages (i.e., weddings) per 1,000 population in 1950 to just 7.8 in 2004.

2. The divorce rate is higher today than in 1950 when there were 2.6 divorces per 1,000 population. In 2004, that figure was 3.7. With ups and downs, the U.S. divorce rate had climbed since the nineteenth century. In the 1920s, the divorce rate accelerated somewhat, and by the mid-1970s divorces reached an all-time high. Although the rate has declined since then, it remains higher than it was sixty years ago.

3. The birth rate has steadily declined since 1950—from 24.1 births per 1,000 population in 1950 to 14.0 in 2004.[1]

These three indicators—marriage, divorce, and birth rates—present a changing picture of marriage over the past sixty years. Today fewer than two-thirds (59 percent) of U.S. adults are currently married (U.S. Census Bureau 2007a, Table 54)—a proportion that has been slowly declining over the past several decades. Although this situation results partly from a continuing trend of generally rising divorce rates from the beginning of the twentieth century, it also marks a fairly dramatic change from just a few decades ago (Coontz 1992, 2005b). Throughout the first half of the twentieth century, the trend was for more and more people to marry and at increasingly younger ages.[2] Moreover,

Marking a couple's commitment, weddings are public events because the community has a stake in marriage as a social institution. Publicly proclaiming commitment to the marriage premise helps to enforce a couple's mutual trust in the permanence of their union.

© Royalty-Free Image Source, London

about 80 percent of those unions lasted until the children left home (Scanzoni 1972). In the 1960s that trend reversed, and since that time the tendency has been for smaller and smaller proportions of Americans to be married. "Facts About Families: Marital Status—The Increasing Proportion of Unmarrieds" further explores marital status in the United States today.

One reason for these changes—perhaps seeming ironic at first glance—is that we increasingly expect to find love in marriage. How would expecting to find love in marriage be associated with fewer of us being married? The following sections answer this question. To begin, we examine the time-honored marriage premise, with its expectations for permanence and sexual exclusivity.

---

[1] Rates per 1,000 population are not the ideal way to present these data, because population characteristics, such as the fact that the U.S. population has gotten older, are not taken into account. However, rates per 1,000 population are the only data available for presenting this long-term, historical comparison.

[2] For men, median age at first marriage in 1890—the year when the government first began to calculate and report this statistic—was 26.1. For both women and men, median ages at first marriage fell from 1890 until 1960, when they began to rise again. Around 1950, family sociologists described a standard pattern of marriage at about age twenty for women and twenty-two for men (Aldous 1978).

Marital Status—The Increasing Proportion of Unmarrieds

The proportion of unmarrieds over age seventeen climbed from 28 percent of the total population in 1970 to 41 percent in 2005 (U.S. Census Bureau 2007a, Table 54). Figure 7.2 compares marital status proportions for non-Hispanic white, Hispanic, African American, and Asian women and men. As you can see in Figure 7.2, Asian Americans are most likely to be married and least likely to be divorced. African Americans are most likely to be never-married and least likely to be married. The percentage for Hispanics falls somewhere between that for Asians and African Americans.

African Americans are slightly more likely than non-Hispanic whites to be divorced; the proportion divorced is lower among Hispanics, an indication of their strong cultural commitment to lifelong marriage, among other possible reasons (Oropesa, Lichter, and Anderson 1994). The fact that Hispanics are less likely to be widowed reflects the fact that, as a category, they are younger, on average, than either non-Hispanic whites or African Americans.

The Never-Married There is a growing tendency for young adults to postpone marriage until they are older. By 2005, the median age at first marriage for both men and women had risen, to 25.8 for women and 27.1 for men (Bergman 2006a). These figures are as high as any ever recorded.

As a consequence of postponing marriage, the number of singles in their twenties has risen dramatically. In 1970, 36 percent of women age twenty through twenty-four were never-married; by 2005, that figure had risen to 75 percent. The ranks of never-married men age twenty through twenty-four have increased from 55 percent in 1970 to 86 percent in 2005 (Saluter and Lugaila 1998; U.S. Census Bureau 2007a, Table 55).

This proportion of unmarrieds is striking when compared with the 1950s, but not so unusual in a broader time frame. That is, the percentage of never-married men and women age twenty through twenty-four today is comparable to the proportion of young adults never married at the turn of the twentieth century (Arnett 2004).

The Divorced The growing divorce rate has contributed to the increased number of singles. In 2005, 8.8 percent of men and 11.5 percent of women age eighteen and over were divorced. These proportions show a sharp increase from 1980, when 3.9 percent of adult men and 6 percent of adult women were divorced (U.S. Census Bureau 2000, Table 53; U.S. Census Bureau 2007a, Table 54). Although the divorce rate is no longer rising, it is stable at a high level, and the divorced will continue to be a substantial component of the unmarried population. Chapter 16 addresses divorce.

The Widowed Unlike the other unmarried categories, the proportion of widowed women and men has remained about the same since 1980—between 2 and 3 percent for men, and between 10 and 12 percent for women (U.S. Census Bureau 2007a, Table 54). Death rates declined throughout the twentieth century, reducing the chances of widowhood for the young and middle-aged—although the September 11, 2001, attack on New York City's Twin Towers and the resulting wars in Afghanistan and Iraq remind us that the widowed can be young as well. Meanwhile, the proportion of older people in the population has increased, and an older person has a greater risk of losing a spouse. Furthermore, widows (though not widowers) find it difficult to remarry, due to the significantly higher number of older women than older men, a situation discussed in Chapter 18.

Cohabitors, more fully explored in Chapter 8, may be never married, divorced, or widowed.

Critical Thinking

How do you think the growing number of unmarrieds has affected American society in general and marriage in particular? What changes in cultural attitudes have helped to cause the high proportion of unmarrieds today? What structural factors have helped to cause the high proportion of unmarrieds?

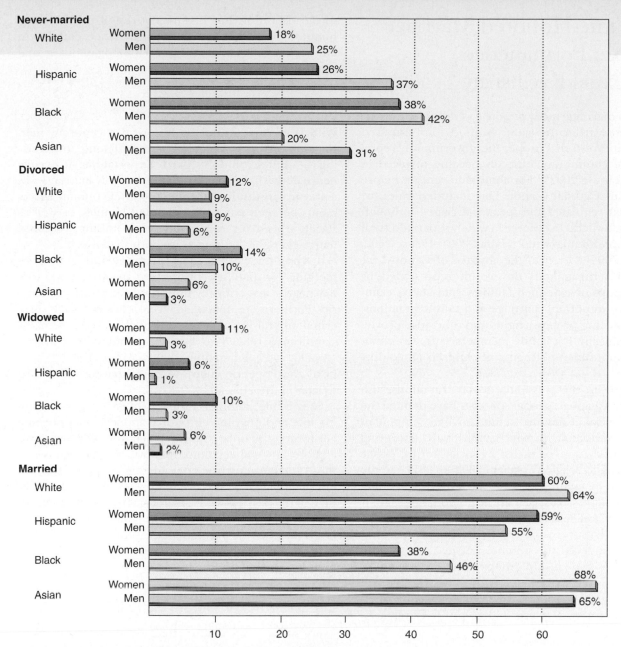

Never-married

White — Women 18%
White — Men 25%

Hispanic — Women 26%
Hispanic — Men 37%

Black — Women 38%
Black — Men 42%

Asian — Women 20%
Asian — Men 31%

Divorced

White — Women 12%
White — Men 9%

Hispanic — Women 9%
Hispanic — Men 6%

Black — Women 14%
Black — Men 10%

Asian — Women 6%
Asian — Men 3%

Widowed

White — Women 11%
White — Men 3%

Hispanic — Women 6%
Hispanic — Men 1%

Black — Women 10%
Black — Men 3%

Asian — Women 6%
Asian — Men 2%

Married

White — Women 60%
White — Men 64%

Hispanic — Women 59%
Hispanic — Men 55%

Black — Women 38%
Black — Men 46%

Asian — Women 68%
Asian — Men 65%

NOTE: Hispanics can be of any race. Unmarried cohabitors can be never-married, divorced, or widowed.

Figure 7.2 Marital Status of the U.S. Population, age 18 and over, 2004, by race/ethnicity and age.

Source: U.S. Census Bureau 2007a, Table 54.

The Time-Honored Marriage Premise: Permanence and Sexual Exclusivity

Why does a marriage today require a wedding, witnesses, and a license from the state? Around four hundred years ago in Western Europe, the government, representing the community, officially became involved in marriage (House 2002). For about one century before that, Roman Catholic Canon Law included rules, or canons, that regulated European marriage—although the canons, difficult to enforce in widely separated rural villages, were often ignored (Halsall 2001; House 2002; Therborn 2004).[3] Even in the absence of Canon Law, communities throughout the world, represented by kinship groups or extended families, had always claim stake in two important marriage and family functions: (1) guaranteeing property rights and otherwise providing economically for family members, and (2) assuring the responsible upbringing of children (Ingoldsby 2006a).

Partly due to these essential social functions, also discussed in Chapter 2, social scientists have defined the family as a **social institution**—a fundamental component of social organization in which individuals, occupying defined statuses, are "regulated by social norms, public opinion, law and religion" (Amato 2004, p. 961).[4] In the vast majority of cultures around the world, a wedding marked a couple's passage into institutionalized family roles, usually well monitored by in-laws and extended kin.

Marriage marked the joining, not just of two individuals, but of two kinship groups (Sherif-Trask 2003). From the couple's perspective, marriage had much to do with "getting good in-laws and increasing one's family labor force" (Coontz 2005b, p. 6). Family as a social institution has historically rested on the time-honored **marriage premise** of permanence, coupled in our society with expectations for monogamous sexual exclusivity.

Expectations of Permanence

With few cross-cultural or historical exceptions, marriages have been expected to be lifelong undertakings—"until death do us part." **Expectations of permanence** derive from the fact that historically marriage was a practical institution (Coontz 2005b). Economic agreements between partners' extended families, as well as society's need for responsible child raising, required marriages to be "so long as we both shall live."

In the United States today, marriage seldom involves merging two families' properties. In other ways, too, marriage is less critically important for economic security. Furthermore, marriage today is less decisively associated with raising children, although marriage remains significantly related to better outcomes for children (Amato 2005; Furstenberg 2003; Waite 1995; Whitehead and Popenoe 2006)—a point that we will return to later in this chapter.

Meanwhile, another function of marriage—providing love and ongoing emotional support—has become key for most people (Cherlin 2004; Coontz 2005b). We explore how expectations for love in marriage affect those for permanence later in this chapter. Here we note that marriage is considerably less permanent now than in the past. However, marriage in the United States today, more than any other non-blood relationship, holds the hope for permanence. At this point, we'll turn to the second component of the time-honored marriage premise—sexual exclusivity.

Expectations of Sexual Exclusivity

Every society and culture that we know of has exercised control over sexual behavior. Put another way, sexual activity has virtually never been allowed simply on impulse or at random. Meanwhile, an amazing array of permissible sexual arrangements has been found by anthropologists. **Polygamy** (having more than one spouse) is culturally accepted in many parts of the world.[5] However, marriage in the United States legally requires monogamy, along with **expectations of sexual exclusivity**, in which spouses promise to have sexual

---

[3] The Netherlands first enacted a civil marriage law in 1590 (Gomes 2004). England passed its first Marriage Act in 1653 but did not require a legal marriage license until 1754 (House 2002). Shortly after Europeans established colonies in the United States, they enacted rules for marriage similar to those that they had known in Europe (Cott 2000). In the four hundred years since then, our federal and state governments have generated a massive number of marriage-related laws and court decisions. For instance, polygamy has been illegal in the United States since 1878, and due to laws enacted at the turn of the twentieth century, unmarried cohabitation is still illegal in some states, although the laws are seldom enforced (Hartsoe 2005). Also, before issuing a marriage license, some states require blood tests for various communicable diseases. Many states have waiting periods, ranging from seventy-two hours to six days, between the license application date and the wedding ("Chart: State Marriage License" 2006).

[4] Social scientists typically point to five major social institutions: family, religion, government or politics, the economy, and education.

[5] Polygamy can be divided into two types. **Polygyny**, a form of polygamy whereby a man can have multiple wives, "is a marriage form found in more places and at more times than any other" (Coontz 2005b, p. 10). However, polygyny is not always that frequent, because many men cannot afford multiple wives. Polyandry is rare (Stephens 1963).

Although a very substantial majority of Americans value monogamy as a cultural standard, there are subcultural exceptions. This box looks at three of these subcultural exceptions, each one very different from the others—polygamy, polyamory, and swinging.

Polygamy

Polygamy has been illegal in the United States since 1878, when the U.S. Supreme Court ruled that freedom to practice the Mormon religion did not extend to having multiple wives (*Reynolds v. United States* 1878). Although a 2006 Gallup poll found that one-quarter of Americans think that most Mormons endorse polygamy (Carroll 2006), this is not the case. The Church of Jesus Christ of Latter-day Saints (LDS) no longer permits polygamy. Nevertheless, there are dissident Mormons (not recognized as LDS by the mainstream church) who follow the traditional teachings and take multiple wives (Woodward 2001, p. 50). Some multiple wives have argued that polygyny is a feminist arrangement because the sharing of domestic responsibilities benefits working women (Johnson 1991; Joseph 1991). Civil libertarians argue that the Supreme Court should rescind its *Reynolds* decision on the grounds that the right to privacy permits this choice of domestic lifestyle as much as any other (Slark 2004).

Polyamory

Polyamory means "many loves" and refers to marriages in which one or both spouses retain the option to sexually love others in addition to their spouse (Polyamory Society n.d.).

Deriving their philosophy from the sexually open marriage movement, which received considerable publicity in the late 1960s and 1970s, polyamorous spouses agree that each may have openly

acknowledged sexual relationships with others while keeping the marriage relationship primary. Unlike in swinging, outside relationships can be emotional as well as sexual. Couples usually establish limits on the degree of sexual and/or emotional involvement of the outside relationship, along with ground rules concerning honesty and what details to tell each other (Macklin 1987, p. 335; Rubin 2001). "Polyamorists are more committed to emotional fulfillment and family building than recreational swingers" (Rubin 2001, p. 721).

Some polyamorous couples are raising children. The Polyamory Society's Children Educational Branch offers advice for polyamorous parents and maintains a PolyFamily scholarship fund, as well as the Internet-based "PolyKids Zine,"and "PolyTeens Zine," both designed to present "uplifting PolyFamily stories and lessons about PolyFamily ethical living" (Polyamory Society n.d.). Like polygamy, polyamory has received some media attention in the last several years, and polyamorists are working toward greater social acceptance. Some polyamorists want to establish legally sanctioned group marriages and have begun to organize in that direction (Anderlini-D'Onofrio 2004). Conservative groups, such as the Institute for American Values, see such moves as evidence of an emergent "radical sensibility" that threatens American values and harms children (Marquardt n.d., p. 30; Kurtz 2006).

Swinging

Swinging is a marriage arrangement in which couples exchange partners in order to engage in purely recreational sex. Swinging gained media and research attention as one of several "alternative lifestyles" in the late 1960s and early 1970s (Rubin 2001). At that time it was estimated that about 2 percent of adults

in the United States had participated in swinging at least once (Gilmartin 1977).

Although little research has been done on swinging in the past few decades, "lifestyle practitioners," as some swingers now prefer to be called, still exist as a minority subculture. It has been estimated that there are now about 3 million married swingers in the United States, an increase of about one million since 1990. Some of this growth is probably due to the Internet, which helps to link potential swingers (Rubin 2001).

Interestingly, as a category, swingers tend to be middle-aged, middle-class, and more socially and politically conservative than one might expect (Jenks 1998; Rubin 2001). Swingers emphasize the lifestyle's positive effects—variety, for example. Former swingers who have given up the lifestyle point to problems with jealousy, guilt, competing emotional attachments, and fear of being discovered by other family members, friends, or neighbors (Macklin 1987).

Advocacy of swinging is largely a product of the pre-AIDS era. Today, a couple considering a sexually nonexclusive marriage must take into account not only personal values and relationship management challenges but also the increased risk of being infected with HIV/AIDS. However, condoms are typically available at swing clubs, and "the fear of disease has apparently not inhibited the recent growth of swinging" (Rubin 2001, p. 723).

Critical Thinking

What do you think about these exceptions to monogamy? Do you see them as threatening to American values? If so, why? If not, why not? Does one or more of them seem reasonable to you while others do not? If so, why? If not, why not?

relations only with each other. (There are exceptions to our cultural expectation for monogamy, however, and three of these exceptions are touched on in "Issues for Thought: Three Very Different Subcultures with Norms Contrary to Sexual Exclusivity.")

In Europe, requirements for women's sexual exclusivity emerged in order to maintain the patriarchal line of descent; the bride's wedding ring symbolized this expectation. The Judeo-Christian tradition eventually extended expectations of sexual exclusivity to include not only wives but also husbands. Over the last century, as "the self-disclosure involved in sexuality [came to] symbolize the love relationship," couples began to see sexual exclusivity as a mark of romantic commitment (Reiss 1986, p. 56).

Today expectations of sexual exclusivity have broadened from the purely physical to include expectations of emotional centrality, or putting one's partner first. Indeed, some marriage counselors now speak of "emotional affairs" (Herring 2005). With well over 90 percent of us believing an affair is morally wrong, Americans are less accepting of extramarital sex than are people in many monogamous societies. (Nevertheless, although the vast majority of Americans say that they disapprove of extramarital sex [Gallup 2003], in practice the picture is somewhat different. Sexual infidelity is explored in Chapter 6.)

To summarize, the marriage premise has changed somewhat over the past century. Expectations for permanence have diminished while those for sexual exclusivity have been extended to include not just physical sex but also emotional centrality. The following section explores how these changes came about.

From "Yoke Mates" to "Soul Mates"—A Changing Marriage Premise

Chapter 1 points to an individualist orientation in our society. In eighteenth-century Europe, **individualism** emerged as a way to think about ourselves. No longer were we necessarily governed by rules of community. Societies changed from **communal**, or **collectivist**, to **individualistic**. In individualistic societies, one's own self-actualization and interests are a valid concern. In collectivist societies, people identify with and conform to the expectations of their extended kin. Western societies are characterized as individualistic, and individualism is positively associated with valuing romantic love (Dion and Dion 1991; Goode 2007 [1982]). (By *Western* we mean the culture that developed in Western

Europe and now characterizes that region and Canada, the United States, Australia, New Zealand, and other societies.)

The Industrial Revolution and its opportunities for paid work outside the home, particularly in the growing cities and independent of one's kinship group, gave people opportunities for jobs and lives separate from the family. In Europe and the North American colonies, people increasingly entertained thoughts of equality, independence, and even the radically new idea that individuals had a birthright to "the pursuit of happiness" (Coontz 2005b). These ideas were manifested in dramatically unprecedented political events of the late 1700s, such as the U.S. Declaration of Independence and the French Revolution.

The emergent individualistic orientation meant a generally diminished obedience to group authority, because people increasingly saw themselves as separate individuals, rather than as intrinsic members of a group or collective. Individuals began to expect self-fulfillment and satisfaction, personal achievement, and happiness. With regard to marriage, an emergent individualist orientation resulted in three interrelated developments:

1. The authority of kin and extended family weakened.

2. Individuals began to find their own marriage partners.

3. Romantic love came to be associated with marriage.

Weakened Kinship Authority

Kin, or **extended family**, include parents and other relatives, such as in-laws, grandparents, aunts and uncles, and cousins. Some groups, such as Italian Americans, African Americans, Hispanics, and gay male and lesbian families, also have "fictive" or "virtual" kin—friends who are so close that they are hardly distinguished from actual relatives (Furstenberg 2005; Sarkisian, Gerena, and Gerstel 2006). In collectivist, or communal, cultures, kin have exercised considerable authority over a married couple. For instance, in traditional African societies, a mother-in-law may have more to say about how many children her daughter-in-law should bear than does the daughter-in-law herself (Caldwell 1982).

In Westernized societies, however, kinship authority is weaker. By the 1940s in the United States, at least among white, middle-class Americans, the husband–wife dyad was expected to take precedence over other family relationships. Sociologist Talcott Parsons noted that the American kinship system was not based on extended family ties (1943). Instead, he saw U.S. kin-

The Dinner Quilt, *Faith Ringgold, 1986.*

However, like the Italians that Gans (1982 [1962]) studied in the 1960s, many Mexican Americans and other Hispanics live in comparatively large, reciprocally supportive kinship networks (Sarkisian, Gerena, and Gerstel 2006; Lugo Steidel and Contreras 2003). For example, many Puerto Rican families have lived in "ethnically specific enclaves" and may rely more on extended kin than on conjugal ties (Wilkinson 1993). Recent Asian immigrants are also likely to emphasize extended kin ties over the marital relationship (Glick, Bean, and Van Hook 1997). Among Chinese and Japanese Americans, expectations of *hsiao* require that an adult child, especially a son, provide aid and affection to parents even when this might conflict with marital obligations (Lin and Liu 1993).

We can sometimes get a glimpse of mainstream American individualism through the eyes of fairly recent immigrants from more collectivist societies. For instance, here a Vietnamese refugee describes his reaction to U.S. housing patterns, which reflect nuclear, rather than extended-family, norms:

> Before I left Vietnam, three generations lived together in the same group. My mom, my family including wife and seven children, my elder brother, his wife and three children, my little brother and two sisters—we live in a big house. So when we came here we are thinking of being united in one place. But there is no way. However, we try to live as close as possible. (quoted in Gold 1993, p. 303)

American housing architecture is similarly discouraging to many Muslim families—from India, Pakistan, or Bangladesh, for example—who would prefer to live in extended-family households (Nanji 1993).

All this is not to say that extended-family members are irrelevant to non-Hispanic white families in the United States. Nuclear families maintain significant emotional and practical ties with extended kin and parents-in-law (Lee, Spitze, and Logan 2003). A qualitative study with a sample that was 95 percent white showed that uncles often mentor nephews or nieces (Milardo 2005). Extensive data from the Longitudinal Study of Generations show that young adults today highly value their parents and extended families (Bengston, Biblarz, and Roberts 2007). However, as individuals and couples increasingly become more urban—and more geographically mobile—the power of kin to exercise social control over

ship as comprised of "interlocking conjugal families" in which married people are members of both their **family of orientation** (the family they grew up in) and their **family of procreation** (the one formed by marrying and having children). Parsons viewed the husband–wife bond and the resulting family of procreation as the most meaningful "inner circle" of Americans' kin relations, surrounded by decreasingly important outer circles. However, Parsons pointed out that his model mainly characterized the American middle class. Recent immigrants and lower socioeconomic classes, as well as upper-class families, still relied on meaningful ties to their extended kin.

Although the situation is changing, the extended family (as opposed to the married couple or nuclear family) has been the basic family unit in the majority of non-European countries (Ingoldsby and Smith 2006). In the United States, extended families continue to be important for various European ethnic families, such as Italians, and for Native Americans, blacks, Hispanics, and Asian Americans, as well as other immigrant families.

Norms about extended-family ties derive both from cultural influences and from economic or other practical circumstances (Hamon and Ingoldsby 2003). Immigrants from many less-developed nations work in the United States and send money to extended kin in their home countries (Ha 2006). Among Hispanics, *la familia* ("the family") means the extended as well as the nuclear family. More and more Hispanics today value the primacy of the conjugal bond (Hirstch 2003).

family members declines. If an individualist orientation has weakened kinship authority, it has also led to the desire to find one's own spouse.

Finding One's Own Marriage Partner

Arranged marriage has characterized collectivist societies (Hamon and Ingoldsby 2003; Sherif-Trask 2003). Because a marriage joined extended families, selecting a suitable mate was a "huge responsibility" not to be left to the young people themselves (Tepperman and Wilson 1993, p. 73). Although arranged marriage is still practiced, the custom is waning with globalization. But arranged marriage was observed throughout most of the world into the twentieth century—and in Western Europe well into the eighteenth century. As pointed out in "My Family: An Asian Indian–American Student's Essay on Arranged Marriages," we can still find arranged marriages in many parts of the less-industrialized world today.

Analyzing arranged marriage in contemporary Bangladesh, sociologist Ashraf Uddin Ahmed notes that an individual's finding of his or her own spouse "is thought to be disruptive to family ties, and is viewed as a child's transference of the loyalty from a family orientation to a single person, ignoring obligations to the family and kin group for personal goals" (1993, p. 76). Moreover, there is concern that an infatuated young person might choose a partner who would make a poor spouse.

Ahmed argues that the arranged-marriage system has functioned not only to consolidate family property but also to keep the family's traditions and values intact. But as urban economies developed in eighteenth-century Europe and more and more young people worked away from home, arranged marriages gave way to those in which individuals selected their own mates. Love rather than property became the basis for unions (Coontz 2005b).

Love—and Marriage

If someone had all the qualities you desired, would you marry that person if you were not in love with him or her? Researchers put this question to male and female urban university undergraduates in ten countries and Hong Kong (Levine et al. 1995). The results are pre-

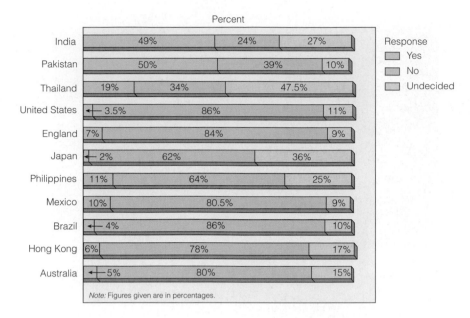

Figure 7.3 Responses to question: "If a man (woman) had all the other qualities you desired, would you marry this person if you were not in love with him (her)?"

Source: Adapted from "Love and Marriage in Eleven Cultures," by R. Levine, S. Sato, T. Hasimoto, and J. Verma, 1995, *Journal of Cross-Cultural Psychology*, 26 (5), pp. 554–71. Copyright © 1996 by Sage Publications, Inc. Reprinted by permission.

sented in Figure 7.3. As you can see from that figure, of the eleven societies sampled, students in Pakistan were most likely to answer yes; 50 percent of them did so.

In the United States, often considered the most individualistic society in the world, only 3.5 percent of the students said that they would marry someone with whom they were not in love, and the highest proportion (86 percent) said no, they would not. That marriages should involve romance and lead to personal happiness is a uniquely modern idea. The strong emotional and personal qualities of romantic love were in keeping with the individual freedom from family supervision that accompanied industrializing and urbanizing Western Europe (Coontz 2005b; Stone 1980).

Throughout the first five thousand years of human history in all the world's cultures that we know of, people probably fell in love, but they weren't *expected* to do so with their spouses. Marriage was thought to be "too vital an economic and political institution to be entered into solely on the basis of something as irrational as love" (Coontz 2005b, p. 7). Love—an intense, often unpredictable, and possibly transitory emotion—was viewed as threatening to the practical institution of marriage. Valuing romance could lead individuals to ignore or challenge their social responsibilities.

Courtly Love An interesting way that Europe's twelfth- and thirteenth-century noblemen and women managed

My Family

An Asian Indian-American Student's Essay on Arranged Marriages

The college student who wrote the following essay is the daughter of Asian Indian immigrants to California. Her essay points out that arranged marriages are experienced by some people in the United States today and that arranged marriage is changing.

Normally [in the United States] when two people decide whether to get married they think about how much they love each other. This, however, is not the case in arranged marriages. . . . I interviewed my parents and my friend who have had marriages arranged for them. After interviewing these people I realized that not all arranged marriages work the same way. . . .

My parents had an arranged marriage twenty-three years ago and are still married to this day. Their wedding day was the first time they saw each other, and even then it was just a quick glance. A mutual friend of both families mentioned . . . that their kids would be a good match. So my mom's parents . . . interviewed my dad. My grandparents took into consideration various things like my dad's height, weight, education, family background, age, income, house, and health. . . .

My dad's parents did the same thing to my mom. They went to see . . . whether they liked her. One of their main concerns was what their grandchildren would look like. So they wanted a tall, pretty, healthy wife for their son. Both sets of parents agreed to the other's child, and the deal was made. Both sets of my grandparents went home to tell their son and daughter that they were getting married. There were no questions asked by my parents. Out of respect for their parents, they agreed to be mar-

ried. Actually, this is incorrect, because they didn't really agree; they couldn't have agreed [because] they were never asked. Basically they weren't given an option. However, neither of my parents argued; they just went along with their parents' wishes.

When I asked my parents if they were disappointed when they first saw each other on their wedding day, they said no. They did not fall in love at first sight either, but they thought their parents did a good job in finding them a spouse. . . .

Neither of my parents regret[s] marrying each other even though they really didn't have much of a choice. They are happy with their lives, their children, and each other. . . .

Arranged marriages in the East Indian culture are a lot different today than they were [twenty-three years ago]. I have friends my own age who have had arranged marriages. Now they get the opportunity to actually meet the person whom their parents have in mind for them. Better yet, they get to decide whether or not they want to marry that person.

A friend of mine just went to India with her parents to get married. Once she got there she discovered that her family members had already picked out about fifteen different men from whom she could choose. She interviewed all of them with her parents. She crossed off the names of the ones she wasn't interested in and had a second interview with the remaining men on her list. With three men left on her list after the second interview, her parents decided that she could meet these men alone without any parent chaperons. . . .

She ended up liking one of them. She said she was very attracted to him. He was a dentist, tall, had a nice body, very polite, and treated her like a princess. She married this guy and brought him over to California. She couldn't be happier. She told me that she doesn't think that she would have ever been able to find such a wonderful husband without the help of her family. She is very grateful to them.

As for my two brothers and me, my parents have not necessarily expected us to have an arranged marriage. But before we do get married they want us to possess the best qualities, mainly a high education, good manners, respect for others, and high self-esteem, which will enable us to choose a partner of equal qualities. . . . I did not have an arranged marriage. I married my husband because I truly loved him. However, before I made the decision to get married, I did try to make sure that we would be compatible and have similar goals.

I sometimes wonder what it would be like to have an arranged marriage. What would the wedding night be like? How could two people who don't really know each other or love each other make love? I did not feel comfortable enough to ask my parents or my friend about this. But it is something that I wonder about.

Critical Thinking

How do the arranged marriages that this student describes illustrate a collectivist society? What are some advantages of arranged marriage? Some disadvantages? How do you think arranged marriage is changing, as a result of Westernization?

love's threat to marriage as a social institution was the practice of **courtly love**. As we have seen, most marriages in the upper levels of society during this period were based on pragmatic considerations, not love. But, as the saying went then, "marriage is no real excuse for not lov-

ing" (quoted in Coontz 2005b, p. 6). Among Europe's noblemen and women, romantic love was expressed in relationships outside marriage in which a knight worshipped his lady, and ladies had their favorites. These relationships involved a great deal of idealization and could be adulterous but were not necessarily sexually consummated (Stone 1980). The distinction between romance and marriage was also evident in the lower classes: "Many of the songs and stories popular among peasants in medieval Europe mocked married love" (Coontz 2005b, p. 7).

However, with time, the ideology of romantic love associated with courtly love became adapted to a situation for which it was probably much less suitable—marriage. In family historian Stephanie Coontz's words, basing marriage on love and companionship

> represented a break with thousands of years of tradition. . . . Critics of the love match argued . . . that the values of free choice and egalitarianism could easily spin out of control. If the choice of a marriage partner was a personal decision, . . . what would prevent young people . . . from choosing unwisely? If people were encouraged to expect marriage to be the best and happiest experience of their lives, what would hold a marriage together if things were "for worse" rather than "for better"? (2005b, pp. 149–50)

To use Coontz's metaphor, couples were no longer yoked together (like field oxen). "Where once marriage had been seen as the fundamental unit of work and politics, it was now viewed as a place of refuge from work, politics, and community obligations—a haven in a heartless world" (Coontz 2005b, p. 146; Lasch 1977). A successful marriage came to be measured by how well the union met its members' emotional needs.

To summarize this section, emergent individualism in eighteenth-century Europe meant that people, increasingly valuing personal satisfaction and happiness, began to associate romantic love with marriage and, hence, to want to find their own marriage partners, a practice that both resulted from and further caused weakened kinship authority. Couples were no longer bound by the yoke of kin control. As you might guess, the nature of marriage changed. We'll explore that change next.

Deinstitutionalized Marriage

In the subtitle of her recent book, Coontz asserts that love and expectations for intimacy have "conquered marriage" (2005b). What does she mean? Coontz is talking about what family sociologist Andrew Cherlin (2004) has called the **deinstitutionalization of marriage**—a situation in which time-honored family definitions and social norms "count for far less" than in the past (p. 853). The following sections present and expand upon Cherlin's analysis of the shift from *institutional* to *companionate* to *individualized* marriage. As we discuss these three kinds of marriage, we need to remember that they are abstractions, or *ideal types*.[6] In reality, marriages approximate these types to varying degrees.

Institutional Marriage

We have witnessed a gradual historical change in Western and Westernized societies away from **institutional marriage**—that is, marriage as a social institution based on dutiful adherence to the time-honored marriage premise, particularly the norm of permanence (Cherlin 2004; Coontz 2005b). Once ensconced in societal mandates for permanence and monogamous sexual exclusivity, the institutionalized marriage in the United States

> represented the age-old tradition of a family organized around economic production, kinship network, community connections, the father's authority, and marriage as a functional partnership rather than a romantic relationship. . . . Family tradition, loyalty, and solidarity were more important than individual goals and romantic interest. (Doherty 1992, p. 33)

Institutional marriage generally offered practical and economic security, along with the rewards that we often associate with custom and tradition (knowing what to expect in almost any situation, for example). Meanwhile, with few exceptions over the past five thousand years, institutional marriage was organized according to patriarchal authority, requiring a wife's obedience to her husband and the kinship group. It is also true that, legally, institutional marriage could involve what today we define as wife and child abuse or neglect.

Across cultures, the strength and scope of patriarchal authority varied, however. As an extreme example, in ancient Rome the *paterfamilias* (family father), having absolute authority over his wife and children, could legally kill them or sell them into slavery.[7] No matter how old they were, sons were subject to the authority of the *paterfamilias* until he died. A daughter lived under her father's rule until she married, when her father's authority over her was legally transferred to her husband

---

[6] In this context the word *ideal* indicates that a type exists as an idea, not that it is necessarily good or preferable.

[7] The occasions on which the *paterfamilias* actually exercised his authority to kill family members were probably uncommon, however (Thompson 2006).

The married couple embedded in this family of Eastern European immigrants who arrived in New York City in 1832 may be in love, but they were not *expected* to find love in marriage. Instead, their union is held together by strong expectations of permanence, bolstered by the social control of the kinship group.

(Long 1875; Thompson 2006). In the United States, of course, patriarchal authority never approached anything near that of the ancient Roman *paterfamilias*. Nevertheless, although they existed, child and wife abuse were not recognized as social problems in this country until the 1960s and 1970s, respectively.

Companionate Marriage

By the 1920s in the United States, family sociologists had begun to note a shift away from institutional marriage, and, in 1945, the first sociology textbook on the American family (by Ernest Burgess and Harvey Locke) was titled *The Family: From Institution to Companionship*. By **companionate marriage**,

> Burgess was referring to the single-earner, breadwinner-homemaker marriage that flourished in the 1950s. Although husbands and wives in the companionate marriage usually adhered to a sharp division of labor, they were supposed to be each other's companions—friends, lovers—to an extent not imagined by the spouses in the institutional marriages of the previous era. . . . Much more so than in the 19th century, the emotional satisfaction of the spouses became an important criterion for marital success. However,

through the 1950s, wives and husbands tended to derive satisfaction from their participation in a marriage-based nuclear family. . . . That is to say, they based their gratification on playing marital roles well; being good providers, good homemakers, and responsible parents. (Cherlin 2004, p. 851)

With companionate marriage, middle-class Americans often dreamed of attaining "the white picket fence." That is, they saw marriage as an opportunity for idealized domesticity within the "haven" of their own single-family home.[8] (This is why we have drawn a picket fence to symbolize the companionate marriage bond in Figure 7.4 on page 167). Meanwhile, women's increasing educational and work options, coupled with expectations for marital love and happiness, sowed the seeds for the demise of companionate marriage (Cherlin 2004; Coontz 2005c).

An individualistic orientation views each person (both husband *and* wife) as having talents that deserve to be actualized. In this climate, women in companionate marriages began to pursue opportunities for self-actualization, as well as to expect a husband's expressive support for their doing so (Jackson 2007). Furthermore, women challenged centuries of previously ignored domestic violence. Given the tension between gender inequality and expectations for emotionally supported self-actualization, the companionate marriage "lost ground" (Cherlin 2004, p. 852).

By the 1970s observers noted a movement away from people's finding of personal satisfaction primarily in acceptable role performance—for example, in the role of husband/breadwinner or wife/homemaker. Research on college students showed a shift in self-orientation away from defining themselves according to the roles they played. More and more, they identified themselves in terms of their individual personality traits. But appreciation for "the esteem that goes with high role adequacy buttresses the institutional structure" (Turner

---

[8] Companionate marriages of the 1950s "were exceptional in many ways. Until that decade, relying on a single breadwinner had been rare. For thousands of years, most women and children had shared the tasks of breadwinning with men. . . . Also new in the 1950s was the cultural consensus that everyone should marry, and that people should do so at a young age. The baby boom of the 1950s was likewise a departure from the past, because birthrates in Western Europe and North America had fallen steadily during the previous 100 years" (Coontz 2005c).

1976, p. 1011; Babbitt and Burbach 1990; Snow and Phillips 1982). As one result, critics began to warn that American culture was becoming "narcissistic": Individuals appeared less focused on commitment or concern for future generations (Bellah et al. 1985; Lasch 1980).

Feminists defined this situation somewhat differently: Attention to domestic abuse, unequal couple decision making, and unfair division of household labor—as well as a wife's ability more easily to leave an intolerable situation through divorce—could be good things (Hackstaff 2007). Some celebrated the fact that finally American culture would begin to make room for "thinking beyond the heteronormative family" (Roseneil and Budgeon 2004, p. 136; Stacey 1996). Coontz summarizes the situation more neutrally: "For better or worse," over the past thirty years, "all the precedents established by the love-based male breadwinner family were . . . thrown into question" (2005b, p. 11; 2005c). However one saw it, by the late 1980s, companionate marriage—which had lasted for but a minute in the long hours of human history—had largely given way to its successor, individualized marriage.

As an ideal type, the *companionate marriage* that characterized most of the twentieth century emphasized love and compatibility, as well as separate gender roles. However, in reality couples represent this ideal type to varying degrees. Although this Russian immigrant couple, who own and operate a small Los Angeles grocery store, illustrate companionate marriage in *some* ways, they do not fit the definition of companionate marriage in at least one important way: They share the family provider role.

Individualized Marriage

Four interrelated characteristics distinguish **individualized marriage**:

1. It is optional.
2. Spouses' roles are flexible—negotiable and renegotiable.
3. Its expected rewards involve love, communication, and emotional intimacy.
4. It exists in conjunction with a vast diversity of family forms.

Individualized marriage is op-tional. Getting married is now one choice among many others. We began this chapter by noting that the proportion of unmarried Americans today is large and growing. As one result, this textbook devotes an entire chapter (Chapter 8) to alternatives to marriage, and each time that we, the authors, write a new edition, we find that yet more options have emerged. Clearly, being married is optional (Cherlin 2004; Willetts 2006).

Partly because marriage is optional today, brides, grooms, and long-\married couples have come to expect different rewards from marriage than people did in the past. They continue to value being good partners and, perhaps, parents. However, today's spouses are less likely to find their only, or definitive, rewards in performing these roles well. More than in companionate marriages, partners now expect love and emotional intimacy, open communication, role flexibility, gender equality, and personal growth (Cherlin 2004). Over the course of about three centuries, couples have moved "from yoke mates to soul mates" (Coontz 2005b, p. 124).

Intense romantic feelings are associated with greater marital happiness and may serve to get a married couple through bad times (Udry 1974; Wallerstein and Blakeslee 1995). But there can be a downside to all this. The idealization and unrealistic expectations implicit in individualized marriage can cause problems. Social theorist Anthony Giddens argues that expectations for a relationship based on intimate communication to the extent that "the rewards derived from such communication are the main basis for the relationship to continue" often lead to disappointment: "[M]ost ordinary relationships don't come even close" (Giddens 2007, p. 30). Giddens may be overstating the case. Probably many

Figure 7.4 a The Institutional Marriage bond. Couples are "yoked" together by high expectations for permanence, bolstered by the strong social control of extended kin and community.

Figure 7.4 b The Companionate Marriage bond. Couples are bound together by companionship, coupled with a gendered division of labor, pride in performing spousal and parenting roles, and hopes for "the American dream"—a home of their own and a comfortable domestic life together.

Figure 7.4 c The Individualized Marriage bond. Spouses in individualized marriages remain together because they find self-actualization, intimacy, and expressively communicated emotional support in their unions.

marriages do come close. However, the fact remains that such high expectations may be associated with the following results:

1. A person's deciding not to marry, because she or he can't find a "soul mate" who can promise this level of togetherness

2. A high divorce rate (although assuredly there are other reasons for divorce, too, as described in Chapter 16)

3. A lower birth rate as individuals focus on options in addition to raising children, a topic addressed in Chapter 10

One theme of this text is that society influences people's options and thereby impacts their decisions. To the extent that they are legally, financially, and otherwise able, people today organize their personal, romantic, and family lives as they see fit. Some engage in "dyadic innovation" (Green 2006, p. 182)—that is, they fashion their relationships with little regard to traditional norms. "How good is your relationship?" is often a question equal in importance to "Are you married?" (Giddens 2007).

In this climate a wide variety of family forms emerge. What today we call the **pluralistic family**, or *postmodern* family, characterized by "tolerance and diversity, rather than a single family ideal," takes many forms (Doherty 1992, p. 35). As noted in Chapter 1, some observers view the deinstitutionalization of marriage as a loss for society, a "decline" that hopefully can be turned around (e.g., Whitehead and Popenoe 2006). Others see the deinstitutionalization of marriage simply as an inevitable historical change (e.g., Coontz 2005b, 2005c).

Individualized Marriage and the Pluralistic Family—*Decline* or Inevitable *Change?*

Those who view individualized marriage as *decline* assert that our culture's unchecked individualism has caused widespread moral weakening and self-indulgence. They say that Americans, more self-centered today, are less likely than in the past to choose marriage, are more likely to divorce, and are less child-centered (Blankenhorn 1995; Stanton 2004a, 2004b; Marquardt nd; Whitehead and Popenoe 2006). From this point of view, the American family has broken down.

Others, in contrast, see the deinstitutionalization of marriage as resulting from inevitable social *change*. These thinkers point out that, for one thing, people who look back with nostalgia to the good old days may be imagining incorrectly the situation that characterized

marriage throughout most of the nineteenth and twentieth centuries. For instance, large families with many children and higher death rates for parents with young children meant that many children were not raised in two-parent households (Coontz 1992). Moreover, we cannot go back:

> [J]ust as we cannot organize modern political alliances through kinship ties or put the farmers' and skilled craftsmen's households back as the centerpiece of the modern economy, we can never reinstate marriage as the primary source of commitment and caregiving in the modern world. For better or worse, we must adjust our personal expectations and social support systems to this new reality. (Coontz 2005c)

In a climate characterized by debate between spokespersons from these opposing perspectives, researchers and policy makers examine the social consequences of deinstitutionalized marriage.

Deinstitutionalized Marriage: Examining the Consequences

In her seminal 1995 presidential address to the American Population Association, family demographer Linda Waite (1995) asked rhetorically, "Does Marriage Matter?" She concluded that indeed it does, for both adults and children. After thoroughly reviewing prior research that compared the well-being of family members in married unions with that of those in unmarried households, Waite reported that, as a category, spouses:

- had greater wealth and assets
- earned higher wages
- had more frequent and better sex
- had overall better health
- were less likely to engage in dangerous risk-taking
- had fewer alcohol-related problems
- had lower rates of marijuana use
- were more likely to engage in generally healthy behaviors
- evidenced an "orderly life style."

Comparing children's well-being in married families with that of those in one-parent families, Waite found that, as a category, children in married families:

- were about half as likely to drop out of high school
- reported more frequent contact and better-quality relationships with their parents
- were significantly less likely to live in poverty.

Since her address, many sociologists and policy makers have further researched and debated Waite's findings. In the section following this one, we will examine the responses of policy makers. Here we review a sampling of demographic data and research findings on the question, "Does marriage matter?"

National income and poverty data apparently support Waite's argument that marrieds are financially better off. As Table 7.1 indicates, the median income for married-couple families in 2004 was $63,630, compared with just $40,293 and $26,964 for unmarried, male- and female-headed households, respectively. Even when a wife is not in the labor force, married-couple households earn, on average, about $2,000 more annually than do unmarried male householders (U.S. Census Bureau 2007a, Table 680). Clearly, these data support the argument that higher income is positively associated with marriage. Furthermore, since Waite's address, studies have continued to find that, compared to unmarrieds, spouses have better physical and mental health (Kim and McKenry 2002; Murphy, Glaser, and Grundy 1997; Stack and Wasserman 1993; Wickrama et al. 1997).

However, research also suggests that the association between marriage and positive outcomes is more complex than Waite indicated. For example, marrieds, on average, are less often depressed than the widowed and the divorced. But marrieds are not less depressed than either the remarried or the never-married (Bierman, Fazio, and Milkie 2006). Then, too, in addition to being married, education, a comfortable income, and not having to suffer from society-wide racism improve mental health (Bierman, Fazio, and Milkie 2006; Ostrove, Feldman, and Adler 1999; Williams and Williams-Morris 2000). And, finally, marrieds have more frequent sex that unmarrieds when all unmarrieds are categorized together, but they do not have more frequent sex than cohabiting couples (Waite 1995).

An early criticism of Waite's claims was that much—although not all—of the association between marriage and positive outcomes was due to *selection effects*. In researchers' language, people may "select" themselves into a category being investigated—in this case, mar-

riage—and this self-selection can yield the results that the researcher was testing for. Increasingly, individuals with superior education, incomes, and physical and mental health, as well as lower rates of childhood sexual abuse, are more likely to marry (Bierman, Fazio, and Milkie 2006; Cherlin et al. 2004; DeLeire and Kalil 2005; McLanahan 2004; Schoen and Cheng 2006). The **selection hypothesis** posits that many of the benefits associated with marriage—for example, higher income and wealth, along with better health—are therefore actually due to the personal characteristics of those who choose to marry (Cherlin 2003). For example, married women are more likely than those who are cohabiting or heading single-family households to inherit wealth (Ozawa and Lee 2006). Being positioned to inherit wealth from one's family of origin is a personal characteristic that *precedes* getting married.

Nevertheless, not all the benefits associated with marriage are accounted for by selection effects. In contrast to the selection hypothesis, the **experience hypothesis** holds that something about the *experience* of being married itself causes these benefits—a point that we will return to at the end of this chapter. Meanwhile, considerable research has focused on examining the relationships between marriage and the consequences for children.

Child Outcomes and Marital Status: Does Marriage Matter?

FOCUS ON CHILDREN   The proportion of children under age eighteen living with two married parents declined steadily over the past thirty years—from 85 percent in 1970 to 67 percent in 2005 (U.S. Federal Interagency Forum on Child and Family Statistics 2006). More than one-quarter of children (26 percent) live in single-parent households (Kreider and Fields 2005, p. 2). Nearly half (48 percent) of all single-parent families are non-Hispanic white. Blacks comprise just under one-third of single-parent families (31 percent), and Hispanics, 17 percent (U.S. Census Bureau 2007a, Table 62).

Table 7.1 Median Income of Families by Types of Family in Constant (2004) Dollars: 1980 to 2004

	All Married-Couple Families	Married-Couple Families; Wife in Paid Labor Force	Married-Couple Families; Wife Not in Paid Labor Force	Unmarried Male Householder	Unmarried Female Householder
1980	$50,245	$58,396	$41,193	$38,038	$22,599
1990	55,910	65,555	42,414	40,706	23,729
2000	64,825	75,943	43,856	41,382	28,208
2004	63,630	76,814	42,221	40,293	26,964

Source: U.S. Census Bureau, 2007a, Table 680.

As shown in Table 7.2, the 20.5 million children living with an unmarried parent comprise 28.4 percent of all U.S. children. Of children under age eighteen, 5.4 percent, or approximately 4 million, live in unmarried-partner, or cohabiting, households. Of those living with cohabiting couples, about half (1.8 million) live with both of their (unmarried) biological parents (Kreider and Fields 2005, p. 2).

Considerable research supports Waite's overall conclusion that growing up with married parents is better for children. For instance, studies that compared economically disadvantaged six- and seven-year-olds from families of various types found fewer problem behaviors among children in married families (Ackerman et al. 2001). Furthermore, when compared with teens in married, two-biological-parent homes, those in single-parent and cohabiting families are more likely to experience earlier premarital intercourse, lower academic achievement, and lower expectations for college, together with higher rates of school suspension and delinquency (Albrecht and Teachman 2003; Brown 2004; Carlson 2006; Manning and Lamb 2003; McLanahan and Sandefur 1994; VanDorn, Bowen, and Blau 2006).

Other research has found that, among couples with comparable incomes, cohabiting parents spend less on their children's education and more on alcohol and tobacco than do married parents (DeLeire and Kalil 2005). As the experience hypothesis would suggest, one reason that, as a category, children with married parents evidence better outcomes may be the *experience* of growing up in a married-couple household. With its presumption of permanent commitment to the family as a whole, marriage "allows caregivers to make relationship-specific investments in the couple's children—investments of time and effort that, unlike strengthening one's job skills, would not be easily portable to another relationship" (Cherlin 2004, p. 855).

Meanwhile, as with the benefits of marriage for adults, researchers, working to unravel the statistical correlation between marriage and positive child outcomes, have uncovered complexities. For instance, findings differ according to how the variables *marriage* and *children* are defined. Recent research has refined the variable *marriage* so that, for example, an investigator might compare the effects of having two biological, continuously married parents with those of having a remarried stepparent. Using data from the National Longitudinal Survey of Youth, one study (Carlson 2006) compared outcomes for adolescents in several family structures. Similar to prior research, this study found fewer behavior problems among teens who lived with their continuously married biological parents. However, adolescents born outside of marriage but whose biological parents later married or were cohabiting, or whose mother married a stepfather, had more behavior problems than teens whose biological parents were continuously married.

Researchers have also refined the variable *children* in order to differentiate between teens and younger children. Working with data from the National Survey of America's Families, sociologist Susan Brown (2004) found that—consistent with other research—adolescents in two-biological-parent, married families had fewer emotional, behavior, or school-related problems. However, her analysis further showed that, for six- to eleven-year-olds, poor emotional, behavior, and school outcomes were more strongly related to poverty, together with parents' low education levels, poor psychological health, and ineffective parenting practices.

Table 7.2 U.S. Children Under Age 18 by Parents' Presence and Marital Status, by Poverty Status, 2001

Child's Living Arrangement	Number	%	Number Below Poverty	% Below Poverty
Living with married parents	**49,987**	**67.6**	**4,948**	**10.1**
Living with an unmarried parent	**20,598**	**28.4**	**5,850**	**33.6**
Living with parent and unmarried partner	3,889	5.4	1,214	31.2
Biological mother and father	1,817	2.5	509	28.0
Biological mother, partner	1,400	1.9	542	38.7
Biological father, partner	304	0.4	72	24.0
Parent has no partner	16,709	23.0	5,715	34.2
Living with biological mother	14,580	20.1	5,307	36.4
Living with biological father	1,778	2.5	1,778	14.7
Living with neither parent	**2,917**	**4.0**	**904**	**31.0**

Source: Adapted from Kreider and Fields 2005, Table 2.

© Westend61/Jupiter Images

Although Hispanics and African Americans have higher percentages, or rates, of mother-headed, single-parent families, the majority of mother-headed, single-parent families are non-Hispanic white. Also, Hispanics and African American families have higher poverty rates, but the majority of families in poverty are non-Hispanic white. Furthermore, although more than one-third of mother-headed, single-parent families live below the official poverty level, nearly two-thirds do not.

In addition to refining the variables *marriage* and *children*, researchers have proposed additional or alternative causes for children's marriage-associated benefits. As an example, a study found that *father involvement*—the extent to which a biological father is engaged with his child—is important regardless of whether he is married to his child's biological mother (Carlson 2006).

Other researchers have suggested that ethnic differences need to be taken into account when measuring children's outcomes. For instance, sociologist Leslie Gordon Simons and her colleagues distinguished between what they call the *marriage perspective* and the *two-caregivers perspective*. "What we label the marriage perspective rests on the assumption that children are

most likely to display healthy growth and development when they are raised by married parents." In contrast, the two-caregivers perspective contends that children do best when raised by two caregivers rather than by a single caregiver (Simons et al. 2006, p. 805).

Analyzing data on 867 African American children from the Family and Community Health Study, Simons and her colleagues found that "child behavior problems were no greater in either mother-grandmother or mother-relative families than in those in intact nuclear families." At least among blacks, these researchers found mother-grandmother families to be "functionally equivalent" (Simons et al. 2006, p. 818). (For more on blacks and marriage, see "A Closer Look at Family Diversity: African Americans and 'Jumping the Broom.'")

Finally, in a study focused on Hispanic children, researchers first noted that, as shown in Figure 7.2, the Hispanic marriage rate (59 percent for women and 55 percent for men) is not much lower than that for non-Hispanic whites (about 62 percent). Nevertheless, 29 percent of Hispanic children live below poverty level, compared with 14 percent of non-Hispanic white children (U.S. Census Bureau 2007a, Table 693). Why does marriage not relate to lower poverty levels among Hispanics to the extent that it does among non-Hispanic whites? To answer this question, researchers added the variable *number of children* to their analysis. Their findings showed that, for Mexican American children, poverty is related to a combination of marital status and the number of children in the household, the latter "an important predictor of poverty regardless of marital status" (Crowley, Lichter, and Qian 2006). This study is one in a growing body of research that examines the relationship between marriage and child poverty, an issue explored later in this chapter.

As with the benefits of marriage for adults, researchers hypothesize that selection effects explain much—although not all—of marriage's advantage for children. We've seen that, on average, individuals who marry are better educated and have higher incomes. As parents, they live in neighborhoods more conducive to successful child raising. Less likely to be stressed due to financial problems, they are more likely to practice effective parenting skills (Manning and Brown 2006). In her address to the American Population Association, Waite acknowledged the contribution of selection effects to child outcomes. She added, however, that "we have been too quick to assign *all* the responsibility to selectivity here, and not quick enough to consider the possibility that marriage *causes* some of the better outcomes we see . . ." (1995, p. 497, italics in original).

To summarize, a large body of research shows that marriage is associated with benefits for adults and children. However, this relationship is complex, and much

Nationally representative surveys show that, among African Americans, husbands and wives are more likely than unmarrieds to report being "very happy" and satisfied with their finances and family life (Blackman et al. 2006). Meanwhile, Figure 7.2 shows that—with 46 percent of black men and 38 percent of black women currently married—African Americans are considerably less likely to be wed than are other U.S. racial/ethnic groups. A large body of literature, written by both blacks and whites, is accumulating on the structural–cultural reasons for this situation (McAdoo 2007; Saad 2006c; Wilson 2002). Chapter 3 explores this literature.

Nonetheless, among the college educated, the *marriage disparity* between the proportion of blacks who are married and other racial/ethnic groups is far less dramatic. According to a recent Gallup poll, 55 percent of college-educated African Americans are married, compared with 57 percent of Hispanics and 65 percent of non-Hispanic whites (Saad 2006c). Furthermore, attitude surveys consistently show that African Americans value marriage, perhaps more than non-Hispanic whites do (Bramlett and Mosher 2001; Saad 2006c; Staples 1999a).

In a recent poll, 69 percent of African Americans said that it is "very important" for a couple to marry when they plan to spend the rest of their lives together. Asked, "When an unmarried man and woman have a child together, how important is it to you that they legally marry?" college-educated African Americans were *more* inclined than either Hispanics or non-Hispanic whites to say that marrying in this situation is "very important." The figures were 55 percent of blacks, 46 percent of Hispanics, and 37 percent of non-Hispanic whites (Saad 2006c).

The news media have focused so frequently on poverty-level African Americans and on the relatively low proportion of married blacks that we may forget about the 10.3 million African Americans who *are* married (U.S. Census Bureau 2007a, Table 54). But google "African American marriage" and you'll find several websites marketing wedding products and services to middle-class blacks. One book, *Jumping the Broom* (Cole 1993) is a wedding planner for American blacks. If you're not African American, there's a fairly good chance that you have not heard of jumping the broom. What is it?

For African Americans the significance of the broom originated among the Asante in what is now the West African country of Ghana. Used to sweep courtyards, the handmade Asante broom was also symbolic of sweeping away past wrongs or warding off evil. Brooms played a part in Asante weddings as well. To culminate their wedding ceremony, a couple might jump over a broom lying on the ground or leaning across a doorway. Jumping the broom symbolized the wife's commitment to her new household, and it was sometimes said that whoever jumped higher over the broom would be the family decision maker (DiStefano 2001).

Among slaves brought to the Americas, jumping the broom continued. Not allowed to marry legally, slaves sometimes jumped a broom as an alternative ceremony to mark their marital commitment. The association of jumping the broom with slavery has stigmatized the tradition for some African Americans. However, the ritual is coming back as more middle-class blacks seek culturally relevant wedding celebrations (African Wedding Guide n.d.; Anyiam 2002; Cole 1993; DiStefano 2001).

Jumping the broom today is often used to symbolize sweeping out the old and welcoming the new. Websites give advice on how to jump the broom. The

Although somewhat controversial because it can be a reminder of slavery, jumping the broom at African American weddings is going through some revival as black couples plan wedding celebration rituals designed to incorporate their cultural heritage.

advice? Ask a prospective guest to serve as narrator. Then, "[s]uggest that the narrator explain to guests that you are re-creating the ceremony as a way to represent the joining together of two lives and the need for support of the marriage from the entire community" ("How to Jump" (n.d.)).

Critical Thinking

How do you think that jumping the broom might be used to symbolize the time-honored marriage premise? Why would it be important to incorporate traditions that are relevant to one's own culture into a wedding ceremony? Why do you think we hear relatively little about African Americans' weddings or marriages?

of it may be due to variables other than marital status as well as to selection effects. One theme of this text is that research findings expand our knowledge so that we can better make decisions knowledgeably. One thing that the research implies is that, although marriage is advantaged, it is not explicitly clear how much this is so, or why. Consequently, if one wants to marry—or is already in a supportive marriage—this can be a positive thing.

At the same time, you may be in a position to—and want to—consider the pros and cons of one or more alternatives to marriage, described in Chapter 8. Then too, whether we choose to be married or not, we need to think about what factors help us to maintain a supportive marriage or relationship. Throughout this text, we make suggestions. For example, Chapter 13 presents research and advice on how best to communicate in relationships. As we continue to make choices throughout our lives, we can follow through on what we learn with action to enhance our chances for marriage or relationship success.

Meanwhile, if researchers have responded in various ways to Waite's address, policy makers have had conflicting reactions. Socioeconomically conservative policy leaders, associated with the *decline* and "family breakdown" perspective, hope to effect a "family turnaround" (Whitehead and Popenoe 2003). They note "a greater emphasis on short-term gratification and on adults' desires rather than on what is good for children" that typically they attribute to government welfare programs and to decreased attention to fundamentalist Christian principles (Giele 2007, p. 76). On the other hand, policy makers who see marriage simply as *changing* recognize that many families are struggling but criticize the solutions offered by conservatives and propose their own. The following section explores this policy debate.

Working Toward a Family "Turnaround"— The Policy Debate

Policy advocates from a marital *change* perspective are mainly concerned about the high number and proportions of parents and children living in poverty. They view poverty as causing difficult child-raising environments with resulting negative outcomes for some—though not all—of America's children. From this viewpoint, family struggle results from structural conditions, such as a changing economy. Accordingly, these spokespersons argue for structural, or ecological (such as neighborhood-level), solutions.

From the *decline* perspective, on the other hand, concerns about "family breakdown" include the high number of federal dollars spent on "welfare" for poverty-level single mothers, coupled with the irresponsible socialization of children (Giele 2007). They define the causes for these concerns as primarily cultural, such as changes in individuals' values and attitudes regarding marriage. Therefore, they offer motivational and educational programs to effect a family "turnaround."

Policies from the Family Decline Perspective

An important goal from the *decline* perspective is to return to a society more in line with the values and norms of companionate marriage. As means to that end, advocates have established programs to encourage marital permanence. Many religions insist on premarital counseling as a way to dissuade couples in inappropriate matches from marrying and to encourage those who do marry to stay together (Nock 2005; Ooms 2005).

Covenant Marriage Some conservative Christian organizations and legislators advocate **covenant marriage**. Covenant marriage is a fairly new type of legal marriage in which partners agree to be bound by a marriage "covenant" (stronger than an ordinary contract) that will not let them get divorced as easily as is presently allowed ("Covenant Marriages Ministry" 1998). About ten years ago, three states enacted covenant marriage laws—Louisiana, Arizona, and Arkansas. Many other states have considered, but failed to pass, covenant marriage laws (Gardiner et al. 2002). Relatively few couples in the states where it is available have opted for covenant marriage ("More Binding Marriage" 2004; Sanchez et al. 2002).

How does covenant marriage work? Before their wedding, couples choose between two marital contracts, conventional or covenant. If legally bound by a marriage covenant, couples are required to get premarital counseling and may divorce only after being separated for at least two years or if imprisonment, desertion for one year, adultery, or domestic abuse is proved in court. In addition, a covenant couple must submit to counseling before a divorce (Brown and Waugh 2004).

Typically, fundamentalist Christian religions are enthusiastic about covenant marriage, while feminists and other critics are not ("Couple Support" 2006; Hawkins et al. 2002; Sanchez et al. 2002). For instance, critics point out that proving adultery or domestic abuse in court may be difficult and expensive, while living in a violent household can be deadly (Gelles 1996). Moreover, some religious authorities have expressed concern that covenant marriage laws, in effect, set up a two-tiered marriage structure that makes a noncovenant marriage second class, however valid and sacramental it may be. The Catholic Church has declined to endorse covenant marriage for this reason. In addition to covenant marriage, the Healthy Marriage Initiative encourages not only the permanence but also the formation of marriages.

The Healthy Marriage Initiative Fairly recently, states have promoted marriage education, some offering money incentives for couples to participate. Other state initiatives include home visitation programs for families that might be targeted for a variety of reasons, such as a birth to a teenager or an unstable marriage; mentoring, marriage counseling, communication skills, and anger management workshops; state-funded resource centers that provide information on marriage; and state websites that include marriage enrichment information and links to service-related sites (Dion 2005; Ooms 2005). West Virginia policy makers determined to offer women receiving welfare a $100 monthly bonus if they marry (Cherlin 2003).

These programs largely began after 1996, when Congress passed the Personal Responsibility and Work Opportunity Reconciliation Act. That federal law authorized the **Temporary Assistance for Needy Families (TANF)**, or "welfare reform," program and stated the following family-related goals:

1. End the dependence of needy parents on government benefits by promoting job preparation, work, and marriage.

2. Prevent and reduce the incidence of out-of-wedlock pregnancies.

3. Encourage the formation and maintenance of two-parent families (U.S. Department of Health and Human Services 2004).[9]

"Welfare reform" was partly motivated by the belief that cutting welfare aid to single mothers would result in fewer female-headed families (Meckler 1999). In 2003, President George W. Bush proclaimed a week in October as "Marriage Protection Week," to help "focus our efforts on . . . building strong and healthy marriages in America" (Bush 2003). The following year, as part of TANF's required reauthorization, President Bush introduced the **Healthy Marriage Initiative (HMI)**. Pro-

ponents argued that "accurate information on the value of marriage in the lives of men, women, and children," along with marriage-skills education, would

> enable couples to reduce conflict and increase the happiness and longevity of their relationship. . . . The marriage program will encourage couples to reexamine and improve their relationships and plan wisely for the future. . . . The program will also provide marriage-skills education to married couples to improve their relationships and to reduce the probability of divorce. (Rector and Pardue 2004)[10]

From a total of $1.5 billion in federal monies, states were allotted funds to create state marriage initiatives, characterized by workshops on listening, communication, and problem-solving skills, as well as presentations on the value of marriage (Dion 2005; U.S. Department of Health and Human Services 2004). Because marriage initiatives proceed from the TANF legislation, their focus has been on low-income Americans.[11] Often programs are targeted to specific racial or ethnic groups; examples are the African American Healthy Marriage Initiative (AAHMI) and the Hispanic Healthy Marriage Initiative (HHMI).

Making the general point that "good marriages are good for people," these programs may offer participants hope that their relationships can succeed. HMI programs further appear to produce at least short-term improvements in communication and problem solving. It is possible that they may also help to reduce domestic violence (Ooms 2005). Evaluation research projects are planned to assess how well these programs work to encourage getting married or to reduce divorce, but the results will not be available for several years (Dion 2005).

Meanwhile, demographic data show that TANF and the Healthy Marriage Initiative have met with some success in decreasing the incidence of single-parent households. Between 1997 and 2002, the percentage of single-mother households declined by just under 4 percentage points. Meanwhile, the proportion of married-parent families increased by 2.5 percentage points. (Cohabit-

---

[9] The 1996 Personal Responsibility and Work Opportunity Reconciliation Act, or "welfare reform bill," effectively ended the federal government's sixty-year guarantee of assisting low-income mothers and children. The federal Aid to Families with Dependent Children (AFDC) program ended in 1997, and a different federal program, **Temporary Assistance for Needy Families (TANF)**, ensued. Under the new legislation, assistance is limited to five years for most families, with most adult recipients required to find work within two years.

[10] In 2005, responding to concerns raised by feminists and others, the Administration for Children and Families published the following caveat: "The [Healthy Marriage] Initiative is not about:

- Trapping anyone in an abusive or violent relationship.
- Forcing anyone to get or stay married.
- Running a federal dating service.
- Withdrawing supports from or diminishing in any way, either directly or indirectly, the important work of single parents" (U.S. Department of Health and Human Services 2005).

[11] Originally developed for middle-class couples, many of these programs may be inadequate for low-income recipients (Ooms 2005). However, program developers have begun to design curricula better suited to the situations of low-income couples (Dion 2005).

Courtesy of FUTURE—Families United Through Understanding Relationships and Empowerment, Chicago Illinios

Under TANF (Temporary Assistance for Needy Families), these individuals have completed an HMI (Healthy Marriage Initiative) program. Federally conceived and government funded, Healthy Marriage Initiatives supports the formation and permanence of marriage through various educational programs that include mentoring, counseling, building communication skills, and anger-management workshops.

ing households increased by 1.2 percentage points [Acs and Nelson 2003].)

Criticisms of the Healthy Marriage Initiative Policy advocates from the *change* point of view typically see the Healthy Marriage Initiative as ill-advised. They argue the following four points:

1. Low-income Americans value marriage and would like to marry, but for many of them marriage is a goal that is difficult to achieve.

2. Given their options, remaining unmarried may be the most rational decision for many low-income women.

3. If TANF recipients do marry, many of their unions are unlikely to look like the "good marriages" envisioned by the Healthy Marriage Initiative.

4. Building healthy marriages presumes relieving poverty, and relieving poverty will require solutions other than—or at least in addition to—the Healthy Marriage Initiative.

We'll look briefly at each of these points.

Low-income Americans value marriage and would like to marry, but for many of them marriage is a goal that is difficult to achieve. For rich and poor alike, a wedding today symbolizes personal achievement (Cherlin 2004). Upon extensively interviewing women in low-income neighborhoods, researchers have concluded that for poor women marriage

has become an elusive goal—one they feel ought to be reserved for those who can support . . . a mortgage on a modest row home, a car and some furniture, some savings in the bank, and enough money left over to pay for a "decent" wedding. (Edin and Kefalas 2007, p. 508)

Additionally, like many of their middle-class counterparts, poor women see the need to gain personal economic independence before marrying, as "insurance against a marriage gone bad" (Edin and Kefalas 2007, p. 509). Marriage is an elusive goal inasmuch as many low-income men and women do not have the money to meet these prerequisites.

Given their options, remaining unmarried may be the most rational decision for many low-income women. Sometimes government regulations actually work against the goals of the Healthy Marriage Initiative. For instance, a woman who marries a man who earns modest wages can lose Medicaid for her children (Carasso and Steuerle 2005). In addition, many poverty-level women are leery about making marriage vows, given the pool of potential husbands available to them.[12] "It is still the norm that a man must be able to provide a steady income to be seen as a good prospect for marriage. He no longer need earn all the family's income, but he must make a substantial, stable contribution" (Cherlin 2005, p. 49). However, due to declining work opportunities for the less well educated and consequent high unemployment rates for men in poor neighborhoods, many potential mates in these communities cannot promise a steady income (Oppenheimer 2003; Uchitelle and Leonhardt 2006). "Two incomes are better than one, but one income for two (a mother and child) is better than one for three (add a husband, who cannot find or hold a job)" (Huston and Melz 2004, p. 955).

Furthermore, low-income women's romantic relationships may be marked by wariness. Their "mistrust is often spawned by chronic violence and infidelity, drug and alcohol abuse, criminal activity, and the threat of imprisonment" (Edin and Kefalas 2007, p. 509).[13] However, like their middle-class counterparts, low-income women would like to find happiness and emotional support in marriage. As one participant in an HMI marriage-education program said to her interviewer:

> Here's what troubles me. I am enjoying these exercises, and I agree our society has too much divorce, but it doesn't seem right to me that a woman should stick with a man when she's miserable, or settle for one who doesn't make her happy. Why isn't it better to be alone? (in Huston and Melz 2004, p. 954)

If TANF recipients do marry, many of their unions are unlikely to look like the "good marriages" envisioned by the Healthy Marriage Initiative. We have seen that selection effects account for at least some of the benefits associated with marriage. If those with relatively low earnings, less education, lower literacy levels, and generally poorer parenting skills are persuaded to marry, there is little reason to believe that their family lives will resemble

those of the presently married (Amato 2005; Cherlin 2003; Manning and Brown 2006). For one thing, the maxim that "two parents are better than one" rests on the assumption that they work together cooperatively. But how couples co-parent has seldom been researched (Furstenberg 2005), and the extent to which, as a category, poorly educated couples engage in positively cooperative parenting is not known.

In addition, increased social support from friends and extended family is positively associated with the benefits of marriage. But data from the Michigan Women's Employment Survey, designed to assess social support among TANF recipients, show that TANF mothers, "embedded in networks whose members are marginally connected to the labor market and who are also poor," would be less likely to get the support characteristic of current marriages (Henly, Danziger, and Offer 2005, p. 123). Moreover, as qualitative researchers Ted Huston and Heidi Melz (2004) observed, some HMI participants did marry as a result of the program they attended. However, they did not marry the biological fathers of their children. As we've seen, research shows that, as a category, stepfamilies do not give children the same benefits offered by continuously married biological parents (Amato 2005; Carlson 2006). In sum, it is questionable whether marriages that are prompted by HMI participation will have the hoped-for positive outcomes for children.

Building healthy marriages presumes relieving poverty, and relieving poverty will require solutions other than—or at least in addition to—the Healthy Marriage Initiative. Nearly 12 million U.S. children under age eighteen live below poverty level (Kreider and Fields 2005, Table 2). This number represents approximately 17 percent of all children in the United States, and children comprise 36 percent of the poor (U.S. Census Bureau 2007a, Tables 693, 694). In recent years, poverty rates have declined for African Americans and Hispanics. Nevertheless, about one-third of African American and more than a quarter of Hispanic children live in poverty (Proctor and Dalaker 2003). Figures like these may lead us to think of family poverty in terms of black or Hispanic families, but even more poor families are non-Hispanic white. Despite lower *rates* of poverty, non-Hispanic white families predominate in sheer numbers, comprising nearly 68 percent of all poor families (U.S. Census Bureau 2007a, Table 696).

Regardless of their parents' marital status, children growing up in poverty often do not have enough nutritious food; are more likely to live in environmentally unhealthy neighborhoods; have more physical health, socio-emotional, and behavioral problems; must travel farther to attain health care; attend poorly financed schools; do less well academically; and are more likely

---

[12] Research in social psychology shows that individuals who are encouraged to choose from what they perceive as undesirable options limit their commitment to the selection (Lawler, Thye, and Yoon 2006). Hence, encouraging poor women to select husbands from what they perceive as a less than desirable pool is probably unlikely to result in many permanent unions.

[13] Although domestic violence is not confined to poor families and occurs in all social classes, there "does appear to be an association between lower income and increased risk for family violence" (Schumacher et al. 2001).

to drop out (Barbassa 2004; Borrell et al. 2004; Pathman, Konrad, and Schwartz 2001; Seccombe 2000; White and Rogers 2000). Furthermore, the rate of severe violence toward children is about 105 per 1,000 in families below the poverty line, compared to about 30 per 1,000 children in other families (Gelles and Cavanaugh 2007).

As noted in the discussion of ecological theory in Chapter 2, economic hardship in childhood, even in a two-parent married family, particularly when it lasts for a long time or occurs in adolescence, is related to lowered emotional well-being in early adulthood. Not having enough money causes stress, which often leads to marital conflict. Marital conflict, in turn, is associated with lower parent–child (especially teen) relationship quality, a situation that results in a child's lower psychological well-being (Sobolewski and Amato 2005).

Data that relate child poverty rates to children's living arrangements show that residing with married parents significantly lessens the likelihood of growing up in poverty. As you can see from Table 7.2, 10.1 percent of children under age eighteen who live with married parents are in poverty. This figure compares to 31.2 percent who are living with a cohabiting biological parent. Of children residing in single-parent households, 34.2 percent live below poverty level (Kreider and Fields 2005, Table 2).

Using computer simulations that paired individuals, similar in education and earnings, to form virtual marriages, one study found that encouraging people to get married would eliminate some poverty (Thomas and Sawhill 2005). We can conclude that encouraging people to get married would work *somewhat* to lessen poverty (Amato 2005). However, similar to the relationship between income and marriage for adults, the association between having unmarried parents and growing up in poverty is apparent but not the whole story. As you can also see from Table 7.2, a little more than 10 percent of children living with married parents do—and about two-thirds of those residing with an unmarried parent do not—live below the official poverty line. We must conclude that marriage contributes to children's economic well-being. Nevertheless, having married parents is not absolutely necessary in order to grow up above the poverty line. Indeed, children who live "with one well-educated parent may be doing better than comparable children a few decades ago" (Cherlin 2005, p. 49).

Moreover, marriage alone is not sufficient to alleviate child poverty. For one thing, as shown in Table 7.2, nearly 5 million of the 12 million American children below poverty level live with their married parents. The Healthy Marriage Initiative ignores these children, who represent nearly 42 percent of all children in poverty.

In addition to marital status, low wages for women contribute to poverty (Ozawa and Lee 2006). As Table 7.2 also shows, 36.4 percent of children in single-parent families headed by a mother live in poverty, compared with 14.7 percent of those in father-headed, single-parent homes.

Policies from the Family Change Perspective

Many policy makers maintain that family formation and maintenance are not simply a question of values or motivation. Instead, families are struggling with economic and time pressures that get in the way of their ability to realize family values (Yorburg 2002). These policy leaders argue that public policy shifts toward greater personal responsibility have not worked either to significantly reduce poverty or to bolster family life (Ozawa and Lee 2006).

As remedies for poverty, policy leaders in this camp propose structural solutions. As Figure 7.5 illustrates, the child poverty rate was about 27 percent in 1959, but beginning with President Lyndon Johnson's War on Poverty[14] in the 1960s, it dropped consistently during the 1970s to a low of about 14 percent. A decade later, a series of economic recessions occurred, along with the phasing out of many War on Poverty measures. As a result, the child poverty rate began to rise in the late 1970s, fell again after about 1993, and was 17.8 percent in 2004 (Proctor and Dalaker 2003; U.S. Census Bureau 2007a, Table 694).

The War on Poverty offered *structural* strategies to decrease poverty, such as community meal programs and health centers, legal services, summer youth programs, senior centers, neighborhood development, adult education, job training, and family planning (Garson n.d.). Commitment to the War on Poverty diminished after the 1970s. By 1996, a gradual public policy shift toward greater individual responsibility (Ozawa and Lee 2006) culminated in the Personal Responsibility and Work Opportunity Reconciliation Act, which would—in then president Bill Clinton's words—"end welfare as we know it."

Today, however, policy makers are again insisting that the United States must pay attention to ecological and structural supports for families—such as increased investment in and support for education, job training, drug rehabilitation, improved job opportunities, a

---

[14] War on Poverty measures, first proposed in 1964 by President Lyndon Johnson and enacted by Congress in the subsequent Economic Opportunity Act, allocated federal funds to reduce poverty. You may have heard of War on Poverty programs, such as the Job Corps or the Neighborhood Youth Corps, Head Start, or Adult Basic Education. Although the majority of War on Poverty measures have ended, Head Start and the Job Corps continue to exist.

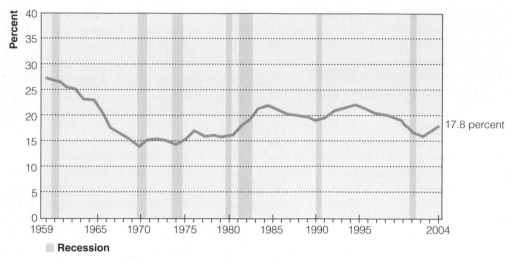

Figure 7.5 U.S. Poverty Rate for Children Under Age 18, 1959 to 2004.
Sources: Proctor and Dalaker, 2003; U.S. Census Bureau 2007a, Table 694.

federally legislated minimum wage adequate to lift full-time workers out of poverty, neighborhood improvements, small-business development, and parenting-skills education (Amato 2005; Brown 2004; Ozawa and Lee 2006). Indeed, "[l]ow-income communities have been neglected for so long that the resources needed to rebuild them will require a major shift in public priorities over an extended period of time, possibly generations" (Huston and Melz 2004, p. 956). In the words of demographer Frank Furstenberg,

> Restoring marriage to an institution of enduring, compassionate relationships will require more than sanctimonious calls for traditional, communitarian, and family values. We should back up our words with resources. . . . Otherwise, the institution of marriage as we knew it in [the twentieth] century will in the 21st century become a practice of the privileged. (2003, p. 177)

We end this section with an invitation to "consider some questions to which many of us offer differing answers" (Huston and Melz 2004, p. 944). Afterward we'll see how marriage matters for personal happiness and life satisfaction. First, the questions:

- Is the proposition that *marriage is good for people* grounded securely enough in research to justify promoting marriage over other adult lifestyles?
- What constitutes a "good marriage" or a "good enough marriage"?
- Are all (or most) marriages salvageable?
- Can all (or most) people be molded into good marriage material?
- What constitute "legitimate" personal reasons for terminating a marriage?

- Whose well-being should be considered first in these matters, and how much weight should be accorded the needs of the adults involved, their children, their extended family, the community, and the society?
- Can the attractiveness of marriage be increased by ameliorating poverty and its presumed common manifestations, such as crime, out-of-wedlock childbearing, low educational attainment, drug abuse, and alcoholism?
- Should we attempt to relieve single mothers' burdens by encouraging them to marry?
- Should the government be involved in encouraging marriage and discouraging divorce, and, if so, what kinds of government efforts are likely to benefit society the most? (Huston and Melz 2004, p. 944)

Having explored research and policy on the question whether marriage matters, we can conclude that marriage does matter, at least for those who can afford to get married. We end this chapter with a discussion of how marriage contributes to spouses' happiness and life satisfaction.

Happiness and Life Satisfaction: How Does Marriage Matter?

No longer a "marker of conformity," a wedding today marks a couple's public announcement that they have chosen marriage, among other available options, as a way to define and live their lives (Cherlin 2004, p. 856). Chapter 5 explores why love is increasingly important in an impersonal society. Marriage, more than any other

As an effort to improve family life, this neighborhood restoration project involves the community in effecting structural, as opposed to cultural or attitudinal, change.

relationship, promises to shore up that love, helping partners to keep it, once discovered.

Polls show that both male and female spouses are far more likely than others to say that they are "very happy." Nearly two-thirds (62 percent) of marrieds say they are "very happy," compared to less than half (45 percent) of unmarrieds (Carroll 2005; Lyons 2003; Saad 2004a; Taylor, Funk, and Craighill 2006). What is it about the experience of being married that works to create this difference?

For one thing, there are some pragmatic reasons that spouses (as well as cohabitors, albeit to a lesser degree) benefit from an *economy of scale*. Think of the saying, "Two can live as cheaply as one." Although this principle is not entirely true, some expenses, such as rent, do not necessarily increase when a second adult joins the household (Thomas and Sawhill 2005; Goode 2007 [1982]; Waite 1995). Then, too, the promise of permanence associated with the marriage premise accords spouses the security to develop some skills and to neglect others because they can count on working in complementary ways with their partners (Goode 2007 [1982]; Nock 2005). Furthermore, "[s]pouses act as a sort of small insurance pool against life's uncertainties, reducing their need to protect themselves *by themselves* from unexpected events" (Waite 1995, p. 498).

In addition, marriage offers enhanced social support (Manning and Brown 2006). Marriage connects people to in-laws and a widened extended family, who may be able to help when needed—for instance, with child care, transportation, a down payment on a house, or just an emotionally supportive phone call. The enhanced social support that typically accompanies marriage works to encourage the union's permanence (Giddens 2007). For example, family and friends send anniversary cards, celebrations of the years the couple has spent together and reminders of the couple's vow of commitment. Beginning with a public ceremony, marriage makes for what sociologist Andrew Cherlin (2004) calls *enforced trust*:

Marriage still requires a public commitment to a long-term, possibly lifelong relationship. This commitment is usually expressed in front of relatives, friends, and religious congregants. . . . Therefore, marriage . . . lowers the risk that one's partner will renege on agreements that have been made. . . It allows individuals to invest in the partnership with less fear of abandonment. (p. 854)

Furthermore, marriage offers *continuity*, the experience of building a relationship over time and resulting in a uniquely shared history. And, finally, marriage provides individuals with a sense of obligation to others, not only to their families but also to the broader community (Goode 2007 [1982]). This, in and of itself, gives life meaning (Waite 1995, p. 498). Chapter 9 addresses finding a marriage partner with whom to create such life-meaning. The following chapter describes alternatives to marriage.

Summary

- The marriage premise involves permanence and—for Western societies—monogamous sexual exclusivity.
- New norms for love-based marriage gradually became prevalent in Europe throughout the 1700s and 1800s.
- Expectations for personal happiness and love in marriage have changed the marriage premise over the past three hundred years.
- Marriages and families have become deinstitutionalized.
- Marriage has changed from institutionalized, to companionate, to individualistic.

© Corbis/ Jupiter Images

Because, more than others, a married couple can count on continuity, bolstered by enforced trust, spouses are freer to plan for a future together.

- The pluralistic family, characterized by tolerance for a diversity of family forms, characterizes American society today.

- Overall, researchers consistently find a significant correlation between marriage and many positive outcomes for both adults and children, but the relationship is more complicated than it first appears.

- Some of the benefits associated with marriage are due to selection effects.

- Scholars and policy makers who view individualized marriage and the pluralistic family as indications that the institution of marriage and family is in "decline" and "breakdown" have proposed ways to effect a turnaround—such as covenant marriage and the Healthy Marriage Initiative.

- Scholars and policy makers who view individualized marriage and the pluralistic family as results of inevitable historical change, resulting in struggle for some families more than for others, have proposed structural solutions to poverty and family struggle—such as higher wages for women, neighborhood development, an adequate minimum wage, and more employment opportunities.

- Optional and less permanent than in the past, marriage continues to offer benefits; married adults are more likely than others to say that they are happy with their lives.

- Although marriage has been deinstitutionalized, being married continues to help bolster the marriage premise, due largely to family and community social support that results in enforced trust.

Questions for Review and Reflection

1. Discuss the marriage premise, with its expectations of permanence and sexual exclusivity. Describe how love has changed the marriage premise over the past three centuries. What does family demographer Stephanie Coontz mean when she says that "love conquered marriage"?

2. Pointing out the pros and cons of each, compare and contrast companionate marriage and individualized marriage.

3. Explain the connection between federal "welfare reform" and the National Marriage Initiative.

4. Recognizing the possibility of selection effects, what are some ways that the experience of being married can enhance happiness and life satisfaction?

5. **Policy Question.** Are you more inclined to agree with policy leaders from the family decline or from the family change perspective? Using research evidence from this chapter, explain the reasons for your answer.

Key Terms

collectivist society 160
communal society 160
companionate marriage 1+65
courtly love 163
covenant marriage 173
deinstitutionalization of marriage 164
expectations of permanence 158
expectations of sexual exclusivity 158
experience hypothesis 169
extended family 160
family of orientation 161
family of procreation 161
Healthy Marriage Initiative (HMI) 174
individualism 160
individualistic society 160

individualized marriage 166
institutional marriage 164
kin 160
la familia 161
marriage premise 1658
pluralistic family 168
polyamory 159
polyandry
polygamy 158
polygyny 158
selection hypothesis 169
social institution 158
swinging 159
Temporary Assistance for Needy Families (TANF) 174

Online Resources

Companion Website for This Book

www.thomsonedu.com/sociology/lamanna

Visit the book companion website, where you will find flash cards, practice quizzes, Internet links, suggested readings, InfoTrac College Edition exercises, and more to help you study.

ThomsonNOW™ for Marriage and Family

Spend time on what you need to master rather than on information you already have learned. Take a pre-test for this chapter, and ThomsonNOW will generate a personalized study plan based on your results. The study plan will identify the topics you need to review and direct you to online resources such as videos, narrated learning modules, and interactive activities to help you master those topics. You can then take a post-test to help you determine the concepts you have mastered and what you will still need to work on. Try it out! Go to **www .thomsonedu.com/login** to sign in with an access code or to purchase access to this product.

Nonmarital Living Arrangements: Living Alone, Cohabitation, Same-Sex Couples, and Other Options

8

Reasons for the Increasing Proportion of Unmarrieds

Demographic, Economic, and Technological Changes

Cultural Changes

The Various Living Arrangements of Nonmarrieds

Living Alone

Living Alone Together

Living with Parents

Group or Communal Living

Cohabitation and Family Life

Cohabitation as an Acceptable Living Arrangement

Alternative to Unattached Singlehood and to Marriage

A Closer Look at Family Diversity: The Meaning of Cohabitation for Puerto Ricans, Compared to Mexican Americans

The Cohabiting Relationship

Focus on Children Cohabitating Families and Raising Children

As We Make Choices: Some Things to Know about the Legal Side of Living Together

Same-Sex Couples and Family Life

The Same-Sex Couple's Relationship

Facts About Families: Same-Sex Couples and Legal Marriage in the United States

Focus on Children: Same-Sex Partners and Raising Children

The Debate over Legal Marriage for Same-Sex Couples

The Unmarried and Life Satisfaction

Maintaining Supportive Social Networks

As one journalist put it, "The unmarried are showing up all over" (A. Roberts 2005, p. H1). For probably the first time in history, the majority of U.S. women (51 percent)—and about half of U.S. men—are living without a spouse (S. Roberts 2007a; Zernike 2006). Yes, a smaller percentage of Americans are married now than fifty years ago, but this situation does not mean that families are less meaningful to us today. A 2003 Gallup poll asked Americans how important were various aspects of their lives. The highest proportion of respondents—96 percent—said that their family was either extremely or very important to them. (After their families, people rank-ordered their health, work, friends, money, and religion [Moore 2003].)

Our families are important to us, but they are likely to be different from the "traditional" family of the 1950s. As we saw in Chapter 7, today's family is pluralistic—characterized by a diversity of family forms. As we look at the various living arrangements of unmarrieds in this chapter, we will examine several of these family forms. In the process we will find that the distinction between being **single** and being married is not that sharp today. Many people who are legally single are embedded in families of one form or another.

Besides a variety of living arrangements, factors such as age, sex, residence, religion, and economic status contribute to the diversity and complexity of single life. An elderly man or woman existing on Social Security payments and meager savings has a vastly different lifestyle from two unmarried professionals living together in an urban area. Also, the experience of being unmarried differs according to whether one is single by choice or involuntarily.

Many college students today think of "being single" as not being in a romantic relationship. By this way of thinking, a person in a dating relationship or cohabiting would not be single. To social scientists, however, *single* still means *unmarried,* and researchers tend to use these terms interchangeably. In this chapter we will examine what social scientists know about the large and growing number of singles: the never-married, the divorced, and the widowed. We'll discuss various nonmarital living arrangements. We'll look at living alone, residing with one's parents, and living in groups or communally. We will explore cohabitation, as well as same-sex families. To begin, we'll examine some reasons for the increasing proportion of unmarrieds in our society today.

Reasons for the Increasing Proportion of Unmarrieds

Chapter 7's Figure 7.2 shows the proportions of singles—the never-married, the divorced, and the widowed—by

various racial/ethnic categories. These percentages are considerably higher than in past decades. In 1970, less than 28 percent of U.S. adults were single. Today that number is about 41 percent (Saluter and Lugaila 1998, Figure 1; U.S. Census Bureau 2007a, Table 54). Much of this change is due to a growing proportion of widowed elderly (Bronson and Merryman 2006). However, the high proportion of singles also results from a high divorce rate and young adults' postponing of marriage, together with a dramatically growing incidence of cohabitation. Several social factors—demographic, economic, technological, and cultural—encourage Americans to postpone marriage, not to marry at all, or to choose to divorce rather than stay married.

Demographic, Economic, and Technological Changes

One reason for the growing proportion of singles is *demographic*, or related to population numbers. A high rate of heterosexual marriage presumes that there are matching numbers of marriage-age males and females in the population. Therefore, the **sex ratio**—the number of men to women in a given society or subgroup—influences marital options and singlehood.[1] Throughout the nineteenth and early twentieth centuries, the United States had more men than women, mainly because more men than women migrated to this country and, to a lesser extent, because a considerable number of young women died in childbirth. Today this situation is reversed due to changes in immigration patterns and greater improvement in women's health. In 2004, there were about 97 men for every 100 women. In 1910 there were nearly 106 men for every 100 women. The sex ratio was 100, or "even," a few years after the end of World War II, in about 1948 (U.S. Census Bureau 2006c, Table 11).

Today, beginning with middle age, there are increasingly fewer men than women in every racial/ethnic category. Sex ratios differ somewhat for various racial/ethnic categories, however. For instance, at younger ages the sex ratio is lower for blacks and Native Americans than for Hispanics or non-Hispanic whites. Moreover, incarceration rates as well as employment prospects also affect individuals' odds of marrying (Harris and Miller 2003).

In addition to demographic factors, widening *economic* opportunities for some have increased the proportion of nonmarrieds. Expanded educational and career options

---

[1] The sex ratio is expressed in one number: the number of males for every 100 females. Thus, a sex ratio of 105 means that there are 105 men for every 100 women in a given population. More specialized sex ratios may be calculated—for example, the sex ratio for specific racial/ethnic categories at various ages or the sex ratio for unmarried people only.

for college-educated women over the past several decades have encouraged many of them to postpone marriage:

> With so many options open to them, and with so little pressure on them to marry by their early twenties, the lives of young American women today have changed almost beyond recognition from what they were 50 years ago. And most of them take on their new freedoms with alacrity, making the most of their emerging adult years before they enter marriage and parenthood. (Arnett 2004, p. 7)

In addition, middle-aged, divorced women with careers tend to look on marriage skeptically, viewing it as a bad bargain once they have gained financial and sexual independence (Swartz 2004; Zernike 2006).

At the same time, growing economic disadvantage and uncertainty appear to have made marriage less available to many who might want to marry but feel that they can't financially afford it. The fact that many men's earning potential has declined, relative to women's, may make marriage less attractive to both genders (Huston and Melz 2004; McLanahan 2004; Raley and Bratter 2004; Sassler and Goldscheider 2004).

Furthermore, *technological* changes over the past sixty years have influenced the proportion of singles. Beginning with the introduction of "the pill" in the 1960s, improved contraception contributed to the decision to delay or forego marriage. With effective contraception, sexual relationships outside marriage and without great risk of unwanted pregnancy became possible (Gaughan 2002; Coontz 2005b). Moreover, new conception technologies, such as artificial insemination, offer the possibility for planned pregnancy to unpartnered heterosexual women as well as to same-sex couples. In addition to these structural reasons for the increasing proportion of nonmarrieds, cultural changes have played a part.

Cultural Changes

Several related cultural changes over the past few decades help to account for the growing proportion of nonmarrieds. First, attitudes toward nonmarital sex have changed dramatically over past decades. "[I]t is now widely accepted that young people will have sexual relations, including sexual intercourse, before marriage" (Arnett 2004, p. 85). Second, as American culture gives greater weight to personal autonomy, many find that—at least "for now"—singlehood is more desirable than marriage (Cherlin 2005; Thornton and DeMarco 2001). As one young man explains:

> It would kind of bum me out to be married. One day I was at work and my friend called me up from Florida and said, "what are you doing?" I'm like, "Just working," and he said, "Can you come down?" I'm like, "When?"

© Asia Images/ Jupiter Images

The increase in the number and proportion of unmarrieds in our society is a result of many factors, including unfavorable sex ratios, especially in older age categories; economic constrictions; improved contraception; and changing attitudes toward marriage and singlehood, which have resulted in more young adults postponing marriage.

and he's like, "Tomorrow," and I'm like, "Well, let me see what I can do." So I took a week off all of a sudden and went down to Florida. And I know I'd never be able to do that if I was married. (in Arnett 2004, p. 101)

A young woman evidences a similar attitude:

> I hope to be married by the time I'm 30. I mean, I don't see it being any time before that. I just think I have a lot of life left in me, and I want to enjoy it. There's so much out there, not that you couldn't see it with your husband, but why have to worry "Is he going to get mad at this?" Just go out and enjoy life and then settle down, and you'll know you've done everything possible that you wanted to do, and you won't regret getting married. (in Arnett 2004, p. 103)

In addition, being unmarried has become an acceptable option, rather than the deviant lifestyle that it was once thought to be. During the 1950s, people (including social scientists) tended to characterize the never-married as selfish, neurotic, or unattractive. That view has changed so much that today the popular press enthusiastically runs stories about those who are "embracing the solo life" (Hurwitt 2004; Sanders 2004).

Furthermore, cohabitation is emerging as a socially accepted alternative to marriage (Arnett 2004; Willetts 2006). Among today's teens, nearly 70 percent say it's okay for couples to live together before they get married, and only about half think that it is "morally wrong" to have a baby outside of marriage (Lyons 2002, 2004). Although beliefs such as these are less likely among many recent immigrants and members of some religions, in general young adults experience less parental pressure to marry than in the past (Arnett 2004; Bumpass, Sweet, and Cherlin 1991).

In addition, getting married is no longer virtually the only way to gain adult status. Before about 1940, the most legitimate reason for leaving home, at least for women, was to get married. Today, 45 percent of young men and 39 percent of young women say that they first left home for other reasons, often to attend college and/or "to gain independence." As more and more young adults choose to claim independence simply by moving, marriage loses its monopoly as the way to claim adulthood (Arnett 2004; Furstenberg et al. 2004). The nationwide General Social Survey (GSS), conducted by the National Opinion Research Center (NORC), found that people now see becoming self-supporting as the first transition to adulthood, followed by no longer living with one's parents, having a full-time job, completing school, being able to support a family financially, and—sixth on the list—getting married (T. Smith 2003).

Finally, the changing nature of marriage itself may render marriage less desirable now than in the past. Marriage has become less strongly defined as permanent, while historically the expectation of permanence offered a significant benefit to getting married. If marriage is losing its permanent status, then

> [i]ndividuals, as a result, have less faith that a successful marriage is possible, and they transfer support for marriage into support for other coupling arrangements, such as cohabitation—arrangements that are easier to dissolve if (and when) problems arise. (Willetts 2006, p. 125)

In sum, it appears that much of the increase in singlehood results from (1) low sex ratios, particularly in certain regions and among specific age and racial/ethnic groups (2) increasing educational and economic options for some, on the one hand, and growing financial disadvantage for others; (3) technological changes regarding pregnancy; and (4) changing cultural attitudes toward marriage and singlehood. Related reasons for the increase in the number and proportion of unmarrieds include the high likelihood of cohabitation, discussed later in this chapter, as well as a high divorce rate (see Chapters 7 and 16). We can apply the exchange theoretical perspective (see Chapter 2) to this question of less-compelling reasons to get married. Overall, as people weigh the costs against the benefits of being married, marriage offers fewer benefits now, relative to being unmarried, than in the past (McGinnis 2003; Seltzer 2000; Willetts 2006). If more Americans are unmarried today, what are their various living arrangements?

The Various Living Arrangements of Nonmarrieds

As unmarrieds make choices about how to live, we see the variety of singles' lives. Some live alone; others, with parents; still others, in groups or communally. Some unmarrieds cohabit with partners of the same or opposite sex.

Living Alone

The number of one-person households has increased dramatically over past decades. Individuals living alone now make up over one-quarter of U.S. households—up from just 8 percent in 1940 (U.S. Census Bureau 1989, Table 61; Bergman 2006a). Figure 8.1 gives the percentage of people over age nineteen living alone, by race/ethnicity. As you can see from the figure, the likelihood of living alone increases with age in all racial/ethnic groups and is markedly higher for older women than for older men (U.S. Census Bureau 2007a, Table 52). Asians and Hispanics of all ages are less likely to live alone than are blacks or non-Hispanic whites. Significantly less likely to be married than other racial/ethnic groups (see Figure 7.2), blacks are more likely than other groups to be living by themselves, particularly in older age groups. More collectivist Asian and Hispanic cultures help to discourage living alone in these ethnic groups. Some who live alone are actually engaged in long-term committed relationships.

Living Alone Together

An emerging alternative to marriage is *living alone together*. Here a couple is engaged in a long-term relationship, but each partner also maintains a separate dwelling (A. Roberts 2005). The number of these relationships is difficult to ascertain, because the U.S. Census Bureau does

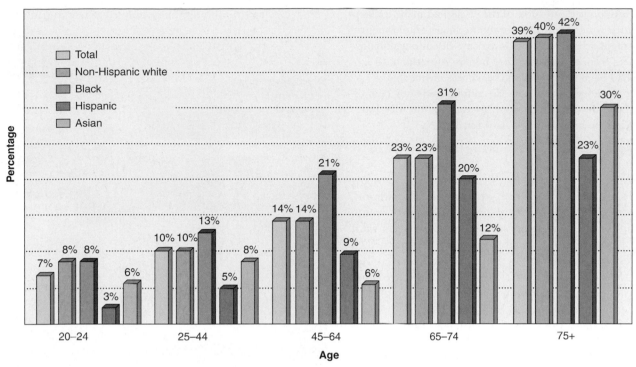

Figure 8.1 Percentage of people over 19 years old living alone, by race/ethnicity, 2004.

Source: Calculated from U.S. Census Bureau 2006c, Table 52.

not measure them. However, British survey data have uncovered this family form. David Popenoe, codirector of the National Marriage Project at Rutgers University, has noted that living alone together is clearly a trend in the United States. We know this partly from anecdotal evidence and "partly [from] the fact that every other significant European trend in family life has turned out to be happening in America" (Popenoe, quoted in Brooke 2006). Although we know little about this family form, it is apparently at least partly motivated by a desire to retain autonomy. As one woman said, "I like my own life, my own identity and want to keep it. I like having the things I love around me." As one man put it, "I am as devoted as any husband to her, . . . but I like my alone time and being around my stuff, not [hers]" (in Brooke 2006). Some young adults in relationships like these actually reside with their parents (S. Smith 2006).

Living with Parents

A large proportion of young adults today are living with one or both parents (Settersten, Furstenberg, and Rumbaut 2005). In Table 8.1, we see that the percentage of young adults living at home has increased moderately since 1960. In 2003, 55 percent of men and 46 percent of women age eighteen through twenty-four lived with

their parents (Fields 2004, p. 13). Because norms prohibiting nonmarital sex have relaxed since the 1960s, it is more likely now that young adults will engage in sexually intimate relationships while living "at home" (S. Smith 2006).

In 1940, the proportion of adults under age thirty living with their parents was quite high. Sociologists Paul Glick and Sung-Ling Lin suggest why:

Table 8.1 Young Adults Living with One or Both Parents, by Age, United States, 1960, 1995, and 2003

PERCENTAGE LIVING WITH THEIR PARENTS SEX AND YEAR		
	Age 18–24	Age 25–34
Men		
1960	52	11
1995	58	15
2003	55	14
Women		
1960	35	7
1995	47	8
2003	46	7

Sources: U.S. Census Bureau 1988, Table A–6, and 1997 Table 65; Bianchi and Casper 2000, Figure 4; Fields 2004, p. 13.

The economic depression of the 1930s had made it difficult for young men and women to obtain employment on a regular basis, and this must have discouraged many of them from establishing new homes. Also, the birth rate had been low for several years; this means that fewer homes were crowded with numerous young children, and that left more space for young adult sons and daughters to occupy. (Glick and Lin 1986, p. 108)

These same reasons apply to many young people today (Cohen and Casper 2002).

Housing in urban areas may be too expensive for many singles to maintain their own apartments. In addition, demographer Frank Furstenberg explains that young single adults are "accurately seeing that if they ever want to buy a house, if they're ever going to get married, if they even want a car, they're going to have to save. And, in effect, their families [with whom they reside] are subsidizing that saving" (quoted in De Vise 2004; Pisano 2005; Settersten, Furstenberg, and Rumbaut 2005).

Although many observers focus on economic reasons as primary causes for living with parents, some others see this trend as resulting from changed attitudes on the part of both young adults and their parents. Young adults "have a greater sense of entitlement these days," according to some counseling psychologists. Psychologist Tova Rubin partly blames "an indulgent parenting style marked by low demandingness and high attentiveness" (in Pisano 2005). Sometimes conflict with parents precipitates the decision to move out and take up residence with a romantic partner (Sassler 2004).

We need to note here that living with parents can occur in a variety of circumstances. Some ethnic groups, such as the Hmong, expect single women to reside with their parents until marriage. Unmarried women who have babies, especially those who became mothers in their teens, may be living with parents (London 1998). Formerly married young men and women may return to their parental home after divorce. Interestingly, singles are less likely to return home when their parents have been divorced or remarried (Goldscheider and Goldscheider 1998).

Just as economic considerations, the need for emotional support, or the need for help with child raising may lead young singles to live with parents, similar pressures may encourage singles to fashion group or communal living arrangements.

Group or Communal Living

Groups of adults and perhaps children may live together. Often these are simple roommate arrangements. But some group houses purposefully share aspects of their lives in common. **Communes**—that is, situations or places characterized by group living—have existed in

Co-housing started in Denmark and spread to the United States in the early 1980s. Residents own their own homes, with residences clustered closely to leave open space, which is community owned. Co-housing complexes, which typically combine private areas with communal kitchens—and, often with community gardens—offer alternative living arrangements and can be a way to cope with some of the problems of aging, unattached singlehood, or single parenthood.

American society throughout its history and have widely varied in their structure and family arrangements.[2]

Living communally has declined in the United States since its highly visible and idealized status in

[2] In some communes, such as the Israeli kibbutzim (Spiro 1956) and nineteenth-century American groups such as the Shakers and the Oneida colony (Kephart 1971; Kern 1981), all economic resources are shared. Work is organized by the commune, and commune members are fed, housed, and clothed by the community. Other communes may have some private property; even some Israeli farming cooperatives that superficially resemble kibbutzim have private land plots, although members share a communal life (Schwartz 1954). Sex-

the 1960s, but many communes that were established then still exist (Miller 1999). Also, new, small-scale and nonideological versions of communal living have surfaced (Jacobs 2006). Communal living, either in single houses or in co-housing complexes that combine private areas with communal kitchens and "family rooms," may be one way to cope with some of the problems of aging, unattached singlehood, or single parenthood ("Cohousing" 2006). In a small but growing number of co-housing complexes, people of diverse races and ethnicities and ages choose to reside together, sharing some meals and recreational activities. Communal living is designed to provide enhanced opportunities for social support and companionship. More commonly, financial considerations and the desire for companionship encourage romantically involved singles to share households. We turn now to a discussion of cohabitation, or living together.

Cohabitation and Family Life

Cohabitation, or nonmarrieds' living together, gained widespread acceptance over the past fifty years and is "widely viewed as one of the most important changes in family life in the past 40 years, dramatically altering the marital life course by offering a prelude to or a replacement for marriage" (S. Smith 2006, p. 7). Not only in the United States but in other industrialized nations as well, "living together" has dramatically increased. In this country, the cohabitation trend spread widely in the 1960s, took off sharply in the 1970s, and has risen steadily ever since, as Figure 8.2 illustrates. Today about 5.5 million U.S. heterosexual couples cohabit (U.S. Census Bureau 2007a, Table 61). This number may be an undercount, because cohabitors do not necessarily move into separate housing. Instead, they may live together in a parental home or reside with roommates and therefore would not be included in a census count (Manning and Smock 2005).

About 9 percent of U.S. women age fifteen through forty-five are currently cohabiting with a male partner, and 50 percent have cohabited at some time in their lives—an increase from 41 percent in 1995 (Chandra et al. 2005, Table 47). At about 4 percent, the proportion of teenage cohabitors is fairly small. Nevertheless,

ual arrangements also vary among communes, ranging from celibacy to monogamous couples (the kibbutzim and some communes in the United States) to the open sexual sharing found in both the Oneida colony and some modern American groups. Children may be under the control and supervision of a parent, or they may be more communally reared, with a de-emphasis on biological relationships and responsibility for discipline and care vested in the entire community.

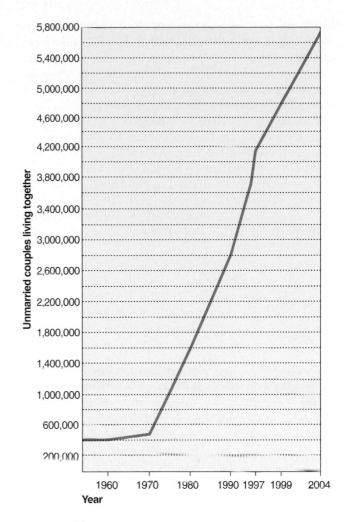

Figure 8.2 Unmarried couples living together in the United States, 1960–2004.

Sources: Glick and Norton 1979; Schneider 2003; Simmons and O'Connell 2003; U.S. Census Bureau 2007a, Table 61.

the likelihood that a fifteen- to nineteen year-old is currently cohabiting nearly tripled since 1982 (Houseknecht and Lewis 2005). The incidence of cohabitation is expected to escalate further as future generations become still more accepting of this family form (Lyons 2004). Furthermore, new generations are growing up in cohabiting families and thereby may be socialized to take cohabiting for granted (Seltzer 2004).

Although approximately 75 percent of cohabitants are under age forty-five, the proportion of middle-aged cohabitors has increased over the past two decades. Middle-aged cohabitors are currently in relationships of longer duration, and—as you might expect—they are more likely to be divorced (King and Scott 2005). Approximately 5 percent of cohabitants are age sixty-five and over—a 50 percent increase since 1990 ("Numbers" 2004; U.S. Census Bureau 2000, Table 57). Older couples have found that living together absent legal marriage may be economically advantageous, because they can retain some financial benefits that are contingent on not being married (King and Scott 2005).

Comparing marrieds to cohabitors, analyses of data from several sources find cohabitors to be younger, less educated, earning less income, less likely to own their own homes, more likely to be nonwhite, and more likely to have been sexually abused in childhood (Chandra et al. 2005, Table 47; Cherlin et al. 2004; DeLeire and Kalil 2005; Schoen and Cheng 2006). Nevertheless, people from all social classes and educational categories have cohabited.

Some couples begin to live together shortly after their first date; others wait for months or longer (Sassler 2004). Accounts of how cohabitation begins suggest that cohabiting does not always result from a well-considered decision. As one twenty-three-year-old woman who had been living with her parents explained,

> I was looking for my own apartment at this time. . . . He was like, "Why don't you just move in with me?" I was like, "Let's give it some time," or whatever. So I dated him for like a month and then finally all my stuff ended up in his house. (in Sassler 2004, p. 496)

Cohabitation as an Acceptable Living Arrangement

As "A Closer Look at Family Diversity" suggests, cohabiting means different things to different people. Generally, though, "[c]ohabitation is very much a family status, but one in which the levels of certainty about commitment are less than in marriage" (Bumpass, Sweet, and Cherlin 1991, p. 913; see also Bianchi and Casper 2000; Willetts 2006). British demographer Kathleen Kiernan (2002) has described a four-stage process through which cohabitation becomes a socially acceptable living arrangement, equal in status to marriage.

In the first stage, the vast majority of people marry without living together first. We saw this stage in the United States until the late 1970s. In the second stage, more people live together but mainly as a form of courtship before marriage, and almost all of them marry with pregnancy. Today some cohabitants consider their lifestyle a means of courtship, or *premarital cohabitation,* as they seek to test their compatibility before deciding whether to marry. As one young woman explained, "We wanted to try it out and see how we got along, because I've had so many long-term relationships. I just wanted to make sure we were compatible. And he's been married before, and he felt the same way" (in Arnett 2004,

p. 108). Living together as courtship is explored further in Chapter 9.

In the third stage, cohabiting becomes a socially acceptable alternative to marriage. A couple no longer feels it necessary to marry with pregnancy or childbirth, and people routinely take an unmarried partner to work or family get-togethers. Nevertheless, in stage three, legal and social differences remain between marriage and "just" living together. In the fourth stage, cohabitation and marriage become virtually indistinguishable legally and socially. In this stage, the numbers of married and cohabiting couples are about equal, and a cohabiting couple may have several children (Kiernan 2002).

Social historian Stephanie Coontz (2005b) characterized the United States as "transitioning from stage two to stage three at the end of the twentieth century" (p. 272).[3] Perhaps in some large metropolitan areas of this country, cohabitation has fully reached stage three. According to Coontz, Sweden is an example of a society in stage four. Will the United States ever get to stage four? Coontz is skeptical, because "people [in the United States] still place much more importance on getting married than Swedes do" (p. 272). "As We Make Choices: Some Things to Know about the Legal Side of Living Together" discusses the legal implications of cohabiting in the United States today.

Alternative to Unattached Singlehood and to Marriage

Some cohabitants view living together as an alternative to dating or unattached singlehood (Hueveline and Timberlake 2004; Manning and Smock 2005). As one respondent told her interviewer:

> Um, he had came over, and we had talked and we had, he had spent the night and then from then on he had stayed the night, so basically . . . he just honestly never went home. I guess he had just got out of a relationship, the person he was living with before, he was staying with an uncle and then once we met, it was like love at first sight or whatever and um, he never went home, he stayed with me. (in Manning and Smock 2005, p. 995)

Psychologist Jeffrey Arnett (2004) has dubbed those who live together as an alternative to being single *uncommitted cohabitors.*

---

[3] Due to laws enacted at the turn of the twentieth century, unmarried cohabitation has remained illegal in some states, although the laws are seldom enforced (Jayson 2005a). The American Civil Liberties Union is suing to overturn anticohabitation laws in states where they still exist (Hartsoe 2005).

You probably have an idea of what cohabitation means to you, and you may assume that living together signifies the same thing to all of us. But researchers who have analyzed national survey data in order to study cohabitation among various racial/ethnic groups have uncovered interesting differences (Castro Martin 2002; Manning 2004). Cohabiting means different things to different people—and to different categories of people.

For instance, Puerto Rican women have a long history of **consensual marriages** (heterosexual, conjugal unions that have not gone through a legal marriage ceremony). The tradition of consensual marriages probably began among Puerto Ricans due to lack of economic resources necessary for marriage licenses and weddings: "Although nonmarital unions were never considered the cultural ideal, they were recognized as a form of marriage and they typically produced children" (Manning and Landale 1996, p. 65). Therefore, for Puerto Ricans in the continental United States, cohabitation symbolizes a committed union much like marriage, and they don't necessarily feel the need to marry legally should the woman become pregnant because they have already defined themselves as (consensually) married. Compared to Mexican Americans, Puerto Ricans are more likely to agree that "[i]t's all right for an unmarried couple to live together if they have no plans to marry" (Oropesa 1996).

Meanwhile, compared to Puerto Ricans (and to non-Hispanic whites), Mexican Americans were more likely to agree that "[i]t is better to get married than go through life being single." Mexican Americans weigh marriage very positively, and a couple's having plans to marry significantly increases Mexican Americans' approval of cohabitation. These findings are especially strong for foreign-born Mexican Americans. However, economic barriers to marriage (discussed in Chapter 7) apparently induce many low-income Mexican Americans to continue to cohabit, rather than to marry, and to raise several children in cohabiting families (Lloyd 2006; Wildsmith and Raley 2006). Furthermore, as a result of their exposure to general cultural values and attitudes in the United States, we can expect second- and third-generation Mexican Americans to embrace cohabitation in increasing proportions (Oropesa and Landale 2004).

For Puerto Ricans, "living together" is likely to symbolize a committed union, virtually equal to marriage. Among Mexican Americans, cohabitation is less valued than marriage but allowable if the couple plans to marry—although economic barriers to marriage can thwart those plans. Our diverse American society encompasses many ethnic groups with family norms that sometimes differ from one another. Together with structural/economic factors, cultural meaning systems play a part in how people define cohabitation.

Critical Thinking

The U.S. Census Bureau groups Puerto Ricans and Mexican Americans, along with other Hispanics, into one ethnic category. What does the information above tell you about diversity *within* the ethnic category Hispanic? Would you suppose that the various groups of Asians, such as the Hmong or Asian Indians, who are also categorized together, differ as well? What about African Americans, or whites?

Other cohabitors view living together as an alternative to marriage (Booth and Crouter 2002; Heuveline and Timberlake 2004; Willetts 2006). We can think of these couples as *committed cohabitors* (Arnett 2004). As one explained.

> We've been together 10 years. We met at college. . . . We graduated and started living together. . . . We never say never, but we certainly don't have any plans to [marry]. We're very happy being unmarried to each other. (in Sachs, Solot, and Miller 2003)

People's reasons for living together as an alternative to marrying legally often include the belief that marriage signifies loss of identity or stifles partners' communication and equality (Steinhauer 1995; Moore, McCabe, and Brink 2001; Willetts 2003). In the United States today this view is unusual among young adults, and committed cohabitors are generally older (Arnett 2004).

The Cohabiting Relationship

Compared to research on marrieds, research on cohabiting relationships is relatively new and undeveloped. Here we present what we know. We should note that some of this research pertains to people who were cohabiting during Kiernan's second stage, described earlier. To what extent, if any, these findings will continue to apply as more and more Americans choose to cohabit is unknown.

Today cohabiting couples differ from marrieds in several ways. First, cohabitors are less homogamous, or alike in social characteristics, than are marrieds (Jepsen and Jepsen 2002). Cohabiting couples are twice as likely as marrieds to be interracial (Fields and Casper 2001, Table 8). Compared with married women, cohabiting women are more likely to be several years older than and to earn more than their partners. About 17 percent of wives earn at least $5,000 more annually than

As We Make Choices   Some Things to Know about the Legal Side of Living Together

When unmarried partners decide to move in together, they may encounter regulations, customs, and laws that cause them problems, especially if they're not prepared (Demian 2006c; Fenton 2004; Skinner and Kohler 2002). Consulting a lawyer is advised. There are no absolutely firm legal guidelines to follow. State laws vary, and new court decisions may effect changes. But a look at some of the potential trouble spots may help.

Domestic Partners

Over the past decade, more cities, states, federal agencies, businesses, and major corporations have established *domestic partner* policies and offer this status and accompanying benefits to their members/ employees (Demian 2006a; Solmonese 2006). Unmarried couples may register their partnership and then enjoy some (although not necessarily all) rights, benefits, and entitlements that have traditionally been reserved for marrieds, such as access to joint health insurance and family or bereavement leave. The definition of **domestic partner** usually includes criteria of joint residence and finances, plus a statement of loyalty and commitment. Between 70 and 90 percent of domestic partnerships involve heterosexual couples. However, domestic partner laws are particularly helpful to same-sex couples who are not allowed to marry legally.

Residence

When renting an apartment or house, renters usually must sign a lease. This is a legal contract, and failure to abide by it can result in eviction. Many leases specify how many people will live in the rental unit. For a single person who later decides to take in a friend, an objecting landlord may prove troublesome.

When two or more unmarried people are renting, landlords may ask each of them to sign the lease so that everyone is held responsible. Conversely, if an unmarried partner's name is not on

the lease, she or he may not be entitled to live in the rental unit if something happens to the named renter.

Bank Accounts

Any couple can open a joint bank account, but it's important to realize that one of the couple may then withdraw all the money without the other's approval.

Power of Attorney for Finances

"One simple thing that all [cohabiting] couples should do is prepare a durable power of attorney for finances," advises Pam Rhode, president of Myvesta, a nonprofit consumer education organization. "Otherwise, if you get sick it's up to a court to decide who is in control of your finances. And quite often it's not someone you would have picked" (quoted in "Financial Agreements" 2004). Among other things, a power of attorney for finances allows the authorized partner to make payments on outstanding bills, run the partner's business, file taxes, and write checks on the partner's account (Demian 2006c).

Credit Cards and Charge Accounts

If a company agrees to issue a joint account to an unmarried couple, both partners are legally responsible for all charges made by either of them, even if the relationship has ended. And creditors generally will not remove one person's name from an account until it is paid in full.

Property

When unmarrieds purchase a house or other property such as home furnishings together, it is a good idea to have a written agreement about what happens should one partner die or the couple break up. If the property is held in "joint tenancy with the right of survivorship" and one dies, the other would take ownership without probate.

Alternatively, the couple can hold property as "tenants in common," which

means that the property would go into the estate to be distributed according to a will. Except for a very small number of states that allow for inheritance without a will, surviving partners who do not have legal title to the couple's assets must establish a legal right to ownership in order to keep the property (Demian 2006c). "Inheritance rights are a particularly sticky issue" (Fenton 2004). Check with a lawyer to be sure that each partner will be entitled to assert ownership of joint property upon the death of other. Meanwhile, keep in mind that under joint title ownership, creditors could take one partner's property if the other partner gets into problems with debts.

Insurance

Anyone may buy life insurance and name anyone else as the beneficiary. However, insurance companies sometimes require an "insurable interest," generally interpreted to mean a conventional family tie. Moreover, the routine extension of auto and home insurance policies to "residents of the household" cannot be presumed to include nonrelatives; one should check with the company about terms of the policy. Domestic partner laws and company policies frequently extend health insurance coverage to an employee's partner.

Wills and Living Trusts

If you have no will or living trust when you die, your property will pass to those people named by law as intestate heirs— usually legal spouses, children, parents, and other [blood] relatives. As a result, your surviving partner may end up with nothing, and even lose property he or she paid for. (Demian 2006c)

Telling relatives or friends what to do in case of your death may not work out. Because handwritten wills are not recognized in some states, it's good to obtain a lawyer's advice.

An alternative to a traditional will is a living trust. This is a legal document naming yourself as the trustee and sole controller of your own property but also providing for a cotrustee, who would only take over the property upon your death or disability.

> Living trusts offer a number of estate planning benefits unavailable with wills. . . . [They can be] advantageous to same-sex couples because, in most states, a trust need not be publicly recorded as a will must be. Consequently, it can provide some protection against contests by hostile blood relatives. (Demian 2006c)

Health Care Decision Making

Any individual has the right to refuse treatment, but anyone too ill to be legally competent must have an agent to act for him or her in medical decision making. Many cohabitants want their partners to play this role. The catch is that to hospitals and doctors, "family" may mean spouses, parents, adult children, or siblings but not unmarried partners or close friends. However, a person may designate a decision maker through use of a "durable power of attorney for health care." Among other rights and responsibilities, the person designated may authorize medical treatment if you are incapacitated and be given first priority in visitation if you become a patient (Demian 2006c). Check local laws for specifics.

Children

With the 1972 case of *Stanley v. Illinois* (405 U.S. 645), an unmarried mother is no longer entitled to sole disposition of the child in many states. Although the courts have placement discretion, unmarried couples should stipulate in writing that custody is to go to the partner if the other parent dies. Note also that financial obligations for child support do not depend on marital status.

A relatively new area for court determination of child custody is that regarding children of unmarried parents who separate. Some courts are treating nonmarital relationships, whether same-sex or heterosexual, as "sufficiently marriage-like" for marital law to apply (Judge Heather Van Nuys in "Court Treats" 2002). In making these custody (and property, child support, and visitation) decisions, courts may disregard actual biological relationship to a child (American Civil Liberties Union 2004; Biskupic 2003; "Court Treats" 2002; Finz 2003).

Not all courts make such rulings, and there is substantial opposition to the courts' becoming involved in the custody issues of unmarried parents. However, as the dean of the Duke University Law School, Katherine Bartlett, remarked: "Courts aren't trying to contribute to the demise of traditional families. But they recognize the reality of families today and functional parents" (Biskupic 2003, p. 2A).

Some courts permit a lesbian partner to adopt the biological child of the other partner or will grant joint adoption to same-sex couples, ensuring legal parenthood to both members of the couple raising a child (Human Rights Campaign 2007). The law remains somewhat unsettled as new cases proceed through the courts. Some states have prohibited adoption by gays, but where the practice has not been made illegal, a majority of adoption agencies will place a child with gay or lesbian parents (Peterson 2003).

Some—but not all—court jurisdictions grant visitation rights to a nonbiological, same-sex co-parent should the relationship end (Demian 2006c). Unmarried parents to one partner's child should consider the following three documents:

- a Co-parenting Agreement that spells out the rights and responsibilities of each partner
- a Nomination of Guardianship that adds language to a will or living trust

- a Consent to Medical Treatment form that gives the co-parent the right to authorize medical procedures for a child (Demian 2006c)

Breaking Up

An advantage that people sometimes see in cohabiting is avoiding legal hassles in the event of a breakup. However, if couples do not take care to stipulate in writing—and preferably with an attorney's assistance—paternity, property, and other agreements, legal hassles *may* result (G. Greenstein 2001). In fact, the parties may find that they have legal obligations typically associated with marriage (*Marvin v. Marvin* 1976). The *Marvin* case established that nonmarital partners may claim property and support if their explicit or implicit contract (the verbal or written understanding underlying their union) established these obligations. It is important to note that child support can never be determined by contract; it is considered an unqualified entitlement of the child.

It is important to see an attorney about the laws in your state. See also the following websites: Human Rights Campaign, www.hrc.org; Lambda Legal, www.lambdalegal.org; and ACLU, www.aclu.org. Also, at www.buddybuddy.com, read "Legal Precautions to Protect Your Relationship" (Demian 2006c) and "Domestic Partnership Benefits" (Demian 2006a). Finally, search the Internet for online publications or software for purchase regarding the legal side of unmarried living together and cohabitation agreements.

Critical Thinking

Are you cohabiting, or do you have friends who are living together? If so, to what extent would you say your or their decisions have been and are being made knowledgeably? Does having to worry about the legal aspects of cohabitation lessen what appear to be some of the advantages of living together, do you think? Why, or why not?

their husbands, compared with 23 percent of cohabiting women (Fields 2004). Cohabitors have been more likely than marrieds to be nontraditional in many ways, including attitudes about gender roles, and to have parents with nontraditional attitudes and/or who have divorced (Baxter 2005; Booth and Amato 1994; Cunningham 2005; Teachman 2004).

On average, cohabiting relationships are relatively short-term. Half last less than one year, because the couple either break up or marry (Bumpass and Lu 2000). However, one national survey found that 39 percent of unmarried couples were still together after five to seven years (Bianchi and Casper 2000, p. 17). Still, "[c]ompared with married couples, cohabitors are much more likely to break up" (Seltzer 2000, p. 1252). Reasons include the fact that, for the most part, cohabiting partners are not committed to their relationship in the same way that marrieds are. Then, too, cohabitation may not include widely held norms to guide behavior to the degree that marriage does. As a result, the relationship may suffer as partners struggle to define their situation. Finally, lack of social support may negatively impact the stability of cohabitation "as members of the network . . . provide the partners possibilities for other intimate relationships" (Willetts 2006, p. 114).

Uncertainty about commitment, together with less well-defined norms for the relationship, may be reasons that, compared to marrieds, cohabitants pool their finances to a lesser extent (Kenney 2004; King and Scott 2005); are less likely to say that they are happy with their relationships and find them less fair (Skinner et al. 2002); report a higher incidence of depression than marrieds (Kim and McKenry 2002; Lamb, Lee, and DeMaris 2003); and have more sex outside the relationship than marrieds do (Treas and Giesen 2000).

Evidence also exists of considerable domestic violence in cohabiting relationships (Brownridge and Halli 2002; DeMaris 2001)—more than among marrieds or dating partners. This situation may also be due to a combination of relatively low commitment (M. Johnson and Ferraro 2000) and conflict over "rights, duties, and obligations" (Magdol et al. 1998, p. 52). In addition, selection effects—the situation in which individuals "select" themselves into a category being investigated (in this case, cohabitation)—probably help to account for these findings. That is, as we have seen, cohabiting couples tend to be less well educated and poorer than marrieds, and—although domestic violence occurs at all economic and education levels—low income and education are statistically associated with higher levels of domestic violence (Schumacher et al. 2001).

On a different note, recent research that analyzed data from the National Survey of Families and Households (NSFH) has found that the relationship quality

According to Pamela J. Smock, associate director at the Institute for Research at the University of Michigan, Ann Arbor, cohabiting "has become the typical and, increasingly, the majority experience of persons before marriage and after marriage" (quoted in "What Happened? . . ." 2003). On average, cohabiting relationships are relatively short-term. Half last less than one year, because the couple either break up or marry. Cohabiting men with intentions to marry their partner are likely to do more housework than other cohabiting males.

of "long-term" cohabiting couples who were together for at least four years differed little from marrieds in conflict levels, amount of interaction together, or relationship satisfaction. One thing did differ, however: For both marrieds and long-term cohabitors, relationship satisfaction declined with the addition of children to the household. But for cohabitors, this decline was more pronounced (Willetts 2006). Other research has found that, compared with younger cohabitors, older cohabiting couples generally report higher relationship quality. Among younger cohabitors, lack of plans for marriage is associated with lower relationship satisfaction (King and Scott 2005). One study found that cohabiting men with intensions to marry their partner do more housework than do other cohabiting males (Ciabattari 2004).

Research on the economic consequences of cohabitors' breaking up finds similarities to getting divorced. On average, men experience moderate financial decline, while women's economic decline is more pronounced (Avellar and Smock 2005). Counselors stress the importance of being fairly independent before deciding to cohabit, understanding one's motives, having clear goals and expectations, and being honest with and sensitive to the needs of both oneself and one's partner. This is especially necessary when children are involved.

Cohabiting Families and Raising Children

FOCUS ON CHILDREN Today, between 10 and 15 percent of all first births occur to a cohabiting mother (Chandra et al. 2005, Table 16). About half of all nonmarital births occur to cohabiting couples (Dye 2005; B. Hamilton et al. 2006). Perhaps the majority of births to cohabitors are planned (Manning 2001). As shown in Figure 8.3, more than 40 percent of cohabiting heterosexual households contain children under age eighteen—a proportion that approaches the percentage of married-couple households with children (Fields 2004). Currently, about 6 percent of children under age eighteen are living with a cohabiting parent (Lugaila and Overturf 2004, Table 3). About half of these children, or 2 million, live with both of their (unmarried) biological parents (Kreider and Fields 2005, p. 2). Perhaps one in four American children "will live in a family headed by a cohabiting couple at some point during childhood" (Graefe and Lichter 1999, p. 215).

Although a large majority of cohabiting couples with children have one child, a significant number (about 1.5 million cohabiting couples) are raising two or more children (Chandra et al. 2005, Table 9). Research from at least three national samples has found this situation to be more characteristic of black and Hispanic cohabitors than of non-Hispanic whites, who are more likely to marry upon becoming pregnant (Chandra et al. 2005, Table 18; Manning 2004; Musick 2002).

Having a child while cohabiting does not necessarily increase a couple's odds of staying together. However, conceiving a child during cohabitation and then marrying before the baby is born apparently does increase union stability. Why would this be? "Although birth in cohabitation indicates a decision to remain together during pregnancy, it also represents a decision not to com-

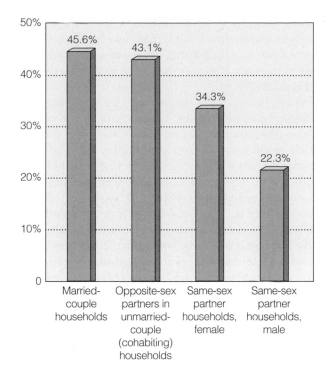

Figure 8.3 Percentage of U.S. households with children under age 18, 2000.

Note: Unmarried partners' children refers to sons/daughters of householder and to other children not related to the household.

Sources: Fields 2004; Simmons and O'Connell 2003; "What Happened?" 2003.

mit to marriage" (Manning 2004, p. 677). Lower commitment is associated with decreased union stability.

For many families, "[c]ohabitation may not be an ideal childrearing context precisely because of the stress associated with the uncertainty of the future of the union" (S. Brown 2004, p. 353). Because cohabiting couples are significantly less likely to stay together than marrieds, it has been noted that many children in cohabiting-couple families will experience a series of changes in their family's living arrangements (Graefe and Lichter 1999; Raley and Wildsmith 2004). "Residential and other household changes associated with the formation of new partnerships may disrupt well-established patterns of [parental] supervision" (Thomson et al. 2001, p. 378).

Accordingly, some family scholars have expressed concern regarding outcomes for adolescents and younger children living in cohabiting families (Booth and Crouter 2002; S. Brown 2004). For example, research that compared economically disadvantaged six- and seven-year-olds from families of various forms found more problem behaviors among children in various types of unmarried families, including cohabiting unions (Ackerman et al. 2001; M. J. Carlson 2006). Other research has found that, among couples with comparable incomes, cohabiting parents spend less on their children's education than do marrieds (DeLeire and Kalil 2005).

When compared to those in married, two-biological-parent families, adolescents who have lived with a cohabiting parent are more likely to experience earlier premarital intercourse, higher rates of school suspension, and antisocial and delinquent behaviors, coupled with lower academic achievement and expectations for college (Albrecht and Teachman 2003; S. Brown 2004; M. J. Carlson 2006; Manning and Lamb 2003). Interestingly, having a cohabiting male in the household who is not the biological father appears not to enhance adolescents' outcomes when compared with living in a single-mother household (Manning and Lamb 2003). Nevertheless, research also shows that, compared to growing up in a single-parent home, children do benefit economically from living with a cohabiting partner, provided that the partner's financial resources are shared with family members (Manning and Brown 2006). As cohabitation becomes increasingly common, we become more aware that today's pluralistic family is comprised of many forms. We turn now to another relationship type that exemplifies the pluralistic family—same-sex couples.

Same-Sex Couples and Family Life

Google GLBT (gay, lesbian, bisexual, and transgendered) organizations, and you'll find websites for blacks, Latinos/as, Jews, and Muslims, among others. Lesbian and gay singles make up a diverse category of all ages and racial/ethnic groups. In 2003, there were approximately 700,000 same-sex households in the United States, about evenly divided between gay-male and lesbian couples (U.S. Census Bureau 2007a, Table 61).[4]

Same-sex couples often find community in urban areas that have high concentrations of gays and lesbians, along with strong activist organizations. But lesbians and gays also live in the suburbs and smaller towns (Oswald and Culton 2003). The Internet has changed life for many gay men and lesbians, especially those living in more rural areas. Accessing websites such as PlanetOut.com, homosexuals from all over the world can meet and chat online regardless of geographical boundaries (Gudelunas 2006).

From a variety of national surveys, demographers estimate that about 28 percent of gay men and 44 percent of lesbians are partnered, many in long-term, committed relationships (Black et al. 2000, p. 143; Seidman 2003).[5] Some have married legally in the state of Massachusetts, although there are legal challenges to their marital status (LeBlanc 2006b). (See "Facts About Families: Same-Sex Couples and Legal Marriage in the United States.")

In the absence of access to legal marriage, partners may publicly declare their commitment in ceremonies among friends or in some congregations and churches, such as the Unitarian Universalist Association or the Metropolitan Community Church, the latter expressly dedicated to serving the gay community (Demian 2005b; Suter et al. 2006). Catholics have access to a union ceremony designed by Dignity, a Catholic support association, although these unions are not recognized by the Catholic Church ("What Is Dignity?" 2004). Secular commitment ceremonies for gay men and lesbians have become common enough to have sparked a number of "wedding"-planning businesses for same-sex couples (e.g., Two Brides 2004). Registering as domestic partners (described in "As We Make Choices: Some Things to Know about the Legal Side of Living Together") can have emotional significance for same-sex couples who may do so partly as a way of publicly expressing their commitment (Willetts 2003).

The Same-Sex Couple's Relationship

In many respects, same-sex relationships are similar to heterosexual ones. Research indicates that the need to resolve issues of sexual exclusivity, division of labor, and power and decision making is not much different in same-sex pairings than among heterosexual partners (Kurdek 1995a, 2006). Psychologist Lawrence Kurdek compared gay-male and lesbian couples, and found the latter to have "enhanced relationship quality." Similar to prior researchers (Blumstein and Schwartz 1983), Kurdek attributes lesbians'

---

[4] Until the 2000 census, the census definition on which calculations of unmarried couples were based did not include same-sex partners. Therefore, comparing estimates from before 2000 with census data thereafter is inappropriate.

[5] Same-sex couples living together in long-term, committed relationships is not a recent development. According to social historian Samuel Kader (1999), same-sex committed couples date back to the Old Testament, and commitment ceremonies between same-sex partners were not unknown in early Christianity. More recently, scholars "have uncovered a long and complicated history of gay relationships in nineteenth-century America. Sometimes women passed as men to form straight-seeming relationships; sometimes men or women lived together as housemates but were really lovers; sometimes individuals would marry but still carry on romantic, sometimes life-long same-sex intimate relationships" (Seidman 2003, p. 124).

Same-Sex Couples and Legal Marriage in the United States

The 1974 U.S. Supreme Court decision in *Singer v. Hara* defined marriage as a union between one man and one woman (*Singer v. Hara* 1974). Nevertheless, the federal government has traditionally recognized the right of individual states to create, interpret, and enforce laws regarding marriage and families. Consequently, the battle over legal marriage for same-sex couples has largely been fought within individual state courts and legislatures.

Lawsuits Claiming Discrimination and Varied State Responses

Beginning in the late 1990s, same-sex couples in several states filed lawsuits claiming that barring lesbians and gays from legal marriage is unconstitutional because it discriminates against same-sex couples. Some (although not all) courts have agreed and ordered their state legislatures to address this problem by passing new, nondiscriminatory laws. Results have been varied. In 2004, Massachusetts allowed gay and lesbian couples to marry legally, although this situation could change due to pending legal challenges to the law. Connecticut and Vermont passed *civil union* laws.

Civil unions allow any two single adults—including same-sex partners or blood relatives, such as siblings or a parent and adult child—to have access to virtually all marriage rights and benefits on the state level, but none on the federal level (Demian 2006a, 2006b). For instance, a couple would have state-regulated rights to joint property and tenancy, inheritance without a will, and hospital visitation and health care decisions for their partners. However, they cannot collect federal Social Security benefits upon a partner's death, nor can a non-U.S. partner become a U.S. citizen upon joining a civil union.

The Federal Defense of Marriage Act (DOMA)

States usually recognize one another's legal decisions. This *principle of reciprocity* would require a state to recognize a legal marriage performed in another state. However, in order to allow states *not* to follow the principle of reciprocity regarding same-sex marriages, the United States passed the 1996 **Defense of Marriage Act (DOMA)**. The Defense of Marriage Act is a federal statute declaring marriage to be a "legal union of one man and one woman" and relieving states of the obligation to grant reciprocity to marriages performed in another state. As a result of the Defense of Marriage Act, a large majority of states have passed laws refusing to recognize a marriage obtained by same-sex couples in another state.

A Proposed Federal Amendment to the U.S. Constitution

A proposed federal amendment to the U.S. Constitution would define marriage as between one man and one woman and ban same-sex marriage in the United States while allowing states to create civil unions or domestic partnerships (M. Allen and Cooperman 2004; Page and Benedetto 2004). Because the originators of the U.S. Constitution intended for amendments not to be undertaken lightly, they made them very difficult to pass. Passing a U.S. constitutional amendment requires a two-thirds majority in both the U.S. House of Representatives and Senate. Then the amendment must be approved by three-fourths of the states. A constitutional amendment that would define marriage as between one man and one woman has not passed in Congress.

This range—from legal marriage for same-sex couples in Massachusetts to a possible federal constitutional amendment that would ban same-sex marriages across the country—points up the serious public divide in the United States regarding same-sex marriage. For further details on legal marriage for same-sex couples in the United States and throughout the world, see Demian (2006), "Legal Marriage Report: Global Status of Legal Marriage," Partners Task Force for Gay and Lesbian Couples (http://www.buddybuddy.com); and/or DOMA Watch (http://www.domawatch .org).

Critical Thinking

Today it would be difficult to escape the public debate over whether, on the one hand, the family as institution is inappropriately threatened or, on the other hand, tolerance for diversity is fitting when the issue is legal marriage for same-sex couples. What do you think? Is the institution of marriage and family threatened by same-sex marriage? Why or why not? Can you back up your opinion with facts?

greater relationship satisfaction, stronger liking of their partners, greater trust, and more frequent shared decision making . . . to *both* partners having been socialized to define themselves in terms of relationships with others, to regulate interactions with others on the basis of care and nurturance, to be sensitive to the needs and feelings of others and to suppress aggressive and competitive urges which may result in social isolation. (Kurdek 1989, p. 55)

Same-sex partners of both genders are likely to evidence more equality and role sharing than couples in heterosexual marriages (Kurdek 1998; Reimann 1997; Rosenbluth 1997).

Daily, same-sex couples are faced with the need to negotiate their private relationship within a heterosexual world (Suter et al. 2006). Discrimination against same-sex couples may add stress to their relationship and result in lowered relationship quality (Otis et al. 2006). In addition, the potential for discrimination gives partners unique avenues for dealing negatively with couple conflict. "For example, 'outing' one's partner is not an issue for heterosexuals but is a surprisingly common weapon for gay people in an abusive relationship" (Burke and Owen 2006, p. 6).

Stress resulting from the effects of discrimination may be one reason that statistics point to higher rates of domestic violence among same-sex couples than among heterosexual couples. This "problem is exacerbated by the current political climate, which treats gays and lesbians as a marginalized population" (Burke and Owen 2006, p. 7). Gay activists argue that domestic-violence laws need to specifically include lesbian and gay partners, and police must be trained to more effectively address intimate-partner violence among same-sex couples.

Increasingly, major corporations, as well as federal agencies and local and state governments, are offering the option for same-sex or heterosexual couples to register as domestic partners. A domestic-partner certificate usually indicates joint residence and finances, as well as including a statement of loyalty and commitment, and grants unmarried partners some legal rights traditionally restricted to marrieds.

Same-Sex Partners and Raising Children

FOCUS ON CHILDREN

Enough same-sex couples are establishing families with children that by the early2000s, observers noted a "gay baby boom" (S. Johnson and O'Connor 2002). According to the 2000 census (see Figure 8.3), more than one-third (34.3 percent) of female, and close to one-quarter (22.3 percent) of male, same-sex couple households now include children under age eighteen—some born to the union and many others from prior heterosexual relationships. Despite this situation, "little is known about the impact of child rearing on same-gender couples compared to the literature examining the impact of children on traditional married couples across the family life cycle" (Means-Christensen, Snyder, and Negy 2003).

Same-sex parents have not only become more visible but have also increased in number (M. Bell 2003). A sig-

nificant number have been married, and some have children from those marriages. Same-sex families include lesbian co-parents, as well as an array of combinations of lesbian mothers and biological fathers, surrogate mothers, and gay biological fathers (less frequent) (C. Patterson 2000). A family studies professor describes the diversity apparent in her own lesbian family as follows:

> My partner and I live with our two sons. Our older son was conceived in my former heterosexual marriage. At first, our blended family consisted of a lesbian couple and a child from one partner's previous marriage. After several years, our circumstances changed. My brother's life partner became the donor and father to our second son, who is my partner's biological child. My partner and I draw a boundary around our lesbian-headed family in which we share a household consisting of two moms and two sons, but our extended family consists of additional kin groups. For example, my former husband and his wife have an infant son, who is my biological son's second brother. All four sets of grandparents and extended kin related to our sons' biological parents are involved in all our lives to varying degrees. These kin comprise a diversity of heterosexual and gay identities as well as long-term married, ever-single, and divorced individuals. (K. R. Allen 1997, p. 213)

In addition to raising children from a prior marriage, same-sex couples become parents through adoption, foster care, planned sexual intercourse, or artificial insemination (M. Bell 2003; Gomes 2003). Religions vary in their policies regarding such families. For example, the Catholic Church officially opposes adoption by same-sex couples (Buchanan 2006b; LeBlanc 2006a). Courts also vary in their receptiveness to same-sex families. Some courts have permitted a lesbian co-parent to adopt a biological child born to her partner. Many courts grant joint adoption to gay male couples. However, some states prohibit same-sex couples from adopting children. Florida, for example, prohibits same-sex couple adoption, although it does allow them to serve as foster parents (Demian 2006c; Waddell 2005).

Among lesbian couples, one partner may give birth to a child that both partners parent. When a couple decides to follow this course, the women face a series of decisions: Who will be the biological mother? How will a sperm donor be chosen? What will they call themselves as parents? How will they negotiate parenthood within a heterosexual society? Where and from whom will they find support? (Chabot and Ames 2004). "Living in a

Lesbian couples may take advantage of AID (artificial insemination by donor) technology so that one partner gives birth to a baby they both want. Research indicates that children of lesbian or gay male parents are generally well adjusted and have no noticeable differences from children of heterosexual parents.

society fixated on labels and family terminology," lesbian couples are often asked, 'Who is the real mom?' One nonbiological mother illustrates this point:

> I think a lot of people have issue with that . . . you're not *really* the mother if you're not the biological mother. You're just sort of playing this role, or something. Maybe you're just the one who's also responsible, but you're not "*the mom*." We don't care what anybody else thinks. We both are the moms. (in Chabot and Ames 2004, p. 354)

As with research on heterosexual cohabitors, the number of studies on same-sex couples is small compared to that on heterosexual marrieds. One study has found that lesbian partners who become parents are more likely than wives to remain committed to full-time work as well as to motherhood (Peplau and Fingerhut 2004). Another study (Goldberg and Sayer 2006) focused on the relationship quality of twenty-nine committed lesbian couples who gave birth to their first child by means of artificial insemination. These researchers found that, similar to heterosexual couples, lesbian partners' relationship satisfaction declined with the transition to parenthood. This situation was largely due to having less time to be alone as a couple after the baby was born. Then, too, issues of support from the couple's extended families may cause tension:

> Biological mothers' families may undermine the nonbiological mother's relationship to the child, seeing her as "less of a mother." . . . Another possibility is that biological mothers' families . . . meet or even surpass nonbiological mothers' expectations for support, but their frequent presence or greater involvement ultimately causes conflict between the partners. (Goldberg and Sayer 2006, p. 97)

Research from an accumulation of more than one hundred studies finds children of gay male and lesbian parents to be generally well adjusted, with no noticeable differences from children of heterosexual parents in cognitive abilities, behavior, or emotional development. There is no evidence that children of same-sex parents are confused about their gender identity, either in childhood or adulthood, or that they are more likely to be homosexual (Meezan and Rauch 2005; Patterson 2000; Perrin 2002; Stacey and Biblarz 2001).

Although not necessarily refuting these findings, sociologists note that the research methodologies of many of these studies are not rigorous, largely because it is very difficult to locate representative samples of gay male and/or lesbian parents. The research that we do have—which is largely on lesbian, white, and middle- or upper-middle class parents—concludes that same-sex parents are much like others in their parenting practices

(Meezan and Rauch 2005; Stacey and Biblarz 2001). Its members having themselves reviewed the literature, the American Academy of Pediatrics officially supports gay male and lesbian couples' adopting, bearing, and raising children (Perrin 2002).

Same-sex parents emphasize their similarity to heterosexual parents: "We go to story time at the library and worry about all the same food groups" (in M. Bell 2003). Meanwhile, like children of other minority groups, those in same-sex families may experience prejudice from friends, classmates, or teachers. Regarding relationships with schools, the Family Pride Coalition urges same-sex parents to

> [t]ell the teachers who is in your family and names your children use to identify them, and provide a glossary of correct terms for lesbian and gay families. Give the library a list of books, videos and other resource materials . . . , and encourage school administrators and librarians to purchase these materials for the school. (Brickley et al. 1999)

In many cities there are workshops for lesbians wanting to get pregnant, for gays and lesbians who want to parent together, and for gay male parents. There are also discussion groups on raising children, along with play groups and organized events for children of same-sex parents. In addition, "[c]ontrary to stereotypes of these families as isolated from families of origin, most report that children had regular (i.e., at least monthly) contact with one or more grandparents, as well as with other adult friends and relatives of both genders" (Patterson 2000, p. 1062).

Children of same-sex parents have formed a support group called COLAGE (Children of Lesbians and Gays Everywhere) and maintain a website (www.colage.org). Their purpose is to "engage, connect, and empower people to make the world a better place for children of lesbian, gay, bisexual, and/or transgender parents and families." Being allowed to marry legally might be a benefit to children being raised in same-sex households, because marriage is associated with increased "durability and stability of the parental relationship" as well as enhanced in-law, grandparent, and other extended-family investment (Meezan and Rauch 2005, p. 108). We turn now to the debate over legal marriage for same-sex couples.

The Debate over Legal Marriage for Same-Sex Couples

In 2000, the Netherlands became the first country to allow same-sex partners to marry.[6] Some other European countries, as well as Canada, now allow same-sex marriage (Demian 2006b).[7] Meanwhile, the United

Nations Commission on Human Rights has not been able to pass a resolution to add sexual preference as a reason that people's human rights must not be violated. The motion was dropped "in the midst of intense pressure" from the Vatican and the Conference of Islamic States ("United Nations Drops" 2004). We can conclude that the **culture war**—deep conflict over matters concerning human sexuality and gender—is global.

"Take a Stand for Marriage!" urges the conservative Family Research Council website (http://www.frc.org), one of several that speak out against same-sex marriage. Other websites, such as Gay and Lesbian Advocates and Defenders (GLAD), the Partners Task Force for Gay and Lesbian Couples, or the National Black Justice Coalition advocate for the other side. (www.glad.org; www.buddybuddy.com; www.nbjcoalition.org). Having first emerged as a remote possibility in the 1970s, legal marriage for gay and lesbian couples "became a front-line issue" after 1991 when gay activists formed the Equal Rights Marriage Fund (Seidman 2003). "Facts about Families: Same-Sex Couples and Legal Marriage in the United States" outlines political developments regarding legal marriage for same-sex couples.

Attitudes toward gay rights generally have become became more accepting since the early 1990s. Gallup polls have shown a gradual increase—from 38 percent in 1992 to 54 percent in 2006—in agreement with the idea that being gay or lesbian is an "acceptable alternative lifestyle" (Buchanan 2006c; Newport 2001; Saad 2006a). As shown in Figure 8.4, more than half of Americans (53 percent) favor allowing same-sex couples to enter into legal agreements, such as civil unions and domestic partnerships, that would give them many of the same rights as married couples. Our country is about evenly split between those who favor (46 percent) and who oppose (48 percent) allowing gays and lesbians to adopt children. About 40 percent of Americans say that they favor legal marriage for same-sex couples (Pew Research Center 2006). What are the arguments against and for legal marriage for same-sex partners?

---

[6] For a detailed account of developments regarding same-sex legal marriage around the world, see Demian(2006), "Legal Marriage Report: Global Status of Legal Marriage," Partners Task Force for Gay and Lesbian Couples.

[7] U.S. citizens are allowed to marry in Canada. However, upon their return to the United States, their unions are unlikely to be recognized by either the federal government or the vast majority of state governments. "Another complication arises if a couple wishes to divorce. They would not be able to do so in their resident state if their state did not recognize the marriage in the first place. To get a divorce, one of the partners would need to reside in Canada for a year" (Demian 2004a, 2005a, 2006c). For these reasons, gay rights activists have published Internet advisories for U.S. citizens deciding about going to Canada to wed.

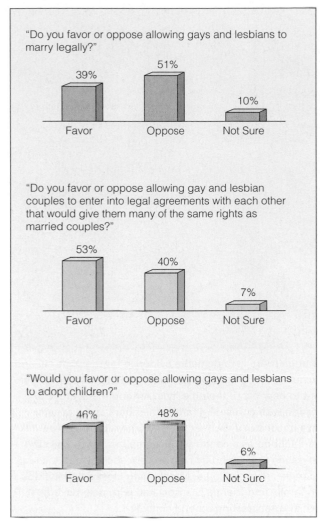

Figure 8.4 American public opinion regarding legal marriage, domestic partnerships/civil unions, and adoption for same-sex couples, 2006.
Source: Pew Research Center 2006

Arguments for Legal Marriage as Heterosexual Only Not all religions or religious leaders oppose legal same-sex marriage (Chadwick 2005; Goodstein 2006; Ontario Consultants on Religious Tolerance 2006). As one example, Christian social psychologist David Myers, making a "Christian Case for Gay Marriage," argues that if marriage is good for people and society, as discussed in Chapter 7, then marriage should be an option for everyone, including lesbians and gays (Myers and Scanzoni 2006). However, for religious fundamentalists and other conservative groups, the move to legalize marriage is an "attempt to deconstruct traditional morality" (Smolowe 1996a; J. Wilson 2001). Those who favor defining legal marriage as only heterosexual argue that only heterosexual marriage has deep roots in history, as

well as in the Judeo-Christian and other religious traditions (Dalley 2004; Hartocollis 2006).

They further claim that only heterosexual married parents can provide the optimum family environment for raising children and that legalizing same-sex marriage would weaken an institution already threatened by single-parent families, cohabitation, and divorce (McClusky 2004; Seidman 2003). Some contend that "[e]ven more ominously, permitting gays to marry would open the door for all sorts of people to demand the right to marry—polygamists, children, friends, kin—even more than two partners" (Seidman 2003, p. 128).[8] Finally, they argue that legal marriage for same-sex couples is unnecessary, given "compromise" legislation, such as **civil unions** in a few states, which give virtually all the rights of marriage to same-sex couples without the title "married" or "spouse" (Seidman 2003).

Arguments for Legal Same-Sex Marriage Those who favor legalized same-sex marriage argue that denying lesbians and gays the right to marry legally violates the U.S. Constitution because it discriminates against a category of citizens. Legal marriage yields economic and other practical advantages. For instance, if one spouse dies or is disabled, the other is entitled to Social Security benefits; legal partners can inherit from one another without a will; the immigrant spouse of a U.S. citizen can, more readily than otherwise, become a citizen. The U.S. General Accounting Office has identified more than one thousand federal laws in which marital status is a factor, including veterans' benefits, for example (Butz 2004; U.S. General Accounting Office 1997). Furthermore, proponents of gay and lesbian rights argue that creating domestic partnerships or civil unions, instead of allowing marriage for same-sex partners, creates "second-class citizens" (Belluck 2004; Leff 2006; Seidman 2003). Many children of same-sex couples view the legalization of same-sex marriage as giving them security and comfort (P. L. Brown 2004).

Gay men and lesbians themselves have been divided somewhat on the desirability of legalized same-sex marriage, at least for themselves ("Gays Want the Right" 2004). Interestingly, although many lesbians and gays support the claim for same-sex marriage in principle, in Massachusetts, where same-sex marriage became legal

[8] This fear is not entirely unfounded. In 2004, attorneys filed suit in Utah, arguing that the state's ban on polygamy violated Mormons' First Amendment right to practice their religion. Although struck down in 2005, the suit was under appeal at this writing. In 2003, the U.S. Supreme Court had struck down laws criminalizing sodomy. At that time, the Supreme Court ruled that individuals have "the full right to engage in private conduct without government intervention." The Utah suit requests the same considerations for proponents of bigamy (Kurtz 2006; Sage 2004; Soukup 2006).

in 2004, less than 20 percent of same-sex couples have chosen to marry (Foust 2006).

Dissenting Arguments among Lesbians and Gay Men
Although probably less true today than fifteen or twenty years ago, some gays and lesbians have themselves opposed legal same-sex marriage. Generally, they have objected to mimicking a traditionally patriarchal institution based on property rights and institutionalized husband–wife roles and characterized by a high divorce rate.[9] Opponents have also objected to giving the state power to regulate primary adult relationships (Peele 2006). Furthermore, they have stressed that legalizing same-sex unions would further stigmatize any sex outside marriage, with unmarried lesbians and gay men facing heightened discrimination ("Monogamy: Is It for Us?" 1998; Seidman 2003).

The extent to which allowing same-sex couples to legally marry would increase their personal life satisfaction is a matter for future research. In the following section, we turn to a discussion of life satisfaction among the unmarried.

The Unmarried and Life Satisfaction

As pointed out in Chapter 7, polls consistently find that marrieds are more likely to say that they are "very happy." Sixty-two percent of spouses report being "very happy," compared with 45 percent of unmarrieds (Carroll 2005; Lyons 2003; Saad 2004a; Taylor, Funk, and Craighill 2006). Nevertheless, more than eight in ten Americans say that they are satisfied with the way things are going in their personal lives (Carroll 2005). And regardless of marital status, 62 percent of us are "highly satisfied" with our families (Saad 2004c).

Perhaps not surprisingly, life satisfaction is associated with income as well as marital status (Taylor, Funk, and Craighill 2006). Many single parents, particularly women, just do not make enough money (Barbassa 2004; Borrell et al. 2004; U.S. Census Bureau 2007a, Table 693). Many work more than one low-paying job, then take care of their homes and children (Huston and Melz 2004). For them, "career advancement"

© Joel W. Rogers/CORBIS

Although there is undeniable evidence for the physical and psychological benefits of marriage, unattached singles do point to benefits of their lifestyle. Among these are less irritation with coresident family members and a greater sense of control over their lives. Moreover, when we think of singlehood as a continuum, we realize that not all singles—even those who live alone—are socially unattached, disconnected, or isolated. Maintaining close relationships with family and friends is associated with positive adjustment and satisfaction among singles.

means hoping for a small raise or just hanging on to a job in the face of growing economic insecurity. Pursuing higher educational opportunities means rushing to class one evening a week after working all day. Moreover, research shows that poor women have less-effective private safety nets than do others, because their families and friends are also very likely to be poor and overburdened financially and emotionally (Harknett 2006). These women are dealing with work, parenting, and low-income issues, not enjoying the stereotypical "swinging singles" lifestyle characterized by personal freedom and consumerism.

Economics notwithstanding, how do nonmarrieds maintain life satisfaction? In one sentence, the answer involves establishing connection with others and maintaining a network of socially supportive relationships. Although probably not sufficient by themselves, web-based chat rooms can add support for some. Today you

---

[9] With irony, San Francisco columnist Mark Morford questions why same-sex couples would *want* to marry: "Show me a single scientific experiment where fully 50 percent of the results turn out negative and induce collapse and emotional breakdown and childhood therapy and Xanax and alcoholism and screaming, and I'll show you a scientist who will quickly scrap the whole thing and start over" (Morford 2006).

can find chat rooms on virtually any subject, from unattached singlehood to co-housing to cohabiting to same-sex family living.

If we think of the various living arrangements of unmarrieds as forming a *continuum of social attachment* (Ross 1995), we realize that not all singles are socially unattached, disconnected, or isolated. In sociologist Catherine Ross's (1995) research with a nationally representative sample of about two thousand adults who were interviewed in 1990, people in close relationships—whether married or not and whether living alone or not—were significantly less depressed than those with no intimate partner at all. Moreover (and this is important!), the relationship between being involved and not being depressed held *only* for those in happy, or supportive, arrangements (see also Wickrama et al. 1997).

One young woman, single by choice, actually planned her own wedding ceremony—to herself. She wore white, carried a bouquet, and invited about twenty friends. She "chose to join herself in matrimony" a few days after her thirtieth birthday. Her friend, serving as officiator, asked, "Do you promise to love, honor, and respect yourself from this day forward for as long as you live?" "I do," answered the woman. She was subsequently declared "wedded to life" (Seligman 2006). Those who view themselves as "wedded to life"—by choice—are probably more satisfied with their lives than are those who are single against their wishes.

Meanwhile, for unattached singles, living alone can be lonesome. However, we need to remember that aloneness (being by oneself) and loneliness (a subjective sensation of distress) are different. Moreover, living alone does not necessarily imply a lack of social integration or meaningful connections with others (Ross 1995; Trimberger 2005). Nevertheless, unattached singles have tended to report feeling lonely more often than have marrieds (Kim and McKenry 2002). Poor and older singles are especially likely to be lonely, perhaps because the low incomes and ill health that tend to accompany old age make socializing very difficult. Besides age and income, being single as a result of divorce apparently affects loneliness.

A book by sociologist E. Kay Trimberger (2005) addresses the challenges of unattached singlehood for women between ages thirty and sixty. Trimberger argues that the "heaviest thing" for unattached, middle-aged women is the "idea of the couple, and that's so internalized." However, according to this author, it is time to recognize unattached singlehood as a "full lifestyle" (Trimberger, in A. Roberts 2005). Trimberger identifies the following "pillars of support" for unattached single women: a nurturing home, satisfying work, satisfaction with their sexuality, connections to the next generation,

a network of friends and possibly family members, and a feeling of community.

Some research has found cohabitants to be midway between unattached singles and marrieds in mental and physical well-being (Kurdek 1991), while other studies have shown no difference between cohabitants and other singles, "suggesting that the protection effects of marriage are not as applicable to cohabitation" (Kim and McKenry 2002, p. 905). However, marriage also involves a set of obligations and the responsibility of coping with both the burdens of other family members and the disappointments that come with family life. Valuing personal autonomy, Americans may find these obligations emotionally stressful (Gove, Style, and Hughes 1990). Hughes and Gove (1989) note that social scientists have tended to focus on the benefits of social integration while ignoring the costs. There are some areas in which nonmarrieds may feel better off than the married. Less irritation and a greater sense of control over one's life can be among the advantages of being single (Hughes and Gove 1989).

Maintaining Supportive Social Networks

All of us need support from people whom we are close to and who care about us. Isolation increases feelings of unhappiness, depression, and anxiety (Umberson et al. 1996), whereas being socially connected "seems to keep stress responses . . . from running amok," according to UCLA psychologist Shelley Taylor (quoted in "Save the Date" 2004). Perhaps the greatest challenge to unmarrieds is the development of strong social networks. Maintaining close relationships with parents, siblings, and friends is associated with positive adjustment and life satisfaction among nonmarrieds (Kurdek 2006; Spitze and Trent 2006; Weaver, Coleman, and Ganong 2003).

A crucial part of one's support network is valued same-sex friendships (Cotton 1999). Despite changing gender roles, men remain less likely than women to cultivate psychologically intimate relationships with siblings or same-sex friends (Weaver, Coleman, and Ganong 2003). Males may believe that they shouldn't bother other men when they feel low, or they may fear that intimate sharing with another man might be interpreted as gay behavior (Monroe, Baker, and Roll 1997). Indeed, a man may be more open and disclosing with a woman friend (Wagner-Raphael, Seal, and Ehrhardt 2001). In general, "[t]he thinness of men's friendships with each other [compared to women's] and the ways that they seem to be constantly undermined through competition and jealousy are distinctive features of modern society" (Seidler 1992, p. 17; see also D. Levy 2005). One study of men in the construction industry found that many of them, rather than

For singles, it's important to develop and maintain supportive social networks of friends and family. Single people place high value on friendships, and they are also major contributors to community services and volunteer work.

building truly supportive friendships, talked instead about horseplay, alcohol consumption, risk-taking, and physical prowess, and generally engaged in one-upmanship (Iacuone 2005). Men (as well as women) who do not establish friendships based on emotional honesty run the risk of feeling socially isolated.

In addition to friendships, other sources of support for singles include group-living situations, religious fellowships, and volunteer work (Lyons 2003; Mustillo, Wilson, and Lynch 2004). Singles also reach out to their families of origin (Arnett 2004; Bengston, Biblarz, and Roberts 2002). Barbara Simon (1987), who studied fifty never-marrieds old enough to be retired, found that they received a great deal of support from their families, especially in middle and old age. Families helped in crises, whether of health, disability, or economic loss.

In later life, single women were likely to set up joint living arrangements with siblings. Twenty-three of the fifty women whom Simon studied were living with a brother or sister in retirement. But ties outside the family remained important. Simon found that "perhaps the most common thread of identity" the women whom she interviewed shared was "their view of themselves as members of a group *larger than* their own families." Asked what had given their lives meaning, forty-five emphasized religious, political, or humanitarian volunteer work. One woman who had been a Big Sister to sixteen Puerto Rican children over the previous twenty-three years explained

proudly that "all Puerto Rican kids are *my* family. . . . Of those sixteen children I have been a buddy to over the years, not one of them has gotten into trouble" (quoted in B. Simon 1987, p. 54). Contributing an average of eighteen hours weekly, these women thought of themselves

as members of an integrated moral world in which their commitments to their work, their family, their friends, their neighborhood, and their society flow from one passion—the desire to be a responsible and responsive actor in the world. (B. Simon 1987, p. 56)

Social support is necessary for feeling positive about and generally satisfied with being single, whether living alone or not. In his review of this textbook, Peter Stein (2001) noted that

[m]uch has changed in [the singles] population since I first wrote about single women and men, but the major issues of acceptance, friendship, loneliness, and community are still there. Yet this continues to be an under-researched area of sociology!

However one chooses to live the single life, establishing a sense of belonging by maintaining supportive social networks is important. As we've seen, much of the increase in the number of singles is due to young adults' postponing of marriage. The next chapter explores the process of choosing a marriage partner as well as the first years of marriage.

Summary

- Since the 1960s, the number of unmarrieds has risen dramatically. Much of this increase is due to young adults' postponing of marriage, coupled with the rise in the incidence of cohabitation.

- One reason people are postponing marriage today is that increased job and lifestyle opportunities may make marriage less attractive.

- The low sex ratio—fewer men for women of marriageable age—has also caused some women to postpone marriage or put it off entirely.

- Attitudes toward marriage and singlehood have changed, so that being unmarried is more often viewed as preferable, at least "for now."

- More and more young unmarrieds are living in their parents' homes, usually at least partly as a result of economic constraints.

- Some unmarrieds have chosen to live in communal or group homes.
- A substantial number and growing percentage of heterosexual unmarrieds are cohabiting.
- As heterosexual cohabitation becomes more acceptable, more and more cohabiting households include children either born to the union or from a previous relationship.
- The relative instability of heterosexual cohabiting unions has led to some, apparently warranted, concern for the outcomes of children living in cohabiting families.

- Some unmarrieds live together in gay male or lesbian unions; a little more than one-third of lesbian and nearly one-quarter of gay male households include children either from the same-sex union or from a previous (often heterosexual) relationship.
- Congruent with the emergence of the pluralistic family, we are witnessing a national and global debate over whether legal marriage should be extended to include lesbians and gay men.
- However one chooses to live the single life, it is important to maintain supportive social networks.

Questions for Review and Reflection

1. Individual choices take place within a broader social spectrum—that is, within society. How do social factors influence an unmarried individual's decision regarding his or her living arrangements?
2. What do you see as the advantages and disadvantages of cohabitation compared to marriage?
3. What does current research tell us about the outcomes generally of children raised in married, two-biological-parent families, compared to those raised in cohabiting families?
4. On average, do the outcomes of children raised by heterosexual parents differ from the outcomes of those raised by same-sex couples?
5. **Policy Question.** Do you think that legalizing same-sex marriage is a good idea? Give arguments based on facts to support your opinion.

Key Terms

civil union 201
cohabitation 189
commune 188
consensual marriage 191
culture war 200

Defense of Marriage Act (DOMA) 197
domestic partner 192
sex ratio 184
single 184

Online Resources

Companion Website for This Book

www.thomsonedu.com/sociology/lamanna

Visit the book companion website, where you will find flash cards, practice quizzes, Internet links, suggested readings, InfoTrac College Edition exercises, and more to help you study.

ThomsonNOW™ for Marriage and Family

Spend time on what you need to master rather than on information you already have learned. Take a pre-test for this chapter, and ThomsonNOW will generate a personalized study plan based on your results. The study plan will identify the topics you need to review and direct you to online resources such as videos, narrated learning modules, and interactive activities to help you master those topics. You can then take a post-test to help you determine the concepts you have mastered and what you will still need to work on. Try it out! Go to **www.thomsonedu.com/login** to sign in with an access code or to purchase access to this product.

Choosing a Marriage Partner, and the First Years of Marriage

Mate Selection and Marital Stability

Attachment Theory

Age at Marriage and Marital Stability

The Intergenerational Transmission of Divorce Risk

Minimizing Mate Selection Risk

The Marriage Market

Arranged and Free-Choice Marriages

The Marital Exchange

Homogamy: Narrowing the Pool of Eligibles

Reasons for Homogamy

Examples of Heterogamy—The Statistical Exceptions

Heterogamy and Marital Stability

Heterogamy and Human Values

Developing the Premarital Relationship and Moving Toward Marital Commitment

Issues for Thought Date or Acquaintance Rape

Physical Attractiveness and Rapport

Defining the Relationship

As We Make Choices Harmonious Needs in Mate Selection

Dating Violence—A Serious Sign of Trouble

The Possibility of Breaking Up

Cohabitation and Marital Quality and Stability

As We Make Choices Some Advice on Breaking Up

Marital Satisfaction and Choices Throughout Life

Preparation for Marriage

The First Years of Marriage

Creating Couple Connection

Creating Adaptable Marriage Relationships

Some Things to Talk About

© RubberBall/Alamy

Marrying involves selecting someone with whom to become emotionally and sexually intimate and, often, with whom to raise children. Marrying holds the promise that we will establish a permanent, loving, and supportive relationship with our selected spouse. Accordingly, the choice of a marriage partner is a major life-course decision. Attention to the high rate of divorce in the United States has led sociologist Norval Glenn (2002), among others, to make "a plea for greater concern about the quality of marital matching." In Chapter 1, Figure 1.2, "The Cycle of Knowledgeable Decision Making," illustrates that making knowledgeable decisions requires an awareness of one's personal beliefs and values, as well as conscious consideration of alternatives and serious thought about the probable consequences. You may want to refer to Figure 1.2 as you study this chapter.

You'll recall that Chapter 5 examines discovering and keeping a loving relationship. In this chapter we'll recall some of the ideas in Chapter 5 as we examine ways that we select marriage partners. Research suggests that the best way to choose a spouse is to look for a socially responsible, respectful, and emotionally supportive mate who demonstrates good communication and problem-solving skills and who is committed both to the relationship and to the value of marriage itself (Bradbury and Karney 2004; Hetherington 2003).

Equally important, research findings also point to looking for a mate with values that resemble one's own, because similar values and attitudes are strong predictors of marital happiness and stability (Cobb, Larson, and Watson 2003; Gaunt 2006). Although romantic love is usually an important ingredient, successful marriages

are based also on such qualities as partners' common goals and needs, their maturity, qualities of friendship or pragmatic love, and the soundness of their reasons for marrying (Lacey et al. 2004).

In this chapter we'll look at some things that influence both the choice of a spouse and marital satisfaction. We will examine how a relationship develops and proceeds from first meeting to commitment to marital commitment. We'll examine research on how cohabiting before marriage affects marital stability. We will also discuss interracial and interreligious and interclass unions. In addition, we'll explore aspects of the first years of marriage. We need to note here that, although more than three-quarters of divorced Americans remarry within ten years (Bramlett and Mosher 2001), research tends to focus on choosing a spouse for a first marriage. Much of what is said in this chapter can probably be applied to remarriages, however, and research specifically related to choosing a spouse for remarriage is explored in Chapter 17. To begin this chapter, we look more closely at what we know about mate selection and marital stability.

Mate Selection and Marital Stability

Figure 9.1 depicts a model of factors that affect **marital stability**—whether spouses remain married or divorce.[1] Marital stability depends upon how satisfied the spouses

[1] Figure 9.1 is designed to apply to same-sex unions as well as to heterosexual marriages (Kurdek 2006).

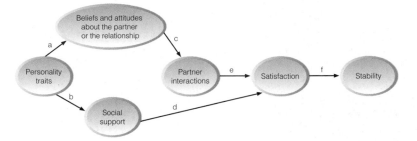

FIGURE 9.1

A time-ordered sequential model of relationship outcomes. "The model has six components that form a time-ordered sequence of six linkages (letters a through f). The [personality traits] component refers to personality traits partners bring to their relationships that affect both the manner in which the relationship events are appraised (. . . [beliefs and attitudes about the relationship]; Link a) and the quality of perceived social support that is received (Link b). . . . The [beliefs and attitudes about the partner or the relationship] component refers to beliefs and attitudes about the partner or the relationship that affect how partners interact with each other (Link c). . . . The component social support

underscores the view that intimate relationship coexist with other personal relationships, particularly those involving friends and family members. . . . The partner interactions component represents how partners behave toward one another and [along with social support, Link d] forms another basis for overall satisfaction with the relationship (Link e). . . . Relationship satisfaction refers to the overall level of positive affect experienced in the relationship and the extent to which important personal needs are being met in the relationship and is one determinant of relationship stability (Link f)" (adapted from Kurdek 2006, pp.510–11).

are with their marriage. Marital happiness and satisfaction, in turn, depend upon how the partners interact with one another as well as on the perceived social support the couple receives from family members, friends, and the community in general. How partners interact with one another, in turn, depends upon "beliefs and attitudes about the partner or the relationship." And these beliefs and attitudes depend, in turn, at least partly upon the personality traits that each partner brings to the union (Kurdek 2006, p. 510).

As an example, let's say that Angel and Maria are considering marriage. Each wonders about the odds of staying married (marital stability). First, Maria and Angel need to take their personality traits into account. Is Angel thoughtful, dependable, reliable, and honest? Is Maria? Is one or both prepared to support a family? What beliefs and attitudes do they have about one another and about their relationship? Does Angel believe that his marriage to Maria is likely to result in marital satisfaction? Or is he marrying Maria despite misgivings about her or their relationship? Does Maria believe that marital stability is likely for her? Or does she see this marriage as likely to end in divorce but "worth a try" anyway? Positive attitudes about the relationship, coupled with realistically positive assessments of a prospective spouse's personality traits, are important to marital stability.

According to this model, Maria and Angel's respective personality traits influence the degree of social support that they will receive—and believe that they receive—from family members and friends. More perceived social support will result in greater marital satisfaction. Then too, Angel and Maria's beliefs and attitudes about each other and about their relationship will affect how they interact with one another. Will they—do they now—interact primarily in supportive ways? Do they handle conflict well? Supportive interaction results in greater marital satisfaction. Greater marital satisfaction, in turn, results in the greater likelihood of marital stability.

Other chapters in this text focus on various aspects of partner interactions and social support. Here we focus on choosing a spouse who is best predisposed psychologically to maintain a stable and committed relationship.

Psychologists and counselors advise choosing a mate who is integrated into society by means of school, employment, a network of friends, and/or family ties and who demonstrates a sense of self-worth (not narcissism, as discussed in Chapter 5) as well as supportive communication and problem-solving skills (Cotton, Burton, and Rushing 2003). "Heavy or risky drinking is associated with a host of marital difficulties including infidelity, divorce, violence and conflict" (L. Roberts 2005, p. F13). The same can be said for other forms of substance abuse (Kaye 2005, F15). Sociological research

shows that marriages are more likely to be stable when partners are in good psychological health, when they are in their mid-twenties or older, and when the spouses' parents have not been divorced. We'll explore these points in this section. To begin, we will look at attachment theory, also discussed in Chapter 5.

Attachment Theory

Attachment theory posits that during infancy and childhood, individuals develop a general style of attaching to others (Bowlby 1969, 1982; Fletcher 2002). Children who trust that their needs will be met form a secure attachment style; children who feel abandoned are likely to acquire an insecure/anxious or an avoidant attachment style. By adulthood, these attachment styles—partly conscious and partly unconscious—have generated broad expectations about oneself and one's partner in close relationships. Adults with a secure attachment style are inclined to trust that their relationships will provide ongoing emotional support. Adults with an insecure/anxious attachment style worry that their beloved will leave, betray, or seriously disappoint them, a situation often described as "fear of abandonment." Adults with an avoidant attachment style duck, or evade, emotional closeness (Fletcher 2002; Main 1996; Simpson and Rholes 1998).

Applying attachment theory to choosing a spouse, we might presume that people with more secure attachment styles would have less ambivalence about emotional closeness and commitment. "Secure attachment, in part, depends on regarding the relationship partner as being available in times of need and as trustworthy" (Kurdek 2006, p. 510). In Figure 9.1, attachment style is incorporated in *beliefs and attitudes about the partner or the relationship*.

Attachment theory leads us to conclude that those with a secure attachment style are better marriage-partner prospects. Meanwhile, one study has found that the attachment style of one's spouse can either magnify or lessen the effects of one's own attachment style. For example, if both spouses are insecure and anxious, the marriage will be characterized that way as well. On the other hand, a person with an insecure attachment style who marries someone with a secure attachment style may gradually learn to feel more secure (Banse 2004). In addition to attachment style, how does age at marriage affect marital stability?

Age at Marriage and Marital Stability

Marriages that occur when individuals are over twenty-five are happier and more stable than those that take place between individuals in their early twenties, but the most significant distinction is between teenage and all other marriages (Heaton 2002; McGinn 2006b). Ten years after the wedding, 40 percent of women who were eighteen or nineteen years old on their wedding day were divorced, compared to 24 percent of women at least twenty-five years old at marriage (Bramlett and Mosher 2001).

Low socioeconomic origins, premarital pregnancy, lack of interest in school, and economic struggles are associated with marrying early (J. Larson and Hickman 2004). Research generally shows that people who marry young are more emotionally immature and impulsive, as well as less apt to be educationally, financially, or psychologically prepared to responsibly select a mate or to perform marital roles (Clements, Stanley, and Markman 2004; Martino, Collins, and Ellickson 2004). (However, a study of Hmong Americans [Hutchinson and McNall 1994] suggested that this overall conclusion may not apply to all ethnic groups; ethnic groups that encourage early marriage and are psychologically supportive and economically helpful to newlyweds may not experience such negative consequences of young marriages.) What if a prospective spouse is from a divorced family?

© Corbis/Jupiter Images

Marriages between individuals with a relatively secure attachment style, that take place after about age twenty-five and are between partners who grew up in intact (nondivorced) families are the most likely to be satisfying and stable. But having grown up as a child of divorce does *not* mean that an individual will *necessarily* have an unhappy or unstable marriage.

The Intergenerational Transmission of Divorce Risk

Either because they know the statistics, have divorced friends, or have experienced their parents' divorce, many young adults are cautious about getting married and possibly going through the pain and economic upheaval of divorce, especially if they plan to have children (Arnett 2004). It is important to remember that assuredly not all children of divorced parents will themselves divorce. No one is suggesting that a child of divorced parents be automatically rejected as a future spouse. However, "[s]tudies based on large national samples consistently show that parental divorce increases the risk of marital instability in offspring" (Hetherington 2003, p. 325; Teachman 2004). When both spouses come from divorced families, the probability of their own divorce is still higher (Amato and DeBoer 2001; Hetherington 2003; Wolfinger 2005). Family scholars refer to this phenomenon as the **inter-**

generational transmission of divorce risk: A divorced parental family transmits to its children a heightened risk of getting divorced. Noting that "apparently, there is something in the divorce experience beyond that of parental conflict that exacerbates problems in stability in intimate relations in offspring" (Hetherington 2003, p. 326), researchers have suggested the following four hypotheses to explain the intergenerational transmission of divorce risk. Children of divorce are themselves more likely to get divorced because they have:

1. more—and more serious—personality problems
2. neither been exposed to nor learned supportive communication or problem-solving skills
3. less commitment to the relationship
4. more accepting attitudes toward divorce (Dunne, Hudgins, and Babcock 2000; Hetherington 2003; Hetherington and Kelly 2002; Wolfinger 2005)

We might also hypothesize that children of divorce, as a category, are less likely to have developed a secure attachment style.

After what we've said here, it's important to emphasize that it is not true that children of divorce will themselves *necessarily* divorce (Zimmerman and Thayer 2004). Research shows that a supportive, well-adjusted partner "can play a protective role" in minimizing the intergenerational transmission of divorce risk. Prominent researcher on children of divorce E. Mavis Hetherington (2003) has described her findings on this point:

> Under conditions of low stress with a supportive partner, there was no difference in couple instability between the offspring of divorced and nondivorced parents. For these well-married youths in a benign environment, no intergenerational transmission of marital instability was found. Under conditions of high stress, there was a marginally significant trend for the offspring of divorced parents, even with a supportive partner, to show somewhat more marital instability than those from nondivorced families. (p. 328)

Mate Selection Risk Mate selection plays a part in the intergenerational transmission of divorce risk because individuals from divorced families are themselves more inclined to have the characteristics described earlier and to choose partners who have them. Hetherington (2003) reports her findings concerning **mate selection risk** as follows:

> Youths from divorced families were more likely to select high-risk partners who were also from divorced families and who were impulsive, socially irresponsible, and had a history of antisocial behaviors such as alcohol and drug abuse, minor misdemeanors, troubles with the law, problems in school and at work, fighting, and an unstable job history. (p. 328)

Other research has found that *mate selection risk* may apply to adult children of alcoholics as well as to those of divorce (Olmsted, Crowell, and Waters 2003; Watt 2002). What can one do to minimize mate selection risk?

Minimizing Mate Selection Risk

A first step in minimizing mate selection risk is to let go of misconceptions we might have about love and choosing a partner. Selecting a partner wisely involves balancing any insistence on perfection against the need to be mindful of one's real needs and desires (Cobb, Larson, and Watson 2003). In the absence of adequate role models for maintaining a supportive marriage, many of us may embrace misconceptions about finding a partner. For instance, we might believe that "I can be happy with anyone I choose to marry, if I work hard enough," or that "Falling in love with someone is sufficient reason for me to marry that person" (Cobb, Larson, and Watson 2003, p. 223). However, working things out requires both partners' willingness and ability to do so; just one's own willingness to work hard at a marriage is not enough. Furthermore, if having fallen in love is assumed to be enough to make a marriage last, then other, potentially detrimental partner charac-

teristics may be minimized. Generally, marriages built on "respect, mutual support and affirmation of each other's worth are more likely to survive" (Hetherington 2003, p. 322).

Later in this chapter, the section "Some Things to Talk About" gives other ideas on assessing your own and a prospective spouse's values and attitudes. Of course, it's important to be truthful when relating with a potential spouse, as well as ascertain how truthful one's partner is being (S. Campbell 2004). Before they decide definitely to marry, some couples go to counseling to assess their future compatibility and commitment to marriage (Marech 2004a), a point that we will return to later in this chapter. At this point, we turn to the social science analogy of choosing a mate in the *marriage market*.

The Marriage Market

Imagine a large marketplace in which people come with goods to exchange for other items. In nonindustrialized societies, a person may go to market with a few chickens to trade for some vegetables. In modern societies, people attend hockey-equipment swaps, for example, trading outgrown skates for larger ones. People choose marriage partners in much the same way: They enter the **marriage market** armed with resources—their (or their children's in the case of arranged marriages) personal and social characteristics—and then they bargain for the best "buy" that they can get.

Arranged and Free-Choice Marriages

As discussed in Chapter 7, in much of the world, particularly in parts of Asia and Africa that are less Westernized, parents have traditionally arranged their children's marriages. In **arranged marriage**, future spouses can be brought together in various ways. For example, in India parents typically check prospective partners' astrological charts to assure future compatibility. Traditionally, the parents of both prospective partners (often with other relatives' or a paid matchmaker's help) worked out the details and then announced the upcoming marriage to their children. The children may have had little or no say in the matter, and they may not have met their future spouse until the wedding. However, today it is more common for the children to marry only when they themselves accept their parents' choice. Unions like these, sometimes called "assisted marriages," can be found among some Muslim groups and other recent immigrants to the United States (Ingoldsby 2006b; D. Jones 2006; MacFarquhar 2006; Smith-Hefner 2005).

The fact that marriages are arranged doesn't mean that love is ignored by parents. Indeed, marital love may be highly valued. However, couples in arranged marriages are expected to develop a loving relationship *after* the marriage, not before (Tepperman and Wilson 1993). A study that compared marital satisfaction among arranged marriages in India to those more freely chosen in the United States found no differences in marital satisfaction between the two groups. According to the authors, "Although this is not a case in favor of arranged marriages, it provides no support for a position opposing this tradition" (Myers, Madathil, and Tingle 2005, p. 189). Meanwhile, with global Westernization, arranged marriages are less and less common, especially among the more highly educated (D. Jones 2006; Hoelter, Axinn, and Ghimire 2004; Sherif-Trask 2003).

The United States is an example of what cross-cultural researchers call a **free-choice culture**: People choose their own mates, although typically they seek parents' and other family members' support for their decision. Immigrants who come to the United States from more collectivist cultures, in which arranged marriages have been the tradition, face the situation of living with a divergent set of expectations for selecting a mate. Some immigrant parents from India, Pakistan, and other countries arrange for spouses from their home country to marry their offspring. This is one type of **cross-national marriage**. Either the future spouse comes to the United States to marry the young person, or the young person travels to the home country for the wedding ceremony, after which the newlyweds usually live in the United States (Dugger 1998). In this case, the marriage is typically characterized by the greater Westernization of one partner (the young person who has lived in the United States) and the spouse's simul-

Although the arranged marriage of this couple in Northern India (right) may seem to be a world apart from the more freely chosen marriage of this couple in the United States (left), bargaining has occurred in both of these unions. In arranged marriages, families and community do the bargaining, based on assets such as status, possessions, and dowry. In freely chosen marriages, the individuals perform a more subtle form of bargaining, weighing the costs and benefits of personal characteristics, economic status, and education.

taneous need to adjust not only to marriage but also to an entirely new culture (Cottrell 1993).

The incidence of cross-national marriages like these may decline as the required visa for an immigrating spouse is far harder to come by now than prior to September 11, 2001. Furthermore, increasingly, American-born children of immigrants may see themselves as too Americanized for this approach to finding a partner (MacFarquhar 2006). Whether marriages are arranged or not, we can think of choosing a marital partner as taking place in a "marriage market."

Regarding arranged marriages, parents go through a bargaining process not unlike what takes place at a traditional village market. They make rationally calculated choices after determining the social status or position, health, temperament, and, sometimes, physical attractiveness of their prospective son- or daughter-in-law. Professional matchmakers often serve as investigators and go-betweens, just as we might engage an attorney or a stockbroker in an important business deal.

Sometimes, as in the Hmong culture, the exchange involves a **bride price**, money or property that the future groom pays the future bride's family so that he

The man on the decorated horse is an investment banker from New York who has traveled to Jaipur, India, to marry a native Asian Indian woman. The marriage had been arranged in India by the groom's mother. The couple will return to New York to live. "I always knew I'd probably end up getting married to someone who wasn't very American, because I'm not myself in some ways," he said.

can marry her. More often the exchange is accompanied by a **dowry**, a sum of money or property brought to the marriage by the female. As one example, Asian Indians have traditionally practiced the dowry system, now illegal there but still widespread (Srinivasan and Lee 2004). A woman with a large dowry can expect to marry into a higher-ranking family than can a woman with a small dowry, and dowries are often increased to make up for qualities considered undesirable (M. Kaplan 1985, pp. 1–13). For instance, parents in eighteenth-century England increased the dowries of daughters who were pockmarked.

With arranged marriage, the bargaining is obvious. The difference between arranged marriages and marriages in free-choice cultures may seem so great that we are inclined to overlook an important similarity: *Both* involve bargaining. What has changed in free-choice societies is that individuals, not family members, do the bargaining.

The Marital Exchange

The ideas of bargaining, market, and resources used to describe relationships such as marriage come to us from **exchange theory**, discussed in Chapter 2. Recall

that the basic idea of exchange theory is that whether or not relationships form or continue depends on the rewards and costs they provide to the partners. Individuals, it is presumed, want to maximize their rewards and avoid costs, so when there are choices, they will pick the relationship that is most rewarding or least costly.

The analogy is to economics, but in romantic and marital relationships individuals are thought to have other sorts of resources to bargain besides money: physical attractiveness, intelligence, educational attainment, earning potential, personality characteristics, family status, the ability to be emotionally supportive, and so on. Individuals may also have costly attributes, such as belonging to the "wrong" social class, religion, or racial/ethnic group, being irritable or demanding, and being geographically inaccessible (a major consideration in modern society).

The Traditional Exchange Historically, women have traded their ability to bear and raise children, coupled with domestic duties, sexual accessibility, and physical attractiveness, for a man's protection, status, and economic support. This traditional exchange characterizes marriages in many immigrant groups that have recently arrived in the United States (Hill, Ramirez, and Dumka 2003). Evidence from classified personal ads shows that the traditional exchange still influences heterosexual relationships in general. Men are more likely to advertise for a physically attractive woman; women, for an economically stable man. Although increasingly women have their own employment and income, as a category women continue to expect greater financial success from prospective husbands than vice versa (Buss et al. 2001). Therefore, men without stable or promising work have disadvantages. National data that looked at black, Hispanic, and white males found that the probability of a man's getting married largely depends on his earning power (Edin and Reed 2005; Lichter, Qian, and Mellott 2006; McLanahan 2004; Oppenheimer 2003; Schoen and Cheng 2006).

Bargaining in a Changing Society "As gender differences in work and family roles blur, individuals' criteria for an acceptable mate are likely to change" (Raley and Bratter 2004, p. 179). For instance, research that looked at mate preferences in the United States over the past sixty years showed that men and women—but especially men—have increased the importance that they put on potential financial success in a mate, while domestic skills in a future wife have declined in importance (Buss et al. 2001; M. Siegel 2004; Sweeney and Cancian 2004). One study indicates that, for today's young man, a woman's high socioeconomic status increases her sexiness (J. L. Martin 2005).

Some observers point out that as gender roles become more alike, exchange between partners may increasingly include "expressive, affective, sexual, and companionship resources" for both partners. In fact, a high-earning woman might bargain for a nurturing, housework-sharing husband, even if his earning potential appears to be lower than hers (Press 2004; Sprecher and Toro-Morn 2002). As college-educated young women approach occupational and economic equality with potential mates, the exchange becomes more symmetrical than in the past, with both genders increasingly looking for emotional sensitivity and earning potential in one another (Buss et al. 2001). Marriages based on both partners' contributing roughly equal economic and status resources are more egalitarian. Changes in men's roles toward greater emotional expressiveness may improve marital communication and satisfaction.

Desiring wives who can make good money, college-educated men are now much more likely than a few decades ago to marry college-educated women (Raley and Bratter 2004). In fact, there is some evidence that today *both* men and women prefer "to marry someone with more education or who earns more money" than they do (Raley and Bratter 2004, p. 175).[2] The fact that college-educated women and men tend to marry each other points to another concept associated with mate selection—assortative mating.

Assortative Mating—A Filtering Process Individuals gradually filter, or sort out, those who they think would not make the best spouse. Research has consistently shown that people are willing to date a wider range of individuals than they would live with or become engaged to, and they are willing to live with a wider range of people than they would marry (Jepsen and Jepsen 2002). For instance, one study has found that women are less likely to consider the economic prospects of their male partners when deciding whether to cohabit than when deciding about marriage (Manning and Smock 2002). Social psychologists call this process **assortative mating**. Assortative mating raises another factor shaping marital choice—the tendency of people to marry others with whom they share certain social characteristics. Social scientists term this phenomenon **homogamy**.

Homogamy: Narrowing the Pool of Eligibles

Americans, like others, tend to make marital choices in socially patterned ways, viewing only certain others as potentially suitable mates. The market analogy would be to choose only certain stores at which to shop. For each shopper there is a socially defined **pool of eligibles**: a group of individuals who, by virtue of background or birth, are considered most likely to make compatible marriage partners.

Americans tend to choose partners who are like themselves in many ways. This situation is called *homogamy*: People tend to marry people of similar race, age, education, religious background, and social class. As an example, traditionally the Protestant, Catholic, and Jewish religions, as well as the Muslim and Hindu religions, have all encouraged **endogamy**: marrying within one's own social group.

The opposite of endogamy is **exogamy**, marrying outside one's group, or **heterogamy**, marrying someone dissimilar in race, age, education, religion, or social class. Age and educational heterogamy have been more pronounced among blacks than among whites, partly

---

[2] As a result of this situation, finding an acceptable spouse could prove problematic for both women and men. "If both sexes are looking to marry ['up,' or] hypergamously, there is a mismatch between the preferences of men and women" (Raley and Bratter 2004, p. 168).

These Hmong immigrants in St. Paul, Minnesota, are celebrating the Hmong New Year, which also serves as a courting ritual. As in Laos, teenagers line up—boys on one side, girls on the other—and play catch with desirable potential mates. Catching the ball begins conversation. Tossing the ball gives girls a chance to meet boys under conditions approved by their parents. In Minnesota, however, the traditional Laotian black cloth ball is often replaced with a fluorescent tennis ball (Hopfensperger 1990, p. 1B). Because virtually all participants are Hmong, the ritual helps to ensure racial/ethnic homogamy.

2005). About 60 percent of Asian Americans and 75 percent of Hispanics marry within their group (del Pinal and Singer 1997; Lee and Edmonston 2005). However, nearly 54 percent of Native Americans marry outside their race, and more than 80 percent of Arab Americans marry outside their ethnicity, mostly to whites (Pollard and O'Hare 1999; Kulczycki and Lobo 2002).

With regard to socioeconomic class, sociologists point out that although people today are marrying across small class distinctions, they still are not doing so across large ones. For instance, individuals of established wealth seldom marry the poor. All in all, an individual is most likely to marry someone who is similar in basic social characteristics. We'll look at a hypothetical case to see why this is so.

Reasons for Homogamy

Andrea is attracted to Alex (and vice versa), who is a college student like herself. Andrea's parents are upper-middle class. They live in the expensive section of her hometown, have a housekeeper, drink wine with their meals, and frequently have parties by their pool. Catholic, they go to Mass every Sunday. Alex's parents are working class. They are separated. His mother lives in an apartment and works as a checker in a supermarket. The family drinks soft drinks at mealtime, then watches TV. They believe in "being good people," but do not belong to any organized religion.

How likely is it that Andrea and Alex will marry? If they do marry, what sources of conflict might occur? We can help to answer these questions by exploring four related elements that influence both initial attraction and long-term happiness. These elements—geographic availability, social pressure, feeling at home, and a fair exchange—are important reasons that many people are homogamous.

Geographic Availability Geographic availability (traditionally known in the marriage and family literature as *propinquity*, or *proximity*) has typically been a reason that people tend to meet others who are a lot like themselves

because an "undersupply" of educated black men prompts black women to marry men with less education and to partner with considerably older or younger men (Surra 1990).

In spite of a trend toward less religious homogamy and a lessened tendency of European Americans—such as Irish, Italians, or Poles—to marry within their own ethnic group, homogamy is still a strong force (Kalmijn 1998).[3] In 2005, about 7.5 percent of U.S. marriages involved spouses of different races or a Hispanic married to a non-Hispanic (U.S. Census Bureau 2007a, Table 58). More than 90 percent of non-Hispanic and of black couples are racially homogeneous (Lee and Edmonston

[3] "It often comes as a surprise to whites born after 1980 that crossing the ethnic boundaries to date or marry had social consequences in recent American ethnic history. The dating and marriage of, for example, an Italian-American and an Irish-American [in the first half of the twentieth century] not only raised eyebrows in each community but often brought disappointment and even estrangement from family members" (C. Gallagher 2006, p. 143).

(Harmanci 2006; Travis 2006). Geographic segregation, which can result from either discrimination or strong community ties, contributes to homogamous marriages (C. Gallagher 2006). Intermarriage patterns within the American Jewish community are an example. Only about 6 percent of Jews married non-Jews in the late 1950s. Now that the barriers that used to exclude Jews from certain residential areas and colleges are gone, about half marry Gentiles (Gary Stern 2003; Sussman 2006).Geographic availability also helps to account for educational (G. Stevens 1991) and social-class homogamy. Middle-class people tend to socialize together and send their children to the same schools; upper- and lower-class people do the same. Unless they had met in a large, public university or online, it is unlikely that Alex and Andrea would have become acquainted at all.

Today, first encounters may occur in cyberspace, and people meet others as far away as other countries. Curiously, however, the Internet may actually encourage homogamy among some ethnic groups, such as Jews or Muslims, who can advertise online for dating partners of the same ethnicity (e.g., www.jewishconnect .com). Moreover, online daters' mutual ability to access the Internet and then to travel, if necessary, to meet each other face-to-face assures some degree of educational and/or financial homogamy. On the other hand, websites such as InterRacialMatcher.com facilitate heterogamy. We know of no research on the effect of the Internet on marital homogamy, and we'd like to suggest that this question would be a good one for future research—perhaps yours.

Social Pressure A second reason for homogamy is social pressure. Inter-ethnic relationships are more likely to develop when young adults are relatively independent of parental influence and/or when one's parents have an ethnically diverse network of friends (Clark-Ibanez and Felmlee 2004; Rosenfeld and Byung-Soo 2005). Meanwhile, for the majority of us, cultural values encourage marrying someone who is socially similar to ourselves. Andrea's parents, friends, and siblings are unlikely to approve of Alex because he doesn't exhibit the social skills and behavior of their social class (Blackwell 1998). Meanwhile, Alex's mother and friends may say to him, "Andrea thinks she is too good for us. Find a girl more like our kind."

Sometimes, social pressure results from a group's concern for preserving its ethnic or cultural identity. When young Jews, particularly college students, began to intermarry more often in the 1960s, Jewish leaders became concerned (Stern 2003; "Tracing" 2003). Recent immigrants, such as various Arab, Asian, or Hispanic groups, may pressure their children to marry within their own ethnic group in order to preserve their ethnic

culture (Kitano and Daniels 1995; S. M. Lee 1998; "One Hundred Questions" n.d.). Whether blatant or subtle, social pressure toward homogamy can be forceful. Making knowledgeable choices involves recognizing the strength of social pressure and deciding whether to act in accordance with others' expectations.

Feeling at Home People often find it easier to communicate and feel more at home with others from similar education, social class, and racial/ethnic backgrounds (Lewin 2005). Alex is likely to have attitudes, mannerisms, and vocabulary different from those of Andrea. Each may feel out of place in surroundings that the other considers natural.

If meeting in the marriage market can sound like a job interview, maybe that's because in at least one important way it is: The goal is to strike a fair exchange. And even without the benefit of interviews, people learn to discern the social class of others through mannerisms, language, dress, and a score of other cues.

We've discussed some reasons for homogamy, but not all marriages are homogamous, of course. *Heterogamy* refers to marriage between those who are different in race, age, education, religious background, or social class.

Examples of Heterogamy— The Statistical Exceptions

How does marrying someone from a different religion, social class, or race/ethnicity affect a person's chances for a happy union? In general, marriages that are homogamous are more likely to be stable because partners are more likely to share the same values and attitudes when they come from similar backgrounds (Furstenberg 2005; Gaunt 2006). In this section, we examine the relationship between heterogamy and marital success in more detail. We will first discuss interfaith marriages, then look at interclass partnerships, and finally review interracial and interethnic unions.

Interfaith Marriages It is estimated that about 30 percent of Jewish, 20 percent of Catholic, 30 percent of Mormon, 40 percent of Muslim, up to 40 percent of Catholic, and a higher percentage of Protestant adults and children in the United States live in interfaith or interdenominational households (D'Antonio et al. 1999). Being highly educated seems to lessen individuals' commitment to religious homogamy (Petersen 1994). Religions that see themselves as the one true faith and people who adhere to a religion as an integral component of their ethnic/cultural identity (for example, some Catholics, Jews, and Muslims) are more likely to encourage homogamy, sometimes by pressing a prospective spouse to convert (Bukhari 2004; Smits, Ultee, and Lammers 1998). Often, religious bodies are concerned that children born into the marriage will not be raised in their religion (Adler 1997a; "Getting It Right" 1995; Kahn n.d.; Sussman 2006).

Some switching, no doubt, also takes place because partners agree with the widely held belief that interreligious marriages tend to be more stressful and less stable than homogamous ones—a belief supported by research (Maneker and Rankin 1993; Mahoney 2005). One probable reason that religious homogamy improves chances for marital success involves value consensus. Religion-based values and attitudes may come into play when negotiating leisure activities, child-raising methods, investments and expenditures of money, and appropriate roles for wives and husbands (Curtis and Elison 2002; Heaton and Pratt 1990). Meanwhile, analysis of data from a national random telephone survey of Protestant and Catholic households concluded that although marital satisfaction was less for interdenominational couples, the difference disappeared when the interdenominational couple had generally similar religious orientations, good communication skills, and similar beliefs about child raising (Hughes and Dickson 2005; Williams and Lawler 2003).

One study conducted with homogamously married Christian, Jewish, and Islamic couples found strong religious beliefs to be associated with less couple conflict. Shared religiosity gave them a shared sense of purpose and commitment to permanence, coupled with a willingness to forgive the spouse when conflicts emerged (Lambert and Dollahite 2006). One research team has attributed differences in marital happiness associated with religious homogeneity almost entirely to the positive effect of church attendance: Homogamously married partners go to church more often and at similar rates and, as a result, show higher marital satisfaction and stability (Heaton and Pratt 1990). Meanwhile, another study (Sheehan, Bock, and Lee 1990) used General Social Survey data from the National Opinion Research Center to compare Catholics in heterogeneous marriages with those in homogamous ones. Heterogamously married Catholics went to Mass less frequently, but this did *not* reduce marital satisfaction. These researchers concluded that

> the effect of church attendance on marital satisfaction in the general population may be due more to the integrative properties of couple-centered organizational participation than to the religious nature of the activity. Heterogamous couples in which one spouse is Catholic are unlikely to attend church together, and may compensate for this by engaging in other couple-centered activities that are equally effective in promoting marital solidarity. (p. 78)

Some recent research shows a declining effect of religious differences on marital satisfaction over the past several decades due to the greater effect of couples' gender, work, and co-parenting concerns (Myers 2006; Williams and Lawler 2003). In general, however, religious homogamy may "create a more integrated social network of relatives, friends, and religious advisors" (Heaton and Pratt 1990, p. 192). This is also true, as is pointed out later in this section, for interracial marriages.

Interclass Marriages What about the marital satisfaction of partners in interclass unions? Researchers have tended to ignore this question in recent decades, focusing instead on interracial and interethnic unions (Kalmijn 1998). However, they have defined the concept of **hypergamy**—improving one's social and/or economic status by marrying up. (The opposite, **hypogamy**, involves marrying down.) One study of marriage in urban Chicago (Pearlin 1975) found that partners experienced more stress in class-heterogamous unions. Maybe not surprisingly, the spouse who had married down was more stressed than the one who had married up. However, it is important to note that the relationship between stress and marrying down existed only when status striving was important to the individual. Those people for whom status was important and who had married down perceived their marriages more negatively—as less reciprocal, less affectionate, less emotionally supportive, and with less value consensus—than did those who had married up. For people for whom status was *not* important, neither marrying up nor down produced any difference in their evaluation of their marriages.

Interracial/Interethnic Marriages **Interracial marriages** include unions between partners of the white, black, Asian, or Native American races with a spouse outside their own race. As defined by the U.S. Census Bureau, Hispanics are not a separate race but, rather, an ethnic group. Unions between Hispanics and others, as well as between different Asian/Pacific Islander or Hispanic ethnic groups (such as Thai–Chinese or Puerto Rican–Cuban), are considered **interethnic marriages**.

In June 1967 *(Loving v. Virginia)*, the U.S. Supreme Court declared that interracial marriages must be considered legally valid in all states. At about the same time, it became impossible to gather accurate statistics on interracial marriages. Many states no longer require race information on marriage registration forms, so these data are incomplete at best.

Available statistics show that the proportion of interracial and interethnic marriages is fairly small (about 7.5 percent, or 4.5 million couples) (U.S. Census Bureau 2007a, Table 58). However, this proportion has steadily increased since 1970 when the proportion was just 1 percent (Lee and Edmonston 2005). If we count cohabiting couples, the percentage would be somewhat higher because cohabiting couples are less homogamous than married couples (Batson, Qian, and Lichter 2006; Joyner and Kao 2005).

As shown in Figure 9.2, of all interracial (this does not count Hispanic–non-Hispanic) marriages in 2005, about 19 percent (422,000 couples) were black–white (Lee and Edmonston 2005, p. 14; U.S. Census Bureau 2007a, Table 58).[4] The vast majority of the remainder were combinations of whites with Asians, Native Americans, and others. Sixty-eight percent of black–white marriages involved black men married to white women (U.S. Census Bureau 2007a, Table 58).

Much attention has been devoted to why people marry interracially. One apparent reason among racial/ethnic groups that are relatively small in number is simply that they are more likely than larger racial/ethnic groups to interact with others of different races. This situation explains much of the reason why Asian Americans, for example, have lower homogamy rates than do whites, blacks, or Hispanics (Hwang and Aguirre 1997). Similarly, black–white marriages may be more numerous today simply because the races are interacting more (Staples 1999b; "Why Interracial" 1996; Yancey and Yancey 1998).

Another explanation is the **status exchange hypothesis**—the argument that an individual might trade his or her socially defined superior racial/ethnic status for the

economically or educationally superior status of a partner in a less-privileged racial/ethnic group (Kalmijn 1998). In this regard, racial stereotypes may play a part:

> [A] society dominated by Euro-Americans will unsurprisingly privilege a standard of beauty and cultural styles that is a mirror image of itself, even if that image is a media distortion. . . . [I]nterviews with Asian men and women [found] that a sizable minority of respondents preferred whites as potential or current mates because of their preference for "European" traits including tallness, round eyes, buffness for men and more ample breasts for women. (C. Gallagher 2006, p. 150)

Applying the status exchange hypothesis to black–white intermarriage would suggest marrying "up" socioeconomically on the part of a white person who, in effect, trades socially defined superior racial status for the economically superior status of a middle- or upper-middle-class black partner. Little research has been done to test this hypothesis, but a recent study of intermarriage among native Hawaiians, Japanese, Filipinos, and Caucasians in Hawaii supports the hypothesis (Fu and Heaton 2000).[5]

---

[4] Native-born African Americans are significantly more likely to intermarry racially than are black recent immigrants from the West Indies or Africa (Batson, Qian, and Lichter 2006).

[5] As a result of historical events and cultural definitions, native Hawaiians and Filipinos have lower ethnic status in Hawaii than do Japanese or Caucasians. Examining marriage certificates in Hawaii from 1983 to 1994, the researchers found that to marry a Caucasian or a Japanese, native Hawaiians and Filipinos had to have higher economic or educational status than those who married within their own ethnic group. At the same time, Japanese and Caucasians who married native Hawaiians or Filipinos were "of lower status in their own group" (p. 53).

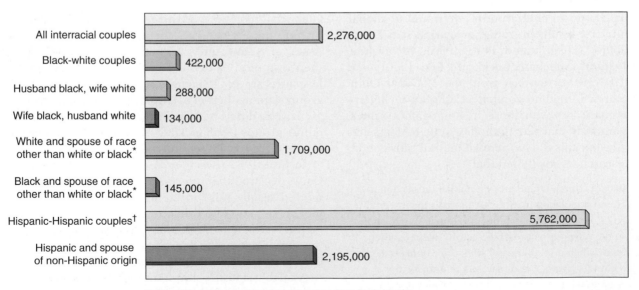

*Neither white nor black, but Asian, Native American, Aleut, Pacific Islander.

†Persons of Hispanic origin may be of any race.

FIGURE 9.2 Number of interracial and Hispanic–non-Hispanic married couples, 2005.

Source: U.S. Census Bureau 2007a, Table 58.

Some people believe that those with privileged racial/ethnic status marry interracially because of rebellion and hostility, guilt, or low self-esteem. Such explanations smack of racism and are not supported by research (J. R. Davidson 1992). Meanwhile, some African American sociologists have expressed concern about black men—especially educated black men—choosing spouses from other races (Crowder and Tolnay 2000; Staples 1994, 1999a). For example, Robert Davis, a past president of the Association of Black Sociologists, believes that black men are inclined to see white women as "the prize" (Davis, quoted in "Why Interracial" 1996). Meanwhile, some African American women view black males' interracial relationships as "selling out"—sacrificing allegiance to one's racial heritage in order to date someone of higher racial status (Paset and Taylor 1991). In a paper on this topic, a Latina student wrote the following:

> It is not just in the African-American community that this is happening. . . . I have noticed when a Mexican-American man gets educated, he usually ends up dating and marrying an Anglo female. Being with an Anglo female is more of a trophy to the Mexican man. . . . I would like to meet an educated Mexican male and date him but there are not that many around. I am not totally set on just dating a Mexican male, but you hardly see white males dating other races. Sometimes it seems there is little hope for Hispanic and African-American females to ever find a good partner. (Torres 1997)

Having said this, we note that research on interracially married couples has generally found that "with few exceptions, this group's motives for marriage do not appear to be any different from those of individuals marrying . . . within their own race." The most common motives by far were love and compatibility (E. Porterfield 1982, p. 23).

Heterogamy and Marital Stability

Marital success can be measured in terms of two related, but different factors: (1) stability— whether or how long the union lasts, and (2) the happiness of the partners. Marital stability is not synonymous with marital happiness because, in some instances, unhappy spouses remain married, whereas less-unhappy partners may choose to separate. In general, social scientists find that marriages that are homogamous in age, education, religion, and race are the most stable (Larson and Hickman 2004).

Just as information on interracial/interethnic marriages is incomplete, so is information on their divorces. Only about half the states and the District of Columbia report race/ethnicity on divorce records. What evidence we have is conflicting on whether interracial/interethnic marriages are more or less stable than intraracial/

intraethnic unions. And although we have some census data on Hispanics who marry outside their ethnic group (see Figure 9.2), we do not know the divorce rates for these interethnic couples.

We can offer at least three explanations for any differences in marital stability that may exist. First, significant differences in values and interests between partners can create a lack of mutual understanding, resulting in emotional gaps and increased couple conflict. Second, such marriages may create conflict between the partners

Some ethnic groups, particularly those consisting of a large proportion of recent immigrants, strongly value homogamy. Nevertheless, an increasing number of Americans enter into ethnically heterogamous unions. This trend toward greater interethnic heterogamy has also occurred in other nations, such as the United Kingdom, where this photo was taken of a British woman being married to a man from Bengal, a region shared by Bangladesh and India. Although "feeling at home"—a factor that encourages homogamy—may be difficult at first, some individuals thrive on the cultural variety characteristic of interracial or inter-ethnic relationships.

and other groups, such as parents, relatives, and friends. Continual discriminatory pressure from the broader society may create undue psychological and marital distress (Bratter and Eschbach 2006). If they lack a supporting social network, partners may find it more difficult to maintain their union in times of crisis. Finally, a higher divorce rate among heterogamous marriages may reflect the fact that these partners are likely to be less conventional in their values and behavior, and unconventional people may divorce more readily than others.

Heterogamy and Human Values

One recent study of (unmarried) interracial couples in college found not only no significant differences in conflict but also *higher* relationship satisfaction compared to same-race couples (Troy, Lewis-Smith, and Laurenceau 2006). Whether these findings would apply to interracially married couples today is unknown. In any case, it is important to note the difference between scientific information and values. Social science can tell us that the stability of heterogamous marriages may be lower than that of homogamous marriages, but many people do not want to limit their social contacts—including potential marriage partners—to socially similar people. Although many people may retain a warm attachment to their racial or ethnic community, and some ethnic groups strongly value homogamy, social and political change has been in the direction of breaking down those barriers. People committed to an open society find intermarriage to be an important symbol, whether or not it is a personal choice, and do not wish to discourage this option (Dunleavy 2004; Moran 2001).

From this perspective, we can think of the negative data on heterogamy and marital stability not as discouragements to marriage but in terms of their utility in helping couples be aware of possible challenges. Intermarrying couples such as Alex and Andrea may anticipate and talk through the differences in their lifestyles.

The data on heterogamy may also be interpreted to mean that common values and lifestyles contribute to stability. A heterogamous pair may have common values that transcend their differences in background. Some problems of interracial (or other heterogamous) marriages have to do with social disapproval and lack of social support from either race (Felmlee 2001; Gullickson 2006). But individuals can choose to work to change the society into one in which heterogamous marriage will be more accepted and hence will pose fewer problems.

Moreover, opinion polls and other research show that Americans are becoming less disapproving of interracial dating (Arnett 2004; J. Jones 2005). Among both blacks and whites, a minority of individuals strongly disapprove

of interracial marriage (Jacobson and Johnson 2006). To the degree that racially, religiously, or economically heterogamous marriages increase in number, they are less likely to be troubled by the reactions of society. Again, we see that private troubles—or choices—are intertwined with public issues. Some ethnic groups strongly value homogamy. Meanwhile, it is also true that if people are able to cross racial, class, or religious boundaries and at the same time share important values, they may open doors to a varied and exciting relationship. Chapter 11 discusses raising children in interracial families.

Falling in love in our society, which generally emphasizes individual choice of marriage partners, whether homogamous or heterogamous, typically involves developing an intimate relationship and establishing mutual commitment. The next section examines these processes.

Developing the Premarital Relationship and Moving Toward Marital Commitment

Social scientists have been interested in how relationships develop during **courtship**, an old-fashioned term that is still used by social scientists to mean the process through which a couple develops mutual commitment and progresses toward marriage. What first brings people together? What keeps them together?

Young people today "meander toward marriage," feeling that they'll be ready to marry when they reach their late twenties or so (Arnett 2004, p. 197). Experiencing unprecedented freedom, today's young adults often express the need to explore as many options as possible before "settling down." As one young woman explained:

> I think everyone should experience everything they want to experience before they get tied down, because if you wanted to date a Black person, a white person, an Asian person, a tall person, short, fat, whatever, as long as you know you've accomplished all that, and you are happy with who you are with, then I think everything would be OK. I want to experience life and know that when that right person comes, I won't have any regrets. (in Arnett 2004, p. 113)

Some young couples "hook up" for nonrelationship sex or find sexual pleasure in "friends with benefits" as they experiment with many relationships before they think about looking for a spouse (Hughes, Morrison, and Asada 2005; Kan and Cares 2006; Manning, Giordano, and Longmore 2006). (Unfortunately, casual dating such as this can be associated with date or acquain-

Issues for Thought

Date or Acquaintance Rape

Contrary to the impression that we are likely to get from the media, most rape victims know their rapists (G. Cowan 2000). **Date** or **acquaintance rape**—being involved in a coercive sexual encounter with a date or other acquaintance—emerged as an issue on college campuses over the past two decades, but date rape no doubt plagued the dating scene for a long time before that (Friedman, Boumil, and Taylor 1992).

Often, excessive use of alcohol is involved (Cue, George, and Norris 1996; Peralta and Cruz 2006). Findings from various research studies over the past decade show that sexually coercive men tend to dismiss women's rejection messages regarding unwanted sex and differ from noncoercive men in their approach to relationships and sexuality: They date more frequently; have higher numbers of sexual partners, especially uncommitted dating relationships; prefer casual encounters; and may "take a predatory approach to their sexual interactions with women."

Closely related to the concept of date rape is *sexual coercion* (Ryan and Mohr 2005). Some researchers have noted the existence of female-initiated sexual coercion—although significantly fewer women than men are sexually coercive, and when they are coercive, they use less forceful techniques. Men's experiences with being coerced most often do not advance beyond kissing or fondling, whereas women's most often result in unwanted, sometimes violent intercourse (Christopher and Sprecher 2000).

Many female victims blamed themselves at least partially—a situation that can result in still greater psychological distress (Breitenbecher 2006). One reason victims blame themselves has to do with **rape myths**: beliefs about rape that function to blame the victim and exonerate the rapist (G. Cowan 2000). Rape myths include the ideas that (1) the rape was somehow provoked by the victim (for example, she "led him on" or wore provocative clothes); (2) men cannot control their sexual urges, a belief that consequently holds women responsible for preventing rape; and (3) rapists are mentally ill, a belief that encourages potential victims to feel safe with someone they know, no matter what (G. Cowan 2000). Increasingly, college men report that they recognize the male's responsibility for rape; this finding may be evidence that campus rape-prevention information and workshops make a difference (Domitrz 2003).

Critical Thinking

What can you do to help prevent date rape? What should you do if you or a friend is raped by an acquaintance? What would or should you do if a friend or acquaintance of yours was known to be the perpetrator of a date or acquaintance rape?

TODAY'S GREEKS CALL IT DATE RAPE.

At its 1985 national convention, members of Pi Kappa Phi fraternity unanimously adopted a resolution not to tolerate any form of sexually abusive behavior on the part of their members. The fraternity also produced this poster and distributed it to all its chapters. The illustration is a detail from the painting *The Rape of the Sabine Women*. Beneath the large message a smaller one reads, "Just a reminder from Pi Kappa Phi. Against her will is against the law."

---

tance rape, as discussed in "Issues for Thought: Date or Acquaintance Rape.")

The majority of couples meet for the first time in face-to-face encounters, such as at school, work, a game, or a party. But today, more and more couples, especially those who are older, meet through singles ads, video-dating services, or online (Cullen 2004; "Online Dating Attracts" 2006). However individuals meet, what is it that draws one to another?

Physical Attractiveness and Rapport

When the first meeting is face-to-face, very often the answer is physical attractiveness. Both women and men tend to believe that they find more socially desirable personality traits in those who are physically attractive. An examination of research studies on mate preferences since 1939 shows that physical attractiveness increased as a value over the past century. Physical attractiveness is especially important in the early stages of a relationship (Buss et al. 2001; Malakh-Pines 2005).

Whether an initial interest develops into a prolonged attachment depends not only on whether one is ready to consider marriage but also on whether the two develop rapport: Do they feel at ease with each other? Are they free to talk spontaneously? Do they feel that they understand each other? At this point, common values begin to play an important role (Malakh-Pines 2005). Couples also tend to be matched on sex drive and attitudes about sex (Lally and Maddock 1994; Murstein 1980), suggesting that these are important sorting factors.

Development of a face-to-face romantic relationship moves from initial encounter to discovery of similarities and self-disclosure (Knobloch, Solomon, and Theiss 2006). However, meeting for the first time online is a bit different (Kopytoff 2005; Mulrine 2003). Internet relationships—sometimes coupled with background checks—progress through "an inverted developmental sequence." That is, without first seeing one another, two people who find each other intriguing gradually get to know one another through keyboard discussions. Then, too, emerging niche websites introduce people who share specific characteristics, such as not wanting children, or being dog owners or vegetarians (Kirby 2005). This development makes it possible to establish the groundwork for rapport from the beginning, rather than having rapport develop as people gradually discover more about each other. Over time e-mails become more intimate, and a powerful connection may be established (Merkle and Richardson 2000).

The wheel theory of love, described in Chapter 5, explains the role of rapport in the development of a relationship. It suggests that mutual disclosure, along with feelings of trust and understanding, are necessary early steps. As you may recall, this theory also posits that an important phase in developing love is "mutual need satisfaction" and resultant interdependence (Anderson and Sabatelli 2007). Along this line, social scientist Robert Winch (1958) once proposed the **theory of complementary needs**, whereby we are attracted to partners whose needs complement our own (Malakh-Pines 2005). Sometimes people take this idea to mean that "opposites attract." This may make intuitive sense to some of us, but needs theorists more often argue that

we are attracted to others whose strengths are *harmonious* with our own (Klohnen and Mendelsohn 1998; P. Schwartz 2006). "As We Make Choices: Harmonious Needs in Mate Selection" further explores these ideas. As partners develop mutual need satisfaction and interdependence, they gradually define their relationship.

Defining the Relationship

From an interactionist theoretical perspective (see Chapter 2), qualitative research with seriously dating couples shows that they pass through a series of fairly predictable stages (Sniezek 2002, 2007). Hinting, testing, negotiating, joking, and scrutinizing the partner's words and behavior characterize this process. As one example, a thirty-two-year-old emergency room worker described reading her partner's joking about marriage—and his use of the word *yet*—as a possible sign that he had considered marrying her.

> It was right here in our kitchen I put it (the food) down on his plate and I'm like "prison food." And he said "Um gee and we're not even married yet." And that was like the first joke. It stuck in my mind. (Sniezek 2007)

As the relationship progresses toward an eventual wedding, the "marriage conversation" is introduced. In the research being described here, women were more likely to initiate marriage talk—cautiously and indirectly: "Yeah it's like so what are you thinking? Where is this relationship heading?" In other cases, the marriage conversation began more directly. One woman raised the question of marriage when her partner suggested that they live together.

> When he asked me to move in with him, I told him I felt uncomfortable living with someone and not being married—a moral issue for me. So we talked about [the probability of getting married] at that time. (Sniezek 2007)

Once marriage talk is initiated, the couple faces negotiating a joint definition of the relationship as premarital. If the idea that the relationship should lead to marriage is rejected by one partner, several responses can occur. In some cases, one partner's marriage hopes may be relinquished, although the relationship continues. In other cases, a partner may deliver an ultimatum. Sometimes an ultimatum results in marriage; in other cases, stating an ultimatum causes an irreparable rift in the relationship.

Finally, most couples do not define themselves as "really" engaged until one or more ritualized practices take place—buying rings, setting a wedding date, public announcements to family and friends, holding engagement parties, and so on. These practices make

As We Make Choices Harmonious Needs in Mate Selection

Finding a spouse with needs that are in harmony with one's own means matching different (but complementary) needs in some cases. In other cases, finding the "right" partner involves matching similar needs. The following three areas in which couples' needs should be similar are suggested by prominent sociologist Pepper Schwartz (2006) as important for a happy, long-term match:

1. **Personal Energy.** Your marriage may have more chance for success when your general energy level matches your partner's. "Whenever a couple spends time together their energy levels come into play. . . . While lovers may be willing to accommodate a leisurely stroll along the beach or a speed walk up the nearest mountain, at the end of the day, constant accommodation can be taxing and frustrating" (P. Schwartz 2006, p. 17).

2. **Outlook.** "People's attitudes and mood ranges from cheerful and upbeat to serious and earnest. . . . There is nothing wrong with either of these two emotional approaches to the world, but [it can be frustrating] if one person always feels the other is 'raining on her parade.' . . . Meanwhile, the partner's take on this may be to see that kind of optimism as simplistic or even scary . . . [and to] stop trusting their partners' instinctive impulse to see the brightest side of everything" (P. Schwartz 2006, p. 18).

3. **Predictability.** "If you draw comfort from surrounding yourself with familiar patterns and places, you are not going to be happy with someone for whom the very thought of predictable days, weeks, and places fills them with an urge to run. . . . The opposite of this need for predictabil-

ity is the passion for variety. . . . [I]f the person who craves variety and the person who craves predictability find themselves together, they are going to feel betrayed and angry and worst of all, trapped" (P. Schwartz 2006, p. 21).

Critical Thinking

Do you agree with Pepper Schwartz that couples' needs should be similar in these three areas? Can you think of examples that would support Schwartz's points? Can you think of exceptions? Can you think of other situations in which the best match would be between partners with similar needs? Can you think of areas in which partners' different needs might complement one another?

the redefinition of the relationship increasingly public and "hardened" (Sniezek 2007).

In another qualitative study on this subject, two social scientists conducted lengthy interviews with 116 individuals in premarital relationships. They examined the process by which these partners gradually committed to marriage (Surra and Hughes 1997). From the interviews, the researchers classified the respondents' relationships in two categories: *relationship-driven* and *event-driven*.

Relationship-driven couples followed the rationally evolving pattern described earlier. But in event-driven relationships, partners vacillated between commitment and ambivalence. Often they disagreed on how committed they were as well as why they had become committed in the first place. The researchers called this relationship type event-driven because events—fighting, discussing the relationship with one's own friends, and making up—punctuated each partner's account.

It's probably no surprise that event-driven couples' satisfaction with the relationship fluctuated over time. Although often recognizing their relationships as rocky, they do not necessarily break up, because positive events (for example, a discussion about getting married or an expression of approval of the relationship from others)

typically follow negative ones. At least some event-driven couples would probably be better off not getting married. We turn now to an even more serous issue—that of dating violence.

Dating Violence—A Serious Sign of Trouble

Sometimes courtship involves the need to make decisions about continuing or ending a relationship that is characterized by physical violence and/or verbal abuse. Physical violence occurs in 20 to 40 percent of dating relationships (DeMaris 2001; Luthra and Gidycz 2006)—a high, "most surprising incidence" (Johnson and Ferraro 2000, p. 951). Most incidents of aggression involve pushing, grabbing, or slapping. Between 1 and 3 percent of college students have reported experiencing severe violence, such as beatings or assault with an object. Researchers are concerned that dating violence among teens is widespread and that many teens—as well as others—apparently minimize violence or view it as to-be-expected in certain situations (Perry and Fromuth 2005; Prospero 2006; Sears et al. 2006).

Both genders engage in physical aggression (Lento 2006; Perry and Fromuth 2005). However, by far the more serious injuries result from male-to-female violence (Johnson and Ferraro 2000). Furthermore, women are more inclined to "hit back" once a partner has precipitated the violence, rather than to physically strike out first (Luthra and Gidycz 2006).

Dating violence typically begins with and is accompanied by verbal or psychological abuse (Hogben and Waterman 2000; Lento 2006; White, Merrill, and Koss 2001) and tends to occur over jealousy, with a refusal of sex, after illegal drug use or excessive drinking of alcohol, or upon disagreement about drinking behavior (Cogan and Ballinger 2006; Makepeace 1981, 1986).

Researchers have found it discouraging that about half of abusive dating relationships continue rather than being broken off (Few and Rosen 2005). Given that the economic and social constraints of marriage are not usually applicable to dating, researchers have wondered why these relationships persist. Evidence suggests that having experienced domestic violence in one's family of origin is significantly related to both being abusive and to accepting abuse as normal (Cyr, McDuff, and Wright 2006; Dutton 2003; Few and Rosen 2005). A recent qualitative study of twenty-eight female undergraduates in abusive dating relationships found that some of these women felt "stuck" with their partner (Few and Rosen 2005). A majority had assumed a "caretaker identity," similar to martyring, discussed in Chapter 5. As one explained,

> I always was a rescuer in my family. I felt that I was rescuing him [boyfriend] and taking care of him. He never knew what it was like to have a good, positive home environment, so I was working hard to create that for him. (p. 272)

Others felt stuck because they wanted to be married, and their dating partner appeared to be their only prospect: "I think near the end, one of the reasons I was scared to let go was: 'Oh, my God, I'm 27.' I was worried that I was going to be like some lonely old maid" (p. 274).

What are some early indicators that a dating partner is likely to become violent eventually? A date who is likely to someday become physically violent often exhibits one or more of the following characteristics:

1. Handles ordinary disagreements or disappointments with inappropriate anger or rage

2. Has to struggle to retain self-control when some little thing triggers anger

3. Goes into tirades

4. Is quick to criticize or to be verbally mean

5. Appears unduly jealous, restricting, and controlling

6. Has been violent in previous relationships (Island and Letellier 1991, pp.158–66)

Courtship violence is never acceptable. Making conscious decisions about whether to marry a certain person raises the possibility of not marrying him or her. Letting go of a relationship can be painful. Next, we'll look at the possibility of breaking up.

The Possibility of Breaking Up

According to the exchange perspective, couples choose either to stay committed or to break up by weighing the rewards of their relationship against its costs. As partners go through this process, they also consider how well their relationship matches an imagined, ideal one. Partners also contemplate alternatives to the relationship, the investments they've made in it, and barriers to breaking up. (We will see in Chapter 16 that this perspective is also used when examining people's decisions about divorce.) Using this scheme, Kurdek developed a questionnaire to measure a couple's relationship commitment. The following are some questions from psychologist Lawrence Kurdek's measure (respondents could strongly agree, agree, remain neutral, disagree, or strongly disagree):

Rewards:
One advantage to my relationship is having someone to count on.

Costs:
It takes a lot for me to be in my relationship.

Match to Ideal Comparison Level:
My current relationship comes close to matching what I would consider to be my ideal relationship.

Alternatives:
As an alternative to my current relationship, I would like the freedom to do what I want to do whenever I want to do it.
As an alternative to my relationship, I would like to date someone else.

Investments:
I've put a lot of energy and effort into my relationship.
A part of me is tied up in my relationship.

Barriers to Breaking Up:
It would be difficult to leave my partner because of the emotional pain involved.
I would find it difficult to leave my partner because I would feel obligated to keep the relationship together. (1995a, p. 263)

When a partner's rewards are higher than the costs, when there are few desirable alternatives to the relationship, when the relationship comes close to one's ideal, when one has invested a great deal in the relationship,

"Put me on your do-not-call list."

and when the barriers to breaking up are perceived as high, an individual is likely to remain committed. However, when costs outweigh rewards, when there are desirable alternatives to the relationship, when one's relationship does not match one's ideal, when little has been invested in the relationship in comparison to rewards, and when there are fewer barriers to breaking up, couples are more likely to do so. "As We Make Choices: Some Advice on Breaking Up" gives suggestions regarding ending a dating relationship.

Having examined the processes through which individuals and couples move as they select a spouse, we turn to a discussion of cohabitation as a form of courtship.

Cohabitation and Marital Quality and Stability

As discussed in Chapter 8, cohabitation serves different purposes for different couples: Living together "may be a precursor to marriage, a trial marriage, a substitute for marriage, or simply a serious boyfriend–girlfriend relationship" (Bianchi and Casper 2000, p. 17). Since the 1970s, the proportion of marriages preceded by cohabitation has grown steadily, and by 1995, a majority of marriages followed this pattern (Bumpass and Lu 2000). This section addresses cohabitation as courtship. Specifically we will explore this question: How does cohabiting affect subsequent marital quality and stability?

During the 1990s, the proportion of cohabitors who eventually married their partners declined (Seltzer 2000, p. 1252). This situation largely results from the fact that cohabiting has become more socially acceptable, a cultural change that "contributes to a decline in cohabiting partners' expectations about whether

marriage is the 'next step' in their own relationship" (p. 1249). Another reason that fewer cohabitors are marrying has to do with economics: Poor cohabiting couples are less likely to marry (Lichter, Qian, and Mellott 2006). One study found that cohabitors "who had talked about future marriage plans have generally been living with their partners for about two years, indicating that the issue of greater permanence in their relationships surfaces over time" (Sassler 2004, p. 501).

Many people today follow the intuitive belief that "cohabitation is a worthwhile experiment for evaluating the compatibility of a potential spouse, [and therefore] one would expect those who cohabit first to have even more stable marriages than those who marry without cohabiting" (Seltzer 2000, p. 1252; see also J. Jones 2002). Perhaps surprisingly, however, there has been little research on whether cohabitation that is limited only to one's future spouse increases the odds of marital success. At this time, we can report that analysis of a nationally representative sample of 6,577 women who married for the first time between 1970 and 1995 has found that premarital cohabitation that was limited to the woman's future husband did not increase the couple's likelihood of divorce (Teachman 2003).

Meanwhile, research over the past twenty years has consistently shown that generally marriages (including remarriages) that are preceded by more than one instance of cohabitation are *more* likely to end in separation or divorce than are marriages in which the spouses had not previously cohabited at all (DeMaris and MacDonald 1993; Dush, Cohan, and Amato 2003; Seltzer 2000; Teachman 2003; Xu, Hudspeth, and Bartkowski 2006). However, one study shows that these findings apply to non-Hispanic whites but not to African Americans or Mexican Americans, for whom cohabiting may be a more normative life-course event, as discussed in Chapter 8 (Phillips and Sweeney 2005). Why might serial cohabitation before marriage be related to lower marital stability? Hypotheses to answer this question can be divided into two categories, both of which are supported to some degree by research.

First, the **experience hypothesis** posits that cohabiting experiences themselves affect individuals so that, once married, they are more likely to divorce (Seltzer 2000). For example, serial cohabitation may adversely affect subsequent marital quality and stability inasmuch as the experiences actually weaken commitment because "'successful' cohabitation demonstrates that reasonable alternatives to marriage exist" (Thomson and Colella 1992, p. 377). There is also evidence that "young adults become more tolerant of divorce as a result of cohabiting, whatever their initial views were," possibly because "cohabiting exposes people to a wider range of attitudes about family arrangements than those who marry without first

As We Make Choices   Some Advice on Breaking Up

Although breaking up is hard to do at any time, breakups before marriage are nearly always less stressful than divorce. Nevertheless, the act of breaking up can be an ordeal (Amatenstein 2002). Sometimes a breakup is followed by unwanted phone calls, unwanted in-person encounters, or stalking. As you might guess, those who initiate the breakup are less likely to engage in these behaviors than are those who have been left behind (Langhinrichsen-Rohling et al. 2000). Sociologist David Knox (1975), in a classic statement mirrored by contemporary counselors, offers the following guidelines for ending a relationship:

1. Decide that terminating the relationship is what you really want to do.

2. Assuming you have definitely determined to break up, prepare yourself for wavering—but don't change your mind.

3. Plan the breakup discussion with your partner in person, but at a location from which you can readily withdraw.

4. Explain your reasons for breaking up in terms of your own values, rather than pointing out what you think is wrong with the other person.

5. Seek out new relationships.

Item 5 is also good advice for those who have recently been broken up with. A few recent studies have found that some ex-partners forge supportive postdat-

ing relationships that satisfy legitimate needs, such as friendship and shared history (Foley and Fraser 1998; Langhinrichsen-Rohling et al. 2000).

Critical Thinking

Under what circumstances do you think that breaking up with a dating partner would be acceptable? Under what circumstances do you believe that ending an engagement would be the right thing to do? Which do you think would be more difficult: going through a breakup or living with an emotionally or physically abusive partner? Which do you think would be more difficult: being single or living with an emotionally or physically abusive partner?

---

living together" (Seltzer 2000, p. 1253; see also Dush, Cohan, and Amato 2003; Popenoe and Whitehead 2000). A related hypothesis suggests that some cohabiting couples, who would not have married if they had been simply dating but not living together, do end up marrying just because getting married seems to be the expected next thing to do. Choosing by default, they "slide" from cohabiting into marrying, rather than making more deliberative decisions (Stanley, Rhoades, and Markman 2006).

Second, the **selection hypothesis** assumes that individuals who choose serial cohabitation (or who "select" themselves into cohabiting situations) are different from those who do not; these differences translate into higher divorce rates. For instance, one study has found that people who cohabit have less-effective problem-solving and communication skills (Cohan and Kleinbaum 2002). Why this is so is unclear. Furthermore, those who choose serial cohabitation before they marry may have more negative attitudes about marriage in general and more accepting attitudes toward divorce.

An important recent international study lends considerable support to the selection hypothesis (Liefbroer and Dourleijn 2006). This study looked at the effects of cohabitation on marital stability in several countries and found that cohabiting had no negative effect on marital stability in countries such as Norway, where cohabiting is more common than in the United States.

The researchers reasoned that in societies where cohabitation is about as common as marriage, those who live together before marrying would not be significantly different from those who do not. Therefore, no selection effect would be operating. The fact that this research found no negative effect of cohabitation on marital stability in societies where there would be little selection effect supports the selection hypothesis. Other support for the selection hypothesis is the finding that negative effects of cohabitation apply more strongly for non-Hispanic whites than for blacks or Mexican Americans, the latter two racial/ethnic groups having a higher percentage of cohabitors (Phillips and Sweeney 2005). To this point we have been discussing why and how relationships proceed to marriage. We turn now to a discussion of marital satisfaction and decisions made, not only in choosing a partner, but in other areas as well.

Marital Satisfaction and Choices Throughout Life

Our theme of making choices throughout life surely applies both to couples anticipating marriage as well as to decisions made during the early years of marriage. We'll examine these topics now.

Preparation for Marriage

Given today's high divorce rate, clergy, teachers, parents, policy makers, and others have grown increasingly concerned that individuals be better prepared for marriage. High school and college family life education courses are designed to prepare individuals of various racial/ethnic groups for marriage (DeMaria 2005; Fincham, Hall, and Beach 2006). Premarital counseling, which often takes place at churches or with private counselors, is specifically oriented to couples who plan to marry. For example, many Catholic dioceses require premarital counseling before a couple may be married by a priest. Other religions and denominations require premarital counseling as well. Moreover, illustrating the connection between private lives and public interest, a few states now legally require premarital counseling (Huston and Melz 2004; Murray 2006).

Premarital counseling has four goals:

1. To evaluate the relationship with the possibility of a couple's deciding against marriage

2. To help the couple to develop a realistic, yet hopeful and positive vision of their future marriage

3. To sensitize partners to potential problems

4. To teach positive ways of communicating about and resolving conflicts

Although common sense suggests that these kinds of programs enhance subsequent unions, they are just beginning to be scientifically evaluated in terms of measurable outcomes (Murray and Murray 2004; Ooms 2005; Rowden, Harris, and Stahmann 2006). One finding is that these programs can't necessarily work miracles: Among other factors, success depends upon the personality characteristics of each partner, as well as on couple characteristics, such as the interactional styles with which they begin the program, influences from their families of origin, and their motivation to learn something from the program (C. Murray 2004). Overall, however, family experts see these programs as important, especially for adult children of troubled or divorced families (Burchard et al. 2003; Markman, Stanley, and Blumberg 2001; D. Olson 1994; F. Russo 1997). Psychologist Scott Stanley identifies four benefits of premarital education:

> (a) it can slow couples down to foster deliberation, (b) it sends a message that marriage matters, (c) it can help couples learn of options if they need help later, and (d) there is evidence that providing some couples with some types of premarital training . . . can lower their risks for subsequent marital distress or termination. (2001, p. 272)

Premarital education or counseling may help make the first years of marriage go more smoothly.

The First Years of Marriage

In the 1950s, marriage and family texts characteristically referred to the first months and years of marriage as a period of adjustment, after which, presumably, spouses had learned to play traditional marital roles. Today we view early marriage more as a time of role-*making* than of role-*taking*.

Role-making refers to modifying or adjusting the expectations and obligations traditionally associated with a role. Role-making involves issues explored more fully in other chapters of this text. Newlyweds negotiate expectations for sex and intimacy (Chapter 6), establish communication (Chapter 13) and decision-making patterns (Chapter 14), balance expectations about marital and job or school responsibilities (Chapter 12), and come to some agreement about becoming parents (Chapter 10) and how they will handle and budget their money (Knudson-Martin and Mahoney 1998; Burke and Cast 1997). When children are present, role-making involves negotiation about parenting roles (Chapter 11). Role-making issues peculiar to remarriages are addressed in Chapter 17. Generally, role-making in new marriages involves creating, by means of communication and negotiation, identities as married persons (Rotenburg, Schaut, and O'Connor 1993). The time of role-making is not a clearly demarcated period but rather continues throughout marriage.

Although the early stages of marriage are not a distinct period, social scientists and others continue to talk and write about them as such (Bulcroft, Smeins, and Bulcroft 1999). One thing we know is that this period tends to be the happiest, with gradual declines in marital satisfaction afterward (Bradbury and Karney 2004). Why this is true is not clear. One explanation points to life-cycle stresses as children arrive and economic pressures intensify; others simply assume that courtship and new marriage are periods of emotional intensity from which there is an inevitable decline (Glenn 1998; Whyte 1990). We do know something about the structural advantages of the early years of marriage, and it is likely that these contribute to high levels of satisfaction. For one thing, partners' roles are relatively similar or unsegregated in early marriage. Spouses tend to share household tasks and, because of similar experiences, are better able to empathize with each other.

But early marriage is not characterized only by happiness. Couples must also accomplish certain tasks during this period. In general, "the solidarity of the new couple relation must be established and competing interpersonal ties modified" (Aldous 1978, p. 141; Rotenberg,

The early stages of marriage tend to be the happiest, partly because partners' roles are relatively similar in early marriage. As newlyweds come to view themselves as a couple, they address potentially problematic topics, such as balancing job and family, negotiating sexual frequency, and agreeing on how much time to spend together.

Schaut, and O'Connor 1993). Getting through this stage requires making requests for change and negotiating resolutions, along with renewed acceptance of each other. Indeed, recent research by psychoanalyst John Gottman shows that communication as newlyweds tends to influence the later happiness—and even the permanence—of the marriage (Gottman et al. 1998). The couple constructs relationships and interprets events in a way that reinforces their sense of themselves as a couple (Wallerstein and Blakeslee 1995).

A national study undertaken by family researchers at Creighton University in Omaha identified three main, potentially problematic topics for couples in first marriages: (1) money—balancing job and family, dealing with financial debt brought into the marriage by one or both spouses, and what to do with money income; (2) sexual frequency; and (3) agreeing on how much time to spend together—and finding it! Challenges associated with learning to balance work and/or college courses and a marital relationship are real (Christopherson 2006). Feeling supported by parents and extended kin helps (Kurdek 2005). Other issues mentioned by the couples in the Creighton study involved expectations about who would do household tasks (and how well),

communication challenges, and problems with in-laws (Brennan 2003; Risch, Riley, and Lawler 2004). A more general, necessary goal for couples in early marriage is to create couple connection.

Creating Couple Connection

Partners who desire enduring emotional relationships must keep their relationship as a high priority. Some research suggests that, on average, today's marriages are happier when both spouses are employed (Schoen, Rogers, and Amato 2006). Also, husbands and wives who engage in supportive communication and who together pursue leisure activities that they both enjoy are more compatible and satisfied with their marriage (Crawford et al. 2002; Johnson et al. 2005; Kurdek 2005). Remember the discussion in Chapter 5 about the biochemistry of new experiences and how novel experiences precipitate the secretion of dopamine, associated with the sensation of pleasure? Other research on marital satisfaction also suggests that novelty-seeking spouses—those who make time for shared new experiences—are more happily married (Burpee and Langer 2005).

Assuredly for wives, time spent together is important to marital happiness (Gager and Sanchez 2003). An important psychologist and expert on marital communication, John Gottman, offers this advice:

> Happy, solid couples nourish their marriages with plenty of positive moments together. . . . Too often, families lead complex—even grueling—lives in which they sacrifice the happy times for more materialistic, fleeting goals. . . . Sundays at the office take the place of Sundays at the park. But if you want to keep your marriage alive, it's essential to rediscover—or perhaps simply make time for—those experiences that make you feel good about your spouse and your marriage. (1994, p. 223)

Comparative analysis of data collected from national samples in 1980 and 2000 revealed that spouses spend less time interacting with each other now than they did twenty-five years ago. (However, their reported marital satisfaction had not declined significantly, partly because they were more satisfied with the decision-making equality in their marriage [Amato et al. 2003].) Nevertheless, increased emphasis on other matters, such as job pressures and long work hours or children's needs, can result in exhaustion and slow emotional erosion (Roberts and Levenson 2001; Sternberg 1988b). Noting that "[l]ove is not an express lane concept," observers suggest creating daily "connecting moments" when you can be alone together and pay attention to your relationship (Brennan 2003; Brotherson 2003).

Keeping one's marriage vital requires that partners consciously and continuously strive to maintain intimacy, which can entail "an enormous investment: in time, effort, and priorities. In other words, an emotionally meaningful relationship does not develop 'by drift or default'" (Cuber and Harroff 1965, pp.142–45). Clearly, satisfaction with the marital relationship has a great deal to do with the choices that partners make. One important set of decisions involves practicing positive communication skills (Wegner 2005). Research that followed 135 Denver couples over thirteen years, from the time they were engaged and into their marriages, concluded that "the seeds of marital distress and divorce are sown for many couples before they say 'I do.' . . . [N]egative premarital and early marital interactions . . . prime a marriage for the erosion of positivity over time" (Clements, Stanley, and Markman 2004, p. 621). Building better communication skills is addressed in Chapter 13.

We have seen that the kind of relationship a couple shares is largely a product of the partners' values and emotional health, their attitudes about one another and about marriage itself, and the conscious attention that they give to their relationship. One way to design and retain the kind of relationship that spouses want is to be adaptable.

Creating Adaptable Marriage Relationships

For years, wrote psychoanalyst Sidney Jourard thirty years ago, spouses go to sleep night after night, with their relationship patterned one way, a way that perhaps satisfies neither—too close, too distant, boring, or suffocating—and on awakening the next morning, they reinvent their relationship *in the same way* (1976, p. 231). Jourard's point remains true today. People change, and—if the marriage is to be permanent—spouses need to envision marriage as able to allow for such change.

An option is to actively pursue an **adaptable marriage relationship**, one that allows and encourages partners to grow and change. In an adaptable marriage, spouses' roles may be renegotiated as the needs of each change (Scarf 1995). Some people may have an intuitive knack for achieving this kind of marriage. But again, we want to stress that in the absence of conscious reflection, decisions are often made by default. Hence, we would encourage spouses to talk to each other about the questions in the following section at various times throughout their marriage.

Talking about the marriage that you and your partner want and expect may point up differences, many of which can be worked out. Also, if dating or engaged couples uncover basic value differences and cannot work them out—for example, about whether or not to have children—it would probably be better to end their relationship before marriage than to commit themselves to a union that cannot satisfy either of them. Openly and honestly discussing matters like the ones that follow is important in maintaining a mutually supportive relationship (Pendley 2006).

Some Things to Talk About

1. When should a marriage be dissolved and under what circumstances? How long and in what ways would you work on an unsatisfactory relationship before dissolving it? If you live in a state where it is available, might the two of you consider a covenant marriage—or not? Why?

2. What are your expectations, attitudes, and preferences regarding sex?

3. Do you want children? If so, how many? Whose responsibility is birth control? What are your values regarding a possible unplanned or unwanted pregnancy?

4. If you have children, how will you allocate child-rearing responsibilities and tasks? What are some of your values about child raising? Do the two of you agree on child-raising practices, such as how strict to be or whether to spank a child?

5. Will major decisions be made equally? Will there be a principal breadwinner, or will partners equally share responsibility for earning money? How will funds be allocated? Will there be his, her, and our money? Or will all money be pooled? Who is the owner of family property, such as family businesses, farms, or other partnerships?

6. Will there be a principal homemaker, or will domestic chores be shared?

7. What about religious values? Do you expect your partner to share yours? Will you attend religious services together? How often? If you are of a religion different from that of your mate, where will you worship on special religious holidays? What about the children's religion?

8. What are your educational goals? How about your prospective spouse's?

9. How will each of you relate to your own and to your spouse's relatives? Do you value sharing many or most activities with relatives? Or do you prefer more couple togetherness, discouraging activities with relatives?

10. How much time and how much intimate information will you share with friends other than your partner?

11. What is your attitude toward friendships with people of the opposite sex? How about Internet (cyberspace) friends? Would you ever consider having sex with someone other than your mate? If so, under what circumstances? How would you react if your partner were to have sex with another person?

12. How much time alone do you need? How much are you willing to allow your partner? Will you buy a larger house or rent a bigger apartment so that each partner may have private space?

13. Will you purposely set aside time to talk to each other? What topics do you like to talk about? What topics do you dislike? Are you willing to try to become more comfortable about discussing these? If communication becomes difficult, will you go to a marriage counselor? If so, what percentage of your income would you be willing to pay for marriage counseling?

14. What kinds of vacations will you take? Will you take couple-only vacations? Would you ever consider taking separate vacations? If so, under what circumstances?

15. What are your own and your partner's personal definitions of *intimacy, commitment,* and *responsibility*?

In talking with each other, partners need to try to keep an open mind and use their creativity. Maintaining a happy marriage is challenging, if only because two people, two imaginations, and two sets of needs are involved. Differences *will* arise because no two individuals have exactly the same points of view.

Getting married can encourage partners to commit themselves to building an ongoing love relationship and history together. Marital relationships can more often be permanently satisfying, counselors advise, when spouses learn to care for the "unvarnished" other, not a "splendid image" (Van den Haag 1974, p. 142). In this regard, sociologist Judith Wallerstein, reflecting on her own marriage of fifty years, writes:

> I certainly have not been happy all through each year of my marriage. There have been good times and bad, angry and joyful moments, times of ecstasy and times of quiet contentment. But I would never trade my husband, Robert, for another man. I would not swap my marriage for any other. This does not mean that I find other men unattractive, but there is all the difference in the world between a passing fancy and a life plan. For me, there has always been only one life plan, the one I have lived with my husband. (Wallerstein and Blakeslee 1995, p. 8)

Choosing a supportive partner is an important factor in developing this kind of long-term marital love and satisfaction.

Summary

- Three factors related to marital stability are partners' attachment style, age at marriage, and mate selection risk, due to one or both partners' having experienced parental divorce.

- Whether marriage partners are arranged, "assisted," or more freely chosen, social scientists typically view people as choosing marriage partners in a marriage market; armed with resources (personal and social characteristics), they bargain for the best deal they can get.

- Historically, in Western cultures, marriages were often arranged in the marriage market, as business deals. In some of the world that is less Westernized, some marriages are still arranged. Some immigrant groups in the United States (and other Westernized societies) today practice arranged or "assisted" marriage.

- Although gender roles and expectations are certainly changing, some aspects of the traditional marriage exchange (a man's providing financial support in exchange for the woman's childbearing and child-rearing capabilities, domestic services, and sexual availability) remain.

- Nevertheless, couples today are increasingly likely to value both partners' potential for financial contribution to the union.

- An important factor shaping marital choice is homogamy, the tendency of people to marry others with whom they share certain social characteristics. Despite the trend toward declining homogamy, it is still a strong force, encouraged by geographical availability, social pressure, and feeling at home with people like ourselves.

- Physical attractiveness is important in first encounters and helps to explain our attraction to others.

- The courtship process develops through the building of rapport and gradually negotiating the relationship as premarital and leading to marriage.

- Some courting relationships will end in breakups.

- Serial cohabiting (although not necessarily cohabiting before marriage only with one's future spouse) has been shown to increase the likelihood of divorce. The suggested reasons for this involve the *selection hypothesis* and the *experience hypothesis.*

- There is society-wide concern about preparation for marriage. Premarital counseling and family life education are two approaches that have been developed, but we need more research data on their effectiveness.

- Partners change over the course of a marriage, so a relationship needs to be adaptable if it is to continue to be emotionally satisfying.

- Spouses in the first years of marriage engage in role-making, a process that includes—among other things—negotiating issues surrounding money, sexual frequency, and time together.

Questions for Review and Reflection

1. In your own words, explain Figure 9.1. Try to think of your own examples to describe each concept.

2. Explain reasons why marriages are likely to be homogamous. Why do you think homogamous marriages are more stable than heterogamous marriages? How might the stability of interracial or interethnic marriages change as society becomes more tolerant of these heterogamous unions?

3. If possible, talk to a few married couples you know who lived together before marrying, and ask them how their cohabiting experience influenced their transition to marriage. How do their answers compare with the research findings presented in this chapter?

4. This chapter lists topics that are important to discuss before and throughout one's marriage. Which do you think are the most important? Which do you think are the least important? Why?

5. **Policy Question.** What social policies, if any, presently exist to discourage couples who are experiencing courtship or dating violence from getting married? What new policies might be enacted to further discourage dating and/or courtship violence?

Key Terms

adaptable marriage relationship 229
arranged marriage 211
assortative mating 214
bride price 213
courtship 220
cross-national marriage 212
date rape (acquaintance rape) 221
dowry 213
endogamy 214
exchange theory 213
exogamy 214
experience hypothesis 225
free-choice culture 212
geographic availability 215
heterogamy 214

homogamy 214
hypergamy 217
hypogamy 217
interethnic marriage 217
intergenerational transmission of divorce 210
interracial marriage 217
marital stability 208
marriage market 211
mate selection risk 211
pool of eligibles 214
rape myth 221
role-making 227
selection hypothesis 226
status exchange hypothesis 218
theory of complementary needs 222

Online Resources

Companion Website for This Book

www.thomsonedu.com/sociology/lamanna

Visit the book companion website, where you will find flash cards, practice quizzes, Internet links, suggested readings, InfoTrac College Edition exercises, and more to help you study.

ThomsonNOW™ for Marriage and Family

Spend time on what you need to master rather than on information you already have learned. Take a pre-test for this chapter, and ThomsonNOW will generate a personalized study plan based on your results. The study plan will identify the topics you need to review and direct you to online resources such as videos, narrated learning modules, and interactive activities to help you master those topics. You can then take a post-test to help you determine the concepts you have mastered and what you will still need to work on. Try it out! Go to **www.thomsonedu.com/login** to sign in with an access code or to purchase access to this product.

To Parent or Not to Parent

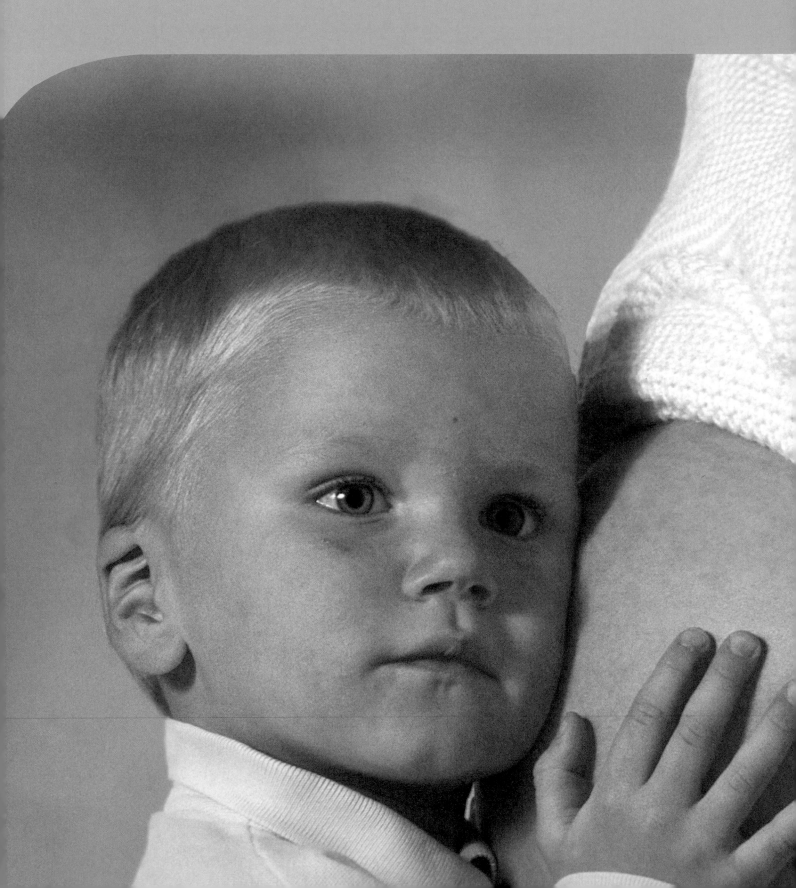

10

Fertility Trends in the United States

Family Size

Differential Fertility Rates

A Closer Look at Family Diversity: Choosing Large Families in a Small Family Era

Facts about Families: Race/Ethnicity and Differential Fertility Rates

The Decision to Parent or Not to Parent

Social Pressures to Have Children

Is American Society Antinatalist?

Motivation for Parenthood

Costs of Having Children

How Children Affect Marital Happiness

Remaining Child-Free

Having Children: Options and Circumstances

The Timing of Parenthood

The One-Child Family

Nonmarital Births

Stepparents' Decisions about Having Children

Multipartnered Fertility

Preventing Pregnancy

Abortion

The Politics of Abortion

The Safety of Abortions

Involuntary Infertility and Reproductive Technology

The Social and Biological Context of Infertility

Infertility Services and Reproductive Technology

Reproductive Technology: Social and Ethical Issues

Reproductive Technology: Making Personal Choices

Facts about Families: "Test-Tube" Babies Grow Up

Adoption

The Adoption Process

Adoption of Racial/Ethnic Minority Children

Adoption of Older Children and Children with Disabilities

International Adoptions

© IT Stock International/Creatas

There may be someone in your class who has been adopted, perhaps by parents of another race. There may be someone in your class who is thinking about infertility treatment. Or who is thinking about having an abortion. Or about having a first child. Or about whether to have children ever. Or about having and raising an only child, or a larger family. All these decisions focus on some aspect of whether (or how) to become a parent. They are very personal choices, but in this chapter we'll see that they are nevertheless influenced by the society around us.

Significant changes have taken place in American childbearing patterns in the decades since World War II. For one thing, the average number of children an American woman bears has declined. For another, women are having children at later ages. And finally, childlessness—by choice or circumstance—is more common today.

The U.S. **total fertility rate (TFR)**—the number of births a typical woman will have over her lifetime[1]—dropped sharply from a high of more than 3.5 at the peak of the baby boom (the post–World War II spurt in fertility) to the lowest level ever recorded: 1.738 in 1976. In recent years, the total fertility rate has fluctuated around 2.0; on average, American women are now having around two children each (J. Martin et al. 2005, Table 4; Hamilton, Martin, and Ventura 2007, Table 1;

Family Group by Henry Spencer Moore, 1947.

and see Figure 10.1). At the same time, choosing not to be a parent is more acceptable today.

As overall fertility[2] levels have dropped, childbearing has increasingly shifted to later ages. Teen birthrates have declined. Married women are waiting longer

---

[1] The total fertility rate (TFR) for a given year is an artificial figure arrived at through complex mathematical calculations. In common-sense terms, the TFR indicates how many children an average woman would have if present trends continue. It is the figure most used in this textbook to grasp trends in fertility and family size. The total fertility rate and other birth rates may be computed for various sectors of the population, for example, unmarried women, white women, adolescent women, and so forth.

[2] The term **fertility** is used by demographers to refer to actual births. In everyday language we use the term *fertility* to mean ability to reproduce. However, the technical social science term for reproductive capacity is **fecundity**.

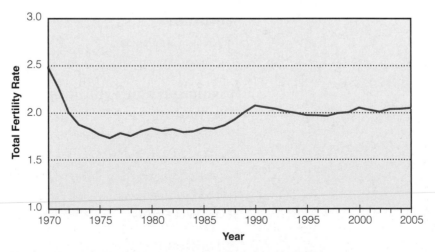

Figure 10.1 Total fertility rates, United States, 1970–2005.

Sources: Martin et al. 2006, Table 4; Hamilton, Martin, and Ventura 2007, Table 1.

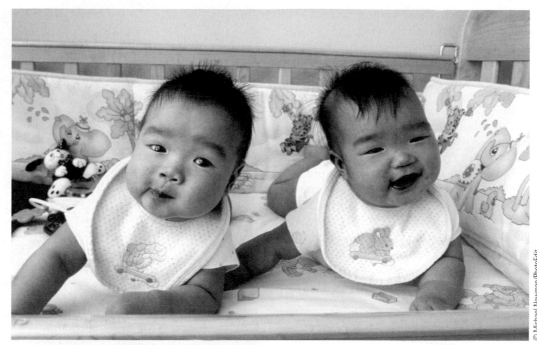

The numbers of twins, triplets, and higher-order births have increased dramatically since 1980. Families raising two or more children who are the same age gain the attention of onlookers when they are out-and-about—and they face challenges at home. As their numbers have grown, so have organizations to bring them together to share common concerns and joys.

to have their first babies. Women in their thirties who had postponed parenthood are now having first, second, and, in some cases, third children, and some are becoming mothers for the first time in their forties. The 2005 birthrate for women in their thirties was the highest in almost forty years (Hamilton, Martin, and Ventura 2007). The multiple birthrate (twins, triplets, and higher order births) is also higher, as more use is made of reproductive technology (Martin, Hamilton, Sutton, Ventura, Menacker, and Kirmeyer 2006, pp. 3, 23).

At the same time, childlessness is higher for women now than in the recent past. In 2004, 19 percent of women age forty through forty-four were childless, almost twice the percentage of childless women in that age group in 1976 (Dye 2005, Table 6). Twenty-two percent of men age forty through forty-four reported that they were childless (in 2002; Martinez et al. 2006, p. 1).

These points describe the sum total of many couple and individual decisions. Throughout this chapter we'll be looking at the choices that individuals and couples have to make about whether to have children and, if so, how many. Among other things, we'll see that modern scientific and technological advances have both increased people's options and added new wrinkles to their decision making. We'll see, too, that technological progress

does not mean that people can exercise complete control over their fertility. To begin, we'll review fertility trends in the United States in more detail. Then we'll examine the decision whether or not to become a parent.

Fertility Trends in the United States

Lower U.S. fertility appears to be a major change when we compare current birthrates to those of the 1950s. But the decline in fertility is actually a continuation of a long-term pattern dating to about 1800. Alternatives to the motherhood role began to open up with the Industrial Revolution and the resulting creation of a labor force that worked in production outside the home. Previously, in a preindustrial economy, women could combine productive work on the farm or home artisan shop with motherhood. But when work moved from home to factory, the roles of worker and mother were not so compatible. Consequently, as women's employment increased, fertility declined.

Another change affecting fertility over time has been declining infant mortality, a result of improved health and living conditions. Gradually, it became unnecessary to bear so many children to ensure the survival of a few. Changes in values accompanying these transformations made large numbers of children more costly economically and less satisfying to parents.

In the face of the long-term decline over the past two centuries, it is the upswing in fertility in the late 1940s and 1950s (the baby boom) that requires explanation. It appears that those who had grown up during the Great Depression, when family size was limited by economic factors, found themselves in an affluent postwar economy as adults. They were able to fulfill dreams of a happy and abundant family life to compensate for deprivations suffered as children (Easterlin 1987). Marriage and motherhood became dominant cultural goals for American women; men also concentrated their attention on family life. Couples in this generation had more than three children, on average, and some had more.

Family Size

Today two children constitute Americans' ideal family size (Hagewen and Morgan 2005). In 2004, only 11 percent of women who had completed their childbearing had four or more children, compared to more than three times that percentage in 1976 (Dye 2005, Table 6). Support for those who choose to have four or more children appears to be declining (Hagewen and Morgan 2005; Mueller and Yoder 1999). See "A Closer Look at Family Diversity: Choosing Large Families in a Small-Family Era" for a discussion of this viewpoint.

U.S. fertility is above **replacement level** (2.1).[3] The total fertility rate in the United States has never dropped as low as those of some European and Asian countries (Hagewen and Morgan 2005, Figure 1; Population Reference Bureau 2001). So a current question regarding American fertility is this: Why does the United States have higher fertility than other countries with parallel levels of economic development and better family support policies?

Historically, America's fertility was higher than that of Europe (Weeks 2002, p. 236), so there may be cultural factors at work that make the United States exceptional. The United States appears to have strong fertility norms encouraging at least two children and discouraging childlessness and one-child families. The pattern of two-child preference has been consistent for over

[3] *Replacement level* is the level of fertility necessary for a society to replenish its population. For each two adults, two children are needed to replace them. The total fertility rate is pegged at 2.1 to take into account that some women will die before reaching reproductive age, some will be biologically unable to reproduce or choose not to, and some will be institutionalized or in religious orders mandating celibacy.

The ideal family size in the United States is now two children.

thirty years. Looking back, demographers now interpret the 1970s–1980s drop in fertility as not really a fertility decline but, rather, a postponement of births (Hagewen and Morgan 2005; Mueller and Yoder 1999).

Differential Fertility Rates

Not surprisingly, fertility rates vary among segments of the U.S. population. Usually, more highly educated and well-off families have fewer children, and that is true of current fertility rates (Chandra et al. 2005; Dye 2005). Although better-off families have more money, their children are also more costly, for these parents expect to send their children to college and to provide them with expensive experiences and possessions. Moreover, people with high education or income have options other than parenting. They may be involved in demanding careers or enjoy travel, activities that they weigh against the investment of time and money required in parenting more children (Weeks 2007).

Choosing Large Families in a Small Family Era

Large families of four or more children are a distinct minority in the United States today—and have been for some time. In 2002, only 15 percent of women who had completed their childbearing had four or more children (Chandra et al. 2005, Table 2).

The U.S. family size ideal for thirty years has been two children, with the three-child family next most popular. Families of four or more are thought better than childless or only-child families. But favorable opinion of this large a family size has been declining, dropping by half (20 percent to 10 percent) between 1970–1974 and 2000–2002 (Hagewen and Morgan 2005). "Being a good parent is now [perceived as] largely inconsistent with having more than a small number of children" (Morgan 2003, p. 593).

A qualitative study of sixty women who have chosen various family sizes—childless, only child, the "normative" family size of two or three, and "supernormative" families of four or more—suggests that views of large families have become negative and involve significant stereotyping. Mothers of large families report that they are stigmatized, seen as uneducated, insufficiently attentive to their children, messy housekeepers, ignorant of birth control, and experiencing unintended pregnancies (Mueller and Yoder 1999; Hagewen and Morgan 2005). Although experiencing pressures to limit family size that began, in some

cases, after their second child was born, the majority of these mothers of large families also received some positive feedback.

Where do we find large families? Women with no high school diploma are most likely (21 percent) to have borne four or more children, dropping off to 11 percent for high school graduates, 8 percent of those women with some college, and only 3 percent of women who hold a bachelor's degree or more (Chandra et al. 2005, Table 2). Mothers of large families are less likely to be in the labor force.

Demographers differ as to the likely future of large families. With high rates of remarriage, couples who already have children may decide to have a baby together, increasing their family size beyond two or three (Mueller and Yoder 1999). On the other hand, delayed childbearing may put biological limits on family size regardless of remarriage or if an empty nest begins to feel lonely (Hagewen and Morgan 2005).

"The acceptable/normative family may very well vary from culture to culture, such that women having family sizes considered deviant in some segments of the U.S. population may experience acceptance within their own culture" (Mueller and Yoder 1999, p. 918). Some commentators note higher fertility rates in the Great Plains and Southwest regions (D. Brooks 2004). The southeast Asian Hmong ethnic group

(Fadiman 1998), some Pacific Islander groups (Harris and Jones 2005; U.S. Census Bureau 1993); and the Amish, among others, favor large families.

There is in fact a pro–large family movement termed "Quiverfull," whose families aim for six or more children. "Quiverfull mothers think of their children as . . . an army they're building for God" (A. Joyce 2006, p. St-1). This movement is situated in fundamentalist churches. Quiverfull mothers homeschool their children, accept male headship, and make no attempt to control family size or timing.

But a desire for large families, though not common, is not limited to conservative religious sectors of American society:

> We come from all different faiths and some of us are not religious at all. We are well-to-do and of modest means. We are home schoolers, public schoolers, and private schoolers. We are stepparents, adoptive parents, and foster parents. . . . We are a diverse bunch, but the one thing we at largerfamilies.com all have in common is that we love our kids. (Francis 2007)

Critical Thinking

What do you see as the advantages and disadvantages of large families? Small families? What is *your* family size ideal? Why?

Women who are not in the labor force have higher birthrates and a larger completed family size on average than employed women. This may be intentional; women may shape their employment commitments to their birth intentions and vice versa (Dye 2005, p. 6).

Differential birthrates also reflect the fact that beliefs and values about having children vary among cultures—see "Facts About Families: Race/Ethnicity and Differen-

tial Fertility Rates" for a discussion of fertility among the diverse racial/ethnic groups of the United States.

Decision making about having children now takes place at a time of more reproductive options than ever before. This observation highlights the point that in the early twenty-first century, parenthood is a choice, made in a social context. We now focus on people as they make their decisions about becoming parents.

Race/Ethnicity and Differential Fertility Rates

As Figure 10.2 shows, women in the various U.S. racial/ethnic groups vary quite a bit in the number of children they have. Here we look at fertility patterns among the major American racial/ethnic groups.

Fertility Rates among Non-Hispanic Whites

Fertility patterns of the non-Hispanic white population are similar to those described for the total population, although slightly lower. The total fertility rate for whites in 2005 was 1.844 compared to 2.054 for the total population (Hamilton, Martin, and Ventura 2007, Table 1). Because the white population was historically such a large part of the total population, explanations offered for historical changes in fertility apply to changes in fertility among non-Hispanic whites.

Fertility Rates among African Americans

Some racial/ethnic minority populations in the United States have fertility rates that are higher than those of non-Hispanic whites, and that is true of African American women at the present time. Earlier in our history, in the late eighteenth century, white and black women appeared to have borne children at approximately the same rates. At about that time, the white population began to reduce its fertility, and by the end of the nineteenth century, childbearing among whites had declined sig-

nificantly. The birthrate among blacks did not decline much until after 1880, when it began to drop rapidly.

When individuals have satisfying options other than parenthood, they typically choose to limit their childbearing. The differences in timing of the fertility decline of white and black populations in this country suggest that although education and other opportunities opened up for whites with the Industrial Revolution earlier in the nineteenth century, they did not do so for blacks until well after the Civil War. By the 1930s, the black fertility rate was close to that of whites. Through the 1940s, 1950s, and after, trends in black fertility generally paralleled those among whites, though at a higher level.

With regard to the current fertility rate among black Americans, the same differential opportunity explanation holds true as an explanation for blacks' higher fertility. Nevertheless, African American fertility rates declined by almost 25 percent in the 1990s and into the current century. The total fertility rate for non-Hispanic African Americans was 2.019 in 2005 (Hamilton, Martin, and Ventura 2007, Table 1; Martin et al. 2006, Table 8).

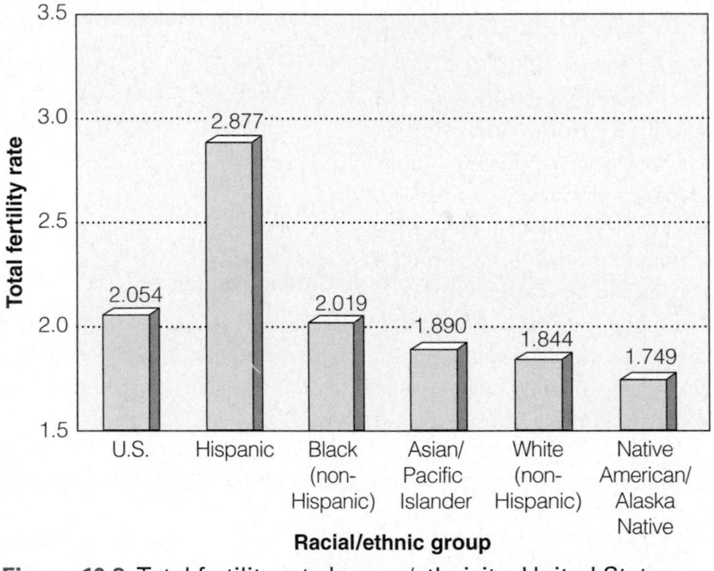

Fertility Rates among Latinos

Latinos (termed *Hispanics* in government statistical documents) have the highest fertility rate of any U.S. racial/ethnic group. Their total fertility rate (TFR) of 2.877 in 2005 was over 50 percent higher than that of non-Hispanic white women. The TFR for Mexican American women is the highest among Hispanics

Figure 10.2 Total fertility rate by race/ethnicity, United States, 2005.

Source: Hamilton, Martin, and Ventura 2007, Table 1.

(3.021), while women of Puerto Rican (2.057) and Cuban background (1.733) have moderate or low total fertility rates. Women of other Central American and South American background have fertility rates just slightly lower than those of Mexican American women (Hamilton, Martin, and Ventura 2007, Table 1; Martin et al. 2006, Table 8).

Reasons for the high birthrates include the fact that Hispanics migrate from nations that have high birthrates and Catholic and rural traditions that value large families. Large families may serve important functions, especially in poorer families. Children might be an insurance policy against a parent's old age in a society that lacks adequate welfare or retirement systems. Even while children are growing up, their earnings might be an important part of the family income. Large-family norms based on these needs may be carried over to the United States (P. H. Collins 1999, p. 202).

Moreover, the lifetime fertility of Latinas varies strongly with their educational attainment, and Latinas are relatively more concentrated in the lower educational categories. Similarly, on average (Cubans excepted), Latino families have lower incomes and higher rates of poverty than the non-Hispanic white population, also factors associated with higher fertility.

Finally, Latinos are younger, with more concentration in childbearing ages. Latinas, especially Mexican Americans, typically begin having children at younger ages. Latinas in their early twenties have a much higher fertility rate than women this age in other racial/ethnic groups (Downs 2003).

Native American women who live on reservations have significantly higher fertility than those who do not. Differential birthrates reflect the fact that people in various cultures have different beliefs and values about having children.

Fertility Rates among Asian Americans/Pacific Islanders

Asian American/Pacific Islander and Native American births are a relatively small proportion of U.S. births. Asian/Pacific Islander women had a comparatively low total fertility rate (1.890) in 2005 (Hamilton, Martin, and Ventura 2007, Table 1), but there is wide variation by country of origin. As Asian/Pacific Islander immigrants assimilate, their birthrates tend to converge with those of whites (Hwang and Saenz 1997).

Fertility Rates among Native Americans/Alaska Natives

Fertility rates of Native Americans/Alaska Natives have declined by over 20 percent since 1990 to a total fertility rate of 1.749 in 2005 (Hamilton, Martin, and Ventura 2007, Table 1; Martin et al. 2006, Table 4). Native American women who live on reservations have significantly higher fertility than those who do not (Taffel 1987), probably because of the limited educational and economic opportunities noted earlier.

Critical Thinking

The total fertility rate, which is an approximation of average family size, is lower in all racial/ethnic groups than it was during the baby boom era (1946–1964). Why do you think this is so? Does it have to do with economic pressures? Changing attitudes toward children? Or something else?

The Decision to Parent or Not to Parent

The variations in birthrates just described reflect decisions shaped by values and attitudes about having children. In traditional society, having children was not viewed as a matter for decision; couples didn't decide to have children. Children just came, and preferring not to have any was unthinkable. Now couples and individuals planfully consider becoming parents.

Early family planning efforts focused on the timing of children and family size. Now choices include "whether" to have children, not only "when," "how many," and "how." Although social change and technology provide more choices, they also present dilemmas. It is not always easy to choose whether to have children, how many to have, when to have them, and when to use reproductive technology. Not all choices can be realized, whether they reflect a desire to have children or to avoid having children.

The extent to which people today consciously choose (or reject) parenthood or experience it as something that simply happens to them is uncertain. Because people have more control over their lives generally, many now approach parenthood as a conscious choice. Among others—teenagers, for example—parenthood is often less thought out. Moreover, some people may be philosophically disinclined to plan their lives (Luker 1984). For whatever reason, in a 2002 survey, women respondents reported that over one-third of their recent births were unintended—14 percent unwanted and 21 percent mistimed (Chandra et al. 2005, p. 1).[4] Nevertheless, more so than in the past, our society presents the possibility of choice and decision making about parenthood.

In the following pages, we'll look more closely at some of the factors involved in an individual's or couple's decision making about whether to become a parent: first, the social pressures, and then the personal pros and cons.

Social Pressures to Have Children

Social pressures to have children exist in our society: "strong norms against childlessness persist" (Hagewen and Morgan 2005, p. 512). Social scientists refer to this cultural phenomenon as a **pronatalist bias**. Having children is taken for granted, whereas not having children seems to need a justification. Eighty-three percent of American women say being or becoming a mother is important to their identity (Center for the Advancement of Women 2003, p. 8). Negative stereotypes of the voluntarily child-free were apparent at least through the 1970s (Mueller and Yoder 1999).

Some scholars believe pronatal pressures are becoming stronger now that the countercultural trends of the 1960s and 1970s have been replaced by an emphasis on "family values" (Bulcroft and Teachman 2004; Park 2002). But demographers who have reviewed survey data on this point argue that the expectation for married couples to have children is much less pronounced than in the past. "Negative views toward voluntary childlessness . . . may be changing" (Hagewen and Morgan 2005, p. 513). The term *child-free* is often used now instead of the more negative-sounding term *childless*.[5]

Is American Society Antinatalist?

Some observers, in fact, argue that U.S. society has become antinatalist—that is, slanted against having children or, at least, not doing all it can to support parents and their children. These family policy scholars view American society as characterized by **structural antinatalism** (Huber 1980), insufficiently supportive of parents and children. Critics point out that compared to other nations at our economic level, nutrition, social service, financial aid, and education programs directly affecting the welfare of children are not adequate (Children's Defense Fund 1998; Hewlett and West 1998). Nor do we provide paid parental leave or other support for parents of young children as many other countries do. Children in the United States are more likely to be poor than in comparable countries, and the United States ranks twentieth out of twenty-one in overall child well-being among advanced industrial nations (UNICEF 2007, p. 1).

Other features of our society make parenthood difficult. Some municipalities keep taxes down by restricting housing size to discourage families with children from living there, meanwhile providing tax breaks and housing preferences for the elderly (C. Jones 2004; Mansnerus 2003; Peterson 2005a). There has been a pushback against "family friendly" policies in the workplace, as workers who do not have children challenge policies that support parents (Burkett 2000). As fewer people are active parents, some advocates anticipate political reverberations that will disadvantage child-rearing families—less willingness of communities to support good schools, for example. As a numerical minority, parents may experience "a growing sense of

---

[4] See Santelli et al. 2003 for a discussion of how *unintended* has been defined and the limitations of research on unintended pregnancy.

[5] Each term conveys an inherent bias. For that reason and because there are no easy-to-use substitute terms, we use both *childless* and *child-free* in this text.

isolation from the American mainstream" (Whitehead and Popenoe 2006).

At the same time, nonparents may perceive that *they* are the less-favored group and resent what they see as assertions of privilege on the part of parents. Sidewalk standoffs, where parents pushing supersized strollers meet adult pedestrians who decline to give way, represent the "latest fissure in a long-standing divide between parents and non-parents over who has made the right choice in life" (Rosenbloom 2005, pp. ST1-2).

Of course, those choices that people make about becoming parents reflect not only external social pressures or cultural moments but also their own needs, values, and attitudes. Still, given "strong antinatalist forces" that include direct and indirect costs and responsibilities for parents, some scholars have asked this question: "Why do people choose to have any children?" (Hagewen and Morgan 2005, p. 513). In the next sections, we will look at some of the rewards and costs associated with parenthood.

Motivation for Parenthood

FOCUS ON CHILDREN

Traditionally, children were viewed as economic assets—more hands added to the work that could be produced in the fields and kitchens. The shift from an agricultural to an industrial society and the development of compulsory education transformed children from economic assets to economic liabilities. But as their economic value declined, children's emotional significance to parents increased, partly because declining infant mortality rates made it safe to become attached to children. Parents' desire was for "a child to love" (Zelizer 1985, p. 190).

Children bring many emotional benefits and other satisfaction to parents. Although less true for today's adults (see Chapter 2), becoming a parent can certify one's attainment of adulthood. For men as well as women, parenthood represents an important personal identity (Hagewen and Morgan 2005). When parents are interviewed, they often express their desire "'to have a child to love'" and talk about the "'joy that comes from watching a child grow'" (Morgan and King 2001, p. 11). Parenthood can give one a sense of commitment and meaning in an uncertain social world (McMahon 1995 in Morgan and King 2001, p. 11).

In having children, parents can find a satisfaction that is lacking in their jobs. Family life also offers an opportunity to exercise a kind of authority and influence that one may not have at work. Children add considerable liveliness to a household, and they have fresh and novel responses to the joys and vexations of life. In sum, children "are capable of bringing profound meaning and purpose into people's lives" (Groat et al. 1997, p. 571). This idea that children bring unique benefits to parents has been termed the **value of children perspective** on motivation for parenthood (Hoffman and Manis 1979; Lamanna 1977).

The *value of children perspective* has recently been supplemented by a **social capital perspective**[6] on the benefits of parenthood:

> Parenthood intensifies interaction with, and assistance from, other family members. It facilitates exchanges with neighbors and other community members. . . . [P]arenthood can bring parents into an extensive and supportive network. (Schoen and Tufis 2003, p. 1032)

Research suggests that the anticipated social capital benefits of parenthood may be one motivation for childbearing, not only for married but also for unmarried prospective parents. Analysis of responses from 1,155 unmarried women in the National Survey of Families and Households (NSFH) found that nonmarital conceptions occurred more often to women who anticipated social capital benefits from children (Schoen and Tufis 2003).

© Beth Huber

Children can bring vitality and a sense of purpose into a household. Having a child also broadens a parent's role in the world: Mothers and fathers become nurturers, advocates, authority figures, counselors, caregivers, and playmates.

[6] We usually think of *capital* as money. But more generally, the term refers to a resource that can be used to one's benefit. Social capital, then, refers to social ties that are or can be helpful resources.

Costs of Having Children

Although the benefits of having children can be immeasurable, children are costly. On a purely financial basis, children decrease a couple's level of living considerably. In husband–wife families with two children, an estimated 42 percent of household expenditures are attributable to children. The average cost of raising a child born in 2001 to age eighteen is estimated at $231,470 for middle-income families (Lino 2002, Tables 11, 12).

Added to the direct costs of parenting are **opportunity costs**: the economic opportunities for wage earning and investments that parents forgo when rearing children. These costs are more often felt by mothers. A woman's career advancement may suffer as a consequence of becoming a mother, especially in a society that does not provide adequate day care or a flexible workplace. A couple in which one partner quits work to stay home with a child or children faces loss of up to half or more of its family income (Longman 1998). The spouse (more often the woman) who quits work also faces lost

A military wife displays the ultrasound image she has sent to her husband in Iraq so he can keep a photo of their baby-to-be with him.

Kirk Condyles/The New York Times/ Redux

pension and Social Security benefits later. All in all, in our society there is "a heavy financial penalty on anyone who chooses to spend any serious amount of time with children" (Crittenden 2001, p. 6).

Conversely, loss of free time and increased stress are two important costs of trying to lead two lives, as a family person and as a career person. Parents generally experience a loss of freedom of activity and schedule flexibility with the arrival of a first child (Hagewen and Morgan 2005).

All in all, "from the day children are born they become a source of joy and a source of burdens for their parents" (Nomaguchi and Milkie 2003, p. 372). Still, a large proportion of men (68 percent) and women (70 percent) surveyed in 2002 who have children answered "strongly agree" to this statement: "The rewards of being a parent are worth it despite the cost and work it takes"; only 2 to 3 percent disagreed (Martinez et al. 2006, Figure 25).

How Children Affect Marital Happiness

Marital strain is considered a common cost of having children. Evidence shows that children, especially young ones, stabilize marriage; that is, parents are less likely to divorce. But a stable marriage is not necessarily a happy one: "[C]hildren have the paradoxical effect of increasing the stability of the marriage while decreasing its quality" (Bradbury, Fincham, and Beach 2000, p. 969). A major review of the research in this area finds that not only do parents report lower marital satisfaction than nonparents, but the more children there are, the lower marital satisfaction is (Twenge, Campbell, and Foster 2003). Parents are also more likely to experience depression than are nonparents (Evenson and Simon 2005).

Spouses' reported marital satisfaction tends to decline over time whether they have children or not. But serious conflicts over work, identity, and domestic responsibilities can erupt with the arrival of children. A study that followed Swedish couples through the parenting years found that though at any one time the majority of parents described their marriages favorably, the marital relationship became less harmonious over time, disharmony peaking at the child's ages of ten through twelve (Stattin and Klackenberg 1992). The couple's relationship is especially affected if one or both partners are not cooperative in their parenting (Belsky and Hsieh 1998).

When they have children, spouses may find that they begin responding to each other in terms of more traditional role obligations, and that in turn affects marital happiness negatively (Coltrane 1990; Nock 1998b). Spouses, who now are not only busier as parents but also more dissimilar in their dominant roles, begin to do fewer things together and to share decision making less (Bird 1997). Although parenthood is viewed positively and increases life satisfaction, research indicates that positive feelings about children are not sufficient to offset the negative effects on marital happiness of changes in marital structure brought about by the arrival of children (Tsang et al. 2003; White, Booth, and Edwards 1986). Dissatisfaction with one's marriage after the arrival of the first child seems more pronounced and longer lasting for wives than for husbands (Glenn 1990, p. 825). Some 38 percent of mothers of infants have high marital satisfaction, while 62 percent of childless women do (Twenge, Campbell, and Foster 2003).

Twenge, Campbell, and Foster's comprehensive review of the research (2003) noted that the negative effects of children on marital satisfaction seem to be stronger for younger cohorts. Perhaps couples today experience a greater "before–after" contrast when children arrive. They have often married and become parents later in their lives, and so experienced a great deal of personal freedom and a career focus for many years. Women's roles, especially, change with parenthood, leaving a big gap between the child-free working-woman's lifestyle and that of a new mother. Moreover, the increased individualism of our culture may make day-to-day responsibility for the care of young children seem less natural than in the 1950s, when social obligations were culturally dominant (Turner 1976).

Even though the addition of a child necessarily influences a household, the arrival of a child is less disruptive when the parents get along well and have a strong commitment to parenting. One longitudinal study shows that the drop in marital satisfaction is less for couples who were happy before the birth and actively planned for the infant (Cowan and Cowan 1992). New friendship networks, such as with other parents, may provide some of the social support previously given by one's spouse. (Chapter 11 looks more closely at the relationships between parents and their children.)

Remaining Child-Free

We have been discussing factors that influence the decision whether to have children (or not). Involuntary childlessness, the result of infertility or other adverse circumstances, is discussed later in this chapter. Here we examine **voluntary childlessness**, the choice reported by

6 percent of American women in a 2002 survey (Chandra et al. 2005, Table B and p. 8).

There is often some ambiguity about the "decision" to remain child-free. For many, it is a gradual decision over time. For others, it is a decision by default, as age or relationship status lead eventually to realization that one will not have children. For an increasing number of younger women, it represents an early commitment not to have children. "Firm choices to have no children may signal an increasing proportion of women who see the costs of childbearing as too high" (Hagewen and Morgan 2005, p. 522).

An increase in voluntary childlessness is ascribed to the social changes of recent decades. The rise of feminism challenged the inevitability of the mother role. More than 70 percent of women surveyed in 2001 said no to the question of whether "a woman need[s] the experience of motherhood to have a complete life," including 69 percent of mothers (Center for the Advancement of Women 2003, p. 8). Greater ability to control fertility; greater participation of women in paid employment; concern about overpopulation and the environment; or an ideological rejection of the traditional family provide a social context for some people's decisions (Gillespie 2003; Paul 2001).

The Lives of the Child Free The voluntarily childless have more education and are more likely to have managerial or professional employment and higher incomes. They are more urban, less traditional in gender roles, less likely to have a religious affiliation, and less conventional than their counterparts. They are also more likely to be white (Abma and Martinez 2006; Park 2005).

Child-free women tend to be attached to a satisfying career. Childless couples value their relative freedom to change jobs or careers, move around the country, and pursue any endeavor they might find interesting (Dalphonse 1997; Park 2005). Most studies have found child-free couples to be more satisfied with their relationship than parenting couples are. The childless elderly are as satisfied with their lives and less stressed than parents. They seem to have developed social support networks in lieu of children (Park 2005).

Men's and Women's Motives for Childlessness An earlier review of the literature by Sharon Houseknecht (1987), summarized by Park (2005), found the most important motive for voluntary childlessness to be "freedom from child care responsibilities and greater opportunity for self-fulfillment and spontaneous mobility," reported in 79 percent of the studies and true of both men and women. "Higher marital satisfaction" was reported as a motive for remaining childless in 62 percent of the studies and was important to both sexes. Men were more affected by "monetary advantages," reported in 55 percent of studies, while women stated that "female career considerations" (55 percent) shaped their decisions to be childless (Park 2005, p. 379). Noting the connection between childlessness and career commitment, Abma and Martinez (2006) also hypothesize that voluntarily childless women are simply satisfied with their lives as they are and are not necessarily driven by a need to sacrifice for their careers.

Having Children: Options and Circumstances

Discussions about having children often evoke images of a young, newly married couple. More and more, however, as the discussion of the changing life course in Chapter 2 suggests, decisions about becoming parents are being made in a much wider variety of circumstances. In this section we address childbearing with reference to postponing parenthood; the one-child family; nonmarital childbearing; decisions about having children in stepfamilies; and multipartnered fertility. Gay and lesbian parenthood is discussed in Chapter 8.

The Timing of Parenthood

Births to women in their twenties, the primary ages for childbearing, constitute just over half of all births in the United States. Teen birthrates have declined to the lowest ever recorded in 65 years of record keeping. Meanwhile, birthrates for women in their thirties and forties have increased dramatically; the rate for women thirty-five through thirty-nine is the highest recorded since 1965. Birthrates for men forty-five through forty-nine—that is, the rate at which older men have fathered children—have increased by over 20 percent since 1980 (Hamilton, Martin, and Ventura 2007; Martin, Hamilton, Sutton, Ventura, Menacker, and Kirmeyer 2006). What are the factors producing this change, and how do early and late parenthood look as choices at the present time?

Postponing Parenthood Later age at marriage and the desire of many women to complete their education and become established in a career appear to be important factors in the high levels of postponed childbearing. Both sexes remain longer in the "emerging adulthood" stage of the life course, enjoying a greater degree of personal freedom and ability to concentrate on career than is possible after family responsibilities are assumed. Moreover, with the availability of reliable contraception

Many couples today are postponing parenthood into their thirties, sometimes later.

and the promise of assisted reproduction technology, people can now plan their parenthood for earlier or later in their adult lives. In addition to delayed first-time parenthood, some births to older women (and men) follow the breakup of marriage or other relationships followed by new pairings and the desire to have children with the new partner (S. Brown 2000; Carnoy and Carnoy 1995).

But fertility declines with age, for men as well as women, although less dramatically for men. Older male age also increases the likelihood of having children with genetic abnormalities or other conditions. "'I think what we're saying is that men, too, need to be concerned about their aging,'" says Dr. Brenda Estenazi of the University of California School of Public Health (Rabin 2007, p. 6).

It has been known for some time that older mothers have higher rates of premature or low-weight babies and multiple births—all risks for learning disabilities and health problems. Older mothers also have higher rates of miscarriage, as well as health problems such as diabetes and hypertension (Martin et al. 2006; D. Williams 2006). Physicians nevertheless advise that pregnancy risk factors should not deter women who want children from having them at older ages: "The take-home message is that while a lot of complications of labor and pregnancy are increased . . . the vast majority of [older mothers] do perfectly fine" (Dr. William Gilbert, quoted in "Older Moms" 1999).

Still, a more intense public concern about the dangers for women of postponing parenthood emerged with the publication of economist Sylvia Ann Hewlett's book *Creating a Life* (2002) based on her survey of 1,168 older "high achieving career women" (women in the top 10 percent of earners). Hewlett found a high rate of childlessness among successful managerial and professional career women, most of whom had not intended to be childless. Hewlett faults women for focusing on careers based on an assumption that it would be easy enough to have children later in life. To avoid childlessness, Hewlett goes so far as to suggest that women start their families earlier by planfully seeking a husband while in their twenties "even if this involves surrendering part of one's ego" (p. 199).

Although Hewlett's advice is questionable, her caution about the limits of reproductive technology are valid (Dunson, Colombo, and Baird 2002). But critics note that she has overgeneralized from a small segment of women at a particular point in their lives. Although her description of high-achieving women at ages twenty-eight through thirty-five is accurate, by age forty, high-achieving women are *more* apt to be married and mothers than are other employed women (Boushey 2005b). Boushey and other critics (e.g., Pollitt 2002) argue that the real problem is the failure of policy support for working families. The implication that women need to minimize their career interests is surprising in this era of generally advancing gender equality.

Needless to say, it is also uncertain whether a "let's get married now" agenda would result in a good marriage.

Early and Late Parenthood Now that postponing parenthood to the thirties is increasingly common, early parenthood tends to be seen as the more difficult path (Jong-Fast 2003). Choosing early parenthood means more certainty of having children, but young parents may have to forgo some education and get a slower start up the career ladder. Early parenthood can create strains on a marriage if the breadwinner's need to support the family means little time to spend at home or if young parents lack the maturity needed to cope with family responsibility (Poniewozik 2002). Moreover, couples who have children early usually start late on saving for college or retirement and must work harder and longer to meet family needs if they have low incomes (Strauss 2002; Tyre 2004). Early mothers' identities seemed much more dominated by their maternal role,

while later mothers' identities were more variegated (Walter 1986).

Parenting early means greater freedom later. The Brewers, a young college couple, were twenty-two and twenty when they married, and they had two children in the next few years. "Believe it or not, the couple planned all this. Three months after their first date, they both knew they wanted the same thing. . . . Have some kids in their 20s and happily wave them off to college in their early 40s" (Christopherson 2006).

Women who postponed parenthood found that combining established careers with parenting created unforeseen problems. Career commitments may ripen just at the peak of parental responsibilities. On the other hand, late mothers had more confidence in their ability to manage their changed lives because of the organizational skills they had developed in their work. They also had more money with which to arrange support services, and they felt confident of their ability as parents (Walter 1986). Psychiatrists speak of the maturity, patience, and good parenting skills of later-life parents (Tyre 2004).

A book based on interviews with a nonrandom set of older fathers, mostly white and middle class, found that men who had children in later life expressed a great deal of joy in parenthood, particularly if they had given priority to jobs with earlier-born children (Carnoy and Carnoy 1995). They saw themselves as more patient with children (Vinciguerra 2007).

Early mothers felt that they had had more spontaneity as youthful parents (Walter 1986). "'We wanted to be young parents [said one mother]. . . . We didn't want to be 60 when they got out of high school'" (Poniewozik 2002, pp. 56–57). In a study based on interviews with 114 Canadian expectant mothers, the younger pregnant women (in their twenties) spoke of their physical health as an asset, as well as the health of their parents—they expected to rely on parents' help with the children. They were also pleased to think that as younger parents there would be less of a "generation gap" between themselves and their children (Dion 1995).

Older expectant mothers in this study (in their thirties) looked to friendship networks for support, including a sense of being "on time" in attaining parenthood—since they had friends who had also delayed parenthood (Dion 1995). They spoke of having needed a period of time for personal development—not just career development—for themselves and their spouses. They felt that delaying parenthood meant greater maturity and preparation for parenthood.

Older parents worry about their physical limitations. And for older parents, there is a sense of limited time with children that both increases pleasure in parenting—

"Everything is more precious"—and creates anxiety about the future—"That he could die before his daughter reaches adulthood 'is a reality that I live with,'" said one father who was fifty-nine when his daughter was born (Vinciguerra 2007, p. ST-1). That he may not live to see grandchildren is another reality.

Being born to older parents affects children's lives as well. They usually benefit from the financial and emotional stability that older parents can provide and the attention given by parents who have waited a long time to have children. But children of older parents often experience anxiety about their parents' health and mortality (Vinciguerra 2007). Their parents may become frail before they have established themselves in their adult lives. Not only does having children later in life put the burden of elderly parent care on their children at a younger age, but it also limits their children's children's years with grandparents.

For prospective parents who seek to time their parenthood to be early or later in life, it's important to have an awareness of the trade-offs—plus an understanding that having children is a challenge at any age!

The One-Child Family

Some prospective parents consider the challenges of parenthood daunting, but also reject the idea of childlessness. For them, the solution is the one-child family. In 2004, 17 percent of women age forty through forty-four had just one child (Dye 2005).

The proportion of one-child families in America appears to be growing due to at least three factors: (1) women's increasing career opportunities and aspirations in a context of inadequate domestic support; (2) the high cost of raising a child through college; and (3) peer support: the choice to have just one child becomes easier to make as more couples do so. Divorced people who do not remarry or form a new reproductive partnership may end up with a one-child family because the marriage ended before more children were born.

Negative stereotypes present only children as "socially unskilled, dependent, anxious, and generally maladjusted" (Hagewen and Morgan 2005, p. 514). To find out whether there was any basis for this image, psychologists in the 1970s produced a staggering number of studies that generally concluded that no negative effects of being an only child could be found (Pines 1981, p. 15; see also Falbo 1976 and Hawke and Knox 1978). Research has sharply diminished since then, but current scientific conclusions do suggest that only children may be less able to make friends, more distressed, more self-centered, and less cooperative (Hagewen and Morgan 2005, p. 514). One recent study of kindergartners concluded that sibling relationships foster the develop-

Some families choose to have only one child, a decision that can ease time, energy, and economic concerns. There may be extra pressure on only children, and they do not experience sibling relationships. But only children tend to receive more personal attention from parents, and parents may enjoy their child more when they do not feel so overwhelmed as they might with more offspring to care for.

ment of interpersonal skills, although the difference of children with sibs and only children is small (Downey and Condron 2004).

Research reports only children to be more intelligent and mature, with more leadership skills, and better health and life satisfaction (as adults; Hagewen and Morgan 2005). In a 1998 survey using a national sample of more than 24,000 eighth-graders, sociologist Douglas Downey (1995) found that only children were significantly more likely to talk frequently with their parents; to have attended art, music, or dance classes outside of school; and to have visited art, science, or history museums.

Advantages Parents with only one child report that they can enjoy parenthood without feeling overwhelmed and tied down. They have more free time and are better off

If these sisters get along well—as they appear to—they can provide companionship and support for each other as they go through life. Over 700,000 siblings shared a residence in 2000 (C. Lee 2006).

financially than they would have been with more children (Downey 1995). Researchers have found that family members shared decisions more equally and could afford to do more things together (Hawke and Knox 1978).

Research shows that the child in a one-child family has some advantages over children with siblings. Parents of only children had higher educational expectations for their child, were more likely to know their child's friends and the friends' parents, and had more money saved for their child's college education.

Disadvantages There are disadvantages, too, in a one-child family. For the children, these include the obvious lack of opportunity to experience sibling relationships, not only in childhood but also as adults. The 2000 census indicated that some 700,000 siblings live together. Siblings may provide social support, as well as exchanges of material assistance and someone to rely on in emergencies (C. Lee 2006; Riedmann and White 1996).

Only children may face extra pressure from parents to succeed, and they are sometimes under an uncomfortable amount of parental scrutiny. As adults they have no help in caring for their aging parents. Disadvantages for parents include the fear that the only child might be seriously hurt or might die and the feeling, in some cases, that they have only one chance to prove themselves good parents.

Nonmarital Births

In 2005, 37 percent of all births were to unmarried women. Nonmarital births take place in many different contexts in terms of parents' relationship status, age, financial resources, and so forth. We will first look at general trends in nonmarital births, as well as at racial/ethnic variation. We will then touch on births in cohabiting families, in "fragile families," to older single mothers, and to adolescent women.

After declining during the 1990s, nonmarital birthrates have risen again to an all-time high (Hamilton, Martin, and Ventura 2007). Meanwhile, childbearing in marriage has declined, leaving births outside of marriage a larger proportion of total births (Martin et al. 2006, Table C). From 1940 till the early 1960s, only 4 to 5 percent of all births were to unmarried women; as recently as 1980, 18 percent were (Martin et al. 2006, Table C; Thornton and Freedman 1983, p. 21).

The current figure represents a profound change in our society of the context of parenthood. Public attitudes correspond to these behavioral trends. Although

67 percent of those responding to a Gallup poll in 2006 thought it "very important" for a couple to marry if they planned to spend their lives together, only 37 percent felt marriage was "very important" "when a couple has a child together" (Saad 2006b).

Biologically, women mature earlier today, but they marry later and are more likely to divorce than in the past, so they spend more years at risk of a nonmarital pregnancy. They are much less likely now to marry upon the discovery of a nonmarital pregnancy. In 2002, 60 percent of women experiencing a first birth were married to the father, and another 12 percent were living with the father without being married. The remainder of first-time mothers were not married or cohabiting with the father (Dye 2005, p. 9).

Just under 40 percent of births to unmarried women in 2004 were to non-Hispanic white mothers (Martin et al. 2006, Table 18). But when we look at the *proportion* of nonmarital births in each racial/ethnic category, the picture looks somewhat different. As Figure 10.3 shows, in 2005, 70 percent of African American births, 63 percent of American Indian/Alaska Native births, 48 percent of Hispanic births, 25 percent of non-Hispanic white births, and 16 percent of Asian/Pacific Islander births occurred outside marriage (Hamilton, Martin, and Ventura 2007, Table 1).

The nonmarital birthrate of African American women has declined substantially and was 25 percent lower in 2004 than at its 1989 peak (Martin et al. 2006, Table 19). This decline has reduced the difference between black and white rates considerably, although African American nonmarital birthrates remain well above those of white women.

Despite the decline in the nonmarital birthrate, the *proportion* of nonmarital births among African American women remains high for several reasons. First, the overall length of time that African American women spend in marriage has shortened dramatically; that is, fewer black women are married throughout their childbearing years. Second, fertility has declined more among married than among unmarried black women, which results in a shift in the proportion of total births that are to unmarried women. For many black women, marriage and parenthood have become separate experiences (Martin et al. 2003; Ventura and Bachrach 2000).

Nonmarital birthrates of Hispanic women are highest of any racial/ethnic group, but so are marital births, so nonmarital births remain a smaller proportion of the total. Nonmarital births to Hispanic women often take place in cohabiting unions (Manning 2001; Ventura et al. 1998; Wildsmith and Raley 2006).

Births to Cohabitants "Fertility during cohabitation continues to account for almost all of the recent increases in nonmarital childbearing. . . . Cohabitation . . . has increasingly become . . . a two-parent family union in which to have and raise children outside of marriage" (Manning 2001, p. 217). Forty percent of nonmarital births are to heterosexual cohabiting women, and birthrates for never-married cohabitants are virtually the same as those for married women (Dye 2005, p. 7; Chandra et al. 2005). Cohabiting families (heterosexual and same-sex) are discussed in Chapter 8.

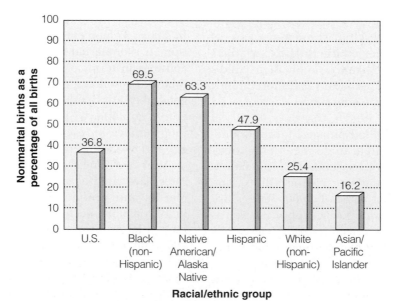

Figure 10.3 Births to unmarried women as a percentage of all births, by race and ethnicity, United States, 2005.

Source: Hamilton, Martin, and Ventura 2007, Table 1.

Births to "Fragile Families" It is now realized that less visibly attached unmarried parents, including those not living together, may have a more regular relationship than previously thought. The Fragile Families study (McLanahan et al. 2001; McLanahan and Carlson 2002) found in an analysis based on 1,764 new mothers in seven cities that the vast majority of new parents described themselves as "romantically involved on a steady basis," with 50 percent cohabiting and 33 percent "visiting." These fathers helped the mother during pregnancy and/or visited the hospital. Nearly 100 percent expressed a desire to be involved in the child's life, and 93 percent of mothers agreed. "The myth that unwed fathers are not around at the time of the birth could not be further from the truth" (McLanahan et al. 2001, p. 217). Nevertheless, involvement of these fathers is likely to decline over time, given their limited resources (McLanahan et al. 2001; Wu and Wolfe 2001). McLanahan and her research colleagues encourage policy support for these "fragile families."

Births to Older Single Mothers Although unwed birthrates are highest among young women in their twenties, they have increased dramatically for older women in recent years. The increase in childbearing by single women in their thirties is largely a white phenomenon. Black nonmarital birthrates in this age group have declined, while those of Hispanic women have not risen nearly as much as those of non-Hispanic white women (Martin et al. 2006, Table 19).

As opportunities grow for women to support themselves and as the permanence of marriage becomes less certain, there is less motivation for a woman to avoid giving birth out of wedlock because she cannot count on lifetime male support for the child even if she marries. Furthermore, stigma and discrimination against unwed mothers have lessened. Seventy percent of women and 59 percent of men surveyed believe it is "okay for an unmarried woman to have a child" (Martinez et al. 2006, p. 29.) Still, because the burden of responsibility for support and care of the child remains on the mother, overall, "the economic situation of older, single mothers is closer to that of teen mothers than that of married childbearers the same age" (Foster, Jones, and Hoffman 1998, p. 163).

There is a category of older single mothers who may be better off than that—termed **single mothers by choice**. The image is that of an older woman with an education, an established job, and economic resources, who has made a choice to become a single mother. Not having found a stable life partner, yet wanting to parent, a woman makes this choice as she sees time running out on her "biological clock."

Whether this is a significant development in terms of numbers is uncertain (Musick 2002). But it has drawn the attention of researchers. Sociologist Rosanna Hertz (2006) interviewed sixty-five single mothers who had their first child at age twenty or older and who, more significantly, are self-sufficient economically. Not having the "chance" to be in stable, child-rearing marriages, they became mothers through various routes: accidental biological pregnancy, artificial insemination by known or unknown donor, or adoption.

"For the women in this study, single motherhood was never a snap decision" (Hertz 2006, p. 26):

"I always had in the back of my mind that if I was thirty and not married, then I'd have children on my own. Then it was when I was thirty-two. Then it was when I went back to school at Princeton to get my master's degree. Then it was thirty-six and I had just broken up with another man." (p. 26)

Women were often surprised to find themselves taking what they saw as an unconventional step:

"Daring to consider getting pregnant on my own just seemed like such an outrageous thing to do. And from that point of thinking about it, to doing it, was the longest stretch because I was kind of shocked that I would think that way, and I wasn't sure of what I really wanted to do." (p. 27)

Once a mother, the parenting practices of single mothers by choice and their sense of family were very traditional. In fact, they saw themselves as exemplifying family values by having chosen parenthood.

Similarly, in two smaller studies of single mothers by choice (Bock 2000; Mannis 1999), researchers interviewed women who adopted children or who purposefully became pregnant. These mothers, usually over age thirty, saw themselves as responsible, emotionally mature, and financially capable of raising a child. Rather than viewing themselves as alternative lifestyle pioneers, they saw their choice as conforming to normal family goals. In fact, their decisions to become single mothers were well accepted by their family, friends, employers, clergy, and physicians.

These were white, middle-class, educated women who insisted on the great difference between themselves and "welfare" or teen mothers. What, in fact, are the realities of teen parenthood today?

Births to Adolescents Public concerns about outcomes for the children of unmarried parents intensify when the mother is a teenager. The words *teenage pregnancy* have been associated with the word *problem* since most of us can remember. Adolescent birthrates rose in the late 1960s as sexual behavior liberalized. However, by the time a "teen pregnancy epidemic" was identified, adolescent birthrates had already begun to decline (see Figure 10.4). Declines in the adolescent birthrates have been especially large for young black women. Teens are using contraception more regularly, and sexual activity has leveled off. The teen abortion rate has dropped also. Teen pregnancies are "at an historic low for the nation" (Ventura et al. 2006; Martin et al. 2006).

Nevertheless, the United States still has by far the highest teen pregnancy, abortion, and birthrates of any industrialized country (Abma et al. 2004), and teen pregnancy is still problematic. In the 1950s, when teen birthrates were actually higher, most teen mothers were already married or they married before the child's birth, and a strong economy provided young fathers with jobs that could support a family.

Now, as Figure 10.4 indicates, most teen women giving birth are not married, and so they lack the economic support of a spouse and the support of a co-parent. Women as well as men need more education in today's world, and women are expected to seek employment. Teenage parents, especially those with more than one child, face a bleak educational future, limited job prospects, and a very good chance of living in poverty, compared to peers who do not become parents as teen-

agers (Nock 1998a; Zabin et al. 1992). Prospects for the children of teen parents have included lower academic achievement and a tendency to repeat the cycle of early unmarried pregnancy (Alexander and Guyer 1993; Hayes 1987).

Yet we have begun to recognize that economic and/or racial/ethnic disadvantage may be playing a larger role than age in shaping a teen mother's limited future (Geronimus 1991; Gueorguieva et al. 2001; Mauldon 2003; Turley 2003). Moreover, outcomes of teen parenthood vary and are not by any means uniformly negative. One longitudinal study of black teen mothers from low-income families in Baltimore concluded that

> while early childbearing increases the risk of ill effects for mother and child, it is unclear that the risk is so high as to justify the popular image of the adolescent mother as an unemployed woman living on welfare with a number of poorly cared-for children. To be sure, teenage mothers do not manage as well as women who delay childbearing, but most studies have shown that there is great variation in the effects of teenage childbearing. (Furstenberg, Brooks-Gunn, and Morgan 1987, p. 142)

Similarly, a careful study based on national sample data sets finds that "teen childbearing plays no causal role in children's test scores and in some behavioral outcomes of adolescence." Research on other outcomes is inconclusive. "We . . . suggest caution in drawing conclusions about early parenthood's overarching effects" (Levine, Emery, and Pollack 2007, p. 105).

Stepparents' Decisions about Having Children

When people remarry or form a new committed partnership, they have decisions to make about having children together. Does it make a difference whether one or both partners already have children? The answer to that question is yes.

A study of more than two thousand couples drawn from a national sample—the National Survey of Families and Households—found that individuals living with a second spouse or partner were most likely to want to have a child if there were no stepchildren of either partner (S. Stewart 2002). Desire for another child was lower for cohabiting couples than for married ones. If *both* partners already had children, an intention to have another child was especially low, with one exception. Because of the symbolic importance of joint parenthood, if the couple did not have a biological child, they were very likely to intend to have one.

"Increasing numbers of children are being born into complex living arrangements" (S. Stewart 2005b, p. 470).

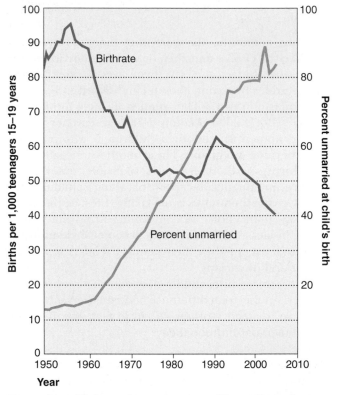

Figure 10.4 Birthrate for teen women fifteen through nineteen years and percentage of teen births that are to unmarried teen women, 1950–2005.

Sources: Ventura, Mathews, and Hamilton 2001, Figure 1; Downs 2003, Figure 1; Martin et al., Tables A, 17; Hamilton et al. 2005; Hamilton, Martin, and Ventura 2007, Tables 1, 2.

The motivation of the parents is often to integrate the stepfamily around a new child who is biologically related to all family members. In fact, there is little firm knowledge about the impact on a stepfamily of a new biological child. Stewart urges more research on the long-term effects of adding children to a stepfamily.

Multipartnered Fertility

Multipartnered fertility is a new interest and a very new area of research for family social scientists. Researchers participating in the Fragile Families and Child Well-being Study of urban parents at the time of their first birth realized in follow-up that some of those parents, particularly those unmarried at the birth, went on to have children with new partners.

How frequent is multipartnered fertility? What are the implications for family life and, especially, for the well-being of children? Research has begun, and we offer some information that is just the beginning of what is likely to become an extensive area of research.

The Fragile Families study is a national longitudinal study conducted in twenty large U.S. cities. It comprised, initially, a sample of 3,700 children born between 1998 and 2000 to unmarried parents and 1,200 born to married parents. Follow-up and reviews of fertility history found that three-fourths of the mothers had children by only one father. Most of the others had children by two fathers, a few by three or four fathers.

Multipartnered fertility is most common in nonmarital families as these have a high rate of breakup; moreover, the participants tend to be younger with more of their lives ahead of them. Black (non-Hispanic) men and women are more likely than other racial/ethnic groups to have children by more than one partner (Carlson and Furstenberg 2006; "Urban Parents" 2006).

Multipartnered fertility seems likely to lead to very complex family systems and weaker ties with extended families. Indeed multipartnered fertility is associated with less financial, housing, and child-care support from kin networks (Carlson and Furstenberg 2006; Harknett and Knab 2007).

Another study using data from the National Longitudinal Study of Adolescent Health (Guzzo and Furstenberg 2007) paid particular attention to the policy implications of multipartnered fertility. "On the one hand, having children by different fathers can present daunting challenges for young mothers. Having to negotiate paternal support and involvement with different men is stressful and may result in different levels of involvement for children who live in the same household but do not share the same father" (p. 37). On the other hand, social welfare authorities can hardly expect these very young women not to have additional children if their first relationship breaks up after only one child.

Much of the foregoing discussion of fertility issues, and especially reports of declining birthrates in some sectors, leads us to the question of preventing unwanted pregnancies.

Preventing Pregnancy

Falling birthrates from the nineteenth century onward indicate that people did not always want to have as many children as nature would make possible. As early as 1832, a book describing birth control techniques and devices was published in the United States. The diaphragm was invented in 1883 and was a common method of birth control for married couples (Weeks 2002, pp. 180–81; 530–31), as was the condom. But it was not until the contraceptive pill became available in the 1960s that women could be more certain of controlling fertility and did not need male cooperation to do so.

Female surgical sterilization has now become the most common method of birth control, primarily for women in their thirties and older; younger women more commonly rely on the pill. Thirteen percent of men age fifteen through forty-four have had vasectomies, a form of birth control more commonly used by whites than other racial/ethnic groups (U.S. Census Bureau 2007a, Table 95). The long-awaited male pill is still on the drawing board ("The Quest Is On" 2004). (Appendix F, "Contraceptive Techniques," describes the various methods of birth control, their effectiveness, and any risks associated with them.)

Whatever methods are available, use of contraception takes place in a relationship context that affects not only choice of methods but also whether contraception is used at all. As one example, teenagers who had a long relationship before commencing a sexual relationship were more apt to use contraception at first sex (Manlove, Ryan, and Franzetta 2003).

The physical and opportunity costs of children tend to be higher for women than for men, whether married or unmarried, and family planning services have always been oriented to women as a clientele. More recently, family planning organizations have realized that they need to reach out to men in order to provide them with contraceptive and health information and so influence couple decisions. So far there are few such programs, and men are typically unaware of their availability where they do exist (Finer, Darroch, and Frost 2003). New research and services have targeted adolescent young men as an approach to adolescent pregnancy prevention (Marsiglio 2003; Marsiglio and Hutchinson 2002).

Abortion

Effective contraception prevents the potential problems associated with pregnancy outside marriage. When contraception is not used or fails, however, many women who do not want to remain pregnant decide to have an abortion. We will look next at this option, a controversial social issue.

The term **abortion** is used for the expulsion of the embryo or fetus from the uterus either naturally (*spontaneous abortion* or *miscarriage*) or medically (surgically or drug-induced abortion). This section addresses **induced abortion**—that is, purposefully obtained abortion, which is what we usually mean in discussions of "abortion."

Thirty percent of American women have had an induced abortion at some point in their lives (Henshaw 1998, p. 24). Abortion decisions are primarily made within the context of unmarried, accidental pregnancy or a failed relationship. However, some married couples may consider aborting an unwanted pregnancy if, for example, they feel that they have already completed their family or could not manage or afford to raise another child. About 40 percent of unintended pregnancies are aborted (Guttmacher Institute 2006). The question of abortion can also arise for couples who, through prenatal diagnosis techniques, find out that a fetus has a serious defect.

Around a quarter of pregnancies ended in abortion in 2002. Around 1.3 million abortions were performed in the United States in that year, down from a peak of about 1.6 million in 1990. The rate of abortions per 1,000 women of childbearing age has been falling since 1980 (U.S. Census Bureau 2007a, Tables 96 and 97). Abortions take place much earlier in pregnancy than in the past—more than half occur within the first nine weeks of pregnancy, and only 11 percent after thirteen weeks or more (U.S. Census Bureau 2007a, Table 97).[7]

Reasons for abortion reported in surveys and interviews at abortion sites include the following: having a child would interfere with the woman's education, work, or ability to care for dependents (74 percent); not being able to afford a baby at this time (73 percent); not wishing to be a single mother or having relationship problems (48 percent); and the woman or couple had completed childbearing (38 percent) or were not ready to have a child (almost one-third; Finer et al. 2005; Boonstra et al. 2006, pp.8–9). A Guttmacher Institute report concluded that "[a]lthough women who have abortions

[7] In 2002, more than four-fifths of abortions were obtained by unmarried women. More than half (56 percent) were obtained by women in their twenties, 17 percent by teens. White women account for the greatest number of abortions (41 percent of total abortions, compared to 32 percent for blacks, 20 percent for Hispanics, 6 percent for Asian/Pacific Islanders, and 1 percent for Native Americans (Jones, Darroch, and Henshaw 2002, Table 1). But the percentage of pregnancies that are terminated by abortion (the *abortion ratio*) is highest among black and Asian/Pacific Islander women. Researchers conclude that "women who have abortions are diverse, and unintended pregnancy leading to abortion is common in all population subgroups" (Jones, Darroch, and Henshaw 2002, p. 232). Still, women in poverty account for a disproportionate share of abortions (Boonstra et al. 2006). Just under half (46 percent) have had a previous abortion (U.S. Census Bureau 2007a, Table 97).

In our society, sexuality and reproduction have become increasingly politicized. Nowhere is this more apparent than in the intensely heated pro-life/pro-choice debate over abortion, one of the most polarizing issues in America today.

and women who have children are often perceived as two distinct groups, in reality they are the same women at different points in their lives" (2006, p. 9).

Less than 1 percent report that an abortion decision was the result of pressure from parents or partners. Sixty percent had consulted someone, usually a husband or partner, in making the decision (Boonstra et al. 2006; Finer et al. 2005). The "right" of the male partner to compel completion of the pregnancy arises regularly as an issue in the media or the courts (Conley 2005; Nolan 1998). U.S. Supreme Court decisions (e.g., *Planned Parenthood v. Danforth* 1976) have made clear that an abortion decision is the woman's, not that of her husband, her parents, or her reproductive partner.

The Politics of Abortion

Throughout world history, abortion has been a way of preventing birth. The practice was not legally prohibited in the United States until the mid-nineteenth century. Laws prohibiting abortion stood relatively unchallenged until the 1960s, when an abortion reform movement succeeded in modifying some state laws to permit abortions approved by physicians on a case-by-case basis. The movement culminated in the 1973 U.S. Supreme Court decision *Roe v. Wade,* which legalized abortion throughout the United States.[8]

As virtually everyone is aware, pro-choice and pro-life activists—those who favor or oppose legal abortion—have made abortion a major political issue. Legislation and other public policy responses to abortion have been shaped by this struggle, as has been the availability of abortion services. Abortion was never widely available outside urban areas. Now states have placed various restrictions on access to abortion including a ban on a certain procedure commonly termed *partial birth abortion,* used later in a pregnancy (*Gonzalez v. Carhart* 2007; Stout 2007). Moreover, the scaling back of training in abortion procedures in medical education as a consequence of political pressures means that as current providers age out or become discouraged by social pressures and threats to their lives, the practical effect is to reduce abortion options. Although clinic violence is down, women arriving for abortion appointments must usually pass a gauntlet of picketers.

Although the Supreme Court has upheld many state restrictions on abortion, it has not outlawed the procedure—at least not yet. Nor has a constitutional amendment to criminalize abortion made it through Congress. The result is that abortion continues to be legally available, as pro-choice advocates wish, while the goals of pro-life advocates have been partially reached through legal and practical restrictions on abortion availability. This has some correspondence with the centrist position of the American public, which favors abortion under certain circumstances.

According to 2005–2006 Gallup polls, 53 percent of respondents described themselves as pro-choice, while 42 percent chose the pro-life label. The majority of Americans (68 percent) believe that *Roe v. Wade* should remain the law of the land. Support for abortion is heavily qualified, however, with only 30 percent believing that abortion should be legal in all circumstances, 53 percent in some circumstances, and 15 percent believing abortion should be illegal in all circumstances (Gallup Poll News Service 2007). Table 10.1 shows the particular circumstances that influence people's attitudes about abortion.

Public opinion approval of abortion differs sharply by the trimester of pregnancy. First-trimester abortion was approved by two-thirds of poll respondents, while later-stage abortions were disapproved by more than two-thirds (Saad 2003). Few abortions (0.17 percent) take place in the third trimester of pregnancy (Jones, Darroch, and Henshaw 2002).

Approval of abortion seems to be decreasing among younger people. A 2003 national survey of college freshmen conducted by UCLA found that 55 percent support legal abortion, compared to 64 percent ten years earlier: "'We're the first generation to be more pro-life than our parents,'" said one freshman (Rosenberg 2004).

The Safety of Abortions

National Right to Life claims that abortion is a threat to both medical and physical health, including threats to future reproductive capacity and an increased risk of breast cancer (National Right to Life 2005; 2006).

[8] *Roe v. Wade* did not legalize any and all abortions in any and all situations. *Roe v. Wade* allows abortion to be obtained without question in the first trimester of pregnancy. But abortion is subject to regulation of providers and procedure in the second trimester and may be outlawed by states after fetal viability (the point at which the fetus is able to live outside the womb), which occurs in the third trimester.

Table 10.1 Percentage of U.S. Adults Approving of Abortion under Certain Circumstances

ABORTION SHOULD BE LEGAL . . .	
When the woman's life is endangered	85%
When the woman's physical health is endangered	77
When the pregnancy was caused by rape or incest	76
When the woman's mental health is endangered	63
When there is evidence that the baby may be physically impaired	56
When there is evidence that the baby may be mentally impaired	55
When the woman or family cannot afford to raise the child	35

Source: Gallup poll, January 10–12, 2003 (Saad 2003).

Abortions and Physical Health The evidence indicates that abortion is a safe medical procedure. According to the American College of Obstetricians and Gynecologists (n.d.), a surgical abortion "is a low risk procedure. . . . An early abortion has less risk than carrying a pregnancy to term." The safety of the less common RU-486 (pill) method of abortion remains under investigation (U.S. Food and Drug Administration 2006).

Research indicates that abortion has no impact on the ability to become pregnant—sterility following abortion is very uncommon—and there is virtually no risk to future pregnancies from a first-trimester abortion of a first pregnancy (Boston Women's Health Book Collective 1998, p. 407).

A panel assembled by the National Cancer Institute to review the research concluded that there is no association between induced abortion and breast cancer (Collaborative Group on Hormonal Factors in Breast Cancer 2004; U.S. National Cancer Institute 2003; see also Bakalar 2007).

Abortions and Psychosocial Outcomes It is safe to say that for most women (and for many of their male partners), abortion is an emotionally charged, often upsetting, experience. Some women report feeling guilty or frightened, a situation that can be heightened by demonstrators outside abortion clinics. Emotional stress is more pronounced for second-trimester than earlier abortions and for women who are uncertain about their decision (Boston Women's Health Book Collective 1998, pp. 406–8). Women from religious denominations or ethnic cultures that strongly oppose abortion may have more negative and mixed feelings after an abortion, but outcomes are more complex than that, as they seem to depend also on the woman's emotional well-being prior to having the abortion (Russo and Dabul 1997).

Some women have reported that the decision to abort enhanced their sense of personal empowerment (Boston Women's Health Book Collective 1998, pp. 406–7). Research has found positive educational, economic, and social outcomes for young women who resolve pregnancies by abortion rather than giving birth. In one study, "those who obtained abortions did better economically and educationally and had fewer subsequent pregnancies than those who chose to bear children" (S. Holmes 1990). A more recent study, done in New Zealand, also reports these outcomes, but finds most of these benefits of abortion to be related to preexisting circumstances of the women. Choosing abortion did result in enhanced educational outcomes (Fergusson, Boden, and Horwood 2007).

The decision to abort is often very difficult to make and act on. But it is important to make a distinction between negative feelings and psychiatric problems. "Having an emotion is not the same as having a mental disorder" (Rubin and Russo 2004, p. 74). The consensus at present is that there is no clear relationship of abortion to mental health (E. Lee 2003).

According to a longitudinal study of almost 5,000 black and white women, the emotional distress involved in making the decision and having the abortion does not typically lead to severe or long-lasting psychological problems (Adler et al. 1992; Boonstra et al. 2006, pp. 22–24; O'Malley 2002; Russo and Dabul 1997; Russo and Zierk 1992; Rubin and Russo 2004). The American Psychological Association (2005a) has taken the position that "[a]bortion is a safe procedure that carries few . . . psychological risks."[9]

Women (and men) making decisions about abortions are most likely to make them in accordance with their values. A detailed review of religiously or philosophically grounded moral and ethical perspectives on abortion is outside the scope of this text, but as we note in Chapter 1, values provide the context for such decisions.

Involuntary Infertility and Reproductive Technology

For some, concern about fertility means avoiding unwanted births. Other couples and individuals face a different problem. They want to have a child, but either they cannot conceive or they cannot sustain a full-term pregnancy. We turn now to the issue of involuntary infertility.

The Social and Biological Context of Infertility[10]

As medically defined, **involuntary infertility** is the condition of wanting to conceive and bear a child but being physically unable to do so. It is usually diagnosed in terms of unsuccessful efforts to conceive for at least

---

[9] The New Zealand study of women who had an abortion prior to age twenty-one and were followed to age twenty-five did find some mental health impact (Fergusson, Horword, and Ridder 2006). It is difficult to evaluate this study vis-à-vis American comparisons because in New Zealand, permission for an abortion requires demonstrating a physical or mental health need for an abortion in the first place. The age range is also somewhat limited. Fergusson et al. simply note that this study contradicts the APA conclusion and advises that the issue remain open for further research. Rubin and Russo (2004) meanwhile note that a pro-life framing of the issue and other movement tactics could induce guilt and other negative feelings, and they provide advice to therapists who are working with women who have had abortions.

[10] The physiology of conception, pregnancy, and childbirth is described in Appendix E, "Conception, Pregnancy, and Childbirth." For a more detailed technical discussion of infertility, see Becker 2000; Greenberg, Bruess, and Haffner 2002; or current books on the subject addressed to a lay (nonmedical) audience.

twelve months. A related concept, **impaired fertility,** describes the situation of a woman or a couple who has a physical barrier to pregnancy or who has not been able to carry a pregnancy to full term. *Subfecundity* or *secondary infertility* describes a situation in which a woman or a couple has had children previously, but now cannot. We will use the term *infertility* for all the situations in which a woman or a couple is not able to have a desired child. Around 12 percent of American women have impaired fertility, while 7 percent of married women are infertile (Chandra, Martinez, Mosher, Abma, and Jones 2005, pp. 21–22).

Infertility has become more visible because the present tendency to postpone childbearing until one's thirties or even forties creates a class of infertile potential parents who are intensely hopeful and financially able to seek treatment. "For most women and their partners, infertility is a major life crisis" (Boston Women's Health Book Collective 1998, p. 532).

Many couples only gradually become aware that unlike other couples they know who are happily planning their pregnancies without apparent difficulty, they themselves remain without desired children. It is at this point that couples are likely to seek a medical solution to their problem (Matthews and Matthews 1986).

Infertility Services and Reproductive Technology

News media reported that in 2006, Louise Brown, the first "test-tube" baby, gave birth to *her* first child ("World's First" 2007). This look back reminds us of how astonishing were the first developments in reproductive technology. Now, more and more, **assisted reproductive technology (ART)** has become an accepted reproductive option. In 2004, there were 128,000 ART procedures, which resulted in almost 50,000 infants (U.S. Centers for Disease Control and Prevention 2006a).

This quote from a six-year-old "dreaming of motherhood" suggests just how normalized ART has become: "'Mommy, Mommy, when I grow up, I want to be a mommy just like you. I want to go to the sperm bank just like you and get some sperm and have a baby just like me'" (in Ehrensaft 2005, p. 1).

Almost half (44 percent) of women with fertility problems sought medical help in 1995 (the latest year for which detailed data are available). They were more often white (75 percent) and typically older (twenty-five through forty-four), married, better educated, and with higher family incomes than those not seeking treatment. But 20 percent of those using infertility services were not married, and 11 percent were poor (Chandra and Stephen 1998). With regard to race and ethnicity, little social science data exist.

"So you're having trouble conceiving. Have you tried sex?"

Medical procedures involving drug therapies, donor insemination, in vitro fertilization, and related techniques are discussed in Appendix G, "High-Tech Fertility." Fertility treatment is stressful. The procedures can be uncomfortable. Scheduling sex for the main purpose of reproduction can feel depersonalizing and can add conflict to a relationship (Becker 1990, 2000). As one wife explained:

> "All the things you read about—that men feel like they are just a tool. You have to have an erection and ejaculate at a certain time whether you want to or not. He has said to me in times out of genuine anger, 'I feel like all you want me for is to make a baby. You don't really want me, you just want me to do it.'" (Becker 1990, p. 94)

Anthropologist Gay Becker undertook an ethnographic study of infertility treatment, conducting five hundred interviews and doing field observation over a four-year period. The study included 143 women and 134 men and is a good source of information about the experience of infertility and its treatment.

When faced with involuntary infertility, an individual or a couple experiences a loss of control over life plans and may feel helpless, defective, angry, and often guilty. Although men and women may differ in their specific responses to infertility, both are very affected emotionally by the challenge to taken-for-granted life plans and their sense of manhood or womanhood (Becker 2000). The psychological burden of infertility may fall especially hard on professional, goal-oriented individuals. These people "have learned to focus all their energies on a particular goal. When that goal becomes a pregnancy that they cannot achieve, they see themselves as failures in a global sense" (Berg 1984, p. 164). Besides having an effect on each partner's self-esteem, the situation can hurt their relationship (Becker 2000).

Going through infertility treatment is costly. A current controversy involves whether employee health insurance should cover it. As of this writing, only fourteen states require insurance companies to offer policies that cover infertility treatment (American Society for Reproductive Medicine 2007).

Infertility treatment can be successful, but often it is not. When it is not, couples are faced with yet another decision—whether, or when, to quit trying. Said one husband, "The technology . . . has given us so many options that it is hard to say no" (quoted in Stolberg 1997, p. A1).

Reproductive Technology: Social and Ethical Issues

Reproductive technologies enhance choices and can reward infertile couples with much-desired parenthood. They enable same-sex couples or uncoupled individuals to become biological parents. But reproductive technologies have tremendous social implications for the family as an institution and raise serious ethical questions as well.

The following sections explore the commercialization of reproduction, inequality of access to reproductive technology, and the sometimes confusing and ambiguous parent–child relationships created by reproductive technology.

Commercialization of Reproduction A general concern is that the new techniques, when performed for profit, commercialize reproduction. Prospective parents and their bodies are treated as products and thereby dehumanized (Rothman 1999). Examples include the selling of eggs or sperm to for-profit fertility clinics and the marketing of sperm or eggs with certain donor characteristics such as intelligence, physical attractiveness, and athletic ability.

Reports of fraud, overstatement of positive outcomes, failure to warn about the risk of multiple births, and other professional violations (Leigh 2004) make it important to understand that an individual seeking treatment is in fact a consumer and should interview the doctor and investigate the facility. There has been little attempt by the government to regulate assisted reproductive technology in the same way that adoption, for example, is regulated. The federal government does require annual reports of procedures and success rates, but no licensing is required (Skloot 2003). Clients may not realize that the average success rate (a baby) is around 27 percent. That varies with the type of procedure and with age; chances are much less for women over forty and as low as 1 percent for women age forty-six (Spar 2006, Table 2.2).

Inequality Issues Reproductive technologies raise social class and other inequality issues. Assisted reproductive technology is usually not affordable by those with low incomes. By and large, after initial diagnosis, lower-income couples do not go on to more advanced (and expensive) treatment. Said one woman, "There need to be some options for people like us who don't have money sitting in the bank" (Becker 2000, p. 20).

Who Is a Parent? Reproductive technology creates "family" relationships that depart considerably from what is possible through unassisted biology—some men and at least one woman have become parents after death ("Kids Conceived" 2004; Weiss 1998).

Surrogacy, along with embryo transfer, creates the possibility that a child could have three mothers (the genetic mother, the gestational mother, and the social mother), as well as two fathers (genetic and social). In such a situation, how do courts define the "real" parents (L. Schwartz 2003)?

An interesting recent development is the emergence of sperm donors as putative fathers, sought out by their "children" as they enter adolescence or young adulthood (Harmon 2005b; 2007). Many states have laws by which sperm donors, with the exception of the husband, have no parental rights, but this barrier between sperm donors and their biological children is gradually being broken.[11]

What Kind of Child? As technology advances, the potential to create a child with certain traits expands. Embryo screening—a technology for examining fertilized eggs before implantation to choose or eliminate certain ones—is a boon for prospective parents whose family heritage includes disabling genetic conditions (Harmon 2006). But embryo screening also raises the possibility of sex selection (Grady 2007; Marchione and Tanner 2006) and perhaps selection for other traits. Those using sperm donors are already scanning the records to find evidence of traits they would like in their children. Philosophers ponder the implications for parents and children when children are made-to-order!

---

[11] Legislation in Sweden and court decisions in the United Kingdom have given children in those countries the right to obtain identifying information about a donor. Some American sperm clinics have responded to the *identity release movement* by developing *open sperm donor* programs, which agree to make information available to the child at eighteen; offer photos of the donor; or, at a minimum, offer genetic/health information. Some previously anonymous donors and their biological offspring have met, arranging meetings through the clinic when there is mutual agreement to do so (Villarosa 2002a; Talbot 2001).

The American Society for Reproductive Medicine recommends against secrecy: "It's no longer possible to think of sperm donation without thinking of what the child it produces may someday want" (Talbot 2001, p. 88).

We should note that these concerns about reproductive technology are primarily articulated by medical and public health professionals, academics, policy analysts, and ethicists. For the most part, prospective parents themselves are more focused on their desire for a child and not so inclined to view ART with a critical eye—at least not initially.

Reproductive Technology: Making Personal Choices

Choosing to use reproductive technology depends on one's values and circumstances. Religious beliefs and cultural values influence decisions.[12] Fertility treatment can be financially, physically, and emotionally draining. The need for frequent physician's visits can interfere with job obligations, and infertility treatment can lead to tensions in a marriage.

There are certain situations in which the need for reproductive technology can be anticipated. Men or women undergoing medical treatments that will leave them infertile may bank sperm or eggs, and couples may take similar action regarding freezing embryos. In the last few years, men going off to war in Iraq have banked sperm, anticipating contact with hazardous materials—or death. Indeed, a baby was recently born to a father who was killed in Iraq two years ago (Oppenheim 2007).

Those whose use of ART is successful are euphoric. Children born by means of in vitro fertilization or donor sperm seem thoroughly normal, as the research reported in "Facts About Families: 'Test-Tube' Babies Grow Up" shows us.

For others who had hoped to become parents, infertility treatment eventually became the problem instead of the solution. Coming to terms with infertility has been likened to the grief process, in which initial denial is followed by anger, depression, and usually ultimate acceptance: "When I finally found out that I absolutely could not have children . . . it was a tremendous relief. I could get on with my life" (Bouton 1987, p. 92). Some people gradually choose to define themselves as permanently and comfortably child-free.

A second way to get on with life yet retain the hope of parenthood is through adoption. Indeed, some couples explore adoption options even as they continue infertility treatments (Becker 2000).

The comment of author Debora Spar about her study of the reproductive technology business (2006) can apply equally well to adoption. When asked what most surprised her in research for her book *The Baby Business* (2006), Spar reflected: "'Everyone I spoke to who had gone through these difficult processes came out with a child that they were convinced was the only child that they were ever destined to have. . . . To me it shows that there's something in humans that connects us to our children and it goes even deeper than genetics alone'" (quoted in Dreifus 2006).

Adoption

The U.S. census looked at adoption for the first time in 2000. In that year, there were more than two million adopted children in U.S. households, about 2.5 percent of all children. In terms of *numbers*, there are more adopted children in non-Hispanic white families (more than 70 percent of all adopted children). But Asian/Pacific Islander families have the highest *rate* of adoption relative to their population. More girls than boys are adopted. Women, especially single women, prefer to adopt girls, and girls are more likely to be available for adoption. Ninety-five percent of Chinese babies available for adoption, for example, are girls (Fields 2001; Kreider 2003; U.S. Census Bureau 2007a, Table 65).

© Jeff Beiermann/ Omaha World Herald

In this photo, taken in Plainview, Nebraska, four-year-old adopted daughter Natalie has just been sworn in as a new U.S. citizen. Since 2001, children adopted internationally by U.S. citizens receive their American citizenship automatically.

---

[12] The Catholic Church prohibits all forms of reproductive technology, including artificial insemination by the husband (Congregation for the Doctrine of the Faith 1988; McCormick 1992). The Jewish tradition requires physical union for adultery and so does not define donor insemination (DI) as adulterous. But Judaism does view masturbation as sinful. Hence, a man's obtaining sperm either to sell or to artificially inseminate his wife is morally problematic; this is true of Catholic teaching as well (Newman 1992). Some interpretations of Protestantism, on the other hand, note that the Bible sees infertility as cause for sorrow and exalts increasing human freedom beyond natural barriers (Meilander 1992).

"Test-Tube" Babies Grow Up

Louise Brown, the first baby conceived through in vitro fertilization (IVF), turned twenty-five in 2003. Elizabeth Carr, the first American IVF baby, is now twenty-two and a college graduate. In vitro fertilization and other assisted reproductive technologies are the "new normal." There are now more than one million living IVF children, and almost 50,000 are born worldwide every year (Szabo 2004; Weiss 2002). "New reproductive technologies . . . have come to be viewed as simply another means of conception" (Becker 2000, p. 19).

How normal are the children produced by the use of such assisted reproductive technology (ART) as in vitro fertilization (IVF), donor insemination (DI), egg donation, and embryo transfer? Medically, the use of ART involves a greater risk of low birth weight, birth defects, developmental delay, or a greater, though infrequent, incidence of some rare diseases ("Abnormalities Cause" 2003; D. Brown 2002; Kolata 2002b; Schieve et al. 2002; Strömberg et al. 2002; Weiss 2002). Nevertheless, 94 percent of all full-term IVF singletons had normal birth weight and 91 percent, no major birth defects. "The absolute risks are low," reports Dr. Mark Walker, who conducted a study of 61,000 Canadian ART births (Marchione 2007).

One may especially want to know what assisted reproduction children are like psychosocially. And are their parents able to relate to them in a "normal" way? Major longitudinal studies of in vitro fertilization and donor insemination children have been conducted in Britain and in some other European countries. The researchers followed the children to age twelve and compared IVF and DI children to adopted and naturally conceived children. On a variety of measures obtained from parents, teachers, and the children themselves, the researchers concluded that the reproductive technology children were functioning well and did not differ from naturally conceived or adopted children in their psychosocial adjustment (Golombok, Brewaeys et al. 2002; Golombok et al. 1995; Golombok, MacCallum, and Goodman 2001; Golombok, MacCallum et al. 2002; McMahon et al. 2003; see also Chan, Raboy, and Patterson 1998).

All in all, careful, well-designed longitudinal studies of ART children and their families conducted by different sets of researchers are unanimous in finding ART children to be thoroughly normal. "Test-tube" babies are developing normally as they grow into adolescence and beyond.

Critical Thinking

Do you know anyone who is an ART child and has discussed it with you? Do you know any parents or would-be parents who have used reproductive technology? What were their experiences with ART?

Census data do not distinguish adoptions by biological relatives or stepparents from non-relative adoptions. But earlier research found that a majority of adopted children were related to their adoptive parents by blood or marriage. Most commonly, those who adopted unrelated children have no other children, have impaired fertility, and have used infertility services. They are more likely to be older and highly educated and to have higher incomes (Chandra et al. 1999; Kreider 2003; U.S. Census Bureau 2007a, Table 65). A study in one U.S. county found adoption applicants drawn to adoption by their pronatalist beliefs (the importance of children and parenting) and their exposure to adoption (through friends and family members) (Bausch 2006).

To encourage adoption, there is now a federal tax credit of $10,000 toward adoption expenses for low- and middle-income parents. Corporations sometimes subsidize employees' adoptions. One survey of one thousand companies of various sizes found that 44 percent offered paid leave to newly adoptive parents, while 83 percent assisted with finances (Clemetson 2006b).

Some children are adopted informally—that is, the children are taken into a parent's home, but the adoption is not legally formalized. **Informal adoption** is most common among Alaska Natives, blacks, and Hispanics (Kreider 2003).

Adoptions increased through much of the twentieth century, reaching a peak in 1970, but the number has declined since (Bachrach et al. 1990). Fewer infants are available due to more effective contraception and legalized abortion. And white unmarried mothers, those most likely to relinquish their infants in the past, are now likely to keep their babies (Tarmann 2002).

Some couples pursue international adoption. A second option is to adopt "special needs" children—those who are older, are nonwhite, come with siblings, and/or are disabled.

The Adoption Process

The experience of legal adoption varies widely across the country, partly because it is subject to differing state laws. Adoptions may be public or private. *Public adoptions* take place through licensed agencies. *Private adoptions* (also called *independent adoptions*) are arranged between the adoptive parent(s) and the birth mother, usually through an attorney. Legal fees and the birth mother's medical costs are usually paid by the adopting couple.

More and more, adoptions are open; that is, the birth and adoptive parents meet or have some knowledge of each other's identities. Even when an adoption is closed, as adoptions used to be, some states now have laws permitting the adoptee access to records at a certain age or under specified conditions.

A concern that arose in recent decades because of some high-profile cases is whether birth parents can claim rights to a biological child after the child has been adopted. In those cases, a nonmarital biological father had not given consent or even been notified, and he was able to assert his parental rights (Burbach and Lamanna 2000). States have begun to reexamine laws requiring birth fathers to register with a "putative father registry" if they wish to have a role in decisions about the child's future (that is, with regard to relinquishment for adoption). Often the time window is very short, and the registries are not well publicized; legal challenges by biological fathers are in the works (Lewin 2006d). However, of all domestic adoptions in the recent past, fewer than 1 percent have been contested by biological parents (Ingrassia 1995).

Another concern of prospective adoptive parents has to do with the adjustment of adopted children—are they likely to have more problems than other children? Research suggests that adopted children, especially males, are at higher risk of problems in school achievement and behavior, psychological well-being, and substance use. A recent careful study, based on a large, nationally representative sample, confirms earlier findings of small to moderate differences between adopted and nonadopted children (those living with biological and/or stepparents; B. Miller et al. 2000). As can be the case in social science, a different research review concluded that the overall body of research supports "the view that most adoptive families are resilient" and that positives outweigh negatives (O'Brien and Zamostny 2003, p. 679).

Adoption of Racial/Ethnic Minority Children

Today, 15 percent of adopted children are of a different race than one or both of their parents, and 6 percent differ as to Hispanic ethnicity (U.S. Census Bureau 2007a, Table 65). The family diversity created by transracial adoption seems in tune with the increasing diversity of American society (Pertman 2000). Yet it has been controversial.

In 1971, agencies placed more than one-third of their black infants with white parents (Nazario 1990). At that time, the number of black adoptive homes was much smaller than the number of available children, while the reverse was true for whites. But interracial adoptions, having increased rapidly in the 1960s and early 1970s, were much curtailed after 1972, when the National Association of Black Social Workers strongly objected. Suggesting that transracial adoption amounted to cultural genocide, racial/ethnic minority advocates expressed concern about identity problems and the loss of children from the black community (Simon and Altstein 2002). Native American activists have successfully asserted tribal rights and collective interest in Indian children. In addition to identity concerns, they expressed the fear that coercive pressures might be put on parents to relinquish their children in order to provide adoptable children to white parents. Indeed, this practice had been pervasive through the 1960s (Fanshel 1972).[13]

As a result of this controversy, adoption agencies shied away from transracial adoption for many years. In the late 1980s, only about 8 percent of adoptions were interracial, usually adoption by white parents of mixed-race, African American, Asian, or Native American children (Bachrach et al. 1990). Congress has had the last word on this matter, however. The Multiethnic Placement Act (1994) and the Adoption and Safe Families Act (1997) prohibit delay or denial of adoption based on race, color, or national origin of the prospective adoptive parents. But there are still some racial issues that arise in adoption decisions. Joseph Crumble typifies the concerns of some black social workers: "'For blacks, it's about how confident whites can be with the issues of race when their race is in conflict with the race of the child'" (Clemetson and Nixon 2006, p. A18).

Long-term studies suggest that transracial adoption has proven successful for most parents and children, including with regard to racial issues. Sociologist Rita Simon and social work professor Howard Altstein followed

---

[13] The Indian Child Welfare Act of 1978 requires that "adoptive placement be made with (1) members of the child's extended family, (2) other members of the same tribe, or (3) other Indian families" so as "to protect the rights of the Indian child as an Indian and the rights of the Indian community and tribe in retaining its children in its society." In practice, outcomes of contested adoption cases have depended on the parents' attachment to the reservation and other circumstances. Tribes have also agreed to placements with white guardians or adoptive parents when they have believed it to be in the child's best interest.

interracial adoptees from their infancy in 1972 to adulthood. They were able to locate eighty-eight of the ninety-six families from the 1984 phase of the study for their latest book (2002). They concluded that as adolescents and later, transracially adopted children "clearly were aware of and comfortable with their racial identity" (p. 222).

Another longitudinal study of transracial (white parents and African American, Asian, and Latino children) and in-race adoptions (white parents, white children) followed the children from the mid-1970s to 1993, when they were in their early twenties. There were no differences in general adjustment or problem behavior between the two groups. Such adjustment difficulties as did exist among the transracially adopted children tended to be connected to racial issues—discrimination and "differentness" of appearance. Not surprisingly then, researchers found that neighborhood made a difference within the transracial adoptee group; those who were reared in mixed-race neighborhoods were more confident in their racial identity (Feigelman 2000).

Some researchers have suggested that rather than causing serious problems, transracial adoptions may produce individuals with heightened skills at bridging cultures. "The message of our findings is that transracial adoption should not be excluded as a permanent placement when no appropriate permanent inracial placement is available" (Simon 1990).

Adoption of Older Children and Children with Disabilities

Together with certain racial/ethnic minorities, children who are no longer infants and children with disabilities make up the large majority of youngsters now handled by adoption agencies (Finley 2000). Special needs adoptions are pursued not only by couples who are infertile but also for altruistic motives. Gay men have adopted infants with HIV/AIDS, for example (Morrow 1992). In some cases, lesbian and gay male or older couples adopt such hard-to-place children because law or adoption agency policy denies them the ability to adopt other children.

The majority of adoptions of older children and children with disabilities work out well. But disruption and dissolution rates rise with the child's age at adoption. Among adoptions generally, only about 2 percent of agency adoptions end up being *disrupted adoptions* (the child is returned to the agency before the adoption is legally final) or *dissolved adoptions* (the child is returned after the adoption is final). But 4.7 percent of adoptions of children age three to five at adoption, 10 percent of those age six to eight years, and perhaps as high as 40 percent of children adopted between the ages of twelve

and seventeen are disrupted or dissolved (Barth and Berry 1988; Sachs 1990; Seelye 1998).

What causes these disrupted and dissolved adoptions? For one thing, some children available for adoption may be emotionally damaged or developmentally impaired due to drug- or alcohol-addicted biological parents, physical abuse from biological or foster parents, or previous broken attachments as they have been moved from one foster home to another. Some develop **attachment disorder**, defensively shutting off the willingness or ability to make future attachments (Barth and Berry 1988). Observers have seen attachment disorder among adoptees from Romania and other Eastern European orphanages (Mainemer, Gilman, and Ames 1998).

Adoption professionals point out that parents are willing to adopt children with problems as long as they know what they are getting into (Groze 1996). Agencies have increasingly tried to gain information about the circumstances of the pregnancy and the child's early life and to match children's backgrounds with couples who know how to help them (M. Ward 1997).

International Adoptions

International adoption has grown dramatically in recent years; about 18,000 adoptions in 2000 were of children from outside the country. Half of all children adopted from overseas by American parents from 1990 to 2005 were from Asia, especially from Korea and China; 18 percent from Latin America and the Caribbean; 31 percent from Europe, primarily Russia and Rumania; and 1 percent from Africa (Clemetson and Nixon 2006).

Parents who have adopted internationally have encountered all kinds of difficulties: the expense of travel to a foreign country—and getting time off from work to go to the child's country for an extended stay; difficulty with negotiations and paperwork in a foreign language, and the need to rely on translators and brokers; the uncertainty about being able to choose a child, as opposed to having one thrust upon the parent; the occasional unexpected expansion of adoption fees or expected charitable contributions; the ambivalence and reluctance of a nation to place its children abroad; and the complete failure to bring home a child.

The biological mother's consent is an issue in overseas adoptions because it is more difficult to be sure that the mother has willingly placed her child for adoption rather than being coerced or misled by a baby broker. Romania recently placed a moratorium on adoptions, fearing corruption of their entire system. Russia has placed a temporary moratorium on adoption applications, and Guatemala is revising its process to comply with the Hague Convention on Intercountry Adoption. (The United States plans to ratify this treaty in 2007.)

China is moving to impose new rules on foreign adoptions, including not only establishing an age requirement for adoptive parents (under fifty) and stable marriage specifications but also ruling out obese prospective parents! (Belluck and Yardley 2006; Clemetson 2007; J. Gross 2007; N. Knox 2004; Lacey 2006; Yin 2007).

International adoptions can pose some of the same problems as the adoption of older children. Conditions in homes and institutions overseas may not be ideal beginnings, and children may have health problems or suffer from attachment disorder (Elias 2005; J. Gross 2006c). But the vast majority of international adoptions are successful (Tanner 2005). A meta-analysis of around one hundred studies found that adopted children are referred to mental health services more often than non-adoptees are, perhaps a function of adjustment concerns and high-income parents more than troubling behavior. "Most international adoptees are well adjusted" (Juffer and van IJzendoorn 2005, p. 2501). They "are underrepresented in juvenile court and adult mental health placements," according to Dr. Laurie C. Miller, editor of the *Handbook of International Adoptive Medicine* (Miller 2005b, p. 2533; see also Miller 2005a).

Those who adopt internationally say they made this choice for several reasons. They are more apt to be able to adopt a healthy infant, with a shorter wait and often fewer limits in terms of age or marital status. The adoption is perceived to be less risky in that there is little likelihood of a birth mother seeking to reclaim the child (Clemetson 2006a; Zuang 2004). To what degree racial preferences enter into the choice of international adoption is difficult to determine.

Today, there are not only more agencies for arranging international adoptions but also more resources for coping with any post-adoption difficulties. There are now specialists in "adoption medicine" who can address medical and cognitive problems of children adopted overseas, as well as psychologists who are prepared to address international or transracial adoption issues (J. Gross 2006c; Tuller 2001). There are "culture camps" (Chappell 1996), schools (Zhao 2002), parent groups (Clemetson 2006a), and other resources for bridging the cultural gap for a child raised in America but conscious of having started life in another country. Most parents try very hard to maintain a bicultural identity for the child (Brooke 2004), and some undertake travel to the child's country of origin. Sometimes, though, internationally adopted children just want to simply be the American child that they also are (Dewan 2000).

International adoption produces more and more multicultural families in an increasingly multicultural America. The many media photos of happy adoptive parents and children tell a story of hopes for parenthood that are realized.

Contemporary society offers many choices about whether to have children and how many. In addition, modern technology has increased people's options about *how* to have children. New trends in adoption, such as international adoption, have added still more options and precipitated more decisions. As this text has often suggested, the best way to make decisions about whether to parent or not is to make them knowledgeably.

Summary

- Today, individuals have more choice than ever about whether and when to have children and how many to have.

- Although parenthood has become a choice, the majority of Americans continue to value parenthood. Only a small percentage expect to be childless by choice.

- Nevertheless, it is likely that changing values concerning parenthood, the weakening of social norms prescribing marriage and parenthood, a wider range of alternatives for women, the desire to postpone marriage and childbearing, and the availability of modern contraceptives and legal abortion will result in a higher proportion of Americans remaining childless or having only one child in the future.

- Some observers believe that societal support for children is so lacking in the United States that it amounts to *structural antinatalism*. They point to the absence of a society-wide program of health insurance and health care for children, to workplace inflexibility, to the lack of affordable quality day care, and to the absence of paid maternal or paternal leave, as is provided in Europe and elsewhere.

- Children can add a fulfilling and highly rewarding experience to people's lives, but they also impose complications and stresses, both financial and emotional.

- Birthrates have declined for married women, and many women are waiting longer to have their first child. Although other nonmarital birthrates have risen in recent decades, teen birthrates have declined. Pregnancy outside of marriage has become increasingly acceptable, but some unmarried pregnant women choose abortion.

- Deciding about parenthood today can include consideration of postponing parenthood, having a one-child family, engaging in nonmarital births, having new biological children in stepfamilies, adopting, and taking advantage of infertility treatment.

Questions for Review and Reflection

1. What are some reasons that there aren't as many large families now as there used to be?

2. Discuss the advantages and disadvantages of having children. Which do you think are the strongest reasons for having children? Which do you think are the strongest reasons for *not* having children?

3. How would you react to becoming the parent of twins? Triplets? More? If your choice is to take fertility treatments that pose a risk of multiple births or to not have children at all, what would you do—and why?

4. Which reproductive technology would you be willing to use? In what circumstances?

5. **Policy Question.** How is a pronatalist bias shown in our society? Are there antinatalist pressures? What policies might be developed to support parents? Are there any special policy needs of nonparents? Why might a society's social policies favor parents over nonparents?

Key Terms

abortion 252
assisted reproductive technology (ART) 255
attachment disorder 260
fecundity 234
fertility 234
impaired fertility 255
induced abortion 252
informal adoption 258
involuntary infertility 254
multipartnered fertility 251

opportunity costs (of children) 242
pronatalist bias 240
replacement level (of fertility) 236
single mothers by choice 249
social capital perspective (on parenthood) 241
structural antinatalism 240
total fertility rate (TFR) 234
value of children perspective (on parenthood) 241
voluntary childlessness 243

Online Resources

Companion Website for This Book

www.thomsonedu.com/sociology/lamanna

Visit the book companion website, where you will find flash cards, practice quizzes, Internet links, suggested readings, InfoTrac College Edition exercises, and more to help you study.

ThomsonNOW™ for Marriage and Family

Spend time on what you need to master rather than on information you already have learned. Take a pre-test for this chapter, and ThomsonNOW will generate a personalized study plan based on your results. The study plan will identify the topics you need to review and direct you to online resources such as videos, narrated learning modules, and interactive activities to help you master those topics. You can then take a post-test to help you determine the concepts you have mastered and what you will still need to work on. Try it out! Go to **www .thomsonedu.com/login** to sign in with an access code or to purchase access to this product.

Raising Children
in a Multicultural Society

11

Parents in Modern America

Issues for Thought Parent Job Description

The Transition to Parenthood

Mothers and Fathers: Images and Reality

Old and New Images of Parents

Mothers and Fathers: What Do They Do?

Facts about Families Fathers as Primary Parents

Sharing Parenthood

Authoritative Parenting

Issues for Thought Growing Up in a Household Characterized by Conflict

As We Make Choices Communicating with Children—How to Talk So Kids Will Listen and Listen So Kids Will Talk

Is Spanking Ever Appropriate?

The Resilient Child

Social Class and Parenting

The Working Poor

Middle- and Upper-Middle-Class Parents

Racial/Ethnic Diversity and Parenting

African American Parents and Children

Native American Parents and Children

Hispanic Parents and Children

Asian American Parents and Children

Parents and Multiracial Children

Religious Minority Parents and Children

Raising Children of Racial/Ethnic Identity in a Racist and Discriminatory Society

Grandparents as Parents

Foster Parents

Parents and Young Adult Children

Independent Adults and Their Parents

Toward Better Parent–Child Relationships

© Christoph Wilhelm/CORBIS

"Whoever came up with the Peace Corps motto, 'The toughest job you'll ever love,' probably wasn't a parent" (Picker 2005, p. 46). Unlike today, for most of human history, adults raised children simply by living with them and thereby providing examples and socialization into adult roles. From an early age, children shared the everyday world of adults, working beside them, dressing like them, sleeping near them.

At least in Europe, the concept of childhood as different from adulthood did not emerge until about the seventeenth century, according to historian Phillipe Ariès (1962). As education became available to all children, not just those of the wealthy, and as they spent more of their time in school, children gradually spent less time participating in the everyday lives of adults. One result is that today we regard children as people who need special training, guidance, and care (Mintz 2004).[1]

But at the same time, our society does not offer parents, stepparents, or others acting as parents much psychological or social support. Indeed, American society often seems indifferent to the needs of parents, including the economic support of families with children (Erickson and Aird 2005; "Parents Want More" 2005). For instance, the rate of child poverty in the United States exceeds that of the nation as a whole and is considerably higher than in other wealthy industrialized nations (U.S. Census Bureau 2007a, Table 694).

In this chapter, we will discuss a range of parenting issues. We'll begin by looking at some difficulties of parenting. Next, we'll examine the roles of mothers and fathers, describe parenting styles, then examine parenting over the life course. We'll see that parenting takes place in social contexts that vary with regard to parents' social class and racial/ethnic background. We'll describe grandparents who serve as parents, and we'll discuss foster parents. (Issues specifically related to same-sex parenting and to children in cohabiting families are addressed in Chapter 8. Combining work and parenting roles is addressed in Chapter 12. The special concerns of divorced single parents are discussed in Chapter 16; those of stepfamilies are considered in Chapter 17.) Here we discuss some common parenting issues and consider how parents can make relationships with their children more satisfying.

Parents in Modern America

Although raising children may be a joyful and fulfilling enterprise, parenting today takes place in a social

context that can make child raising an enormously difficult task. (See "Issues for Thought: Parent Job Description.") Today's parents face a myriad of questions and dilemmas that parents just a few decades ago would not have imagined: Should I have my baby boy circumcised? Can I trust my child's babysitter? How much fast food is too much? Should I believe the teacher who says my child needs medication? Should I homeschool my child? Does my pre-teen spend too much time on a cell phone? Playing video games? What if I discover that my child is using illegal drugs? Should I "snoop" into what my teenager is doing on MySpace.com? What should I tell my child about terrorism?

We would not want to point out the difficulties of today's parents without first noting some advantages. In many respects, technology has vastly improved health care over the past several decades, and parents now have higher levels of education and are likely to have had some exposure to formal knowledge about child development and child-raising techniques. Advances in technology allow parents to keep more vigilant track of their children (Tovia Smith 2006)(although experts and parents vary on whether such surveillance is always a good idea). Many fathers are more emotionally involved than they were several decades ago (Bianchi, Robinson, and Milkie 2006; Gerson 1997). The Internet offers countless sources of information for parents dealing with virtually any situation. E-mail can make keeping in touch with children, parents, and extended family both easier and more likely.

Nevertheless, the family ecology theoretical perspective (see Chapter 2) also leads us to point to ways that the larger environment makes parenting especially difficult today. Here we list five features of the social context of child raising that can make modern parenting difficult and stressful:

1. In our society, the parenting role conflicts with the working role, and employers typically place work demands first (Barnett and Gareis 2006; Williams and Cooper 2004). In one national survey, two-thirds of a representative sample of American parents with children between ages five and seventeen said that they worry either "some" or "a lot" about juggling the demands of work and family (see Figure 11.1). (Chapter 12 presents work–family conflicts in more detail.) In another national survey, more than half (53 percent) of the mothers said they wished they could spend more time with their children (Erickson and Aird 2005, Figure 5).

2. Today's parents raise their children in a pluralistic society, characterized by diverse and conflicting values (Rigby 2006). Parents are only one of several influences on children. Others are older siblings, schools, peers, television, movies, music, books, the

---

[1] A tragic exception to this statement involves the use of children as soldiers, chronicled by historians in the case of the thirteenth-century "Children's Crusade" in Europe and apparent today in many parts of the developing world (Beah 2007).

This piece was written by columnist Annette Clifford. It appeared in the Florida Today *newspaper in Melbourne, Florida.*

Job Description:

Long-term, team players needed for challenging permanent work in an often chaotic environment. Candidates must possess excellent communication and organizational skills and be willing to work variable hours, which will include evenings and weekends and frequent 24-hour shifts on call. Some overnight travel required, including trips to primitive camping sites on rainy weekends and endless sports tournaments in far away cities! Travel expenses not reimbursed. Extensive courier duties also required.

Responsibilities:

The rest of your life. Must be willing to be hated, at least temporarily, until someone needs $5. Must be willing to bite tongue repeatedly. Also, must possess the physical stamina of a pack mule and be able to go from zero to 60 mph in three seconds flat in case, this time, the screams from the backyard are not someone just crying wolf. Must be willing to face stimulating technical challenges, such as small gadget repair, mysteriously sluggish toilets and stuck zippers. Must screen phone calls, maintain calendars and coordinate production of multiple homework projects. Must have ability to plan and organize social gatherings for clients of all ages and mental outlooks. Must be willing to be indispensable one minute, an embarrassment the next. Must handle assembly and product safety testing of a half million cheap, plastic toys, and battery operated devices. Must always hope for the best but be prepared for the worst. Must assume final, complete accountability for the quality of the end product. Responsibilities also include floor maintenance and janitorial work throughout the facility.

Possibility for Advancement and Promotion

None. Your job is to remain in the same position for years, without complaining, constantly retraining and updating your skills, so that those in your charge can ultimately surpass you.

Previous Experience:

None required unfortunately. On-the-job training offered on a continually exhausting basis.

Wages and Compensation:

Get this! You pay them! Offering frequent raises and bonuses. A balloon payment is due when they turn 18 because of the assumption that college will help them become financially independent. When you die, you give them whatever is left. The oddest thing about this reverse-salary scheme is that you actually enjoy it and wish you could only do more.

Benefits:

While no health or dental insurance, no pension, no tuition reimbursement, no paid holidays and no stock options are offered, this job supplies limitless opportunities for personal growth and free hugs for life if you play your cards right.

Critical Thinking

Are you a parent? If so, how well does this job description fit your experience? What might you add?

Source: Annette Clifford, "Parent Job Description" from the *Florida Today* newspaper, Melbourne, FL, 1999. Reprinted by permission of the author.

Internet, travel, and, yes, drug dealers. As Figure 11.1 shows, 73 percent of American parents today say they worry "some" or "a lot" about negative messages in the media. More than half worry a lot about protecting their children from drugs and alcohol. Three-quarters worry about the negative influence of other kids on their child (Farkas, Johnson, and Duffett 2002). In addition, one-quarter worry about their children's physical safety at school (Saad 2006d). About two-thirds of parents monitor their teenagers' Internet use (Wang, Bianchi, and Raley 2005).

3. Various experts have publicized the fact that parents influence their children's health, weight, eating habits, math and language abilities, behaviors, and self-esteem (Brazelton 1997; L. Burney 2005;

Koplan, Liverman, and U.S. Institute of Medicine 2005; Nash 1997). Although much child-parenting advice is useful, the emphasis on how parents influence their children can lead us to feel anxious about our performance as parents.[2]

[2] Today you can read about how to raise "respectful" (Cartmell 2006; Rigby 2006), "happy" (Adkins 2007; Biddulph and Biddulph 2007), optimistic and "depression-proofed" (Murray and Fortinberry 2006), "successful" (Brodkin 2006; Burt and Perlis 2006), "well-adjusted" (Gangstad 2006), "confident" (Apter 2007), "socially skilled" (Markway and Markway 2006), "charitable" (Weisman 2006), "kind" (Siegel 2006), "resourceful" (Nelsen, Erwin, and Duffy 2007), "generous" (Gallo and Gallo 2005), and "balanced" kids (Campbell and Suggs 2006). You can read about how to raise kids who "make a change" (Tim Smith 2006), kids destined for "true greatness" (Kimmel 2006)—even "athletic stars" (Dance and Place 2006). *(continued)*

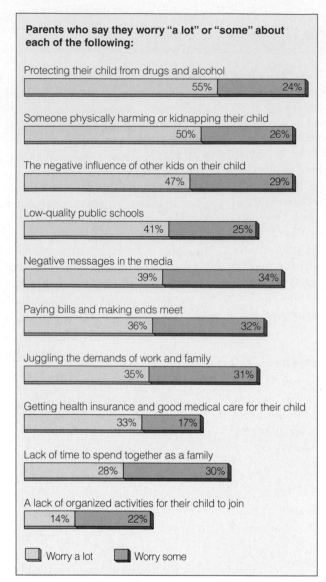

Parents who say they worry "a lot" or "some" about each of the following:

Protecting their child from drugs and alcohol
55% | 24%

Someone physically harming or kidnapping their child
50% | 26%

The negative influence of other kids on their child
47% | 29%

Low-quality public schools
41% | 25%

Negative messages in the media
39% | 34%

Paying bills and making ends meet
36% | 32%

Juggling the demands of work and family
35% | 31%

Getting health insurance and good medical care for their child
33% | 17%

Lack of time to spend together as a family
28% | 30%

A lack of organized activities for their child to join
14% | 22%

☐ Worry a lot   ▨ Worry some

FIGURE 11.1 Parents who say they worry "a lot" or "some" about each of these potential hazards.

Source: Steve Farkas, Jean Johnson, and Ann Duffett. 2002. *A Lot Easier Said Than Done: Parents Talk About Raising Children in Today's America.* Public Agenda: Report prepared for State Farm Insurance Companies. Reprinted by permission of Public Agenda Foundation, Inc.

[2] *(continued)* Advice may be specifically directed to parents who are raising boys (Cox 2006; M. Jones 2006; Lewis 2007), girls (Preuschoff 2006; Trevathan and Goff 2007), twins (Gottesman 2006; Heim 2007), children who are deaf (Marschark 2007), children with special needs (Winter 2006), and "gifted" children (Klein 2007), as well as those who are "strong-willed" (Pickhardt 2005), shy (Markway and Markway 2006), or "spirited" (Kurcinka 2006).

You can learn to raise great children properly by using "6 keys" (Leman 2006), "8 steps" (Gallo and Gallo 2005), "12 secrets" (Wright 2006a), "13 dynamics" (Inman and Koenig 2006), "52 brilliant ideas" (Dosani and Cross 2007), "101 truths" (Scott 2006), or "135 tools" (Arnall and Elicksen 2007).

4. The myriad of today's child-raising experts disagree among themselves (Murkoff 2000; Rankin 2005a, 2005b). One example of disagreement concerns spanking, an issue that we return to later in this chapter. Then, too, over the years, experts have changed their recommendations regarding some child-raising techniques. One example is whether babies should sleep alone or with their parents (Brant and Kuchment 2006).

5. Today's parents are given full responsibility for raising successful or good children, but their authority is often questioned. For example, the state may intervene in parental decisions about schooling, discipline and punishment, medical care, and children's safety as automobile passengers ("HPV Policy" 2007; Jervey 2004).

As a result of these factors, being a parent today can be far more difficult than many nonparents may realize. Also, fighting depression or other illnesses while raising children, as well as raising a child with special needs, add parenting stresses peculiar to these situations (Thomas and Dowling 2006; T. Thompson 2006; Winter 2006).

The Transition to Parenthood

Interviews in two hospitals' labor and delivery units with eighty-eight mothers and seventy-five fathers of firstborns found that "nearly all of the fathers" and two-thirds of the mothers expressed worry or concern about becoming parents: "[T]he concerns voiced by the greatest number of fathers related to his ability to 'take good enough care' of his child . . . and his ability to 'keep [his] kids safe.' . . . Among mothers, concerns about safety and finding childcare predominated" (Fox, Bruce, and Combs-Orme 2000, p. 126).

Once they get their babies home, new fathers and mothers report being bothered by the baby's interruption of their sleeping, going places, and expressing themselves sexually. Disconnected from friends and others, new mothers may feel isolated (Paris and Dubus 2005). When a new mother's expectations about how much the father will be involved with the baby are met, the transition to parenthood is easier (Fox et al. 2000). And when married parents rate their relationship quality as high, the transition to parenthood is easier, even with an unusually fussy baby (Schoppe-Sullivan et al. 2007).

Forty years ago, in what has become a classic analysis that still applies, social scientist Alice Rossi (1968) analyzed the **transition to parenthood**, comparing the circumstances involved in assuming the parent role with those of other adult roles, such as worker or spouse. The transition to parenthood, Rossi asserts, is more difficult than the transition to either of these other roles for several reasons:

One survey shows that given work and other demands, more than half of mothers wish they had more time with their children. One way that these Colorado mothers cope with time pressures is by taking their toddlers to their yoga class. One thing that may be sacrificed, however, is mom's time for personal relaxation.

1. Cultural pressure encourages adults to become parents even though they may not really want to. But once a baby is born to married or, to a lesser degree, to cohabiting couples, there is little possibility of undoing the commitment to parenthood.

The transition to parenthood can be difficult for a number of reasons, including upset schedules and lack of sleep. It can help to remember that babies have different temperaments: some are "easy," others "difficult." Many fathers today are more involved with day-to-day parenting activities than in the past—a situation that increases marital satisfaction and both parents' confidence.

2. Most first parents approach parenting with little or no previous experience in child care. This is particularly true for fathers who, as boys, were less likely than girls to have babysat (Parke and Buriel 1998).

3. Unlike other adult roles, the transition to parenting is abrupt. New parents suddenly are on twenty-four-hour duty, caring for a fragile, mysterious, and utterly dependent infant.

4. Adjusting to parenthood necessitates changes in the couple's emotional and sexual relationship (Savage 2003). In general, husbands can expect to receive less attention from their wives. Employed wives who have established fairly egalitarian relationships with their husbands may find themselves in a different role, particularly if they quit working to become full-time homemakers (see Chapter 12).

Research supports the continued validity of Rossi's analysis (Wallace and Gotlib 1990; Youngs, Heim, and Youngs 2006). [3] Along with other factors, the difficulties associated with the transition to parenthood result in postpartum depression in about 10 percent of new mothers (Formichelli 2001). It helps to know that babies are different from one another even at birth; the fact that a baby cries a lot does not necessarily mean that she or he is receiving the wrong kind of care (Rankin 2005b). Infants may have different "readabilities"—that is, varying clarity in the messages or cues they give to tell caregivers how they feel or what they want (R. Bell 1974).

Although new parents' attitudes, overall mood, and self-esteem influence how they view their babies, it also appears that babies have varied temperaments at birth (Komsi et al. 2006; Lindsey, Caldera, and Colwell 2005; Roisman and Fraley 2006). Some are "easy," responding positively to new foods, people, and situations, and transmitting consistent cues (such as tired cry or hungry cry). Other infants are more "difficult." They have irregular habits of sleeping or eating that sometimes extend into childhood; they may adapt slowly to new situations and stimuli; and they may cry endlessly, for no apparent reason.

Still other babies are neither easy nor particularly difficult (Crouter and Booth 2003; Thomas, Chess, and Birch 1968). In any event, it may help to keep in mind that "it appears that after an initial disruption, most couples . . . seem to be doing well" (Demo and Cox 2000, p. 878). Feeling support of family and friends helps (Bost, Cox, and Payne 2002).

Mothers and Fathers: Images and Reality

If we look at men and women as parents, we find a range of ideas and practices.

Old and New Images of Parents

Our cultural tradition stipulates that mothers assume primary responsibility for child raising (Cancian and Oliker 2000). In the United States, the mother is generally expected to be the child's primary *psychological parent*, assuming the major emotional responsibility for the safety and upbringing of her children (Ridgeway and Correll 2004). The "enduring image of motherhood" includes the idea that "[a] woman enjoys and intuitively knows what to do for her child; she cares for her child without ambivalence or awkwardness" (Thompson and Walker 1991, p. 91). She is "perfect"—self-sacrificing virtually without limit. This image of motherhood persists, even when Mom is employed (Schafer 2006; Warner 2005). And what about fathers?

Good Dad—Bad Dad Fathers were once expected to be mainly providers or breadwinners, not necessarily competent in or desirous of nurturing children on a day-to-day basis (Gerson 1997). Succeeding the breadwinner-only father, we now have the opposite images of the *good dad* and the *bad,* or "deadbeat," *dad* (Furstenberg 1991). "Good" fathers not only take financial responsibility for their children but also are actively involved in child care (Crosby, Williams, and Biernat 2004).

An opposite image is of "deadbeat dads." From this vantage point, a growing category of men "are eschewing even minimal responsibility for their children" (Gerson 1997, p. 119; see also Blankenhorn 1995). However, unwed, non-custodial, poverty-level fathers may not have the means to support their children financially. In addition,

[c]hild support policy does not allow fathers to substitute the provision of in-kind services when circumstances prevent their economic support. For example, absent, unemployed fathers are not permitted to provide child care that might allow the mother to continue working and reduce the cost of such care to her in place of their child support payment. . . . The potential use and effect of alternative forms of support by the absent father is unknown. . . . Thus, the role of breadwinner is the most visible socially prescribed duty of the paternal role in the American construction of fatherhood. While its successful performance is critical to the economic well-being of children, its primacy tends to relegate [poverty-level] fathers to a peripheral function in their child's development. (Kost 2001)

Furthermore, racial/ethnic stereotyping gives us an exaggerated, negative image of African Americans and Latinos as parents: black matriarchs; aloof or absent black fathers; macho, authoritarian Latino fathers (Cose 1994b; Robert Hill 2004). But, because they are exaggerated, "these images are myths: black couples share child raising no less, and perhaps more, than white couples, and black husbands are as intimately involved with their children as white husbands" (Thompson and Walker 1991, p. 91).

Recent research, especially on fathers, has "alerted us to the historical flexibility of fatherhood" (Marsiglio et al. 2000, p. 1175) and of motherhood as well (Arendell 2000). In other words, throughout history parents have never completely conformed with dominant cultural images. Contrary to stereotypes, there are women who do not want to be involved in the daily care of children, "and many men [who] do" (Cancian and Oliker 2000, p. 48). (See "Facts about Families: Fathers as Primary Parents.") With an idea of our varied cultural images of fathers and mothers, we'll look briefly at what mothers and fathers actually do.

Mothers and Fathers: What Do They Do?

Mothers typically engage in more hands-on parenting and take primary responsibility for children, whereas fathers are often viewed as helping (Cancian and Oliker 2000). As Figure 11.2 makes clear, "Despite much attention in recent years to the so-called 'new, nurturing father' and some change on men's part, women still do most child raising (and homemaking)" (Arendell 2000, p. 1198; Bianchi, Robinson, and Milkie 2006). As one example, mothers in two-parent families are far more likely than fathers to attend school conferences and class events and to serve as school volunteers (U.S. Census Bureau 2003a, Table 234). In addition, a mother may try to manage her child(ren)'s relationship with their father

Fathers as Primary Parents

Some fathers who serve as primary, or principal, parents are single, usually divorced but also possibly never-married or widowed. A single custodial father may be cohabiting or not. Other men serving as primary parents are stay-at-home married fathers with wives in the labor force. Compared to mothers, the proportion of fathers who serve as the principal parent is small. However, their numbers have significantly increased over the past twenty years. Take a look at the following facts:

1. About 5 percent of all U.S. children under age fifteen—or 3.3 million children—are living with single fathers (Fields 2003, p. 5).

2. About 1.1 million children under age fifteen live with a single father who is cohabiting (Fields 2003, p. 5).

3. About 5 percent of black and Hispanic children live with single fathers, compared to 4 percent of non-Hispanic white children and 2 percent of Asian and Pacific Islander children (Fields 2003, Figure 1).

4. Another 1.5 million children under age fifteen are living in two-parent families with a stay-at-home father (Fields 2003, p. 10).

5. Among these children, about 336,000 had fathers who told the U.S. Census Bureau that their primary reason for staying home was to "care for home and family" (Fields 2003, Table 5).

6. Some stay-at-home, married fathers have been laid off and decided to stay out of the workforce. Others have wives who earned more than they did and began to question the logic of spending money on day care and sending the children away to day care when the father could stay at home. Others are "trailing husbands," who follow their wives to new career positions (Conlin 2001).

7. Some fathers who are primary parents and their children are homeless ("Homeless Fathers with Children" n.d.).

8. Whether married or single, whether poor or financially better off, fathers as primary parents report facing isolation and stereotyping (Allen 2001).

9. In response, primary-parent fathers have begun to organize support groups, often on the Internet (www.dadstayshome.com; http://slowlane.com).

Critical Thinking

How might the higher visibility of fathers as primary parents change neighborhoods? What might be some similarities between single-parent fathers and single-parent mothers? Some differences?

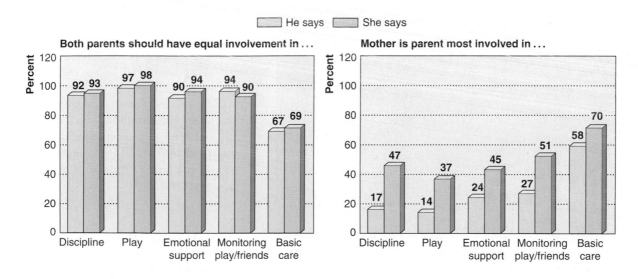

FIGURE 11.2 Who *should do* vs. who *does* the most parenting?

Source: M. Milkie, S. M. Bianchi, M. Mattingly, and J. Robinson. 2000. "Fathers' Involvement in Childrearing: Ideals, Realities, and Their Relationship to Parental Well-Being." Revised version of a paper presented at the American Association for Public Opinion Research, Portland, Oregon, May 18–21.

by encouraging father–child activities and constructing for them a positive image of him (Seery and Crowley 2000). The intense daily contact with children is viewed ambivalently by many mothers: as a source of great life satisfaction but also a source of a great deal of frustration and stress (Warner 2006).

In the past, research on parent roles viewed fathers as financial providers, disciplinarians, and "playmates," while mothers were seen mainly as "caregivers and comfort givers" (Thompson and Walker 1991, pp. 91–92). But as women have entered the labor force in greater numbers, many men have been encouraged by their family's need and the redefinition of male roles to want to play a larger part in the day-to-day care of the family (Bianchi, Robinson, and Milkie 2006; Bulanda 2004). Doing errands, planning, sharing activities, and teaching their children, married fathers are increasingly invested in their children (Strand 2004; Yeung et al. 2001). When mothers see fathers as competent parents—and when fathers believe that their wives have confidence in them— fathers are more likely to be highly involved (Fagan and Barnett 2003; Pasley, Futris, and Skinner 2002).

Sharing Parenthood

A recent national survey shows that about two-thirds of married couples report that they share parental responsibilities (Erickson and Aird 2005, Table 2). Diane Ehrensaft (1990) searched for these "new" parents to learn more about them. Interviewing and observing forty

Many relationship dynamics affect parenting. Fathers and mothers not only relate individually to their children and to each other but also relate in a *parenting alliance*—that is, as co-parents to their children. Authoritative co-parents are emotionally involved with their children, setting limits while encouraging them to develop and practice their talents.

shared-parenting couples, she defined **shared parenting** not in terms of time, but rather as an identity. Her central question was this: Were both father and mother **primary parents**—a couple "mothering together"—rather than one parent and one helper?

Three factors affected parents' commitment to shared parenting. First, many couples were strongly influenced by the feminist movement. Second, many of the fathers were in occupations related to children, such as child psychology. Finally, both parents tended to have good job security, so they could risk the displeasure of their supervisors in giving time to parenthood. Nevertheless, there was a tendency to backslide as the husband's income outpaced the wife's. Mothers, more than fathers, engaged in "worrying" (anticipating and coping with problems) and gave more attention to the "psychological management" of children. They devoted more attention than their husbands did to the child's clothing or birthday parties, for example. There was a tendency for mothers to "take over" in these areas.

Despite the fact that they reported having little time alone together, the couples in Ehrensaft's study felt that their relationship was strengthened by shared parenting. Moreover, research generally shows that shared parenting decreases children's behavior problems (Amato and Rivera 1999) and increases partners' feelings of competence as parents and spouses' marital satisfaction (Ehrenberg et al. 2001; Kluwer, Heesink, and Van de Vliert 2002). An interesting study of two-parent Mexican American families concluded that when the **parenting alliance**—that is, the degree to which partners agree with and support each other as parents—is strong, both children and parents are happier (Formoso et al. 2007).

As discussed in "Issues for Thought: Growing Up in a Household Characterized by Conflict," being raised in a family with ongoing conflict is statistically related to less-desirable outcomes for children. Shared parenting is probably more satisfying for parents and effective for children when both parents use an authoritative parenting style (Lindsey and Mize 2001).

Authoritative Parenting

Children's needs differ according to their age. For instance, in order to establish the basic human trust that is

A home characterized by significant, ongoing conflict has a negative impact on the couple's children (J. Siegel 2000). Researchers divide children's behavior problems into two categories: externalizing (aggression, lying, cheating, running away from home, disobeying at school, delinquency) and internalizing (withdrawal, depression, and anxiety). At least since the 1980s, researchers have consistently found a link between marital conflict and both types of behavior problems in children (Dukes 2003; Gerard, Krishnakumar, and Buehler 2006).

One study (Buehler et al. 1998) sampled 337 sixth- through eighth-grade girls and boys, age ten through fifteen, in Utah and Tennessee. Three-quarters of the children were non-Hispanic white, 12 percent were Hispanic, and 13 percent represented other racial/ethnic groups. Most families were middle class; 85 percent of the children had their own bedroom, for example. The parents of 87 percent of the children in the sample were married. The parents' average education level was somewhere between high school graduate and some college.

The students were asked to fill out questionnaires that assessed their behavior and any conflict between their parents. Externalizing behavior problems were measured by students' agreeing or disagreeing with statements such as "I cheat a lot" or "I tease others a lot." Internalizing behavior problems were measured by students' agreeing or disagreeing with statements such as "I am unhappy a lot" or "I worry a lot." The children were also asked how often their parents disagreed on certain topics. Then they were asked about the style

of their parents' conflict. Overt parental conflict styles involved such things as the parents' calling each other names, telling each other to shut up, or threatening each other in front of the child. Covert parental conflict styles included such things as trying to get the child to side with one parent and asking the child to relay a message from one parent to the other because the parents didn't want to talk to each other.

The researchers found that conflict between parents was far from the only cause of children's behavior problems. Nevertheless, for both girls and boys, the researchers did find a strong correlation between interparental conflict and behavior problems. This relationship held true regardless of whether the parents were married or divorced. When parents displayed an overt conflict style, the youth were more likely to report externalizing behavior problems; this relationship was stronger for fifth graders than it was for eighth graders. When parents displayed a more covert conflict style, the youth were more likely to report internalizing behavior problems. In the researchers' words, "The results of our study confirm previous findings that hostile and sometimes violent ways of managing interparental disagreements place youth at risk for problem behaviors" (p. 130).

In another study of fifty-five Caucasian middle- and upper-middle-class five-year-olds (twenty-six girls and twenty-nine boys) and their married mothers, the mothers completed questionnaires on parent–child relations and interparental arguing that were mailed to them at home. Later, the mothers took

their children to be observed in a university laboratory setting. The researchers found that marital discord was positively related both to children's externalizing and internalizing behavior problems. However, this research also showed that the interparental conflict influenced a child's behavior *indirectly:* Marital discord negatively affected parental discipline and the parent–child relationship more generally; this situation negatively affected the child's behavior. The researchers concluded that "if parents are able to maintain good relations with children in the face of marital conflict, the children may be buffered from the potential emotional fallout of the conflict" (Harrist and Ainslie 1998, p. 156; see also Buehler and Gerard 2002).

Generally, these two studies and others (Cummings et al. 2002; Katz and Woodin 2002) show that choices about one's marital conflict styles affect not only spouses but their children as well. Furthermore, "unlike children of divorce, children with parents in conflicted marriages (who do not divorce) may be unable to escape from their parents' marital problems—even into adulthood" (Amato and Afifi 2006, p. 222). Whether children are better off in two-parent conflict habituated households or in single-parent households is discussed in Chapter 16.

Critical Thinking

In your opinion, which is more stressful—growing up in a conflict-habituated, two-parent home, or growing up in a single-parent household as a result of divorce? Why?

---

a prelude to normal development, infants need to bond with a consistent and dependable caregiver (Brazelton and Greenspan 2000; Karen 1994). Like anyone else, they need positive, affectionate, intimate relationships as well as encouragement, conversation, and variety in

their environment in order to develop emotionally and intellectually (Brazelton and Greenspan 2000; Khaleque and Rohner 2002; Rankin 2005b). (Discipline is never appropriate for babies.) Preschool children need opportunities to practice motor development as well as wide exposure to language, especially when people talk directly to them (Cowley 2000). They also need consistent, clear definitions of what behavior is unacceptable (Del Vecchio and O'Leary 2006; Dorman 2006; Junn and Boyatzis 2005).

School-age children need to practice accomplishing goals appropriate to their abilities (Hofferth and Sandberg 2001) and to learn how to get along with others. In order to better accept criticism as they get older, they need realistic feedback regarding task performance, not exaggerated praise (Dinkmeyer, McKay, and Dinkmeyer 1997; Jayson 2005b). They also need to feel that they are contributing family members by being assigned tasks and taught how to do them. (Those who are not given responsibility for their share of household chores may have trouble feeling that they belong, or they may become demanding because they have learned to belong as consumers rather than as productive family members [Dinkmeyer, McKay, and Dinkmeyer 1997].)

Although the majority of teenagers do not cause familial "storm and stress" (Kantrowitz and Springen 2005), the teen years do have the special potential of creating conflict between parent and child (Booth, Carver, and Granger 2000). Adolescents need firm guidance, coupled with parental accessibility and emotional support, as they search for identity and begin to define who they are and will be as adults (W. Collins 1990; Guilamo-Ramos et al. 2006; D. Walsh 2004, 2007). They also need to learn effective methods for resolving conflict (Tucker, McHale, and Crouter 2003). Throughout this period, it's important for parents to remember "the obvious fact that most adolescents make it to adulthood relatively unscathed and prepared to accept and assume adult roles" (Furstenberg 2000, p. 903).

Despite age-related differences in children's needs, virtually all children benefit from authoritative parenting (Junn and Boyatzis 2005). From one point of view, there are as many parenting styles as there are parents. Nevertheless, parents and stepparents will gradually establish a **parenting style**—a general manner of relating to and disciplining their children. We can distinguish among authoritarian, laissez-faire, and authoritative parenting styles (Baumrind 1978). The **authoritarian parenting style** is characterized as low on emotional nurturing and support but high on parental direction and control. The authoritarian parent's attitude is "I am in charge and set/enforce the rules, no matter what." Characterized as emotionally aloof or harsh, parents using this style often use physical or otherwise harsh punishment (Manisses Communications Group 2000).

In contrast, the **laissez-faire parenting style** is permissive, allowing children to set their own limits with little or no parental guidance. This parenting style, although low on parental direction or control, may be high on parental emotional nurturing—a situation that "leads to the classic 'spoiled child.'" This parenting style is characterized by the statement "I often give in to my child's arguing, whining, and other demands." A variant of the laissez-faire parenting style is low on both parental direction and emotional support—a situation of emotional neglect. This style is characterized by the statement "I spend little time with my child" or "I feel overwhelmed and am almost ready to give up on my child" (Manisses Communications Group 2000, p. S1). Both authoritarian and laissez-faire parenting styles are associated with children's and adolescents' depression and otherwise poor mental health, low school performance, behavior problems, high rates of teen sexuality and pregnancy, and juvenile delinquency (Longmore, Manning, and Giordano 2001; Morris et al. 2002; Parcel and Dufur 2001).

Child psychologists prefer the **authoritative parenting style**. This style, described as "warm, firm, and fair" (Gray and Steinberg 1999), combines emotional nurturing and support with parental direction. Authoritative parenting involves encouraging the child's individuality and accepting the child's personality, talents, and emerging independence, while also consciously setting limits and enforcing rules (Brooks and Goldstein 2001; Ginott, Ginott, and Goddard 2003).[4] The authoritative parent monitors the child's activities and behavior, and gives appropriate consequences for misbehavior.

As the child grows older, the authoritative parent increasingly considers the child's point of view when setting rules. I-statements (see Chapter 13) from parent to child can help. For example, "I get angry when you leave the car without gas in it, and I go out to work and find the tank empty." Or "I was worried because I hadn't heard from you and you weren't answering your cell phone." ("As We Make Choices: Communicating with Children—How to Talk So Kids Will Listen and Listen So Kids Will Talk" offers some important advice on parenting.)

Authoritative parents would agree with the statements "I communicate rules clearly and directly," "I consider my child's wishes and opinions along with my own when making decisions," "I value my child's school achievement and support my child's efforts," and "I expect my child to act independently at an age-appropriate level" (Manisses Communications Group 2000, p. S1). Believ-

---

[4] Limits are best set as house rules and stated objectively in third-person terms. A parent may say, for example, "Chairs are for sitting in, not for jumping on." With preschoolers, limits need to be set and stated very clearly: A parent who says "Don't go too far from home" leaves "too far" to the child's interpretation. "Don't go out of the yard at all" is a wiser rule. As the child learns to distinguish what is "too much," limits may be more flexible.

As We Make Choices

Communicating with Children—How to Talk So Kids Will Listen and Listen So Kids Will Talk

There are more and less effective ways to communicate with children, and a knowledgeable choice would probably involve more effective ways. What are some of these methods?

Helping Children Deal with Their Feelings

Children—including adult children—need to have their feelings accepted and respected.

1. *You can listen quietly and attentively.*

2. *You can acknowledge their feelings with a word.* "Oh . . . mmm . . . I see. . . ."

3. *You can give the feeling a name.* "That sounds frustrating!"

4. *You can note that all feelings are accepted, but certain actions must be limited.* "I can see how angry you are at your brother. Tell him what you want with words, not fists."

Engaging a Child's Cooperation

1. *Describe what you see, or describe the problem.* "There's a wet towel on the bed."

2. *Give information.* "The towel is getting my blanket wet."

3. *Describe what you feel.* "I don't like sleeping in a wet bed!"

4. *Write a note* (above towel rack): Please put me back so I can dry. Thanks! Your Towel

Instead of Punishment

1. *Express your feelings strongly—without attacking character.* "I'm furious that my saw was left outside to rust in the rain!"

2. *State your expectations.* "I expect my tools to be returned after they've been borrowed."

3. *Show the child how to make amends.* "What this saw needs now is a little steel wool and a lot of elbow grease."

4. *Give the child a choice.* "You can borrow my tools and return them, or you can give up the privilege of using them. You decide."

Encouraging Autonomy

1. *Let children make choices.* "Are you in the mood for your gray pants today or your red pants?"

2. *Show respect for a child's struggle.* "A jar can be hard to open."

3. *Don't ask too many questions.* "Glad to see you. Welcome home."

4. *Don't rush to answer questions.* "That's an interesting question. What do you think?"

5. *Encourage children to use sources outside the home.* "Maybe the pet shop owner would have a suggestion."

6. *Don't take away hope.* "So you're thinking of trying out for the play! That should be an experience."

Praise and Self-Esteem

Instead of evaluating, describe.

1. *Describe what you see.* "I see your car parked exactly where we agreed it would be."

2. *Describe what you feel.* "It's a pleasure to walk into this room!"

3. *Sum up the child's praiseworthy behavior with a word.* "You sorted out your pencils, crayons, and pens, and put them in separate boxes. That's what I call *organization!*"

Freeing Children from Playing Roles

1. *Look for opportunities to show the child a new picture of himself or herself.* "You've had that toy since you were three, and it looks almost like new!"

2. *Put children in situations in which they can see themselves differently.* "Sara, would you take the screwdriver and tighten the pulls on these drawers?"

3. *Let children overhear you say something positive about them.* "He held his arm steady even though the shot hurt."

4. *Model the behavior you'd like to see.* "It's hard to lose, but I'll try to be a sport about it. Congratulations!"

5. *Be a storehouse for your child's special moments.* "I remember the time you. . . ."

Critical Thinking

What bit of advice given here might you choose to practice when communicating with the child(ren) in your life? Why is it important to encourage children to talk? Why is it important to listen to children? Why does how we talk to children matter?

ing that the parent can be counted on for direction and assistance if needed, the child likely views the authoritative parent as loving, responsive, and involved (Gray and Steinberg 1999). Regardless of ethnicity, parental education, or family structure, authoritative parents tend to have children who do better in school and are socially competent, with relatively high self-esteem and cooperative, yet independent, personalities (Amato and Fowler 2002; Brooks and Goldstein 2001; Crosnoe 2004).

However, we need to note that more and more scholars of color view the authoritarian/laissez-faire/authoritative model as biased and ethnocentric or Eurocentric. For instance, one recent study shows that authoritative parenting is a more important prediction of children's behavior for those of European descent than for the Hmong (Supple and Small 2006). Some scholars argue that the authoritarian/laissez-faire/authoritative model uses European, white, middle-class parenting beliefs, values, and behaviors as the standard to which all others are—usually unfavorably—compared (Greenfield and Suzuki 2001; McLoyd et al. 2000). This point is developed throughout the section "Racial/Ethnic Diversity and Parenting," later in this chapter. The next section focuses on the question of whether spanking is ever appropriate.

Is Spanking Ever Appropriate?

In 2007, a California state legislator proposed legislation that would have outlawed spanking children under three years old. Had the proposal become law, California would have joined the approximately fifteen European nations in which spanking children is illegal (Straus 2007). However, the California-based suggestion met enough negative media response that the idea was dropped, and the proposed bill was revised to involve only more serious forms of corporal punishment, such as kicking or hitting a child with an implement (Steinhauer 2007a; Yi 2007). Whether spanking children is ever a good idea is controversial in the United States.

Spanking refers to hitting a child with an open hand without causing physical injury. It is estimated that between 70 and 90 percent of U.S. parents spank their children, at least occasionally (Benjet and Kazdin 2003). Analysis of data from the 13,000 respondents in the National Survey of Families and Households shows that about one-third of fathers and 44 percent of mothers had spanked their children during the week prior to being interviewed. Boys, especially those under age two, are spanked the most often. Children over age six are spanked less often, but some parents spank their children during early adolescence. Mothers spank more often than fathers. African American mothers, but not fathers, spank more frequently than most other racial/ethnic groups. Younger, less-educated parents in larger households with more children and less social support, parents who argue a lot with their children, and those with a fundamentalist religious orientation are more likely to spank. "It is clear . . . that wide variations in the incidence of spanking and extensive differences in its intensity are certainly prevalent" (Day, Peterson, and McCracken 1998, p. 91).

Pediatricians as well as researchers have conflicting opinions about whether it is appropriate ever to spank a child (Benjet and Kazdin 2003; Larzelere 1996; Saadeh, Rizzo, and Roberts 2002). A leading domestic violence researcher, sociologist Murray Straus (1996, 1999a, 2001), advises parents never to hit children of any age under any circumstances. Research by Straus and his colleagues has shown that children who have been spanked by their parents—even if infrequently and by parents who are otherwise loving—are more likely later to cheat or tell lies, bully or be cruel or mean to others, disobey in school, and misbehave in other ways (Straus and Mouradian 1998).

Furthermore, at least among non-Hispanic white children, being frequently spanked in childhood is linked to later behavior problems, as well as to depression, suicide, alcohol or drug abuse, and physical aggression against one's parents in adolescence and to abusing one's own children and violence against an intimate partner in adulthood (Slade and Wissow 2004; Straus 1999a; Swinford et al. 2000). Straus has argued that spanking teaches children a "hidden agenda"—that it is all right to hit someone and that those who love you hit you. This confusion of love with violence sets the stage for spouse abuse (Straus and Yodanis 1996; Straus 2007). Then, too, especially when a parent spanks in anger—which is never advised—"mild spanking can escalate and apparently does mix in with more severe hitting" (Kazdin and Benjet 2003, p. 102).

However, some researchers contend that Straus and others may be overstating their case (Saadeh, Rizzo, and Roberts 2002). For instance, psychologist Marjorie Gunnoe (cited in S. Gilbert 1997) theorizes that spanking is most likely to result in children's aggressive behavior only when they perceive being spanked as an aggressive act. She hypothesizes that children under age eight tend to think it is their parent's right to spank them; older children, who are less willing to accept parental authority, are more likely to see being spanked as aggressive. Gunnoe also hypothesizes that African American children are more inclined than others to see spanking as acceptable, because spanking is generally accepted in the black community. "It is likely that any effects of parenting discipline practice are moderated by scores of variables related to the child, parent, family, and . . . culture" (Kazdin and Benjet 2003, p. 102).

Nevertheless, child-raising experts find many reasons to discourage spanking. For one thing, physical punishment "may interfere with the development of a child's conscience. *Spanking relieves guilt too easily:* The child, having paid for the misbehavior, feels free to repeat it" (Ginott, Ginott, and Goddard 2003, p. 133, italics in original). Many parents feel that when all else fails, spanking works (although spanking can also encourage a child to misbehave further, even immediately). But research shows that spanking is seldom more effective

Children have a certain degree of resilience, which is enhanced by strong familial bonds. The self-esteem they gain through their family and friends can help them in becoming self-confident adults.

than timeouts or short-term loss of privileges (Kazdin and Benjet 2003).

Straus has argued that spanking usually accompanies other, more effective discipline methods such as explaining or depriving privileges. These nonspanking discipline methods are effective by themselves, and parents should be encouraged to follow the principle of "just leave out the spanking part" (Straus 1999a, p. 8; Straus 2007). Consensus statements drafted at the 1996 Conference of the American Academy of Pediatrics advise that children under two years old and adolescents should *never* be spanked and "recommends that parents be encouraged and assisted in the development of methods other than spanking for managing undesired behavior" (American Academy of Pediatrics 1998).

The Resilient Child

This textbook is written for people interested enough in parenting and family life to take a course. But no one is perfect; most parents have failings of one sort or another. Parents may encounter serious problems in their lives, problems that affect their children: pov-

erty, discrimination, divorce, unemployment, legal and financial conflicts, scandal, sudden change of residence, crime victimization, military service, war, death, mental illness, drug or alcohol abuse, or family violence.

The hope that research in child development offers to parents who make mistakes is that children can be surprisingly resilient (Brooks and Goldstein 2001; Furstenberg and Hughes 1995; L. Rubin 1997). As an example, a long-term study was conducted in Hawaii based on a sample of all the children (698) born on the island of Kauai in 1955—one-half of whom were in poverty, and one-sixth of whom were physically or intellectually handicapped. A smaller group of 225 children was identified as being at high risk of poor developmental outcomes. Researchers found that even one-third of this last group "grew into competent young adults who loved well, worked well, played well, and expected well" (Werner 1992, p. 263). The researchers spoke of a "self-righting tendency" whereby children lucky enough to have certain characteristics—a sociable personality, self-esteem derived from a particular talent, a support network, and, above all, a good relationship with at least one caring adult—emerged into adulthood in good shape (Werner 1992; Werner and Smith 2001).

Risk is risk, but hope is not unrealistic (Brooks and Goldstein 2001). Other research indicates that "[a]dults who acknowledge and seem to have worked through difficulties of their childhood are apparently protected against inflicting them on their children" (Belsky 1991, p. 124). There is also evidence that a conscientious **para-parent**—an unrelated adult who informally plays a parentlike role for a child—can generate a resilient child (Johnson 2000; Soukhanov 1996). One form of para-parent is the "social father"—"a male relative or family associate who demonstrates parental behaviors and is like a father to the child"—and research on social fathers' influence on preschoolers' development found that "male relative social fathers are associated with higher levels of children's school readiness, whereas mothers' romantic partner social fathers are associated with lower levels of emotional maturity" (Jayakody and Kalil 2002, p. 504). We turn next to an examination of parenting differences related to social class.

Social Class and Parenting

As Chapter 3 points out, virtually all life experiences (and opportunities, or "life chances") are mediated or influenced by social class—one's overall status in a society, often measured by educational achievement, occupation, and/or income. Parenting is no exception (Bornstein and Bradley 2003; Furstenberg 2006; Hitlin 2006). You'll recall a theme of this text: Decisions are influenced by social conditions that limit or expand a decision maker's options. This section examines some ways that the conditions of social class affect a parent's options and decisions.

The Working Poor

The majority of poor parents are employed and live in rented homes, apartments, or motel rooms (Ehrenreich 2001). These "working poor" have minimum- or less-than-minimum-wage jobs with irregular and unpredictable hours and no medical insurance or other benefits. Some parents classified as "working poor" have two or three jobs (Ames, Brosi, and Damiano-Teixeira 2006). Working full time at minimum wage does not earn a parent enough money to live above the poverty line.

Nearly 11 percent of all children (8 percent of white, 14 percent of black, and 23 percent of Hispanic children) have no health insurance, either public or private (Cohen and Bloom 2005; U.S. Federal Interagency Forum 2004, Table ECON5.A). Many mothers who have been affected by the **Temporary Assistance for Needy Families (TANF)** Act lack job skills that might yield above-poverty wages, and many more face problems with job, day-care, or transportation availability (Monroe and Tiller 2001). The long-term consequences of TANF remain to be seen (Seccombe 2007). However, many organizations, including the National Coalition for the Homeless, for example, argue that welfare changes have increased poverty and family homelessness ("Homeless Families with Children" 2001; Seccombe 2007).

Meanwhile, children living in poverty—more often disabled or chronically ill than other children—have expensive health care needs that are not always or completely covered by welfare or other social services (Cohen and Bloom 2005; Lukemeyer, Meyers, and Smeeding 2000). Many poor families move often from city to city to move in with relatives or to search for jobs. This makes it difficult for a parent to establish support systems and hinders children's chances for school continuity and success (Molyneux 1995).

Assuredly, raising children in poverty is qualitatively different from doing so otherwise. Poverty-level parents and their children have poorer nutrition; more illnesses such as asthma (Akinbami 2006; Crouter and Booth

Raising children while in poverty is a very different experience from parenting in wealthier social classes. Besides concerns for basic necessities, such as food, clothing, shelter, and health care, poverty-level parents may live in depressingly blighted neighborhoods. When this photo was taken, several months after Hurricane Katrina struck, these children were living in a gutted home in New Orleans.

2004); schools that are less safe; and limited access to quality medical care (Barton 1999; Seccombe 2007). Items that other Americans take for granted, such as relatively safe, gang-free neighborhoods, are often unavailable (O'Hare and Mather 2003), and parental control is harder to achieve in neighborhoods characterized by antisocial behavior (Browning, Leventhal, and Brooks-Gunn 2005; VanDorn, Bowen, and Blau 2006). Given these circumstances, it seems unsurprising that children raised in poverty are significantly more likely (7.8 percent) to have emotional or behavioral difficulties than children raised in families that are not poor (4.6 percent) (Simons et al. 2006, p. 3). Growing up in poverty is associated with emotional and behavioral problems in adolescence, the ramifications of which may persist into adulthood (Sobolewski and Amato 2005; Vandewater and Lansford 2005).

Nevertheless, many working-poor parents *do* promote academic success in their children (Woolley and Grogan-Kaylor 2006). One longitudinal, qualitative study of preschoolers born to low-income adolescent mothers found that children of mothers whose parenting style was generally authoritative made a better adjustment to school (Luster et al. 2000).

Homeless Families Over the past two decades a shortage of affordable housing has helped create a significant and visible number of homeless families—a phenomenon that thirty years ago would have been unthinkable.

> Declining wages have put housing out of reach for many families: in every state, metropolitan area, county, and town, more than the minimum wage is required to afford a one- or two-bedroom apartment at Fair Market Rent. In fact, the median wage needed to afford a two-bedroom apartment is more than twice the minimum wage. ("Homeless Families with Children" 2001).

Partly as a result of changes to the welfare laws (Quindlen 2001; Seccombe 2000), described in Chapter 7, approximately 40 percent of the homeless today are mothers and children, with children under age eighteen making up about one-quarter of the homeless. Fathers who are their children's primary parent are also found among the homeless ("Homeless Fathers with Children" n.d.). Families with children are among the fastest-growing segments of the homeless population ("Who Is Homeless?" 2004).

Homeless parents, especially those who have been without housing for a longer time, move often and have little in the way of a helpful social network ("Homeless Families with Children" 2001). "Length-of-stay restrictions in shelters, short stays with friends and relatives, and/or relocation to seek employment make it difficult for homeless children to attend school regularly" ("Education of Homeless Children and Youth" 2001). (See Chapter 15's "A Closer Look at Family Diversity: Stressor Pile-Up Among Single-Mother Families in Homeless Shelters.")

Middle- and Upper-Middle-Class Parents

Incomes have grown little for middle-class parents, who have experienced increased economic uncertainty: For example, can they pay off their credit card debt or count on continued health insurance or pension benefits (Colliver 2006)? Upper-middle-class parents, on the other hand, may not have significant family wealth but do earn high salaries as corporate executives and professionals: physicians or attorneys, for example. Other professionals, such as college professors, accountants, engineers, architects, and psychotherapists, may not earn quite so much money but have a comfortable income that supports an upper-middle-class lifestyle.

More than 90 percent of households with incomes of $100,000 or more have Internet access, compared with just 31 percent of those making less than $25,000 (Day, Janus, and Davis 2005, Table A). Upper-middle-class parents have the money to fit the idealized cultural image of the self-sufficient nuclear family (Cancian and Oliker 2000). For instance, one married parent in this

social class is more likely than in lower social classes to embrace the option of not working outside the home (Story 2005; Tyre 2006b; Wallis 2004). Indeed, upper-middle-class families have considerably more options than do those in lower social classes.

For instance, they can better afford to choose the neighborhood—and the neighborhood school—in which they want to raise and educate their children (Sweet, Swisher, and Moen 2005). Among other factors, parents' choice of a neighborhood because of school quality is associated with less negative risk-taking behavior among teens (Knoester, Haynie, and Stephens 2006). Upper-middle-class parents can send their offspring away to college and sometimes to private schools. On a different level (but one that points up the myriad of daily-life advantages), upper-middle-class parents can hire personal parenting coaches (K. Harvey 2002) or household help; or they can purchase an automobile for their adolescent so that sharing a parent's car is unnecessary.

Research shows that while working-class parents tend to emphasize obedience and conformity, middle- and upper-middle-class parents more often foster language and critical thinking skills, self-direction, and initiative in their children (Lareau 2006; T. Smith 1999).[5] Tending to adopt a more authoritative parenting style, emphasizing a child's happiness, creativity, achievement, and independence, middle- and upper-middle class parents are generally less restrictive and more "affectionate and responsive" (Belsky 1991, p. 122). As a group, they have the material and educational resources to better prepare their children for occupational success. (For one thing, better-educated parents are more likely to discourage their children from watching television while encouraging them to read or study [Hofferth and Sandberg 2001].)

The "Hurried Child" Although there is some recent evidence that tightly scheduling a child may not be harmful (Cloud 2007), at least some critics argue that many parents, especially those in the middle and upper-middle classes, place too many demands on their children by engaging them in all sorts of private lessons, extracurricular activities associated with school or church, and organized recreational programs—even encouraging them

---

[5] During the second half of the twentieth century, child development advice became widely dispersed through the popular media. Despite a convergence of available professional information about child raising across social classes, educational, neighborhood/community, and extended-family differences continue to result in different social classes' receiving of different information regarding child rearing. Also, parents in different social classes may interpret the same professional advice in different ways (W. Walsh 2002).

to compete for places in the most preferred preschools (Saulny 2006). According to critics, such parents may be determined to raise "trophy kids" (Kirn and Cole 2001; E. Zimmerman 2004).

But, as developmental psychologist David Elkind (1988) first warned in the 1980s, "scheduled hyperactivity" (Kantrowitz 2000b)—or "hyper-parenting" (Rosenfeld and Wise 2001)—can produce the "hurried child," not to mention frazzled parents (Warner 2006). The over-scheduled or "hurried child" is forced to assume too many challenges and responsibilities too soon (Elkind 2007a, 2007b; Rosenfeld and Wise 2001). Hurried children may achieve in adult ways at a young age, but they also suffer the stress induced by the pressure to achieve (Anderson and Doherty 2005). Or they may "drop out" and abandon goal-directed academic and/or extracurricular activity. A related issue involves schools' hurrying of children with the increased use of standardized testing and decreased emphasis on music, art, or time for spontaneity and play (Cloud 2007; Trudeau 2006; Tyre 2006a).

Parents can help to relieve this situation by checking on whether they have realistic expectations for their children and by moderating unreasonable outside demands. Some parents have created an organization called "Family Life 1st!" that encourages and supports parents who want to do less carpooling to children's organized activities and have more unscheduled family time (Kantrowitz 2000b).

This section has described various parenting issues associated with different social classes, regardless of ethnicity. The next section addresses racial/ethnic diversity with regard to raising children.

"So many toys—so little time."

Racial/Ethnic Diversity and Parenting

Chapter 3 points out that social class may be more important than race in terms of parental values and interactions with children (Lareau 2003b). At the same time, social scientists do look at how various U.S. ethnic groups evidence culturally specific parenting styles (Cohen, Tran, and Rhee 2007; Giles-Sims and Lockhart 2005). The major focus of this section, however, is on the particular challenges faced by racial/ethnic minority parents in the United States today.

As a beginning, we need to note that there is considerable overlap among class and racial/ethnic categories. The upper class is almost entirely white. The upper-middle class, still largely white, now includes substantial numbers of people of color, particularly Asians. Other Asians, especially Southeast Asians, remain in lower social classes. Many African American families are now solidly middle class. Meanwhile, African Americans, Native Americans, Latinos, and some Asians are heavily represented in the working class and overrepresented in the poverty ranks. Within the broad "poverty" category, blacks are much more likely to live in neighborhoods of "extreme poverty," those where two-fifths of the population is poor. It is important to remember, though, that a majority of African Americans are now members of the working or middle class.

African American Parents and Children

Evidence suggests that African American (as well as Hispanic and Asian American) parents' attitudes, behaviors, and hopes for their children are similar to those of other parents in their social class (Julian, McKenry, and McKelvey 1994; Peters 2007). Middle-class parents of all racial/ethnic groups are more alike than different, and so are poverty-level parents. Upper-middle-class black parents perform their role differently than do working-class black parents (Bluestone and Tamis-LeMonda 1999) or those living below poverty level.

Nevertheless, the impact of race remains important. For instance, even when social class is taken into account, it appears that more African American parents than parents in other ethnic groups spank their children. But comparing African American parents to other ethnic groups can be seen as Eurocentric. For instance, spanking may not have the same negative effects on African American children as it does on European American children. Among African Americans, physical punishment is more acceptable and hence more likely to be viewed as an appropriate display of positive parenting both by the parent and by the child (Robert Hill 2004; McLoyd et al. 2000; Peters 2007).

Besides putting up with research findings that are possibly biased against them (Dodson 2007; Pyke 2000), parents of color face additional challenges. The African American middle class remains vulnerable to discrimination in employment and housing. The status of middle-class black parents does not suffice to protect them from demeaning or suspicious behavior on the part of whites (Peters 2007; Welborn 2006). Even so simple a matter as buying toys becomes problematic. Black dolls only? Should the child choose? What if the choice is a white Barbie doll?

Native American Parents and Children

Native American parents have been described as exercising a laissez-faire parenting style that some critics view as bordering on neglectful. However, describing Native American parenting in this way may smack of Eurocentrism. Traditionally, Native American culture has emphasized personal autonomy and individual choice, even for children. Before the arrival of Europeans and for some time thereafter, Native Americans successfully raised their children by using example and "light discipline" and by "persuasion, ridicule, or shaming in opposition to corporal punishment or coercion." Native Americans continue to "respect children enough to allow them to work things out in their own manner" (R. John 1998, p. 400).

Given the problems of substance abuse and high teenage suicide rates documented among Native American youth ("American Indians" 1992; R. John 1998), we might conclude that the traditional method of raising Native American children is no longer effective, due to changes in the broader society:

> Back when [today's] elders were growing up, the family was much closer, was more organized and protective, combined discipline with permissiveness better than today, and had the advantage of having parents (particularly the mother) around the home. (R. John 1998, p. 401)

However, valuing their cultural heritage, many Native Americans have been reluctant to assimilate into the broader society—and this reluctance may mean a rejection of the authoritative parenting style advised by European American psychologists. Meanwhile, suicide prevention has become a top priority in many tribes, with the use of tribal elders "to help mitigate the loss of parental involvement and early nurturant figures in the lives of Native American adolescents" (R. John 1998, p. 404).

African American parents' attitudes, behaviors, and hopes for their children are similar to those of other parents in their social class. Many African American families are now solidly middle- or upper-middle class, but they and their children continue to be vulnerable to discrimination, a situation that virtually all parents in racial/ethnic groups face.

Hispanic Parents and Children

Mexican American parents teach their children the traditions and values of their cultures of origin (McLoyd et al. 2000) while often coping with a generation gap that includes differential fluency and different attitudes toward speaking Spanish (Anti-Defamation League of B'nai B'rith 1981; Gonzales et al. 2006). As in other bicultural families, conflicts may extend into many matters of everyday life: "My mother would give me these silly dresses to wear to school, not jeans," complained a fifteen-year-old Mexican American female (Suro 1992, p. A-11).

Hispanic parents have been described as more authoritarian than white parents. However, as with African Americans, it may be that this description is Eurocentric and therefore inaccurate. The concept of **hierarchical parenting**, which combines warm emotional support for children with a demand for significant respect for parents and other authority figures, including older extended-family members, may more aptly apply to Hispanic parents. Hierarchical parenting is designed to instill in children a more collective value system rather than the relatively high individualism favored by European Americans (McLoyd et al. 2000, p. 1082).

Asian American Parents and Children

Compared to the average of 27.6 percent for all Americans over twenty-four years old, 50.1 percent of Asians have completed four years of college or more (U.S. Census Bureau 2007a, Table 214). Ironically, the Asian American parenting style, characterized by some researchers as authoritarian (Greenfield and Suzuki 2001) and even hostile (McBride-Chang and Chang 1998), has not generally been credited with children's educational success. So researchers have explained Asian American children's high school performance by arguing that peers in their ethnic group strongly support academic success (McBride-Chang and Chang 1998; McLoyd et al. 2000).

Finding this explanation inadequate and ethnocentric, a few Asian American social scientists have offered alternative concepts that emphasize the indigenous **Confucian training doctrine**, named after the sixth-century Chinese social philosopher Confucius, who stressed (among other things) honesty, sacrifice, familial loyalty, and respect for parents and all elders. Like the hierarchical parenting concept suggested for Hispanic parents, the Confucian training doctrine blends parental love, concern, involvement, and physical closeness with strict and firm control (Chao 1994; McBride-Chang and Chang 1998).

Because Asian American children have achieved above-average educational levels in the United States and have done relatively well in the professions, they are thought to have few problems. Like other ethnic minorities, however, they have suffered from discrimination (Lau, Takeuchi, and Alegria 2006; Tong 2004). Furthermore, Asian American youths must contend with high expectations created by the stereotyping of Asians as a "super-minority" (Abboud 2006; Wong et al. 1998).

Parents and Multiracial Children

According to the 2000 census, which was the first to offer citizens the option of identifying themselves as more than one race, there are nearly 7 million Americans of mixed race (Roth 2005). Of those, more than 40 percent are children under age eighteen. Chapter 9 explores homogamy versus heterogamy in marriage; as racial heterogamy slowly loses its taboo, the number of multiracial births is expected to climb (Dunnewind 2003). The greatest number of multiracial births is to black–white couples, followed by Asian–white and then

Native American–white couples. Other interracial births occur as well, of course, such as babies born to Native American–black or Native American–Asian couples (Kalish 1995).

Raising biracial or multiracial children has challenges peculiar to it, although it is not without rewards as well (Rockquemore and Laszloffy 2005). One challenge may be tension between parents—and between parents and children—over cultural values and attitudes: "Black parents may teach their biracial children to grow up to be Black and proud, but society teaches that to be Black is to be an inferior person" (Luke 1994, p. 58). Then, too, many white parents, particularly white single mothers who are living in mostly white communities, find that "[y]ou have to seek, to go out of your way to give them that African American side" (respondent, quoted in O'Donoghue 2005, p. 148).

Some Caucasian parents, particularly those who identify as white ethnics, such as Italian American or Irish American, also work to instill pride in their own ethnicity in their multiracial children (O'Donoghue 2005). Yet a white parent may have trouble doing so. As one wife and mother put it, "In this racist society I'm not even permitted to feel good about being white and teach my child that it's okay that he has a part of whiteness in him as well" (Luke 1994, p. 58, citing Ladner 1984).

> [C]ontradictory identity positions that parents in fact embody, illustrate the conflicts and paradoxes many interracial parents face. Hence, the complexity of parenting . . . is a profoundly different emotional, cultural, and political experience for either parent, particularly when the family includes biracial and monoracial children. (Luke 1994, p. 58)

A small, qualitative study of eleven East Coast white women who were raising multicultural teens unexpectedly found that—because their physical characteristics made it possible—some adolescents (three females) chose to embrace a Latina identity as a way to deal with racial ambiguity (O'Donoghue 2005).

One psychologist surveyed multiracial adults and asked whether they thought that their parents had been prepared to raise children of mixed race. The majority did not believe so (Dunnewind 2003). Today, however, many schools are more sensitive to the needs of multiracial children (Wardle 2000), and more resources are available for parents raising multiracial children. The following are four tips from one of these resources:

- Encourage children to be proud of all their racial background. Encouraging them to identify with only one race "is all but guaranteed to set them up for a state of inner turmoil and identity problems over the long haul."

- Watch for two pivotal "pressure points" children will face: grade school (usually third or fourth grade), when teasing starts and multiracial children realize that others see them as different; and the early teen years, as they struggle to fit in socially and find their identities.

- Understand that racial identity is fluid during adolescence, with a teen changing from one primary racial affiliation to another. [Among other reasons,] this is a way to fit into racial groupings at school.

- Stress the positives. Multiracial children often demonstrate greater creativity and flexibility because they use more than one culture's approach to life's challenges. (Dunnewind 2003, citing and quoting Nakazawa 2003)

To finish this section, we quote the conclusions of a recent Population Reference Bureau publication on intermarriage:

At this festival marking Eid, the end of Ramadan, this Muslim community in central Texas gathers for afternoon prayers. Muslim parents hope that their children will remain true to their religious tradition. Meanwhile, like parents of other minority religions in the United States, they must help their children face fear of ridicule and actual discrimination.

Intermarried couples, intermarried families, and multiracial and multiethnic children increasingly populate the American landscape. In some communities, especially in Hawaii and California, it would not be surprising if the average person were to conclude that intermarriage and multiracial and multiethnic children are the norm. . . . As intermarriage continues to increase, further blurring racial and ethnic group boundaries, Americans' notions of race and ethnicity will sure change. (Lee and Edmonston 2005, p. 33)

For other heterogeneously paired parents, the challenge may be about what religion the children will be raised in or how to teach the children one's native tongue: "As the trend toward increased rates of racial and ethnic intermarriage continues, it will become increasingly important to understand what factors promote resilience among such families, given the unique challenges they confront" (McLoyd et al. 2000, p. 1074).

Religious Minority Parents and Children

Ethnicity is often associated with religious belief. Chinese Americans may be Buddhists, for example, and Asian Indian Americans may be Hindu or Sikh. In a dominant Christian culture, diverse ethno-religious affiliations affect parenting for many Americans. For instance, Muslims have their own holy days, such as

Ramadan, which are seldom, if ever, taken into account in public schools' scheduling. In addition, traditional Muslims, particularly women, dress differently than do the majority of Americans. Wearing flowing robes and, more often, headscarves or veils (called *hijab*), Muslims report that they fear ridicule and face discrimination from employers and others (Harden and Sengupta 2001; "Muslim Parents Seek" 2005).

Parents of minority religions in America hope that their children will remain true to their religious heritage, even amid a majority culture that seldom understands ("Muslim Parents Seek . . ." 2005) and, in fact, is sometimes threatening (F. R. Lee 2001).[6] One solution has been the emergence of religion-based summer camps for children of Jewish, Buddhist, Muslim, Hindu, Sikh, and Zoroastrian parents (Lieblich 1998).

Raising Children of Racial/Ethnic Identity in a Racist and Discriminatory Society

Whatever its social class, the family of racial/ethnic identity—whether black, Native American, Hispanic, Asian American, or multiracial—must serve as an insu-

[6] This desire that their children maintain their ethno-religious heritage is a principal reason for some immigrant parents' preference that their children marry homogamously, sometimes in arranged marriages (see Chapter 9).

lating and advocating environment, as much as possible shielding children from and/or confronting racial slurs and injustices (Cohen, Tran, and Rhee 2007). Raising children in a white-dominated society creates situations that white families never encounter, regardless of their social class (Coles 2006; Coll and Szalacha 2004). For instance, various forms of racism persist in our nation's schools ("Black Parents Fight" 2004; Owo 2004). On a more personal level, a parent of a child of color must decide whether to warn the youngster who is going off to school for the first time about the possibility of classmates' racial slurs (Ambert 1994).

As a result, parents are acutely concerned about the need to develop adequate self-esteem in their children, along with pride in their cultural heritage (Umana-Taylor, Bhanot, and Shin 2006). Some parents in families of racial/ethnic identity decide not to discuss racism or discrimination with their children; they do not want them to become unnecessarily bitter or resentful. Instead, these parents prepare to help their offspring cope with racism when it arises (T. Moore 1993; J. E. White 1993). Others believe it is important to teach their youngsters the history of discrimination against them (Peters 2007).

Parents do not necessarily agree on the best approach to racial issues. About one-third of African American parents do not attempt any explicit racial socialization. Others differ as to whether they emphasize forewarning or take a more militant position toward the elimination of social inequality (McLoyd et al. 2000). We might conclude that

> [i]n the socialization of children there is some tension between teaching an unclouded knowledge of racism's realities and communicating a sense of personal strength and capability. Black children should be taught that there are major barriers, but they also need to be taught that they can be overcome—a difficult balancing act for parents. (Feagin and Sikes 1994, p. 314)

A dilemma faced by all parents of racial/ethnic identity is to address the balance between loyalty to one's ethnic culture and individual advancement in the dominant society. For instance, in many ethnic families the dialect or language spoken at home is neither used nor respected in the larger society. Hence, in order to succeed educationally and occupationally, children must become bilingual or forsake the language of their ancestors.

Valuing one's cultural heritage, while simultaneously being required to deny or "rise above" it in order to advance, poses problems both for individuals and between parents and their children. Native Americans must choose between the reservation and its high poverty level (some have 90 percent unemployment

[Bedard 1992, p. 99; Seccombe 2007]) and an urban life that is perhaps alienating but presents some economic opportunity. Latinos may see a threat to deeply cherished values of family and community in the competitive individualism of the mainstream American achievement path (McLoyd et al. 2000). Asian Americans may live out the "model minority" route to success but experience emotional estrangement from still-traditional parents or identity problems as they feel pressured to cultivate their Asian ethnicity but also to downplay it (Kibria 2000). And Asian American parents may be dismayed by their children's lack of interest in the history of their homeland or failure to respect their elders (Gorman 1998).

Having explored the class and racial/ethnic diversity of U.S. parents, we turn now to a discussion of grandparents as parents.

A dilemma faced by all parents of racial/ethnic identity—whether African American, Native American, Hispanic, Asian American, or multiracial—is to address the balance between loyalty to one's ethnic culture and individual advancement in the dominant society. Native Americans must choose between the reservation and its high poverty level and an urban life that is perhaps alienating but presents some economic opportunity.

Grandparents as Parents

More than 3.6 million children under age eighteen are living in a grandparent's household. These grand-children—and great-grandchildren—represent about 5 percent of all children under eighteen (Fields 2003, Table 3). Some experts predict that these figures will rise as changes in welfare laws, discussed earlier in this chapter, limit parents' welfare benefits. In accordance with "welfare reform," several states require single teen mothers to reside with their parents (the baby's grand-parents) in order to receive government assistance (McDonald and Armstrong 2001):

> In the context of marital instability . . . , it is clear that grandparents and step-grandparents are becoming increasingly important family connections. . . . Two-fifths of divorced mothers move during the first year of the divorce . . . , and most of these move in with their parents while they make the transition to single parent-ing. (Bengston 2001, p. 7)

Individuals who have grandchildren living in their homes are not always primary parents; single mothers who also reside in the household usually assume the role of primary parent (Caputo 2001; and see Fields 2003, Table 3). Nevertheless, many grandparents do serve as the grandchild's principal parent. A grandpar-ent's assuming the role of primary parent may often be viewed as a family crisis; handling family crises creatively is addressed in Chapter 15. Abuse of alcohol and drugs, particularly crack cocaine, along with the rapid spread of AIDS, combined with teen pregnancy, abuse, neglect, abandonment, incarceration, and sometimes murder, account for a very large majority of **grandparent fami-lies** (Holloway 1994; Toledo and Brown 1995).

Compared to other parents, grandparents who are raising their grandchildren tend to be "less educated, much younger at the time of the birth of their first child, and 2 to 4 times as likely to be female, single, black, poor and unemployed" (Caputo 2001, p. 541; Geen 2004; Simmons and Dye 2003). About one-fifth of those who are raising grandchildren live below poverty level (Haskell 2003). However, contrary to stereotypes, a grandparent's (often a single grandmother's) assum-ing full-time responsibility for a grandchild's upbring-ing is limited neither to racial/ethnic minorities nor to inner-city settings (Hayslip and Hicks-Patrick 2006).

Sylvie de Toledo is a social worker whose nephew was raised by her mother after her sister's suicide. As a result of this experience, Toledo founded a support group called Grandparents as Parents (GAP).

> Sometimes the call comes at night, sometimes on a bright morning. It may be your child, the police, or child protective services. "Mama, I've messed up . . ." "We're sorry. There has been an accident . . ." "Mrs. Smith, we have your grandchild. Can you take him?" Sometimes you make the call yourself—reporting your own child to the authorities in a desperate attempt to protect your grandchild from abuse or neglect. Often the change is gradual. At first your grandchild is with you for a day, then four days, a month, and then two months as the parents slowly lose control of their lives. You start out baby-sitting. You think the arrangement is temporary. You put off buying a crib or moving to a big-ger apartment. Then you get a collect call from jail—or no call at all. (Toledo and Brown 1995, p. 9)

At other times the change is more sudden, as when a grandchild's parents are killed in an auto accident (Landry-Meyer and Newman 2004).

Becoming a primary parent requires adjustment for grandparents (Houtman 2006). Their circle of friends may change or dwindle because few or perhaps no oth-ers in the grandparents' peer group have children, and the grandparents are older than most parents with children. And living with children in the house is an adjustment after years of not doing so (Dolbin-MacNab 2006). Moreover, a grandmother's work life may change. She may retire early, reduce her work hours, or try to negotiate more flexible ones. On the other hand, she may return to work to have money to raise the child. In either case, the grandparents' finances may suffer, although states offer some financial compensation to grandparents who are officially serving as foster par-ents. Realizing that "the social problems that led to the phenomenon of grandparents raising grandchildren are not likely to disappear in the near future," social service agencies across the country are initiating edu-cational and coping programs for often stressed grand-parents acting as parents (Dolbin-MacNab 2006; Ross and Aday 2006). In 2007, U.S. Senators Hillary Rodham Clinton, Olympia Snowe, and Thad Cochran proposed the Kinship Caregiver Support Act, which would autho-rize federal payment to grandparents who are raising children to the same degree that foster parents are paid by federal funding ("It Takes a Family" 2007).

Foster Parents

Every state government has a department that moni-tors parents' treatment of their children. An example is California's Department of Child Protective Services. When state or county officials determine that a child is being abused or neglected, they can take temporary or permanent custody of the child and remove her or him from the parental home to be placed in **foster care**.

Some foster care takes place in **group homes**, where several children are cared for around the clock by paid professionals who work in shifts and live elsewhere.

A significant portion of foster care is **family foster care**—foster care that takes place in a trained and licensed foster parent's home. The goal of family foster care is to provide "planned, time-limited, substitute family care for children who cannot be adequately cared for at home" (Baum, Crase, and Crase 2001, p. 202). Some specialized foster family homes are available for children with specific and complex emotional or medical needs (J. Ward 1998). **Formal kinship care**, a development in foster parenting since the 1980s, is out-of-home placement with biological relatives of children who are in the custody of the state (Robert Hill 2004). Kinship foster placements are mostly with grandparents, the remainder often with aunts (Geen 2004; Robert Hill 2004).

It is estimated that more than 500,000 children are in foster care (U.S. Department of Health and Human Services 2006). There would be more children in foster homes, but there are not enough foster parents to fill current needs, especially for openly gay youth or children of racial/ethnic minorities ("Foster Care" 2005; Wingett 2007). Largely due to the effects of parental drug abuse on the child before and/or after the child's birth, a disproportionately high percentage of children living below or near the poverty level are foster children. Foster children have up to seven times more serious chronic health, emotional, developmental, and cognitive problems than poor children not in foster care (Baum, Crase, and Crase 2001; "Foster Care" 2005). Foster parents may be married or single, are of all social classes, and may or may not be employed outside the home (Foster Care Project 1998). Among others, motivations for becoming a foster parent include fulfilling religious principles, wanting to help fill the community's need for foster homes, enjoying children and hoping to help them, providing a companion for one's only child or for oneself, and earning money. Some foster parents had childhood experiences with foster care: They were foster children themselves, or their own parents fostered children.

Some foster parents see fostering as a step toward adopting either the child they are fostering or a different child (Baum, Crase, and Crase 2001). Although family reunification is the goal in foster parenting, many children—for the most part, older youth and the developmentally neediest—remain in foster care until they "age out" of the system (Chipungu and Bent-Goodley 2004; Wulczyn 2004). Some foster children are available for adoption; more than half of all foster teens who get adopted are adopted by their foster parents (A. Hamilton 2006; Massinga and Pecora 2004). (Adoption of children with special needs is addressed in Chapter 10.)

As wards of the court, foster children are financially supported by the state. Technically not salaried, foster parents are "reimbursed" in regular monthly stipends by the government. Although there is a popular belief that foster families "do it just for the money," the reimbursement is not large and is even inadequate for many foster parents, who report spending significant amounts of their own money to get needed clothes, toys, and services for their foster children (Barton 1999). In the case of kinship foster care, relatives often need tangible items such as beds, food, and clothing as foster care begins. Ongoing needs include information regarding how the case is progressing through the child welfare agencies involved, day care, and counseling for the child (Geen 2004).

Meanwhile, as many as 40 percent of foster parents stop fostering within their first year. There are several reasons for this. First, some foster parents report difficulties in dealing with the bureaucracy of the social services system (Badeau 2004). Second, even trained and licensed foster parents are not always equipped to handle the children's demanding needs (Harden 2004). Third, there is little distinction, or social respect, associated with being a foster parent (Rindfleisch 1999). We end this section with the words of Jo Ann Wentzel, senior editor of the magazine *Parenting Today's Teen* and foster mother to more than seventy-five children over the course of her career:

> I don't regret anything I've ever done for any of my [foster] kids. I do not for one minute believe I replaced their parents. When they left our house to return to their birth parents, they may have soon forgot me, but some of them never did. . . . Every once in a while, a kid will track me down and leave a cryptic message on my answering machine, which says, I know I was a pain-in-the-butt when I lived with you but I really learned a lot from you. . . . Or maybe they will tell me about their successes and claim it was because of something we did or said. They tell me they called because they wanted us to know they turned out good [sic] or because they respected our opinion on something. (Wentzel 2001, p. 2)

The next section explores relationships between parents and adult children.

Parents and Young Adult Children

Parenting does not end when a child reaches eighteen, twenty-one, or even twenty-five or older; children benefit from parents' emotional support and encouragement through their twenties and after (Arnett 2004; Kantrowitz and Tyre 2006). One study that analyzed National Survey of Families and Households (NSFH) data concluded that as adolescents make the transition to adult roles, parent–child relations grow closer, more supportive, and less conflicted (Aquilino 1997). At the same time, concerns over young adults' having gained access to health or auto insurance—or perhaps their request that a parent co-sign on a loan—can cause parental ambivalence or conflict (Quinn 2006).

Perhaps not surprisingly, research shows that having an adult child who is experiencing problems—with health, the law, keeping a job, or alcohol or substance abuse, for instance—can result in lower feelings of well-being for parents as well as in poor parent-child relationship quality (Greenfield and Marks 2006). Just listening and using other positive communication skills (described in Chapter 13) can help. (It also helps not to jump to conclusions. A child who calls in desperation because his or her marriage is breaking up may *not* be asking to move home.) Parents can help to replenish self-confidence in frustrated children by reminding them of their past successes and commenting on the strength and skills they demonstrated (Haines and Neely 1987). A parent might say, for example, "I remember your persistence as you worked toward first chair in band." A grieving young adult will need to be informed that what she or he is feeling is normal.

At times, parents may choose to confront their adult children: "It sounds as if drinking is beginning to cause problems for you," or "It sounds as if you feel stuck in a job you don't like." Serious problems, such as dealing with an adult child's chronic depression or chemical addiction, require counseling and/or support groups designed for this purpose.

Despite their best efforts, upper-middle-class parents cannot ensure that each child will eventually enjoy a position in the upper-middle class. An executive's child will more than likely have to finish college and maybe even attain a higher degree in order to match the parent's occupational status. Related to this is the problem of how to teach a child raised in relative affluence to live in less-luxurious conditions should she or he be unable to afford luxury in adulthood (LeMasters and DeFrain 1989).

Sharing the Household More and more young adult children either do not leave the family home or return to it—after college, after divorce, or upon finding first jobs unsatisfactory (Kantrowitz and Tyre 2006). As discussed in Chapter 8, 55 percent of men and 47 percent of women between ages eighteen and twenty-four live with their parents. Of adults between ages twenty-five and thirty-four, 14 percent of men and 7 percent of women reside with parents (Fields 2004). Unemployment and underemployment, along with a decline in affordable housing, make launching oneself into independent adulthood difficult today (Cohen and Casper 2002; Settersten, Furstenberg, and Rumbaut 2005). Some research also indicates that today's young adults lack a sense of urgency when it comes to establishing independence (Arnett 2004; Nevius 2006).

Are they spongers? Some psychologists think so ("It's the Kids" 2005). Kids have a greater sense of entitlement these days, says psychologist Susan Jennings. "It's possible that this is just a continuation of what the parents had done from the beginning, buying their kids the expensive shoes because everybody has them. . . . At 25, they are adolescents with no restrictions and more money" (Jennings, in Pisano 2005).

Also, in the past two generations, kids and parents got to be pals, so kids think of themselves as having more privileges and authority than they probably should. "Kids learn to punish their parents by bad behavior. When they get what they want, they're all sweetness. Parents have the attitude that they should do all they can for their children or they'll be selfish" (Jennings, in Pisano 2005).

> Parents are not doing their children a favor when they make it too easy. They are not teaching their children the lessons they learned when they were growing up and working hard. In trying to spare their children the hard times they had they are undermining their children's sense of self-efficacy and self-worth. They are also instilling a narcissism or sense of entitlement in their children to think that they deserve to receive without having to give. (Rubin, in Pisano 2005)

Adults living with their parents can feel this ambivalence as well. One recent college grad who returned home while looking for a job said, "I'm not ready to accept responsibility for paying for my health insurance and blah, blah, blah right now. So I guess it's kind of like a double-edged sword thing. Like, I want them to think of me as being an adult and independent, but I also don't want to be fully independent" (quoted in Arnett 2004, p. 60).

Parents who anticipated increased intimacy or personal freedom may be disappointed when the nest doesn't empty. When parents share their homes with adult children, the relationship is often characterized by ambivalence (Luscher 2002; Pillemer and Suitor 2002), but it will probably be enhanced if parents relinquish at least some parental authority and recognize that their children's attitudes and values may differ from their own (Arnett 2004). However, relinquishing parental authority does *not* mean allowing absolutely any behavior to go on in the family home. For instance, parents who believe that premarital sex or alcohol or other drug usage is always unwarranted have the right to disallow it under their roof ("Not in Our House" 2001). The relationship will probably be more positive when the adult child is in school or employed (White and Rogers 1997). In general, parents should feel comfortable in setting reasonable household expectations. One way to do this is to negotiate a parent–adult child residence-sharing agreement.

Parent–Adult Child Residence-Sharing Agreements Following are some issues to negotiate.

1. How much money will the adult child be expected to contribute to the household? When is it to be paid? Will there be penalties for late payment?

2. What benefits will the child receive? For example, will the family's laundry soap or anything in the refrigerator be at the child's disposal?

3. Who will have authority over utility usage? Who will decide, for instance, when the weather warrants turning on an air conditioner or where to set the thermostat?

4. What are the standards for cleanliness and orderliness? For instance, what precisely is the definition of "leaving the bathroom (or kitchen) in a mess"?

5. Who is responsible for cleaning what and when? What about yard work?

6. Who is responsible for cooking what and when? Will meals be at specified times? Will the adult child provide his or her own food?

7. How will laundry tasks be divided?

8. If the adult child owns a car, where will it be parked? Who will pay the property taxes and insurance?

9. What about noise levels? How loud may music be played and when? If the noise associated with an adult child's coming home late at night disturbs sleeping parents, how will this problem be solved?

10. What about guests? When are they welcome, with how much notice, and in what rooms of the house? Will the home be used for parties? (First, though, what *is* a party? Three guests? Six? Five hundred?)

11. What arrangement will be made for informing other household members if one will be unexpectedly late? (As an adult, the child should have a right to come and go as he or she pleases. But courtesy requires informing others in the household of the general time when one may be expected home. This avoids unnecessary phone calls to every hospital emergency room in the region.)

12. What about using the personal possessions of other members of the household? May a mother borrow her adult daughter's clothes without asking, for example?

13. If the adult child has returned home with children, who is responsible for their care? How often, when, and with how much notice will the grandparents babysit? Who in the household may discipline the children? How, when, and for what?

Although a residence-sharing agreement can help temporarily, the goal of the majority of parents is for their adult children to move on. Accomplishing this may be complicated by differing ideas on just what a parent owes an adult child. Our culture offers few guidelines about when parental responsibility ends or how to withdraw it.

Independent Adults and Their Parents

Relationships between parents and their children last a lifetime. In discussing child raising throughout this chapter, we have taken the perspective of the older generation looking at the younger. But as parents and their children grow older, things change.

Marriage, and then parenthood, redefine the relationship between parents and children. Typically, the parent–child tie moves gradually from one of dependence to interdependence at this point (Arnett 2004). Adults' relationships with their parents range from tight-knit, to intimate but distant, to nonintimate but sociable, to obligatory, to detached (Silverstein and Bengston 1997). In some families the reality of past abuse, a conflict-filled divorce, or simply fundamental differences in values or lifestyles make it seem unlikely that parents and children will spend time together (Kaufman and Uhlenberg 1998; Kutner 1990a). Money matters can also cause tension (Greenfield and Marks 2006; Kutner 1990b. For many mothers and daughters, motherhood for the daughter creates a closer bond than had existed in adolescence—perhaps ever—as these women, who may have very different views and styles, may now have something very important in common (Kutner 1990d).

Toward Better Parent–Child Relationships

Studies generally show that optimal parenting involves at least five factors: (1) adequate economic resources; (2) workplace and other social policies that would improve the work/family balance and better support parents

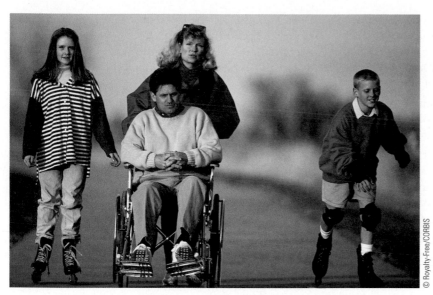

Good parenting involves having adequate economic resources, being involved with the child, using supportive communication, and having support from family and/or friends. There is evidence that using supportive parenting techniques is intergenerationally transmitted, or passed on from parent to adult child.

in other ways as well (Abel 2007; Williams and Cooper 2004); (3) being involved in a child's life and school; (4) using supportive, rather than negative, family communication (Hofferth and Sandberg 2001); and (5) having support from family and/or friends (Bynum and Brody 2005; Lindsey, Caldera, and Colwell 2005). We might also add recognizing and valuing being "good enough" parents while not trying to be perfect—and not competing with other parents over who is more perfect—and having some fun with your kids (Quindlen 2005).

Over the past several decades, many national organizations have emerged to help parents with the parent–child relationship. For example, various intervention programs are designed to help teenage and/or substance-abusing parents (Middlemiss and McGuigan 2005; Suchman et al. 2006; Tolan, Szapocznik, and Sambrano 2007). Other programs serve parents more generally (Keith n.d.). One of these is Thomas Gordon's Parent Effectiveness Training (PET), which applies the guidelines for no-win intimacy to the parent–child relationship (Gordon 2000). Another is Systematic Training for Effective Parenting (STEP) (Center for the Improvement of Child Caring n.d.). Both STEP and PET combine instruction on effective communication techniques with emotional support for parents. These programs are offered in many communities, and related books are also available. In addition to national organizations, countless local and community programs, as well as professional websites, have emerged that teach various facets of parent education, particularly for teen and low-income parents and for grandparents as parents. Some of these programs are especially designed by and intended for particular racial/ethnic groups (Kumpfer and Tait 2000).

In addition to learning and practicing good parenting techniques, parents might consider involving other members of their communities in child raising (Scanzoni 2001b). "Pediatrics is politics," the late pediatrician Benjamin Spock once said (quoted in Maier 1998). He meant that good parenting makes for better communities—and more supportive communities make for better parents.

Then, too, parents can not only encourage more cooperation among friends and neighbors but also work together toward creating safer, more child-friendly neighborhoods (Furstenberg 2001a). For instance, parents might exchange homework help—"I'll help Johnny with math on Tuesday evenings if you'll help Mary with English"—and, of course, form carpools for children's lessons and activities. Such practical exchanges provide the occasion for children to form supportive relationships with other adults, who serve as para-parents or mentors (Bould 2003). Another source of support is the community itself: teachers, school counselors and principals, police officers, adolescents' employers, the library, the Internet, and the public in general (McCurdy and Daro 2001; C. Miller 2003; Warren and Cannan 1997).

Summary

- The family ecology theoretical perspective reminds us that society-wide conditions influence the parent–child relationship, and these factors can place extraordinary emotional and financial strains on parents.

- This chapter began by presenting five reasons why parenting can be difficult today. Some things noted are that work and parent roles often conflict.

- Although more fathers are involved in child care today, mothers are the primary parent in the vast majority of cases and continue to do the majority of day-to-day child care.

- Not only mothers' but fathers' roles can be difficult, especially in a society like ours, in which attitudes have changed so rapidly and in which there is no consensus about how to raise children and how mothers and fathers should parent.
- Child psychologists prefer the authoritative parenting style, although some scholars of color describe the authoritarian/laissez-faire/authoritative parenting style model as ethnocentric or Eurocentric.
- The need for supportive—and socially supported— parenting transcends social class and race or ethnicity. At the same time, we have seen that parenting differs in some important ways, according to economic resources, social class, and whether parent and child suffer discrimination due to religion, racial/ethnic status, or sexual orientation of the parents.
- Raising children while in poverty is a very different experience than parenting in wealthier social classes.

Besides concerns for basic necessities, such as food, clothing, shelter, and health care, poverty-level parents may live in depressingly blighted neighborhoods.

- A trend over the past several decades has been for an increasing number of grandparents to be serving as primary parents, often as a result of some crisis in the child's immediate family.
- More than 500,000 children are in foster care today, many of them in kinship foster care.
- To have better relationships with their children, parents need to recognize their own needs and to avoid feeling unnecessary guilt; to accept help from others (friends and the community at large as well as professional caregivers); and, finally, to try to build and maintain flexible, intimate relationships using the techniques suggested in this chapter, along with those suggested in Chapter 13.

Questions for Review and Reflection

1. Describe reasons why parenting can be difficult today. Can you think of others besides those presented in this chapter?
2. Compare these three parenting styles: authoritarian, authoritative, and laissez-faire. What are some empirical outcomes of each? Which one is recommended by most experts? Why?
3. How does parenting differ according to social class? Use the family ecology theoretical perspective to explain some of these differences.
4. What unique challenges do African American, Native American, Hispanic, and/or Asian American parents face today, regardless of their social class? How would *you* prepare an immigrant child or a child of color to face possible discrimination?
5. **Policy Question.** Describe some social policies that could benefit the children who are being raised by their grandparents. What about foster children?

Key Terms

authoritarian parenting style 274
authoritative parenting style 274
Confucian training doctrine 282
family foster care 286
formal kinship care 286
foster care 285
grandparent families 285
group home 286
hierarchical parenting 281

laissez-faire parenting style 274
para-parent 277
parenting alliance 272
parenting style 274
primary parent 272
shared parenting 272
Temporary Assistance for Needy Families (TANF) 278
transition to parenthood 268

Online Resources

Companion Website for This Book

www.thomsonedu.com/sociology/lamanna

Visit the book companion website, where you will find flash cards, practice quizzes, Internet links, suggested readings, InfoTrac College Edition exercises, and more to help you study.

ThomsonNOW™ for Marriage and Family

Spend time on what you need to master rather than on information you already have learned. Take a pre-test for this chapter, and ThomsonNOW will generate a personalized study plan based on your results. The study plan will identify the topics you need to review and direct you to online resources such as videos, narrated learning modules, and interactive activities to help you master those topics. You can then take a post-test to help you determine the concepts you have mastered and what you will still need to work on. Try it out! Go to **www.thomsonedu.com/login** to sign in with an access code or to purchase access to this product.

Work and Family

© Ariel Skelley/GettyImages/Taxi

12

Women in the Labor Force
Women's Entry into the Labor Force

Women's Market Work

The Wage Gap

Opting Out, Stay-at-Home Moms, and Neotraditional Families

Men's Market Work
The Provider Role

Why Do Men Leave the Labor Force?

Two-Earner Marriages—Work/Family Options
Two-Career Marriages

Part-Time Employment

Shift Work

Doing Paid Work at Home

A Closer Look at Family Diversity: Diversity and Child Care

Leaving the Labor Force and Reentry

Unpaid Family Work
Caring for Dependent Family Members

Housework

Juggling Employment and Family Work
Work, Family, and Leisure: Attitudes and Time Allocation

Facts about Families: Where Does the Time Go?

How Are Children Faring?

How Are Parents Faring?

Social Policy, Work, and Family
What Is Needed to Resolve Work–Family Issues?

As We Make Choices: Child Care and Children's Outcomes

As We Make Choices: Selecting a Child-Care Facility

Who Will Provide What Is Needed to Resolve Work–Family Issues?

The Two-Earner Marriage and the Relationship
Gender Strategies

Maintaining Intimacy While Negotiating Provider Roles and the Second Shift

Providing and caring for all family household members, including dependents and the elderly, is integral to our definition of families. Until recently, historically speaking, cooperative labor for survival was the dominant purpose of marriage. Women as well as men engaged in economically productive labor not limited to the personal care of family members.

"Where do you work?" is a new question in human history. Only since the Industrial Revolution has working been considered separate from family living, and only since then have the concepts "employed" and "unemployed" emerged. With the Industrial Revolution, economic production moved outside the household to factories, shops, and offices. Although human beings have always worked, it was not until the industrialization of the workplace in the nineteenth century that people characteristically became wage earners, hiring out their labor to someone else and joining a **labor force.**[1]

First men and now women have become workers in the labor force. How has that affected family life? In this chapter we'll look at the interrelationship of work and family roles for both women and men. We'll look at market work (paid employment) and unpaid household work. We'll consider how people use their time to meet work and family responsibilities and consider whether time spent with children has been cut short. And we'll look at the strategies and choices partners use to manage their work and their family relations.

Women in the Labor Force

As the Industrial Revolution got under way, women by and large remained in the home, depending on social class, of course. Women of lower social classes, immigrant women, women of color, and widowed women often supported themselves and their families by taking in laundry, marketing baked goods, working as domestics in other people's homes, and housing boarders; before they married, they may have worked in factories. Still, it was largely men who held "jobs" and were visible in economic production.

Women's Entry into the Labor Force

As family size declined and especially as the need for clerical workers and light factory workers expanded, women began to enter the labor force. As Figure 12.1 shows, women's participation in the labor force has increased greatly since the beginning of the nineteenth

[1] The term *labor force* refers to those persons who are employed or who are looking for a paid job.

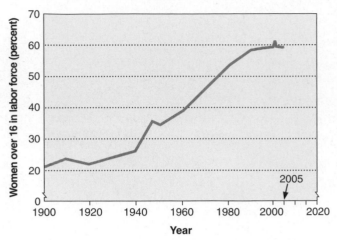

Figure 12.1 The participation of women over age sixteen in the labor force, 1900–2005.

Sources: Thornton and Freedman 1983; U.S. Census Bureau 1998, 2007a, Table 583.

century. Industrialization gave rise to bureaucratic corporations, which depended heavily on paperwork. Clerical workers were needed, and not enough men were available. Textile industries sought workers with a dexterity thought to be possessed by women. The expanding economy needed more workers, and women were drawn into the labor force in significant numbers beginning around 1890.

This trend accelerated during World War I, the Great Depression, and World War II, then slowed following the war. As soldiers came home, the government encouraged women to return to their kitchens. Despite these cultural pressures, the number of wage-earning women rose again. Material expectations increased for housing and consumer goods, and families became more likely to think of college education for the kids.

Beginning in about 1960, the number of employed women began to increase rapidly. As the 1970s brought a decline or stagnation of men's earnings and economic uncertainty spread to sectors that had been doing relatively well, more families turned to a second earner. The growth in the divorce rate left women uncertain about the wisdom of remaining out of the labor force and, hence, dependent on a husband's earnings. The Women's Movement emerged and was a strong force for anti–sex discrimination laws that opened formerly male occupations to women. The movement also altered attitudes about careers for women. By 1979, a majority of married women were employed outside the home.

At first, the largest group of wage-earning women were young unmarried women; relatively few women

Women have entered the labor force in greater and greater numbers since the 1960s.

worked during child-rearing years. Although many mothers remained at home while children were small, by 1970, half of wives with children between ages six and seventeen earned wages, and that figure increased to 75 percent in 2005 (U.S. Census Bureau 2007a, Table 584).

Mothers of young children were the last women to move into employment outside the home. In 2005, 60 percent of wives with children under age six were paid employees. In fact, 56 percent of married mothers of children under age one had joined the labor force. Even larger proportions of single women were employed: 80 percent of those with children age six to seventeen, and 68 percent of those with children under six (U.S. Census Bureau 2007a, Tables 584, 585).

The *rate* of increase in employment has been greater for white women than black women, who historically had been more likely to work for wages (England, Garcia-Beaulieu, and Ross 2004). Now, white women—with a labor force participation rate of 60 percent—are catching up to black women at 62 percent. Fifty-eight percent of Asian women and 55 percent of Hispanic women are employed (U.S. Census Bureau 2007a, Table 574). Atti-

tudes changed along with behavior. By the late 1990s, fewer than 20 percent of women and men disapproved of married women working (Sayer, Cohen, and Casper 2004, Table 1).

Women's Market Work

Working for pay—in contrast to unpaid labor in the home—is **market work**. What kinds of jobs do women hold? Occupational distribution of women differs from that of men, as Figure 12.2 indicates.

The pronounced tendency for men and women to be employed in different types of jobs is termed **occupational segregation**. Figure 12.2 depicts the major occupational categories of employed women for 2005. As you can see, 22 percent of all employed women were office or service workers. Only 13 percent of employed women were in management, business, or finance positions, while 25 percent were in professional work (U.S. Bureau of Labor Statistics 2006d, Table 10). Asian American women (45 percent) were the most likely to hold managerial or professional jobs, compared to white (29 percent), black (30 percent), and Hispanic women (22 percent; U.S. Bureau of Labor Statistics 2006d).

Jobs typically held by men and women differ *within* major occupational categories, with men more likely to hold the upper-level jobs within each sector. Even though women are proportionately more likely to be professionals than men, they occupy the lower-paying ranks. For example, women are 30 percent of lawyers, but 86 percent of paralegals and legal assistants; 32

Women in blue-collar jobs are still a minority, although more women are entering these jobs, which tend to pay better than traditional women's jobs in service or clerical work.

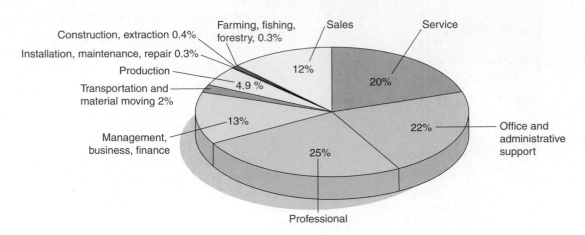

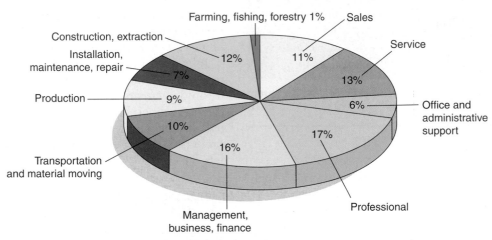

Figure 12.2 The jobs held by women and men, 2005. The percentages in each sector of the pie charts tell us what percentages of women and what percentages of men hold certain jobs. For example, 25 percent of women have professional employment while 20 percent are in service occupations. Seventeen percent of men are in professional jobs, while 13 percent are service workers.

Source: Based on data from U.S. Bureau of Labor Statistics 2006d, Table 10.

[a]Percentages may not add to 100 percent due to rounding.

percent of physicians, but 92 percent of nurses (U.S. Bureau of Labor Statistics 2006d, Table 11). This occupational segregation contributes to the difference between men's and women's average earnings.

The Wage Gap

Differences in earnings persist in comparisons of employed women and men. Women who worked full time in 2006 earned eighty-one cents for every dollar earned by men (U.S. Bureau of Labor Statistics 2007). The **wage gap** (the difference in earnings between men and women) varies considerably depending on occupation and tends to be greater in the more elite, higher-paying occupations (Weinberg 2004). For instance, in 2000, in the highest-paying occupation, that of physician, women made $80,000 while men earned $140,000 on average (Weinberg 2004). The difference is thought to be related to choice of occupational specialty and practice setting (for example, pediatrics, which pays less, is a popular choice of female physicians). To some extent, men's and women's employment remains segmented into dual labor markets, with women in a narrower range of jobs offering fewer benefits and advancement opportunities.

Men continue to dominate corporate America. In 2000, only 5.2 percent of the highest-earning executives in Fortune 500 companies were women ("Women Still Lag" 2004). Although racism blocks the path to management for nonwhite or Hispanic men, both racism and sexism block the path for nonwhite and Hispanic women, who hold only 1.3 percent of executive positions (Solis and Oldham 2001).

Occupational segregation (that is, differentiation in jobs of men and women) declined from 1960 to 1990 at all levels of the occupational range. The decline was most pronounced for the college educated. "But it is also clear that men and women continue to occupy separate spheres in the world of work. It is also clear that the pace of change has slowed" (Cotter, Hermsen, and Vanneman 2004, pp. 13–14). Another important point is the growing divide among women (and men) who have or do not have a college education. Increasingly, the earnings of less-educated men and women, especially men, are falling behind those of more highly educated individuals (Blau and Kahn 2006).

Whether the wage gap is due to discrimination or represents "the personal choices of some men and many women who want or need a job that fits their family obligations" is disputed (Boraas and Rodgers 2003, p. 14). Do women's family responsibilities lower their career achievement, and, if so, is the pay gap a result of personal choice? We have discussed the wage gap more generally in Chapter 4. Here we focus on the relationship between lesser earnings and women's motherhood role.

The concept of the **motherhood penalty** describes the fact that motherhood has a tremendous negative lifetime impact on earnings, the "long-term earnings gap" (Budig and England 2001, p. 208). "Women still earn a small proportion of what men earn [over a lifetime] . . . and remain financially dependent on men for income during the child-rearing years and indeed throughout much of their adult lives" (Hartmann, Rose, and Lovell 2006, p. 125). Furthermore, the motherhood penalty has not declined over time despite women's increasing education, their attachment to the labor force, and, presumably, less discrimination and more opportunities for women to advance their careers (Budig and England 2001; Avellar and Smock 2003).

A study conducted by the U.S. General Accounting Office (2003) for the years 1983–2000 did find that work patterns accounted for much of the difference between the earnings of women and men. Women had fewer years of work experience, worked fewer hours per year, were less likely to work full time, and left the labor force for longer periods than men.

Work productivity may be affected by a mother's sense of constant responsibility for children. One mother says that no matter what she is doing at work, "I'm thinking, 'Is Colin going to eat lunch?' 'Is Kara going out on the playground and does she have the right coat?'" (interview in Orenstein 1998, p. 48). Mothers may be tired, worried, distracted, or saving up energy for the home front (Budig and England 2001).

But 20 percent of the difference between men's and women's earnings was left unexplained when relevant variables were taken into account. The researchers concluded that "[i]t is difficult to evaluate this remaining portion. . . . [A]n earnings difference that results from individuals' decisions about how to manage work and family responsibilities may not necessarily indicate a problem unless these decisions are not freely made. On the other hand, an earnings difference may result from discrimination in the workplace or subtler discrimination about what types of career or job choices women can make" (U.S. General Accounting Office 2003, p. 3).

The relative share of child care and domestic work carried by men and women (to be discussed later in this chapter) plays a role. "Until men take on close to an equal role at home, the pattern will be difficult to break," comments economist Anne Preston, author of yet another study finding a motherhood penalty (in Kleiman 2003, p. D-1). Researchers Michelle Budig and Paula England point out that society as a whole benefits from mothers' work:

> Good parenting . . . increases the likelihood that a child will grow up to be a caring, well-behaved, and productive adult. This lowers crime rates, increases the level of care for the next generation, and contributes to economic productivity [which benefits the whole society]. . . . [M]others pay a price in lowered wages for doing childrearing, while most of the rest of us are "free riders" on their labor. (2001, p. 205)

The future is difficult to predict. On the one hand, women's increased entry into professional and managerial tracks suggests more substantial future advancement. Yet the difficulty of combining work and family responsibilities, a burden that most often falls unevenly on women, still seems to present a formidable barrier to equal occupational status and income.

Opting Out, Stay-at-Home Moms, and Neotraditional Families

"The housewife" has vanished, more or less. That would be a woman who views her adult role as one devoted to the home, while she remains economically dependent on the earnings of her husband, the breadwinner. Today, though, over 70 percent of women with children under eighteen are in the labor force, 68 percent of married mothers (U.S. Bureau of Labor Statistics 2006d, Table 6). Are there no traces left of the housewife?

It's been noted that the movement of women into the labor force has plateaued, and even dropped a percentage point or so from its 2000 peak (see Figure 12.1). The percentage of mothers who return to work within the year after a birth has dropped from a 1998 peak of 59 percent (Dye 2005, Figure 2).

About 25 percent of married women (in 2003) with children under fifteen gave as their reason for not participating in the labor force "to care for home and family." Most of them had employed husbands who worked fifty-two weeks in the last year. Generally, the higher the family income, the more likely this was (Fields 2004, Table 5).

We don't know from these bare-bones data whether these mothers plan to remain out of the labor force, having made a commitment to being a full-time mom, or whether they plan to return to work. We also don't know what their occupations are, although highly educated mothers and those with higher-level occupations are more likely to be employed, and they return to the labor force more quickly after giving birth (Johnson and Downs 2005).

Opting Out Some journalists have concluded that such "career" women are now **opting out** of the labor force. A feature article by *New York Times* reporter Lisa Belkin (2003) called this the "Opt-Out Revolution," and her article was followed by "Stretched to Limit, Women Stall March to Work" (Porter 2006b), "Many Women at Elite Colleges Set Career Path to Motherhood" (Story 2005), and more.

Belkin interviewed Ivy League women who had established impressive professional and managerial careers after graduation. Yet they were now leaving employment to enjoy children, domesticity, and a less hectic life. As one of them said, "I wish it had been possible to be the kind of parent I want to be and continue with my legal career. But I wore myself out trying to do both jobs well." Said another, "I like life's rhythms when I'm nurturing a child." Another journalist concluded that her interviewees "will happily play a traditional female role, with motherhood their main commitment" (Story 2005, p. A1).

Opting out was conceived of in more limited terms than a complete withdrawal from the labor force, as the young women interviewed or informally surveyed spoke of part-time jobs or leaving the labor force for a few years. Little evidence exists that substantial "opting out" has in fact occurred. Economist Heather Boushey of the Cen-

ter for Economic and Policy Research (2005a; 2006) suggests, based on her analysis, that a weak labor market since 2001 has led women, as well as men, to evidence a very slight downturn in labor force participation. Labor force participation of single women and of high school dropouts has continued to grow (Porter 2006b).

Black women "are opting out of the 'opt-out' debate" (Clemetson 2006d, p. St-1). Interviews with African American women lawyers, technology experts, corporate managers, and entrepreneurs indicate that they are not focused on working- versus stay-at-home-mother issues. Rather, black women are more concerned about the need to build financial security for their families and, often, the need to help extended-family members.

A closer look at the choices of women graduates of elite universities found that these women did not leave the workforce, at least not for very long—58 percent were never out of the job market for more than six months, and on average the women spent 1.6 years out of the labor force. Most married and had children (Goldin 2006). "Among highly educated women aged 25 to 45, the effect of having children on women's labor force participation has been negligible since 1984, and remains so today" (Boushey 2006).

Stay-at-Home Moms In 2006, almost 25 percent of mothers of children under fifteen in married-couple families were stay-at-home mothers, wives of steadily employed men, who remained out of the labor force for the entire year, giving as their reason "taking care of home and family" (U.S. Fertility and Family Statistics Branch 2006, Table SHP-1). These data give no indication of whether this arrangement is temporary or permanent. Given that most women leave the labor force for relatively short periods over a lifetime, "stay-at-home mom" is a status that is temporary for the majority of women. But what would women prefer?

The Gallup Poll has been asking that question for many years. In 1978, a decisive majority favoring employment over the traditional homemaker role of women appeared in poll data for the first time. "Since then, no clear consensus in either direction has emerged, with small majorities of women sometimes opting for working outside the home and, as measured in the latest [2005] Gallup survey, small majorities sometimes favoring the traditional role of family caretaker. . . . [This suggests] a mostly divided opinion among women" as to what they would prefer "if they were free to choose" (Moore 2005).

Neotraditional Families There are families, termed **neotraditional families** (Wilcox 2004, pp. 209–211), for whom a traditional division of labor is the ideal:

Noah Berger/The New York Times/ Redux

Some women have chosen to opt out of the labor force to raise their children at home. This former executive may return to the labor force eventually.

This [neotraditional] order is appealing to men and women who are discontented with . . . family modernization, the lack of clarity in gender roles . . . , and the pressures associated with combining two full-time careers. It is also appealing to women who continue to identify with the domestic sphere, who wish to see homemaking and nurturing accorded high value, and who wish to have husbands who share their commitment to family life. . . . Men who continue to seek status as domestic patriarchs who have the primary earning responsibility and at least titular authority over their families are also attracted to this order. (Wilcox 2004, p. 209)

Wilcox associates this family model with evangelical Christianity, as well as Orthodox Judaism, traditional Catholicism, and Mormonism. It is most likely to be found in the middle and working classes of the outer suburbs and in rural areas (Wilcox 2004, p. 210).

Wilcox found active conservative Protestants more likely than mainline Protestants to agree that men should be breadwinners and women homemakers. Interestingly, all groups showed a decline in this viewpoint from the 1970s to the 1990s, though "active conservative Protestants" remain at almost 60 percent support for this model (Wilcox 2004, Figure 3.3). Probably economic pressures force many neotraditional women into the labor force, though they are likely to organize

that work as much as possible around part-time or in-home work or take substantial time out of the labor force when children are small.

Men's Market Work

We tend to forget that not all men are doctors, lawyers, and executives. Figure 12.2 shows us that the work situations of men are many and varied.

Many of the blue-collar jobs that paid good wages to earlier generations of men have vanished, and non–college graduate men have experienced eroding incomes. "'In the past guys could drop out of school after finishing high school, or even without finishing, and go into a factory and get a steady job with benefits. . . . But there has been a deterioration in young men's economic position'" (sociologist Valerie Oppenheimer, quoted in Porter and O'Donnell 2006). Between 1979 and 2003, there was no gain for those with some college but no degree, while high school grads' earnings declined 8 percent. Young black men have been "left behind," with high unemployment rates and low earnings (Mincy 2006).

Women without college degrees fared better, because the service sector where they tended to be employed was more resilient. The earnings of women with some college rose 20 percent and those of high school graduates 12 percent (Porter and O'Donnell 2006).

Yet, the provider role is an important one for men of all social classes. What is the present state of the provider?

The Provider Role

What sociologist Jessie Bernard terms the **good provider role** for men emerged in this country during the 1830s. Before then, a man was expected to be "a good steady worker," but "the idea that he was *the* provider would hardly ring true" (Bernard 1986, p. 126) because in a farm economy both husband and wife had roles in producing the family's income. The provider role (and its counterpart, the housewife role) lasted into the late 1970s. The proportion of married-couple families in which only the husband worked gradually declined from 42 percent in 1960 to 19 percent in 2004 (Wilkie 1991; U.S. Bureau of Labor Statistics 2006d, Table 23; and see Figure 12.3).

As Figure 12.3 indicates, in the vast majority (57 percent) of married couples, both husband and wife are now employed. In 5 percent of married couples, only the wife is employed. Although the role of family wage earner is no longer reserved for husbands, many Americans still believe that the man should be the principal provider for his family, and it works out that way in practice to some degree.

Overall, whether single or married, parent or not, men work more hours than women and are more likely (90 percent) to work full time than are women (75 percent). Employed wives contribute about a third (35 percent) of a family's income (U.S. Bureau of Labor Statistics 2006d,

Tables 20, 23). Men continue to be primary breadwinners in the majority of couples, and most men (in all racial/ethnic groups) identify with this role (Coltrane 2000).

> [S]ocietal notions of the meaning of work for men and women are still quite distinctive. Both men and women may view working as a choice for women, even when the woman has no real alternative to being employed. In contrast, there is a strong societal imperative for men to be employed outside the home, and those who choose not to do so are viewed skeptically. (Taylor, Tucker, and Mitchell-Kernan 1999, p. 756)

In fact, men's success—as measured in terms of employment and higher earnings—still seems to be important in "facilitating marriage and enhancing marital stability" (Bianchi and Casper 2000, p. 31).

It is difficult to live up to societal expectations that may not mesh with the reality of economic opportunities. This situation is especially applicable to blue-collar and racial/ethnic minority husbands in the late twentieth- and early twenty-first-century economy (Gerson 1993; Grimm-Thomas and Perry-Jenkins 1994). Moreover, husbands who want to share household work and child care will not find it easy to do so while continuing as the primary breadwinner. For this reason, partners who want to create new options for themselves need to work for changes in the public and corporate spheres, an option explored later in this chapter.

Some husbands today are rejecting the idea that dedication to one's job or occupational achievement is the ultimate indicator of success (Booth and Crouter 1998). Some are choosing less-competitive careers and are spending more time with their families. Four-fifths of men age twenty through thirty-nine who were interviewed in 2000 rated a work schedule that would give them more family time as a more desirable job quality than challenging work or high income. Seventy percent of these younger men said they would exchange money for time with their families—compared to 26 percent of men over sixty-five. This suggests an important generational change, and one that might be happening because a substantial majority of the younger men (70 percent) had working mothers (Grimsley 2000).

Meanwhile, there is an effort on the part of some social scientists (e.g., Christiansen and Palkovitz 2001) to change the *meaning* of the standard male provider role so that it is seen to be as much a form of family work and fathering as "hands-on" parenting. Men with children work increased hours compared to childless men, on average.

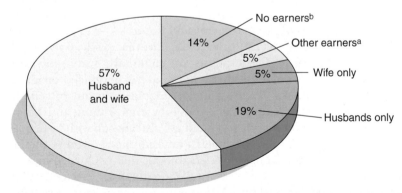

Figure 12.3 Married-couple families by number and relationship of earners, 2004.

Source: U.S. Bureau of Labor Statistics 2006d, Table 23.

[a]Includes husband and other family member(s); wife and other family member(s); other earners, neither husband nor wife.

[b]The spouses may be unemployed, retired, disabled, institutionalized, or imprisoned. (The term *unemployed* refers to persons who are in the labor force and are looking for work but who presently have no job.)

Many men today expect to work at home doing child care or domestic work, as well as holding a job.

Anthropologist Nicholas Townsend (2002) interviewed thirty-nine men who graduated from the same northern California high school in the 1970s; thirty were non-Hispanic white, while six were Hispanic and three, Asian American. Regardless of ethnicity, the men described their lives and goals in terms of "the package deal," which was composed of marriage, children, home ownership, and a steady job. Work was seen to be part of being a good father: "Everybody has a purpose in life. It's the same basic, mundane thing. You get up, you go to work, you come home. Your purpose is to provide for your family" (Skip, quoted on p. 117). Although these men desired to spend more time with their children and thought that important, in reality their time was devoted to paid work—many had two jobs or put in extensive overtime.

Still, it appears that there are two distinct models for the father-as-provider role. Some fathers (*good providers*) work *more* hours than childless men, while others (*involved fathers*) work *fewer* hours. A man's ideological commitment to one or the other role makes a difference. And "it seems clear that a shift away from the provider role and toward the involved father role [has occurred] in recent years" (Kaufman and Uhlenberg 2000, p. 934). Thus, some fathers try to decrease the demands of the workplace in order to participate more at home.

Why Do Men Leave the Labor Force?

Men may relinquish employment as a positive choice: the desire to spend more time with their children. But they may also not be employed because of poor health or disability, or their loss of a job may have developed into long-term unemployment.

Men may be dissatisfied with the competitive grind or the nature of their work, and find themselves in a situation—a working wife who earns enough to support the family or an early retirement package—that permits them to seek new options (Hagenbaugh 2002; Shellenbarger 2002; Tyre and McGinn 2003). Some couples may size up the situation and recognize that the woman is more desirous of pursuing a career, or has a higher-earning career, and/or is more successful than the man, and they can decide as a couple to reverse roles. In 25 percent of couples, wives earn more than their husbands (U.S. Bureau of Labor Statistics 2006d, Table 25). For a variety of reasons, including the demise of secure employment at all economic levels, labor force participation rates have fallen for men (A. Krueger 2004).

Although they are a small minority, some men have relinquished breadwinning to become **househusbands**: men who stay home to care for the house and family while their wives work. About 160,000 fathers with children under fifteen remained out of the labor force for that purpose in 2005 (U.S. Census Bureau 2006b, Table FG8). The Census Bureau only considers those whose wives worked full time as **stay-at-home dads**. Although few men—0.4 percent—are stay-at-home dads by this definition (Fields 2004, Table 5), some 20 percent of fathers of preschool children whose mothers were employed were principle caregivers (J. Johnson 2005, Table 2).

Gay male couples with children often (26 percent) include a stay-at-home parent: "To some gay men, the idea of entrusting the care of a hard-won child to someone else seems to defeat the purpose of parenthood" (Bellafante 2004). These couples will, of course, have a male earner, which underscores the fact that the options for men who would like to give more time to their families are limited because men in our society typically earn more than women do. Consequently, whatever their preferences, many heterosexual couples find themselves needing to encourage the man's dedication to his job or career in the interests of the family's overall financial well-being (Casper and O'Connell 1998).

Although fathers who are primary parents express more sense of isolation than stay-at-home mothers and may experience the loss of a career-based identity, being a househusband is not the lonely choice it once was. Local groups, national organizations, and Internet chat rooms bring househusbands together, and mothers at home are more welcoming of their male counterparts than they used to be.

As with many aspects of family life, choice is the key to a man's satisfaction with the househusband role, as is mutual understanding by the couple about the specifics of their division of labor (Eveld 2003; Marin 2000; Shellenbarger 2002; Spragins 2002).

Some dual-earner couples choose to work together in a joint business.

Gordon M. Grant/The New York Times/ Redux

Two-Earner Marriages— Work/Family Options

As recently as 1968, there were equal proportions of dual-earner and provider–housewife couples: 45 percent of each (Hayghe 1982). Today, **two-earner marriages**, in which both partners are in the labor force, are the statistical norm among married couples.

Even though we may tend to think of two-earner couples as ones in which both partners are employed nine to five, spouses display considerable flexibility in how they design their two-earner unions. (Single-parent-headed households, of course, have more constraints on their choices.) These arrangements are ever-changing and flexible, varying with the arrival and ages of children and with both spouses' job opportunities and working conditions, and involving experimentation with different solutions to managing work and family commitments.

Although these work–family arrangements are fluid, we have observed certain patterns. In this section we examine some ways in which couples choose to structure their work commitments and family life: the two-career marriage, part-time employment, shift work, working at home, and temporarily leaving the labor force.

Two-Career Marriages

Careers differ from *jobs* in that they hold the promise of advancement, are considered important in themselves—not just a source of money—and demand a high degree of commitment. Career men and women work in occupations that usually require education beyond the bachelor's degree, such as medicine, law, academia, financial services, and corporation management.[2]

The vast majority of two-earner marriages would not be classified as *dual career* because the wife's or the husband's employment does not have the features of a *career*. Nevertheless, the dual-career couple is a powerful image. Most of today's college students view the **two-career marriage** as an available and workable option.

For two-career couples with children, family life can be hectic, as partners juggle schedules, chores, and child care. Career wives, in particular, often find themselves in a paradoxical situation. The career world tends to view the person who splits time between work and family as less than professional, yet society encourages working women to do exactly that (Hochschild 1997). Two-career families often outsource domestic work and are likely to employ an in-home caregiver, a **nanny.** Managing the relationship with the nanny adds another complication to the two-career choice (see "A Closer Look at Family Diversity: Diversity and Child Care").

[2] Higher-income men tend to be married to higher-income women, as the tendency to marry homogamously (see Chapter 9) would suggest. One effect of the trend toward dual-earner families is increasing inequality between families with two high-status, high-paying careers and those with two poorly paid jobs (Paul 2006; Schwartz and Mare 2005). Families depending on one woman's income fare even worse.

Part-Time Employment

Twenty-five percent of women worked part time in 2005 (compared to 11 percent of men; U.S. Bureau of Labor Statistics 2006d, Table 20). Many mothers scale back their employment while children are preschoolers. Fewer than half of all mothers of preschool children worked full time in 2004 (Dye 2005, Figure 3). "Most married mothers have not traded raising their own children for paid work" (Bianchi and Casper 2000, p. 33).

Research shows that mothers employed part time are more traditional and more similar to full-time homemakers than to full-time employed mothers in their attitudes about wife and mother roles (Glass 1992; Muller 1995), although some women are channeled into part-time work because they cannot find full-time jobs and/or adequate child care.

Greater family and personal time is a clear benefit of part-time employment, but there are costs. As it exists now, part-time work seldom offers job security or benefits such as health insurance. And part-time pay is rarely proportionate to that of full-time jobs. For example, a part-time teacher or secretary usually earns well below the wage paid to regular staff. In higher-level professional/managerial jobs, a different problem appears. To work "part time" as an attorney, accountant, or aspiring manager is to forgo the salary, status, and security of a full-time position and still to put in forty hours a week (Abelson 1998).

Shift Work

Sometimes one or both spouses engage in **shift work**, defined by the Bureau of Labor Statistics as any work schedule in which more than half an employee's hours are before 8 a.m. or after 4 p.m. It has been estimated that in one-quarter of all two-earner couples, at least one spouse does shift work; one in three if they have children (Presser 2000). Some spouses use shift work for higher wages or to ease child-care arrangements. Thirty-six percent of fathers who spend time in child care of preschoolers worked non-day shifts (J. Johnson 2005, Table 2).

Shift workers not only face physical stress with night work or frequently changing schedules; shift work also reduces the overlap of family members' leisure time, and that can affect the marriage: "To the extent that social interaction among family members provides the 'glue' that binds them together, we would expect that the more time spouses have with one another, the more likely they are to develop a strong commitment to their marriage and feel happy with it" (Presser 2000, p. 94). Analysis of responses of 1,668 individuals in a national survey found that—all things equal—a partner's doing shift work reduced satisfaction with the sexual relationship and increased the probability of divorce (White and Keith 1990). A later study also found shift work associated with a higher risk of divorce, though only for couples with children and only for work at late-night hours (Presser 2000).

Doing Paid Work at Home

Home-based work (working from home, either for oneself or for an employer) has increased dramatically over the past decades—a 55 percent increase between 1990 and 2000 (Bergman 2004).

Home-based work used to involve *piecework*, sewing or flower making, for example. This mode of home production is declining due to competition from low-wage workers overseas. It still exists, particularly in the assembly of medical kits, circuit boards, jewelry, and some textile work. Nowadays, some states regulate home-based piecework and require payment of workers' compensation and unemployment benefits ("At-

A San Francisco choreographer goes back to work, taking her new baby to a ballet rehearsal—another way to combine work and family.

© Photo by Andrea Flores

FOCUS ON CHILDREN

Every weekday evening in affluent homes across America, two groups of women trade places. Mothers who follow careers come home and the women who are paid to care for their children prepare to depart or step aside. . . .

For Ruth Sarfaty, 31 years old, a Manhattan public relations executive with a 2½-year-old daughter, the other woman is Cheryl Ryan, 40, a mother of five from Trinidad. "I'm completely dependent on her," said Ms. Sarfaty, whose husband is a real estate broker. "She's in my home more than I am. We could not earn a living without her." Yet, fundamental as these arrangements may be, there are few working relationships that are more ambiguous, complex or ultimately fragile. . . . There are rarely credentials or contracts. Many caregivers are . . . [undocumented immigrants] who are grateful for work that is paid for off the books.

A Gamble, and for Low Pay

[In-home caregivers are poorly paid, on average]. . . . Sixty-two percent leave their jobs each year. "It's a gamble," Professor [Edward] Zigler said, "If you get a

wonderful one, it's like having a new, valued family member. If you get an awful one, you and your child are in trouble." But for women who pursue demanding careers that involve long workdays and irregular hours or travel, in-home care is more than a luxury. . . . [Thus, c]aregivers can wield tremendous power over these women: "You think, if the nanny is happy, the baby is happy. If the baby's happy, you're happy. If you're happy, your husband's happy."

When problems come up, they can throw a family into chaos. Stories of caregivers' abrupt departures abound. . . . Even if the arrangement is running smoothly, women who employ caregivers often wonder about their influence. . . . "You're always re-evaluating the choice," said Rhea Paul, a professor of speech and hearing science at Courtland State University, Oregon, who has hired a grandmother from the Netherlands to care for her three children. "Every day you come home and ask yourself: 'Am I doing the right thing?'" . . .

Special Fabrics of Living

Women who strive to be model mothers learn to make accommodations as their children and caregivers develop their

own rituals. Amy Samuelson's 3-year-old son, Zachary, has looked forward to weekly outings to McDonald's with his caregiver. Ms. Samuelson, who is a nutritionist, said, "It's not my favorite place, but it's important to Zachary. . . ."

Such domestic arrangements, while unfamiliar to many professional women, have long been a part of the fabric of life for the wealthiest Americans and for white Southern families. . . . Today, while there are no reliable estimates of the number of in-home caregivers, it seems clear that not enough skilled ones are available. Caregivers often tell of being approached in playgrounds with their charges by other mothers seeking to lure them away from their employer.

Yet for all the demand, many caregivers complain bitterly about how they are treated. "In this country baby sitting is not seen as a job," said a Jamaican caregiver who keeps a photograph of her employer's child on her dresser at home along with a photograph of her own son. . . .

"It's long hours," said Marie Gaston, 50, who works as a live-in caregiver in Aspen, Colorado. "When you travel with them, it's 24 hours. Sometimes it's two or three weeks before you get time off. There's no overtime." . . .

Home Workers" 2003). Other home-based businesses include the direct selling of cosmetics, kitchenware, and other products, as well as working as an independent contractor to handle customer service calls (Armour 2006).

Home-based work now includes working from home for an employer, perhaps through telecommuting—connecting to the office, customers, clients, or others by the Internet, telephone, videoconferencing, or other means. In 2004, 15 percent of workers worked at home as part of their primary job, and 34 percent of them were self-employed. Two-thirds were managerial or professional employees. A little over half of home-based workers are women (U.S. Bureau of Labor Statistics 2005; U.S. Census Bureau 2007a, Table 592).

The reason women give most often for working at home is "competing domestic demands, such as taking care of children or household chores" ("Both Sexes" 1990). One study (Hill, Hawkins, and Miller 1996) compared 157 home-based teleworkers for a major corporation with 89 office workers from the same company. Almost three-quarters of the teleworkers reported benefiting from the arrangement. Remarking on the advantages of flexibility, mothers of young children were the most likely to be favorable: "I can take care of the sick child and get my work done. A win–win situation" (p. 297).

As the author of a study of women in a home-based direct-selling business noted, however, "many women soon discovered . . . that they had exchanged one set of challenges for another. Mothers employed at home

In some cases, such employment can lead to legal status in the United States, but even that has its drawbacks, according to one caregiver. "They seem nice at first. . . . [T]hen when they know they're going to sponsor you they start to treat you differently because they know if you don't work with them you're going to have to start over with someone else again. Some of them treat you like a slave." . . . Caroline Brownell, who directs an employment agency in San Rafael, California, said she recently decided to stop placing caregivers because of the unrealistic demands of "corporate mothers."

. . . [E]fforts are under way to introduce standards. Mary Starkey, who runs a placement agency in Denver, helped found the 300-member International Nanny Association to seek better pay and working conditions. . . . Her efforts are focused partly on drawing attention to the widespread avoidance of such legal requirements that employers face as Social Security payments, workmen's compensation, unemployment insurance, and reporting earnings to the Internal Revenue Service.

In New York, the 92nd Street Y in Manhattan started what may be the first support and education course for caregivers. Roanna Shorofsky, director of the nursery school there, said, "I realized what was happening when I looked down the hallway one day and saw all the caregivers picking up the kids." Of the 150 children enrolled in the nursery school last year, a third had in-home care. Among the caregivers in last year's course were women from Ireland, Haiti, West Germany, Brazil, China and Jamaica. With the prevalence of foreign-born caregivers, many children move in and out of distinctly different cultural worlds.

"There is no Mary Poppins," said a 39-year-old Manhattan advertising sales executive who interviewed 50 women before she found a 50-year-old woman from Trinidad, who has worked for her for seven years and now attends to a 7-year-old and a 4-year-old. "You have to constantly make compromises. . . . This is one of the most important relationships I'll have in my entire life. I work at it all the time." . . .

Sometimes no effort can keep arrangements from falling apart. That was the experience of Ms. Samuelson, 38, a corporate nutritionist who lives in Riverdale with her husband, a college professor, and Zachary, their son. The first woman she hired had taken excellent care of a friend's children but became pregnant in the Samuelson's employ and left after seven months. . . . The second woman, whom Ms. Samuelson found through an advertisement in *The Irish Echo* newspaper, lasted one week. A third woman left after six months to return to her native Jamaica to care for her sick mother. Finally, nearly two years ago, Ms. Samuelson found a 35-year-old Jamaican who was devoted to Zachary. But three months ago the woman announced that she was five months pregnant and not sure she would continue working after she had the baby.

"When child care breaks down," Ms. Samuelson said, "everything else breaks down."

Critical Thinking

What family theory or theories could you use to analyze this situation?

Source: Abridged from Sara Rimer, "Diversity and Childcare," © *New York Times,* Dec. 26, 1988, p. A-1. Copyright © 1988 by the New York Times Co. Reprinted by permission. For additional information on this topic, see Hondagneu-Sotelo 2001; Lipman 1993; MacDonald 1998; and Romero 1992.

report problems with interruptions . . . ; they are often asked to . . . run errands for relatives, to watch neighbors' children when bad weather closes the school, or to keep an eye out for the older kids" (Kutner 1988).

A study comparing office-based employees to teleworkers found that teleworkers were no more likely than the office workers to feel they had enough time for family life. Some said that they tended to work more hours than they would otherwise, "instead of taking time to enjoy the family" (Hill, Hawkins, and Miller 1996, p. 297). Indeed, work–family flexibility may be a double-edged sword. The families of some teleworkers "struggled because workplace and schedule flexibility blurred the boundaries between work and family life" (p. 293). Home-based workers faced the same tension between career-advancement—which required putting in long work hours—and family time as did employees working in a more conventional setting (Berke 2003).

Leaving the Labor Force and Reentry

One way a woman may deal with the demands of work and family is to leave paid employment in order to spend some years at home raising children:

Distrustful of dawn-to-dusk child care and unable to negotiate flexible work schedules, a growing number of women are conducting their lives in chapters, devoting their adulthood largely to careers but taking time off to be full-time mothers while their children are young. (Uchitelle 2002, p. C1)

These **"sequencing moms"** (Armour 2004) describe staying at home as "a phase in a life that gives equal importance to paid employment" (Uchitelle 2002, p. C1). This is especially possible for those whose husbands earn enough to support the family during the wife's at-home phase.

> A younger generation of workers watched their mothers strive to raise children while ascending the corporate ladder, but they've decided they don't want the same stress. Many still want a career *and* a family. But unlike the Baby Boom women before them, they don't want them at the same time. (Armour 2002, p. B-1)

There may be additional reasons for a mother's putting her career on hold. Lack of society-wide support for employed women—in terms of parental leave for pay, flexible time schedules, or reasonable work expectations—makes combining work and family difficult. This situation is aggravated by the lingering inequality between spouses regarding housework and child care (Rose and Hartmann 2004).

Job dissatisfaction may be a reason for leaving the labor force. Barriers to career advancement remain, and may prove frustrating to a highly educated and able woman. In our society, becoming a mother gives women an option that men are less likely to see as possible: "[W]hen a man gets dissatisfied with his job, he has to stick it out" (Belkin 2003, p. 58).

Sequencing moms who've been interviewed by journalists report being pleased with their decision. As one explained, "[W]e had money, but someone else was raising our kids. . . . I just feel like a new person. After working so hard and being so stressed for years, I really appreciate the small things in life, like the first smile" (Armour 2002, p. B-2). Those "opting out" mothers who plan to eventually return to work fit the leaving work and returning pattern: As one explained, "'You're working. Then you're not working. Then maybe you're working part-time or consulting. Then you go back. [Staying home] . . . is a chapter, not the whole book'" (Belkin 2003, p. 58).

The down side to exercising the sequencing-mom alternative involves concerns about career reentry. The women interviewed lost 18 percent of their earning capacity, and some were not able to get full-time jobs. A lot depends on the economy and the need for workers. It may be that with the education and skill levels that characterize women who can choose this option, employers will adapt to the sequencing-mom pattern. In fact, some companies are beginning to develop reentry programs or "on-ramps" for women who want to resume their careers (Joyce 2005a, 2007b; McGinn 2006a).

Meanwhile, a majority of first-time mothers (65 percent) return to work within the first year after their baby is born. Older mothers, college graduates, and non-Hispanic white women are likely to return to work earlier than their counterparts (Johnson and Downs 2005).

Unpaid Family Work

Unpaid family work involves the necessary tasks of attending both to the emotional needs of all family members and to the practical needs of dependent members (such as children or elderly parents), as well as maintaining the family domicile.

Caring for Dependent Family Members

Our cultural tradition and social institutions give women principal responsibility for raising children (Cancian and Oliker 2000). Moreover, our culture designates women as "kinkeepers" (Hagestad 1986), whose job it is to keep in touch with—and, if necessary, care for—parents, adult siblings, and other relatives. The vast majority of informal elderly care is provided by female relatives, usually daughters and (albeit less often) daughters-in-law (Keith 1995; Globerman 1996).

Family responsibilities and resources in meeting the needs of elderly, ill, or disabled family members are topics included in Chapters 15 and 18, while many of the chapters deal with the emotional aspects of family life. In this chapter we look more closely at housework and child care.

Housework

Utopians and social engineers alike once shared a hope that advancing technology and changed social arrangements would make obsolete the need for families to

Doris Lee (1905–1983), *Thanksgiving*, 1935. Oil on canvas.

cook, clean, or mind children (D. Hayden 1981). But collective arrangements proposed by utopians and early feminists never caught on. Servants, who had done much of the work for earlier middle-class housewives, entered factory work or took other, better jobs, and middle-class women were left to do their own housework (Cowan 1983). Technology seems merely to have raised the standards rather than making housework less time-consuming. For example, instead of changing clothes at infrequent intervals, we now do so daily (Cowan 1983).

The Second Shift Housework—even with the decline—remains substantial. Including child care, many employed wives (and some husbands) put in what sociologist Arlie Hochschild calls a **second shift** of unpaid family work that amounts to an extra month of work each year (Hochschild 1989).

Increased immigration has provided a class of women who will do child care and cleaning for affluent, dual-career families. But despite changing attitudes among couples and media portrayals of two-earner couples who share housework, women in fact continue to do more of it. Although the gap has lessened (Artis and Pavalko 2003), data from about 8,500 participants in a University of Michigan study showed that women, on average, spend twenty-seven hours a week on housework (compared to forty hours in 1965), while men increased their housework time from twelve hours in 1965 to sixteen hours in 1999 (Institute for Social Research 2002).

Women's revolutionary entry into the labor force would seem to require a concurrent restructuring of household labor. Husbands *are* doing somewhat more around the house than they did twenty years ago. But "women continue to feel responsible for family members' well-being and are more likely than men to adjust their work and home schedules to accommodate others" (Coltrane 2000, p. 1212).

Economics plays a role. When we consider men's and women's paid and unpaid work, it becomes apparent that a **reinforcing cycle** emerges: For a number of reasons, which we have already explored, men employed full time average higher earnings than women employed full time. Because most husbands actually or potentially earn more than their wives, couples allow her paid work role to be more vulnerable to family demands than his. This situation, in turn, has the effects of lowering the time and energy a wife spends in the labor force and of giving employers reason to pay women less than men. This lower pay, coupled with society's devaluation of family in favor of job demands, encourages couples to give priority to husbands' work. Disproportionately burdened with household labor, wives find it difficult to invest themselves in the labor force to the same degree that husbands do (Zvonkovic et al. 1996).

Who Does the Housework? A researcher commenting on the Michigan study said: "Women have shown a massive decline in the time spent in housework and a massive increase in paid work. Men have picked up a bit of the slack at home, but at some point have said, 'I've put the dishes in the dishwasher five nights this week. What else do you want from me?'" (K. Peterson 2002, p. D-06). Husbands are typically more willing to do child care—especially "fun" activities—than housework (S. Berk 1985; Hochschild 1989).

Participation in household labor is generally related to the degree of equality of earnings between the spouses and the proportionate share of those earnings produced by the wife. But when men are unemployed they may actually do less (Coltrane 2000). It may be that being a breadwinner is so symbolically important that unemployed family men are reluctant to do anything that might seem to undermine their manhood, such as labor traditionally considered women's work (Shelton and John 1993). This pattern of less housework time also characterizes those men whose wives earn more than they do, perhaps for the same reason (Brines 1994; Hochschild 1989; Tichenor 1999; see also Kroska 1997).

Ways in which individual families manage vary. Some wives scale back their paid work, and others quit entirely. These may seem the best choices, given the options. But the reality is that "no-fault divorce laws combined with rising divorce rates have substantially increased the risks for women [who remain out of the labor force or reduce their employment options]" (R. Peterson 1989, p. 2). Another strategy is to lower housework standards and food preparation time after a wife becomes employed (Shelton 1990).

Some two-earner couples hire household help, especially in upper-income white families, and purchase the services of immigrant, racial/ethnic minority, and working-class people for housekeeping and child-care work or other chores (Coltrane 2000). Researchers note that women more often coordinate paid services as well as do more housework themselves (L. Thompson 1991).

Another housework option might appear to be help from children. Some studies find that children in single-parent families, especially, help significantly with housework, while others find that children in married-couple families do more work. In any case, "while many children do some household labor . . . their contribution is typically occasional and their time investment small" (Shelton and John 1996, p. 311; see also Coltrane 2000, pp. 1225–26).

Generally, husbands follow "the path of least resistance" (Peterson and Gerson 1992, p. 532). To secure her spouse's help with the second shift, a wife must take the initiative. She must be willing to truly share decisions

Children do some household labor, but it is more often a socialization device or family group activity than a substantial sharing of parents' household tasks.

about children and housework. Some wives are reluctant to relinquish the centrality and decision-making role or to loosen their standards and preferences for how things should be done, and that may discourage husband participation (Allen and Hawkins 1999).

Another issue is that housework can have a meaning beyond simple household maintenance. Performing certain household tasks considered traditionally feminine (or masculine) may reinforce a masculine or feminine gender identity (Coltrane 2000, p. 1213). "Housework is not just the performance of basic household tasks but it is also a symbolic expression of gender relations, particularly between wives and husbands" (Artis and Pavalko 2003, p. 748). For some women, homemakers, the perception of "home" is of "the world where we carry out the private search for intimacy" (Nippert-Eng 1996, p. 22). Their enjoyment of domestic work relates to their belief that "perform-

ing family work is a way of showing care for loved ones" (Grote, Naylor, and Clark 2002, p. 520). Gender ideology plays a role for more traditional women—for them, housework has a "moral quality" (Stevens, Kiger, and Riley 2001, p. 524).[3]

Still, the Michigan researchers believe that "the gap will continue to close as society moves closer to the notion that there is not men's work and women's work, but just different kinds of work that is shared by both sexes" (in K. Peterson 2002, p. D-06).

Race/Ethnicity and Other Factors In some ethnic groups, such as Vietnamese and Laotian, housework is significantly shared, if not by husbands, by household members other than the wife/mother (P. Johnson 1998). Among blacks, adult children living at home, extended kin, and nonresident fathers are likely to share housework and child care (Coltrane 2000). The latter may provide child care or help with repairs.

Research on racial/ethnic differences finds that the pattern of men's spending less time than women in housework occurs in white, black, and Hispanic families. However, black men spend more time in unpaid family work than do white men (Shelton and John 1993; John, Shelton, and Luschen 1995; Orbuch and Eyster 1997). One explanation offered for black men's greater participation in housework is that they have more egalitarian attitudes, at least in this domain, and that African American wives are more likely to be employed and to have earnings that are closer to equality compared to their husbands than is true for other groups (Coltrane 2000). However, when factors other than race/ethnicity that affect men's household labor were taken into account—such as age, number of children, sex-role attitudes, and wives' sex-role attitudes—race/ethnicity was no longer so significantly associated with household labor time (Shelton and John 1993). In other words, the differences among white, black, and Hispanic men's household labor time may reflect other differences among them, as well. Further research will be needed to resolve the differences among these studies.

Research regarding Latino couples is mixed, with some studies showing no difference from the white division of household labor and others showing that Latino men do slightly more (Coltrane 2000). Blue-collar men do more housework than middle-class white-collar men despite being more likely to express a traditional gender ideology—the wife's earnings are more essential to the family (Hochschild 1989).

---

[3] See Artis and Pavalko 2003, pp. 747–48, or Coltrane 2000, pp. 1212–17, for a more comprehensive discussion than we can present here.

Is Housework Vanishing? One of the ways in which families have adjusted to women's entry into the labor force is to scale down what is thought necessary—assisted by microwaves, fast food, and so forth, and sometimes by paid services. The University of Michigan researchers use the term *vanishing housework* in noting that as men and women are both putting in more hours of employment, the total amount of time a couple spends on housework has declined (Institute for Social Research 2002).

> There's . . . reason to believe . . . low levels of family-performed housework will persist . . . since our research shows that most people rate routine housework as the least enjoyable use of their time. (researcher Frank Stafford, in K. Peterson 2002, p. D-06)

Another reason for the decline in housework may be a related change in culture. A study which looked at different cohorts of women found that younger women do less housework, suggesting that "socialization about family life, gender, and household labor may have been

After a long day on the job, Cabral and Denys get some sleep on the seventeen-mile shuttle bus trip from the plant to Moline, Illinois, where they live. Longer hours of employment mean that time families spend on housework is "vanishing."

© The Modesto Bee

substantially different for newer cohorts" (Artis and Pavalko 2003, p. 758).

The Leisure Gap Women interviewed by sociologist Arlie Hochschild

> tended to talk more intently about being overtired, sick, and "emotionally drained." . . . They talked about how much [sleep] they could "get by on.". . . These women talked about sleep the way a hungry person talks about food. (Hochschild 1989, p. 9)

She and other researchers concluded that the second shift for women means a "**leisure gap**" between husbands and wives, as women sacrifice leisure—and sleep—to accomplish unpaid family work.

But according to recent research, the leisure gap seems to have vanished, at least so far as work demands are concerned. In their research based on time diaries, Bianchi, Robinson, and Milkie (2006) add employment hours and household work hours to get total time spent in work for men and women. Men, it is true, spend fewer hours in housework, but they spend more in paid employment. A University of Michigan time study also found gender equity in work time; women averaged fifty-one hours, while men averaged fifty-three in total hours spent on employment plus domestic work (D. Johnson 2002).

Still, women have half an hour less than men of leisure time. Moreover, a lot depends on what is meant by "leisure." "Because women tend to be the coordinators of family life, it is often difficult for them to take time for themselves independent of household responsibilities" (Mattingly and Bianchi 2003, p. 1001). What counts as leisure time for women often involves their organizing of family activities for others. For example, while a mother is enjoying a child's birthday party, she is simultaneously managing the occasion. Mothers' ostensibly "leisure" time includes time spent with children and a great deal of multitasking, or "contaminated" leisure, as they do household tasks or supervise children while engaging in recreational activities. Free time away from the household is less available to women than men (Mattingly and Bianchi 2003).

Fairness and Marital Happiness A conclusion easily drawn from research is that employed women are carrying an unfair share of domestic tasks. But do couples themselves see it that way? That depends on the meaning of household work to the couple and what they consider "fair."

Although, overall, unequal shares of household labor are associated with marital dissatisfaction, this relationship is altered by perceptions of fairness. Citing a number of studies, Michelle Frisco and Kristi Williams (2003) found perceived fairness to be more strongly associated with marital happiness (and, in their own study, with the likelihood of divorce) than differences in actual hours spent in domestic work. To a wife or woman partner, a man's taking up *some*, if not an equal share of, household tasks may signify caring.

Interesting is that men and women perceive "fair share" differently. Of those men in dual-earner families who perceived that they were doing *more than their fair share*, 43 percent were actually doing *less than half* the housework. In other words, they did not think it would be fair for them to do as much as half the housework. Meanwhile, of women who perceived themselves to be doing a *fair* share, almost two-thirds were doing *all or more* of the housework. An uneven split seemed fair to them (Frisco and Williams 2003 [the Frisco and Williams study used the *Marital Instability Over the Life Course* data set]; White and Booth 1991.) Probably both men and women have in mind as a standard of comparison the breadwinner–housewife model. Men, then, are doing more, while women are unloading some of their former responsibility. That seems "fair." And men may lump housework and employment together and add that up to feel the total burden of family responsibility is a fair one (Lavee and Katz 2002). The relatively comparable men's and women's total hours of paid and household

The second shift is probably more enjoyable when shared by both partners.

work reported by Bianchi, Robinson, and Milkie (2006) would support this conclusion.

Gay Men, Lesbians, and Housework Given that gay couples are composed of persons of the same gender, how does their household division of labor work out and what impact does it have on the relationship?

A small qualitative study of forty-three gay male and thirty-six lesbian couples explored these questions. Each partner was employed full time, and there were no children residing with the couples (which is the majority pattern among gay/lesbian couples). The study looked at who performed some traditionally female tasks—it provides some interesting insights, though given the small sample, it cannot be conclusive.

Partners were asked how often they performed six tasks compared to how often their partner did. Generally, lesbian couples' division of labor was more egalitarian than that of gay male couples. The researcher was most interested in the impact on the relationship. Perceived equality was closely tied to relationship satisfaction and that, in turn, to relationship stability (Kurdek 2007).

In the next section, we will examine how partners juggle household labor demands, along with employment.

Juggling Employment and Family Work

The concept of juggling implies a hectic and stressful situation. A great deal of research and other writings on the subject suggest that today's typical dual-earner or single-working-parent family is a hectic one (e.g., Hochschild 1989, 1997). This is particularly true when there are children in the home, and more so for single men and married and single women than for married men due to the greater "role overload" of the first three groups (Kiecolt 2003, p. 34).

Work, Family, and Leisure: Attitudes and Time Allocation

American workers lead the industrial world in the number of hours worked (Jacobs and Gerson 2004, pp. 128–34). About 28 percent of all employees now work more than forty hours per week. Just over 5 percent of the labor force held two or more paid jobs in 2005, with slightly higher proportions of women than men (U.S. Census Bureau 2007a, Tables 588, 591).

An influential study of changes in time at work concluded that working people are spending significantly more hours at work than in the recent past (Schor 1991). In their book based on data from the Current

Population Survey, sociologists Jerry Jacobs and Kathleen Gerson affirmed this conclusion. They point to an "increasing mismatch between our economic system and the needs of American families" (Jacobs and Gerson 2004, back cover). However, Bianchi, Robinson, and Milkie (2006) present time diary data that show only a small increase in work hours since 1976. Government data on work hours indicate that men's hours have increased 2 percent over this period, women's 6 percent. Employed women work an average of 36 hours a week, men 41.8—but when agricultural workers are taken out of the calculation, men work, on average, less than forty hours a week (U.S. Bureau of Labor Statistics 2006d, Table 21).

This does not mean the combination of work and family responsibilities is stress free or free of time pressure. Virtually every researcher studying work–family time hears expressions of time pressure, of feeling rushed and stressed (e.g., Jacobs and Gerson 2004; Bianchi, Robinson, and Milkie 2006). Yet Bianchi and her colleagues argue that such stress in concentrated in the children's early years and especially for women with demanding careers, as well as for single mothers, while Jacobs and Gerson see more pervasive problems for working families. These different conclusions as to whether work hours have increased are difficult to resolve, but they seem to reflect methodological differences. Bianchi and her colleagues argue that their time diary methodology is the more accurate because it is specific and timely—study participants are "walked" through activities of the preceding twenty-four hours. Jacobs and Gerson point to the small size of time diary samples and to other methodological issues and argue the merits of their Current Population Survey data.

Jacobs and Gerson do a careful analysis of theirs and the time diary studies and conclude that each is measuring different things. The hours worked per week by each employee have not changed much over recent decades. But the weeks devoted to work by family members have increased dramatically because of women's entry into the labor force. Total hours of work are expanded by the increasing tendency for women to work full time and not leave the labor force for an extended period.

Table 12.1 reports a Gallup poll that asked individuals whether they have enough time to do what they want. About 60 percent of those age eighteen through forty-nine—the ages of employment and active parenting—say they do not have enough time (Saad 2004b). For a majority of Americans, rest and relaxation time, time for friends and hobbies, and even time for sleep is not what they would like it to be (Saad 2004b; and see Table 12.1). "Facts About Families: Where Does the Time Go?" reports data from a major government sur-

vey on how employed parents spend their time on an average day.

Some interesting research has been designed to assess the impact of women's entry into the labor force on health, marital quality, and marital stability. One such study has found women to have increasingly good (self-reported) health as labor force participation and working hours have increased. Both women's increased education and their employment have contributed to better health, contrary, perhaps, to expectation. Although there was a short-term diminishment of health attributed to the stress of coping with work and family in children's younger years, once children entered

Table 12.1 Do Americans Feel That They Have Enough Time, or Not?

GALLUP POLL RESPONSES TO THE FOLLOWING QUESTION: GENERALLY SPEAKING, DO YOU HAVE ENOUGH TIME TO DO WHAT YOU WANT TO THESE DAYS, OR NOT?			
December 2003	Right Amount	Too Little	Too Much
In general	52%	48%	—
Your family	66%	29%	4%
Friendships or other personal relationships	58%	37%	4%
Sleep	57%	39%	4%
Household chores	55%	27%	17%
Internet use (users only)	55%	26%	17%
Your job (emploed only)	54%	4%	41%
Relaxing or doing nothing	45%	44%	11%
Hobbies	40%	51%	5%
Reading	38%	54%	7%
Personal exercise and recreation	37%	59%	3%
Watching television	50%	16%	32%

Data were collected by the Gallup Poll from a national sample of 1,011 adults, December 11–14, 2003.

Source: Adapted from Saad 2004b.

"Hey Baby, I just dropped off the kids at school, and now I'm going to the grocery store, and then I'm going home and unloading the car—am I making you hot?"

Where Does the Time Go?

We've talked about employment and household labor. What do people do with the rest of their time?

An American Time Use Survey was conducted in 2003 by the U.S. Bureau of Labor Statistics (2004). Some 21,000 people were asked to keep time diaries, recording what activities they engaged in and for how much time. The reports of these many individuals were averaged to come up with typical days for different groups. Let's look at employed parents of children under eighteen and see what happens in an average day.

First there are the basics. Just over an hour (1.12 hours) was spent in *eating and drinking*. Around nine hours (8.97) were spent in such *personal care* activities as sleeping, bathing, dressing, and health care.

Work averaged six and a half hours (6.49) for men, and four and a half (4.64) for women (remember that some people work part time and that all days are not work days). On average, employed women spent over two hours (2.05) on *household activities*—the domestic labor—while these tasks occupied almost an hour and a quarter (1.22) of men's time.

These totals did not include child care, which fell into the category of *caring for and helping household members,* a category that also included helping adult members of the household, perhaps with medical needs. Women spent an hour and a half (1.56) on caring for household members, while men spent less than an hour (.85).

Shopping—*purchasing goods and services,* as the survey termed it—took almost an hour of an employed mother's daily time (.91), while fathers devoted two-thirds of an hour to shopping (.65). Men were able to devote more of their time to *leisure and sports* (4.07 hours) than were women (3.49 hours). The most common use of leisure time for all was watching television.

Men and women participated in *organizational, civic, and religious activities* at about the same rate, each spending about a third of an hour on an average day. Men and women alike spent an average of .18 hour in *caring for and helping nonhousehold members* and in *educational activities. Telephone calls, mail, and e-mail* communication rounded out the day (at .07 hour for men and .14 hour for women), while some time (.14 hour) was spent on unspecified *other activities.*

So what does it all mean? Despite amounts of time in some categories so small as to seem trivial, we can see some interesting things in these figures. The American Time Use Survey shows that women spend 75 percent more time than men in the care of the household and its members, adding one more study to those that show a gender disparity. However, men spent 40 percent more time working than did women.

In other areas, there is little difference in time use between men and women. The time men and women devote to organizational, civic, religious, and educational activities and to helping nonhousehold members is similar. Still, men have more leisure time, while women do more shopping (more likely to be grocery shopping than "fun" shopping). Women spend twice as much time as men in communication activities and more time on personal care, a large portion of which is sleeping.

Critical Thinking

How do you spend *your* time? Has the time you spend in various activities changed throughout your life? These data are for employed people who have children at home. If your situation is different, is your time use different as well?

Source: U.S. Bureau of Labor Statistics 2004, Tables 1, 6.

school, superior health rebounded. Overall, women have gained in health as employment has become the norm (Schnittker 2007).

Another study using a national data set found that "wives' full-time employment is associated with greater marital stability" while not affecting quality one way or the other (Schoen, Rogers, and Amato 2006). Still another study looked at gender changes and marital quality and found that most gender-related changes had no negative impact on marital quality, but there was increased marital conflict attributable to "work-family demands based on the combination of wives' employment and preschool-age children" (Rogers and Amato 2000, p. 747). This suggests, once again, that perhaps the negatives for families of women's employment are focused on the preschool years of those with children.

There is some indication that younger workers have different attitudes toward work–family balance than did their predecessors. Social scientists see a "gender convergence" in attitudes and values regarding work/family roles. Both men and women want a balance of work and family in their lives (Cohen 2007b, p. A13; Monahan Lang, and Risman 2007).

A 2002 study sponsored by the American Business Collaboration (composed of such prominent corporations as IBM and Johnson and Johnson, with additional support from the Ford Foundation) and conducted by the Families and Work Institute surveyed some 2,800 adults from four generations of workers: "Matures" (born 1945 and earlier); "Baby Boomers" (born 1946–64), "Generation X" (born 1965–79) and "Generation Y" (born 1980–94). Respondents were asked if they put work before family ("work-centric"), put family before work ("family-centric"), or prioritized both equally ("dual-centric").

As Figure 12.4 indicates, a majority of the two youngest generations described themselves as family-centric, some as dual-centric, with few likely to style themselves as work-centric. Their predecessors, the baby boomers, were comparatively more work oriented and less family oriented, although the dual-centric and family-centric orientations together were selected by a majority of Boomers. Matures (not included in Figure 12.4) were similar to Generation X and Y in being less work-centric, but were also less family-centric than all other generational groups. A majority were dual-centric (Families and Work Institute 2004).

We will look now at how children in two-earner marriages are doing, and then at parents.

How Are Children Faring?

Before women with children entered the

FOCUS ON CHILDREN work force in large numbers, working mothers were considered problematic by child develop-

"Quality time? Do I have to?"

ment experts and the public. Now they are taken for granted. A 2001 survey of women (not all of them mothers) found more than 90 percent in agreement with the statement that a woman can be a good mother and have a successful career (Center for the Advancement of Women 2003). A recent study draws the conclusion that maternal employment does not cause behavior problems in children (Vander Ven et al. 2001), and another study of more than 6,000 children studied at age twelve found no difference between the children whose mothers were employed or not employed during the child's first three years (E. Harvey 1999).

Overall, this continues to be the prevailing view. Furthermore, the economic benefit to children of working mothers cannot be overlooked. Family income tends to be favorably associated with various child outcome measures. Important for parents, though, is keeping their child's needs in the forefront in the face of daily pressures. Recent studies have found that mothers who work part time are better at this than those who work full time—and may indeed spend more time helping their children with homework than even full-time homemakers (Muller 1995). Before the era of working mothers, so-called full-time mothers did not spend all their time with children, but devoted more time than today's mothers to household work or volunteer work. And some of those mothers—of larger families, especially—made use of paid help in caring for children.

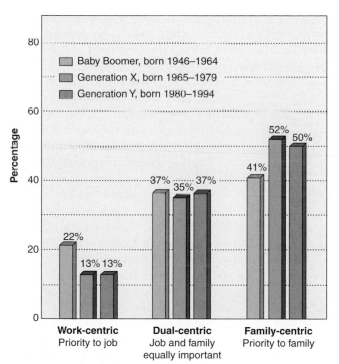

Figure 12.4 Priority given to work, family, or both by 2,800 workers surveyed in 2002: Generational differences.
Source: Families and Work Institute 2004.

"The puzzling thing about the reallocation of mothers' time to market work is that it appears to have been accomplished with little effect on children's well-being," noted sociologist Suzanne Bianchi in her presidential address to the Population Association of America (Bianchi 2000). A variety of studies indicate that parents today spend as much or more time with children as in the past (Milkie et al. 2004; Bianchi, Robinson, and Milkie2006; and see Figures 12.5 and 12.6). Figure 12.5 presents total weekly hours parents spent with children in 1975 and 2000. That time has increased for married

fathers and married mothers. It has, however, decreased for single mothers, though it remains substantial.

The data on "total time" reflect the time a parent spends in the presence of children. Figure 12.6 presents the time parents spend in "primary child care," that is, active caretaking, whether that takes the form of routine care or enrichment activities. Mothers and fathers spent more time in child care in 2000 than did parents in previous measured years going back to 1965. (Time spent doing child care was measured in time diary studies done by various universities using samples ranging from 1,200 to over 5,000 (Bianchi, Robinson, and Milkie 2006, Chapter 2).

How did mothers, especially, accomplish an increase in time with children while at the same time dramatically increasing employment hours? (Incidentally, time spent in personal care [sleeping, grooming and eating] and free time remained relatively stable) (Bianchi, Robinson, and Milkie 2006, Figure 5.1). They cut back on housework and spent somewhat less time doing things just with spouses. In part, they multitasked; parents spent time with children (and often each other) in children's activities or those of the parents. Today's families are smaller, so that parental attention is less divided; moreover, the increase in father's time with children (for married parents) means increased total attention for children.

These results present an optimistic and reassuring view of how children of working parents are faring as mothers have entered the labor force. Several concerns remain. One concern is that "as parents' lives have become more hectic, those of their children are becoming more tightly organized." Children are spending more time on school, organized sports, chores, and going with their parents on errands rather than engaging in unstructured play or organizing their own activities with other children (S. Holmes 1998).

The divergence in parental attention to children in two-parent families and those in single-parent families (which may have other problems and pressures) is another concern. And though married-couple families are virtually equal in total workweek time—fathers spending more hours in employment and mothers on the "second shift"— employed mothers still seem more stressed and time pressured. For one thing, they more often must "orchestrate family life" (Bianchi, Robinson, and Milkie 2006 p. 171). Because wives more often adjust employment hours during children's preschool years, they

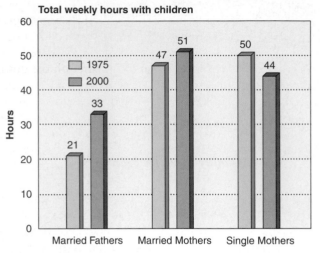

Total weekly hours with children

Figure 12.5 Total weekly hours spent with children for married fathers, married mothers, and single mothers, 1975 and 2000.

Source: From Bianchi, Milkie, and Robinson, *The Changing Rhythms of American Family Life,* Fig. 4.1, p. 63. Reprinted by permission of the Russell Sage Foundation.

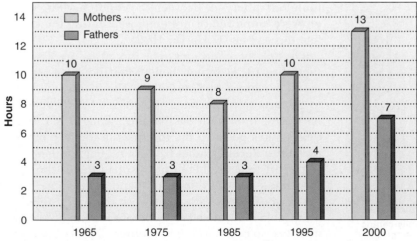

Primary Child Care, Average Weekly Hours

Figure 12.6 Primary child care, average weekly hours, mothers and fathers, 1965–2000.

Source: From Bianchi, Milkie, and Robinson, *The Changing Rhythms of American Family Life,* Fig. 4.3, p. 72. Reprinted by permission of the Russell Sage Foundation.

run a risk of lower pensions and inadequate support should the marriage break up, and they may not have the careers they might have had otherwise. This leads us to the issue of how parents are faring as they juggle paid and unpaid work.

How Are Parents Faring?

This chapter focuses on work and family in marriages (rather than other family forms) for two reasons. First, the vast majority of research on the interface between paid employment and family labor concerns marrieds. Second, single parenting is addressed in some detail in Chapter 16.

> Although the rough edges of the work–family conflict may be particularly sharp for single parents, two-earner marriages assuredly have them also. Whether one is single or married, "career and family involvement have never been combined easily in the same person." (Hunt and Hunt 1986)

An ideal for the baby boom and younger husband is to share wage-earning and family responsibilities on an equal basis and especially to be an involved father. Indeed, more fathers are taking off work following the birth of a child, and they are more visible in parenting classes, in pediatricians' offices, and dropping off and picking up children in day-care centers.

The man who gives family priority may have to deal with challenges to his masculinity or resentment from coworkers, whether parents or not. Employers may not see unpaid family work as important or believe that employees, especially males, should allow family responsibilities to interfere with labor force involvement (Hochschild 1997). As a result, workers report that they are reluctant to take advantage of family benefits that are theoretically available (Jacobs and Gerson 2004, p. 6). Some husbands report having lied to bosses or taken other evasive steps at work to hide conflicts between job and family. One man told his boss that he has "another meeting" so that he can leave the office each day at 6 p.m.: "I never say it's a meeting with my family."

The previous discussion applies to working parents generally. In the next section, we will look at some stresses peculiar to *two-career* marriages—keeping in mind the distinction between *two-earner* couples and *two-career* couples made earlier in the chapter.

Two-Career Marriages Some decades ago as the two-career marriage was emerging as an ideal lifestyle available to all young couples, Hunt and Hunt (1977) noted that dual-career families require a support system of child-care providers and household help that depends heavily on ability to pay. That means it is inherently limited to a small number of families. Moreover, the success of today's two-career union is premised on the existence of a labor pool of low-paid, but highly dependable, household help. The vast majority of such help is provided by women, many of whom have their own families to worry about (Romero 1992). Even parents who can afford to pay for it find that locating such help may be difficult.

Two careers requiring travel may present added problems as parents "scramble to patch things together" for overnight child care (Shellenbarger 1991a). Two-career partners need the dexterity to balance not only career and family life but also her and his careers so that both spouses prosper professionally in what they see as a fair way. The balance between partners may be upset by career fluctuations as well as family time allocations. The contrast between one career that is going well and one that is not may be hard on the partner on the down side. But the marriage may "operate as a buffer, cushioning the negative impacts of failures or reversals in one or the other career" (Hertz 1986, p. 59). When the marriage is rewarding, compromises, such as turning down opportunities that would require relocation, are acceptable because of the importance given to marriage as well as career.

Sociologist Rosanna Hertz (1986) found that the two-career couples she studied were realistic, though sometimes regretful, about some benefits of the traditional relationships they are giving up. Although men acknowledged that their wives provided less support, they appreciated the excitement, and the status, associated with an achieving wife. Some of them had considered or made career changes that would not have been possible if wives had not been successful wage earners. Both partners claimed fulfillment from and assigned emotional meaning to an egalitarian dual-career marriage: "She has a sense of a full partnership and she should" (in Hertz 1986, p. 75).

Commitment was perceived as truer: "Working . . . has decreased my dependence. . . . That makes it into much more of a voluntary relationship" (in Hertz 1986, p. 75). Very visible to Hertz was the way in which communication was enhanced by similar lives, making possible a higher level of mutual support than in conventional couples: "These couples . . . [had] a different level of understanding about each other's lives, a level that is intimate and empathic" (p. 77).

The couples studied by Hertz did report conflict over balancing time, commitment, and career moves. Indeed, the geography of two careers presents a significant challenge to couples.

The Geography of Two Careers Because career advancement often requires geographic mobility—and even international transfers—juggling two careers may prove difficult for marrieds or committed partners. A career move for one may make the other a **trailing spouse** who relocates to accommodate the partner's career. Increasingly, couples turn down transfers because of two-career issues. As a result, some large companies now offer career-opportunity assistance to a trailing spouse, such as hiring a job search firm, facilitating intercompany networking, attempting to locate a position for the spouse in the same institution, or providing career counseling (Lublin 1992).

Although wives still move for their husband's career more often than the reverse, the number of trailing husbands has increased. Counselors who work with trailing husbands note that these men have few role models and must confront norms and social pressures that conflict with their decisions. Financial pressures, when a trailing spouse cannot find a job, may intensify the strain (Hendershott 1995). But more two-career marriages today are based on a conscious mutuality to which partners have become accustomed by the time a career move presents itself. Such couples are less likely to have problems with a female-led relocation than are more traditional marrieds. For many spouses, trailing is preferable to commuting, another solution to the problem of career opportunities in two locations.

To Commute or Not to Commute? Social scientists have called marriages in which spouses live apart **commuter marriages**. The vast majority of commuting couples would rather not do so, but endure the separation for the sake of career or other goals. Since research began on commuter marriages in the early 1970s, social scientists have drawn different conclusions. Some studies suggest that the benefits of such marriages—greater economic and emotional equality between spouses—counter their drawbacks. Other research focuses on difficulties in managing the lifestyle. One conclusion to be drawn from the research is that commuters who are able to have frequent reunions are happier with the lifestyle than those who cannot.

One study (Bunker et al. 1992) compared life satisfaction for 90 commuting and 133 single-resident, two-career couples. Almost three-fourths of the commuters saw their partner weekly. The researchers were surprised to find that the commuters experienced less stress and overload than the single-residence couples: "Perhaps there is some restructuring in the commuting two-residence couple that simplifies life or perceptions of it. Perhaps short separations facilitate compartmentalization, allowing commuters to keep work life and family life in well-separated spheres, and to confront the demands of each role in alternation rather than simultaneously" (p. 405). Then, too, the commuter couples had significantly fewer babies and young children than did single-residence couples; commuter marriages

probably work better in the absence of dependent children (G. Stern 1991).

Generally, the researchers concluded that commuting has both rewards and costs. Commuters reported more satisfaction with their work life than did single-residence, two-career respondents, but commuters were significantly less satisfied with their partner relationships and family life (Bunker et al. 1992). Some commuters say they can put their respective careers first for only so long before their relationship frays: "Career-wise it was absolutely fantastic," said one spouse who had given it up. "Personally, it was absolutely horrible" (in G. Stern 1991, p. B3).

Couples who have been married for shorter periods seem to have more difficulties with commuter marriages. Perhaps because of their history of shared time, more established couples in commuter marriages have a greater "commitment to the unit" (H. Gross 1980; Rhodes 2002).

Social Policy, Work, and Family

Despite the benefits of employment to women and their families, and despite societal pressures and gender-role changes leading to high female employment, neither public policy nor families have fully adapted to this change. This section examines policy issues regarding work and family. Policy issues center on two questions: "What is needed?" and "Who will provide it?"

What Is Needed to Resolve Work–Family Issues?

Researchers and other work–family experts are in general agreement that single-parent and two-earner families are in need of more adequate provisions for child and elder care, family leave, and flexible employment scheduling.

Child Care Policy researchers define **child care** as the full-time care and education of children under age six, care before and after school and during school vacations for older children, and overnight care when employed parents must travel. Child care may be paid or unpaid and provided by relatives or others, including one of the parents.

In her study of dual-earner couples, sociologist Rosanna Hertz (1997) explored parents' approaches to child care and found they fell into three categories. One was the **mothering approach to child care**, whereby the couple preferred that the wife care for the children. An initial strategy of overtime or a second job for the husband often proved to be unworkable, so the wife did have to enter the labor force. But the couple maintained as traditional a division of labor as they could, with the mother working as much as possible during hours the children were sleeping or in school.

In the **parenting approach to child care**, family care was shared by parents, who structured their work to this end. They accepted part-time work, for example, and the lower incomes that went with it. But primarily these were "labor force elites" (Hertz 1997, p. 370), who could be sure of commanding a full-time job when they wanted to, or whose part-time earnings produced substantial income. In blue-collar or lower-income families, shift care or the periodic unemployment of men produced a parenting approach. In 2003, 32 percent of fathers worked late-evening or night shifts and were principle sources of child care for preschoolers during mothers' working hours (J. O. Johnson 2005).

In the **market approach to child care**, career-oriented couples hired other people to care for their children. We now look at child care in this sense. There are essentially three types of nonrelative child care. Paid care may be provided in the child's home by a nanny, an **in-home caregiver** who lives in or comes to the house daily (see "A Closer Look at Family Diversity: Diversity and Child Care" p. 304). The term **family child care** refers to care provided in a caregiver's home, often by an older woman or a mother who has chosen to remain out of the labor force to care for her own children. Parents who prefer family day care seem to be seeking a family-like atmosphere, with a smaller-scale, less-routinized setting. Perhaps they also desire social similarity of caregiver and parent to better ensure that their children are socialized according to their own values (Greathouse 1996).

Center care provides group care for a larger number of children in child-care centers. The use of child care centers has increased rapidly, partly because of the growing scarcity of in-home caregivers, as relatives or neighbors who formerly cared for children now join the labor force themselves. Increased use of center care is also due to the perception that it offers greater safety and a strong preschool curriculum.[4]

By the time they enter school, an estimated 44 percent of children have been in a nonrelative child-care arrangement. This is more common for black and non-Hispanic white children, a little less so for Asian or Pacific Islander children, and least common among Hispanics (Dye and Johnson 2007, Table 2). Black

mothers, who relied heavily on kin networks in the past, saw that option decline by the 1990s as grandmothers and other relatives entered the labor force themselves (Brewster and Padavic 2002). Nonrelative care is also more common for children in families above the poverty level than for those in lower-income families (Dye and Johnson 2007, Table 3).

Of children of employed mothers, 24 percent were in organized care—day-care centers, Head Start, or preschool. Six percent had in-home care; 10 percent, family day care; and the remainder, other arrangements, no care, or multiple arrangements. Relative care was heavily used—28 percent of children were in the care of grandparents, with 25 percent cared for by fathers; sibs or other relatives cared for 11 percent; and mothers themselves, 5 percent (by bringing children to the office or other work site, including self-employment work at home; J. O. Johnson 2005, Tables 1 and 2).

Now there is extensive research on the developmental outcomes of various child-care arrangements. See "As We Make Choices: Child Care and Children's Outcomes" for a discussion of this research.

About 40 percent of children age twelve to fourteen and 8 percent of those age five to eleven whose mothers were employed were in **self-care**—that is, without adult supervision—for an average of seven hours a week (J. O. Johnson 2005, Table 5). Self-care is more common in white upper middle- and middle-class families than in black, Latino, or low-income settings, perhaps because of differences in neighborhood safety (Casper and Smith 2002).

Low-income, single-parent, rural, and Hispanic parents are especially likely to have relatives take care of their children (Phillips and Adams 2001). Hispanic parents seem to prefer either relative or family day care rather than center care, a choice attributed to wanting a "warm and family-like atmosphere" rather than a "formal and cold" child-care center. Family day care may also be seen as providing a personal relationship between the parent and the caregiver and, perhaps, a bilingual setting (Chira 1994).

African American parents prefer a center for its perceived educational benefits, while white parents' preference is more likely to be for the social interaction experiences a center provides for children. Some families may seek a provider of their own racial/ethnic group who will maintain the cultural context children have at home or, at a minimum, a white caregiver or center that will provide "racial safety"—that is, will not act in a racist way with their children (Uttal 2004).

Research by the Families and Work Institute has found four sources of parental stress regarding child care: (1) it is difficult to find, (2) some arrangements are of lower quality than others, (3) child care is expensive,

---

[4] With regard to safety, it is important to note that despite a smattering of confirmed cases, concerns about abuse of children in day care have largely proved unfounded; studies indicate that children are at greater risk of abuse in their own homes (Finkelhor, Hotaling, and Sedlak 1991). "Overall, child care is quite safe" (Wrigley and Dreby 2005, p. 729), and center care is safer than care in private homes.

As We Make Choices   Child Care and Children's Outcomes

FOCUS ON CHILDREN

Parents who have to make decisions about child care want to know two things: What are the characteristics of quality child care? And what effect does being in child care have on children? We address child-care quality in "As We Make Choices: Selecting a Child-Care Facility." Here we look at outcomes for children who have spent time in child care in their early years.

Psychologist Jay Belsky drew considerable attention when he reported an early finding that infants in their first year who are in nonparental care for twenty or more hours per week "are at elevated risk of being classified as insecure in their *attachments* to their mothers at 12 or 18 months of age" (Belsky 1990, p. 895).[a] This set off the "day care wars" (Carey 2007), in which Belsky has continued to engage in dialogue with other child-care researchers about whether time in child care is harmful to children and in what circumstances (2002).

A multiple-site longitudinal study, organized by the National Institute of he Child Health and Human Development (NICHD), began in 1991 and has now followed more than 1,300 children from

---

[a] "**Attachment** represents an active, affective, enduring, and reciprocal bond between two individuals that is believed to be established through repeated interaction over time" (Coleman and Watson 2000, p. 297, citing Ainsworth et al. 1978).

---

shortly after birth through sixth grade (Belsky et al. 2007). The study looks at the impact of various types of child care compared to maternal care. (Commentators on the NICHD research find it noteworthy that the focus of the NICHD study is on *mothers*. A child is considered to be in care when not with the mother—i.e., care by the father is considered "child care"; U.S. National Institute of Child Health and Human Development 2002). Professor Belsky was one of the thirty researchers initially involved in the study, and has continued to participate. He is one of the authors of the latest report on the NICHD study.

The conclusion first drawn from NICHD research was that children in nonrelative care and children cared for by their own parents differed little in development and emotional stability at fifteen months and three years (U.S. National Institute of Child Health and Human Development 1999b). Yet, at the three-year point, child care did have a negative relationship to maternal sensitivity ("how attuned the mother is to the child's wants and needs") and child engagement ("how connected or involved a child appeared to be when relating to his or her mother"). But that finding did not hold for children in *quality care* (NICHD Early Child Care Research Network 1999a; U.S. National Institute of Child Health and Human Development 1999).

Moreover, favorable outcomes in terms of cognitive and linguistic skills

were associated with *quality* of care, described as "when child care providers talk to children, encourage them to ask questions, respond to children's questions, read to them, challenge them to attend to others' feelings, and to different ways of thinking" (U.S. National Institute of Child Health and Human Development 1999; NICHD Early Child Care Research Network 1999b).

As the children approached age five and entered kindergarten, those who had spent longer hours in child care over time were found to have more behavior problems and conflicts with adults (as reported by parents, teachers, and the children themselves). That was true even when quality and type of care were taken into account (NICHD Early Child Care Research Network 2003a).

Although the results were made much of by Professor Belsky, his coresearchers argued that these were not serious problems—that, in fact, more serious behavior problems were evidenced by children who had not been in day care at all. They also pointed to the fact that problem behavior was confined to a minority of day-care children—more than 80 percent of children long in care did *not* exhibit any behavior problems ("Day-Care Researchers" 2001). In this view, the findings had a "lack of clinical significance" (Dworkin 2002, p. 167), meaning that they did not signal a level of trouble that should cause concern.

---

and (4) "parents are forced to put together a patchwork system of care that tends to fall apart" (Galinsky and Stein 1990, pp. 369–70).

In 2002, the average cost of child care was $95 a week, and about 6 percent of parents had government assistance with the cost (J. O. Johnson 2005, Tables 6, 7). About half of parents using paid care change their arrangements each year because a caregiver quits, the cost is too high, the hours or location are inconvenient,

the child is unhappy, or the parent dislikes the caregiver (Shellenbarger 1991b). As they struggle to find quality, affordable child care, many parents must make more than one arrangement for each child. As they patch together a series of child-care arrangements, the system becomes increasingly unpredictable.

Family day care and many child-care centers are usually open weekdays only and close by 7 p.m. Some parents, such as single mothers on shift work or those

Moreover, children in high-quality center care outperformed children not in care in measures of cognitive skills and language development (NICHD Early Child Care Research Network 2000b). Family background factors and maternal sensitivity were more important in their impact on children's adjustment than was time in child care (NICHD Early Child Care Research Network 2003a). The small size of the negative effects, the good adjustment of the preponderance of children, and the greater importance of parental influence in terms of the effects of extended child care were reassuring.

Research continued through the first $4^1/_2$ years of the children's lives, their day-care years. The latest report on the NICHD study (Belsky et al. 2007) assesses the situation of these children since entering school and draws the following conclusions.

1. Change over time has seen some earlier negative or positive effects vanish, while others take their place. This report, too, captures only one point in time in an ongoing process.

2. Children with more experience in child-care center settings continued to evidence more behavior problems. Why this is so remains a mystery, but the researchers speculate that it may be peer interaction in a center group setting that elicits disruptive behavior.

3. Nonrelative care, mostly center care, is associated with negative effects.

4. High-quality care of any kind is associated with better vocabulary.

5. "[P]arenting quality proved to be a far stronger and more consistent predictor of tested achievement and teacher-reported social functioning than was child-care experience" (p. 696).

6. The developmental impact of child care on individual children may thus not be so significant, because child development outcomes of child care are "smaller in size and less pervasive than those associated with families and parenting" (p. 698). But the "*collective consequences*" of a certain amount of problem behavior associated with children's child care experience can affect "classrooms, schools, communities, and society at large" (p. 698).

There continue to be criticisms of the study, most notably, the question of a "selection effect." The researchers were not, of course, able to assign families randomly to each type of child care; the choices of the parents may reflect something distinctive about the family that is the key factor affecting outcomes. A different and later study took advantage of developments in methodology to counter the effect of selection bias. The focus of this study was on only the first year of the child's life. Results indicated that the mother's working full-time in the first year was associated with negative cognitive and behavioral outcomes; these negative outcomes did not occur

when mothers worked part-time in the first year, postponed work, or did not work for the first three years (J. Hill et al. 2005).

Child-care researchers consider the policy implications of the research. Belsky (2002) argues for tax or other policies to support full-time parental care in the home, especially during the first year. In the most recent report, the NICHD researchers suggest that intervention programs might be effective in enhancing the parenting skills that their research suggests is more important for development than whether or not the child spends time in day care (Belsky et al. 2007).

Other child-care scholars agree with the NICHD researchers that subsidies should be available to permit parents to cut back work hours. At the same time, they urge attention to improving the quality of out-of-home care. They also believe child care can make a positive contribution to social development if done well (Maccoby and Lewis 2003).

Critical Thinking

If you were the mother of a new baby, would you find this research useful in making your decision about returning to work? Or would you be more inclined to rely on the advice of family members or other parents—or your child's reactions to child care? What would you like researchers to find out about children in child care?

who travel, need access to twenty-four-hour care centers. Child care is difficult to find for mildly ill youngsters too sick to go to their regular day-care facility, although there are now centers beginning to fill this need (Galinsky and Stein 1990). Adding to the difficulty of finding day care is parents' need for *quality child care*. "As We Make Choices: Selecting a Child-Care Facility" offers guidelines for evaluating the quality of a child-care setting.

Elder Care There are some parallels between workers' responsibility for child care and for elder care. **Elder care** involves providing assistance with daily living activities to an elderly relative who is chronically frail, ill, disabled, or just in need of assistance. Many parents of the large baby boom generation are in their eighties and may live far away from their adult children. An estimated 20 million employees have ailing parents. Some workers have retired early or just quit in order to care

As We Make Choices   Selecting a Child-Care Facility

FOCUS ON CHILDREN Universal, comprehensive, government-funded day care does not exist in the United States today. Although some parents have access to child-care facilities through government programs or their employers, many parents are on their own in selecting a child-care facility.

Some parents arrange their work schedules to care for their children, while others hire a nanny or recruit relatives into this role. Here we make some suggestions to parents who are choosing from commercially available child care.

State laws, which vary in both provisions and enforcement, establish minimal standards, and professional organizations like the American Academy of Pediatrics have developed guidelines for quality child care. We outline some of the things we think parents should consider when exploring and choosing child care for their children, drawing on the American Academy of Pediatrics guidelines as well as other sources.

Some criteria are very tangible and specific, like the ratio of children to adults. Some are more qualitative and can best be judged by the parent during visits, including post-placement visits, to the child-care facility. Some are only applicable to center care, while others are relevant to family day care as well.

- *Low child-to-staff ratio.* Positive caregiving is associated with a low child-to-staff ratio, especially for very young children. State guidelines vary, but experts believe they tend to be too minimal. Best would be six to eight infants per two caregivers, six to twelve 1- to 2-year-olds per three teachers, and fourteen to twenty older preschoolers per two teachers.

- *Stable staff.* Some staff turnover is inevitable, but it should not exceed 25 percent a year. If children must constantly adjust to changes in person-

Child-care centers and preschools provide care for many children during the workday. Although children may not receive as much adult attention as they might with a single caregiver or with family day care, they benefit from greater interaction with other children and a preschool curriculum.

nel, they cannot build the warm and trusting relationships that they need with caregivers. It is also important to learn how much attention is given to preparing children for a caretaker's departure and to helping them adjust to new staff.

- *A well-trained staff.* Trained staff members are likely to be more responsive, more stimulating, and more creative in their activities with children. Because child-care workers are poorly paid, it is difficult to find centers with staff members who are highly educated or trained in early childhood education. The ideal situation is for staff to be knowledgeable about child development and to participate in workshops or other ongoing training in best practices. Ask about staff education and plans for further training. In family day-care settings, ask whether other family members or others who are not formally "staff" are nevertheless involved in caring for the children.

- *Cultural sensitivity.* Caregivers should be knowledgeable about the di-

verse racial/ethnic, religious, and social class cultures of this society and should be aware that children may come from various types of families, such as traditional nuclear, dual-earner, gay/lesbian, single-parent, divorced, or remarried.

- *Other staff qualities.* A warm personality and interpersonal sensitivity are essential. Caregivers who let children express their feelings and who will take their views into account are desirable. Because staff members will have an influence on the child's language acquisition, being verbally fluent and well-spoken is an asset. Some parents may have specific preferences, such as male or female caregivers or both, or minority or bilingual staff. Parents seeking family child care may have a specific type of home environment in mind and should consider how well their values and lifestyle match those of the caretaker.

- *Age-appropriate attention.* Babies need a responsive adult who coos and talks to them. One-year-olds need a staff member who will name things for them. Two-year olds need someone who reads to them. Older children can profit from social interaction and activities with other children as well as with adult caregivers.

- Adults should be responsive to children and interact with them, not limit themselves to a directive, organizing role. Do they greet the child warmly? Do they seem interested in what the child is doing or saying? They should make eye contact and perhaps bend to their level when speaking with children, not brush the children off or have a ho-hum attitude. How staff members interact with children can best be ascertained by observation in visits to the center.

- *Age-appropriate and stimulating activities and play spaces.* Experts differ on how academic a preschool program should be, and parents differ in how "educational" a program they are looking for. Look for a facility that also fosters play and community activities such as trips to the zoo or fire station—and one that prepares children for learning rather than offering a first-grade program in preschool. In any case, parents should pick a child-care facility that is a good match for their values in this regard. You should find that staff members have a well-thought-out rationale for their program that they can easily describe.

- On the negative side, avoid child-care centers or family day-care environments that seem to provide only custodial care or allow lots of TV watching. What kinds of indoor and outdoor spaces are there for constructive and imaginative child play? What toys, books, and games are available? What are the ages of the other children who will be with your child in care?

- *Discipline.* Inquire about how staff handle the minor behavior problems that inevitably arise with children. "Time out" is typically recommended by child experts, with physical discipline to be avoided. States vary in their laws regarding whether child caretakers are permitted to spank children. Where this is legally permissible, there may be centers or family caretakers who are indeed committed to the use of physical discipline—of course, parents may vary in terms of whether this is acceptable to them. You should both inquire and observe how "incidents" are handled, and ascertain whether the child-care facility's policy and practice match what you want for your children. Use of physical discipline suggests that the caretakers are not well trained in handling problems and may create a somewhat fearful atmosphere for children as well.

- *A relationship with parents. Parent–caregiver relationships* will vary depending on whether the child is in family day care or a center. Any child-care facility should welcome parental involvement, in the form of visits at a minimum; be wary of facilities that do not allow unannounced visits. You should feel supported in your parental role by the family caretaker or center staff (rather than distanced or unduly criticized). You should feel included in the child's daily life in child care. Especially important is how and how well family caretakers or center staff members communicate with you about problems.

- *Practical and financial considerations. You* will be told the basic hours and fees, but you also need to know what happens when the child is sick or the family leaves town and the child does not attend as usual. Can arrange-

ments be made to have children arrive earlier or leave later than normal center hours on occasion? Regularly? Is transportation provided? If so, how costly is it, and how reliable?

- *Recommendations from other parents.* Talk to other parents about the facility. If you don't know any parents with children in the center, ask for names and phone numbers of parents who have children enrolled there, and talk to them about the facility. If a center declines to give you this information, try to determine whether a privacy policy adopted by their board to protect parents is the reason or whether the management is being elusive and defensive.

- *Visits.* Visit the day-care center as often as you can—and, if possible, unannounced—both before and after selecting a facility.

- *Accreditation.* The National Association for the Education of Young Children (NAEYC) is an accrediting agency for child-care centers. If you plan to use center care, you might want to check the association's website (www.naeyc.org) for listings of accredited centers in your state. Although not all good child-care centers have taken this step, accreditation by the NAEYC is a good sign.

Critical Thinking

What qualities do you think are most important in choosing a child-care center? How would you compare in-home care, family day care, or center care on the qualities you think are important?

Sources: American Academy of Pediatrics 1992; Coordinated Access for Child Care 2001; Find Care 2002; Galinsky 2001; NICHD Early Child Care Research Network 2000a, 2003b; Phillips and Adams 2001; U.S. National Institute of Child Health and Human Development 2002; Watson 1984; Working Moms Refuge 2001.

for parents, while others have turned down promotions, switched to part-time work, taken leaves of absence, or simply taken time off from work (Gross 2006a).

The need for companies to offer employees help with elderly dependents beyond unpaid family leave is just beginning to be recognized. Supervisors may offer flexibility on an individual basis, but formal programs of assistance for elder care are in the beginning stages. Some 27 percent of companies now offer elder care benefits (Joyce 2007a). Care of the elderly is discussed in more detail in Chapter 18.

Family Leave **Family leave** involves an employee being able to take an extended period of time from work, either paid or unpaid, for the purpose of caring for a newborn, for a newly adopted or seriously ill child, for an elderly parent, or for their own health needs, with the guarantee of a job upon returning. The concept of family leave incorporates maternity, paternity, ill-child, and elder-care leaves.

The 1993 Family and Medical Leave Act mandates up to twelve weeks of unpaid family leave for workers in companies with at least fifty employees. But unpaid leave will not solve the problem for a vast majority of employees, as most working parents need the income. More employers are now offering paid maternity leave, and 42 percent of first-time mothers who had worked during pregnancy took paid leave (maternity leave, sick leave, or vacation), while 45 percent took unpaid leave. Another 7 percent took disability leave. Twenty-six percent of these first-time mothers quit their jobs, while 2 percent were let go (Johnson and Downs 2005).

Some 15 percent of companies now offer paid paternity leave, around twenty-five days on average. "'Gen X and Gen Y men [men born later than 1964] are demanding to have the ability to play a larger role in family life than their fathers did," states Joan Williams, director of Work/Life Law at American University ("More New Dads" 2005, p. Bus. 1).

Flexible Scheduling About 28 percent of full-time workers have flexible schedules (U.S. Bureau of Labor Statistics 2006d, Table 29). **Flexible scheduling** includes such options as **job sharing** (two people share one position), working at home or telecommuting, compressed workweeks, flextime, and personal days (days off for the purpose of attending to a personal matter such as a doctor's appointment or a child's school program). Compressed workweeks allow an employee to concentrate the workweek into three or four or sometimes slightly longer days. **Flextime** involves flexible starting and ending times, with required core hours.

Flexible scheduling, although not a panacea, can help parents share child care or be at home before and after an older child's school hours. Some types of work do not lend themselves to flexible scheduling (Christensen and Staines 1990), but the practice has been adopted by the federal government and by some companies because it offers employee-recruiting advantages, prevents turnover, and frees up office space when some employees work at home. Even when not formally offered, it may be possible. In a survey of employees in 1997, almost half reported that they had some choice in when to begin and end the workday, and 19 percent did some work at home (Lewin 1998).

Employees who have flexible hours report enhanced job satisfaction and loyalty to the employer, but they find that flextime does not alleviate all or even most family–work conflicts. For one thing, women are slightly less likely to have this option than men are, though they are more in need of it given the typical division of labor in the home (U.S. Bureau of Labor Statistics 2006d, Table 29).

Who Will Provide What Is Needed to Resolve Work–Family Issues?

Policy experts, lawmakers, employers, parents, and citizens disagree over who has the responsibility to provide what is needed regarding various work–family solutions. A principal conflict concerns whether such solutions as child care or family leave should be government policy or constitute privileges for which a worker must negotiate.

The countries of northwestern Europe, which have a more pronatalist and social-welfare orientation than the United States, tend to view family benefits as a right (Glass and Estes 1997). There is "the pervasive belief . . . that children are a precious national resource for which society has collective responsibility" (Clinton 1990, p. 25). Putting this belief into practice, most European countries are committed to *paid* maternity (or parental) leave for up to at least six months and usually much longer (Waldfogel 2001). Accustomed to a lack of family policy at the federal level, American parents sometimes turn their attention to local schools as a source of help for the care of older children in after-school programs and younger children in preschool programs and all-day kindergarten.

Some large corporations demonstrate interest in effecting **family-friendly workplace policies** that are supportive of employee efforts to combine family and work commitments. Such policies include on-site child-care centers, sick-child care, subsidies for child-care services or child-care locator services, flexible schedules, parental or family leaves, workplace seminars and counseling programs, and support groups for employed parents. Such research as exists on outcomes for employers suggests that these policies help in recruitment, reduce employee stress and turnover, enhance morale, and thus increase productivity (Galinsky and Stein 1990; Glass and Estes 1997; Shellenbarger and Trost 1992).

But family-friendly policies are hardly available to all American workers. Professionals and managers are much more likely than technical and clerical workers to have access to leave policies, telecommuting, or flexible scheduling (Christensen and Staines 1990). "At the high end, the big corporations are stepping up to provide benefits to help families, and at the lower end, as women leave welfare, there's now much more support for the idea that they deserve help with child care. But the blue-collar families, the K-Mart cashier, get nothing" (work–family policy expert Kathleen Sylvester, quoted in Lewin 2001b).

An estimated 40 percent of the workforce is made up of unmarried people. Single individuals or childless workers have begun to complain about what they see as the privileging of parents of young children when they themselves may have family caregiving needs: for elderly parents, siblings, or friends with whom they maintain caregiving relationships. They may find it onerous to cover for coworkers who are on leave or out of the office. They may feel that simple fairness should permit some flexibility in their schedules as well, for personal needs. Some companies have begun to accommodate these workers by instituting sabbaticals, "flexible culture," and "employee friendly" policies, redefining policies previously characterized as "family friendly" (Joyce 2006; 2007a).

We have devoted attention to work–family policies because these issues so strongly influence the options and choices of individual families. We would like to think that family-friendly companies represent the future of work. After all, "children . . . are 'public goods'; society profits greatly from future generations as stable, well-adjusted adults, as well as future employees and tax payers" (Avellar and Smock 2003, p. 605). Nevertheless, these voluntary programs and benefits do depend on cost constraints and corporate self-interest and are not likely to be so available during economic downturns or restructuring. Moreover, family-friendly programs need to be more comprehensive in terms of benefits and more widely available to all echelons of workers. However, keep in mind that most workers need extensive family support only during the period in which they are parenting young children. From that perspective, the challenge looks less daunting (Glass and Estes 1997).

Entering the political arena to work toward the kinds of changes families want is one aspect of creating satisfying marriages and families. But employed couples also want to know what *they* can do themselves to maintain happy marriages. We now turn to that topic.

The Two-Earner Marriage and the Relationship

We have been addressing problems associated with two-earner marriages. But research shows that, provided there is enough time to accomplish things, a person's having multiple roles (such as employee/spouse/parent) does not add to stress and in fact may enhance personal happiness (O'Neil and Greenberger 1994; Roxburgh 1997). Research also points to the heightened satisfaction, excitement, and vitality that two-earner couples can have because these partners are more likely to have common experiences and shared worldviews than do traditional spouses, who often lead very different everyday lives (Chafetz 1989; Hughes, Galinsky, and Morris 1992). At the same time, conflict may arise in two-earner marriages as couples negotiate the division

This couple seems happy with their work as welders and happy with each other.

of household labor and more generally adjust to changing roles (Orbuch and Custer 1995; Hondagneu-Sotelo and Messner 1999; P. Johnson 1998).

Gender Strategies

How a couple allocates paid and unpaid work and then justifies that allocation can be thought of as a *gender strategy*, a way of working through everyday situations that takes into account an individual's beliefs and deep feelings about gender roles, as well as her or his employment commitments (Hochschild 1989). In today's changing society, conscious beliefs and deeper feelings about gender may conflict. For example, a number of men in Hochschild's study of working couples articulated egalitarian sentiments, but had clearly retained gut-level traditional feelings about sex differences. Tensions exhibited by many of Hochschild's respondents were a consequence of "faster-changing women and slower-changing men" (p. 11).

Even when spouses share similar attitudes about gender, circumstances may not allow them to act accordingly. In one couple interviewed by Hochschild, both partners held the traditional belief that a wife should be a full-time homemaker. Yet because the couple needed the wife's income, she was employed, and they shared housework on a nearly equal basis. How couples manage their everyday lives in the face of contradictions reflects a consciously or unconsciously negotiated gender strategy.

One gender strategy used by wives who would like their husband to do more, but know he won't and are reluctant to insist, is to compare their husbands to other men "out there" who apparently are doing even less. A common gender strategy, according to Hochschild (1989), is to develop *family myths*—"versions of reality that obscure a core truth in order to manage a family tension." For example, when a husband shares housework in a way that contradicts his traditional beliefs and/or feelings, couples may develop a myth alleging the wife's poor health or incompetence in order to protect the man's image of himself. A common family myth defines the wife as an organized and energetic superwoman who has few needs of her own, requires little from her husband, and congratulates herself on how much she can accomplish.

Sociologist Bradford Wilcox (2004) uses the term *"enchanted" economies of gratitude* (p. 137, referencing Hochschild) in his study of evangelical families (to explain evangelical husbands' greater than average expressions of appreciation for their wives' household work. The commitment of the couple to a religiously based traditional division of labor is an anomaly in the context of today's ideal of egalitarian sharing. The evangelical wife's greater household labor is a "gift" that has symbolic significance for their religious and family world, and the husband reciprocates with "emotion work" (Wilcox 2004, Chapter 5).

Maintaining Intimacy While Negotiating Provider Roles and the Second Shift

Two kinds of changes are involved in moving toward more egalitarian family roles: Women come to share the provider role, while men take greater responsibility for household work. In considering the provider role, we turn to the notion of *meaning* again: Is women's sharing of the provider role a *threat*, so that men fear losing masculine identity, women's domestic services, and power? Or is a woman's sharing the provider role a *benefit*, because men benefit materially from wives' employment and earnings and from a partner's enthusiasm for the wider world? Recent research suggests that men are more apt to see women's employment as a benefit. As a result, there is an "ideological shift of men toward egalitarianism" (Zuo and Tang 2000).

Household work seems to be the greater arena for stress and conflict as roles change. Study after study shows that marital satisfaction is greater when wives feel that husbands share fairly in the household work. But a woman's employment does not necessarily lead to a husband's sharing of household work.

Although husbands may now carry a greater share of the family work than in the past, getting comfortable with transitions in marital roles is not a quick and easy process. But when the transition proceeds from a mutual commitment to achieve an equitable relationship, the result may be greater intimacy. It follows from the general principle articulated in Chapter 1 that initial choices may need to be revisited over the life cycle. Gender issues may be revisited as partners adjust to changing work–family realities and as children enter the picture and then grow older. A first step is to address conflict.

Accept Conflict as a Reality The idea that marital partners may sometimes have competing interests departs from the more romanticized view that sees marriages and families as integrated units with shared desires and goals. As a first step toward maintaining intimacy during role changes, partners need to recognize their possibly competing interests and to expect conflict (Paden and Buehler 1995).

Accept Ambivalence After accepting conflict as a reality, the next step in maintaining intimacy as spouses adjust to two-earner marriages is for both to recognize that each may have ambivalent feelings. The following excerpt from one young husband's essay for his English composition class is illustrative of a man's dilemma in assessing fairness in the division of labor: "I'm in school six days a week. My wife works between 40 to 50 hours a week. So I do the majority of the cooking, cleaning, and laundry. To me this is not right. But am I wrong to think so?" Women may also be ambivalent. They want their husbands to be happy, they want their husbands to help and support them, they feel angry about any past inequalities, and they feel guilty about their declining interest in housekeeping and their decreasing willingness to accommodate their husbands' preferences. Furthermore, men who participate have opinions about how child rearing or housework should be done. As a husband begins to pitch in, his wife may resent his intrusion into her traditional domain.

Empathize A next step is to empathize. This may be difficult, for it is tempting instead to point out where a partner falls short. But if couples are to maintain intimacy, they must make sure that *both* partners "win." Wives are often irritated by observing that husbands may underestimate the number of hours that household labor takes (Wilkie, Ferree, and Ratcliff 1998). It is never easy to adjust to new roles, and men especially may feel they have a lot to lose. Men can gain, too, of course: They develop domestic skills, their marriage is enhanced, there is more money, and they benefit from spending time with their children. In Hochschild's study (1989), some fathers who felt they had been emotionally deprived in relationships with their own fathers took great pleasure in creating more satisfying family relationships with and for their children.

As husbands empathize, they need to be aware that their willingness to participate in household tasks is vitally important to wives, especially to employed wives (McHale and Crouter 1992). A husband's sharing carries a symbolic meaning for a wife, indicating that her work is recognized and appreciated and that her husband cares.

Strike an Equitable Rebalance Researchers who studied 153 Pennsylvania couples with children in school concluded the following: "Our data imply that the adjustment of individual family members, as well as harmonious family relationships, requires a *balance* among the very different and often conflicting needs and goals of different family members" (McHale and Crouter 1992, pp. 545–46, italics in original). Once equity is habitual, calculation and constant comparison are no longer necessary; some observers point out that the balance need not be an exactly calculated 50–50 split.

Show Mutual Appreciation Once partners have committed themselves to striking a balance, they need to create ways to let each know the other is loved. Traditional role expectations were relatively rigid and limiting, but they could be a way of expressing love and caring. When a wife cooked her husband's favorite meal or a husband could pay for family travel, each felt cared about. As spouses relinquish some traditional behaviors, they need to create new ways of letting each other know they care. Many people have noted the potential of shared work and of shared provider and caregiving roles for enriching a marriage (Beeghley 1996; Risman and Johnson-Sumerford 1998).

This discussion of the second shift has been framed in terms of marriage, the relationships of husbands and wives as they negotiate this marital challenge. Marriage *is* most likely to draw on cultural expectations of a traditional division of labor. But the second shift exists in other family forms. In heterosexual cohabiting couples, the woman does less household labor and the man more than in marriage, while in gay and lesbian couples the domestic division of labor is rather egalitarian. Single women and men also have work to do to maintain their households, especially if they are parents. Single men tend to do more than married men, while single women do less than married women. Interestingly, remarried couples are more likely to share housework than are men and women in a first marriage (Coltrane 2000; Patterson 2000), as are couples who cohabited before marriage (Batalova and Cohen 2002). We should keep in mind that employees are embedded in diverse families and that partners may come up with a variety of ways of accomplishing providing and caregiving.

Despite the unresolved tensions of the second shift, research by sociologist K. Jill Kiecolt (2003) suggests that employed men and women are largely happy with their home lives. She set out to explore a thesis developed by Arlie Hochschild (1997) in her study of workers at one company. Hochschild concluded that family life for employed people is so hectic that work becomes a refuge, a place where individuals would prefer to be. Hochschild's was a case study, so no statistical conclusions could be drawn.

Testing this thesis with General Social Survey data from NORC over the period 1973–1994, Kiecolt found that only 13 percent of workers saw it that way. In the most recent year she studied, over 40 percent of respondents had "high work-home satisfaction," while for another 40 percent plus, home was viewed as a haven.

The next chapter examines communication and managing conflict in families, skills that can smooth the negotiation of work–family roles.

Summary

- We look at men's and women's "market work," that is, their participation in the labor force. Traditionally, the husband's job was as provider, the wife's as homemaker. These roles changed as more and more women entered the workforce. Women remain segregated occupationally, and they earn lower incomes than men, on average.

- We have seen that paid work is not usually structured to allow time for household responsibilities and that women, more than men, continue to adjust their time to accomplish both paid and unpaid work. Many wives would prefer shared roles, and negotiation and tension over this issue can cast a shadow on a marriage. An incomplete transition to equality at work and at home affects family life profoundly. However, in recent years, men have been increasing their share of the housework and men and women now have a balance in total work hours, with men spending more time in paid employment than women, while women spend more time in domestic work than men.

- Household work and child care are pressure points as women enter the labor force and the two-earner marriage becomes the norm. To make it work, either the structure of work must be changed, social policy must support working families, or women and men must change their household role patterns—very probably all three.

- We have emphasized that both cultural expectations and public policy affect people's options. As individuals come to realize this, we can expect pressure on public officials and corporations to meet the needs of working families by providing supportive policies: parental leave, child care, and flextime.

- To be successful, two-earner marriages will require social policy support and workplace flexibility. But there are some things couples themselves can do to better manage a working-couple family. Recognition of both positive and negative feelings and open communication between partners can help working couples cope with an imperfect social world.

Questions for Review and Reflection

1. Discuss to what extent distinctions between husbands' and wives' work are disappearing.

2. What do you see as the advantages and disadvantages of men being househusbands? Discuss this from the points of view of both men and women.

3. What are some advantages and disadvantages of home-based work?

4. What work–family conflicts do you see around you? Interview some married or single-parent friends of yours for concrete examples and for some suggestions for resolving such conflicts.

5. **Policy Question.** What family-friendly workplace policies would you like to see instituted? Which would you be likely to take advantage of?

Key Terms

attachment 318
center care 317
child care 316
commuter marriage 316
elder care 319
family child care 317
family-friendly workplace policies 322
family leave 322
flexible scheduling 322
flextime 322
good provider role 300
househusband 301
in-home caregiver 317
job sharing 322
labor force 294
leisure gap 309
market approach to child care 317
market work 295

motherhood penalty 297
mothering approach to child care 316
nanny 302
neotraditional families 298
occupational segregation 295
opting out 298
parenting approach to child care 317
reinforcing cycle 307
second shift 307
self-care 317
sequencing mom 306
shift work 303
stay-at-home dad 301
trailing spouse 316
two-career marriage 302
two-earner marriage 302
unpaid family work 306
wage gap 296

Online Resources

Companion Website for This Book

www.thomsonedu.com/sociology/lamanna

Visit the book companion website, where you will find flash cards, practice quizzes, Internet links, suggested readings, InfoTrac College Edition exercises, and more to help you study.

ThomsonNOW™ for Marriage and Family

Spend time on what you need to master rather than on information you already have learned. Take a pre-test for this chapter, and ThomsonNOW will generate a personalized study plan based on your results. The study plan will identify the topics you need to review and direct you to online resources such as videos, narrated learning modules, and interactive activities to help you master those topics. You can then take a post-test to help you determine the concepts you have mastered and what you will still need to work on. Try it out! Go to **www .thomsonedu.com/login** to sign in with an access code or to purchase access to this product.

Communication
in Marriage and Families

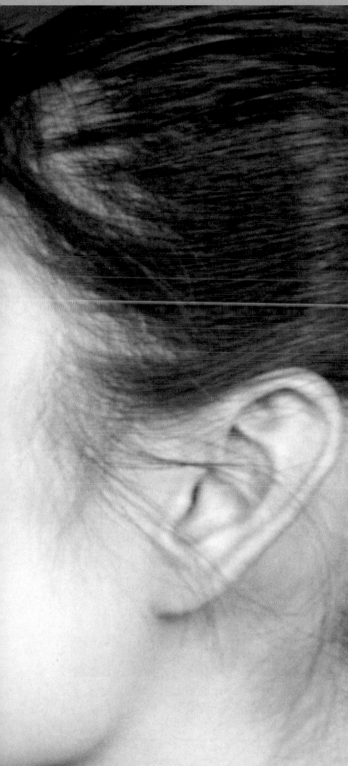

© Ron Chapple/Getty Images/Taxi

13

Communication and Couple Satisfaction
Facts about Families: Six Characteristics of Cohesive Families
Let Your Partner Know That You're Listening
Show Interest in What Your Partner Is Telling You
Have Some Fun Together
As We Make Choices: Ten Rules for a Successful Relationship

Conflict and Love
Denying Conflict: Some Results

Supportive Couple Communication and Conflict Management
The Four Horsemen of the Apocalypse
Issues for Thought: A Look Behind the Scenes at Communication Research
What Is Supportive Communication?
Gender Differences in Couple Communication
Avoiding the Four Horsemen of the Apocalypse

Bonding Fights—Ten Guidelines
Guideline 1: Level with Each Other
Guideline 2: To Avoid Attacks, Use I-Statements When You Can
Guideline 3: Avoid Mixed, or Double, Messages
Guideline 4: Choose the Time and Place Carefully
Guideline 5: Focus Anger Only on Specific Issues
Guideline 6: Ask for a Specific Change, but Be Open to Compromise
Guideline 7: Be Willing to Change Yourself
Guideline 8: Don't Try to Win
Guideline 9: Remember to End the Argument
Guideline 10: Be Willing to Forgive

Toward Better Communication
The Myth of Conflict-Free Conflict

Providing emotional security and feelings of belonging is an important function of today's families. Virtually nowhere else in our society is there such power to support, hurt, comfort, denigrate, reassure, ridicule, hate, and love. It follows that the emotional tone of a couple's everyday communication is very important.

Research makes it clear that the expression of positive feelings is critical to marital and family happiness (Gottman and Levenson 2000; Roberts 2000). Couples who communicate mutual affection create a contagious "spiraling effect" so that the household atmosphere becomes one of emotional support, affecting their children as well (L. White 1999). Distressed couples, on the other hand, tend toward negative exchanges that put their marriages on a downward spiral (Driver and Gottman 2004; Marchand and Hock 2000). Although conflict is a natural part of every relationship, it is imperative to think about how we communicate with our loved ones on a daily basis. Developing positive communication skills can help to create **family cohesion**—the emotional bonding of family members.

There are several ways to look at couples' communication. For example, psychologists might look at how partners' individual personality characteristics influence their communication and marital satisfaction. One study like this (Bouchard, Lussier, and Sabourin 1999) found that partners who are agreeable, imaginative, intellectually curious, liberal in their attitudes, and conscientious are more likely to have better communication and marital adjustment. On the other side of this coin, depressed and chronically worried or anxious, guilt-ridden, and perfectionist personalities are associated with poorer couple communication and less marital satisfaction (Haring, Hewitt, and Flett 2003). A second way to look at couple communication and satisfaction is through the ecology perspective (see Chapter 3), whereby family interaction is seen as influenced by outside stressors such as economic uncertainty or racism.

This chapter will focus on couple communication using mainly an interactionist perspective—looking at patterns of interaction between partners. We will discuss some healthy attitudes and propose some guidelines for communicating affection. Also, we'll see that boredom in intimate relationships often results from partners' attempts to deny or ignore conflict, and we'll examine several other outcomes of refusing to deal openly with conflict. We will explore ten guidelines for addressing conflict in ways that can actually enhance the bond between partners. To begin, we'll look at the relationship between communication and couple satisfaction.

Communication and Couple Satisfaction

One prominent researcher on marital communication, Mary Anne Fitzpatrick (1995), has found variation among happy couples in their marital ideology—ideas about the roles they should play, expectations for closeness and/or distance, and attitudes toward conflict. Some of the couples in Fitzpatrick's sample expected to engage in conflict only over big issues. Other couples were more open to conflict and argued more often. Still others expected a relationship that largely avoided not only conflict but also demonstrations of affection.

Fitzpatrick found that all couple types could be satisfied with their relationship. What mattered was whether the partners' actual interaction matched their marital ideology. For instance, the marital happiness of the more interdependent couples depends on their level of sharing and disclosure, whereas "separates" were more satisfied if they avoided jarring conflicts. A piv-

Even the happiest and most committed couples experience conflict. Meanwhile, research shows that an essential characteristic of happy couples involves disclosure of feelings and partners' showing affection for one another.

otal task for all marrieds is to balance each partner's need for autonomy with the simultaneous need for intimacy and togetherness. The happiest couples are those who manage to do this—by negotiating personal and couple boundaries through supportive communication (S. Marks 1989; Scarf 1995). Fitzpatrick's research also uncovered "mixed couples." In this case, spouses had dissimilar ideologies of marriage; they differed in their expectations for closeness and attitudes toward conflict. Not surprisingly, couples who differ in these ways are unlikely to be very satisfied with their marriages (Weigel, Bennett, and Ballard-Reisch 2006a).

Furthermore, unhappy marriages such as these do tend to have some common features: less positive and more negative verbal and nonverbal communication, together with more reciprocity of negative—but not of positive—communication (Noller and Fitzpatrick 1991; Gottman and Levenson 2000). Among other things, Fitzpatrick's research pointed out that all couples—even the happiest of them—experience conflict. Later in this chapter, we will explore the topic of managing conflict in marriages and other relationships.

First, however, we want to point out that research overwhelmingly supports what may be intuitively obvious: Disclosing one's feelings and conveying affection for one's partner are very important determinants of marital and family happiness and cohesion, as well as of each partner's psychological well-being (Bradbury and Karney 2004; Cotton, Burton, and Rushing 2003). "Facts about Families: Six Characteristics of Cohesive Families" describes ways to make your relationship more cohesive.

Positive affect involves the expression, either verbal or nonverbal, of one's feelings of affection toward another. Having gathered data on couples, researchers Ted Huston and Heidi Melz (2004) classified marital relationships into four types: *Warm*, or friendly; *Tempestuous*, or stormy; *Bland*, or empty shell; and *Hostile*, or distressed (p. 951). As indicated in Figure 13.1, warm relationships are high on showing signs of love and affection while low on antagonism. Tempestuous unions are high on both affection and antagonism. Bland marriages are low on showing signs of affection as well as on antagonism. Hostile marriages are low on love and affection but high on antagonism.

We can assume that warm and friendly unions best fill the family function of providing emotional security. We can also conclude that hostile marriages are undesirable. Huston and Melz called both Bland and Tempestuous unions "mixed blessing marriages" because these two marriage types evidenced only one of two desirable attributes. Although Bland marriages experience little antagonism, they lack displays of affection. Although Tempestuous couples intermittently show affection,

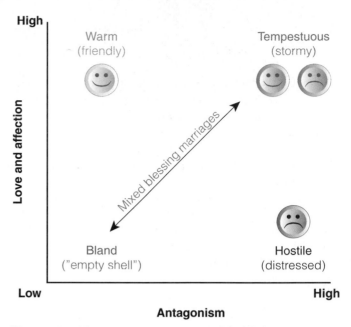

Figure 13.1 The emotional climates of marital relationships. This figure depicts the classification of marital emotional climates along two dimensions: (1) love and affection, and (2) antagonism. Warm marital relationships are high on love and affection while low on antagonism. Tempestuous unions are high on love and affection but also on antagonism. Bland marriages are low on love and affection as well as on antagonism. Hostile marriages are low on love and affection but high on antagonism. Why do you think Tempestuous and Bland marriages are called "mixed blessing" marriages?

Source: From Huston and Melz, "The Case for (Promoting) Marriage: The Devil is in the Details," *Journal of Marriage and the Family* 66(4): 942–953, 2004. Reprinted by permission of Blackwell Publishing.

they deal with conflicts in aggressive, or antagonistic, ways.

In general, Huston and Melz found that after the honeymoon stage there is a "coming down to earth" in a marriage. Interestingly, however, in the years after "the honeymoon's over," couples did not necessarily fight more. Instead, their marriages showed a decline in signs of love and affection. "One year into marriage, the average spouse says 'I love you,' hugs and kisses their partner, makes their partner laugh, and has sexual intercourse about half as often as when they were newly wed." Although marriages do not necessarily "become more antagonistic as time passes, the unpleasant exchanges that *do* occur are embedded in a less affectionate context, and thus, the spouses are likely to come to feel that their marriage is less of 'a haven in a heartless world'" (p. 951).

If our goal is to identify the early signs of a marital rupture, our research suggests that we look to the loss of

Six Characteristics of Cohesive Families

To find out what makes families cohesive, social scientist Nick Stinnett researched 130 "strong families" in rural and urban areas throughout Oklahoma (Stinnett 1985, 1997). Obviously, this limited sample, selected with help from home economics extension agents, has no claim to representativeness. The concept of "strong family" is equally subjective. Various individuals or groups have their own ideas about just what a "strong family" is. But Stinnett's research helped to advance ideas about what makes for marital happiness and cohesion.

When Stinnett made his observations, the following six qualities stood out:

1. Family members often communicated their *appreciation for one another.* They "built each other up psychologically" (Stinnett 2003, p. 25). One way of doing this is to express affection for one's partner by touching or hugging (Mackey, Diemer, and O'Brien 2000).

2. Members of cohesive families had a *high degree of commitment* to promoting one another's happiness and welfare and to the family group as a whole. They invested time and energy in the family group. When life got so hectic that members didn't have enough time for their families, they listed the activities they were involved in, found those that weren't worth their time, and scratched them off their lists, leaving more free time for their families (Stinnett 2003).

3. On a regular basis, family members *arranged their personal schedules* so that they could do things together. For example, they might agree to save Saturday or Sunday afternoons for one another. Then, too, what families do together at home doesn't have to be routine, habitual, or boring: They might have a winter picnic in front of the fireplace, for example.

4. These families had *positive communication* patterns (Stinnett, Hilliard, and Stinnett 2000). They argued, but they did so openly, sharing their feelings and talking over alternative solutions to their problems. And when they were *not* arguing, they took time to talk with and listen to one another, conveying respect and interest (see also Finkenauer et al. 2004).

5. Stinnett found that strong families were able to *deal positively with crises.* Family members were able to see something good in bad situations, even if it was just gratitude that they had each other and were able to face the crisis together (Stinnett 2003). (Chapter 15 discusses in detail the process of dealing creatively with stress and crises.)

6. Many of the families that Stinnett studied had a *spiritual orientation.* Although they were not necessarily members of any organized religion, they did have a sense of some power and purpose greater than themselves and typically evidenced a "hopeful attitude toward life" (DeFrain 2002).

In general, Stinnett's families took the initiative in structuring their lifestyles to enhance family relationships. Instead of drifting into family relationships by default, they made knowledgeable choices, each member playing an active part in carrying out the family commitments.

Critical Thinking

In your opinion, which of Stinnett's research findings deserve further investigation, and why? Which of Stinnett's findings might you want to better incorporate into your own family-living situation? In what specific ways might you do that?

---

love and affection early in marriage as symptomatic. . . . This loss of good feelings, rather than the emergence of conflict early in marriage, seems to be what sends relationships into a downward spiral, no doubt eventually leading to increased bickering and fighting and, ultimately, to the collapse of the union. (Huston and Melz 2004, pp. 951–52).

Showing signs of affection—both verbal and nonverbal—is important throughout a marriage. Relatedly, research conducted by highly esteemed communication psychologists has found that "[t]he absence of positive affect and not the presence of negative affect . . . was most predictive of later divorcing" (Gottman and Levenson 2000, p. 743). An important way to show positive affection is to let your partner know that you are truly listening.

Let Your Partner Know That You're Listening

Really listening is basic to an emotionally bonded relationship. According to the late sociologist/counselor Carlfred Broderick, good listening has the following important positive results:

"Why won't you cuddle?"

1. The attitude of listening itself shows love, concern, and respect. . . . Any act that expresses a positive attitude is likely to trigger a sequence of positive responses back and forth. . . .

2. The avoidance of interrupting and criticism prevents the sending of negative messages such as "I don't care how you feel or what you think." "You're not worth listening to."

3. You discover how things actually look from your spouse's or partner's point of view. There's a risk, because what you hear may be surprising and even unsettling. But it is nearly always worth it. In fact, it's hard to imagine how any couple can become close without achieving insight into each other's feelings.

4. You lose your status as chief expert on what your spouse really thinks, wants, fears, and feels. Instead, your spouse takes over as the final authority on his or her own feelings. . . . [Furthermore,] if you listen sympathetically to your spouse, he or she is able to develop greater clarity in areas that may have been confused and confusing. . . .

5. You set an example for your spouse to follow in listening to your . . . feelings. (Broderick 1979a, pp. 40–41)

We all want to be heard and feel understood. With both words and gestures, happy couples typically let each other know that they are listening (Weger 2005). They do this by using what communication researchers call **listener backchannels**—"the usual brief vocalizations, head nods, and facial movements that convey to the speaker that the listener is tracking" (Gottman et al. 1998, p. 17). Gottman further argued that, at least for middle-class couples in his sample, he could pre-dict a couple's later divorce by examining how well the spouses listened to each other when they talked about everyday things:

> In a careful viewing of the videotapes, we noticed that there were critical moments during the events-of-the-day conversation that could be called either "requited" [returned, acknowledged, or reciprocated] or "unre-quited" interest and excitement. For example, in one couple, the wife reported excitedly about something their young son had done that day, but she was met with her husband's disinterest. After a time of talking about errands that needed doing, he talked excitedly about something important that happened to him that day at work, but she responded with disinterest and irrita-tion. No doubt this kind of interaction pattern carried over into the rest of their interaction, forming a pattern for "turning away" from one another. (Gottman and Levenson 2000, p. 744)

The preceding scenario suggests a second important way that couples communicate positive affect: They show genuine interest in one another.

Show Interest in What Your Partner Is Telling You

UCLA psychologist Shelly Gable studied how one partner responds when something positive happens to the other one, such as a promotion at work (Gable et al. 2004). A partner might respond enthusiastically ("That's wonderful, and it's because you've had so many good ideas in the past few months."). But he or she could instead respond in a less-than-enthusiastic man-ner ("Hmmm, that's nice."), seem uninterested ("Did you see the score of the Yankees game?"), or point out the downsides ("I suppose it's good news, but it wasn't much of a raise."). According to Gable's research, the only "correct" reaction—the response that's correlated with intimacy, satisfaction, trust, and continued com-mitment—is the first response: the enthusiastic, active one (W. Lawson 2004a).

Have Some Fun Together

Social psychologist John Crosby points out that people may misinterpret the idea of "working at" marriage: "Instead of working *at* marriage we may, with all good intentions, end up making work *of* marriage" (J. Crosby 1991, p. 287). At least sometimes, being happily mar-ried involves play—humor, spontaneity, and fun (Wood and Duck 2006). Being able to feel playful and behave playfully involves feeling safe in the presence of a part-ner. "As We Make Choices: Ten Rules for a Successful Relationship" gives some good ideas for positive couple

As We Make Choices   Ten Rules for a Successful Relationship

Research consistently shows that expressions of positive interest and affection are related to happy marriages. Psychologists Nathaniel Branden and Robert Sternberg, both of whom are mentioned in our discussion about love in Chapter 5, have developed some rules for nourishing a romantically loving relationship. Here are ten:

1. *Express your love verbally.* Say "I love you" or some equivalent (in contrast to the attitude, "What do you mean, do I love you? I married you, didn't I?").

2. *Be physically affectionate.* This includes making love sexually as well as handholding, kissing, cuddling, and comforting—with a cup of tea, a pillow, or a woolly blanket.

3. *Express your appreciation and even admiration.* Talk together about what you like, enjoy, and cherish in each other.

4. *Share more about yourself with your partner than you do with any other person.* In other words, keep each other primary (see Chapter 8).

5. *Offer each other an emotional support system.* Be there for each other in times of illness, difficulty, and crisis; be generally helpful and nurturing—devoted to each other's well-being.

6. *Express your love materially.* Send cards or give presents, big and small, on more than just routine occasions. Lighten the burden of your part-

ner's life once in a while by doing more than your agreed-upon share of the chores.

7. *Accept your partner's demands and put up with your partner's shortcomings.* We are not talking here about putting up with physical or verbal abuse. But demands and shortcomings are part of every happy relationship, and so is the grace with which we respond to them. Love your partner, not an unattainable idealization of him or her.

8. *Make time to be alone together.* This time should be exclusively devoted to the two of you as a couple. Understand that love requires attention and leisure.

9. *Do not take your relationship for granted.* Make your relationship your first priority and actively seek to meet each other's needs.

10. *Do unto each other as you would have the other do unto you.* Unconsciously, we sometimes want to give less than we get, or to be treated in special ways that we seldom offer our mate. Try to see things from your lover's viewpoint so that you can develop the empathy that underlies every lasting close relationship.

Critical Thinking

Often we read a list like the one above and think about whether our partner is

doing them, not whether we ourselves are. Chapter 5's discussion of love suggests that we pay attention to giving, as well as to receiving, love. How many of the items on the above list do you yourself do? Which two or three items might you work to incorporate into a relationship?

Sources: Branden 1988, pp.225–28; Sternberg 1988b, pp.272–77; see also Gottman and Silver 1999; Gottman and DeClaire 2001; Markman, Stanley, and Blumberg 2001.

communication. Conflicts do arise, however, and how they are addressed has much to do with how secure the mates feel in their relationship. We turn to an exploration of the relationship between conflict and love.

Conflict and Love

Marital anger and conflict are necessary forces and challenges to be met rather than avoided (Schechtman and Schechtman 2003). Although this may be especially

true in the early years of marriage, when individuals may be still in the process of getting to know each other (Driver and Gottman 2004), conflicts arise throughout marriage.

Sociologist Judith Wallerstein (Wallerstein and Blakeslee 1995) conducted lengthy interviews with fifty predominantly white, middle-class couples in northern California. The shortest marriage was ten years and the longest forty years. In order to participate, both husband and wife had to define their marriage as happy. When discussing what she found, Wallerstein wrote this:

[E]very married person knows that "conflict-free marriage" is an oxymoron. In reality it is neither possible nor desirable. . . . [I]n a contemporary marriage it is expected that husbands and wives will have different opinions. More important, they can't avoid having serious collisions on big issues that defy compromise. (p. 143)

The couples in Wallerstein's research quarreled on issues such as personal autonomy, who should handle the money and how it ought to be spent, how much a spouse should work, and whether the wife should be employed at all. Some fought over smoking and drinking:

In one marriage the husband and wife sat in the car to argue, to avoid upsetting the children. She told him that passive smoke was a proven carcinogen, and while the children were young he could not smoke in their home. He could do what he wanted outside. The man admitted that the request was reasonable, but he was furious. He punished her by not talking to her except when absolutely necessary for three months. Then he accepted the injunction on his smoking and they resumed their customary relationship. (p. 148)

Wallerstein concluded that

[T]he happily married couples I spoke with were frank in acknowledging their serious differences over the years. . . . What emerged from these interviews was not only that conflict is ubiquitous but that these couples considered learning to disagree and to stand one's ground one of the gifts of a good marriage. (p. 144)

Denying Conflict: Some Results

Many committed couples are reluctant to argue, even to share situations that might lead to an argument or a partner's negative response. For instance, a business person may keep her or his failing financial situation from a partner, fearing that the partner might think her or him a failure. But failing to talk about money leaves the spouse in the dark and the partner might continue to spend, driving the couple into bankruptcy that could have been avoided had the two only communicated the truth about the situation (Glink 2001). Reluctance to argue may also have other destructive effects on the partners as individuals and on their relationship, as we discuss next.

The majority of us know when we're angry, but many of us may feel uncomfortable about expressing that anger directly. Through years of being socialized to avoid getting mad or letting others know that they are angry, some people learn not to make an issue of things.

Learning to express anger and dealing with conflict early in a relationship are challenges to be met rather than avoided. Acknowledging and resolving conflict is painful, but it often strengthens the couple's union in the long run. A key to effective conflict management is to share everyday—and positive—events in friendly, supportive ways so that arguments occur within an overall context of couple satisfaction and mutual trust.

One result is that they may resort to anger substitutes, rather than dealing directly with their emotions.

One substitute for directly expressed anger is **passive-aggression**. When a person expresses anger at someone but does so indirectly rather than directly, that behavior is called passive-aggression. People use passive-aggression for the same reasons they use other anger substitutes—they are reluctant to engage in direct conflict, often because they are afraid of it.

Chronic criticism, nagging, nitpicking, and sarcasm are all forms of passive-aggression. Procrastination, especially when you have promised a partner that you will do something, may be a form of passive-aggression (Ferrari and Emmons 1994). These behaviors create unnecessary distance and pain in relationships. For instance, most people use sarcasm unthinkingly, and they often aren't aware of its effect on a partner. But being the target of a sarcastic remark can be painful; it may also result in partners feeling alienated from each other.

Sex becomes an arena for ongoing conflict when mates habitually withhold it or use it as passive-aggressive behavior. For example, a partner makes a disparaging comment in front of company. The hurt spouse says nothing at the time but rejects the other's sexual advances later that night because "I'm just too tired." It is much better to express anger at the time that an incident occurs. Otherwise, the anger festers and contaminates other areas of the relationship.

Other forms of passive-aggression are sabotage and displacement. In **sabotage**, one partner attempts to spoil or undermine some activity the other has planned. The husband who is angry because his wife invited friends over when he wanted to relax may sabotage her evening by acting bored. In **displacement**, a person directs anger at people or things that the other cherishes. A wife who is angry with her husband for spending too much time and energy on his career may hate his expensive car, or a husband who feels angry and threatened because his wife returned to school may express disgust for her books and "clutter." Sometimes child abuse, discussed in Chapter 14, can be related to displaced aggression felt by a parent.

Another possible consequence of suppressing anger over a long period of time can be indifference toward one's partner, as opposed to either love or hate (J. Crosby 1991). Therapists report that one of the most common complaints they hear from married couples these days is that "we don't feel much like having sex anymore" (Masters, Johnson, and Kolodny 1994). Repressing one's anger may contribute to this sexual boredom. When partners do not express anger toward each other (in positive—and always nonviolent—ways), their penalty may be emotional detachment: "[P]eople may stay together but become emotionally detached, postponing divorce until their loneliness becomes unbearable and the need to remain married (e.g., to raise children) becomes less compelling" (Gottman and Levenson 2000, p. 738).

Although suppressing anger may be a source of boredom and emotional detachment, partners can of course go too far in the opposite direction and habitually or violently hurt each other in angry outbursts (Berns, Jacobson, and Gottman 1999). Chapter 14 addresses spouse abuse as the extreme of destructive conflict. In this chapter, we look at what some social psychologists and family therapists can teach us about communication and conflict management in general. We turn now to what some recent communication research has to say about resilient unions.

Supportive Couple Communication and Conflict Management

Social psychologist John Gottman (1979, 1994, 1996; Gottman et al. 1998; Gottman and DeClaire 2001; Gott-

man and Notarius 2000, 2003) has made his reputation in the field of marital communication. In the 1970s, applying an interactionist perspective to partner communication, he began studying newly married couples in a university lab while they talked casually, discussed issues that they disagreed about, or tried to solve problems. Video cameras recorded the spouses' gestures, facial expressions, and verbal pitch and tone. Since he began this research, Gottman has kept in contact with more than 650 of the couples, some for as many as fourteen years. Typically, the couples were videotaped intermittently. Some couples volunteered for laboratory observation that monitored shifts in their heart rate and chemical stress indicators in their blood and urine as a result of their communicating with each other (Gottman 1996).

Studying marital communication in this detail, Gottman and his colleagues were able to chart the effects of small gestures. For example, early in his career he reported that when a spouse—particularly the wife—rolled her eyes while the other was talking, divorce was likely to follow sometime in the future, even if the couple was not thinking about divorce at the time (Gottman and Krotkoff 1989). Gottman's research has been challenged recently and may apply only to middle-class, married couples (see "Issues for Thought: A Look Behind the Scenes at Communication Research"). Recognizing the need for continued research in this area, we present Gottman's highly influential findings here.

The Four Horsemen of the Apocalypse

Gottman's research (1994) showed that conflict and anger themselves did not predict divorce, but processes that he called the **Four Horsemen of the Apocalypse** did.[1] The Four Horsemen of the Apocalypse are contempt, criticism, defensiveness, and stonewalling. Rolling one's eyes indicates **contempt**, a feeling that one's spouse is inferior or undesirable. **Criticism** involves making disapproving judgments or evaluations of one's partner. **Defensiveness** means preparing to defend oneself against what one presumes is an upcoming attack. **Stonewalling** is resistance, refusing to listen to one's partner, particularly to a partner's complaints. In study after study, these behaviors identified those who would divorce, with an unusually high accuracy of about 90 percent.

---

[1] The word *apocalypse* refers to the biblical idea that the world is soon to end, being destroyed by fire. The Four Horsemen are allegorical figures representing war, famine, and death, with the fourth uncertain (*Concise Columbia Encyclopedia* 1994, p. 309). Gottman used the phrase to indicate attitudes and behaviors that foreshadow impending divorce.

An important scientific norm requires that research findings be critically reviewed by others in order to help ensure that they are accurate. The purpose "is not to attack, . . . but to ensure that the methods used in research can stand up to close, careful examination" (Neuman 2000, p. 9).

One way to follow this norm is for subsequent studies to try to reproduce, or *replicate,* the findings of an earlier researcher—that is, follow the first researcher's design and methods over again to discern whether the same findings emerge. If a study replicates well (the same findings show up), we can be better assured that the research is to be taken seriously. If the study does not replicate (the same findings do not emerge in both studies), then we cannot be certain what to think until even more studies are done.

In 2007, a team of researchers (Kim, Capaldi, and Crosby 2007) sought to reproduce findings from the much publicized earlier research of well-known and highly respected social psychologist John Gottman and his colleagues (Gottman et al. 1998). The research that sought to reproduce Gottman's findings used observation methods similar to Gottman's. However, the sample used by Kim and colleagues was purposefully different. Gottman had used a sample of child-free Seattle newlyweds who had been married for the first time within the previous six months and who answered media ads that requested their participation. Most of these couples were middle-class college graduates. Kim, Capaldi, and Crosby (2007) used a sample of young adults who had grown up in poor neighborhoods in Oregon and who, by their twenties, were unlikely to have graduated from college. Furthermore, Kim and colleagues' research used a sample that included both married and cohabiting couples, many of whom had children. Kim and colleagues used a different sample in order to discern whether Gottman's findings could be applied to other than middle-class marrieds.

As described in more detail elsewhere in this chapter, one thing that Gottman and his colleagues had found was that a serious communication problem faced by couples occurs when the wife raises complaints to her husband in ways that he perceives as abrasive or attacking. The husband then withdraws and apparently ignores her. (This situation is commonly known among researchers and therapists as the *female-demand/male-withdraw communication* pattern.) Based on their findings, Gottman and his colleagues suggested that therapists should focus on gender differences when counseling (heterosexual) couples' communication. Therapists were encouraged to help wives to raise issues more gently and husbands to be more willing to be influenced by their wives (Gottman et al. 1998).

The later researchers pointed out that Gottman and his colleagues had published advice to therapists without the qualification that it might only apply to middle-class, married couples. Therefore, they argued that Gottman's research needed to be further examined in order to see whether his findings applied to couples who were not middle class and/or were not married, but cohabiting. The replication researchers further argued that, "given the fact that low-socioeconomic status populations have been underrepresented in research on couples, testing the generalizability of [Gottman's study] to couples with lower socioeconomic backgrounds is especially valuable" (Kim, Capaldi, and Crosby 2007, p. 57).

This story might not be news if Kim and colleagues had successfully reproduced Gottman's findings. However, this was not the case. For one thing, the later researchers' findings did not support the female-demand/male-withdraw gender differences described by Gottman. In a published response Gottman argued, among other things, that his research was not necessarily meant to apply to cohabiting couples (Coan and Gottman 2007). Nevertheless, Kim and colleagues agued that their failure to replicate Gottman's findings

> calls into question the extent to which [Gottman and his colleagues'] findings . . . should be used as a basis for recommendation for therapy and interventions with young couples and in general provides a caution against translating empirical findings to treatment recommendations without replication. (Kim, Capaldi, and Crosby 2007, p. 66)

When researchers fail to replicate another's findings, "it is often difficult for readers to know what to conclude." Therefore, we need to be "cautious with initial findings until they are replicated" (Heyman and Hunt 2007, p. 84) and tested in many different samples.

Critical Thinking

Given Kim, Capaldi, and Crosby's (2007) failure to reproduce the findings of Gottman et al. (1998) in a sample that was not primarily middle-class and included cohabiting couples, what do you think about the generalizability of Gottman's suggestions to therapists? How might yet another research team further investigate Gottman's findings?

Later, after more research, Gottman added **belligerence**, "a behavior that is provocative and that challenges the spouse's power and authority. For example: 'What can you do if I do go drinking with Dave? What are you going to do about it?'" (Gottman et al. 1998, p. 6). Still later, Gottman and his colleagues identified similar patterns among gay and lesbian couples (Gottman et al. 2003). In sum, contempt, criticism, defensiveness, stonewalling, and belligerence characterize unhappy marriages and may signal impending divorce (Gottman and Levenson 2002). Supportive communication characterizes happier, stable unions, but what exactly is supportive communication?

What Is Supportive Communication?

Gottman and his colleagues videotaped 130 newlywed couples as they discussed for fifteen minutes a problem that caused ongoing disagreement in their marriage (Gottman et al. 1998). Each couple's communication was coded in one-second sequences, then synchronized with each spouse's heart-rate data, which was being collected at the same time. The heart-rate data would indicate each partner's physiological stress.

The researchers examined all the interaction sequences in which one partner first expressed *negative affect:* anger, sadness, whining, disgust, tension and fear, belligerence, contempt, or defensiveness. Belligerence, contempt, and defensiveness (three of Gottman's indicators of impending divorce) were coded as *high-intensity, negative affect.* The other emotions listed above (anger, sadness, whining, etc.) were coded as *low-intensity negative affect.*

Next, the researchers watched what happened immediately after a spouse had expressed negative affect or raised a complaint. Sometimes the partner reciprocated with negative affect in kind, either low or high intensity. For example, she whines, and he whines back; he expresses anger, and she responds with tension and fear; or she is contemptuous, and he immediately becomes defensive.

At other times, one partner's first negative expression was reciprocated with an escalation of the negativity. For example, she whined, and he grew belligerent; or he expressed anger, and she became defensive. Gottman and his colleagues called this kind of interchange *refusing-to-accept-influence,* because the spouse on the receiving end of the other's complaint refuses to consider it and, instead, escalates the fight.

Meanwhile, still other couples were likely to communicate with *positive affect,* responding to each other warmly with interest, affection, or shared (not mean or contemptuous) humor. Positive affect typically de-escalated conflict (Gottman and Levenson 2000, 2002).

Gottman and his colleagues found that "[t]he only variable that predicted both marital stability and marital happiness among stable couples was the amount of positive affect in the conflict" (1998, p. 17). In stable, happy couples, shared humor and expressions of warmth, interest, and affection were apparent even in conflict situations and, therefore, de-escalated the argument.

Second, the researchers "found no evidence . . . to support the [idea that] anger is the destructive emotion in marriages" (1998, p. 16). Instead, they found that contempt, belligerence, and defensiveness were the destructive attitudes and behaviors. Specifically, they concluded that the interaction pattern that best predicts divorce is a wife's raising a complaint, followed by her husband's refusing-to-accept-influence, followed, in turn, by the wife's reciprocating her husband's escalated negativity, and the absence of any de-escalation by means of positive affect. Gottman and his colleagues went on to make suggestions for better couple communication, and their advice for wives is different than that for husbands.

Gender Differences in Couple Communication

Deborah Tannen's book *You Just Don't Understand* (1990) argued that men typically engage in **report talk**, conversation aimed mainly at conveying information. Women, on the other hand, are likely to engage in **rapport talk**, speaking to gain or reinforce rapport or intimacy. One result can be "men and women talking at cross-purposes" (p. 287).

A review of research on couple communication in the 1990s (Gottman and Notarius 2000; Bradbury, Fincham, and Beach 2000) strongly suggests that men and women differ in their responses to negative affect in close relationships. When faced with a complaint from their partner, men tend to withdraw emotionally whereas women do not. This pattern is so common that therapists have named it the **"female-demand/male-withdraw communication pattern."**[2] In distressed marriages, this pattern becomes a repeated cycle of negative verbal expression by a wife and withdrawal by the husband (Kurdek 1995b; Gottman et al. 1998).

[2] Many researchers who study couple communication agree that generally there is a "female-demand/male-withdraw pattern" (Gottman and Levenson 2000, p. 738; Gottman and Notarius 2000, p. 940; Bradbury, Fincham, and Beach 2000, p. 967; Miller and Roloff 2005; Weger 2005). However, an alternative view argues that "it is not gender per se but the nature of the marital discussion—for example, whether it is the wife or the husband who desires a change—that may determine who is demanding and who is withdrawing" (Roberts 2000, p. 702; also see Kim, Capaldi, and Crosby 2007).

© Royalty-Free/Mediolmages/Index Stock Imagery

What can couples do to make conflict management easier on them—and on their relationship? According to John Gottman, wives generally can learn to raise issues in more gentle ways, whereas husbands generally need to learn to accept their partner's influence rather than escalating the argument. This advice may be applied to either partner, of course. Whoever is voicing a complaint might do so gently, whereas the receiver needs to be willing to listen. Indeed, both partners need to do what they can to de-escalate the fight—but not to avoid their conflict altogether.

Which came first is hard to say. Some researchers speculate that wives, being more expressive, attuned to the emotional quality of a marriage and often having less power, attempt to bring conflict out into the open by initiatives that have an attention-getting negative tone (Cui et al. 2005). Husbands try to minimize conflict by conciliatory gestures (Real 2002; L. Rubin 2007). Either a healthy problem-solving dialogue may ensue, or, more likely, the husband's minimization of conflict may seem to the wife to be a lack of recognition of her emotional needs and her concern about the marriage (Noller and Fitzpatrick 1991; Canary and Dindia 1998). As one husband described his situation:

> The more I try to be cool and calm her the worse it gets. I swear, I can't figure her out, I'll keep trying to tell her not to get so excited, but there's nothing I can do. Anything I say just makes it worse. So then I try to keep quiet, but . . . wow the explosion is like crazy, just nuts. (in L. Rubin 2007, p. 323).

We might compare this to a wife, who told her interviewers that,

> I can't stand that he's so damned unemotional and expects me to be the same. He lives in his head all of

[the] time, and he acts like anything that's emotional isn't worth dealing with. (in L. Rubin 2007, p. 322)

Obviously, the demand/withdraw interaction pattern leads to both partners' feeling misunderstood, thereby decreasing marital satisfaction (Weger 2005). Gottman and his colleagues (1998) concluded that wives and husbands have different goals when they disagree:

> The wife wants to resolve the disagreement so that she feels closer to the husband and respected by him. The husband, though, just wants to avoid a blowup. The husband doesn't see the disagreement as an opportunity for closeness, but for trouble. (p. 17)

In one husband's words, "I just got mad and I'd take off—go out with the guys and have a few beers or something. When I'd get back, things would be even worse." From his wife's perspective, "The more I screamed, the more he'd withdraw, until finally I'd go kind of crazy. Then he'd leave and not come back until two or three in the morning sometimes" (L. Rubin 1976, pp. 77, 79).

Gottman and his colleagues sought to better understand this female-demand/male-withdraw pattern. You'll recall that the researchers monitored spouses' heart rates as indicators of physiological stress during conflict. They found that, although the final word is not yet in, "it is likely that the biological, stress-related response of men is more rapid and recovery is slower than that of women, and that this response is related to the greater emotional withdrawal of men than women in distressed families" (Gottman et al. 1998, p. 19). That is, when confronted with conflict from an intimate, men may experience more intense and uncomfortable physical symptoms of stress than women do. Therefore, men are more likely than women to withdraw emotionally and/or physically.

An alternative—or complementary—view is that men have been socialized to withdraw. The cultural options for masculinity include "no 'sissy' stuff," according to which men are expected to distance themselves from anything considered feminine. We guess this could include a wife's complaints. In two books on men and communication, the first called *I Don't Want to Talk*

About It, therapist Terrence Real (1997, 2002) attributes males' withdrawal to a "secret legacy of depression," brought on by men's traditional socialization, particularly society's refusal to let them grieve over losses (e.g., "Don't cry over nothing"). It is likely that physiology and culture interact to create the female-demand/male-withdraw pattern.

In line with the view that social factors influence divergent communication patterns for men and women is research that compares communication patterns among husbands of various racial/ethnic groups (Mackey and O'Brien 1998). In one such study of sixty non-Hispanic white, African American, and Mexican American couples whose marriages had lasted at least twenty years, social work professors Richard Mackey and Bernard O'Brien found that African American husbands were much less likely to withdraw from conflict than were non-Hispanic white or Mexican American husbands. Mackey and O'Brien speculated that the historical social context of black men has affected their conflict management styles at home:

> It was dangerous for most of these black men to assert themselves in conflict situations with white people. As a consequence, the home may have been one of the few safe places for African American men to deal openly with interpersonal conflict. (p. 138)

What Wives Can Do In the following discussion, the term *soothe* indicates things that people do to reduce physical stress symptoms. Although both spouses benefit from being soothed, Gottman and his colleagues go so far as to say that "[m]arriages will work to the extent that they provide for soothing of the male" (Gottman et al. 1998, p. 20). "Soothing of the male" can involve self-soothing—for example, he takes a timeout or tells his wife that "I just can't talk about it now, but I will later" (and means it). Also, soothing may imply soothing of the male by the female.

This process involves two things: (1) using positive affect, such as shared humor and expressions of affection, to de-escalate negativity; and (2) the wife's softening the way she brings up complaints. Gottman does not mean to discourage wives from raising disagreeable topics, but rather to "soften" their confrontations by using less-negative communication styles. For example, a wife who often voices complaints by whining or with a tone of contempt might try to speak more gently.

What Husbands Can Do Reminding us that fighting per se ("negative affect reciprocity in kind") is not the problem, Gottman and his colleagues argue that the husband's escalation of negativity is the real problem.

The researchers view this escalation as a symptom of the husband's refusal to accept influence from his wife or to share power with her:

> Usually the wife brings marital issues to the table for discussion, and she usually brings a detailed analysis of the conditions in which this problem occurs, its history, and suggestions for a solution. Some men, those whose marriages wind up stable and happy, accept influence from their wives, and some do not. . . . Our data suggest that only newlywed men who accept influence from their wives are winding up in happy and stable marriages. (1998, pp. 18–19)

Unfortunately, newspapers publicized this research with headlines such as "'Honey, just be a yes man'" and "Marriage lasts if husband gives in." But *sharing* power is not the same as how one journalist described it: "Just do what your wife says. Go ahead, give in to her" (Maugh 1998). Sharing power involves the willingness to be influenced—to negotiate or compromise, sometimes giving in and sometimes not (Gottman and DeClaire 2001). The real message to husbands is not to respond to their wife's complaints by escalating the argument with defensiveness, contempt, or belligerence.

What Couples Can Do The general conclusion of Gottman's research on communication and conflict management among married couples is as follows:

1. Partners, especially wives, need to try to be more gentle when they raise complaints.

2. Partners, especially wives, can help soothe their spouse by communicating care and affection.

3. Partners, especially husbands, can learn self-soothing techniques.

4. Partners, especially husbands, need to be willing to accept influence from their wives.

5. Both partners need to do what they can—perhaps using authentic, shared humor, kindness, and other signs of affection—to de-escalate the argument. (It is important to recognize that this does not mean avoiding the issue altogether.)

Finally, Gottman and his colleagues (1998) suggest that, as we have already seen, it is probably important for couples to think about communicating with positive affect more often in their daily living and not just during times of conflict (Gottman and DeClaire 2001). ("As We Make Choices: Ten Rules for a Successful Relationship" suggests ways to do this.) Communicating with positive affect, of course, implies avoiding the Four Horsemen of the Apocalypse.

"I agreed to 'for better' and 'for worse,' but never to 'for mysterious' and 'withholding.'"

Avoiding the Four Horsemen of the Apocalypse

Consider the following exchange:

PARTNER A: I can't find my cell phone.

PARTNER B: What do you mean, you can't find it? Don't accuse me of taking it. It's never on when I try to call you anyway.

PARTNER A: What's that got to do with anything, Stupid?

PARTNER B: So look for it.

PARTNER A: I thought maybe you could help me since you're not doing anything important right now anyway.

PARTNER B: You're just like your dad—always expecting somebody to wait on you.

PARTNER A: So?

PARTNER B: Your father's a jerk.

PARTNER A: At least my mother's not a snoop!

PARTNER B: Her hair is ridiculous!

PARTNER A: It wouldn't hurt if you did something with *your* hair.

PARTNER B: Not that there's room in the bathroom with your stuff scattered all over.

In this scenario, Partner A mentions having misplaced a cell phone, and a fight ensues. Some might find this couple's exchange humorous. But this is not the kind of communication that bonds couples and helps to keep them together. This fight reveals three of Gottman's Four Horsemen of the Apocalypse—contempt, defensiveness, and criticism—along with belligerence, the sign that Gottman added later as predictive of divorce.

When Partner A announces the need for the cell phone, Partner B becomes defensive: "Don't accuse me of taking it." At this point, Partner B raises a complaint: "It's never on when I try to call you anyway." In a less-distressed couple, Partner A might respond to Partner B's complaint. But Partner A fails to de-escalate the interchange and does not acknowledge Partner B's complaint. Instead, Partner A calls Partner B stupid. Name-calling is typically contemptuous; counselors encourage us to avoid it. A less-distressed couple might stop this negative communication with shared humor or some sign of affection. Partner A subsequently requests that Partner B help look for the cell phone. Partner B's reply is contemptuous and critical: "You're just like your dad—always expecting somebody to wait on you." Again, the couple fails to de-escalate the negative affect. This time Partner A responds with belligerence: "So?" The couple continues to criticize and show mutual contempt, while neither spouse de-escalates the argument. It probably goes without saying that we are advised to avoid this kind of couple interaction. Moreover, it appears the couple has forgotten what the fight is about. In fact, one wonders whether they ever knew what the fight was about.

Counselors point out that distressed couples, like the one depicted here, often do not know what they are really fighting about. Fighting over petty annoyances, such as who should have put gas in the car, is healthy and can even be fun as an essentially harmless way to release tension (Fitzpatrick 1995). But partners sometimes unconsciously allow trivial issues to become decoys so that they evade the real area of conflict and leave it unresolved. For example, an annoyed spouse who consistently complains about the other's "ex" may really be experiencing feelings of anxiety or insecurity about the current marriage. We turn now to take a closer look at Gottman's fourth Horseman of the Apocalypse—stonewalling, or refusing to listen to a partner's complaints.

Stonewalling Avoiding or evading a fight is an example of stonewalling. Stonewallers react to their partner's attempts to raise disputed or tension-producing issues by refusing to engage with the partner's initiatives. They fear conflict and hesitate to accept their own and others' hostile or angry emotions. Fight evaders use several tactics to avoid fighting, such as the following:

1. Leaving the house or the scene when a fight threatens

2. Turning sullen and refusing to argue or talk

3. Derailing potential arguments by saying, "I can't take it when you yell at me"

4. Using the "hit and run" tactic of filing a complaint, then leaving no time for an answer or for a resolution

5. Saying "OK, you win," giving in verbally, maybe even promising to "do better next time," but without meaning it

Stonewallers may argue that they avoid conflicts because the issue raised is silly or they don't want to hurt their partners. Often, however, they are really trying to protect themselves: "A great deal of dishonesty that ostensibly occurs in an effort to prevent pain actually occurs as we try to protect and shield ourselves from the agony of feeling our own pain, fear, fright, shame, or embarrassment" (J. Crosby 1991, pp.159–60). Stonewalling can make partners who need to raise and resolve differences feel worse, not better.

In addition, stonewalling may encourage one's partner to engage in "gunnysacking"—keeping one's grievances secret while tossing them into an imaginary gunnysack that grows heavier and heavier over time. Martyring (see Chapter 5) is often accompanied by gunnysacking. When marital complaints are toted and nursed along quietly in a gunnysack for any length of time, they "make a dreadful mess when they burst out" (Bach and Wyden 1970, p. 19).

Research psychologists and family counselors agree that strong, or resilient, families are not without conflict. Cohesive families have fights. But arguments do not necessarily pull a union apart. We turn to what may at first seem like a strange idea—that some arguments, or ways to fight, may actually bring a couple or other family members closer together (H. Lerner 2001).

Bonding Fights— Ten Guidelines

Some goals and strategies can help make conflict management productive rather than destructive. This kind of fighting, which brings people closer rather than pushing them apart, has been called **bonding fighting**. The key to creating a bonding fight is for partners to try to build up, not tear down, each other's self-esteem, even as they argue.

Social groups within the United States vary considerably in the endorsement their cultures give to the open expression of emotion, which may make arguing constructively more or less difficult for people within or across cultures (see, for example, Hirsch 2003). Deborah Tannen's (1990) book *You Just Don't Understand*, which drew wide attention for its comparison of men's and women's communication styles, also points out cultural communication differences among, for example, New Yorkers, Californians, New Englanders, and Midwesterners, and among Scandinavians, Canada's native peoples, and Greeks. Nevertheless, there are better (and not-so-good) ways that virtually all couples and family members can resolve differences. Now we turn to ten specific guidelines for constructive conflict management.

© Noel Hedrickson/Getty Images/Digital Vision

Chronic stonewallers may fear rejection or retaliation and therefore hesitate to acknowledge their own or their partner's angry emotions. Examples of stonewalling include saying things like, "I can't take it when you yell at me," or turning sullen and refusing to talk. It may sound impossible to fight more fairly when you're angry, but "practice makes better." Using I-statements, avoiding mixed messages, focusing your anger on specific issues, and being willing to change are some guidelines worth trying.

Guideline 1: Level with Each Other

Partners need to be as (gently, kindly) candid as possible; counselors call this **leveling**—being transparent, authentic, and explicit about how one feels, "especially concerning the more conflictive or hurtful aspects" of an intimate relationship (Bach and Wyden 1970, p. 368; J.Block 2003; H. Lerner 2001). Leveling is self-disclosure in action.

Various studies indicate that—often because of the mistaken impression that one partner already knows how the other feels—partners overestimate how accurately their mate understands them and then fail to understand their partner. Underlying conflicts often go unresolved because partners fail to voice their feelings, irritations, and preferences—and neither is aware that the other is holding back. Remember: It's unfair to expect your mate to read your mind (Bernstein and Magee 2004). The solution to this problem is to air grievances: to candidly explain where one stands and how one feels about a specific situation. Being candid does not mean the same thing as being mean or unnecessarily critical. Leveling is never intentionally hurtful.

Guideline 2: To Avoid Attacks, Use I-Statements When You Can

Attacks are insults, or assaults on a partner's character or self-esteem. Needless to say, attacks do not help to bond a couple. Neither does blame (Sinclair and Monk 2004). We have seen that contemptuous remarks are destructive fighting tactics. A rule in avoiding attack is to use *I* rather than *you* or *why*. The receiver usually perceives I-statements as an attempt to recognize and communicate feelings, but you- and why-statements are more likely to be perceived as attacks—whether or not they are intended as such. For example, instead of declaring, "You're late," or asking "Why are you late?"—both of which can smack of blame—a statement such as "I was worried because you hadn't arrived" may allow for more positive dialogue.

I-statements are most effective if they are communicated in a positive way. A partner should express his or her anger directly, but it will seem less threatening if he or she conveys positive feelings at the same time that negative emotions are voiced. The message comes across, but it's not as bitter as when only angry feelings are expressed.

Making I-statements can be difficult, of course, and may be too much to ask in the heat of an argument. One social psychologist has admitted what many of us may already know: "It is impossible to make an 'I-statement' when you are in the 'hating-my-partner, wanting-revenge, feeling-stung-and-needing-to-sting-back' state of mind" (quoted in Gottman et al. 1998, p. 18). Of course, this is partly the point. Keeping in mind the possibility of expressing a complaint— at least *begin-*

ning a confrontation—with an I-statement can discourage partners from getting to that wanting-revenge state of mind in the first place.

Guideline 3: Avoid Mixed, or Double, Messages

A third tip for fighting in a more positive way is to avoid using **mixed, or double, messages**: simultaneous messages that contradict each other.[3] Contradictory messages may be verbal, or one may be verbal and one nonverbal. For example, a spouse agrees to go out to eat with a partner but at the same time yawns and says that he or she is tired and has had a hard day at work. Or a partner insists, "Of course I love you" while picking an invisible speck from her or his sleeve in a gesture of indifference.

Communication also involves both a sender and a receiver. Just as the sender gives both a verbal message and a nonverbal metamessage, so also does a receiver give nonverbal cues about how seriously she or he is taking the message. For example, listening while continuing to do chores sends the nonverbal message that what is being heard is not very important.

Senders of mixed messages may not be aware of what they are doing, and mixed messages can be very subtle. They usually result from just not paying attention to one's relationship or from simultaneously wanting to recognize and to deny conflict or tension. In the latter case, mixed messages allow senders to let other people know they are angry at them and at the same time to deny that they are. A classic example is the *silent treatment*. A spouse becomes aware that she or he has said or done something and asks what's wrong. "Oh, nothing," the partner replies, without much feeling, but everything about the partner's face, body, attitude, and posture suggests that something is indeed wrong (H. Lerner 2001).

Besides the silent treatment, other ways to indicate that something is wrong while denying it include making a partner the butt of jokes, using subtle innuendos rather than direct communication, and being sarcastic (also defended as "just a joke" by mixed-message senders). Sarcasm and other mixed messages create distance and cause pain and confusion, for they prevent honest communication from taking place. Expressing anger in as positive a way as possible is better, because it opens the way for solutions.

---

[3] Communication scholars and counselors point out that there are two major aspects of any communication: *what* is said (the verbal message) and *how* it is said (the nonverbal "metamessage"). The metamessage involves tone of voice, inflection, and body language. In a mixed message, the verbal message does not correspond with the nonverbal metamessage.

Guideline 4: Choose the Time and Place Carefully

Fights may be nonconstructive if the complainant raises grievances at the wrong time. One partner may be ready to argue about an issue when the other is almost asleep or working on an important assignment, for instance. At such times, the person who picked the fight may get more than he or she bargained for.

Partners might try to negotiate *gripe hours* by pinning down a time and place for a fight. Fighting by appointment may sound silly and may be difficult to arrange, but it has two important advantages. First, complainants can organize their thoughts and feelings more calmly and deliberately, increasing the likelihood that their arguments will be persuasive. Second, recipients of complaints have time before the fight to prepare themselves for some criticism.

Guideline 5: Focus Anger Only on Specific Issues

Constructive fighting aims at resolving specific problems that are happening *now*—not at gunnysacking. Recipients of complaints need to feel that they can do something specific to help resolve the problem raised. This will be difficult if they feel overwhelmed. Noted marriage communication researcher Andrew Christensen advises that

> If you're angry and resentful, requests for change will be met with resistance and countercharge efforts: "It's not my problem; it's your problem." But if you learn to approach each other with acceptance and empathy, you can create a collaborative context, and often people will make spontaneous changes. ("Loving Your Partner . . ." 2000)

Then, too, if things seem to be getting out of hand, call for a timeout.

Guideline 6: Ask for a Specific Change, but Be Open to Compromise

Initially, complainants should be ready to propose at least one solution to the problem. Recipients might come up with possible solutions. If they can keep proposed solutions pertinent to the issue at hand, partners might be able to negotiate alternatives.

Resolving specific issues involves bargaining and negotiation. Partners need to recognize that there are probably several ways to solve a particular problem, and backing each other into corners with ultimatums and counter-ultimatums is not negotiation but attack. John Gottman found that happily married couples reach agreement rather quickly. Either one partner gives in to the other without resentment, or the two compromise. Sometimes compromise involves one's rethinking the complaint—that is, asking oneself "How important is it?" (Sanford 2006). Unhappily married couples tend to continue in a cycle of stubbornness and conflict (Gottman and Krotkoff 1989).

Guideline 7: Be Willing to Change Yourself

Communication, of course, needs to be accompanied by action. One counselor team (Christensen and Jacobson 1999) has suggested "acceptance therapy," helping partners accept their spouses as they are instead of demanding change, although they suggest that, paradoxically, acceptance is also the basis for obtaining behavior change. Meanwhile, the romantic belief that couples should accept each other *completely* as they are is often merged with the view that people should be exactly what they choose to be. The result is an erroneous assumption that if a partner loves you, he or she will accept you just as you are and not ask for even minor changes. On the contrary, partners need to be willing to change themselves, to be changed by others, and to be influenced by their partner's feelings and rational arguments. Defensiveness, resentments, and refusing to change are dysfunctional responses that contribute to marital deterioration (Gottman and Silver 1999; H. Lerner 2001). Every intimate relationship involves negotiation and mutual compromise; partners who refuse to change, or who insist they cannot, are in effect refusing to engage in an intimate relationship. Therapists note that in some couples, each partner expects the other one to do the changing ("You have to understand, she's [or he's] impossible to live with.") (Ball and Kivisto 2006, p. 155). But being willing to change ourselves is key.

Guideline 8: Don't Try to Win

Partners must not compete in fights. American society encourages people to see almost everything they do in terms of winning or losing. Yet research clearly indicates that the tactics associated with winning in a particular conflict are also those associated with lower marital satisfaction (Noller and Fitzpatrick 1991; Holmes and Murray 1996; Klein and Johnson 1997; Zak 1998).

Bonding fights, like dancing, can't involve a winner and a loser. If one partner must win, then the other obviously must lose. But losing lessens a person's self-esteem and increases resentment and strain on the relationship. This is why in intimate fighting there can never be one winner and one loser—only two losers. Both partners lose if they engage in destructive conflict. Both win if they become closer and settle, or at least understand, their differences. Being willing to negotiate, rather than to win, is a way to demonstrate love (Carroll, Badger, and Yang 2006).

Guideline 9: Remember to End the Argument

The happily married couples that Wallerstein (Wallerstein and Blakeslee 1995) interviewed (described earlier in this chapter) tried to fight only about big issues and knew how and when to stop fighting. However, if a couple cannot designate a winner and a loser, they may be at a loss to know how to end a fight. Ideally, a fight ends when there has been a mutually satisfactory airing of each partner's views.

Sometimes when partners are too hurt or frightened to continue they need to stop arguing before they reach a resolution. Women may cry as a signal that they've been hit below the beltline or that they feel too frustrated or hurt to go on fighting. Men experience the same feelings, but they have learned from childhood not to cry. Hence, they may hide their emotions, or they may erupt angrily. In either case, it would help to bargain about whether the fight should continue. The partner who is not feeling so hurt or frightened might ask, "Do you want to stop now or to go on with this?" If the answer is "I want to stop," the fight should be either terminated or interrupted for a time.

Guideline 10: Be Willing to Forgive

In recent years a growing number of therapists have suggested that being willing to forgive one's partner is critical to ongoing satisfying relationships (Fincham, Hall, and Beach 2006). Forgiveness "is the idea of a change whereby one becomes less motivated to think, feel, and behave negatively (e.g., retaliate, withdraw) in regard to the offender." Forgiveness is not something to which the offender is necessarily entitled, but it is granted nevertheless. Contrary to what many folks believe, forgiveness does not require that the offended partner minimize the offense. Rather, "an individual forgives despite the wrongful nature of the offense and the fact that the offender is not entitled to forgiveness." Forgiveness differs from condoning or excusing an offense. Further, "forgiveness is distinct from denial (an unwillingness to perceive the injury) . . . or forgetting (removes awareness of offence from consciousness)" (p. 416). Forgiveness is often a process that takes time, rather than one specific decision or act of the will. Being willing to forgive has been associated in research with marital satisfaction, lessened ambivalence toward a partner, conflict resolution, enhanced commitment, and greater empa-

thy. Reconciliation may follow forgiveness, but not necessarily (Fincham, Hall, and Beach 2006).

We've looked at ten specific guidelines for fighting more positively, even having fights that can bring a couple closer together. Realizing that there are ways to fight that can actually be "bonding" might help to overcome what some of us experience as fear of anger and conflict. The assumption that conflict and anger don't belong in healthy relationships exists in many couples and families. This assumption is based partly on the idea that love is the polar opposite of hate (J. Crosby 1991). But emotional intimacy necessarily involves feelings of both wanting to be close and needing to be separate, of agreeing and disagreeing (Scarf 1995). Gottman and his colleagues would not have done all their research or spent so much time reporting it both in scholarly journals and in more-popular books if they did not believe that individuals and partners could change their fighting habits for the better. The next section explores this idea.

Toward Better Communication

Social scientist Suzanne Steinmetz traced in fifty-seven intact urban and suburban families the patterns of how families resolve conflict. Her research shows that families assume consistent patterns or habits for facing conflict, and these patterns are passed from one generation to the next (Steinmetz 1977). Subsequent research has reached similar conclusions (Conger and Conger 2002; VanLear 1992). Although the generalization that communication patterns are transmitted from parents to children is correct, it's important to note variations from this pattern (Rovers 2006). VanLear (1992) found that young married men tend to rebel against their parents' marital conflict style. (Women are more apt to follow their parents' lead.) VanLear's comparison of married couples in their late twenties to parental couples in their fifties found that the younger married men tended to choose different conflict styles from their parents. Most often, that meant they evidenced less conflict avoidance. These men also married women very different in conflict style from their own mothers. Moreover, the younger couples also reported more sharing and disclosure than was characteristic of the parental generation (VanLear 1992). Despite its fairly small sample size (fifty-eight families), VanLear's study signals hope for future generations as they learn more about fighting fairly.

Couples can consciously act to change marital interaction patterns. A study in Germany found that couples establish conflict resolution styles during the first year of marriage and then gradually make them habitual

Couples *can* change their fighting habits. The key to staying happily together is to make knowledgeable choices—about not avoiding conflict but dealing with it openly, or directly, and in supportive ways. Doing so involves listening—without judgment, without formulating a response while the other talks, and without interrupting. The goal isn't necessarily agreement, but acknowledgment, insight, and understanding.

(Schneewind and Gerhard 2002). However, couples can change. By making knowledgeable decisions rather than resorting to old habits by default we can unlearn less-effective ways of communicating (Wright 2006b).

Some training programs in couple empathy and communication, conducted by psychologists, have proven quite effective in helping people change these behaviors (Long et al.1999). One such program for married couples is ENRICH, developed by social psychologist David Olson (1994) at the University of Minnesota. A similar important program is PREP (the Prevention and Relationship Enhancement Program), developed by marital communication psychologists Scott Stanley and Howard Markman, with the overall aim of strengthening marriages and preventing divorce (Markman, Stanley, and Blumberg 2001). Marriage Encounter and similar organizations offer weekend workshops, designed for mostly satisfied couples who want to improve their relationship (Yalcin and Karaban 2007). The following ideas may help people work for change on their own.

A first step in improving one's marital communication may be to set realistic expectations about the relationship (Cloud and Townsend 2005). As one married woman put it,

> You just have this idealized version of getting married, you know, everybody plays it up as so romantic and so wonderful and sweet. Now that I am married and now that I have gotten older and hit the real world I'm kind of like. . . . It's a lot more hands-on, you know, getting stuff done . . . than it is that idealized romantic notion that you get as a girl. (in Fairchild 2006, p. 13)

Besides "getting stuff done," spouses need to accept the reality of conflict. A second step is to begin to use the guidelines for bonding fighting that we have described. Often, as partners grow more accustomed to voicing grievances regularly and in more respectful or caring ways, their fights may hardly seem like fights at all: Partners will gradually learn to incorporate many irritations and requests into their normal conversations. Partners adept at constructive fighting often argue in normal tones of voice and even with humor. In a very real sense, their disagreements are essential to their intimacy.

Partners who are just learning to manage their conflicts constructively may be anxious or insecure. Some ways to begin are by writing letters or e-mails, or recording a complaint that one's partner can listen to later. In this way the complainant is not inhibited or stopped by a mate's interruption or negative nonverbal cues. Later, the mate can read or listen to the other's complaints in privacy when she or he is ready to listen.

Another idea is to videotape a fight and play it back later. This exercise can help spouses look at themselves objectively. Interestingly, when researchers videotaped couples who were fighting, the couples were surprised at their own behavior: They had underestimated their displays of hostility (Cui et al. 2005). Watching a videotape in order to improve their fighting behaviors, couples can ask themselves whether they really listened, stuck to specifics, or resorted to hurtful fight tactics.

Although these suggestions may help, learning to fight fair is not easy. Sometimes couples feel that they need outside help with their fighting, and they may decide to have a marriage counselor serve as referee. See Appendix H, "Marriage and Close Relationship Counseling," which is available on the Internet, for a discussion of this alternative. A number of books and Internet resources are available to those who want to improve their relationships, and many of these appear in the Suggested Readings section for this chapter, to be found on the website that accompanies this textbook.

The Myth of Conflict-Free Conflict

By now, enough attention has been devoted to the bonding capacity of intimate fighting that it may seem as if conflict itself can be free of conflict. It can't. Even the fairest fighters hit below the belt once in a while, and just about all fighting involves some degree of frustration and hurt feelings. After all, anger is anger, and hostility is hostility—even between partners who are very close to each other.

Moreover, some spouses are married to mates who don't want to learn to fight positively. In marriages in which one partner wants to change and the other doesn't, sometimes much can be gained if just one partner begins to communicate more positively. Other times, however, positive changes in one spouse do not spur growth in the other. Situations like this may end in divorce.

Even when both partners develop constructive habits, all their problems will not necessarily be resolved (Booth, Crouter, and Clements 2001; Driver and Gottman 2004). Even though a complainant may feel that he or she is being fair in bringing up a grievance and discussing it openly and calmly, the recipient may view the complaint as critical and punitive, and it may be a blow to that partner's self-esteem. The recipient may not feel that the time is right for fighting and may not want to bargain about the issue. Finally, sharing anger and hostilities may violate what the other partner expects of the relationship.

Studies comparing mutually satisfied couples with those experiencing marital difficulties found that when couples are having trouble getting along or are stressed, they tend to interpret each other's messages and behavior more negatively. Satisfied partners did not differ from distressed ones in how they intended their behavior to be received by mates. But distressed partners interpreted their spouse's words and behavior as being more harsh and hurtful than was intended (Gottman 1979; Noller and Fitzpatrick 1991).

Not all negative facts and feelings need to be communicated. Before offering negative information, it is important to ask yourself why you want to tell it (to win?) and whether the other person really needs to know the information. Moreover, not every conflict can be resolved, even between the fairest and most mature fighters. If an unresolved conflict is not crucial to either partner, then they have reached a stalemate. The two may simply have to accept their inability to resolve that particular issue.

Communication between mates is addressed throughout this text. Chapter 8 discusses negotiating flexible marriage agreements. Domestic violence, which can be the unfortunate, even tragic, result of poorly managed conflict, is addressed at length in Chapter 14. Like love, fair fighting doesn't conquer all. But it can certainly help partners who are reasonably well matched and who want to stay together. Success in marriage has much to do with a couple's gentleness—and humor!—in relating to each other—perhaps much more than the social similarity, financial stress, and age at marriage often emphasized by social scientists in earlier studies of marital adjustment (Gottman et al. 1998). Finally, you may recall that Chapter 5 discusses not just discovering love but also keeping it. Keeping love, marital communication research informs us, largely involves letting our loved ones know how much we care about and appreciate them—a task largely accomplished by little gestures of appreciation, such as a touch or hug, and also simply by listening with genuine interest.

Summary

- Research on couple communication indicates the importance to relationships of both positive communication and the avoidance of a spiral of negativity.

- Although some family interaction tactics may reach the point of pathology, family conflict itself is an inevitable part of normal family life.

- Research psychologists and family counselors point out that to deny conflict may be destructive to both individuals and relationships.

- Although arguing is a normal part of the most loving relationships, there are better and worse ways of managing conflict.

- Alienating practices, such as belligerence and the Four Horsemen of the Apocalypse—contempt, criticism, defensiveness, and stonewalling—should be avoided.

- Bonding fights may often resolve issues and bring partners closer together by improving communication.

- Bonding fights may be characterized by attitudes of and efforts at gentleness, soothing, and de-escalation of negativity. In bonding fights, both partners win.

- There is no such thing as conflict-free conflict.

Questions for Review and Reflection

1. Explain why families are powerful environments. What are the advantages and disadvantages of such power in family interaction?

2. Explain the interactionist theoretical perspective on families, and show how John Gottman's research illustrates this perspective.

3. Describe the Four Horsemen of the Apocalypse. If someone you care for treated you this way in a disagreement, how would you feel? What might you say in response?

4. Discuss your reactions to each of the ten guidelines proposed in this chapter for bonding fights. What would you add or subtract?

5. **Policy Question.** Besides the suggestions in "As We Make Choices: Ten Rules for a Successful Relationship," what *society-wide* ideas might you offer for keeping love in one's long-term relationship?

Key Terms

belligerence 338
bonding fighting 342
contempt 336
criticism 336
defensiveness 336
displacement 336
family cohesion 330
female-demand/male-withdraw communication
    pattern 338
Four Horsemen of the Apocalypse 336

leveling 342
listener backchannel 333
mixed, or double, messages 343
passive-aggression 335
positive affect 331
rapport talk 338
report talk 338
sabotage 336
stonewalling 336

Online Resources

Companion Website for This Book

www.thomsonedu.com/sociology/lamanna

Visit the book companion website, where you will find flash cards, practice quizzes, Internet links, suggested readings, InfoTrac College Edition exercises, and more to help you study.

ThomsonNOW™ for Marriage and Family

Spend time on what you need to master rather than on information you already have learned. Take a pre-test for this chapter, and ThomsonNOW will generate a personalized study plan based on your results. The study plan will identify the topics you need to review and direct you to online resources such as videos, narrated learning modules, and interactive activities to help you master those topics. You can then take a post-test to help you determine the concepts you have mastered and what you will still need to work on. Try it out! Go to **www .thomsonedu.com/login** to sign in with an access code or to purchase access to this product.

Power and Violence in Families

14

What Is Power?

What Does Marital Power Involve?

Power Bases

The Dynamics of Marital Power

Classical Perspectives on Marital Power

Current Research on Marital Power

The Future of Marital Power

AS WE MAKE CHOICES Peer Marriage

Power Politics versus No-Power Relationships

Power Politics in Marriage

Alternatives to Power Politics

AS WE MAKE CHOICES Disengaging from Power Struggles

MY FAMILY An Ice Skating Homemaker in a My-or-Him Bind

The Role That Marriage Counselors Can Play

Family Violence

Major Sources of Data on Family Violence

Intimate Partner Violence

Gender Issues in Intimate Partner Violence

Abuse among Lesbian, Gay Male, and Bisexual Couples

Stopping Relationship Violence

Violence Against Children

Child-to-Parent Abuse

- Sarah gets a chance for a promotion at work, but accepting it will mean moving to another city; Sarah's spouse does not want to relocate.

- Antonio wants a new stereo for his truck; his partner would prefer to spend the money on ski equipment.

- Marietta would like to talk to her husband about what he does (and doesn't do) around the house, but he is always too busy to discuss the issue.

- Greg feels that he gives more and is more committed to his marriage than his wife is.

This chapter examines power in relationships, particularly marriage and intimate partner relationships. We will discuss some classic studies of marital decision making and look at what contemporary social scientists say about marital power. We will discuss why playing power politics is harmful to intimacy and explore an alternative. Finally, we will explore one tragic result of the abuse of power in families—family violence between intimate partners and violence involving children. We begin by defining power.

What Is Power?

Power may be defined as the ability to exercise one's will. There are many kinds of power. Power exercised over oneself is *personal power,* or autonomy. Having a comfortable degree of personal power is important to self-development. *Social power* is the ability of people to exercise their wills over the wills of others. Social power may be exerted in different realms, including within the family. Parental power, for instance, operates between parents and children. (In this chapter we focus more on the general dynamics of power in *couple* relationships, rather than parent–child relationships, but we do include child abuse and neglect in the section on family violence.)

The analysis of power in couples originally focused on marriage, but it has been extended to include couples who are not married, both heterosexual cohabitors and same-sex partners. We will use the term **intimate partner power** in referring to unmarried couples or to unmarried *and* married couples, when discussing both together. But because much research on relationship power still focuses on married couples, we will often be discussing **marital power**, with the partners described as husbands and wives.

What Does Marital Power Involve?

Marital power is complex and has several components. First, marital power involves *decision making:* Who gets to make decisions about everything from where the couple will live to how they will spend their leisure time? Second, marital power involves the *division of labor:* Who earns money? Who does the work around the house? A third arena of marital power is the *allocation of money* earned by either or both partners. Who controls spending for the household? Who has access to personal spending money? Finally, marital power involves a partner's *sense of empowerment, being able to influence* one's partner and feeling free to raise complaints to one's spouse about the relationship.

In addition to the components of marital power, the concept involves both *objective measures of power* (who actually makes more—or more-important—decisions, etc.) and a *subjective measure of fairness* in the marriage. These two concepts may be related, but not necessarily. For example, a husband who makes virtually all the important decisions and does relatively little housework may perceive the relationship as fair, whereas a wife who has a larger role in decision making and whose husband shares the housework may nevertheless feel that the relationship is unfair, depending on her expectations.

Judging fairness can be grounded in an **equality** standard—both partners should share equally in the rights and responsibilities of the relationship. Or fairness can be thought of in terms of **equity**—are the rewards and privileges of the relationship proportional to the contributions of the partners? The difference between these concepts will be discussed later, when we analyze how gender plays out in marital and intimate partner power relationships.

Both objective measures of *actual* equality and partners' subjective *perceptions* of fairness influence marital satisfaction, marital commitment, and the risk of disruption, but the perception of fairness is generally more powerful. Furthermore, when partners perceive themselves as reciprocally respected, listened to, and supported by the other, they are more apt to define themselves as equal partners. They are also less depressed, generally happier, and more satisfied with their marriage (Amato et al. 2003; Coltrane 2000; DeMaris 2007; Frisco and Williams 2003; and Weigel, Bennett, and Ballard-Reisch 2006b).

Understanding that marital power is a complex concept, we turn to an examination of the sources of marital power.

Power Bases

Two psychologists (French and Raven 1959) developed a typology of six bases, or sources, of social power: coercive, reward, expert, informational, referent, and legitimate power. These bases of social power can be applied to the family, and we use them in this chapter in analyzing couple power relationships (see Table 14.1).

Table 14.1 Bases of Social Power as Applied to the Family

Type of Power	Source of Power	Example
Coercive Power	Ability and willingness to punish the partner	Partner sulks, refuses to talk, and withholds sex; physical violence
Reward Power	Ability and willingness to give partner material or nonmaterial gifts and favors	Partner gives affection, attention, praise, and respect to partner, and assists him or her in realizing his or her goals; takes over unpleasant tasks; gives material gifts
Expert Power	Knowledge, ability, judgment	Savings and investment decisions shaped by partner with more education or experience in financial matters
Informational Power	Knows more about a consumer item, childrearing, travel destination, housing market, health issue	Persuades other parent about most effective mode of child discipline, citing experts' books
Referent Power	Emotional identification with partner	Partner agrees to purchase of house or travel plans preferred by the other because she or he wants to make partner happy
Legitimate Power	Society and culture authorize the power of one or the other partner, or both	In traditional marriage, husband has final authority as "head" of household; current ideal is that of equal partners

Source: Typology of power concepts from French and Raven (1959). Specific wording of definitions and the examples are the authors' (Lamanna/Riedmann).

Coercive power is based on the dominant person's ability and willingness to punish the partner either with psychological–emotional abuse or physical violence or, more subtly, by withholding favors or affection. Slapping a mate and spanking a child are examples of *coercive power*; so is refusing to talk to the other person—the silent treatment. **Reward power** is based on an individual's ability to give material or nonmaterial gifts and favors, ranging from emotional support and attention to financial support or recreational travel.

Expert power stems from the dominant person's superior judgment, knowledge, or ability. Although this is certainly changing, our society traditionally attributed expertise in such important matters as finances to men, while women were attributed special knowledge of children and expertise in the domestic sphere. **Informational power** is based on the persuasive content of what the dominant person tells another individual. A husband may be persuaded to stop smoking by his wife's giving him information on smoking's health dangers.

Referent power is based on a person's emotional identification with the partner. In feeling part of a couple or group, such as a family, whose members share a common identity, an individual gets emotional satisfaction from thinking as the more dominant person does. Alternatively, *referent power* might be a source of influence for the partner who is generally less dominant, for the dominant partner may gain satisfaction in behaving as the "referent" individual wishes. A husband who attends a social function when he'd rather not "because my wife wanted to go and so I wanted to go too" has been swayed by *referent power*. In happy relationships, *referent power* increases as partners grow older together (Raven, Centers, and Rodrigues 1975).

Finally, **legitimate power** stems from the dominant individual's ability to claim authority, or the right to request compliance. *Legitimate power* in traditional marriages involves acceptance by both partners of the husband's role as head of the family. Although this is not the case for all families in the United States, the current ideal in mainstream culture is an egalitarian couple partnership.

Throughout this chapter we will see the various power bases at work. The consistent research finding, for instance, that the economic dependence of one partner on the other results in the dependent partner's being less powerful may be explained by understanding the interplay of both *reward power* and *coercive power*. If I can reward you with financial support—or threaten to take it away—then I am more able to exert power over you.

The Dynamics of Marital Power

We turn now to look more specifically at research on marital power and the theoretical perspectives used to explain couple power relationships.

Native Man and Woman by unidentified Native artist, Chukotka Peninsula, Russia. Artist workshop, Uelen.

Classical Perspectives on Marital Power

Research on marital power began in the 1950s. At that time—before the feminist movement of the 1970s—interest in marital power was more academic than political. Social scientists Robert Blood and Donald Wolfe were curious about how married couples made decisions. Their book *Husbands and Wives: The Dynamics of Married Living* (1960) was based on interviews with wives only. Nevertheless, it was a significant piece of research and shaped thinking on marital power for many years.

Egalitarian Power and the Resource Hypothesis Blood and Wolfe began with the assumption that although the American family's forebears were patriarchal, "the predominance of the male has been so thoroughly undermined that we no longer live in a patriarchal system" (pp. 18–19). They reasoned that the relative power of wives and husbands results from their relative resources. The **resource hypothesis** holds that the spouse with more resources has more power in marriage. Resources include education and earnings; within marriage, a spouse's most valuable resource would be the ability to provide money. Another resource would be good judgment, probably enhanced by education and experience. (Note that the resource hypothesis is a variation on *exchange theory,* presented in Chapter 2)

To test their resource hypothesis, Blood and Wolfe interviewed about 900 wives in greater Detroit and asked who made the final decision in eight areas, such as what job the husband should take, what car to buy, whether the wife should work, and how much money the family could afford to spend per week on food. From their

interviews they drew the conclusion that most families (72 percent) had a "relatively egalitarian" decision-making structure (that is, the spouses held roughly equal power, whether that involved separate areas of decision making or joint decisions). However, there were families in which the husband made the most decisions (25 percent), and a few wife-dominated families (3 percent).

The resource hypothesis was supported by the finding that the relative resources of wives and husbands were important in determining which partner made more decisions. Wage and salary earnings or other individual income was a major source of decision-making power. Older spouses and those with more education also made more decisions. Blood and Wolfe also found the relative power of a wife to be greater after she no longer had young children (and was less dependent on her husband) or when she worked outside the home and thereby gained wage-earning resources for herself.

The Blood and Wolfe study had the effect of encouraging people to see marital power as shared rather than patriarchal and resting on their individual attributes or resources rather than on social roles. But this study was strongly criticized.

Criticism of the Resource Hypothesis One criticism concerns Blood and Wolfe's criteria for attributing power to husbands or wives. The decisions made by wives (such as how much to spend on food) were generally less important than those typically made by husbands (which city the couple should live in): "Having the power to make trivial decisions is not the same as having the power to make important ones" (Brehm et al. 2002, p. 321). And there were important areas of family life that were not included in the Blood and Wolfe study—such as sexual life, how many children to have, and how much freedom partners might have for same- or opposite-sex friendships.

Critics stated that power between spouses involves far more than which partner makes the most *final* decisions—deciding what *alternatives* are going to be considered may be the real decision. Moreover, the person who seems to be making a decision may in fact be acting on a delegation of power from the other partner (Safilios-Rothschild 1970). For example, a husband might ask his wife to make vacation arrangements, specifyng that it be a skiing vacation.

Another criticism of the resource hypothesis concerns its narrow focus—on individuals' background characteristics and abilities—but does not take into account their personalities and the way they interact (Brehm et al. 2002). And finally, marital power is more than decision making; it also implies the relative autonomy of wives and husbands, along with the division of labor in marriages (Safilios-Rothschild 1970).

Blood and Wolfe came under heaviest fire for their conclusion that a patriarchal power structure had been replaced by egalitarian marriages.

Resource and Gender Feminist Dair Gillespie (1971) pointed out that power-giving resources tend to be unevenly distributed between the sexes. Husbands usually earn more money even when wives work, so husbands have access to more economic *resources*. Husbands are often older (and at the time of the study were often better educated than their wives). So husbands are more likely to have more status, and they may be more knowledgeable, or seem to be (*expert* or *informational power*). Even their greater physical strength may be an important resource (*coercive power;* Collins and Coltrane 1995), although it can be a destructive one, as we will see later in this chapter.

Women are likely to have fewer alternatives to the marriage than their husbands, especially if wives cannot support themselves or are responsible for the care of young children. Moreover, men can remarry more readily than women. Consequently, according to Gillespie, the resource hypothesis, which presents resources as neutral and power as gender-free, is simply "rationalizing the preponderance of the male sex." Marriage is hardly a "free contract between equals" (p. 449).

Current research tends to support Gillespie's insight that American marriages continue to be inegalitarian even though they are no longer traditional (Rosenbluth, Steil, and Whitcomb 1998; Wilkie, Ferree, and Ratcliff 1998). True, resources make a difference, and an important factor in marital power is whether or not a wife is employed. Wage-earning wives have more to say in important decisions (Blumberg and Coleman 1989) and in the division of household labor (Risman and Johnson-Sumerford 1998).

One way in which women come to have fewer resources is through their reproductive roles and resulting economic dependence. Just after marriage the relationship is apt to be relatively egalitarian, with the husband only moderately more powerful than the wife—if at all. Often at this point the wife has considerable economic power in relation to her husband because she is employed and may even have a well-paying career. But relationships tend to become less egalitarian with the first pregnancy and birth (Coltrane and Ishii-Kuntz 1992).

During the childbearing years of the marriage, the practical need to be married is felt especially strongly by women, who are more often than not the primary caregivers as well as bearers of children (Johnson and Huston 1998). A divorce would likely mean that the woman must parent and support small children alone. Women engaged in reproduction and child rearing may have less energy to resist dominance attempts. On the other hand, a mother may exert power over her husband by threatening to leave and take the infant with her (LaRossa 1979).

As we noted, working contributes to marital power. But working for wages or even outearning a husband does not necessarily give a wife full status as an equal partner (Coltrane 2000; Risman and Johnson-Sumerford 1998; Tichenor 2005). Even though a working wife is, in theory, less obliged to defer to her husband and has greater authority in making family decisions, she does not necessarily participate equally in decision making in fact, and she is still unequally burdened with housekeeping and child rearing.

Researchers have come to realize that resource theory does not fully explain marital power. Although women's employment rates, occupational status, and income have increased in recent decades, their share of household work has not declined to a similar degree (Coltrane 2000). This "failure of resource and exchange perspectives to explain marital power dynamics in two-earner couples" (Tichenor 1999, pp. 638–39; 2005) has led scholars to turn to other theoretical perspectives.

Resources in Cultural Context Studies comparing traditional societies with more modern ones suggest that in a traditional society, norms of patriarchal authority may be so strong that they override personal resources and give considerable power to all husbands (Safilios-Rothschild 1967; Blumberg and Coleman 1989). Put another way, in a traditional society, male authority is *legitimate power*. This perspective, termed **resources in cultural context**, stresses the idea that resources are not effective in conferring marital power in traditional societies that legitimate male dominance with a patriarchal norm.

This situation may be especially true for immigrant families from traditional societies, such as in Asia or Central and South America, at least for those who are newly arrived. However, subsequent generations may be expected to adopt the more common American pattern. The generation born in the United States has moved to a **transitional egalitarian situation** regarding marital power, typical of the rest of the country, in which "husband–wife relationships are more flexible and negotiated . . . [and] socioeconomic achievements become the basis for negotiation within the family" (Cooney et al. 1982, p. 622).

Even among native-born Americans, however, we must recognize the continuing salience of tradition and the assumption that it is legitimate to some degree for husbands to wield authority in the family (Komter 1989). The continued importance of the legitimation of husbands' authority is apparent in religious groups that accept the principle of male headship of the family (Wilcox 2004). Although egalitarianism is undoubtedly the most sought after mode among American couples generally, whether an **egalitarian norm** of marital power is fully realized in any sector of American society is a question we will discuss throughout this chapter. Presently it seems those most likely to have attained this idea are lesbian couples, in which the resources, for example, that each brings to the relationship do not affect each person's power (Blumstein and Schwartz 1983).

In sum, the cultural context conditions resource theory. Resource theory explains marital power only when there is no overriding egalitarian norm or **patriarchal norm of marital power**. Put another way, if traditional norms of male authority are strong, husbands will almost inevitably dominate regardless of personal resources. Similarly, if an egalitarian norm of marriage were completely accepted, then a husband's superior economic achievements would be irrelevant to his decision-making power because both spouses would have equal power. It is only in the present transitional egalitarian situation, in which neither patriarchal norms nor egalitarian norms are firmly entrenched, that marital power is negotiated by individual couples, and the power of husbands and wives may be a consequence of their resources (Cooney et al. 1982; Rodman 1972).

Love, Need, and Power Some have argued that a primarily economic analysis does not do justice to the complexities of marital power. Perhaps a wife has considerable power through her husband's love for her, what we have termed *referent power*. Generally, however, the wife holds the less-powerful position even in this reckoning. In our society, women value close emotional relationships more than men do (Coltrane 1998, p. 202). They are encouraged to express their feelings, while men are less likely to articulate their feelings for their partners. Overt dependency affects power: "A woman gains power over her husband if he clearly places a high value on her company or if he expresses a high demand or

Although an older generation may hold to traditional patriarchal power, the next generation may renegotiate and consciously change those roles, especially as women assume more autonomy and make gains in the workplace. In this photo, the classic game of mahjong and the Chinese vase and screen in the background suggest a world of traditional authority, a man's *legitimate power* as head of the family. The posture and clothing of the younger family members suggest more casual and democratic family relations.

need for what she supplies. . . . If his need for her and high evaluation of her remain covert and unexpressed, her power will be low" (Cancian 1985, p. 258).

But another way of looking at it is that men are less relatively powerful in the private, intimate sphere than they are in the public world because the private world is more likely to give priority to *referent power*. Therapists and mass media, and, to an increasing degree, the public, support women's desire for more expression of feelings. Men have been much influenced by the expectation that they should respond favorably to wives' influence (Gottman 1998). They are encouraged to engage in "emotion work," "to express emotion to their wives, to be attentive to the dynamics of their relationship and the needs of their wives, [and] . . . to set aside time for activities focused especially on the relationship" (Wilcox and Nock 2006, p. 1322).

We have spent some time on earlier theory and research because these lead to issues of marital power that are still current.

Current Research on Marital Power

The first research on marital power by Blood and Wolfe focused solely on decision making. A later research project by sociologists Philip Blumstein and Pepper

Schwartz (1983) covered other aspects of couple relationships—money and sex, for example—and it compared married couples to heterosexual cohabiting couples and gay male and lesbian couples. As a major step forward in the study of couple relationships, this study is still cited (Christopher and Sprecher 2000).

One reason for its longevity may be that social scientists had seemed to lose interest for a time in researching "marital power." Instead they pursued marital and partner equality issues indirectly, by examining women's expanding entry into the labor force and related issues of who does the unpaid labor of household and child care. Recently, however, the word *power* has begun to reappear in journal articles and books examining couples' allocation of money, their capacity to influence each other and to raise touchy issues, and, still, the question of fairness (or not) in the division of household labor.

Equality, equity, and *gender* and their interrelationship are themes of current thinking about marital and other intimate partner power. Are men and women now equal in their family relationships? If not, why not?

Social scientists generally agree that the cultural ideal today is one of spousal and partner equality and of shared work and family roles. According to the resource hypothesis, as wives entered the labor force and began earning substantial income, they would be able to bargain for equality at home based on their resources. By and large, this vision of equality has not been attained in a number of respects.

> Feminists and scholars assumed that women's moving into the labor force and becoming important co-breadwinners would increase their power in the family—especially in terms of control over money management and decision making. However, the marital power literature over the last several decades has not borne this assumption out. Women's power in decision-making has increased somewhat, but not to a degree commensurate with the level of income many of them have been earning. In short, their income does not seem to buy them the same . . . power that men have typically enjoyed. (Tichenor 2005, p. 91)

We examine the complexities of partner equality by looking at current research on couples and their unpaid household work, control over money, decision making, and the expression of grievances and management of emotions. We draw on a number of studies (research reviews, quantitative and qualitative studies) of varying methodologies, sample sizes, and social locations.[1]

---

[1] In this limited space it becomes impossible to discuss the details of the research methodology of each source cited. For more detail, consult the original sources.

Gay and lesbian couples are more likely to share domestic duties than are heterosexual couples, although attainment of an egalitarian ideal eludes many gay/lesbian couples as well. In marriages, men's participation in housework has increased, although wives continue to do more.

We then look at where things stand regarding gender equality in the family and consider the future of family power.

Household Work and Leisure Time Virtually all research indicates that women's satisfaction with the fairness of their partners' contributions to household work is strongly associated with women's (and sometimes men's) relationship happiness, marital commitment, and depression and with the risk of marital disruption. Where women have more egalitarian expectations than men fulfill, there is often marital conflict (Coltrane 2000; DeMaris 2007; Frisco and Williams 2003).

Fairness of the division of household labor is not usually evaluated on a 50–50 standard. What's "fair" to a man may be less than half, while a woman has to be doing all or almost all the housework to find it "unfair" (Frisco and Williams 2003). "[U]nequal divisions of labor are accepted as normal" (Coltrane 2000, p. 1223).

Women whose husbands work more hours are less apt to see the division of household labor as unfair. So are more traditional women (Coltrane 2000), perhaps because their expectations are shaped by a religious doctrine of separate spheres and male headship (Wilcox 2004). Still, even in evangelical couples there is an implicit acknowledgment of a norm of equality in the attention given by evangelical men to expressing great appreciation for their wives' doing the preponderant share of housework. In the context of a societal egalitarian ideal, the additional domestic work of evangelical wives becomes a "gift," which is reciprocated by the husband's emotional work of expressed appreciation in an "economy of gratitude" (Wilcox 2004, p. 154, referencing Hochschild 1989).

In American society more generally, there has been a significant increase in men's share of housework (Amato et al. 2003). Although that share still does not approach equality, the increase since 1965 is quite dramatic. In 1965, women did seven hours of housework

for every hour that men put in; in 1999, it was one and a half hours (see Figure 14.1).

Social scientists now tend to use housework as one criterion of power (on the assumption that no one really wants to do it). The current situation—women do one and one half times what men do in housework—can be seen as a metaphor for their relative marital power. Women have gained men's participation in housework—and gained in power—but have not achieved absolute equality.

There also continues to be a "leisure gap." Although in formal terms, women have only one-half hour less of leisure time than men have, what is labeled "leisure" for women is often indirectly child care and household management (Bianchi, Robinson, and Milkie 2006; Jacobs and Gerson 2004).

Some women see their greater responsibility in household work as enabling the acquisition of some measure of power at the practical level (Tichenor 2005):

> As wives gather information in preparation for having some kind of discussion, they often form opinions about what . . . they would prefer to happen. They are then free to present the information . . . in such a way that makes what they want to do seem like the . . . most reasonable course of action. . . .
>
> [This] suggests that information is an important source of power in these relationships. While women carry a tremendous burden in terms of managing household responsibilities, that work . . . gives women access to knowledge that either gives them direct control or sometimes allows them an extra measure of influence in joint decision making. Most important is that women are often completely aware of this power and use it consciously to their advantage. (Tichenor 2005, p. 96)

Thus, women's *informational power* can offset men's *resource* or *legitimate power* or enable them to have the influence that their own *resource power* apparently does not. Of course, it must be exercised clandestinely.

Control Over Money Research on couples' **allocation systems**—whether they pool their money and who controls pooled or separate money—is relatively recent. British social policy scholar Jan Pahl (1989) developed a typology of allocation systems that has been used or adapted by subsequent researchers.

In the industrial era, a family's allocation system was typically one of complete control of his earnings by the male breadwinner, who doled out a housekeeping allowance to his homemaker wife. The allowance was often rather skimpy, while the husband was privileged to take money "off the top" for personal spending and recreation.

Even before the emergence of feminism, this system began to be seen as inappropriate to a companionate

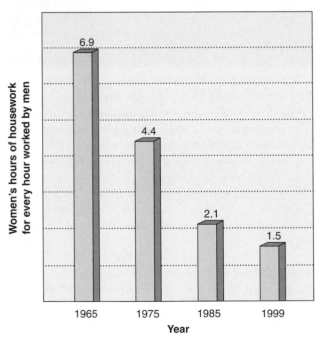

Figure 14.1 Trends in average weekly housework[a] hours for women and men (ages twenty-five through fifty-four), 1965–1999 (ratio of women's hours to men's hours).

[a]"Housework" includes "core housework" (cooking meals, meal cleanup, housecleaning, laundry, and ironing) as well as "other housework" (outdoor chores, repairs, gardening, animal care, bills, other financial).

Source: Adapted from Sayer, Cohen, and Casper 2004, Table 3.

model of marriage in which men and women were seen as equal, though with different family roles. To resolve the tension between a theoretical equality of men and women in the family, but their much different worth in the market economy, the typical marital allocation system became one of pooled resources. The husband's earnings were deposited into an account maintained in both names and controlled jointly by the spouses—at least, that was the theory. Given male dominance in decision making in this era, the pooled account was usually controlled by the husband. Moreover, non-earning women typically felt uncomfortable making decisions about "his" earnings. In reality, the joint account was not jointly controlled.

Feminists began to criticize the joint pool system. Women were now earning money as well. Separate financial accounts and control began to be seen as a favored alternative, with equal contributions made by each spouse or partner to the running of the household. But in another iteration, scholars and feminists have pointed out that equal household contributions may not be equitable when women typically earn less than men—their contribution to household expenses represents a larger proportion of their earnings (Kenney 2006; Tichenor 2005; V. Zelizer 1994).

A variety of allocation systems operate in American (and European) marriages at present, involving two dimensions: whether to pool and who controls—man, woman, or both?). There continues to be a tension in many marriages and other partner relationships between the communal values of the couple relationship and the individualism of the market, in which each person may have a very different level of earned income (Vogler 2005). Cohabitants and those who have been previously divorced are especially likely to maintain separate money (Kenney 2006).

Gender still plays a strong role, and men seem to retain more control over the family's income no matter who earns it. They are especially likely to retain personal spending money and/or to feel free to spend the family's income on personal and recreational desires without consulting their partner. Women may spend some of their "personal" money on household needs. And even otherwise egalitarian men may assume they have "veto power" over major decisions (Nyman 1999; Tichenor 2005). This would seem to be an example of traditional *legitimate power* ascribed to a male, overriding the wife's *resource power*.

Power and Decision Making Here, we look at decision making and marital power in general terms rather than in the specific domains of spending and housework. Using a national-sample survey to compare decision making in 1980 and 2000, Amato, Johnson, Booth, and Rogers found that in 2000 "respondents were significantly more likely to report equal-decision-making" (2003, p. 9). Even wives in evangelical families often have more decision-making power than their formal

This couple seems to be sharing control over their money on an equal basis.

submission to the male family head would indicate (Gallagher and Smith 1999; Bartkowski 2001).

Power asymmetry was found more often among dissatisfied couples. Men's power may not be visible, as they may have the ability to suppress issues so that they never arise overtly (Tichenor 2005, p. 25). "The spouse with less power [usually the wife] typically spends more time aligning emotions with [the spouse's] expectations" (Coltrane 1998) rather than risking confrontation. This increases emotional pressure. Coltrane notes that some men may *feel* powerless despite their greater power:

> Men's subjective sense of powerlessness—of lost or slipping privilege—is often a precursor to wife-beating or sexual abuse. . . . This does not mean that these men are less powerful than their wives. . . . This contradictory co-existence of felt powerlessness and actual (if latent) power is quite common for men. (Coltrane 1998, p. 201)

Women, on the other hand, may fear appearing too powerful. "For some women, expressing or exercising power seems threatening either to their relationships or to their gender identities. Some wives speak openly of the danger that power poses for them" (Tichenor 2005, p. 110). They are concerned about their husbands' sense of masculinity, as well as their gender identity (p. 114).

Bases of Marital Power To sum up, in these discussions of marital power and decision making, we see the interplay of three bases of social power: *resource power*, *legitimate power*, and *informational power*.

Resource power traditionally gave provider husbands greatest power in marital decision making, including the capacity to keep troubling issues and decisions from even arising. But the equation of resources (i.e., earnings) with power hasn't worked in the same way for women. A study of wives who earn more than their husbands suggests that "the gender structure exerts an influence that is independent of breadwinning or relative financial contributions" (Tichenor 2005, p. 117). A residual sense of the propriety of traditional male privilege—that is, *legitimate power*—ascribed more authority to men even in situations where they lacked *resource power*: "Just as women's income does not buy them either relief from domestic labor or greater financial power . . . , it does not give them dominion in decision making" (p. 117).

In an interesting twist, women can sometimes gain power from their greater knowledge of the household. They can use this *informational power* to shape decisions about purchases and household arrangements, as we noted earlier.

Equality, Equity, and Gender Spouses are usually aware of imbalances in marital power. Wives typically have a greater sense of unfairness because they are so often disadvantaged (DeMaris 2007, p. 192). From 1980 to 2000 there has been a "shift toward more egalitarian marital relations" (Amato et al. 2003, p. 9). At the same time, wives seem to have gained in average marital happiness. "Wives were less happy than husbands in both surveys, but the gap between husbands and wives grew smaller between 1980–2000. The narrowing of the gender gap in happiness may be attributable to more egalitarian marital relations" (p. 11).

The Future of Marital Power

Power disparities discourage intimacy, which is based on honesty, sharing, and mutual respect. For most, therefore, attainment of the American ideal of equality in marriage would seem to support the development of intimacy in marital relationships.

Yet the United States is a pluralistic society, and so we may expect to find varied visions of the future of marital power. Whether they reflect an egalitarian ideal or not, they generally take into account an egalitarian norm of marital power. We first sketch out this diversity, then look at some of the specific marriage models envisioned by scholars as they ponder the direction of change.

The Road to the Future One way to bring varied visions of the future together is to imagine couples driving along an interstate highway that leads to gender equality. Some couples are committed to getting there fast, and they take the express lane directly to shared and equal roles and power.

Most of the couples remain on the main interstate and are not completely sure if they want to travel all the way to the end. They keep consulting their maps to see if there is a stopping point they would like better, a mix of equality and gender identity.

A few couples exit the interstate, looking for a setting, perhaps a small town, where they can reproduce the more differentiated gender roles of the mid-twentieth century, though with some respect for equality in the relationship.

Some couples pull into a rest stop to continue the quarrel that has sprung up—she prefers a greater degree of sharing of power and household work than he does. After some negotiation, they reach at least a temporary compromise and continue on their way.

Finally, some couples have a complete breakdown and are waiting along the road for assistance, to return home and then move into separate lives.

Mutually Economically Dependent Spouses or Other Egalitarian Relationships Sociologist Steven Nock sees the future as one of *mutually economically dependent*

Breakfast in a household where roles may be somewhat differentiated by gender, but there is no sharp difference in status and power between the adults.

spouses "What I propose [as] . . . the emerging form of American marriage [is] a relationship in which couples are equally dependent on one another's earnings" (2001, p. 755). He defines *MEDS*, or **mutually economically dependent spouses,** as dual-earner couples in which each spouse earns between 40 and 59 percent of the family's income. Examining data from the 1999 Current Population Survey, he finds that presently just under one-third of all dual earners (some 20 percent of all couples) are mutually economically dependent. This pattern occurs at all economic levels (Nock 2001).

Nock not only sees equality in this arrangement but also finds it less threatening to marriage than one might think. True, an independent income increases the risk of divorce on the part of wives who are dissatisfied with household contributions of their husbands. At the same time, in a MEDS marriage, the two would become equally dependent financially, which could strengthen commitment if husbands change to contribute more household work.

This is a complex argument and rests on the thought that a marriage would be grounded in "extensive dependencies by both partners," as was the case in traditional society. As Nock sees it, the decline in divorce rates since the early 1980s may reflect "the gradual working out of the gender issues first confronted in the 1960s. If so, this implies that young men and women are forming new types of marriages that are based on a new understanding of gender ideals" (Nock 2001, p. 774). Men growing

up today, often with working mothers, are more likely to adapt to changing gender roles. "We are still at the early stages of a fundamental realignment of gender in our society" (p. 773).

Another possibility is that *norms of equality* may come to be so strong that men and women will have equal power in marriage regardless of resources. *Legitimate power* would endorse women's equality with men in the family. Pepper Schwartz's research on *peer marriage* offers an example of a strong equality norm at work (1994; 2001). She studied couples who do attempt to make their marriage according to this ideal. "As We Make Choices: Peer Marriage" describes this research.

Neotraditional Families In a pluralistic society, there are alternative visions of the family model. Among evangelical Christians and other conservative religious sectors, a gendered division of labor, formal male dominance in decision making, and an egalitarian spirit combine in the **neotraditional family**.

Although a husband's dominant power is legitimated in this milieu, in practice marital power is often negotiated. The "mutual submission" (of husband and wife to each other) justifies the shared decision making that characterizes many evangelical marriages (Bartkowski 2001). Another way in which a norm of equality is represented in these ostensibly husband-dominant marriages is in the emotional "economy of gratitude" (Wilcox

As We Make Choices   Peer Marriage

A piece of research by Pepper Schwartz paints a picture of couples who have developed egalitarian marriages, or tried to. Schwartz followed up her earlier research on couples with an exploration of the factors that facilitate **peer marriage** (1994, 2001): "I began looking for couples who had worked out no worse than a 60–40 split on childrearing, housework, and control of discretionary funds, and who considered themselves to have 'equal' status or standing in the relationship" (2001, p. 182). The study was based on fifty-seven egalitarian couples, with some additional interviews with couples considered **near peers** and **traditionals** for comparison.

Near peers believed in equality, but the combination of the arrival of children and the desire to maximize income meant that the husband did not participate as much as the couple's egalitarian ideals required. *Traditionals* were those marriages in which males dominated decision making except regarding children, but both parties were OK with this—the wife did not seek equality.

Peer marriages did not necessarily stem from a feminist ideology. Only 40 percent of women and 20 percent of men in peer marriages cited feminism as a motive. The rest gave other reasons for wanting a peer marriage: a rejection of negative parental models (women resented their father's dominance of their mothers; men wished for more involvement as parents); a desire to undertake co-parenting; and, in some cases, a period of serious tension in the marriage that required renegotiation of roles. However, for men especially, partner's preference was what led their marriage in an egalitarian direction. In an interesting twist on the expressive role of women, "[m]any of these men told me they had always expected a woman to be the emotional architect of a relationship and were predisposed to let her set the rules" (p. 183).

There was "no single blueprint" (p. 189), nor were these peer marriage couples high-earning "yuppies" or academics with flexible schedules. Peer marriage seemed, in the long run, to require an intense desire to have such a marriage and a persistent willingness to forgo male career advancement and income. Everyday responsibilities also had to be constantly monitored and renegotiated. Over time, the peer marriage couples evolved strong egalitarian norms that overrode the surrounding structure and typical power processes, much as Blumstein and Schwartz had earlier found in their lesbian couples (and sociologist Barbara Risman [1998] found in her research on "fair" marriages). The couple's respect for each other as described in Schwartz's study of peer marriage is essentially a "no-power" relationship.

Critical Thinking

Do you see peer marriages as an ideal for yourself, or not? How common do you think peer marriages will become in the future?

Source: Pepper Schwartz 1994.

2004, p. 154), as husbands display appreciation for their wives' "gift" of household work. Evangelical couples *are* committed to a headship model of marital power, yet this has an "enchanted" quality, symbolic of the religious commitment of the couple. In many ways, then, the edges of difference and dominance are softened in the neotraditional family, as the title of sociologist Bradford Wilcox's book—*Soft Patriarchs*—suggests.

A Gender Model of Marriage Writing from a perspective somewhat different than Nock's MEDS vision, Wilcox and Nock (2006) suggest that the egalitarian, equal-resource model of marriage does not represent what most couples want, at least at present, or what makes them happy with their marriage. Instead, they construct a **gender model of marriage**.

Wilcox and Nock see the egalitarian definition of marital power as circumscribed by the symbolic importance of maintaining gender boundaries. Couples want to construct conventional relationships and marriages

in which they are comfortable. Compromise with an egalitarian ideal occurs "as spouses work together to construct appropriate gender identities and maintain viable marriages" (Tichenor 2005, p. 32).

> Because wives—even wives with egalitarian attitudes—have been socialized to value gender-typical patterns of behavior, wives will be happier in marriages with gender-typical practices in the division of household labor, work outside the home, and earnings. Because husbands—even husbands with egalitarian attitudes—have been socialized to value gender-typical patterns of behavior, husbands will be happier in marriages that produce gender-typical patterns and will be more inclined to invest themselves emotionally in their marriages than husbands organized along more egalitarian lines. (Wilcox and Nock 2006, p. 1328)

In their study of over 5,000 couples drawn from the second wave of the National Survey of Families and Households (1992–94), Wilcox and Nock did find support for the hypothesis that "the gendered character of marriage seems to remain sufficiently powerful as a tacit ideal among women to impact women's marital quality" (pp. 1339–40). Nevertheless, when men's household work departed from the expectations of more egalitarian wives, marital quality was also affected. "'Her' marriage is happiest when it combines elements of the new and old" (p. 1321).

Power Politics versus No-Power Relationships

Marriage and other intimate partner relationships that partners find fair and equitable are generally more apt to be stable and satisfying. Social scientist Peter Blau terms this situation *no power*. **No-power** does not mean that one partner exerts little or no power; it means that each partner has the ability to mutually and reciprocally influence and be influenced by the other (Gottman et al. 1998; Schwartz 1994). We turn now to a discussion of the process of changing power relationships in marriage.

A fair division of household labor is not the only standard by which women and men judge the equality or lack of equality in their marriage. The respect one has for the other's views is extremely important; that is a central element in a no-power conceptualization of marriage and other partner relations. As we use the term, *no-power* also implies that partners do not seek to exercise their relative power over each other. No-power partners seek to negotiate and compromise, not to win (see Chapter 13). They are able to avoid **power politics**.

Power Politics in Marriage

As gender norms move from traditional toward egalitarian, all family members' interests and preferences gain legitimacy, not only or primarily those of the husband

"I'm trying to look at it from my point of view."

or husband/father. For example, the man's occupation is no longer the sole determining factor in where the family will live or how the wife will spend her time. This means that decisions formerly made automatically, or by spontaneous consensus, must now be consciously negotiated. A possible outcome of such conscious negotiating, of course, is greater intimacy; another is locking into power politics and conflict.

In the worst case, both equal and unequal partners may engage in a cycle of devitalizing power politics. Partners come to know where their own power lies, along with the particular weaknesses of the other. They may alternate in acting sulky, sloppy, critical, or distant, or even hint at leaving the marriage (Blumberg and Coleman 1989; Chafetz 1989). The sulking partner carries on this behavior until she or he fears the mate will "stop dancing" if it goes on much longer; then it's the other partner's turn. This kind of seesawing may continue indefinitely, with partners taking turns manipulating each other. However, the cumulative effect of such power politics is to create distance and loneliness for both spouses.

Few couples knowingly choose power politics, but this is an aspect of marriage in which choosing by default may occur. Our discussion of power in marriage is designed to help partners become sensitive to these issues so that they can avoid such a power spiral, or reverse one if it has already started.

Alternatives to Power Politics

There are alternatives to this kind of power struggle. Robert Blood and Donald Wolfe (1960) proposed one in which partners grow increasingly separate in their decision making; that is, they take charge of separate domains: one buying the car, perhaps the other taking charge of disciplining their children. This alternative is a poor one for partners who seek intimacy, however, for it enforces separateness rather than the sharing of important decisions.

A second, more viable alternative to perpetuating an endless cycle of power politics is for one partner to disengage from power struggles, as described in "As We Make Choices: Disengaging from Power Struggles." This includes a third, perhaps best, alternative, which is for the more powerful partner to consciously relinquish some power in order to save or enhance the marriage. We saw in Chapter 13, for instance, that marriage communication expert John Gottman and his colleagues (Gottman et al. 1998) advise husbands to be willing to share power with their wives if they want happy, stable marriages (pp. 18–19).

The Importance of Communication As we've noted earlier, partners who see themselves as mutually respected,

As We Make Choices Disengaging from Power Struggles

The late Carlfred Broderick, sociologist and marriage counselor, offered the following exercise to help people disengage from power struggles. The object of this exercise is to get you out of the business of monitoring everyone else's behavior and free you from the unrewarding power struggles resulting from that assignment. Here is the exercise:

1. Think of as many things as you can that your spouse or children should do, ought to do, and would do if they really cared, but don't do (or do only grudgingly because you are always after them). Write them down in a list.

2. From your list, choose three or four items that are especially troublesome right now. Write each one at the head of a sheet of blank paper. These are the issues that you, considerably more than your spouse, want to resolve (even though he or she, by rights, should be the one to see the need for resolution). Right now you are locked in a power struggle over each one, leading to more resentment and less satisfaction all around.

3. In this step you'll consider, one by one, optional ways of dealing with these issues without provoking a power struggle. Place an A, B, C, and D on each sheet of paper at appropriate intervals to represent the four options listed below. Depending on the nature of the issue, some of these options will work better than others, but for a start write a sentence or paragraph indicating how each one might be applied in your case. Even if you feel like rejecting a particular approach out of hand, be sure to write something as positive as possible about it

Option A: Resign the Crown

Swallow your pride and cut your losses by delegating to the other person full control and responsibility for his or her own life in this area. Let your partner reap his or her own harvest, whatever it is. In many cases, your partner will rise to the occasion, but if this doesn't happen, resign yourself to suffering the consequences.

Option B: Do It Yourself

There's an old saying: "If you want something done right, do it yourself." Accordingly, if you want something done, and if the person you feel should do it doesn't want to, it makes sense to do it yourself the way you'd like to have it done. After all, who ever said someone should do something he or she doesn't want to do just because you want him or her to do it?

Option C: Make an Offer Your Partner Can't Refuse

Too many interpret this, at first, as including threats of what will happen if the partner doesn't shape up. The real point, however, if you select this approach, is to find out what your partner would really like and then offer it in exchange for what you want him or her to do. After all, it's your want, not your spouse's, that is involved. Why shouldn't you take the responsibility for making it worth your spouse's while?

Option D: Join with Joy

Often the most resisted task can become pleasant if one's partner shares in it, especially if an atmosphere of play or warmth can be established. This calls for imagination and goodwill, but it can also be effective in putting an end to established power struggles.

Critical Thinking

Have you ever tried any of these in a couple situation? If so, how did it work out? Would these principles be useful, do you think, in other relationships, such as with children, extended family, or coworkers?

Source: Broderick 1979a, pp. 117–23.

equally committed, and listened to when they raise concerns are more likely to see their relationship as egalitarian and are more satisfied overall with their relationship.

Meanwhile, unequal relationships discourage closeness between partners: Exchange of confidences between unequals may be difficult, especially when self-disclosure is seen to indicate weakness. Men more than women have been socialized not to reveal their emotions (Henley and Freeman 1995). Women, feeling less powerful and more vulnerable, may resort to pretense and the withholding of sexual and emotional response (Blumberg and Coleman 1989).

Nevertheless, trying to change the balance of marital power may bring the risk of devitalizing a relationship, depending on how partners go about it. Mates who try to disengage from power struggles, without explaining what they are doing and why, risk estrangement. The reason is that dominant partners may have taken a mate's compliance as evidence of love rather than fear. If this deference is withdrawn, a dominant partner may conclude that "she (or he) doesn't love me anymore" and escalate efforts at control, contributing to a spiral of alienation and estrangement that is not acknowledged or discussed openly. "My Family: An Ice-Skating Homemaker in a Me-or-Him Bind" illustrates this pattern.

My Family   An Ice-Skating Homemaker in a Me-or-Him Bind

Joan is an attractive, full-time homemaker who has been married nineteen years. Recently, she began taking courses at a local university and became involved in learning to figure skate.

Interviewer: When did you begin ice-skating?

Joan: Well, I took one year when I was a kid, but I had to ride the bus and the streetcar and all that. . . . And then I didn't skate again until last year. I've been skating for two years now and I just love it. I'm getting better. I can do three turns real well and three of the very basic dances. . . .

I try to skate twice a week. But it's created a problem with Chuck. Last year he was working days during the skating season. But now he works midnight to eight and he just hates for me to go there during the day. . . . I don't know whether it's because I like it real well or what it is. But he doesn't like it. When he works midnight to eight, he knows every time I go. When he was working days and I went, as long as my work was done and I had dinner on the table, there was no problem when he came home from work.

Now he knows every time I leave this house. Every place I go he knows. Every time the garage door opens, it wakes him up. It's almost like being in prison without the doors being locked. . . . One time I stayed too late, I got home at 5:30. My brother was there—I got home at 5:30 and no dinner or nothing. He told

me, he said, "If you ever do this again—there's no dinner—if you ever do this again, I'm going to cut your skates." Oh boy! So I try to avoid doing that. I come home about four o'clock, so I can get dinner on okay. But the trouble [with the ice-skating] is that I can go there and it's almost like on that ice nothing—I just get totally absorbed in it and I forget I'm a mother, forget I'm a wife, I forget everything, I'm just there. I felt that way about golf and waterskiing too, but those things didn't bother Chuck because I was doing them with him, I think. Skating excludes him. . . .

At first I thought it was jealousy. No, it's not jealousy. It's possessiveness. He wants to control what I do: . . . "This is a possession now; I own this person; I can control her mind and body."

My daughter's starting to want to skate now too. The rink is open for the public this summer and I'm not going to be skating very much because I'd have to go in the evenings and that's just not going to work out with our schedule. But I'll try to go. Like this weekend, Chuck will be out of town, so I'm going to go then. Anyway, my daughter's going to go with me when she's out of school. She's getting so she can skate pretty well and she's starting to like it. So she wants a pair of skates. Now he won't buy her the skates. He says, "No, we're not going to spend the money on something like that." Now I think that's terrible. . . .

I could just go buy them because I definitely bought my own skates. I just

went out and bought them. And then at first I lied to him—this is awful—I told him, "Oh, these are just my sister-in-law's skates. . . ." Then finally once I told him they were my own. He said, "Oh! You can afford those skates and I can't afford a jacket." I said, "You can afford a jacket. Go buy one if you want. . . ."

A lot of times he'll say, "What are you going to do today?" And I say, "Well, it's Tuesday and I skate on Tuesday." He's known that all year, but every time he wants to take me to lunch or go somewhere, it is always on Tuesday. . . . One time I said, "Why can't we do it on Monday or Wednesday?" He said, "Oh, I never thought about that. . . ." He gets mad about everything I really like. Like when I started bowling and I really liked that, he gave me a hard time. It's really not just the skating. If he took the ice-skating away, and I replaced it with something else I liked equally well, that would be the thing he'd be against.

This case—about whether a spouse is free to spend time in self-actualizing pursuits—reflects a marital power struggle. Joan is relying on latent *referent power,* while Chuck is exercising *coercive power* in threatening to cut Joan's skates.

Critical Thinking

Do you think these kinds of issues—independent activities for spouses—remain possible areas of conflict in couple relationships? How would you handle this situation?

The Change At a No-Power Relationship Changing power patterns can be difficult, even for couples who talk about it, because these patterns usually have been established from the earliest days of the relationship. From the interactionist perspective, certain behaviors come not only to be expected but also to have symbolic meaning. In addition, sociologist William Goode had an insight that continues to be relevant for many couples.

He wrote about the important change in men's position as women gain equality in society and in the family. According to Goode:

Men have always taken for granted that what they were doing was more important than what the other sex was doing, that where they were, was where the action was. Men occupied the center of the stage, and women's attention was focused on them. . . . [But] the center of attention shifts to women more now than in the past. I believe that this shift troubles men far more, and creates more of their resistance, than the women's demand for equal opportunity and pay in employment. (Goode 1982, p. 140)

One small study of twelve fairly equal newlywed couples found that some of them either consciously or unconsciously avoided issues about marital power and developed a "myth of equality" (Knudson-Martin and Mahoney 1998). Sometimes this seems to work—but only for a while. The best way to work through power changes is to openly discuss power and to fight about it fairly, using the techniques and cooperative attitudes we describe in Chapter 13. The partner who feels more

© David Young-Wolff / PhotoEdit

Doing laundry does not seem to have become the site of a power struggle for this couple, but rather it is just something that needs to be done. Partners in a no-power relationship work at doing things on equal terms and seek to negotiate and compromise, thus avoiding deadly power games.

uncomfortable can bring up the subject, sharing his or her anger and desire for change but also stressing that he or she still loves the other. Indeed, research suggests that spouses think of their marital relationship as fair when they feel listened to and emotionally supported (Risman and Johnson-Sumerford 1998; Wilkie, Ferree, and Ratcliff 1998).

Meanwhile, partners need to remember that managing conflict about power in a positive way is easier said than done. Attempts at communication—and open communication itself—do not solve all marital problems. Changing a power relationship is a challenge to any marriage. It can be painful for both partners, though promising a more rewarding relationship in the long run. One option for handling power and gender role change is to seek the help of a qualified marriage counselor or counselor team (see Appendix H: "Marriage and Close Relationship Counseling," on the *Marriages and Families* website).

The Role That Marriage Counselors Can Play

Today, many marriage counselors are committed to viewing couples as two human beings who need to relate to each other as equals. In other words, they are committed to helping couples develop no-power relationships. They realize that once both spouses admit—to themselves and to each other—that they do in fact love and need each other, the basis for power politics is gone. On this assumption, counselors help spouses learn to respect each other as people and not to engage in coercive withdrawal.

Couples need to be aware that, like everybody in society, marriage counselors have internalized their own perspectives on gender roles—and these may not match the goals of the couple. There may be issues concerning potential racial and cultural bias on the part of therapists (Taylor et al. 1990) or simple lack of awareness of cultural differences in communication style or other matters. Choosing (or retaining) an appropriate counselor should involve an assessment of the counselor's sensitivity to the values, goals, and needs of the couple.

The counselor's gender may be an issue for some couples as they explore power and gender issues. A dominant husband, fearful that "it's going to be two against one," may feel threatened by a female counselor. On the other hand, a wife may fear that a male counselor will be too traditional or unable to relate to her. In this situation, counselors sometimes work as a team, woman and man. In any case, it is important that both partners feel comfortable with a counselor or counseling team from the beginning.

Whether on their own or with the help of counselors, partners can choose to emphasize no-power over the politics of power. No marriage—indeed, no relationship of any kind—is entirely free of power politics. But as

Chapter 13 points out, the politics of love requires managing conflict in such a way that both partners win.

When, on the other hand, power politics triumphs over no-power, one result may be family violence—psychological (emotional) and/or physical.

Family Violence

The use of physical violence to gain or demonstrate power in a family relationship has occurred throughout history, but only recently has family violence been labeled a social problem.[2]

The identification of child abuse as a social problem in the 1960s was followed in the 1970s by attention to wife abuse. With the 1980s came concern about elder abuse, as well as husband abuse. More recently, attention has been given to youth dating violence, to violence in adult dating and cohabiting relationships, including same-sex relationships, sexual coercion in marital and nonmarital relationships, sibling violence, and child-to-parent violence. We discuss many of these forms of violence in this chapter; dating violence and acquaintance rape are discussed in Chapter 9 and elder abuse and neglect in Chapter 18.

Major Sources of Data on Family Violence

There are several major sources of current data on family violence. Probably the best for our purposes is the National Crime Victimization Survey, conducted every two years by the Bureau of Justice Statistics. This is a national-sample survey that asks respondents about all violence they have experienced, their relationship if any to the perpetrator, and whether the violence was reported to the police. Violent acts covered by the survey include assault and rape/sexual assault, as well as other crimes not relevant to family violence. Although murder is obviously not included in the victimization survey, other data on homicides are included in Bureau of Justice Statistics reports on **intimate partner violence**. Spouses, ex-spouses, and current or former boyfriends or girlfriends, including same-sex partners, are considered *intimate partners*.

Other relevant government data include the Uniform Crime Reports of the FBI based on the National Incident-Based Reporting System (NIBRS). Data on criminal incidents reported to the police are compiled from records submitted by many (though not all) local law enforcement agencies (Durose et al. 2005). A weakness of these data is that many crimes are not reported to the police, including an estimated one-half of intimate partner violent crimes (Rennison and Welchans 2000). However, because most homicides are reported, the homicide data are more valid (e.g., Fox and Zawitz 2004).

A third major source of data on family violence is the National Violence Against Women Survey (Tjaden and Thoennes 1998, 2000), commissioned by the National Institute of Justice and the Centers for Disease Control and Prevention and conducted in1995–96. The survey employed a modified version of Murray Straus's Conflict Tactics Scale rather than asking about "crimes."

The work of Murray Straus, Richard Gelles, and their colleagues in their National Family Violence Surveys pioneered the scientific study of family violence. Before we examine current patterns of family violence, let us look at the work of this early research group.[3]

The National Family Violence Surveys The early and continuing research of Straus, Gelles, and their colleagues shaped the social science study of family violence. This research group undertook a household survey in 1975 followed by a 1985 telephone survey; together, the surveys produced data from more than 8,000 husbands, wives, and cohabiting individuals (Straus, Gelles, and Steinmetz 1980; Straus and Gelles 1986, 1988, 1995; Gelles and Straus 1988).

The authors defined violence as "an act carried out with the intention, or perceived intention, of causing physical pain or injury to another person." This definition is synonymous with the legal concept of assault.

Researchers developed a measure of family violence termed the **Conflict Tactics Scale**. Respondents were asked about the following acts: threw something at the other; pushed, grabbed, or shoved; slapped or spanked; kicked, bit, or hit with a fist; hit or tried to hit with something; beat up the other; burned or scalded (children) or choked (spouses); threatened with a knife or gun; and used a knife or gun (Straus and Gelles 1988, p. 15). *Severe violence* was defined as acts that have a relatively high probability of causing an injury: kicking, biting, punching, hitting with an object, choking, beating, threatening with a knife or gun, using a knife or gun—and, for violence by parents against children, burning or scalding the child (Straus and Gelles 1988, p. 16).

---

[2] Dr. C. Henry Kempe and his colleagues are credited with the "discovery" of child abuse. They published an article on the "battered child syndrome" based on their observation of hidden injuries to children revealed by X-rays (Kempe et al. 1962). Social scientists took note, and then pursued their interest in child abuse and other forms of family violence. The discovery of child abuse was somewhat like Columbus's discovery of America in that the phenomenon was always there but had not been noticed or taken seriously by academics or authorities.

[3] Murray Straus still leads the Family Violence Research Program at the University of New Hampshire's Family Research Laboratory. Many of the colleagues he has co-published with are there. Richard Gelles is now at the University of Pennsylvania.

Later modified somewhat (Straus et al. 1996), the Conflict Tactics Scale is different from and broader than the crime categories of assault and homicide that form the basis of criminal justice system statistics. It has been used by many other family violence researchers.

The 1975 and 1985 National Family Violence Surveys found that in 16 percent of the couples surveyed, at least one of the partners had engaged in a violent act against the other during the previous year. Considering the entire length of the marriage rather than just the previous year, respondent reports indicated that a violent act occurred in 28 percent of couples. National Family Violence Survey data also yielded information on violence directed toward children by parents and siblings. The National Family Violence Surveys explored social variation in family violence and some of the circumstances thought to be associated with family violence, such as stress and alcohol use.

Having presented some major sources of data on family violence, we examine the circumstances and outcomes of spouse or partner abuse in more detail in the next sections.

Intimate Partner Violence

Intimate partner violence—the physical or emotional abuse of spouses, cohabiting or noncohabiting relationship partners, or former spouses or intimate partners—is a serious and significant problem. First identified in terms of *wife abuse,* the growing practice of cohabitation places many unmarried women in similar situations. Husbands or male partners may also be subject to abuse from intimate partners as may same-sex partners of gay males and lesbians. Employing the term *intimate partner violence,* the federal government now includes all these forms of couple violence in its reports on domestic violence.

We will focus primarily on marital violence in analyzing the dynamics of intimate-partner violence, but it is worth noting that the rate of violence between cohabiting partners is higher than that of spouses (Magdol et al. 1998). As the proportion of cohabiting couples in the population increases, this setting becomes of greater importance in an overall perspective on domestic violence. That is, if cohabiting couples have higher rates of domestic violence and if there come to be more of them, theories of domestic violence may need to be modified to take this group into greater account.

We focus on physical abuse, but verbal abuse (such as name-calling, demeaning verbal attacks), and other kinds of emotional abuse (such as threats to take children away, threats to the victim's extended family or friends, and threats or attacks on pets) virtually always occur along with physical aggression (Stets 1991) and may be part of a pattern of control and domination.

Intimate partner violence can indeed result in serious injuries. National Crime Victimization Survey data

Local advocacy groups draw attention to efforts to prevent domestic violence and to the need for more resources. In many localities there are still not enough shelters to meet the needs of battered women and their children.

indicate that for the period 1993 to 2004, 5 percent of female victims of intimate-partner abuse and 5 percent of male victims were seriously injured. More women (43 percent) than men (31 percent) had minor injuries (Catalano 2006). Another source of injury data is the Study of Injured Victims of Violence (SIVV), which is a count of emergency room admissions attributable to family or nonfamily violence. In 1994, there were more emergency room admissions due to serious family violence (not only intimate partner violence) than reported in the National Crime Victimization Survey. However, the emergency room study was small and the two data sources are not truly comparable (Durose et al. 2005, p. 72).

Who Are the Victims of Intimate Partner Violence? According to a report based on the National Crime Victimization Survey, there were over 600,000 "victimizations" by intimate partners in 2004. One-third of these were serious violent crimes: rapes, sexual assaults, and aggravated assaults, and/or crimes involving serious injuries, weapons, or sexual offenses. The other two-thirds were lesser offenses, mostly simple assaults (Catalano 2006).

Women are the primary victims of intimate partner violence reported in the National Crime Victimization Survey. Over 75 percent of the victims of nonfatal victimizations were women, and women were also 75 percent of homicide victims. In every racial/ethnic category (see Figure 14.2), women have higher rates of victimization than men. Although intimate partners commit only 5 percent of murders of men, they account for 30 percent of homicides of women (Catalano 2006).

Younger women (twenty through twenty-four) are more likely to have experienced intimate partner victimization, as are those women who are separated or divorced (although some experts question the lower rates of marital violence, arguing that married women are simply less likely to acknowledge their victimization; Catalano 2006; "Domestic Violence Decline" 2006).

As Figure 14.2 indicates, rates of intimate partner violence vary greatly by race/ethnicity. Victimization rates are strikingly higher (18.2 per 1,000) for Native American women. Black women's rates are high (8.2), but still less than one-half the rate for Native American women. White and Hispanic females have moderate rates (6.3 and 6.0, respectively), while Asian females, as well as Asian males, have very low rates of intimate partner violence victimization (1.5 and 0.1, respectively). White, black, and Hispanic male victimization rates are also low, while those of Native American men are relatively high.

Multiple studies have demonstrated that cohabiting partners have higher rates of intimate partner violence than married couples (Brownridge and Halli 2002). A variety of explanations have been offered, but none conclusively proven. Overall, cohabitors are younger, less integrated into family and community, and more likely to have psychobehavioral problems such as depression and alcohol abuse—all factors associated with family violence (Stets 1991). Another possibility is that there is less institutional control over cohabiting relationships than

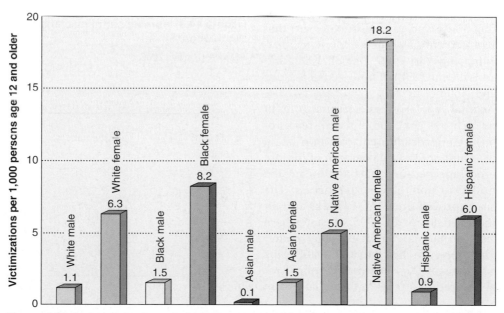

Figure 14.2 Intimate partner victimization rate (nonfatal) by gender, race, and Hispanic origin, 1993–2004.

Source: Catalano 2006.

over marriage (Ellis 2006; Nock 1995). Still another thesis is that the less-violent cohabiting couples end up getting married while more-violent married couples get divorced, sharpening the difference between the two groups (Kenney and McLanahan 2006).

Several recent studies have reported that pregnancy increased the likelihood of physical violence by intimate partners (Burch and Gallup 2004; S. Martin et al. 2004). None of these studies used a representative sample. Earlier studies using national samples found that when age was controlled, there was no increased risk with pregnancy. Still, the many studies, however imperfect, that have found an association between pregnancy and violence have kept this hypothesis alive, along with a possible explanation— jealousy, specifically that the new baby would interfere with the wife's attention to and care of the man. What is known with more certainty is that those pregnant women who are abused seek medical care later in pregnancy and are more likely to have preterm and low-birth-weight babies (Kantor and Jasinski 1998, pp. 31–33).

Substance abuse, especially of alcohol, is often cited as a factor in male violence against women. That seems to be true of heavy use of alcohol and binge drinking, though not necessarily for other patterns of alcohol use. Alcohol is implicated in violence through cognitive impairment, impulsivity, and a tendency to perceive threats (Kantor and Jasinski 1998, pp. 20–23; Kaukinen 2004). Drinking may also serve as a rationalization and excuse for violence that would have occurred in any case (Gelles 1974).

Marital Rape Wife and female-partner abuse may take the form of sexual abuse and rape. Estimates are that between 10 and 14 percent of women experience marital rape (Finkelhor and Yllo 1985; Russell 1990; and see Mahoney and Williams 1998). These sexual assaults often involve other violence as well.

The issue of **marital rape** arose as a feminist one in the 1970s and as such was conceptualized in terms of the law of *marriage*. Under traditional common law, a husband's sexual assault or forceful coercion of his wife was not considered rape because marriage meant the husband was entitled to unlimited sexual access. The legal situation has improved since the 1970s as a result of feminist political activity. As of 1993, all states have provisions against marital rape in their legal codes[4] (National Clearinghouse on Marital and Date Rape 2005). More research is needed in this area; the "lack of empirical and theoretical attention to sexual assault

and coercion in marriage . . . is striking" (Christopher and Sprecher 2000, p. 1007). Data on sexual assault of women intimate partners, married or nonmarried, are collected as part of the federal government's documentation of intimate partner violence.

Intimate Partner Violence is Declining The preceding data show us how significant the problem of intimate partner violence still is. Yet, the direction of change gives us some indication that efforts to combat domestic violence are paying off. Intimate partner violence declined dramatically from 1993 to 2004, as Figures 14.3 and 14.4 indicate. Although the rate of nonfatal victimization was relatively stable for men, it declined 40 percent for women. Intimate partner homicide rates declined 45 percent for men and 26 percent for women (Catalano 2006).

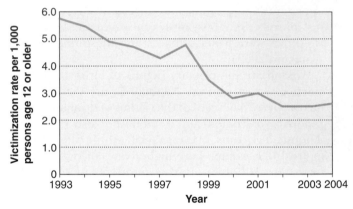

Figure 14.3 Intimate partner victimization rate (nonfatal), 1993–2004.
Source: Catalano 2006.

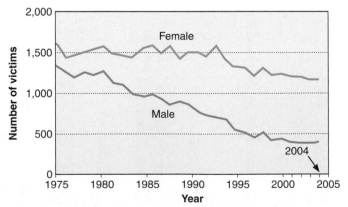

Figure 14.4 Homicides of intimates by gender of victim, 1976–2004.
Source: Catalano 2006.

---

[4] There are some exemptions in the laws of thirty of the states. One common example is that if a wife is asleep or unconscious, thus legally unable to consent, a husband may be exempt from prosecution (National Clearinghouse on Marital and Date Rape 2005).

Shannan Catalano, author of the Bureau of Justice Statistics intimate partner violence study, cites experts' opinions that stronger law enforcement, increased education, and expanded services for battered partners have led to this decline. A cautious note is also sounded: "[T]he apparent decline could [also] mean that women are choosing to suffer in silence rather than seek help ("Domestic Violence Decline" 2006).

As we go on to explore gender issues in intimate partner violence, we will consider why women may not seek help or leave their marital or other relationships—and why and how they do. We'll also consider whether men are equally victims of domestic violence.

Gender Issues in Intimate Partner Violence

Three questions arise regarding gender and intimate partner violence: Why do men beat their wives and partners? Why do women live with it? And what about husband or male partner abuse?

Why Do Men Do It? From data in the National Crime Victimization Survey, we find that men committed 78 percent of all heterosexual intimate partner victimizations in 2004 (calculated from Catalano 2006).

Richard Gelles (1994, 1997) lists "risk factors" for men who abuse women: those who are between eighteen and thirty years old; unemployed; users of illicit drugs or abusers of alcohol; and high school dropouts. This suggests that men who beat their wives or partners might be attempting to compensate for general feelings of powerlessness or inadequacy—in their jobs, in their marriages, or both. As Chapter 4 indicates, our cultural images and socialization processes encourage men to appear strong and self-sufficient.

Men's feelings of powerlessness may stem from an inability to earn a salary that keeps up with inflation and the family's standard of living—or from the stress of a high-pressure occupation, which is not necessarily a high-status one. Men may use physical expressions of supremacy to compensate for their lack of occupational success, prestige, or satisfaction (K. Anderson 1997). Research using the National Survey of Families and Households found that financial adequacy reduced the risk of couple violence. Employment in low-status and unpleasant jobs that increased irritability, on the other hand, was associated with man-to-woman violence, a stress explanation of family violence (Fox et al. 2002). The husband's unemployment is also associated with domestic violence (Gelles and Cavanaugh 2005).

In terms of relative status, a woman's risk of experiencing severe violence is greatest when she is employed and her husband is not. Much research has found violence associated more generally with status reversal, where the woman is superior in some way to the man in terms of employment, earnings, or education (Kaukinen 2004). A man's loss of status upon immigration—when jobs commensurate with education or expectations do not measure up, economic hardship is the family's lot, and wives, children, and people in general do not accord a male the respect he is accustomed to in a more hierarchical society—can lead to family conflict and violence (Min 2002).

Absent a *reward power* base for family power, some men resort to *coercive power*: "[V]iolence will be invoked by a person who lacks other resources to serve as a basis for power"—it is the "ultimate resource" (Goode 1971, p. 628; see also Allen and Straus 1980, p. 190, in Fox et al. 2002). Men may use violence to attempt to maintain control over wives or partners trying to become independent of the relationship (Dutton and Browning 1988). Figure 14.5, developed by staff members of a program for male batterers in Duluth, Minnesota (Pence and Paymar 1993), illustrates how a male partner's need for power and control may result in both psychoemotional and physical violence. This type of family violence has been called *patriarchal terrorism* (M. Johnson 1995) and will be discussed in a subsequent section of this chapter.

Why Do Women Continue to Live With It? Women do not like to get beaten up. However, they may stay married to husbands or remain with violent male partners who beat them repeatedly. For the most part, battered wives leave and/or seek divorce only after a long history of severe violence and repeated conciliation. There are several reasons for this, and they all point to those women's lack of personal resources with which to take control of their own lives.

Fear Battered women's lack of personal power begins with fear (DeMaris and Swinford 1996). "First of all," reports social scientist Richard Gelles, "the wife figures if she calls police or files for divorce, her husband will kill her—literally" (Gelles, quoted in C. Booth 1977, p. 7). This fear is not unfounded. An estimated 75 percent of murders of women by their male partners occurred in response to the woman's attempt to leave (de Santis 1990). Husbands or ex-husbands have shown enormous persistence in stalking, pursuing, and beating or killing women who try to leave an abusive situation (Johann 1994; U.S. Department of Justice 1998b). Fear of reprisals by the batterer continues to be a barrier to seeking police intervention, according to recent studies (M. Anderson et al. 2003; Wolf et al. 2003).

Cultural Norms Historically women were encouraged to put up with abuse. English common law, the basis of the American legal structure, asserted that a husband

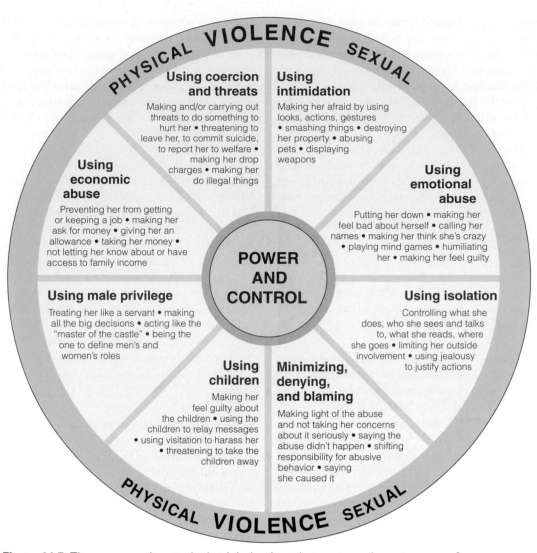

Figure 14.5 The power and control wheel: behaviors that some male partners use for coercive power and control.

Source: Domestic Abuse Intervention Program, Duluth Model, Minnesota Program Development Organization, Duluth, MN.

had the right to physically "chastise" an errant wife. Although the legal right to physically abuse women has long since disappeared, our cultural heritage continues to have an influence on seeking help and getting it (Torr and Swisher 1999). For some women of color, hesitancy to call the police may derive from historic tensions between racial/ethnic communities and the police force (Wolf et al. 2003, p. 124).

What is true of America's English cultural legacy may be even more true of some immigrant or refugee communities, when "family honor, reputation, and preserving harmony" are primary values, impeding help-seeking. Immigrant women may have limited language skills, and they may be socially isolated from family and community. Or they may be living with in-laws who sup-

port the abusive husband. For that matter, a woman's own family may urge her to remain in the marriage despite the abuse. And if the victim is not yet a citizen or legal resident, to seek help carries the risk of deportation; legal status may be dependent on the marriage (Childress 2003; Mehrota 1999; Menjívar and Salcido 2002; Yoshioka et al. 2003).

Programs are beginning to emerge to assist immigrant women (Abraham 1995, 2000). Moreover, in some immigrant communities, the word has spread that wife abuse (and harsh physical discipline of children) is not the way things are done in America. Here community social control has thus shifted from protecting abusive husbands to admonishing them ("Old Ways" 2003).

Love, Economic Dependence, and Hopes for Reform Women may live with abuse because they love their husbands or partners, depend on their economic resources, and/or hope they will reform. In one study of 485 women who had entered a domestic victims' advocacy shelter but returned home, researchers found that the most common reasons for returning were the male partner's promise to change (71 percent) and his apology (60 percent; M. Anderson et al. 2003).

This same study found that lack of money (40 percent) and nowhere to go (28 percent) were also important reasons. Battered women who stay with their partners may fear the economic hardship or uncertainty that will result if they leave. They hesitate to summon police or to press charges not only out of fear of retaliation but also because of the loss of income or damage to a husband's professional reputation that could result from his incarceration. Fear of economic hardship is heightened when children are involved. For a mother, leaving requires being financially able to take along her children and support them—or leaving them behind, where they may also be in danger.

A new wrinkle in economic dependency has emerged with the passage of welfare reform legislation in 1996. Studies show that 20 to 30 percent of women on welfare are in situations of risk for domestic violence. Some men become abusive when the woman gets a job, which may threaten his control. Compliance with the requirement to report paternity of children may also trigger retaliation by a man, who now will be pursued for child support. Although the law contains a waiver provision directed at exactly these problems, it is not certain that women are being informed or that the provision is implemented. Some women will find it difficult to comply with welfare requirements because of the objections and control tactics of men in their lives (Riger, Staggs, and Schewe 2004). Cut off from welfare, they become even more dependent on violent men (Ooms 2001; Scott, London, and Meyers 2002).

Apart from such special circumstances, it is possible that though a dramatic rise in women's employment and earnings may prove threatening to low-earning husbands in the short run, in the long run, mutual awareness of a woman's potential economic independence may deter wife abuse by changing the family power dynamic (Blumberg and Coleman 1989).

Gendered Socialization Another factor that helps perpetuate abuse is the cultural mandate that it is primarily a woman's responsibility to keep a marriage or relationship from failing. Believing this, wives are often convinced that their emotional support may lead husbands to reform. Thus, wives often return to violent mates after leaving them (Herbert, Silver, and Ellard 1991).

Childhood Experiences Research suggests that people who experience violence in their parents' home while growing up may regard beatings as part of married life (Torr and Swisher 1999), and this is another factor associated with women's living with abuse. Men, as well as women, are more likely to be victims of intimate partner violence as adults if they were exposed to child abuse or witnessed parental interpersonal violence as children (Heyman and Slep 2002).

Low Self-Esteem Finally, unusually low self-esteem interacts with fear, depression, confusion, anxiety, feelings of self-blame (Andrews and Brewin 1990), and loss of a sense of personal control (Umberson et al. 1998) to create the *battered woman syndrome*, in which a wife cannot see a way out of her situation (L. Walker 1988; Johann 1994).

A Way Out: Shelters and Domestic Violence Programs A woman in such a position needs to redefine her situation before she can deal with her problem, and she needs to forge some links with the outside world to alter her circumstances. This usually occurs over time, with some unsuccessful attempts to leave as part of the process.

Although there are not enough of them, a network of shelters for battered women provides a woman and her children with temporary housing, food, and clothing to alleviate the problems of economic dependency and physical safety. These organizations also provide counseling to encourage a stronger self-concept so that the woman can view herself as worthy of better treatment and capable of making her way alone in the outside world if need be. Finally, shelters provide guidance in obtaining employment, legal assistance, family counseling, or whatever practical assistance is required for a more permanent solution.

This last service provided by shelters—obtaining help toward longer-range solutions—is important. Two face-to-face interviews with the same 155 wife-battery victims (a "two-wave panel study") were conducted within eighteen months during 1982 and 1983 in Santa Barbara, California. Each of the women interviewed had sought refuge in a shelter. Findings showed that victims who were also taking other measures (for example, calling the police, trying to get a restraining order, seeking personal counseling or legal help) were more likely to benefit from their shelter experience: "Otherwise, shelters may have no impact or perhaps even trigger retaliation (from husbands) for disobedience" (Berk, Newton, and Berk 1986, p. 488). As the researchers conclude,

> The possibility of perverse shelter effects for certain kinds of women poses a troubling policy dilemma. On the one hand, it is difficult to be enthusiastic about an

intervention that places battered victims at further risk. On the other hand, a shelter stay may for many women be one important step in a lengthy process toward freedom, even though there may also be genuine short-run dangers. (p. 488)

As with some other decisions discussed in this text, social scientists have applied *exchange theory* to an abused woman's decision to stay or leave (Choice and Lamke 1997). As Figure 14.6 illustrates, an abused wife weighs such things as her investment in the relationship, her (dis)satisfaction with the relationship, the quality of her alternatives, and her beliefs about whether it is appropriate for her to leave ("subjective norm") against such questions as whether she will be better off if she leaves (might her husband retaliate, for example?) and whether she can actually do it. The woman's personal resources along with community (structural) resources, such as whether shelters or other forms of assistance are available, further affect her decision. Personal barriers might involve not having either a job with adequate pay or an extended family that could help. Structural barriers might include the lack of community systems for practical help.

Michael Johnson and Kathleen Ferraro (2000) answer the question "Why do they stay?" with: "The truth is, they don't stay." Instead, abused women went "through a process of leaving and returning, each time gaining more psychological and social resources . . . until they escaped from the web" (pp. 956–57).

Men as Victims of Intimate Partner Abuse Both women and men sometimes resort to violence. A major question regarding family violence is whether female-to-male violence is trivial in numbers and effects or should be regarded as a serious social problem.

The early National Family Violence Surveys reported approximately equal amounts of both minor and serious partner violence on the part of men and women. Researcher Murray Straus and his colleagues continue to point to data indicating comparable levels of male and female intimate partner violence (Straus 1999b; 2005). A number of other studies and research reviews also find that comparable numbers of males and females have engaged in physical violence (e.g., K. Anderson 2002; Archer 2000). Although the National Family Violence Survey is a national-sample survey, many of the other studies cited as evidence for gender symmetry are convenience samples, studies of college students, or clinical samples of couples who have sought help for their marital problems (Kimmel 2002)—in other words, not so strong methodologically.

Crime victimization data, including carefully done, large-sample surveys, indicate that women are overwhelmingly the victims of intimate partner violence. These conflicting reports set off a dispute, still not resolved, as to whether intimate partner violence is *asymmetrical*—with women primarily victims of male aggression—or whether couple violence is *symmetrical*—both men and women engage in intimate partner violence and at similar rates.

The first assumption—that violence against partners is primarily perpetrated by males—underlies policy directed toward providing resources for women victims; it is a strongly held feminist perspective. If, on the contrary, women are as likely as men to perpetrate intimate partner violence, then they begin to look less like victims and more like aggressors.

Differences in conclusions may simply arise from methodological differences. Critics of the National Crime Victimization Survey (which finds *asymmetric*

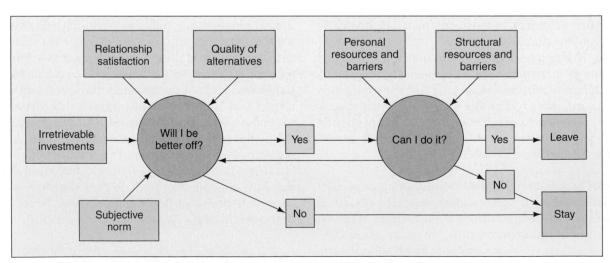

Figure 14.6 Conceptual model of abused women's stay/leave decision-making process.
Source: Choice and Lamke 1997, p. 295.

violence) point out that "crime" terminology may dampen reports of less-serious female-to-male violence because those acts may not seem to be crimes to those interviewed. Questions on the Conflict Tactics Scale (CTS) include a broader range of actions that may be characterized by the survey respondent as family conflict and violence, but not criminal victimization (Straus 1999b, 2005). A key problem with the Conflict Tactics Scale (used in many studies that find *symmetric violence*), however, is that sexual assault, a substantial part of male-to-female violence, was not included in the first version of the CTS used in the 1975/1985 National Family Violence Surveys. (The later modification of the CTS does include sexual assault [Straus et al. 1996].)

The Conflict Tactics Scale, used by many researchers and most associated with findings of gender-balanced violence, has been widely criticized for lack of context. In reporting lifetime or annual incidence of violence, a single, never-repeated act could be equated with a marriage-long pattern of abuse. Feminist critics assert that the context of violence is ignored in simple counts of male and female violence: Where does a particular violent act fit into the couple relationship? Who initiated the violence? Was it in self-defense? (Kurz 1993; Kimmel 2002; Loseke and Kurz 2005).

Recent reviewers of the literature have tried to make distinctions that might explain the contradictory conclusions about who is violent. Definitions and measurements of violence continue to be relevant, as does whether a survey asks about victimization only or also asks whether the respondent has been a perpetrator of violence (Tjaden and Thoennes 2000). The most convincing explanations for contradictory findings—that men are the more violent sex (asymmetrical violence) or that men and women are both violent (symmetrical violence)—are (1) sample differences, (2) measures, and (3) typologies of intimate partner violence (to be discussed momentarily).

Studies and research reviews (e.g., Archer 2000) that are dominated by samples of younger people may accurately reflect the behavior of that age group. But they cannot claim to be representative of the general adult population in their findings of symmetrical violence. They capture a life course stage in which women are more likely to strike out in an argument and/or to be living in less-stable cohabiting relationships (Tjaden and Thoennes 2000). National sample surveys that reach a broader and more representative range of respondents (the National Crime Victimization Survey and the National Violence Against Women Survey) more often find a pattern of much higher rates of victimization and more serious levels of violence directed against women.

The question of whether wives' violence toward husbands is mostly in self-defense, as feminist violence researchers argue, is part of the debate. Demie Kurz (1993; Loseke and Kurz 2005) offers evidence that intimate partner violence by women is largely in self-defense, or at least retaliation, rather than the initiation of a violent attack. Other data support the defensive character of women's violence against male partners (Kimmel 2002). Kimmel speculates that women may be inclined to overstate their responsibility for a violent exchange, and men understate it.

Straus (2005) claims that better data indicate that wives often strike out first and that the data do "not support the hypothesis that assaults by wives are primarily acts of self-defense or retaliation" (Straus 1993, p. 76). Moreover, he argues, though women's violence produces fewer serious injuries and deaths than men's, these are substantial enough in numbers to challenge any minimization of women's intimate partner violence (Straus 2005). Straus and Gelles have argued their position, that couple violence is gender symmetrical, as one that ultimately benefits women despite the criticism they have received from feminists:[5]

> Let us assume that most of the assaults by women are of the "slap the cad" genre and are not intended to and do not physically injure the husband. The danger to women of such behavior is that it . . . provides the justification for him to hit her. . . . Unless women . . . forsake violence in their relationships with male partners and children, they cannot expect to be free of assault. (Straus and Gelles 1988, pp. 25–26)

Straus would like to see abuse prevention programs directed toward girls and treatment programs developed for women perpetrators of family violence.

Two other well-known researchers, Neil Jacobson and John Gottman, strongly object to this line of reasoning. In their sample, women rarely initiated a violent sequence. Should a woman do so in the form of punching, pushing, or throwing something, the man quite rightly could defend against it—at the same level of violence. Such minor violence on the part of women should not be taken to be "provocation" of severe violence by men. Instead, men must be held accountable for their own violence if things are to change (2001, pp. 482–83).

The root explanation for contradictory research results may be that there are two forms of heterosexual violence against women—"patriarchal terrorism" and

---

[5] Straus has sometimes been verbally harassed when he has presented at professional meetings. Criticism from feminist scholars has discouraged some researchers from publishing articles on battered husbands (Gelles and Conte 1990, p. 1046).

"common couple violence" (M. Johnson 1995).[6] **Patriarchal terrorism** refers specifically to abuse that is almost entirely male and that is oriented to controlling the partner through fear and intimidation. Physical abuse is but one of the tools used by the terrorist; emotional abuse is frequent as well. Patriarchal terroristic violence is not focused on a particular matter of dispute between the partners, but is intended to establish a general pattern of dominance in the relationship. This form of intimate partner violence occurs more often in marriage than in cohabitation. It includes more incidents, is likely to escalate, and is more likely to produce serious injury.

Common couple violence refers to mutual violence between partners that often occurs in conjunction with a specific argument. It involves fewer instances, is not likely to escalate, and tends to be less severe in terms of injuries (M. Johnson 1995; Johnson and Ferraro 2000). Common couple violence appears to be perpetrated by women as well as men and may be more common than patriarchal terrorism, producing the gender-balanced rates found in some studies.

On the other hand, there is "compelling evidence that men's and women's experiences with violence at the hands of marital and cohabiting partners differ greatly" (Tjaden and Thoennes 2000, p. 156). The overwhelming victimization of women shown by crime victimization data, including data on homicides, suggests that women are victims of the most serious violence. Related research-based points are as follows:

1. Husbands or other male partners have higher rates of inflicting the most dangerous and injurious forms of violence, such as severe beatings (Kurz 1993, p. 90; U.S. Department of Justice 1998a). Female victims report more threats to life and fear of bodily injury (Tjaden and Thoennes 2000).

2. Violence by husbands or male partners does more damage, even if it is an exchange of slaps or punches, because of a man's generally greater physical strength; therefore, the woman is more likely to be seriously injured (Jacobson and Gottman 2001). Women who were physically assaulted were significantly more likely than men to be injured, to

receive medical treatment, to be hospitalized, and to lose more time from work (Rennison and Welchans 2000). Moreover, a study that explored the consequences of male and female violence in the context of mutual violence found that "the negative consequences of intimate partner violence [depression and substance abuse] are more likely to be experienced by women" (K. Anderson 2002, p. 861).

3. Violent acts by men are more frequent, tending to be repeated over time (Tjaden and Thoennes 2000).

4. Husbands are more apt to leave an abusive relationship within a short time. Having more resources, men rarely face women's dilemma of choosing between poverty (for their children as well as themselves) and violence (Straus, Gelles, and Steinmetz 1980).

Despite his strong assertion that both men and women may be violent in the family, Murray Straus takes this position: "[T]he first priority in services for victims and in prevention and control must continue to be directed toward assaults by men because these tend to result in greater physical, financial, and emotional injury" (2005, p. 69).

Yet there may be a need for some programmatic support for male victims of spouse abuse: "Compassion for victims of violence is not a zero sum game.... Reasonable people would rationally want to extend compassion, support, and intervention to all victims of violence" (Kimmel 2002, p. 1354). Indeed, the male victim of violence has few resources and often little sympathy (Cose 1994a).

Abuse among Lesbian, Gay Male, and Bisexual Couples

We discuss gay male, lesbian, and bisexual intimate partner violence apart from our discussion of married-couple and heterosexual cohabitants violence because the analysis of heterosexual intimate partner violence is largely based on gender *difference*. In fact, it was initially assumed that the likely greater similarity in power of same-sex couples would deter couple violence—unfortunately not.

Domestic violence has long been one of the lesbian and gay communities' "nastiest secrets" (Island and Letellier 1991, p. 36; Obejas 1994, p. 53). Lesbians may have denied the issue because they believe in the inherent goodness of lesbian relationships or are afraid of giving fuel to homophobia. As for violence in the relationships of gay men, there may be even more silence and denial (Island and Letellier 1991).

Research on lesbian, gay male, and bisexual relationship violence was initially scanty, but more research and service-oriented articles and books have appeared

---

[6] Johnson now uses the gender-neutral term *intimate terrorism* and points to its existence in lesbian as well as heterosexual couples (Johnson and Ferraro 2000). However, we believe the original term best captures the typical male-to-female abuse represented by this pattern.

Johnson has added two more types that we do not include here as they are not yet fully developed or sufficiently researched (M. Johnson 2001; Johnson and Ferraro 2000). These are *violent resistance* and *mutual violent control*. Johnson considers the latter to be rare, which we see as confirming the decision to retain a gendered definition of the control-oriented form of intimate partner violence.

in the last few years. Studies done to date suggest that violence between same-sex partners occurs at the same or greater rate as in heterosexual relationships (Potoczniak et al. 2003). One large-sample study of 499 couples found that 9 percent reported physical violence in current couple relationships, and 32 percent in past relationships (Turrell 2000).

As is also true for straights, domestic violence may be found in all racial/ethnic categories, social classes, education levels, and age groups. Among lesbians, neither "butch/femme" roles nor the women's physical size has been found to figure into violence (Obejas 1994).

Some of the relationship dynamics in same-sex abusive partnerships are similar to those in abusive straight relationships (Kurdek 1994). An "intense dependency" (Renzetti 2001, p. 455) often characterizes the batterer. Batterers may use drugs or alcohol or a history of childhood exposure to violence to enable and excuse attacks on the partner. The abusive partner uses violence or threats of violence to keep the partner from leaving. Furthermore, the couple is likely to deny or minimize the violence, along with believing that the violence is at least partly the victim's fault (Island and Letellier 1991; Renzetti 1992, 2001).

Other relationship dynamics are specific to same-sex domestic abuse. It is more difficult to attribute same-sex violence to theories of patriarchy and culturally influenced gender roles, the primary perspectives developed to explain men's abuse of women. Lesbians as well as gay men may fight back more often than do heterosexual women, a situation that leads to confusion about who is the battered and who is the batterer. Furthermore, some lesbians and gay men who are battered in one relationship may become batterers in another relationship (Island and Letellier 1991; Obejas 1994; Potoczniak et al. 2003).

Lesbian violence is different in still other respects. For one thing, according to psychologist Vallerie Coleman, who works with battered lesbians, heterosexual men tend to feel they have a right to abuse their mates, whereas lesbians do not (Obejas 1994). A greater proportion of lesbian batterers seek help than do heterosexual male abusers. Lesbians are more likely to go into treatment on their own, according to Coleman: "Heterosexual men go in because they're court-mandated" (quoted in Obejas 1994).

A special problem for lesbian and gay male domestic-violence victims is that few resources exist to serve their needs. The availability of legal protection is problematic in many states (e.g., American Civil Liberties Union 2000). Some states specifically exclude same-sex couples from domestic violence laws, and in many other states the law or its enforcement is ambiguous.

Gay/lesbian/bisexual individuals may be afraid to go to the police—or to use any domestic violence intervention services—for fear of having their gay identity revealed or receiving a hostile response. Although lesbians do seek help from the same services as heterosexual women, they find friends, counselors, and relatives the most helpful sources of support. Gay men find friends, counselors, and support groups of greatest help. Domestic violence services oriented to gay men, lesbians, and bisexuals are now somewhat available in larger cities with substantial gay/lesbian communities (Potoczniak et al. 2003).

Stopping Relationship Violence

The debate over whether women are as violent as men—or not—may be resolved at the practical level by noting that the interests of men as a group converge with those of women in curbing spousal violence—not only in hopes of having viable relationships but simply for survival. Even though men kill wives and girlfriends at a much higher rate than women kill husbands and boyfriends, some victimized women do murder or seriously injure their male partners. Progress in stopping intimate partner violence will benefit both sexes.

We have already discussed the shelter movement. Other approaches involve (1) counseling and group therapy directed toward abusive male partners (or the couple) and (2) the criminal justice system.

Counseling and Group Therapy Counseling and group therapy were earlier thought to be ineffective for male abusers. That may have been partly due to the inapplicability of general programs to this specific problem.

A number of male batterer intervention programs have now been developed. Many abusing husbands and male partners have difficulty controlling their response to anger and frustration, dealing with problems, and relinquishing their excessive control over their partner. Even though many, perhaps most, abusers are not reachable and may drop out of treatment (Brown, O'Leary, and Feldbau 1997), other men have a sincere desire to stop. Group therapy reduces stigma and provides a setting in which abusers can learn more-constructive ways of both coping with anger and balancing autonomy and intimacy, often another area of difficulty. Some men's therapy groups have emerged in which former batterers help lead male abusers toward recovery (Allen and Kivel 1994).

It is difficult to evaluate the level of success of male batterer intervention programs because of design problems, low response rates, and high program dropout rates and because programs do not always follow the research protocol (Hamby 1998; Jackson et al. 2003). From what we know, it appears that "[o]verall, batterers intervention program outcomes are modest" (Bennett and Williams 1999, p. 242). Two recent and rigorously designed evaluations sponsored by the National Institute of Justice were conducted on intervention programs in Broward County in Florida and in Brooklyn, New York. The researchers concluded that the programs had "little or no effect" (Jackson et al. 2003). But though they may be ineffective on a large scale, such programs may work for some men, and that's all to the good. A study conducted in Maine found "conflicting evidence on whether programs were effective, though . . . men who completed a batterers' intervention program were less likely to re-offend than men who dropped out (Hench 2004).

Often male batterers are court-ordered into treatment. Sometimes one option is an anger management program, but these have been criticized by victim advocates as ineffective. The Federal Office on Violence Against Women now agrees, and prohibits federal funds being used for anger management programs that do not specifically deal with domestic violence (Hench 2004). "'All of us are angry at some point during our day; violence, on the other hand, is very different. It's an action,'" says one director of a program that offers both kinds of treatment to varied clients. Another says, "'The issue regarding domestic violence is power and control. The offender is likely to beat or abuse the victim whether or not he or she is angry'" (in Hench 2004).

In the past decade, some couples' therapy programs have emerged to treat wife abuse (Johannson and Tutty 1998). Typically, such programs counsel husbands and wives—or just husbands—separately over a period of up to six months. After this first treatment phase, couples are counseled together and are taught anger-management techniques, along with communication, problem-solving, and conflict-resolution skills.

Couples' therapy programs designed to stop domestic violence are somewhat controversial because they proceed from the premise that a couple's staying together without violence after an abusive past is possible. Feminist scholars have expressed concern that therapists underestimate the danger that women face in violent relationships (Hansen, Harway, and Cervantes 1991). There is some evidence that negative social sanctions from either partner's relatives or friends may help stop wife abuse (Lackey and Williams 1995).

The Criminal Justice Response There was little legal protection for battered women in the past. The street wisdom among police, as well as those who worked with battered women, was that calling the police was an ineffective strategy and posed some risk to the woman.

Arresting an abusive partner or pressing charges would only aggravate the situation and result in escalating violence later. Officers also felt themselves to be at risk in responding to domestic violence calls.

Police officers typically avoided making arrests for assault that would be automatic if the man and woman involved were not married. The laws themselves contributed to police reluctance: Statutes might require a police officer to witness the act before making an arrest at the scene, or more severe injury might be required for prosecution for battery. In some cases, restraining orders required additional court action before they could be enforced.

However, a sociological experiment in Minneapolis in the 1980s obtained results indicating that mandatory arrest could be an effective deterrent to future violence (Sherman and Berk 1984).[7] As a consequence of this experiment, laws have been changed to make arrests for domestic violence more feasible, and some states or jurisdictions have policies that mandate arrest in certain situations involving family violence (Buzawa and Buzawa 1990, p. 96).

Most subsequent replications of the arrest experiment did not get the same result. It now appears that arrest will deter future violence only on the part of men who are employed and married, men with a "stake in conformity." Other men, those who are unemployed and/or not married to the woman they abused, may react to arrest by *increased* violence (Sherman 1992).

An even more serious problem of the arrest strategy has been that a literal reading of a mandatory arrest law has resulted in the arrest of victims, along with perpetrators, when the victim has resisted with violent force (Goldberg 1999). Women also fear that reporting domestic violence to the police will risk contact with Child Protective Services and the removal of their children from the home. Some women who did contact police reported that the batterer was not arrested, as they had expected, and that the police sometimes trivialized their situation. In some cases women claimed that the exchange between the perpetrator and the police officer was characterized by "male bonding," in which the perpetrator's story overrode the woman's complaint of violence.

Some women reported positive and protective experiences to researchers: "[S]o when the police did intervene that night, they made it pretty clear that I didn't deserve it (the abuse). . . . [T]hey talked to me and I

---

[7] In the Minneapolis experiment, officers were randomly assigned to respond by arresting the (presumably male) perpetrator, by counseling the parties, or simply by separating them for a cooling-off period. A six-month follow-up by telephone and an examination of police call records indicated that arrest was the most effective response in deterring subsequent violence (Sherman and Berk 1984).

filed a report . . . and that's the last I saw of my husband" (M. Wolf et al. 2003).

This seems a good time to remind ourselves of the good news that appears in recent reports. Both fatal and nonfatal violence against intimate partners has declined since 1993, and that may well be a consequence of the support and treatment programs we have described.

The drop in the male homicide rate is attributed to the greater availability of options for abused women. When women kill a partner, it is usually out of desperation to exit a violent relationship. The shelter programs and other resources that now exist have given battered women escape routes so that they are less likely to kill spouses or partners in an attempt to stop the violence.

Shelter options, women's increased ability to support themselves, a cultural change that takes domestic violence seriously and endorses women's taking self-protective actions, and increased interest in and understanding of domestic violence on the part of law enforcement agencies are all developments that may account for the decrease in fatal and nonfatal violence against women by their intimate partners.

We turn now to another type of family violence in which the more powerful abuse the less powerful—child abuse.

Violence Against Children

FOCUS ON CHILDREN Perceptions of what constitutes child abuse or neglect have differed throughout history and in various cultures.[8] Practices that we now consider abusive were accepted in the past as the normal exercise of parental rights or as appropriate discipline.

Even today, standards of acceptable child care vary according to culture and social class. What some groups consider mild abuse others consider right and proper discipline. In 1974, however, Congress provided a legal definition of *child maltreatment* in the Child Abuse Prevention and Treatment Act. (The federal government and some researchers use the umbrella term *child maltreatment* to cover both abuse and neglect.)

The act defines child abuse and neglect as the "physical or mental injury, sexual abuse, or negligent treatment of a child under the age of 18 by a person who is responsible for the child's welfare under circumstances that indicate that the child's health or welfare is harmed or threatened" (U.S. Department of Health, Education, and Welfare 1975, p. 3).

Child Abuse and Neglect People use the term **child abuse** to refer to overt acts of aggression—excessive verbal derogation (emotional child abuse) or physical child abuse such as beating, whipping, punching, kicking, hitting with a heavy object, burning or scalding, or threatening with or using a knife or gun. (By current American standards, spanking or hitting a child with a paddle, stick, or hairbrush is not "abuse," although it is in Sweden and several other countries [Straus and Donnelly 2001]; and see Chapter 11 of this text.)

Child neglect includes acts of omission—failing to provide adequate physical or emotional care. Physically neglected children often show signs of malnutrition, lack immunization against childhood disease, lack

Child abuse is not specific to the United States. This pamphlet was produced by social service agencies in Hong Kong.

---

[8] A dramatic example of cultural difference in defining child abuse is the controversy surrounding *female genital mutilation (FGM)*. Some sub-Saharan African and Muslim cultures practice FGM, which is the surgical removal of the clitoris and other external female genital organs, and suturing of the vaginal opening until marriage. In those cultures, FGM is an important rite of passage for young girls and considered necessary to make them eligible to marry. (It does not seem to be a Muslim religious teaching, however.) FGM has been brought to the United States by some immigrants as part of their cultural heritage. It has been outlawed in the United States since 1996 and is now prohibited in some African countries. FGM is still practiced clandestinely here (Renteln 2004, pp. 51–53).

proper clothing, attend school irregularly, and need medical attention for such conditions as poor eyesight or bad teeth. Often these conditions are grounded in parents' or guardians' economic problems (Baumrind 1994; J. Brown et al. 1998; Kruttschnitt, McLeod, and Dornfeld 1994), but child neglect may also be willful neglect (Gillham et al. 1998).

Emotional child abuse or neglect involves a parent's often being overly harsh and critical, failing to provide guidance, or being uninterested in a child's needs. Emotional child abuse might also include allowing children to witness violence between parents—there were children in residence in 40 percent of households where intimate partner violence took place (Catalano 2006). Although emotional abuse may occur without physical abuse, physical abuse results in emotional abuse as well.

Child Sexual Abuse Another form of child abuse is **sexual abuse**: a child's being forced, tricked, or coerced into sexual behavior—exposure, unwanted kissing, fondling of sexual organs, intercourse, rape, and incest—with an older person (Gelles and Conte 1990). Eight percent of children (of all ages) in a national-sample survey reported being sexually abused (Finkelhor et al. 2005).

Incest involves sexual relations between related individuals. The most common forms are father–daughter incest and incest involving a girl and her stepfather or older brother. The definition of child sexual abuse *excludes* mutually desired sex play between or among siblings close in age, but coerced sex by strong and/or older brothers is sexual abuse and may be more widespread than parent–child incest (Canavan, Meyer, and Higgs 1992). Incest is the most emotionally charged form of sexual abuse; it is also the most difficult to detect. Incest appears to be in the background of a variety of sexual, emotional, and physical problems among adults who were abused as children (Bell and Belicki 1998; Browning and Laumann 1997; Luster and Small 1997).

We see occasional media stories about female sex abusers, but research indicates that sexual abuse is almost entirely perpetrated by males (U.S. Children's Bureau 2000). Data on sexual exploitation indicate that 47 percent of sexual assaults on children were by relatives; 49 percent by others such as teachers, coaches, or neighbors; and only 4 percent by strangers (Hernandez 2001). Sexual abuse by paid caregivers and by mentors such as teachers, coaches, youth program directors, and clergy is a problem being addressed by policy makers and child-care professionals. Sexual exploitation of homeless children is yet another abuse problem (Shamin and Chowdhury 1993).

Research by social psychologists finds lower self-esteem and greater incidences of depression among adults who have been victims of child abuse (Downs and Miller 1998; Silvern et al. 1995). A study of nearly 43,000 adolescents found that those who had been physically and/or sexually abused were more prone to binge drinking and thoughts of suicide. However, high levels of supportive interest and monitoring from at least one parent decreased the risk for these outcomes among sexually abused adolescents (Luster and Small 1997).

Sibling Violence Sibling violence is often overlooked and rarely studied (K. Butler 2006a; Finkelhor et al. 2005) even though the early National Family Violence Survey found it to be the most pervasive form of family violence (Straus, Gelles, and Steinmetz 1980).

Nor is it only of the "harmless" teasing variety (Wiehe 1997; "UF Study" 2004). A national-sample study found that 35 percent of children had been hit or attacked by siblings in the previous year. Fourteen percent were repeatedly attacked, 5 percent hard enough to have injuries such as bruises, cuts, chipped teeth, and sometimes broken bones. Two percent were hit with rocks, toys, broom handles, shovels, or knives (K. Butler 2006a).

Child psychologist John Caffaro (in K. Butler 2006a) sees sibling abuse as situational, not personality driven. When parents are frequently physically or emotionally absent from the home, or when they have their own problems, sibling violence is more apt to occur. Failure to intervene effectively also plays a part, as does parental favoritism of one child over another. Trauma, anxiety, and depression are likely to result from experiencing sibling violence, as well as an increased likelihood to perpetrate violence as an adult and to have relationship problems (K. Butler 2006a; Hoffman and Edwards 2004; Noland et al. 2004).

Perpetrators of sibling violence are more likely than others to become perpetrators of dating violence, according to a study of more than 500 men and women at a Florida community college. "Siblings learn violence as a form of sibling manipulation and control as they compete with each other for family resources. . . . They carry these bullying behaviors into dating, the next peer relationship in which they have an emotional investment" (researcher Virginia Noland in "UF Study" 2004; Noland et al. 2004). Yet sibling violence has received comparatively little research attention and even less attention has been given to preventive or therapeutic responses. Noland recommends that sibling violence be taken more seriously and that anger management programs be implemented while these violent individuals are still kids ("UF Study" 2004).

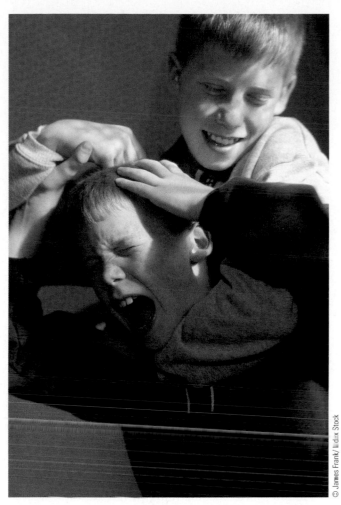

Sibling violence is not "kid stuff." This under-the-radar form of violence is rather frequent and can be quite injurious.

Abused children live in families of all socioeconomic levels, races, nationalities, and religious groups, although child abuse is reported more frequently among poor and nonwhite families than among middle- and upper-class white families. Families below the poverty line have three times the rate of severe violence to children. Differences in rates may be partly due to differences in reporting—children of the poor are more apt to be seen in the emergency room or by social welfare authorities (Gelles and Cavanaugh 2005). Another reason may be unconscious racial discrimination on the part of physicians and others who report abuse and neglect (Lane et al. 2002). Experts believe there are also real differences, however (Gelles and Cavanaugh 2005), and a stress explanation is often offered.

In 2005, according to government data, 50 percent of the victims of child maltreatment were white, 25 percent African American, 17 percent Hispanic, 2 percent American Indian/Alaska Native, and 1 percent Asian/Pacific Islander. When the size of each racial/ethnic group is taken into account, it appears that African American, American Indian, and Pacific Islander children had the highest victimization rates; Hispanics and whites had moderate levels of victimization; and Asian American children had low rates of child maltreatment (U.S. Department of Health and Human Services 2007).

The percentages of male (47 percent) and female (51 percent) victims were not very different. The youngest children (through age three) were more vulnerable than older children (U.S. Department of Health and Human Services 2007). A child faces the greatest risk of becoming a victim of homicide during the first year of life (Collymore 2002).

Eighty-four percent of abused children were mistreated by at least one parent; in 40 percent of cases by mother only; in 18 percent of cases by father only;

How Extensive is Child Abuse? Rates of child physical abuse and child sexual abuse declined in the 1990s and in the first years of the twenty-first century (Finkelhor and Jones 2004, 2006; U.S. Department of Health and Human Services 2007). These are apparently "real" declines, not artifacts of reporting standards or bureaucratic processes.

Current estimates from the federal report *Child Maltreatment 2005* are based on state reports of child abuse. Of the reported cases of child maltreatment, 63 percent are of neglect; 17 percent, of physical abuse; 9 percent, of sexual abuse; 7 percent, of psychological mistreatment; and 2 percent, of medical neglect. (The remainder are cases that include multiple factors or unspecified maltreatment.)[9] An estimated 1,460 children died from abuse or neglect in 2005 (U.S. Department of Health and Human Services 2007).

[9] A controversy has arisen over accusations of child sexual and other abuse in the context of a child custody dispute. On the one hand, parents alleging child abuse (usually mothers) have been accused of fabricating the charge to gain an advantage in the custody determination (Childress 2006). On the other, those parents have claimed that their intent is to protect the child from real abuse by the other parent (usually fathers).

A study of over 9,000 contested divorces found that only 1 to 8 percent involved allegations of child abuse (Goldstein and Tyler 1998; McDonald 1998; citing Thoennes and Tjaden 1990). Half the allegations were considered "founded," that is, found to be true. In 33 percent of the cases, no abuse was found, and in 17 percent it could not be determined if child abuse had occurred or not.

The key point about fraudulent reports is that only 14 percent were "deliberate false accusations" (Goldstein and Tyler 1998, p. 1). The remainder of the "unfounded" cases were sincerely made reports that were later found to be in error, typically due to misunderstandings of children's behavior or statements.

and in 17 percent of cases by both mother and father. In 11 percent of cases, children were mistreated by other caregivers: foster parents or legal guardians, day-care workers, or unmarried partners of a parent (U.S. Department of Health and Human Services 2007).

The most common forms of maltreatment by female parents were "neglect" and "medical neglect." In presenting statistics that evidence a greater likelihood of mothers than fathers to abuse or neglect children, we should note that when responsibility for child care is taken into account, males are more abusive or there is no difference (Black, Heyman, and Slep 2001; Margolin 1992).

Abuse versus "Normal" Child Rearing It is too easy for parents to go beyond reasonable limits when angry or distraught or to include as "discipline" what most observers would define as abuse (Baumrind 1994; Whipple and Richey 1997). Hence, child abuse must be seen as a potential behavior in many families—even those we think of as "normal" (Straus 1994).

Immigrant families may come from cultures where rather severe physical punishment is considered necessary for good child rearing. Those parents may not be aware that what they are doing by way of parental discipline is illegal in this country. They may instead view themselves as very responsible parents (Renteln 2004, pp. 54–57).[10]

Risk Factors for Child Abuse Consider the following society-wide beliefs and conditions that, when exaggerated, may encourage even well-intentioned parents to mistreat their children:

- A belief in physical punishment is a contributing (but not sufficient) factor in child abuse. Abusive parents have learned—probably in their own childhood—to view children as requiring physical punishment (Gough and Reavey 1997).
- Parents may have unrealistic expectations about what the child is capable of; often, they lack awareness and knowledge of the child's physical and emotional needs and abilities (Gough and Reavey 1997). For example, slapping a bawling toddler to stop her

or his crying is completely unrealistic, as is too-early toilet training.

- Parents who abuse their children were often abused or neglected themselves as children. Violent parents are likely to have experienced and thereby learned violence as children. Whether victims of child abuse or witnesses of adult interpersonal violence, those exposed to family violence in childhood are more likely than others to abuse their own children, and their wives as well (Heyman and Slep 2002). This does not mean that abused children are predestined to be abusive parents or partners. Gelles and Cavanaugh (2005) report an intergenerational transmission rate of 30 percent. That is much higher than the general average of 2 to 4 percent; nevertheless, "[t]he most typical outcome for individuals exposed to violence in their families of origin is to be nonviolent in their adult families. This is the case for both men and women" (Heyman and Slep 2002, p. 870).
- Parental stress and feelings of helplessness play a significant part in child abuse (Rodriguez and Green 1997). "Economic adversity and worries about money pervade the typical violent home" (Gelles and Straus 1988, p. 85). Overload, often related to family problems, also creates stress that may lead to child abuse (J. Brown et al. 1998). Other causes of parental stress are children's misbehavior, changing lifestyles and standards of living, and a parent's feeling pressure to do a good job but being perplexed about how to do it.
- Families have become more private and less dependent on kinship and neighborhood relationships (Berardo 1998). Hence, parents are alone with their children, shut off at home from the "watchful eyes and sharp tongues that regulate parent–child relations in other cultures" (Skolnick 1978, p. 82). In neighborhoods that have support systems and tight social networks of community-related friends—where other adults are somewhat involved in the activities of the family—child abuse and neglect are much more likely to be noticed and stopped (Gelles and Straus 1988).
- Other circumstances that are statistically related to child maltreatment include parental youth and inexperience, marital discord and divorce, and unusually demanding or otherwise difficult children (Baumrind 1994; J. Brown et al. 1998). Other risk factors involve parental abuse of alcohol or other substances (Fleming, Mullen, and Bammer 1996); a mother's cohabiting with her boyfriend (who is more likely than a child's male relative to abuse the child; Margolin 1992); and having a stepfather (because stepfathers are more likely than biological fathers to abuse their children; Daly and Wilson 1994).

[10] Immigrant parents may be mistakenly identified as having abused children because of certain cultural practices not initially understood in this country. There are healing practices in certain cultures that can produce what looks like evidence of injuries to an American doctor or social service worker. Southeast Asians employ a practice known as "coining" whereby they rub the edge of a coin along the skin. This leaves marks that can appear to be those of a whip (Child Abuse Protection Council of Sacramento n.d.). Similarly, Asian children may have "Mongolian spots" on their skin, a natural phenomenon, but one that appears as bruising to the unaware health practitioner (Families with Children from China 1999).

Combating Child Abuse Three major approaches to combating child abuse and willful neglect are the punitive approach, which views abuse and neglect as crimes for which parents should be punished; the therapeutic approach, which views abuse as a family problem requiring treatment; and the social welfare approach, which looks to stress factors and the family's social context.

The Criminal Justice Approach Those who favor the punitive approach believe that one or both parents should be held legally responsible for abusing a child.

A complicated issue emerging with regard to this approach involves holding battered women criminally responsible for "failing to act" to prevent such abuse at the hands of their male partners. Feminist legal advocates have begun to question whether the law should hold a battered woman responsible for failing to prevent harm to her children when, as a battered woman, she cannot even defend herself: "When the law punishes a battered woman for failing to protect her child against a batterer, it may be punishing her for failing to do something she was incapable of doing. . . . She is then being punished for the crime of the person who has victimized her" (Erickson 1991, pp. 208–9). Legal experts note that fathers are typically *not* held accountable for child abuse committed by female partners (Liptak 2002).

The courts are starting to recognize this paradox. The Illinois Supreme Court overturned such a mother's conviction in 2002, and courts have ruled in favor of mothers who lost custody or had children removed from the home, citing the mothers' domestic violence victimization (Liptak 2002; *Nicholson v. Scopetta* 2004; Nordwall and Leavitt 2004).

The Therapeutic Approach All states have criminal laws against child abuse. But the approach to child protection has gradually shifted from punitive to therapeutic. Not all who work with abused children are happy with this shift. These critics prefer to hold one or both parents clearly responsible. They reject the family system approach to therapy because it implies distribution of responsibility for change to all family members (M. Stewart 1984). Nevertheless, social workers and clinicians—rather than the police and the court system—increasingly investigate and treat abusive or neglectful parents.

The therapeutic approach involves two interrelated strategies: (1) increasing parents' self-esteem and their knowledge about children and (2) involving the community in child rearing (Goldstein, Keller, and Erne 1985). A typical voluntary program holds regular meetings to enhance self-esteem and educate abusive parents. Programs may attempt to reach stressed parents before they hurt their children, and many operate a twenty-four-hour hotline for parents under stress. High school classes on family life, child development, and parenting are now virtually universal and are thought to reduce child abuse by giving future parents an understanding of what they can expect from children at different ages.

Involving the community means getting people other than parents to help with child rearing. There are options such as *supplemental mothers,* who are available to babysit regularly with potentially abused children. Another community resource is the *crisis nursery,* where parents may take their children when they need to get away for a few hours. Ideally, crisis nurseries are open twenty-four hours a day and accept children at any hour without prearrangement.

One form of protection for abused or neglected children is to remove them from their parents' homes and place them in foster care. This practice is controversial, as foster parents have been abusive in some cases, and in many regions of the country there are not enough foster parents to go around. Moreover, removal from the home can be quite traumatic to children, who are often very attached to their parents despite the abuse (Kaufman 2006). They may blame themselves for the breaking up of the family (Gelles and Cavanaugh 2005).

An alternative is **family preservation**, whereby a Child Protective Services worker is able to "leave the child with an impoverished or troubled family and provide support in the form of housekeeping help or drug treatment, and then visit frequently to monitor progress" (Kaufman 2006, p. A12). The family preservation approach would not be appropriate if harm to the child appears imminent. Family preservation is a controversial strategy (Gelles 2005; Wexler, 2005), but both removal of the child from the home and a family preservation approach carry risk.[11]

The Social Welfare Approach The social welfare approach overlaps with the therapeutic approach but takes note of the social, cultural, and economic context of child maltreatment to provide services and parent education that may make child abuse less likely. Housing assistance and subsidized child care, for example, might prevent a low-income or socially isolated parent's taking the risk of leaving children alone while working.

Parent education directed toward new immigrant parents might mitigate the development of situations that end in removal of children from the home. For

[11] For detailed discussions of this controversy see articles by Richard Wexler ("Family Preservation Is the Safest Way to Protect Most Children") and Richard Gelles ("Protecting Children Is More Important Than Preserving Families") in Loseke, Gelles, and Cavanaugh (2005).

example, if some immigrant families do not realize that their traditional disciplinary practices constitute criminal child abuse in the United States, parent education offered through refugee service centers could anticipate that problem. The same is true regarding leaving children alone at home. This may be customary and perfectly safe in a small tribal village but not so safe in the United States; moreover, it is illegal (Gonzalez and O'Connor 2002; Renteln 2004, pp. 54–58).

Commercial Sexual Exploitation of Children We close this section on child maltreatment with a look at a form of child abuse that is not, strictly speaking, family violence, but which is often set in motion by developments in seriously troubled families—that is the commercial sexual exploitation of children. Researchers Richard J. Estes and Neil Weiner of the University of Pennsylvania go beyond family violence per se to look at society-wide organized sexual exploitation of children. Their study was based on interviews with victims and child welfare workers in twenty-eight cities in the United States, Mexico, and Canada (Estes and Weiner 2002; Hernandez 2001; Memmott 2001). Based on this research, they estimate that as many as 300,000 to 400,000 children a year are molested or used in pornography or prostitution.

Family dynamics often place children in harm's way. Typically, victims of organized sexual exploitation are runaways, "throwaways" (children who have been kicked out of the home by parents), or other homeless children who trade or sell sex to meet their basic survival needs. Some sexually exploited children live at home but are offered for sexual purposes by their families in exchange for money, drugs, or other benefits (Hernandez 2001; Memmott 2001).

We are much more aware of parents' abuse of children than we are of children's abuse of parents, but it does happen. Sometimes it is an outgrowth of earlier child abuse. We turn now to the topic of child-to-parent abuse.

Child-to-Parent Abuse

The discussion of **child-to-parent abuse** is brief because not much research has been done (Cottrell and Monk 2004). Yet, like other forms of family violence, child-to-parent abuse has been there all along.

This section relies heavily on a review article by Cottrell and Monk (2004). Data suggest that 9 to 14 percent of parents have been abused by adolescent children, with injuries that include bruises, cuts, and broken bones. Types of assaults have included kicking, punching, biting, and weapons. Mothers, especially single mothers, and elderly parents of youth are the most frequent victims.

Adolescent boys are the most frequent perpetrators, and their growth in size and strength is associated with increases in violence. Although there are no clear findings of differences in race/ethnicity or social class, poverty and other family stressors are associated with this form of violence.

Abusive children may exhibit diminished emotional attachments to parents. The child may have been abused by the parent or witnessed intimate partner abuse in the household. Overly permissive parents and those who abandon their authority in response to the violence tend to see more of it. Parents whose child-rearing styles contradict each other are also at risk. Drug use by the adolescent may play a role.

Parents who are victims of assaults by their adolescent children often engage in denial. Unfortunately, at the moment, few if any support services exist, and the criminal justice system has not responded systematically (Cottrell and Monk 2004).

Generally, we see any form of family violence as more likely to occur in situations of unequal rather than equal power. We close this chapter with a reminder of everyone's basic right to be respected—and not to be physically, emotionally, or sexually abused—in any relationship. And we end on an optimistic note, as most forms of family violence show evidence of declining rather than increasing.

Summary

- Power, the ability to exercise one's will, may rest on cultural authority, on economic and personal resources that are gender-based and/or involve love and emotional dependence, on interpersonal dynamics, or on physical violence.

- Marital power or power in other intimate partner relationships includes decision making, control over money, the division of household labor, and a sense of empowerment in the relationship. American marriages experience a tension between egalitarianism on the one hand and, on the other, gender identities that in effect preserve male authority.

- The relative power of a husband and wife within a marriage or other intimate partnership varies by education, social class, religion, race/ethnicity, age, immigration status, and other factors. It varies by whether or not the woman works and with the presence and age of children. Studies of married couples, cohabiting couples, and gay and lesbian couples illustrate the significance of economically based power and of norms about who should have power.

- Couples can consciously work toward more egalitarian marriages or intimate partner relationships and relinquish "power politics." Changing gender roles, as they affect marital and intimate-relationship power, necessitate negotiation and communication.

- Physical violence is most commonly used in the absence of other resources.

- Researchers do not agree on whether intimate partner violence is primarily perpetrated by males or whether males and females are equally likely to abuse their partners. The effects of intimate partner violence indicate that victimization of women is the more crucial social problem, and it has received the most programmatic attention. Recently, some programs have been developed for male abusers. Studies suggesting that arrest is *sometimes* a deterrent to further wife abuse illustrate the importance of public policies in this area.

- Economic hardships and other stress factors (among parents of all social classes and races) can lead to physical and/or emotional child abuse as can lack of understanding of children's developmental needs and abilities. One difficulty in eliminating child abuse is drawing a clear distinction between "normal" child rearing and abuse.

- Physical, verbal, and emotional abuse, as well as sexual abuse and child neglect, are forms of violence against children. Sibling violence is an often overlooked form of child abuse.

- Criminal justice, therapeutic, and social welfare approaches are ways of addressing the problem of child maltreatment.

- Child-to-parent abuse is a recently "discovered" form of family violence. It may grow out of previous abuse of a child.

Questions for Review and Reflection

1. How is gender related to power in marriage? How do you think ongoing social change will affect power in marriage?

2. Do you think that power in a marriage or other couple relationship depends on who earns how much money? Or does it depend on emotions? Is it possible for a couple to develop a no-power relationship?

3. Looking at domestic violence, why might women remain with the men who batter them? Do you think

that shelters provide an adequate way out for these women? What about arresting the abuser? Should intimate partner violence against men receive more attention in the form of social programs? Why or why not?

4. What factors might play a role when well-intentioned parents abuse their children?

5. **Policy Question.** What can we as a society do to combat child neglect that is really due to family poverty?

Key Terms

allocation systems 358
child abuse 379
child neglect 379
child-to-parent abuse 384
coercive power 353
common couple violence 376
Conflict Tactics Scale 367
egalitarian norm (of marital power) 356
emotional child abuse or neglect 380
equality 352
equity 352
expert power 353
family preservation 383
gender model of marriage 362

incest 380
informational power 353
intimate partner power 352
intimate partner violence 367
legitimate power 353
marital power 352
marital rape 370
mutually economically dependent spouses (MEDS) 361
near peer marriage (Schwartz's typology) 362
neotraditional family 361
no-power 363
patriarchal norm (of marital power) 356
patriarchal terrorism 376
peer marriage (Schwartz's typology) 362

power 352
power politics 363
referent power 353
resource hypothesis 354
resources in cultural context 355

reward power 353
sexual abuse 380
sibling violence 380
traditionals (Schwartz's typology) 362
transitional egalitarian situation (of marital power) 355

Online Resources

Companion Website for This Book

www.thomsonedu.com/sociology/lamanna

Visit the book companion website, where you will find flash cards, practice quizzes, Internet links, suggested readings, InfoTrac College Edition exercises, and more to help you study.

ThomsonNOW™ for Marriage and Family

Spend time on what you need to master rather than on information you already have learned. Take a pre-test for this chapter, and ThomsonNOW will generate a personalized study plan based on your results. The study plan will identify the topics you need to review and direct you to online resources such as videos, narrated learning modules, and interactive activities to help you master those topics. You can then take a post-test to help you determine the concepts you have mastered and what you will still need to work on. Try it out! Go to **www.thomsonedu.com/login** to sign in with an access code or to purchase access to this product.

Family Stress, Crisis, and Resilience

15

Theoretical Perspectives on Family Stress and Crises

What Precipitates a Family Crisis?

Types of Stressors

Issues for Thought: Caring for Patients at Home—A Family Stressor

Stressor Overload

The Course of a Family Crisis

The Period of Disorganization

Recovery

A Closer Look at Family Diversity: Stressor Pile-Up Among Single-Mother Families in Homeless Shelters

Family Stress, Crisis, Adjustment, and Adaptation: A Theoretical Model

Stressor Pile-Up

Appraising the Situation

Crisis-Meeting Resources

Meeting Crises Creatively

A Positive Outlook

Spiritual Values and Support Groups

Open, Supportive Communication

Adaptability

Informal Social Support

An Extended Family

Community Resources

Crisis: Disaster or Opportunity?

Issues for Thought: When a Parent Is in Prison

It is said that "the only things a person can be sure of in this world are death and taxes. It should be noted that a third sure thing exists. This third reality is family stress . . ." (National Ag Safety Database n.d.). We can think of the family as a group that is continually balancing the demands put upon it against its capacity to meet those demands. As sociologist Pauline Boss (1997) reminds us,

> Perhaps the first thing to realize about stress is that it's not always a bad thing to have in families. In fact it can make family life exciting—being busy, working, playing hard, competing in contests, being involved in community activities, and even arguing when you don't agree with other family members. Stress means change. It is the force exerted on a family by demands. (p. 1)

Family stress is a state of tension that arises when demands test, or tax, a family's capabilities. Situations that we think of as good, as well as those that we think of as bad, are all capable of creating stress in our families. Moving to a different neighborhood, taking on a new job, and bringing a baby home are examples of situations that create family stress. Family stress might be caused by financial pressures such as finding adequate housing on a poverty budget or financing children's education on a middle-class income. A family member's injury or a death in the family is a source of family stress. Responding to the needs of aging parents is stressful for a family (see Chapter 18).

Family stress calls for family adjustment (Patterson 2002b). In response to financial pressures, for instance, middle-class family members might adjust their budget, cutting back spending on clothing, recreation, travel, or eating out. They might cope with time pressures by reducing their responsibilities or by arranging for someone outside the immediate family to help.

When adjustments are not easy to come by, family stress can lead to a **family crisis**: "a situation in which the usual behavior patterns are ineffective and new ones are called for immediately" (National Ag Safety Database n.d., p. 1; Patterson 2002b). We can think of a family crisis as a sharper jolt to a family than more ordinary family stress. The definition of *crisis* encompasses three interrelated ideas:

1. Crises necessarily involve change.
2. A crisis is a turning point with the potential for positive effects, negative effects, or both.
3. A crisis is a time of relative instability.

Family crises are turning points that require some change in the way family members think and act in order to meet a new situation (Hansen and Hill 1964; McCubbin and McCubbin 1991; Patterson 2002b). In the words of social worker and crisis researcher Ronald Pitzer,

> *Crisis* occurs when you or your family face an important problem or task that you cannot easily solve. A crisis consists of the problem and your reaction to it. It's a turning point for better or worse. Things will never be quite the same again. They may not necessarily be worse; perhaps they will be better, but they will definitely be different. (Pitzer 1997a, p. 1)

We point out in several places throughout this text that families are more likely to be happy when they work toward mutually supportive relationships—and when they have the resources to do so. Nowhere does this become more apparent than in a discussion of how families manage stress and crises. Among other topics, this chapter examines how families can cope with stress and crises creatively. We'll discuss what precipitates family stress or crisis, then look at how families define or interpret stressful situations and how their definitions affect the course of a family crisis. To begin, we'll review some theoretical perspectives on the family and see how these can be applied to family stress and crises.

Theoretical Perspectives on Family Stress and Crises

We saw in Chapter 2 that there are various theoretical perspectives concerning marriages and families. Throughout this chapter, we will apply several of these theoretical perspectives to family stress and crises. Here we give a brief review of several theoretical perspectives that are typically used when examining family stress and crises.

You may recall that the *structure–functional* perspective views the family as a social institution that performs essential functions for society—raising children responsibly and providing economic and emotional security to family members. From this point of view, a family crisis threatens to disrupt the family's ability to perform these critical functions (Patterson 2002b).

The *family development*, or *family life course*, perspective sees a family as changing in predictable ways over time. This perspective typically analyzes **family transitions**—expected or *predictable* changes in the course of family life—as family stressors that can precipitate a family crisis (Carter and McGoldrick 1988). For example, having a first baby or sending the youngest child off to college taxes a family's resources and brings about significant changes in family relationships and expectations. Over the course of family living, people may form cohabiting relationships, marry, become parents, break up or divorce, remarry, and make transitions to retirement and widowhood or widowerhood. All these transitions are stressors.

"Sgt. Michael Buyas, with sons Jaiden (left) and Justin, says that in his dreams he still has legs. In waking moments, he worries about how he'll teach his three boys wrestling, his favorite sport in high school. Michael's legs were blown off by an improvised explosive device just before Christmas 2004 in Iraq" (Ryan 2006). A crisis necessarily involves change. The *family ecology* perspective focuses on how factors external to the family, such as the war in Iraq, can result in family crisis. From a *family systems* perspective, all the members in this family must adapt to their father's injuries.

Chronicle photo by Michael Macor

(Voydanoff 2002). Changes in the national welfare laws have caused stress or crisis for many families (Dyk 2004; Edin and Kefalas 2007). The September 11, 2001, attacks on New York City and Washington, DC, were environmental factors that dramatically affected our families, creating family stress. Natural disasters, such as tornadoes, hurricanes, or earthquakes, create family stress and crises (Sattler 2006). Moreover, as we'll see later in this chapter, our family's external environment offers or denies us resources for dealing with stressors.

The *family system* theoretical framework looks at the family as a system—like a computer system or an organic system, such as a living plant or the human body. In a system, each component or part influences all the other parts. For example, changing a piece of code in a computer program will affect the entire program. Similarly, one family member's changing her or his role requires all the family members to adapt and change as well. As an example, when a family member becomes addicted to alcohol, the entire family system is affected (El-Sheikh and Flanagan 2001).

Furthermore, like any system, a family has boundaries. Family members need to know "who is in and who is outside the family" (Boss 1997, p. 4). We'll return to this point later in this chapter.

Finally, exploring the discussions, gestures, and actions that go on in families, the *interactionist perspective* views families as shaping family traditions and family members' self-concepts and identities. By interacting with one another, family members struggle to create shared family meanings that define stressful or potentially stressful situations—for example, as good or bad, disaster or challenge, someone's fault or no one's fault. As we will explore later in this chapter, "a family's shared meanings about the demands they are experiencing can render them more or less vulnerable in how they respond" (Patterson 2002b, p. 355).

In addition, the family development perspective focuses on the fact that predictable family transitions, such as an adult child's becoming financially independent, are expected to occur within an appropriate time period (see, for example, Furstenberg et al. 2004). Transitions that are "outside of expected time" create greater stress than those that are "on time" (Hagestad 1996; Rogers and Hogan 2003). Partly for this reason, teenage pregnancy is often a family stressor. Another example, explored in Chapter 11, involves a grandparent's filling the parent role.

The *family ecology* perspective explores how a family influences and is influenced by the environments that surround it. From this point of view, many causes of family stress originate outside the family—in the family's neighborhood, workplace, and national or international environment (Boss 2002). Living in a violent neighborhood causes family stress and has potential for sparking family crises (Fox 2000; Koblinsky 2001). Conflict between work and family roles that is largely created by workplace demands is another example of an environmental factor that may cause family stress

What Precipitates a Family Crisis?

Demands put upon a family cause stress and sometimes precipitate a family crisis. Social scientists call such demands **stressors**—a precipitating event or events that create stress. Stressors vary in both kind and degree, and their nature is one factor that affects how a family responds. In general, stressors are less difficult to cope with when they are expected, are brief, and gradually improve over time.

Types of Stressors

There are several types of stressors, as Figure 15.1 shows. We will briefly examine eight of them here.

1. Addition of a Family Member Adding a member to the family—for example, through birth, adoption (Bird, Peterson, and Miller 2002), marriage, remarriage, or the onset of cohabitation—is a stressor. You may recall the discussion in Chapter 11 on why the transition to parenthood is stressful. The addition of adult family members may bring into intimate social contact people who are very different from one another in values and life experience. Then, too, not only are in-laws (and increasingly stepparents, step-grandparents, and step-siblings) added through marriage but also a whole array of *their* kin come into the family. Adding a family member is stressful because doing so involves family boundary changes; that is, family boundaries have to shift to include or "make room for" new people or to adapt to the loss of a family member (Boss 1980).

2. Loss of a Family Member The death of a family member is, of course, a stressor. The likelihood of death in our society influences how we define a death in the family. Under the mortality conditions that existed in this coun-

try in 1900, half of all families with three children could expect to have one die before reaching age fifteen. Social historians have argued that parents defined the loss of a child as almost natural or predictable and, consequently, may have suffered less emotionally than do parents today (Wells 1985, pp. 1–2). Family members who lose a child today do so "outside of expected time," a situation that exacerbates, or adds to, their grief. Moreover, when an only child dies, parents must adjust to the sudden loss of an important role as well as grieving their child. The long-term effects of grieving such a loss may negatively affect marital intimacy (Gottlieb, Lang, and Amsel 1996).

Loss of potential children through miscarriage or stillbirth has the possible added strain of family disorientation. Attachment to the fetus may vary substantially so that the loss may be grieved greatly or little. Add to that the generally minimal display of bereavement customary in the United States and the omission of funerals or support rituals for perinatal (birth process) loss, and "all these ambiguities mean that a family may have to cope with sharply different feelings among family members . . . [and] the family as a whole may have to cope with the fact that they as a family have a very different reaction to loss than do the people around them" (Rosenblatt and Burns 1986, p. 238).

In fact, a study of fifty-five instances of perinatal loss found that grief was still felt by some parents forty years later, whereas the majority reported no long-term grief; some had always defined their loss as a medical problem rather than a child's death. Men and women may have different reactions to their pregnancy loss and a different sensibility about the expression of feelings (Stinson et al. 1992).

In addition to permanent loss, the temporary loss of a family member, such as through hospitalization or military deployment, is a stressor. Temporary losses like these, creating changes in family structure as well as fear of the unknown, are a form of ambiguous loss (Huebner et al. 2007; Whealin and Pivar 2006).

| Addition of a family member | Loss of a family member | Ambiguous loss | Sudden unexpected change | Ongoing family conflict | Caring for a dependent, ill or disabled family member | Demoralizing event | Daily family hassles |

FIGURE 15.1 Types of stressors.

3. Ambiguous Loss The loss of a family member is *ambiguous* when it is uncertain whether the family member is "really" gone (Boss 2007).

> Ambiguous loss is a loss that remains unclear. . . . [U]ncertainty or a lack of information about the whereabouts or status of a loved one as absent or present, as dead or alive, is traumatizing for most individuals, couples, and families. The ambiguity freezes the grief process and prevents cognition, thus blocking coping and decision-making processes. Closure is impossible. (Boss 2007, p. 105)

Having a family member who has been called to war or who is missing in action are situations of ambiguous loss (Pittman, Kerpelman, and McFadyen 2004; Boss 2007).

In addition, a family member may be physically present but psychologically absent, as in the case of alcoholic or mentally ill family members, those suffering from Alzheimer's disease or who have experienced brain injury, or children with cognitive impairment or severe disabilities (Blieszner et al. 2007; Roper and Jackson 2007). The ambiguity of postdivorce family boundaries can be stressful. Unmarried fathers whose relationship with the pregnant mother—and hence with their future child—is uncertain can experience ambiguous loss (Leite 2007).

From the family systems perspective, ambiguous loss is uniquely difficult to deal with because it creates family **boundary ambiguity** (see Figure 15.2)—"confused percep-

tions about who is in or out of a particular family" (Boss 2004, p. 553; Carroll, Olson, and Buckmiller 2007).

With a clear-cut loss, there is more clarity—a death certificate, mourning rituals, and the opportunity to honor and dispose [of the] remains. With ambiguous loss, none of these markers exists. The clarity needed for boundary maintenance (in the sociological sense) or closure (in the psychological sense) is unattainable. . . . [P]arenting roles are ignored, decisions are put on hold, daily tasks are undone, family members are ignored or cut off, and rituals and celebrations are canceled even though they are the glue of family life. (Boss 2004, p. 553)

4. Sudden, Unexpected Change A sudden, unexpected change in the family's income or social status may also be a stressor. The losses associated with the shooting deaths of more than thirty students and professors at Virginia Tech University in April 2007 were exacerbated by the abrupt and unanticipated nature of the event. As another example, natural disasters, mentioned earlier, cause sudden change. Most people think of stressors as being negative, and some sudden changes are. But positive changes, such as winning the lottery (don't you wish?) or getting a significant promotion can cause stress too.

5. Ongoing Family Conflict Ongoing, unresolved conflict among members may be a stressor (Hammen, Brennan, and Shih 2004). For example, deciding how children should be disciplined may bring to the surface divisive differences over parenting roles. The role of an adult child living with parents is often unclear and can be a source of unresolved conflict. If children of teenagers or of divorced adult children are involved, the situation becomes even more challenging. For a grandmother, watching her married child go through family conflict may be a stressor (Hall and Cummings 1997).

6. Caring for a Dependent, Ill, or Disabled Family Member Caring for a dependent or disabled family member is a stressor (Berge and Holm 2007; Patterson 2002a). An example involves being responsible for an adult child or a sibling with mental illness and/or physical or developmental disabilities (Nachshen, Woodford, and Minnes 2003; Rogers and Hogan

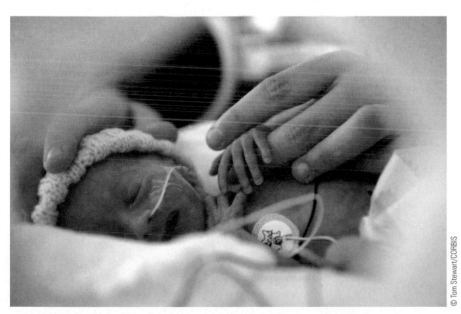

© Tom Stewart/CORBIS

Sometimes a situation may be classified as more than one type of stressor. Due to advancing medical technology, for instance, more newborns today survive low birth weight or birth defects but may need ongoing remedial attention. Therefore, adding a baby to the family may also mean caring for a medically fragile child.

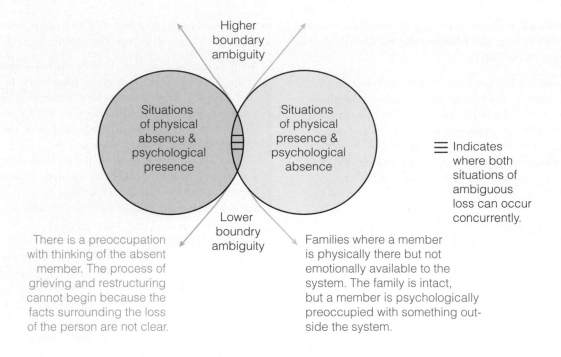

Higher boundary ambiguity

Situations of physical absence & psychological presence

Situations of physical presence & psychological absence

≡ Indicates where both situations of ambiguous loss can occur concurrently.

Lower boundry ambiguity

There is a preoccupation with thinking of the absent member. The process of grieving and restructuring cannot begin because the facts surrounding the loss of the person are not clear.

Families where a member is physically there but not emotionally available to the system. The family is intact, but a member is psychologically preoccupied with something outside the system.

Catastrophic and unexpected situations

- war (missing soldiers)
- natural disaster (missing persons)
- kidnapping, hostage-taking, terrorism
- incarceration
- desertion, mysterious disappearance
- missing body (murder, plane crash, etc.)

- Alzheimer's disease and other dementias
- chronic mental illness
- addictions (alcohol, drugs, gambling, etc.)
- traumatic head injury, brain injury
- coma, unconsciousness

More common situations

- divorce
- military deployment
- young adults leaving home
- elderly mate moving to a nursing home

- preoccupation with work
- obsession with computer games, Internet, TV

FIGURE 15.2 High boundary ambiguity—two forms: (1) a family member's physical absence coupled with psychological presence, and (2) a family member's physical presence coupled with psychological absence. "Sometimes a family experiences an event or situation that makes it difficult—or even impossible—for them to determine precisely who is in their family system" (Boss 1997, pp. 2–3).

Sources: Adapted from Boss 1997, pp. 2–3; and Boss, Pauline. 2004, "Ambiguous Loss Research, Theory, and Practice: Reflections after 9/11." *Journal of Marriage and Family* 66 (3), p. 555. Used by permission of Blackwell Publishing.

2003). Due mainly to advancing medical technology, the number of dependent people and the severity of their disabilities have steadily increased over recent decades. For instance, more babies today survive low birth weight and birth defects. Also, more people now survive serious accidents, and many seriously injured soldiers in Iraq have survived. These family members may require ongoing care and medical attention. "Issues

"It's very important that you try very, very hard to remember where you electronically transfered Mommy and Daddy's assets."

for Thought: Caring for Patients at Home—A Family Stressor" discusses how recent technological advances, coupled with the goal of containing medical-care costs, have created new stressors for families who are increasingly expected to care for very ill patients at home.

In addition, parents may be raising children with chronic physical conditions, such as asthma, diabetes, epilepsy, or autism (O'Brien 2007). Families may need to see their children through bone marrow, kidney, or liver transplants, sometimes requiring several months' residence at a medical center away from home (LoBiondo-Wood, Williams, and McGhee 2004). Adults with advanced AIDS may return home to be taken care of by family members. Caring for a terminally ill family member is, of course, another stressor—for young children, who may exhibit behavior problems as a response, as well as for the adults in the household (Seltzer and Heller 1997).

7. Demoralizing Events Stressors may be demoralizing events—those that signal some loss of family morale. Demoralization can accompany the stressors already described (see, for example, Early, Gregoire, and McDonald 2002). But, among other things, this category also includes job loss, poverty, homelessness, having one's child placed in foster care, juvenile delinquency or criminal prosecution, scandal, family violence, mental illness, alcoholism, drug abuse, incarceration, or suicide (Grekin, Brennan, and Hammen 2005; Hammack et al. 2004; Wadsworth and Berger 2006). Being the brunt of racist treatment is potentially demoralizing (Murry et al. 2001; "Poor People . . ." 2003). Grandparents' raising grandchildren is a situation that is often—although not always—associated with demoralizing events (Ross and Aday 2006; G. Warren 2003).

Physical, mental, or emotional illnesses or disorders can be demoralizing. Alzheimer's disease or brain injury, in which a beloved family member seems to have become a different person, can be heartbreaking. In military personnel who have served during wartime, posttraumatic stress disorder (PTSD) can be demoralizing, causing "family members [to] feel hurt, alienated, or discouraged, and then become angry or distant toward the partner" ("PTSD and Relationships . . ." 2006). Some illnesses can be especially demoralizing when they are associated with the possibility of being socially stigmatized. HIV/AIDS, attention deficit hyperactivity disorder (ADHD) (K. Wells et al. 2000), anorexia nervosa, or bulimia are examples.

8. Daily Family Hassles Finally, daily family hassles are stressors. Examples are balancing employment against family demands (O'Laughlin and Bischoff 2005;

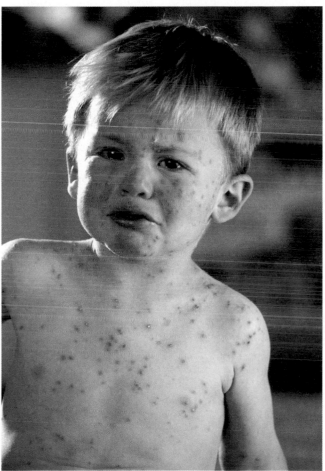

Daily family hassles, such as a child's coming down with chicken pox, put demands on a family. Sometimes everyday hassles pile up to result in what social scientists call "stressor overload." This is especially true when a new stressor is added to already difficult daily family life.

"The philosophy of ambulatory or community care, coupled with economic preoccupation over growing health care budgets in a period of economic restraint, have led to reduced hospital stays for many patient populations, resulting in longer periods of convalescence at home. This shift has been made possible thanks to medical innovations in both surgical techniques and postoperative care making early discharge an option. We are thus witnessing a spectacular increase in day surgeries and, more generally, in care that was previously only offered in a hospital setting being offered in the patient's home by public, private, or community home care professionals and even by the patients themselves or by members of their families. . . .

"It is taken for granted that [family] caregivers are ready to help others, be it through love or obligation, and that they automatically possess the necessary resources and skills to do so, at least in the vast majority of situations. . . .

"The research on which this article is based . . . sought to understand how sick people and their caregivers were managing this transfer; their difficulties, their questions, and their preoccupations. . . . The study is thus qualitative. . . . A convenience sample of 119 patients and/or caregivers was referred to the research team. . . . [T]he majority of interviews were with the patients themselves, although in many cases the main caregiver or another member of the family was present for at least part of the interview. . . .

"One of the main issues raised by patients and caregivers was related to a certain lack of sensitivity on the part of hospital staff . . . to the implications of transferring care to a setting that is very different from a hospital. . . .

"It appears that information given at the hospital is mostly technical and consists of explanations of how to perform various procedures. . . . [S]peaking of dealing with an IV patient, one caregiver stated, 'You think it's easy to inject someone, but when you've never done it . . . and then you try for the first time, you're suddenly all thumbs. It's hard! I really found it stressful! You can do it, but it's very stressful.'. . .

"It is somewhat disconcerting to imagine an activity taking place in the hospital and then displacing this same activity to the home. In the hospital, patients are put into hospital gowns on beds with sheets which are often changed daily. The patient is in a supposedly sterile environment. Diet and medications are completely controlled by hospital staff. Indeed, a patient who asks to keep and self-administer his or her medications is refused. An interdisciplinary professional team is present, and when any one member is confronted with a problem (leaking IV tube, patient discomfort, apparatus malfunction), the members of the team are backed up by specialists (IV technicians, specialized doctors, technicians, etc.) and by a team of people responsible for the organization of the instrumental activities of daily living (meals, toileting). Staff members are generally dressed in some form of uniform and must wear gloves, and sometimes masks, when entering a patient's room.

Voydanoff 2002); working odd hours (Coles 2004); being regularly stuck in traffic on long commutes to work, arranging child care or transportation among low-income families (Roy, Tubbs, and Burton 2004); or protecting children from danger, especially in neighborhoods characterized by violence (Jarrett and Jefferson 2004). Although we may tend to think of work–family tensions as a middle-class issue, research points to serious stress involved in balancing jobs and family roles among the working poor as well (Blalock 2003; Dolan, Braun, and Murphy 2003; Reschke 2003).

Some scholars have investigated everyday stressors that are unique to certain professions. For instance, especially in recent years military families "are subjected to unique stressors, such as repeated relocations that often include international sites, frequent separations of service members from families, and subsequent reorganizations of family life during reunions" (Drummet, Coleman, and Cable 2003, p. 279; see also Bowen et al. 2003).

And families of Protestant clergy experience not only the stressors of ministry demands but also family criticism and situations in which members of the congregation "intrusively assume that the minister will fulfill their expectations without due consideration of the minister's priorities" (Lee and Iverson-Gilbert 2003, p. 251).

You may have noted as you read this section that sometimes a single event can be classified as more than one type of stressor. For instance, the September 11, 2001, attack on New York City and Washington, DC, was an event that can be classified as a sudden change in our family environments—a change that, among other things, sparked parents' need to consider how to talk with their children about terrorism (Myers-Walls 2002; Walsh 2002b). For many, the attack was a demoralizing event. For others, the event not only was sudden and demoralizing but also sadly marked the loss of one or more family members. Many who had a family member in the Twin Towers on September 11 experienced

"Now transfer this to the home setting. The patient comes home and puts on the pajamas they were wearing before hospital admission. They move freely from room to room, hug and kiss family members, and handle the family pet. Having lived on hospital food for the past week, they are ready for home cooking. Their caregiver quarrels with them as he or she feels responsible for ensuring that the patient follow the diet outlined by the hospital. In the excitement of returning home, the patient forgets to take his or her morning medications. A day after returning home, the patient has trouble with his or her IV catheter. The IV pole is squeezed in between the bed and the night table, and there is almost no room to move because of the addition of a small table that is used to lay out equipment. The patient frequently gets caught in the line and loosens the catheter in his or her vein. When it starts bleeding at the site, the home care nurse has already come and gone. What to do? The caregiver makes an adjustment. He or she is abused for hurting the patient, but the IV starts to flow again and the bleeding stops. There is another dispute between patient and caregiver concerning hygiene around the IV. What does keeping a sterile area mean? Can the dog sit on the bed? Does the caregiver have to wear gloves? Are these questions important enough to disturb medical personnel for answers? Who should be called—the hospital, the home care nurse, or the 24-hour medical-information line? . . .

"[P]erhaps the most unsettling aspect of the transfer of care responsibilities to patients and their families is the anxiety and insecurity of assuming this care without sufficient supervision and emergency backup. In the hospital, you have an emergency call button if something goes wrong. But what replaces this button when you are being cared for at home? Indeed, the home is psychologically, and sometimes physically, very far from immediate help in the case of an emergency or an unforeseen development. The majority of patients and caregivers assuming complex care felt alone and abandoned, causing high levels of stress and anguish and conflicts within couples and within families.

"As one caregiver stated,

It's a huge responsibility. You think, what if something were to happen and you don't know what to do. Who's going to live with that on their conscience for the rest of their life. Not the hospital. Not the nurse. Not the guy with the pencils trying to save money. It's the person who will have had to live through that. . . .

"Our data reveal that this transfer of responsibility to patients is underscored by a growing trivialization of medical and nursing activities that now, it seems, can be accomplished by anybody. . . . Based on our study, we raise serious questions about the legitimacy of the transfer of high-tech care to the family."

Source: Excerpted from N. Guberman, E. Gagnon, D. Cote, C. Gilbert, N. Thivierge, and M. Tremblay, "How the Trivialization of the Demands of High-Tech Care in the Home Is Turning Family Members into Para-Medical Personnel," *Journal of Family Issues* 26 (2) (March 2005): 247–72.

ambiguous loss as they searched for missing relatives (Boss 2004).

Sometimes a single event combines stressor types. For example, adopting a child with special needs often involves both adding a family member and caring for a disabled child (Schweiger and O'Brien 2005). As another example, a birth to an unmarried teen may combine the addition of a family member with family conflict, particularly if this situation is defined as a demoralizing event.

Stressor Overload

A family may be stressed not just by one serious, chronic problem but also by a series of large or small, related or unrelated stressors that build on one another too rapidly for the family members to cope effectively (McCubbin, Thompson, and McCubbin 1996). This situation is called *stressor overload*, or **pile-up**:

Even small events, not enough by themselves to cause any real stress, can take a toll when they come one after another. First an unplanned pregnancy, then a move, then a financial problem that results in having to borrow several thousand dollars, then the big row with the new neighbors over keeping the dog tied up, and finally little Jimmy breaking his arm in a bicycle accident, all in three months, finally becomes too much. (Broderick 1979b, p. 352)

Characteristically, stressor overload creeps up on people without their realizing it. Even though it may be difficult to point to any single precipitating factor, an unrelenting series of relatively small stressors can add up to a crisis. In today's economy, characterized by longer working hours, two-paycheck marriages, fewer high-paying jobs, fewer benefits, and less job security, stressor overload may be more common than in the past. ("A Closer Look at Family Diversity: Stressor Pile-Up Among

Single-Mother Families in Homeless Shelters" on page 400 illustrates stressor overload.) Another example of stressor overload is the addition of depression to an earlier stressor, such as chronic poverty or an adolescent family member's living with epilepsy (Seaton and Taylor 2003). We'll return to the idea of stressor pile-up shortly. Now, however, with an understanding of the various kinds of events that cause family stress and can precipitate a family crisis, we turn to a discussion of the course of a family crisis.

The Course of a Family Crisis

Family stress "is simply pressure put on the family"; in a family crisis, there is an "imbalance between pressure and supports" (Boss 1997, p. 1). A family crisis ordinarily follows a fairly predictable course, similar to the truncated roller coaster shown in Figure 15.3. Three distinct phases can be identified: the event that causes the crisis, the period of disorganization that follows, and the reorganizing or recovery phase after the family reaches a low point. Families have a certain level of organization before a crisis; that is, they function at a certain level of effectiveness—higher for some families, lower for others. Families that are having difficulties or functioning less than effectively before the onset of additional stressors or demands are said to be **vulnerable**; families capable of "doing well in the face of adversity" are called **resilient** (Patterson 2002b, p. 350).

In the period of disorganization following the crisis, family functioning declines from its initial level. Families reorganize, and after the reorganization is complete, (1) they may function at about the same level as before; (2) they may have been so weakened by the crisis that they function only at a reduced level—more often the case with vulnerable families; or (3) they may have been stimulated

by the crisis to reorganize in a way that makes them more effective—a characteristic of resilient families.

At the onset of a crisis, it may seem that no adjustment is required at all. A family may be confused by a member's alcoholism or numbed by the new or sudden stress and, in a process of denial, go about their business as if the event had not occurred. Gradually, however, the family begins to assimilate the reality of the crisis and to appraise the situation. Then the **period of family disorganization** sets in.

The Period of Disorganization

At this time, family organization slumps, habitual roles and routines become nebulous and confused, and members carry out their responsibilities with less enthusiasm. Although not always, this period of disorganization may be "so severe that the family structure collapses and is immobilized for a time. The family can no longer function. For a time no one goes to work; no one cooks or even wants to eat; and no one performs the usual family tasks" (Boss 1997, p. 1). Typically, and legitimately, family members may begin to feel angry and resentful.

Expressive relationships within the family change, some growing stronger and more supportive perhaps, and others more distant. Sexual activity, one of the most sensitive aspects of a relationship, often changes sharply and may temporarily cease. Parent–child relations may also change.

Relations between family members and their outside friends, as well as the extended kin network, may also change during this phase. Some families withdraw from all outside activities until the crisis is over; as a result, they may become more private or isolated than before the crisis began. As we shall see, withdrawing from friends and kin often weakens rather than strengthens a family's ability to meet a crisis.

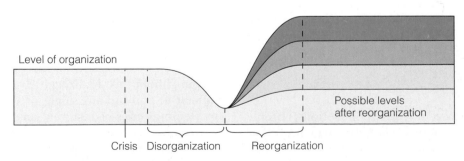

FIGURE 15.3 Patterns of family adaptation to crisis.
Source: Adapted from Hansen and Hill 1964, p. 810.

At the **nadir**, or low point, of family disorganization, conflicts may develop over how the situation should be handled. For example, in families with a seriously ill member, the healthy members are likely either to overestimate or to underestimate the sick person's incapacitation and, accordingly, to act either more sympathetically or less tolerantly than the ill member wants (Conner 2000; Pyke and Bengston 1996). Reaching the optimal balance between nurturance and encouragement of the ill person's self-sufficiency may take time, sensitivity, and judgment.

During the period of disorganization, family members face the decision of whether to express or to smother any angry feelings they may have. As Chapter 13 points out, people can express their anger either in primarily bonding ways or in alienating ways. Expressing anger as blame will usually sharpen hostilities; laying blame on a family member for the difficulties being faced will not help to solve the problem and will only make things worse (P. Stratton 2003). At the same time, when family members opt to repress their anger, they risk allowing it to smolder, thus creating tension and increasingly strained relations. How members cope with conflict at this point will greatly influence the family's overall level of recovery.

Recovery

Once the crisis hits bottom, things often begin to improve. Either by trial and error or (when possible) by thoughtful planning, family members usually arrive at new routines and reciprocal expectations. They are able to look past the time of crisis to envision a return to some state of normalcy and to reach some agreements about the future.

Some families do not recover intact, as today's high divorce rate illustrates. Divorce (or the breakup of a cohabiting relationship) can be seen both as an adjustment to family crisis and as a family crisis in itself (Figure 15.4).

Other families stay together, although at lower levels of organization or mutual support than before the crisis. As Figure 15.3 shows, some families remain at a very low level of recovery, with members continuing to interact much as they did at the low point of disorganization. This interaction often involves a series of circles in which one member is viewed as deliberately causing the trouble and the others blame that individual and nag him or her to stop. This is true of many families in which one member is an alcoholic or otherwise chemically dependent, an overeater, or a chronic gambler, for example. Rather than directly expressing anger about being blamed and nagged, the offending member persists in the unwanted behavior.

Some families match the level of organization they had maintained before the onset of the crisis, whereas others rise to levels above what they experienced before the crisis (M. McCubbin 1995). For example, a family member's attempted suicide might motivate all family members to reexamine their relationships.

Reorganization at higher levels of mutual support may also result from less-dramatic crises. For instance, partners in midlife might view boredom with their relationship as a challenge and revise their lifestyle to add some zest—by traveling more or planning to spend more time together rather than in activities with the whole family, for example.

Now that we have examined the course of family crises, we will turn our attention to a theoretical model specifically designed to explain family stress, crisis, adjustment, and adaptation.

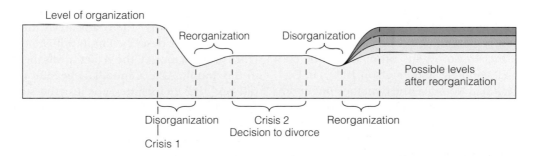

FIGURE 15.4 Divorce as a family adjustment to crisis and as a crisis in itself.

Homeless families, mostly single mothers with children, constitute about one-third of the U.S. homeless population. Up to one-half of these families became homeless when the mothers fled abusive relationships. Other causes include job loss, eviction due to inability to pay rent or other conflicts with landlords, mother's or partner's substance abuse, and conflict with relatives or friends with whom the family was staying prior to becoming homeless (Torquati 2002).

Social scientist Elizabeth Lindsey (1998) analyzed interviews from seventeen Georgia and North Carolina mothers who had stayed in a homeless shelter with at least one of their children. Participants ranged in age from nineteen to fifty-two. Twelve were African American, and five were white. The families had from one to five children, between six months and sixteen years of age;

they had stayed in shelters between two weeks and eight months.

Lindsey noted that although these families had many past and present stressors, they also evidenced important strengths: pride, determination, a positive orientation, clarity of focus, commitment to parenting and other personal relationships, finding purpose in helping others, and a moral structure used to guide their lives: "It is also important to note that women who enter shelters with their children have managed to maintain enough stability to avoid having the children placed into foster care" (p. 244).

These families obviously benefited from being sheltered. However, shelter life itself often added stress, partly because the shelters usually held families to the same rules as singles. For example, the mothers objected strongly to requirements that they and their chil-

dren leave the shelter during the day, regardless of the weather: "How can this mother go out and look for a job or even look for a place to live when she's got three kids, and it's raining, or it's cold?" (p. 248).

Other problematic rules involved bedtimes, mealtimes, keeping their children quiet, and the requirement that children be with their parents at all times:

> They have a bedtime for the children, 8:00. . . . And if you can't get them in the bed, they require that you put them in the room if you can, and keep them occupied until they're sleepy. Which, you know, they need those rules with that many people. (p. 249)

Other stressors occurred as well. One mother told of a single male resident's "getting fresh with my older girl"

Family Stress, Crisis, Adjustment, and Adaptation: A Theoretical Model

Several decades ago, sociologist Reuben Hill proposed the ABC-X family crisis model, and much of what we've already noted about stressors is based on the research of Hill and his colleagues (R. Hill 1958; Hansen and Hill 1964). The **ABC-X model** states that **A** (the stressor event) interacting with **B** (the family's ability to cope with a crisis, their crisis-meeting resources) interacting with **C** (the family's appraisal of the stressor event) produces **X** (the crisis) (see Sussman, Steinmetz, and Peterson 1999). In Figure 15.5 on page 402, A would be the demands put upon a family, B would be the family's capabilities—resources and coping behaviors—and C would be the meanings that the family creates to explain the demands.

As Figure 15.5 illustrates, families continuously balance the demands put upon them against their capabilities to meet those demands. When demands become

heavy, families engage their resources to meet them while also appraising their situation—that is, they create meanings to explain and address their demands. When demands outweigh resources, family adjustment is in jeopardy, and a family crisis may develop. Through the course of a family crisis, some level of adaptation occurs (Patterson 2002b).

Stressor Pile-Up

Building on the ABC-X model, Hamilton McCubbin and Joan Patterson (1983) advanced the *double* ABC-X model to better describe family adjustment to crises. In Hill's original model, the *A* factor was the stressor event; in the double ABC-X model, *A* becomes *Aa*, or "family pile-up." *Pile-up* includes not just the stressor but also previously existing family strains and future hardships induced by the stressor event.

When a family experiences a new stressor, prior strains that may have gone unnoticed—or been barely managed—come to the fore. Prior strains might be any residual family tensions that linger from unresolved

(p. 249). Another mother expressed concern about changes in her son:

> My 12-year-old, oh gosh! He was so depressed. . . . His personality changed, and I had to learn how to deal with that. And it was so tough because he had always been such a sweet child . . . but his attitude became rotten. He was fed up with the rules. . . . (p. 250)

However, Lindsey found that perhaps the most troublesome aspect of shelters for the mothers was the prohibition against any type of corporal punishment: "Parents were expected to make their children behave but were not allowed to use their main form of discipline. At times, shelter staff corrected the mothers in front of their children, undermining their parental authority" (p. 248).

Some mothers described the stress they felt. One said she was in a daze. . . . I really didn't know where to turn. My nerves were gone. I couldn't sleep. I was about afraid to close my eyes, and I didn't feel safe when I first got there. . . . I had a 3-year-old, and I was like panicking. "What am I going to do?" (p. 249)

Beginning in their own childhoods, these mothers' stresses had gradually piled up.

Lindsey's findings were not all negative. Many of the younger children liked the security and attention they received from shelter residents and staff. Some mothers said that they and their children had grown closer at the shelter. Nevertheless, this research shows that shelter life itself can add to stressor pile-up for homeless families.

Suggestions for lessening family stress while at homeless shelters include allowing parents as much control as possible over bedtimes and eating arrangements, as well as providing offspring day care and keeping shelters open to families during the day. Furthermore, since "punitive approaches toward parents who rely on corporal punishment do not necessarily prevent parents from spanking," shelter staff need to be supportive in helping parents learn and use other forms of discipline (Lindsey 1998, p. 251; see also Torquati 2002).

Source: "The Impact of Homelessness and Shelter Life on Family Relationships," by Elizabeth W. Lindsey, *Family Relations, 47 (3): 243–52.* Copyright © 1998 by the National Council on Family Relations.

---

stressors or are inherent in ongoing family roles, such as being a single parent or a spouse in a two-career family. For example, ongoing-but-ignored family conflict may intensify when parents or stepparents must deal with a child who is underachieving in school, has joined a criminal gang, or is abusing drugs. As another example, financial and time constraints typical of single-parent families may assume crisis-inducing importance with the addition of a stressor, such as caring for an injured child.

An example of future demands precipitated by the stressor event would be a parent's losing a job, a stressor followed by unpaid bills. A study about parenting a disabled child found that the child's rehabilitation often led to parental job changes, severe financial problems, and sleep deprivation (Rogers and Hogan 2003; S. Porterfield 2002).

The pile-up concept of family-life demands, or stressors (similar to the concept of stressor overload described earlier), is important in predicting family adjustment over the course of family life. Social scientists believe that, generally, an excessive number of life changes and strains occurring within a brief time, perhaps a year, are more likely to disrupt a family.[1] Put another way, pile-up renders a family more vulnerable to emerging from a

[1]The Holmes–Rahe Social Readjustment Rating Scale, developed in 1967, provides a way to measure an individual adult's or child's stress level. Many of the scale items, such as death of a spouse, death of a parent, divorce, divorce of parents, marital separation, death of a close family member, marriage, marital reconciliation, change in health of a family member, pregnancy, fathering an unwed pregnancy, gaining a new family member, child leaving home, and trouble with in-laws, are actually family stressors and result not only in individual stress but also in family stress or crisis.

The authors rank various life events according to how difficult they are to cope with. For instance, death of a spouse, the most stressful life event on the adult scale, is equivalent to 100 *life change units.* Getting married, the most stressful life event on the scale designed for children age eighteen and under, is equivalent to 101 life change units. For adults, divorce is equivalent to 73 life change units, while trouble with in-laws is equivalent to 29. For children, divorce of parents is equivalent to 77 life change units, while hospitalization of a parent is equivalent to 55 life change units and loss of a job by a parent is equivalent to 46. You can find the Holmes–Rahe Social Readjustment Rating Scale on the Internet.

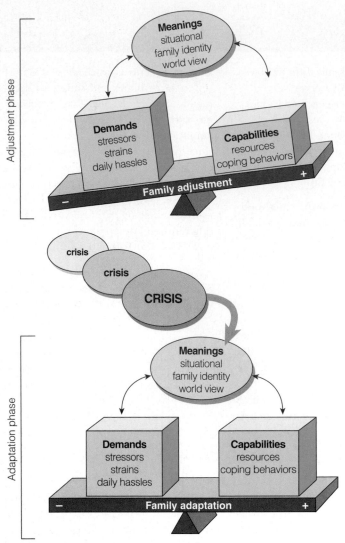

FIGURE 15.5 Family Stress, Crisis, Adjustment, and Adaptation. Families continuously balance the demands put upon them against their capabilities to meet those demands. When demands become heavy, families engage their resources to meet them while also appraising their situation—that is, they create meanings to explain and address their demands. When demands outweigh resources, family adjustment is in jeopardy, and a family crisis may develop. Through the course of a family crisis, some level of adaptation occurs (Patterson 2002b).

Source: From Joan M. Patterson, "Integrating Family Resilience and Family Stress Theory," *Journal of Marriage and Family* 64 (2), p. 351. Reprinted by permission of Blackwell Publishing.

Note: Previously adapted from "Families Experiencing Stress: The Family Adjustment and Adaptation Response Model," by J. M. Patterson, 1988, *Family Systems Medicine* 6 (2), pp.202–37. Copyright © 1988 by Families, Systems & Health, Inc.

crisis at a lower level of effectiveness (McCubbin and McCubbin 1989).

We have examined various characteristics of stressor demands put upon a family. Next we will look at how the family makes meaning of, defines, or appraises those demands. We'll look at crisis-meeting resources and coping behaviors after that.

Appraising the Situation

From an interactionist perspective, the meaning that a family gives to a situation—how family members appraise, define, or interpret a crisis-precipitating event—can have as much or more to do with the family's ability to cope as does the character of the event itself (McCubbin and McCubbin 1991; Patterson 2002a, 2002b). For example, a study of families faced with caring for an aging family member (Pyke and Bengston 1996) found that some families felt more ambivalent or negative about having to provide care than did others, who saw caregiving as one more chance to bring the family together.

Several factors influence how family members define a stressful situation.[2] One is the nature of the stressor itself. For instance, sometimes in the case of ambiguous loss, families do not know whether a missing family member will ever return or whether a chronically ill or a chemically dependent family member will ever recover. Being in limbo this way is very difficult.

In addition to the nature of the stressor itself, a second factor is the degree of hardship or the kind of problems the stressor creates. Temporary unemployment is less a hardship than is a layoff in an area where there are few job prospects or a loss of a job at age fifty-five. Being victimized by a crime is always a stressful event, but coming home to find one's house burglarized may be less traumatic than being robbed at gunpoint.

A third factor is the family's previous successful experience with crises, particularly those of a similar nature. If family members have had experience in nursing a sick member back to health, they will feel less bewildered and more capable of handling a new, similar situation. Believing from the start that demands are surmountable, and that collectively the family has the ability to cope, may make adjustment somewhat easier (Pitzer 1997b; Wells, Widmer, and McCoy 2004). Family

---

[2] Although we are discussing the family's definition of the situation, it is important to remember the possibility that each family member experiences a stressful event in a unique way: "These unique meanings may enable family members to work together toward crisis resolution or they may prevent resolution from being achieved. That is, an individual's response to a stressor may enhance or impede the family's progress toward common goals, may embellish or reduce family cohesion, may encourage or interfere with collective efficacy" (Walker 1985, pp.832–33).

This family survived Hurricane Katrina and has begun to rebuild in New Orleans. This crisis certainly qualifies as causing stressor overload. Nevertheless, as much as possible, families with strong crisis-meeting resources appraise their situation in a way that encourages them to find the potential positive amid their troubles and work together so as not to make the demands that they are confronting even worse. Later on the afternoon that this photo was taken, the family planned to attend a Mardi Gras parade. You can see that the little girl is already wearing her Mardi Gras beads.

members' interpretations of a crisis event shape their responses in subsequent stages of the crisis. Meanwhile, the family's crisis-meeting resources affect its appraisal of the situation.

A fourth, related factor that influences a family's appraisal of a stressor involves the adult family members' legacies from their childhoods (Carter and McGoldrick 1988).[3] For example, growing up in a family that tended to define anything that went wrong as a catastrophe or a "punishment" from God might lead the family to define the current stressor more negatively. On the other hand, growing up in a family that tended to define demands simply as problems to be solved or as challenges might mean defining the current stressor more positively.

Crisis-Meeting Resources

A family's crisis-meeting capabilities—resources and coping behaviors—constitute its ability to prevent a stressor

[3] In their model of family stress and crisis, social workers Betty Carter and Monica McGoldrick (1988) see "family patterns, myths, secrets [and] legacies" as *vertical stressors*—because they come down from previous generations. These authors call the type of stressors that we have been discussing in this chapter *horizontal stressors* (p. 9).

from creating severe disharmony or disruption. We might categorize a family's crisis-meeting resources into three types: personal/individual, family, and community.

The personal resources of each family member (for example, intelligence, problem-solving skills, and physical and emotional health) are important. At the same time, the family *as family* or family system has a level of resources, including bonds of trust, appreciation, and support (family harmony); sound finances and financial management and health practices; positive communication patterns; healthy leisure activities; and overall satisfaction with the family and quality of life (Boss 2002; Patterson 2002b).

Family rituals are resources (Boss 2004). A study of alcoholic families found that adult children of alcoholics who came from families that had maintained family dinner and other rituals (or who married into families that did) were less likely to become alcoholics themselves (Bennett, Wolin, and Reiss 1988; Goleman 1992).

And, of course, *money* is a family resource (Seaton and Taylor 2003). For instance, the breadwinner's losing his or her job is less difficult to deal with when the family has substantial savings (A. Bryant 2001). In a qualitative study among U.S. working-poor rural families, one respondent explained that "I had absolutely nothing after I paid my bills to feed my kids. I scrounged just so that they could eat something, and I had to short change my landlord so that I could feed them, too, which put me behind in rent." Another said, "I felt overwhelmed and stressed because every time I get paid, I just don't have money for everything . . . because I have two . . . children [with medical problems]" (Dolan, Braun, and Murphy 2003, p. F14).

The family ecology perspective alerts us to the fact that *community resources* are consequential as well. Increasingly aware of this, medical and family practice professionals have in recent years designed a wide variety of community-based programs to help families adapt to medically related family demands, such as a partner's cancer or a child's diabetes, congenital heart disease, and other illnesses (P. Peck 2001; Tak and McCubbin 2002). In fact, in many instances family members have become community activists, working to create community resources to aid them in dealing with a particular family stressor or crisis. Parents have been "a driving force" in shaping services and laws related to individuals with mental retardation (Lustig 1999). As a second example, parent groups helped to pass the Americans with Disabilities Act (Turnbull and Turnbull 1997).

Vulnerable versus Resilient Families
Ultimately the family either successfully adapts or becomes exhausted and vulnerable to continuing crisis. Family systems may be high or low in vulnerability, a situation that affects how positively the family faces demands; this enables us to predict or explain the family's poor or good adjustment to stressor events (Patterson 2002b).

A positive outlook, spiritual values, supportive communication, adaptability, public services, and informal social support—all these, along with an extended family and community resources, are factors in family resilience, or meeting a crisis creatively.

More prone to poor adjustment from crisis-provoking events, vulnerable families evidence a lower sense of common purpose and feel less in control of what happens to them. They may cope with problems by showing diminished respect or understanding for one another. Vulnerable families are also less experienced in shifting responsibilities among family members and are more resistant to compromise. There is little emphasis on family routines or predictable time together (McCubbin and McCubbin 1991).

From a social psychological point of view, resilient families tend to emphasize mutual acceptance, respect, and shared values. Family members rely on one another for support. Generally accepting difficulties, they work together to solve problems with members, feeling that they have input into major decisions (McCubbin et al. 2001). It may be apparent that these behaviors are less difficult to foster when a family has sufficient economic resources. The next section discusses factors that help families to meet crises creatively.

Meeting Crises Creatively

Meeting crises creatively means that after reaching the nadir in the course of the crisis, the family rises to a level of reorganization and emotional support that is equal to or higher than that which preceded the crisis. For some families—for example, those experiencing the crisis of domestic violence—breaking up may be the most beneficial (and perhaps the only workable) way to reorganize. Other families stay together and find ways to meet crises effectively. What factors differentiate resilient families that reorganize creatively from those that do not?

A Positive Outlook

In times of crisis, family members make many choices, one of the most significant of which is whether to blame one member for the hardship. Casting blame, even when it is deserved, is less productive than viewing the crisis primarily as a challenge (P. Stratton 2003).

Put another way, the more that family members can strive to maintain a positive outlook, it helps a person or a family to meet a crisis constructively (Thomason 2005). Electing to work toward developing more open, supportive family communication—especially in times of conflict—also helps individuals and families meet crises constructively (Stinnett, Hilliard, and Stinnett 2000). Families that meet a crisis with an accepting attitude, focusing on the positive aspects of their lives, do better than those that feel they have been singled out for misfortune. For example, many chronic illnesses have downward trajectories, so both partners may realistically expect that the ill mate's health will only grow worse. Some couples are remarkably able to adjust to this, "either because of immense closeness to each other or because they are grateful for what little life and relationship remains" (Strauss and Glaser 1975, p. 64).

Spiritual Values and Support Groups

"Spirituality, however the family defines it, can be a strong comfort during crisis" (Thomason 2005, p. F11). Some researchers have found that strong religious faith is related to high family cohesiveness (Stinnett 2003) and helps people manage demands or crises, partly because it provides a positive way of looking at suffering (Wiley, Warren, and Montanelli 2002). A spiritual outlook may be fostered in many ways, including through Buddhist, Christian, Muslim, and other religious or philosophical traditions. However, a sense of spirituality—that is, a conviction that there is some power or entity greater than oneself—need not be associated with membership in any organized religion. Self-help groups, such as Alcoholics Anonymous or Al-Anon for families of alcoholics, incorporate a "higher power" and can help people take a positive, spiritual approach to family crises.

Open, Supportive Communication

Families whose members interact openly and supportively meet crises more creatively (Orthner, Jones-Sanpei, and Williamson 2004). For one thing, free-flowing communication opens the way to understanding (Thomason 2005). As an example, research shows that expressions of support from parents help children to cope with daily stress (Valiente et al. 2004). As another example, the better-adjusted husbands with multiple sclerosis believed that even though they were embarrassed when they fell in public or were incontinent, they could freely discuss these situations with their families and feel confident that their families understood (P. Power 1979). And as a final example, talking openly and supportively with an elderly parent who is dying about what that parent wants—in terms of medical treatment, hospice, and burial—can help (Fein 1997).

Knowing how to indicate the specific kind of support that one needs is important at stressful times. For example, differentiating between—and knowing how to request—just listening as opposed to problem-solving discussion can help reduce misunderstandings among family members—and between family members and others as well (Stinnett, Hilliard, and Stinnett 2000; Tannen 1990). Families whose communication is characterized by a sense of humor, as well as a sense of family history, togetherness, and common values, evidence greater resilience in the face of stress or crisis (Thomason 2005).

Adaptability

Adaptable families are better able to respond effectively to crises (Boss 2002). And families are more adaptable when they are more democratic and when conjugal power is fairly egalitarian. In families in which one member wields authoritarian power, the whole family suffers if the authoritarian leader does not make effective decisions during a crisis—and allows no one else to move into a position of leadership (McCubbin and McCubbin 1994). A partner who feels comfortable only as the family leader may resent his or her loss of power, and this resentment may continue to cause problems when the crisis is over.

Family adaptability in aspects other than leadership is also important (Burr, Klein, and McCubbin 1995). Families that can adapt their schedules and use of space, their family activities and rituals, and their connections with the outside world to the limitations and possibilities

Many—although not all—turn to their extended family for social support in times of stress. This may be less true than researchers once thought, but kin may provide emotional support, monetary support, and practical help.

© Image100/Jupiter Images

posed by the crisis will cope more effectively than families that are committed to preserving sameness. For example, a study of mothers of children with developmental disabilities found that mothers who worked part time had less stress than those who worked full time or were not employed at all (Gottlieb 1997). As another example, a study of married parents caring for a disabled adult child found that when their division of labor was adapted to feel fair, both parents experienced greater marital satisfaction and less stress (Essex and Hong 2005).

Informal Social Support

It's easier to cope with crises when a person doesn't feel alone (see, for example, Bowen et al. 2003; Tak and McCubbin 2002). It may go without saying that spouses do better when they feel supported or validated by their partners (Franks et al. 2002). Families may find helpful support in times of crisis from kin, good friends, neighbors, and even acquaintances such as work colleagues. Analysis of data from the National Study of Black Americans found that in times of crisis many of them received support from fellow church members (Taylor, Lincoln, and Chatters 2005). These various relationships provide a wide array of help—from lending money in financial emergencies to helping with child care to just being there for emotional support. Research on families in poverty shows that, although the informal social support that they receive rarely helps to lift them out of poverty, it does help them to cope with their economic circumstances (Henly, Danziger, and Offer 2005).

Even continued contact with more-casual acquaintances may be helpful, as often they offer useful information, along with enhancing one's sense of community (Orthner, Jones-Sanpei, and Williamson 2004). And, of course, the Internet offers information and support for virtually any stressor conceivable. A qualitative study that recruited participants by means of web pages asked the seventy-seven respondents who answered an Internet-based survey about the advantages and disadvantages of Internet support, compared with face-to-face social networks (Colvin et al. 2004). Respondents mentioned two main Internet advantages—anonymity and the ease of connecting with others in the same situation despite geographical distance. Disadvantages related to lack of physical contact: "No one can hold your hand or give you a Kleenex when the tears are flowing" (p. 53).

An Extended Family

Sibling relationships and other kin networks can be a valuable source of support in times of crisis (J. Johnson 2000; Weaver, Coleman, and Ganong 2003). Grand-parents, aunts, uncles, or other relatives may help with health crises or with more common family stressors, like running errands or helping with child care (Milardo 2005). Families going through divorce often fall back on relatives for practical help and financial assistance. In other crises, kin provide a shoulder to lean on—someone who may be asked for help without causing embarrassment—which can make a crucial difference in a family's ability to recover.

Although extended families as residential groupings represent a small proportion of family households, kin ties remain salient (Furstenberg 2005). One aspect of all this that is beginning to get more research attention involves reciprocal friendship and support among adult siblings (White and Riedmann 1992; Spitze and Trent 2006; Weaver, Coleman, and Ganong 2003). In times of family stress or crisis, new immigrants (as well as African Americans) may rely on **fictive kin**—relationships based not on blood or marriage but rather on "close friendship ties that replicate many of the rights and obligations usually associated with family ties" (Ebaugh and Curry 2000).

We need to be cautious, though, not to overestimate or romanticize the extended family as a resource. For instance, a study that compared mothers who had children with more than one father found that the women received less support from their kin networks than did single mothers who did not have multipartnered births. The researchers concluded that "smaller and denser kin networks seem to be superior to broader but weaker kin ties in terms of perceived instrumental support" (Harknett and Knab 2007). Among the poor, extended kin may not have the resources to offer much practical help (Henly, Danziger, and Offer 2005).

Moreover, along with some previous research, a small study of low-income families living in two trailer parks along the mid-Atlantic coast concluded that "low-income families do not share housing and other resources within a flexible and fluctuating network of extended and fictive kin as regularly as previously assumed." Extended family members may not get along, or individuals may be too embarrassed to ask their kin for help. One woman explained that neither her parents nor any one of her five siblings could help her because "they all have problems of their own." A Hispanic mother told the interviewer, "I know you've probably heard that Hispanic families are close-knit, well, hmmph! No, we take care of ourselves" (Edwards 2004, p. 523). Then, too, among some recent immigrant groups, such as Asians or Hispanics, expectations of the extended family may clash with the more-individualistic values of Americanized family members (Kamo and Zhou 1994).

Community Resources

The success with which families meet the demands placed upon them also depends on the community resources available to help (Trask et al. 2005).

> Community-based resources are all of those characteristics, competencies and means of persons, groups and institutions outside the family which the family may call upon, access, and use to meet their demands. This includes a whole range of services, such as medical and health care services. The services of other institutions in the family's . . . environment, such as schools, churches, employers, etc.[,] are also resources to the family. At the more macro level, government policies that enhance and support families can be viewed as community resources. (McCubbin and McCubbin 1991, p. 19)

Among others, community resources include social workers and family welfare agencies; foster child care; church programs that provide food, clothing, or shelter to poor or homeless families; twelve-step and other support programs for substance abusers and their families; programs for crime or abuse victims and their families; support groups for people with serious diseases such as cancer or AIDS, for parents and other relatives of disabled or terminally ill children, or for caregivers of disabled family members or those with cancer or Alzheimer's disease; and community pregnancy prevention and/or parent education programs. An Oregon study of non-Hispanic white and Hispanic teen mothers found that a government-funded home-visitation program increased family functioning, especially for the Hispanics in this sample (Middlemiss and McGuigan 2005).

A unique example of parent education programs, mandated by the U.S. government in 1995, involves federal prison inmates. Parent inmates learn general skills, such as how to talk to their child. They also learn ways to create positive parent–child interaction from prison—such as games they can play with a child through the mail—as well as suggestions on what to do when returning home upon release (Coffman and Markstrom-Adams 1995). ("Issues for Thought: When a Parent Is in Prison" on page 408 further describes some of these programs.)

A more familiar community resource is marriage and family counseling. Counseling can help families after a crisis occurs; it can also help when families foresee a family change, or future new demands. For instance, a couple might visit a counselor when expecting or adopting a baby, when deciding about work commitments and family needs, when the youngest child is about to leave home, or when a partner is about to retire. Increasingly, counselors and social workers emphasize empowering families toward the goal of enhanced resilience—that

is, emphasizing and building upon a family's strengths (Power 2004; F. Walsh 2002a, 2004). Family counseling is not just for relationships that are in trouble but is also a resource that can help to enhance family dynamics (see Appendix H, available on the Internet).

We also need to note here the countless resources available online. Indeed, families with an infinite variety of stressors—from involuntary infertility (www.resolve.org); to having a disabled child (www.supportforfamilies.org); to experiencing the death of a child (http://compassionatefriends.org); to having a family member in prison (http://prisontalk.com)—can participate in web-based virtual communities and access information from experts as well as from others who are experiencing similar family demands. Unfortunately, many families feel stigmatized by the stressors that they are experiencing (such as epilepsy, money problems, or a diagnosis of mental illness, for example) and therefore are reluctant to seek informal and community support (Arditti 2003; Edwards 2004; Hinshaw 2003; Seaburn and Erba 2002). Because people can seek help anonymously, online resources may be especially useful (Colvin et al. 2004).

Crisis: Disaster or Opportunity?

A family crisis is a turning point in the course of family living that requires members to change how they have been thinking and acting (McCubbin and McCubbin 1991, 1994). We tend to think of *crisis* as synonymous with *disaster*, but the word comes from the Greek for *decision*. Although we cannot control the occurrence of many crises, we can decide how to cope with them.

Most crises—even the most unfortunate ones—have the potential for positive as well as negative effects. For example, Professor Joan Patterson, a recognized expert in the field of family stress, has observed that many parents who are raising children with "complex and intense" medical needs

> seem to find new meaning for their life. Having a child with such severe medical needs and such a tenuous hold on life shatters the expectations of most parents for how life is supposed to be. It leads to a search for meaning as a way to accept their circumstances. When families get to this place, they not only accept their child and their family's life, but they often experience a kind of gratitude that those of us who have never faced this level of hardship can't really understand. (2002a, p. F7)

Whether a family emerges from a crisis with a greater capacity for supportive family interaction depends at least partly on how family members choose to define

Some children have parents who are in jail or prison—a demoralizing family stressor event, coupled with boundary ambiguity. Incarceration rates began to increase dramatically in the 1970s and have risen even more sharply since 1990 (Arditti 2003). Rates are especially high for young minority men but have increased more rapidly for women than for men (Mumola 2000).

"The impact of strict and severe sentencing has meant that increasing numbers of children are affected by the imprisonment of their parents" (Enos 2001, p. 1). Estimates are that about a million and a half children have parents behind bars, and about half of those children had lived with their incarcerated parent. Some 78 percent of women prisoners and 64 percent of men are parents. But there is a crucial gender difference. Prior to imprisonment, 79 percent of mothers were living with their children compared to 53 percent of fathers, and mothers were usually the primary caretakers (Federal Resource Center for Children of Prisoners 2004; Mumola 2000).

While mothers were in prison, 35 percent of white children, 24 percent of Hispanic children, and 19 percent of African American children lived with their fathers. Grandparents cared for 57 percent of black children, 55 percent

of Hispanic children, and 41 percent of white children. White children were more likely to be in nonfamily foster care (see Chapter 11's discussion on foster parenting) than were African American or Hispanic children (13 percent compared to 6 percent). This may be because black and Hispanic communities have had more of a tradition of shared care of children (e.g., Stack 1974), a situation facilitating making arrangements that place children with adult relatives, often grandparents (Poehlmann 2005). White parenthood has been more "privatized," so white mothers have fewer resources in a crisis situation (Enos 2001, especially p. 38).

Children's visiting an incarcerated parent can be expensive and otherwise difficult to arrange, because prisons are often far from the homes of children (McManus 2006). One study found that half of children of women prisoners did not visit at all during their mother's incarceration. However, including phone calls and letters, 78 percent of mothers and 62 percent of fathers had at least monthly contact with children (Mumola 2000).

Then, too, the children's caregivers often

feel compelled to lie about their loved one's whereabouts. If the children are young, their mother may explain the father's absence

by saying that "Daddy's away on a long trip" or "He's working on a job in another state." One caregiver . . . explained to her nephews that their father was away at "super-hero school." Older children who know the truth may feel that they need to be careful not to discuss it at school or with friends. (Arditti 2003, p. F15)

More and more, policy makers have realized that disrupted family ties have a severe and negative impact on the next generation (Arditti 2003; Poehlmann 2005). Consequently, a number of correctional systems, including the Federal Bureau of Prisons, have developed visitation programs to facilitate parent–child contact. Many correctional facilities have returned to an earlier practice of permitting babies born in prison to remain with their mothers for a time. Although visitation programs were initially oriented solely to mothers, prisons have more recently developed programs for fathers as well (Amnesty International 1999; Enos 2001). The National Fatherhood Initiative has developed an educational program, called "Inside/Out Dad," for imprisoned fathers (McManus 2006).

Visitation programs try to normalize parent–child contact. The Nebraska women's correctional facility, for

the crisis. A major theme of this text is that, given the opportunities and limitations posed by society, people create their families and relationships based on the choices they make. Families whose members choose to be flexible in roles and leadership meet crises creatively.

However, even though they have options and choices, family members do not have absolute control over their

lives (Coontz 1997b; Kleber et al. 1997). Many family troubles are really the results of public issues. For example, the serious family disorganization that results from poverty is as much a social as a private problem (Trask et al. 2005). Also, most American families have some handicaps in meeting crises creatively. The typical American family is under a high level of stress at all times. Providing family members with emotional secu-

Having a family member in prison or jail is a crisis faced by a small but growing number of families today. Family stress and adjustment experts tell us that virtually all family crises have some potential for positive as well as negative effects. Can you think of any possible positive effects in this case? What community supports might help this family? What might be some alternatives to incarcerating parents who have been actively involved in raising their children?

wire fences and uniformed guards at the Indiana Women's Prison, where a summer day camp strives to preserve family ties among inmates and their loved ones. ("Prison Day Camp . . ." 2001)

Because there may be opposition to benefiting parents who have been convicted of crimes, it is important to note that the effects of parent-in-prison programs are to improve behavior in prison and to reduce recidivism after release, and to provide hope for the next generation: "It's about the children bonding with their parents [said one mother] . . . more so than the parents bonding with the children" (Goldyn 2001, p. 17)

We focus here on children's needs, but imprisonment demoralizes spouses and other family members as well and usually has a negative economic impact on all family members, not only when the prisoner has been an essential breadwinner but also due to costs associated with visiting the prisoner and making long-distance family telephone calls, among others (Arditti, Lambert-

Shute, and Joest 2003). Moreover, due to "the stigma of incarceration, families of prisoners receive little social support" (Arditti 2003, p. F15).

However, strong marital and family bonds appear to reduce children's negative behaviors (Poehlmann 2005), although "incarceration can undermine social bonds, [and] strain marital and other family relationships. . . . Without assistance for families disrupted by incarceration, the negative social effects of the penal system may aggravate the problems it was designed to solve" (Western and McLanahan 2000, p. 323). A family member's imprisonment is damaging to white-collar families as well as to those at lower social levels (Mason 2000, p. 325).

Policy analysts close to this topic argue that "[a]n over reliance on incarceration as punishment, particularly for nonviolent offenders, is not good family policy" (Arditti 2003, p. F17). They propose alternatives to incarceration, such as home confinement with work release. Meanwhile, some officials have begun to act on the idea that it is important for society to make family relations as good as they can be under the circumstances of incarceration and to aid with the parenting of the 2 percent of America's children who have parents in prison (Cose 2000; Enos 2001; Gardiner et al. 2002).

instance, permits overnight stays of five days for children age one through eight. In an Indiana women's prison day camp,

> [visiting] children snack on snow cones, line up for pony rides, and bond with their families. . . . But [these activities] can't hide razor-

rity in an impersonal and unpredictable society is difficult even when things are running smoothly. Family members are trying to do this while holding jobs and managing other activities and relationships.

Moreover, many family crises are more difficult to bear because communities lack adequate resources to help families meet them (Coontz 1997b; Mason, Skolnick, and Sugarman 1998). One response to this situa-

tion is to engage in community activism. For example, one couple, frustrated by the lack of organized community support available to them and their autistic child, founded Autism Speaks. One project of Autism Speaks is "to develop a central database of 10,000-plus children with autism that will provide, for the first time, the standardized medical records that researchers need to conduct accurate clinical trials" (S. Wright 2005, p. 47).

When families act collectively toward the goal of obtaining the resources they need for effectively meeting the demands placed upon them, family adjustment can be expected to improve overall.

Summary

- Throughout the course of family living, *all* families are faced with demands, transitions, and stress.

- Family stress is a state of tension that arises when demands test, or tax, a family's resources.

- A sharper jolt to a family than more-ordinary family stress, a family crisis encompasses three interrelated factors: (1) family change, (2) a turning point with the potential for positive and/or negative effects, and (3) a time of relative instability.

It's important to remember that not all stressors are unhappy ones. Happy events, such as moving into a new house, can be family stressors too.

- Demands, or stressors, are of various types and have varied characteristics. Generally, stressors that are expected, brief, and improving are less difficult to cope with.

- The predictable changes of individuals and families—parenthood, midlife transitions, post-parenthood, retirement, and widowhood and widowerhood—are all family transitions that may be viewed as stressors.

- A common pattern can be traced in families that are experiencing family crisis. Three distinct phases can be identified: (1) the stressor event that causes the crisis, (2) the period of disorganization that follows, and (3) the reorganizing or recovery phase after the family reaches a low point.

- The eventual level of reorganization a family reaches depends on a number of factors, including the type of stressor, the degree of stress it imposes, whether it is accompanied by other stressors, the family's appraisal or definition of the crisis situation, and the family's available resources.

- Meeting crises creatively means resuming daily functioning at or above the level that existed before the crisis.

- Several factors can help families meet family stress and/or crises more creatively: a positive outlook, spiritual values, the presence of support groups, high self-esteem, open and supportive communication within the family, adaptability, counseling, and the presence of a kin network.

Questions for Review and Reflection

1. Compare the concepts *family stress* and *family crisis*, giving examples and explaining how a family crisis differs from family stress.

2. Differentiate among the types of stressors. How are these single events different from stressor overload? How might living in poverty cause stressor overload?

3. Discuss issues addressed in other chapters of this text (e.g., work–family issues, parenting, divorce,

and remarriage) in terms of the ABC-X model of family crisis.

4. What factors help some families recover from crisis while others remain in the disorganization phase?

5. **Policy Question.** In your opinion, what, if anything, could/should government do to help families in stress? In crisis?

Key Terms

ABC-X model 400
boundary ambiguity 393
family crisis 390
family stress 390
family transitions 390
fictive kin 406

nadir of family disorganization 399
period of family disorganization 398
pile-up (stressor overload) 397
resilient families 398
stressor 392
vulnerable families 398

Online Resources

Companion Website for This Book

www.thomsonedu.com/sociology/lamanna

Visit the book companion website, where you will find flash cards, practice quizzes, Internet links, suggested readings, InfoTrac College Edition exercises, and more to help you study.

ThomsonNOW™ for Marriage and Family

Spend time on what you need to master rather than on information you already have learned. Take a pre-test for this chapter, and ThomsonNOW will generate a personalized study plan based on your results. The study plan will identify the topics you need to review and direct you to online resources such as videos, narrated learning modules, and interactive activities to help you master those topics. You can then take a post-test to help you determine the concepts you have mastered and what you will still need to work on. Try it out! Go to **www.thomsonedu.com/login** to sign in with an access code or to purchase access to this product.

Divorce: Before and After

16

Today's High U.S. Divorce Rate

Why Are Couples Divorcing?

Economic Factors

High Expectations of Marriage

Decreased Social, Legal, and Moral Constraints

Intergenerational Transmission of Divorce

Other Factors Associated with Divorce

Thinking about Divorce: Weighing the Alternatives

Marital Happiness, Barriers to Divorce, and Alternatives to the Marriage

"Would I Be Happier?"

Is Divorce a Temporary Crisis or a Permanent Stress?

Getting the Divorce

The Emotional Divorce

The Legal Divorce

The Community Divorce

The Economic Consequences of Divorce

Divorce, Single-Parent Families, and Poverty

Husbands, Wives, and Economic Divorce

Child Support

Divorce and Children

The Various Stresses for Children of Divorce

My Family: How It Feels When Parents Divorce

Custody Issues

A Closer Look at Family Diversity: A Noncustodial Mother Tells Her Story

Parent Education for Co-Parenting Ex-Spouses

His and Her Divorce

Her Divorce

His Divorce

Some Positive Outcomes?

Facts about Families: Postdivorce Pathways

Adult Children of Divorced Parents and Intergenerational Relationships

Should Divorce Be Harder to Get?

Is Divorce Necessarily Bad for Children?

Is Making Divorce Harder to Get a Realistic Idea?

Surviving Divorce

Social Policy Support for Children of Divorce

The Good Divorce

My Family: The Postdivorce Family as a Child-Raising Institution

As We Make Choices: Ten Keys to Successful Co-Parenting

Divorce has become a common experience in the United States for all social classes, age categories, and religious and ethnic groups. Over 40 percent of recent first marriages are likely to end in divorce (Teachman, Tedrow, and Hall 2006).[1] In this chapter, we'll examine factors that affect people's decisions to divorce, the experience itself, and ways the experience may be made less painful and become the prelude to the future, alone or in a new marriage. We'll also analyze why so many couples in our society decide to divorce and examine the debate over whether a divorce should be harder to get than it is today. We'll begin by looking at divorce rates in the United States, which are among the highest in the world (Mackay 2000, pp. 38–39).

Today's High U.S. Divorce Rate

The divorce rate started its upward swing in the nineteenth century (Amato and Irving 2006; Teachman, Tedrow, and Hall 2006, Figure 4.1).[2] The frequency of divorce increased throughout most of the twentieth century, as Figure 16.1 shows, with dips and upswings surrounding historical events such as the Great Depression and major wars. Between 1960 and its peak in 1979, the **refined divorce rate** more than doubled. Then the *refined divorce rate* declined throughout the nineties.

We can extend the time line to 2005 if we use the **crude divorce rate** (see Figure 16.2). The crude divorce rate has declined almost 30 percent since 1979 and has not been so low since around 1970 (Stevenson and Wolfers 2007; U.S. Census Bureau 2007a, Table 76).[3]

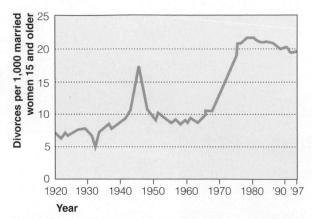

FIGURE 16.1 Divorces per 1,000 married women age fifteen and older in the United States, 1920–1997. This includes the latest data available for the refined divorce rate.

Source: U.S. National Center for Health Statistics 1990a, 1998, p. 3.

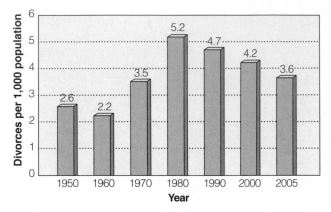

FIGURE 16.2 Divorces per 1,000 population, 1950 to 2005 (crude divorce rate).

Source: Adapted from U.S. Census Bureau 2003a, Table 83; U.S. National Center for Health Statistics 2006, Table A.

---

[1] For years estimates were that as many as 50 percent of first marriages would end in divorce. Experts now think marital dissolutions never reached 50 percent and likely never will (Hurley 2005 citing Rose Kreider of the U.S. Census Bureau). As of 2001, the estimated percentages of marriages ending in divorce for men and women now in their fifties were 41 percent for men and 39 percent for women (Kreider 2005).

[2] See Paul. R. Amato and Shelley Irving's chapter in *Handbook of Divorce and Relationship Dissolution* (2006) for a presentation of divorce rates, divorce law, and attitudes toward divorce in various eras of American history.

[3] The *refined divorce rate* is the number of divorces per 1,000 married women. The refined divorce rate compares the number of divorces to the number of women at risk of divorce (i.e., married women). It is a more valid indicator of the rate at which marriages are dissolved than the crude divorce rate.

The *crude divorce rate* is the number of divorces per 1,000 population. This rate includes portions of the population—children and the unmarried—who are not at risk for divorce. Despite its limitations, the crude divorce rate is used for comparisons over time because these data are the only long-term annual data available. The federal

The decline in divorce rates varies by social category. It has declined dramatically for women college graduates, while less-educated women have experienced virtually stable divorce rates (Martin 2006; Martin and Parashar 2006). This has produced what sociologist Steven Martin calls the **divorce divide** (in Hurley 2005). Predictions are that only 25 percent of college women who married in the early 1990s will divorce, while over 50 percent of less-educated women will experience a divorce.

government discontinued compilation of the refined divorce rate in the midnineties (Broome 1995).

In lieu of detailed government data, we also rely on national-sample surveys—including the Census Bureau's Current Population Survey—for individuals' reports of their current or cumulative experience of divorce. These divorce data are *not* collected annually, but less frequently.

Divorces occur relatively early in marriage. The median length of a first marriage that ends in divorce is about eight years. The proportion of divorces for couples married twenty years or more has increased, however (Kreider 2005).

Most observers (though not all)[4] conclude that the divorce rate has stabilized for the time being. Probably the most significant reason is the rise in the age at marriage. Fewer people are marrying at the vulnerable younger ages. Those who wait are likely to make better choices and to have the maturity and commitment to work through problems (Heaton 2002; Teachman, Tedrow, and Hall 2006).

Another reason is that better educated and better-off working couples have had the economic tide in their favor. According to public policy professor Andrew Cherlin, "'Families with two earners with good jobs have seen an improvement in their standard of living, which leads to less tension at home and lower probability of divorce'" (in "Divorce Rate" 2007). Also, some societal adjustment to women's employment and dual-earner families now seems to have occurred (Teachman, Tedrow, and Hall 2006). Spouses "are learning how to negotiate marriages based on less rigid gender roles than in the past" (historian Stephanie Coontz in "Divorce Rate" 2007).

Some credit marriage education programs funded by the federal government for falling divorce rates. For poorer families, who could not afford family counseling on their own, the programs may have helped couples manage their marital relationships (Crary 2007; "Divorce Rate" 2007). Moreover, some observers think they note an increased determination on the part of children of a divorcing generation to make their own marriages work (Crary 2007; Teachman, Tedrow, and Hall 2006).

On a less-enthusiastic note, demographers point out that divorce rates may have stabilized or declined because cohabitation has increased—if riskier relationships never become marriages, they never become divorces either. The fact remains that since around 1980, there has been an unanticipated decline in divorce rates. Nevertheless, divorce rates remain high by historical standards.

Historians also point to the fact that marriage can be dissolved by death as well as divorce. The longer lifespan attained in the twentieth century gives people who remain married more time together. Married couples are now much more likely to reach their fortieth anniversary than they were at the beginning of the twentieth

Deciding to divorce is difficult. Couples struggle with concerns about the impact on children and feelings about their past hopes and current unhappiness.

century, and children are less likely to be bereft of both parents (Skolnick 2001).

Still, the continuation of a high incidence of divorce contributes to the increased prevalence of single-parent families. Children's living arrangements vary greatly by race and ethnicity, as Figure 16.3 indicates. Asian and non-Hispanic white children are most apt to be living in two-parent families (with biological parents or a parent and stepparent). A majority of Hispanic, American Indian/Alaska Native, and Hawaiian/Pacific Islander children live with two parents, while just under a majority of black children are living in a single-mother household (Lugaila and Overturf 2004).

In summing up the statistics, we need to note that a high divorce rate does not mean that Americans have given up on marriage. It means that they find an unhappy marriage intolerable and hope to replace it with a

[4] See Schoen and Canudas-Romo 2006; Teachman, Tedrow and Hall 2006; and a comment by sociologist Andrew Cherlin in Hurley 2005, p. A7).

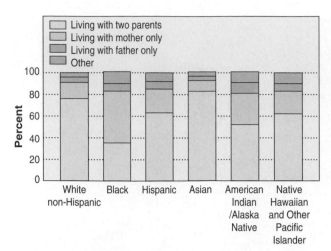

FIGURE 16.3 Living arrangements of children under eighteen by race/ethnicity, 2000. *Other* includes children who are living in the homes of relatives, in foster homes, or with other nonrelatives, or who are heads of their own households.

Source: Adapted from Lugaila and Overturf 2004, Table PHC-T-30b.

happier one. But a consequence of remarriages—which have higher divorce rates than first marriages—is an emerging trend of **redivorce.** Many who divorce—and their children—can expect several emotionally significant transitions in family structure and lifestyle. (The stability of remarriages is addressed in greater detail in Chapter 17.)

In a context of a high though declining divorce rate, along with a positive view of marriage, why is it that married couples do divorce?

Why Are Couples Divorcing?

Various factors can bind married couples together: economic interdependence; legal, social, and moral constraints; and the spouses' relationship itself. Yet the binding strength of some of these factors has lessened. "[A]ll Western [and some non-Western] countries have been moving toward a less familistic set of attitudes and toward greater individual investments in self, career, and . . . personal growth and goals" (Goode 1993, p. 81).

Economic Factors

Traditionally, as we've seen, the family was a self-sufficient productive unit. Survival was far more difficult outside of families, so members remained economically bound to one another. But today, because family members no longer need one another for basic necessities, they are freer to divorce than they once were (Coontz 1997b).

Families are still somewhat interdependent economically. As long as marriage continues to offer practical benefits, economic interdependence will help hold marriages together. The economic practicality of marriages varies according to several conditions.

Divorce and Social Class The higher the social class as defined in terms of education, income, and home ownership, the less likely a couple is to divorce. Income loss has been found to increase the likelihood of divorce (White and Rogers 2000). Both the stress of living with inadequate finances and the failure to meet expectations for economic or educational attainment seem to contribute to marital instability (White 1990). This situation, together with the tendency of low-income groups to marry relatively early, helps explain why less-well-off families have the highest rates of marital disruption, including divorce, separation, and desertion.

Wives in the Labor Force The upward trend of divorce and the upward trend of women in the labor force have accompanied each other historically. But are they causally connected?

Much research, though not all, indicates that wives' employment in itself makes no difference in marital quality (S. Rogers 1999; Sayer and Bianchi 2000). As Chapter 12 points out, whether husbands are supportive of their wives' employment and share in housework *does* relate to wives' marital satisfaction. *Conflict theorists* hypothesize and research confirms that marital conflict may increase if women go into the job market but their husbands do not take over an equitable share of the domestic tasks.

Although it may not affect marital quality, employment might nevertheless contribute to a divorce by giving an unhappily married woman the economic power, the increased independence, and the self-confidence to help her decide on divorce—called the **independence effect** (Sayer and Bianchi 2000). Some economists and sociologists posit that marriages are most stable and cohesive when husbands and wives have different and complementary roles—the husband the primary earner, while the wife bears and rears children and is the family's domestic and emotional specialist. Drawing on *exchange theory,* they assert that economic interdependency in marriage is a strong bond holding a marriage together (Becker 1991; Oppenheimer 1997).

But much recent research does *not* support the premise that specialized roles and economic interdependence are necessary to marital stability (Schoen et al. 2002). Moreover, there is an **income effect** to women's employment. Among low-income couples, a wife's earnings may actually help to hold the marriage together by counteracting the negative effects of poverty and economic insecurity on marital stability (Sayer and Bianchi 2000).

The effects of women's employment on marriage may depend on gender ideology. "[T]he sharp rise in the rates of divorce between 1965 and 1980 may have been at least partly a function of disjuncture between the expectations of spouses [at the time] and the reality of wives' labor market activities" (Teachman, Tedrow, and Hall 2006, p. 71). But for couples today, expectations of role sharing are common. To explore whether wives' employment has positive or negative effects on divorce proneness, researchers Sayer and Bianchi (2000) analyzed a national sample survey based on 3,339 female respondents interviewed around 1988 and again around 1994. When gender ideology and other variables related to likelihood of divorce were taken into account, there was no direct effect of women's employment on divorce. The desirability of the marriage relationship was a much more important factor in predicting divorce.

It is probably the case that there is considerable variety in the impact of women's employment and earnings on a marriage. It is also likely that the effect of wives' employment on marital stability is in transition (Teachman, Tedrow, and Hall 2006). Moreover, women's educational gains seem to be a stabilizing factor in marriage (Heaton 2002). Researchers Robert Brennan, Rosalind Barnett, and Karen Gareis (2001), in a study conducted in the Boston area, concluded that "times have changed and the theories may need to change" (p. 179)—role specialization is no longer so important to couple solidarity.

High Expectations of Marriage

Some observers attribute our high divorce rate to the view that Americans' expectations are too high. People increasingly expect marriage to provide a happy, emotionally supportive relationship. This is an essential family function, yet too-high expectations for intimacy between spouses may push the divorce rate upward (Glenn 1996; see also VanLaningham, Johnson, and Amato 2001). Research has found that couples whose expectations are more practical are more satisfied with their marriages than are those who expect completely loving and expressive relationships (Troll, Miller, and Atchley 1979; see also White and Booth 1991). Although many couples part for serious and specific reasons, others may do so because of unrealized expectations and general discontent.

Decreased Social, Legal, and Moral Constraints

"**Barriers to divorce** function to keep marriages intact even when attractiveness of the marital relationship is low and the attractiveness of alternatives to the relation-

ship is high" (Knoester and Booth 2000, p. 81). But the social constraints that once kept unhappy partners from separating operate less strongly now.

The official posture of many—though not all—religions in the United States has become less critical of divorce than in the past. **No-fault divorce** laws, which exist in all fifty states,[5] have eliminated legal concepts of guilt and are a symbolic representation of how our society now views divorce. But it does not appear that changes in the law have themselves led to more divorce (Wolfers 2006). Rather, legal change seems to have followed the trajectory of cultural attitudes and behavioral practice regarding divorce.[6]

To say that societal constraints against divorce no longer exist would be an overstatement; nevertheless, barriers have weakened. Knoester and Booth (2000) go so far as to conclude that "perhaps the concept of barriers has outlived its usefulness" (p. 98).

Attitudes Toward Marriage Virtually no respondents in a study of marital cohesion mentioned stigma or disapproval as a barrier to divorce (Previti and Amato 2003). Emphasis on the emotional relationship over the institutional benefits of marriage results in marriage being viewed as not necessarily permanent (Glenn 1996). Friedrich Engels, a colleague of Karl Marx and an early family theorist, noted: "If only the marriage based on love is moral, then also only the marriage in which love continues" (1942 [1884], p. 73). The changing nature of marriage is a worldwide phenomenon as far as the industrialized world is concerned (Giddens 2007).

Self-Fulfilling Prophesy Defining marriage as semipermanent can become a self-fulfilling prophecy, says Joshua Goldstein, a Princeton professor of sociology and public affairs: "'Expectations of high divorce rates

---

[5] Some authorities say that "most states" have no-fault divorce laws (Buehler 1995; Stevenson and Wolfers 2007), while others cite all fifty states (Nakonezny, Shull, and Rodgers 1995). There is a gray area in that some "no-fault" divorce laws may require a specific period of separation rather than just a declaration by one of the parties that the marriage is over (Hakim 2006). Moreover, some states have retained fault divorce alongside no-fault. In those states, a spouse may choose to file for divorce under a fault provision, alleging that the other partner has committed whatever statutory faults are relevant to the state's marital dissolution laws.

[6] Nakonezny, Shull, and Rodgers (1995) published an article purporting to prove that no-fault divorce laws have played a causative role in increasing divorce rates. Sociologist Norval Glenn (1997) responded with an effective critique of their methodology, concluding that "the adoption of no-fault divorce in itself had very little direct effect on divorce rates" (p. 1023; and see Rodgers, Nakonezny, and Shull's 1997 response). Further research supports the view that the passage of "unilateral" divorce laws does not account for divorce trends (Wolfers 2006).

are in some ways self-fulfilling. . . . [T]hat's a partial explanation for why the rates went up in the 1970s.'" If partners behave as if their marriage could end, it is more likely that it will. But "as word gets out that rates have tempered or even begun to fall, '[i]t could lead to a self-fulfilling prophecy in the other direction'" (in Hurley 2005; see also Goldstein 1999).

Marital Conversation—More Struggle and Less Chitchat

If barriers can no longer be counted on to preserve marital stability, the quality of the relationship becomes central to the survival of a marriage (Knoester and Booth 2000). That will "heighten the need for individuals to be committed to the union and the need to make a good marital match—with someone with whom it is possible to negotiate the details of everyday life without relying on the structural constraints generated by a highly gendered division of labor" (Teachman, Tedrow, and Hall 2006, p. 71). No longer are the normative role prescriptions for wives, husbands, or children taken for granted. Consequently, marriage entails continual negotiation and renegotiation among members about trivial matters as well as important ones. As one divorced woman put it,

> It had taken Howard and me only about ten minutes to pronounce the "I do's," but we would spend the next ten years trying to figure out who, exactly, was supposed to do what: Who was responsible for providing child care, finding babysitters and tutors, driving car pools, for which periods and where? (Blakely 1995, p. 37)

Intergenerational Transmission of Divorce

As discussed in Chapter 9, having parents who divorced increases the likelihood of divorcing (Amato and DeBoer 2001; Teachman, Tedrow, and Hall 2006). Researchers are not certain of the reasons for this. It is possible that (1) divorcing parents are models of divorce as a solution to marital problems or (2) children of divorced parents are more likely to exhibit personal behaviors that interfere with maintaining a happy marriage. There is also evidence that children of divorced parents marry at younger ages and are more likely to experience premarital cohabitation and births; these factors are associated with higher divorce rates (Heaton 2002; Teachman 2002a).

In a test of the two major hypotheses about **intergenerational transmission of divorce**, using longitudinal data, Amato and DeBoer (2001) found support for the *commitment to marriage* hypothesis. When parents remained married, they served as models of optimism about solving marital problems.

A hypothesis about the importance of *parents as models of relationship skills and interpersonal behavior* was not sup-

ported in this study (although there is other evidence for it—e.g., Amato 1996). The conclusion of Amato and DeBoer's study is that "it is actual termination of the marriage rather than the disturbed family relationships that affects children. Divorce, rather than conflict, undermines children's faith in marriage" (p. 1049).

As more parents divorce, more offspring would seem to be vulnerable to the intergenerational transmission of divorce. Yet research spanning the period 1973–1996 finds a decline of almost 50 percent in the rate of intergenerational transmission of divorce. It may be that acceptance of divorce is now so widespread that having parental models is less significant for marital stability (Wolfinger 1999). It would be nice to conclude on that hopeful note. But analysis of data from the Marital Instability Over the Life Course study suggests that "divorce has consequences for subsequent generations, including individuals not yet born at the time of the original divorce" (Amato and Cheadle 2005, p. 191). Problems evident in the grandchildren of the original divorcing couple include less education, more marital conflict, and poorer relationships with their parents.

Other Factors Associated with Divorce

Thus far in this section we have looked at sociohistorical, cultural, and intrafamilial factors that encourage high divorce rates. Another way to think about divorce is to recognize that certain demographic and behavioral factors might be related to divorce rates. These include the following:

- *Remarried mates are more likely to divorce.*

- *Premarital sex and cohabitation before marriage increase the likelihood of divorce, but only when these take place with someone other than the future marital partner* (Heaton 2002; Teachman 2003). "There is evidence that the relationship between premarital cohabitation and divorce is waning" (Teachman, Tedrow, and Hall 2006, p. 74).

- *Premarital pregnancy and childbearing usually increase the risk of divorce in a subsequent marriage* (Heaton 2002; Teachman 2002b). However, if the biological parents marry, and especially if the birth occurred during cohabitation, "it might simply represent the continued evolution of the process of mate selection" (Teachman, Tedrow, and Hall 2006, p. 75).

- Young children stabilize marriage (Hetherington 2003). Hence, *remaining child-free is associated with a higher likelihood of divorce.*

- *Race and ethnicity are differentially associated with the chances of divorcing.* But "racial differences in dissolution are not well understood . . . and we know little about the underlying processes that may generate differences in divorce rates among racial and ethnic groups" (Teachman, Tedrow, and Hall 2006, p. 76).

A government survey reported that as of 2001 (latest detailed data) the duration of marriage to particular anniversary dates was lower for black, Asian, and Hispanic women than for non-Hispanic whites. If, on the other hand, you look at lifetime experience of divorce for those over age fifteen (see Table 16.1), blacks have a relatively low percentage "ever divorced," while that of whites is the highest (Kreider 2005, p. 12 and Appendix Table 1).

This discrepancy results from several patterns. Asian and Latino populations are relatively young, so they have not been married and at risk of divorce for as long. Their ultimate divorce rates are difficult to predict.

The black population is also younger than the white non-Hispanic population. But the percentage of blacks who have "ever divorced" is low in large part because of the black "retreat from marriage." "Blacks who marry are an increasingly select subgroup of all blacks . . . who are committed to marriage and therefore less likely to divorce" (Teachman 2002b, p. 345; see also Stevenson and Wolfers 2007). Economic and educational factors seem to play a much more significant role in marital stability among African Americans than in other racial/ethnic groups (Sweeney and Phillips 2004).

- Not surprisingly, *when marital partners are emotionally mature and possess good interpersonal communication skills, "they are better able to deal with the bumps along the road to marital survival"* (Hetherington 2003, p. 322).

The preceding are the connections scholars have made between divorce and other factors. Marital complaints given by the divorced themselves include the partner's infidelity, alcoholism, drug abuse, jealousy, moodiness, violence, and, much less often, homosexuality, as well as perceived incompatibility and growing apart (Amato and Rogers 1997; Amato and Wallin 2001; Kitson 1992). Counselors suggest that some common complaints—about money, sex, and in-laws, for example—are really arenas for acting out deeper conflicts, such as who will be the more powerful partner, how much autonomy each partner should have, and how emotions are expressed. A general conclusion to be drawn from research is that deficiencies in the emotional quality of the marriage lead to divorce. "In Western cultures, happiness and satisfaction are integral to relationships and are thought to guide decisions regarding their future" (Rodrigues, Hall, and Fincham 2006, p. 97). The personal decision about divorce involves a process of balancing alternatives against the practical and emotional satisfactions of one's present union.

Thinking about Divorce: Weighing the Alternatives

Not everyone who thinks about divorce actually gets one. As divorce becomes a more available option, spouses may compare the benefits of their union to the projected consequences of not being married.

Marital Happiness, Barriers to Divorce, and Alternatives to the Marriage

One model of deciding about divorce, derived from exchange theory (see Chapter 2) by social psychologist George Levinger, posits that spouses assess their marriage in terms of the *rewards* of marriage, *alternatives* to the marriage (possibilities for remarriage or fashioning a satisfying single life), and *barriers* to divorce (Levinger 1965, 1976). Here we look at **Levinger's model of divorce decisions** from the perspective of the person considering divorce.

Respondents to the Marital Instability Over the Life Course surveys named children, along with religion and lack of financial resources, as *barriers* to divorce in open-ended interviews (Previti and Amato 2003). Indeed, another study found that both mothers and fathers anticipated that "divorce would worsen their economic situation and their abilities to fulfill the responsibilities of being a parent" (Poortman and Seltzer 2007, p. 265). However, when researchers Chris Knoester and Alan Booth (2000) examined *quantitative data* from these Marital Instability Over the Life Course surveys, they found that only three of nine barriers studied were associated with a lower likelihood of divorce: (1) when

Table 16.1 Percentage of Men and Women (Fifteen Years and Older) Ever Divorced, by Race/Ethnicity and Gender, 2001

RACE/ETHNICITY	MEN	WOMEN[a]
White, non-Hispanic	23.3%	25.4%
Black[b]	18.8	20.1
Asian	8.8	10.4
Hispanic	12.7	15.9

[a]Women's rates of divorce are higher because they have usually married younger and so are at greater risk of experiencing a divorce than are men of the same ages.

[b]Over 40 percent of black men and women have never married, so are not at risk of divorce.

Source: Adapted from Kreider 2005, Table 1.

the wife's income was a smaller percentage of the family income, (2) when church attendance was high, or (3) when there was a new child.

Other research evidence shows that young children do serve as a barrier to divorce, especially when one of the children is a boy (Leonhardt 2003). Anticipated economic loss was not as important as parenting concerns. Affection for their children and concern about the children's welfare after divorce discourage some parents from dissolving their marriage. This concern sometimes leads to delaying an intended divorce (Furstenberg and Kiernan 2001; Heaton 2002; Poortman and Seltzer 2007).

Long marriages are less likely to end in divorce. One reason for this, in addition to the marital bond itself, is that common economic interests and friendship networks increase over time and help stabilize the marriage at times of tension (Kurdek 1998; White and Booth 1991;). When divorce does occur in a longer marriage, it may be partly related to dissatisfaction with one's marital relationship at the onset of the empty nest (Hiedemann, Suhomlinova, and O'Rand 1998).

When parents consider divorce, they often think about the potential impact on their children—and that is a barrier to divorce.

Although some barriers do seem to have an impact on decisions to divorce, it is the *rewards* of marriage—love, respect, friendship, and good communication—that are most effective in keeping marriages together. "Generally, marriages that have built up positive emotional bank accounts through respect, mutual support, and affirmation of each person's worth are more likely to survive" (Hetherington 2003, p. 322).

"Would I Be Happier?"

Alternatives, the third element of Levinger's theory, was found to be the least important in decisions to divorce (Previti and Amato 2003). Yet, some married people may ask themselves whether they would be happier if they were to divorce. This is not an easy question to answer. Some people may prefer to stay single after divorce, but many partners probably weigh their chances for a remarriage.

Some research finds that leaving a bad marriage may have a positive outcome regardless of whether the individual remarries. A British study found people to be less happy one year after separation, but by one year after the divorce, both men and women were happier than they had been while married (Gardner and Oswald 2006).

A study of 1,755 whites in Detroit found that higher levels of depression among the divorced were not apparent among those who saw themselves as escaping marriages with serious, long-term problems (Aseltine and Kessler 1993). Other research (Ross 1995) used data from a national sample of 2,031 adults to compare depression levels among those with no partners and those in relationships of varying quality. As Figure 16.4 shows, people without a partner are likely to be depressed—but those in unhappy relationships are likely to be even more depressed. Compared to unhappily married people, divorced individuals display generally better physical and emotional health and higher morale (Wickrama et al. 1997). Marriage can and often does provide emotional support, sexual gratification, companionship, and economic and practical benefits, including better health. But unhappy marriages do not provide all (or in some cases, any) of these benefits (Wickrama et al. 1997) and may be a factor in poorer health (Elias 2004). "[I]t appears that at any particular point in time most marriages are 'good marriages' and that such marriages have a strong positive effect on well-being and that 'bad marriages' have a strong negative effect on well-being" (Gove, Style, and Hughes 1990, p. 14).

Can This Marriage Be Saved? In some cases, partners might be happier trying to improve their relationship rather than divorcing. "Can This Marriage Be Saved?" is the title of a series that ran in the *Ladies Home Jour-*

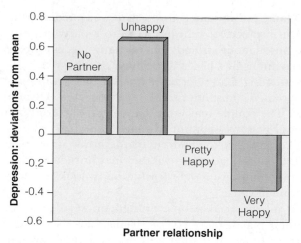

FIGURE 16.4 Depression levels of people with no partner and in relationships of varying quality. Depression is measured by a modified Center for Epidemiological Studies Depression Scale (CES-D), and scores are calculated in terms of deviation from the mean (average) rating of depression in the sample. Married and unmarried partners' scores were similar for each relationship status, so they were combined. Those with *unhappy* relationships were more depressed than those with *no partner*, while those in *very happy* relationships had the lowest levels of depression.

Source: From "Reconceptualizing Marital Status as a Continuum of Social Attachment" by C. E. Ross, 1995, *Journal of Marriage and the Family,* 57, pp. 129–140, fig. 2. Copyright © 1995. Reprinted by permission of Blackwell Publishing.

nal beginning in the 1950s—articles about couples in troubled marriages who were counseled about how to save their marriages. In this spirit, sociologist Linda Waite reports that couples may be in the lowest grouping on marital satisfaction, yet, if they don't divorce, five years later two thirds of the unhappily married couples she and her colleagues studied described themselves as "very happy." Those who divorce do not report themselves as very happy later: "If you are playing the odds in favor of happiness, . . . 'staying married is the better bet'" (Waite, quoted in Peterson 2001, p. 8D).

Improvements in those marriages came about through the passage of time (children got older, job or other problems improved); because partners' efforts to work on problems, make changes, and communicate better were effective; or because individual partners made personal changes (travel, work, hobbies, or emotional disengagement) that enabled them to live relatively happily despite an unsatisfying marriage (Waite et al. 2002).

One must decide, then, whether divorce represents a healthy step away from an unhappy relationship that can-

not be satisfactorily improved or is an illusory way to solve what in reality are personal problems. Going to a marriage counselor may help partners become more aware of the consequences of divorce so that they can make this decision more knowledgeably and not by default.

Marital Separation Some marital partners who have separated do make efforts to reconcile. Little research has been done on marital separation. But "each year [it appears] that a substantial number of separated women try to save their marriage" (Wineberg 1996, p. 308). Wineberg's study, using a sample of white women from the 1987 National Survey of Families and Households, found that 44 percent of the separated women attempted reconciliation. Half of the resumptions of marriage that followed took place within a month, suggesting that those separations may have been impulsive and soon regretted. Virtually no marriages were resumed after eight months of separation.

Only one-third of the reconciliations "took"—that is, resulted in a continued marriage (Wineberg 1996). For a majority of individuals, first separation from the spouse denoted permanent dissolution (Binstock and Thornton 2003). Researcher Howard Wineberg cautions that "not all separated couples should be encouraged to reconcile since a reconciliation does not ensure a happy marriage or that the couple will be married for very long" (p. 308).

Stable Unhappy Marriages From time to time researchers have taken up the question of what happens to couples who are distanced, unhappy, or in conflict if they don't divorce (e.g., Heaton and Albrecht 1991; LeMasters 1959). It is, however, "surprising" that "long-term low quality marriage . . . has received relatively little attention" (Hawkins and Booth 2005, p. 451). Hawkins and Booth's study followed unhappy marriages for twelve years and compared people in unhappy marriages to divorced single and remarried individuals. "Divorced individuals who remarry have greater overall happiness, and those who divorce and remain unmarried have greater levels of life satisfaction, self-esteem, and overall health than unhappily married people. . . . We suggest that unhappily married people who dissolve low-quality marriages likely have greater odds of improving their well-being than those remaining in such unions" (p. 468).

Is Divorce a Temporary Crisis or a Permanent Stress?

Initially, studies portrayed divorce as a temporary crisis, with adjustment completed in two to four years. Some scholars now consider divorce to be a lifetime chronic stress for both children and adults (Wallerstein, Lewis, and Blakeslee 2000). Although outcomes vary, divorce researcher E. Mavis Hetherington maintains that 70 percent of those who obtain a divorce have a "good enough" postdivorce adjustment (Hetherington and Kelly 2002). "Most men, women, and childen adapt to their new lives reasonably well within 2–3 years if they are not confronted with continued or additional stresses" (Hetherington 2003, p. 322).

It appears likely that both temporary crisis and chronic stress are outcomes of divorce—some divorced people are rather permanently derailed from an economically and emotionally comfortable life, while others are mostly recovered after several years. Of the latter—those who may be considered "recovered"—some have diminished well-being in some respects, while others arrive at a higher level of life satisfaction (Amato 2000, 2003a; Hetherington and Kelly 2002). Difficulties and adjustments don't seem to vary much by race or ethnicity (Amato 2000). They do vary by whether or not the couple are parents. "Generally . . . [for childless couples] recovery is almost always rather swift" (Braver, Shapiro, and Goodman 2006, p. 313).

Getting the Divorce

One of the reasons it feels so good to be engaged and newly married "is the rewarding sensation that out of the whole world, you have been selected. One of the reasons that divorce feels so awful is that you have been de-selected" (Bohannan 1970b, p. 33). Anthropologist Paul Bohannan analyzed the divorce experience in terms of six different facets, or "stations": the emotional, the legal, the community, the psychic, the economic, and the co-parental divorce. Experience in each of these realms varies from one individual to another; some stations, such as the co-parental, do not characterize every divorce. Yet the six stations capture the complexity of the divorce experience. In this section, we will examine the first three stations just listed; we will explore the economic and co-parental aspects of divorce in greater detail later in this chapter, and then make brief mention of the psychic divorce.

The Emotional Divorce

Emotional divorce involves withholding positive emotions and communications from the relationship (Vaughan 1986), typically replacing these with alienating actions and words. Partners no longer reinforce but, rather, undermine each other's self-esteem through endless large and small betrayals: responding with blame rather than comfort to a spouse's disastrous day, for instance, or refusing to go to a party given by the spouse's family, friends, or colleagues. As emotional divorce intensifies, betrayals become greater.

In a failing marriage, both spouses feel profoundly disappointed, misunderstood, and rejected (Brodie 1999). The couple may want the marriage to continue for many reasons—continued attachment, fear of being alone, obligations to children, the determination to be faithful to marriage vows—yet they may hurt each other as they communicate their frustration by look, posture, and tone of voice.

Not all divorced people wanted or were ready to end their marriage, of course. It may have been their spouse's choice. Initiating and noninitiating partners tend to talk about their reasons in different terms. The initiator of the divorce typically invokes a "vocabulary of individual needs" while the noninitiating partner speaks in terms of "familial commitment" (Hopper 1993).[7]

Women are more often the initiators of a divorce (Brinig and Allen 2000). The initiator describes many and ongoing complaints that essentially reprise the issues and events described in this chapter and others: conflict over sharing domestic work; infidelity, physical and emotional abuse, alcoholism, political differences, recreational differences, sexual tensions, disagreements about children, and so on. Whatever the specifics, the initiator decides that the marriage will never be what she or he wants: "'My needs were not being met'; 'I wasn't being fulfilled'" (Hopper 1993, p. 807). The noninitiating partner, who may have been fairly ambivalent and uncertain about the marriage as well, begins to point to the good in the marriage: "'You need to do something to keep this relationship going'; 'you tell someone you're going to be there forever, then you're going to work on it'" (p. 809).

Not surprisingly, research shows that the degree of trauma a divorcing person suffers usually depends on whether that person or the spouse wanted the dissolution because the one feeling "left" experiences a greater loss of control and has much mourning yet to do—the divorce-seeking spouse may have already worked through his or her sadness and distress (Amato 2000; Braver, Shapiro, and Goodman 2006). Even for those who actively choose to divorce, however, divorce and its aftermath may be unexpectedly painful.

---

[7] This analysis references sociologist C. Wright Mills's *vocabularies of motive*, (1940), a concept that students of sociology or communication may have encountered before. The idea is that individuals construct accounts to justify their actions. These are not necessarily their actual motives, of which they may be somewhat unaware, but narratives of explanation.

The Legal Divorce

A **legal divorce** is the dissolution of the marriage by the state through a court order terminating the marriage. The principal purpose of the legal divorce is to dissolve the marriage contract so that emotionally divorced spouses can conduct economically separate lives and be free to remarry.

Two aspects of the legal divorce make marital breakup painful. First, divorce, like death, creates the need to grieve. But the usual divorce in court is a rational, unceremonial exchange that takes only a few minutes. Divorcing individuals may feel frustrated by their lack of control over a process in which the lawyers are the principals. In one study of divorced women, virtually all had complaints about their lawyers and the legal system (Arendell 1986).

A second aspect of the legal divorce that aggravates conflict and misery is the adversary system. Under our judicial system, a lawyer advocates his or her client's interest only and is eager to "get the most for my client" and "protect my client's rights." Opposing attorneys are not trained to and ethically are not even supposed to balance the interests of the parties and strive for the outcome that promises most mutual benefit.

No-Fault Divorce A major change in the legal process of divorce has been the introduction of no-fault divorce. This revision of divorce law was intended to reduce the hostility of the partners and to permit an individual to end a failed marriage readily. Before the 1970s, the fault system predominated. A party seeking a divorce had to prove that she or he had "grounds" for divorce, such as the spouse's adultery, mental cruelty, or desertion. Obtaining a divorce might require falsifying these facts.

A fault divorce required a legal determination that one party was guilty and the other innocent. The one judged guilty rarely got custody of the children, and the judgment largely influenced property settlement and alimony awards, as well as the opinion of friends and family (Weitzman 1985). Such a protracted legal battle of adversaries increased hostility and diminished chances for a civil postdivorce relationship and successful co-parenting.

Beginning with California in 1970 and continuing until all states passed no-fault legislation, divorce was redefined as "marital dissolution" and no longer required a legal finding of a "guilty" party and an innocent one. Instead, a marriage became legally dissolvable when one or both partners declared it to be "irretrievably broken" or characterized by "irreconcilable differences." No-fault divorce is sometimes termed **unilateral divorce** because one partner can secure the divorce even if the other wants to continue the marriage.

A final note on the legal divorce is that, by definition, it applies only to marriage. There is no legal forum in which cohabitants, whether heterosexual or gay/lesbian, may obtain a divorce. Some couples may be cohabiting precisely to avoid the prospect of going to court should their relationship sour. However, they are likely to find that the absence of a venue in which to resolve separation-related disputes in a standardized way is also a problem. (The legal side of living together is discussed in more detail in Chapter 8.)

Courts in some states are beginning to grant orders of legal separation or orders of dissolution of civil unions to the nonmarried (Hartocollis 2007; "Iowa Supreme Court" 2007). These may apply the same principles of property arrangements, child custody, and child support to nonmarital cohabiting relationships (Hartocollis 2007). Cohabiting couples may also avail themselves of mediation services.

Divorce Mediation Divorce mediation is an alternative, nonadversarial means of dispute resolution by which a couple, with the assistance of a mediator or mediators (frequently a lawyer–therapist team), negotiate the settlement of their custody, support, property, and visitation issues. In the process, it is hoped that they learn a pattern of dealing with each other that will enable them to resolve future disputes. Mediation is recommended or mandatory in all states for child custody and visitation disputes before litigation can be commenced (Comerford 2006).

Early research indicated that couples who use divorce mediation have less relitigation, feel more satisfied with the process and the results, and report better relationships with ex-spouses (Marlow and Sauber 1990) and children (Beck and Blank 1997). Recent research summaries are less enthusiastic: "Overall, the corpus of available research does not indicate that mediation (relative to more traditional litigation) serves to either increase or decrease general psychological distress or . . . improve co-parenting relations." However, people were more satisfied with mediation than litigation in child custody cases: "Your feelings were understood" and "Your rights were protected" (Sbarra and Emery 2006, pp. 556–557).

There are arguments for and against mediation in child custody. Women's advocacy groups have claimed that mediation may be biased against females in that they may be less assertive in negotiations. It is also argued that mediators take insufficient account of prior domestic violence (Comerford 2006). Judith Wallerstein believes that the positive effects of divorce mediation for children may be overstated (2003, p. 80). Yet it does seem that "[m]ediation produces higher levels of compliance [with court decisions] and lower relitigation rates than litigation or attorney-negotiated settlement." It is less costly and generally less time-consuming than litigation (Comerford 2006).

The Community Divorce

Marriage is a public announcement to the community that two individuals have joined their lives. Marriage usually also joins extended families and friendship networks and simultaneously removes individuals from the world of dating and mate seeking. The **community divorce** refers to ruptures of relationships and changes in social networks that come about as a result of divorce. At the same time, divorce provides the opportunity for forming new ties.

Divorce affects the extended family as well as the nuclear one. In some families, grandparents may lose touch with grandchildren, while in others they may become more central figures of support and stability.

© Paul Barton/ CORBIS

Kin No More? Given the frequency of divorce, most extended families find themselves touched by it. Grandparents fear losing touch with grandchildren, and this does happen. In response, all fifty states have passed grandparent visitation laws. However, a Supreme Court decision struck down Washington's law (*Troxel v. Granville* 2000) because it was considered to interfere with parents' rights to determine how their children are to be raised. The status of other states' laws is uncertain; some courts have allowed grandparents visitation rights in certain circumstances (Dao 2005; Henderson and Moran 2001; Hsia 2002; Stoddard 2006).

In favorable circumstances, grandparents very commonly become closer to grandchildren, as adult children turn to grandparents for help (Coleman, Ganong, and Cable 1997) or grandchildren seek emotional support (Spitze et al. 1994). Researchers and therapists have concluded that

> these relationships work best when family members do not take sides in the divorce and make their primary commitment to the children. Grandparents can play a particular role, especially if their marriages are intact: symbolic generational continuity and living proof to children that relationships can be lasting, reliable, and dependable. Grandparents also convey a sense of tradition and a special commitment to the young.
> . . . Their encouragement, friendship, and affection has special meaning for children of divorce; it specifically

counteracts the children's sense that all relationships are unhappy and transient. (Wallerstein and Blakeslee 1989, p. 111)

Indeed, children who were close to their grandparents had fewer problems adjusting to their parents' divorce (Lussier et al. 2002).

Of course, more and more grandparents' own marriages are not intact today. Nevertheless, one can assume that even a loving, divorced grandparent could add to the support system of a grandchild of divorce.

Women are more likely than men to retain in-law relationships after divorce, particularly if they had been in close contact before the divorce and if the in-law approves of the divorce (Serovich, Price, and Chapman 1991). Relationships between former in-laws are more likely to continue when children are involved. In any event, grandchildren were most likely to remain closest to maternal grandparents, as mothers typically grew closer to and relied more on their parents after divorce (Lussier et al. 2002).

Divorce and remarriage tend to connect chains of people in complex kinship systems (Bohannan 1970a). One study looked at the general character of postdivorce extended-kin relationships. This study found that in half the cases, the kinship system included **relatives of divorce** and *relatives of remarriage* (C. Johnson 1988, p. 168). These would be familial connections established through networks of marriage and remarriage: grandparents of half siblings, for example. A photo in this chapter portrays a young boy with his *eight* grandparents, all in attendance at his basketball game (Harmon 2005a).

After divorce, adult children's relationships with their own parents may change. According to one study:

> Members of both generations had to revise their expectations of the other, and members of the older generation found themselves in a situation of having to give more of themselves to a child than they had expected to do at their stage of life. They were often forced into a parenting role, and this greater involvement provided more opportunity to observe and comment on their adult child's life. . . . Adult children were more likely to feel that parents should be available to help them with their emotional problems than their parents felt was appropriate. Divorcing children did not want their parents to interfere in childrearing or offer unsolicited advice, while their parents felt they could voice their concerns. (C. Johnson 1988, pp.190–91)

There was considerable variation in these relationships within the sample of fifty-two adult–child dyads followed over several years in Johnson's study. But most older parents espoused "modern values of personal freedom and self-fulfillment" (p. 191); that is, they did not criticize the decision to divorce from a traditional perspective.

Friends No More? A change in marital status is likely to mean changes in one's community of friends. Divorced people may feel uncomfortable with their friends who are still married because activities are done in pairs; the newly single person may also feel awkward. Couple friends may fear becoming involved in a conflict over allegiances, and they may experience their own sense of loss. Moreover, if married friends have some ambivalence about their own marriages, a divorce in their social circle may cause them to feel anxious and uncomfortable. A common outcome is a mutual withdrawal.

Like many newly married people, those who are newly divorced must find new communities to replace old friendships that are no longer mutually satisfying. The initiative for change may in fact come not only from rejection or awkwardness in old friendships but also from the divorced

person's finding friends who share with him or her the new concerns and emotions of the divorce experience. Priority may also go to new relationships with people of the opposite sex; for the majority of divorced and widowed people, building a new community involves dating again.

Deciding knowledgeably whether to divorce means weighing what we know about the consequences of divorce. The next section examines the economic consequences of divorce.

The Economic Consequences of Divorce

Social scientists and policy makers worry about the economic consequences of divorce, especially for children, but also for women and men.

Divorce, Single-Parent Families, and Poverty

Figure 16.5 displays the proportions of children who were living in poverty in 2003 for the largest racial/ethnic groups, comparing poverty rates by family type. As you can see, 42 percent of all children who reside in mother-only, single-parent families live in poverty. This compares to 9 percent of those living in married-couple families. The relationship between family type and poverty is consistent across racial/ethnic categories.

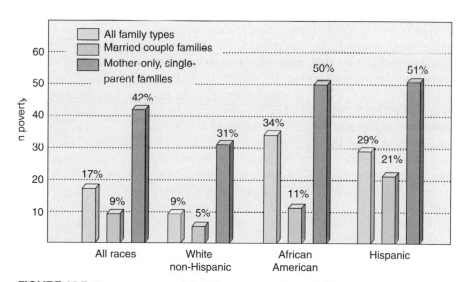

FIGURE 16.5 Poverty status of families with children under eighteen by race/ethnicity and type of family, 2003 (percentage of families with incomes below the poverty level).

Source: Adapted from U.S. Federal Interagency Forum on Child and Family Statistics 2005, Table ECON1A.

Another consistent research finding is that divorce is related to a woman's and sometimes a man's lowered economic status. "Divorce carr[ies] economic costs" (Sayer 2006, p. 392).

Husbands, Wives, and Economic Divorce

Upon divorce, a couple undergoes an **economic divorce** in which they become distinct economic units, each with its own property, income, control of expenditures, and responsibility for taxes, debts, and so on.

Women Lose Financially in Divorce Sociologist Lenore Weitzman addressed the financial plight of divorced women and their children in her landmark book *The Divorce Revolution* (1985). She compared the postdivorce economic decline of women with children to the improved standard of living of ex-husbands.[8] Women and their children experience declines in family income of between 27 percent and 51 percent (depending on the research study). An even more telling statistic is the **income-to-needs ratio**—that is, how well income meets financial needs. Women and their children experience a decline of 20 to 36 percent in their income-to-needs ratio (Sayer 2006).

A study that compared former spouses in terms of their postdivorce economic situations found that wives with custody of children had only 56 percent of the income-relative-to-needs that noncustodial fathers had (Bianchi, Subaiya, and Kahn 1999). What accounts for this situation? A fundamental reason for the income disparity between ex-husbands and their former wives is men's and women's unequal wages and different work patterns (Smock 1993). Despite women's greater participation in the labor force, any reduction in employment during childbearing and child-raising years means they have forgone opportunities for career development. "[A]lthough women are moving toward greater equality with men in the labor market, they remain more economically vulnerable when marriages end" (Bianchi, Subaiya, and Kahn 1999, p. 196).

It is also the case that women who are custodial parents must depend on child support from the other parent to meet their new single-parent family's expenses. Child support amounts are set relatively low, and much child support remains unpaid (as discussed in a later section of this chapter).

A third reason has to do with the typical division of property in divorce. Most state laws require a division of

Women and their children experience a substantial decline in their standard of living after a divorce. They may need to move to less-expensive—and less-desirable—housing and away from their former neighborhood, school, and friends. Many men also experience a decline in standard of living.

property that is specified as "equitable" (Buehler 1995). Behind the idea of a fair property settlement run two legal assumptions: The first is that marriage is an economic partnership. A man could not earn the money he earns without the moral support and domestic work of his wife, whether or not she was employed during the marriage. A minority of states have community property laws based on the premise that family property belongs equally to both partners. The remaining states, the majority, have laws promising a divorced wife either an equitable (fair) or an equal (exactly the same) share of the marital property.

But a second assumption is that property consists of such tangible items as a house or money in the bank, or other investments. Yet, except for very wealthy people, the valuable "new property" (Glendon 1981) in today's society is the earning power of a professional degree, a business or managerial position, work experience, a skilled trade, or other human capital. When property is divided in divorce, the wife may get an equal share of tangible property, such as a house or savings, but usually that does not put her on an equal footing with her former husband for the future. An even split of the marital property may not be truly equitable if one partner has stronger earning power and benefits than the other, and if the parent with custody of the children has a heavier child support burden in actuality (even paid-up child support is typically not adequate to meet children's

---

[8] Weitzman's book brought attention to the different economic outcomes of divorce for men and women. Her specific figures were later proven to be erroneous, but a reanalysis of her data still showed a substantial loss for divorced women compared to a slight gain for men (R. Peterson 1996).

expenses). Put another way, dividing property may be easy compared to ensuring that both partners and their children will have enough to live on comfortably after divorce or at least will be on a similar financial footing. "Most women would have to make heroic leaps in the labor or marriage market to keep their losses as small as the losses experienced by the men from whom they separate" (McManus and DiPrete 2001, p. 266).

In part, this situation results from the assumption of legislators and the courts that women and men would come to have equal earning power. When divorce laws were reformed in the 1970s, self-support for both parties was presumed. Some financially dependent spouses have been awarded short-term **spousal support** or *maintenance*[9] in the form of *rehabilitative alimony*, in which the ex-husband pays his ex-wife maintenance for a few years while she prepares to reenter the job market. In many, perhaps most, cases, this is not truly enough to enable the woman to reestablish herself financially, and it is not that commonly awarded in any case (Buehler 1995).

Some activists have argued that wives who left the labor force to raise children or to help with their husband's career deserve not alimony but an *entitlement*, the equivalent of severance pay for the work they did at home during the length of a marriage (Weitzman 1985). (Social Security provisions do allow an ex-wife who had been married at least ten years to collect 50 percent of the amount paid her ex-husband.) Given the risk of divorce, a recent spate of books have warned today's career women not to "opt out" of the labor force to nurture small children, but to maintain employability (Bennetts 2007; Hirschman 2006). In the future, more women who are divorced *will* have a history of almost continual employment and a current job, although they are still likely to have the heavier expenses of a custodial parent.

Anticipating the difference that the stronger labor force attachment and likely higher earnings of younger women may make, one review article takes the position that the long-term divorce disadvantage for women compared to men is, or at least will be, less striking than it now appears (Braver, Shapiro, and Goodman 2006). These authors argue that more research using long-term data is needed and should include custodial and noncustodial parents' differences in tax status and a father's expenses during visitation. They argue that "[i]t is premature to say exactly how the two parents compare in [postdivorce] economic well-being" (p. 324).

Some Men Win, Most Lose Financially in Divorce In fact, the postdivorce economic situation of men has undergone some rethinking. Circumstances have changed since the 1970s, and men and women are both likely to be family earners now. A study covering the years 1980–1993 (McManus and DiPrete 2001) found that most men lose economically in divorce (or in a separation from a cohabiting union). The chief reason for their declining standard of living is the loss of the partner's income. Depending on the study, married men experience a decline in *family income* of from 8 percent to 41 percent; cohabiting men's drop in income is comparable (Sayer 2006).

However, though family income drops for a man when he is no longer part of a couple, so do his expenses; his household is now smaller. Consequently, his *income-to-needs ratio* rises anywhere from 8 percent to 41 percent, even taking child support into account (Sayer 2006). But usually, that is not enough to maintain his previous standard of living and quality of material life.

To sum up, though there are no women "winners" in divorce, a majority of men lose, too. Only men who had contributed at least 80 percent of their family's predivorce income in a traditional marriage gain economically in divorce. Still, to continue the gender comparison, "[s]tudies that focus on women's outcomes have yet to unearth any comparable core of women who gain financially following union dissolution" (McManus and DiPrete 2001, p. 266).

Child Support

Child support involves money paid by the noncustodial to the custodial parent to support the children of a now-ended marital, cohabiting, or sexual relationship. Because mothers retain custody in the preponderance of cases, the vast majority of those ordered to pay child support are fathers.

For many years, the child support awarded to the **custodial parent** was often not paid, and states made little effort to collect it on the parent's behalf. Policy makers' concerns about child poverty, the economic consequences of divorce for women, and welfare costs led to a series of federal laws that have changed that situation

---

[9] These terms have replaced *alimony* to describe a former spouse's support payment to his or her ex-spouse following divorce. Historically, alimony was a payment of husband to wife resting on the assumption that the contract of marriage included a husband's lifetime obligation to support his wife and children. Traditionally, of course, the wife had not been employed, but instead had primary responsibility for making a home and bearing and raising children. Popular myth had it that ex-wives lived comfortably on high alimony awards. But in reality, courts awarded alimony to only a small minority of wives.

In 1979 the U.S. Supreme Court determined that laws against sex discrimination should make alimony gender-neutral—in essence, transforming the basis for spousal support from the common-law tradition of husbands' and wives' specialized roles into an economic partnership model. Along with this and other reforms of divorce law came a presumption that spouses should be self-supporting after divorce (Buehler 1995, pp. 102–11).

considerably.[10] In recent years government authorities have been more successful at securing payment, and at standardized amounts that are often higher than previously. With better child support enforcement, the poverty of custodial parents and their children dropped from 33 percent in 1993 to 26 percent in 2003 (Grall 2006).

Nevertheless, child support awards have historically been and continue to be small. In 2003, 60 percent of custodial parents had child support awards, and three-fourths of those received payments. Only 45 percent received full payment of what was due, however, and the amounts involved are not very impressive, averaging $3,500. Some noncustodial parents do make additional contributions in the form of gifts, clothes, food, medical costs (beyond health insurance), and camp or child care (Grall 2006).

Some research suggests that the principal reason for a noncustodial parent's failure to pay is unemployment or underemployment (Meyer and Bartfeld 1996). Among families in which the absent parent has been employed during the entire previous year, payment rates are 80 percent or more. Not so when unemployment is involved. "The key to reducing poverty [among single-parent families] thus appears to be the old and unglamorous one, of solving un- and underemployment, both for the fathers and the mothers" (Braver, Fitzpatrick, and Bay 1991, pp.184–85).

Some noncustodial fathers provide support in ways other than money (Teachman 1991), such as child care: "In some cases attempts to locate and require payments from such fathers may result in severing these ties" (Peterson and Nord 1990, p. 539). Compliance may be related to the noncustodial parent's involvement in the child's life. Seventy-nine percent are in compliance when they have either joint custody or visitation arrangements, only 63 percent when the parent has neither (Grall 2006).

---

[10] The Child Support Amendments (1984) to the Social Security Act, the Family Support Act (1988), and the child support provisions of the Personal Responsibility and Work Opportunity Reconciliation Act (1996) did the following: (1) encouraged the establishment of paternity and consequent child support awards, (2) required states to develop numerical guidelines for determining child support amounts, (3) required periodic review of award levels to amend them for inflation and to ensure that the noncustodial parent continued to pay an appropriate share of his or her income, and (4) enforced payments through locator services to find nonpaying noncustodial parents. States were required to implement automatic wage withholding of child support, and some states imposed penalties such as revoking a driver's license, seizing a delinquent payer's assets, or garnishing his or her wages ("Child Support Collected" 1995; Garfinkel, Meyer, and McLanahan 1998; Pirog-Good and Amerson 1997). Perhaps the most interesting collection device is that of the state of Maine, where child support must be paid before worm digging or moose hunting licenses will be issued (Koch 2006).

Two suggested solutions to the problem of nonpayment of child support are guaranteed child support and a children's allowance. Both are based on the principle of society-wide responsibility for all children. With **guaranteed child support**, a policy adopted in France and Sweden, the government sends to the custodial parent the full amount of support awarded to the child. It then becomes the government's task to collect the money from the parent who owes it. A second alternative, a **children's allowance**, provides a government grant to all families—married or single-parent, regardless of income—based on the number of children they have. All industrialized countries except the United States have some version of a children's allowance. In the present political and economic climate in the United States, it seems unlikely that such measures would be adopted.

As another approach to securing payment of child support, some states have begun experimenting with "responsible fatherhood" programs, often supported by government grants. Low-income fathers are typically expected to pay a higher portion of their income in child support than are middle-class fathers, resulting in a spiral of expanded debt and often withdrawal from their children (Bianchi, Subaiya, and Kahn 1999). Recognizing that there are low-income fathers who want to provide support for their children but lack the income to do so, these multifaceted programs provide employment services, family support, and mediation services. Results thus far are only modest. Some increase in child support payments has occurred, though not yet enough to produce the dramatic improvement in the lives of men and their children that program designers had hoped for (Johnson, Levine, and Doolittle 1999; Pearson et al. 2003; Reichert 1999).

We have been speaking of child support in the context of marriage and divorce, but some courts have awarded child support when same-sex couples who have been raising children together break up (Kravets 2005; "State Court Orders" 2005).

We turn now from the economics of postdivorce family support to a broader examination of the aftermath of divorce for children.

Divorce and Children

FOCUS ON CHILDREN

More than half of all divorces involve children under eighteen, and about 40 percent of children born to married parents will experience marital disruption (Amato 2000). How do separation and divorce affect children? There is strong disagreement on the answer to this question. One research review spoke of the "polemical nature of divorce scholarship" (Amato 2000, p. 1270).

Outcomes for children depend a great deal on the circumstances before and after the divorce. Although the divorce experience is psychologically stressful and, in most cases, financially disadvantageous for children, children in high-conflict marriages seem to benefit from a divorce. Living in an intact family characterized by unresolved tension and alienating conflict can cause as great or greater emotional stress and a lower sense of self-worth in children than living in a supportive single-parent family (L'Heureux-Dubé 1998). But when the conflict level in the home has been low, children have poorer postdivorce outcomes. They are likely taken by surprise by a divorce and seem to suffer more emotional damage. Among other things, it is difficult for them to see the divorce as necessary in this situation (Amato and Booth 1997; Booth and Amato 2001).

The Various Stresses for Children of Divorce

We begin this section with the research of Judith Wallerstein and her colleagues. This group's research has been very influential in defining the situation of children of divorce for both professionals and the public.

The Wallerstein Research In their longitudinal study of children's postdivorce adjustment, psychologists Judith Wallerstein and Joan Kelly interviewed all of the members of some sixty families with one or more children who had entered counseling at the time of the parents' separation in 1971. Wallerstein and her colleagues reinterviewed children at one year, two years, five years, ten years, and, in some cases, fifteen years later and finally again at the twenty-five year point (Wallerstein, Lewis, and Blakeslee 2000).

In the initial aftermath of the divorce, children appeared worst in terms of their psychological adjustment at one year after separation. By two years postdivorce, households had generally stabilized. At five years, many of the 131 children seemed to have come through the experience fairly well: 34 percent "coped well"; 29 percent were in a middle range of adequate, though uneven, functioning; and 37 percent were not coping well, with anger playing a significant part in the emotional life of many of them (Wallerstein and Kelly 1980). If the middle group is considered to be well enough adjusted, one can say that two-thirds of these children emerged from the divorce intact.

Nevertheless, children whose parents have divorced will more than likely have less money available for their needs. This is especially significant because some of the negative impact of divorce can be attributed to economic deprivation (McLanahan and Sandefur 1994).

Wallerstein found considerable deprivation among even middle-class children compared to what they could have expected had their parents remained married. Because divorce settlements seldom include arrangements to pay for children's college education[11] and family savings are often eroded by divorce, financing higher education is especially problematic. Wallerstein, who followed her sample into young adulthood, was surprised at the extent of their educational downward mobility. Sixty percent of the study children were likely to receive less education than their fathers; 45 percent were likely to receive less than their mothers. Even divorced fathers who had retained close ties, who had the money or could save it, and who ascribed importance to education seemed to feel less obligated to support their children through college (Wallerstein and Blakeslee 1989; Wallerstein, Lewis, and Blakeslee 2000).

After following their sample of children of divorce for ten years, Wallerstein and her colleagues found the majority to be approaching economic self-sufficiency, to be enrolled in educational programs, and, in general, to be responsible young adults. Even so, the overall impression left by the Wallerstein research is one of loss. Children may lose fathers, who become uninterested and detached; they may lose mothers, who are overwhelmed by the task of supporting the family and managing a household alone and who either see little chance of happiness for themselves or are busy pursuing their "second chance." Children of divorce experience the loss of daily interaction with one of their parents. Boys, especially, seem to find it difficult to establish themselves educationally, occupationally, or maritally (Wallerstein and Blakeslee 1989). Wallerstein found that half of the children in her study had experienced a second divorce of one or both parents. ("My Family: How It Feels When Parents Divorce," illustrates many points raised in this section.)

The Wallerstein study has methodological problems: a small, unrepresentative sample recruited by offering free counseling to the family; lack of a control group; and difficulty separating family troubles and mental health concerns that predate the separation and divorce from those that might be effects of divorce. It has been challenged by studies with more representative samples. These studies reach less-negative conclusions. Some critics have also noted that in the early 1970s, when the study began, women were less likely to be in the labor force. The need for an inexperienced mother to enter the labor force created an adjustment problem in the 1970s that would be less of a stress now. Another methodological problem, although one shared by other longitudinal studies, is that continual interviewing of

---

[11] Some divorce agreements provide for support of children through college, provided they are doing well and advancing toward the goal of graduation. It has happened occasionally, but rarely, that courts have ordered such support against the wishes of a parent.

My Family How It Feels When Parents Divorce

In the following excerpts, four children of divorce tell their own stories. As you will see, they talk about issues raised in this chapter.

Zach, Age 13

Even though I live with my Dad and my sister lives with my Mom, my parents have joint custody, which means we can switch around if we feel like it. I think that's the best possible arrangement because if they ever fought over us, I know

I would have felt I was like a check in a restaurant—you know, the way it is at the end of a meal when two people are finished eating and they both grab for the check . . . but secretly neither one really wants it, they just go on pretending until someone finally grabs it, and then that one's stuck. . . .

My parents knew they couldn't live together, but they also knew it was nobody's fault. It was as if they were mag-

nets—as if when you turn them the opposite way they can't touch. . . . Neither of them ever blamed the other person, so they worked it out the best they could—for their sakes and ours, too.

Nevertheless, it's very sad and confusing when your parents are divorced. I think I was five when they separated. . . .

When my parents first split up, it affected me a lot. . . . I got real fat and my grades went way down, so I went to a psychologist. She made me do a lot of things which seemed dumb at the time—like draw pictures and answer lots of silly questions. . . . My school work suffered because I was so distracted thinking about my situation that I couldn't listen very well, and for a long time I didn't work nearly as hard as I should have. Everyone told me I was an underachiever, and my parents tell me I still am, but I don't think so. What I do think is that I am a lot more independent—a go-out-and-do-it-yourself person. . . .

I've heard about kids who are having all these problems because their parents are getting divorced, but I can't understand what the big deal is. I mean, it's upsetting, sure, but just because your parents are separated it doesn't mean you're going to lose anybody. . . . It's not something I talk about very much. Most of my friends would rather talk about MTV than talk about divorce.

Ari, Age 14

When my parents were married, I hardly ever saw my Dad because he was always busy working. Now that they're divorced, I've gotten to know him more because I'm with him every weekend. And I really look forward to the weekends because it's kind of like a break—it's like going to Disneyland because there's no set schedule, no "Be home by five-thirty" kind of stuff. It's open. It's free. And my father is always buying me presents.

FIGURE 16.6.a and FIGURE 16.6.b Professional counselors often use art to gain insight into children's feelings about how divorce affects their family. The first drawing reveals the creative coping of a child whose parents are divorcing. She has figured out a way to *include* her father while keeping within the bounds of reality as she knows it. Her sister, on the other hand, used a jagged line to *separate* her father from the rest of the family.

Source: From *The Difficult Divorce: Therapy for Children and Families*, by Marla Beth Isaacs, Braulio Montalvo, and David Abelsohn Copyright © 1986 by Basic Books, Inc. Reprinted by permission of Basic Books, a member of Perseus Books, L.L.C.

My mom got remarried and divorced again, so I've gone through two divorces so far. And my father's also gotten remarried—to someone I don't get along with all that well. It's all made me feel that people shouldn't get married—they should just live together and make their own agreement. Then, if things get bad, they don't have to get divorced and hire lawyers and sue each other. And, even more important, they don't have to end up hating each other.

I'd say that the worst part of the divorce is the money problem. It's been hard on my Mom because lots of times she can't pay her bills, and it makes her angry when I stay with my father and he buys me things. She gets mad and says things like, "If he can buy you things like this, then he should be able to pay me." And I feel caught in the middle for two reasons: First, I can't really enjoy whatever my Dad does get for me, and second, I don't know who to believe. My Dad's saying, "I don't really owe her any money," and my Mom's saying he does. Sometimes I fight for my Mom and sometimes I fight for my Dad, but I wish they'd leave me out of it completely.

Caleb, Age 7

My parents aren't actually divorced yet. But they're getting one soon. They stopped living together when I was one and a half, and my Dad moved next door. Then, when I was five, he moved to Chicago, and that hurt my feelings because I realized he was really leaving and I wouldn't be able to see him every day. My father's an artist, and when he lived next door to us in New York, I used to go to his studio every day and watch him when he was welding. I had my own goggles and tools, and we would spend many an hour together. I remember when I first heard the bad news that he was moving away, because I almost flipped my lid. My father said he

would be divorcing my Mom but that he wouldn't be divorcing me and we'd still see each other a lot—but not as often. I started crying then and there, and ever since then I've been hoping every single second that he'd move back to New York and we'd all live together again. I don't cry much anymore because I hold it back, but I feel sad all the same.

I get to visit my father quite often. And Shaun. He's my collie. My cat lives in New York with me and Mom. Whenever I talk with Daddy on the phone I can hear Shaun barking in the background. The hardest thing for me about visiting my father is when I have to leave, and that makes me feel bad—and mad—inside. I still wish I could see him every day like I did when I was little. It's hard to live with just one person, because you don't have enough company, though my Mom has lots of great babysitters and that helps a little.

Tito, Age 11

It seems like my parents were always fighting. The biggest fight happened one night when we were at a friend's house. Mommy was inside the house crying, and Daddy was out on the sidewalk yelling and telling my mother to come down, and my little sister, Melinda, and I were outside with a friend of my father's. We were both crying because we were so frightened. Then Daddy tried to break the door down, so Mommy came downstairs. And then the police cars came and Daddy begged Mommy to stay quiet and not say anything and to give him another chance, but she was so unhappy that she got into one of the cars. I was only four but I remember everything. We stayed with our cousin for about two months, and during this time I saw my father whenever he visited us at my grandmother's house. . . . I was always happy to see him, but sometimes it made me feel sad, too, because I would look

forward to our visits so much, and then when we were together it could never be as perfect as I was hoping it would be. He was still so angry at Mommy's leaving him that it was hard for him to feel anything else for anybody. . . .

About the time of the divorce I started to get into fights with other kids, and my mother got worried. She thought I must be feeling very angry and having a hard time expressing my feelings, so she took me to a therapist. . . . We got really close and he'd talk to me about my problems with my Dad. This went on for about two years, and during that time he helped me realize that the divorce was better for me in the long run because our home was more relaxed and there wasn't so much tension in the air.

The other thing that happened around this time was that my mother found out about an organization called Big Brothers, where I could have another male figure in my life. . . . They paired me off with a guy named Pat Kelly, and we've been getting together every weekend for a couple of years. . . . Pat and I do a lot of things like play baseball or video games and eat hot dogs. But the best thing we do is talk—like when I do something good in school I can tell him, and if I feel sad I can talk about that, too. His parents got divorced when he was twelve, and so we have a lot of the same feelings.

Critical Thinking

Overall, do you see these stories as hopeful, dismaying, or both? Why? Were there any particular points that you found surprising or interesting? What do these stories suggest to divorcing parents about how they might help their children cope with divorce?

Source: Excerpts from *How It Feels When Parents Divorce*, by Jill Krementz. Copyright © 1984 by Jill Krementz. Reprinted by permission of Alfred A. Knopf a division of Random House, Inc.

children about the impact of the divorce might create a mind-set in which any problems are given a divorce-generated interpretation (Ahrons 1994; Cherlin 1999, 2000; Coontz 1997a).

Still, other researchers have come to think, like Wallerstein, that divorce has long-term effects (Cherlin 2000; Amato 2000; Amato and Sobolewski 2001). Divorce is a "risk factor for multiple problems in adulthood" (Amato 2000, p. 1279). Children of divorce continue to have lower outcomes than children from intact families in the areas of academic success, conduct, psychological adjustment, social competence, and self-concept, and they have more troubled marriages and weaker ties to parents, especially fathers (Amato 2000, 2003; Kelly and Emery 2003).

Reasons for Negative Effects of Divorce on Children
Researchers and theorists offer a variety of explanations for why and how divorce could adversely affect children. Amato (1993) has summarized five theoretical perspectives concerning the reasons for negative outcomes. We present his typology, along with some relevant research by others. Then we introduce an additional theoretical perspective.

1. The **life stress perspective** assumes that, just as divorce is known to be a stressful life event for adults, it must also be so for children. Furthermore, divorce is not one single event but a process of associated events that may include moving—often to a poorer neighborhood—changing schools, giving up pets, and losing contact with grandparents and other relatives (Lorenz et al. 1997; Morrison and Cherlin 1995; South, Crowder, and Trent 1998). This perspective holds that an accumulation of negative stressors results in problems for children of divorce.

2. The **parental loss perspective** assumes that a family with both parents living in the same household is the optimal environment for children's development. Both parents are important resources, providing children love, emotional support, practical assistance, information, guidance, and supervision, as well as modeling social skills such as cooperation, negotiation, and compromise. Accordingly, the absence of a parent from the household is problematic for children's socialization.

3. The **parental adjustment perspective** notes the importance of the custodial parent's psychological adjustment and the quality of parenting. Supportive and appropriately disciplining parents facilitate their children's well-being. However, the stress of divorce and related problems and adjustments may impair a parent's child-raising skills, with probably negative consequences for children. Divorced parents do spend less time with children. Divorced parents, compared to married parents, are "less supportive, have fewer rules, dispense harsher discipline, provide less supervision, and engage in more conflict with their children" (Amato 2000, p. 1279).

4. The **economic hardship perspective** assumes that economic hardship brought about by marital dissolution is primarily responsible for the problems faced by children whose parents divorce (Amato 2000). Indeed, economic circumstances do condition diverse outcomes for children—perhaps accounting for one-half the differences between children in divorced compared to intact two-parent families. But differences in outcomes exist *within* social class groupings. Children in better-off remarried or single-parent families still lag behind children from two-parent families on various outcome indicators (McLanahan and Sandefur 1994; Parke 2003).

5. The **interparental conflict perspective** holds that conflict between parents is responsible for the lowered well-being of children of divorce. Many studies, including that of Wallerstein, indicate that some negative results for children may not be simply the result of divorce per se, but are also generated by exposure to parental conflict prior to, during, and subsequent to the divorce (Amato 2000; Barber and Demo 2006; Hetherington 1999; Wallerstein and Kelly 1980).

   Visitation is one frequent arena of postdivorce parental disputes. The child isn't ready to go when visitation time starts, or the visiting parent brings the child home late. Child support is another. The Stanford Child Custody Project, which followed over one thousand parents and children, found that a quarter of parents had a conflicted co-parenting relationship three and a half years after the divorce (M-Y. Lee 2002).

The factors that seem to affect co-parenting success are rather straightforward: a previous good co-parenting relationship during the marriage; a mediated rather than hostile divorce process; a reasonably good postdivorce relationship between ex-spouses; and length of time since the divorce. Research on the relationship between good co-parenting and type of custody is inconclusive except that a joint custody arrangement chosen by the parents is much more conducive to good co-parenting than one imposed by the courts. Research on the effect of remarriage on co-parenting is not sufficiently developed for conclusions to be drawn (Adamsons and Pasley 2006).

Multiple Transitions and Children's Outcomes The **family instability perspective** is an additional theory of children's negative outcomes of divorce that has emerged since Amato's original article. The **instability hypothesis** stresses that *transitions* in and out of various family settings are the key to children's adjustment. (Barber and Demo 2006; Hetherington 2005). The logic of the instability hypothesis is this:

> Transitions may include parents' separation; a cohabiting romantic partner's move into, or out of, the home of a single parent; the remarriage of a single (noncohabiting) parent[;] or the disruption of a remarriage. The underlying assumption is that children and their parents, whether single or partnered, form a functioning family system and that repeated disruption of this system may be more distressing than its long-term continuation. . . . Stable single-parent households or stepfamilies, in contrast, do not require that children readjust repeatedly to the loss of coresident parents and parent-figures or the introduction of cohabiting parents and stepparents. (Fomby and Cherlin 2007, p. 182)

Paula Fomby and Andrew Cherlin (2007) tested the *instability hypothesis,* as well as a competing *selection hypothesis,* to assess whether the number of transitions produces lower cognitive (academic) outcomes or behavior problems or whether preexisting characteristics of the mother explain both household instability and the effects of that instability on children. They used the National Longitudinal Survey of Youth waves of 1979–2000 and a supplemental survey of the original respondents' children.

Multiple transitions did not seem to impact black children. The researchers were not able to determine why from the data they had, but speculate that black children may have more support from the extended family. It may also be the case that other stresses on many black families are so overwhelming as to overshadow changes in family structure.

Multiple transitions did not seem the key to explaining white children's *academic outcomes.* But the number of transitions *did* seem related to white children's *behavioral problems.* Even so, multiple transitions did not seem so powerful a negative influence as living in a single-parent, mother-only family in a child's early years.

A More Optimistic Look at Children in Divorce Having considered reasons for the negative effects of divorce on children, we now try to assess just how important divorce is in the lives of affected children. We've given considerable attention to the research of Wallerstein and her colleagues because it has been very influential. "Judith Wallerstein's research on the long-term effects of divorce on children has had a profound effect on scholarly work, clinical practice, social policy, and the general public's views of divorce" (Amato 2003, p. 332). In fact, this is not a definitive study, and the strongly negative conclusions about divorce that Wallerstein presents seem overstated. "Many of Wallerstein's conclusions about the long-term consequences of dissolution on children are more pessimistic than the evidence warrants" (Amato 2003, p. 332).

Nevertheless, concern that children of divorce are disadvantaged does not rest solely on Wallerstein's research and what many see as her exaggerated presentation of the dangers of divorce (Cherlin 1999). A "persuasive body of evidence supports a moderate version of [her] thesis" (Amato 2003, pp. 338–39; Hetherington 2005). The remaining question, then, is this: *How much does divorce affect children?*

E. Mavis Hetherington has been studying divorcing families for about the same length of time as Judith Wallerstein, and she has a much more optimistic view of the outcomes for children—and adults. Starting in 1974 in Virginia with forty-eight divorced and forty-eight married-couple families, parents of four-year-olds, her research ultimately included 1,400 stable and dissolved marriages and the children of those marriages, some followed for almost thirty years. Hetherington found that 25 percent of these children of divorce had long-term social, emotional, or psychological problems, compared to 10 percent of those whose parents had not divorced. However, in assessing the impact of divorce, she would emphasize the 75 to 80 percent of children who are coping reasonably well (Hetherington and Kelly 2002).

> Researchers have clearly demonstrated that, on average, children benefit from being raised in two biological or adoptive parent families rather than separated; divorced; or never married single-parent households. . . . But . . . there is considerable variability, and the differences between groups, while significant, are relatively small. Indeed, despite the well-documented risks associated with separation and divorce, the majority of divorced children as young adults enjoy average or better social and emotional adjustment. (Kelly and Lamb 2003, p. 195, citations omitted; see also Kelly and Emery 2003)

Other scholars agree: "On average, parental divorce and remarriage have only a small negative impact on the well-being of children" (Barber and Demo 2006, p. 291; see also Demo, Aquilino, and Fine 2005, p. 125). All in all, divorce researchers seem to be moving to a middle ground in which they acknowledge that children of divorce are disadvantaged compared to those of married parents—and that those whose parents were not engaged in serious marital conflict have especially lost the advantage of an intact parental home. But many have moved away from simplistic or overly negative views of the outcomes of divorce.

From studies that reach different conclusions about overall outcomes, we can still learn much that is potentially useful about what postdivorce circumstances are most beneficial to children's development and what pitfalls to avoid. A good mother–child (or custodial parent–child) bond and competent parenting by the custodial parent seem to be the most significant factors (Wallerstein and Blakeslee 1989; Tschann et al. 1989). Another highly important factor in children's adjustment to divorce is the divorced parents' relationship with each other (Ahrons 2004; Kelly and Emery 2003; Wallerstein 2003). And good nonresident parental relationships are also a positive influence on outcomes (Amato and Gilbreth 1999).

We now turn to issues of custody, the setting in which children will live after the divorce.

Custody Issues

A basic issue in a divorce of parents is the determination of which parent will take **custody**—that is, assume primary responsibility for caring for the children and making decisions about their upbringing and general welfare.

Custody After Divorce As formalized in divorce decrees, child custody is most commonly an extension of traditional gender roles. Divorced fathers typically have legal responsibility for financial support, while divorced mothers continue the physical, day-to-day care of their children. Eighty-three percent of custodial parents are mothers; 17 percent are fathers (Grall 2006). (Not all "custodial mothers" in these government statistics have been divorced; 31 percent were never married.)

Custody patterns and preferences in law have changed over time. As part of a patriarchal legal system, fathers were automatically given custody until the mid-nineteenth century. Then the first wave of the Women's Movement made mothers' parental rights an issue. Emerging theories of child development also lent support to a presumption that mother custody was virtually always in the child's best interest, the so-called "tender years" doctrine (Depner 1993; Erickson and Babcock 1995).

In the 1970s, states' reforms of divorce law incorporated new ideas about men, women, and parenthood; custody criteria were made gender neutral. Under current laws, a father and a mother who want to retain custody have theoretically equal chances. Judges try to assess the relationship between parents and children on a case-by-case basis. But because mothers are typically the ones who have physically cared for the child, and because many judges still have traditional attitudes

"So what's your custody deal?"

about gender, some courts continue to give preference to mothers (Bauserman 2002). The "best interests of the child" or the more recent "primary caretaker" standard was often assumed by judges to signal a choice of the mother (Erickson and Babcock 1995).[12]

When both parents seek custody, the odds of father custody are slightly higher when the children are older (Fox and Kelly 1995). Judges may have become more favorable to father custody, but there are no definitive studies on whether fathers are now winning more contested custody cases. One study found that by 1995, court decisions were almost equalized, with 45 percent

---

[12] Several new legal approaches have appeared in recent child custody cases. One is the *friendly parent* concept, the idea that custody should favor the parent who is more likely to grant access to the child and foster the child's relationship with the other parent. Many states have incorporated the friendly parent doctrine into their statutory standards for custody as one factor among many or as the determining factor.

"There is, however, a small but growing movement to reject the friendly parent statute or limit its application" (Dore 2004, p. 43). This is because in practice it has generated hostility and litigation, as competing parents denigrate each other and sometimes try to provoke the other parent into behavior that will look bad in court. It has also made parents hesitant to raise legitimate child abuse or domestic violence allegations for fear of appearing critical of the other parent. Some courts have rejected the friendly parent doctrine, and some states are modifying their laws (W. Davis 2001; Dore 2004).

A second concept is that of *parental alienation syndrome*, originated by psychiatrist Richard Gardner. This is the idea that one parent has turned the child against the other parent without cause and that a parent may raise false allegations of child abuse (Lavietes 2003). This concept is most often introduced by fathers seeking custody.

Parental alienation syndrome has not received legal acceptance nor is it accepted by the American Psychiatric Association, the American Medical Association, or the American Psychological Association (American Psychological Association 2005b; Lavietes 2003). Courts have not to date permitted it to enter into consideration (e.g., *People v. Michael Fortin* 2000).

of mothers and 42 percent of fathers awarded sole custody and 9 percent sharing custody in disputed cases (Mason and Quirk 1997). Other data, taking as a starting point the original hope of each parent, found that "fathers get the arrangement they prefer less often than mothers do" (Braver, Shapiro, and Goodman 2006, p. 317).

It may be the case that mothers have become less inclined to insist on sole custody. Fatherhood scholar James Levine thinks that "[w]e're seeing some weakening of the constraints on women to feel they can only be successful if they are successful mothers," so they are more willing to concede custody to willing fathers (quoted in Fritsch 2001, p. 4). As with mothers, not all custodial fathers are or were married; in 2003, 20 percent were never married (Grall 2006).

Generally, studies have found nothing to preclude father custody or to prefer it (Buchanan, Maccoby, and Dornbusch 1996; Luepnitz 1982). Neither does whether the custodial parent is the same sex as the child seem to make a difference in a child's adjustment (Powell and Downey 1997).

Noncustodial Mothers With unpromising economic prospects and in the context of changing attitudes about gender roles, some mothers are relinquishing custody. There are more than two million noncustodial mothers (Sousa and Sorensen 2006), concentrated in the twenty-five to forty-five age range and lower- to middle-class economic level. Some of those mothers have lost custody of children due to their abuse or neglect, while others have voluntarily surrendered custody or lost a custody contest to the other parent (Eicher-Catt 2004b).

In an earlier study of noncustodial mothers based on interviews with more than 500 mostly white women in forty-four states, only 9 percent reported losing their children in a court battle or ceding custody to avoid a custody fight. The others voluntarily agreed to father custody and gave as reasons: money (30 percent); child's choice (21 percent); difficulty in handling the children (12 percent); avoidance of moving the children (11 percent); and self-reported instability or problems (11 percent; Greif and Pabst 1988, p. 88; see also Depner 1993).

More than 90 percent of mothers in the Greif and Pabst study reported that the experience of becoming the noncustodial parent was stressful. So was maintaining a relationship with the child. Deborah Eicher-Catt's qualitative study of noncustodial mothers (2004b) found that the minority of mothers whose custody was abrogated by the courts were restricted in their contact, perhaps permitted only supervised visitation with their children. The larger group who voluntarily relinquished custody found it hard to achieve a workable relationship with the child as well. They were unable to be traditional mothers, but found a "mother-as-friend" role insufficient and uncomfortable. Eicher-Catt advises noncustodial mothers to focus on building a relationship, rather than thinking in terms of the traditional maternal role. "A Closer Look at Family Diversity: A Noncustodial Mother Tells Her Story" describes one mother's struggle to perform the mother role in this challenging context.

Judith Fisher, who also studied noncustodial mothers, believes that women should not relinquish custody just because they feel inadequate in comparison to their successful husbands. At the same time, she strongly supports the freedom of men and women to make choices about custody—including the woman's choice to live apart from her children—without guilt or stigma. She urges

> the negation of the unflattering stereotypes of noncustody mothers; . . . supportiveness of the woman's choice when it appears to have been well thought out; and . . . [not] blaming the mother when others (the children, the children's father, the courts) decide that the children should live apart from her. (1983, p. 357)

The Visiting Parent To date, most research and discussion on visiting parents has been about fathers, but one study did compare the two sexes. Nonresidential mothers were more apt to telephone and to engage in extended visits with children. But nonresidential mothers and fathers had essentially similar levels of visitation in terms of frequency and activities during the visit. Both were more likely to engage in only leisure activities with their children rather than spending time helping with homework or going to school activities. In reality, less frequent and more recreational visitation seem to be a result of structural factors: distance from the child's home; the difficulty of finding an appropriate setting for the visit; and the wish not to engage in conflict or disciplinary actions in the limited time spent with the child (S. Stewart 1999).[13]

[13] There are some special situations of visitation. In some communities, courts and social workers have developed programs to offer *supervised visitation* between a noncustodial parent and his or her offspring. In this situation, parent–child contact occurs only in the presence of a third party, such as a social worker or a court employee. Supervised visitation is often mandated in situations of alleged domestic violence, drug abuse, long absenteeism, or past imprisonment. Although no doubt a warranted precaution in many cases, supervision is also a hardship on the parent, who must not only visit in a strained situation but also cover the financial cost. Some fathers must forgo visits they desire because they lack money to pay the typical $100 a visit (Kaufman 2007).

As I fold the last batch of warm clothes from the dryer, I glance over at the kitchen clock on the wall. Oh dear . . . it's almost four-thirty. . . . It's Sunday and I need to get the guys ready to go home to their dad's. . . .

Nowadays, I live [in a room] in someone else's house, see my kids every other weekend, and pay child support. How can I continue to call myself a mother when I no longer provide their regular care and nurturance? Unlike some mothers . . . who lose custody of their children . . . I voluntarily chose my status. . . . With little money coming in as a full time student, I am unable to provide adequately for them. Like other mothers I've interviewed, making the difficult decision to leave the care of my chidren to someone else because I deemed it "in their best interest" is not a decision reached lightly. . . . I suddenly realize that it's awfully quiet in the house. "Ty . . . Zachary," I call out, with the basket of clothes now resting on one hip. No response. All I hear is the low drone of a televised basketball game coming from the . . . living room. That's odd, I wonder where they could be. . . . I'm sure they were here just a minute ago.

Have I been too involved in cleaning up our breakfast mess or doing laundry to notice that they'd disappeared? It is a rarity that my boys, Ty, age ten, and Zac, age six, would be unaccounted for during a weekend visit. After all, I consider our time together precious time, although very much punctuated and measured according to planned activities and events. Granted, I have been daydreaming about how good this weekend with them has been. I think I've managed to keep them sufficiently "entertained. . . ." I know that's not my only goal while they're with me, but I do want them to enjoy coming to see me.

Yes, let's see. Friday night we went to the movies. Yesterday afternoon I took them roller skating. . . . We stayed up late last night and watched a rented movie. Dare I say it felt like "family time," if only temporarily? This morning our time together was more improvised. . . . Zac talked me into making waffles for breakfast. How long has it been since I did that? Seldom do I cook anymore.

[After breakfast] I helped Ty finish some homework and talked with him about dealing with his math teacher, whom he hates. I must admit the "down time" with them has been nice. . . . It's the routine patterns of being together, the sense of everydayness, that we miss the most. . . .

Muffled voices outside my window bring me back from my thoughts. They must be outside. . . . "Mom, come here, quick!" Ty yells excitedly . . . [and Zac explains]: "[W]e're building a fort!"

"Well, that sounds pretty good guys, but it's almost time to go and you still haven't packed up yet. Your dad's expecting you for dinner, remember?" "Ah, Mom, can't we stay a little longer," Ty insists, "we just got started." "I know, honey, but this project will be here when you come to visit next time. . . . " I hear myself reluctantly saying. . . . I'm immediately filled with mixed emotions. Although I'm happy to see them finally comfortable enough to make some aspect of this experience their own, I have to begin the departure process. . . . If I don't get them moving now, I won't keep my agreed-on visitation schedule with their dad.

We've entered the kitchen and the door slams behind us, as if to punctuate my words and mark the beginning of our "departure routine." The three of us take the cue and scatter to make preparations.

Source: Adapted from Eicher-Catt 2004a. Deborah Eicher-Catt is assistant professor of Communication Arts and Sciences at Pennsylvania State University.

Noncustodial fathers, like noncustodial mothers, find it difficult to construct a satisfying parent–child relationship. During the marriage, a father's authority in the family gave weight to his parental role, but this vanishes in a nonresidential situation. Geographical distance and conflict with the mother may also be barriers to frequent contact. Custodial mothers are effectively gatekeepers, facilitating, or not, the noncustodial father's relationship with his children (Adamsons and Pasley 2006; Leite and McKenry 2002).

A related issue is **interference with visitation**, discussed earlier in conjunction with conflict between parents. Such a situation can be very frustrating for fathers who do want to maintain close contact with their children (Perrine 2006). In 1998 Congress passed the Visitation Rights Enforcement Act, which requires states to recognize and enforce visitation orders of another state. The earlier Family Support Act of 1988 authorized court intervention programs such as intensive case supervision, mediation, parent education and so on, but so far experimental programs to address interference with visitation have had disappointing results (Pearson and Anhalt 1994; Turkat 1997). As a last resort, courts can order a change of custody.

A new marriage or cohabiting relationship was not itself a factor in decreasing visitation, but the presence of children in a new family, particularly biological children, did lead to a decline. Fathers seemed to find it difficult to parent their children across two families (Manning and Smock 1999). Be that as it may, the situation of noncustodial fathers seems to have improved since earlier research found that many had detached from their children. Noncustodial fathers now spend more time with their children; 35 to 40 percent have at least weekly contact. Few drop out entirely (Kelly and Lamb 2003). In Ahrons's longitudinal study of postdivorce families, 62 percent of now-adult children reported that their relationships with their father got better or at least stayed the same over the twenty years since the divorce (Ahrons and Tanner 2003).

A father's minimal or decreased visiting may be painful for children, and so are visits that alienate rather than bond the child and the noncustodial parent. In one example, described in the Wallerstein study,

> [a]lmost always, there would be other adults around or adult activities planned. Carl watched hundreds of hours of television at his father's house, feeling more and more alone and removed from his earlier visions of family life. (Wallerstein and Blakeslee 1989, p. 79)

Children often forgave geographically distant fathers who did not appear frequently, but were very hurt by those nearby fathers who rarely visited.

The visitation of fathers does not always affect children positively (Marsiglio et al. 2000). In extreme cases—where there is verbal, physical, or sexual abuse— father contact may actually be damaging to children (King 1994). We've seen that some divorces are precipitated by alcoholism, drug abuse, or domestic violence; in such cases, visitation is not necessarily in the best interest of a child.

When the father enacts an authoritative parenting style (see Chapter 11) and when the visit does not lead to conflict between the parents, it has a favorable impact on the child's adjustment. The most recent studies do show a higher level of paternal parenting skills, so perhaps younger divorced fathers have been more involved with children in the marriage and have a better mastery of parenting during visitation.

Good relationships with noncustodial fathers foster better outcomes for children (Carlson 2006; White and Gilbreth 2001). Contact is a threshold requirement for a father's positive influence. Relationship quality and responsive parenting (that fathers consider the child's point of view and explain decisions) were found to have a positive effect regarding adolescents' "internalizing" (depression) and "externalizing" (aggressive and antisocial behavior) problems. Adolescents' relationships with their mothers were a more powerful influence on well-being, however. Noteworthy is that if an adolescent had a poor relationship with his or her mother, a good one with a nonresidential father seemed to make a difference. Adolescents with poor relationships with both custodial mothers and nonresidential fathers were, not surprisingly, at greatest disadvantage in terms of adjustment (King and Sobolewski 2006; Sobolewski and King 2005).

A custodial parent's moving away has become a significant postdivorce visitation issue, to be discussed later in this section. In some moving cases, as well as others, judges have ordered "electronic communication" or "virtual visits," by video conferencing, instant messaging, webcam setups, and the like. Although they can be costly, these virtual visits allow the noncustodial parent to talk, play chess, view art projects or at-home dance or music performances, and the like over the Internet. On the whole, such electronic communication enhances contact between parents and children. There is some concern that courts will come to rely on electronic visitation rather than the real thing: "'You can't virtually hug your child'" (Clemetson 2006c).

Child Abduction At the other extreme from dissociating from children is kidnapping one's children from the other parent. A study sponsored by the Justice Department reports that over 200,000 children were abducted by family members in 1999 (Hammer, Finkelhor, and Sedlak 2002). Fifty-three percent were taken by biological fathers, 25 percent by biological mothers, 24 percent by grandparents, and the rest by siblings, aunts, uncles, or mothers' boyfriends. Younger children (under six) are most apt to be abducted; there is no difference in the numbers of boys or girls. Most of the children abducted by family members were returned or located.

Child snatching is frightening and confusing for the child, may be physically dangerous, and is usually detrimental to the child's psychological development. Yet for years the abduction of a child by a biological parent (without custody) was not legally considered kidnapping—or at least not prosecuted as such. Now, however, due to the passage of the Uniform Child-Custody Jurisdiction and Enforcement Act and the Parental Kidnapping Prevention Act, states must recognize out-of-state custody decrees and do more to find the child and prosecute offenders (Fass 2003).

Another form of child-snatching is international abduction, increasingly common when cross-cultural marriages fail and a parent has transnational ties. Retrieving a child from another country is very difficult, despite the Hague Convention (an international treaty that requires countries to recognize original custody determinations). Advocates argue that the U.S. government has not been sufficiently aggressive in pursuing such cases, and parents often turn to private services that attempt re-abduction of the child back to the parent in the United States (Alvarez 2003; Sapone 2000).

Child abduction is an extreme act, but it points up the frustration involved in arrangements regarding sole custody, or, in some cases, a lack of attention to the noncustodial parent's allegations of child abuse (Johnston and Girtner 2001).

Joint Custody California was the first state to enact a statute on joint custody. "Currently joint custody is either recognized, presumed, or mandated in most states [and] provinces of the United States and Canada" (M-Y. Lee 2002, p. 672).

In **joint custody**, both divorced parents continue to take equal responsibility for important decisions regarding the child's general upbringing. When parents live close to each other and when both are committed, joint custody can bring the experiences of the two parents closer together, providing advantages to each. Both parents may feel they have the opportunity to pass their own beliefs and values on to their children. In addition, neither parent is overloaded with sole custodial responsibility. Joint custody gives each parent some downtime from parenting (M-Y. Lee 2002).

Joint custody agreements have two variations. One is *joint legal and physical custody,* in which parents or children move periodically so that the child resides with each parent in turn on a substantially equal basis. The second variation is *joint legal custody*—in which both parents have the right to participate in important decisions and retain a symbolically important legal authority—with physical custody (that is, residential care of the child) going to just one parent. Parents with higher incomes and education are more likely to have joint custody (Wallerstein 2003).

Table 16.2 lists advantages and disadvantages of joint custody from a father's perspective. Shared custody gives children the chance for a more realistic and normal relationship with each parent (Arditti and Keith 1993). It results in more father involvement and in closer relationships with both parents (M-Y. Lee 2002.)

The parents of Zach, whose story is included in "My Family: How It Feels When Parents Divorce," have joint custody; this may be one reason for his conclusion that "just because your parents are separated it doesn't mean you're going to lose anybody."

The high rate of geographic mobility in the United States can make joint physical custody difficult. Even without that, some children who have experienced joint custody report feeling "torn apart," particularly as they get older. Although some youngsters appreciate the contact with both parents and even the "change of pace" (Krementz 1984, p. 53), others don't. The following account from eleven-year-old Heather shows both sides of a joint physical custody arrangement:

> The way it works now is we switch houses every seven days—on Friday night at five-thirty. . . . [E]ach of our parents likes to help us with our homework and when we stay with them for a week at a time it's easier for them to keep up with what we're doing. . . . And as long as they're divorced, I don't see any alternative because it wouldn't seem right to live with either parent a hundred percent of the time and only see the other one on weekends. But switching is definitely the biggest drag in my life. . . . My rooms are so ugly because I never take the time to decorate them—I can't afford enough posters and I don't bother to set up my hair stuff in a special way because I know that I'll have to take it right back down and bring it to the next house. Now I'm thinking that I'll try to make one room my real room and have the other one like camping out. I can't buy two of everything, so I might as well have one good room that's really mine. (quoted in Krementz 1984, pp. 76–78)

Table 16.2 Advantages and Disadvantages of Joint Custody from a Father's Perspective

ADVANTAGES	DISADVANTAGES
Fathers can have more influence on the child's growth and development—a benefit for men and children alike.	Children lack a stable and permanent environment, which can affect them emotionally.
Fathers are more involved and experience more self-satisfaction as parents.	Children are prevented from having a relationship with a "psychological parent" as a result of being shifted from one environment to another.
Parents experience less stress than sole-custody parents.	Children have difficulty gaining control over and understanding of their lives.
Parents do not feel as overburdened as sole-custody parents.	Children have trouble forming and maintaining peer relationships.
Generally, fathers and mothers report more friendly and cooperative interaction in joint custody than in visitation arrangements, mostly because the time with children is evenly balanced and agreement exists on the rules of the system.	Long-term consequences of joint custody arrangements have not been systematically studied.
Joint custody provides more free social time for each single parent.	
Relationships with children are stronger and more meaningful for fathers.	
Parental power and decision making are equally divided, so there is less need to use children to barter for more.	

Source: Adapted from *The Developing Father: Emerging Roles in Contemporary Society* by B. E. Robinson and R. L. Barret, 1986, p. 89. Copyright © 1986 Guilford Publications. Adapted by permission.

Joint custody is expensive. Each parent must maintain housing, equipment, toys, and often a separate set of clothes for the children and must sometimes pay for travel between homes if they are geographically distant. Mothers, more than fathers, would find it difficult to maintain a family household without child support, which is often not awarded when custody is shared. There may be situations—an abusive parent, other domestic violence, or extremely high levels of parental conflict, for example—where sole custody is preferable (Hardesty and Chung 2006).

Research does not consistently support the presumption that joint custody is always best for children of divorced parents. The Stanford Child Custody Study (Maccoby and Mnookin 1992) found that children in mother custody did as well as those in joint custody: "'[T]he welfare of kids following a divorce did not depend on who got custody, but on how the household was managed and how the parents cooperated'" (psychologist Eleanor Maccoby in Kimmel 2000, p. 141; see also Ahrons 2004). One reviewer of the research literature concluded that there is "no consistent evidence of the superiority of one arrangement over another" (M-Y. Lee 2002, p. 673).

Another review of thirty-three studies of joint and sole custody (Bauserman 2002) did find that children in joint custody arrangements had superior adjustment. In fact, "joint custody and intact family children did not differ in adjustment" in terms of general adjustment, family relationships, self-esteem, emotional and behavioral adjustment, and divorce-specific adjustment (p. 98). This finding of the advantages of joint custody applies to *legal joint custody* as well as to *legal and physical joint custody*. Sole custody was not necessarily bad, but joint custody was simply better in terms of child outcomes.

When a Custodial Parent Wants to Move The desire of a joint custodian or a parent with sole custody to move and take the children "is the hottest issue in the divorce courts at the moment," according to Judith Wallerstein (in Eaton 2004, p. A-1). Some divorce decrees mandate judicial consent and/or the consent of the other parent for a move to another locality. Other cases have gone to court as a result of a parent's initiating legal action to prevent a move.

In deciding these cases, judges have difficult issues to sort out: "Does the parent who wants to move have a compelling reason, or is she just trying to keep the child away from the father? Does the parent who opposes the move really want to be involved with the child, or is he just trying to control his ex-wife?" (Eaton 2004, p. A-1). Judges in different jurisdictions have rendered varying decisions.

Some state laws or court decisions have prohibited custodial parents from moving if they want to retain custody or share joint custody (Cooper 2004; *Navarro v. LaMusga* 2004). "As a result, women have been torn between their wish to remarry or otherwise rebuild their lives and their wish to have their children reside in their homes at least part-time. . . . In checking with legal experts, I found no instance where the father's wish to move was contested" (Wallerstein and Blakeslee 2003, p. 201).

Some judges do see a constitutional issue in the right to move, especially in this "highly mobile society" (Elrod and Spector 2002, p. 595). Or they wish to balance the needs of all family members and consider the benefits, as well as costs, involved in a parent's relocation—a child may benefit from a parent's increased earning power, for example, or may gain a two-parent family if the move is related to remarriage (S. Downey 2000). Courts are now more inclined to permit moves for remarriage or economic reasons than they were in the 1980s and 1990s (Kelly and Lamb 2003).

Judith Wallerstein has appeared in court in support of relocating parents, and her opinion has proven very influential. She takes the position that the well-being of the custodial parent and that parent's relationship with the child are the most important factors in adjustment, trumping the question of contact with the other parent. Another divorce researcher, Richard Warshak, presents the opposite point of view in advocating that attention be paid to the importance of a child's maintaining contact with each parent (Eaton 2004). There is little research to date on the issue of parental relocation and none yet on the adjustment of young children to parental relocation.

Parent Education for Co-Parenting Ex-Spouses

Several states have begun to offer or require parent education for divorcing parents. In some communities, the children also meet in groups with a teacher or mental health professional (Geasler and Blaisure 1998; Lewin 1995). The idea is that parents will continue to raise their children as **co-parents,** and they are likely to need help in meeting this new challenge. Evaluation forms completed after the sessions have shown predominantly positive responses. But "there has been no evaluation of whether the information provided is actively employed by parents in their relationship with each other or with the child or whether, indeed, there is any change in the child's well-being" (Wallerstein 2003, p. 86).

Parents in many states are now required to negotiate a "parenting plan" before their divorce is approved. Again, we have no research yet as to the effectiveness of this requirement in facilitating cooperative postdivorce parenting.

This discussion of mothers' and fathers' custody, visitation, and child support issues suggests that being divorced is in many ways a very different experience for men and women.

His and Her Divorce

Perhaps nowhere is this difference more evident than in the debate over which partner—the ex-wife or the ex-husband—is the primary victim of divorce. Both are affected by the divorce, but often in different ways.

The first year after divorce is especially stressful for both ex-spouses. Divorce wields a blow to each one's self-esteem. Both feel they have failed as spouses and, if there are children, as parents (Brodie 1999). They may question their ability to get along well in a remarriage. Yet each has particular difficulties that are related to the sometimes different circumstances of men and women. In this discussion, we are primarily speaking of divorced men and women who are parents.

Her Divorce

Women who were married longer, particularly those oriented to traditional gender roles, lose the identity associated with their husband's status. Getting back on their feet may be particularly difficult for older women, who usually have few opportunities for meaningful career development and limited opportunities to remarry (Choi 1992). Women of the baby boom generation and later have usually had significant work experience, so they may find it easier to reenter the work world, if they are not already there.

Divorced mothers who retain sole custody of their children often experience severe overload as they attempt to provide not only for financial self-support but also for the day-to-day care of their children. Monitoring and supervising children as a single parent is especially difficult (Braver, Shapiro, and Goodman 2006). Mothers' difficulties are aggravated by lingering gender discrimination in employment, promotion, and salaries and by the high cost of child care. They may have less education and work experience than their ex-husbands. All in all, custodial mothers frequently feel alone as they struggle with money, scheduling, and discipline problems. Objective difficulties are reflected in decreased psychological well-being (Doherty, Su, and Needle

"Her" divorce often involves financial worries and task and emotional overload as she tries to be the complete parent for the children.

© Rameshwas Das

1989; Ross 1995). An encouraging note, though, is that the poverty rate of single custodial mothers dropped significantly between 1993 and 2005, although at 26 percent, it remains higher than that of custodial fathers (Grall 2006).

Although those experiencing marital dissolution are less happy than those who are married, another comparison gives us a picture of "her" divorce that is a bit brighter. A majority of women respondents to the National Survey of Families and Households (1992–1993) who compared their lives before and after marital separation perceived improvement in overall happiness, home life, social life, and parenting, although not in finances or job opportunities (Furstenberg 2003, Figure 1, p. 172). Women, compared to men, are more likely to have built social support networks, and they do show greater emotional adjustment and recovery than men (Braver, Shapiro, and Goodman 2006).

His Divorce

Divorced men miss having daily contact with their children and are concerned about possible qualitative changes in their parent–child relationships as well (Braver, Shapiro, and Goodman 2006). In some ways, divorced noncustodial fathers have more radical readjustments to make in their lifestyles than do custodial mothers. In return for the responsibilities and loss of freedom associated with single parenthood, custodial mothers escape much of the loneliness that divorce might otherwise cause and are rewarded by social approval for raising their children (M. Myers 1989).

"His" divorce involves loss of time with children, as well as a more general loneliness. Being the "visiting parent" is often difficult, but maintaining the father–child bond is significant in a child's adjustment to divorce.

Many children of divorce, especially daughters, developed closer relationships with their mothers after the divorce (Amato 2000).

Custodial fathers, like custodial mothers, are under financial stress. Noncustodial fathers often retain the financial obligations of fatherhood while experiencing few of its joys (Arendell 1995). Whether it takes place in the children's home, the father's residence, or at some neutral spot, visitation is typically awkward and superficial. The man may worry that if his ex-wife remarries, he will lose even more influence over his children's upbringing. For many individuals, parenthood plays an important role in adult development: "Removed from regular contact with their children after divorce, many men stagnate" (Wallerstein and Blakeslee 1989, p. 143).

Ex-husbands' anger, grief, and loneliness may be aggravated by the traditional male gender role, which discourages them from sharing their pain with other men (Arendell 1995). Sociologist Catherine Ross (1995) compared levels of psychological distress for men and women in four different categories: marrieds, cohabitors, those who were dating, and those with no partner. Ross found that divorced men had the lowest levels of emotional support of any group, while emotional support among divorced women was "not that much lower than married women's" (p. 138). In situations of isola-

tion and depression, men are more likely than women to be vulnerable to substance abuse and alcoholism (Braver, Shapiro, and Goodman 2006). Yet in most cases, men still hold the keys to economic security, and ex-wives suffer financially more than do ex-husbands.

The fact is that both men's and women's postdivorce situations would be somewhat alleviated by eliminating the economic discrimination faced by women, especially women reentering the labor force, by strong child support enforcement, and by constructing co-parenting relationships that give fathers the sense of continuing involvement as parents that most would like.

Some Positive Outcomes?

First came *Creative Divorce*. As divorce rates rose steeply in the 1960s and into the 1970s, many were heartened by Mel Krantzler's 1973 book, which offered the hope that some good would come of this painful experience.

The eighties and nineties saw an accounting of the all too real problems of divorce for children and adults. "Creative divorce" seemed not only ironic but almost maliciously misleading to those making the difficult decision of whether to divorce.

Another swing of the pendulum seems to be taking place. Researchers have begun to explore positive outcomes of divorce. Scholars and clinicians have begun to talk about **stress-related growth** (for children as well as adults). There is now more emphasis on the diversity of outcomes of divorce.

Those studying positive outcomes have connected this line of research to other research on stress-related growth. Stress-related growth can take different paths. A *crisis-related pathway* is marked when a traumatic event generates an ultimate result that makes the person stronger. (See Chapter 15, "Family Stress, Crises, and Resilience," for a more general discussion of these ideas as applied to the family.) A *stress-relief pathway* occurs, when, for example, the end of a marriage and its problems brings relief to one or both of the partners. Kinds of growth include growth in the self; growth in interpersonal relationships (closer to family and friends); and growth or change in philosophy of life. The specifics are as yet a little vague, and more research is needed. Yet, scholars reviewing the literature conclude that

[r]esearch on stress-related growth indicates that most individuals who have experienced traumatic events

Postdivorce Pathways

Not all divorces have the same outcomes, as research by E. Mavis Hetherington and her colleagues demonstrates. These researchers developed a typology to describe the adjustment to divorce of 238 divorced women and 216 men whom they had interviewed regularly over a ten-year period in the Virginia Longitudinal Study of Divorce and Remarriage. The variability of outcomes is striking.

The Virginia researchers developed a typology based on a cluster analysis of eleven adjustment measures: neuroticism, antisocial behavior, social maturity/responsibility, health, achievement, well-being and satisfaction, self-efficacy, autonomy, parenting competence, social relations, and self-esteem. Six patterns of adjustment emerged from the analysis: Figure 16.7 presents the percentages of men and women in each category at the ten-year point.

Enhancers composed 20 percent of the sample, with more women than men in the group. These individuals "grew more competent, well adjusted, and fulfilled" (Hetherington 2003, p.

324) and had good success at work, in social relations, as parents, and often in remarriages. Some had had a good start in terms of their predivorce qualities, while others were "women who looked ordinary until the stresses of divorce and the challenges of being a single parent activated competencies or forced them to seek out additional resources" (p. 324).

Goodenoughs "had some vulnerabilities, some strengths, some successes, and some problems. They fell in the middle on most personal characteristics. . . . Ten years after divorce, the goodenoughs' postdivorce life looked like their old predivorced life" (p. 324). At 40 percent, the Goodenoughs were the largest group, almost equally divided between men and women.

Seekers were those who "were eager to find a new mate as quickly as possible." They are hard to quantify because they dropped out of this category once they repartnered. Seekers had less self-esteem and independence, and the men "required a great deal of affirmation. . . . [If

not remarried, Seeker men] succumbed to anxiety, depression, and sometimes sexual dysfunction" (p. 324). They were very dependent on their partners, both old and new. Haste to remarry meant that they sometimes did not make good choices in remarriage partners.

Swingers were a predominantly male group that also declined in numbers over time as the attraction of a libertine lifestyle waned. At the ten-year point, fewer than 10 percent of the divorced people studied were Swingers.

More women than men were *Competent Loners*. "Healthy, well-adjusted, self-sufficient, and socially skilled, competent loners often had gratifying careers, active social lives, and a wide range of hobbies and interests. . . . [They] were often involved [in] intimate relationships, but these relationships were not enduring . . . [as competent loners] had little interest in permanently committing to share their lives with anyone" (p. 325). Hetherington characterizes Competent Loners, along with Enhancers, as "divorce winners" (p. 325).

---

report positive life changes. . . . One thing that is clear from the existing research . . . is that it is at least as common to experience positive outcomes following divorce as negative one[s], and that positive outcomes can coexist with even substantial pain and stress. (Tashiro, Frazier, and Berman 2006, pp. 362, 364)

Another way of looking at stress-related growth—as well as less happy outcomes—comes from E. Mavis Hetherington's Virginia Longitudinal Study of Divorce and Remarriage. She and her colleagues followed 144 couples for twenty years; half were divorced initially, and half not. Additional families were added as time went by. Families were interviewed at various points, but our interest here is in the ten-year point. A previously developed typology of postdivorce adaptive patterns was used to assess the adjustment of divorced adults. Hetherington found 20 percent of those studied to have

"enhanced" lives, while 40 percent had "good enough adjustment" (Hetherington and Kelly 2002; Hetherington 2003). "Facts about Families: Postdivorce Pathways" provides more details about this important study.

Perhaps the best overall assessment of the outcomes of divorce is that of Paul Amato:

On one side are those who see divorce as an important contributor to many social problems. On the other side are those who see divorce as a largely benign force that provides adults with a second chance for happiness and rescues children from dysfunctional and aversive home environments. . . . Based on . . . research . . . it is reasonable to conclude that . . . [d]ivorce benefits some individuals, leads others to experience temporary decrements in well-being that improve over time, and forces others on a downward cycle from which they might never fully recover. (Amato 2000, p. 1282)

Defeated individuals, a little over 10 percent of the divorced group at the ten-year point, had low social responsibility and self-esteem and high depression and antisocial behavior. In essence, they did not have satisfying lives.

Hetherington remarks that in analyzing divorce, many commentators assume that the "defeated" type is the "standard outcome of a marital breakup"—but this is not the case (p. 325). "When marriages dissolve, there is no one adaptive pathway adults follow. Some pathways may be destructive, others may be constructive and enhancing" (p. 329).

Critical Thinking

Hetherington and her colleagues have provided us with a set of types. How well do these types of postdivorce adjustment apply to situations that you may have witnessed or personally experienced?

Source: Hetherington 2003.

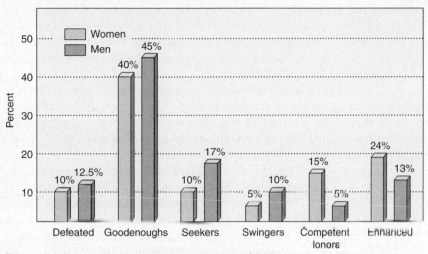

Figure 16.7 Postdivorce adaptive patterns of 216 men and 238 women at the ten-year point: Virginia Longitudinal Study of Divorce and Remarriage.

Source: From Hetherington, 2003, "Intimate Pathways: Changing Patterns in Close Personal Relationships Across Time," *Family Relations*, 52(4): 318–331, Figure 3. Reprinted by permission of Blackwell Publishing.

Adult Children of Divorced Parents and Intergenerational Relationships

We have talked about the general effect of divorce on children, but what do we specifically know about how a parental divorce affects adult children's married and family lives? Marital stability for adult children of divorce is discussed earlier in this chapter, as well as in Chapter 9. Here we address the topic of the quality of intergenerational relationships between adult children and their divorced parents.

There is evidence that adult children of divorced parents have probably come to accept their parents' divorce as a desirable alternative to ongoing family conflict (Ahrons 2004; Amato and Booth 1991). Neverthe-

less, a number of studies point to one conclusion: Ties between adult children and their parents are generally weaker (less close, less supportive) when the parents are divorced (Aquilino 1994a, b; Szinovacz 1997; L. White 1994). The effect for divorced parents is stronger for fathers, usually the noncustodial parent, but the relationship has been found for mothers as well.

Sociologist Lynn White (1994) analyzed data from 3,625 National Survey of Families and Households respondents to examine the long-term consequences of childhood family divorce for adults' relationships with their parents. Using a broad array of indicators of family solidarity—relationship quality, contact frequency, and perceived and actual social support (doing favors, lending and giving money, feeling that one can call on the parent for help in an emergency)—White found that those raised by single parents reported lowered solidarity with them. As adults, they saw their parents less often, had poorer-quality relationships, felt less able to count on parents for help and emotional support, and actually received less support. White found these negative effects to be stronger regarding noncustodial parents (usually the father) but not limited to them.

In another study, sociologist William Aquilino (1994a) analyzed National Survey of Families and Households data from 3,281 young adults between ages nineteen and thirty-four. All grew up in intact families and had therefore lived with both biological parents from birth to age eighteen, but in about 20 percent of the sample, their parents had subsequently divorced. Aquilino found that even when parents divorce after the child is eighteen, the divorce seems to negatively affect the quality of their relationship. Children of divorced parents were in contact with their parents less often and reported lower relationship quality overall. These findings applied to both mothers and fathers, although the effect was much stronger for fathers.

Generally, evidence suggests that adult children of divorced parents feel less obligation to remain in contact with them and are less likely to receive help from them or to provide help to them. Social scientists (Lye et al. 1995) have posited four reasons for these findings:

1. Children raised in divorced, single-parent families may have received fewer resources from their custodial parent than did their friends in intact families, and thus they may feel less obliged to reciprocate.

2. Strain in single-parent families, deriving from the single parent's emotional stress or economic hardship or both, may weaken subsequent relations between adult children and their parents.

3. The reciprocal obligations of family members in different generations may be less clear in single-parent, postdivorce families.

4. Adult children raised in divorced, single-parent families may still be angry, feeling that their parents failed to provide a stable, two-parent household.

Remarriage and stepfamily relationships may generate similar tensions (remarriage and stepfamilies are discussed in Chapter 17).

Should Divorce Be Harder to Get?

In reviewing the process of divorce and its effects, this question arises: Should divorce be harder to get? Some Americans and some family scholars and policy makers think so. At the same time, the American public holds somewhat ambivalent attitudes about divorce. In one poll, one-half of those surveyed thought divorce should be harder to get (Thornton and Young-DeMarco 2001, p. 1021). It also appears that some unhappily married individuals postponed divorce until their children were older (American Association of Retired Persons 2004). Yet one poll found most people saying that they do want divorce laws to be tougher—but not when the divorce is their own ("The Divorce Dilemma" 1996).

Some family scholars argue that our high divorce rate signals the decline of the American family (see Chapter 1). To address this situation, policy makers have proposed changes in state divorce laws so that divorces would be more difficult to get than they have been since the 1970s. As noted earlier, with no-fault divorce laws, a marriage can be dissolved simply by *one* spouse's testifying in court that the couple has "irreconcilable differences" or that the marriage has suffered an "irretrievable breakdown."

Concerned about the sanctity of marriage, the impact on children of marital impermanence, and what seems to some a lack of fairness toward the spouse who would like to preserve the marriage, some states have developed—or at least considered—laws and policies that would make divorce harder to obtain. Three states—Louisiana (in 1997), Arizona (in 1998), and Arkansas (in 2001)—have enacted covenant marriage laws. Such laws have been proposed in a number of other states but not enacted (Zurcher 2004).

Covenant marriage, also discussed in Chapter 7, is an alternative to standard marriage that couples may select at the time of marriage or later. It is essentially a return to fault-based divorce because it requires spouses to prove fault (adultery, physical or sexual abuse, imprisonment for a felony, or abandonment) or to live apart for a substantial length of time in order to obtain a divorce or to do both. Premarital counseling and counseling directed toward saving the marriage are also required. Although a poll indicates that one-half of Americans say they support covenant marriage (Thornton and Young-DeMarco 2001), only a small minority of couples have chosen this option—less than 2 percent in Louisiana (Nock et al. 2003). "Overall, covenant marriage has not proved as popular as supporters have hoped" (Zurcher 2004, p. 288), although those who have chosen covenant marriage are very satisfied (Nock et al. 2003). Chapter 7 discusses covenant marriage and other marriage support programs in detail.

Those who believe divorce is too readily available have proposed other restrictions on divorce or postdivorce arrangements. These have included the restoration of fault for all divorces; a waiting period of as long as five years; a two-tier divorce process, with a more extensive process for divorces involving children; prioritization of children's needs in postdivorce financial arrangements; requirement of a "parenting plan" to be negotiated prior to granting a divorce; and publicizing research that would convince the public of the risks of divorce (Hewlett and West 1998, pp.242–43; Waite and Gallagher 2000, pp.188–99). Many states and cities have established premarital counseling, marriage education, marriage counseling, or some combination of the three as either required or elective for couples planning to marry. Some locales require divorcing parents to attend a parent education program. Few object to such programs when voluntary, though some have objected to their being required. Research is lacking on their effectiveness in preventing divorce (Belluck 2000; Lewin 1995).

Opposition to restrictions on divorce centers around various points. First, divorce is not always or necessarily bad for children. Second, some marriages—those involving physical violence or overt conflict or both—are harmful to children and to one or both spouses. Divorce provides an escape from marital behaviors, such as a parent's alcoholism or drug abuse, that may be more harmful than divorce itself (Coontz 1997a). An interesting study by economists Betsey Stevenson and Justin Wolfers (2004) found that no-fault divorce was associated with a decline in suicide rates for women, as well as a decline in domestic violence against both men and women, and a decline in intimate-partner homicides of women. The existence of an escape route seems to change the balance of power and reduce violence.

It also appears that staying married would not necessarily provide economic stability for women and children. Those women who obtain divorces would be better off economically if they remained married, but they would not be as well off as that portion of the population that has not divorced; there are differences between the two groups in economic resources quite apart from divorce (Smock, Manning, and Gupta 1999).

Those who oppose restoration of fault divorce point to the fraudulent practices that characterized the divorce process under fault statutes. Seldom was either party truly "innocent" of contributing to the marital difficulties, although one party had to pose as such. "Mental cruelty" was the most easily proven grounds for divorce, but the "evidence" for this was often exaggerated at best and completely trumped up at worst. In New York State—where adultery was the only grounds for divorce—"adultery" was often staged, in a drama organized by lawyers and colluded in by both spouses.

Is Divorce Necessarily Bad for Children?

Having thoroughly reviewed the literature and conducted longitudinal research on the subject, sociologists Paul Amato and Alan Booth (1997) conclude that children whose parents were continuously and happily married are indeed the most successful in adulthood. Children of divorce or those whose parents remained unhappily married were less successful. Amato and Booth note the significant role that level of parental conflict plays in conclusions about benefit or harm to children from divorce. They divide divorce outcomes into two classes: In one-third of the cases, marital conflict is so serious and so affects children that they are much better off if the parents divorce. But in two-thirds of the cases—in these researchers' opinion—conflict is low-level and not very visible to children. Then the children seem better off if the parents remain married. Amato and Booth present their conclusions as informative, not as advocacy for legal restrictions on divorce.

Is Making Divorce Harder to Get a Realistic Idea?

Noting that divorce is "an American tradition" that began in colonial times and has grown more prevalent with industrialization and urbanization, historian Glenda Riley, among others, argues that making divorce harder to get will not change this trend (Riley 1991; Coontz 1997b; Skolnick 1997).

Given the likelihood that the restrictions on divorce that some reformers would like to see put in place are unlikely to become law, what may be done to address the negative consequences of divorce for children and to help postdivorce families more generally?

Surviving Divorce

Studies in other countries suggest that policy remedies can make divorce less fraught with hardship. And there is research on "the good divorce," one that provides a workable family in the aftermath of divorce.

Social Policy Support for Children of Divorce

A cross-cultural study gives insight into what the wider U.S. society might do to help. Sociologists Sharon Houseknecht and Jaya Sastry (1996) examined the relationship between "family decline" and child well-being in four industrialized countries: Sweden, the United States, the former West Germany, and Italy. These researchers' measures of family decline included nonmarital birth and divorce rates, the proportion of one-parent households with children, and the percentage of employed mothers with children under three years old. Child well-being was measured by six factors: educational performance, the percentage of children in poverty, infant deaths from child abuse, teenage suicide rates, juvenile delinquency rates, and juvenile drug offense rates. The researchers found that "Sweden, which has the highest family decline score, does not demonstrate a high level of negative outcomes for children compared with other countries with lower levels of family decline. It looks much better than the U.S., which ranks the lowest on child well-being" (p. 736).

What makes the difference between child well-being in the United States and in Sweden? Sweden's welfare policies are "egalitarian and generous" when compared to those of the United States (p. 737). Sweden's society-wide willingness to support children's needs by paying relatively high taxes translates into significantly less child poverty, fewer working hours for parents, and more family support programs, such as paid parental leave. This situation results in relatively high levels of child well-being despite high proportions of nonmarital births, mother employment, divorces, and single-parent households. A review of policies and outcomes in Nordic countries by sociologist William Goode reached similar conclusions (Goode 1993).

The Good Divorce

Is there such a thing as a "good divorce"? That depends on expectations. Against the assumption that divorce is a disaster and solidifies a lasting enmity between the part-

ners to the detriment of their children, one can indeed find a different pattern, whereby couples maintain civility and cooperative parenting, and perhaps even spend some holidays together with their children (Scelfo 2004). "My Family: The Postdivorce Family as a Child-Raising Institution" describes a couple that continued to parent their children together after divorce, with the assistance of a counselor and after some turmoil.

The Binuclear Family Study The Binuclear Family Study, led by sociologist Constance Ahrons (1994), interviewed ninety-eight divorcing couples approximately one year after their divorce. Ninety percent of them were followed to the five-year point, in a total of three interviews each. These were primarily white, middle-class couples from one Wisconsin county.

At the one-year point, 50 percent of the ex-spouses had amicable relations while the other 50 percent did not. In half the cases, the divorce was a bad one and harmful to family members; in the other half, the divorcing spouses had "preserved family ties and provided children with two parents and healthy families" (p. 16):

> In a good divorce a family with children remains a family. The family undergoes dramatic and unsettling

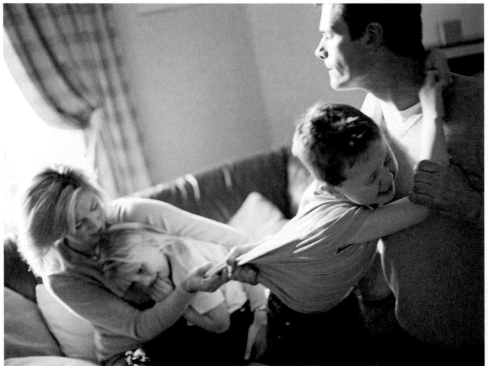

When divorcing parents continue to engage in conflict and especially when children are drawn into it, a child's adjustment is poorer. Interparental conflict does tend to diminish with the passage of time.

My Family | The Postdivorce Family as a Child-Raising Institution

Jo Ann is thirty-eight and has been divorced for six years. She has five children. Gary, nineteen, her oldest, lives with his father, Richard. At the time of this interview, Jo Ann and Richard and their children had recently begun family counseling. The purpose, Jo Ann explained, was to create for their children a more cooperative and supportive atmosphere. Jo Ann and Richard do not want to renew an intimate relationship, but they and their children are still in many ways a family fulfilling traditional family functions.

We've been going to family counseling about twice a month now. The whole family goes—all five kids, Richard, and me. The counselor wants to have a videotaping session. He says it would help us gain insights into how we act together. The two older girls don't want any part of it, but the rest of us decided it might be really good for Joey to see how he acts [Joey's] the reason we're going in the first place. At the first counseling sessions, he sat with his coat over his head. . . .

Joey's always been a problem. He's used to getting his own way. Some people want all the attention. They will do anything to get it. I guess I never knew

how to deal with this. . . . He drives us nuts at home. He calls me and the girls names. . . . He was disrupting class and yelling at the teacher. And finally they expelled him. . . . Joey gets anger and frustration built up in him.

So I took him to a psychologist, and the psychologist said he'd like the whole family to come in, including Richard. Well, Richard still lives in this city and sees all the kids, so I asked him about it. And he said okay. . . .

In between sessions, the counselor wants us to have family conferences with the seven of us together. One day I called Richard and asked him over for supper. In the back of my mind I thought maybe we could get this family conferencing started.

Well, after dinner Joey, our eleven-year-old, started acting up. So I went for a walk with him. We must have walked a mile and a half, and Joey was angry the whole time. He told me I never listen to him; I never spend time with him. Then he started telling me about how he was mad at his dad because his dad won't listen to him.

He said his dad tells all these dumb jokes that are just so old, but he just

keeps telling them and telling them. So when we got home, I saw Richard was still there, and I asked Joey, "Would you like to have a family conference? Maybe tell your dad some of the things that are bothering you?" And he said, "Could we?" . . . [During the conference] Joey talked first. Then everybody had a chance to say something. There was one time I was afraid it was going to get out of hand. Everybody was interrupting everybody else. But the counselor had told me you have to set up ground rules. This is where we learned that we got some neat kids because when I said "Let somebody else talk," everybody did! So it went real well. . . . And then finally Richard said, "I think it's time for us to come to a conclusion." I said, "Well, you're right."

Critical Thinking

How might this divorced family differ from the same family before divorce? How is it the same? Even though Jo Ann and Richard's family is no longer intact, what functions does it continue to perform for its members? For society?

changes in structure and size, but its functions remain the same. The parents—as they did when they were married—continue to be responsible for the emotional, economic, and physical needs of their children. (Ahrons 1994, p. 3)

The ninety-eight couples represented a broad range of postdivorce relationships. In 12 percent of the cases, couples were what Ahrons termed *Perfect Pals*—friends who called each other often and brought their common children and new families together on holidays or for outings or other activities. This was a minority pattern among the "good divorces." More often (38 percent), the couples were *Cooperative Colleagues*, who worked well together as co-parents but did not attempt to share holidays or be in constant touch—occasionally, they might share children's important events such as birthdays. Ex-spouses might talk about extended family, friends, or

work. They still had areas of conflict but were able to compartmentalize them and keep them out of the collaboration that they wanted to maintain for their children (Ahrons 1994). "As We Make Choices: Ten Keys to Successful Co-Parenting" provides some general guidelines for divorcing parents who want to cooperate in parenting their children.

Other divorcing couples were the *Angry Associates* (25 percent) or *Fiery Foes* (25 percent) that we often think of in conjunction with divorce. Over time, one-quarter of the Cooperative Colleagues drifted into one of these more antagonistic categories.[14]

[14] Ahrons (1994) identified a fifth type of postdivorce couple relationship, the *Dissolved Duo*. These are couples who have completely lost touch with each other. Because Ahrons's specification of her sample required that a divorced couple have children and be in touch, there were no instances of Dissolved Duos in her sample.

As We Make Choices — Ten Keys to Successful Co-Parenting

Melinda Blau, author of *Families Apart: Ten Keys to Successful Co-parenting*, observes that "[d]ivorce ends a marriage—it does not end a family; we got divorced; our children didn't" (1993, p. 16). Here are her general guidelines for those who hope to accomplish the "heroic feat" of co-parenting after divorce (pp. 16–17):

Key #1: Heal yourself—so that you can get on with your life without leaning on your kids.

Key #2: Act maturely—whether or not you really *feel* it; you and your co-parent are the adults, with the responsibility to care for your kids and to act in their best interest.

Key #3: Listen to your children; understand their needs.

Key #4: Respect each other's competence as parents and love for the children.

Key #5: Divide parenting time—somehow, in some way, so that the children feel they still have two parents.

Key #6: Accept each other's differences—even though one of you is a health-food nut and the other eats Twinkies, one is laidback and the other a disciplinarian, one's fanatically neat, the other is a slob.

Key #7: Communicate about (and with) the children directly, not *through* them.

Key #8: Step out of traditional gender roles. Mom learns how to fix a bike and knows what the "first down" is if her son's into football, and Dad can take his daughter shopping and talk with her about dates.

Key #9: Recognize and accept that change is inevitable and therefore can be anticipated.

Key #10: Know that co-parenting is forever; be prepared to handle holidays, birthdays, graduations, and other milestones in your children's lives with a minimum of stress and encourage your respective extended families to do the same.

Critical Thinking

Do you agree or disagree with the advice presented here?
Source: Blau 1993.

These divorced parents have both come to meet with their child's teacher. When parents work together to co-parent their children, they continue to have a sense of "family."

Ahrons's overall point is that the "good divorce" does not end a family but instead produces a **binuclear family**—two households, one family. She argues that we must "recognize families of divorce as legitimate." To encourage more "good divorces," it is important to dispel the "myth that only in a nuclear family can we raise healthy children" (p. 4). People often find what they expect, and social models of a functional postdivorce family have been lacking.

Ahrons (2004) recently reinterviewed 173 children from eighty-nine of the original families in her Binuclear Family Study. Now averaging thirty-one years of age, they had been six through fifteen at the time of the marital separation. At present—twenty years later—79 percent think that their parents' decision to divorce was a good one, and 78 percent feel that they are either better off than they would have been, or else not that affected. Twenty percent, however, did not do so well, with "emotional scars that didn't heal" (p. 44). Ahrons judges that the prime factor affecting outcomes was how the parents related to each other in terms of avoiding conflict. The title of Ahrons's most recent book—*We're Still Family* (2004)—characterizes the positive outcomes of divorce that she has found among many of the families she studied.

Attachment Between Former Partners A more controversial outcome of the "good divorce," and perhaps even some bad ones, is continuing attachment between ex-spouses. One of Paul Bohannon's "stations of divorce" is the psychic divorce, marking the end of the divorce process. **Psychic divorce** refers to the regaining of psychological autonomy through emotional separation from the personality and influence of the former spouse. In Bohannon's view, one must distance oneself from the still-loved aspects of the spouse, from the hated aspects, and "from the baleful presence that led to depression and loss of self-esteem" (Bohannan 1970b, p. 53).

By this standard, attachment between former spouses had been seen as a failure of adjustment. But now, clinicians and social scientists are beginning to rethink this stance. "[A]ttachment may be a natural outcome of shared parenting" (Madden-Derdich and Arditti 1999, p. 243). Ahrons and others have written favorably about continuing attachment in the context of co-parenting and maintenance of a family identity and activities.

But what about the postdivorce partner bond as an end in itself? Not only has it been "underacknowledged" but "the nonparenting aspect of ex-spousal relationships has been considered synonymous to psychological maladjustment" (Masuda 2006, pp. 114; 117).

Taking a positive view of former partners who redefine their relationship as friendship, Masahiro Masuda points out that there can be other than parenting elements in a continued attachment. Exploratory research

found some interesting themes that point to good reasons ex-partners might maintain a degree of attachment. What these ex-partners, now friends, talked about was that he or she is "part of my life." They had shared experiences with the former partner that they did not want to consign to limbo. They also claimed to have had a "clean breakup" and that "we're different now." In other words, there were boundary markers that would make sure the past relationship did not prevent formation of new serious relationships despite the continuation of a friendship.

Masuda studied young people and had a sample of limited size—thirty-four college students. But journalists have reported on later-life playing out of postdivorce couple attachments. It appears that it is not unusual for one divorced spouse to provide assistance to the other who needs it at the end of life:

> Hospice workers, academics, and doctors say they are seeing more such cases. . . . Often a person feels deep ties to a former husband or wife or feels a responsibility born of common experience and childrearing. . . . "They are acting more like a brother or sister, or cousin, or extended family member" [said the CEO of a public policy hospice group]. (Richtel 2005, p. ST1-2)

The Divorce-Extended Family A continued postdivorce partner connection can result in a much expanded family. Ahrons, author of *The Good Divorce*, offers a number of suggestions that she believes would contribute to good divorce outcomes and successful binuclear families. One suggestion is that the parent "accept that your child's family will expand to include nonbiological kin" (p. 252). Indeed, divorce and the new relationships that follow can produce a **divorce-extended family**.

A surprising phenomenon encountered by those who do research on divorced families is the expansion of the kinship system that is produced by links between ex-spouses and their new spouses and significant others and beyond to *their* extended kin. Sociologist Judith Stacey (1990) speaks of a divorce-extended family (p. 61) and quotes writer Delia Ephron's apt observation:

> It occurred to me . . . that the extended family is in our lives again. . . . Your basic extended family today includes your ex-husband or -wife, your ex's new mate, your new mate, possibly your new mate's ex, and any new mate that your new mate's ex has acquired. It consists entirely of people who are not related by blood, many of whom can't stand each other. (Ephron 1988, frontleaf)

Ephron's version may be out of date in one respect. Some postdivorce extended families find they can enjoy and benefit from connections to one another even when there had earlier been conflict and old tensions sometimes resurface (Kleinfield 2003). Stacey's research described a Silicon Valley family that functioned as a mutual aid society in times of crisis and happily shared good times and special occasions as well.

Therapists claim to see "a new norm" of rapport and social contact among the divorce-extended family that is "becoming part of the culture" (Dr. Harvey Ruben, professor of clinical psychiatry at Yale School of Medicine, quoted in Kuczynski 2001, pp. 9-1, 9-6). In this spirit, "[n]o longer are the names of exes unmentioned at the dinner table. No longer are the details of passing children between homes confined to emotionless e-mail messages. Family therapists, sociologists, and journalists note that 'family members who 25 years ago might not have had anything to do with one another are finding it desirable to stay connected'" (Kuczynski 2001, p.9-1).

These eight grandparents, all connected to the young basketball player by marriage, divorce, and remarriage, come together to cheer him on and enjoy his game.

To the extent that relationships between ex-spouses are cordial and the ties of a divorce-extended family come to seem natural, tension for children moving between families should be reduced. Familial occasions such as graduations and weddings that bring everyone together should be less strained. New research finds that good relationships between children and noncustodial fathers *and* residential stepfathers make independent contributions to good child outcomes (White and Gilbreth 2001). If the therapists are right about "new norms," what we could see in the future would be an institutionalization of the "good divorce"—perhaps not attainable for all, but recognized as "normal" for those who do.

That change involves incorporating remarriage bonds into the original family. We turn in Chapter 17 to a consideration of that common step for many divorced people: remarrying.

Summary

- Divorce rates rose sharply in the twentieth century, and divorce rates in the United States are now among the highest in the world. Since around 1980, however, they have declined substantially.

- Among the reasons divorce rates have increased to the present level are changes in society. Economic interdependence and legal, moral, and social constraints are lessening. Expectations for intimacy have risen, while expectations of permanence are declining.

- People's personal decisions to divorce involve weighing the advantages of the marriage against marital complaints in a context of weakening barriers to divorce and an assessment of the possible consequences of divorce.

- Two consequences that receive a great deal of consideration are how a divorce will affect any children and whether it will cause serious financial difficulties.

- Bohannan has identified six "stations of divorce," or aspects of the divorce process and adjustment to divorce. These are: the emotional divorce, the legal divorce, the community divorce, the psychic divorce, the economic divorce, and the co-parental divorce.

- The economic divorce is typically more disastrous for women than for men, and this is especially so for custodial mothers. Over the past twenty-five years, child support policies have undergone sweeping changes. The results appear to be positive, with more child support being collected. Fathers' chief concern is maintaining a relationship with their children, so visitation, joint custody, and the moving away of custodial mothers are their chief legal and policy issues.

- Researchers have proposed six possible theories to explain negative effects of divorce on children. These include the life stress perspective, the parental loss perspective, the parental adjustment perspective, the economic hardship perspective, the interparental conflict perspective, and the family instability perspective.

- Husbands' and wives' divorce experiences are typically different. Both the task overload and financial decline that characterize the wife's divorce and the loneliness that often accompanies the husband's might be mitigated by less-gender-differentiated postdivorce arrangements. Joint custody offers the opportunity of greater involvement by both parents, although there are some concerns about joint custody as a universal remedy.

- Debate continues among family scholars and policy makers concerning how important a threat divorce is to children today. Some call for return to a fault system of divorce or other restrictions on divorce. Others see divorce as part of a set of broad social changes, the implications of which must be addressed in ways other than turning back the clock. Now there is also a centrist view of the impact of divorce on children: Yes, there is some disadvantage; no, divorce is not the most powerful influence on children's lives.

- New norms and new forms of the postdivorce family seem to be developing. Some postdivorce families can share family occasions and attachments and work together civilly and realistically to foster a "good divorce" and a binuclear family.

Questions for Review and Reflection

1. What factors bind marriages and families together? How have these factors changed, and how has the divorce rate been affected?

2. How is "his" divorce different from "her" divorce? How are these differences related to society's gender expectations? In your observation, are the descriptions given in this chapter accurate assessments of divorce outcomes for men and women today?

3. In what situation(s), in your opinion, would divorce be the best option for a family and its children?

4. Do you think couples are too quick to divorce? What are your reasons for thinking so?

5. **Policy Question.** Should divorced parents with children be required to remain in the same community? Permitted to move only by court authorization? Be free to choose whether to be geographically mobile?

Key Terms

barriers to divorce 417
binuclear family 449
child support 427
children's allowance 428
community divorce 424
co-parents, co-parenting 439
covenant marriage 444
crude divorce rate 414
custodial parent 427
custody 434
divorce divide 414
divorce-extended family 449
divorce mediation 423
economic divorce 426
economic hardship perspective (on children's adjustment to divorce) 432
emotional divorce 422

family instability perspective (on children's adjustment to divorce) 433
guaranteed child support 428
income effect 416
income-to-needs ratio 426
independence effect 416
instability hypothesis 433
interference with visitation 436
intergenerational transmission of divorce 418
interparental conflict perspective (on children's adjustment to divorce) 432
joint custody 438
legal divorce 423
Levinger's model of divorce decisions: barriers, rewards, alternatives 419
life stress perspective (on children's adjustment to divorce) 432

no-fault divorce 417

parental adjustment perspective (on children's
    adjustment to divorce) 432

parental loss perspective (on children's adjustment
    to divorce) 432

psychic divorce 449

redivorce 416

refined divorce rate 414

relatives of divorce 424

selection hypothesis 433

spousal support 427

stress-related growth 441

unilateral divorce 423

Online Resources

Companion Website for This Book

www.thomsonedu.com/sociology/lamanna

Visit the book companion website, where you will find
flash cards, practice quizzes, Internet links, suggested
readings, InfoTrac College Edition exercises, and more
to help you study.

ThomsonNOW™ for Marriage and Family

Spend time on what you need to master rather than on
information you already have learned. Take a pre-test for
this chapter, and ThomsonNOW will generate a personalized study plan based on your results. The study plan
will identify the topics you need to review and direct you
to online resources such as videos, narrated learning
modules, and interactive activities to help you master
those topics. You can then take a post-test to help you
determine the concepts you have mastered and what
you will still need to work on. Try it out! Go to **www
.thomsonedu.com/login** to sign in with an access code
or to purchase access to this product.

Remarriages and Stepfamilies

17

Remarriage: Some Basic Facts

Facts about Families: Remarriages and Stepfamilies—Diversity by Race/Ethnicity and Sexual Orientation

Remarriage, Stepfamilies, and Children's Living Arrangements

Choosing Partners the Next Time: Variations on a Theme

Remarriage Advantages for Women and Men

Homogamy in Remarriage

Spouses' Happiness/Satisfaction and Stability in Remarriage

Happiness/Satisfaction in Remarriage

The Stability of Remarriages

Negative Stereotypes and Remarital Satisfaction and Stability

My Family: My (Step)Family

The Various Types of Remarried and Stepfamilies

Differences Between First Marriages with Children and Stepfamilies

Stepfamilies and Ambiguous Norms

Stepfamily Boundary Ambiguity

A Closer Look at Family Diversity: Immigrant Stepfamilies

Kin Networks in Stepfamilies

Family Law and Stepfamilies

Children's Well-Being in Stepfamilies

Stepparenting: A Challenge in Remarriage

Some Reasons Stepparenting Is Difficult

Stepmothers

As We Make Choices: Some Stepparenting Tips

Stepfathers

Having a Mutual Child

My Family: From Stepfather to Father—Creating a Resilient Stepfamily

Creating Supportive Stepfamilies

© Michelle D. Bridwell/PhotoEdit

Today remarriages make up approximately half of all marriages (Coleman, Ganong, and Fine 2000). And "one in three Americans are now stepparents, stepchildren, stepsiblings, or living in a stepfamily" (Dawn Miller 2004). Enough remarriages involve stepchildren that travel packages market the "familymoon"—that is, a honeymoon that includes the entire new stepfamily (Greenberg and Kuchment 2006). This chapter explores remarriages and stepfamilies.

More and more stepfamilies today result from cohabitation rather than from legal remarriage. Although studies are accumulating on cohabitation in general, relatively little research has been done on how cohabiting *stepfamilies* function (Ganong and Coleman 2004; S. Stewart 2007). Consequently, many of the researchers' findings and therapists' suggestions in this chapter were meant to apply to **remarried families**. The extent to which they apply to *cohabiting* stepfamilies is uncertain.

Many remarried people are happy with their relationships and lives. Much of what we have said throughout this book—about good parenting practices, for example, and about positive ways for couples to communicate or how best to handle family stress—applies to remarriages and stepfamilies. At the same time, partners and children in stepfamilies experience unique challenges, because stepfamilies are different from first-marriage families in several important ways (Ganong and Coleman 2004).

In this chapter, we will discuss choosing a remarriage partner. We'll examine happiness and stability in remarriage, as well as the adjustment and well-being of children in stepfamilies. We'll examine two challenges that are typically associated with remarriages and stepfamilies.

Finally, we will explore ideas for creating happy and supportive remarriages and stepfamilies. We'll begin with an overview of remarriage in the United States today.

Remarriage: Some Basic Facts

Unfortunately, the U.S. Census Bureau stopped compiling remarriage statistics in 1988. Today we rely on survey data from national random samples (Bramlett and Mosher 2002; Kreider and Fields 2005). Based on survey data, we can estimate today's situation. We know, for instance, that **remarriages** (marriages in which at least one partner had previously been divorced or widowed) are assuredly more frequent in the United States today, compared to the middle decades of the twentieth century. The remarriage rate rose sharply during World War II, peaking as the war ended. During the 1950s, both the divorce rate and the remarriage rate declined and remained relatively low until the 1960s, when they began to rise again. The remarriage rate peaked again in about 1972 but has declined somewhat since then (Bianchi and Casper 2000, Figure 2).

One reason for the decline in remarriage rates is that many divorced people who would have remarried in the past are now cohabiting (S. Stewart 2007). A second reason for the decline may be economic constraints and uncertainties, which discourage divorced men, in particular, who may already be paying child support, from assuming financial responsibility for a new family.[1]

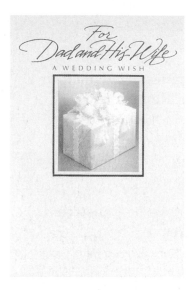

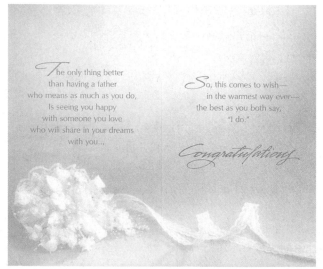

About half of all marriages today are remarriages, a fact that greeting card companies acknowledge.

---

[1] Some states, concerned about child support, passed legislation in the 1970s designed to prevent the remarriage of people whose child support was not paid up. But the Supreme Court ruled in *Zablocki v. Redhail* (1978) that marriage—including remarriage—was so fundamental a right that it could not be abridged in this way.

"*Well, the children are grown up, married, divorced, and remarried. I guess our job is done.*"

vorce, then remarry again. But a majority of remarriages are second marriages. ("Facts about Families: Remarriages and Stepfamilies—Diversity by Race/Ethnicity and Sexual Orientation" gives further statistics regarding remarriages.)

Remarriages have always been fairly common in the United States. However, well into the twentieth century almost all remarriages followed widowhood. Today, the vast majority of remarrieds have been divorced (S. Stewart 2007). Remarriage is much more likely to occur, age for age, among divorced women than among widowed women (Talbott 1998). Figure 17.1 contrasts the marriage rates of divorced men and women with those of the widowed and illustrates change over time.

Although remarriages represent approximately half of all marriages today, when compared with first-marriage families, remarried families continue to be stereotyped as other than "normal" (Ganong and Coleman 2004). As discussed in Chapter 3's "Issues for Thought: Studying Families and Ethnicity," research can be undertaken from the cultural equivalent, cultural deviant, or cultural variant approach. For the most

Nevertheless, about three-quarters of divorced women remarry within ten years (Bramlett and Mosher 2001, Table 7). Some people divorce, remarry, redi-

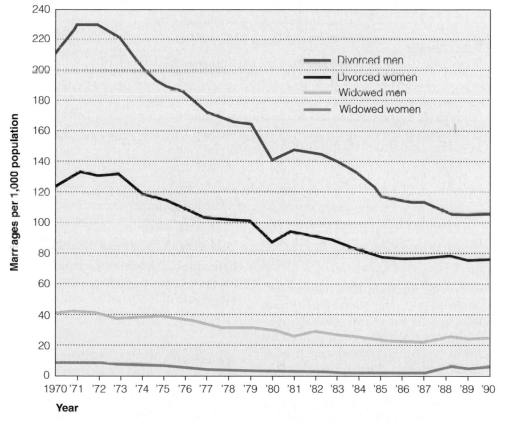

Figure 17.1 Marriage rates of divorced and widowed men and women, 1970–1990. Marriage rates presented here are number of marriages per 1,000 population in the specified marital status category. These data are from the 1990 national census—the latest statistics available.

Sources: U.S. National Center for Health Statistics 1990b, Table 5; Clarke 1995, Table 6.

Remarriages and Stepfamilies—Diversity by Race/Ethnicity and Sexual Orientation

The average divorced person who remarries does so within four years after divorce; 30 percent do so within one year (Coleman, Ganong, and Fine 2000). However, rapidity—and overall probability—of remarriage vary for women of different ethnic origins. About 42 percent of non-Hispanic white women remarry within three years after divorce, compared with 23 percent of non-Hispanic black women and 29 percent of Latinas. Analogous percentages for five years after dissolution are 58 percent for non-Hispanic whites, 32 percent for non-Hispanic blacks, and 44 percent for Latinas (Bramlett and Mosher 2001, Table 8).

Stepfamilies and Racial/Ethnic Diversity

The living arrangements of children who are residing with two parents are also differentially distributed by race and Hispanic origin.* Among non-Hispanic white children who live in two-parent families, 88 percent reside with both biological parents and another 8 percent live with their biological mother and a stepfather. For Hispanics, those figures are 90 percent and 8 percent, respectively. Among Asian Americans, 95 percent of children in two-parent families live with both of their biological parents, and 2 percent reside with their biological mother and a stepfather. Among African American children who live in two-parent families, 82 percent reside with both biological parents, and 13 percent live with their biological mother and a stepfather. These figures compare to 88 percent and 9 percent, respectively, for all races taken together (Kreider and Fields 2005, Table 1).

Gay and Lesbian (GL) Stepfamilies

A gay or lesbian (GL) stepfamily is "any GL couple in which at least one of the partners has at least one child from a prior marriage or partnership (heterosexual or homosexual); the child may reside with the couple full- or part-time, and the couple may have formalized their relationship as a civil union . . . or may simply cohabit" (van Eeden-Moorefield, Henley, and Pasley 2005, p. 231).

It is difficult to get accurate statistics on GL stepfamilies, but the "best guess" of some experts is that "there are millions" of gay and lesbian stepfamilies in the United States today. The number is expected to increase, given current separation rates and the significant number of GL couples who are raising children (van Eeden-Moorefield, Henley, and Pasley 2005).

Critical Thinking

What do you think might be some policy implications of some of the statistics presented here?

*Note that this discussion is about the distribution of children, not in *all* households with children, but only in *two-parent* households.

---

part, research on stepfamilies has proceeded from the cultural deviant perspective—that is, researchers look at ways that stepfamilies deviate from the "normal," first-married family.

Meanwhile, there is no question that remarriages' and stepfamilies' increasing numbers and visibility have led to their somewhat greater social and cultural acceptance. In line with this development, communications professor Paul Schrodt (2006) has created a measure of stepfamily life from the cultural variant approach—that is, Schrodt investigates stepfamilies on their own terms without comparing them to other family forms. Here are some sample statements to which a respondent can agree or disagree:

- I have a peaceful stepfamily.
- Members of my stepfamily respect each other.
- We honor everyone's birthday in my stepfamily.

- My stepfamily tries new ways of dealing with family problems. (Schrodt 2006, pp.436–37)

In the future, should researchers use Schrodt's measure, we can expect to learn more about everyday stepfamily life. We turn now to an examination of children's living arrangements in stepfamilies.

FOCUS ON CHILDREN

Remarriage, Stepfamilies, and Children's Living Arrangements

One result of the significant number of remarriages and the growing incidence of cohabitation after divorce is that more Americans are parenting other people's biological children. In U.S. households, a little over 5 percent of children under age eighteen are stepchildren, and almost 6 percent of adult children (eighteen years old and over) who are living "at home" are doing so in stepfamily households (Kreider 2003, Table 1). As you can see in Figure 17.2, 88 percent of children under age eighteen in married-couple or cohabiting households are the biological offspring of both parents. Another 8 percent of children in two-parent households are the biological offspring of the mother and stepchildren of the father. About 2 percent of children in two-parent households are biological children of the father and stepchildren of the mother (Kreider and Fields 2005, Table 1).

Figure 17.2 points up the fact that stepfamilies are not all alike: A stepparent may be mother or father (although usually the father). Furthermore, a stepfamily may or may not contain biological children of both remarried parents. At least 4 percent and perhaps up to 10 percent of households with children are *joint biological-step*—that is, at least one child is a *mutual child*—the biological child of both parents—and at least one other child is the biological child of one parent and the stepchild of the other parent (Kreider 2003, Table 8). In some stepfamilies, both parents are stepparents to their spouse's biological children.

Then, too, as we have already mentioned, stepfamilies do not always result from remarriage: "Approximately 25% of the 3.7 million cohabiting couples in the United States are households in which at least one adult brings children from prior relationships, thereby creating cohabiting stepfamily households" (Coleman, Ganong, and Fine 2000, p. 1290; see also Simmons and O'Connell 2003, Table 4).

The remainder of this chapter explores what family life is like for children—and their parents—who are living in stepfamilies. We begin with a question about courtship before remarriage. Do people choose partners differently the next time around?

Choosing Partners the Next Time: Variations on a Theme

Courtship for remarriage has not been a major topic for research. Nevertheless, counselors note that people who ended troubled first marriages through divorce are often still experiencing personal conflicts (Bray 1999; Hetherington 1989) that they need to resolve before they can expect to fashion a supportive, stable second marriage. Counselors advise waiting until one has worked through grief and anger over the prior divorce before entering into another serious relationship (Marano 2000).

Meanwhile, courtship before remarriage may differ in many respects from courtship before first marriage. It may proceed much more rapidly, with the people involved viewing themselves as mature adults who know what they are looking for—or it may be more cautious, with the partners needing time to recover from their previous marital experience or being wary of repeating it. A second courtship may include both outings with the children and evenings at home as partners seek to recapture their accustomed domesticity. It may have a sexual component that is hidden from the children through a series of complex arrangements. "A common courtship pattern is as follows: (a) male partner spends a few nights per week in the mother's household, followed by (b) a brief period of full-time living together, followed by (c) remarriage" (Coleman, Ganong, and Fine 2000, p. 1290). Next we'll look at two topics that we also discuss in Chapters 7 and 9: (1) the relative advantages of marriage—in this case, remarriage—for men and for women, and (2) homogamy.

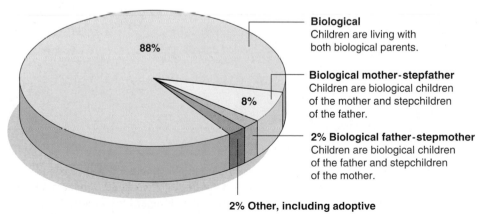

Figure 17.2 Children under age eighteen living with two parents, by their biological, step, and adoptive status, 2001.
Source: Kreider and Fields 2005, Table 1.

Remarriage Advantages for Women and Men

Economists and other social scientists point out that, as a group, ex-wives, but not ex-husbands, are likely to gain financially by being remarried. A longitudinal study by sociologists Donna Morrison and Amy Ritualo (2000) used National Longitudinal Survey of Youth (NLSY) data to track the financial well-being of children of divorced mothers and their custodial children. The children had been born to a married couple who later divorced. Some of the custodial mothers remained single, others remarried, and still others formed cohabiting stepfamilies. The finances of mothers who remarried greatly improved. Mothers who began cohabiting also saw an increase in finances, although not as great. We can conclude that, in general, remarriage is financially advantageous to divorced mothers and their children (Morrison and Ritualo 2000). This situation would change, of course, if women's earnings were to catch up with men's. Chapter 16 addresses the economic plight of divorced women in more detail.

This uneven situation—that is, that remarrying women, on average, benefit financially more than do remarrying men—is one reason that women's remarriage rate is considerably lower than men's. In part, this statistic is a consequence of the very low remarriage rate of widows, for whom few partners are available in later life (Moorman, Booth, and Fingerman 2006). But even comparing only divorced people, men's remarriage rates are substantially higher, particularly after age thirty. At least two factors work against women's remarriage.

Age and the Odds of Remarriage Remarriages increased among older adults over the past several decades. Currently about a half million people over age sixty-five remarry annually, and about 4 percent of older adults who do not remarry choose to cohabit (Coleman, Ganong, and Fine 2000). Nevertheless, age may work against both women's and men's remarriage. Older people may face considerable opposition to remarriage—both from restrictive pension and Social Security regulations and from their friends and children. Although some peers or grown children may be supportive of a remarriage, others may find it inappropriate. Adult children may worry about the biological parent's continued interest in them, or, ultimately, they may be concerned about their inheritance (Pasley 1998b; Rosenfeld 1997).

© Walter Hodges/GettyImages/Riser

As Americans live longer, many of them are finding that love and intimacy can occur at any age. People tend to choose partners a bit differently the second time around; for one thing, remarriages tend to be less homogeneous with regard to religion than are first marriages. And although remarriage rates are relatively low for those over sixty-five, some do find happiness in a late remarriage.

Specifically concerning women, age reduces the odds of remarrying. Although the pattern of remarriage since 1960 has been similar for all age categories, the remarriage rate for younger women is consistently higher than for older women (Moorman, Booth, and Fingerman 2006). As discussed in Chapter 8, women live longer, on average, than men do: By about age sixty-five, there are approximately eighty men for every one hundred women (U.S. Census Bureau 2007a, Table 11). Then, too, the *double standard of aging* works against women in the remarriage market: In our society, women are considered to be less physically attractive with age, and they may also be less interested in fulfilling more-traditional gender-role expectations.

Children and the Odds of Remarriage "Children lower the likelihood of remarriage for both men and women, but the impact of children is greater on women's probability of remarriage" (Coleman, Ganong, and Fine 2000, p. 1289). As we see in Chapter 16, the woman usually retains custody of children from a previous marriage. As a result, a prospective second partner may look on her family as a financial—and an emotional and psychological—liability. Interestingly, a recent study that analyzed data from the National Survey of Families and Households (NSFH) found that custodial fathers are significantly more likely to marry women with children than are other men (Goldscheider and Sassler 2006). This situation exemplifies the "traditional exchange," discussed in Chapter 9, according to which women trade child raising for enhanced economic security. We might also define this situation as a form of homogamy in remarriages.

Homogamy in Remarriage

We see in Chapter 9 that homogamy is important in both the choice of a first marriage partner and in subsequent marital stability. Does homogamy play a similar role in remarriages? Unfortunately, there has not been much research on this question. However, available data suggest that remarriages are somewhat less homogeneous than first unions. When they do remarry, older people, particularly those who are widowed, are likely to choose homogamous spouses. Sometimes the new partner is someone who reminds them of their first spouse or is someone they've known for years. But this rule does not apply to middle-aged or younger people who choose remarriage partners.

Choosing a remarriage partner differs from making a marital choice the first time inasmuch as there is a smaller pool of eligibles with a wider range on any given attribute. As prospective mates move from their late twenties into their thirties and forties, they affiliate in occupational circles and interest groups that assemble people from more diverse backgrounds. As a result, remarriages have been less homogamous than first marriages, with partners differing more in age, educational background (U.S. National Center for Health Statistics 1990b), and religion.

Because homogamy increases the likelihood of marital stability, the increased heterogamy characteristic of remarriage has been offered as a partial explanation for the fact that the divorce rate is higher for remarriages (Booth and Edwards 1992). We turn now to a discussion of remarried spouses' happiness and the stability of remarriages.

Spouses' Happiness/Satisfaction and Stability in Remarriage

As pointed out elsewhere in this text, marital happiness, or satisfaction, and marital stability are not the same. *Marital happiness* and *marital satisfaction* are synonymous phrases that refer to the quality of the marital relationship whether or not it is permanent; *marital stability* refers simply to the duration of the union. We'll look at both ways of evaluating remarriage.

Happiness/Satisfaction in Remarriage

In general, research shows little difference in spouses' overall well-being (Demo and Acock 1996) or in marital happiness between first and later unions (Ihinger-Tallman and Pasley 1997; Skinner et al. 2002). For one thing, as we see in Chapters 12 and 14, wives' satisfaction with the division of household labor is important to marital satisfaction. Some evidence shows that there is more equity, or fairness, in remarriages than in first marriages (Buunk and Mutsaers 1999) because remarried husbands contribute somewhat more to housework than do husbands in first marriages. This situation may be especially true for older remarried couples (Clarke 2005). Interestingly, one study found that this appears to have more to do with an ex-wife's less-than-satisfactory experience in her first marriage, and subsequent partner selection for remarriage, than with remarried men's resolution to do more around the house than they did in their first marriage (Sullivan 1997). On the other hand, a small study based on extensive interviews with fifteen adult stepchildren found "the persistence of traditional gender practices in the parenting and stepparenting of children" (Schmeeckle 2007, p. 174).

Whatever may be the case regarding gender roles in remarriages and stepfamilies, considerable research shows that remarrieds experience more tension and conflict than do first marrieds, usually on issues related to stepchildren—discipline or distribution of resources to stepchildren (Coleman, Ganong, and Fine 2000). Nevertheless, it is probably safe to conclude that support from friends and families of origin and supportive family communication are more important to marital satisfaction than whether the union is a first marriage or a remarriage (Golish 2003).

The Stability of Remarriages

"Remarriages dissolve at higher rates than first marriages, especially for remarried couples with stepchildren" (Coleman, Ganong, and Fine 2000, p. 1291; see also Bramlett and Mosher 2001). According to the Stepfamily Association of America, about 60 percent of remarriages end in divorce, compared with about half of all first marriages ("Stepfamily Facts" 2003). As a result, a "conservative estimate is that between 20 percent and 30 percent of stepchildren will, before they turn eighteen, see their custodial parent and stepparent divorce" (Mason 1998, p. 99).

There are several reasons for the generally lower stability of remarriages. You may recall Chapter 8's discussion about how cohabiting—at least serial cohabiting—before marriage generally increases the odds of divorce. Interestingly, a study that analyzed more than 3,000 remarried respondents from National Survey of Families and Households (NSFH) data found that, similarly, postdivorce cohabitation is positively associated with remarital instability (Xu, Hudspeth, and Bartkowski 2006). The authors of the study suggest that *selection* (the idea that divorced people who "select" themselves into cohabitation are different from those who don't) may explain this situation. For one thing, people who divorce in the first place—and those who cohabit—are disproportionately from lower-middle- and lower-class groups, which generally have a higher tendency to divorce or redivorce.

A second reason that remarriages are more likely to end in divorce may be that people who remarry after divorce are, as a group, more accepting of divorce and may have already demonstrated that they are willing to choose divorce as a way of resolving an unsatisfactory marriage. Third, remarrieds may receive less social support from their families of origin and are generally less integrated with parents and in-laws, thus not having the advantage of relationships that can act as a barrier to divorce (Coleman, Ganong, and Fine 2000).

Perhaps the most significant factor in the comparative instability of remarriages is the presence of stepchildren. One important study on a national sample of black and white couples concluded that stepchildren are *not* necessarily associated with more frequent marital conflict. Moreover, it's important to note that the negative impact of stepchildren declines with the length of the remarriage (MacDonald and DeMaris 1995). "My Family: My (Step)Family" illustrates these points.

However, sociologists Lynn White and Alan Booth interviewed a national sample of more than 2,000 married people under age fifty-five in 1980 and reinterviewed four-fifths of them in 1983. During that interval, **double remarriages**, in which both partners had been married before, were twice as likely to have broken up as marriages of people in their first marriage. **Single remarriages**, in which only one partner had been previously married, did not differ significantly from first marriages in their likelihood of divorce.

It is estimated that about one-fifth of all marriages today are double remarriages. Approximately another one-fifth of all marriages are single remarriages (Clarke 1995, p. 4). In White and Booth's study, double remarriage increased the probability of divorce by 50 percent over what it would have been otherwise, and having stepchildren in the home increased it an additional 50 percent. Although the presence of stepchildren did not make so much difference in single remarriages, double remarriages involving stepchildren have a very elevated risk of dissolution. Of course, these are the most-complex family types in a society that has not yet developed a normative structure for stepfamilies.

Nevertheless, White and Booth found that *marital quality* does not vary greatly between first marriages and single or double remarriages. Rather, *satisfaction with family life* is generally affected:

> Since they report only modestly lower marital happiness, we interpret this as evidence that the stepfamily, rather than the marriage, is stressful. . . . These data suggest that . . . if it were not for the children these marriages would be stable. The partners manage to be relatively happy despite the presence of stepchildren, but they nevertheless are more apt to divorce because of child-related problems. (White and Booth 1985, p. 696)

Negative Stereotypes and Remarital Satisfaction and Stability

Remarital satisfaction is influenced by the wider society through the negative stereotyping of remarriages (Ganong and Coleman 2004; S. Stewart 2007). Some religions, such as Catholicism, do not recognize a remarriage after divorce unless the first marriage has been annulled (Hornik 2001). Historically (R. Phillips 1997), and today, society is beset with such potentially harmful myths as "a stepfamily can never be as good as

My Family   My (Step)Family

The following essay was written for a marriage and family course by a young college student named David.

I'm writing this paper about my family. My family is made up of my family that I reside with and then my dad, stepmother, and half-sister that I visit. My family I reside with is who I consider my real family. We are made up of five girls and three boys, a cat and a dog, my mom and stepfather. The oldest is Harry, then down the line goes Diane, Barbara Ann, Kathy, Debi, Mel, Sharon, and myself. My sister Debi and I are the only kids from my mom's original marriage, so as you can see my mom was taking a big step facing six new kids. (My mom has guts!)

I still consider my dad "family," but I don't come into contact with him that much now. I would like to concentrate on my new "stepfamily," but I really don't like that word for it. My family is my family. My brothers and sisters are *all* my brothers and sisters whether they are step or original. My stepfather, although I don't call him "dad," is my father. My grandparents, step or original, are my grandparents. I can honestly say I love them all the same.

It all began when I was four. I don't remember much about my parents' divorce. The one real memory I have is sleeping with my dad downstairs while my sister slept upstairs with my mom. . . .

My mom met my stepfather, Harry, through mutual friends who went to our church. I was in first grade, and I don't really remember much about their dating. All I knew was either these strange kids came over to my house or I went over to theirs. They were married [when] I was five. At the reception I got to see all my relatives, old and new. . . . After my parents got married, we moved. We didn't move into my stepfather's and his kids' house but to a new house altogether for everyone. I still live there. I love it there and probably will live in that area all my life. . . .

Well, we moved into our new house, and I had to change schools. I had to leave all my old friends and make some new ones. I did make new friends, and what was neat was that our two football teams played each other every year. So I got to play against my old friends with my new friends. When I got into high school, we were all united again. So I had gotten a new family, a new house, and a new school with new friends. I would have to say it was a major life transition. . . .

Both my parents agreed about most issues (discipline, for example), and this led to smooth communication between our parents and us kids. The only thing detrimental I can think of that came out of being in a large family was that I had poor study habits as a young child. The problem was my stepfather can watch TV, listen to the radio, and prepare a balance sheet all at the same time. So he let his kids listen to the radio or watch TV while they did their homework. My mom didn't agree with this, but it was too hard for her to enforce not watching TV with so many kids already used to doing it. . . .

I love all my brothers and sisters very much and would do anything for them.

It is neat to see them get married and have kids. I have three nieces and five nephews. It is very exciting to get the whole family together. A lot of my family, nuclear and extended, live in our area. My grandparents, aunts and uncles, cousins, three sisters, and their kids all live within twenty minutes of our house. Having roots and strong family connections are two things I'm very thankful for. These are things I received from my stepfather because if I lived with my dad, I would be on what I consider his nomadic journey: he moves about every three years.

I think I'm very lucky. I had a solid upbringing and relatively few problems. I owe my stepfather a lot. He has given me clothes and food, taught me important lessons, instilled in me a good work ethic, and seen to it that I get a good education—all the way through college. Without him a lot of these things would not be possible; I am grateful for everything he has done for me. I'm happy with the way things turned out, and I love my family dearly.

Critical Thinking

What might be a reason that David does not like to apply the term *stepfamily* to his own family? Divorce and remarriage may be thought of as transitions or crises or both, the subjects of Chapter 15. In what ways does David's essay illustrate meeting crises creatively, as discussed in that chapter? If you live in a stepfamily, how does David's experience compare to your own?

---

a family in which children live with both natural parents" (Kurdek and Fine 1991, p. 567). In an interesting small study, 211 university students were asked to examine an eight-year-old child's report card. All the students saw the same report card, but some were told that the child lived with his biological parents while others were told that he lived with his mother and stepfather. Asked about their impressions of the child, male (but not female) students rated stepchildren less positively than biological children with respect to social and emotional behaviors (Claxton-Oldfield et al. 2002).

In other words, the stigma associated with stepfamilies may influence our appraisal of stepfamily members' functioning (Jones and Galinsky 2003).[2] Furthermore, "When stepfamilies are not stigmatized, they are often invisible to social systems—the policies and practices of schools and youth organizations create barriers to participation by stepfamily members because they are based on models of first-marriage families" (Coleman, Ganong, and Fine 2000, p. 1299).

In a study of thirty-one white, middle-class spouses in stepfather families, researchers found, especially among the wives, that believing in none or very few of these negative myths and having high optimism about the remarriage were related to high family, marital, and personal satisfaction (Kurdek and Fine 1991). Therapist Anne Bernstein (1999) proposes that we all begin "deconstructing the stories of failure, insufficiency, and neglect" and, instead, "collaboratively reconstruct stories that liberate steprelationships" from this legacy (p. 415).

The Various Types of Remarried and Stepfamilies

When neither spouse enters a remarriage with children, the couple's union is usually very much like a first marriage. But when at least one spouse has children from a previous marriage, family life often differs sharply from that of first marriages.

Remarried families with children are of various types. The simplest is one in which a divorced or widowed spouse with one child remarries a never-married childless spouse. In the most complex type, both remarrying partners bring children from previous unions and have a mutual child or children together. If a remarriage is followed by redivorce and a subsequent remarriage, the new remarried family structure is even more complex (Trost 1997). Moreover,

[E]x-spouses remarry, too, to persons who have spouses by previous marriages, and who also have mutual children of their own. This produces an extraordinarily complicated network of family relationships in which adults have the roles of parent, stepparent, spouse, and ex-spouse; some adults have the role of custodial parent and others have the role of noncustodial, absent parent. The children all have roles as sons or daughters, siblings, residential stepsiblings, nonresidential stepsiblings, residential half-siblings, and nonresidential half-

---

[2] As a unique form of stepfamilies, many gay and lesbian families are "triple-stigmatized" for being (1) gay, (2) gay parents, and (3) stepfamilies (R. Berger 2000; Erera and Fredriksen 1999; Lynch and Murray 2000).

siblings. There are two subtypes of half-sibling roles: those of children related by blood to only one of the adults, and the half-sibling role of the mutual child. Children also have stepgrandparents and ex-stepgrandparents as well as grandparents. (Beer 1989, p. 8)

Stepgrandparents are addressed in Chapter 18.

"I come from a family that has two sets of stepfamilies," wrote one of our students in a recently assigned essay. The complexity of stepfamily structure is further illustrated in Table 17.1. The table compares stepfamilies with consistently married nuclear families. ("A Closer Look at Family Diversity: Immigrant Stepfamilies" explores an even more complex stepfamily system.) The sequential transitions from one family structure to another create a prolonged period of upheaval and stress. Furthermore, enough adjustment to a single-parent household may have occurred that a new, subsequent adaptation to a two-parent stepfamily becomes all the more difficult.

Differences Between First Marriages with Children and Stepfamilies

We can point to the following differences between stepfamilies and first marriages with children. In stepfamilies:

1. "There are different structural characteristics" (see Table 17.1). Therefore, the first-married, nuclear family model is not valid.

2. "There is a complicated 'supra family system,'" including family members from one or more previous marriages.

3. "Children [may] have more than two parenting figures."

4. "There [may be] less family control because there is an influential parent elsewhere or in memory."

5. "There [may be] preexisting parent–child coalitions."

6. "There have been many losses for all individuals."

7. "There are ambiguous family boundaries with little agreement as to family history."

8. At least initially, "there is little or no family loyalty."

9. "There is a long integration period. . . ."

10. Prior to possible integration, family members must recover from previous transitional stresses.

11. Because "society compares stepfamilies negatively to first-married families," individuals need validation as members of a worthwhile family unit.

12. The balance of power is different: Stepparents have relatively little authority initially, and children generally wield more power than in first-married families.

Table 17.1 Major Structural Characteristics of Stepfamilies versus Consistently Married Families

Stepfamilies	Consistently Married Families
Biological parent is elsewhere.	Both biological parents are present.
Virtually all members have recently sustained a primary relationship loss.	
Relationship between one adult (parent) and child predates the marriage.	Spousal relationship predates parental ones.
Children are members in more than one household.	Children are members in only one household.
One adult (stepparent) is not legally related to a child (stepchild).	Parents and child(ren) are legally related.

Source: Adapted with permission from *Stepfamilies: A Guide to Working with Stepparents and Stepchildren* by Emily B. Visher and John S. Visher, 1979. Copyright © 1979. Used by permission of Routledge, Taylor, & Francis Group.

13. A good couple relationship does not necessarily make for good stepparent–stepchild relationships. (Visher and Visher 1996, pp. 41–42)

Throughout the remainder of this chapter, we address many of these characteristics and what can be done to meet the challenges that they create.

Stepfamilies and Ambiguous Norms

Society offers members of stepfamilies an underdeveloped **cultural script**, or set of socially prescribed and understood guidelines, for relating to each other or for defining responsibilities and obligations (Ganong and Coleman 2000). Because of the cultural ambiguity of stepfamily relationships, social scientist Andrew Cherlin (1978) thirty years ago called the remarried family an **incomplete institution**. For the most part, researchers continue to view the situation this way (Ganong and Coleman 2004; Marsiglio 2004a). Social work professor Irene Levin (1997) has argued that "the nuclear family has a kind of model monopoly when it comes to family forms" (p. 123). According to this **nuclear-family model monopoly**, the first-marriage family is the "real" model for family living, with all other family forms "seen as deficient alternatives." This "prejudice" affects everyone's understanding of stepfamilies—researchers and stepfamily members alike—so that we incorrectly expect a second marriage to be "more or less the same as the first" (p. 124).

Although society tends to broadly apply the rules and assumptions of first marriages to remarriages, these rules ignore the complexities of remarried families and leave many questions unanswered (Ganong and Coleman 2004). We'll explore three areas in which the stepfamily as an incomplete institution, with ambiguous norms, is most apparent: (1) boundary ambiguity, (2) relationships with kin, and (3) family law.

Stepfamily Boundary Ambiguity

You may recall that *family boundary ambiguity*, also discussed in Chapter 15, is a "state when family members are uncertain in their perception of who is in or out of the family or who is performing what roles and tasks within the family system" (Boss 1987, quoted in S. Stewart 2005a, p. 1003). Sociologist Susan D. Stewart discusses stepfamily boundary ambiguity as follows:

Family definitions in stepfamilies are dynamic and changeable. One stepfamily member, a wife and mother who complains about never knowing how much to fix for dinner on any given day, describes her family as an "accordion" that "shrinks and expands alternately" [Berger 1998, quoted in S. Stewart 2007, p. 38]. . . . Interviews with stepfamily members reveal that definitions of family often differ between parents and children and between siblings. . . . Boundary ambiguity is higher in nontraditional stepfamilies involving cohabitation, part-time residence, and more complex parenting configurations. (S. Stewart 2007, p. 38)

Stewart analyzed national data from the National Survey of Families and Households (NSFH). The data

"Oh, perfect. I can't remember what I wanted from the basement, and you've remarried."

Social scientists typically research the topics of remarriage and immigration separately, but social work professor Roni Berger (1997) points out that the two situations can occur simultaneously, making for extra family stress.

In the transition from their country of origin to the new society, immigrants experience loss of a familiar physical, social, and cultural environment, destruction of significant relationships, and a loss of language, belief system, and socioeconomic status. Immigration often means also the bitter loss of a dream because of discrepancies between pre-immigration expectations and the reality of life in the new country. . . .

Immigration and remarriage are similar in that both involve multiple losses, discrepancy between expectations and reality, and integration of two cultures within one unit. Therefore, both processes shake the individual and family foundation of identity and require flexibility in adapting to a totally new situation. . . .

In immigration the family culture may serve as a support and in remarriage the cultural context may do the same. However, when remarriage and immigration coincide, families lose the stability of their anchors and the stresses exacerbate each other. For example, it has been recognized that one source of difficulty in remarriage stems from reactivation of previous losses caused by divorce or death. Immigration is an additional link in the chain of losses that intensifies the already heavy history of losses typical to all stepfamilies. . . .

Case Example

Igor, 15, was referred by the school he attends because of acting out behaviors in school. At the time of his referral the boy had been in the United States for six months and lived with his divorced and subsequently remarried mother, his stepfather, his four-year-old half-sis-

ter, and his maternal grandparents. All these six people are crowded in a one-bedroom apartment.

Igor's biological parents lived in Moscow. They married when both of them were 29, . . . and they eventually divorced when Igor was five years old. However, they continued to live in the same apartment because of housing difficulties. As both parents worked, Igor's maternal grandmother was the main parenting figure, a common practice in Soviet families.

When Igor was nine his father moved in with another woman, a single mother of a boy the same age as Igor. They had together two daughters, married, and emigrated to the United States, where Igor's biological father secured a high engineering position and is financially very successful. For five years Igor had no contact with his biological father and his new family. His mother remarried and had a daughter with her new husband, who had never been married before. A year ago the family renewed the contact with Igor's biological father, who sponsored their emigration. Igor's stepfather has been unemployed for most of the last year and Igor's mother works off the books in child care.

His mother and stepfather reported that until the immigration Igor was a "model child." He excelled in school, was popular with friends, involved in extra-curricular activities, played the violin, [was] active in sports and was cooperative and pleasant. During all these years Igor's grandmother remained the major parental figure while practically no relationship developed between him and his stepfather. The troubles started a short time after the family came to the United States. Igor was enrolled in a public school with mostly immigrant Black and Hispanic students. He excelled in mathematics and physics which he studied in a bilingual program and in sports. His language skills were very limited and so were his social rela-

tionships. The family's squeezed housing conditions fostered tension and conflicts. Igor's grandmother does not speak any English and could not therefore continue to negotiate with school and social agencies for him anymore, forcing his mother to take on more of a parental role.

The main issues that Igor brought up with the therapist related to his natural father and to his parents' divorce which he returned to time and again. His mother and stepfather were annoyed with his behavior, blamed him for being ungrateful, and used him as a target for all their frustrations and disappointments with the hardships in the new land. Igor felt rejected, idealized his biological father, and blamed his mother and stepfather of being unjust and not understanding. Everybody in the family felt deprived, treated unfairly, disappointed, and angry.

It seemed that while the divorce occurred 15 years earlier and the actual separation four years later, family stresses related to the remarriage of both parents and the birth of the half-sibling gradually piled up. Subsequently the immigration reactivated the experiences of loss and triggered reactions of mourning, accusation, anger, and guilt that have been building up for a long time. . . .

Igor's situation reveals multiple forces operating simultaneously. . . . Systematic research is much needed to study the combined effects of immigration and step-relationships, the issues caused by this combination of stresses, coping mechanisms that help families with this pile up of stresses, and effective strategies to promote the welfare and well being of immigrant stepfamilies (pp. 362, 364–369).

Source: Roni Berger. "Immigrant Stepfamilies." *Contemporary Family Therapy.* Sept. 1997, vol. 19, Issue 3, pp. 361–370. Reprinted by permission of Springer Science and Business Media.

included 2,313 stepfamilies, defined as "married or cohabiting couples in which at least one partner has a biological or adopted child from a previous union living inside or outside the household" (S. Stewart 2005a, p. 1009). Stewart operationally defined *boundary ambiguity* as "any discrepancy in spouses' or partners' reports of shared children (the biological or adopted children of both partners) and/or stepchildren (biological or adopted children from previous unions" (S. Stewart 2005a, p. 1009).

Stewart found evidence of boundary ambiguity among 25 percent of parents with stepchildren. When one or more stepchildren lived outside the family household, boundary ambiguity rose to 54 percent. When one or more children of both partners lived outside the family household, boundary ambiguity rose still further—to nearly 80 percent (S. Stewart 2005a, p. 1015, Table 1). Cohabiting stepfamilies are more likely to experience boundary ambiguity than are remarried stepfamilies (S. Stewart 2005a, p. 1015, Table 1).

> Results indicate that boundary ambiguity may negatively affect relationship quality and stability, but only for wives or female partners. . . . Because women are generally more relationship centered than men, wives or female partners may experience greater distress from boundary ambiguity than husbands or male partners.
>
> It is also important to consider that family boundary ambiguity may affect stepfamily relationships other than that between spouses and partners (e.g., biological parent-child, stepparent-stepchild, and between step[,] half-, and full siblings). Researchers should examine the effect of boundary ambiguity on the full array of stepfamily relationships. Although boundary ambiguity did not have strong effects on couples' relationships, the presence of stepchildren was associated with more disagreements and an increase in couples' perceptions that they may separate and that things would improve for their partner if they did. These findings are consistent with former work suggesting that the stresses of raising stepchildren may be responsible for high rates of divorce among remarried couples. (S. Stewart 2005a, p. 1025)

Kin Networks in Stepfamilies

Relationships with kin outside the immediate remarried family are complex and uncharted as well (Ganong and Coleman 2004). We have few mutually accepted ways of dealing with the new extended and ex-kin relationships that result from remarriage (S. Stewart 2007). One indication of this situation is that our language has not caught up with the proliferation of new family roles.[3] As family members separate and then join new

families formed by remarriage, the new kin do not so much *replace* as *add to* kin from the first marriage (White and Riedmann 1992). What are the new relatives to be called? There may be stepparents, stepgrandparents, and stepsiblings, but what, for instance, does a child call the new wife that her or his noncustodial father has married (Ganong and Coleman 1997, pp. 89–90). Or if a child alternates between the new households or remarried parents in a joint custody arrangement, what does he or she call "home," and where is his or her "family"? A further example of ambiguity regarding stepfamilies is the lack of legal definitions for roles and relationships.

Family Law and Stepfamilies

Because family law assumes that marriages are first marriages, few legal provisions exist for several remarried-family challenges—for example, balancing husbands' financial obligations to their spouses and children from current and previous marriages, and defining wives' obligations to husbands and children from current and the former marriages. For instance, "in most states, stepparents are not required to support their spouses' children financially, although most voluntarily choose to provide contributions" (Malia 2005, p. 302). (Interestingly, college financial aid applications require information on a stepparent's income in order to calculate student need.) As a result of such ambiguities, including the absence of family legislation for concerns such as providing stepchildren with health insurance, stepfamilies are left to draft individual solutions based on expediency:

> Children receive medical benefits from whichever parent has the more generous plan, or any plan at all. Sometimes, it is the noncustodial parent who offers this advantage, and in one case, it was the cohabiting girlfriend of the noncustodial parent whose plan somehow included the nonresidential children of her partner. Still, a number of stepchildren have currently or at some point in the past been considered dependents of their stepparents for these purposes. (Mason et al. 2002, p. 516)

---

[3] Stepmother Beth Bruno (2001) tells of her experience shortly after her marriage to a man with two daughters:

> We hated the words that described our connection after their dad and I married; the words "stepmother" and "stepdaughter" seemed like flashing neon signs that said, "not-real-mother" and "not-real-daughter." It had been much easier for them to introduce me as their Dad's friend, Beth, and for me to introduce them as Gordon's daughters, Terry and Cindy. Yet I was proud to be legally related to these two wonderful children, who have enriched my life since the day we met. . . . We've come to terms with these complexities over the years.

Incidentally, research suggests that, though remarrieds often share their economic resources, they also take care to protect their individual interests and those of their biological children (Mason et al. 2002). Moreover, in some states, stepparents do not have the authority to see the school records of stepchildren or make medical decisions for them. The preservation of stepparent–stepchild relations when death or divorce severs the marital tie is also a serious issue.

Some stepparents do continue relationships with their stepchildren after divorce (Dickinson 2002). Visitation rights (and corresponding support obligation) of stepparents are just beginning to be legally clarified (Hans 2002; Mason, Fine, and Carnochan 2001). When a custodial, biological parent dies, the absence of custodial preference for stepparents over extended kin may result in children's being removed from a home in which they had close psychological ties to a stepparent. If a stepparent dies without a will, stepchildren are not legally entitled to any inheritance. The only way to be certain that situations like these do not occur is for the stepparent to legally adopt the stepchild, and this situation may be virtually impossible due to the noncustodial, biological parent's objections (Malia 2005; Mason et al. 2002).[4] People who remarry are advised to check with an attorney regarding applicable laws in their state.

The vast majority of legislation that is meant to address stepfamilies proceeds primarily from the government's concern over children's well-being. We turn to that topic now.

Children's Well-Being in Stepfamilies

How does membership in a stepfamily affect children's well-being? Considerable research has found that, on average, stepchildren of all ages have higher rates of juvenile delinquency (Pasley 2000), do less well in school (Jeynes 2000), may experience more family conflict, and are somewhat less well-adjusted than children in first-marriage families (Coleman, Ganong, and Fine 2000; Kirby 2006). "Studies consistently indicate . . . that children in stepfamilies exhibit more problems than do children with continuously married parents and about the same number of problems as do children with single parents" (Amato 2005, p. 80).

[4] Stepchild adoption generally requires the waiver of parental rights by the biological parent, who may be actively involved with the child (Malia 2005) and—understandably!—may not want to do so. When the nonresident parent is actively involved, adoption is seldom given serious consideration by either the remarried adults or the children (Pasley 1998a). Children above a certain age, perhaps fourteen, may or must give their consent to stepparent adoption in some states, and even younger children may need to agree to the adoption.

However, because many of the small, negative outcomes for stepchildren are also associated with divorce,

> it is difficult to know the relative contribution of parental remarriage to poor child adjustment. It may well be that most of the negative effects can be attributed to predivorce conditions . . . or postdivorce effects (e.g., reduced income, multiple transitions that accompany divorce), of which parental remarriage is only one. (Ihinger-Tallman and Pasley 1997, p. 31)

Some social scientists have asked whether remarriage can lessen some of the negative effects of divorce for children. One researcher has concluded that, in general, "[c]hildren of stepfamilies don't do better than children of mothers who never marry" (McLanahan and Sandefur 1994, p. 51; see also M. Carlson 2006). However, other researchers (Zill, Morrison, and Coiro 1993) have concluded that remarriage lessens some negative effects for children—but only for those who experienced their parents' divorce at an early age and when the remarriage remained intact (see also Arendell 1997, pp.186–88). Additional research shows that younger children adjust better to a parent's remarriage than do older children, especially adolescents (Amato 2005; Coleman, Ganong, and Fine 2000).

Research consistently shows that stepfamilies are less stable than nuclear families and that, in general, children in stepfamilies have more problems than those in intact, nuclear families. However, research also indicates that the quality of the communication and relationships among family members—and the extent to which children are monitored—may be more important to positive child outcomes than is family structure itself.

Although we note the preceding findings, we also recognize another aspect of this story. According to several studies, family structure (whether the family is first-marriage, cohabiting, divorced, or remarried) is not as important to stepchildren's well-being or future outcomes as is the quality of the communication and relationships among family members (Davis and Friel 2001; White and Gilbreth 2001). Furthermore, the extent to which parents or stepparents monitor their children's comings and goings is probably more important to positive child outcomes than is family structure itself (Fisher et al. 2003). Recent research shows that a close, non-conflictual relationship with a stepfather enhances the overall well-being of adolescents, and this is especially true when the child has a similar relationship with the biological mother (Yuan and Hamilton 2006).

Just as social scientists debate whether the family is in "decline" (see Chapters 1 and 7), they disagree on how to interpret findings about stepchildren's well-being. Social scientists working from a biosocial perspective (see Chapter 2) argue that biological forces make genetically related families more functional for children than do other family types (Popenoe 1996). According to this view, bioevolutionary forces encourage parents to favor their genetic offspring (Case, Lin, and McLanahan 2000). This situation puts stepchildren at risk and perhaps even jeopardizes their safety. For instance, evidence exists that the incidence of child abuse, including sexual abuse, is higher for stepfathers than for biological fathers (Giles-Sims 1997).[5] From this perspective, characterized by family law expert Mary Ann Mason (1998) as *negativist*, the formation of stepfamilies should be discouraged (Popenoe 1998).

However, the vast majority of social scientists reject the idea that stepfamily formation should be discouraged. Sociologist Jean Giles-Sims (1997) points out that although child abuse rates are higher among stepfamilies, this situation assuredly "does not mean that all stepfamilies are at risk" (p. 227). In fact, "a low percent of stepchildren are physically or sexually abused" (p. 220; see also Claxton-Oldfield 2003).

In sum, research findings can hardly be characterized as rosy, but we can still conclude that most children "eventually adapt to life in a stepfamily and emerge as reasonably competent individuals" (Hetherington and Jodl 1994, p. 76). Moreover, "[u]nderstanding how

families manage change and supporting all families to provide good enough parenting is likely to be a better investment for children than cataloguing disadvantages and difficulties and denigrating different family structures" (De'Ath 1996, p. 82).

Stepparenting: A Challenge in Remarriage

Although they are developing, cultural norms do not clearly indicate how stepparents should play their role (Ganong and Coleman 2004). With few clear guidelines or norms regarding what responsibilities a stepparent has, it may not be surprising that for a remarried spouse, stepchildren and finances present the greatest challenges (Visher and Visher 1996).

Some Reasons Stepparenting Is Difficult

"Crucial to children's overall well-being and development in remarriage and stepparent families, as in divorced and intact families as well, is the *quality* of parenting" (Arendell 1997, p. 187). Meanwhile, there are special difficulties associated with bringing families together under the same roof. For one thing, it is likely that children are influenced not only by their residential parents but also by their relationship with their noncustodial biological parent (S. Stewart 2003). For another thing, stepsiblings may not get along with each other (A. Bernstein 1997; Ganong and Coleman 2004).

Over the past thirty years, researchers and family therapists have consistently reported an array of challenges specific to stepfamilies. For instance, ties with the noncustodial parent may create a triangle effect that makes the spouse's previous marriage seem "more real" than the second union. The children, upset after visits with the noncustodial parent, may make life difficult for everyone else. Stepchildren in joint custody arrangements (see Chapter 16) may regularly move back and forth between two households with two sets of rules.

Family-rule differences, along with disruptions associated with one or more family members' coming and going, may be stressful (Kheshgi-Genovese and Genovese 1997). And the biological parents may feel caught between loyalties to their biological child and the desire to please their partner (Bray 1999; Visher and Visher 1996)—and between other loyalties as well. As one stepparent puts it,

> When you become a stepparent, you find yourself not just playing Piggy in the Middle between your partner and his/her children, but often between your partner

[5] "Unfortunately, given how abuse data are recorded, it is sometimes difficult to determine whether the perpetrator of child abuse is a stepparent or another adult. For example, mothers' boyfriends and legally remarried stepfathers are often categorized as one group. Children are more at risk for abuse if they live in a household with an adult who is not their genetic parent, but the extent to which stepchildren are at greater risk for being abused by a step-parent continues to be debated" (Ganong and Coleman 2000, p. 1295).

and his/her ex, your partner and your ex, your partner and your children, your children and your partner's children. The combinations are endless! (J. Andersen 2004)

Three major parenting challenges can be identified in remarried families with stepchildren: (1) financial strains, (2) role ambiguity, and (3) negative feelings of the children, who may not want the new family to work (Kheshgi-Genovese and Genovese 1997).

Financial Strains The particular challenges that characterize stepfamilies often begin with the previous divorce. This is especially evident in the case of finances (Mason, Fine, and Carnochan 2001). Frequently, money problems arise from two sources: financial obligations from first marriages and stepparent role ambiguity.

A remarried spouse (usually the husband) generally is financially accountable by law for children from the first union *and* financially responsible—sometimes legally[6]—for stepchildren (Hans 2002; Manning, Stewart, and Smock 2003). Whether legally required to or not, "many stepparents do in fact help to support the stepchildren with whom they reside, either through direct contributions to the child's personal expenses or through contributions to general household expenses such as food and shelter" (Mahoney 1997, p. 236; see also Mason et al. 2002).[7] Even though disproportionately more second wives are employed outside their homes than are first wives, remarried husbands report feeling caught between the often impossible demands of both their former family and their present one.

Meanwhile, stepmothers often spend their own money on stepchildren—usually for incidentals during visitation periods (Engel 2000). Then, too, mothers with children from a former marriage worry about receiving regular child support from their ex-husband (Manning, Stewart, and Smock 2003; Mason et al. 2002). Some second wives—more often, those without children of their own—feel resentful about the portion of the husband's income that goes to his first wife to help support his children from that marriage (Engel 2000). Or a second wife may feel guilty about the burden of support that her own children place on their stepfather (Barash 2000). For some remarried couples, the financial stress

associated with stepchildren's expenses is a determining factor in the decision not to have a mutual child (Engel 2000).

Role Ambiguity Relatively low role ambiguity has been associated with higher remarital satisfaction, especially for wives, and with greater parenting satisfaction, especially for stepfathers (Kurdek and Fine 1991). Hence, another challenge to remarried families is that roles of stepchild and stepparent are not well defined, clearly understood, or fully agreed upon by the stepfamily members themselves (Bray 1999; Ganong, Coleman, and Fine 2000). "The role of the stepparent is precarious; the relationship between a stepparent and stepchild only exists in law as long as the biological parent and stepparent are married" (Beer 1989, p. 11).

Although some stepchildren certainly do maintain relations with a stepparent after a stepparental divorce, doing so requires forging personalized ways to do this in the absence of commonly understood norms (Dickinson 2002). Legally, the stepparent is a nonparent with no prescribed rights or duties (Mason, Fine, and Carnochan 2001). Indeed, the term *stepparent* originally meant a person who replaces a dead parent, not an *additional* parent figure (Bray 1999). Uncertainties arise when the role of parent is shared between the stepparent and the noncustodial natural parent (MacDonald and DeMaris 2002). Stepparents aren't "real" parents, but "the culture so far provides no norms to suggest how they are different" (Bohannan 1970a, p. 119; see also Fine, Coleman, and Ganong 1999).

One result of role ambiguity is that society—and, hence, the members of the stepfamily itself—seems to expect stepparents and children to love one another in much the same way as biologically related parents and children do. In reality, however, this is not often the case, and therapists point out that stepparents and stepchildren should not expect to feel the same as they would if they were biologically related (Barash 2000; Visher and Visher 1996). Therapists advise—and research shows—that a stepparent's waiting through a period of family adjustment before becoming an active disciplinarian is usually a good idea (Visher and Visher 1996; Ganong and Coleman 2000). Of course, children's attitudes as well as their power can have an impact on the new marriage.

Stepchildren's Hostility A third reason for the difficulty in stepparent–child relationships lies in children's lack of desire to see them work. After age two or three (Gamache 1997), children often harbor fantasies that their original parents will reunite (Bray 1999; Burt and Burt 1996). Children who want their natural parents to remarry may feel that sabotaging the new relation-

---

[6] Some states (about seventeen) have passed legislation that holds stepparents responsible for the support of stepchildren during the marriage, although not afterward, as would be the case for biological children after divorce (Hans 2002; Malia 2005).

[7] Even though the stepfamily may come to rely on such financial support, if the remarriage ends in divorce, the stepparent is not legally responsible for child support unless he or she has formally adopted the stepchildren or signed a written promise to pay child support in the event of divorce (Malia 2005).

ship will help achieve that goal (Kheshgi-Genovese and Genovese 1997).

Furthermore, "[s]tepchildren may feel they are betraying their biological parent of the same sex as the stepparent if they form a friendly relationship with the stepparent" (Kheshgi-Genovese and Genovese 1997, p. 256). As one of our students wrote in an essay for this chapter: "Since I [had] idolized my father for so many years, I didn't want to accept my stepfather. I didn't like the fact that someone else was sleeping with my mother and touching her." (This student gradually changed his attitude, however: "The thing that won me over was [my stepfather's] support of everything that we did. Whenever we went to any of our sporting events he was there to help us.") In the case of remarriage after widowhood, children may have idealized, almost sacred, memories of the parent who died and may not want another to take his or her place (J. D. Andersen 2002; Barash 2000).

Many adolescents blame their parents or themselves, or both, because the first marriage broke up. The stepparent becomes a convenient scapegoat for their hostilities (Warshak 2000). As a result, stepchildren, especially adolescents, may prove to be hostile adversaries. Our discussion of power in Chapter 14 focuses on marital power, but we're reminded that adolescent stepchildren wield considerable family power (Visher and Visher 1996). Then, too, the desire of the remarried parents to create a cohesive family may conflict with an adolescent's normal need to express independence (Kheshgi-Genovese and Genovese 1997) or with the "substantial degree of autonomy" that they experienced in their former single-parent family or with both (Amato 2005, p. 81). ("As We Make Choices: Some Stepparenting Tips" contains advice that can make stepparenting easier.)

Sociologists Lynn White and Alan Booth's (1985b) analysis of stability in remarriages, discussed earlier, considered one additional point: that family tension may be resolved by the child's rather than the partner's exit from the home. Speculating that children might be moved out by sending them to live with the other parent or forcing them to become independent, White and Booth found that older teenage and young adult children in stepfamilies do indeed leave home at significantly lower ages than do teens in intact families. Furthermore, parents in stepfamilies are less likely than those in first marriages to feel an obligation to help support their young adult children (Aquilino 2005).

Not all teen or young adult stepchildren who leave home early do so for the reasons that White and Booth suggest (Ganong and Coleman 2005). However, subsequent research supports White and Booth's findings, and today we have a word for this situation—**extrusion**, "defined as individuals' being 'pushed out' of their households earlier than normal for members of their cultural group, either because they are forced to leave or because remaining in their households is so stressful that they 'choose' to leave" (Crosbie-Burnett et al. 2005, p. 213). Based on research findings and various theories,

[w]e would conclude that the probability of extrusion in a stepfamily increases (a) when the adolescent cannot communicate effectively about family issues, . . . particularly feelings about a new stepparent entering the family . . . ; (b) when the stepparent and biological parent cannot communicate effectively with the adolescent . . . ; (c) when the biological parent fears losing the relationship with the stepparent if the adolescent remains in the home . . . ; (d) when the biological parent has an insecure, dismissing attachment style, making him or her more likely to "let go of" the adolescent . . . ; (e) when the adolescent reports physical or sexual abuse . . . ; (f) when the stepparent is male, as men tend to have more power than women in conjugal relationships and are more likely to be abusive . . . ; (g) when the stepparent is bringing more resources into the family than the biological parent, giving him or her more power to effect the extrusion . . . ; (h) when the adolescent is not heterosexual . . . ; and (i) when the family is from the mainstream individualist American culture as opposed to a culture strong in familism. (Crosbie-Burnett et al. 2005, pp. 228–29)

Although stepchildren, their biological parents, and stepparents may be uncomfortable with aspects of their family roles, certain difficulties are more likely to trouble stepmothers, and others are more common to stepfathers. We'll look at each of these roles and the problems associated with them in more detail.

Stepmothers

A small study asked 265 stepmothers about their expectations of the stepmother role. The researchers found

As We Make Choices　Some Stepparenting Tips

Preparing to Live in Step

In a stepfamily, at least three (and often more) individuals struggle to form new familial relationships while coping with grief, pain, reminders of the past, or all three. Each family member brings to the situation expectations and attitudes that are as diverse as the personalities involved. The task of creating a successful stepfamily, as with any family, will be easier for all concerned if each member tries to understand the feelings and motivations of the others as well as his or her own.

It is important to discuss the realities of living in a stepfamily before the marriage, when problems that are likely to arise can be foreseen and examined theoretically. If you are contemplating entering a steprelationship, here are some key points to consider.

1. *Plan ahead.* Consider attending an "education for remarriage" workshop, offered by many religious and other community organizations. "Read and understand basic child development so you don't mistake developmentally normal behaviors as inappropriate, uncooperative or as personally against you" (Lavin 2003).

2. *Examine your motives and those of your future spouse for marrying.* Get to know him or her as well as possible under all sorts of circumstances. Consider the possible impact of contrasting lifestyles.

3. *Discuss the modifications that will be required in bringing two families together.* Compare similarities and differences in your concepts of child raising.

4. *Explore with your children the changes remarriage will bring:* new living arrangements, new family relationships, the effect on their relationship with their noncustodial parent.

5. *Give your children ample opportunity to get to know your future spouse well.* Consider your children's feelings, but don't allow them to make your decision about remarriage.

6. *Discuss the disposition of family finances with your future spouse.* An open and honest review of financial assets and responsibilities may reduce unrealistic expectations and resultant misunderstandings.

7. *Understand that there are bound to be periods of doubt, frustration, and resentment.*

Living in Step

Any marriage is complex and challenging, but the problems of remarriage are more complicated because more people, relationships, feelings, attitudes, and beliefs are involved than in a first marriage. The two families may have differing roles, standards, and goals. Because its members have not shared past experiences, the new family will need to redefine rights and responsibilities to fit both individual and combined needs.

Time and understanding are key allies in negotiating the transition from single-parent to stepfamily status. Consideration of the following points may ease the transition process.

1. *Let your relationship with stepchildren develop gradually.* Don't expect too much too soon—from the children or yourself. Children need time to adjust, accept, and belong. So do parents.

2. *Don't try to replace a lost parent; be an additional parent.* Children need time to mourn the parent lost through divorce or death.

3. *Expect to deal with confusing feelings—* your own, your spouse's, and the children's.

Anxiety about new roles and relationships may heighten competition among family members for love and attention; loyalties may be questioned. Your children may need to understand that their relationship with you is valued but different from that of your relationship with your spouse and that one cannot replace the other. You love and need them both, but in different ways.

4. *Recognize that you may be compared to the absent partner.* Be prepared to be tested, manipulated, and challenged in your new role. Decide, with your mate, what is best for your children, and stand by it.

5. *"Discuss discipline and make sure the biological parent is the one carrying out the discipline of his or her child"* (Lavin 2003)—at least, at first.

6. *Understand that stepparents "do not have the power or authority to 'fix' their stepchildren or the family.* Only a biological parent has that ability"* (Lavin 2003). Understand, too, that stepparents need support from biological parents on child-raising issues. Raising children is tough; helping to raise someone else's can seem tougher.

7. *Acknowledge periods of cooperation among stepsiblings.* Try to treat stepchildren and your own with equal fairness. Communicate! Don't pretend that everything is fine when it isn't. Acknowledge problems immediately, and deal with them openly.

8. *Admit that you need help if you need it.* Don't let the situation get out of hand. Everyone needs help sometimes. Join an organization for stepfamilies; seek counseling.

Source: U.S. Department of Health, Education, and Welfare 1978; Lavin 2003; Van Pelt 1985; see also Jeannette Lofas (n.d.), "10 Steps for Steps," The Stepfamily Foundation (www.stepfamily.org/ten_steps_for_stepfamilies.htm).

that stepmothers expect to be included in stepfamily activities but certainly do not see themselves as replacing the stepchild's mother. The more time a stepmother spent with her stepchildren, the more she expected to be included in stepfamily functions and decisions, and the more she behaved as concerned parent, rather than friend (Orchard and Solberg 2000). The stepmother role is thought by social scientists to be more difficult than the stepfather role (Coleman and Ganong 1997; L. White 1994). One important reason for this is a contradiction in expectations for the stepmother role:

> Whether mothers or stepmothers, . . . the women's roles are very similar. Irrespectively, they take care of children and housework. The *step*mother role does not expect her to do such tasks. On the contrary; the stepparent role expects a certain distance, the female role the opposite. Between the two roles there is a dilemma. One cannot be distant and close at the same time. (Levin 1997, p. 132)

The stepmother role has been described as the **stepmother trap**: On the one hand, society seems to expect romantic, almost mythical loving relationships between stepmothers and children (D. Smith 1990). On the other hand, stepmothers are seen and portrayed as cruel, vain, selfish, competitive, and even abusive (remember Snow White's, Cinderella's, and Hansel and Gretel's).

Maureen McHugh (2007) is a stepmother who writes for the website Second Wives Café: Online Support for Second Wives and Stepmoms (http:secondwivescafe.com). Here's an excerpt from her online article "The Evil Stepmother":

> My nine year-old stepson Adam and I were coming home from Kung Fu. "Maureen," Adam said—he calls me "Maureen" because he was seven when Bob and I got married and that was what he had called me before. "Maureen," Adam said, "are we going to have a Christmas Tree?"
>
> "Yeah," I said, "of course." After thinking a moment, "Adam, why didn't you think we were going to have a Christmas Tree?"
>
> "Because of the new house," he said, rather matter-of-fact. "I thought you might not let us."
>
> It is strange to find that you have become the kind of person who might ban Christmas Trees.

Some stepmothering situations can make the role especially complicated (Coleman and Ganong 1997). Special problems accompany the role of *part-time*, or "weekend," *stepmother* when women are married to noncustodial fathers who see their children regularly. The part-time stepmother may try to establish a loving relationship with her husband's children only to be openly rejected, or she may feel left out by the father's ongoing relationship with his offspring. Part-time stepmothers may also feel left out by the father's continued relationship with his ex-wife (Barash 2000). Noncustodial fathers may spend long hours on the telephone with their ex-wives discussing their children's school problems, orthodontia, illnesses, and even household maintenance and repairs.

Meanwhile, *residential stepmothers* may face somewhat different challenges. Social worker and stepmother Emily Bouchard tells her story:

> When I moved in with my husband and his two teenage daughters, he had a real "hands off" approach. . . . Sparks began to fly as soon as I asserted what I needed to be different . . . For example, when I noticed that my car had been "borrowed" (the odometer was different) without my knowledge or permission, I had to show up as a parent the way I needed to parent—setting limits, confronting the greater issues of lying and sneaking, and asserting the natural consequences for unacceptable behavior. This method was foreign to their family, and there were reactions all the way around! Thankfully, my husband supported me in front of his daughter, and then we discussed our differences privately and came to a mutual understanding about how to handle parenting together from then on. (Bouchard n.d.)

One explanation for the greater difficulty of the residential stepmother role involves the fact that stepmother families, more than stepfather families, begin after difficult custody battles or have a history of particularly troubled family relations or both.

Stepfathers

Men who decide to marry a woman with children come to their new responsibilities with varied emotions, typically far different from those that motivate a man to assume responsibility for his biological children. "I was really turned on by her," said one stepfather of his second wife. "Then I met her kids." This sequence is a fairly common "situation of many stepparents whose primary focus may be the marriage rather than parenting" (Ceballo et al. 2004, p. 46). A new husband may have negative reactions, such as fright, as well as positive feelings.

Research into the stepfather role shows that many children do have positive relationships with their stepfathers and that a good relationship is associated with better child outcomes (White and Gilbreth 2001). Probably not surprisingly, stepfathers who adopt their stepchildren tend to be more involved with them than those who don't (Schwartz and Finley 2006). Children and their stepfathers are more likely to feel positive about their relationship when the role expectations are clear, when the stepfather assumes a parental identity, when his parenting behavior meets his own and other family members' expectations, and when his parental demands are not challenged by an involved nonresidential, biological father (Coleman, Ganong, and Fine 2000; MacDonald and DeMaris 2002; Marsiglio 2004a).

However, when a mother and her children make up a single-parent family, the woman tends to learn autonomy and self-confidence, and her children may do more work around the house and take more responsibility in family decisions than do children in two-parent households. These are positive developments, but to enter such a family, a stepfather must work his way into a closed group (Cherlin and Furstenberg 1994). For one thing, the mother and children share a common history, one that does not yet include a new stepfather.

The **hidden agenda** is one of the first difficulties a stepfather encounters: The mother, her children, or both may have expectations about what the stepfather will do but may not think to give the new husband a clear picture of those expectations. The stepfather may have a hidden agenda of his own. For example, he may see his new stepchildren as unruly and decide they need discipline. In a time of increased ethnic and cultural diversity, as well as increasing interethnic and interreligious marriages, a new stepfather may feel out of place not only because of his different background but also because he has a different perspective on family life. A part of the stepchildren's hidden agenda involves the extent to which they will let the new husband play the father role. Children may be adamant in their distaste for or jealousy of the stepfather, or they may be ready and anxious to accept the stepfather as a new dad. This last is particularly true of young children.

Research shows that both stepmothers and stepfathers play their roles with more distance than do biological parents—as more like friends than monitoring parents (Ganong and Coleman 2000). Meanwhile, stepfathers tend to be more distant and detached than stepmothers, especially when they have biological children of their own (Coleman and Ganong 1997). Young adult children tend to think of the new addition to the family primarily as their mother's husband rather than as a stepfather.

Discipline is likely to be a particularly tricky aspect of both the children's and the parents' hidden agendas. A few challenges are notable:

1. There are now two parents rather than one to establish house rules and to influence children's behavior, but the parents may not agree.

2. There may be three or four parents instead of two—especially if the noncustodial parent sees the children regularly; sometimes the noncustodial biological parent may have more influence than the stepparent.

3. After developing considerable independence and responsibility in single-parent families, stepchildren may be reluctant to go back to being subject to adult direction.

Stepfathers may react to these difficulties in several different ways:

1. The stepfather may be driven away, with the stepfamily ultimately being dissolved.

2. The stepfather may take control, establishing himself as undisputed head of the household and forcing the former single-parent family to accommodate his preferences.

3. The stepfather may be assimilated into a family with a mother at its head and have relatively little influence on the way things are done.

© David Young-Wolff/PhotoEdit

Conflicting expectations concerning a stepfather's— or stepmother's—role may make it stressful. When stepparents can ignore the myths and negative images of the role and maintain optimism about the remarriage, they are more likely to have high family, marital, and personal satisfaction.

4. The stepfather, his new wife, and her children may all negotiate new ways of doing things (Isaacs, Montalvo, and Abelsohn 1986, pp.248–64).

This last possibility is the most positive alternative for everyone, and it is further addressed in the final section of this chapter. First, though, we'll look at what the research has to say about having a mutual child.

Having a Mutual Child

Biological children of both partners in a stepfamily are called *mutual, shared,* or *joint* children (S. Stewart 2007). Although some remarried men decide to have children later in life (Campbell 2004), other remarried men, especially those who are older, make it a condition of their remarriage to a younger woman that she relinquish the idea of having children together (Brooke 2002). However, some couples in a stepfamily do decide to have one or more children together, a decision addressed in Chapter 10. Research shows that a principal reason for choosing to have a child together involves hope that the mutual child will "cement" the remarriage bond (Ganong and Coleman 2004). Some women with children feel obliged to give a childless husband a son or daughter of his own. Another cause is perceived social pressure to be like "a normal family."

Some research has found that having a mutual child is associated with increased marital happiness and stability (Pasley and Lipe 1998). However, experts have expressed concern about the impact on remarriage of having a child early in what is bound to be a complex adjustment (A. Bernstein 1997). A new child may diminish parental attention to the children already in the stepfamily (S. Stewart 2005b). Believing that they will now be ignored by the stepparent—or seeing the mutual child as having a privileged place in the family—the stepchildren may feel threatened, jealous, or resentful (Barash 2000; Pasley and Lipe 1998).

Moreover, although joint children

> have both of their biological parents present in the household, they must still deal with the complications of stepfamily life. . . . Qualitative work suggests that children born into stepfamilies face a unique set of challenges. William Beer (1992) reveals that mutual children occupy a privileged yet pressure-filled position [referred to as] the hub. On one hand, the child is related to everyone in the family by blood, so he or she gets more attention and has more control in the family than the other children. On the other hand, this child feels constant pressure to ensure that everyone gets along. (S. Stewart 2007, pp. 70–71)

More research is needed on how adding a mutual child to a stepfamily impacts all the children (S. Stewart 2005b, 2007). We turn now to a look at what family therapists can tell us more generally about creating supportive stepfamilies.

This family portrait is of a mother and stepfather of two full sisters, along with a baby son from the new union. The remarried family structure, which is complex and has many unique characteristics, has no accepted cultural script. When all members are able to work thoughtfully together, adjustment to a new family life can be easier.

© Laura Dwight

My Family   From Stepfather to Father—Creating a Resilient Stepfamily

At the groom's dinner the night before my marriage to Jack, there was much good-natured bantering. My children were happy that my grief over the death of their father had finally run its course. They savored the sight of their mother filled with joy over a new love.

Jack, a genuine, never-been-married bachelor, received their mock gratitude for taking me off their hands. They congratulated him on his good fortune in acquiring them as family now that they were all grown up rather than during their teen years when they had been really rotten. I laughed with them, remembering those earlier times. At the nuptial Mass the next morning, I thanked God for this man and all he would bring to the family.

Honeymoon's End

Jack was elated over this new family of his—a wife, four children aged nineteen to twenty-four, a son-in-law, and two grandchildren—though he did wince the first few times the little ones called him "Grumpa." That discomfort eased when I reminded him that he would now be sharing his life with a grandmother.

The new relationship between Jack and his stepfamily began smoothly enough. We left the offspring behind at their various apartments and campuses when we relocated from Minnesota to Houston because of Jack's job. But a series of harried phone calls caused the rosy family picture to fade. One of the

brood had spent tuition money repairing a car that she had not maintained. Then another neglected to wrap water pipes at the family homestead before a fierce storm. The frozen lines ruptured, requiring major replacement work.

Another's car died. Though I would have preferred to send flowers, a loan was more to the point. We weren't optimistic about repayment. As each new problem unfolded, I saw the light dim in Jack's eyes. These kids he had gotten so easily were *not* all grown up.

Meanwhile, the tales he brought home about co-workers' children bore a common thread: achievement! One father, with all due modesty, reported on the winning touchdown made by his high school junior, whose coach, of course, saw potential for the pros. Another's daughter had graduated Phi Beta Kappa and was breezing through a prestigious M.B.A. program.

Before Jack became part of the "Dad Derby," such tales hadn't affected him. But as a new parent, he was listening to the daily achievement litany as other parents paraded the most recent honors bestowed upon brilliant kids. And Jack had no one to brag about. I felt responsible both for my kids' failures and for his disillusionment.

The Truth

In despondent moments I thought about family friends back home. They had all had problems similar to mine

with nearly-adult children. How did I know that? I wondered. Ah, yes, I'd heard the misadventures from other mothers—not fathers.

The next time we dined with friends of Jack's, I paid close attention. It was the men who reported accomplishments. Mothers mostly remained quiet or cautiously changed the subject. On another dinner date, the conversation predictably progressed to children, theirs then mine—"*our* children," I hastily corrected. But what wondrous tale could I spin about my splendid, overachieving children? What story could I tell that would make Jack glow with pride over his new heirs?

A little voice in my heart said, "Forget it, Mary. It won't work." So I told the truth—the latest dumb thing that had happened back home.

There was just the briefest moment of silence, a collective sigh, and then came the response. "You think that's bad? Well, wait till you hear about *our* kids' latest exploits." I sat back and enjoyed watching Jack's stunned expression as the stories spilled across the table. See, I wanted to say, mine aren't so bad. At least they're normal. I finally felt vindicated.

Family Triangle

There was still a bumpy road ahead for this family. My kids were my kids. Jack was accepting them as that and was beginning to acknowledge that they really were pleasant young people. And they thought he was great as Mom's husband. But there remained distance.

Toward the end of the first year, one son quit college and decided that Houston, where Mom and Jack lived, had better job potential than the old hometown. He was taking us up on the promise that our home would always be his. This was the kid who had quit talking to the family for five years when he reached thirteen. The same one who couldn't wait to be old enough to get away from his parents.

Now there was a triangle in the house, a disruption of the still-delicate relationship Jack and I were working out together. I felt caught between the two males, serving as a messenger, carrying subtle little missives between them. When the star boarder found a good job within a few weeks, I was relieved. But, of course, he had to stay on for a bit to build financial reserves. I finally gave him a little nudge; it was time he settled into a place of his own. I had been struggling on the family bridge long enough.

Trial by Fire

Two years later the same son was stricken with a rare form of meningitis. It was scary watching his body and his mind atrophy while neurologists struggled to diagnose him. Meanwhile, I fell into near despair, terrified that his brain would be destroyed before they found a treatment.

Jack, a fitness buff, decided that disuse had caused the wasting away of his stepson's body and mind. "He needs to get out of that hospital bed and move around to regain strength in his muscles." But he was unable to stand or sit unsupported. "He needs to make himself eat to rebuild his stamina." But he couldn't hold a fork anymore; he vomited whatever he could swallow.

We were with him and his future bride the evening his neurologist came in with the final test results, which we all hoped would bring an answer. But the tests hadn't isolated his specific kind of meningitis.

"We have come to the wall," the doctor said. "We have no choice but to schedule a cranial biopsy for tomorrow morning." We were stunned. The surgery would involve drilling a hole the size of a quarter through his skull to reach the meninges, the membranes surrounding the brain, for tissue samples.

After reading and signing the papers, I looked at Jack. He had moved to the bedside. He was looking down, oblivious to the tears dripping off his cheeks, at my son—*our* son. I saw nothing short of pure love in his face, his touch, his heart. Jack became a dad that night.

Real Love

The surgery solved the mystery, and medication miraculously brought on a quick return of full brain function, though it was several years before our son's body

returned to normal. Meanwhile, there were other minor crises with each child. And each time, sharing both the problem and the solution created deeper bonds. Through these experiences, Jack has learned and taught both of our sons that it is okay to cry and to hug another man—their stepdad and each other, for starters.

The whole gang has learned to trust this man, knowing they can rely on him without doubt or fear. We know that Jack loves us all, even with our many warts. We are a family.

Critical Thinking

What principles discussed in this chapter are illustrated in this woman's essay? What factors helped to make this remarried family a resilient one?

Source: From "From Stepfather to Father," by Mary Zimmeth Shomaker, 1994, *Liguorian.* (June) pp. 54–56. Copyright © 1994 by Liguori Publications. Reprinted by permission

Creating Supportive Stepfamilies

Creating a supportive stepfamily is not automatic. One stepfamily scholar (Papernow 1993) has suggested a **seven-stage model of stepfamily development:**

1. *Fantasy*—adults expect a smooth and quick adjustment while children expect that the stepparent will disappear and their parents will be reunited.

2. *Immersion*—tension-producing conflict emerges between the stepfamily's two biological "subunits."

3. *Awareness*—family members realize that their early fantasies are not becoming reality.

4. *Mobilization*—family members initiate efforts toward change.

5. *Action*—remarried adults decide to form a solid alliance, family boundaries are better clarified, and there is more positive stepparent–stepchild interaction.

6. *Contact*—the stepparent becomes a significant adult family figure, and the couple assumes more control.

7. *Resolution*—the stepfamily achieves integration and appreciates its unique identity as a stepfamily.

Therapists have condensed this model to four (easier to remember) consecutive stages: the fantasy stage, the confusion stage, the conflict stage, and the comfort stage ("Stepfamily Stages: A Thumbnail Sketch" n.d.). Therapists tend to agree that getting from fantasy to comfort takes time—from four to seven years!—and "is one of the most difficult tasks that families can face" (Wark and Jobalia 1998, p. 69; see also Lavin 2003).

The transition to successful remarriage requires considerable adjustment on the part of everyone involved. From a family systems perspective,

> shifting roles and relationships is necessary when a new member is introduced into the family system by remarriage. The family has to struggle with the role of the new family member while allegiances, loyalties, and daily relationship patterns undergo transition. For many families, just as they are adjusting to one new member, the other exspouse remarries, which causes another transition requiring a shift in the family's tentative equilibrium. (Ahrons and Rodgers 1997, p. 187)

It helps to remember that the (unrealistic) "urge to blend the two biological families as quickly as possible" may lead to disappointment when one or more adult or child members "resist connecting" (Wark and Jobalia 1998, p. 70). (You may have noticed that we have not used the once-familiar term *blended family* in this chapter. That's because family therapists and other stepfamily experts have concluded that stepfamilies do not readily "blend.")[8]

A principal challenge in creating supportive stepfamilies stems from society's nuclear-family model monopoly, discussed earlier in this chapter. Remarrieds often unconsciously try to approximate the nuclear-family model, but "this model does not work for most remarried families" (Wark and Jobalia 1998, p. 70) because, as we have seen, stepfamilies differ from first-marriage families in important ways (Ganong and Coleman 2004). It may help to think of a stepfamily as a **binuclear family**—a new family type that includes members of the two (or more) families that existed before the divorce and remarriage (Ahrons 2004).

Nevertheless, as "My Family: From Stepfather to Father—Creating a Resilient Stepfamily" illustrates, people can and do create supportive, resilient remarriages and stepfamilies (Ahrons 2004). For instance, the Binuclear Family Study (Ahrons and Miller 1993) collected data from ninety-eight pairs of Wisconsin families at one, three, and five years after divorce. At three years, remarried biological parents and their new partners had high rates of **co-parenting**—shared decision making and parental supervision in such areas as discipline and schoolwork or shared holidays and recreation—with 62 percent of stepmothers and 73 percent of stepfathers reporting joint involvement in seven of ten areas of child raising.

Meanwhile, counselors remind remarrieds not to forget their couple relationship. Because stepfamilies—once called "instant families" (R. Phillips 1997)—have children from the start, spouses have little time or privacy to adjust to each other as partners. Furthermore, the relationship between biological parent and child predates the remarriage and may be stronger than the marital relationship. Therefore, "the couple relationship needs to be a priority in the family's life" (Kheshgi-Genovese and Genovese 1997, p. 260). In many locations, prospective spouses can participate in remarriage preparatory courses to alert remarrying couples to

---

[8] In fact, Dr. Marjorie Engel (2003), president of the Stepfamily Association of America, warns that "[c]ouples with 'blended' as their objective tend to have the most problematic households and those are the couples most likely to leave the stepfamily because some or all of the members won't buy into the blended concept." Playing with the language, stepmother and online columnist Dawn Miller refers to stepfamily living as "life in a blender" (Miller, "Surviving" n.d.).

common problems and to help them find ways to discuss inevitable conflicts. Openly discussing upcoming changes prior to the remarriage can help.

In a clever play on words, online columnist and stepmother Dawn Miller (n.d.) titled one of her essays "Don't Go Nuclear—Negotiate." Chapter 9 presents some things for couples to talk about when forging an adaptable, supportive marriage relationship. Many of those questions also apply to remarriages. But there are additional things to talk about regarding stepfamilies, such as what will be the household rules, expectations for a stepparent's financial support of stepchildren, how emergency medical care will be handled if the biological parent isn't there to sign a release, questions of inheritance, and perhaps whether there will be a mutual child or children (Lavin 2003).

Chapter 15 points out that life transitions, such as remarriage or the transition to stepparent, are family stressors. That chapter explains that resilient families deal with family transitions creatively by emphasizing mutual acceptance, respect, and shared values (Ahrons 2004). You may also recall that Chapter 13 presents several guidelines for bonding fights—all applicable in stepfamilies.

As the number of stepfamilies increases, they have access to more resources than in the past. For instance, several online websites by stepfamily counselors and well-respected researchers are designed to give advice and report research findings concerning stepfamilies. Examples are thestepfamilylife.com, and the website of the Stepfamily Association of America (www.saafamily .org). There are also more and more books written by psychologists and others for remarrieds and stepfamily members. One of these, directed to teens, is *Stepliving for Teens: Getting Along with Step-Parents, Parents and Siblings* (Block and Bartell 2001). And stepfamily enrichment programs, support groups, and various other group-counseling resources for stepfamilies are becoming available in more and more communities. One example is the Active Parenting for Stepfamilies program (Popkin and Einstein 2006).

In general, counselors and other stepfamily experts advise the following: "Don't resent the custody situation—deal with it. Form realistic expectations, and don't be afraid to establish new traditions" (Miller, "Surviving" n.d.). Researchers and family therapists tend to agree that "it is neither the structural complexity nor the presence/absence of children in the home *per se* that impacts the marital relationship. Rather, the ways in which couples interact around these issues are the key to understanding marital relationships in general

and marital relationships in remarriages specifically" (Ihinger-Tallman and Pasley 1997, p. 25). Interacting in positive ways in remarriages and stepfamilies involves making knowledgeable choices.

We close this chapter with the paragraph that stepfamily scholar Susan Stewart uses to close her book, *Brave New Stepfamilies* (2007):

> One might conclude that Americans can maximize their well-being by getting married, staying married, reproducing their own biological offspring, and toughing it out. Yet an increasing number of Americans live increasing portions of their lives in increasingly diverse families that do not align with this idea. Perhaps Americans might do better by admitting the emerging normality of stepfamilies and building institutional support to make their brave new stepfamilies strong. (p. 224)

Summary

- Remarriages have always been fairly common in the United States but are more frequent now than they were earlier in this century, and they follow divorce more often than widowhood.

- The courtship process by which people choose remarriage partners has similarities to courtship preceding first marriages, but the basic exchange often weighs more heavily against older women, and homogamy tends to be less important.

- Remarriages are usually about as happy as first marriages, but they tend to be slightly less stable.

- One reason for relative remarital instability is lack of a cultural script for living in remarriages or stepfamilies.

- Relationships in immediate remarried families and with kin are often complex, yet there are virtually no social prescriptions and few legal definitions to clarify roles and relationships.

- The lack of cultural guidelines is most apparent in the stepparent role.

- Stepparents are often troubled by financial strains, role ambiguity, and stepchildren's hostility.

- Marital happiness and stability in remarried families are greater when the couple has strong social support, high expressiveness, a positive attitude about the remarriage, low role ambiguity, and little belief in negative stereotypes and myths about remarriages or stepfamilies.

Questions for Review and Reflection

1. Discuss the similarities and differences between courtship before remarriage and courtship before first marriage.

2. The remarried family has been called an incomplete institution. What does this mean? How does this affect the people involved in a remarriage? Include a discussion of kin networks and family law. Do you think this situation is changing?

3. What evidence can you gather from observation or your own personal experience or both to show that stepfamilies (a) may be more culturally acceptable today than in the past and (b) remain negatively stereotyped as not as functional or as normal as first-marriage, nuclear families?

4. What are some problems faced by both stepmothers and stepfathers? What are some problems faced particularly by stepfathers? Why might the role of stepmother be more difficult than that of stepfather? How might these problems be resolved or alleviated?

5. **Policy Question.** In terms of social policy, what might be done to increase the stability of remarriages?

Key Terms

binuclear family 478
co-parenting 478
cultural script 465
double remarriage 462
extrusion 471
hidden agenda 474
incomplete institution 465

nuclear-family model monopoly 465
remarriages 456
remarried family 456
seven-stage model of stepfamily development 478
single remarriage 462
stepmother trap 473

Online Resources

Companion Website for This Book

www.thomsonedu.com/sociology/lamanna

Visit the book companion website, where you will find flash cards, practice quizzes, Internet links, suggested readings, InfoTrac College Edition exercises, and more to help you study.

ThomsonNOW™ for Marriage and Family

Spend time on what you need to master rather than on information you already have learned. Take a pre-test for this chapter, and ThomsonNOW will generate a personalized study plan based on your results. The study plan will identify the topics you need to review and direct you to online resources such as videos, narrated learning modules, and interactive activities to help you master those topics. You can then take a post-test to help you determine the concepts you have mastered and what you will still need to work on. Try it out! Go to **www.thomsonedu.com/login** to sign in with an access code or to purchase access to this product.

Aging Families

18

Our Aging Population

Aging Baby Boomers

Longer Life Expectancy

Racial/Ethnic Composition of the Older American Population

Living Arrangements of Older Americans

Gender Differences in Older Americans' Living Arrangements

Racial/Ethnic Differences in Older Americans' Living Arrangements

Aging in Today's Economy

Older Women's Finances

Marriage Relationships in Later Life

Retirement

Later-Life Divorce, Widowhood, and Remarriage

Widowhood and Widowerhood

Older Parents, Adult Children, and Grandchildren

Older Parents and Adult Children

Grandparenthood

Aging Families and Caregiving

As We Make Choices: Community Resources for Eldercare

Issues for Thought: Child—and Grandchild—Caregivers

Adult Children as Eldercare Providers

Gender Differences in Providing Eldercare

My Family: Looking After—A Son's Memoir

The Sandwich Generation

Eldercare as a Family Process

Elder Abuse and Neglect

Racial/Ethnic Diversity and Family Eldercare

The Changing American Family and Eldercare in the Future

Toward Better Caregiving

In a clever play on words, *Newsweek* magazine announced in 1999 that America was becoming the "home of the gray" (Peyser 1999). The aging of the American population has also been termed a "demographic avalanche" (Conner 2000, p. 6). More and more family members are living longer. This chapter examines families in later life.

As we begin, we need to note that many of the topics explored elsewhere in this text apply to aging families. For instance:

- Older wives—like younger ones—concern themselves with marital equity when it comes to power, decision making, housework, and other/caregiving tasks (Clarke 2005; Essex and Hong 2005).

- Older couples may be caring for disabled adult children (Essex and Hong 2005).

- Older families may be comprised of lesbian or gay male couples (Price 2000).

- As today's adults age, more and more older families will be stepfamilies.

- Communication is as important in older families as in younger ones (Carroll, Badger, and Yang 2006).

However, this chapter focuses on topics specifically related to aging families. We will look at living arrangements of older Americans and at marriage relationships in later life. We'll discuss the grandparent role, then explore issues concerning giving care to older family members. To begin, we'll examine some facts about our aging population.

Our Aging Population

The number of older people in the United States (and all other industrialized nations) is growing remarkably. In 1980 there were 25.5 million Americans age sixty-five or older; today nearly 36.8 million Americans are age sixty-five or older, and that number is expected to double over the next twenty-five years. Regarding Americans age seventy-five and older, in 1980 there were close to 10 million; by 2002 there were more than 18 million. Of those age eighty-five and above, there were 2.2 million in 1980, compared to more than 5 million today. Projections are that by the year 2050, there will be nearly 87 million Americans age sixty-five and older and close to 21 million Americans age eighty-five and over (U.S. Census Bureau 2007a, Tables 11 and 12).

Not just the *number* of elderly has increased but also their *proportion* of the total U.S. population. This is especially true for those in the "older-old" (age seventy-five through eighty-four) and the "old-old" (eighty-five and over) age groups. Those age seventy-five and above are

projected to rise from 4.4 percent in 1980 to 6.1 percent in 2010, while the proportion of Americans age eighty-five and older is projected to rise from 1.0 percent to 2.0 percent over those same years (U.S. Census Bureau 2003a, Table 11; 2007a, Table 12).

Aging Baby Boomers

Between 1946 and 1964, in the aftermath of World War II, more U.S. women married and had children than ever before. The high birthrate created what is commonly called the **baby boom**. Now baby boomers are beginning to retire, and within the next twenty years they will comprise a dramatically large elderly population (see Figure 18.1). Meanwhile, the number of children under age eighteen is about the same today as it has been for several decades (about 70 million). Children now make up a smaller proportion—and older Americans a larger proportion—of the population. The changing American age structure is indicated by the nation's median age; it was 36.2 in 2005—up from 30.0 in 1980 (U.S. Census Bureau 2007a, Table 11). Along with the impact of the baby boomers' aging and the declining proportion of children in the population,[1] longer life expectancy has contributed to the aging of our population.

Longer Life Expectancy

Americans are now living long enough that demographers divide the aging population into three categories: the "young-old" (age sixty-five through seventy-four), the "older-old" (age seventy-five through eighty-five), and the "old-old" (age eighty-five and over). Life expectancy at birth increased from 70.8 in 1970 (67.1 for men and 74.7 for women) to 79.2 in 2004 (75.2 for men and 80.4 for women; U.S. Census Bureau 2007a, Table 98).

Gender and Life Expectancy Women, on average, live about five years longer than men. Consequently, the makeup of the elderly population differs by gender. In 2005, there were 21.4 million women age sixty-five and older, compared to 15.4 million men. For Americans over age eighty-four, there are 3.5 million women and about 1.6 million men (U.S. Census Bureau 2007a, Table 11). This gendered difference in life expectancy means that, among other things, women are more likely to be widowed—and poor in old age—than are men.

Interestingly, however, trends show that the life-expectancy gap between women and men is narrow-

---

[1] The proportion of the U.S. population under age eighteen was about 36 percent in 1960, compared to about 25 percent in 2005 (U.S. Census Bureau 2003a, Table 11; 2007a, Table 11).

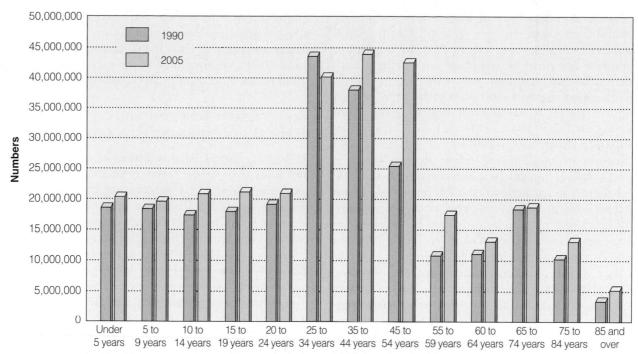

Figure 18.1 Number of Americans in population age groups, 1990 and 2005. The baby boom cohort is represented by the central bars. As this cohort continues to age, we will see a dramatic increase in the elderly population.

Sources: Adapted from www.seniorjournal.com/news/features/06-16-01popgraphs.htm, reprinted with permission; U.S. Census Bureau 2007a, Table 11.

ing. Policy analysts point to at least two implications for women, should this trend continue. For one thing, more elderly women will have spouses who may be able to care for them should they develop chronic illnesses. In addition, a shorter widowhood could mean that older women will be better off financially (Zernike 2006). In addition to differing by gender, life expectancy also differs by race/ethnicity, with Asians and whites having the longest life expectancy.

Race/Ethnicity and Life Expectancy In 2003 the white male life expectancy at birth was 75.3, compared to 69.0 for black males. Among women, the figure was 80.5 for whites, compared to 76.1 for blacks (U.S. Census Bureau 2007a, Table 99). Much of this difference is associated with whites having, on average, higher incomes and lower poverty rates than blacks. Higher incomes, along with higher education levels, are associated with better health and longer life expectancy, largely because people in higher socioeconomic groups have access to better preventive health care and are less likely to work in hazardous environments: "Their educational advantage may also make them more avid consumers of the vast

"Good news, honey—seventy is the new fifty."

amounts of information available on improving health" (Conner 2000, p. 16). Some of the racial/ethnic difference in life expectancy may also be explained by genetics and by discrimination in health care.

Two Family Consequences of Longer Life Expectancy
Demographers point to two general family-related consequences of our living longer. First, because more generations are alive at once, we increasingly have opportunities to maintain ties with grandparents, great-grandparents, and even great-great-grandparents (Bengston 2001). It is estimated that by 2030, more than two-thirds of eight-year-olds will have a living great-grandparent (Rosenbloom 2006).

A second consequence of longer life expectancy is that, on average, Americans spend more years near the end of their lives with chronic health problems (Crimmins 2001). As Americans get older, more and more of us will be called upon to provide care for a parent or other aging relative (Garey et al. 2002). We will return to issues surrounding giving care to aging family members later in this chapter. At this point, it's also nice to note that we can think not just in terms of overall life expectancy but also in terms of **active life expectancy**—the period of life free of disability in activities of daily living, after which may follow a period of being at least somewhat disabled. Today, an American man who is sixty-five can expect to live actively for about another fourteen years, with two years after that at least partly disabled. For females age sixty-five, the numbers are about sixteen more years of active life with about seven additional years at least partly disabled (Manton and Land 2000). We turn now to the racial/ethnic composition of the older American population.

Racial/Ethnic Composition of the Older American Population

As a group, non-Hispanic whites in the United States are older than other racial/ethnic categories. Of the total population, 12.4 percent are currently over age sixty-five, while 24.7 percent of non-Hispanic whites are over sixty-five. This figure compares to just 8 percent of non-Hispanic blacks, 9 percent of Asians, and 5.3 percent of Hispanics (U.S. Census Bureau 2007a, Table 14).

Figure 18.2 looks at the nation's age distribution by race/ethnicity in another way. As you can see from the figure, about 81 percent of the U.S. population over age sixty-four is non-Hispanic white. Another 8 percent is African American, with another 6 percent Hispanic. However, the older population is becoming more ethnically and racially diverse as members of racial/ethnic

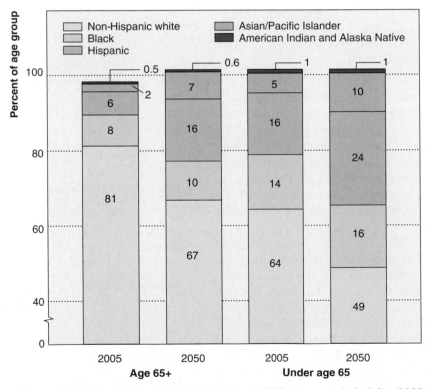

Figure 18.2 U.S. elderly and nonelderly population by race/ethnicity, 2005 and 2050.

Note: Hispanic may be of any race.

Sources: del Pinal and Singer 1997; S. Lee 1998; and calculated from U.S. Census Bureau 2007a, Table 14.

minority groups grow older. As described in Chapter 3, due to immigration and to relatively high birthrates of ethnic and racial minority groups, Hispanic, African American, and Asian populations are growing faster than non-Hispanic whites (del Pinal and Singer 1997; Lee 1998). By 2050, the non-Hispanic white share of the population over age sixty-four is projected to fall to 67 percent: "Some senior centers already offer *tai chi* exercise classes or serve tamales for lunch, a reflection of greater ethnic diversity" (Treas 1995, p. 8).

Living Arrangements of Older Americans

About one-quarter of U.S. households are made up of people living alone. Many of them are older people. This situation represents a growing trend since about 1940. Among Americans age sixty-five and older, approximately 30 percent live alone. Due to the increased likelihood of being widowed, nearly 38 percent of people over age seventy-five live by themselves (U.S. Census Bureau 2007a, Table 56). In the future, an increasing proportion of older Americans is projected to live alone (U.S. Senate Special Committee on Aging 2004).[2]

The high proportion of elderly Americans living alone does not necessarily mean that they are either abandoned by their families or isolated. The elderly who live alone "are usually within a close distance of relatives or only a phone call [or e-mail][3] away. Fewer than one out of twenty are socially isolated, and usually are so because they have lived that way most of their lives" (Moody 2006, p. 331). In fact, historical trends in family living arrangements show a long-term preference for separate households in American society (Haber and Gratton 1994). Some older Americans move to retirement communities in the "Sun Belt"—Florida and the Southwest (Frey 1999). However, for the most part, both adult children and their parents prefer to live near one another, although not in the same residence (Moody 2006, p. 332).

[2] The future increase in the proportion of elderly living alone will be due largely to three factors: first, the relatively high divorce rate for people who are now middle-aged (see Chapter 16); second, an increase in the number of people who never marry (see Chapters 7 and 8); and third, a decline in the proportion of older people living with their adult children due to decreasing economic incentive to share living space (Bianchi and Casper 2000; Novak 1997)—unless there is a very significant and prolonged downturn in our economy.

[3] Although only about one-third of those over age sixty-five use the Internet today, more than two-thirds of those ages fifty through sixty-four have ventured online (Joseph and Stone 2005). Hence, e-mail contact between aged family members and their relatives can only be expected to increase.

Gender Differences in Older Americans' Living Arrangements

Table 18.1 shows the living arrangements of older Americans by gender. Due mainly to differences in life expectancy, older men are much more likely to be living with their spouse than are older women (73 percent of men age sixty-five and older, compared to 41 percent of women). This pattern becomes more pronounced in the older ages (see Table 18.1).

Again, due to life expectancy differences, older women (43 percent) are far more likely than men (14 percent) to be widowed (U.S. Administration on Aging 2006a, Figure 2). Therefore, older women are more than twice as likely to live alone than are older men (40 percent of women, compared to 17 percent of men age sixty-five and older). Of those seventy-five and over, 49 percent of women live by themselves, compared to 21 percent of men.

Finally, from Table 18.1, we can see that older women are significantly more likely than older men to live with people other than their spouse—a pattern that persists into old-old age (Fields and Casper 2001, Table 6). We can conclude from these figures that

[m]en generally receive companionship and care from their wives in the latter stages of life, while women are more likely to live alone, perhaps with assistance from grown children, to live with other family members, or to enter a nursing home. (Bianchi and Casper 2000, p. 10)

Besides gender, race and ethnicity also affect the living arrangements of older Americans.

Racial/Ethnic Differences in Older Americans' Living Arrangements

Due to economic and cultural differences, the living arrangements of older Americans vary according to race and ethnicity. For instance, Asian and Central and

Table 18.1 Living Arrangements of People Sixty-five Years Old and Over, by Gender, 2000

	Living Arrangement	Men %	Women %
65 years old and over	Alone	17	40
	With spouse	73	41
	With other people	10	19
65–74 years old	Alone	14	31
	With spouse	77	53
	With other people	10	16
75 years old and over	Alone	21	49
	With spouse	67	29
	With other people	12	22

Source: Adapted from Fields and Casper 2001, Table 6.

South American immigrant parents are more likely than non-Hispanic whites to reside with adult children who provide most of the household income (Glick and Hook 2002). Table 18.2 compares the living arrangements of non-Hispanic white, black, Asian, and Hispanic adults age sixty-five and older.

One generalization that we can make from the statistics in Table 18.2 is that African Americans, Asian Americans, and Hispanics are far more likely than whites to live with people other than their spouse—grown children, siblings, or other relatives (Karasik and Hamon 2007). Partly as a result of economic necessity, coupled with social norms involving family members' obligations to one another (Bianchi and Casper 2000), older Asian Americans and Hispanics are less likely than non-Hispanic whites to live alone. This is true for Hispanics even though they are also less likely than non-Hispanic whites to live with a spouse.[4]

Table 18.2 Living Arrangements of People Sixty-five Years Old and Over, by Race/Ethnicity, 2005

	Living Arrangement	65–74 Years Old %	75 and Older %
Total Population	Alone	23	38
	With spouse	64	45
	With other people	13	17
Non-Hispanic White	Alone	23	39
	With spouse	67	47
	With other people	10	14
Non-Hispanic Black	Alone	32	42
	With spouse	40.5	25
	With other people	27	33
Asian American	Alone	12.5	23
	With spouse	68	46
	With other people	19	30
Hispanic Origin[a]	Alone	19	27
	With spouse	56	38
	With other people	25	34

[a]People of Hispanic origin may be of any race.
Source: Calculated from U.S. Census Bureau 2007a, Table 56.

[4] Older African Americans and Hispanics are less likely than non-Hispanic whites to live with a spouse for two reasons. First, due to differences in patterns of marriage and divorce, African Americans are more likely than whites to enter older ages without a spouse. Second, gender differences in life expectancy (with women living longer than men) are slightly higher among blacks and Hispanics (about seven years) than among non-Hispanic whites (about five years) (U.S. Census Bureau 2007a, Table 98).

Among older Americans without partners, living arrangements depend on a variety of factors, including the status of one's health, the availability of others with whom to reside, social norms regarding obligations of other family members toward their elderly, personal preferences for privacy and independence, and economics (Bianchi and Casper 2000). We will look at all these factors in various sections of this chapter. Here we note that older Americans with better health and higher incomes are more likely to live independently, a situation that suggests strong personal preferences for privacy and independence. Meanwhile, those in financial need are more likely to live with relatives (Bianchi and Casper 2000).

Aging in Today's Economy

Today's older Americans live on a combination of Social Security benefits, private pensions from employers, personal savings, and social welfare programs designed to meet the needs of the poor and disabled. About 40 percent of the income of people age sixty-five and older is from Social Security benefits and related federal programs, such as Medicare, Medicaid, and Supplemental Security Income (SSI).[5] Social Security benefits are the only source of income for one-fifth of Americans over age sixty-five (He et al. 2005, pp. 95, 97).

Growth in Social Security benefits has resulted in dramatic changes in U.S. poverty rates over the last several decades. Before Social Security was initiated, the elderly were disproportionately poor (Meyer and Bellas 2001). But poverty has declined sharply for those age

[5] During the Great Depression of the 1930s, millions of Americans lost their jobs and savings. In response, the federal government passed the 1935 Social Security Act, a dramatically new program designed to assist the elderly. The Social Security Act established the collection of taxes on income from one generation of workers to pay monthly pensions to an older generation of nonworkers. Initially, only those who contributed to Social Security were eligible to receive benefits, but over the years the U.S. Congress has extended coverage to spouses and to the widowed, as well as to the blind and permanently disabled.

Medicare, begun in 1965, is a compulsory federal program that does not provide money but does offer health care insurance and benefits to the aged, blind, and permanently disabled. Before the program began, just 56 percent of the aged had hospital insurance. In 1992, at least 97 percent of all older people in the United States had coverage because all who qualify for Social Security are eligible for Medicare.

In 1965, intending to provide health care to poor Americans of all ages, Congress created the Medicaid program in conjunction with Medicare. Eligibility for Medicaid is based on having virtually no family assets (saving and checking accounts, stocks, bonds, mutual funds, and any form of property that can be converted to cash) and very little income. In 1972, Congress created the federal Supplemental Security Income program (SSI), a "welfare" program that provides monthly income checks to poverty-level older Americans and the disabled (Meyer and Bellas 2001).

sixty-five and over—from 36 percent in 1959 to about 10 percent today. Due partly to older Americans' lobbying to protect Social Security benefits, the poverty rate for those over age sixty-four is now about one-half that of children (U.S. Census Bureau 2007a, Table 694).

Largely due to Social Security pensions and Medicare health insurance, "today we have the most affluent generation of older people America has ever seen" (Conner 2000, p. 10). Then, too, older Americans today benefit from what was a generally stable or rising economy during most of their working years and have also gained from the appreciated value of their homes. Overall, the improvements in the financial status, as well as the health, of older Americans over the past several decades have resulted in "a revolution in lifestyles and living arrangements among the elderly" (Bianchi and Casper 2000, p. 9).

However, having noted that today's older Americans are better off than generations preceding them, we need to acknowledge that, on average, their income declines by up to one-half upon retirement and that the retired spend considerably more of their incomes on health care (DeNavas-Walt, Cleveland, and Webster 2003, Table 3; "Spending Patterns" 2000). Health costs are rising dramatically, and health insurance programs, including Medicaid and Medicare, are unlikely to keep up (Meyer and Bellas 2001). Serious illness can erode the savings and income of the elderly and their families.

Furthermore, one-tenth of older adults *are* living in poverty (U.S. Administration on Aging 2006b). They, along with the "near poor" (those with incomes at or below 125 percent of the poverty level, who make up another 7 percent of the elderly), as well as others with relatively low incomes, are hardly enjoying the comfortable, leisurely lifestyle that we might think of when we imagine retirement.[6]

Older Women's Finances

Older men are considerably better off financially than are older women. In 2005, the median income of individual Americans age sixty-five and older was $21,784 for males and $12,495 for females (U.S. Administration on Aging 2006b). This dramatically unequal situation is partly due to the fact that throughout their employment years, men averaged higher earnings than women did (see Chapter 12). Consequently older women today have smaller (if any) pensions from employers. Furthermore, older women on average did not begin to save for retirement as early as did men (Even and Macpherson 2004).

[6] For instance, Medicaid recipients (see footnote 5) living in nursing homes are wards of the state. Hence, their entire monthly income, except for a small personal-needs allowance, goes toward nursing home costs (Meyer and Bellas 2001).

Social Security and Medicare have raised the incomes of older Americans, beginning in 1940, so that today the proportion of elderly in the United States living in poverty has declined and is less than that of children. Nevertheless, 3.6 million, or 10 percent of older Americans—disproportionately the unmarried and women—are living in poverty. Another 2.3 million of the elderly are classified as "near poor," with income up to 125 percent of the poverty level (U.S. Administration on Aging 2006b).

Moreover, women's Social Security benefits average about 76 percent of men's. Maximum Social Security benefits (about $2,000 monthly) are available only to workers with lengthy and continuous labor force participation in higher-paying jobs (U.S. Social Security Administration 2007). This situation works against older women today, who either did not participate in the labor force at all or are likely to have dropped in and out of the labor force while taking lower-paying jobs (Vartanian and McNamara 2002). "Thus, women are penalized for conforming to a role that they are strongly encouraged to assume—unpaid household worker—and their disadvantaged economic position is carried into old age" (Meyer and Bellas 2001, p. 193). An older wife married for at least ten years to a now-retired worker can receive a spousal "allowance," but it is equal to one-half of her husband's benefits.[7]

[7] Employed women may qualify on the basis of either their own or their husband's work records, although they cannot receive benefits under both categories. It is a statement of the gendered inequality in earnings, described in Chapter 12, that about half of women who are dually entitled today receive greater benefits from qualifying as their husband's spouse than on their own work history (Meyer and Bellas 2001).

Ex-spouses qualify for one-half the amount of their ex's Social Security benefits, provided the marriage lasted at least ten years. Compared to widows, divorced and separated women are worse off, and many need to work for several years after traditional retirement age. Together with other factors, "[p]oorly constructed divorce settlements . . . can cripple [divorced] women's finances" (Block 2000, p. 1B).

Having looked at the economic situation of older Americans, together with their living arrangements, we turn to an examination of marriage and other family relationships in later life.

Marriage Relationships in Later Life

Only about 4 percent of women and of men over sixty-five today have never married (U.S. Administration on Aging 2006b, Figure 2). Some later-life marriages are remarriages, but the majority of older married couples have been wed for quite some time—either in first or second marriages.

Most older married couples place intimacy as central to their lives and describe their unions as happy (Szinovacz and Schaffer 2000; A. Walker et al. 2001). On average, older couples report having fewer disagreements, and marital happiness often increases in later life, when couples have the time, energy, and financial resources to invest in their couple relationship (Hatch and Bulcroft 2004). This is not to say that all older couples are happy together. One study of national data shows that, among the aged, marrieds who felt unfairly treated by their mates were more distressed than were singles of the same age (Hagedoorn et al. 2006). Another study found that later-life couples who hold more egalitarian attitudes toward gender roles report significantly higher levels of marital happiness than do those with more traditional attitudes (Kaufman and Taniguchi 2006). Also, health is an important factor in morale in later life, and it has a substantial impact on marital quality as well as other social contacts (Atchley 1997; Wickrama et al. 1997).

Older Americans continue to be interested in sex, even into old-old age and even in nursing homes (Purdy 1995; Talbott 1998). According to sociologist Andrew Greeley, "It may be that the last great American taboo is passion among the elderly" (quoted in "Happiest Couples in Study" 1992). However, the fact that the large baby boom cohort is aging means that we now see many more books about sex in later life. And the overall conclusion of these books is that—as one author titles hers—the old folks are "still doing it" (Sachs 2001).

Chapter 6 points out that though health does affect sexual performance, sex does indeed continue into late life. A national survey sponsored by AARP (formerly the American Association of Retired Persons) of Americans age forty-five and older found that more than half of men and women with partners in all age groups had regular sexual intercourse. Even including those age seventy-five and older, more than half of men and 85 percent of women said that their sex lives were unimpaired by illness. Asked what would most improve their sex lives, people age forty-five through fifty-nine most often said "less stress" and "more free time." "Better health" headed the list for men sixty and older, "better health for partner" headed the list for women sixty through seventy-four, and "finding a partner" was the most frequent answer for women seventy-five and older (Jacoby 1999).

Although older and elderly women may be interested in sex, lack of a partner can be a problem (Talbott 1998). Jacoby (1999) refers to this situation as the "partner gap." We have seen that, as they age, women are far more likely than men to be widowed. Moreover, as they grow older, women are adversely affected by the *double standard of aging* (Sontag 1976); that is, men aren't considered old or sexually ineligible as soon as women are. In our culture, being physically attractive is far more important in attracting a mate for women than for men. Beauty, "identified, as it is for women, with youthfulness, does not stand up well to age" (Sontag 1976, p. 352). So in our society, women become sexually ineligible much earlier than men do. An attractive man can remain eligible well into old age and is considered an acceptable mate for a younger woman. For older single women, this situation can exacerbate more general feelings of loneliness.

All of this is not to imply that there are no sexual problems in later marriages. A husband's having difficulty with erection, which can begin to happen in late middle age, may decrease his sexual motivation. However, it is also true that a husband's having difficulty with erection may result in his slowing down sexually and making sex more exciting for his partner (Sachs 2001).

As discussed in Chapter 6, long-term partners have to deal with habituation, or declining interest in sex due to greater accessibility. But habituation effects seem to be more prevalent in the first year of marriage. Indeed, marrieds of all ages tend to report high satisfaction with their sex lives, perhaps because increasingly they see sex as a "pleasure bond" (see Chapter 6). According to psychiatrist Stephen Levine, "Over age 50, the quality of sex depends much more on the overall quality of a relationship than it does for young couples" (quoted in Jacoby 1999, p. 42).

Retirement

Just as the concept *labor force* is an invention of industrialization, so too is the idea of retirement.

> Retirement as a time of leisure is feasible only with a certain degree of wealth. From a historical standpoint, widespread retirement first became possible when the industrial economy was productive enough to support sizable numbers of nonworking adults. At the same time, the economy no longer needed so many workers in the labor force, and companies believed that older workers were not as quick or as productive as the young. Governments, corporations, labor unions, and older workers themselves found retirement to be a desirable policy, and it soon became the normal practice. (Moody 2006, p. 234)

Although most older people retire, some do not—and many of those who don't are employed into their seventies and eighties. Not wanting to retire is one reason for continuing to work. Another reason, particularly applicable to divorced older women, is being unable to afford to retire (Atchley 1997). In fact, even among middle-class Americans,

> [t]here is evidence that the long post–World War II trend of earlier retirement may now be coming to an end. For instance, labor participation rates in later life have . . . increased a bit in recent years. More older people are working than earlier trends would have predicted. Some surveys suggest that new attitudes may be developing about work late in life. An AARP-Roper survey in 1997 revealed that up to 80% of aging baby boomers expect to work at least part-time after what used to be normal retirement age. (Moody 2006, pp. 240–41)

Regarding those who do retire, we tend to think of retiring as an abrupt event. However, many people retire gradually by steadily reducing their work hours or intermittently leaving, then returning to the labor force before retiring completely (Kim and DeVaney 2005). Even when it is not an abrupt event, retirement represents an important change for individuals and couples.

One small study of 228 couples (Smith and Moen 1998) found that the decision to retire is influenced by one's spouse—although for both husbands and wives, personal satisfaction in retirement is associated with *not* having been influenced by one's partner. Interestingly—and in line with traditionally gendered power relations in marriage—wives more often than husbands are motivated to retire by their spouse's wanting them to do so (Smith and Moen 2004).

Most older couples describe their marriages as happy. A retired husband may choose to spend more time doing homemaking tasks and give increased attention to being a companionate spouse. Role sharing, feeling that work is fairly shared, and having supportive communication predict good adjustment for retiring couples.

We know most about the retirement experience of men. A retired husband may choose to devote more attention to family roles such as being a companionate husband and grandparent; he might spend more time in homemaking tasks, especially if his wife is still employed (Szinovacz 2000). However, doing this can be problematic for men who cling to the traditional masculine role that highly values paid employment and achievement (Aldous 1978; Moody 2006).

Social scientist David Ekerdt (2006) notes that "a society that traditionally identifies work and productivity as a wellspring of virtue would seem to need some justification for a life of pensioned leisure. How do retirees and observers alike come to feel comfortable with a 'retired' life? . . . I suggest that retirement is . . . legitimated on a day-to-day basis in part by an ethic that esteems leisure that is earnest, occupied, and filled with activity—a 'busy ethic' [analogous to the 'work ethic'] (p. 254).

A husband's retirement requires homemaking wives to adjust as well. Full-time homemakers may find it difficult to share the house that had become their exclusive territory during the day. Even employed wives may have trouble sharing control over what had previously been their territory—the kitchen cupboards, for example. This situation may be partly why some research has found that husbands are happier with wives' retirement than vice versa (Smith and Moen 2004). When both partners are employed, simultaneous retirement or the retirement of the wife before the husband may cause fewer relationship problems (Brubaker 1991; Davey and Szinovacz 2004). For both wives and husbands, role flexibility is important to successful adjustment.

Later-Life Divorce, Widowhood, and Remarriage

Although the majority of couples who divorce do so before their retirement years, some couples do divorce in later life. Older-age divorces may be prompted by a husband's falling in love with a younger woman or by an older wife's tiring of being what she considers an unappreciated caregiver (Springen 2000). Little research has been done on the topic, but we might hypothesize that later-life divorces are not necessarily easy on the couple's adult children. For one thing, family rituals, such as birthday parties or Thanksgiving dinner are disrupted (Pett, Lang, and Gander 1992). An adult child's graduation or wedding arrangements can be difficult when forced to accommodate hostile, divorced parents. Then, too, adult children of divorcing parents may worry about having to become full-time caregivers to an aging parent in the absence of the parent's spouse. Nevertheless, although some later-life marriages end in divorce, the vast majority do so with the death of a spouse.

Widowhood and Widowerhood

Adjustment to widowhood or widowerhood is an important and common family transition in later life. We saw earlier in this chapter that, because women's life expectancy is longer and older men remarry far more often than women do, widowhood is significantly more common than widowerhood in our society. As Table 18.1 shows, nearly three-quarters of men age sixty-five and over live with their spouse, but fewer than half (41 percent) of women live with theirs. Widowhood is usually a permanent status for older women. Indeed, for some women, widowhood may last longer than the child-rearing stage of life. Nevertheless, we are reminded that widowhood does not, of course, happen only to women (Atchley 1997). In 2000, for instance, nearly one-third of men age seventy-five and older were widowed (Fields and Casper 2001, Table 6).

Typically, widowhood and widowerhood begin with **bereavement**, a period of mourning, followed by gradual adjustment to the new, unmarried status and to the loss. Bereavement manifests itself in physical, emotional, and intellectual symptoms (Figley et al. 1998). Recently widowed people perceived their health as declining and reported depressive symptoms (Brubaker 1991). Both men and women experience emotional reactions—anger, guilt, sadness, anxiety, and preoccupation with thoughts of the dead spouse—but these responses tend to diminish over time (Doka, Breaux, and Gordon 2002). Social support, adult children's help with housework and related tasks, and activities with friends, children, and siblings help (Utz et al. 2004).

There is some evidence that being single in old age is more detrimental, physically and emotionally, for men than for women (Peters and Liefbroer 1997). Women more often have social support outside the family, whereas men are typically more dependent on family for support.

> [Both] men and women experience similar physical and emotional difficulties initially, but after a time seem to cope with the loss of a spouse. . . . [B]oth establish new [single] lifestyles based on their past patterns of interaction. For both, their financial [and health] situation is related to their feelings of well-being. (Brubaker 1991, p. 233)

A spouse's death brings the conjugal unit to an end—often a profoundly painful event. For some, remarriage promises resumed intimacy and companionship. Far more widowers than widows remarry, a situation explained by the facts that (1) considerably fewer men are available as new partners, and (2) women appear to be less interested than men in late-life remarriage (Moorman, Booth, and Fingerman 2006). Research shows that the myth that widowers are quick to replace a deceased wife is just that—an exaggerated stereotype. "Men with high levels of social support from friends are no more likely than women to report interest in repartnering" (Carr 2004, p. 1065). During later life, morale and well-being frequently derive from relations with siblings, as well as from friends, neighbors, and other social contacts (Eriksen and Gerstel 2002). Furthermore, particularly for women, relationships with adult children and grandchildren continue to be important.

Older Parents, Adult Children, and Grandchildren

More often than spousal relationships, those between parents and their biological children last a lifetime (Kaufman and Uhlenberg 1998). In this section, we examine older parent–adult child and grandparent relations.

Older Parents and Adult Children

Chapter 11 mentions that adults' relationships with their parents can be classified as *tight-knit, sociable, obligatory, intimate but distant,* or *detached.* Here we will expand our discussion of this typology. Sociologists Merril Silverstein and Vern L. Bengston (2001) developed six indicators of relationship solidarity, or connection: geographic proximity, contact between members in a relationship, emotional closeness, similarity of opinions, providing care, and receiving care. Based on survey evidence and using these six indicators, Silverstein and Bengston developed a typology of five kinds of parent–adult child relations (see Table 18.3).

Parent–adult child relations vary depending on how family members combine—or, in the case of the detached relationship style, do not combine—the six indicators. For instance, in tight-knit relations, the parent and the adult child live near each other (geographic proximity), feel emotionally close, share similar opinions, and help each other (give and receive assistance). Sociable relations involve all these characteristics except that the parent and adult child do not exchange assistance. Table 18.3 defines all five relationship types.

Research shows that there is no one typical model for parent–adult child relationships (Arnett 2004; Silverstein and Bengston 2001). Furthermore, parent–adult child relations might change over time, moving from one relationship type to another depending on the par-

Table 18.3 Types of Intergenerational Relations

Class	Definition
Tight-knit	Adult children are engaged with their parents based on geographic proximity, frequency of contact, emotional closeness, similarity of opinions, and providing and receiving assistance.
Sociable	Adult children are engaged with their parents based on geographic proximity, frequency of contact, emotional closeness, and similarity of opinions but not based on providing or receiving assistance.
Obligatory	Adult children are engaged with their parents based on geographic proximity and frequency of contact but not based on emotional closeness and similarity of opinions. Adult children are likely to provide or receive assistance or both.
Intimate but distant	Adult children are engaged with their parents based on emotional closeness and similarity of opinions but not based on geographic proximity, frequency of contact, providing assistance, and receiving assistance.
Detached	Adult children are not engaged with their parents based on any of these six indicators of solidarity.

Source: Adapted from Silverstein and Bengston 2001, p. 55.

ent's and the adult child's respective ages, the parent's changed marital status, and the presence or absence of grandchildren, among other factors. For instance, to be nearer to their aging parents, adult children sometimes return to the area in which they grew up, or retired grandparents may decide to relocate in order to be near their grandchildren. Both of these situations could move an intimate-but-distant relationship to a tight-knit one. Then, too, a parent–adult child relationship might change depending only on emotional factors, such as when an adult child chooses to forgive an aging parent for some past transgression, or vice versa.

Using national survey data from a sample of 971 adult children who had at least one surviving noncoresident parent, Silverstein and Bengston (2001) made the following findings (among others):

- The majority of relations were neither tight-knit nor detached, but "variegated"—one of the three relationship styles in between (see Table 18.3). Variegated relations characterized 62 percent of adult children's interaction with their mothers and 53 percent with their fathers.

- Tight-knit relations are more likely to occur among lower socioeconomic groups and racial/ethnic minorities.

- Non-Hispanic whites were more likely than African Americans to have detached relationships with their parents and more likely than blacks or Hispanics to have obligatory relationships with their mothers.

- The most common relationship between a mother and her adult child was tight-knit. The next most common was sociable, followed by intimate-but-distant, obligatory, and, finally, detached.

- The most common relationship between a father and his adult child was detached, followed by sociable, tight-knit, obligatory, and intimate-but-distant. Almost four times as many adult children reported being detached from their fathers as from their mothers.

- Daughters were more likely than sons to have tight-knit relations with their mothers.

- Sons were more likely than daughters to have obligatory relations with their mothers.

Financially independent adults' relationships with a parent can be of several types: tight-knit, sociable, obligatory, intimate-but-distant, or detached. Then too, today's parents can find themselves in the "senior sandwich generation"— paying for a child's college tuition, worrying about the financial burden of eldercare for aging parents, while trying to save for their own retirement.

- Adult children were more likely to have obligatory or detached relations with divorced or separated mothers than with married mothers.

- Adult children were more likely to have detached relations with divorced or separated fathers than with consistently married fathers.

From these findings we can conclude that daughters are more likely than sons to have close relationships with their parents, especially with their mothers. Even for mothers, a parent's divorce or separation often weakens the bond with adult children. However, having detached relations with one's adult children after divorce is nearly five times greater for fathers than for mothers. Partly, at least, this is true because a divorced father is less likely than either a consistently married father or a divorced mother to live with his biological children and more likely to remarry (Silverstein and Bengston 2001).

In some families, the reality of past abuse, a conflict-filled divorce, or simply fundamental differences in values or lifestyles makes it seem unlikely that parents and children will spend time together (Kaufman and Uhlenberg 1998). Money matters can also cause tension. This is especially true in stepfamilies where "[a]dult children can feel resentful when they see a stepparent spending what they consider as their rightful inheritance" (Sherman 2006, p. F8). Overall, however, the majority of adult children's relationships with parents, though not necessarily tight-knit, continue to be meaningful.

Grandparenthood

Partly due to longer life expectancy, which creates more opportunity for the role, grandparenting (and great-grandparenting) became increasingly important to families throughout the twentieth century (Bengston 2001; Rosenbloom 2006). This is true despite urbanization's changing the grandparent role somewhat, with rural grandchildren more likely to have regular contact with their grandparents (King et al. 2003). Among both rural and urban grandparents, some are raising grandchildren, as explored in Chapter 11. The discussion in this section focuses on grandparents who are not primarily responsible for raising their grandchildren.

Young-old grandparents are typically employed and often married, while old-old grandparents may be physically disabled, so younger grandparents' experiences with their grandchildren are typically quite different from those of older grandparents (Silverstein and Marenco 2001). Meanwhile, declining birthrates have decreased the number of available grandchildren (Conner 2000).

Besides (and in accordance with) these demographic changes, the twentieth century saw increased emphasis on affection and companionship with grandparents.

Many grandparents find the role deeply meaningful: Grandchildren give personal pleasure and a sense of immortality. Some grandfathers see the role as an opportunity to be involved with babies and very young children, an activity that may have been discouraged when their own children were young (Cunningham-Burley 2001). Overall, the grandparent role is mediated by the parent; not getting along with the parent dampens the grandparent's contact and, hence, the relationship with her or his grandchildren (Mueller and Elder 2003).

Grandparents continue to provide practical help (King et al. 2003). They may serve as valuable "family watchdogs," ready to provide assistance when needed (Troll 1985). In low-income and ethnic-minority families, parents and children readily rely on grandparents and other kin for child care and other help. A recent *New York Times* article features several upper-middle-class grandparents who commute by plane weekly to help with childcare; they say it's "cheaper than getting a nanny" (Lee 2007). Even among white, middle-class families, it is not unusual for grandparents to help with child care or contribute to the cost of a grandchild's schooling, wedding, or first house. If an adult child of divorced parents becomes divorced, assistance may be more readily available from a grandparent (Vandell et al. 2003).

Grandparenting Styles Grandparents often adopt a grandparenting style similar to the one they experienced as grandchildren with their own grandparents (King and Elder 1997; Mueller and Elder 2003). Of course, grandparenting styles are also shaped by the grandparent's age, health, employment status, and personality (Silverstein and Marenco 2001). Among those who are not playing parentlike roles to their grandchildren, three general styles of grandparenting have been identified: remote, companionate, and involved (Cherlin and Furstenberg 1986). About one-third of grandparents have *remote* relationships with their grandchildren, often because they live far away. About half of grandparent–grandchild relationships are *companionate*. In this case, grandparents do things with their grandchildren but exercise little authority and allow the parent to control access to the youth. Companionate grandparents are often involved in work, leisure, or social activities of their own. Other grandparents are more *involved*, probably living with or near their grandchildren and frequently initiating interaction with their grandchild.

A grandparent may have different relationship styles with different grandchildren. Although some of them prefer to interact with their teenage grandchildren, grandparents generally are most actively involved with preadolescents, particularly preschoolers. Preschoolers are more available and respond most enthusiastically to a grandparent's attention. There is also evidence that

"Your're real good with kids, Grandma . . . you ought to have some of your own."

© George Crenshaw 1995. Reprinted by permission.

after a typically uninterested adolescence, adults renew relationships with grandparents (Cherlin and Furstenberg 1986).

Race/Ethnicity and Grandparenting Although there is relatively little research on the subject, we do know some ways in which race/ethnicity affects grandparenting (Karasik and Hamon 2007). For instance, one study found that 87 percent of black grandparents felt free to correct a grandchild's behavior, compared to 43 percent of white grandparents. As one black grandmother said of her fourteen-year-old grandson, "He can get around his mother, but he can't get around me so well" (quoted in Cherlin and Furstenberg 1986, p. 128; see also Flaherty, Facteau, and Garver 1999).

As another example, Native American elders may serve as *cultural conservator grandparents*—actively seeking contact and temporary coresidence with their grandchildren "for the expressed purpose of exposing them to the American Indian way of life" (Weibel-Orlando 2001, p. 143, quoted in Karasik and Hamon 2007, p. 145). Maintaining an ethnic-minority culture into future generations may be of particular concern for ethnic-minority grandparents. One study, for instance, found that "the erosion of traditional cultural language, values, and practices" negatively affected grandparent relationships in Mexican American families (Silverstein and Chen 1999, p. 196).

Divorce, Remarriage, and Grandparenting How does an adult child's divorce affect the grandparent relationship? Evidence suggests that the news hits hard, and grandparents worry over whether to intervene on behalf of the grandchildren. As might be expected, effects of the divorce are different for the **custodial grandparent**

(parent of the custodial parent) than for the **noncustodial grandparent** (parent of the noncustodial parent), with noncustodial grandparents significantly less likely to see their grandchildren as often as they had before the divorce (Cherlin and Furstenberg 1986; Spitze et al. 1994). With the current trends in child custody, the most common situation is for maternal grandparent relationships to be maintained or enhanced while paternal ones diminish (Mills, Wakeman, and Fea 2001).

Because of pressure from noncustodial grandparents, all fifty states have passed laws intended to give grandparents the right to seek legalized visitation rights, but courts are reluctant to do so when parents object. "The focus on grandparent visitation rights largely has centered on this legal question: Should the government intrude upon the fundamental rights of parents to allow grandparents to visit their grandchildren?" (Henderson 2005a, p. 640). Grandparents who go to court to seek visitation rights are successful between 30 and 40 percent of the time (Henderson 2005b). When courts do recognize visitation rights for grandparents in spite of parental objections, the reason usually involves the best interests of the child (Henderson 2005a, 2005b).

Then, too, remarriages (and re-divorces) create step-grandparents (and ex-stepgrandparents; Ganong and Coleman 2004). Very little information exists on step-grandparents, but available data suggest that stepgrandparents tend to distinguish their "real" grandchildren from those of remarriages, while younger stepgrandchildren and those who live with the grandparent's adult child are more likely to develop ties with the stepgrandparent (Cherlin and Furstenberg 1986; Coleman, Ganong, and Cable 1997).

To close this section, we quote sociologist Vern L. Bengston (2001) as he notes the importance of grandparents to younger family members' well-being:

> Grandparents provide many unacknowledged functions in contemporary families. They are important role models in the socialization of grandchildren. They provide economic resources to younger generation family members. They contribute to cross-generational solidarity and family continuity over time. They also represent a bedrock of stability for teenage moms raising infants [as well as for other family members]. (p. 7)

We turn now to an examination of caregiving to aging family members.

Aging Families and Caregiving

When we associate caregiving with the elderly, we may tend to think only in terms of older generations as care recipients and younger generations as caregivers. How-ever, older Americans give to their communities and assist their adult children financially and in many other ways as well (Caputo 2005; Ingersoll-Dayton, Neal, and Hammer 2001). Many older Americans are volunteers in hospitals and countless other settings. For example, in some communities, older people mentor troubled youth (Donahoe 2005). As another example, you can go online for advice from the Elder Wisdom Circle, a group of "cyber-grandparents" who volunteer to offer guidance to younger people (Adler 2006). In this section, however, we focus on **eldercare**—that is, care provided to the elderly. About 20 percent of Americans age seventy-five and older are engaged in some form of caregiving, whether child care or eldercare (Shapiro 2006b).

Eldercare involves emotional support, a variety of services, and, sometimes, financial assistance. A growing number of tax-funded, charity, and for-profit services provide eldercare. Nevertheless, the persisting social expectation in the United States is that family members will either care for elderly relatives personally or organize and supervise the care provided by others (Conner 2000). At least one-quarter of American households are involved in eldercare to some extent, with the average caregiver providing eighteen hours of assistance each week (Cancian and Oliker 2000; Gavin 2003). The vast majority of eldercare is **informal caregiving**—unpaid and provided personally by a family member as a form of unpaid family work, discussed in Chapter 12.

Being concerned about an elderly family member might involve nothing more than making a daily phone call to make sure that he or she is okay or stopping by for a weekly visit. However, **gerontologists**—social scientists who study aging—more specifically define **caregiving** as "assistance provided to persons who cannot, for whatever reason, perform the basic activities or instrumental activities of daily living for themselves" (Uhlenberg 1996, p. 682). Caregiving may be short term (taking care of someone who has recently had joint-replacement surgery, for example) or long term. The majority of the young-old need almost no help at all, but as an elderly person continues to age, she or he may require ongoing help with tasks such as paying bills and, later, eating or bathing. About 54 percent of those over age eighty-five need assistance in meeting their daily needs. This compares to 22 percent of those between seventy-five and eighty-four, and 8 percent of those sixty-five through seventy-four (Conner 2000). Severely ill or disabled older people often need a great deal of care over a long period. "As We Make Choices: Community Resources for Eldercare" describes eldercare options.

A number of eldercare givers are relatively young—in their thirties, with some in their twenties, partly because children born to older parents begin elder-

As We Make Choices Community Resources for Eldercare

Financial resources enhance options when dealing with the stress or crisis of providing eldercare. Today, more older Americans and their care providers are turning to professional eldercare service providers for help. A few will arrange a house call from a dentist or look after the cat when someone goes to the hospital. Nurses provide medical care; home health aides assist with personal care like bathing (Shapiro 2001b, p. 61). With growing numbers of elderly today, there are more and more community services for eldercare and, consequently, more options (Greenwald 1999). The table in this box describes several options. Several experts offer advice on steps in coping with an aging parent:

1. *Don't wait.* Exploring options before they're needed helps all family members know what to expect and begin to prepare for the future (Greenwald 1999, p. 53).

2. *Seek support.* Eldercare givers need to seek all the help they can get. For example, geriatric social workers can help to assess an elderly person's needs and develop action plans: "Such people may be especially helpful in those painful cases when children must take needed steps in spite of the objections of mentally declining parents" (Greenwald 1999, p. 53).

3. *Shop around.* Most providers of senior housing are businesses, not charities, and their products should be scrutinized for cost and quality. Families should visit as many facilities as they can on different days of the week and hours of the day. Ask for references (Shapiro 2001b, p. 60).

The Options	What Is It?
Home care	Wide range of services, including shopping and transportation, health aides who give baths, nurses who provide medical care, and physical therapy brought to the home
Adult day care	A place to get meals and spend the day, usually run by not-for-profit agencies
Congregate housing	A private home within a residential compound, providing shared activities and services
Assisted living	Residential units offering private rooms, meals, twenty-four-hour supervision, and other assistance
Continuing care facility	A variety of housing options and a continuum of services all in one location
Nursing home	Residential medical care for the aged who need continual attention

Sources: Greenwald 1999, pp. 54–55; Moody 2006, pp.290–93; Shapiro 2001a, b; also see "Glossary of Senior Housing Terms" (2007) at http://senioroutlook.com/glossary.asp.

care at younger ages (Dellmann-Jenkins, Blankemeyer, and Pinkard 2000; "When Elder Care Falls" 2001). As described in "Issues for Thought: Child—and Grandchild—Caregivers," some family caregivers are children. However, the mean age for caregivers is fifty-seven; more than one-third (35 percent) are over age sixty-five and may themselves be in poor health or beginning to suffer from age-related disabilities (Himes 2001). The National Long-Term Care Survey conducted in 1982 by the federal Department of Health and Human Services found that most long-term caregivers had provided help for between one and four years, and 20 percent had been caring for the disabled person for five years or more. Almost all caregivers in this survey provided assistance seven days a week for an average of four hours daily (Cancian and Oliker 2000).

Which family members more often provide eldercare and how much they provide depend on the care receiver's preference as well as the family's understanding of who is primarily responsible for giving the care. The first choice for a caregiver is an available spouse, followed by adult children, siblings, grandchildren, nieces and nephews, neighbors and friends, and, finally, a formal service provider (Cantor 1979; Horowitz 1985).[8]

Older Americans provide a considerable amount of eldercare to one another. Up to 40 percent of eldercare is provided by the elderly care receiver's spouse (Novak 1997). Caregiving and receiving are expected components of the marital relationship for most of today's older couples, who have developed a relationship of mutual exchange over many years (Huyck 1996; Machir 2003). A qualitative study of seventy-five spouse

[8] M. H. Cantor (1979) termed this system of elderly care receivers' preference for caregivers the *hierarchical compensatory model* of caregiving.

When we think about giving care to other family members, especially to elderly family members, we probably assume that the caregiver is a middle-aged or older adult—often the child of the care recipient. But according to a national survey by the National Alliance for Caregiving:

- About 1.4 million U.S. children between the ages of eight and eighteen are caring for another family member, usually a parent or grandparent.

- Three of every ten child caregivers are between ages eight and eleven.

- Almost four of every ten child caregivers are ages twelve to fifteen.

- About three-quarters of child caregivers are not the only ones providing care to the recipient; they say that someone else helps, too.

- More than half of child caregivers help with at least one activity of daily living, such as bathing, dressing, or feeding.

- Almost all young caregivers help with keeping the recipient company, shopping, preparing meals, or doing other household tasks.

- One in six child caregivers helps the recipient to communicate with doctors or nurses.

- Fifteen percent of child caregivers who are age twelve or older make phone calls and otherwise help make arrangements for other people to work with the care recipient.

- As you might expect, child caregivers have less time for themselves than do other children.

- It's hard to say whether it's "good or bad" for a child to be a caregiver; there is not enough research on the topic to draw conclusions.

- One thing that professionals do know is that child caregivers need breaks, as well as support groups specifically designed for them. One idea is to organize support groups at schools during lunch hours.

Besides children under age eighteen, young adult grandchildren may be providing eldercare. Although some ethnic-minority cultures in the United States expect that grandchildren will provide eldercare when needed, "grandparent care is a relatively new phenomenon in American culture and has not been the focus of caregiving literature" (Fruhauf, Jarrott, and Allen 2006, p. 888). A future research topic for you?

Critical Thinking

How is the fact that some children and young adult grandchildren are providing care for adults an example of family change? What characteristics of our society might add to the challenges of child/grandchild caregivers? What might our society do to offer social support to young caregivers?

Sources: Hunt, Levine, and Naiditch 2005; Shapiro 2006a.

caregivers found that those in longer, emotionally close marriages with little ongoing conflict evidenced better overall well-being (Townsend and Franks 1997).

After spouses, adult children are most likely to be providing eldercare. Especially for the unmarried and child-free, an older American's siblings are important in mutual caregiving (Eriksen and Gerstel 2002).

Adult Children as Eldercare Providers

Motivated both by **filial responsibility** (a child's obligation to parents) and, often, by affection, adult children care for their folks "because they're my parents" (C. Stein et al. 1998; see also Gans and Silverstein 2006). Adults who care for aging parents often provide the vast majority of care themselves, but they also enlist their siblings when possible or seek assistance from formal service providers or do both (Wolf, Freedman, and Soldo 1997).

A small study of 387 elderly parents in Florida found that principles of reciprocity are at work regarding family eldercare. Parents expected help from their adult children in proportion to the aid that the parents had once given to their children (Lee, Netzer, and Coward 1994). In other research, adult children who had received considerably more financial help from their parents were more likely than their siblings to be engaged in caring for the parent in old age (Henretta et al. 1997).

Today it's often the case that siblings have geographically moved away from each other and from their aging parents. Even when siblings live near an elderly parent, however, the burden of eldercare does not always fall upon each equally—a situation that causes added stress for the principal or sole caregiver. A study based on forty focus groups asked eldercare givers with siblings to describe how they felt about this situation:

> Siblings who described an imbalance in caregiving responsibilities reported feeling considerable distress. . . . One participant confessed that she was straddling a "real thin line between just taking her [barely participating sister's] head off some day, because I'm so mad at the inequity of it." (Ingersoll-Dayton et al. 2003, p. 205)

In addition, the participants sought to define the situation as more-or-less fair. To do so, they took into

Aging and failing health can create stress both individually and within a marriage, but many spouses draw on deep reserves of affection and love to find the patience and willingness to care for the other.

account such things as a sibling's geographical distance from the aging parent, employment responsibilities, and other family obligations. Interestingly, some participants (both men and women) called upon gendered expectations to help justify women's inequitable eldercare responsibilities. "I guess it's my gender," said a woman whose brother did little to help. "It's just natural." Participants also explained that their parents preferred the help of their daughters. A son-in-law explained his wife's caring for her mother this way: "I think gender has a lot to do with it . . . that's traditionally . . . been the way it goes. Mom just, I think, calls on her more, so that's the way. . . . It's not that the brothers wouldn't help at all, but it's just . . . she gets called on more" (p. 207).

Gender Differences in Providing Eldercare

Women account for about two-thirds of all unpaid caregivers (Johnson and Wiener 2006). An analysis of Internet hits on the website of the Michigan Office of Services to the Aging found that, when using e-mail to request information, women are more active in eldercare (Ellis 1999). Since about 1990, women have spent more years caring for an elderly relative than caring for young chil-

dren (Abel 1991). These figures do not mean that men are uninvolved in eldercare. We need to remember that about one-third of unpaid caregivers are male. And, as only-child sons become middle-aged with aging parents, it is likely they will be involved in caregiving.

"More than 9 out of 10 frail older care recipients who are married obtain help from their spouses," themselves often in poor health (Johnson and Wiener 2006). Among marrieds, far more unpaid caregivers are wives. This situation is mostly due to women's living longer; feelings of obligation to care for an elderly disabled spouse are fairly equal between husbands and wives. Husband-caregivers may see their role as an extension of the traditionally masculine one of provider and protector (Bowers 1999). However, gender makes a significant difference in adult children's caregiving obligations (Cancian and Oliker 2000).

Norms in many Asian American families designate the oldest son as the responsible caregiver to aging parents (Kamo and Zhou 1994; Lin and Liu 1993). Except in this case, the adult child involved in a parent's care is more likely to be a daughter (or even a daughter-in-law) than a son. This situation—one that raises issues of gender equity similar to those of parenting and domestic work discussed in Chapters 11 and 12—is partly due to ongoing employment differences between women and men (Sarkisian and Gerstel 2004). Then, too, in accordance with the findings (discussed earlier) that parent–daughter relations are more often tight-knit than parent–son relations, sons tend to provide eldercare only in the absence of available daughters (Lee, Spitze, and Logan 2003).

Nevertheless, the proportion of sons involved in eldercare is expected to increase in the relatively near future due to the growing number of only-child sons, smaller sibling groups from which to draw care providers, and changing gender roles that make caregiving an expectation for adult male behavior (B. Harris 1998). "My Family: Looking After—A Son's Memoir" is one son-caregiver's story.

When siblings share in caring for aging parents, daughters do more than sons, on average, as measured by time spent. Furthermore, men and women tend to provide care differently—in ways that reflect socially gendered expectations and increase females' caregiver fatigue (Raschick and Ingersoll-Dayton 2004). Sons, grandsons, and other male caregivers (although not husbands) tend to perform a more limited range of occasional tasks, such as cleaning gutters or mowing the lawn, while daughters more often provide consistently required routine services like housekeeping, cooking, or doing laundry.

A son is more likely than a daughter to enlist help from his spouse, the eldercare receiver's daughter-in-law.

My Family   Looking After—A Son's Memoir

Daughters are far more likely than sons to be personal caregivers. However, some men do give more personal or intimate kinds of care. In the following essay, author John Daniel describes providing intimate care for his elderly mother.

I never looked forward to helping my mother with her shower. She wasn't the least self-conscious about baring her body in my presence, but something in me shrank from it. To be with her in her nakedness seemed too intimate for a grown son. And some other part of me, the child who wants always to be cared for and never burdened with responsibility, felt put upon and put out. Why was I having to do this? . . .

Talking her into it was the first challenge. "Oh, I don't need a shower," she would say. "I just had one yesterday, didn't I?"

"You haven't had one for a week."

"But I don't *do* anything. Why do I need a shower?"

It wasn't only bad memory and lapsing judgment that made her resist, of course. It was also that the shower was strenuous for her, and she didn't want to acknowledge, or couldn't, that she

needed help with anything so simple. In her own mind, the mind I believe she inhabited most of the time, she was perfectly capable of taking a shower by herself if she wanted to. In this mind she was still the woman she had been five years ago, a woman who came and went and drove a car. . . .

But in her present mind she knew, whenever she leaned far forward in a chair and tried to stiff-arm herself to her feet, whenever she steadied herself with a hand on the wall as she shuffled to the bathroom, just how incapable she had become. She knew, and she hated it. How could she not have hated it? And if she had to bear it, she didn't want me . . . to have to bear it. She wanted to carry herself on her own stooped shoulders. . . .

She squeezed her eyes shut as I rinsed her hair in the shower stream. She scrunched up her face, stuck her lips out, and sputtered through the soapy runoff. It was in that recurring moment of her life with us, her hair flattened to her head, darkened a little with the soaking spray, that I could almost see my mother as a girl—swimming the

cold swells off Hancock Point, splashing and laughing, shouting something toward shore, laying into the water with strong even strokes that would take her where she wanted to go.

She would let me stop rinsing only when she could rub a bit of her hair between finger and thumb and make it squeak. Then I would steady her out of the shower stall, her two hands in mine. It felt at that moment like a kind of dance, a dance that maybe I knew how to do and needed to do. . . .

I guess I came out of the bathroom cleaner of spirit myself. . . . I appreciate now what a privilege it was to help my mother with her shower. I wish I'd seen it more clearly at the time. We don't get to choose our privileges, and the ones that come to us aren't always the ones we would choose, and each of them is as much burden as joy. But they do come, and it's important to know them for what they are. . . .

Source: From *Looking After: A Son's Memoir* by John Daniel. Copyright © 1997 by John Daniel. Reprinted by permission of Counterpoint Press, a member of Perseus Books, L.L.C.

Furthermore, sons more often serve as organizers, negotiators, supervisors, and intermediaries between the care receiver and formal service providers (Raschick and Ingersoll-Dayton 2004). "Providing intimate, hands-on care is culturally defined as feminine, [and the] dirty parts of care work are mainly women's work" (Isaksen 2002, pp. 806, 809).

The Sandwich Generation

Many daughter-caregivers have children under age eighteen living at home. Indeed, it looks as if "the presence of children in the household connects parents to kin," including aging parents who may need eldercare (Gallagher and Gerstel 2001, p. 272). National surveys show that 37 percent of Americans between ages fifty-three and sixty-one have at least one living parent and one dependent child. More than one-quarter have a grand-

child as well (Kolata 1993). About twenty years ago, journalists and social scientists took note of an emerging **sandwich generation**: middle-aged (or older) individuals, usually women—although not always (Harris and Bichler 1997)—who are sandwiched between the simultaneous responsibilities of caring for their dependent children and aging parents.

Although some demographers believe that the popular press has exaggerated the burdens of the sandwich generation (Bengston, Rosenthal, and Burton 1996), the sandwich generation does indeed experience all the hectic task juggling discussed in Chapters 11 and 12 (Kaplan-Leiserson 2003). Stress builds as family members handle not only employment and child care but also parent care (Ingersoll-Dayton, Neal, and Hammer 2001). Recently, gerontologist Neal Cutler, who studies the effect of aging on finances, coined the term *senior sandwich generation*. These folks are "at least 60 years old and facing the ultimate financial trifecta: college for their kids (either current tuition bills or paying back borrowed money), retirement for themselves and at-home or nursing-home care for one or more parents. All at the same time" (Chatzky 2006).

Eldercare as a Family Process

Sociologists Francesca Cancian and Stacey Oliker (2000) write,

> Contrary to the myth that Americans are increasingly abandoning older people to institutional care, families continue to provide most care for frail or disabled elders, except for financial support. Only 5 percent of all older people live in nursing homes, and the figure was only slightly lower in the 1950s. (p. 65)

In accordance with the interactionist theoretical perspective, we can envision eldercare as an interactive process during which family members struggle to negotiate various caregiving decisions. Social scientists have noted a **caregiving trajectory** through which the process of eldercare proceeds.

First, the caregiver becomes concerned about an aging family member, and often she or he expresses this concern to others, although not necessarily to the older family member. Later, still concerned, the caregiver begins to give advice to the older family member, such as "Don't forget to take your medicine" or "You should get an appointment for new glasses." Still later, the caregiver takes action to provide needed services (Cicirelli 2000). Throughout this trajectory, family members may be called upon for advice and counsel in making medical or other significant decisions. A family's decision to move an elderly parent to a nursing home is particularly painful, with concern for the aged parent continuing thereafter (Keefe and Fancey 2000).

As they make decisions about the elderly family member's condition, disagreements may arise between the caregiver(s) and the receiver as well as among family caregivers themselves (Mills and Wilmoth 2002). Such issues as whether the elderly family member is able to drive safely or should undergo major surgery are examples. And families "are often forced to make urgent, complex decisions for loved ones in intensive care units" (M. Siegel 2004). All else being equal, the caregiving experience is less stressful and more positive when conflict is low and family members can agree on issues such as these (Conner 2000; Scharlach, Li, and Dalvi 2006). Put another way, families that have developed a shared understanding of the caregiving situation make more effective caregiving teams (Pruchno, Burant, and Peters 1997).

Caregiving parent–child relations—like some other family relationships—might best be characterized by ambivalence (Fingerman, Hay, and Birditt 2004; Willson, Shuey, and Elder 2003). Older people are often uncomfortable and sometimes angry or stubborn about receiving help, for it represents a threat to their autonomy and self-esteem, especially if the caregiver is controlling or if earlier conflicts reemerge (Brubaker, Gorman, and Hiestand 1990).

Parents may become more controlling as they grow older, a common reaction to loss of bodily and social power with aging and retirement. One in-depth study, however, suggests that adult children caregivers may expect a certain amount of deference, or courteous submission to their opinions and decisions, from the aging parent for whom they are caring—and when this does not occur, "intergenerational relations become strained, and children are likely to set limits on their caregiving" (Pyke 1999, p. 661). Meanwhile, frail and fearful parents may make unreasonable demands.

Caregiver Stress Providing eldercare may enhance one's sense of purpose and overall life satisfaction due to the self-validating effects of helping another person, enhanced intimacy, and the belief that helping others may result in assistance with one's own needs when the time arrives (Marks, Lambert, and Choi 2002).

Nevertheless, "providing help can overwhelm caregivers" (Johnson and Wiener 2006). Caregiving is stressful and can be physically (Christakis and Allison 2006), financially, and emotionally costly. Employed caregivers not only spend their own money but (especially women) may also pass up promotions or take extended time off

© Bill Anon/PhotoEdit

The majority of elderly Americans maintain their own homes. However, many of the frail elderly depend on, or live with, family members. Although care for an aging parent—most often by daughters—is often given with fondness and love, it can also bring stress, conflicting emotions, and great demands on time, energy, health, and finances.

from work or take early retirement to engage in eldercare (Cancian and Oliker 2000; Dentinger and Clarkberg 2002). In addition, providing eldercare may be socially isolating, often brings on depression, and may further strain one's own health (Machir 2003; Marks, Lambert, and Choi 2002). Younger caregivers experience limitations on dating and other relationships. As one twenty-six-year-old explained to a research team, "I would like to go camping with my husband once in a while, but I can't just get up and go away, because of taking care of my grandparents" (in Dellmann-Jenkins, Blankemeyer, and Pinkard 2000, p. 181).

Caregiver stress among Americans results partly from the fact that ours is an individualist, rather than a collectivist, culture, where adult children are expected to establish lives apart from their parents and to achieve success as individuals rather than (or as well as) working to benefit the family system (Killian and Ganong 2002). "The most problematic aspect of individualism and caregiving is that there is no formal mechanism to ensure that there will be support, and expectations are vague at best" (Fry 1996, p. 134).

Furthermore, because the chronically ill or disabled of all ages are decreasingly cared for in hospitals, today's informal caregivers are asked to perform complicated care regimens that have traditionally been handled only in hospitals by health care professionals (Guberman et al. 2005). This situation places added demands on a family caregiver's time, energy, and emotional stamina, a situation that not infrequently leads to caregiver depression (Dwyer, Lee, and Jankowski 1994).

One study of caregivers found that when the relationship feels more reciprocal, with the caregiver feeling that he or she is getting something in return, the caregiver is less often depressed (LeBlanc and Wright 2000). Furthermore, receiving adequate training and learning specific caregiver skills can lessen caregiver stress, as do various forms of social support—including finding information and connecting with other caregivers either in face-to-face support groups or on the Internet (Colvin et al. 2004; "Learning Skills" 2003; Smerglia et al. 2007). Research with one hundred African American wife caregivers found that receiving support from their churches lessened their stress and helped their marriage relationships (Chadiha, Rafferty, and Pickard 2003). Meanwhile, elder abuse and neglect in families often—although not always—results from caregiver stress (Conner 2000).

Elder Abuse and Neglect

Parallel to child abuse and neglect, discussed in Chapter 14, **elder abuse** involves overt acts of aggression, whereas **elder neglect** involves acts of omission or failure to give adequate care. Elder abuse by family members may include physical assault, emotional humiliation, purposeful social isolation (for example, forbidding use of the telephone), or financial exploitation (Henningson 1997; Tatara and Blumerman 1996).

As with other forms of domestic abuse, the development of accurate statistics has been a gradual process, as formal reports to state agencies miss the many unreported instances of elder abuse. Various studies have concluded that between 1 and 10 percent of individuals over age sixty are abused or neglected. In 1996, the federal government sponsored the National Elder Abuse Incidence Study, a random sample survey of counties, which combined reports from Adult Protective Services with interviews with "sentinels," people in the community who have contact with the elderly. Estimates from this study are that 450,000 individuals over sixty living in domestic settings were abused or neglected; if self-neglect is included, the total rises to 551,000 ("Fact Sheet: : Elder Abuse Prevalence and Incidence" 2005). Neglect is the most common form of elder maltreatment (55 percent in the 1996 study). Of the remaining study participants, 15 percent experienced physical abuse; 12 percent, exploitation; 8 percent, emotional abuse; and 0.3 percent, sexual abuse (Tatara, Kuzmeskus, and Duckhorn 1997).

The emerging profile of the abused or neglected elderly person is of a female, seventy years old or older, who has physical, mental, or emotional impairments or a combination of all three and is dependent on the abuser/caregiver for both companionship and help with daily living activities. Studies have found that the *neglected* elderly are older and have more physical and mental difficulties (and, hence, are more burdensome to care for) than are elder *abuse* victims (Pillemer 1986; Whittaker 1995).

There are many parallels between elder maltreatment and other forms of family violence. In fact, "there is reason to believe that a certain proportion of elder abuse is actually spouse abuse grown old" (L. Phillips 1986, p. 212; see also Zink et al. 2006). In some cases, marital violence among the elderly involves abuse of a caregiving partner by a spouse who has become ill with Alzheimer's disease (Pillemer 1986). Spouses, though, are 16 percent of abusers, while adult children make up 37 percent of perpetrators. Males and females appear equally likely to abuse the elderly (Tatara et al. 1997).

The social context of elders who are abused by family members or others includes stress from outside sources, such as financial problems or a caregiver's job conflicts, and lack of the elderly person's connectedness with friends and community. As discussed in Chapter 14, these factors are also associated with child abuse.

Elder-abuse victims, in contrast to the neglected, are relatively healthy and able to meet their daily needs.

The common denominators in cases of physical elder abuse are shared living arrangements, the abuser's poor emotional health (often including alcohol or drug problems), and a pathological relationship between victim and abuser (Anetzberger, Korbin, and Austin 1994). Indeed, data from one study of 300 cases of elder abuse in the Northeast found that an abuser (frequently an adult son) was likely to be financially dependent on the elderly victim. Abusive acts may be "carried out by abusers to compensate for their perceived lack or loss of power" (Pillemer 1986, p. 244). Moreover, "[i]n many instances, both the victim and the perpetrator were caught in a web of interdependency and disability, which made it difficult for them to seek or accept outside help or to consider separation" (R. Wolf 1986, p. 221; 1996).

Researching and combating elder abuse generally proceed from either of two models: the *caregiver model* or the *domestic violence model*. The **caregiver model of elder abuse and neglect** views abusive or neglectful caregivers as individuals who are simply overwhelmed by the requirements of caring for their elderly family members. Burdens associated with caring for an older person may sometimes cause the caregiver to lose control and verbally or physically abuse the receiver. Professional care providers employed by community agencies are often trained to recognize potentially abusive family situations and can work to reduce dangerous levels of caregiver stress that may trigger abuse.

In contrast, the **domestic violence model** views elder abuse and neglect as one form of family violence and focuses on characteristics of abusers, on situations that put potential victims at increased risk (see Finkelhor and Pillemer 1988; Whittaker 1995), and on a possible criminal justice response (Brownell 1998). Because financial gain is one motive for elder abuse by adult children or other caregivers, a criminal justice response seems important, and it is being pursued in some jurisdictions. Orange County, California, undertook sixty prosecutions in one year and got convictions in 90 percent of them (Gross 2006b). We have examined providing eldercare as a general process. We turn next to a discussion of racial/ethnic diversity and eldercare.

Racial/Ethnic Diversity and Family Eldercare

Adult children of all races and ethnicities feel responsible for their aging parents (Eggebeen and Davey 1998) and to their siblings, with whom they may share eldercare obligations (C. Stein et al. 1998). However, racial/ethnic differences do exist regarding eldercare. For instance, Asians have traditionally tended to emphasize the centrality of filial obligations over conjugal relationships (Burr and Mutchler 1999). In addition, older

blacks are more likely than non-Hispanic whites to expect their adult children to personally care for them in old age (Lee, Peek, and Coward 1998). Blacks and Hispanics (Burr and Mutchler 1999), as well as Asian Americans, are more likely than non-Hispanic whites to expect to share a residence if necessary. Table 18.2 shows that they do.

Fictive kin (family-like relationships that are not based on blood or marriage but on close friendship ties) are often resources for eldercare-giving help among African Americans (sometimes called "going for sisters"), Hispanics (*compadrazgos*), Italians (*compare*), and other ethnic groups as well (Ebaugh and Curry 2000). Meanwhile, racial/ethnic minorities have not been as likely as non-Hispanic whites to use community-based services, such as senior centers, or to receive government assistance. This discrepancy occurs because of language barriers (U.S. House of Representatives Select Committee on Aging 1992), because individuals don't know that they qualify for government-funded services, or because they are reluctant to include paid service providers as members of their caregiving team (Riekse and Holstege 1996; Treas 1995).

Partly because of differences like these, the cultural assumption, or myth, exists that minority ethnic communities rely only on their own family members for support. We may have an idealized view of minority families' providing eldercare with little stress or need for public or community assistance (Connor 2000). Research shows that this is an exaggerated stereotype. Minority families providing eldercare do experience stresses and often need to rely on community services (Dilworth-Anderson, Williams, and Cooper 1999).

> Assumptions that ethnic minorities take care of their own with little need for community assistance may be used by the larger community to relieve itself of responsibility for providing access to services and designing services to meet the needs of the minority community. [These stereotypical assumptions] can also give a false sense that older people in these communities do not need care and attention from the larger society and result in further isolation and alienation of minority group Americans. (Conner 2000, p. 164)

Moreover, among many immigrant ethnic groups, **acculturation** (the process whereby immigrant groups adopt the beliefs, values, and norms of their new culture) affects norms of filial obligation. Among immigrant groups, younger generations are more likely than their elders to become acculturated—a situation that creates the potential for intergenerational conflict (Silverstein 2000; Silverstein and Chen 1999).

A study of older Puerto Ricans found that filial obligation has declined in the younger generations. Hence, older Puerto Ricans in this study "strive to retain some measure of self-management and to more flexibly integrate informal and formal services, creating a dynamic and individualized plan of care for themselves" (Zsembik and Bonilla 2000, p. 652). And research on ethnic Chinese immigrant families in California found that sons often outsourced elder care:

> "I told her that I hire you to help me achieve my filial duty," Paul Wang, a 60-year-old Taiwanese immigrant owning a software company in Silicon Valley, California, described . . . his conversation with the in-home care worker he employed for his mother suffering from Alzheimer's disease. (Lan 2002, p. 812)

Acculturation has also meant that more elderly immigrants today than in the past live in housing designed for the elderly, rather than with their grown children: "As norms change, more retirement homes have miso soup on the menu" (Kershaw 2003, p. A10).

The Changing American Family and Eldercare in the Future

As America ages, providing eldercare has become "a central feature of American family life" (Conner 2000, p. 88; White House Conference on Aging 2005). At the same time, the American family is changing in structure and form, as we have seen throughout this text. Because these changes could result in a diminishing caregiver "kin supply" (Bengston 2001, p. 5), many policy makers have become concerned about the family's capability to provide eldercare in the future (U.S. Senate Special Committee on Aging 2002; White House Conference on Aging 2005).

For one thing, women's increased participation in the labor force decreases the time that women, the principal providers of eldercare, have available to engage in eldercare. Furthermore, the greater geographical mobility of family members is likely to negatively affect family members' face-to-face support (Himes 2001). Moreover, families on average are smaller today than in the past. Hence, the ratio of adult children to elderly parents is declining (Bengston 2001). Research shows that the more living children a person has, the more care from family members he or she is likely to receive (Spitze and Logan 1990).

More siblings ease the burden of each one because they can share in the caregiving (Wolf, Freedman, and Soldo 1997). However, today and increasingly in the future, there are and will be fewer adult siblings available to share in the care of their elderly parents. Furthermore, today's older Americans are likely to have siblings who can help them, but as more younger par-

ents today choose to have fewer or only children, more elderly in the future will have fewer or no siblings.

> Policy makers' concerns about providing eldercare involve other family-structure changes as well, such as higher rates of individuals' remaining single and/or child-free and higher rates of cohabitation, divorce and repartnering. For one thing, the child-free and unmarried populations will increase among future elderly generations, and being child-free or without a spouse "eliminates the two most important caregiving resources—spouse and adult child." (Conner 2000, p. 14)

Moreover, a high sense of filial obligation in a family has been positively related to actual caregiving and support (Ikkink, Tilburg, and Knipscheer 1999). But divorce among the older generation seems to reduce the younger generation's feelings of filial obligation. Research suggests that a daughter's being divorced does *not* decrease her help to her parents—although divorce probably does decrease help from an ex-daughter-in-law (Spitze et al. 1994). Meanwhile, research also shows that—particularly for fathers—being divorced reduces parents' intergenerational exchanges with adult children. Exchanges at the end of the life course continue to be negatively affected (Pezzin and Schone 1999).

We are just beginning to understand the ramifications of remarriage for eldercare. In one qualitative study of late-life remarried caregivers,

> [w]ives revealed how little support or assistance they received from adult stepchildren for their ailing father. Often these caregivers endured a kind of amplified stress, isolation, and conflict in their caregiving role, which they attributed to their remarried, stepmother status. By the same token, adult children and stepchildren are not always granted access to the critical decision-making or caretaking. (Sherman 2006, p. F8)

In general, research shows that people without a spouse or adult children get less personal eldercare and have a higher rate of nursing-home residency than do elderly people with children (Conner 2000). However, singles in the future may be increasingly creative in providing alternatives for themselves.

As an example, "[f]amilies of older gay and lesbian people have many of the same strengths and deal with the same issues as other families. But along with getting older, they also have to face the prejudices of being gay or lesbian." For instance, public retirement housing often does not allow "unrelated adults" to live together. Then, too, "nursing homes and private retirement centers . . . [often] make assumptions that their residents are heterosexual and structure activities on the basis of these assumptions" (Powell 2004, p. 60). Partly so as not to be separated from their partners by well-meaning relatives who may put them in separate nursing homes, gay men and lesbian couples (who can afford it) have begun to create old-age and retirement communities of their own (Nystrom and Jones 2003; Rosenberg 2001).

Siblings, nieces, and nephews can fulfill the obligations of children for the child-free elderly (Penning 1990). We can also imagine that, especially among women, child-free and single elderly will fashion "families" of mutually caring friends. The extent to which one's cohabiting partner participates in eldercare is a matter for future research.

Although many policy analysts express concern, some demographers conclude that intergenerational relations "generally possess the potential to serve their members' needs" (Silverstein and Bengston 1997). They point to the **latent kin matrix**, defined as "a web of continually shifting linkages that provide the potential for activating and intensifying close kin relationships" (Riley 1983, p. 441). An important feature of the latent matrix is that family relations, although they may remain dormant for long periods, emerge as a resource when the need arises (Silverstein and Bengston 2001).

Moreover, while family structure and forms become increasingly diverse, so may ways that members of the postmodern family deal with eldercare. For instance, in research involving in-depth interviews with forty-five older respondents, a sixty-seven-year-old separated wife, whose husband had become diabetic and asthmatic and

had heart trouble, reported that she still loved him very much: "If something happened to him and this gal [his new romantic partner] didn't take care of him, I would go and take care of him myself" (quoted in K. R. Allen et al. 1999, p. 154).

Toward Better Caregiving

Family sociologist and demographer Andrew Cherlin (1996) distinguishes between the "public" and the "private" face of families. The family's **private face** "provides individuals with intimacy, emotional support, and love" (p. 19). Social scientists who work with the family development model (see Chapter 2) argue that developing *family integrity*—"the ultimate, positive outcome of an older adult's developmental striving toward meaning, connection, and continuity within his or her multigenerational family"—is the final developmental concern for the majority of us (King and Wynne 2004, p. 7). Family integrity can be recognized in:

> (a) the transformation of relationships over time in a manner that is dynamic and responsive to the changing life cycle needs of individual family members, (b) the resolution or acceptance of past losses or family conflicts, with the dead as well as the living, and (c) the shared creation of meaning by passing on individual and family legacies within and across generations. (King and Wynne 2004, p. 7)

© Nancy Pastor, Hayward Daily Review

Many older Americans remain active even into old-old age, as has this water-skier, who is eighty-two. Nonetheless, the aging of the American population raises concerns about how a changing family structure will be able to care for them and to what extent community and government resources can or will be engaged to help.

One thing that younger eldercare givers can do to facilitate family integrity is to examine their own attitudes for evidence of ageism. One idea of psychologists, for instance, is that younger people often harbor prejudice against their "feared future [elderly] self" (Nelson 2005).

The family's **public face** produces public goods and services by educating their children, caring for their ill, and helping their elderly members: "While serving each other, members of the 'public' family also serve the larger community" (Conner 2000, p. 36; Gross 2004). The public family saves millions of dollars annually for the taxpayer. In this context, sociologist Arlie Hochschild (1997, p. 168) has suggested that family and friends may be considered "as an informal domestic 'welfare system.'"

Meanwhile, government leaders tend to emphasize the "paramount importance" of "personal responsibility and accountability for planning for one's longevity" (White House Conference on Aging 2005, p. 18). However, the costs of providing good care for ill and disabled family members are often too high for family caregivers to manage without help. The relatively few employers who offer benefits to help employees with elderly parents are finding these benefits increasingly costly, while employees complain that work-related programs are inadequate (Gross 2006a). People who are not poor enough to receive Medicaid and are not wealthy may be the most strapped. Then, too, people who are ill or disabled may need special care that the family cannot provide.

Furthermore, caregiving, as we have seen, is stressful. Many point to their need for services that temporarily replace the caregiver, such as transportation, personal care services, and adult day care. However, existing centers in the United States can be expensive, and they are not subsidized by Medicare (Cancian and Oliker 2000). "Although we have shelves full of books that address work/family problems, we still have not named the burdens that affect most of America's working families. Call it the care crisis" (Rosen 2007, p. 11).

Unlike other Western democracies, the U.S. government restricts its social insurance programs to elderly people (Achenbaum 2005). Social Security and Medicare have indeed improved the economic status of the aged, as we saw earlier in this chapter. However, it is estimated that Medicare pays for less than half of all old-age health care costs: "A fragmented old-age welfare state places much of the responsibility for the care of older people on the shoulders of family members, mainly women" (Meyer and Bellas 2001, p. 199; see also Caputo 2005).

Sociologists and policy analysts Francesca Cancian and Stacey Oliker (2000) argue that men ought to be encouraged to be as responsible as women for eldercare. Also, they ask rhetorically whether the wider community, as well as the individual family, is not responsible for eldercare. In fact, "this country's family policies lag far behind those of [many nations in] the rest of the world."

> The media constantly reinforce the conventional wisdom that the care crisis is an individual problem. Books, magazines and newspapers offer American women an endless stream of advice about how to maintain their "balancing act," how to be better organized and more efficient or how to meditate, exercise and pamper themselves to relieve their mounting stress. Missing is the very pragmatic proposal that American society needs new policies that will restructure the workplace and reorganize family life. (Rosen 2007, p. 13)

Cancian and Oliker (2000) have proposed the following strategies for moving our society toward better eldercare coupled with greater gender equity in providing eldercare:

1. Provide government funds that support more care outside the family, such as government-funded daycare centers for the elderly and respite (time off) services for caregivers.

2. Increase social recognition of caregiving—both paid and unpaid—as productive and valuable work.

3. Make caregiving more economically rewarding or, at least, less economically costly to caregivers. (p. 130)

How these policy changes might be accomplished may be difficult to imagine, but this fact negates the utility neither of the vision nor of the political debate that needs to emerge (Gross 2007). Across the world and throughout history, families have been expected to provide eldercare, and they did so until about the twentieth century in industrialized countries without help from government or community services or resources. However, at least in the industrialized world, that time has passed (Achenbaum 2005; Conway-Giustra, Crowley, and Gorin 2002). Eldercare (as well as child care) is indeed a responsibility not only of individual families but of an entire society.

Summary

- The *number* of elderly, as well as their *proportion* of the total U.S. population, is growing.
- Along with the impact of the baby boomers' aging and the declining proportion of children in the population, longer life expectancy has contributed to the aging of our population.

- For the most part, both adult children and their parents prefer to live near each other, although not in the same residence.

- Due mainly to differences in life expectancy, older men are much more likely to be living with their spouse than are older women.

- Among older Americans without partners, living arrangements depend on one's health, the availability of others with whom to reside, social norms regarding obligations of other family members toward their elderly, personal preferences for privacy and independence, and economics.

- Growth in Social Security benefits has resulted in dramatic reductions in U.S. poverty rates for the elderly over the last several decades, although 11 percent of older adults are living in poverty.

- Due to differences in work patterns, wage differentials, and Social Security regulations, older men are considerably better off financially than are older women.

- Most older married couples place intimacy as central to their lives, describe their unions as happy, and continue to be interested in sex, even into old age.

- Even when it is not an abrupt event, retirement represents a great change for individuals and couples, particularly for males who have embraced the traditional masculine gender role.

- Adjustment to widowhood or widowerhood is an important family transition that often must be faced by married couples in later life. Bereavement manifests itself in physical, emotional, and intellectual symptoms.

- Daughters are more likely than sons to have close relationships with their parents, especially with their mothers. However, even among mothers, a parent's divorce or separation often weakens the bond with adult children.

- Partly due to longer life expectancy, grandparenting (and great-grandparenting) became increasingly important to families throughout the twentieth century.

- As members of our families age, eldercare is becoming an important feature in family life, with women providing the bulk of it.

- After spouses, adult children (usually daughters) are a preferred choice of an older family member as eldercare providers.

- Eldercare in families typically follows a caregiving trajectory as the care receiver ages, and it involves not only benefits but also stresses for the caregiver(s).

- Elder abuse and neglect exist in some aging families and can be explained and addressed in public policy by either the caregiver model or the domestic violence model.

- There are empirically noted racial/ethnic differences in eldercare, but this does not negate that racial/ethnic minorities—as well as non-Hispanic whites—need community and government assistance in providing eldercare.

- Changes in the American family lead some policy analysts to be concerned that families will have greater difficulty in the future providing eldercare. However, others point out that family relationships, though latent for long periods, can be activated when needed.

- Better eldercare in the future will necessitate involving more men as caregivers and developing public policy that adequately supports expanded community services to assist families in providing eldercare.

Questions for Review and Reflection

1. Discuss ways that society's age structure today affects American families.

2. Describe the living arrangements of older Americans today, and give some reasons for these arrangements.

3. Give some facts concerning family relationships—for example, between spouses or between older parents and their adult children—in later life.

4. Apply the exchange, interactionist, structure-functionalist, or ecological perspective (Chapter 2) to the process of providing eldercare.

5. **Policy Question.** Describe two suggestions for policy changes that would make family eldercare less difficult.

Key Terms

acculturation 503
active life expectancy 486
baby boom 484
bereavement 492
caregiver model of elder abuse and neglect 503
caregiving 496
caregiving trajectory 501
custodial grandparent 495
domestic violence model of elder abuse and neglect 503
elder abuse 502
elder neglect 502

eldercare 496
fictive kin 503
filial responsibility 498
gerontologist 496
informal caregiving 496
latent kin matrix 505
noncustodial grandparent 496
private face of family 505
public face of family 506
sandwich generation 500

Online Resources

Companion Website for This Book

www.thomsonedu.com/sociology/lamanna

Visit the book companion website, where you will find flash cards, practice quizzes, Internet links, suggested readings, InfoTrac College Edition exercises, and more to help you study.

ThomsonNOW™ for Marriage and Family

Spend time on what you need to master rather than on information you already have learned. Take a pre-test for this chapter, and ThomsonNOW will generate a personalized study plan based on your results. The study plan will identify the topics you need to review and direct you to online resources such as videos, narrated learning modules, and interactive activities to help you master those topics. You can then take a post-test to help you determine the concepts you have mastered and what you will still need to work on. Try it out! Go to **www.thomsonedu.com/login** to sign in with an access code or to purchase access to this product.

Glossary

ABC-X model A model of family crisis in which A (the stressor event) interacts with B (the family's resources for meeting a crisis) and with C (the definition the family formulates of the event) to produce X (the crisis).

abortion See **induced abortion**.

abstinence The standard that maintains that nonmarital intercourse is wrong or inadvisable for both women and men regardless of the circumstances. Many religions espouse abstinence as a moral imperative, while some individuals are abstinent as a temporary or permanent personal choice.

acculturation The process whereby immigrant groups adopt the beliefs, values, and norms of their new culture and lose their traditional values and practices.

acquaintance rape Forced or unwanted sexual contact between people who know each other, often—although not necessarily—taking place on a date. See also **date rape.**

active life expectancy The period of life free of disability in activities of daily living, after which may follow a period of being at least somewhat disabled.

adaptable marriage relationship A marital relationship that allows and encourages partners to grow and change.

A-frame relationship A relationship style (symbolized by the capital letter *A*) in which partners have a strong couple identity but little self-esteem; therefore, they are dependent on each other rather than interdependent. See also **H-frame relationship, M-frame relationship**.

agape The love style that emphasizes unselfish concern for the beloved, in which one attempts to fulfill the other's needs even when that means some personal sacrifice. See also **eros, ludus, mania, pragma, storge.**

agentic (instrumental) character traits Traits such as confidence, assertiveness, and ambition that enable a person to accomplish difficult tasks or goals.

agreement reality Knowledge based on agreement about what is true.

AIDS See **HIV/AIDS**.

allocation systems The arrangements couples make for handling their income, wealth, and expenditures. Allocation systems may involve pooling partners' resources or keeping them separate. Who controls pooled resources is another dimension of an allocation system.

arranged marriage Unions in which parents choose their children's marriage partners.

asexual, asexuality A person who is asexual does not experience sexual desire. This is different from abstinence or celibacy, which is a choice to not engage in sexual activity despite feelings of sexual desire. Asexuality may be considered a sexual orientation.

assisted reproductive technology (ART) Advanced reproductive technology, such as artificial insemination, in vitro fertilization, or embryo transplantation, that enables infertile couples or individuals, including gay and lesbian couples, to have children.

assortative mating Social psychological filtering process in which individuals gradually filter out those among their pool of eligibles who they believe would not make the best spouse.

attachment "An active, affective, enduring, and reciprocal bond between two individuals that is believed to be established through repeated action over time" (Coleman and Watson 2000, p. 297, citing Ainsworth et al. 1978).

attachment disorder An emotional disorder in which a person defensively shuts off the willingness or ability to make emotional attachments to anyone.

attachment theory A psychological theory that holds that, during infancy and childhood, a young person develops a general style of attaching to others; once an individual's attachment style is established, she or he unconsciously applies that style to later, adult relationships. The three basic styles are **secure, insecure/anxious,** and **avoidant**.

authoritarian parenting style All decision making is in parents' hands, and the emphasis is on compliance with rules and directives. Parents are more punitive than supportive, and use of physical punishment is likely.

authoritative parenting style Parents accept the child's personality and talents and are emotionally supportive. At the same time, they consciously set and enforce rules and limits, whose rationale is usually explained to the child. Parents provide guidance and direction and state expectations for the child's behavior. Parents are in charge, but the child is given responsibility and must take the initiative in completing schoolwork and other tasks and in solving child-level problems.

avoidant attachment style One of three attachment styles in **attachment theory**, this style avoids intimacy either by evading relationships altogether or by establishing considerable distance in intimate situations.

baby boom The unusually large cohort of U.S. children born after the end of World War II, between 1946 and 1964.

barriers to divorce Impediments to a decision to divorce, such as concern about children, religiously grounded objections to divorce, or financial concerns or dependencies.

belligerence A negative communication/relationship behavior that challenges the partner's power and authority.

bereavement A period of mourning after the death of a loved one.

bicultural families See **Miller's typology of urban Native American families**.

binational family An immigrant family in which some members are citizens or legal residents of the country they migrate to, while others are **undocumented**—that is, they are not legal residents.

binuclear family One family in two household units. A term created to describe a postdivorce family in which both parents remain involved and children are at home in both households.

biosocial perspective Theoretical perspective based on concepts linking psychosocial factors to anatomy, physiology, genetics, and/or hormones as shaped by evolution.

bisexual A person who is sexually attracted to both males and females.

bonding fighting Fighting that brings intimates closer together rather than leaving them just as far apart or pushing them even farther apart.

borderwork Interaction rituals that are based on and reaffirm boundaries and differences between girls and boys.

boundary ambiguity When applied to a family, a situation in which it is unclear who is in and who is out of the family.

bride price Money or property that the future groom pays the future bride's family so that he can marry her.

caregiver model of elder abuse and neglect A view of elder abuse or neglect that highlights stress on the caregiver as important to the understanding of abusive behavior.

caregiving "Assistance provided to persons who cannot, for whatever reason, perform the basic activities or instrumental activities of daily living for themselves" (Cherlin 1996, p. 762).

caregiving trajectory The process through which eldercare proceeds, according to which, first, the caregiver becomes concerned about an aging family member, then later begins to give advice to the older family member, and still later takes action to provide needed services.

case study A written summary and analysis of data obtained by psychologists, psychiatrists, counselors, and social workers when working directly with individuals and families in clinical practice. Case studies may be used as sources in scientific investigation and have played a role in the development of certain family theories.

center care Group child care provided in day-care centers for a relatively large number of children.

checking it out A communication or fighting technique in which a person asks the other whether her or his perceptions of the other's feelings or thoughts are correct.

child abuse Overt acts of aggression against a child, such as beating or inflicting physical injury or excessive verbal derogation. Sexual abuse is a form of physical child abuse. See also **emotional child abuse or neglect.**

child care The care and education of children by people other than their parents. Child care may include before- and after-school care for older children and overnight care when employed parents must travel, as well as day care for preschool children.

child neglect Failure to provide adequate physical or emotional care for a child. See also **emotional child abuse or neglect.**

child support Money paid by the noncustodial parent to the custodial parent to financially support children of a former marital, cohabiting, or sexual relationship.

child-to-parent abuse A form of family violence involving a child's (especially an adolescent's) physical and emotional abuse of a parent.

children's allowance A type of child support that provides a government grant to all families—married or single-parent, regardless of income—based on the number of children they have.

Chodorow's theory A theory of gender socialization that combines psychoanalytic ideas about identification of children with parents with an awareness of those parents' social roles in our society.

choosing by default Making semiconscious or unconscious choices when one is not aware of all the possible alternatives or when one pursues the path of least resistance. From this perspective, doing nothing about a problem or issue, or making no choice, is making a choice—the choice to do nothing.

choosing knowledgeably Making choices and decisions after (1) recognizing as many options or alternatives as possible, (2) recognizing the social pressures that can influence personal choices, (3) considering the consequences of each alternative, and (4) becoming aware of one's own values.

civil union Legislation like that in Hawaii or Vermont that allows any two single adults—including same-sex partners or blood relatives, such as siblings or a parent and adult child—to have access to virtually all marriage rights and benefits on the state level, but none on the federal level. Designed to give same-sex couples many of the legal benefits of marriage while denying them the right to legally marry.

co-dependents "Persons who gravitate toward relationships with exploitative or abusive partners around whom they organize their lives and to whom they remain strongly committed despite the absence of any identifiable rewards or personal fulfillment for themselves" (Wright and Wright 1999, p. 528).

coercive power One of the six power bases, or sources of power. This power is based on the dominant person's ability and willingness to punish the partner either with psychological–emotional or physical abuse or with more subtle methods of withholding affection.

cohabitation Living together in an intimate, sexual relationship without traditional, legal marriage. Sometimes referred to as *living together* or *marriage without marriage.* Cohabitation can be a courtship process or an alternative to legal marriage, depending on how partners view it.

collectivist society A society in which people identify with and conform to the expectations of their relatives or clan, who look after their interests in return for their loyalty. The group has priority over the individual. A synonym is *communal society.*

commitment (to intimacy) The determination to develop relationships in which experiences cover many areas of personality, problems are worked through, conflict is expected and seen as a normal part of the growth process, and there is an expectation that the relationship is basically viable and worthwhile.

commitment (Sternberg's triangular theory of love) The short-term decision that one loves someone and the long-term commitment to maintain that love; one dimension of the triangular theory of love.

common couple violence Mutual violence between partners in conjunction with a specific argument.

common law marriage A legal concept whereby cohabiting partners are considered legally married if certain requirements are met, such as showing intent to enter into a marriage and living together as husband and wife for a certain period. Most states have dropped common law marriage, but cohabiting relationships may sometimes have a similar effect on property ownership and custody rights.

communal (expressive) character traits Traits that foster relationships with others, such as warmth, sensitivity, the ability to express tender feelings, and the desire to place concern about others' welfare above self-interest.

communal society See **collectivist society.**

commune A group of adults and perhaps children who live together, sharing aspects of their lives. Some communes are group marriages, in which members share sex; others are communal families, with several monogamous couples, who share everything except sexual relations and their children.

community divorce Ruptures of relationships and changes in social networks that come about because of divorce.

commuter marriage A marriage in which the two partners live in different locations and commute to spend time together.

companionate marriage The single-earner, breadwinner–homemaker marriage that flourished in the 1950s. Although husbands and wives in the companionate marriage usually adhered to a sharp division of labor, they were supposed to be each other's companion—friends, lovers—in a realization of trends beginning in the 1920s.

conflict perspective Theoretical perspective that emphasizes social conflict in a society and within families. Power and dominance are important themes.

Conflict Tactics Scale A scale developed by sociologist Murray Straus to assess how couples handle conflict. Includes detailed items on various forms of physical violence.

Confucian training doctrine Concept used to describe Asian and Asian American parenting philosophy that emphasizes blending parental love, concern, involvement, and physical closeness with strict and firm control.

consensual marriage Heterosexual, conjugal unions that have not gone through a legal marriage ceremony.

consummate love A complete love, in terms of Sternberg's triangular theory of love, in which the components of passion, intimacy, and commitment come together.

contempt One of the **Four Horsemen of the Apocalypse** (which see), in which a partner feels that his or her spouse is inferior or undesirable.

co-parenting, co-parents Shared decision making and parental supervision in such areas as discipline and schoolwork or shared holidays and recreation. Can refer to parents working together in a marriage or other ongoing relationship or after divorce or separation.

courtly love Popular during the twelfth century and later, courtly love is the intense longing for someone other than one's marital partner—a passionate and sexual longing that ideally goes unfulfilled. The assumptions of courtly love influence our modern ideas about romantic love.

courtship The process whereby a couple develops a mutual commitment to marriage.

covenant marriage A type of legal marriage in which the bride and groom agree to be bound by a marriage contract that will not let them get divorced as easily as is allowed under no-fault divorce laws.

criticism One of the **Four Horsemen of the Apocalypse** (which see) that involves making disapproving judgments or evaluations of one's partner.

cross-national marriage Marriage in which spouses are from different countries.

crude divorce rate The number of divorces per 1,000 population. See also **refined divorce rate.**

cultural deviant perspective A theoretical framework that emphasizes those features of racial/ethnic minority families that distinguish them from white, usually middle-class, families. In the cultural deviant perspective, those different qualities of minority families are viewed negatively.

cultural equivalent perspective A theoretical framework that emphasizes those features that racial/ethnic minority families have in common with white families.

cultural script Set of socially prescribed and understood guidelines for relating to others or for defining role responsibilities and obligations.

cultural variant perspective A theoretical approach that calls for making contextually relevant interpretations of racial/ethnic minority families. Those families are studied on their own terms, as opposed to making comparisons, favorable or unfavorable, to white families. Instead, within-group comparisons are explored.

culture war Deep cultural conflict, often buttressed by religious belief systems, over matters concerning human sexuality and gender.

custodial grandparent A parent of a divorced, custodial parent.

custodial parent The parent who has legal responsibility for a child after parents divorce or separate. In sole custody, the child resides with the custodial parent. In joint custody, the child may reside primarily with one parent or may live part of the time with each.

custody Primary responsibility for making decisions about a child's upbringing and general welfare.

cyberadultery Marital infidelity or adultery on the Internet.

date rape Forced or unwanted sexual contact between people who are on a date. See also **acquaintance rape.**

Defense of Marriage Act (DOMA) Federal statute declaring marriage to be a "legal union of one man and one woman," denying gay couples many of the civil advantages of marriage and relieving states of the obligation to grant reciprocity, or "full faith and credit," to marriages performed in another state.

defensiveness One of the **Four Horsemen of the Apocalypse** (which see) that means preparing to defend oneself against what one presumes is an upcoming attack.

deinstitutionalization of marriage A situation in which time-honored family definitions are changing and family-related social norms are weakening so that they "count for far less" than in the past.

dependence The general reliance on another person or on several others for continuous support and assurance, coupled with subordination to the other(s). A dependent partner probably has low self-esteem and is having illegitimate needs met by the partner on whom he or she is dependent. See also **independence, interdependence.**

developmental task A challenge that must be mastered in one stage of the family life cycle for a successful transition to the next.

displacement A passive-aggressive behavior in which a person expresses anger with another by being angry at or damaging people or things the other cherishes. See also **passive-aggression.**

divorce divide The gap in divorce rates between college-educated and less-educated women. The divorce rate has declined substantially for college-educated women, but not for less-educated women.

divorce-extended family Kinship ties that form in the wake of a divorce. May include former in-laws, new spouses of one's ex-spouse, and that person's children and kin as part of one kinship system.

divorce mediation A nonadversarial means of dispute resolution by which the couple, with the assistance of a mediator or mediators (frequently a lawyer–therapist team), negotiate the terms of their settlement of custody, support, property, and visitation issues.

domestic partner Partner in an unmarried couple who have registered their partnership with a civil authority and then enjoy some (although not necessarily all) rights, benefits, and entitlements that have traditionally been reserved for marrieds.

domestic violence model of elder abuse and neglect A model that conceptualizes elder abuse as a form of family violence.

double message See **mixed message.**

double remarriage A remarriage in which both partners were previously married.

double standard The standard according to which nonmarital sex or multiple partners are more acceptable for males than for females.

dowry A sum of money or property brought to the marriage by the female.

economic divorce The aspect of divorce that divides the couple into separate economic units, each with its own property, income, control of expenditures, and responsibility for taxes, debts, and so on.

economic hardship perspective (on children's adjustment to divorce) One of the theoretical perspectives concerning the negative outcomes among children of divorced parents. From this perspective, it is the economic hardship brought about by marital dissolution that is primarily responsible for problems faced by children.

egalitarian norm (of marital power) The norm (cultural rule) that husband and wife should have equal power in a marriage.

elder abuse Overt acts of aggression toward the elderly, in which the victim may be physically assaulted, emotionally humiliated, purposefully isolated, or materially exploited.

elder neglect Acts of omission in the care and treatment of the elderly.

eldercare Care provided to older generations.

emerging adulthood The youth and young adult stage of life, which is a period of frequent change and exploration.

emotion A strong feeling arising without conscious mental or rational effort, such as joy, reverence, anger, fear, love, or hate. Emotions are neither bad nor good and should be accepted as natural. People can and should learn to control what they do about their emotions.

emotional child abuse or neglect A parent or other caregiver's being overly harsh and critical, failing to provide guidance, or being uninterested in a child's needs.

emotional divorce Withdrawing bonding emotions and communication from the marital or other relationship, typically replacing these with alienating feelings and behavior.

endogamy Marrying within one's own social group. See also **exogamy.**

equality Power or resources divided between partners so that each has the same amount.

equilibrium The balanced state of a system. If one part of a system changes, other elements must change in order to restore balance in the system.

equity A standard for distribution of power or resources of partners according to the contribution each person has made to the unit. Another way of characterizing an equitable result is that it is "fair."

eros The love style characterized by intense emotional attachment and powerful sexual feelings or desires. See also **agape, ludus, mania, pragma, storge.**

ethnicity A group's identity based on a sense of a common culture and language.

Euro-American families Families whose members are of European ethnic background.

evolutionary heritage In the biosocial perspective, human behavior is encoded in genetic or other biological features that come to us as members of a species.

exchange balance Balance of rewards and costs in a relationship.

exchange theory Theoretical perspective that sees relationships as determined by the exchange of resources and the reward–cost balance of that exchange. This theory predicts that people tend to marry others whose social class, education, physical attractiveness, and even self-esteem are similar to their own.

exogamy Marrying a partner from outside one's own social group. See also **endogamy.**

expectations of permanence One component of the marriage premise, according to which individuals enter marriage expecting that mutual affection and commitment will be lasting.

expectations of sexual exclusivity The cultural ideal according to which spouses promise to have sexual relations with only one another.

experience hypothesis The idea that the independent variable in a hypothesis is responsible for changes to a dependent variable. With regard to marriage, the experience hypothesis holds that something about the experience of being married itself causes certain results for spouses. See also the antonym, **selection hypothesis.**

experiential reality Knowledge based on personal experience.

experiment One tool of scientific investigation, in which behaviors are carefully monitored or measured under controlled conditions. Participants are randomly assigned to treatment or control groups.

expert power One of the six power bases, or sources of power. This power stems from the dominant person's superior judgment, knowledge, or ability.

expressive sexuality The view of human sexuality in which sexuality is basic to the humanness of both women and men, all individuals are free to express their sexual selves, and there is no one-sided sense of ownership.

expressive traits See **communal (expressive) character traits**.

extended family Family including relatives besides parents and children, such as aunts or uncles. See also **nuclear family**.

extrusion "[I]ndividuals' being 'pushed out' of their households earlier than normal for members of their cultural group, either because they are forced to leave or because remaining in their households is so stressful that they 'choose' to leave" (Crosbie-Burnett et al. 2005, p. 213).

familistic (communal) values Values that focus on the family group as a whole and on maintaining family identity and cohesiveness.

family Any sexually expressive or parent–child or other kin relationship in which people live together with a commitment in an intimate interpersonal relationship. Family members see their identity as importantly attached to the group, which has an identity of its own. Families today take several forms: single-parent, remarried, dual-career, communal, homosexual, traditional, and so forth. See also **extended family, nuclear family**.

family boundaries Family members' understandings of who is and who is not in the family. Markers, whether material (e.g., doors, fences, communication devices) or social (e.g., symbols of identity, conversational styles and content, time spent together), indicate the boundaries of the family.

"family change" perspective See **"family decline," "family change" perspectives**.

family child care Child care provided in a caregiver's home.

family cohesion That intangible emotional quality that holds groups together and gives members a sense of common identity.

family crisis A situation (resulting from a stressor) in which the family's usual behavior patterns are ineffective and new ones are called for.

"family decline," "family change" perspectives Some family scholars and policy makers characterize late-twentieth-century developments in the family as "decline," while others describe "change." Those who take the "family decline" perspective view such changes as increases in the age at first marriage, divorce, cohabitation, and nonmarital births and the decline in fertility as disastrous for the family as a major social institution. "Family change" scholars and policy makers consider that the family has varied over time. They argue that the family can adapt to recent changes and continue to play a strong role in society.

family development perspective Theoretical perspective that gives attention to changes in the family over time.

family ecology perspective Theoretical perspective that explores how a family influences and is influenced by the environments that surround it. A family is interdependent first with its neighborhood, then with its social–cultural environment, and ultimately with the human-built and physical–biological environments. All parts of the model are interrelated and influence one another.

family foster care Foster care that takes place in a trained and licensed foster parent's home.

family-friendly workplace policies Workplace policies that are supportive of employee efforts to combine family and work commitments.

family function Activities performed by families for the benefit of society and of family members.

family instability perspective (on children's adjustment to divorce) The thesis that a negative impact of divorce on children is primarily caused by the number of changes in family structure, not by any particular family form. A stable single-parent family may be less harmful to children than a divorce followed by a single-parent family followed by cohabitation, then remarriage, and perhaps a redivorce.

family leave A leave of absence from work granted to family members to care for new infants, newly adopted children, ill children, or aging parents, or to meet similar family needs or emergencies.

family life cycle Stages of family development defined by the addition and subtraction of family members, children's ages, and changes in the family's connection with other social systems.

family of orientation The family in which an individual grows up. Also called *family of origin*.

family of procreation The family that is formed when an individual marries and has children.

family policy All the actions, procedures, regulations, attitudes, and goals of government that affect families.

family preservation A program of support for families in which children have been abused. The support is intended to enable the child to remain in the home safely rather than being placed in foster care.

family stress State of tension that arises when demands tax a family's resources.

family structure The form a family takes, such as nuclear family, extended family, single-parent family, stepfamily, and the like.

family systems theory An umbrella term for a wide range of specific theories. This theoretical perspective examines the family as a whole. It looks to the patterns of behavior and relationships within the family, in which each member is affected by the behavior of others. Systems tend toward equilibrium and will react to change in one part by seeking equilibrium either by restoring the old system or by creating a new one.

family transitions Expected or predictable changes in the course of family life that often precipitate family stress and can result in a family crisis.

family values See **familistic (communal) values**.

fecundity Reproductive capacity; biological capability to have children.

female-demand/male-withdraw communication pattern A cycle of negative verbal expression by a wife and withdrawal by the husband in the face of his partner's demands. In other words, women tend to deal with problems by bringing them into the open through initiatives that have an attention-getting negative tone. Men tend to withdraw emotionally from the disagreement or conflict.

femininities Culturally defined ways of being a woman. The plural conveys the idea that there are varied models of appropriate behavior.

feminist perspective Feminist theories are conflict theories. The primary focus of the feminist perspective is male dominance in families and society as oppressive to women. The mission of this perspective is to end this oppression of women (or related pattern of subordination based on social class, race/ethnicity, age, or sexual orientation) by developing knowledge and action that confront this disparity. See also **conflict perspective**.

fertility Births to a woman or category of women (actual births, not reproductive capacity).

fictive kin Family-like relationships that are not based on blood or marriage but on close friendship ties.

filial responsibility A child's obligation to a parent.

flexible scheduling A type of employment scheduling that includes scheduling options such as **job sharing** or **flextime.**

flextime A policy that permits an employee some flexibility to adjust working hours to suit family needs or personal preference.

formal kinship care Out-of-home placement with biological relatives of children who are in the custody of the state.

foster care Care provided to children by other than their parents as a result of state intervention.

Four Horsemen of the Apocalypse Contempt, criticism, defensiveness, and stonewalling—marital communication behaviors delineated by John Gottman that often indicate a couple's future divorce.

free-choice culture Culture or society in which individuals choose their own marriage partners, a choice usually based at least somewhat on romance.

friends with benefits Sexual activity between friends or acquaintances with no expectation of romance or emotional attachment. Typically practiced by unattached people who want to have a sexual outlet without "complications."

function See **family function.**

gay A person whose sexual attraction is to persons of the same sex. Used especially for males, but may include both sexes. This term is usually used rather than *homosexual.*

gender Attitudes and behavior associated with and expected of the two sexes. The term **sex** denotes biology, while *gender* refers to social role. See also **gendered.**

gender identity The degree to which an individual sees herself or himself as feminine or masculine based on society's definition of appropriate gender roles.

gender role Prescription for masculine or feminine behavior. The masculine gender role demands instrumental character traits and behavior, whereas the feminine gender role specifies expressive character traits and behavior.

gender schema theory of gender socialization A framework of knowledge and beliefs about differences or similarities between males and females. Gender schema shape socialization into gender roles.

gender similarities hypothesis Assertion—backed by research—that there are few gender differences in characteristics and abilities.

gendered The way that aspects of people's lives and relationships are influenced by gender.

geographic availability Traditionally known in the marriage and family literature as propinquity or proximity and referring to the fact that people tend to meet potential mates who are present in their regional environment.

gerontologist A social scientist who studies aging and the elderly.

giving feedback A recommended communication behavior in which a partner repeats in her or his own words what the other has said or revealed.

GLBT An acronym for *g*ay, *l*esbian, *b*isexual, or *t*ransgendered; a term commonly used when discussing sexual minorities.

globalization The interdependency of people, organizations, economies, or governments across national borders.

good provider role A specialized masculine role that emerged in this country around the 1830s and that emphasized the husband as the only or primary economic provider for his family. The good provider role had disappeared by the 1970s as an expected masculine role. See also **provider role.**

grandparent families Families in which a grandparent acts as primary parent to grandchildren.

group home One type of foster-care setting in which several children are cared for around-the-clock by paid professionals who work in shifts and live elsewhere.

guaranteed child support Type of child support (provided in France and Sweden, for example) in which the government sends to the custodial parent the full amount of support awarded to the child and assumes responsibility for collecting what is owed by the noncustodial parent.

habituation The decreased interest in sex over time that results from the increased accessibility of a sexual partner and the predictability of sexual behavior with that partner.

habituation hypothesis Hypothesis that the decline in sexual frequency over a marriage results from habituation.

Healthy Marriage Initiative (HMI). Federal program initiated in 2004 and targeted to TANF ("welfare") recipients, consisting of workshops on listening, communication, and problem-solving skills, as well as presentations on the value of marriage.

hermaphrodite See **intersexual.**

heterogamy Marriage between partners who differ in race, age, education, religious background, or social class. Compare with **homogamy.**

heterosexism The taken-for-granted system of beliefs, values, and customs that places superior value on heterosexual behavior (as opposed to homosexual) and denies or stigmatizes nonheterosexual relations. This tendency also sees the heterosexual family as standard.

heterosexual A person who prefers sexual partners of the opposite sex.

H-frame relationship Relationship that is structured like a capital *H*: Partners stand virtually alone, each self-sufficient and neither influenced much by the other. An example would be a devitalized, dual-career marriage. See also **A-frame relationship, M-frame relationship.**

hidden agenda Associated with stepfathers who, with remarriage, join a single-parent family of a mother and her children. The former single-parent family may have a hidden agenda, or assumptions and expectations about how the stepfather will behave—expectations and assumptions that are often not passed on to the new stepfather.

hierarchical parenting Concept used to describe a Hispanic parenting philosophy that blends warm emotional support for children with demand for significant respect for parents and other authority figures, including older extended-family members.

HIV/AIDS HIV is *human immunodeficiency virus,* the virus that causes AIDS, or *acquired immune deficiency syndrome.* AIDS is a sexually transmitted disease involving breakdown of the immune system defense against viruses, bacteria, fungi, and other diseases.

holistic view of sex The view that marital or other partnered sex is an extension of the whole relationship.

homogamy Marriage between partners of similar race, age, education, religious background, and social class. See also **heterogamy.**

homophobia Fear, dread, aversion to, and often hatred of homosexuals.

homosexual A person who is sexually attracted to persons of the same sex. Preferred terms are *gay* or *gay man* for men and *lesbian* for women. See also **gay, lesbian.**

hooking up A sexual encounter between young people with the understanding that there is no obligation to see each other again or to endow the sexual activity with emotional meaning. Usually there is a group or network context for hooking up; that is, the individuals meet at a social event or have common acquaintances. On some college campuses and elsewhere, hooking up has replaced dating, which is courtship-oriented socializing and sexual activity.

hormonal processes Chemical processes within the body regulated by such hormones as testosterone (a "male" hormone) and estrogen (a "female" hormone). Hormonal processes are thought to shape behavior, as well as physical development and reproductive functions, although experts disagree as to their impact on behavior.

hormones Chemical substances secreted into the bloodstream by the endocrine glands.

household As a Census Bureau category, a household is any group of people residing together.

househusband A man who takes a full-time family-care role, rather than being employed; the male counterpart to a housewife.

hypergamy A marriage in which a person gains social rank by marrying someone of higher rank.

hypogamy Marriage to a partner with lower social and/or economic status than one's own.

identity A sense of inner sameness developed by individuals throughout their lives. They know who they are throughout their various endeavors and pursuits, no matter how different these may be.

illegitimate needs Needs that arise from feelings of self-doubt, unworthiness, and inadequacy. Loving partners cannot fill each other's illegitimate needs no matter how much they try. One fills one's illegitimate needs best by personally working to build one's self-esteem. A first step might be doing something nice for oneself rather than waiting for somebody else to do it.

impaired fertility Describes the situation of a woman who is not able to succeed in having a child due to a physical barrier or an inability to carry a pregnancy to full term.

incest Sexual relations between closely related individuals.

inclusive fitness In evolutionary theories of human behavior, the propensity to advance preservation of one's genes either through direct reproduction (one's own offspring) or through facilitating the survival and reproduction of close relatives.

income effect Occurs when an increase in income contributes to the stability of a marriage by giving it a more adequate financial basis.

income-to-needs ratio An assessment of income as to the degree it meets the needs of the individual, family, or household.

incomplete institution Cherlin's description of a remarried family due to cultural ambiguity.

independence Self-reliance and self-sufficiency. To form lasting intimate relationships, independent people must choose to become interdependent.

independence effect Occurs when an increase in income leads to marital dissolution because the partners are better able to afford to live separately.

individualism The cultural milieu that emerged in Europe with industrialization and that values personal self-actualization and happiness along with individual freedom.

individualistic society Society in which the main concern is with one's own interests (which may or may not include those of one's immediate family).

individualistic (self-fulfillment) values Values that encourage self-fulfillment, personal growth, autonomy, and independence over commitment to family or other communal needs.

individualized marriage Concept associated with the argument that contemporary marriage in the United States and other fully industrialized Western societies is no longer institutionalized. Four interrelated characteristics distinguish individualized marriage: (1) it is optional; (2) spouses' roles are flexible—negotiable and renegotiable; (3) its expected rewards involve love, communication, and emotional intimacy; and (4) it exists in conjunction with a vast diversity of family forms.

induced abortion The scientific term for what is commonly termed *abortion.* The removal of the fetus from the uterus is "induced"; that is, it requires a deliberate surgical or pharmaceutical act. What we commonly call "miscarriage" is termed *spontaneous abortion* in scientific language because it happens without any initiative on the part of individuals or medical personnel and, in fact, is usually not desired.

informal adoption Children are taken into a home and considered to be children of the parents, although the "adoption" is not legally formalized.

informal caregiving Unpaid caregiving, provided personally by a family member.

informational power One of the six power bases, or sources of power. This power is based on the persuasive content of what the dominant person tells another individual.

informed consent A requirement of research involving human subjects;

before agreeing to participate, subjects are told the purpose of the research and the procedure and whether any risk is involved in participation. The process of obtaining informed consent is supervised by an **institutional review board.**

in-home caregiver A caregiver who provides child care in the child's home, either coming in by the day or as a live-in caregiver.

insecure/anxious attachment style One of three attachment styles in attachment theory, this style entails concern that the beloved will disappear, a situation often characterized as "fear of abandonment."

instability hypothesis The idea that the instability of postdivorce family structure(s) can be damaging to children. According to this hypothesis, a stable single-parent family might be better for a child than a single-parent family succeeded by a remarried family.

institution See **social institution.**

institutional marriage Marriage as a social institution based on dutiful adherence to the time-honored **marriage premise** (which see), particularly the norm of permanence. "Once ensconced in societal mandates for permanence and monogamous sexual exclusivity, the institutionalized marriage in the United States was centered on economic production, kinship network, community connections, the father's authority, and marriage as a functional partnership rather than a romantic relationship. . . . Family tradition, loyalty, and solidarity were more important than individual goals and romantic interest" (Doherty 1992, p. 33). Also referred to as *institutionalized marriage.*

institutional review board (IRB) A local body of experts and community representatives established by a university or research organization to scrutinize research proposals for adherence to professional ethical standards for the protection of human subjects.

instrumental traits See **agentic (instrumental) character traits.**

interaction The exchange of conversation, gestures, expressions, and so on as two or more people are engaged with each other face-to-face.

interactionist perspective Theoretical perspective that focuses on internal family dynamics; the ongoing action among and response to one another of family members.

interactionist perspective on human sexuality A perspective, derived from symbolic interaction theory, which holds that sexual activities and relationships are shaped by the sexual scripts available in a culture.

interdependence A relationship in which people who have high self-esteem make strong commitments to each other, choosing to help fill each other's legitimate, but not illegitimate, needs.

interethnic marriage Marriage between spouses who are not defined as of different races but do belong to different ethnic groups.

interference with visitation A legal term for actions of a custodial parent that hinder the noncustodial parent's scheduled visitation with a child. Such interference may consist of alleging (falsely) that the child is too ill to visit, has other plans, is not at home at the pick-up time, and the like. Some states have legislated penalties for interference with visitation, while others make little effort to enforce the noncustodial parent's right to contact with her or his child. Often allegations of interference with visitation are difficult to evaluate.

intergenerational transmission of divorce risk The tendency for children of divorced parents to have a greater propensity to divorce than children from intact families.

internalize Make a part of oneself. Often refers to the socialization process by which children learn their parents' norms and values to the point that they become the child's own views.

interparental conflict perspective (on children's adjustment to divorce) One of the theoretical perspectives concerning the negative outcomes among children of divorced parents. From the interparental conflict perspective, the conflict between parents before, during, and after the divorce is responsible for the lowered well-being of the children of divorce.

interpersonal exchange model of sexual satisfaction A view of sexual relations, derived from exchange theory, that sees sexual satisfaction as shaped by the costs, rewards, and expectations of a relationship and the alternatives to it.

interracial marriage Marriage of a partner of one (socially defined) race to someone of a different race.

intersexual A person whose genitalia, secondary sex characteristics, hormones, or other physiological features are not unambiguously male or female.

intimacy Committing oneself to a particular other and honoring that commitment in spite of some personal sacrifices while sharing one's inner self with the other. Intimacy requires interdependence.

intimate partner power Power in a relationship, whether of married or unmarried intimate partners.

intimate partner violence Violence against current or former spouses, cohabitants, or sexual or relationship partners.

involuntary infertility Situation of a couple or individual who would like to have a baby but cannot. Involuntary infertility is medically diagnosed when a woman has tried for twelve months to become pregnant without success.

job sharing Two people sharing one job.

joint custody A situation in which both divorced parents continue to take equal responsibility for important decisions regarding their child's general upbringing.

kin Parents and other relatives, such as in-laws, grandparents, aunts and uncles, and cousins. See also **extended family.**

labor force A social invention that arose with the industrialization of the nineteenth century, when people characteristically became wage earners, hiring out their labor to someone else.

laboratory observation Observation of behavior, including verbal behavior, in an environment controlled by the researcher. For example, a researcher may ask a father, a mother, and an adolescent to discuss an issue, solve a problem, or play a game and observe their responses and interactions, which may be audio- or video-recorded.

la familia Spanish term that literally means "the family" and, for Hispanics, connotes the extended as well as the nuclear family.

laissez-faire parenting style Overly permissive parenting. Children set their own standards for behavior, with little or no parental guidance or authority. Parents are indulgent but not necessarily involved in a supportive way with the child's everyday activities and problems.

latent kin matrix "A web of continually shifting linkages that provide the potential for activating and intensifying close kin relationships" (Riley 1983, p. 441).

legal divorce The dissolution of a marriage by the state through a court order terminating the marriage.

legitimate needs Needs that arise in the present rather than out of the deficits accumulated in the past.

legitimate power One of the six power bases, or sources of power. Legitimate power stems from the more dominant individual's ability to claim authority, or the right to request compliance.

lesbian A woman who is sexually attracted to other women. This term is usually used rather than *homosexual*.

leveling Being transparent, authentic, and explicit about how one truly feels, especially concerning the more conflictive or hurtful aspects of an intimate relationship. Among other things, leveling between intimates implies self-disclosure and commitment (to intimacy).

Levinger's model of divorce decisions This model, derived from exchange theory, presents a decision to divorce as involving a calculus of the *barriers to* divorce (e.g., concerns about children and finances; religious prohibitions), the *rewards* of the marriage, and *alternatives* to the marriage (e.g., can the divorced person anticipate a new relationship, career development, or a single life that will be more rewarding and less stressful than the marriage?).

life chances The opportunities that exist for a social group or an individual to pursue education and economic advancement, to secure medical care and preserve health, to marry and have children, to have material goods and housing of desired quality, and so forth.

life stress perspective (on children's adjustment to divorce) One of the theoretical perspectives concerning the negative outcomes among children of divorced parents. From the life stress perspective, divorce involves the same stress for children as for adults. Divorce is not one single event but a process of stressful events—moving, changing schools, and so on.

limerence A psycho-emotional situation in which one obsesses about another person (the "limerent object") and yearns for reciprocation but has little, if any, concern for the other person's well-being. Not to be confused with love or the early, anxious stage of discovering love.

listener backchannel Brief vocalizations, head nods, and facial movements that convey to the speaker that the listener is tracking what the speaker is saying.

longitudinal study One technique of scientific investigation in which researchers study the same individuals or groups over an extended period, usually with periodic surveys.

looking-glass self The concept that people gradually come to accept and adopt as their own the evaluations, definitions, and judgments of themselves that they see reflected in the faces, words, and gestures of those around them.

love A deep and vital emotion resulting from significant need for satisfaction, coupled with a caring for and acceptance of the beloved, and resulting in an intimate relationship. Love may make the world go 'round, but it's a lot of work, too.

love style A distinctive character or personality that loving or lovelike relationships can take. One social scientist has distinguished six: **agape, eros, ludus, mania, pragma,** and **storge.**

ludus The love style that focuses on love as play and on enjoying many sexual partners rather than searching for one serious relationship. This love style emphasizes the recreational aspect of sexuality. See also **agape, eros, mania, pragma, storge.**

male dominance The cultural idea of masculine superiority; the idea that men should and do exercise the most control and influence over society's members.

mania The love style that combines strong sexual attraction and emotional intensity with extreme jealousy and moodiness, in which manic partners alternate between euphoria and depression. See also **agape, eros, ludus, pragma, storge.**

manipulating Seeking to control the feelings, attitudes, and behavior of one's partner or partners in underhanded ways rather than by assertively stating one's case.

marginal families See **Miller's typology of urban Native American families.**

marital power Power exercised between spouses.

marital rape A husband's forcing a wife to submit to sexual contact that she does not want or that she finds offensive.

marital stability The quality or situation of remaining married.

market approach to child care Child-care arrangement of working parents; other people are hired to care for children while parents are at their jobs.

market work Employment—that is, work for pay—as contrasted with unpaid household work.

marriage market The sociological concept that potential mates take stock of their personal and social characteristics and then comparison shop or bargain for the best buy (mate) they can get.

marriage premise By getting married, partners accept the responsibility to keep each other primary in their lives and to work hard to ensure that their relationship continues.

martyring Doing all one can for others while ignoring one's own legitimate needs. Martyrs often punish the person to whom they are martyring by letting her or him know "just how much I put up with."

masculinities Culturally defined ways of being a man. The plural conveys the idea that there are varied models of appropriate behavior.

meaning What a given activity or statement conveys symbolically. For example, a woman's domestic work may symbolize love and family caring, or it may symbolize a subservient social status. Meanings can be culturally agreed upon or be the attributions of individuals.

M-frame relationship Relationship based on couple interdependence. Each partner has high self-esteem, but they mutually influence each other and experience loving as a deep emotion. See also **A-frame relationship, H-frame relationship.**

Miller's typology of urban Native American families

> **bicultural:** Families that develop a successful blend of native beliefs and practices with those adaptive to living in urban settings.

marginal: Urban families that have become alienated from both Indian and mainstream American cultures.

traditional: Families that retain primarily Indian ways in their urban environment.

transitional: Families that are tending to assimilate to the white working class.

mixed message Two simultaneous messages that contradict each other; also called a *double message*. For example, society gives us mixed messages regarding family values and individualistic values and about premarital sex. People, too, can send mixed messages, as when a partner says, "Of course I always like to talk with you" while turning up the TV.

modern sexism Sexism that takes the form of (a) denial of the existence of discrimination against women, (b) resentment of complaints about discrimination, and (c) resentment of "special favors" for women.

mothering approach to child care A family's child-care arrangement that gives preference to the mother's caregiving role. A couple balances nonemployment of the mother with extra jobs or hours for the father, or, if the mother must work to maintain the family economically, her employment role is minimized.

multipartnered fertility Having children in more than one marriage or relationship.

mutually economically dependent spouses (MEDS) Describes a dual-earner marriage in which each partner earns between 40 and 59 percent of the family income.

nadir of family disorganization Low point of family disorganization when a family is going through a family crisis.

nanny An in-home child-care worker who cares for a family's children either on a live-in basis or by the day; may include traveling with the family.

narcissism Concern chiefly or only with oneself, without regard for the well-being of others. Narcissism is selfishness, not self-love. People with high self-esteem care about and respect themselves and others. Narcissistic, or selfish, people, on the other hand, have low self-esteem, are insecure, and therefore worry unduly about their own well-being and very little about that of others.

naturalistic observation A technique of scientific investigation in which a researcher lives with a family or social group or spends extensive time with them, carefully recording their activities, conversations, gestures, and other aspects of everyday life.

near peer marriage (Schwartz's typology) Couples who believe in partner equality but fall short of a 60/40 division of household labor, usually because of the need for the husband's higher earnings.

neo-sexism Same as **modern sexism.**

neotraditional families Families that value traditional gender roles and organize their family life in these terms as far as practicable. Formal male dominance is softened by an egalitarian spirit.

no-fault divorce The legal situation in which a partner seeking a divorce no longer has to prove "fault" according to a state's legal definition but only needs to assert "irretrievable breakdown" or "irreconcilable differences." Sometimes termed **unilateral divorce.**

noncustodial grandparent A parent of a divorced, noncustodial parent.

no-power A situation in which partners are equally able to influence each other and, at the same time, are not concerned about their relative power vis-à-vis each other. No-power partners negotiate and compromise instead of trying to win.

normative order The culturally approved sequencing of education, work, marriage, and parenthood in an individual's life.

normative order hypothesis The thesis that to proceed through the family life cycle "on time" provides the best chance for a good adjustment in each family stage. Applies as well to the sequencing of education, job, marriage, and parenthood.

nuclear family A family group comprising only the wife, the husband, and their children. See also **extended family.**

nuclear-family model monopoly The cultural assumption that the first-marriage family is the "real" model of family living, with all other family forms viewed as deficient.

occupational segregation The distribution of men and women into substantially different occupations. Women are overrepresented in clerical and service work, for example, whereas men dominate the

higher professions and the upper levels of management.

"on-time" transition Moving from one family life cycle stage to another according to the most common cultural pattern.

opportunity costs (of children) The economic opportunities for wage earning and investments that parents forgo when raising children.

opting out A woman's leaving the labor force, permanently or temporarily, in order to devote full time to child-raising.

para-parent An unrelated adult who informally plays a parentlike role for a child.

parental adjustment perspective (on children's adjustment to divorce) One of the theoretical perspectives concerning the negative outcomes among children of divorced parents. From the parental adjustment perspective, the parent's child-raising skills are impaired as a result of the divorce, with probable negative consequences for the children.

parental loss perspective (on children's adjustment to divorce) One of the theoretical perspectives concerning the negative outcomes among children of divorced parents. From the parental loss perspective, divorce involves the absence of a parent from the household, which deprives children of the optimal environment for their emotional, practical, and social support.

parenting alliance The degree to which partners agree with and support each other as parents.

parenting approach to child care In this approach, child care is shared by the parents on as equal a basis as possible. Working parents try to restructure their employment arrangements to make this possible.

parenting style A general manner of relating to and disciplining children.

passion (Sternberg's triangular theory of love) The drives that lead to romance, physical attraction, sexual consummation, and so on in a loving relationship; one dimension of the triangular theory of love.

passive-aggression Expressing anger at some person or situation indirectly, through nagging, nitpicking, or sarcasm, for example, rather than directly and openly. See also **displacement, sabotage.**

patriarchal norm (of marital power) The norm (cultural rule) that the man should be dominant in a marital relationship.

patriarchal sexuality The view of human sexuality in which men own everything in the society, including women and women's sexuality. Males' sexual needs are emphasized while females' needs are minimized.

patriarchal terrorism A man's systematic use of verbal or physical violence to gain or maintain control over his female partner.

patriarchy A social system in which males are dominant.

peer marriage (Schwartz's typology) Couples who have a close-to-equal split of household chores and money management and who consider themselves to have equal status in the marriage or cohabiting union.

period of family disorganization That period in a family crisis, after the stressor event has occurred, during which family morale and organization slump and habitual roles and routines become nebulous.

permissiveness with affection The standard that permits nonmarital sex for women and men equally, provided they have a fairly stable, affectionate relationship.

permissiveness without affection The standard that allows nonmarital sex for women and men regardless of how much stability or affection exists in their relationship. Also called the *recreational standard*.

pile-up (stressor overload) Concept from family stress and crisis theory that refers to the accumulation of family stressors and prior hardships.

play As a term used in social theory, *play* references the symbolic interaction theory of George Herbert Mead. Play is not idle time, but a vehicle through which children develop appropriate concepts of adult roles, as well as images of themselves, through acting out social roles and engaging in social interaction.

pleasure bond The idea, from Masters and Johnson's book by the same name, that sexual expression between intimates is one way of expressing and strengthening the emotional bond between them.

pleasuring Spontaneously doing what feels good at the moment during a sexual encounter; the opposite of **spectatoring.**

pluralistic family Term used to designate the contemporary family, characterized by "tolerance and diversity, rather than a single family ideal" (Doherty 1992, p. 35). Taking many forms, the pluralistic family is also referred to as the *postmodern family.*

polyamory A marriage system in which one or both spouses retain the option to sexually love others in addition to their spouses.

polyandry A marriage system in which a woman has more than one spouse.

polygamy A marriage system in which a person takes more than one spouse.

polygyny A marriage system in which one man has multiple wives; a marriage of a woman with plural husbands is termed **polyandry.**

pool of eligibles A group of individuals who, by virtue of background or social status, are most likely to be considered eligible to make culturally compatible marriage partners.

positive affect The expression, either verbal or nonverbal, of one's feelings of affection toward another.

power The ability to exercise one's will. *Personal power,* or *autonomy,* is power exercised over oneself. *Social power* is the ability to exercise one's will over others.

power politics Power struggles between spouses in which each seeks to gain a power advantage over the other; the opposite of a **no-power** relationship.

pragma The love style that emphasizes the practical, or pragmatic, element in human relationships and involves the rational assessment of a potential (or actual) partner's assets and liabilities. See also **agape, eros, ludus, mania, storge.**

primary group A group, usually relatively small, in which there are close, face-to-face relationships or equivalent ties that are technologically mediated. The family and a friendship group are primary groups. See also **secondary group.**

primary parent Parent who takes full responsibility for meeting the child's physical and emotional needs by providing the major part of the child's care directly or by managing the child's care by others or by doing both.

principle of least interest The postulate that the partner with the least interest in the relationship is the one who is more apt to control the relationship and to exploit the other.

private face of family The aspect of the family that provides individuals with intimacy, emotional support, and love.

pronatalist bias A cultural attitude that takes having children for granted.

provider role A term for the family role involving market work to support the family. May be carried out by one spouse or partner only or by both.

psychic divorce Regaining psychological autonomy after divorce; emotionally separating oneself from the personality and influence of the former spouse.

psychic intimacy The sharing of people's minds and feelings. Psychic intimacy may or may not involve sexual intimacy.

public face of family The aspect of the family that produces public goods and services.

race A group or category thought of as representing a distinct biological heritage. In reality, there is only one human race. "Racial" categories are social constructs; the so-called races do not differ significantly in terms of basic biological makeup. But "racial" designations nevertheless have social and economic effects and cultural meanings.

rape myth Belief about rape that functions to blame the victim and exonerate the rapist.

rapport talk In Deborah Tannen's terms, this is conversation engaged in by women aimed primarily at gaining or reinforcing rapport or intimacy. See also **report talk.**

redivorce An emerging trend in U.S. society. Redivorces take place more rapidly than first divorces so that many who divorce (and their children) can expect several rapid and emotionally significant transitions in lifestyle and family unit.

referent power One of the six power bases, or sources of power. In a marriage or relationship, this form of power is based on one partner's emotional identification with the other and his or her willingness to agree to the other's decisions or preferences.

refined divorce rate Number of divorces per 1,000 married women over age fifteen. See also **crude divorce rate.**

reinforcing cycle A cycle regarding women's earnings and paid and unpaid family work in which cultural expectations and persistent discrimination result in employed males receiving higher average earnings than women employed full time and, hence, in women's doing more unpaid family work to the detriment of their careers.

relatives of divorce Kinship ties established by marriage but retained after the marriage is dissolved—for example, the relationship of a former mother-in-law and daughter-in-law.

remarriage Marriage in which at least one partner has already been divorced or widowed. Remarriages are becoming increasingly common for Americans.

replacement level (of fertility) The average number of births per woman (a total fertility rate of 2.1) necessary to replace the population.

report talk In Deborah Tannen's terms, this is conversation engaged in by men aimed primarily at conveying information. See also **rapport talk.**

resilient families Families that emphasize mutual acceptance, respect, and shared values; members rely on one another for emotional support.

resource hypothesis Hypothesis (originated by Robert Blood and Donald Wolfe) that the relative power between wives and husbands results from their relative resources as individuals.

resources In exchange theory or intimate partner power analysis, the assets an individual can bring to the relationship. Resources can be material (e.g., income, gifts) or nonmaterial (e.g., emotional support, practical assistance, personality qualities).

resources in cultural context The effect of resources on marital power depends on the cultural context. In a traditional society, norms of patriarchal authority may override personal resources. In a fully egalitarian society, a norm of intimate partner and marital equality may override personal resources. It is in a transitional society that the resource hypothesis is most likely to shape marital power relations.

reward power One of the six power bases, or sources of power. With regard to marriage or partner relationships, this power is based on an individual's ability to give material or nonmaterial gifts and favors to the partner.

rewards and costs In exchange theory or related theoretical analyses, the benefits and disadvantages of a relationship.

role The expectations associated with a particular position in society or in a family. The mother role, for example, calls for its occupant to provide physical care, emotional nurturance, social guidance, and the like to her children.

role-making Improvising a course of action as a way of enacting a role. In role-making, we may use our acts to alter the traditional expectations and obligations associated with a role. This concept emphasizes the variability in the ways different individuals enact a particular role.

role sequencing Assuming and enacting roles in sequence rather than trying to perform what may be competing roles at the same time. For example, a woman may first adopt a work role, then a domestic role, and then return to educational or career activities.

role-taking Role-taking has two meanings. It can mean playing a role associated with a status one occupies, such as taking the mother role when one has a child. It can also mean acting out a role that is not, or not yet, one's own, as when children play "mommy" or "daddy" or "police officer."

sabotage A passive-aggressive action in which a person tries to spoil or undermine some activity another has planned. Sabotage is not always consciously planned. See also **passive-aggression.**

sandwich generation Middle-aged (or older) individuals, usually women, who are sandwiched between the simultaneous responsibilities of caring for their dependent children (sometimes young adults) and aging parents.

science "A logical system that bases knowledge on . . . systematic observation, empirical evidence, facts we verify with our senses" (Macionis 2006, p. 15).

scientific investigation In social science, the systematic gathering of information—using surveys, experiments, naturalistic observation, archival historical material, and case studies—from which it is often possible to generalize with a significant degree of predictability. Data collection and analysis are usually guided by theory or earlier scientific observations.

They point to theory modification and a greater understanding of the phenomenon being studied.

second shift Sociologist Arlie Hochschild's term for the domestic work that employed women must perform after coming home from a day on the job.

secondary group A group, often large and geographically dispersed, characterized by distant, practical relationships. An impersonal society is characterized by secondary groups and relations. See also the opposite, **primary group.**

secure attachment style One of three attachment styles in attachment theory, this style involves trust that the relationship will provide necessary and ongoing emotional and social support.

segmented assimilation Assimilation may vary within an immigrant stream. Immigrants with professional education and skills or from favored national origin groups or both may do very well economically and socially and become culturally integrated. Other immigrants may not have the educational background or other human capital necessary to advance in the new environment and may even experience downward mobility.

selection hypothesis The idea that many of the changes found in a dependent variable, which might be assumed to be associated with the independent variable, are really due to sample selection. For instance, the selection hypothesis posits that many of the benefits associated with marriage—for example, higher income and wealth, along with better health—are not necessarily due to the fact of being married but, rather, to the personal characteristics of those who choose—or are selected into—marriage. Similarly, the selection hypothesis posits that many of the characteristics associated with cohabitation result not from the practice of cohabiting itself but from the personal characteristics of those who choose to cohabit. See also the antonym, **experience hypothesis.**

self-care An approach to child care for working parents in which the child is at home or out without an adult caretaker. Parents may be in touch by phone.

self-concept The basic feelings people have about themselves, their characteristics and abilities, and their worth; how people think of or view themselves.

self-disclosure Letting others see one as one really is. Self-disclosure demands authenticity. Also see *self-revelation*.

self-identification theory A theory of gender socialization, developed by psychologist Lawrence Kohlberg, that begins with a child's categorization of self as male or female. The child goes on to identify sex-appropriate behaviors in the family, media, and elsewhere and to adopt those behaviors.

self-revelation gradually sharing intimate information about oneself. Also see *self-revelation*.

self-worth Part of a person's self-concept that involves feelings about one's own value; also called *self-esteem*.

sequencing mom A mother who chooses to leave paid employment in order to spend some years at home raising children, but who plans to return to work eventually.

seven-stage model of stepfamily development Model of stepfamily progression that proceeds through the following stages: fantasy, immersion, awareness, mobilization, action, contact, and resolution.

sex Refers to biological characteristics—that is, male or female anatomy or physiology. The term **gender** refers to the social roles, attitudes, and behavior associated with males or females.

sex ratio The number of men per 100 women in a society. If the sex ratio is above 100, there are more men than women; if it is below 100, there are more women than men.

sexual abuse A form of child abuse that involves forced, tricked, or coerced sexual behavior—exposure, unwanted kissing, fondling of sexual organs, intercourse, rape, and incest—between a minor and an older person.

sexual intimacy A level of interpersonal interaction in which partners have a sexual relationship. Sexual intimacy may or may not involve psychic intimacy.

sexual orientation The attraction an individual has for a sexual partner of the same or opposite sex.

sexual responsibility The assumption by each partner of responsibility for his or her own sexual response.

sexual script A *script* is a culturally written pattern or "plot" for human behavior.

A sexual script offers reasons for having sex and designates who should take the sexual initiative, how long an encounter should last, what positions are acceptable, and so forth.

sexually transmitted diseases (STDs) Contagious diseases transmitted from one person to another through sexual contact. They are also termed *sexually transmitted infections*.

shared parenting Mother and father (or two same-sex parents) who both take full responsibility as parents.

shift work As defined by the Bureau of Labor Statistics, any work schedule in which more than half of an employee's hours are before 8 a.m. or after 4 p.m.

sibling violence Family violence that takes place between siblings (brothers and sisters).

single Any person who is divorced, widowed, or never-married.

single mothers by choice Women who planfully become mothers, although they are not married or with a partner. They are typically older, with economic and educational resources that enable them to be self-supporting.

single remarriage A remarriage in which only one of the partners is previously married.

social capital perspective (on parenthood) Motivation for parenthood in anticipation of the links parenthood provides to social networks and their resources.

social class Position in the social hierarchy, such as *upper class*, *middle class*, *working class*, or *lower class*. Can be viewed in terms of such indicators as education, occupation, and income or analyzed in terms of status, respect, and lifestyle.

social institution A system of patterned and predictable ways of thinking and behaving—beliefs, values, attitudes, and norms—concerning important aspects of people's lives in society. Examples of major social institutions are the family, religion, government, the economy, and education.

social learning theory (of gender socialization) According to this theory, children learn gender roles as they are taught or modeled by parents, schools, and the media.

socialization The process by which society influences members to internalize attitudes, beliefs, values, and expectations.

spectatoring A term Masters and Johnson coined to describe the practice of emotionally removing oneself from a sexual encounter in order to watch oneself and see how one is doing.

spousal support Economic support of a separated spouse or ex-spouse by the other spouse ordered by a court following separation or divorce.

status exchange hypothesis Regarding interracial/interethnic marriage, the argument that an individual might trade his or her socially defined superior racial/ethnic status for the economically or educationally superior status of a partner in a less-privileged racial/ethnic group.

stay-at-home dad or mom A marital or cohabiting partner who is not employed but remains at home to take care of children and other domestic responsibilities.

stepmother trap The conflict between two views: Society sentimentalizes the stepmother's role and expects her to be unnaturally loving toward her stepchildren but at the same time views her as a wicked witch.

stonewalling One of the **Four Horsemen of the Apocalypse** (which see) that involves refusing to listen to a partner's complaints.

storge An affectionate, companionate style of loving. See also **agape, eros, ludus, mania, pragma.**

stressor A precipitating event that causes a crisis; it is often a situation for which the family has had little or no preparation. See also **ABC-X model.**

stressor overload A situation in which an unrelenting series of small crises adds up to a major crisis.

stress-related growth Personal growth and maturity attained in the context of a stressful life experience such as divorce.

structural antinatalism The structural, or societal, conditions in which bearing and raising children is discouraged either overtly or—as may be the case in the United States—covertly through inadequate support for parenting.

structure–functional perspective Theoretical perspective that looks to the functions that institutions perform for society and the structural form of the institution.

survey A technique of scientific investigation using questionnaires or brief face-to-face interviews or both. An example is the U.S. census.

swinging A marriage agreement in which couples exchange partners in order to engage in purely recreational sex.

symbiotic relationship A relationship based on the mutual meeting of illegitimate needs. See also **legitimate needs.**

symbolic interaction theory (of gender socialization) Uses the concepts of Charles Cooley (primary group, looking-glass self) and George Herbert Mead ("me" and "I," "play, the game, and the generalized other") to explain how children are socialized into culturally defined gender roles.

system A combination of elements or components that are interrelated and organized as a whole. The human body is a system, as is a family.

Temporary Assistance for Needy Families (TANF) Federal legislation that replaces Aid to Families with Dependent Children and whereby government welfare assistance to poor parents is limited to five years for most families, with most adult recipients required to find work within two years.

theoretical perspective A way of viewing reality, or a lens through which analysts organize and interpret what they observe. Researchers on the family identify those aspects of families that are of interest to them, based on their own theoretical perspective.

theory of complementary needs Theory developed by social scientist Robert Winch suggesting that we are attracted to partners whose needs complement our own. In the positive view of this theory, we are attracted to others whose strengths are harmonious with our own so that we are more effective as a couple than either of us would be alone.

total fertility rate For a given year, the number of births that women would have over their reproductive lifetimes if all women at each age had babies at the rate for each age group that year. Can be calculated for social or age categories as well as for nations as a whole.

traditional families See **Miller's typology of urban Native American families.**

traditional sexism Beliefs that men and women are essentially different and should occupy different social roles, that women are not as fit as men to perform certain tasks and occupations, and that differential treatment of men and women is acceptable.

traditionals (Schwartz's typology) Marriages or domestic partnerships in which the man dominates all areas of decision making except children. He is the primary breadwinner and she is the primary homemaker, even if employed. In Schwartz's typology, both spouses favor this arrangement.

trailing spouse The spouse of a relocated employee who moves with him or her.

transgendered A person who has adopted a gender identity that differs from sex/gender as recorded at birth; a person who declines to identify as either male or female.

transition to parenthood The circumstances involved in assuming the parent role.

transitional egalitarian situation (of marital power) Marriages or domestic partnerships in which neither patriarchal nor egalitarian norms prevail. The couple negotiate relationship power, with the relative resources of each individual playing an important role in the outcome.

transitional families See **Miller's typology of urban Native American families.**

transnational family A family of immigrants or immigrant stock that maintains close ties with the sending country. Identity and behavior connect the immigrant family to the new country and the old, and their social networks cross national boundaries.

transsexual An individual who has begun life identified as a member of one sex, but later comes to believe he or she belongs to the other sex. The person may undertake surgical reconstruction to attain a body type closer to that of the desired sex.

two-career marriage Marriage in which both partners have a strong commitment to the lifetime development of both careers. Also called *dual-career couple* or *dual-career family.*

two-earner marriage Marriage in which the wife as well as the husband is employed, but her work is not viewed as a lifetime career. His may be viewed as a "job" rather than a career, as well. Sometimes termed *dual-earner marriage* or *two-paycheck marriage.*

undocumented immigrant The preferred term for "illegal" immigrants, those who are present in a country but are not citizens or legal residents. The implication of the term *undocumented* (compared to *illegal*) is that immigrants may or should have legitimate claims to asylum or residence even if these have not been formally recognized.

unilateral divorce A divorce can be obtained under the no-fault system by one partner even if the other partner objects. The term *unilateral divorce* emphasizes this feature of current divorce law. See also **no-fault divorce.**

unpaid family work The necessary tasks of attending to both the emotional needs of all family members and the practical needs of dependent members, such as children or elderly parents, and maintaining the family domicile.

value of children perspective (on parenthood) Motivation for parenthood because of the rewards, including symbolic rewards, that children bring to parents.

voluntary childlessness The deliberate choice not to become a parent.

vulnerable families Families that have a low sense of common purpose, feel in little control over what happens to them, and tend to cope with problems by showing diminished respect and/or understanding for each other.

wage gap The persistent difference in earnings between men and women.

wheel of love An idea developed by Ira Reiss in which love is seen as developing through a four-stage, circular process, including rapport, self-revelation, mutual dependence, and personality need fulfillment.

References

AAUW (American Association of University Women). 1992. *The AAUW Report: How Schools Shortchange Girls*. New York: Marlowe.

AAUW Educational Foundation. 1999. *Gender Gaps: Where Schools Still Fail Our Children*. New York: Marlowe.

AAUW Educational Foundation. 2006. *Drawing the Line: Sexual Harassment on Campus Study*. Washington, DC: American Association of University Women. January 26. Retrieved February 5, 2007 (www.aauw.org).

Abboud, Soo Kim. 2006. *Top of the Class: How Asian Parents Raise High Achievers, and How You Can Too*. New York: Berkley Books.

Abel, Emily K. 1991. *Who Cares for the Elderly? Public Policy and the Experiences of Adult Daughters*. Philadelphia, PA: Temple University Press.

Aber, J. Lawrence. 2007. *Child Development and Social Policy*. Washington, DC: American Psychological Association.

Abelson, Reed. 1998. "Part-Time Work for Some Adds Up to Full-Time Job." *New York Times*, November 2, pp. A1, A16.

Abma, Joyce C. and Gladys M. Martinez. 2006. "Childlessness among Older Women in the United States: Trends and Profiles." *Journal of Marriage and Family* 68(4): 1045–56.

Abma, Joyce C., Gladys M. Martinez, William D. Mosher, and D. S. Dawson 2004. "Teenagers in the United States: Sexual Activity, Contraceptive Use, and Childbearing 2002." *Vital Health Statistics* 23(24). Hyattsville, MD: National Center for Health Statistics. December.

"Abnormalities Cause New In Vitro Concern." 2003. *Omaha World-Herald* (*LA Times*), January 24.

Abraham, Margaret. 1995. "Ethnicity, Gender, and Marital Violence: South Asian Women's Organizations in the U.S." *Gender and Society* 9:450–68.

———. 2000. *Speaking the Unspeakable: Marital Violence among South Asian Immigrants in the United States*. New Brunswick, NJ: Rutgers University Press.

"The Abstinence-Only Delusion" (editorial). 2007. *New York Times*, April 28.

Achenbaum, W. Andrew. 2005. *Older Americans, Vital Communities*. Baltimore, MD: Johns Hopkins University Press.

Ackerman, Brian P., Kristen Schoff D'Eramo, Lina Umylny, David Schultz, and Carroll E. Izard. 2001. "Family Structure and the Externalizing Behavior of Children from Economically Disadvantaged Families." *Journal of Family Psychology* 15(2):288–301.

Acs, Gregory and Sandi Nelson. 2003. "The More Things Change? Children's Living Arrangements Since Welfare Reform." Washington, DC: Urban Institute. Retrieved September 25, 2006 (http://www.urban.org).

Adams, Michele and Scott Coltrane. 2004. "Boys and Men in Families." Pp. 189–98 in *Families and Society: Classic and Contemporary Readings*, edited by Scott Coltrane. Belmont, CA: Wadsworth.

Adamsons, Kari and Kay Pasley. 2006. "Coparenting Following Divorce and Relationship Dissolution." Pp. 241–61 in *Handbook of Divorce and Relationship Dissolution*, edited by Mark A. Fine and John H. Harvey. Mahwah, NJ: Erlbaum.

Adkins, Sue. 2007. *Raising Happy Children for Dummies: Hands on Parenting Skills for Happy Families*. Chichester, UK: Wiley.

Adler, Jerry. 1993. "Sex in the Snoring '90s." *Newsweek*, April 26, pp. 55–57.

———. 1997. "A Matter of Faith." *Newsweek*, December 15, pp. 49–54.

Adler, Margot. 2006. "'Dear Elders' Dispense Advice Online." *People and Places*. National Public Radio. March 23. Retrieved March 23, 2006 (http://www.npr.org).

Adler, Nancy E., Henry P. David, Brenda N. Major, Susan H. Roth, Nancy Felipe Russo, and Gail E. Wyatt. 1992. "Psychological Factors in Abortion: A Review." *American Psychologist* 47:1194–1204.

African Wedding Guide. N.d. Retrieved October 15, 2006 (http://www .africanweddingguide.com).

Ahmed, Ashraf Uddin. 1993. "Marriage and Its Transition in Bangladesh." Pp. 74–83 in *Next of Kin: An International Reader on Changing Families*, edited by Lorne Tepperman and Susannah J. Wilson. Englewood Cliffs, NJ: Prentice Hall.

Ahrons, Constance. 1994. *The Good Divorce: Raising Your Family Together When Your Marriage Comes Apart*. New York: HarperCollins.

———. 2004. *We're Still Family: What Grown Children Have to Say about Their Parents' Divorce*. New York: HarperCollins.

Ahrons, Constance and Richard B. Miller. 1993. "The Effect of the Post-divorce Relationship on Paternal Involvement: A Longitudinal Analysis." *American Journal of Orthopsychiatry* 63(3):462–79.

Ahrons, Constance and Roy H. Rodgers. 1997. "The Remarriage Transition." Pp. 185–96 in *Family in Transition*, 9th ed., edited by Arlene S. Skolnick and Jerome H. Skolnick. New York: Addison Wesley Longman.

Ahrons, Constance and Jennifer L. Tanner. 2003. "Adult Children and Their Fathers: Relationship Changes 20 Years after Parental Divorce." *Family Relations* 52:340–51.

Ainsworth, Mary D. S., M. C. Blehar, E. Waters, and S. Wall. 1978. *Patterns of Attachment: A Psychological Study of the Strange Situation*. Hillsdale, NJ: Erlbaum.

Akinbami, Lara J. 2006. "The State of Childhood Asthma, United States, 1980–2005." *Advance Data from Vital and Health Statistics*, No. 381. Hyattsville, MD: National Center for Health Statistics.

Albrecht, Chris and Jay D. Teachman. 2003. "Childhood Living Arrangements and the Risk of Premarital Intercourse." *Journal of Family Issues* 24(7):867–94.

Aldous, Joan. 1978. *Family Careers: Developmental Change in Families*. New York: Wiley.

———. 1996. *Family Careers: Rethinking the Developmental Perspective*. Thousand Oaks, CA: Sage Publications.

Alexander, C. S. and B. Guyer. 1993. "Adolescent Pregnancy: Occurrence and Consequences." *Pediatric Annals* 22:85–88.

Alexander, Deborah. 2003. "Money Spent on Pets Is Nothing to Growl At." *Omaha World-Herald*, May 27.

Ali, Lorraine and Julie Scelfo. 2002. "Choosing Virginity." *Newsweek*, December 9, pp. 61–71.

Allen, C. M. and M. A. Straus. 1980. "Resources, Power, and Husband Wife Violence." Pp. 188–208 in *The Social Causes of Husband-Wife Violence*, edited by Murray A. Straus and Gerald T. Hotaling. Minneapolis, MN: University of Minnesota Press.

Allen, Cheryl. 2001. "Doing the Dad Thing: Real Men Stay at Home." *The Greenville News*. August 6.

Allen, Karen. 2002. "Companion Animals as Part of a Healthy Family Environment" (www.deltasociety.org).

Allen, Katherine R. 1997. "Lesbian and Gay Families." Pp. 196–218 in *Contemporary Parenting: Challenges and Issues*, edited by Terry Arendell. Thousand Oaks, CA: Sage Publications.

Allen, Katherine R., Rosemary Bleiszner, Karen A. Roberto, Elizabeth B. Farnsworth, and Karen L. Wilcox. 1999. "Older Adults and Their Children: Family Patterns of Structural Diversity." *Family Relations* 48(2):151–57.

Allen, Katherine R. and Karen L. Wilcox. 2000. "Gay/Lesbian Families over the Life Course." Pp. 51–63 in *Families Across Time: A Life Course Perspective: Readings*, edited by Sharon J. Price, Patrick C. McKenry, and Megan J. Murphy. Los Angeles, CA: Roxbury.

Allen, Mike. 2002. "Law Extends Benefits to Same-sex Couples." *Washington Post*, June 26.

Allen, Mike, and Alan Cooperman. 2004. "Bush Plans to Back Marriage Amendment." *Washington Post*.

Allen, Robert L. and Paul Kivel. 1994. "Men Changing Men." *Ms.*, September/ October, pp. 50–53.

Allen, Sarah M. and Alan J. Hawkins. 1999. "Maternal Gatekeeping: Mothers' Beliefs and Behaviors That Inhibit Greater Father Involvement in Family Work." *Journal of Marriage and Family* 61:199–212.

Allen, W. 1978. "The Search for Applicable Theories of Black Family

Life." *Journal of Marriage and Family* 40(1):117–31.

Allen, Walter R., Angela D. James, and Ophelia Dana. 1998. "Comparative Perspectives on Black Family Life: Uncommon Explorations of a Common Subject." *Journal of Comparative Family Studies* 29(1):1–11.

Allgeier, A. R. 1983. "Sexuality and Gender Roles in the Second Half of Life." Pp. 135–57 in *Changing Boundaries: Gender Roles and Sexual Behavior*, edited by Elizabeth Rice Allgeier and Naomi B. McCormick. Palo Alto, CA: Mayfield.

Alper, Gerald. 2003. *Knowing If It's the Real Thing: Discovering the Roots of Intimacy*. Lanham, MD: Taylor Trade Publishers.

Altman, Irwin and Dalmas A. Taylor. 1973. *Social Penetration: The Development of Interpersonal Relations*. New York: Holt, Rinehart & Winston.

Altman, Lawrence K. 2004. "Study Finds That Teenage Virginity Pledges Are Rarely Kept." *New York Times*, March 10.

———. 2005. "More Living with H.I.V., But Concerns Remain." *New York Times*, June 14.

Alvarez, Lizette. 2003. "Helping Retrieve Muslim Children, Including Her Own." *New York Times*, June 16.

———. 2006a. "After Loss of a Parent to War, a Shared Grieving." *New York Times*, May 29.

———. 2006b. "Jane, We Hardly Knew Ye Died." *New York Times*, September 24.

Amatenstein, Sherry. 2002. *Love Lessons from Bad Breakups*. New York: Perigee Publishers.

Amato, Paul R. 1993. "Children's Adjustment to Divorce: Theories, Hypotheses, and Empirical Support." *Journal of Marriage and Family* 55(1): 23–28.

———. 1996. "Explaining the Intergenerational Transmission of Divorce." *Journal of Marriage and Family* 58(3):628–40.

———. 2000. "The Consequences of Divorce for Adults and Children." *Journal of Marriage and Family* 62:1269–87.

———. 2003. "Reconciling Divergent Perspectives: Judith Wallerstein, Quantitative Research, and Children of Divorce." *Family Relations* 52:332–30.

———. 2004. "Tension between Institutional and Individual Views of

Marriage." *Journal of Marriage and Family* 66(4):959–65.

———. 2005. "The Impact of Family Formation Change on the Cognitive, Social and Emotional Well-being of the Next Generation." *The Future of Children* 15(2):75–96.

Amato, Paul R. and Tamara D. Afifi. 2006. "Feeling Caught between Parents: Adult Children's Relations with Parents and Subjective Well-Being." *Journal of Marriage and Family* 68(1):222–35.

Amato, Paul R. and Alan Booth. 1991. "The Consequences of Divorce for Attitudes toward Divorce and Gender Roles." *Journal of Family Issues* 12(3):306–22.

———. 1997. *A Generation at Risk: Growing Up in an Era of Family Upheaval*. Cambridge, MA: Harvard University Press.

Amato, Paul R. and Jacob Cheadle. 2005. "The Long Reach of Divorce: Divorce and Child Well-being across Three Generations." *Journal of Marriage and Family* 67(1):191–206.

Amato, Paul R. and Danelle B. DeBoer. 2001. "The Transmission of Marital Instability across Generations: Relationship Skills or Commitment to Marriage?" *Journal of Marriage and Family* 63:1038–51.

Amato, Paul R. and Frieda Fowler. 2002. "Parenting Practices, Child Adjustment, and Family Diversity." *Journal of Marriage and Family* 64(3):703–16.

Amato, Paul R. and Joan G. Gilbreth. 1999. "Nonresident Fathers and Children's Well-Being: A Meta-Analysis." *Journal of Marriage and Family* 61:557–73.

Amato, Paul R. and Shelley Irving. 2006. "Historical Trends in Divorce in the United States." Pp. 41–57 in *Handbook of Divorce and Relationship Dissolution*, edited by Mark A. Fine and John H. Harvey. Mahwah, NJ: Erlbaum.

Amato, Paul R., David R. Johnson, Alan Booth, and Stacy J. Rogers. 2003. "Continuity and Change in Marital Quality between 1980 and 2000." *Journal of Marriage and Family* 65(1):1–22.

Amato, Paul R. and Fernando Rivera. 1999. "Paternal Involvement and Children's Behavior Problems." *Journal of Marriage and Family* 61(2):375–84.

Amato, Paul R. and Stacy J. Rogers. 1997. "A Longitudinal Study of Marital Problems and Subsequent Divorce." *Journal of Marriage and Family* 59(3): 612–24.

Amato, Paul R. and Juliana M. Sobolewski. 2001. "The Effects of Divorce and Marital Discord on Children's Well-Being." *American Sociological Review* 66:900–21.

Amato, Paul R. and Denise Wallin. 2001. "People's Reasons for Divorce: Gender, Social Class, the Life Course, and Adjustment." Presented at the annual meeting of the National Council on Family Relations, November 10, Rochester, NY.

Ambert, Anne Marie. 1994. "A Qualitative Study of Peer Abuse and Its Effects: Theoretical and Empirical Implications." *Journal of Marriage and Family* 56(1): 119–30.

American Academy of Pediatrics. 1992. *Caring for Our Children: National Health and Safety Performance Standards as Guidelines for Out-of-Home Child Care Programs.* Elk Grove Village, IL: American Public Health Association and American Academy of Pediatrics.

———. 1998. "Guidance for Effective Discipline." *Pediatrics* 101:723–28.

American Association of Retired Persons (AARP). 2004. *A Report of Multicultural Boomers Coping with Family and Aging Issues.* Washington, DC: American Association of Retired Persons.

American College of Obstetricians and Gynecologists. N.d. "Induced Abortion." Bethesda, MD: National Institutes of Health. Retrieved March 29, 2007 (www.medem.com).

American Civil Liberties Union. 2000. "Federal Court Rejects HIV-based Job Discrimination, Ties Employment to Individual Capabilities, Not Bias." March 10 (www.aclu.org).

———. 2004. "Washington Appeals Court Allows Non-biological Mother in Same-sex Relationship to Seek Parental Rights after Breakup." Press Release (www.aclu.org).

"American Indians by the Numbers." 1992. *New York Times,* February 26.

American Psychological Association. 2001. "Answers to Your Questions About Sexual Orientation and Homosexuality." APA Online (www.apa.org/pubinfo/orient.html).

———. 2005a. "The Impact of Abortion on Women: What Does the Psychological Research Say?" APA Briefing Paper. Washington, DC: American Psychological Association. January 31. Retrieved November 10, 2006 (www.apa.org).

———. 2005b. "Statement on Parental Alienation Syndrome." Press Release. Washington, DC: American Psychological Association. October 28. Retrieved May 15, 2007 (www.apa.org).

———. 2007. "Answers to Your Questions about Sexual Orientation and Homosexuality." Washington, DC: American Psychological Association. Retrieved June 12, 2007 (www.apa.org).

American Psychological Association. Committee on Lesbian and Gay Concerns. 1991. "Avoiding Heterosexual Bias in Language." *American Psychologist* 46:973–74.

American Society for Reproductive Medicine (ASRM). 2007. "Frequently Asked Questions about Infertility." Birmingham, AL: American Society for Reproductive Medicine. Retrieved March 29, 2007 (www.asrm.org).

American Sociological Association. 2002. "Statement of the American Sociological Association on the Importance of Collecting Data and Doing Social Science Research on Race." Washington, DC: American Sociological Association. Retrieved August 28, 2006 (www.asanet.org).

American Veterinary Medical Association. 2002. *U.S. Pet Ownership and Demographics Sourcebook.* Schaumberg, IL: American Veterinary Medical Association/Center for Information Management.

AmeriStat Staff. 2001. "Racial Identity in the U.S. Hispanic/Latino Population." June (www.prb.org).

Ames, Barbara D., Whitney A. Brosi, and Karla M. Damiano-Teixeira. 2006. "'I'm Just Glad My Three Jobs Could Be during the Day': Women and Work in a Rural Community." *Family Relations* 55(1):119–31.

Amnesty International. 1999. *"Not Part of My Sentence": Violations of the Human Rights of Women in Custody.* New York: Amnesty International.

Anderlini-D'Onofrio, Serina. 2004. "Introduction to Plural Loves: Bi and Poly Utopias for a New Millennium." *Journal of Bisexuality* 4(3/4):2–6.

Andersen, Jan. 2004. "Stepfamilies—How to Live in Harmony." SelfGrowth.com. Retrieved September 21, 2004 (http://www.selfgrowth.com).

Andersen, Julie Donner. 2002. "His Kids: Becoming a W.O.W. Stepmother." SelfGrowth.com (http://www.selfgrowth.com/articles/Andersen3.html).

Andersen, Margaret L. 1988. *Thinking about Women: Sociological Perspectives on Sex and Gender.* 2nd ed. New York: Macmillan.

Andersen, Margaret L. and Patricia Hill Collins. 2007. "Why Race, Class, and Gender Still Matter." Pp. 1–16 in *Race, Class and Gender: An Anthology,* 6th ed., edited by Margaret L. Andersen and Patricia Hill Collins. Belmont, CA: Wadsworth.

Anderson, Jared R. and William J. Doherty. 2005. "Democratic Community Initiatives: The Case of Overscheduled Children." *Family Relations* 54(5):654–65.

Anderson, Kristin L. 1997. "Gender, Status, and Domestic Violence: An Integration of Feminist and Family Violence Approaches." *Journal of Marriage and Family* 59(3):655–69.

———. 2002. "Perpetrator or Victim: Relationships between Intimate Partner Violence and Well-Being." *Journal of Marriage and Family* 64:851–63.

Andersen, Margaret L., and Howard F. Taylor. 2002. *Sociology: Understanding A Diverse Society,* 2nd ed. Belmont, CA: Wadsworth.

Anderson, Michael A., Paulette Marie Gillig, Marilyn Sitaker, Kathy McCloskey, Katherine Malloy, and Nancy Grigsby. 2003. "'Why Doesn't She Just Leave?' A Descriptive Study of Victim Reported Impediments to Her Safety." *Journal of Family Violence* 18:151–55.

Anderson, Stephen A. and Ronald M. Sabatelli. 2007. *Family Interaction: A Multigenerational Developmental Perspective,* 4th edition. Boston, MA and New York: Pearson.

Andrews, Bernice and Chris R. Brewin. 1990. "Attributions of Blame for Marital Violence: A Study of Antecedents and Consequences." *Journal of Marriage and Family* 52(3): 757–67.

Anetzberger, Georgia, Jill Korbin, and Craig Austin. 1994. "Alcoholism and Elder Abuse." *Journal of Interpersonal Violence* 9(2):184–93.

Ansay, Sylvia J., Daniel F. Perkins, and Colonel John Nelson. 2004. "Interpreting Outcomes: Using Focus Groups in Evaluation Research." *Family Relations* 53(3):310–16.

Anti-Defamation League of B'nai B'rith. 1981. "The American Story: The Hernandez Family." Video. New York: Anti-Defamation League.

Anyiam, Thony. 2002. "Who Should Jump the Broom?" Retrieved October 2, 2006 (http://www.anyiams.com/jumping_the _broom).

Apter, T. E. 2007. *The Confident Child: Raising Children to Believe in Themselves.* New York: W. W. Norton.

Aquilino, William S. 1994a. "Later Life Parental Divorce and Widowhood: Impact on Young Adults' Assessment of Parent–Child Relations." *Journal of Marriage and Family* 56(4):908–22.

———. 1994b. "Impact of Childhood Family Disruption on Young Adults' Relationships with Parents." *Journal of Marriage and Family* 56(2):295–313.

———. 1997. "From Adolescent to Young Adult: A Prospective Study of Parent–Child Relations during the Transition to Adulthood." *Journal of Marriage and Family* 59:670–86.

———. 2005. "Impact of Family Structure on Parental Attitudes toward the Economic Support of Adult Children over the Transition to Adulthood." *Journal of Family Issues* 26(2):143–67.

Archer, John. 2000. "Sex Differences in Aggression between Heterosexual Partners: A Meta-Analytic Review." *Psychological Bulletin* 126:651–80.

Arditti, Joyce A. 2003. "Incarceration Is a Major Source of Family Stress." *Family Focus* (June):F15–F17. Minneapolis, MN: National Council on Family Relations.

Arditti, Joyce A. and Timothy Z. Keith. 1993. "Visitation Frequency, Child Support Payment, and the Father–Child Relationship Postdivorce." *Journal of Marriage and Family* 55(3):699–712.

Arditti, Joyce A., Jennifer Lambert-Shute, and Karen Joest. 2003. "Saturday Morning at the Jail: Implications of Incarceration for Families and Children." *Family Relations* 52(3):195–204.

Arendell, Terry. 1986. *Mothers and Divorce: Legal, Economic, and Social Dilemmas.* Berkeley, CA: University of California Press.

———. 1995. *Fathers and Divorce.* Thousand Oaks, CA: Sage Publications.

———. 1997. "Divorce and Remarriage." Pp. 154–95 in *Contemporary Parenting: Challenges and Issues,* edited by Terry Arendell. Thousand Oaks, CA: Sage Publications.

———. 2000. "Conceiving and Investigating Motherhood: The Decade's

Scholarship." *Journal of Marriage and Family* 62(4):1192–1207.

Arenson, Karen W. 2005. "Little Advance Is Seen in Ivies' Hiring of Minorities and Women." *New York Times,* March 1.

Arias, Elizabeth. 2004. "United States Life Tables, 2001." *National Vital Statistics Reports* 52(14). Hyattsville, MD: National Center for Health Statistics. February 11.

Ariès, Phillipe. 1962. *Centuries of Childhood: A Social History of Family Life.* New York: Knopf.

Armour, Stephanie. 2002. "More Moms Make Kids Their Career of Choice." *USA Today,* March 12.

———. 2004. "Moms Find It Easier to Pop Back into Work Force." *USA Today,* September 23.

———. 2006. "Cost-effective 'Homesourcing' Grows." *USA Today,* March 13.

Armstrong, Larry. 2003. "Your Mouse Knows Where Your Car Is." *Business Week* 16.

Arnall, Judy and Debbie Elicksen. 2007. *Discipline without Punishment: 135 Tools for Raising Caring, Responsible Children without Time-Out, Spanking, Punishment, or Bribery.* Calgary, Canada: Professional Parenting Canada.

Arnett, Jeffrey Jensen. 2000. "Emerging Adulthood: A Theory of Development from the Late Teens through the Twenties." *American Psychologist* 55(5):469–80. Retrieved March 28, 2003 (PsycARTICLES 0003-006X).

———. 2004. *Emerging Adulthood: The Winding Road from the Late Teens through the Twenties.* London, England: Oxford University Press.

Arnott, Teresa and Julie Matthaei. 2007. "Race, Class, and Gender and Women's Works." Pp. 283–92 in *Race, Class, and Gender,* 6th ed., edited by Margaret Andersen and Patricia Hill Collins. Belmont, CA: Wadsworth.

Aron, Arthur, Christina C. Norman, Elaine N. Aron, Colin McKenna, and Richard E. Heyman. 2000. "Couples' Shared Participation in Novel and Arousing Activities and Experienced Relationship Quality." *Journal of Personality and Social Psychology* 78(2):273–84.

Aronson, Pamela. 2003. "Feminists or 'Postfeminists'? Young Women's Attitudes toward Feminism and Gender Relations." *Gender and Society* 17:903–22.

Artis, Julie E. and Eliza K. Pavalko. 2003. "Explaining the Decline in Women's Household Labor: Individual Change and Cohort Differences." *Journal of Marriage and Family* 65:746–61.

Aseltine, Robert H., Jr. and Ronald C. Kessler. 1993. "Marital Disruption and Depression in a Community Sample." *Journal of Health and Social Behavior* 34(September):237–51.

Ashmun, Joanna M. 2004. "Narcissistic Personality Disorder." Retrieved August 16, 2006 (http://www.halcyon .com/jmashmun/npd).

Atchley, Robert C. 1997. *Social Forces and Aging.* Belmont, CA: Wadsworth.

"At-Home Workers Are Vanishing." 2003. *Omaha World-Herald* (*Wall Street Journal*), August 4.

Avellar, Sarah and Pamela J. Smock. 2003. "Has the Price of Motherhood Declined Over Time? A Cross-Cohort Comparison of the Motherhood Wage Penalty." *Journal of Marriage and Family* 65:597–607.

———. 2005. "The Economic Consequences of the Dissolution of Cohabiting Unions." *Journal of Marriage and Family* 67(2):315–27.

Babbie, Earl. 1992. *The Practice of Social Research.* 6th ed. Belmont, CA: Wadsworth.

———. 2007. *The Practice of Social Research.* 11th ed. Belmont, CA: Wadsworth.

Babbitt, Charles E. and Harold J. Burbach. 1990. "A Comparison of Self-orientation among College Students across the 1960s, 1970s and 1980s." *Youth & Society* 21(4):472–82.

Baca Zinn, Maxine, Pierette Hondagneu-Sotelo, and Michael A. Messner. 2004. "Gender through the Prism of Difference." Pp. 166–74 in *Race, Class, and Gender,* 5th ed., edited by Margaret L. Andersen and Patricia Hill Collins. Belmont, CA: Wadsworth.

———. 2007. "Sex and Gender through the Prism of Difference." Pp. 147–55 in *Race, Class, and Gender: An Anthology,* 6th ed, edited by Margaret L. Andersen and Patricia Hill Collins. Belmont, CA: Wadsworth.

Baca Zinn, Maxine and Angela Y. H. Pok. 2002. "Tradition and Transition in Mexican-Origin Families." Pp. 79–100 in *Minority Families in the United States,* 3rd ed., edited by Ronald L. Taylor. Upper Saddle River, NJ: Prentice Hall.

Baca Zinn, Maxine and Barbara Wells. 2007. "Diversity within Latino Families: New Lessons for Family Social Science." Pp. 422–47 in *Family in Transition*, 14th ed., edited by Arlene S. Skolnick and Jerome H. Skolnick. Boston, MA: Allyn and Bacon.

Bach, George R. and Peter Wyden. 1970. *The Intimate Enemy: How to Fight Fair in Love and Marriage.* New York: Avon.

Bachrach, Christine, Patricia F. Adams, Soledad Sambrano, and Kathryn A. London. 1990. "Adoption in the 1980's." *Advance Data*, No. 181. Hyattsville, MD: U.S. National Center for Health Statistics, January 5.

Badeau, Susan H. 2004. "Five Commentaries: Looking to the Future: Commentary 1." *The Future of Children* 14(1):175–178.

Bailey, J. Michael, David Bobrow, Marilyn Wolfe, and Sarah Mikach. 1995. "Sexual Orientation of Adult Sons of Gay Fathers." *Developmental Psychology* 31:124–29.

Bakalar, Nicholas. 2007. "Breast Cancer Not Linked to Abortion, Study Says." *New York Times*, April 24.

Ball, Derek and Peter Kivisto. 2006. "Couples Facing Divorce." Pp. 145–61 in *Couples, Kids, and Family Life*, edited by Jaber F. Gubrium and James A. Holstein. New York: Oxford University Press.

Bandura, Albert and Richard H. Walters. 1963. *Social Learning and Personality Development.* New York: Holt, Rinehart & Winston.

Banerjee, Neela. 2006a. "Clergywomen Find Hard Path to Bigger Pulpit." *New York Times*, August 26.

———. 2006b. "A Woman Is Installed as Top Bishop of the Episcopal Church." *New York Times*, November 5.

Banse, Rainer. 2004. "Adult Attachment and Marital Satisfaction: Evidence for Dyadic Configuration Effects." *Journal of Social and Personal Relationships* 21(2): 273–82.

Barash, Susan Shapiro. 2000. *Second Wives: The Pitfalls and Rewards of Marrying Widowers and Divorced Men.* Far Hills, NJ: New Horizon.

Barber, Bonnie L. and David H. Demo. 2006 "The Kids Are Alright (at Least Most of Them): Links between Divorce and Dissolution and Child Well-Being." Pp. 289–311 in *Handbook of Divorce and Relationship Dissolution*, edited by Mark A. Fine and John H. Harvey. Mahwah, NJ: Erlbaum.

Barbassa, Juliana. 2004. "The Obesity Paradox: Poorer People Pay a Price in Pounds." Associated Press, March 4.

Barker, Susan E. N.d. "'Cuddle Hormone': Research Links Oxytocin and Sociosexual Behaviors." Retrieved August 30, 2006 (http://www.oxytocin.org/cuddle-hormone/).

Barnett, Rosalind Chait and Karen C. Gareis. 2006. "Parental After-School Stress and Psychological Well-Being." *Journal of Marriage and Family* 68(1):101–8.

Barth, Richard P. and Marianne Berry. 1988. *Adoption and Disruption: Rates, Risks, and Responses.* New York: Aldine.

Bartkowski, John P. 2001. *Remaking the Godly Family: Gender Negotiation in Evangelical Families.* Piscataway, NJ: Rutgers University Press.

Barton, Sharon J. 1999. "Promoting Family-centered Care with Foster Families." *Pediatric Nursing* 25(1):57–62.

Basow, Susan H. 1992. *Gender: Stereotypes and Roles.* 3rd ed. Pacific Grove, CA: Brooks/Cole.

Batalova, Jeanne A. and Philip N. Cohen. 2002. "Premarital Cohabitation and Housework: Couples in Cross-national Perspective." *Journal of Marriage and Family* 64:743–55.

Batson, Christie D., Zhenchao Qian, and Daniel T. Lichter. 2006. "Interracial and Intraracial Patterns of Mate Selection among America's Diverse Black Populations." *Journal of Marriage and Family* 68(3):658–72.

Baum, Angela C., Sedahlia Jasper Crase, and Kirsten Lee Crase. 2001. "Influences on the Decision to Become or Not Become a Foster Parent." *Families in Society* 82(2):202–21.

Baumrind, Diana. 1978. "Parental Disciplinary Patterns and Social Competence in Children." *Youth and Society* 9:239–76.

———. 1994. "The Social Context of Child Maltreatment." *Family Relations* 43(4):360–68.

Bausch, Robert S. 2006. "Predicting Willingness to Adopt a Child: A Consideration of Demographic and Attitudinal Factors." *Sociological Perspectives* 49(1):47–65.

Bauserman, Robert. 2002. "Child Adjustment in Joint-Custody versus Sole Custody Arrangements: A Meta-Analytic Review." *Journal of Family Psychology* 16:91–102.

Baxter, Janeen. 2005. "To Marry or Not to Marry: Marital Status and the Household Division of Labor." *Journal of Family Issues* 26(3):300–321.

Beah, Ishmael. 2007. *A Long Way Gone: Memoirs of a Boy Soldier.* New York: Sarah Crichton Books.

Beaman, Lori G. 2001. "Molly Mormons, Mormon Feminists and Moderates: Religious Diversity and the Latter Day Saints Church." *Sociology of Religion* 62:65–86.

Bean, Frank D., Jennifer Lee, Jeanne Batalova, and Mark Leach. 2004. *Immigration and Fading Color Lines in America.* New York: Russell Sage.

Bearman, Peter S. and Hannah Brückner. 2001. "Promising the Future: Virginity Pledges and First Intercourse." *American Journal of Sociology* 106:859–912.

Beavers, Laura and Jean D'Amico. 2005. *Children in Immigrant Families: U.S. and State-level Findings from the 2000 Census.* Washington, DC: Annie E. Casey Foundation and Population Reference Bureau. January.

Beck, Peggy and Nancee Blank. 1997. "Broadening the Scope of Divorce Mediation to Meet the Needs of Children." *Mediation Quarterly: Journal of the Academy of Family Mediators* 14(3):179–85.

Becker, Gary S. [1981] 1991. *A Treatise on the Family.* 2nd ed. Cambridge, MA: Harvard University Press.

Becker, Gay. 1990. *Healing the Infertile Family.* New York: Bantam.

———. 2000. *The Elusive Embryo: How Women and Men Approach New Reproductive Technologies.* Berkeley and Los Angeles, CA: University of California Press.

Bedard, Marcia E. 1992. *Breaking with Tradition: Diversity, Conflict, and Change in Contemporary Families.* Dix Hills, NY: General Hall.

Beeghley, Leonard. 1996. *What Does Your Wife Do? Gender and the Transformation of Family Life.* Boulder, CO: Westview.

Beer, William R. 1989. *Strangers in the House: The World of Stepsiblings and Half Siblings.* New Brunswick, NJ: Transaction Books.

———. 1992. *American Stepfamilies.* New Brunswick, NJ: Transaction Books.

Begley, Sharon. 1998. "You're OK, I'm Terrific: 'Self-Esteem' Backfires." *Newsweek,* July 13, p. 69.

———. 2007. "Just Say No to Bad Science." *Newsweek,* May 7, pp. 57–58.

Belcastro, Philip A. 1985. "Sexual Behavior Differences between Black and White Students." *Journal of Sex Research* 21(1):56–67.

Belkin, Lisa. 2003. "The Opt-Out Revolution." *New York Times Magazine,* October 26, pp. 42–47, 58, 85–86.

Bell, Alan P., Martin S. Weinberg, and Sue Kiefer Hammersmith. 1981. *Sexual Preference: Its Development in Men and Women.* Bloomington, IN: University of Indiana Press.

Bell, Diane and Kathy Belicki. 1998. "A Community-based Study of Well-being in Adults Reporting Childhood Abuse." *Child Abuse & Neglect* 22(7):681–85.

Bell, Maya. 2003. "More Gays and Lesbians Than Ever Are Becoming Parents." Knight Ridder/Tribune News Service, October 1.

Bell, Richard Q. 1974. "Contributions of Human Infants to Caregiving and Social Interaction." Pp. 11–19 in *The Effect of the Infant on Its Care Giver: Origins of Behavior Series.* Vol. 1, edited by Michael Lewis and Leonard A. Rosenblum. New York: Wiley.

Bellafante, Ginia. 2004. "Two Fathers, with One Happy to Stay at Home." *New York Times,* January 12.

Bellah, Robert N., Richard Madsen, William M. Sullivan, Ann Swidler, and Steven M. Tipton. 1985. *Habits of the Heart: Individualism and Commitment in American Life.* Berkeley and Los Angeles, CA: University of California Press.

Belluck, Pam. 2000. "States Declare War on Divorce Rates Before Any 'I Dos.'" *New York Times,* April 21.

———. 2004. "Gays Win the Right to Marry." *Oakland Tribune,* February 5.

Belluck, Pam and Jim Yardley. 2006. "China Tightens Adoption Rules for Foreigners." *New York Times,* December 20.

Belsky, Jay. 1990. "Parental and Nonparental Child Care and Children's Socioemotional Development: A Decade in Review." *Journal of Marriage and Family* 52(4):885–903.

———. 1991. "Parental and Non-Parental Child Care and Children's Socioemotional Development." Pp. 122–40 in *Contemporary Families: Looking Forward, Looking Back,* edited by Alan Booth. Minneapolis, MN: National Council on Family Relations.

———. 2002. "Quantity Counts: Amount of Child Care and Children's Socioemotional Development." *Developmental and Behavioral Pediatrics* 23:167–70.

Belsky, Jay and K. H. Hsieh. 1998. "Patterns of Marital Change during the Early Childhood Years: Parent Personality, Coparenting, and Division-of-Labor Correlates." *Journal of Family Psychology* 12:511–26.

Belsky, Jay, Deborah Lowe Vandell, Margaret Burchinal, Alison Clarke-Stewart, Kathleen McCartney, Margaret Tresch Owen, and the NICHD Early Child Care Research Network. 2007. "Are There Long-term Effects of Early Child Care?" *Child Development* 78(2):681–701.

Belt, Nancy. 2000. "Bargaining Power." *Washington University Magazine,* Spring, pp. 22–24.

Bem, Sandra Lipsitz. 1981. "Gender Schema Theory: A Cognitive Account of Sex Typing." *Psychological Review* 88:354–64.

Bengston, Vern L. 2001. "Beyond the Nuclear Family: The Increasing Importance of Multigenerational Bonds." *Journal of Marriage and Family* 63(1):1–16.

Bengston, Vern L., Timothy J. Biblarz, and Robert E. L. Roberts. 2002. *How Families Still Matter: A Longitudinal Study of Youth in Two Generations.* Cambridge, UK: Cambridge University Press.

———. 2007. "How Families Still Matter: A Longitudinal Study of Youth in Two Generations." Pp. 315–24 in *Family in Transition,* 14th ed., edited by Arlene S. Skolnick and Jerome H. Skolnick. Boston, MA: Allyn and Bacon.

Bengston, Vern L., C. Rosenthal, and L. Burton. 1996. "Paradoxes of Families and Aging." Pp. 245–53 in *Handbook of Aging and the Social Sciences,* edited by R. H. Binstock and L. K. George. New York: Academic.

Benjet, Corina and Alan E. Kazdin. 2003. "Spanking Children: The Controversies, Findings, and New Directions." *Clinical Psychological Review* 23(2):197–224.

Bennett, Larry W. and Oliver J. Williams. 1999. "Men Who Batter." Pp. 227–59 in

Family Violence: Prediction and Treatment, 2nd ed., edited by Robert L. Hampton. Thousand Oaks, CA: Sage Publications.

Bennett, Linda A., Steven J. Wolin, and David Reiss. 1988. "Deliberate Family Process: A Strategy for Protecting Children of Alcoholics." *British Journal of Addiction* 83:821–29.

Bennetts, Leslie. 2007. *The Feminine Mistake: Are We Giving Up Too Much?* New York: Voice.

Benoit, D. and K. Parker. 1994. "Stability and Transmission of Attachment across Three Generations." *Child Development* 65:1444–56.

Berardo, Felix M. 1998. "Family Privacy." *Journal of Family Issues* 19(1):4–19.

Berg, Barbara. 1984. "Early Signs of Infertility." *Ms.,* May, pp. 68ff.

Berg, S. J. and K. E. Wynne-Edwards. 2001. "Changes in Testosterone, Cortisol, and Estradiol Levels in Men Becoming Fathers." *Mayo Clinic Proceedings* 76:582–92.

Berge, Jerica M. and Kristen E. Holm. 2007. "Boundary Ambiguity in Parents with Chronically Ill Children: Integrating Theory and Research." *Family Relations* 56(2):123–34.

Berger, Peter L., Brigitte Berger, and Hansfried Kellner. 1973. *The Homeless Mind: Modernization and Consciousness.* New York: Random House.

Berger, Peter L. and Hansfried Kellner. 1970. "Marriage and the Construction of Reality." Pp. 49–72 in *Recent Sociology No. 2,* edited by Hans Peter Dreitzel. New York: Macmillan.

Berger, Roni. 1997. "Immigrant Stepfamilies." *Contemporary Family Therapy* 19(3):361–70.

———. 1998. *Stepfamilies: A Multi-dimensional Perspective.* New York: Haworth.

———. 2000. "Gay Stepfamilies: A Triple-Stigmatized Group." *Families in Society* 81(5):504–16.

Bergman, Mike. 2004. "Census Bureau Releases Information on Home Workers." Press Release CB04-183, October 20. Washington, DC: U.S. Census Bureau.

———. 2006a. "Americans Marrying Older, Living Alone More, See Households Shrinking, Census Bureau Reports." Press Release CB06-83, May 25. Washington, DC: U.S. Census Bureau.

————. 2006b. "Census Bureau Data Underscore Value of College Degree." Press Release CB06-159. Washington, DC: U.S. Census Bureau.

————. 2006c. "Dramatic Changes in U.S. Aging: Highlighted in New Census, NIH Report." Press Release CB06-36, March 9. Washington, DC: U.S. Census Bureau.

————. 2006d. "Growth of Hispanic-owned Businesses Triples the National Average." Press Release, March 21. Washington, DC: U.S. Census Bureau.

Berk, Richard A., Phyllis J. Newton, and Sarah Fenstermaker Berk. 1986. "What a Difference a Day Makes: An Empirical Study of the Impact of Shelters for Battered Women." *Journal of Marriage and Family* 48:481–90.

Berk, Sarah Fenstermaker. 1985. *The Gender Factory: The Apportionment of Work in American Households.* New York: Plenum.

Berke, Debra L. 2003. "Coming Home Again: The Challenges and Rewards of Home-based Self-Employment." *Journal of Family Issues* 24:513–46.

Bernard, Jessie. 1986. "The Good-Provider Role: Its Rise and Fall." Pp. 125–44 in *Family in Transition: Rethinking Marriage, Sexuality, Child Rearing, and Family Organization,* 5th ed., edited by Arlene S. Skolnick and Jerome H. Skolnick. Boston, MA: Little, Brown.

Berns, Sara B., Neil S. Jacobson, and John M. Gottman. 1999. "Demand–Withdraw Interaction in Couples with a Violent Husband." *Journal of Consulting and Clinical Psychology* 67(5):666–74.

Bernstein, Aaron. 2004. "Shaking Up Trade Theory." *Business Week,* December 6, pp. 116–20.

Bernstein, Anne C. 1997. "Stepfamilies from Siblings' Perspectives." Pp. 153–75 in *Stepfamilies: History, Research, and Policy,* edited by Irene Levin and Marvin B. Sussman. New York: Haworth.

————. 1999. "Reconstructing the Brothers Grimm: New Tales for Stepfamily Life." *Family Process* 38(4):415–30.

Bernstein, Fred A. 2004. "On Campus, Rethinking Biology 101." *New York Times,* March 7.

Bernstein, Jeffrey and Susan Magee. 2004. *Why Can't You Read My Mind? Overcoming the 9 Toxic Thought Patterns That Get in the Way of a Loving Relationship.* New York: Marlowe.

Bernstein, Nina. 2004a. "More Teenagers Are Striving for Restraint." *New York Times,* March 7.

————. 2004b. "Study of Immigrant Children Finds Surprising Health Benefit." *New York Times,* October 6.

————. 2005. "Caught between Parents and the Law." *New York Times,* February 17.

————. 2006. "A Climate of Fear as Immigration Agents Raid New York Farms." *New York Times,* December 24.

Bernstein, Robert. 2003. "Two Married Parents the Norm." Press Release, January 12. Washington, DC: U.S. Census Bureau.

————. 2005a. "Hispanic Population Passes 40 Million, Census Bureau Reports." Press Release CB05-77, June 9. Washington, DC: U.S. Census Bureau.

————. 2005b. "Texas Becomes Nation's Newest 'Majority-Minority' State, Census Bureau Announces." Press Release CB05-118, August 11. Washington, DC: U.S. Census Bureau.

Berridge, K. and T. Robinson. 1998. "What Is the Role of Dopamine in Reward: Hedonic Impact, Reward Learning, or Incentive Salience?" *Brain Research Review* 28(3):309–69.

Beutel, Ann M. and Margaret Mooney Marini. 1995. "Gender and Values." *American Sociological Review* 60(3):436–49.

Bianchi, Suzanne M. 2000. "Maternal Employment and Time with Children: Dramatic Change or Surprising Continuity?" *Demography* 37:401–14.

Bianchi, Suzanne M., and Lynne M. Casper. 2000. "American Families." *Population Bulletin* 55(4). Washington, DC: Population Reference Bureau.

Bianchi, Suzanne M., John P. Robinson, and Melissa A. Milkie. 2006. *Changing Rhythms of American Family Life.* New York: Russell Sage.

Bianchi, Suzanne M., Lekha Subaiya, and Joan P. Kahn. 1999. "The Gender Gap in the Economic Well-being of Nonresident Fathers and Custodial Mothers." *Demography* 36:185–203.

Biddulph, Steve, and Shaaron Biddulph. 2007. *Raising a Happy Child.* London: Doring Kindersley.

Bierman, Alex, Elena M. Fazio, and Melissa A. Milkie. 2006. "A Multifaceted Approach to the Mental Health Advantage of the Married." *Journal of Family Issues* 27(4):554–82.

"Big (Lack of) Men on Campus." 2005. *USA Today,* September 23.

Billingsley, Andrew. 1968. *Black Families in White America.* Englewood Cliffs, NJ: Prentice Hall.

————. 1992. *Climbing Jacob's Ladder: The Enduring Legacy of African-American Families.* New York: Simon and Schuster.

Binstock, Georgina and Arland Thornton. 2003. "Separations, Reconciliations, and Living Apart in Cohabiting and Marital Unions." *Journal of Marriage and Family* 65:432–43.

"Biology of Social Bonds." 1999. *Science News,* August 7.

Bird, Chloe E. 1997. Gender Differences in the Social and Economic Burdens of Parenting and Psychological Distress." *Journal of Marriage and Family* 59(4):809–23.

Bird, Gloria W., Rick Peterson, and Stephanie Hotta Miller. 2002. "Factors Associated with Distress among Support-Seeking Adoptive Parents." *Family Relations* 51(3):215–20.

Bird, Mark H. 2006. "Sexual Addiction and Marriage and Family Therapy: Facilitating Individual and Relationship Healing through Couple Therapy." *Journal of Marital and Family Therapy* 32(3):297–311.

Biskupic, Joan. 2003. "Same-sex Couples Are Redefining Family Law in USA." *USA Today,* February 18.

Black, D. A., Richard E. Heyman, and Amy M. Smith Slep. 2001. "Risk Factors for Child Physical Abuse." *Aggression and Violent Behavior* 6:121–88.

Black, Dan, Gary Gates, Seth Sanders, and Lowell Taylor. 2000. "Demographics of the Gay and Lesbian Population in the United States: Evidence from Available Systematic Data Sources." *Demography* 37:139–54.

"Black Parents Fight Racial Discrimination in Schools." 2004. PR Web. July 27. (http://www.prweb.com/releases/2004).

Blackman, Lorraine, Obie Clayton, Norval Glenn, Linda Malone-Colon, and Alex Roberts. 2006. *The Consequences of Marriage for African Americans: A Comprehensive Literature Review.* New York: Institute for American Values.

Blackwell, Debra L. 1998. "Marital Homogamy in the United States: The Influence of Individual and Paternal Education." *Social Science Research* 27(2):159–64.

Blakely, Mary Kay. 1995. "An Outlaw Mom Tells All." *Ms.*, January/February, pp. 34–45.

Blalock, Lydia B. 2003. "Poverty Exacerbates Work/Family Tensions." *Family Focus* (June):F11–F13. Minneapolis, MN: National Council on Family Relations.

Blanchflower, David G. and Andrew J. Oswald. 2004. "Money, Sex and Happiness: An Empirical Study." Working Paper 10499. Cambridge, MA: National Bureau of Economic Research.

Blankenhorn, David. 1995. *Fatherless America: Confronting Our Most Urgent Social Problem.* New York: Basic Books.

Blau, Francine D., Mary C. Brinton, and David B. Grusky, eds. 2006. "The Declining Significance of Gender?" Pp. 3–34 in *The Declining Significance of Gender*, edited by Francine D. Blau, Mary C. Brinton, and David B. Grusky. New York: Russell Sage.

Blau, Francine D. and Lawrence M. Kahn. 2006. "The Gender Pay Gap: Going, Going, but Not Gone." Pp. 37–66 in *The Declining Significance of Gender*, edited by Francine Blau, Mary C. Brinton, and David B. Grusky. New York: Russell Sage.

Blau, Melinda. 1993. *Families Apart: Ten Keys to Successful Co-Parenting.* New York: Perigee.

Blee, Kathleen M. and Ann R. Tickamyer. 1995. "Racial Differences in Men's Attitudes about Women's Gender Roles." *Journal of Marriage and Family* 57:913–25.

Blieszner, Rosemary, Karen A. Roberto, Karen L. Wilcox, Elizabeth J. Barham, and Brianne L. Winston. 2007. "Dimensions of Ambiguous Loss in Couples Coping with Mild Cognitive Impairment." *Family Relations* 56(2):196–209.

Blinn-Pike, Lynn. 1999. "Why Abstinent Adolescents Report They Have Not Had Sex: Understanding Sexually Resilient Youth." *Family Relations* 48:295–301.

Block, Joel D. 2003. *Naked Intimacy: How to Increase True Openness in Your Relationship.* Chicago, IL: Contemporary Books.

Block, Sandra. 2000. "Golden Years Bleak for Divorcees." *USA Today*, August 8.

———. 2002. "Pet Insurance Can Save Owners from Wrenching Decisions." *USA Today*, February 19.

Block, Joel D., and Susan S. Bartell 2001. *Stepliving for Teens: Getting along with Step-parents, Parents, and Siblings.* New York: Penguin Young Readers Group.

Blood, Robert O., Jr. and Donald M. Wolfe. 1960. *Husbands and Wives: The Dynamics of Married Living.* New York: Free Press.

Blow, Adrian J. and Kelley Hartnett. 2005. "Infidelity in Committed Relationships II: A Substantive Review." *Journal of Marital and Family Therapy* 31(2):217–33.

Bluestone, Cheryl and Catherine S. Tamis-LeMonda. 1999. "Correlates of Parenting Styles in Predominantly Working- and Middle-Class African American Mothers." *Journal of Marriage and Family* 61(4):881–93.

Blum, Deborah. 1997. *Sex on the Brain: The Biological Differences between Men and Women.* New York: Penguin.

Blumberg, Rae Lesser and Marion Tolbert Coleman. 1989. "A Theoretical Look at the Gender Balance of Power in the American Couple." *Journal of Family Issues* 10:225–50.

Blumer, Herbert. 1969. *Social Interactionism: Perspective and Method.* Berkeley, CA: University of California Press.

Blumstein, Philip and Pepper Schwartz. 1983. *American Couples: Money, Work, Sex.* New York: Morrow.

Bly, Robert. 1990. *Iron John: A Book about Men.* Reading, MA: Addison-Wesley.

Bock, Jane D. 2000. "'Doing the Right Thing?' Single Mothers by Choice and the Struggle for Legitimacy." *Gender and Society* 14:62–86.

Bogaert, Anthony F. 2004. "Asexuality: Prevalence and Associated Factors in a National Probability Sample." *Journal of Sex Research* 41(3):279–83.

Bogenschneider, Karen. 2000. "Has Family Policy Come of Age? A Decade Review of the State of U.S. Family Policy in the 1990s." *Journal of Marriage and Family* 62:1136–59.

———. 2006. *Family Policy Matters: How Policymaking Affects Families and What Professionals Can Do.* 2nd ed. Mahwah, NJ: Erlbaum.

Bogle, Kathleen A. 2004. "From Dating to Hooking Up: The Emergence of a New Sexual Script." Unpublished PhD dissertation, Department of Sociology, University of Delaware. Newark, DE.

Bohannan, Paul. 1970a. "Divorce Chains, Households of Remarriage, and Multiple Divorces." Pp. 113–23 in *Divorce and After*, edited by Paul Bohannan. New York: Doubleday.

———. 1970b. "The Six Stations of Divorce." Pp. 29–55 in *Divorce and After*, edited by Paul Bohannan. New York: Doubleday.

Bolzendahl, Catherine I. and Daniel J. Myers. 2004. "Feminist Attitudes and Support for Gender Equality: Opinion Change in Women and Men, 1974–1998." *Social Forces* 83(2):759–90.

Boonstra, Heather D., Rachel Benson Gold, Cory L. Richards, and Lawrence B. Finer. 2006. *Abortion in Women's Lives.* New York: Guttmacher Institute.

Booth, Alan and Paul R. Amato. 1994. "Parental Gender Role Nontraditionalism and Offspring Outcomes." *Journal of Marriage and Family* 56(4):865–77.

———. 2001. "Parental Predivorce Relations and Offspring Post-Divorce Well-being." *Journal of Marriage and Family* 63:197–212.

Booth, Alan, Karen Carver, and Douglas A. Granger. 2000. "Biosocial Perspectives on the Family." *Journal of Marriage and Family* 62(4):1018–34.

Booth, Alan and Ann C. Crouter, eds. 1998. *Men in Families: When Do They Get Involved? What Difference Does It Make?* Mahwah, NJ: Erlbaum.

———. 2001. *Does It Take a Village? Community Effects on Children, Adolescents, and Families.* Mahwah, NJ: Erlbaum.

———. 2002. *Just Living Together: Implications of Cohabitation for Children, Families, and Social Policy.* Mahwah, NJ: Erlbaum.

Booth, Alan, Ann C. Crouter, and Mari Clements, eds. 2001. *Couples in Conflict.* Mahwah, NJ: Erlbaum.

Booth, Alan and James Dabbs. 1993. "Testosterone and Men's Marriages." *Social Forces* 72:463–77.

Booth, Alan and John N. Edwards. 1992. "Starting Over: Why Remarriages Are More Unstable." *Journal of Family Issues* 13(2):179–94.

Booth, Alan, David R. Johnson, and Douglas A. Granger. 2005. "Testosterone, Marital Quality, and Role Overload." *Journal of Marriage and Family* 67(2):483–98.

Booth, Alan, David R. Johnson, Lynn K. White, and John N. Edwards. 1985. "Predicting Divorce and Separation." *Journal of Family Issues* 6:331–46.

Booth, Cathy. 1977. "Wife-Beating Crosses Economic Boundaries." *Rocky Mountain News,* June 17.

Boraas, Stephanie and William R. Rodgers III. 2003. "How Does Gender Play a Role in the Earnings Gap? An Update." *Monthly Labor Review,* March, pp. 9–15.

"Born Again Adults Less Likely to Cohabit, Just as Likely to Divorce." 2001. Ventura, CA: Barna Research Group (Barna Research Online). August 6 (www .barna.org/cgi-binPagePressRelease).

"Born Again Adults Remain Firm in Opposition to Abortion and Gay Marriage." 2001. Ventura, CA: Barna Research Group (Barna Research Online). July 23 (www.barna.org/ cgi-bin/PagePressRelease).

Bornstein, Marc H. and Robert H. Bradley, eds. 2003. *Socioeconomic Status, Parenting, and Child Development.* Mahwah, NJ: Erlbaum.

Borrell, Luisa N., Pam Factor-Litvak, Mary S. Wolff, Erza Susser, and Thomas D. Matte. 2004. "Effect of Socioeconomic Status on Exposures to Polychlorinated Biphenyls (PCBs) and Dichlorodiphenyldichloroethylene (DDE) among Pregnant African-American Women." *Archives of Environmental Health* 59(5):250–56.

Bosman, Julie. 2006. "Hey, Just Because He's Divorced Doesn't Mean He Can't Sell Things." *New York Times,* August 17.

Boss, Pauline. 1980. "Normative Family Stress: Family Boundary Changes across the Lifespan." *Family Relations* 29:445–52.

———. 1987. "Family Stress." Pp. 695–723 in *Handbook of Marrage and Family,* edited by M.B. Sussman and Suzanne K. Steinmets. New York: Plenum.

———. 1997. "Ambiguity: A Factor in Family Stress Management." University of Minnesota Extension Service (http:// www.extension.umn.edu).

———. 2002. *Family Stress Management.* 2nd ed. Newbury Park, CA: Sage Publications.

———. 2004. "Ambiguous Loss Research, Theory, and Practice: Reflections after 9/11." *Journal of Marriage and Family* 66(3):551–66.

———. 2007. "Ambiguous Loss Theory: Challenges for Scholars and Practitioners." *Family Relations* 56(2):105–111.

Boss, Pauline G., William J. Doherty, Ralph La Rossa, Walter R. Schumm, and Suzanne K. Steinmetz, eds. 1993. *Sourcebook of Family Theories and Methods.* New York: Plenum.

Bossard, James H. and E. S. Boll. 1943. *Family Situations.* Philadelphia, PA: University of Pennsylvania Press.

Bosse, Irina. 1999. "Oxytocin: A Hormone for Love." *Futureframe: International Webzine for Science and Culture.* Retrieved August 30, 2006 (http://www .morgenwelt.de/futureframe/ 9908-oxytocin.htm).

Bost, Kelly K., Martha J. Cox, and Chris Payne. 2002. "Structural and Supportive Changes in Couples' Family and Friendship Networks across the Transition to Parenthood." *Journal of Marriage and Family* 64(2):517–31.

Boston Women's Health Book Collective. 1998. *Our Bodies, Ourselves for the New Century.* New York: Touchstone/Simon and Schuster.

———. 2005. *Our Bodies, Our Selves: A New Edition for a New Era.* New York: Simon and Schuster.

"Both Sexes Are Drawn to Working at Home." 1990. *Wall Street Journal,* May 24.

Bouchard, Emily. N.d. "Navigating Parenting Differences." SelfGrowth.com. Retrieved September 21, 2004. (http:// www.selfgrowth.com/articles/Bouchard2 .html).

Bouchard, Genevieve, Yvan Lussier, and Stephane Sabourin. 1999. "Personality and Marital Adjustment: Utility of the Five-Factor Model of Personality." *Journal of Marriage and Family* 61(3):651–60.

Boushey, Heather. 2005a. "Are Women Opting Out? Debunking the Myth." Briefing Paper. Washington, DC: Center for Economic and Policy Research. November. Retrieved March 28, 2007 (www.cepr.net).

———. 2005b. "'Baby Panic' Book Skews Data, Misses Actual Issue." *Viewpoints,* July 12. Washington, DC: Economic Policy Institute. Retrieved June 16, 2005 (www.epinet.org).

———. 2006. "Are Mothers Really Leaving the Workplace?" Issue Brief. Chicago, IL: Council on Contemporary Families. Retrieved March 28, 2007 (www.contemporaryfamiiles.org).

Bould, Sally. 2003. "Caring Neighborhoods: Bringing Up the Kids Together." *Journal of Family Issues* 24:427–47.

Bouton, Katherine. 1987. "Fertility and Family." *Ms.,* April, p. 92.

Bowen, Gary L., Jay A. Mancini, James A. Martin, William B. Ware, and John P. Nelson. 2003. "Promoting the Adaptation of Military Families: An Empirical Test of a Community Practice Model." *Family Relations* 52(1):33–44.

Bowers v. Hardwick. 1986. 478 U.S. 186, 92 L.Ed.2d 140, 106 S. Ct. 2841.

Bowers, Susan P. 1999. "Gender Role Identity and the Caregiving Experience of Widowed Men." *Sex Roles* 41(9/10):645–55.

Bowlby, John. 1969. *Attachment and Loss.* New York: Basic Books.

———. 1982. *Attachment and Loss.* 2nd ed. New York: BasicBooks.

Bowser, Benjamin P. 1999. "African-American Male Sexuality through the Early Life Course." Pp. 127–50 in *Sexuality across the Life Course,* edited by Alice S. Rossi. Chicago, IL: University of Chicago Press.

"Boys' Academic Slide Calls for Accelerated Attention." 2003. *USA Today,* December 22.

"Boys' Turn: Now *They* Need Help Getting into Colleges." 2006. *USA Today,* April 3.

Bradbury, Thomas N., Frank D. Fincham, and Steven R. H. Beach. 2000. "Research on the Nature and Determinants of Marital Satisfaction: A Decade in Review." *Journal of Marriage and Family* 62(4):964–80.

Bradbury, Thomas N. and Benjamin R. Karney. 2004. "Understanding and Altering the Longitudinal Course of Marriage." *Journal of Marriage and Family* 66(6):862–79.

Bramlett, Matthew D. and William D. Mosher. 2001. "First Marriage Dissolution, Divorce, and Remarriage: United States." *Advance Data from Vital and Health Statistics,* No. 323. Hyattsville, MD: U.S. National Center for Health Statistics.

———. 2002. "Cohabitation, Marriage, Divorce, and Remarriage in the United States." *Vital and Health Statistics* 23(22). Hyattsville, MD: U.S. National Center for Health Statistics. July.

Branden, Nathaniel. 1988. "A Vision of Romantic Love." Pp. 218–31 in *The Psychology of Love,* edited by Robert J. Sternberg and Michael L. Barnes. New Haven, CT: Yale University Press.

———. 1994. *Six Pillars of Self-Esteem.* New York: Bantam.

Brant, Martha and Anna Kuchment. 2006. "The Little One Said 'Roll Over.'" *Newsweek,* May 29, pp. 54–55.

Braschi v. Stahl Associates Company. 1989. 74 N.Y.2d 201.

Bratter, Jenifer L. and Karl Eschbach. 2006. "'What About the Couple?' Interracial Marriage and Psychological Distress." *Social Science Research* 35(4):1025–47.

Braver, Sanford, Jennesa R. Shapiro, and Matthew R. Goodman. 2006. "Consequences of Divorce for Parents." Pp. 313–37 in *Handbook of Divorce and Relationship Dissolution,* edited by Mark A. Fine and John H. Harvey. Mahwah, NJ: Erlbaum.

Braver, Sanford L., Pamela J. Fitzpatrick, and R. Curtis Bay. 1991. "Noncustodial Parent's Report of Child Support Payments." *Family Relations* 40(2):180–85.

Bray, James H. 1999. "From Marriage to Remarriage and Beyond." Pp. 253–71 in *Coping with Divorce, Single Parenting and Remarriage,* edited by E. Mavis Hetherington. Mahwah, NJ: Erlbaum.

Brazelton, T. Berry. 1997. "Building a Better Self-Image." *Newsweek* Special Issue, Spring/Summer, pp. 76–79.

Brazelton, T. Berry, and Stanley Greenspan. 2000. "Our Window to the Future." *Newsweek* Special Issue, Fall/Winter, pp. 34–36.

Brehm, Sharon S., Rowland S. Miller, Daniel Perlman, and Susan M. Campbell. 2002. *Intimate Relationships.* 3rd ed. New York: McGraw-Hill.

Breitenbecher, Kimberly Hanson. 2006. "The Relationships among Self-blame, Psychological Distress, and Sexual Victimization." *Journal of Interpersonal Violence* 21(5):597–611.

Brennan, Bridget. 2003. "No Time. No Sex. No Money." *First Years and Forever: A Monthly Online Newsletter for Marriages in the Early Years.* Chicago, IL: Archdiocese of Chicago, Family Ministries. Retrieved September 8, 2006 (http://www .familyministries.org).

Brennan, Robert T., Rosalind Chait Barnett, and Karen C. Gareis. 2001. "When He Earns More Than She Does: A Longitudinal Study of Dual Earner Couples." *Journal of Marriage and Family* 63:168–80.

Brenner, N., L. Kann, R. Lowry, H. Wechsler, and L. Romero. 2006. "Trends in HIV-related Risk Behaviors among High School Students—United States, 1991–2005." *Morbidity and Mortality Weekly Review* 55(31):851–54.

Brewster, Karin L. and Irene Padavic. 2002. "No More Kin Care? Change in Black Mothers' Reliance on Relatives for Child Care, 1977–94." *Gender and Society* 16:546–63.

Brickley, Margie, Aimee Gelnaw, Hilary Marsh, and Daniel Ryan. 1999. "Opening Doors: Lesbian and Gay Parents and Schools." Educational Advocacy Committee of the Family Pride Coalition (http://www.familypride.org).

Brines, Julie. 1994. "Economic Dependency, Gender, and the Division of Labor at Home." *American Journal of Sociology* 100(3):652–88.

Brinig, Margaret F. and Douglas W. Allen. 2000. "'These Boots Are Made for Walking': Why Most Divorce Filers Are Women." *American Law and Economics Review* 2(1):126–69.

Britz, Jennifer Delahunty. 2006. "To All the Girls I've Rejected." *New York Times,* March 23.

Broder, John M. 2006. "Immigrants and the Economics of Hard Work." *The Nation,* April 2.

Broderick, Carlfred B. 1979a. *Couples: How to Confront Problems and Maintain Loving Relationships.* New York: Simon and Schuster.

———. 1979b. *Marriage and the Family.* Englewood Cliffs, NJ: Prentice Hall.

———. 1993. *Understanding Family Process: Basics of Family Systems Theory.* Thousand Oaks, CA: Sage Publications.

Brodie, Deborah. 1999. *Untying the Knot: Ex-Husbands, Ex-Wives, and Other Experts on the Passage of Divorce.* New York: St. Martin's Griffin.

Brodkin, Adele M. 2006. *Raising Happy and Successful Kids: A Guide for Parents.* New York: Scholastic Books.

Brody, Jane E. 2001. "V.I.P. Medical Treatment Adds Meaning to a Dog's (or Cat's) Life." *New York Times,* August 14.

———. 2003a. "Adoptions from Afar: Rewards and Challenges." *New York Times,* July 22.

———. 2003b. "Empowering Children to Thwart Abductors." *New York Times,* January 28.

———. 2004. "Abstinence-Only: Does It Work?" *New York Times,* June 3.

Brodzinsky, David M., Daniel. W. Smith, and Anne B. Brodzinsky. 1998. *Children's Adjustment to Adoption.* Thousand Oaks, CA: Sage Publications.

Bronfenbrenner, Urie. 1979. *The Ecology of Human Development: Experiments by Nature and Design.* Cambridge, MA: Harvard University Press.

Bronson, Po and Ashley Merryman. 2006. "Has Being Married Gone Out of Style?" *Time,* October 18. Retrieved November 8, 2006 (http://www.time.com).

Brooke, Jill. 2002. "A Promise to Love, Honor, and Bear No Children." *New York Times,* October 13.

———. 2004. "Close Encounters with a Home Barely Known." *New York Times,* July 22.

———. 2006. "Home Alone Together." *New York Times,* May 4. Retrieved May 7, 2006 (http://www.nytimes.com).

Brooks, Clem. 2002. "Religious Influence and the Politics of Family Decline Concern: Trends, Sources, and U.S. Political Behavior." *American Sociological Review* 67:191–211.

Brooks, David. 2004. "The New Red-Diaper Babies." *New York Times,* December 7.

———. 2006. "Immigrants to Be Proud Of." *New York Times,* March 30.

Brooks, Robert and Sam Goldstein. 2001. *Raising Resilient Children: Fostering Strength, Hope, and Optimism in Your Child.* New York: Contemporary Books.

Broome, Claire V. 1995. "Change in the Marriage and Divorce Data Available from the National Center for Health Statistics." *Federal Register* 60, No. 241: 64437–38.

Brotherson, Sean. 2003. "Time, Sex, and Money: Challenges in Early Marriage." *The Meridian.* Retrieved September 8, 2006 (http://www.meridianmagazine .com).

Brown, Dave and Phil Waugh. 2004. *Covenant vs. Contract.* New York: Franklin, Son Publishers.

Brown, David. 2002. "Studies: Test-Tube Babies Face Higher Health Risks." *Washington Post,* March 7.

Brown, Jocelyn, Patricia Cohen, Jeffrey G. Johnson, and Suzanne Salzinger. 1998. "A Longitudinal Analysis of Risk Factors for Child Maltreatment: Findings of a

17-Year Prospective Study of Officially Recorded and Self-reported Child Abuse and Neglect." *Child Abuse & Neglect* 22(11):1065–78.

Brown, Pamela D., K. Daniel O'Leary, and Shari R. Feldbau. 1997. "Dropout in a Treatment Program for Self-referring Wife Abusing Men." *Journal of Family Violence* 12(4):365–87.

Brown, Patricia Leigh. 2001. "Heavy Lifting Required: The Return of Manly Men." *New York Times,* October 28.

——. 2004. "For Children of Gays, Marriage Brings Joy." *New York Times,* March 19.

——. 2006. "Supporting Boys or Girls When the Line Isn't Clear." *New York Times,* December 4.

Brown, Susan L. 2000. "Fertility Following Marital Dissolution: The Role of Cohabitation." *Journal of Family Issues* 21:501–24.

——. 2004. "Family Structure and Child Well-Being: The Significance of Parental Cohabitation." *Journal of Marriage and Family* 66(2):351–67.

Brownell, Patricia J. 1998. *Family Crimes against the Elderly: Elder Abuse and the Criminal Justice System.* New York: Taylor and Francis.

Browning, Christopher R. and Edward O. Laumann. 1997. "Sexual Contact between Children and Adults: A Life Course Perspective." *American Sociological Review* 62:540–60.

Browning, Christopher R., Tama Leventhal, and Jeanne Brooks-Gunn. 2005. "Sexual Initiation in Early Adolescence: The Nexus of Parental and Community Control." *American Sociological Review* 70(5):758–79.

Brownridge, Douglas A. and Shiva Halli. 2002. "Understanding Male Partner Violence against Cohabiting and Married Women: An Empirical Investigation with a Synthesized Model." *Journal of Family Violence* 17(4):341–61.

Brubaker, Ellie, Mary Anne Gorman, and Michele Hiestand. 1990. "Stress Perceived by Elderly Recipients of Family Care." Pp. 267–81 in *Family Relationships in Later Life,* 2nd ed., edited by Timothy H. Brubaker. Newbury Park, CA: Sage Publications.

Brubaker, Timothy H. 1991. "Families in Later Life: A Burgeoning Research Area." Pp. 226–48 in *Contemporary Families: Looking Forward, Looking Back,* edited by

Alan Booth. Minneapolis, MN: National Council on Family Relations.

Bruno, Beth. 2001. "A New National Holiday: Stepparents Day." SelfGrowth. com (http://www.selfgrowth.com/articles/Bruno1.html).

Bryant, Adam. 2001. "Drowning in a Sea of Debt." *Newsweek,* February 5, p. 43.

Bubolz, Margaret M. and M. Suzanne Sontag. 1993. "Human Ecology Theory." Pp. 419–48 in *Sourcebook of Family Theories and Methods: A Contextual Approach,* edited by Pauline G. Boss, William J. Doherty, Ralph LaRossa, Walter R. Schumm, and Suzanne K. Steinmetz. New York: Plenum.

Buchanan, Christy M., Eleanor E. Maccoby, and Sanford M. Dornbusch. 1996. *Adolescents After Divorce.* Cambridge, MA: Harvard University Press.

Buchanan, Wyatt. 2006a. "Catholic Charity Might Stop Adoptions, Vatican Prohibits Placement with Same-sex Couples." *San Francisco Chronicle,* March 11.

——. 2006b. "Poll Finds U.S. Warming to Gay Marriage." *San Francisco Chronicle,* March 23.

Budig, Michelle J. and Paula England. 2001. "The Wage Penalty for Motherhood." *American Sociological Review* 66:204–55.

Buehler, Cheryl. 1995. "Divorce Law in the United States." Pp. 99–120 in *Families and Law,* edited by Lisa J. McIntyre and Marvin B. Sussman. New York: Haworth.

Buehler, Cheryl and Jean M. Gerard. 2002. "Marital Conflict, Ineffective Parenting, and Children's and Adolescents' Maladjustment." *Journal of Marriage and Family* 64(1):78–92.

Buehler, Cheryl, Ambika Krishnakumar, Gaye Stone, Christine Anthony, Sharon Pemberton, Jean Gerard, and Brian K. Barber. 1998. "Interpersonal Conflict Styles and Youth Problem Behaviors." *Journal of Marriage and Family* 60(1):119–32.

Bukhari, Zahid Hussain. 2004. *Muslims' Place in the American Public Square: Hope, Fears, and Aspirations.* Walnut Creek, CA: AltaMira.

Bulanda, Ronald E. 2004. "Paternal Involvement with Children: Influence of Gender Ideologies." *Journal of Marriage and Family* 66(1):40–45.

Bulcroft, Kris, Linda Smeins, and Richard Bulcroft. 1999. *Romancing the Honeymoon:*

Consummating Marriage in Modern Society. Thousand Oaks, CA: Sage Publications.

Bulcroft, Richard. 2000. "The Management and Production of Risk in Romantic Relationships: A Postmodern Paradox." *Journal of Family History* 25(1):63–92.

Bulcroft, Richard and Jay Teachman. 2004. "Ambiguous Constructions: Development of a Childless or Child-free Life Course." Pp. 116–35 in *Handbook of Contemporary Families: Considering the Past; Contemplating the Future,* edited by Marilyn Coleman and Lawrence H. Ganong. Thousand Oaks, CA: Sage Publications.

Bumpass, Larry L. and Hsien-Hen Lu. 2000. "Trends in Cohabitation and Implications for Children's Family Contexts in the United States." *Population Studies* 54:29–41.

Bumpass, Larry L., James A. Sweet, and Andrew Cherlin. 1991. "The Role of Cohabitation in Declining Rates of Marriage." *Journal of Marriage and Family* 53(4):913–27.

Bunker, Barbara B., Josephine M. Zubek, Virginia J. Vanderslice, and Robert W. Rice. 1992. "Quality of Life in Dual-career Families: Commuting versus Single-residence Couples." *Journal of Marriage and Family* 54(3):399–407.

Burbach, Mary and Mary Ann Lamanna. 2000. "The Moral Mother: Motherhood Discourse in Biological Father and Third Party Cases." *Journal of Law and Family Studies* 2:153–97.

Burch, Rebecca and Gordon G. Gallup, Jr. 2004. "Pregnancy as a Stimulus for Domestic Violence." *Journal of Family Violence* 19:243–47.

Burchard, Glenice A., Mark A. Yarhouse, Marcus K. Killian, Everett L. Worthington, Jr., Jack W. Berry, and David E. Canter. 2003. "A Study of Two Marital Enrichment Programs and Couples' Quality of Life." *Journal of Psychology and Theology* 31(3):240–53.

Burgess, Ernest and Harvey Locke. [1945] 1953. *The Family: From Institution to Companionship.* New York: American.

Burkett, Elinor. 2000. *The Baby Boon: How Family-friendly America Cheats the Childless.* New York: Free Press.

Burke, Peter J. and Alicia D. Cast. 1997. "Stability and Change in the Gender Identities of Newly Married Couples." *Social Psychology Quarterly* 60(4):277–90.

Burke, Tod W. and Stephen S. Owen. 2006. "Same-sex Domestic Violence: Is Anyone Listening?" *Gay and Lesbian Review Worldwide* 13(1):6–7.

Burney, Lucy. 2005. *Boost Your Child's Immune System: A Program and Recipes for Raising Strong, Healthy Kids.* New York: Newmarket Press.

Burney, Robert. 1995. "Learning to Love Our Self." Retrieved August 16, 2006 (http://www.silcom.com/~joy2meu/loveself.html).

Burns, A. and R. Homel. 1989. "Gender Division of Tasks by Parents and Their Children." *Psychology of Women Quarterly* 13:113–25.

Burpee, Leslie C. and Ellen J. Langer. 2005. "Mindfulness and Marital Satisfaction." *Journal of Adult Development* 12(1):1281–87.

Burr, Jeffrey A. and Jan E. Mutchler. 1999. "Race and Ethnic Variation in Norms of Filial Responsibility among Older Persons." *Journal of Marriage and Family* 61(3):674–87.

Burr, Wesley R., Shirley Klein, and Marilyn McCubbin. 1995. "Reexamining Family Stress: New Theory and Research." *Journal of Marriage and Family* 57(3):835–46.

Burt, Marla S. and Roger B. Burt. 1996. *Stepfamilies: The Step by Step Model of Brief Therapy.* New York: Brunner/Mazel.

Burt, Sandra and Linda Perlis. 2006. *Raising a Successful Child: Discover and Nurture Your Child's Talents.* Berkeley, CA: Ulysses/Enfield Publishers Group.

Buscaglia, Leo. 1982. *Living, Loving, and Learning.* New York: Holt, Rinehart & Winston.

Bush, George W. 2003. "Marriage Protection Week, 2003." The White House. Retrieved October 12, 2006 (http://www.whitehouse.gov/news/releases).

Bushman, Brad J. and Roy F. Baumeister. 1998. "Threatened Egoism, Narcissism, Self-esteem, and Direct and Displaced Aggression: Does Self-love or Self-hate Lead to Violence?" *Journal of Personality and Social Psychology* 75(1):219–30.

Buss, D. M., Todd K. Shackelford, Lee A. Kirkpatrick, and Randy J. Larsen. 2001. "A Half Century of Mate Preferences: The Cultural Evolution of Values." *Journal of Marriage and Family* 63(2):491–503.

Bussey, K. and A. Bandura. 1999. "Social Cognitive Theory of Gender Development and Differentiation." *Psychological Review* 106:676–713.

Butler, Amy C. 2005. "Gender Differences in the Prevalence of Same-sex Sexual Partnering: 1998–2002." *Social Forces* 84(1):421–39.

Butler, Judith. 1990. *Gender Trouble: Feminism and the Subversion of Identity.* New York: Routledge.

Butler, Katy. 2006a. "Beyond Rivalry: A Hidden World of Sibling Violence." *New York Times,* February 28.

———. 2006b. "Many Couples Must Negotiate Terms of 'Brokeback' Marriages." *New York Times,* March 7.

Butz, Tim. 2004. "Marital Amendment Would Discriminate." *Omaha World-Herald,* March 12.

Buunk, Bram and Wim Mutsaers. 1999. "Equity Perceptions and Marital Satisfaction in Former and Current Marriage: A Study among the Remarried." *Journal of Social and Personal Relationships* 16(1):123–32.

Buzawa, Eve S. and Carl G. Buzawa. 1990. *Domestic Violence: The Criminal Justice Response.* Newbury Park, CA: Sage Publications.

Byers, E. Sandra. 2005. "Relationship Satisfaction and Sexual Satisfaction: A Longitudinal Study of Individuals in Long-term Relationships." *Journal of Sex Research* 42(2):113–18.

Bynum, Mia Smith and Gene H. Brody. 2005. "Coping Behaviors, Parenting, and Perceptions of Children's Internalizing and Externalizing Problems in Rural African American Mothers." *Family Relations* 54(1):58–71.

Caldera, Y. M., A. C. Huston, and M. O'Brien. 1989. "Social Interactions and Play Patterns of Parents and Toddlers with Feminine, Masculine, and Neutral Toys." *Child Development* 60:70–76.

Caldwell, John. 1982. *Theory of Fertility Decline.* London, England: Academic Press.

Call, Vaughn, Susan Sprecher, and Pepper Schwartz. 1995. "The Incidence and Frequency of Marital Sex in a National Sample." *Journal of Marriage and Family* 57(3):639–52.

Campbell, Bernadette, E. Glenn Schellenberg, and Charlene Y. Senn. 1997. "Evaluating Measures of Contemporary Sexism." *Psychology of Women Quarterly* 1(1):89–102.

Campbell, Kim. 2004. "Men Decide It's Never Too Late to Have Kids." *Christian Science Monitor.* September 1.

Campbell, Mary. 2002. "What About the Children? The Psychological and Social Well-being of Multiracial Adolescents." Presented at the annual meeting of the American Sociological Association, August, Chicago, IL.

Campbell, Ross and Rob Suggs. 2006. *How to Really Parent Your Teenager: Raising Balanced Teens in an Unbalanced World.* Nashville, TN: W Publishing Group.

Campbell, Susan. 1991. "Male Day-Care Workers Face Prejudice." *Omaha World-Herald,* July 14.

———. 2004. *Truth in Dating: Finding Love by Getting Real.* Tiburon, CA: H. J. Kramer/New World Library.

Campbell, W. Keith. 2005. *When You Love a Man Who Loves Himself.* Naperville, IL: Sourcebooks.

Campbell, W. Keith, Craig A. Foster, and Eli J. Finkel. 2002. "Does Self-love Lead to Love for Others? A Story of Narcissistic Game Playing." *Journal of Personality and Social Psychology* 83(2):340–54.

Canary, D. J. and K. Dindia. 1998. *Sex Differences and Similarities in Communication.* Mahwah, NJ: Erlbaum.

Canary, D. J. and Tara M. Emmers-Sommer. 1997. *Sex and Gender Differences in Personal Relationships.* New York: Guilford.

Canavan, Margaret M., Walter J. Meyer III, and Deborah C. Higgs. 1992. "The Female Experience of Sibling Incest." *Journal of Marital and Family Therapy* 18(2):129–42.

Cancian, Francesca M. 1985. "Gender Politics: Love and Power in the Private and Public Spheres." Pp. 253–64 in *Gender and the Life Course,* edited by Alice S. Rossi. New York: Aldine.

———. 1987. *Love in America: Gender and Self-Development.* New York: Cambridge University Press.

Cancian, Francesca M. and Stacey J. Oliker. 2000. *Caring and Gender.* Walnut Creek, CA: AltaMira.

Canedy, Dana. 2001. "Often Conflicted, Hispanic Girls Are Dropping Out at High Rates." *New York Times,* March 25.

Cantor, M. H. 1979. "Neighbors and Friends: An Overlooked Resource in the Informal Support System." *Research on Aging* 1:434–63.

Caputo, Richard K. 2001. "Grandparents and Coresident Grandchildren in a Youth Cohort." *Journal of Family Issues* 22(5):541–56.

———. 2005. "Editor's Introduction: Challenges of Aging on U.S. Families: Policy and Practice Implications." *Marriage and Family Review* 37(1/2):3–6.

Carasso, Adam and C. Eugene Steuerle. 2005. "The Hefty Penalty on Marriage Facing Many Households with Children." *The Future of Children* 15(2):157–75.

Carey v. Population Services International. 1977. 431 U.S. 678, 52 L.Ed.2d 675, 97 S. Ct. 2010.

Carey, Benedict. 2004. "Long after Kinsey, Only the Brave Study Sex." *New York Times,* November 9.

———. 2007. "Study Finds Rise in Behavior Problems after Significant Time in Child Care." *New York Times,* March 26.

Carlson, Darren K. 2001. "Over Half of Americans Believe in Love at First Sight." Poll Releases. February 14. Retrieved August 20, 2006 (http://www.gallup.com/poll/releases).

Carlson, Marcia J. 2006. "Family Structure, Father Involvement, and Adolescent Behavior Outcomes." *Journal of Marriage and Family* 68(1):137–54.

Carlson, Marcia J. and Frank F. Furstenberg, Jr. 2006. "The Prevalence and Correlates of Multipartnered Fertility among Urban U.S. Parents." *Journal of Marriage and Family* 68(3):718–32.

Carnoy, Martin and David Carnoy. 1995. *Fathers of a Certain Age: The Joys and Problems of Middle-aged Fatherhood.* Minneapolis, MN: Fairview Press.

Carr, Deborah. 2004. "The Desire to Date and Remarry among Older Widows and Widowers." *Journal of Marriage and Family* 66(4):1051–68.

Carroll, Jason S., Sarah Badger, and Chongming Yang. 2006. "The Ability to Negotiate or the Ability to Love? Evaluating the Developmental Domains of Marital Competence." *Journal of Family Issues* 27(7):1001–32.

Carroll, Jason S., Chad D. Olson, and Nicolle Buckmiller. 2007. "Family Boundary Ambiguity: A 30-Year Review of Theory, Research, and Measurement." *Family Relations* 56(2):210–30.

Carroll, Joseph. 2005. "Society's Moral Boundaries Expand Somewhat This Year." *Public Opinion 2005.* May 16. Retrieved March 2, 2007 (www.gallup.com).

———. 2006. "One in Four Americans Think Most Mormons Endorse Polygamy." The Gallup Poll. September

7. Retrieved September 8, 2006 (http://www.galluppoll.com).

Carter, Betty. 1991. "Children's TV, Where Boys Are King." *New York Times,* May 1, pp. A1, C18.

Carter, Betty and Monica McGoldrick. 1988. *The Changing Family Life Cycle: A Framework for Family Therapy.* 2nd ed. New York: Gardner.

———, 1999. "The Divorce Cycle: A Major Variation in the American Family Life Cycle." Pp. 373–80 in *The Expanded Life Cycle: Individual, Family, and Social Perspectives,* 3rd ed., edited by Betty Carter and Monica McGoldrick. Boston, MA: Allyn and Bacon.

Carter, Steven. 2001. *This Is How Love Works: 9 Essential Secrets You Need to Know.* New York: M. Evans.

Cartmell, Todd. 2006. *Respectful Kids: The Complete Guide to Bringing Out the Best in Your Child.* Colorado Springs, CO: NavPress.

Case, Anne, I-Fen Lin, and Sara McLanahan. 2000. "How Hungry Is the Selfish Gene?" *The Economic Journal* 110(October):781–804.

Casper, Lynne M. and Suzanne M. Bianchi. 2002. *Continuity and Change in the American Family.* Thousand Oaks, CA: Sage Publications.

Casper, Lynne M. and Martin O'Connell. 1998. "Work, Income, the Economy, and Married Fathers as Child-care Providers." *Demography* 35(2):243–50.

Casper, Lynne M. and Kristen E. Smith. 2002. "Dispelling the Myths: Self-care, Class, and Race." *Journal of Family Issues* 23:716–27.

Castro Martin, Teresa. 2002. "Consensual Unions in Latin America: Persistence of a Dual Nuptiality System." *Journal of Comparative Family Studies* 33(1):35–56.

Castro Martin, Teresa and Larry Bumpass. 1989. "Trends in Marital Disruption." *Demography* 26:37–52.

Catalano, Shannan. 2006. *Intimate Partner Violence in the United States.* Washington, DC: U.S. Bureau of Justice Statistics. December 28. Retrieved January 9, 2007 (www.ojp.usdog.gov/bjs).

Cave, Damien. 2006. "New York Plans to Make Gender Personal Choice." *New York Times,* November 7.

Ceballo, Rosario, Jennifer E. Lansford, Antonia Abbey, and Abigail J. Stewart. 2004. "Gaining a Child: Comparing

the Experiences of Biological Parents, Adoptive Parents, and Stepparents." *Family Relations* 53(1):38–48.

Center for the Advancement of Women. 2003. "Progress and Perils: New Agenda for Women." (www.advancewomen.org).

Center for the Improvement of Child Caring. N.d. "Systematic Training for Effective Parenting Programs." Retrieved February 12, 2007 (http://www.ciccparenting.org).

Chabot, Jennifer M. and Barbara D. Ames. 2004. "'It Wasn't "Let's Get Pregnant and Go Do It"': Decision Making in Lesbian Couples Planning Motherhood Via Donor Insemination." *Family Relations* 53(4):348–56.

Chadiha, Letha A., Jane Rafferty, and Joseph Pickard. 2003. "The Influence of Caregiving Stressors, Social Support, and Caregiving Appraisal on Marital Functioning among African American Wife Caregivers." *Journal of Marital and Family Therapy* 29(4):479–90.

Chadwick, Alex. 2005. "Homosexual Policy Could Divide Anglican Church." National Public Radio. Retrieved March 31, 2006 (http://www.npr.org).

Chafetz, Janet Saltzman. 1989. "Marital Intimacy and Conflict: The Irony of Spousal Equality." Pp. 149–56 in *Women: A Feminist Perspective,* 4th ed., edited by Jo Freeman. Mountain View, CA: Mayfield.

Chan, Raymond W., Barbara Raboy, and Charlotte J. Patterson. 1998. "Psychosocial Adjustment among Children Conceived Via Donor Insemination by Lesbian and Heterosexual Mothers." *Child Development* 69:443–57.

Chandra, Anjani, Gladys M. Martinez, William D. Mosher, Joyce C. Abma, and Jo Jones. 2005. "Fertility, Family Planning, and Reproductive Health of U.S. Women: Data from the 2002 National Survey of Family Growth." *Vital and Health Statistics* 23(25). Hyattsville, MD: U.S. National Center for Health Statistics. December.

Chandra, Anjani, Joyce Abma, Penelope Maza, and Christine Bachrach. 1999. "Adoption, Adoption Seeking, and Relinquishment for Adoption in the United States." *Advance Data* No. 306. May 11. Hyattsville, MD: U.S. National Center for Health Statistics.

Chandra, Anjani and Elizabeth Hervey Stephen. 1998. "Impaired Fecundity in the United States: 1982–1995." *Family Planning Perspectives* 30(1):35–42.

Chao, R. K. 1994. "Beyond Parental Control and Authoritarian Parenting Style: Understanding Chinese Parenting through the Cultural Notion of Training." *Child Development* 65(4):1111–19.

Chappell, Crystal Lee Hyun Joo. 1996. "Korean-American Adoptees Organize for Support." *Minneapolis Star Tribune,* December 29, p. E7.

"Chart: State Marriage License and Blood Test Requirements." 2006. Nolo. Retrieved September 7, 2006 (http://www.nolo.com).

Chatzky, Jeann. 2006. "Just When You Thought It Was Safe to Retire. . . . " CNN Money.com. September 21. Retrieved October 29, 2006 (http://money.cnn.com).

Cherlin, Andrew J. 1978. "Remarriage as Incomplete Institution." *American Journal of Sociology* 84:634–50.

———. 1996. *Public and Private Families.* New York: McGraw-Hill.

———. 1999. "Going to Extremes: Family Structure, Children's Well-being, and Social Science." *Demography* 36:421–28.

———. 2000. "Generation Ex-." *The Nation,* December 11 (www.thenation.com).

———. 2003. "Should the Government Promote Marriage?" Contexts 2(4):22–29.

———. 2004. "The Deinstitutionalization of American Marriage." *Journal of Marriage and Family* 66(4):848–61.

———. 2005. "American Marriage in the Early Twenty-First Century." *The Future of Children* 15(2):33–55.

Cherlin, Andrew J., Linda M. Burton, Tera R. Hurt, and Diane M. Purvin. 2004. "The Influence of Physical and Sexual Abuse on Marriage and Cohabitation." *American Sociological Review* 69(6):768–90.

Cherlin, Andrew J. and Frank F. Furstenberg, Jr. 1986. *The New American Grandparent: A Place in the Family, a Life Apart.* New York: BasicBooks.

———. 1994. "Stepfamilies in the United States: A Reconsideration." *Annual Review of Sociology* 20:359–81.

Chesler, Phyllis. 2005 [1972]. *Women and Madness.* New York: Palgrave/Macmillan.

Child Abuse Prevention Council of Sacramento. N.d. "About Child Abuse: Cultural Customs." Retrieved May 5, 2007 (www.capcsac.org).

Child Support Amendments. 1984. Public Law 98-378. Washington, DC: U.S. Congress.

"Child Support Collected: DHHS Press Release." 1995. Family Law List. lawlib.wuacc.edu).

Children's Defense Fund. 1998. *The State of America's Children, Yearbook 1998.* Washington, DC: CDF.

Childress, Sarah. 2003. "9/11's Hidden Toll." *Newsweek,* August 4, p. 37.

———. 2006. "Fighting Over the Kids." *Newsweek,* September 25, p. 35.

Childress, Sarah and Dirk Johnson. 2004. "The Hot Sound of Hate." *Newsweek,* November 21.

Chipungu, Sandra Stukes and Tricia B. Bent-Goodley. 2004. "Meeting the Challenges of Contemporary Foster Care." *The Future of Children* 14(1):75–93.

Chira, Susan. 1994. "Hispanic Families Avoid Using Day Care, Study Says." *New York Times,* April 6.

Chodorow, Nancy. 1978. *The Reproduction of Mothering: Psychoanalysis and the Sociology of Gender.* Berkeley, CA: University of California Press.

Choi, Namkee G. 1992. "Correlates of the Economic Status of Widowed and Divorced Elderly Women." *Journal of Family Issues* 13(1):38–54.

Choice, Pamela and Leanne K. Lamke. 1997. "A Conceptual Approach to Understanding Abused Women's Stay/Leave Decisions." *Journal of Family Issues* 18:290–314.

Christakis, Nicholas A. and Paul D. Allison. 2006. "Mortality After the Hospitalization of a Spouse." *New England Journal of Medicine* 354(7):719–30.

Christensen, Andrew and Neil Jacobson. 1999. *Reconcilable Differences.* London, England: Guilford.

Christensen, Kathleen E. and Graham L. Staines. 1990. "FlexTime: A Viable Solution to Work/Family Conflict?" *Journal of Family Issues* 11(4) 455–76.

Christiansen, Shawn L. and Rob Palkovitz. 2001. "Why the 'Good Provider' Role Still Matters: Providing as a Form of Paternal Involvement." *Journal of Family Issues* 22:84–106.

Christopher, F. Scott and Susan Sprecher. 2000. "Sexuality in Marriage, Dating, and Other Relationships." *Journal of Marriage and Family* 62:999–1017.

Christopherson, Brian. 2006. "Some Buck Trends, Marry Before Finishing College." *Lincoln Journal Star,* October 3. Retrieved October 4, 2006 (http://www.journalstar.com).

Chung, Juliet. 2006. "Hispanic Paradox: Income May Be Lower but Health Better Than Most." *Seattle Times,* August 29. Retrieved February 12, 2007 (www.seattletimes.com).

Ciabattari, Teresa. 2004. "Cohabitation and Housework: The Effects of Marital Intentions." *Journal of Marriage and Family* 66(1):118–125.

Ciaramigoli, Arthur P. and Katherine Ketcham. 2000. *The Power of Empathy: A Practical Guide to Creating Intimacy, Self-Understanding, and Lasting Love in Your Life.* New York: Dutton.

Cicirelli, Victor G. 2000. "An Examination of the Trajectory of the Adult Child's Caregiving for an Elderly Parent." *Family Relations* 49(2):169–75.

Clark-Ibanez, Marisol and Diane Felmlee. 2004. "Interethnic Relationships: The Role of Social Network Diversity." *Journal of Marriage and Family* 66(2):293–305.

Clarke, L. 2005. "Remarriage in Later Life: Older Women's Negotiation of Power, Resources, and Domestic Labor." *Journal of Women and Aging* 17(4):21–41.

Clarke, Sally C. 1995. "Advance Report of Final Marriage Statistics, 1989 and 1990." *Monthly Vital Statistics Report* 43(12), July 14. Washington, DC: U.S. Department of Health and Human Services, National Center for Health Statistics.

Claxton-Oldfield, Stephen. 2003. "Child Abuse in Stepfather Families." *Journal of Divorce and Remarriage* 40(1):17–35.

Claxton-Oldfield, Stephen, Carla Goodyear, Tina Parsons, and Jane Claxton-Oldfield. 2002. "Some Possible Implications of Negative Stepfather Stereotypes." *Journal of Divorce and Remarriage* Spring-Summer: 77–89.

Clayton, Obie and Joan Moore. 2003. "The Effects of Crime and Imprisonment on Family Formation." Pp. 84–102 in *Black Fathers in Contemporary American Society: Strengths, Weaknesses, and Strategies for Change,* edited by Obie Clayton, Ronald B. Mincy, and David Blankenhorn. New York: Russell Sage.

Clements, Mari L., Scott M. Stanley, and Howard J. Markman. 2004. "Before They Said 'I Do': Discriminating among Marital Outcomes over 13 Years." *Journal of Marriage and Family* 66(3):613–26.

Clemetson, Lynette. 2006a. "Adopted in China: Seeking Identity in America." *New York Times,* March 23.

————. 2006b. "Breaking the Biology Barrier." *New York Times,* August 30.

————. 2006c. "Weekends with Dad, Courtesy of D.S.L." *New York Times,* March 19.

————. 2007. "Working on Overhaul, Russia Halts Adoption Applications." *New York Times,* April 12.

Clemetson, Lynette and Ron Nixon. 2006. "Overcoming Adoption's Racial Barriers." *New York Times,* August 17.

Clifford, Annette. 2006. "Parent—Job Description." *Florida Today Newspaper,* Melbourne, FL. Retrieved February 26, 2007 (http://interioroffice.wordpress. com/mom-job-description).

Clinton, Hillary Rodham. 1990. "In France, Day Care Is Every Child's Right." *New York Times,* April 7.

Cloud, Henry and John Sims Townsend. 2005. *Rescue Your Love Life: Changing Those Dumb Attitudes and Behaviors That Will Sink Your Marriage.* Nashville, TN: Integrity Publishers.

Cloud, John. 2007. "Busy Is O.K." *Time,* January 29, p. 51.

Coan, James A. and John M. Gottman. 2007. "Sampling, Experimental Control, and Generalizability in the Study of Marital Process Models." *Journal of Marriage and Family* 69(1):73–80.

Cobb, Nathan P., Jeffry H. Larson, and Wendy L. Watson. 2003. "Development of the Attitudes about Romance and Mate Selection Scale." *Family Relations* 52(3):222–31.

Coburn, Jennifer. 1999. "Motherhood a Key Feminist Issue." *Omaha World-Herald,* April 9.

Cochran, Susan D. and Vicki M. Mays. 1999. "Sociocultural Factors in the Black Gay Male Experience." Pp. 349–56 in *The Black Family: Essays and Studies,* 6th ed., edited by Robert Staples. Belmont, CA: Wadsworth.

Coffman, Ginger and Carol Markstrom-Adams. 1995. "A Model for Parent Education among Incarcerated Adults." Presented at the annual meeting of the National Council on Family Relations, November 15–19, Portland, OR.

Cogan, Rosemary and Bud C. Ballinger III. 2006. "Alcohol Problems and the Differentiation of Partner, Stranger, and General Violence." *Journal of Interpersonal Violence* 21(7):924–35.

Cohan, Catherine L., Alan Booth, and Douglas Granger. 2003. "Gender Moderates the Relationship between Testosterone and Marital Interaction." *Journal of Family Psychology* 17(1):29–40.

Cohan, Catherine L. and Stacey Kleinbaum. 2002. "Toward a Greater Understanding of the Cohabitation Effect: Premarital Cohabitation and Marital Communication." *Journal of Marriage and Family* 64(1):180–92.

Cohen, Patricia. 2007a. "As Ethics Panels Expand Grip, No Research Field Is Off Limits." *New York Times,* February 28.

Cohen, Patricia. 2007b. "Signs of Détente in the Battle between Venus and Mars." *New York Times,* May 31.

Cohen, Philip N. and Lynne M. Casper. 2002. "In Whose Home? Multigenerational Families in the United States, 1998–2000." *Sociological Perspectives* 45(1):1–20.

Cohen, Robin A. and Barbara Bloom. 2005. "Trends in Health Insurance and Access to Medical Care for Children under Age 19 Years: United States, 1998–2003." *Advance Data from Vital and Health Statistics,* No. 355. Hyattsville, MD: U.S. National Center for Health Statistics.

Cohen, Susan Phillips. 2002. "Can Pets Function as Family Members?" *Western Journal of Nursing Research* 24(6):621–38.

"Cohousing in Today's Real Estate Market." 2006. *Cohousing Magazine.* The Cohousing Association of the United States. Retrieved October 3, 2006 (http://www.cohousing.org).

Cole, Harriette. 1993. *Jumping the Broom: The African-American Wedding Planner.* New York: Henry Holt.

Cole, Thomas. 1983. "The 'Enlightened' View of Aging." *Hastings Center Report* 13:34–40.

Coleman, Marilyn and Lawrence H. Ganong. 1997. "Stepfamilies from the Stepfamily's Perspective." Pp. 107–22 in *Stepfamilies: History, Research, and Policy,* edited by Irene Levin and Marvin B. Sussman. New York: Haworth.

Coleman, Marilyn, Lawrence H. Ganong, and Susan M. Cable. 1997. "Beliefs about Women's Intergenerational Family Obligations to Provide Support Before and After Divorce and Remarriage." *Journal of Marriage and Family* 59(1):165–76.

Coleman, Marilyn, Lawrence H. Ganong, and Mark Fine. 2000. "Reinvestigating Remarriage: Another Decade of Progress." *Journal of Marriage and Family* 62:1288–1307.

Coleman, Priscilla and Anne Watson. 2000. "Infant Attachment as a Dynamic System." *Human Development* 43:295–313.

Coles, Clifton. 2004. "Odd Working Hours Cause Family Stress: Need for Night and Weekend Shift Workers Continues to Rise." *The Futurist* 38(3):9–10.

Coles, Roberta L. 2006. *Race and Family: A Structural Approach.* Thousand Oaks, CA: Sage Publications.

Coll, Cynthia and Laura A. Szalacha. 2004. "The Multiple Contexts of Middle Childhood." *The Future of Children* 14(2):81–97.

Collaborative Group on Hormonal Factors in Breast Cancer. 2004. "Breast Cancer and Abortion: Collaborative Reanalysis of Data from 53 Epidemiological Studies, Including 83,000 Women with Breast Cancer from 16 Countries." *Lancet* 363(9414):1007–16.

Collins, Nancy L. and Brooke C. Feeney. 2000. "A Safe Haven: An Attachment Theory Perspective on Support Seeking and Caregiving in Intimate Relationships." *Journal of Social and Personal Relationships* 78(6):1053–73.

Collins, Patricia Hill. 1999. "Shifting the Center: Race, Class, and Feminist Theorizing about Motherhood." Pp. 197–217 in *American Families: A Multicultural Reader,* edited by Stephanie Coontz. New York: Routledge.

Collins, Randall and Scott Coltrane. 1995. *Sociology of Marriage and the Family: Gender, Love, and Property.* 4th ed. Chicago, IL: Nelson-Hall.

Collins, W. A. 1990. "Parent–Child Relationships in the Transition to Adolescence: Continuity and Change in Interaction, Affect and Cognition." Pp. 85–106 in *From Childhood to Adolescence: A Transitional Period? Advances in Adolescent Development.* Vol. 2, edited by R. Montemayor, G. R. Adams, and T. P. Gullotta. Newbury Park, CA: Sage Publications.

Colliver, Victoria. 2006. "Jump in Middle-Income Americans Who Go Without Health Insurance." *San Francisco Chronicle,* April 26. Retrieved April 26, 2006 (http://www.sfgate.com).

Collymore, Yvette. 2002. "Risk of Homicide Is High for U.S. Infants." *Population Today,* May/June, p. 10.

Coltrane, Scott. 1990. "Birth Timing and the Division of Labor in Dual-earner Families: Exploratory Findings and Suggestions for Further Research." *Journal of Family Issues* 11:157–81.

——. 1996. *Family Man: Fatherhood, Housework, and Gender Equity.* New York: Oxford University Press.

——. 1998. "Gender, Power, and Emotional Expression: Social and Historical Contexts for a Process Model of Men in Marriages and Families." Pp. 193–211 in *Men in Families: When Do They Get Involved? What Difference Does It Make?* edited by Alan Booth and Ann C. Crouter. Mahwah, NJ: Erlbaum.

——. 2000. "Research on Household Labor: Modeling and Measuring the Social Embeddedness of Routine Family Work." *Journal of Marriage and Family* 62:1208–33.

Coltrane, Scott and Masako Ishii-Kuntz. 1992. "Men's Housework: A Life Course Perspective." *Journal of Marriage and Family* 54(2):43–57.

Colvin, Jan, Lillian Chenoweth, Mary Bold, and Cheryl Harding. 2004. "Caregivers of Older Adults: Advantages and Disadvantages of Internet-based Social Support." *Family Relations* 53(1):49–57.

Comerford, Lynn. 2006. "The Child Custody Mediation Policy Debate." *Family Focus* (March):F7, F12. National Council on Family Relations. February

Concise Columbia Encyclopedia. 1994. New York: Columbia University Press.

"Conclusions Are Reported on Teaching of Abstinence." 2007. *New York Times,* April 15.

Conger, Rand D. and Katherine J. Conger. 2002. "Resilience in Midwestern Families: Selected Findings from the First Decade of a Prospective, Longitudinal Study." *Journal of Marriage and Family* 64(2):361–73.

Congregation for the Doctrine of the Faith. 1988. "Instruction on Respect for Human Life in Its Origin and on the Dignity of Procreation." Pp. 325–31 in *Moral Issues and Christian Response,* 4th ed., edited by Paul Jersild and Dale A. Johnson. New York: Holt, Rinehart & Winston.

Conley, Dalton. 2005. "A Man's Right to Choose." *New York Times,* December 1.

Conlin, Michelle. 2001. "Look Who's Barefoot in the Kitchen." *Business Week,* September 17.

——. 2003a. "The New Gender Gap." *Business Week,* May 26, pp. 75–82.

——. 2003b. "Unmarried America." *Business Week,* October 20, pp.106–16.

Connell, R. W. 2005. *Masculinities.* 2nd ed. Berkeley: University of California Press.

Conner, Karen A. 2000. *Continuing to Care: Older Americans and Their Families.* New York: Falmer.

Conway-Giustra, Francine, Ann Crowley, and Stephen H. Gorin. 2002. "Crisis in Caregiving: A Call to Action." *Health and Social Work* 27(4):307–12.

Cooley, Charles Horton. 1902. *Human Nature and the Social Order.* New York: Scribner's.

——. 1909. *Social Organization.* New York: Scribner's.

Cooney, Rosemary, Lloyd H. Rogler, Rose Marie Hurrel, and Vilma Ortiz. 1982. "Decision Making in Intergenerational Puerto Rican Families." *Journal of Marriage and Family* 44:621–31.

Coontz, Stephanie. 1992. *The Way We Never Were: American Families and the Nostalgia Trap.* New York: Basic Books.

——. 1997. "Divorcing Reality." *The Nation,* November 17, pp. 21–24.

——. 2005a. "The Heterosexual Revolution." *New York Times,* July 5.

——. 2005b. *Marriage, a History: From Obedience to Intimacy, or How Love Conquered Marriage.* New York: Viking.

——. 2005c. "The New Fragility of Marriage, for Better or for Worse." *Chronicle of Higher Education* 51(35): B7–10. Retrieved September 29, 2006 (http://chronicle.com).

Cooper, Al, ed. 2002. *Sex and the Internet: A Guidebook for Clinicians.* New York: Routledge.

——. 2004. "Online Sexual Activity in the New Millenium." *Contemporary Sexuality* 38:i–vii.

Cooper, Claire. 2004. "Court: Closer Scrutiny in Custody Case Moves." *Sacramento Bee,* April 30. Retrieved June 1, 2004 (www.sacbee.com).

Coordinated Access for Child Care. 2001. "Choosing Quality Child Care" (www.cafcc.on.ca).

Cose, Ellis. 1994a. "Truths about Spouse Abuse." *Newsweek,* August 8, p. 49.

——. 1994b. "The Year of the Father." *Newsweek,* October 31, p. 61.

——. 2000. "The Prison Paradox." *Newsweek,* November 13, pp. 42–49.

Cott, Nancy F. 2000. *Public Vows: A History of Marriage and the Nation.* Cambridge, MA: Harvard University Press.

Cotter, David A., Joan M. Hermsen, and Reeve Vanneman. 2004. *Gender Inequality at Work.* New York: Russell Sage.

Cotton, Sheila R. 1999. "Marital Status and Mental Health Revisited: Examining the Importance of Risk Factors and Resources." *Family Relations* 48(3):225–33.

Cotton, Sheila, R., Russell Burton, and Beth Rushing. 2003. "The Mediating Effects of Attachment to Social Structure and Psychosocial Resources on the Relationship between Marital Quality and Psychological Distress." *Journal of Family Issues* 24(4):547–77.

Cottrell, Ann Baker. 1993. "Cross-National Marriages." Pp. 96–103 in *Next of Kin: An International Reader on Changing Families,* edited by Lorne Tepperman and Susannah J. Wilson. New York: Prentice Hall.

Cottrell, Barbara and Peter Monk. 2004. "Adolescent-to-Parent Abuse: A Qualitative Overview of Common Themes." *Journal of Family Issues* 25(8):1072–95.

"Couple Support." 2006. Covenant Marriage Movement. Retrieved October 16, 2006 (http://www.covenantmarriage .com).

"Court Treats Same-sex Breakup as Divorce." 2002. *Seattle Times,* November 3.

"Covenant Marriages Ministry." 1998. http://www.covenantmarriages.com/ index2.html.

Cowan, C. P. and P. A. Cowan. 1992. *When Partners Become Parents: The Big Life Change for Couples.* New York: Basic Books.

Cowan, Gloria. 2000. "Beliefs about the Causes of Four Types of Rape." *Sex Roles* 42(9/10):807–23.

Cowan, Ruth Schwartz. 1983. *More Work for Mother: The Ironies of Household Technology from the Open Hearth to the Microwave.* New York: Basic Books.

Cowley, Geoffrey. 2000. "For the Love of Language." *Newsweek* Special Issue, Fall/Winter, pp. 12–15.

Cox, Adam J. 2006. *Boys of Few Words: Raising Our Sons to Communicate and Connect.* New York: Guilford.

Craig, Stephen. 1992. "The Effect of Television Day Part on Gender Portrayals in Television Commercials: A Content Analysis." *Sex Roles* 26(5/6):197–211.

Cramer, Duncan. 2003. "Facilitativeness, Conflict, Demand for Approval, Self-esteem, and Satisfaction with Romantic Relationships." *Journal of Psychology* 137(1):85–94.

Crary, David. 2007. "U.S. Divorce Rate Lowest Since 1979." Associated Press, May 10. Retrieved May 10, 2007 (www.breitbart.com).

Cravens, Hamilton. 1997. "Postmodernist Psychobabble: The Recovery Movement for Individual Self-esteem in Mental Health Since World War II." *Journal of Policy History* 9(1):141–53.

Crawford, D., D. Feng, and J. Fischer. 2003. "The Influence of Love, Equity, and Alternatives on Commitment in Romantic Relationships." *Family and Consumer Sciences Research Journal* 31(3):253–71.

Crawford, Duane W., Renate M. Houts, Ted L. Huston, and Laura J. George. 2002. "Compatibility, Leisure, and Satisfaction in Marital Relationships." *Journal of Marriage and Family* 64(2):433–49.

Cresswell, Mark. 2003. "Sex/Gender: Which Is Which? A Rejoinder to Mary Riege Laner." *Sociological Inquiry* 73:138–51.

Crick, Nicki R., Nicole E. Werner, Juan F. Casas, Kathryn M. O'Brien, David A. Nelson, Jennifer K. Grotpeter, and Kirstian Markon. 1999. "Childhood Aggression and Gender: A New Look at an Old Problem." Pp. 75–141 in *Gender and Motivation,* Nebraska Symposium on Motivation, vol. 45, edited by Dan Bernstein. Lincoln, NE. University of Nebraska Press.

Crimes Against Children Research Center (CCRC). University of New Hampshire. 2005. "Fact Sheet: Sexual Assault." Durham, NH: Crimes Against Children Research Center. Retrieved September 14, 2006 (www.unh.edu/ccrc).

Crimmins, Eileen M. 2001. "Americans Living Longer, Not Necessarily Healthier, Lives." *Population Today* (February/March): 1, 8.

Crittenden, Ann. 2001. *The Price of Motherhood: Why the Most Important Job in the World Is Still the Least Valued.* New York: Metropolitan.

Crooks, Robert and Karla Baur. 2005. *Our Sexuality.* 9th ed. Belmont, CA: Wadsworth.

Crosbie-Burnett, Margaret and Edith Lewis. 1999. "Use of African-American Family Structure and Functioning to Address the Challenges of European-American Post-Divorce Families." Pp. 455–68 in *American Families: A Multicultural Reader,* edited by Stephanie Coontz. New York: Routledge.

Crosbie-Burnett, Margaret, Edith A. Lewis, Summer Sullivan, Jessica Podolsky, Rosane Mantilla de Souza, and Victoria Mitrani. 2005. "Advancing Theory through Research: The Case of Extrusion in Stepfamilies." Pp. 213–30 in *Sourcebook of Family Theory and Research,* edited by Vern L. Bengston, Alan C. Acock, Katherine R. Allen, Peggye Dilworth-Anderson, and David M. Klein. Thousand Oaks, CA: Sage Publications.

Crosby, Faye J., John C. Williams, and Monica Biernat. 2004. "The Maternal Wall." *Journal of Social Issues* 60(4):675–82.

Crosby, John F. 1991. *Illusion and Disillusion: The Self in Love and Marriage.* 4th ed. Belmont, CA: Wadsworth.

Crosnoe, Robert. 2004. "Social Capital and the Interplay of Families and Schools." *Journal of Marriage and Family* 66(2):267–80.

Crouter, Ann C. and Alan Booth, eds. 2003. *Children's Influence on Family Dynamics: The Neglected Side of Family Relationships.* Mahwah, NJ: Erlbaum.

———. 2004. *Work-Family Challenges for Low-Income Parents and Their Children.* Mahwah, NJ: Erlbaum.

Crowder, Kyle D. and Stewart E. Tolnay. 2000. "A New Marriage Squeeze for Black Women: The Role of Racial Intermarriage by Black Men." *Journal of Marriage and Family* 62(3):792–807.

Crowley, Martha, Daniel T. Lichter, and Zhenchao Qian. 2006. "Beyond Gateway Cities: Economic Restructuring and Poverty Among Mexican Immigrant Families and Children." *Family Relations* 55(3):345–60.

Cuber, John and Peggy Harroff. 1965. *The Significant Americans.* New York: Random House. (Published also as *Sex and the Significant Americans.* Baltimore, MD: Penguin, 1965.)

Cue, Kelly L., William H. George, and Jeanette Norris. 1996. "Women's Appraisals of Sexual-Assault Risk in Dating Situations." *Psychology of Women Quarterly* 20:487–504.

Cui, Ming, Frederick O. Lorenz, Rand D. Conger, Janet N. Melby, and Chalandra M. Bryant. 2005. "Observer, Self-, and Partner Reports of Hostile Behaviors in Romantic Relationships." *Journal of Marriage and Family* 67(5):1169–81.

Cullen, Lisa T. 2004. "Cupid Academy." *Time,* February 16, p. 67.

Cummings, E. Mark, Marcie C. Goeke-Morey, Lauren M. Papp, and Tammy L. Dukewich. 2002. "Children's Responses to Mothers' and Fathers' Emotionality and Tactics in Marital Conflict in the Home." *Journal of Family Psychology* 16(4): 478–492.

Cunningham, Mick. 2005. "Gender in Cohabitation and Marriage: The Influence of Gender Ideology on Housework Allocation over the Life Course." *Journal of Family Issues* 26(8):1037–61.

Cunningham-Burley, Sarah. 2001. "The Experience of Grandfatherhood." Pp. 92–96 in *Families in Later Life: Connections and Transitions,* edited by Alexis J. Walker, Margaret Manoogian-O'Dell, Lori A. McGraw, and Diana L. G. White. Thousand Oaks, CA: Pine Forge Press.

Curtis, Kristen Taylor and Christopher G. Ellison. 2002. "Religious Heterogamy and Marital Conflict." *Journal of Family Issues* 23(4):551–76.

Cyr, Mireille, Pierre McDuff, and John Wright. 2006. "Prevalence and Predictors of Dating Violence among Adolescent Female Victims of Child Sexual Abuse." *Journal of Interpersonal Violence* 21(8):1000–1017.

Dahms, Alan M. 1976. "Intimacy Hierarchy." Pp. 85–104 in *Process in Relationship: Marriage and Family,* 2nd ed., edited by Edward A. Powers and Mary W. Lees. New York: West.

Dailard, Cynthia. 2002. "Abstinence Promotion and Teen Family Planning: The Misguided Drive for Equal Funding." *The Guttmacher Report on Public Policy* 5(1).

———. 2003. "Understanding 'Abstinence': Implications for Individuals, Programs and Policies." *The Guttmacher Report* 6(5). December (www.agi-usa.org).

Dalley, Timothy J. 2004. "Homosexual Parenting: Placing Children at Risk." Family Research Council. March 25 (http://www.frc.org).

Dalphonse, Sherri. 1997. "Childfree by Choice." *The Washingtonian* 32(5):48–57.

Daly, Martin and Margo I. Wilson. 1994. "Some Differential Attributes of Lethal Assaults on Small Children by Stepfathers versus Genetic Fathers." *Ethology and Sociobiology* 15:207–17.

———. 2000. "The Evolutionary Psychology of Marriage and Divorce." Pp. 91–110 in *The Ties That Bind: Perspectives on Marriage and Cohabitation*, edited by Linda J. Waite. New York: Aldine.

Dance, Theodore and Elizabeth Latrobe Place. 2006. *Raising Athletic Stars*. Erie, PA: First Books.

Dang, Alain and Samjen Frazer. 2004. *Black Same-sex Households in the United States: A Report from the 2000 Census*. New York: National Gay and Lesbian Task Force Policy Institute and National Black Justice Coalition.

D'Antonio, W. V., D. R. Hoge, K. Meyer, and J. D. Davidson. 1999. "American Catholics." *Catholic Reporter*, October 29, p. 20.

Dao, James. 2005. "Grandparents Given Rights by Ohio Court." *New York Times*, October 11.

Darlin, Damon. 2006. "Vet Bills and the Priceless Pet: What's a Practical Owner to Do? *New York Times*. May 13.

Darwin, Charles. [1859] 1977. *On the Origin of Species*. Fulcroft, PA: Fulcroft Library Editions.

Davey, Adam and Maximiliane E. Szinovacz. 2004. "Dimensions of Marital Quality and Retirement." *Journal of Family Issues* 25(4):431–64.

Davey, Monica. 2006. "As Tribal Leaders, Women Still Fight Old Views." *New York Times*, February 4.

David, Deborah S. and Robert Brannon, eds. 1976. *The Forty-nine Percent Majority: The Male Sex Role*. Reading, MA: Addison-Wesley.

Davidson, Jeannette R. 1992. "Theories about Black–White Interracial Marriage: A Clinical Perspective." *Journal of Multicultural Counseling and Development* 20(4):150–57.

Davies, Curt and Jeff Love. 2002. *Tracing Baby Boomer Attitudes Then and Now: A Comparative Look at the Attitudes of Baby Boomers in the 1970s and 2002*. Washington, DC: American Association of Retired Persons.

Davis, Erin Calhoun and Lisa V. Friel. 2001. "Adolescent Sexuality: Disentangling the Effects of Family Structure and Family Context." *Journal of Marriage and Family* 63(3):669–81.

Davis, Fred. [1963] 1991. *Passage Through Crisis: Polio Victims and Their Families*. 2nd ed. New Brunswick, NJ: Transaction Books.

Davis, James. 1991. *Who Is Black? One Nation's Definition*. University Park, PA: Pennsylvania State University Press.

Davis, Wendy. 2001. "Some Lawyers Are Growing Hostile to the 'Friendly Parent' Idea in Custody Fights." *American Bar Association Journal* 87(October):26ff.

Dawkins, Richard. 1976. *The Selfish Gene*. New York: Oxford University Press.

Dawn, Laura. 2006. *It Takes a Nation: How Strangers Became Family in the Wake of Hurricane Katrina*. San Rafael, CA: Earth Aware Editions.

Day, Jennifer Cheesman, Alex Janus, and Jessica Davis. 2005. *Computer and Internet Use in the United States: 2003*. Current Population Reports P23-208. Washington, DC: U.S. Census Bureau. October.

Day, Randal D., Gary W. Peterson, and Coleen McCracken. 1998. "Predicting Spanking of Younger and Older Children by Mothers and Fathers." *Journal of Marriage and Family* 60(1):79–94.

"Day-Care Researchers in Retreat." 2001. *Omaha World-Herald*, April 26.

de la Cruz, Patricia and Angela Brittingham. 2003. "The Arab Population: 2000." Census 2000 Brief C2KBR 23. December.

Dear, Greg E. and Clare M. Roberts. 2002. "The Relationships between Codependency and Femininity and Masculinity." *Sex Roles* 46(5/6):159–65.

De'Ath, Erica. 1996. "Family Change: Stepfamilies in Context." *Children & Society* 10:80–82.

Dee, Jonathan. 2005. "Their Unexpected Adolescence." *New York Times Magazine*. 35-40; 53.

Deen, Michelle Radin. 2005. "Family Values Reconsidered." *Family Focus* (June):F3, F6. Minneapolis, MN: National Council on Family Relations.

DeFrain, John. 2002. *Creating a Strong Family: American Family Strengths Inventory*. Nebraska Cooperative Extension NF01-498 (http://ianrpubs.unl.edu/family/nf498.htm).

DeLamater, John and William N. Friedrich. 2002. "Human Sexual Development." *Journal of Sex Research* 39:10–14.

DeLamater, John D. and Morgan Sill. 2005. "Sexual Desire in Later Life." *Journal of Sex Research* 42(2):138–49.

DeLeire, Thomas and Ariel Kalil. 2005. "How Do Cohabiting Couples with Children Spend Their Money?" *Journal of Marriage and Family* 67(2):286–95.

Dellman-Jenkins, Mary, Maureen Blankemeyer, and Odessa Pinkard. 2000. "Young Adult Children and Grandchildren in Primary Caregiver Roles to Older Relatives and Their Service Needs." *Family Relations* 49(2):177–86.

del Pinal, Jorge and Audrey Singer. 1997. "Generations of Diversity: Latinos in the United States." *Population Bulletin* 52(3). Washington, DC: Population Reference Bureau.

Del Vecchio, Tamara and Susan G. O'Leary. 2006. "Antecedents of Toddler Aggression: Dysfunctional Parenting in Mother-Toddler Dyads." *Journal of Clinical Child and Adolescent Psychology* 35(2):194–202.

DeMaria, Rita M. 2005. "Distressed Couples and Marriage Education." *Family Relations* 54(2):242–53.

DeMaris, Alfred. 2001. "The Influence of Intimate Violence on Transitions out of Cohabitation." *Journal of Marriage and Family* 63(1):235–46.

———. 2007. "The Role of Relationship Inequality in Marital Disruption." *Journal of Social and Personal Relationships* 24(2):177–95.

DeMaris, Alfred and William MacDonald. 1993. "Premarital Cohabitation and Marital Instability: A Test of the Unconventionality Hypothesis." *Journal of Marriage and Family* 55(2):399–407.

DeMaris, Alfred and Steven Swinford. 1996. "Female Victims of Spousal Violence: Factors Influencing Their Level of Fearfulness." *Family Relations* 45(1):98–106.

Demian. 2004a. "Canada Offers Legal Marriage." Partners Task Force for Gay & Lesbian Couples. Retrieved April 3, 2003 (http://www.buddybuddy.com).

———. 2004b. "The Gay Parent: Challenging the Myths." Partners Task Force for Gay & Lesbian Couples. Retrieved October 28, 2006 (http://www.buddybuddy.com).

Demian. 2005a. "Quick Facts on Legal Marriage for Same-sex Couples." Partners Task Force for Gay & Lesbian Couples. Retrieved October 28, 2006 (http://www.buddybuddy.com).

———. 2005b. "Where to Get a Religious Blessing: Gay-Welcoming Denominations in the United States." Partners Task Force for Gay & Lesbian Couples. Retrieved October 28, 2006 (http://www.buddybuddy.com).

———. 2006a. "Domestic Partnership Benefits." Partners Task Force for Gay & Lesbian Couples. Retrieved September 12, 2006 (http://www.buddybuddy.com).

———. 2006b. "Legal Marriage Report: Global Status of Legal Marriage." Partners Task Force for Gay & Lesbian Couples. Retrieved October 29, 2006 (http://www.buddybuddy.com).

———. 2006c. "Legal Precautions to Protect Your Relationship." Partners Task Force for Gay & Lesbian Couples. Retrieved October 29, 2006 (http://www.buddybuddy.com).

D'Emilio, John and Estelle B. Freedman. 1988. *Intimate Matters: A History of Sexuality in America.* New York: HarperCollins.

Demo, David H. and Alan C. Acock. 1996. "Singlehood, Marriage, and Remarriage: The Effects of Family Structure and Family Relationships on Mothers' Well-being." *Journal of Family Issues* 17(3):388–407.

Demo, David H., William S. Aquilino, and Mark A. Fine. 2005. "Family Composition and Family Transitions." Pp. 119–34 in *Sourcebook of Family Theory and Research,* edited by Vern L. Bengston, Alan C. Acock, Katherine R. Allen, Peggye Dilworth-Anderson, and David M. Klein. Thousand Oaks, CA: Sage Publications.

Demo, David H. and Martha J. Cox. 2000. "Families with Young Children: A Review of Research in the 1990s." *Journal of Marriage and Family* 62(4):876–95.

DeNavas-Walt, Carmen, Robert W. Cleveland, and Bruce H. Webster, Jr. 2003. *Income in the United States: 2002.* Current Population Reports P60-221. Washington, DC: U.S. Census Bureau. September.

DeNavas-Walt, Carmen, Bernadette D. Proctor, and Cheryl Hill Lee. 2006. *Income, Poverty, and Health Insurance Coverage in the United States: 2005.* Current Population Reports P60-291. Washington, DC: U.S. Census Bureau. August.

Denizet-Lewis, Benoit. 2003."Double Lives on the Down Low." *New York Times Magazine,* August 3.

———. 2004. "Friends, Friends with Benefits, and the Benefits of the Local Mall." *New York Times,* May 30.

Dentinger, Emma and Marin Clarkberg. 2002. "Informal Caregiving and Retirement Timing among Men and Women." *Journal of Family Issues* 23(7):857–79.

Depner, Charlene E. 1993. "Parental Role Reversal: Mothers as Nonresidential Parents." Pp. 37–57 in *Nonresidential Parenting: New Vistas in Family Living,* edited by Charlene E. Depner and James H. Bray. Newbury Park, CA: Sage Publications.

de Santis, Marie. 1990. "Hate Crimes Bill Excludes Women." *Off Our Backs,* June.

Detzner, Daniel F. and Blong Xiong. 1999. "Southeast Asian Families Straddle Two Worlds." *NCFR Report,* June, pp. 14–15.

De Vise, Daniel. 2004. "Living with Parents Lets Young Adults Build Careers, Savings." Knight Ridder/Tribune Business News, January 11.

Dewan, Shaila K. 2000. "For Adoptees from Overseas, Generations and Worlds Apart." *Omaha World-Herald,* July 26.

Dey, Achintya N. and Jacqueline Wilson Lucas. 2006. "Physical and Mental Health Characteristics of U.S. and Foreign-born Adults: United States, 1998–2003." *Advance Data,* No. 369, March 1. Hyattsville, MD: National Center for Health Statistics.

Dickinson, Amy. 2002. "An Extra-Special Relation." *Time,* November 18, pp. A1+.

Dilworth-Anderson, Peggye, Linda M. Burton, and Eleanor Boulin Johnson. 1993. "Reframing Theories for Understanding Race, Ethnicity, and Families." Pp. 627–46 in *Sourcebook of Family Theories and Methods,* edited by Pauline C. Boss et al. New York: Plenum.

Dinkmeyer, Don, Sr., Gary D. McKay, and Don Dinkmeyer, Jr. 1997. *The Parent's Handbook: Systematic Training for Effective Parenting.* Circle Pines, MN: American Guidance Service.

Dion, Karen K. 1995. "Delayed Parenthood and Women's Expectations about the Transition to Parenthood." *International Journal of Behavioral Development* 18(2): 315-333.

Dion, Karen K. and Kenneth L. Dion. 1991. "Psychological Individualism and Romantic Love." *Journal of Social Behavior and Personality* 6:17–33.

Dion, M. Robin. 2005. "Healthy Marriage Programs: Learning What Works." *The Future of Children* 15(2):139–56.

DiStefano, Joseph. 2001. "Jumping the Broom." Retrieved October 2, 2006 (http://www.randomhouse.com).

"The Divorce Dilemma." 1996. *U.S. News & World Report,* September 30, pp. 58–62.

"Divorce Rate Drops to Lowest Since 1970." 2007. *USA Today,* May 11.

Doble, Richard deGaris. 2006. AbusiveLove.com. Retrieved August 16, 2006 (http://www.abusivelove.com).

Dodson, Jualynne E. 2007. "Conceptualization and Research of African American Family Life in the United States: Some Thoughts." Pp. 51–68 in *Black Families,* 4th ed., edited by Harriette Pipes McAdoo. Thousand Oaks, CA: Sage Publications.

Doherty, William J. 1992. "Private Lives, Public Values." *Psychology Today* 25(3):32–39.

Doherty, William J., Susan Su, and Richard Needle. 1989. "Marital Disruption and Psychological Well-Being: A Panel Study." *Journal of Family Issues* 10:72–85.

Doka, Kenneth J., John Breaux, and Jack D. Gordon. 2002. *Living with Grief: Loss in Later Life.* Washington, DC: Hospice Foundation of America.

Dolan, Elizabeth M., Bonnie Braun, and Jessica C. Murphy. 2003. "A Dollar Short: Financial Challenges of Working-poor Rural Families." *Family Focus* (June): F13–F15. National Council on Family Relations.

Dolbin-MacNab, Megan L. 2006. "Just Like Raising Your Own? Grandmothers' Perceptions of Parenting a Second Time Around." *Family Relations* 55(5):564–75.

DOMA Watch. 2006. Retrieved September 7, 2006 (http://www.domawatch.org).

"Domestic Violence Decline Reported." 2006. *Omaha World-Herald/Los Angeles Times,* December 29.

Domitrz, Michael J. 2003. *May I Kiss You? A Candid Look at Dating, Communication, Respect, and Sexual Assault Awareness.* Greenfield, WI: Awareness Publications.

Donahoe, Elizabeth. 2005. "Using Foster Grandparents as Mentors in Family Drug Court: A Case Study." *Family Focus on . . . Substance Abuse across the Life Span* FF25: F17–F18. National Council on Family Relations.

Dore, Margaret K. 2004. "The 'Friendly Parent' Concept: A Flawed Factor for Child Custody." *Loyola Journal of Public Interest Law* 6:41–56.

Dorman, Clive. 2006. "The Social Toddler: Promoting Positive Behaviour." *Infant Observation* 9(1):95–97.

Dosani, Sabina and Peter Cross 2007. *Raising Young Children: 52 Brilliant Little Ideas for Parenting Under 5s.* Oxford, Canada: Infinite Ideas Press.

Dowd, James J. and Nicole R. Pallotta. 2000. "The End of Romance: The Demystification of Love in the Postmodern Age." *Sociological Perspectives* 43(4):549–80.

Downey, Douglas B. 1995. "When Bigger Is Not Better: Family Size, Parental Resources, and Children's Educational Performance." *American Sociological Review* 60:746–61.

Downey, Douglas B. and Dennis J. Condron. 2004. "Playing Well with Others in Kindergarten: The Benefit of Siblings at Home." *Journal of Marriage and Family* 66(2):333–50.

Downey, Sarah. 2000. "The Moving-Van Wars." *Newsweek,* February 28, p. 53.

Downs, Barbara. 2003. *Fertility of American Women: June 2002.* Current Population Reports P20-548. Washington, DC: U.S. Census Bureau. October.

Downs, Kimberly J. M., Marilyn Coleman, and Lawrence H. Ganong. 2000. "Divorced Families over the Life Course." Pp. 24–36 in *Families Across Time: A Life Course Perspective; Readings,* edited by Sharon J. Price, Patrick C. McKenry, and Megan J. Murphy. Los Angeles, CA: Roxbury.

Downs, William R. and Brenda A. Miller. 1998. "Relationships between Experiences of Parental Violence During Childhood and Women's Self-Esteem." *Violence and Victims* 13(1):63–74.

Doyle, J. 1989. *The Male Experience.* Dubuque, IA: Brown.

Dreifus, Claudia. 2006. "An Economist Examines the Business of Fertility." *New York Times,* February 26.

Driver, Janice L. and John M. Gottman. 2004. "Daily Marital Interactions and Positive Affect During Marital Conflict among Newlywed Couples." *Family Process* 43(3):301–14.

Drummet, Amy R., Marilyn Coleman, and Susan Cable. 2003. "Military Families Under Stress: Implications for Family Life Education." *Family Relations* 52(3):279–87.

Duck, Steve. 1999. *Relating to Others.* 2nd ed. Philadelphia, PA: Open University Press.

Duck, Steve W. and Julia T. Wood. 2006. "What Goes Up May Come Down: Sex and Gendered Patterns in Relationship Dissolution." Pp. 169–99 in *Handbook of Divorce and Relationship Dissolution,* edited by Mark A. Fine and John H. Harvey. Mahwah, NJ: Erlbaum.

Duenwald, Mary. 2005. "For Them, Just Saying No Is Easy." *New York Times,* June 9.

Dugger, Celia W. 1998. "In India, an Arranged Marriage of Two Worlds." *New York Times,* July 20, pp. A1, A10.

Dukes, Howard. 2003. "In Parents' Hands, Children's Development Influenced Profoundly by Marital Conflict, ND Researcher Points Out." *South Bend Tribune,* July 8.

Duncan, Gabriel. 2005. "Don't Follow America: Tribes Should Lift Bans on Gay Marriage." Pacific News Service. Retrieved December 29, 2006 (www.imdiversity.com).

Duncan, Greg J. and Jeanne Brooks-Gunn. 2002. "Family Poverty, Welfare Reform, and Child Development." *Child Development* 71:188–96.

Duncan, Greg J. and P. Lindsay Chase-Lansdale, eds. 2004. *For Better and For Worse: Welfare Reform and the Well-being of Children and Families.* New York: Russell Sage.

Dunleavy, Victoria Orrego. 2004. "Examining Interracial Marriage Attitudes as Value Expressive Attitudes." *The Howard Journal of Communications* 15:21–38.

Dunne, John E., E. Wren Hudgins, and Julia Babcock. 2000. "Can Changing the Divorce Law Affect Post-Divorce Adjustment?" *Journal of Divorce & Remarriage* 33(3):35–55.

Dunnewind, Stephanie. 2003. "Book Helps Impart Coping Skills, Self-esteem to Multiracial Children." Knight Ridder/Tribune News Service, August 5.

Dunphy v. Gregor. 1994. 136 N.J. 99.

Dunson, David B., Bernardo Colombo, and Donna D. Baird. 2002. "Changes with Age in the Level and Duration of Fertility in the Menstrual Cycle." *Human Reproduction* 17(5):1399–1403.

Durkheim, Émile. [1893] 1933. *Division of Labor in Society.* Translated by George Simpson. New York: Macmillan.

———. 1911. Contribution to discussion of "L'Education sexuelle." *Bulletin de la Société française de philosophie* XL, pp. 33–38, 44–47.

Durose, Matthew R., Caroline Wolf Harlow, Patrick A. Langan, Mark Motivans, Ramona R. Rantala, and Erica L. Smith. 2005. *Family Violence Statistics, Including Statistics on Strangers and Acquaintances.* NCJ 207846. June. Washington, DC: Bureau of Justice Statistics.

Dush, Claire M. Kamp, Catherine L. Cohan, and Paul R. Amato. 2003. "The Relationship between Cohabitation and Marital Quality and Stability: Change Across Cohorts?" *Journal of Marriage and Family* 65(3):539–49.

Dutton, Donald G. 2003. *The Abusive Personality: Violence and Control in Intimate Relationships.* New York: Guilford.

Dutton, Donald G. and James J. Browning. 1988. "Concern for Power, Fear of Intimacy, and Aversive Stimuli for Wife Assault." Pp. 163–75 in *Family Abuse and Its Consequences: New Directions in Research,* edited by Gerald T. Hotaling, David Finkelhor, John T. Kirkpatrick, and Murray A. Straus. Newbury Park, CA: Sage Publications.

Duvall, Evelyn M. and Brent C. Miller. 1985. *Marriage and Family Development.* 6th ed. New York: Harper and Row.

Dworkin, Paul H. 2002. "Editor's Note." *Journal of Developmental and Behavioral Pediatrics* 23:167.

Dworkin, Shari L. and Michael A. Messner. 1999. "Just Do . . . What? Sports, Bodies, and Gender." Pp. 341–61 in *Revisioning Gender,* edited by Myra Marx Ferree, Judith Lorber, and Beth. B. Hess. Thousand Oaks, CA: Sage Publications.

Dwyer, J. W., Gary R. Lee, and Thomas B. Jankowski. 1994. "Reciprocity, Elder Satisfaction, and Caregiver Stress and Burden: The Exchange of Aid in the Family Caregiving Relationship." *Journal of Marriage and Family* 56(1):35–43.

Dye, Jane Lawler. 2005. "Fertility of American Women: June 2004." *Current Population Reports* 20-555. December. Washington, DC: U.S. Census Bureau.

Dye, Jane Lawler and Tallese Johnson. 2007. *A Child's Day: 2003.* Current Population Reports P70-109. Washington, DC: U.S. Census Bureau.

Dyk, Patricia H. 2004. "Complexity of Family Life among the Low-income and Working Poor: Introduction to the Special Issue." *Family Relations* 53(2):122–26.

Dziech, Billie Wright. 2003. "Sexual Harassment on College Campuses." Pp. 147–71 in *Academic and Workplace Sexual Harassment: A Handbook of Cultural, Social Science, Management, and Legal Perspectives,* edited by Michele Paludi and Carmen A. Paludi, Jr. Westport, CT: Praeger.

Eagly, Alice, Wendy Wood, and Amanda Diekman. 2000. "Social Role Theory of Sex Differences and Similarities: A Current Appraisal." Pp. 123–74 in *The Developmental Social Psychology of Gender,* edited by Thomas Eckes and Hanns M. Trautner. Mahwah, NJ: Erlbaum.

Early, Theresa J., Thomas K. Gregoire, and Thomas P. McDonald. 2002. "Child Functioning and Caregiver Well-being in Families of Children with Emotional Disorders." *Journal of Family Issues* 23(3):374–91.

Easterlin, Richard. 1987. *Birth and Fortune: The Impact of Numbers on Personal Welfare.* 2nd rev. ed. Chicago, IL: University of Chicago Press.

Eaton, Danice K. et al. 2006. "Youth Risk Behavior Surveillance—United States, 2005." Surveillance Summaries. *Morbidity and Mortality Weekly Report* 55, No. SS-5, June 9.

Eaton, Leslie. 2004. "Divorced Parents Move, and Custody Gets Trickier." *New York Times,* August 8.

Ebaugh, Helen Rose and Mary Curry. 2000. "Fictive Kin as Social Capital in New Immigrant Communities." *Sociological Perspectives* 43(2):189–209.

Eckholm, Eric. 2006. "Plight Deepens for Black Men, Study Warns" *New York Times,* March 20.

———. 2007. "Childhood Poverty Is Found to Portend High Adult Costs." *New York Times,* Jan. 25.

Edgell, Penny. 2006. *Religion and Family in a Changing Society.* Princeton: Princeton University Press.

Edin, Kathryn and Maria Kefalas. 2005. *Promises I Can Keep: Why Poor Women Put Motherhood before Marriage.* Berkeley and Los Angeles, CA: University of California Press.

———. 2007. "Unmarried with Children." Pp. 505–11 in *Family in Transition,* 14th ed., edited by Arlene S. Skolnick and Jerome H. Skolnick. Boston, MA: Allyn and Bacon.

Edin, Kathryn and Joanna M. Reed. 2005. "Why Don't They Just Get Married? Barriers to Marriage among the Disadvantaged." *The Future of Children* 15(2):117–38.

Edmondson, B. and J. Galper. 1998. "Pet Places." *American Demographics.* Cited by S. Cohen (2002), p. 622 (www.demographics.com/publications).

"Education of Homeless Children and Youth." 2001. National Coalition for the Homeless, Fact sheet #10 (http://www.nationalhomeless.org/edchild.html).

Edwards, Cody S. 2006. "Friends with Benefits." Presented at the annual meeting of the Midwest Sociological Society, March 31, Omaha, NE.

Edwards, Margie L. K. 2004. "We're Decent People: Constructing and Managing Family Identity in Rural Working-class Communities." *Journal of Marriage and Family* 66(2):515–29.

Egan, Timothy. 2001. "Loyal, Two-Legged Lobbyists Raise Banner of Dog Rights." *New York Times,* March 25.

Eggebeen, David J. and Adam Davey. 1998. "Do Safety Nets Work? The Role of Anticipated Help in Times of Need." *Journal of Marriage and Family* 60(4):939–50.

Ehrenberg, Marion F., Margaret Gearing-Small, Michael A. Hunter, and Brent J. Small. 2001. "Childcare Task Division and Shared Parenting Attitudes in Dual-earner Families with Young Children." *Family Relations* 50(2):143–53.

Ehrenreich, Barbara. 2001. *Nickel and Dimed: On (Not) Getting By in America.* New York: Henry Holt.

Ehrensaft, Diane. 1990. *Parenting Together: Men and Women Sharing the Care of Their Children.* Urbana: University of Illinois Press.

———. 2005. *Mommies, Daddies, Donors, Surrogates: Answering Tough Questions and Building Strong Families.* New York: Guilford.

Eicher-Catt, Deborah. 2004a. "Noncustodial Mothering: A Cultural Paradox of Competent Performance–Performative Competence." *Journal of Contemporary Ethnography* 33(1):72–108.

———.2004b. "Noncustodial Mothers and Mental Health: When Absence Makes the Heart Break." *Family Focus* (March): F7–F8. National Council on Family Relations.

Eisenberg, Anne. 2005. "Hello Kitty, Hello Clone." *New York Times,* May 28.

Eisenstadt v. Baird. 1972. 405 U.S. 398.

Ekerdt, David J. 2006. "The Busy Ethic: Moral Continuity between Work and Retirement." Pp. 253–61 in *Aging: Concepts and Controversies,* 5th ed., edited by Harry R. Moody. Thousand Oaks, CA: Pine Forge Press.

Elder, Glen H., Jr. 1974. *Children of the Great Depression: Social Change in Life Experience.* Chicago, IL: University of Chicago Press.

Elder, Glen H., Jr., Jacquelynne S. Eccles, Monika Ardelt, and Sara Lord. 1995. "Inner-city Parents under Economic Pressure: Perspectives on the Strategies of Parenting." *Journal of Marriage and Family* 57:771–84.

Elfrink, Tim. 2006. "RX for Deployment Blues." *Omaha World-Herald,* December 4.

Elias, Marilyn. 2003. "Children on Heightened Alert." *USA Today,* March 24.

———. 2004. "Marriage Taken to Heart." *USA Today,* March 4.

———. 2005. "Orphans at Developmental 'Risk.'" *USA Today,* October 11.

Elkind, David. 1988. *The Hurried Child: Growing Up Too Fast Too Soon.* Reading, MA: Addison-Wesley.

———. 2007a. *The Hurried Child: Growing Up Too Fast Too Soon.* 25th anniversary ed. Cambridge, MA: Da Capo Lifelong.

———. 2007b. *The Power of Play: How Spontaneous, Imaginative Activities Lead to Happier, Healthier Children.* Cambridge, MA: Da Capo Lifelong.

Ellis, D. 2006. "Male Abuse of a Married or Cohabiting Female Partner: The Application of Sociological Theory to Research Findings." *Violence and Victims* 4:235–55.

Ellis, R. Darin. 1999. "Patterns of E-Mail Requests by Users of an Internet-based Aging-Services Information System." *Family Relations* 48(1):15–21.

El Nasser, Haya. 2001. "Minorities Make Choice to Live with Their Own." *USA Today,* July 9.

El Nasser, Haya and Lorrie Grant. 2005. "Diversity Tints New Kind of Generation Gap." *USA Today*, June 9.

Elrod, Linda D. and Robert G. Spector. 2002. "A Review of the Year in Family Law: State Courts React to *Troxel*." *Family Law Quarterly* 35(4):577–617.

El-Sheikh, Mona and Elizabeth Flanagan. 2001. "Parental Problem Drinking and Children's Adjustment: Family Conflict and Parental Depression as Mediators and Moderators of Risk." *Journal of Abnormal Child Psychology* 29(5):417–35.

Emlen, Stephen T. 1995. "An Evolutionary Theory of the Family." *Proceedings of the National Academy of Sciences* 92:8092–99.

Enda, Jodi. 1998. "Women Have Made Gains, Seek More." Washington Bureau in Saint Paul, *Minneapolis Pioneer Press*, Early Edition, July 19, pp. 1A, 4A.

Engel, Marjorie. 2000. "The Financial (In)Security of Women in Remarriages." *Research Findings*. Stepfamily Association of America (http://www.saafamilies.org).

———. 2003. "Stepfamily Resources." Retrieved October 5, 2004 (http://www.marriagepreparation.com/stepfamily_resources.html).

Engels, Friedrich. [1884] 1942. *The Origin of the Family, Private Property, and the State*. New York: International.

England, Paula. 2006. "Toward Gender Equality: Progress and Bottlenecks." Pp. 245–64 in *The Declining Significance of Gender?*, edited by Francine D. Blau, Mary C. Brinton, and David B. Grusky. New York: Russell Sage.

England, Paula, Carmen Garcia-Beaulieu, and Mary Ross. 2004. "Women's Employment among Blacks, Whites, and Three Groups of Latinas: Do More Privileged Women Have Higher Employment?" *Gender and Society* 18(4):494–509.

England, Paula and Reuben J. Thomas. 2007. "The Decline of the Date and the Rise of the College Hook Up." Pp. 151–71 in *Family in Transition*, 14th ed., edited by Arlene S. Skolnick and Jerome H. Skolnick. Boston, MA: Allyn and Bacon.

Enos, Sandra. 2001. *Mothering from the Inside: Parenting in a Women's Prison*. Albany: SUNY Press.

Ephron, Delia. 1988. *Funny Sauce: Us, the Ex, the Ex's New Mate, the New Mate's Ex, and the Kids*. New York: Penguin.

Epstein, Cynthia Fuchs. 1988. *Deceptive Distinctions: Sex, Gender, and the Social Order*. New Haven, CT: Yale University Press.

Erera, Pauline and Karen Fredriksen. 1999. "Lesbian Stepfamilies: A Unique Family Structure." *Families in Society* 80(3):263–70.

Erickson, Martha F. and Enola G. Aird. 2005. *The Motherhood Study: Fresh Insights on Mothers' Attitudes and Concerns*. New York: Institute for American Values. www.motherhoodproject.org.

Erickson, Nancy S. 1991. "Battered Mothers of Battered Children: Using Our Knowledge of Battered Women to Defend Them Against Charges of Failure to Act." *Current Perspectives in Psychological, Legal, and Ethical Issues*. Vol. 1A, *Children and Families: Abuse and Endangerment*, pp. 197–218.

Erickson, Rebecca J. and Ginna M. Babcock. 1995. "Men and Family Law: From Patriarchy to Partnership." Pp. 31–54 in *Families and Law*, edited by Lisa J. McIntyre and Marvin B. Sussman. New York: Haworth.

Eriksen, Shelley and Naomi Gerstel. 2002. "A Labor of Love or Labor Itself: Care Work among Brothers and Sisters." *Journal of Family Issues* 23(7):836–56.

Essex, Elizabeth L. and Junkuk Hong. 2005. "Older Caregiving Parents: Division of Household Labor, Marital Satisfaction, and Caregiver Burden." *Family Relations* 54(3):448–60.

Estes, Richard and Neil Weiner. 2002. *The Commercial Sexual Exploitation of Children in the U.S., Canada, and Mexico*. Philadelphia, PA: University of Pennsylvania (www.ssw.upenn.edu/~restes/CSEC).htm.

Etcheverry, Paul E., and Benjamin Le. 2005. "Thinking about Commitment: Accessibility of Commitment and Prediction of Relationship Persistence, Accommodation, and Willingness to Sacrifice." *Personal Relationships* 23 (1): 103-123.

Eveld, Edward M. 2003. "At-home Dads Create Support Systems." *Omaha World-Herald*, September 4.

Even, William E. and David A. Macpherson. 2004. "When Will the Gender Gap in Retirement Income Narrow?" *Southern Economic Journal* 71(1):182–201.

Evenson, Ranae J., and Robin W. Simon. 2005. "Clarifying the Relationship between Parenthood and Depression." *Journal of Health and Social Behavior* 46: 341-358.

"Fact Sheet: Elder Abuse Prevalence and Incidence." 2005. Washington, DC: National Center on Elder Abuse.

Fadiman, Anne. 1998. *The Spirit Catches You and You Fall Down*. New York: Farrar, Straus and Giroux.

Fagan, Jay and Marina Barnett. 2003. "The Relationship between Maternal Gatekeeping, Paternal Competence, Mothers' Attitudes about the Father Role, and Father Involvement." *Journal of Family Issues* 24(8):1020–43.

Fairchild, Emily. 2006. "'I'm Excited to Be Married, But . . .': Romance and Realism in Marriage." Pp. 1–19 in *Couples, Kids, and Family Life*, edited by Jaber F. Gubrium and James A. Holstein. New York: Oxford University Press.

Falbo, T. 1976. "Does the Only Child Grow Up Miserable?" *Psychology Today* 9:60–65.

Families and Work Institute. 2004. *Gender and Generation in the Workplace*. Boston, MA: American Business Collaboration. October 5.

Families with Children from China. 1999. "Mongolian Spots." Retrieved April 26, 2006 (www.fwcc.org).

Family Support Act. 1988. Public Law 100-628. Washington, DC: U.S. Congress.

Fanshel, David. 1972. *Far from the Reservation: The Transracial Adoption of American Indian Children*. Metuchen, NJ: Scarecrow.

Farkas, Steve, Jean Johnson, and Ann Duffett. 2002. "A Lot Easier Said Than Done: Parents Talk about Raising Children in Today's America." *Public Agenda:* A report prepared for State Farm Insurance Companies.

Fass, Paula S. 2003. Review of *Anxious Parents* (www.amazon.com).

Fausto-Sterling, Anne. 2000. "The Five Sexes Revisited." *Sciences*, July/August, pp.19–23.

Feagin, Joe R. and Melvin P. Sikes. 1994. *Living with Racism: The Black Middle-Class Experience*. Boston, MA: Beacon Press.

Fears, Darryl. 2003. "Race Divides Hispanics, Report Says." *Washington Post*, July 13.

———. 2004. "Black Baby Boomers' Income Gap Cited." *Washington Post*, December 17.

Fears, Darryl and Claudia Dean. 2001. "Biracial Couples Report Tolerance: Most Are Accepted by Families." *Washington Post*, July 6.

Fehr, Beverly, and Ross Broughton. 2001. "Gender and Personality Differences in Conceptions of Love: An Interpersonal Theory Analysis." *Personal Relationships* 8 (2): 115-123.

Fehring, Richard and Andrea Matovina Schlidt. 2001. "Trends in Contraceptive Use among Catholics in the United States: 1988–1995." *Linacre Quarterly* (May): 170–85.

Feigelman, W. 2000. "Adjustments of Transracially and Inracially Adopted Young Adults." *Child and Adolescent Social Work Journal* 17:165–83.

Feijoo, Ammie N. 2004. "Trends in Sexual Risk Behavior among High School Students—United States, 1991 to 1997 and 1999 to 2003." Washington, DC: Advocates for Youth. September. Retrieved January 7, 2007 (www.advocatesforyouth.org).

Fein, Esther B. 1997. "Failing to Discuss Dying Adds to Pain of Patient and Family." *New York Times,* March 5, pp. A1, A14.

Feldman, Robert S. 2003. *Development across the Life Span.* 3rd ed. Upper Saddle River, NJ:Prentice Hall.

Felmlee, Diane H. 2001. "No Couple Is an Island: A Social Network Perspective on Dyadic Stability." *Social Forces* 79(4):1259–82.

Fenton, Bruce. 2004. "Cohabitation Raises Legal Issues." *Fenton Report: Wealth Management Magazine,* June 7. Retrieved October 29, 2006 (http://www.fentonreport.com).

Fergusson, David M., Joseph M. Boden, and L. John Horwood. 2007. "Abortion among Young Women and Subsequent Life Outcomes." *Perspectives on Sexual and Reproductive Health* 39(1):6–12.

Fergusson, David M., L. John Horwood, and Elizabeth M. Ridder. 2006. "Abortion in Young Women and Subsequent Mental Health." *Journal of Child Psychiatry and Psychology* 47(1):16–24.

Ferrante, Joan. 2000. *Sociology: The United States in a Global Community.* 4th ed. Belmont, CA: Wadsworth.

Ferrari, J. R. and R. A. Emmons. 1994. "Procrastination as Revenge: Do People Report Using Delays as a Strategy for Vengeance?" *Personality and Individual Differences* 17(4):539–42.

Few, April L. and Karen H. Rosen. 2005. "Victims of Chronic Dating Violence: How Women's Vulnerabilities Link to

Their Decisions to Stay." *Family Relations* 54(2):265–79.

Fields, Jason. 2001. *Living Arrangements of Children: 1996.* Current Population Reports P70-74. Washington, DC: U.S. Census Bureau. April.

———. 2003. *Children's Living Arrangements and Characteristics: March 2003.* Current Population Reports P20-547. Washington, DC: U.S. Census Bureau.

———. 2004. *America's Families and Living Arrangements: 2003.* Current Population Reports P20-553. Washington, DC: U.S. Census Bureau. November.

Fields, Jason and Lynne M. Casper. 2001. *America's Families and Living Arrangements: March 2000.* Current Population Reports P20-537. Washington, DC: U.S. Census Bureau.

Fierstein, Harvey. 2003. "The Culture of Disease." *New York Times,* July 31.

Fiese, Barbara H., Thomas J. Tomcho, Michael Douglas, Kimberly Josphers, Scott Poltrock, and Tim Backer. 2002. "A Review of 50 Years of Research on Naturally Occurring Family Routines and Rituals: Cause for Celebration?" *Journal of Family Issues* 16:381–90.

Figley, Charles, Brian Bride, Nicholas Mazza, and Marcia Egan. 1998. "Death and Trauma: The Traumatology of Grieving." *Health and Social Work* 23(1):186–98.

"Financial Agreements without Saying 'I Do': Publications Outline Options for Same-sex Couples." 2004. *US Newswire,* March 4.

Fincham, Frank D., Julie Hall, and Steven R. H. Beach. 2006. "Forgiveness in Marriage: Current Status and Future Directions." *Family Relations* 55(4):415–27.

Find Care. 2002. "Choosing Quality Child Care" (www/cafcc.on.ca).

Fine, Mark, Marilyn Coleman, and Lawrence H. Ganong. 1999. "A Social Constructionist Multi-Method Approach to Understanding the Stepparent Role." Pp. 273–94 in *Coping with Divorce, Single Parenting, and Remarriage,* edited by E. Mavis Hetherington. Mahwah, NJ: Erlbaum.

Fine, Michelle, Lois Weis, Judi Addelston, and Julia Marusza. 1997. "(In)Secure Times: Constructing White Working-class Masculinities in the Late 20th Century." *Gender and Society* 11:52–68.

Finer, Lawrence B. 2007. "Trends in Premarital Sex in the United States, 1954–2003." *Public Health Reports* 122(January/February):73–78. Retrieved December 20, 2006 (www.publichealthreports.org).

Finer, Lawrence B., Jacqueline E. Darroch, and Jennifer J. Frost. 2003. "Services for Men at Publicly Funded Family Planning Agencies, 1998–1999." *Perspectives on Sexual and Reproductive Health* 35:202–7.

Finer, Lawrence B., Lori Frohwirth, Lindsay A. Dauhiphinee, Sushella Singh, and Ann M. Moore. 2005. "Reasons U.S. Women Have Abortions: Quantitative and Qualitative Perspectives." *Perspectives on Sexual and Reproductive Health* 37(3):110–18.

Fingerman, Karen L., Elizabeth L. Hay, and Kira S. Birditt. 2004. "The Best of Ties, the Worst of Ties: Close, Problematic, and Ambivalent Social Relationships." *Journal of Marriage and Family* 66(3):792–808.

Fink, Paul J. 2003. "Fink! Still at Large: Low Self-esteem and Narcissism." *Clinical Psychiatry News* 31(1):25.

Finkelhor, David, Gerald Hotaling, and Andrea Sedlak. 1991. "Children Abducted by Family Members: A National Household Survey of Incidence and Episode Characteristics." *Journal of Marriage and Family* 53(3):805–17.

Finkelhor, David and Lisa M. Jones. 2004. "Explanations for the Decline in Child Sexual Abuse Cases." NCJ 199298, September. Washington, DC: Office of Juvenile Justice and Delinquency Prevention.

———. 2006. "Why Have Child Maltreatment and Child Victimization Declined?" *Journal of Social Issues* 62(4):685–716.

Finkelhor, David, Richard Ormrod, Heather Turner, and Sherry Hamby. 2005. "The Victimization of Children and Youth: A Comprehensive National Survey." *Child Maltreatment* 10:5–25.

Finkelhor, David and Karl Pillemer. 1988. "Elder Abuse: Its Relationship to Other Forms of Domestic Violence." Pp. 244–54 in *Family Abuse and Its Consequences: New Directions in Research,* edited by Gerald T. Hotaling, David Finkelhor, John T. Kirkpatrick, and Murray A. Straus. Newbury Park, CA: Sage Publications.

Finkelhor, David and Kersti Yllo. 1985. *License to Rape: Sexual Abuse of Wives.* New York: Henry Holt.

Finkenauer, Catrin, Rutger C. M. E. Engels, Susan J. T. Branje, and Wim Meeus. 2004. "Disclosure and Relationship Satisfaction in Families." *Journal of Marriage and Family* 66(1):195–209.

Finley, Gordon E. 2000. "Adoptive Families: Dramatic Changes across Generations." *Family Focus* (June): F10, F12. National Council on Family Relations.

Finz, Stacy. 2003. "Estranged Lesbians Battle for Custody of Twins." *San Francisco Chronicle,* December 5.

Fisher, Judith L. 1983. "Mothers Living Apart from Their Children." *Family Relations* 32:351–57.

Fisher, Philip A., Leslie D. Leve, Catherine C. O'Leary, and Craig Leve. 2003. "Parental Monitoring of Children's Behavior: Variation across Stepmother, Stepfather, and Two-Parent Biological Families." *Family Relations* 52(1):45–52.

Fitzpatrick, Mary Anne. 1995. *Explaining Family Interactions.* Thousand Oaks, CA: Sage Publications.

Flaherty, Sr. Mary Jean, Lorna Facteau, and Patricia Garver. 1999. "Grandmother Functions in Multigenerational Families: An Exploratory Study of Black Adolescent Mothers and Their Infants." Pp. 223–31 in *The Black Family: Essays and Studies,* edited by Robert Staples. Belmont, CA: Wadsworth.

Fleming, Julian, Paul Mullen, and Cabriele Bammer. 1996. "A Study of Potential Risk Factors for Sexual Abuse in Childhood." *Child Abuse & Neglect* 21(1):49–58.

Fletcher, Garth. 2002. *The New Science of Intimate Relationships.* Malden, MA: Blackwell.

Foley, Lara and James Fraser. 1998. "A Research Note on Post-Dating Relationships." *Sociological Perspectives* 41(1):209–19.

Fomby, Paula and Andrew J. Cherlin. 2007. "Family Instability and Child Well-Being." *American Sociological Review* 72(2):181–204.

"Foreign-born Make Up Growing Segment of U.S. Black Population." 2002. *Population Today* (April). Retrieved December 13, 2006 (www.prb.org).

Formichelli, Linda. 2001. "Baby Blues." *Psychology Today* (March/April):24.

Formoso, Diana, Nancy A. Gonzales, Manuel Barrera, Jr., and Larry E. Dumka. 2007. "Interparental Relations, Maternal Employment, and Fathering in Mexican American Families." *Journal of Marriage and Family* 69(1):26–39.

"Foster Care." 2005. *Facts for Families.* American Academy of Child and Adolescent Psychiatry. Retrieved February 19, 2007 (http://www.aacap.org).

Foster Care Project. 1998. "The Foster Care Project: What You May Not Know" (http://www.kidscampaigns .org/fostercare).

Foster, E. Michael, Damon Jones, and Saul D. Hoffman. 1998. "The Economic Impact of Nonmarital Childbearing: How Are Older, Single Mothers Faring?" *Journal of Marriage and Family* 60(1):163–74.

Foster, Joshua D., Ilan Shrira, and W. Keith Campbell. 2006. "Theoretical Models of Narcissism, Sexuality, and Relationship Commitment." *Journal of Social and Personal Relationships* 23(3):367–86.

Foust, Michael. 2006. "Marriage Digest: Homosexuals in No Hurry to Marry, New Study Says." *BP News.* Retrieved October 29, 2006 (http://www.bpnews.net).

Fox, Greer Litton. 2000. "No Time for Innocence, No Place for Innocents: Children's Exposure to Extreme Violence." Pp. 163–81 in *Families, Crime, and Criminal Justice,* edited by Greer Litton Fox and Michael L. Benson. New York: Elsevier Science.

Fox, Greer Litton, Michael L. Benson, Alfred A. DeMaris, and Judy Van Wyk. 2002. "Economic Distress and Intimate Violence: Testing Family Stress and Resources Theory." *Journal of Marriage and Family* 64:793–807.

Fox, Greer Litton, Carol Bruce, and Terri Combs-Orme. 2000. "Parenting Expectations and Concerns of Fathers and Mothers of Newborn Infants." *Family Relations* 49(2):123–31.

Fox, Greer Litton and Robert F. Kelly. 1995. "Determinants of Child Custody Arrangements at Divorce." *Journal of Marriage and Family* 57(3):693–708.

Fox, Greer Litton and Velma McBride Murry. 2000. "Gender and Families: Feminist Perspectives and Family Research." *Journal of Marriage and Family* 62:1160–72.

Fox, James Alan and Marianne W. Zawitz. 2004. *Homicide Trends in the U.S.* Washington, DC: U.S. Bureau of Justice Statistics (www.ojp.usdoj.gov/bjs).

Fracher, Jeffrey and Michael S. Kimmel. 1992. "Hard Issues and Soft Spots: Counseling Men about Sexuality." Pp. 438–50 in *Men's Lives,* 2nd ed., edited by Michael S. Kimmel and Michael A. Messner. New York: Macmillan.

Francis, Meagan. 2007. "About LargerFamilies.com." Retrieved March 23, 2007 (www.largerfamilies.com).

Franks, Melissa M., Tantina B. Hong, Linda S. Pierce, and Mark W. Ketterer. 2002. "The Association of Patients' Psychosocial Well-being with Self and Spouse Ratings of Patient Health." *Family Relations* 51(1):22–27.

French, J. R. P. and Bertram Raven. 1959. "The Basis of Power." In *Studies in Social Power,* edited by D. Cartwright. Ann Arbor: University of Michigan Press.

Frey, Kurt and Mahzad Hojjat. 1998. "Are Love Styles Related to Sexual Styles?" *Journal of Sex Research* 35(3):265–72.

Frey, William H. 1999. "'New Sun Belt' Metros and Suburbs Are Magnets for Retirees." *Population Today* 27(9):1–3.

———. 2002. "The New White Flight." *American Demographics* 24:20–23.

Friedan, Betty. 1963. *The Feminine Mystique.* New York: Dell.

Friedman, Joel, Marcia M. Boumil, and Barbara Ewert Taylor. 1992. *Date Rape: What It Is, What It Isn't, What It Does to You, What You Can Do About It.* Deerfield Beach, FL: Health Communications.

Friedrich, William N., Jennifer Fisher, Daniel Broughton, Margaret Houston, and Constance R. Shafran. 1998. "Normative Sexual Behavior in Children: A Contemporary Sample." *Pediatrics* 104(April):E9 (www.pediatrics.org).

Frisco, Michelle L. and Kristi Williams. 2003. "Perceived Housework Equity, Marital Happiness, and Divorce in Dual Earner Families." *Journal of Family Issues* 24:51–73.

Fritsch, Jane. 2001. "A Rise in Single Dads." *New York Times,* May 20.

Fromm, Erich. 1956. *The Art of Loving.* New York: Harper and Row.

Fruhauf, Christine A., Shannon E. Jarrott, and Katherine R. Allen. 2006. "Grandchildren's Perceptions of Caring for Grandparents." *Journal of Family Issues* 27(7):887–911.

Fry, C. L. 1996. "Age, Aging, and Culture." Pp. 126–34 in *Handbook of Aging and the Social Sciences,* edited by R. H. Binstock and L. K. George. New York: Academic Press.

Frye, Marilyn. 1992. "Lesbian 'Sex.'" Pp. 109–19 in *Essays in Feminism 1976–1992,* edited by Marilyn Frye. Freedom, CA: Crossing.

Fu, Xuanning and Tim B. Heaton. 2000. "Status Exchange in Intermarriage among Hawaiians, Japanese, Filipinos and Caucasians in Hawaii: 1983–1994." *Journal of Comparative Family Studies* 31(1):45–64.

Fuller, T. L. and F. D. Fincham. 1997. "Attachment Style in Married Couples: Relation to Current Marital Functioning, Stability Over Time, and Method of Assessment." *Personal Relationships* 2:17–34.

Furman, W. and A. S. Flanagan. 1997. "The Influence of Earlier Relationships on Marriage: An Attachment Perspective." Pp. 179–202 in *Clinical Handbook of Marriage and Couples Interventions,* edited by W. K. Halford and H. J. Markman. Chichester, UK: Wiley.

Furstenberg, Frank F., Jr. 1991. "As the Pendulum Swings: Teenage Childbearing and Social Concern." *Family Relations* 40:127–38.

———. 2000. "The Sociology of Adolescence and Youth in the 1990s: A Critical Commentary." *Journal of Marriage and Family* 62(4):896–910.

———. 2001a. "The Fading Dream: Prospects for Marriage in the Inner City." Pp. 224–46 in *Problem of the Century: Racial Stratification in the United States,* edited by Elijah Anderson and Douglas S. Massey. New York: Russell Sage.

———. 2001b. "Managing to Make It." *Journal of Family Issues* 22 (2): 150–62.

———. 2003. "The Future of Marriage." Pp. 171–77 in *Family in Transition,* 12th ed., edited by Arlene S. Skolnick and Jerome H. Skolnick. Boston, MA: Allyn and Bacon.

———. 2005. "Banking on Families: How Families Generate and Distribute Social Capital." *Journal of Marriage and Family* 67(4):809–21.

———. 2006. "Diverging Development: The Not-So-Invisible Hand of Social Class in the United States." Network on Transitions to Adulthood Research Network Working Paper. Presented at the biennial meeting of the Society for Research on Adolescence, March 23–26, 2006, San Francisco, CA.

Furstenberg, Frank F., Jr., J. Brooks-Gunn, and S. Philip Morgan. 1987. *Adolescent Mothers in Later Life.* New York: Cambridge University Press.

Furstenberg, Frank F., Jr. Thomas D. Cook, Jacquelynne Eccles, Glen H. Elder, Jr., and Arnold Sameroff. 1999. *Managing to Make It: Urban Families and Adolescent Success.* Chicago, IL: University of Chicago Press. Chapter 4, "How Parents Manage Risk and Opportunity," with Sarah E. Lord, W. Todd Bartko, and Karen Walker; and Chapter 7, "How Do Neighborhoods Matter," with Jeong-Ran-Kim, Wing-Shing Chan, Richard A. Settersten, Jr., and Julien O. Teitler.

Furstenberg, Frank F., Jr. and Mary Elizabeth Hughes. 1995. "Social Capital and Successful Development among At-risk Youth." *Journal of Marriage and Family* 57(3):580–92.

Furstenberg, Frank F., Jr., Sheela Kennedy, Vonnie C. McLoyd, Rubén G. Rumbaut, and Richard A. Settersten, Jr. 2004. "Growing Up Is Harder to Do." *Contexts* 3(3):33–41.

Furstenberg, Frank F., Jr. and Kathleen E. Kiernan. 2001. "Delayed Parental Divorce: How Much Do Children Benefit?" *Journal of Marriage and Family* 63(2):446–57.

Gable, Shelly L., Harry T. Reis, Emily A. Impett, and Evan R. Asher. 2004. "Interpersonal Relations and Group Processes—What Do You Do When Things Go Right? The Intrapersonal and Interpersonal Benefits of Sharing Positive Events." *Journal of Personality and Social Psychology* 87(2):228–45.

Gaffney, Dennis. 2006. "'American Indian' or 'Native American': Which Is Correct?" *Antiques Roadshow* (TV series). Washington, DC: Public Broadcasting System. Retrieved December 2, 2006 (www.pbs.org).

Gager, Constance T. and Laura Sanchez. 2003. "Two as One? Couples' Perceptions of Time Spent Together, Marital Quality, and the Risk of Divorce." *Journal of Family Issues* 24(1):21–50.

Gagnon, John H. and William Simon. 2005. *Sexual Conduct: The Social Sources of Human Sexuality (Social Problems and Social Issues).* 2nd ed. New Brunswick, NJ: Transaction Books.

Galinsky, Ellen. 2001. "Parent Tips." Families and Work Institute (www.familiesandwork.org/ParentTips.htm).

Galinsky, Ellen and Peter J. Stein. 1990. "The Impact of Human Resource Policies on Employees: Balancing Work/Family Life." *Journal of Family Issues* 11(4):368–83.

Gallagher, Charles A. 2006. "Interracial Dating and Marriage: Fact, Fantasy and the Problem of Survey Data." Pp. 141–53 in *African Americans and Whites: Changing Relationships on College Campuses,* edited by Robert M. Moore III. New York: University Press of America.

Gallagher, Maggie. 2004. "Can Government Strengthen Marriage? Evidence from the Social Sciences." New York: National Fatherhood Initiative, Institute for Marriage and Public Policy, Institute for American Values. Retrieved November 15, 2005 (www.marriagemovement.org).

Gallagher, Sally K. 2002. *Evangelical Identity and Gendered Family Life.* New Brunswick, NJ: Rutgers University Press.

———. 2004. "Where Are the Antifeminist Evangelicals? Evangelical Identity, Subcultural Location, and Attitudes toward Feminism." *Gender and Society* 18(4):451–72.

Gallagher, Sally K. and Naomi Gerstel. 2001. "Connections and Constraints: The Effects of Children on Caregiving." *Journal of Marriage and Family* 63(1):265–75.

Gallagher, Sally K. and Christian Smith. 1999. "Symbolic Traditionalism and Pragmatic Egalitarianism: Contemporary Evangelicals, Families, and Gender." *Gender and Society* 13:211–33.

Gallo, Eileen and Jon J. Gallo. 2005. *The Financially Intelligent Parent: 8 Steps to Raising Successful, Generous, Responsible Children.* New York: New American Library.

Gallup, George H., Jr. 2003. "Current Views on Premarital, Extramarital Sex." The Gallup Poll. June 24. Retrieved September 13, 2006 (http://www.galluppoll.com).

Gallup Poll News Service. 2007. "Gallup's Pulse of Democracy: Abortion." Washington, DC: Gallup Poll News Service. Retrieved March 21, 2007 (www.galluppoll.com).

Gamache, Susan J. 1997. "Confronting Nuclear Family Bias in Stepfamily Research." *Marriage and Family Review* 26(1–2):41–50.

Gandy, Kim. 2005. "The Patriarchy Isn't Falling." *USA Today,* September 22.

Gangstad, Jack. 2006. *From Diapers to Diplomas: A Common Sense Approach to Raising Well-Adjusted Children.* Bloomington, IN: AuthorHouse.

Ganong, Lawrence H. and Marilyn Coleman. 1997. "How Society Views Stepfamilies." Pp. 85–106 in *Stepfamilies: History, Research, and Policy,* edited by Irene Levin and Marvin B. Sussman. New York: Haworth.

———. 2000. "Remarried Families." Pp. 155–68 in *Close Relationships: A Sourcebook,* edited by Clyde Hendrick and Susan S. Hendrick. Thousand Oaks, CA: Sage Publications.

———.2004. *Stepfamily Relationships: Development, Dynamics, and Interventions.* New York: Kluwer Academic/Plenum.

———. 2005. "Leaving Whose Home? When Stepchildren Leave Is It Always Extrusion?" Pp. 233–36 in *Sourcebook of Family Theory and Research,* edited by Vern L. Bengston, Alan C. Acock, Katherine R. Allen, Peggye Dilworth-Anderson, and David M. Klein. Thousand Oaks, CA: Sage Publications.

Gans, Daphna and Merril Silverstein. 2006. "Norms of Filial Responsibility for Aging Parents across Time and Generations." *Journal of Marriage and Family* 68(4):961–76.

Gans, Herbert J. [1962] 1982. *The Urban Villagers: Group and Class in the Life of Italian-Americans,* updated and expanded edition. New York: Free Press.

Gardiner, Karen N., Michael E. Fishman, Plamen Nikolov, Asaph Glosser, and Stephanie Laud. 2002. "State Policies to Promote Marriage: Final Report." September. Washington, DC: U.S. Department of Health and Human Services (http://aspe.hhs .gov/hsp/marriage02f).

Gardner, Jonathan and Andrew Oswald. 2006. "Do Divorcing Couples Become Happier by Breaking Up?" *Journal of the Royal Statistical Society,* Series A 169(2):319–36.

Gardner, Saundra. 1990. "Images of Family Life over the Family Life Cycle." *Sociological Quarterly* 31:77–92.

Gardyn, Rebecca. 2002. "Animal Magnetism." *American Demographics* 24(May):30–37.

Garey, Anita I., Karen V. Hansen, Rosanna Hertz, and Cameron MacDonald. 2002. "Care and Kinship." *Journal of Family Issues* 23(6):703–15.

Garfinkel, Irwin, Daniel R. Meyer, and Sara S. McLanahan. 1998. "A Brief History of Child Support Policies in the U.S." Pp. 14–30 in *Fathers Under Fire: The Revolution in Child Support Enforcement,* edited by Irwin Garfinkel, Sara S. McLanahan, Daniel R. Meyer, and Judith A. Seltzer. New York: Russell Sage.

Garson, David G. N.d. "Economic Opportunity Act of 1964." Retrieved October 9, 2006 (http://cwx.prenhall. com).

Gates, Gary J. 2006. *Same-sex Couples and the Gay, Lesbian, and Bisexual Population: New Estimates from the American Community Survey.* Los Angeles, CA: The Williams Institute on Sexual Orientation, Law, and Public Policy, University of California at Los Angeles. October.

Gaughan, Monica. 2002. "The Substitution Hypothesis: The Impact of Premarital Liaisons and Human Capital on Marital Timing." *Journal of Marriage and Family* 64(2):407–19.

Gaunt, Ruth. 2006. "Couple Similarity and Marital Satisfaction: Are Similar Spouses Happier?" *Journal of Personality* 74(5):1401–20.

Gavin, Molly R. 2003. "Elder Care Targeted as Top Employee Benefit." *Healthcare Review* 16(2):11–13.

"Gays Want the Right, but Not Necessarily the Marriage." 2004. *The Christian Science Monitor,* February 12.

Geary, David C. and Mark V. Flinn. 2001. "Evolution of Human Parental Behavior and the Human Family." *Parenting Science and Practice* 1:5–61.

Geasler, Margie J. and Karen R. Blaisure. 1998. "A Review of Divorce Education Program Materials." *Family Relations* 47(2):167–75.

Gecas, Viktor. 1982. "The Self-Concept." *Annual Review of Sociology* 8:1–33.

Geen, Rob. 2004. "The Evolution of Kinship Care: Policy and Practice." *The Future of Children* 14(1):131–53.

Gelles, Richard J. 1974. *The Violent Home: A Study of Physical Aggression between Husbands and Wives.* Beverly Hills, CA: Sage Publications.

———. 1994. "Ten Risk Factors." *Newsweek,* July 4, p. 29.

———. 1996. *The Book of David: How Preserving Families Can Cost Children's Lives.* New York: Basic Books.

———. 1997. *Intimate Violence in Families.* 3rd ed. Thousand Oaks, CA: Sage Publications.

———. 2005. "Protecting Children Is More Important Than Preserving Families." Pp. 329–40 in *Current Controversies on Family Violence,* 2nd ed., edited by Donileen R. Loseke, Richard J. Gelles, and Mary M. Cavanaugh. Thousand Oaks, CA: Sage Publications.

Gelles, Richard J. and Mary M. Cavanaugh. 2005. "Violence, Abuse, and Neglect in Families and Intimate Relationships." Pp. 129–54 in *Families and Change: Coping with Stressful Events and Transitions,* 3rd ed., edited by Patrick C. McKenry and Sharon J. Price. Thousand Oaks, CA: Sage Publications.

Gelles, Richard J. and Jon R. Conte. 1990. "Domestic Violence and Sexual Abuse of Children: A Review of Research in the Eighties." *Journal of Marriage and Family* 52(4):1045–58.

Gelles, Richard J. and Jane B. Lancaster, eds. 1987. *Child Abuse and Neglect: Biosocial Dimensions.* Hawthorne, NY: Aldine.

Gelles, Richard J. and Murray A. Straus. 1988. *Intimate Violence: The Definitive Study of the Causes and Consequences of Abuse in the American Family.* New York: Simon and Schuster.

"Genetically, Race Doesn't Exist." 2003. *Washington University Magazine,* Fall, p. 4.

Gerard, Jean M., Ambika Krishnakumar, and Cheryl Buehler. 2006. "Marital Conflict, Parent-Child Relations, and Youth Maladjustment: A Longitudinal Investigation of Spillover Effects." *Journal of Family Issues* 27(7):951–75.

Geronimus, Arline T. 1991. "Teenage Childbearing and Social and Reproductive Disadvantage: The Evolution of Complex Questions and the Demise of Simple Answers." *Family Relations* 40(4):463–71.

Gerson, Kathleen. 1993. *No Man's Land: Men's Changing Commitments to Family and Work.* New York: HarperCollins, Basic Books.

———. 1997. "The Social Construction of Fatherhood." Pp. 119–53 in *Contemporary Parenting: Challenges and Issues,* edited by Terry Arendell. Thousand Oaks, CA: Sage Publications.

"Getting It Right: Marriage Preparation in the Catholic Church." 1995. Omaha, NE: Creighton University Center for Marriage and Family. Retrieved September 8, 2006 (http://www.usccb.org).

Giddens, Anthony. 2007. "The Global Revolution in Family and Personal Life." Pp. 26–31 in *Family in Transition,* edited by Arlene S. Skolnick and Jerome H. Skolnick. Boston, MA: Allyn and Bacon.

Giele, Janet Z. 2007. "Decline of the Family: Conservative, Liberal, and Feminist Views." Pp. 76–91 in *Family in Transition,* edited by Arlene S. Skolnick and Jerome H. Skolnick. Boston, MA: Allyn and Bacon.

Gilbert, Lucia Albino, Sarah J. Walker, Sherry McKinney, and Jessica L. Snell. 1999. "Challenging Discourse Theories Reproducing Gender in Heterosexual Dating: An Analog Study." *Sex Roles* 41:753–74.

Gilbert, Susan. 1997. "Two Spanking Studies Indicate Parents Should Be Cautious." *New York Times,* August 20.

Giles-Sims, Jean. 1997. "Current Knowledge about Child Abuse in Stepfamilies." Pp. 215–30 in *Stepfamilies: History, Research, and Policy,* edited by Irene Levin and Marvin B. Sussman. New York: Haworth.

Giles-Sims, Jean and Charles Lockhart. 2005. "Culturally Shaped Patterns of Disciplining Children." *Journal of Family Issues* 26(2):196–218.

Gillespie, Dair. 1971. "Who Has the Power? The Marital Struggle." *Journal of Marriage and Family* 33:445–58.

Gillespie, Rosemary. 2003. "Childfree and Feminine: Understanding the Gender Identity of Voluntarily Childless Women." *Gender and Society* 17:122–36.

Gillham, Bill, Gary Tanner, Bill Cheyne, Isobel Freeman, Martin Rooney, and Allan Lambie. 1998. "Unemployment Rates, Single Parent Density, and Indices of Child Poverty: Their Relationship to Different Categories of Child Abuse and Neglect." *Child Abuse & Neglect* 22(2).79–90.

Gilligan, Carol. 1982. *In a Different Voice: Psychological Theory and Women's Development.* Cambridge, MA: Harvard University Press.

Gilligan, Carol, Nona P. Lyons, and Trudy J. Hanmer, eds. 1990. *Making Connections: The Relational Worlds of Adolescent Girls at Emma Willard School.* Cambridge, MA: Harvard University Press.

Gilmartin, B. 1977. "Swinging: Who Gets Involved and How." Pp. 161–85 in *Marriage and Alternatives,* edited by R. W. Libby and R. N. Whitehurst. Glenview, IL: Scott, Foresman.

Gilmore, David D. 1990. *Manhood in the Making: Cultural Concepts of Masculinity.* New Haven, CT: Yale University Press.

Ginott, Haim G., Alice Ginott, and Wallace Goddard. 2003. *Between Parent and Child: The Bestselling Classic That Revolutionized Parent-Child Communication.* New York: Three Rivers Press.

Glass, Jennifer. 1992. "Housewives and Employed Wives: Demographic and Attitudinal Change, 1972–1986." *Journal of Marriage and Family* 54:559–69.

Glass, Jennifer and Sarah Beth Estes. 1997. "The Family Responsive Workplace." *Annual Review of Sociology* 23: 289–313.

Glass, Jennifer and Leda E. Nath. 2006. "Religious Conservatism and Women's Market Behavior Following Marriage and Childbirth." *Journal of Marriage and Family* 68(3):611–29.

Glass, Shirley. 1998. "Shattered Vows." *Psychology Today* 31(4):34–52.

Glassner, Barry. 1999. *The Culture of Fear: Why Parents Are Afraid of the Wrong Things.* New York: Basic Books.

Glendon, Mary Ann. 1981. *The New Family and the New Property.* Toronto: Butterworths.

Glenn, Norval. 1990. "Quantitative Research on Marital Quality in the 1980s: A Critical Review." *Journal of Marriage and Family* 52(November):818–31.

———. 1996. "Values, Attitudes, and the State of American Marriage." Pp. 15–33 in *Promises to Keep: The Decline and Renewal of Marriage in America,* edited by David Popenoe, Jean Bethke Elshtain, and David Blankenhorn. Lanham, MD: Rowman and Littlefield.

———. 1997. "A Reconsideration of the Effect of No-Fault Divorce on Divorce Rates." *Journal of Marriage and Family* 59(4):1023–30.

———. 1998. "The Course of Marital Success and Failure in Five American 10-Year Marriage Cohorts." *Journal of Marriage and Family* 60(3):569–76.

———. 2002. "A Plea for Greater Concern About the Quality of Marital Matching." Pp. 45–58 in *Revitalizing the Institution of Marriage for the Twenty-first Century,* edited by Alan J. Hawkins, Lynn D. Wardle, and David Orgon Coolidge. Westport, CT: Praeger.

Glenn, Norval and Elizabeth Marquardt. 2001. *Hooking Up, Hanging Out, and Hoping for Mr. Right: College Women on Dating and Mating Today.* New York: Institute for American Values.

Glick, Jennifer E., Frank D. Bean, and Jennifer Van Hook. 1997. "Immigration and Changing Patterns of Extended Family Household Structure in the United States: 1970–1990." *Journal of Marriage and Family* 59:177–91.

Glick, Jennifer E. and Jennifer Van Hook. 2002. "Parents' Coresidence with Adult Children: Can Immigration Explain Racial and Ethnic Variation?" *Journal of Marriage and Family* 64(1):240–53.

Glick, Paul C. and Sung-Ling Lin. 1986. "More Young Adults Are Living with Their Parents: Who Are They?" *Journal of Marriage and Family* 48:107–12.

Glick, Paul C. and Arthur J. Norton. 1979. "Marrying, Divorcing, and Living Together in the U.S. Today." *Population Bulletin* 32(5). Washington, DC: Population Reference Bureau.

Glink, Ilyce R. 2001. *50 Simple Things You Can Do to Improve Your Personal Finances.* New York: Three Rivers Press.

Globerman, Judith. 1996. "Motivations to Care: Daughters- and Sons-in-Law Caring for Relatives with Alzheimer's Disease." *Family Relations* 45(1):37–45.

Goffman, Erving. 1959. *The Presentation of Self in Everyday Life.* Garden City, NY: Doubleday.

———. 1961. *Asylums: Essays on the Social Situation of Mental Patients and Other Inmates.* Garden City, NY: Anchor.

Gold, J. M. and J. D. Rogers. 1995. "Intimacy and Isolation: A Validation Study of Erikson's Theory." *Journal of Humanistic Psychology* 35(1):78–86.

Gold, Steven J. 1993. "Migration and Family Adjustment: Continuity and Change among Vietnamese in the United States." Pp. 300–314 in *Family Ethnicity: Strength in Diversity,* edited by Harriette Pipes McAdoo. Newbury Park, CA: Sage Publications.

Goldberg, Abbie E. and Aline Sayer. 2006. "Lesbian Couples' Relationship Quality across the Transition to Parenthood." *Journal of Marriage and Family* 68(1):87–100.

Goldberg, Carey. 1998. "After Girls Get the Attention, Focus Shifts to Boys' Woes." *New York Times,* April 23.

———. 1999. "Crackdown on Abusive Spouses, Surprisingly, Nets Many Women." *New York Times,* November 23.

Goldin, Claudia. 2006. "Working It Out." *New York Times,* March 15.

Goldner, Virginia. 1993. "Feminist Theories." Pp. 623–25 in *Sourcebook of Family Theories and Methods: A Contextual Approach,* edited by Pauline G. Boss, William J. Doherty, Ralph LaRossa, Walter R. Schumm, and Suzanne K. Steinmetz. New York: Plenum.

Goldscheider, Frances K. and Calvin Goldscheider. 1998. "Effects of Childhood Family Structure on Leaving and Returning Home." *Journal of Marriage and Family* 60:745–56.

Goldscheider, Frances and Sharon Sassler. 2006. "Creating Stepfamilies: Integrating Children into the Study of Union Formation." *Journal of Marriage and Family* 68(2):275–91.

Goldstein, Arnold P., Harold Keller, and Diane Erne. 1985. *Changing the Abusive Parent.* Champaign, IL: Research Press.

Goldstein, Joshua R. 1999. "The Leveling of Divorce in the United States." *Demography* 36:409–14.

Goldstein, Joshua R. and Kristen Harknett. 2006. "Parenting across Racial and Class Lines: Assortative Mating Patterns of New Parents Who Are Married, Cohabiting, Dating, or No Longer Romantically Involved." *Social Forces* 85(1):121–43.

Goldstein, Seth and R. P. Tyler. 1998. "Frustrations of Inquiry: Child Sexual Abuse Allegations in Divorce and Custody Cases." *Law Enforcement Bulletin,* July, pp. 1–6.

Goldyn, Cheryl. 2001. "The Mother and Child Reunion." *The Reader,* June 13, pp. 14–17.

Goleman, Daniel. 1985. "Patterns of Love Charted in Studies." *New York Times,* September 10.

———. 1988. "The Lies Men Tell Put Women in Danger of AIDS." *New York Times,* August 14.

———. 1992. "Family Rituals May Promote Better Emotional Adjustment." *New York Times,* March 11.

Golish, T. 2003. "Stepfamily Communication Strengths: Understanding the Ties That Bind." *Human Communication Research* 29(1):41–80.

Golombok, Susan., A. Brewaeys, M. T. Giavazzi, D. Guerra, F. MacCallum, and J. Rust. 2002. "The European Study of Assisted Reproduction Families: The Transition to Adolescence." *Human Reproduction* 17:830–40.

Golombok, Susan, Rachel Cook, Alison Bish, and Clare Murray. 1995. "Families Created by the New Reproductive Technologies: Quality of Parenting and Social and Emotional Development of the Children." *Child Development* 66:285–98.

Golombok, Susan, Fiona MacCallum, and Emma Goodman. 2001. "The 'Test-Tube' Generation: Parent–Child Relationships and the Psychological Well-being of In Vitro Fertilization Children at Adolescence." *Child Development* 72:599–608.

Golombok, Susan, Fiona MacCallum, Emma Goodman, and Michael Rutter. 2002. "Families with Children Conceived by Donor Insemination: A Follow-up at Age Twelve." *Child Development* 73:952–68.

Golombok, Susan and Fiona Tasker. 1996. "Do Parents Influence the Sexual Orientation of Their Children? Findings from a Longitudinal Study of Lesbian Families." *Developmental Psychology* 32:3–11.

Gomes, Charlene. 2003. "Partners as Parents: Challenges Faced by Gays Denied Marriage." *The Humanist* 63(6):14–20.

Gomes, Peter J. 2004. "For Massachusetts, a Chance and a Choice." *Boston Globe,* February 8. Retrieved October 6, 2006 (http://www.boston.com/news/globe).

Gonzales, Nancy A., Julianna Deardorff, Diana Formoso, Alicia Barr, and Manuel Berrara, Jr. 2006. "Family Mediators of the Relation between Acculturation and Adolescent Mental Health." *Family Relations* 55(3):318–30.

Gonzalez v. Carhart. 2007. U.S.S.C. 05-380. April 18.

Gonzalez, Cindy. 2006a. "Latino Leader Urges End to Concept of 'Minorities.'" *Omaha World-Herald,* November 17.

———. 2006b. "Short Supply of Visas Adds to Illegal Immigration." *Omaha World-Herald,* May 16.

Gonzalez, Cindy and Michael O'Connor. 2002. "Dialogue Key in Blending Cultures." *Omaha World-Herald,* May 4.

Goode, Erica. 2002. "Deflating Self-esteem's Role in Society's Ills." *New York Times,* October 1. Retrieved January 14, 2004 (http://web.lexis-nexis.com).

Goode, William J. 1963. *World Revolution and Family Patterns.* New York: Free Press.

———. 1971. "Force and Violence in the Family." *Journal of Marriage and Family* 33:624–36.

———. 1982. "Why Men Resist." Pp. 131–50 in *Rethinking the Family: Some Feminist Questions,* edited by Barrie Thorne and Marilyn Yalom. New York: Longman.

———. 1993. *World Changes in Divorce Patterns.* New Haven, CT: Yale University Press.

———. [1982] 2007. "The Theoretical Importance of the Family." Pp. 14–25 in *Family in Transition,* 14th ed., edited by Arlene S. Skolnick and Jerome H. Skolnick. Boston, MA: Allyn and Bacon.

Goodman, Brenda. 2004. "Forgiveness Is Good, up to a Point." *Psychology Today* (January/February):16.

Goodstein, Laurie. 2001. "New Christian Take on the Old Dating Ritual." *New York Times,* September 9.

———. 2006. "Jewish Panel Delays a Vote on Gay Issues." *New York Times,* March 9.

Gordon, Thomas. 2000. *Parent Effectiveness Training: The Proven Program for Raising Responsible Children.* New York: Three Rivers Press.

Gorman, Jean Cheng. 1998. "Parenting Attitudes and Practices of Immigrant Chinese Mothers of Adolescents." *Family Relations* 47(1):73–80.

Gottesman, Karen. 2006. *Raising Twins After the First Year.* New York: Marlowe.

Gottlieb, Alison Stokes. 1997. "Single Mothers of Children with Developmental Disabilities: The Impact of Multiple Roles." *Family Relations* 46(1):5–12.

Gottlieb, Laurie N., Ariella Lang, and Rhonda Amsel. 1996. "The Long-term Effects of Grief on Marital Intimacy Following an Infant's Death." *Omega* 33(1):1–9.

Gottlieb, Lori. 2006. "How Do I Love Thee?" *Atlantic Monthly,* March, pp. 58–70.

Gottman, John M. 1979. *Marital Interaction: Experimental Investigations.* New York: Academic.

———. 1994. *Why Marriages Succeed or Fail.* New York: Simon and Schuster.

———. 1996. *What Predicts Divorce? The Measures.* Hillsdale, NJ: Erlbaum.

———. 1998. "Toward a Process Model of Men in Marriages and Families." Pp. 149–92 in *Men in Families,* edited by Alan Booth and Ann C. Crouter. Mahwah, NJ: Erlbaum.

Gottman, John M., James Coan, Sybil Carrere, and Catherine Swanson. 1998. "Predicting Marital Happiness and Stability from Newlywed Interactions." *Journal of Marriage and Family* 60(1):5–22.

Gottman, John M. and Joan DeClaire. 2001. *The Relationship Cure: A Five-step Guide for Building Better Connections with Family, Friends, and Lovers.* New York: Crown.

Gottman, John M. and L. J. Krotkoff. 1989. "Marital Interaction and Satisfaction: A Longitudinal View." *Journal of Consulting and Clinical Psychology* 57:47–52.

Gottman, John M. and Robert W. Levenson. 2000. "The Timing of Divorce: Predicting When a Couple Will Divorce Over a 14-Year Period." *Journal of Marriage and Family* 62(3):737–45.

———. 2002. "A Two-factor Model for Predicting When a Couple Will Divorce: Exploratory Analyses Using 14-Year Longitudinal Data." *Family Process* 41(1):83–96.

Gottman, John M., Robert W. Levenson, James Gross, Barbara Frederickson, Leah Rosenthal, Anna Ruef, and Dan Yoshimoto. 2003. "Correlates of Gay and Lesbian Couples' Relationship Satisfaction and Relationship Dissolution." *Journal of Homosexuality* 45(1):23–45.

Gottman, John M. and Clifford I. Notarius. 2000. "Decade Review: Observing Marital Interaction." *Journal of Marriage and Family* 62(4):927–47.

———. 2003. "Marital Research in the 20th Century and a Research Agenda for the 21st Century." *Trends in Marriage, Family, and Society* 25(2):283–97.

Gottman, John M. and Nan Silver. 1999. *The Seven Principles for Making Marriage Work.* New York: Crown.

Gough, Brendan and Paula Reavey. 1997. "Parental Accounts Regarding the Physical Punishment of Children: Discourses of Dis/empowerment." *Child Abuse & Neglect* 21(5):417–30.

Gove, Walter R., Carolyn Briggs Style, and Michael Hughes. 1990. "The Effect of Marriage on the Well-being of Adults." *Journal of Family Issues* 11(1):4–35.

Grady, Denise. 2007. "Girl or Boy? As Fertility Technology Advances, So Does an Ethical Debate." *New York Times,* February 6.

Graefe, Deborah R. and Daniel T. Lichter. 1999. "Life Course Transitions of American Children: Parental Cohabitation, Marriage, and Single Motherhood." *Demography* 36(2):205–17.

Grall, Timothy S. 2006. *Custodial Mothers and Fathers and Their Child Support: 2003.* Current Population Reports P60-230. Washington, DC: U.S. Census Bureau.

Gray, Marjory Roberts and Laurence Steinberg. 1999. "Unpacking Authoritative Parenting: Reassessing a Multidimensional Construct." *Journal of Marriage and Family* 61(3):574–87.

Greathouse, Ann N. 1996. "Quality Child Care from a Parental Perspective." University of Nebraska at Omaha, Omaha, NE. Unpublished M.A. thesis.

Greeley, Andrew. 1989. "Protestant and Catholic." *American Sociological Review* 54:485–502.

———. 1991. *Faithful Attraction: Discovering Intimacy, Love, and Fidelity in American Marriage.* New York: Doherty.

Green, Adam Isaiah. 2006. "Until Death Do Us Part? The Impact of Differential Access to Marriage on a Sample of Urban Men." *Sociological Perspectives* 49(2):163–89.

Greenberg, Jerrold S., Clint E. Bruess, and Debra W. Haffner. 2002. *Exploring the Dimensions of Human Sexuality.* Sudbury, MA: Jones and Bartlett.

Greenberg, Susan H. and Anna Kuchment. 2006. "The 'Familymoon.'" *Newsweek,* January 9, pp. 44–45.

Greenblatt, Cathy Stein. 1983. "The Salience of Sexuality in the Early Years of Marriage." *Journal of Marriage and Family* 45:289–99.

Greenfield, Emily A. and Nadine F. Marks 2006. "Linked Lives: Adult Children's Problems and Their Parents' Psychological and Relational Well-Being." *Journal of Marriage and Family* 68(2):442–54.

Greenfield, Patricia M. and Lalita K. Suzuki. 2001. "Culture and Parenthood." Pp. 20–33 in *Parenthood in America,* edited by Jack C. Westman. Madison: University of Wisconsin Press.

Greenhouse, Steven and David Leonhardt. 2006. "Real Wages Fail to Match a Rise in Productivity." *New York Times,* September 29.

Greenstein, Gregg A. 2001. "Relationships Made Easy by Marital and Cohabitation Agreements" (http://www.frascona.com).

Greenwald, John. 1999. "Elder Care: Making the Right Choice." *Time,* August 30, pp. 52–56.

Greif, Geoffrey and Mary S. Pabst. 1988. *Mothers Without Custody.* Lexington, MA: Heath.

Grekin, E. R., P. A. Brennan, and C. Hammen. 2005. "Parental Alcohol Use Disorders and Child Delinquency: The Mediating Effects of Executive Functioning and Chronic Family Stress." *Journal of Studies on Alcohol* 66(1):14–23.

Grieco, Elizabeth and Rachel Cassidy. 2001. "Census 2000 Shows America's Diversity." Press Release. Washington, DC: U.S. Census Bureau.

Grimm-Thomas, Karen and Maureen Perry-Jenkins. 1994. "All in a Day's Work: Job Experiences, Self-esteem, and Fathering in Working-class Families." *Family Relations* 43:174–81.

Grimsley, Kristen Downey. 2000. "Family a Priority for Young Workers." *Washington Post,* May 3.

Griswold v. Connecticut. 1965. 381 U.S. 479, 14 L. Ed.2d 510, 85 S. Ct. 1678.

Groat, Theodore, Peggy Giordano, Stephen Cernkovich, M. D. Puch, and Steven Swinford. 1997. "Attitudes Toward Childbearing Among Young Parents." *Journal of Marriage and Family* 59:568–81.

Gross, Harriet Engel. 1980. "Dual-career Couples Who Live Apart: Two Types." *Journal of Marriage and Family* 42:567–76.

Gross, Jane. 2002. "U.S. Fund for Tower Victims Will Aid Some Gay Partners." *New York Times,* May 22.

———. 2004. "Alzheimer's in the Living Room: How One Family Rallies to Cope." *New York Times,* September 16.

———. 2006a. "As Parents Age, Baby Boomers and Business Struggle to Cope." *New York Times,* March 25.

———. 2006b. "Forensic Skills Seek to Uncover Hidden Patterns of Elder Abuse." *New York Times,* September 27.

———. 2006c. "Seeking Doctor's Advice in Adoptions from Afar." *New York Times,* January 3.

———. 2006d. "When the Beard Is Too Painful to Remove." *New York Times,* August 3.

———. 2007. "A Taste of Family Life in U.S., but Adoption Is in Limbo." *New York Times,* January 13.

Gross, Michael. 2006. "Bad Advice: How Not to Have Sex in an Epidemic." *American Journal of Public Health* 96(6):964–66.

Grote, Nancy K., Kristen E. Naylor, and Margaret S. Clark. 2002. "Perceiving the Division of Family Labor to Be Unfair: Do Social Comparison, Enjoyment, and Competence Matter?" *Journal of Family Psychology* 16:510–22.

Groze, V. 1996. *Successful Adoptive Families: A Longitudinal Study*. Westport, CT: Praeger.

Guberman, Nancy, Eric Gagnon, Denyse Cote, Claude Gilbert, Nicole Thivierge, and Marielle Tremblay. 2005. "How the Trivialization of the Demands of High-tech Care in the Home Is Turning Family Members into Para-Medical Personnel." *Journal of Family Issues* 26(2):247–72.

Gudelunas, David. 2006. "Who's Hooking Up On-line?" *Gay and Lesbian Review Worldwide* 13(1):23–27.

Gueorguieva, Ralitza V., Randy L. Carter, Mario Ariet, Jeffrey Roth, Charles S. Mahan, and Michael B. Resneck. 2001. "Effect of Teenage Pregnancy on Educational Disabilities in Kindergarten." *American Journal of Epidemiology* 154:212–20.

Guilamo-Ramos, Vincent, James Jaccard, Patricia Dittus, and Alida M. Bouris. 2006. "Parental Experience, Trustworthiness, and Accessibility: Parent-Adolescent Communication and Adolescent Risk Behavior." *Journal of Marriage and Family* 68(5):1229–46.

Gullickson, Aaron. 2006. "Black/White Interracial Marriage Trends, 1850–2000." *Journal of Family History* 31(3):289–312.

Gunderson, Amy. 2006. "What's the Thread Count on My Dog's Bed?" *New York Times*. June 25.

Gurian, Michael. 1996. *The Wonder of Boys: What Parents, Mentors and Educators Can Do to Shape Boys into Exceptional Men*. New York: Putnam.

Guttmacher Institute. 2006. "Facts on Induced Abortion in the United States." New York: Guttmacher Institute. May.

Guzzo, Karen Benjamin and Frank F. Furstenberg, Jr. 2007. "Multipartnered Fertility among Young Women with a Nonmarital First Birth: Prevalence and Risk Factors." *Perspectives on Sexual and Reproductive Health* 39(1):29–38.

Ha, K. Oanh. 2006. "Filipinos Work Overseas, Help Kin." *San Jose Mercury News*, April 4.

Haaga, John. 2002. "How Many Muslims Live in the United States?" Washington, DC: Population Reference Bureau. November. Retrieved March 16, 2004 (www.prb.org).

Haber, C. and B. Gratton. 1994. *Old Age and the Search for Security*. Bloomington, IN: Indiana University Press.

Haberman, Clyde. 2006. "A Battle for Freedom at the Mall." *New York Times*, November 24.

Hacker, Jacob S. 2006. *The Great Risk Shift: The Assault on American Jobs, Families, Health Care, and Retirement—And How You Can Fight Back*. New York: Oxford University Press.

Hackstaff, Karla B. 2007. "Divorce Culture: A Quest for Relational Equality in Marriage." Pp. 188–222 in *Family in Transition*, 4th ed., edited by Arlene S. Skolnick and Jerome H. Skolnick. Boston, MA: Pearson.

Haddad, Yvonne Y. and Jane I. Smith. 1996. "Islamic Values Among American Muslims." Pp. 19–40 in *Family and Gender Among American Muslims: Issues Facing Middle Eastern Immigrants and Their Descendants*, edited by Barbara C. Aswad and Barbara Bilgé. Philadelphia, PA: Temple University Press.

Hagan, Joseph R., Jr. 2005. "Psychosocial Implications of Disaster or Terrorism on Children: A Guide for the Pediatrician." *Pediatrics* 116(3):787–95.

Hagedoorn, Mariet, Nico W. Van Yperen, James C. Coyne, Cornelia van Jaarsveld, Adelita Ranchor, Eric van Sonderen, and Robbert Sanderman. 2006. "Does Marriage Protect Older People from Distress? The Role of Equity and Recency of Bereavement." *Psychology and Aging* 21(3):611–20.

Hagenbaugh, Barbara. 2002. "More Men Just Say No to Working." *USA Today*, February 20.

Hagestad, G. 1986. "The Family: Women and Grandparents as Kin Keepers." Pp. 141–60 in *Our Aging Society*, edited by A. Pifer and L. Bronte. New York: Norton.

———. 1996. "On-Time, Off-Time, Out of Time? Reflections on Continuity and Discontinuity from an Illness Process." Pp. 204–22 in *Adulthood and Aging*, edited by V. L. Bengston. New York: Springer.

Hagewen, Kellie J. and S. Philip Morgan. 2005. "Intended and Ideal Family Size in the United States, 1970–2002." *Population and Development Review* 31(3):507–27.

Haines, James and Margery Neely. 1987. *Parents' Work Is Never Done*. Far Hills, NJ: New Horizon.

Hakim, Danny. 2006. "Panel Asks New York to Join the Era of No-fault Divorce." *New York Times*, February 7.

Hale-Benson, J. E. 1986. *Black Children: Their Roots, Culture, and Learning Styles*. Provo, UT: Brigham Young University Press.

Hall, Edie Jo and E. Mark Cummings. 1997. "The Effects of Marital and Parent–Child Conflicts on Other Family Members: Grandmothers and Grown Children." *Family Relations* 46(2):135–43.

Hall, Elaine J. and Marnie Salupo Rodriguez. 2003. "The Myth of Postfeminism." *Gender and Society* 17:878–902.

Halpern-Felsher, Bonnie L., Jodi L. Cornell, Rhonda Y. Kropp, and Jeanne M. Tschann. 2005. "Oral versus Vaginal Sex among Adolescents: Perceptions, Attitudes, and Behavior." *Pediatrics* 115(4):845–51.

Halsall, Paul. 2001. *Internet Medieval Sourcebook*. Retrieved October 6, 2006 (http:www.fordham.edu).

Hamachek, Don E. 1971. *Encounters with the Self*. New York: Holt, Rinehart & Winston.

———. 1992. *Encounters with the Self*. 4th ed. New York: Holt, Rinehart & Winston.

Hamby, Sherry L. 1998. "Partner Violence: Prevention and Intervention." Pp. 210–58 in *Partner Violence: A Comprehensive Review of 20 Years of Research*, edited by Jana L. Jasinski and Linda M. Williams. Thousand Oaks, CA: Sage Publications.

Hamer, Jennifer. 2001. *What It Means to Be Daddy: Fatherhood for Black Men Living Away from Their Children*. New York: Columbia University Press.

Hamill, Sean. 2006. "Altoona, with No Immigrant Problem, Decides to Solve It." *New York Times*, December 7.

Hamilton, Anita. 2006. "When Foster Teens Find a Home." *Time*, June 5, pp. 58–63.

Hamilton, Brady E., Joyce A. Martin, and Stephanie J. Ventura. 2006. "Births: Preliminary Data for 2005." *National Vital*

Statistics Reports 55(11). Hyattsville, MD: National Center for Health Statistics. December 28.

———. 2007. *Births: Preliminary Data for 2005.* NCHS E-Stats. Hyattsville, MD: National Center for Health Statistics. Retrieved March 18, 2007 (www.cdc.gov/nchs).

Hamilton, Brady E., Joyce A. Martin, Stephanie J. Ventura, Paul D. Sutton, and Fay Menacker. 2005. "Births: Preliminary Data for 2004." *National Vital Statistics Reports* 54(8). Hyattsville, MD: National Center for Health Statistics. December 29.

Hamilton, Brady E., Stephanie J. Ventura, Joyce A. Martin, and Paul Sutton. 2006. *Final Births for 2004.* Health E-Stats. Hyattsville, MD: National Center for Health Statistics. July 6. Retrieved August 1, 2006 (www.cdc.gov/nchs).

Hamilton, W. D. 1964. "The Genetical Evolution of Social Behavior II." *Journal of Theoretical Biology* 7:17–52.

Hammack, Philip L., W. LaVome Robinson, Isiaah Crawford, and Susan T. Li. 2004. "Poverty and Depressed Mood among Urban African-American Adolescents: A Family Stress Perspective." *Journal of Child and Family Studies* 13(3):309–23.

Hammen, Constance, Patricia A. Brennan, and Josephine H. Shih. 2004. "Family Discord and Stress Predictors of Depression and Other Disorders in Adolescent Children of Depressed and Nondepressed Women." *Journal of the American Academy of Child and Adolescent Psychiatry* 43(8):994–1003.

Hammer, Heather, David Finkelhor, and Andrea J. Sedlak. 2002. *Children Abducted by Family Members: National Estimates and Characteristics.* National Incidence Studies of Missing, Abducted, and Throwaway Children (NISMART). Washington, DC: Office of Juvenile Justice and Delinquency Prevention. October. Retrieved May 7, 2007 (www.loffdp.ncjrs.org).

Hamon, Raeann R. and Bron B. Ingoldsby. 2003. *Mate Selection across Cultures.* Thousand Oaks, CA: Sage Publications.

Hanawalt, Barbara. 1986. *The Ties That Bound: Peasant Families in Medieval England.* New York: Oxford University Press.

Hans, Jason D. 2002. "Stepparenting after Divorce: Stepparents' Legal Position Regarding Custody, Access, and Support." *Family Relations* 51(4):301–07.

Hansen, Donald A. and Reuben Hill. 1964. "Families Under Stress." Pp. 782–819 in *The Handbook of Marriage and the Family,* edited by Harold Christensen. Chicago, IL: Rand McNally.

Hansen, Gary L. 1985. "Perceived Threats and Marital Jealousy." *Social Psychology Quarterly* 48(3):262–68.

Hansen, M., M. Harway, and N. Cervantes. 1991. "Therapists' Perceptions of Severity in Cases of Family Violence." *Violence and Victims* 6:225–35.

"Happiest Couples in Study Have Sex After 60." 1992. *New York Times* National Sunday, October 4, p. 13.

Haraway, Donna. 1989. *Primate Visions: Gender, Race, and Nature in the World of Modern Science.* New York: Routledge, Chapman and Hall.

Harden, B. and S. Sengupta. 2001. "Some Passengers Singled Out for Exclusion by Flight Crew." *New York Times,* September 22.

Harden, Brenda Jones. 2004. "Safety and Stability for Foster Children: A Developmental Perspective." *The Future of Children* 14(1):31–47.

Hardesty, Jennifer L. and Grace H. Chung. 2006. "Intimate Partner Violence, Parental Divorce, and Child Custody: Directions for Intervention and Future Research." *Family Relations* 55.200–216.

Haring, Michelle, Paul L. Hewitt, and Gordon L. Flett. 2003. "Perfectionism, Coping, and Quality of Intimate Relationships." *Journal of Marriage and Family* 65(1):143–58.

Harknett, Kristen. 2006. "The Relationship between Private Safety Nets and Economic Outcomes among Single Mothers." *Journal of Marriage and Family* 69(1):172–91.

Harknett, Kristen and Jean Knab. 2007. "More Kin, Less Support: Multipartnered Fertility and Perceived Support among Mothers." *Journal of Marriage and Family*

Harmanci, Reyhan. 2006. "The Neighbordaters." *San Francisco Chronicle Magazine,* February 12, pp. 13–14.

Harmon, Amy. 2005a. "Ask Them (All 8 of Them) about the Grandkids." *New York Times,* March 20.

———. 2005b. "Hello, I'm Your Sister, Our Father Is Donor 150." *New York Times,* November 20.

———. 2006. "Seeking Healthy Children, Couples Cull Embryos." *New York Times,* September 6.

———. 2007. "Sperm Donor Father Ends His Anonymity." *New York Times,* February 14.

Harris, B. 1998. "Listening to Caregiving Sons: Misunderstood Realities." *The Gerontologist* 38:342–52.

Harris, Christine R. 2003a. "A Review of Sex Differences in Sexual Jealousy, Including Self-report Data: Psychophysiological Responses, Interpersonal Violence, and Morbid Jealousy." *Personality and Social Psychology Review* 7(2):102–8.

Harris, Judith Rich. 1998. *The Nurture Assumption: Why Children Turn Out the Way They Do.* New York: Free Press.

Harris, Othello and R. Robin Miller, eds. 2003. *Impacts of Incarceration on the African American Family.* New Brunswick, NJ: Transaction Books.

Harris, Philip M. and Nicholas A. Jones. 2005. *We the People: Pacific Islanders in the United States.* CENSR-26. Washington, DC: U.S. Census Bureau. August. Retrieved December 15, 2006 (www.census.gov).

Harris, Phyllis B. and Joyce Bichler. 1997. *Men Giving Care: Reflections of Husbands and Sons.* New York: Garland.

Harrist, Amanda W. and Ricardo C. Ainslie. 1998. "Marital Discord and Child Behavior Problems." *Journal of Family Issues* 19(2):140–63.

Hartmann, Heidi, Stephen J. Rose, and Vicky Lovell. 2006. "How Much Progress in Closing the Long-term Earnings Gap?" Pp. 125–55 in *The Declining Significance of Gender?* edited by Francine D. Blau, Mary C. Brinton, and David B. Grusky. New York: Russell Sage.

Hartocollis, Anemona. 2006. "Meaning of 'Normal' Is at Heart of Gay Marriage Ruling." *New York Times,* July 8. Retrieved July 11, 2006 (http://www.nytimes.com).

———. 2007. "Married or Not, Gay Couple Are Ruled Legally Separated." *New York Times,* January 9.

Hartog, Henrik. 2000. *Man and Wife in America: A History.* Cambridge, MA: Harvard University Press.

Hartsoe, Steve. 2005. "Shacking Up: N.C. Anti-cohabitation Law Under Legal Attack." *Raleigh News and Observer,* May 9. Retrieved May 11, 2005 (http://www.newsobserver.com).

Harvard University. Mind/Brain/Behavior Initiative. 2005. "The Science of Gender and Science: Pinker vs. Spelke, a Debate." Cambridge, MA. May 16. Retrieved January 1, 2006 (www.edge.org).

Harvey, Elizabeth. 1999. "Short-term and Long-term Effects of Early Parental Employment on Children of the National Longitudinal Survey of Youth." *Developmental Psychology* 35:445–59.

Harvey, Kay. 2002. "Help for Parents a Call Away: Specialists Coach Moms, Dads." *Omaha World-Herald*, November 10, p. E-5.

Haskell, Kari. 2003. "The Neediest Cases: When Grandparents Step into the Child Care Gap, Money Can Be Scarce." *New York Times*, November 30.

Hatch, Laurie R. and Kris Bulcroft. 2004. "Does Long-term Marriage Bring Less Frequent Disagreements?" *Journal of Family Issues* 25(4):465–95.

Haub, Carl. 2006. "Hispanics Account for Almost One-Half of U.S. Population Growth." Washington, DC: Population Reference Bureau. January. Retrieved December 13, 2006 (www.prg.org).

Hawke, Sharryl and David Knox. 1978. "The One-Child Family: A New Life-Style." *Family Coordinator* 27:215–19.

Hawkins, Alan J., Steven L. Nock, Julia C. Wilson, Laura Sanchez, and James D. Wright. 2002. "Attitudes about Covenant Marriage and Divorce: Policy Implications from a Three-State Comparison." *Family Relations* 51(2):166–75.

Hawkins, Daniel N. and Alan Booth. 2005. "Unhappily Ever After: Effects of Long-term, Low-quality Marriages on Well-Being." *Social Forces* 84(1):451–71.

Hayden, Dolores. 1981. *The Grand Domestic Revolution: A History of Feminist Designs for American Homes, Neighborhoods, and Cities.* Cambridge, MA: MIT Press.

Hayes, Cheryl D., ed. 1987. *Risking the Future: Adolescent Sexuality, Pregnancy, and Childbearing.* Vol. 1. Washington, DC: National Academy Press.

Hayghe, Howard. 1982. "Dual Earner Families: Their Economic and Demographic Characteristics." Pp. 27–40 in *Two Paychecks*, edited by Joan Aldous. Newbury Park, CA: Sage Publications.

Haynes, Faustina E. 2000. "Gender and Family Ideals: An Exploratory Study of Black Middle Class Americans." *Journal of Family Issues* 21:811–37.

Hayslip, Bert and Julie Hicks-Patrick. 2006. *Custodial Grandparenting: Individual, Cultural, and Ethnic Diversity.* New York: Springer.

Hazen, C. and P. Shaver. 1994. "Attachment as an Organizing Framework for Research on Close Relationships." *Psychological Inquiry* 5:1–22.

He, Wan, Manisha Sengupta, Victoria A. Velkoff, and Kimberly A. DeBarros. 2005. *65+ in the United States: 2005.* Current Population Reports P23-209. Washington, DC: U.S. Census Bureau. December.

Heaton, Tim B. 2002. "Factors Contributing to Increasing Marital Stability in the United States." *Journal of Family Issues* 23(3):392–409.

Heaton, Tim B. and Stan L. Albrecht. 1991. "Stable Unhappy Marriages." *Journal of Marriage and Family* 53:747–58.

Heaton, Tim B. and Edith L. Pratt. 1990. "The Effects of Religious Homogamy on Marital Satisfaction and Stability." *Journal of Family Issues* 11(2):191–207.

Heim, Susan M. 2007. *It's Twins! Parent-to-Parent Advice from Infancy through Adolescence.* Charlottesville, VA: Hampton Roads.

Hein, Holly. 2000. *Sexual Detours: Infidelity and Intimacy at the Crossroads.* New York: St. Martin's.

Heiss, Jerold. 1991. "Gender and Romantic Love Roles." *Sociological Quarterly* 32:575–92.

Hench, David. 2004. "Is Anger Management a Remedy for Batterers?" *Portland Press Herald* (Maine), October 10.

Hendershott, Anne. 1995. "A Moving Story for Spouses." *Psychology Today* (September/October). Retrieved April 8, 2007 (http://psychologytoday.com/articles).

Henderson, Tammy L. 2005a. "Grandparent Visitation Rights: Justices' Interpretation of the Best Interests of the Child Standard." *Journal of Family Issues* 26(5):638–64.

———. 2005b. "Grandparent Visitation Rights: Successful Acquisition of Court-ordered Visitation." *Journal of Family Issues* 26(1):107–37.

Henderson, Tammy L. and Patricia B. Moran. 2001. "Grandparent Visitation Rights." *Journal of Family Issues* 22(5):619–38.

Hendrick, Clyde, Susan S. Hendrick, and Amy Dicke. 1998. "The Love Attitudes Scale: Short Form." *Journal of Social and Personal Relationships* 15(2):147–59.

Hendrick, Susan S. 2000. "Links between Sexuality and Love as Contributors to Relationship Satisfaction." Presented at the annual meeting of the National Council on Family Relations, November 10–13, Minneapolis, MN.

Henley, Nancy and Jo Freeman. 1995. "The Sexual Politics of Interpersonal Behavior." Pp. 79–91 in *Women: A Feminist Perspective,* 5th ed. Mountain View, CA: Mayfield.

Henly, Julia R., Sandra K. Danziger, and Shira Offer. 2005. "The Contribution of Social Support to the Material Well-being of Low-income Families." *Journal of Marriage and Family* 67(1):122–40.

Henningson, Ellen. 1997. "Financial Abuse of the Elderly." Wisconsin Department of Health and Family Services (www.dhrs.state.wi.us).

Henretta, J. C., M. S. Hill, L. Wei, B. J. Soldo, and D. A. Wolf. 1997. "Selection of Children to Provide Care: The Effect of Early Parental Transfers." *Journal of Gerontology* 52B:110–19.

Henshaw, Stanley K. 1998. "Unintended Pregnancy in the United States." *Family Planning Perspectives* 30:24–29, 46.

Herbert, Tracy Bennett, Roxane Cohen Silver, and John H. Ellard. 1991. "Coping with an Abusive Relationship: How and Why Do Women Stay?" *Journal of Marriage and Family* 53(2):311–25.

Hernandez, Raymond. 2001. "Children's Sexual Exploitation Underestimated, Study Finds." *New York Times*, September 10.

Herring, Jeff. 2005. "Affairs Don't Have to Be Physical." Knight/Ridder Newspapers, November 6.

Hertz, Rosanna. 1986. *More Equal Than Others: Women and Men in Dual Career Marriages.* Berkeley: University of California Press.

———. 1997. "A Typology of Approaches to Child Care." *Journal of Family Issues* 18(4):355–85.

———. 2006. *Single by Chance, Mothers by Choice: How Women Are Choosing Parenthood without Marriage and Creating the New American Family.* New York: Oxford University Press.

Hetherington, E. Mavis. 1989. "Coping with Family Transitions: Winners, Losers, and Survivors." *Child Development* 60:1–14.

———, ed. 1999. *Coping with Divorce, Single Parenting, and Remarriage: A Risk and Resiliency Perspective.* Mahwah, NJ: Erlbaum.

———. 2003. "Intimate Pathways: Changing Patterns in Close Personal Relationships across Time." *Family Relations* 52(4):318–31.

———. 2005. "The Adjustment of Children in Divorced and Remarried Families." Pp. 137–39 in *Sourcebook of Family Theory and Research,* edited by Vern L. Bengston, Alan C. Acock, Katherine R. Allen, Peggye Dilworth-Anderson, and David M. Klein. Thousand Oaks, CA: Sage Publications.

Hetherington, E. Mavis and K. M. Jodl. 1994. "Stepfamilies as Settings for Child Development." Pp. 55–80 in *Stepfamilies: Who Benefits? Who Does Not?* edited by Alan Booth and J. Dunn. Hillsdale, NJ: Erlbaum.

Hetherington, E. Mavis and John Kelly. 2002. *For Better or for Worse: Divorce Reconsidered.* New York: Norton.

Hewlett, Sylvia Ann. 2002. *Creating a Life: Professional Women and the Quest for Children.* New York: Hyperion.

Hewlett, Sylvia Ann and Cornell West. 1998. *The War Against Parents: What We Can Do for America's Beleaguered Moms and Dads.* Boston, MA: Houghton Mifflin.

Heyman, Richard E. and Ashley N. Hunt. 2007. "Replication in Observational Couples Research: A Commentary." *Journal of Marriage and Family* 69(1):81–85.

Heyman, Richard A. and Amy M. Smith Slep. 2002. "Do Child Abuse and Interparental Violence Lead to Adulthood Family Violence?" *Journal of Marriage and Family* 64:864–70.

Heywood, Leslie and Jennifer Drake. 1997. "Introduction." Pp. 1–20 in *Third Wave Agenda: Being Feminist, Doing Feminism,* edited by Leslie Heywood and Jennifer Drake. Minneapolis, MN: University of Minnesota Press.

Hiedemann, Bridget, Olga Suhomlinova, and Angela M. O'Rand. 1998. "Economic Independence, Economic Status, and Empty Nest in Midlife Marital Disruption." *Journal of Marriage and Family* 60(1):219–31.

Hill, Robert B. [1972] 2003. *The Strengths of Black Families.* 2nd ed. with "Epilogue: Thirty Years Later." Lanham, MD: University Press of America.

Hill, Jeffrey E., Alan J. Hawkins, and Brent C. Miller. 1996. "Work and Family in the Virtual Office: Perceived Influences of Mobile Telework." *Family Relations* 45(3):293–301.

Hill, Jennifer L., Jane Waldfogel, Jeanne Brooks-Gunn, and Wen-Juui Han. 2005. "Maternal Employment and Child Development: A Fresh Look Using Newer Methods." *Developmental Psychology* 41(6):833–50.

Hill, Nancy E., Cynthia Ramirez, and Larry E. Dumka. 2003. "Early Adolescents' Career Aspirations: A Qualitative Study of Perceived Barriers and Family Support among Low-income Ethnically Diverse Adolescents." *Journal of Family Issues* 24(7):934–59.

Hill, Reuben. 1958. "Generic Features of Families Under Stress." *Social Casework* 49:139–50.

Hill, Robert B. 2004. "Institutional Racism in Child Welfare." *Race and Society* 7(1):17–33.

Hill, Shirley A. 2004. *Black Intimacies: A Gender Perspective on Families and Relationships.* Lanham, MD: Rowman and Littlefield.

———. 2006. "Marriage among African American Women: A Gender Perspective." *Journal of Comparative Family Studies* 37(3):421–40.

Himes, Christine L. 2001. "Social Demography of Contemporary Families and Aging." Pp. 47–50 in *Families in Later Life: Connections and Transitions,* edited by Alexis J. Walker, Margaret Manoogian-O'Dell, Lori A. McGraw, and Diana L. G. White. Thousand Oaks, CA: Pine Forge.

Hines, Melissa, Susan Golombok, John Rust, Katie J. Johnston, Jean Golding, and the Avon Longitudinal Study of Parents and Children Study Team. 2002. "Testosterone during Pregnancy and Gender Role Behavior of Preschool Children: A Longitudinal Population Study." *Child Development* 73:1678–87.

Hinshaw, Stephen P. 2009. "A Family Perspective on Mental Disorder: Silence, Stigma, Diagnosis, Treatment, and Resilience." *The ADHD Report* 11(6):1–4.

Hirsch, Jennifer S. 2003. *A Courtship after Marriage: Sexuality and Love in Mexican Transnational Families.* Berkeley: University of California Press.

Hirschman, Linda. 2006. *Get to Work: A Manifesto for Women of the World.* New York: Viking.

"Hispanic Nation—Myth and Reality." 2004. *Business Week,* March 15, p. 128.

Hitlin, Steven. 2006. "Parental Influences on Children's Values and Aspirations: Bridging Two Theories of Social Class and Socialization." *Sociological Perspectives* 49(1):25–46.

Hitt, Jack. 2005. "The Newest Indians." *New York Times,* August 21.

Hochschild, Arlie. 1979. "Emotion Work, Feeling Rules, and Social Structure." *American Journal of Sociology* 85:551–75.

———. 1989. *The Second Shift: Working Parents and the Revolution at Home.* New York: Viking/Penguin.

———. 1997. *Time Bind: When Work Becomes Home and Home Becomes Work.* New York: Henry Holt.

———. 2003. *The Commercialization of Intimate Life: Notes from Home and Work.* Berkeley: University of California Press.

Hoelter, Lynette F., William G. Axinn, and Dirgha J. Ghimire. 2004. "Social Change, Premarital Nonfamily Experiences, and Marital Dynamics." *Journal of Marriage and Family* 66(5):1131–51.

Hofferth, Sandra L. and John F. Sandberg. 2001. "How American Children Spend Their Time." *Journal of Marriage and Family* 63(2):295–308.

Hoffman, Kristin and John N. Edwards. 2004. "An Integrated Theoretical Model of Sibling Violence and Abuse." *Journal of Family Violence* 19(3):185–200.

Hoffman, Lois W. and Jean B. Manis. 1979. "The Value of Children in the United States: A New Approach to the Study of Fertility." *Journal of Marriage and Family* 41: 583–96.

Hogan, Dennis P. and Nan M. Astone. 1986. "The Transition to Adulthood." *Annual Review of Sociology* 12:109–30.

Hogben, Matthew and Caroline K. Waterman. 2000. "Patterns of Conflict Resolution within Relationships and Coercive Sexual Behavior of Men and Women." *Sex Roles* 43(5/6):341–57.

Holloway, Lynette. 1994. "A Grandmother Fights for Her Second Generation." *New York Times,* December 12, p. 59.

Holmes, J. G. and S. L. Murray. 1996. "Conflict in Close Relationships." Pp. 622–54 in *Social Psychology: Handbook of Basic Principles,* edited by E. T. Higgins and A. Kruglanski. New York: Guilford.

Holmes, Steven A. 1990. "Day Care Bill Marks a Turn toward Help for the Poor." *New York Times,* January 25.

———. 1998. "Children Study Longer and Play Less, a Report Says." *New York Times,* November 11.

"Homeless Families with Children." 2001. National Coalition for the Homeless, Fact Sheet #7 (http://www.nationalhomeless.org/families.html).

"Homeless Fathers with Children." N.d. Retrieved July 28, 2004 (http://anitraweb.org/homeless/faqs/forfathers/).

"'Hon, I Miss You More Than Anything.'" 2003. *Omaha World-Herald*/Cox News Service, March 27.

Hondagneu-Sotelo, Pierrette. 1996. "Overcoming Patriarchal Constraints: The Reconstruction of Gender Relations among Mexican Immigrant Women and Men." Pp. 184–205 in *Race, Class, and Gender,* edited by Esther Ngan-Ling Chow, Doris Wilkinson, and Maxine Baca Zinn. Newbury Park, CA: Sage Publications.

———. 2001. *Doméstica: Immigrant Workers Cleaning and Caring in the Shadows of Affluence.* Berkeley: University of California Press.

Hondagneu-Sotelo, Pierrette and E. Avila. 1997. "I'm Here but I'm There: The Meaning of Transnational Motherhood." *Gender and Society* 11:548–71.

Hondagneu-Sotelo, Pierrette and Michael A. Messner. 1994. "Gender Displays and Men's Power: The 'New Man' and the Mexican Immigrant." Pp. 200–218 in *Theorizing Masculinity,* edited by Harry Brod and Michael Kaufman. Newbury Park, CA: Sage Publications.

———. 1999. "Gender Displays and Men's Power: The 'New Man' and the Mexican Immigrant Man." Pp. 342–58 in *American Families: A Multicultural Reader,* edited by Stephanie Coontz. New York: Routledge.

Hook, Misty K., Lawrence H. Gerstein, Lacy Detterich, and Betty Gridley. 2003. "How Close Are We? Measuring Intimacy and Examining Gender Differences." *Journal of Counseling and Development* 81(4):462–73.

hooks, bell. 2000. *All About Love.* New York: HarperCollins.

Hopfensperger, Jean. 1990. "A Day for Courting, Hmong Style." *Minneapolis Star Tribune,* November 24, p. 1B.

Hopper, Joseph. 1993. "The Rhetoric of Motives in Divorce." *Journal of Marriage and Family* 55:801–13.

Hornik, Donna. 2001. "Can the Church Get in Step with Stepfamilies?" *U.S. Catholic* 66(7):30–41.

Horowitz, A. 1985. "Sons and Daughters as Caregivers to Older Parents: Differences in Role Performance and Consequences." *The Gerontologist* 25:612–17.

Horowitz, June Andrews. 1999. "Negotiating Couplehood: The Process of Resolving the December Dilemma among Interfaith Couples." *Family Process* 38:303–23.

House, Anthony. 2002. *A Problematic Solution: Responses to the Marriage Reform Act of 1753.* Retrieved October 5, 2006 (http://users.ox.ac.uk).

Houseknecht, Sharon K. 1987. "Voluntary Childlessness." Pp. 369–in *Handbook of Marriage and the Family,* edited by Marvin B. Sussman and Suzanne K. Steinmetz. New York: Plenum.

Houseknecht, Sharon K. and Susan K. Lewis. 2005. "Explaining Teen Childbearing and Cohabitation: Community Embeddedness and Primary Ties." *Family Relations* 54(5):607–20.

Houseknecht, Sharon K. and Jaya Sastry. 1996. "Family 'Decline' and Child Well-Being: A Comparative Assessment." *Journal of Marriage and Family* 58(3):726–39.

Houtman, Sally. 2006. *To Grandma's House, We—Stay: When You Have to Stop Spoiling Your Grandchildren and Start Raising Them.* St. Louis, MO: Quick Publishing.

Houts, Leslie A. 2005. "But Was It Wanted? Young Women's First Voluntary Sexual Intercourse." *Journal of Family Issues* 26(8):1082–1102.

"How Many Muslims Live in the United States?" 2005. Washington, DC: Population Reference Bureau. Retrieved July 5, 2007 (www.prb.org).

"How to Jump the Broom for an African-American Wedding." N.d. Retrieved October 2, 2006 (http://www.ehow.com).

Howard, J. A. 1988. "Gender Differences in Sexual Attitudes: Conservatism or Powerlessness?" *Gender and Society* 2:103–14.

Howard, Theresa. 2005. "Pets Clean Up for the Holidays." 2005. *USA Today,* December 5.

Hoyert, Donna L., Melanie P. Heron, Sherry L. Murphy, and Hsiang-Ching Kung. 2006. "Deaths: Final Data for 2003." *National Vital Statistics Reports* 54(13). Hyattsville, MD: National Center for Health Statistics. April 19.

"HPV Policy Becomes Political Issue." 2007. *Day to Day.* National Public Radio (NPR). February 27.

Hsia, Annie. 2002. "Considering Grandparents' Rights and Parents' Wishes: 'Special Circumstances' Litigation Alternatives." *The Legal Intelligencer* 227(83):7.

Huber, Joan. 1980. "Will U.S. Fertility Decline toward Zero?" *Sociological Quarterly* 21:481–92.

Huebner, Angela J., Jay A. Mancini, Ryan M. Wilcox, Saralyn R. Grass, and Gabriel A. Grass. 2007. "Parental Deployment and Youth in Military Families: Exploring Uncertainty and Ambiguous Loss." *Family Relations* 56(2):112–22.

Hueveline, Patrick and Jeffrey M. Timberlake. 2004. "The Role of Cohabitation in Family Formation: The United States in Comparative Perspective." *Journal of Marriage and Family* 66(5):1214–30.

Hughes, Diane, Ellen Galinsky, and Anne Morris. 1992. "The Effects of Job Characteristics on Marital Quality: Specifying Linking Mechanisms." *Journal of Marriage and Family* 54(1):31–42.

Hughes, Michael and Walter R. Gove. 1989. "Explaining the Negative Relationship between Social Integration and Mental Health: The Case of Living Alone." Presented at the annual meeting of the American Sociological Association, August, San Francisco, CA.

Hughes, Mikayla, Kelly Morrison, and Jean K. Asada. 2005. "What's Love Got to Do with It? Exploring the Impact of Maintaining Rules, Love Attitudes, and Network Support on Friends with Benefits Relationships." *Western Journal of Communication* 69(1):49–67.

Hughes, Patrick C. and Fran C. Dickson. 2005. "Communication, Marital Satisfaction, and Religious Orientation in Interfaith Marriages." *Journal of Family Communication* 5(1):25–41.

Hulbert, Ann. 2006. "Confidant Crisis." *New York Times,* July 16.

Human Rights Campaign. 2005. "Relationship Recognition in the U.S." Washington, DC. Human Rights Campaign. April. Retrieved July 27, 2006 (www.hrc.org).

———. 2006. "The State of the Workplace for Gay, Lesbian, Bisexual and Transgender Americans 2005–2006." Washington, DC: Human Rights Campaign. Retrieved July 27, 2006 (www.hrc.org).

———. 2007. "Which States Permit Same-sex Parents to Be Listed on a Birth Certificate?" Washington, DC: Human Rights Campaign. Retrieved March 30, 2007 (www.hrc.org).

Hunt, Gail, Carol Levine, and Linda Naiditch. 2005. *Young Caregivers in the U.S: Report of Findings September 2005*. National Alliance for Caregiving.

Hunt, Janet G. and Larry L. Hunt. 1977. "Dilemmas and Contradictions of Status: The Case of the Dual-career Family." *Social Problems* 24:407–16.

———. 1986. "The Dualities of Careers and Families: New Integrations or New Polarizations?" Pp. 275–89 in *Family in Transition: Rethinking Marriage, Sexuality, Child Rearing, and Family Organization*, 5th ed., edited by Arlene S. Skolnick and Jerome H. Skolnick. Boston, MA: Little, Brown.

Hunter, Andrea G. and Sherrill L. Sellers. 1998. "Feminist Attitudes among African American Women and Men." *Gender and Society* 12:81–99.

Hurley, Dan. 2005. "Divorce Rate: It's Not as High as You Think." *New York Times,* April 19.

Hurwitt, Sam. 2004. "Meet the Quirkyalones." *East Bay Express,* March 17.

Huston, Ted L. and Heidi Melz. 2004. "The Case for (Promoting) Marriage: The Devil Is in the Details." *Journal of Marriage and Family* 66(4):943–58.

Hutchinson, Ray and Miles McNall. 1994. "Early Marriage in a Hmong Cohort." *Journal of Marriage and Family* 56(3):579–90.

Huyck, M. H. 1996. "Marriage and Close Relationships of the Marital Kind." Pp. 56–67 in *Aging and the Family*, edited by R. Blieszner and V. H. Bedford. London, England: Praeger.

Hwang, Sean-Shong and Benigno E. Aguirre. 1997. "Structural and Assimilationist Explanations of Asian American Intermarriage." *Journal of Marriage and Family* 59:758–72.

Hwang, Sean-Shong and Rogelio Saenz. 1997. "Fertility of Chinese Immigrants in the U.S.: Testing a Fertility Emancipation Hypothesis." *Journal of Marriage and Family* 59:50–61.

Hyde, Janet Shibley. 2005. "The Gender Similarities Hypothesis." *American Psychologist* 60(6):581–92.

Hyde, Janet Shibley, Elizabeth Fennema, and Susan Lamon. 1990. "Gender Differences in Mathematics Performance: A Meta-Analysis." *Psychological Bulletin* 106:139–55.

Hymowitz, Kay. 2006. *Marriage and Caste in America: Separate and Unequal Families in a Post-Marital Age*. Chicago, IL: Ivan R. Dee.

Iacuone, David. 2005. "'Real Men Are Tough Guys': Hegemonic Masculinity and Safety in the Construction Industry." *Journal of Men's Studies* 13(2):247–67.

Ihinger-Tallman, Marilyn and Kay Pasley. 1997. "Stepfamilies in 1984 and Today—A Scholarly Perspective." *Marriage and Family Review* 26(1-2):19–41.

Ikkink, Karen Klein, Theo van Tilburg, and Kees Knipscheer. 1999. "Perceived Instrumental Support Exchanges in Relationships between Elderly Parents and Their Adult Children: Normative and Structural Explanations." *Journal of Marriage and Family* 61(4):831–44.

"Illegal Immigrant Population." 2001. *New York Times*, July 26.

"Improvements in Teen Sexual Risk Behavior Flatline." 2006. Press Release. Washington, DC: Advocates for Youth.

"Incarceration and Fewer Jobs Given as Impeding Black Gains." 2003. *New York Times*, July 21.

Ingersoll-Dayton, Berit, Margaret B. Neal, Jung-Hwa Ha, and Leslie B. Hammer. 2003. "Redressing Inequity in Parent Care among Siblings." *Journal of Marriage and Family* 65(1):201–12.

Ingersoll-Dayton, Berit, Margaret B. Neal, and Leslie B. Hammer. 2001. "Aging Parents Helping Adult Children: The Experience of the Sandwiched Generation." *Family Relations* 50(3):262–71.

Ingoldsby, Bron B. 2006a. "Family Origin and Universality." Pp. 67–78 in *Families in Global and Multicultural Perspective*, 2nd ed., edited by Bron B. Ingoldsby and Suzanna D. Smith. New York: Guilford.

———. 2006b. "Mate Selection and Marriage." Pp. 133–46 in *Families in Global and Multicultural Perspective*, 2nd ed., edited by Bron B. Ingoldsby and Suzanna D. Smith. New York: Guilford.

Ingoldsby, Bron B. and Suzanna D. Smith, eds. 2005. *Families in Global and Multicultural Perspective*. 2nd ed. Thousand Oaks, CA: Sage Publications.

Ingrassia, Michele. 1995. "Ordered to Surrender." *Newsweek*, February 6, pp. 44–45.

Inman, Jessica and Larry J. Koenig. 2006. *Crash Course on Successful Parenting: 13 Dynamics of Raising Great Kids*. Nashville, TN: Countryman Press.

Institute for Social Research. University of Michigan. 2002. "U.S. Husbands Are Doing More Housework While Wives Are Doing Less." Press Release, March 12.

"Iowa Supreme Court Rejects Antigay Activists' Claims in Lesbian Civil Union Dissolution Case; Lambda Legal Declares Victory." 2007. Press Release, February 26. New York: Lambda Legal. Retrieved May 13, 2007 (www.lambdalegal.org).

Isaacs, Marla Beth, Braulio Montalvo, and David Abelsohn. 1986. *The Difficult Divorce: Therapy for Children and Families*. New York: Basic Books.

Isaksen, Lise W. 2002. "Toward a Sociology of (Gendered) Disgust." *Journal of Family Issues* 23(7):791–811.

Ishii-Kuntz, Masako. 2000. "Diversity within Asian American Families." Pp. 274–92 in *Handbook of Family Diversity*, edited by David H. Demo, Katherine R. Allen, and Mark Fine. New York: Oxford University Press.

Island, David and Patrick Letellier. 1991. *Men Who Beat the Men Who Love Them: Battered Gay Men and Domestic Violence*. New York: Haworth

"It Takes a Family." 2007. *San Francisco Chronicle*, February 25, p. E-4.

"It's the Kids: Lock Up the China!" 2005. *New York Times*, July 28.

Jackson, Pamela Braboy. 2004. "Role Sequencing: Does Order Matter for Mental Health?" *Journal of Health and Social Behavior* 45:132–54.

Jackson, Robert Max. 2006. "Opposing Forces: How, Why, and When Will Gender Inequality Disappear?" Pp. 215–44 in *The Declining Significance of Gender?* edited by Francine D. Blau, Mary C. Brinton, and David B. Grusky. New York: Russell Sage.

Jackson, Shelly, Lynette Feder, David R. Forde, Robert C. Davis, Christopher D. Maxwell, and Bruce G. Taylor. 2003. *Batterer Intervention Programs: Where Do We Go from Here?* Washington, DC: U.S. National Institute of Justice.

Jackson, Robert M. 2007. "Destined for Equality." Pp. 109–16 in *Family in Transition*, 14th ed., edited by Arlene S. Skolnick and Jerome H. Skolnick. Boston, MA and New York: Pearson.

Jacobs, Andres. 2006. "Extreme Makeover, Commune Edition." *New York Times*, June 11. Retrieved June 11, 2006 (http://www.nytimes.com).

Jacobs, Jerry A. and Kathleen Gerson. 2004. *The Time Divide: Work, Family, and Gender Inequality*. Cambridge, MA: Harvard University Press.

Jacobson, Cardell K. and Bryan R. Johnson. 2006. "Interracial Friendship and African American Attitudes about Interracial Marriage." *Journal of Black Studies* 36(4):570–84.

Jacobson, Neil S. and John M. Gottman. 2001. "Anatomy of a Violent Relationship." Pp. 475–87 in *Family in Transition*, 11th ed., edited by Arlene S. Skolnick and Jerome H. Skolnick. Boston, MA: Allyn and Bacon.

Jacoby, Susan. 1999. "Great Sex: What's Age Got to Do with It?" *Modern Maturity* (September–October), pp. 41–47.

———. 2005. "Sex in America." *AARP The Magazine*, July/August, pp. 57–62, 114.

Jaksch, Mary. 2002. *Learn to Love: A Practical Guide to Fulfilling Relationships*. San Francisco, CA: Chronicle Books.

Janofsky, Michael. 2001. "Conviction of a Polygamist Raises Fears Among Others." *New York Times*, May 24.

Jaret, Charles, Donald C. Reitzes, and Nadezda Shapkina. 2005. "Reflected Appraisals and Self-Esteem." *Sociological Perspectives* 48(3):403–19.

Jarrett, Robin L. and Stephanie M. Jefferson. 2004. "Women's Danger Management Strategies in an Inner-City Housing Project." *Family Relations* 53(2):138–47.

Jay, David. 2005. "Asexual: A Person Who Does Not Experience Sexual Attraction." Asexual Visibility and Education Network. Retrieved February 22, 2007 (www.asexuality.org).

Jayakody, R. and A. Kalil. 2002. "Social Fathering in Low-income, African American Families with Preschool Children." *Journal of Marriage and Family* 64(2):504–16.

Jayson, Sharon. 2005a. "Cohabiting Americans in 7 States Run Afoul of the Law." *USA Today*, July 17. Retrieved October 29, 2006 (http://www.usatoday.com).

———. 2005b. "Yep, Life'll Burst That Self-esteem Bubble." *USA Today*, February 16.

———. 2006a. "Is 'Failure to Launch' Really a Failure?" *USA Today*, March 16.

———. 2006b. "Outside the Race Box." *USA Today*, February 8.

Jeffries, Vincent. 2000. "Virtue and Marital Conflict: A Theoretical Formulation and Research Agenda." *Sociological Perspectives* 43(2):231–46.

Jenks, R. L. 1998. "Swinging: A Review of the Literature." *Archives of Sexual Behavior* 27:507–21.

Jepsen, Lisa. K. and Christopher A. Jepsen. 2002. "An Empirical Analysis of the Matching Patterns of Same-sex and Opposite-sex Couples?" *Demography* 39(3):435–53.

Jervey, Gay. 2004. "The Bad Mother." *Good Housekeeping*, August, pp. 132–82.

Jeynes, William. 2000. "A Longitudinal Analysis on the Effects of Remarriage Following Divorce on the Academic Achievement of Adolescents." *Journal of Divorce and Remarriage* 33(1/2):131–48.

Jo, Moon H. 2002. "Coping with Gender Role Strains in Korean American Families." Pp. 78–83 in *Contemporary Ethnic Families in the United States*, edited by Nijole V. Benekraitis. Upper Saddle River, NJ: Prentice Hall.

Johann, Sara Lee. 1994. *Domestic Abusers: Terrorists in Our Homes*. Springfield, IL: Thomas.

Johannson, Melanie A. and Leslie M. Tutty. 1998. "An Evaluation of After-treatment Couples' Groups for Wife Abuse." *Family Relations* 47(1):27–35.

John, Daphne, Beth Anne Shelton, and Kristen Luschen. 1995. "Race, Ethnicity, and Perceptions of Fairness." *Journal of Family Issues* 16:357–79.

John, Robert. 1998. "Native American Families." Pp. 382–421 in *Ethnic Families in America: Patterns and Variations*, edited by Charles H. Mindel, Robert W. Haberstein, and Roosevelt Wright, Jr. Upper Saddle River, NJ: Prentice Hall.

Johnson, Colleen L. 1988. *Ex Familia: Grandparents, Parents, and Children Adjust to Divorce*. New Brunswick, NJ: Rutgers University Press.

Johnson, Dirk. 1991. "Polygamists Emerge from Secrecy, Seeking Not Just Peace but Respect." *New York Times*, April 9.

———. 2002. "Until Dust Do Us Part." *Newsweek*, March 25, p. 41.

Johnson, Earl S., Ann Levine, and Fred Doolittle. 1999. *Fathers' Fair Share: Helping Poor Men Manage Child Support and Fatherhood*. New York: Russell Sage.

Johnson, Elizabeth M. and Ted L. Huston. 1998. "The Perils of Love, or Why Wives Adapt to Husbands during the Transition to Parenthood." *Journal of Marriage and Family* 60(1):195–204.

Johnson, Jason B. 2000. "Something Akin to Family: Struggling Parents, Kids, Move in with Their Mentors." *San Francisco Chronicle*, November 10.

Johnson, Julia Overturf. 2005. *Who's Minding the Kids? Child Care Arrangements: Winter 2002*. Current Population Reports P70-101. Washington, DC: U.S. Census Bureau.

Johnson, Julia Overturf and Barbara Downs. 2005. *Maternity Leave and Employment Patterns of First-time Mothers 1961–2000*. Current Population Reports P70-103. Washington, DC: U.S. Census Bureau. October.

Johnson, Kirk. 1998. "Self-image Is Suffering from Lack of Esteem." *New York Times*, May 5, p. B12.

Johnson, Matthew D., Joanne Davila, Ronald D. Rogge, Kieran T. Sullivan, Catherine L. Cohan, Erika Lawrence, Benjamin R. Karney, and Thomas N. Bradbury. 2005. "Problem-solving Skills and Affective Expressions as Predictors of Change in Marital Satisfaction." *Journal of Consulting and Clinical Psychology* 73(1):15–27.

Johnson, Michael P. 1995. "Patriarchal Terrorism and Common Couple Violence: Two Forms of Violence Against Women." *Journal of Marriage and Family* 57(2):283–94.

———. 2001. "Conflict and Control: Images of Symmetry and Asymmetry in Domestic Violence." Pp. 95–104 in *Couples in Conflict*, edited by Alan Booth, Ann C. Crouter, and M. Clements. Hillsdale, NJ: Erlbaum.

Johnson, Michael P. and Kathleen J. Ferraro. 2000. "Research on Domestic Violence in the 1990s: Making Distinctions." *Journal of Marriage and Family* 62(4):948–63.

Johnson, Phyllis J. 1998. "Performance of Household Tasks by Vietnamese and Laotian Refugees." *Journal of Family Issues* 10(3):245–73.

Johnson, Richard W. and Joshua M. Wiener. 2006. "A Profile of Frail Older Americans and Their Caregivers." Urban Institute. March 1. Retrieved May 18, 2007 (http://www.urban .org/publications).

Johnson, Suzanne M. and Elizabeth O'Connor. 2002. *The Gay Baby Boom: The Psychology of Gay Parenthood.* New York: New York University Press.

Johnson, Thomas W. and Patricia Colucci. 1999. "Lesbians, Gay Men, and the Family Life Cycle." Pp. 356–61 in *The Expanded Life Cycle: Individual, Family, and Social Perspectives,* 3rd ed., edited by Betty Carter and Monica McGoldrick. Boston, MA: Allyn and Bacon.

Johnston, Janet and Linda K. Girtner. 2001. *Family Abductions, Descriptive Profiles, and Preventive Interventions.* Juvenile Justice Bulletin. January.

Jones, A. J., and M. Galinsky. 2003. "Restructuring the Stepfamily: Old Myths, New Stories." *Social Work* 48(2):228–37.

Jones, Anne C. 2004. "Transforming the Story: Narrative Applications to a Stepmother Support Group." *Families in Society: The Journal of Contemporary Human Services* 85(1):29–39.

Jones, B. J. 1995. "The Indian Child Welfare Act: The Need for a Separate Law." *GP Solo Magazine.* Chicago, IL: American Bar Association. Fall. Retrieved December 28, 2006 (www.abanet.org/ general practice).

Jones, Charisse. 2004. "Housing Doors Close on Parents." *USA Today,* May 6.

Jones, Del 2006. "One of USA's Exports: Love, American Style." *USA Today.* February 14.

Jones, Jeffrey M. 2002. "Public Divided on Benefits of Living Together Before Marriage." The Gallup Poll. Retrieved September 13, 2006 (http://www .galluppoll.com).

———. 2005. "Most Americans Approve of Interracial Dating." The Gallup Poll. Retrieved November 4, 2006 (http://www.galluppoll.com).

Jones, Matthew D. 2006. *Raising Boys to Become Responsible Men.* New York: iUniverse.

Jones, Nicholas. 2005. *We the People of More Than One Race in the United States.* CENSR22. Washington, DC: U.S. Census Bureau. April. Retrieved April 30, 2005 (www.census.gov).

Jones, Nicholas A. and Amy Symens Smith. 2001. "The Two or More Races Population: 2000." Census 2000 Brief C2KBR/01-6. November.

Jones, Rachel K., Jacqueline E. Darroch, and Stanley K. Henshaw. 2002. "Patterns in the Socioeconomic Characteristics of Women Obtaining Abortions in 2000–2001." *Perspectives on Sexual and Reproductive Health* 34:226–35.

Jong-Fast, Molly. 2003. "Out of Step and Having a Baby." *New York Times,* October 5.

Joseph, Elizabeth. 1991. "My Husband's Nine Wives." *New York Times,* May 23.

Joseph, Nadine and Brad Stone. 2005. "Diagnosis: Internet Phobia." *Newsweek,* April 25, p. 74.

Jourard, Sidney M. 1976. "Reinventing Marriage." Pp. 231–37 in *Process in Relationship: Marriage and Family,* 2nd ed., edited by Edward A. Powers and Mary W. Lees. New York: West.

Joyce, Amy. 2005a. "Time Off for Babies Often Does Not Pay." *Omaha World-Herald (Washington Post).* March. 4.

———. 2005b. "Workplace Improves for Gay, Transgender Employees, Rights Group Says." *Washington Post,* June 6.

———. 2006. "Kid-Friendly Policies Don't Help Singles." *Washington Post,* September 16.

———. 2007a. "Caring for Dear Old Dad Becomes a Little Easier." *Washington Post,* March 4.

———. 2007b. "Developing Boomerang Mothers." *Washington Post,* March 11.

Joyner, Kara and Grace Kao. 2005. "Interracial Relationships and the Transition to Adulthood." *American Sociological Review* 70(4):563–81.

Juffer, Femmie and Marinus H. van Uzendoorn. 2005. "Behavior Problems and Mental Health Referrals of International Adoptees: A Meta-Analysis. *Journal of the American Medical Association* 293(20):2501–15.

Julian, Teresa W., Patrick C. McKenry, and Mary W. McKelvey. 1994. "Cultural Variations in Parenting." *Family Relations* 43:30–37.

Junn, Ellen Nan and Chris J. Boyatzis. 2005. *Child Growth and Development 05/06,* 12th edition. Guilford, CT: McGraw-Hill/Dushkin.

Kader, Samuel. 1999. *Openly Gay, Openly Christian: How the Bible Really Is Gay Friendly.* Leyland Publications.

Kahn, Arif Shamim. N.d. "Marriage between Muslims and Non-Muslims." *Issues in Intermarriages.* Retrieved November 24, 2006 (http://www.admin .muslimonline.com).

Kaiser Family Foundation. 2001. *Inside-OUT: A Report on the Experiences of Lesbians, Gays, and Bisexuals in America and the Public's Views on Issues and Policies Related to Sexual Orientation.* Menlo Park, CA: Kaiser Family Foundation.

Kalish, Susan. 1995. "Multiracial Births Increase as U.S. Ponders Racial Definitions." *Population Today* 23(4):1–2.

Kalmijn, Matthijs. 1998. "Differentiation and Stratification—Intermarriage and Homogamy: Causes, Patterns, and Trends." *Annual Review of Sociology* 24:395–427.

Kamo, Yoshinori and Min Zhou. 1994. "Living Arrangements of Elderly Chinese and Japanese in the United States." *Journal of Marriage and Family* 56(3):544–58.

Kan, Marni L. and Alison C. Cares. 2006. "From 'Friends with Benefits' to 'Going Steady': New Directions in Understanding Romance and Sex in Adolescence and Emerging Adulthood." Pp. 241–58 in *Romance and Sex in Adolescence and Emerging Adulthood: Risks and Opportunities,* edited by Ann C. Crouter and Alan Booth. Mahwah, NJ: Erlbaum.

Kane, Emily W. 2000. "Racial and Ethnic Variations in Gender-related Attitudes." *Annual Review of Sociology* 26:416–39.

Kann, Mark E. 1986. "The Costs of Being on Top." *Journal of The National Association for Women Deans, Administrators, and Counselors* 49:29–37.

Kantor, David and William Lehr. 1975. *Inside the Family: Toward a Theory of Family Process.* San Francisco, CA: Jossey-Bass.

Kantor, Glenda Kaufman and Jana L. Jasinski. 1998. "Dynamics and Risk Factors in Partner Violence." Pp. 1–13 in *Partner Violence: A Comprehensive Review of 20 Years of Research,* edited by Jana L. Jasinski and Linda M. Williams. Thousand Oaks, CA: Sage Publications.

Kantor, Jodi. 2006. "Nanny Hunt Can Be a 'Slap in the Face' for Blacks." *New York Times,* December 26.

Kantrowitz, Barbara. 2000. "Busy around the Clock." *Newsweek,* July 17, pp. 49–50.

Kantrowitz, Barbara and Karen Springen. 2005. "A Peaceful Adolescence." *Newsweek,* April 25, pp. 58–61.

Kantrowitz, Barbara and Peg Tyre. 2006. "The Fine Art of Letting Go." *Newsweek,* May 22, pp. 49–61.

Kaplan, Karen. 2006. "Study Links Male Gays, Birth of Older Brothers." *Los Angeles Times,* June 27.

Kaplan, Marion A., ed. 1985. *The Marriage Bargain: Women and Dowries in European History.* New York: Harrington Park.

Kaplan-Leiserson, Eva. 2003. "Generation Sandwich." *American Society for Training and Development: T&D* 57(2):16–18.

Karasik, Rona J. and Raeann R. Hamon. 2007. "Cultural Diversity and Aging Families." Pp. 136–53 in *Cultural Diversity and Families,* edited by Bahira Sherif Trask and Raeann R. Hamon. Thousand Oaks, CA: Sage Publications.

Karen, R. 1994. *Becoming Attached: Unfolding the Mystery of the Infant–Mother Bond and Its Impact on Later Life.* New York: Warner.

Katz, Jon. 2003. *The New Work of Dogs: Tending to Life, Love, and the Family.* New York: Villard.

Katz, Lillian. 1993. *Distinctions between Self-esteem and Narcissism: Implications for Practice.* ERIC Clearinghouse on Elementary and Early Childhood Education. Retrieved August 16, 2006 (http://www.ericdigests.org/1993/esteem.htm).

Katz, Lynn F. and Erica M. Woodin. 2002. "Hostility, Hostile Detachment, and Conflict Engagement in Marriages: Effects on Child and Family Functioning." *Child Development* 73(2):636–52.

Kaufman, Gayle and Hiromi Taniguchi. 2006. "Gender and Marital Happiness in Later Life." *Journal of Family Issues* 27(6):735–57.

Kaufman, Gayle and Peter Uhlenberg. 1998. "Effects of Life Course Transitions on the Quality of Relationships between Adult Children and Their Parents." *Journal of Marriage and Family* 60(4):924–38.

———. 2000. "The Influence of Parenthood on the Work Effort of Married Men and Women." *Social Forces* 78:931–49.

Kaufman, Leslie. 2006. "Facing Hardest Choice in Child Safety, New York Tilts to Preserving Families." *New York Times,* February 4.

———. 2007. "In Custody Fights, a Hurdle for the Poor." *New York Times,* April 8.

Kaukinen, Catherine. 2004. "Status Compatibility, Physical Violence, and Emotional Abuse in Intimate Relationships." *Journal of Marriage and Family* 66:452–71.

Kaye, Sarah. 2005. "Substance Abuse Treatment and Child Welfare: Systematic Change Is Needed." *Family Focus on . . . Substance Abuse across the Life Span*: FF25: F15–F16. Minneapolis, MN: National Council of Family Relations.

Kazdin, Alan E. and Corina Benjet. 2003. "Spanking Children: Evidence and Issues." *Current Directions in Psychological Science* (March):99–103.

Keefe, Janice and Pamela Fancey. 2000. "The Care Continues: Responsibility for Elderly Relatives Before and After Admission to a Long Term Care Facility." *Family Relations* 49(3):235–44.

Keith, Carolyn. 1995. "Family Caregiving Systems: Models, Resources, and Values." *Journal of Marriage and Family* 57(1):179–89.

Keith, Kimberly K. N.d. "Parenting of K–6 Children." Retrieved February 12, 2007 (http://childparenting.about.com).

Kelly, Joan B. and Robert E. Emery. 2003. "Children's Adjustment Following Divorce: Risk and Resiliency Perspectives." *Family Relations* 52:352–62.

Kelly, Joan B. and Michael E. Lamb. 2003. "Developmental Issues in Relocation Cases Involving Young Children: When, Whether, and How?" *Journal of Family Psychology* 17:193–205.

Kempe, C. Henry, Frederic N. Silverman, Brandt F. Steele, William Droegemuller, and Henry K. Silver. 1962. "The Battered Child Syndrome." *Journal of the American Medical Association* 181:17–24.

Kenney, Catherine. 2004. "Cohabiting Couple, Filing Jointly? Resource Pooling and U.S. Poverty Policies." *Family Relations* 53(2):237–47.

———. 2006. "The Power of the Purse: Allocative Systems and Inequality in Couple Households." *Gender and Society* 20(3):354–81.

Kenney, Catherine and Sara S. McLanahan. 2006. "Why Are Cohabiting Relationships More Violent Than Marriages?" *Demography* 43(1):127–40.

Kent, Mary and Robert Lalasz. 2006. "In the News: Speaking English in the United States." Washington, DC: Population Reference Bureau. Retrieved December 22, 2006 (www.prb.org).

Kent, Mary M., Kelvin M. Pollard, John Hagga, and Mark Mather. 2001. "First Glimpses from the 2000 U.S. Census." *Population Bulletin* 56(2). Washington, DC: Population Reference Bureau.

Kephart, William. 1971. "Oneida: An Early American Commune." Pp. 481–92 in *Family in Transition: Rethinking Marriage, Sexuality, Child Rearing, and Family Organization,* edited by Arlene S. Skolnick and Jerome H. Skolnick. Boston, MA: Little, Brown.

Kern, Louis J. 1981. *An Ordered Love: Sex Roles and Sexuality in Victorian Utopias— The Shakers, the Mormons, and the Oneida Community.* Chapel Hill: University of North Carolina Press.

Kershaw, Sarah. 2003. "Many Immigrants Decide to Embrace Homes for Elderly." *New York Times,* October 20, pp. A1, A10.

———. 2004. "For Native Alaskans, Tradition Is Yielding to Modern Customs." *New York Times,* August 21.

———. 2005. "Crisis of Indian Children Intensifies as Families Fail." *New York Times,* April 5.

Khaleque, Abdul and Ronald P. Rohner. 2002. "Perceived Parental Acceptance-Rejection and Psychological Adjustment: A Meta-Analysis of Cross-cultural and Intracultural Studies." *Journal of Marriage and Family* 64(1):54–64.

Kheshgi-Genovese, Zareena and Thomas A. Genovese. 1997. "Developing the Spousal Relationship within Stepfamilies." *Families in Society* 78(3):255–64.

Kibria, Nazli. 2000. "Race, Ethnic Options, and Ethnic Binds: Identity Negotiations of Second-Generation Chinese and Korean Americans." *Sociological Perspectives* 43(1):77–95.

———. 2007. "Vietnamese Americans and the Rise of Women's Power." Pp. 220–27 in *Race, Class, and Gender: An Anthology,* 6th ed., edited by Margaret L. Andersen and Patricia Hill Collins. Belmont, CA: Wadsworth.

"Kids Conceived after Dad Died to Get Benefits." 2004. *Omaha World-Herald* (*L.A. Times*), June 10.

Kiecolt, K. Jill. 2003. "Satisfaction with Work and Family Life: No Evidence of Cultural Reversal." *Journal of Marriage and Family* 65(1):23–35.

Kiernan, Kathleen. 2002. "Cohabitation in Western Europe: Trends, Issues, and Implications." Pp. 3–31 in *Just Living Together: Implication of Cohabitation on Families, Children, and Social Policy*, edited by Alan Booth and A. C. Crouter. Mahwah, NJ: Erlbaum.

Kilbourne, Jean. 1994. "'Gender Bender' Ads: Same Old Sexism." *New York Times*, May 15, p. F13.

Killian, Timothy and Lawrence H. Ganong. 2002. "Ideology, Context, and Obligations to Assist Older Persons." *Journal of Marriage and Family* 64(4):1080–88.

Kim, Haejeong and Sharon A. DeVaney. 2005. "The Selection of Partial or Full Retirement by Older Workers." *Journal of Family and Economic Issues* 26(3):371–94.

Kim, Hyoun K., Deborah M. Capaldi, and Lynn Crosby. 2007. "Generalizability of Gottman and Colleagues' Affective Process Models of Couples' Relationship Outcomes." *Journal of Marriage and Family* 69(1):55–72.

Kim, Hyoun K., and Patrick C. McKenry. 2002. "The Relationship between Marriage and Psychological Well-Being." *Journal of Family Issues* 23(8):885–911.

Kimmel, Michael S. 1995. "Misogynists, Masculinist Mentors, and Male Supporters: Men's Responses to Feminism." Pp. 561–72 in *Women: A Feminist Perspective*, 5th ed., edited by Jo Freeman. Mountain View, CA: Mayfield.

———. 2000. *The Gendered Society*. New York: Oxford University Press.

———. 2001. "Manhood and Violence: The Deadliest Equation." *Newsday*, March 8, p. A41.

———. 2002. "'Gender Symmetry' in Domestic Violence." *Violence Against Women* 8:1332–63.

Kimmel, Michael S. and Michael A. Messner. 1998. *Men's Lives*. 4th ed. Boston, MA: Allyn and Bacon.

Kimmel, Tim. 2006. *Raising Kids for True Greatness*. Nashville, TN: W Publishing Group.

Kimura, Doreen. 1999. *Sex and Cognition*. Cambridge, MA: MIT Press.

———. 2002. "Sex Differences in the Brain." *Scientific American* 12(1):32–37.

Kindlon, Dan and Michael Thompson. 1999. *Raising Cain: Protecting the Emotional Life of Boys*. New York: Ballantine.

King, Deborah A. and Lyman C. Wynne. 2004. "The Emergence of 'Family Integrity' in Later Life." *Family Process* 43(1):7–21.

King, Valarie and Mindy E. Scott. 2005. "A Comparison of Cohabiting Relationships among Older and Younger Adults." *Journal of Marriage and Family* 67(2):271–85.

King, Valarie. 1994. "Variation in the Consequences of Nonresident Father Involvement for Children's Well-Being." *Journal of Marriage and Family* 56(3):963–72.

King, Valarie and Glen H. Elder, Jr. 1997. "The Legacy of Grandparenting: Childhood Experiences with Grandparents and Current Involvement with Grandchildren." *Journal of Marriage and Family* 59(4):848–59.

King, Valarie, Merril Silverstein, Glen H. Elder, Jr., Vern L. Bengston, and Rand D. Conger. 2003. "Relations with Grandparents: Rural Midwest versus Urban Southern California." *Journal of Family Issues* 24(8):1044–69.

King, Valarie and Juliana M. Sobolewski. 2006. "Nonresident Fathers' Contributions to Adolescent Well-Being." *Journal of Marriage and Family* 68(3):537–57.

Kinsey, Alfred, Wardell B. Pomeroy, and Clyde E. Martin. 1948. *Sexual Behavior in the Human Male*. Philadelphia, PA: Saunders.

———. 1953. *Sexual Behavior in the Human Female*. Philadelphia, PA: Saunders.

Kirby, Carrie. 2005. "Picky Suitors Narrow Search to Niche Sites." *San Francisco Chronicle*, February 14.

Kirby, Douglas. 2001. *Emerging Answers*. Washington, DC: National Campaign to Prevent Teen Pregnancy.

Kirby, Douglas, B. A. Laris, and Lori Rolleri. 2006. *Sex and HIV Education Programs for Youth: Their Impact and Important Characteristics*. Research Triangle Park, NC: Family Health International. May 13.

Kirby, James B. 2006. "From Single-parent Families to Stepfamilies: Is the Transition Associated with Adolescent Alcohol Initiation?" *Journal of Family Issues* 27(5):685–711.

Kirn, Walter and Wendy Cole. 2001. "What Ever Happened to Play?" *Time*, April 30, pp. 54–56.

Kitano, Harry and Roger Daniels. 1995. *Asian Americans: Emerging Minorities*. 2nd ed. Englewood Cliffs, NJ: Prentice Hall.

Kitson, Gay C. 1992. *Portrait of Divorce: Adjustment to Marital Breakdown*. New York: Guilford.

Kleber, Rolf J., Charles R. Figley, P. R. Barthold, and John P. Wilson. 1997. "Beyond Trauma: Cultural and Societal Dynamics." *Contemporary Psychology* 42(6):516–27.

Kleiman, Carol. 2003. "Working Moms See Pay Take a Hit." *Omaha World-Herald*, May 4.

Klein, Barbara Schave. 2007. *Raising Gifted Kids: Everything You Need to Know to Help Your Exceptional Child Thrive*. New York: AMACOM (American Management Association).

Klein, R. C. and M. P. Johnson. 1997. "Strategies of Couple Conflict." Pp. 14–39 in *Handbook of Personal Relationships: Theory, Research, and Interventions*, 2nd ed., edited by S. Duck. New York: Wiley.

Kleinfield, N. R. 2003. "Around Tree, Smiles Even for Wives No. 2 and 3." *New York Times*, December 24.

Kliman, Jodie and William Madsen. 1999. "Social Class and the Family Life Cycle." Pp. 88–105 in *The Expanded Family Life Cycle: Individual, Family, and Social Perspectives*, 3rd ed. Boston, MA: Allyn and Bacon.

Klohnen, Eva C. and Gerald A. Mendelsohn. 1998. "Partner Selection for Personality Characteristics: A Couple-centered Approach." *Personality & Social Psychology Bulletin* 24(3):268–77.

Kluger, Jeffrey. 2004. "The Power of Love." *Time*, January 19.

Kluwer, Esther S., Jose A. M. Heesink, and Evert Van de Vliert. 2002. "The Division of Labor across the Transition to Parenthood: A Justice Perspective." *Journal of Marriage and Family* 64(4):930–43.

Knapp, Caroline. 1999. *Pack of Two: The Intricate Bond between People and Dogs*. New York: Doubleday/Broadway.

Knobloch, Leanne K., Denise H. Solomon, and Jennifer A. Theiss. 2006. "The Role of Intimacy in the Production and Perception of Relationship Talk within Courtship." *Communication Research* 33(4):211–41.

Knoester, Chris and Alan Booth. 2000. "Barriers to Divorce: When Are They Effective? When Are They Not?" *Journal of Family Issues* 21:78–99.

Knoester, Chris and Dana L. Haynie. 2005. "Community Context, Social Integration into Family, and Youth Violence." *Journal of Marriage and Family* 67:767–80.

Knoester, Chris, Dana L. Haynie, and Crystal M. Stephens. 2006. "Parenting Practices and Adolescents' Friendship Networks." *Journal of Marriage and Family* 68(5):1247–60.

Knox, David H., Jr. 1975. *Marriage: Who? When? Why?* Englewood Cliffs, NJ: Prentice Hall.

Knox, Noelle. 2004. "Orphans Caught in the Middle." *USA Today,* May 18.

Knudson-Martin, Carmen and Anne Rankin Mahoney. 1998. "Language and Processes in the Construction of Equality in New Marriages." *Family Relations* 47(1):81–91.

Koblinsky, Sally A. 2001. "A Peaceful Village: Protecting Young Children from Community Violence." *Family Focus* (September):F10. National Council on Family Relations.

Koch, Wendy. 2005. "Despite High-profile Cases, Sex-offense Crimes Decline." *USA Today,* August 25.

———. 2006. "Creative Efforts Ensure Parents Pay." *USA Today,* March 15.

Kohlberg, Lawrence. 1966. "A Cognitive–Developmental Analysis of Children's Sex-role Concepts and Attitudes." Pp. 82–173 in *The Development of Sex Differences,* edited by Eleanor E. Maccoby. Palo Alto, CA: Stanford University Press.

Kolata, Gina. 1993. "Family Aid to Elderly Very Strong, Study Shows." *New York Times,* May 3.

———. 2002a. "Parenthood Help for Men with H.I.V." *New York Times,* April 30.

———. 2002b. "Treatments for Fertility Are Studied for Problems." *New York Times,* March 7.

Komsi, Niina, Katri Raikkonen, Anu-Katriina Pesonen, Kati Heinonen, Pertti Keskivaara, Anna-liisa Japvenpaa, and Timo E. Strandberg. 2006. "Continuity of Temperament from Infancy to Middle Childhood." *Infant Behavior and Development* 29(4):494–508.

Komter, A. 1989. "Hidden Power in Marriage." *Gender and Society* 3:187–216.

Konner, Melvin. 1990. "Women and Sexuality." *New York Times Magazine,* April 29, pp. 24, 26.

Koop, C. Everett. N.d. *Surgeon General's Report on Acquired Immune Deficiency Syndrome.* Washington, DC: U.S. Department of Health and Human Services.

Koplan, Jeffrey, Catharyn T. Liverman, and U.S. Institute of Medicine, National Committee on Prevention of Obesity. 2005. *Preventing Childhood Obesity: Health in the Balance.* Washington, DC: National Academies Press.

Kopytoff, Verne. 2005. "Online Dating Tries to Rekindle the Love." *San Francisco Chronicle,* February 14.

Kosmin, Barry A., Egon Mayer, and Ariela Keysar. 2001. "American Religious Identification Survey, 2001." New York and Hartford, CT: Graduate Center of the City University of New York and the Institute for the Study of Secularism in Society. Retrieved July 5, 2007 (www.trincoll.edu/secularisminstitute)

Kost, Kathleen A. 2001. "The Function of Fathers: What Poor Men Say about Fatherhood." *Families in Society: The Journal of Contemporary Human Services* 82(5):499–15.

Krantzler, Mel. 1973. *Creative Divorce: New Opportunities for Personal Growth.* New York: M. Evans.

Kravets, David. 2005. "Custody, Support Applied to Gays in Calif." *USA Today,* August 23.

Kreider, Rose M. 2003. *Adopted Children and Stepchildren: 2000.* Census 2000 Special Reports CENSR-6. Washington, DC: U.S. Census Bureau. August.

———. 2005. *Number, Timing, and Duration of Marriages and Divorces: 2001.* Current Population Reports P70-97. Washington, DC: U.S. Census Bureau.

Kreider, Rose M. and Jason M. Fields. 2002. *Number, Timing, and Duration of Marriages and Divorces: 1996.* Current Population Reports P70-80. Washington, DC: U.S. Census Bureau. February.

———. 2005. *Living Arrangements of Children: 2001.* Current Population Reports P70-104. Washington, DC: U.S. Census Bureau. July.

Krementz, Jill. 1984. *How It Feels When Parents Divorce.* New York: Knopf.

Krivo, Lauren J. and Robert L. Kaufman. 2004. "Housing and Wealth Inequality: Racial-Ethnic Differences in Home Equity in the United States." *Demography* 41(3):585–605.

Kroska, Amy. 1997. "The Division of Labor in the Home: A Review and Reconceptualization." *Social Psychology Quarterly* 60(4):304–22.

Krueger, Alan. B. 2004. "Economic Scene." *New York Times,* April 29.

Krueger, Joachim. 2003. "Self-esteem as a Social Dilemma." Knight Ridder/Tribune News Service, May 13.

Krugman, Paul. 2006a. "The Great Wealth Transfer." *Rolling Stone,* December 14, pp. 44–48.

———. 2006b. "North of the Border." *New York Times,* March 27.

Kruttschnitt, Candace, Jane D. McLeod, and Maude Dornfeld. 1994. "The Economic Environment of Child Abuse." *Social Problems* 41(2):299–315.

Kuczynski, Alex. 2001. "Guess Who's Coming to Dinner Now?" *New York Times,* December 23.

Kulczycki, Andrzej and Arun Peter Lobo. 2002. "Patterns, Determinants, and Implications of Intermarriage among Arab Americans." *Journal of Marriage and Family* 64(1):202–10.

Kumpfer, Karol and Connie Tait. 2000. *Family Skills Training for Parents and Children.* Juvenile Justice Bulletin. April.

Kurcinka, Mary S. 2006. *Raising Your Spirited Child.* New York: Harper.

Kurdek, Lawrence A. 1989. "Relationship Quality in Gay and Lesbian Cohabiting Couples: A 1-Year Follow-up Study." *Journal of Social and Personal Relationships* 6:35–59.

———. 1991. "The Relations between Reported Well-being and Divorce History, Availability of a Proximate Adult, and Gender." *Journal of Marriage and Family* 53(1):71–78.

———. 1994. "Areas of Conflict for Gay, Lesbian, and Heterosexual Couples: What Couples Argue About Influences Relationship Satisfaction." *Journal of Marriage and Family* 56(4):923–34.

———. 1995a. "Assessing Multiple Determinants of Relationship Commitment in Cohabiting Gay, Cohabiting Lesbian, Dating

Heterosexual, and Married Heterosexual Couples." *Family Relations* 44:261–66.

———. 1995b. "Predicting Change in Marital Satisfaction from Husbands' and Wives' Conflict Resolution Styles." *Journal of Marriage and Family* 57(1):153–64.

———. 1998. "Relationship Outcomes and Their Predictors: Longitudinal Evidence from Heterosexual Married, Gay Cohabiting, and Lesbian Cohabiting Couples." *Journal of Marriage and Family* 60(3):553–68.

———. 2005. "Gender and Marital Satisfaction Early in Marriage: A Growth Curve Approach." *Journal of Marriage and Family* 67(1):68–84.

———. 2006. "Differences between Partners from Heterosexual, Gay, and Lesbian Cohabiting Couples." *Journal of Marriage and Family* 68(2):509–28.

———. 2007. "The Allocation of Household Labor by Partners in Gay and Lesbian Couples." *Journal of Family Issues* 28(1):132–48.

Kurdek, Lawrence A. and Mark A. Fine. 1991. "Cognitive Correlates of Satisfaction for Mothers and Stepfathers in Stepfather Families." *Journal of Marriage and Family* 53(3):565–72.

Kurtz, Stanley. 2006. "Big Love, from the Set." *National Review,* March 13.

Kurz, Demie. 1993. "Physical Assaults by Husbands: A Major Social Problem." Pp. 88–103 in *Current Controversies on Family Violence,* edited by Richard J. Gelles and Donileen R. Loseke. Newbury Park, CA: Sage Publications.

———. 2002. "Poor Mothers and the Care of Teenage Children." Pp. 23–36 in *Child Care and Inequality: Rethinking Care Work for Children and Youth,* edited by Francesca Cancian, Demie Kurz, Andrew S. London, Rebecca Reviere, and Mary C. Tuominen. New York: Routledge.

Kutner, Lawrence. 1988. "Parent and Child: Working at Home; or, The Midday Career Change." *New York Times,* December 8.

———. 1990a. "Parent and Child: Chasms of Pain and Growth; When Generation Gaps Are Too Wide to Leap." *New York Times,* March 8.

———. 1990b. "Parent and Child: Money Matters, for Some as Confidential as Sex, Are Often a Stressful Subject." *New York Times,* January 11.

———. 1990c. "Parent and Child: When a Child Marries; The Pride and the Pitfalls." *New York Times,* May 10.

Lacey, Mary. 2006. "With More Americans Adopting, Guatemala System Is Questioned." *New York Times,* November 5.

Lacey, Rachel Saul, Alan Reifman, Jean Pearson Scott, Steven M. Harris, and Jacki Fitzpatrick. 2004. "Sexual-Moral Attitudes, Love Styles, and Mate Selection." *Journal of Sex Research* 41(2):121–29.

Lackey, Chad and Kirk R. Williams. 1995. "Social Bonding and the Cessation of Partner Violence across Generations." *Journal of Marriage and Family* 57(2):295–305.

Ladner, Joyce A. 1984. "Providing a Healthy Environment for Interracial Children." *Interracial Books for Children Bulletin* 15(6):7–9.

Lally, Catherine F. and James W. Maddock. 1994. "Sexual Meaning Systems of Engaged Couples." *Family Relations* 43:53–60.

Lamanna, Mary Ann. 1977. "The Value of Children to Natural and Adoptive Parents." PhD dissertation, Department of Sociology, University of Notre Dame, Notre Dame, IN.

Lamb, Kathleen A., Gary R. Lee, and Alfred DeMaris. 2003. "Union Formation and Depression: Selection and Relationship Effects." *Journal of Marriage and Family* 65(4):953–62.

Lambert, Nathaniel M. and David C. Dollahite. 2006. "How Religiosity Helps Couples Prevent, Resolve, and Overcome Marital Conflict." *Family Relations* 55(4):439–49.

Lambert, Tracy A., Arnold S. Kahn, and Kevin J. Apple. 2003. "Pluralistic Ignorance and Hooking Up." *Journal of Sex Research* 40(2):129–33.

Lan, Pei-Chia. 2002. "Subcontracting Filial Piety: Elder Care in Ethnic Chinese Immigrant Families in California." *Journal of Family Issues* 23(7):812–35.

Landry-Meyer, Laura and Barbara M. Newman. 2004. "An Exploration of the Grandparent Caregiver Role." *Journal of Family Issues* 25(8):1005–25.

Lane, Wendy G., David M. Rubin, Ragin Monteith, and Cindy Christian. 2002. "Racial Differences in the Evaluation of Pediatric Fractures for Physical Abuse." *Journal of the American Medical Association* 288(13). (www.jama.org).

Laner, Mary Riege. 2003. "A Rejoinder to Mark Cresswell." *Sociological Inquiry* 73:152–56.

Langhinrichsen-Rohling, Jennifer, Russel E. Palarea, Jennifer Cohen, and Martin L. Rohling. 2000. "Breaking Up Is Hard to Do: Unwanted Pursuit Behaviors Following the Dissolution of a Romantic Relationship." *Violence and Victims* 15(1):73–90.

Lareau, Annette. 2002. "Invisible Inequality: Social Class and Childrearing in Black and White Families." *American Sociological Review* 67:747–76.

———. 2003a. "The Long-lost Cousins of the Middle Class." *New York Times,* December 20.

———. 2003b. *Unequal Childhoods: Class, Race, and Family Life.* Berkeley: University of California Press.

———. 2006. "Unequal Childhoods: Class, Race, and Family Life." Pp. 537–48 in *The Inequality Reader: Contemporary and Foundational Readings in Class, Race, and Gender,* edited by David B. Grusky and Szonja Szelenyi. Boulder: Westview.

LaRossa, Ralph. 1979. *Conflict and Power in Marriage: Expecting the First Child.* Newbury Park, CA: Sage Publications.

LaRossa, Ralph and Donald C. Reitzes. 1993. "Symbolic Interactionism and Family Studies." Pp. 135–63 in *Sourcebook of Family Theories and Methods: A Contextual Approach,* edited by Pauline G. Boss, William J. Doherty, Ralph LaRossa, Walter R. Schumm, and Suzanne K. Steinmetz. New York: Plenum.

Larson, Jeffry H. and Rachel Hickman. 2004. "Are College Marriage Textbooks Teaching Students the Premarital Predictors of Marital Quality?" *Family Relations* 53(4):385–92.

Larson, Jeffry H., Shannon M. Anderson, Thomas B. Holman, and Brand K. Niemann. 1998. "A Longitudinal Study of the Effects of Premarital Communication, Relationship Stability, and Self-esteem on Sexual Satisfaction in the First Year of Marriage." *Journal of Sex & Marital Therapy* 24:193–206.

Larzelere, Robert E. 1996. "Presentation: Implications of the Strongest Studies for Discriminating Effective versus Counterproductive Corporal Punishment." *Pediatrics* 98:824–27.

Lasch, Christopher. 1977. *Haven in a Heartless World: The Family Besieged.* New York: Basic Books.

———. 1980. *The Culture of Narcissism.* New York: Warner Books.

Laslett, Peter. 1971. *The World We Have Lost: England Before the Industrial Age.* 2nd ed. New York: Scribner's.

Lau, Anna S., David T. Takeuchi, and Margarita Alegria. 2006. "Parent-to-Child Aggression among Asian American Parents: Culture, Context, and Vulnerability." *Journal of Marriage and Family* 68(5):1261–75.

Laub, Gillian. 2005. "The Young and the Sexless." *Rolling Stone,* June 30–July 14, pp. 103–11.

Laumann, Edward, John H. Gagnon, Robert T. Michael, and Stuart Michaels. 1994. *The Social Organization of Sexuality: Sexual Practices in the United States.* Chicago, IL: University of Chicago Press.

Lauro, Patricia Winters. 2000. "Advertising: The Subject of Divorce Is Becoming More Common as Another Backdrop in Campaigns." *New York Times,* October 12.

Lavee, Yoav and Ruth Katz. 2002. "Division of Labor, Perceived Fairness, and Marital Quality: The Effect of Gender Ideology." *Journal of Marriage and Family* 64:27–39.

Lavietes, Stuart. 2003. "Richard Gardner, 72, Dies; Cast Doubt on Abuse Claims." *New York Times,* June 9.

Lavin, Judy. 2003. "Smoothing the Step-Parenting Transition." SelfGrowth.com. Retrieved April 26, 2007 (http://www.selfgrowth.com).

Lawler, Edward J., Shane R. Thye, and Jeongkoo Yoon. 2006. "Commitment in Structurally Enabled and Induced Exchange Relations." *Social Psychology Quarterly* 69(2):183–200.

Lawrance, K. and E. S. Byers. 1995. "Sexual Satisfaction in Long-term Heterosexual Relationships: The Interpersonal Exchange Model of Sexual Satisfaction." *Personal Relationships* 2:267–85.

Lawrence et al. v. Texas. 2003. 539 U.S. 558.

Lawson, Willow. 2004a. "Encouraging Signs: How Your Partner Responds to Your Good News Speaks Volumes." *Psychology Today* (January/February):22.

———. 2004b. "The Glee Club: Positive Psychologists Want to Teach You to Be Happier." *Psychology Today* (January/February):34–40.

"Learning Skills Greatly Limits Stress for Family Caregivers, Says Stanford Study." 2003. *Mental Health Weekly Digest,* October 13.

LeBlanc, Allen J. and Richard G. Wright. 2000. "Reciprocity and Depression in AIDS Caregiving." *Sociological Perspectives* 43(4):631–49.

LeBlanc, Steve. 2006a. "Boston Catholic Charities Halts Adoptions." Associated Press. *San Francisco Chronicle,* March 10.

———. 2006b. "Massachusetts Lawmakers Delay Action on Gay Marriage Ban." Associated Press. Retrieved November 10, 2006 (http://www.boston.com/news).

Lee, Cameron and Judith Iverson-Gilbert. 2003. "Demand, Support, and Perception in Family-related Stress among Protestant Clergy." *Family Relations* 52(3):249–57.

Lee, Carol E. 2006. "Sibling Seeks Same to Share Apartment." *New York Times,* January 29.

Lee, Ellie. 2003. *Abortion, Motherhood, and Mental Health: Medicalizing Reproduction in the United States and Great Britain.* Hawthorne, NY: Aldine.

Lee, Eunju, Glenna Spitze, and John R. Logan. 2003. "Social Support to Parents-in-Law: The Interplay of Gender and Kin Hierarchies." *Journal of Marriage and Family* 65(2):396–403.

Lee, F. R. 2001. "Trying to Soothe the Fears Hiding Behind the Veil." *New York Times,* September 23.

Lee, Gary R., Julie K. Netzer, and Raymond T. Coward. 1994. "Filial Responsibility Expectations and Patterns of Intergenerational Assistance." *Journal of Marriage and Family* 56(3):559–65.

Lee, Gary R., Chuck W. Peek, and Raymond T. Coward. 1998. "Race Differences in Filial Responsibility Expectations among Older Parents." *Journal of Marriage and Family* 60(2):404–12.

Lee, Jennifer. 2007. "The Incredible Flying Granny Nanny." *New York Times,* May 10. Retrieved May 11, 2007 (http://www.nytimes.com).

Lee, John Alan. 1973. *The Colours of Love.* Toronto: New Press.

———. 1981. "Forbidden Colors of Love: Patterns of Gay Love." Pp. 128–39 in *Single Life: Unmarried Adults in Social Context,* edited by Peter J. Stein. New York: St. Martin's.

Lee, Mo-Yee. 2002. "A Model of Children's Postdivorce Behavioral Adjustment in Maternal- and Dual-residence Arrangements." *Journal of Family Issues* 23(5):672–97.

Lee, Sharon M. 1998. "Asian Americans: Diverse and Growing." *Population Bulletin* 53(2). Washington, DC: Population Reference Bureau.

Lee, Sharon M. and Barry Edmonston. 2005. "New Marriages, New Families: U.S. Racial and Hispanic Intermarriage." *Population Bulletin* 60(2). Washington, DC: Population Reference Bureau.

Leff, Lisa. 2006. "State Lawyer Faces Tough Questions Arguing Against Gay Marriage." Associated Press. July 11. Retrieved July 11, 2006 (http://www.mercurynews.com).

Leigh, Suzanne. 2004. "Fertility Patients Deserve to Know the Odds—and Risks." *USA Today,* July 7.

Leinwand, Donna. 2002. "Kidnapping Problem 'Impossible' to Quantify." *USA Today,* August 15.

Liefbroer, Aart C. and Edith Dourleijn. 2006. "Unmarried Cohabitation and Union Stability: Testing the Role of Diffusion Using Data from 16 European Countries." *Demography* 43(2):203–21.

Leite, Randall. 2007. "An Exploration of Aspects of Boundary Ambiguity among Young, Unmarried Fathers during the Prenatal Period." *Family Relations* 56(2):162–74.

Leite, Randall W. and Patrick C. McKenry. 2002. "Aspects of Father Status and Post-Divorce Father Involvement with Children" *Journal of Family Issues* 23:601–23.

Leland, John. 2006. "A Spirit of Belonging, Inside and Out." *New York Times,* October 8.

Leman, Kevin. 2006. *Single Parenting That Works: Six Keys to Raising Happy, Healthy Children in a Single-parent Home.* Carol Stream, IL: Tyndale House Publishers.

LeMasters, E. E. 1959. "Holy Deadlock: A Study of Unsuccessful Marriages." *The Midwest Sociologist* 21(1):86–91.

LeMasters, E. E. and John DeFrain. 1989. *Parents in Contemporary America: A Sympathetic View.* 5th ed. Belmont, CA: Wadsworth.

Lento, Jennifer. 2006. "Relational and Physical Victimization by Peers and Romantic Partners in College Students." *Journal of Social and Personal Relationships* 23(3):331–48.

Leonhardt, David. 2003. "It's a Girl! (Will the Economy Suffer?)" *New York Times,* October 26.

———. 2006a "The New Inequality. *New York Times Magazine,* December 10.

———. 2006b. "Scant Progress in Closing Gap." *New York Times,* December 24.

Lerner, Barron M. 2003. "If Biology Is Destiny, When Shouldn't It Be?" *New York Times,* May 27.

Lerner, Harriet. 2001. *The Dance of Connection: How to Talk to Someone When You're Mad, Hurt, Scared, Frustrated, Insulted, Betrayed, or Desperate.* New York: HarperCollins.

Lerner, Sharon. 2003. "Making New Efforts to Convince Youths They're Not Invulnerable to H.I.V." *New York Times,* August 5.

"Lesbian and Gay Rights in the 107th Congress." 2001. American Civil Liberties Union (http://www.aclu.org/issues/gay).

"Lesbians' Brains Respond Like Straight Men." CNN.com. May 8. Retrieved May 9, 2006 (http://cnn.worldnews.com).

Letiecq, Bethany L. and Sally A. Koblinsky. 2001. "African American Fathers' Strategies for Protecting Young Children in Violent Neighborhoods." *Family Focus* (September):F7–F8. National Council on Family Relations.

———. 2004. "Parenting in Violent Neighborhoods: African American Families Share Strategies for Keeping Children Safe." *Journal of Family Issues* 25:715–34.

Levin, Irene. 1997. "Stepfamily as Project." Pp. 123–33 in *Stepfamilies: History, Research, and Policy,* edited by Irene Levin and Marvin B. Sussman. New York: Haworth.

Levine, Judith A., Clifton R. Emery, and Harold Pollack. 2007. "The Well-being of Children Born to Teen Mothers." *Journal of Marriage and Family* 69(1):105–22.

Levine, Madeline. 2006. *The Price of Privilege: How Parental Pressure and Material Advantage Are Creating a Generation of Disconnected and Unhappy Kids.* New York: HarperCollins.

Levine, Robert, Suguru Sato, Tsukasa Hashimoto, and Jyoti Verma. 1995. "Love and Marriage in Eleven Cultures." *Journal of Cross-Cultural Psychology* 26(5):554–71.

Levine, Stephen B. 1998. "Extramarital Sexual Affairs." *Journal of Sex & Marital Therapy* 24:207–16.

Levinger, George. 1965. "Marital Cohesiveness and Dissolution: An Integrative Review." *Journal of Marriage and Family* 27:19–28.

Levinger, George. 1976. "A Social Psychological Perspective on Marital Discord." *Journal of Social Issues* 32:21–47.

Levy, Donald P. 2005. "Hegemonic Complicity, Friendship, and Comradeship: Validation and Causal Processes among White, Middle-class, Middle-aged Men." *Journal of Men's Studies* 13(2):199–225.

Lewin, Tamar. 1995. "Now Divorcing Parents Must Learn How to Cope with Children's Needs." *New York Times,* April 24.

———. 1998. "Men Assuming Bigger Share at Home, New Survey Shows." *New York Times,* April 15.

———. 2001a. "Report Looks at a Generation, and Caring for Young and Old." *New York Times,* July 11.

———. 2001b. "Study Says Little Has Changed." *New York Times,* September 10.

———. 2003. "For More People in Their 20s and 30s, Going Home Is Easier Because They Never Left." *New York Times,* December 22.

———. 2005. "A Marriage of Unequals: When Richer Weds Poorer, Money Isn't the Only Difference." *New York Times,* May 19.

———. 2006a. "At Colleges, Women Are Leaving Men in the Dust." *New York Times,* July 9.

———. 2006b. "Boys Are No Match for Girls in Completing High School." *New York Times,* April 19.

———. 2006c. "A More Nuanced Look at Men, Women, and College." *New York Times,* July 12.

———. 2006d. "Unwed Fathers Fight for Babies Placed for Adoption by Mothers." *New York Times,* March 19.

Lewis, Thomas, M.D., Fari Amini, M.D., and Richard Lannon, M.D. 2000. *A General Theory of Love.* New York: Random House.

Lewis, Robert. 2007. *Raising a Modern-day Knight.* Carol Stream, IL: Tyndale House Publishers.

Lewontin, Richard. 2004. "Dishonesty in Science." *New York Review of Books,* November 18, pp. 38–39.

L'Heureaux-Dubé, Claire. 1998. "A Response to Remarks by Dr. Judith Wallerstein on the Long-term Impact of Divorce on Children." *Family and Conciliation Courts Review* 36(3):384–86.

Libby, Roger W. 1976. "Social Scripts for Sexual Relationships." In *Sexuality Today and Tomorrow,* edited by Sol Gordon and Roger W. Libby. North Scituate, MA: Duxbury.

Lichter, Daniel T. and Zhenchao Qian. 2004. *Marriage and Family in a Multiracial Society.* New York: Russell Sage.

Lichter, Daniel T., Zhenchao Qian, and Leanna M. Mellott. 2006. "Marriage or Dissolution? Union Transitions among Poor Cohabiting Women." *Demography* 43(2):223–41.

Lieblich, Julia. 1998. "Non-Christian Summer Camps for Kids Combine Fun, Faith." *Saint Paul Pioneer Press,* July 19, p. 3G.

Liefbroer, Aart C., and Edith Dourleijn. 2006. "Unmarried Cohabitation and Union Stability: Testing the Role of Diffusion Using Data from 16 European Countries." *Demography* 43 (2): 203–221.

"Life Expectancy Increases for H.I.V. Patients." 2006. *New York Times,* November 12.

Lin, Chien and William T. Liu. 1993. "Relationships among Chinese Immigrant Families." Pp. 271–86 in *Family Ethnicity: Strength in Diversity,* edited by Harriette Pipes McAdoo. Newbury Park, CA: Sage Publications.

Lindberg, Laura Duberstein, John S. Santelli, and Susheela Singh. 2006. "Changes in Formal Sex Education: 1995–2002. *Perspectives on Sexual and Reproductive Health* 38(1):182–80.

Lindsey, Elizabeth W. 1998. "The Impact of Homelessness and Shelter Life on Family Relationships." *Family Relations* 47(3):243–52.

Lindsey, Eric W., Yvonne Caldera, and Malinda Colwell. 2005. "Correlates of Coparenting during Infancy." *Family Relations* 54(3):346–59.

Lindsey, Eric W. and Jacquelyn Mize. 2001. "Interparental Agreement, Parent–Child Responsiveness, and Children's Peer Competence." *Family Relations* 50(4):348–54.

Lino, Mark. 2002. "Expenditures on Children by Families, 2001." Annual Report. Washington, DC: U.S. Department of Agriculture, Center for Nutrition Policy and Promotion. Miscellaneous Publication No. 1528-2001.

Lipman, Joanne. 1993. "The Nanny Trap." *Wall Street Journal,* April 14, pp. A1, A8.

Lips, Hilary M. 2004. *Sex and Gender: An Introduction.* New York: McGraw-Hill.

Liptak, Adam. 2002. "Judging a Mother for Someone Else's Crime." *New York Times,* November 27.

Liu, Chien. 2000. "A Theory of Marital Sexual Life." *Journal of Marriage and Family* 62(2): 363-74.

Lloyd, Kim M. 2006. "Latinas' Transition to First Marriage: An Examination of Four Theoretical Perspectives." *Journal of Marriage and Family* 68(4):993–1014.

LoBiondo-Wood, Geri, Laurel Williams, and Charles McGhee. 2004. "Liver Transplantation in Children: Maternal and Family Stress, Coping, and Adaptation." *Journal of the Society of Pediatric Nurses* 9(2):59–67.

Lobo, Susan, ed. 2001. *American Indians and the Urban Experience.* Thousand Oaks, CA: AltaMira.

Lofas, Jeannette. N.d. "Ten Steps for Steps." The Stepfamily Foundation (http://www.stepfamily.org/ten_steps _for_stepfamilies.html).

Loftus, Jeni. 2001. "America's Liberalization in Attitudes toward Homosexuality, 1973 to 1998." *American Sociological Review* 66:762–82.

Lohr, Steve. 2006. "Study Plays Down Export of Computer Jobs." *New York Times,* February 23.

London, Rebecca A. 1998. "Trends in Single Mothers' Living Arrangements from 1970 to 1995: Correcting the Current Population Survey." *Demography* 35(1):125–31.

Long, Edgar C. J., Jeffrey J. Angera, Sara Jacobs Carter, Mindy Nakamoto, and Michelle Kalso. 1999. "Understanding the One You Love: A Longitudinal Assessment of an Empathy Training Program for Couples in Romantic Relationships." *Family Relations* 48(3):235–42.

Long, George. 1875. "Patria Potestas." Pp. 873–75 in *A Dictionary of Greek and Roman Antiquities,* edited by Sir William Smith, William Wayte, and G. E. Marindin.

London, England: J. Murray. Retrieved October 6, 2006 (http://penelope .uchicago.edu).

Longman, Phillip J. 1998. "The Cost of Children." *U.S. News & World Report,* March 30, pp. 51–58.

Longmore, Monica A. and Alfred Demaris. 1997. "Perceived Inequality and Depression in Intimate Relationships: The Moderating Effect of Self-Esteem." *Social Psychology Quarterly* 60(2):172–81.

Longmore, Monica A., Wendy D. Manning, and Peggy C. Giordano. 2001. "Preadolescent Parenting Strategies and Teens' Dating and Sexual Initiation: A Longitudinal Analysis." *Journal of Marriage and Family* 63(2):322–35.

Lorenz, Frederick O., Ronald L. Simons, Rand D. Conger, and Glen H. Elder, Jr. 1997. "Married and Recently Divorced Mothers' Stressful Events and Distress: Tracing Change across Time." *Journal of Marriage and Family* 59(1):219–32.

Loseke, Donileen R., Richard J. Gelles, and Mary M. Cavanaugh, eds. 2005. *Current Controversies on Family Violence.* 2nd ed. Thousand Oaks, CA: Sage Publications.

Loseke, Donileen R. and Demie Kurz. 2005. "Men's Violence toward Women Is the Serious Social Problem." Pp. 79–95 in *Current Controversies on Family Violence,* edited by Donileen R. Loseke, Richard J. Gelles, and Mary M. Cavanaugh. Thousand Oaks, CA: Sage Publications.

Losh-Hesselbart, Susan. 1987. "Development of Gender Roles." Pp. 535–64 in *Handbook of Marriage and the Family,* edited by Marvin B. Sussman and Suzanne K. Steinmetz. New York: Plenum.

Lott, Juanita Tamayo. 2004. "Asian-American Children Are Members of a Diverse and Urban Population." Washington, DC: Population Reference Bureau. January. Retrieved December 13, 2006 (www.prb.org).

Love, Patricia. 2001. *The Truth About Love.* New York: Simon and Schuster.

Loving v. Virginia. 1967. 388 U.S. 1, 87 S. Ct. 1817, 18 L.Ed.2d 1010.

"Loving Your Partner as a Package Deal." 2000. *Newsweek,* March 20, p. 78.

Lowenstein, Roger. 2006. "The Immigrant Equation." *New York Times Magazine,* July 9, pp. 36–43, 69–71.

Lublin, Joann S. 1992. "Spouses Find Themselves Worlds Apart as Global Commuter Marriages Increase." *Wall Street Journal,* August 19, pp. B1, B6.

Luepnitz, Deborah Anne. 1982. *Child Custody: A Study of Families After Divorce.* Lexington, MA: Lexington Books.

Lugaila, Terry and Julia Overturf. 2004. *Children and the Households They Live In: 2000.* Census Special Report CENSR-14. Washington, DC: U.S. Census Bureau. February.

Lugo Steidel, Angel G. and Josefina M. Contreras. 2003. "A New Familism Scale for Use with Latino Populations." *Hispanic Journal of Behavioral Sciences* 25(3):312–30.

Luke, Carmen. 1994. "White Women in Interracial Families: Reflections on Hybridization, Feminine Identities, and Racialized Othering." *Feminist Issues* 14(2): 49–72.

Lukemeyer, Anna, Marcia K. Meyers, and Timothy Smeeding. 2000. "Expensive Children in Poor Families: Out-of-Pocket Expenditures for the Care of Disabled and Chronically Ill Children in Welfare Families." *Journal of Marriage and Family* 62(2):399–415.

Luker, Kristin. 1984. *Abortion and the Politics of Motherhood.* Berkeley: University of California Press.

Lundquist, Jennifer Hickes. 2004. "When Race Makes No Difference: Marriage and the Military." *Social Forces* 83(2):731–57.

Lundquist, Jennifer Hickes and Herbert L. Smith. 2005. "Family Formation among Women in the U.S. Military: Evidence from the NLSY." *Journal of Marriage and Family* 67:1–13.

Luscher, Kurt. 2002. "Intergenerational Ambivalence: Further Steps in Theory and Research." *Journal of Marriage and Family* 63(3):585–93.

Lussier, Gretchen, Kirby Deater-Deckard, Judy Dunn, and Lisa Davies. 2002. "Support across Two Generations: Children's Closeness to Grandparents Following Parental Divorce and Remarriage." *Journal of Family Psychology* 16:363–76.

Luster, Tom, Laura Bates, Hiram Fitzgerald, Marcia Vanderbelt, and Judith Peck Key. 2000. "Factors Related to Successful Outcomes among Preschool Children Born to Low-income Adolescent Mothers." *Journal of Marriage and Family* 62(1):133–46.

Luster, Tom, Kelly Rhoades, and Bruce Haas. 1989. "The Relation between Parental Values and Parenting Behavior: A Test of the Kohn Hypothesis." *Journal of Marriage and Family* 51:139–47.

Luster, Tom and Stephen A. Small. 1997. "Sexual Abuse History and Problems in Adolescence: Exploring the Effects of Moderating Variables." *Journal of Marriage and Family* 59(1):131–42.

Lustig, Daniel C. 1999. "Family Caregiving of Adults with Mental Retardation: Key Issues for Rehabilitation Counselors." *Journal of Rehabilitation* 65(2):26–45.

Luthar, Suniya S. 2003. "The Culture of Affluence: Psychological Costs of Material Wealth." *Child Development* 74:1581–93.

Luthra, Rohini and Christine A. Gidycz. 2006. "Dating Violence among College Men and Women: Evolution of a Theoretical Model." *Journal of Interpersonal Violence* 21(6):717–31.

Lye, Diane N., Daniel H. Klepinger, Patricia Davis Hyle, and Anjanette Nelson. 1995. "Childhood Living Arrangements and Adult Children's Relations with Their Parents." *Demography* 32(2):261–80.

Lyman, Rick. 2006. "Census Reports Slight Increase in '05 Incomes." *New York Times,* August 30.

Lyman, Stanford M. and Marvin B. Scott. 1975. *The Drama of Social Reality.* New York: Oxford University Press.

Lynch, Jean M. and Kim Murray. 2000. "For the Love of the Children: The Coming Out Process for Lesbian and Gay Parents and Stepparents." *Journal of Homosexuality* 39(1):1–24.

Lyons, Linda. 2002. "The Future of Marriage: Part I." The Gallup Poll. July 23. Retrieved September 13, 2006 (http://www.galluppoll.com).

———. 2003. "Who Can't Get No Satisfaction?" The Gallup Poll. February 18. Retrieved September 13, 2006 (http://www.galluppoll.com).

———. 2004. "How Many Teens Are Cool with Cohabitation?" The Gallup Poll. April 13. Retrieved September 13, 2006 (http://www.galluppoll.com).

Maccoby, Eleanor E. 1998. *The Two Sexes: Growing Up Apart, Coming Together.* Cambridge, MA: Belknap/Harvard University Press.

Maccoby, Eleanor E. and Carol Nagy Jacklin. 1974. *The Psychology of Sex Differences.* Stanford, CA: Stanford University Press.

Maccoby, Eleanor E. and Catherine C. Lewis. 2003. "Less Day Care or a Different Day Care?" *Child Development* 74:1069–75.

Maccoby, Eleanor E. and Robert Mnookin. 1992. *Dividing the Child: Social and Legal Dilemmas of Custody.* Cambridge, MA: Harvard University Press.

MacDonald, Cameron L. 1998. "Manufacturing Motherhood: The Shadow Work of Nannies and Au Pairs." *Qualitative Sociology* 21(1):25–53.

MacDonald, William L. and Alfred DeMaris. 1995. "Remarriage, Stepchildren, and Marital Conflict: Challenges to the Incomplete Institutionalization Hypothesis." *Journal of Marriage and Family* 57(2):387–98.

———. 2002. "Stepfather-Stepchild Relationship Quality: The Stepfather's Demand for Conformity and the Biological Father's Involvement." *Journal of Family Issues* 23(1):121–37.

MacFarquhar, Neil. 2006. "It's Muslim Boy Meets Girl, but Don't Call It Dating." *New York Times,* September 19. Retrieved September 19, 2006 (http://www.nytimes.com).

Machir, John. 2003. "The Impact of Spousal Caregiving on the Quality of Marital Relationships in Later Life." *Family Focus* (September):F11–F13. National Council on Family Relations.

Macionis, John J. 2006. *Society: The Basics.* 6th ed. Upper Saddle River, NJ: Prentice Hall.

Mackay, Judith. 2000. *The Penguin Atlas of Human Sexual Behavior.* New York: Penguin Putnam.

Mackey, Richard A., Matthew A. Diemer, and Bernard A. O'Brien. 2000. "Psychological Intimacy in the Lasting Relationships of Heterosexual and Same-gender Couples." *Sex Roles* (August):201–15.

Mackey, Richard A. and Bernard A. O'Brien. 1998. "Marital Conflict Management: Gender and Ethnic Differences." *Social Work* 43(2):128–41.

Macklin, Eleanor D. 1987. "Nontraditional Family Forms." Pp. 317–53 in *Handbook of Marriage and the Family,* edited by Marvin B. Sussman and Suzanne K. Steinmetz. New York: Plenum.

MacQuarrie, Brian. 2006. "Guard Families Cope in Two Dimensions." *Boston Globe,* August 30.

Madden-Derdich, Debra A. and Joyce A. Arditti. 1999. "The Ties That Bind: Attachment between Former Spouses." *Family Relations* 48(3):243–48.

Madrigal, Luke. 2001. "Indian Child and Welfare Act: Partnership for Preservation." *American Behavioral Scientist* 44(9):1505–11.

Magdol, Lynn, Terrie E. Moffitt, Avshalom Caspi, and Phil A. Silva. 1998. "Hitting without a License: Testing Explanations for Differences in Partner Abuse between Young Adult Daters and Cohabitors." *Journal of Marriage and Family* 60(1):41–55.

Mahoney, Annette. 2005. "Religion and Conflict in Marital and Parent-Child Relationships." *Journal of Social Issues* 61(4):689–717.

Mahoney, Margaret M. 1997. "Stepfamilies from a Legal Perspective." Pp. 231–47 in *Stepfamilies: History, Research, and Policy,* edited by Irene Levin and Marvin B. Sussman. New York: Haworth.

Mahoney, P. and L. Williams. 1998. "Sexual Assault in Marriages: Prevalence, Consequences, and Treatment of Wife Rape." Pp. 113–62 in *Partner Violence: A Comprehensive Review of 20 Years of Research,* edited by Jana L. Jasinski and Linda M. Williams. Thousand Oaks, CA: Sage Publications

Maier, Thomas. 1998. "Everybody's Grandfather." *U.S. News & World Report,* March 30, p. 59.

Main, M. 1996. "Introduction to the Special Section on Attachment and Psychopathology: Overview of the Field of Attachment." *Journal of Consulting Clinical Psychology* 64:237–43.

Mainemer, Henry, Lorraine C. Gilman, and Elinor W. Ames. 1998. "Parenting Stress in Families Adopting Children from Romanian Orphanages." *Journal of Family Issues* 19(2):164–80.

Majors, Richard G. and Janet M. Billson. 1992. *Cool Pose: The Dilemmas of Black Manhood in America.* Lexington, MA: Heath.

Makepeace, James M. 1981. "Courtship Violence among College Students." *Family Relations* 30:97–102.

———. 1986. "Gender Differences in Courtship Violence Victimization." *Family Relations* 35:383–88.

Malakh-Pines, Ayala. 2005. *Falling in Love: Why We Choose the Lovers We Choose.* New York: Routledge.

Malia, Sarah E. C. 2005. "Balancing Family Members' Interests Regarding Stepparent Rights and Obligations: A Social Policy Challenge." *Family Relations* 54(2):298–319.

Maneker, Jerry S. and Robert P. Rankin. 1993. "Religious Homogamy and Marital Duration among Those Who File for Divorce in California, 1966–1971." *Journal of Divorce and Remarriage* 19(1–2):233–41.

Manisses Communications Group. 2000. "When It Comes to Handling Your Hard-to-Handle Child, Are You an Authoritative, Authoritarian or Permissive Parent?" *The Brown University Child and Adolescent Behavior Letter* 16(3):S1–S2.

Manlove, Jennifer, Suzanne Ryan, and Kerry Franzetta. 2003. "Patterns of Contraceptive Use within Teenagers' First Sexual Relationships." *Perspectives on Sexual and Reproductive Health* 35:246–55.

Manning, Wendy D. 2001. "Childbearing in Cohabiting Unions: Racial and Ethnic Differences." *Family Planning Perspectives* 33(5):217–34.

———. 2004. "Children and the Stability of Cohabiting Couples." *Journal of Marriage and Family* 66(3):674–89.

Manning, Wendy D. and Susan Brown. 2006. "Children's Economic Well-being in Married and Cohabiting Parent Families." *Journal of Marriage and Family* 68(2):345–62.

Manning, Wendy D. and Kathleen A. Lamb. 2003. "Adolescent Well-being in Cohabiting, Married, and Single-parent Families." *Journal of Marriage and Family* 65(4):876–93.

Manning, Wendy D., Peggy C. Giordano, and Monica A. Longmore. 2006. "Hooking Up: The Relationship Contexts of 'Nonrelationship' Sex." *Journal of Adolescent Research* 21(5):459–83.

Manning, Wendy D. and Nancy S. Landale. 1996. "Racial and Ethnic Differences in the Role of Cohabitation in Premarital Childbearing." *Journal of Marriage and Family* 58(1):63–77.

Manning, Wendy D. and Pamela J. Smock. 1999. "New Families and Nonresident Father–Child Visitation." *Social Forces* 78:87–116.

———. 2002. "First Comes Cohabitation and Then Comes Marriage?" *Journal of Family Issues* 23(8):1065–87.

———. 2005. "Measuring and Modeling Cohabitation: New Perspectives from Qualitative Data." *Journal of Marriage and Family* 67(4):989–1002.

Manning, Wendy D., Susan D. Stewart, and Pamela J. Smock. 2003. "The Complexity of Fathers' Parenting Responsibilities and Involvement with Nonresident Children." *Journal of Family Issues* 24(5):645–67.

Mannis, Valerie S. 1999. "Single Mothers by Choice." *Family Relations* 48(2):121–28.

Mansnerus, Laura. 2003. "Great Haven for Families, but Don't Bring Children." *New York Times,* August 13.

Manton, Kenneth G. and Kenneth C. Land. 2000. "Active Life Expectancy Estimates for the U.S. Elderly Population: A Multidimensional Continuous-mixture Model of Functional Change Applied to Completed Cohorts, 1982–1996." *Demography* 37(3):253–65.

Marano, Hara Estroff. 1997. "Puberty May Start at 6 as Hormones Surge." *New York Times,* July 1, pp. B1, B12.

———. 2000. "Divorced? (Remarriage in America)." *Psychology Today* 33(2):56–60.

Marchand, Jennifer F. and Ellen Hock. 2000. "Avoidance and Attacking Conflict-resolution Strategies among Married Couples: Relations to Depressive Symptoms and Marital Satisfaction." *Family Relations* 49(2):201–06.

Marchione, Marilynn. 2007. "Fertility Treatment Raises Defect Risk." Associated Press, February 9. Retrieved February 11, 2007 (www.lasvegassun.com).

Marchione, Marilynn and Lindsey Tanner. 2006. "Many U.S. Couples Seek Embryo Screening." Associated Press, September 20. Retrieved September 21, 2006 (www.apnews.myway.com).

Marcussen, Kristen. 2006. "Identities, Self-Esteem, and Psychological Distress: An Application of Identity-Discrepancy Theory." *Sociological Perspectives* 49 (1): 1-24.

Marech, Rona. 2004. "To Wed or Not to Wed." *San Francisco Chronicle Magazine,* January 18.

Margolin, Leslie. 1992. "Child Abuse by Mothers' Boyfriends: Why the Overrepresentation?" *Child Abuse & Neglect* 16:541–51.

Marin, Rick. 2000. "At-home Fathers Step Out to Find They Are Not Alone." *New York Times,* January 12.

Markman, Howard, Scott Stanley, and Susan L. Blumberg. 2001. *Fighting for Your Marriage: Positive Steps for Preventing Divorce and Preserving a Lasting Love.* San Francisco, CA: Jossey-Bass.

Marks, Nadine F., James D. Lambert, and Heejeong Choi. 2002. "Transitions to Caregiving, Gender, and Psychological Well-being: A Prospective U.S. National Study." *Journal of Marriage and Family* 64(3):657–67.

Marks, Stephen R. 1989. "Toward a Systems Theory of Marital Quality." *Journal of Marriage and Family* 51:15–26.

———. 2001. "Teasing Out the Lessons of the 1960s: Family Diversity and Family Privilege." Pp. 66–79 in *Understanding Families in the New Millennium: A Decade in Review,* edited by Robert M. Milardo. Lawrence, KS: National Council on Family Relations.

Markway, Barbara and Gregory Markway. 2006. *Nurturing the Shy Child: Practical Help for Raising Confident and Socially Skilled Kids and Teens.* New York: Griffin.

Marlow, Lenard and S. Richard Sauber. 1990. *The Handbook of Divorce Mediation.* New York: Plenum.

Marquardt, Elizabeth. N.d. *The Revolution in Parenthood: The Emerging Global Clash between Adult Rights and Children's Needs.* Commission on Parenthood's Future. Retrieved October 4, 2006 (http://www.americanvalues.org).

"Married Households Rise Again among Blacks, Census Finds." 2003. Associated Press, April 25.

Marriott, Michel. 1995. "Living in 'Lockdown.'" *Newsweek,* January 23, pp. 56–57.

Marschark, Marc. 2007. *Raising and Educating a Deaf Child.* New York: Oxford University Press.

Marshall, Susan E. 1995. "Keep Us on the Pedestal: Women Against Feminism in Twentieth-Century America." Pp. 547–60 in *Women: A Feminist Perspective,* 5th ed., edited by Jo Freeman. Mountain View, CA: Mayfield.

Marsiglio, William. 2003. "Making Males Mindful of Their Sexual and Procreative Identities: Using Self-narratives in Field Settings." *Perspectives on Sexual and Reproductive Health* 35:229–232.

———. 2004. *Stepdads: Stories of Love, Hope, and Repair.* Boulder, CO: Rowman and Littlefield.

Marsiglio, William, Paul Amato, Randal Day, and Michael E. Lamb. 2000. "Scholarship on Fatherhood in the 1990s and Beyond." *Journal of Marriage and Family* 62:1173–91.

Marsiglio, William and Sally Hutchinson. 2002. *Sex, Men, and Babies: Stories of Awareness and Responsibility.* New York: NYU Press.

Martin, C. L. 1989. "Children's Use of Gender-related Information in Making Social Judgments." *Developmental Psychology* 25:80–88.

Martin, John Levi. 2005. "Is Power Sexy?" *American Journal of Sociology* 111(2):408–47.

Martin, Joyce A., Brady E. Hamilton, Paul D. Sutton, Stephanie Ventura, Fay Menacker, and Martha Munson. 2003. "Births: Final Data for 2002." *National Vital Statistics Report* 52(10). Hyattsville, MD: National Center for Health Statistics. December 17.

Martin, Joyce A., Brady E. Hamilton, Paul D. Sutton, Stephanie J. Ventura, Fay Menacker, and Martha L. Munson. 2005. "Births: Final Data for 2003." *National Vital Statistics Report* 54(2). Hyattsville, MD: National Center for Health Statistics. September 8.

Martin, Joyce A., Brady E. Hamilton, Paul D. Sutton, Stephanie J. Ventura, Fay Menacker, and Sharon Kirmeyer. 2006. "Births: Final Data for 2004." *National Vital Statistics Report* 55(1). Hyattsville, MD: National Center for Health Statistics. September 29.

Martin, Philip and Elizabeth Midgley. 2003. "Immigration: Shaping and Reshaping America." *Population Bulletin* 58(2). Washington, DC: Population Reference Bureau. June.

———. 2006. "Immigration: Shaping and Reshaping America." 2nd ed. *Population Bulletin* 61(4). Washington, DC: Population Reference Bureau. December.

Martin, Sandra L., April Harris-Britt, Yun Li, Kathryn E. Moracco, Lawrence L. Kupper, and Jacquelyn C. Campbell. 2004. "Change in Intimate Partner Violence during Pregnancy." *Journal of Family Violence* 19:243–47.

Martin, Steven P. 2006. "Trends in Marital Dissolution by Women's Education in the United States." *Demographic Research* 15(Article 20):537–60. December 13. Retrieved May 10, 2007 (www.demographic-research.org).

Martin, Steven P. and Sangeeta Parashar. 2006. "Women's Changing Attitudes toward Divorce, 1974–2002: Evidence for an Educational Crossover." *Journal of Marriage and Family* 68(1):29–40

Martinez, Gladys M., Anjani Chandra, Joyce C. Abma, Jo Jones, and William D. Mosher. 2006. "Fertility, Contraception, and Fatherhood: Data on Men and

Women from Cycle 6 (2002) of the National Survey of Family Growth." *Vital and Health Statistics* 23(26). May. Retrieved January 27, 2007 (www.nchs.gov).

Martino, Steven C., Rebecca L. Collins, and Phyllis L. Ellickson. 2004. "Substance Use and Early Marriage." *Journal of Marriage and Family* 66(1):244–57.

Marvin v. Marvin. 1976. 18 Cal. 3d 660, 134 Cal. Rptr. 815, 557 P.2d 106.

Masanori, Ishimori, Ikuo Daibo, and Yuji Kanemasa. 2004. "Love Styles and Romantic Love Experiences in Japan." *Social Behavior and Personality* 32(3):265–81.

Maslow, Abraham H. 1943. "A Theory of Human Motivation." *Psychological Review* 50:370–96.

Mason, Heather and Steve Crabtree. 2004. "Marital Morals: Different Standards in U.S., Canada, Britain." November 30. Washington, DC: The Gallup Organization. Retrieved December 1, 2004 (www.gallup .com/poll).

Mason, Karen A. 2000. "They Do Time Too: The Effects of Imprisonment on the Families of White-collar Offenders." Pp. 325–27 in *Families, Crime, and Criminal Justice,* edited by Greer Litton Fox and Michael L. Benson. New York: Elsevier Science.

Mason, Mary Ann. 1998. "The Modern American Stepfamily: Problems and Possibilities." Pp. 95–116 in *All Our Families: New Policies for a New Century,* edited by Mary Ann Mason, Arlene Skolnick, and Stephen D. Sugarman. New York: Oxford University Press.

Mason, Mary Ann, Mark A. Fine, and Sarah Carnochan. 2001. "Family Law in the New Millennium: For Whose Families?" *Journal of Family Issues* 22(7):859–81.

Mason, Mary Ann, Sydney Harrison-Jay, Gloria Messick Svare, and Nicholas H. Wolfinger. 2002. "Stepparents: De Facto Parents or Legal Strangers?" *Journal of Family Issues* 23(4):507–22.

Mason, Mary Ann and Ann Quirk. 1997. "Are Mothers Losing Custody? Read My Lips: Trends in Judicial Decision-making in Custody Disputes—1920, 1960, 1990, and 1995." *Family Law Quarterly* 31:215–36.

Mason, Mary Ann, Arlene Skolnick, and Stephen D. Sugarman, eds. 1998. *All Our Families: New Policies for a New Century.* New York: Oxford University Press.

Massinga, Ruth and Peter J. Pecora. 2004. "Providing Better Opportunities for Older Children in the Child Welfare System." *The Future of Children* 14(1):151–72.

Masters, Coco. 2005. "Let's Pawty." *Time,* April 4. Retrieved June 23, 2007 (www.time.com).

Masters, William H. and Virginia E. Johnson. 1966. *Human Sexual Response.* Boston, MA: Little, Brown.

———. 1976. *The Pleasure Bond: A New Look at Sexuality and Commitment.* New York: Bantam.

Masters, William H., Virginia E. Johnson, and Robert C. Kolodny. 1994. *Heterosexuality.* New York: HarperCollins.

Masuda, Masahiro. 2006. "Perspectives on Premarital Postdissolution Relationships: Account-making of Friendships between Former Romantic Partners." Pp. 113–32 in *Handbook of Divorce and Relationship Dissolution,* edited by Mark A. Fine and John H. Harvey. Mahwah, NJ: Erlbaum.

Mather, Mark and Kerri L. Rivers. 2006. *The Concentration of Negative Child Outcomes in Low income Neighborhoods.* Washington, DC: Annie E. Casey Foundation and Population Reference Bureau. February. Retrieved March 31, 2006 (www.prb.org).

Mathews, T. J. and Brady E. Hamilton. 2005. "Trend Analysis of the Sex Ratio at Birth in the United States." *National Vital Statistics Reports* 53(20). Hyattsville, MD: National Center for Health Statistics. June 14.

Mathews, T. J. and Marian F. MacDorman. 2006. "Infant Mortality Statistics from the 2003 Period Linked Birth/Infant Death Data Set." *National Vital Statistics Reports* 54(16). Hyattsville, MD: National Center for Health Statistics. May 3.

Mattessich, Paul and Reuben Hill. 1987. "Life Cycle and Family Development." Pp. 437–69 in *Handbook of Marriage and the Family,* edited by Marvin B. Sussman and Suzanne K. Steinmetz. New York: Plenum.

Mathews, T. J., Fay Menacker, and Marian F. MacDorman. 2003. "Infant Mortality Statistics from the 2001 Period Linked Birth/Infant Death Data Set." *National Vital Statistics Reports* 52(2). Hyattsville, MD: National Center for Health Statistics. September 14.

Matthews, Ralph and Anne Martin Matthews. 1986. "Infertility and Involuntary Childlessness: The Transition to Nonparenthood." *Journal of Marriage and Family* 48:641–49.

Mattingly, Marybeth J. and Suzanne M. Bianchi. 2003. "Gender Differences in the Quantity and Quality of Free Time: The U.S. Experience." *Social Forces* 81(3):999–1030.

Maugh, Thomas H. 1998. "'Honey, Just Be a Yes Man'—Study: Marriage Lasts if Husband Gives In." *Los Angeles Times,* February 21.

Mauldon, Jane. 2003. "Families Started by Teenagers." Pp. 40–65 in *All Our Families,* 2nd ed., edited by Mary Ann Mason, Arlene Skolnick, and Stephen D. Sugarman. New York: Oxford University Press.

May, Rollo. 1969. *Love and Will.* New York: Norton.

———. 1975. "A Preface to Love." Pp. 114–19 in *The Practice of Love,* edited by Ashley Montagu. Englewood Cliffs, NJ: Prentice Hall.

Mays, Vickie M. and Susan D. Cochran. 1999. "The Black Woman's Relationship Project: A National Survey of Black Lesbians." Pp. 59–66 in *The Black Family: Essays and Studies,* 6th ed., edited by Robert Staples. Belmont, CA: Wadsworth.

McAdoo, Harriette Pipes. 2007. *Black Families,* 4th edition. Thousand Oaks, CA: Sage Publications.

McBride-Chang, Catherine and Lei Chang. 1998. "Adolescent–Parent Relations in Hong Kong: Parenting Styles, Emotional Autonomy, and School Achievement." *Journal of Genetic Psychology* 159(4):421–35.

McClusky, Tom. 2004. "Thirty Years of Marriage on Trial." Family Research Council. March 25 (http://www.frc.org).

McCone, David and Kathy O'Donnell. 2006. "Marriage and Divorce Trends for Graduates of the U.S. Air Force Academy." *Military Psychology* 18(1):61–75.

McCormick, Richard A., S.J. 1992. "Christian Approaches: Catholicism." Presented at the Surrogate Motherhood and Reproductive Technologies Symposium, January 13, Creighton University.

McCubbin, Hamilton I. and Marilyn A. McCubbin. 1991. "Family Stress Theory and Assessment: The Resiliency Model of Family Stress, Adjustment and Adaptation." Pp. 3–32 in *Family Assessment Inventories for Research and Practice,* 2nd ed., edited by Hamilton I. McCubbin and Anne I. Thompson. Madison: University of Wisconsin, School of Family Resources and Consumer Services.

———. 1994. "Families Coping with Illness: The Resiliency Model of Family Stress, Adjustment, and Adaptation." Chapter 2 in *Families, Health, and Illness.* St. Louis: Mosby.

McCubbin, Hamilton I. and Joan M. Patterson. 1983. "Family Stress and Adaptation to Crisis: A Double ABCX Model of Family Behavior." Pp. 87–106 in *Family Studies Review Yearbook.* Vol. 1, edited by David H. Olson and Brent C. Miller. Newbury Park, CA: Sage Publications.

McCubbin, Hamilton I., Anne I. Thompson, and Marilyn A. McCubbin, eds. 1996. *Family Assessment: Resiliency, Coping and Adaptation: Inventories for Research and Practice.* Madison: University of Wisconsin Press.

McCubbin, Hamilton I., Elizabeth Thompson, Anne Thompson, Jo A. Futrell, and Suniya Luthar. 2001. "The Dynamics of Resilient Families." *Contemporary Psychology* 48(2):154–56.

McCubbin, Marilyn A. 1995. "The Typology Model of Adjustment and Adaptation: A Family Stress Model." *Guidance and Counseling* 10(4):31–39.

McCubbin, Marilyn A. and Hamilton I. McCubbin. 1989. "Theoretical Orientations to Family Stress and Coping." Pp. 3–43 in *Treating Families Under Stress,* edited by Charles Figley. New York: Brunner/Mazel.

McCurdy, Karen and Deborah Daro. 2001. "Parent Involvement in Family Support Programs: An Integrated Theory." *Family Relations* 50(2):113–21.

McDermott, Monica and Frank L. Samson. 2005. "White Racial and Ethnic Identity in the United States." *Annual Review of Sociology* 31:245–61.

McDonald, Katrina Bell and Elizabeth M. Armstrong. 2001. "De-Romanticizing Black Intergenerational Support: The Questionable Expectations of Welfare Reform." *Journal of Marriage and Family* 63:213–23.

McDonald, Merrilyn. 1998. "The Myth of Epidemic False Allegations of Sexual Abuse in Divorce Cases." *Court Review* (Spring). Retrieved January 14, 2002 (www.omsys.com).

McGinn, Daniel. 2006a. "Getting Back on Track." *Newsweek,* September 26, pp. 62–64.

———. 2006b. "Marriage by the Numbers." *Newsweek,* June 5, pp. 40–47.

McGinnis, Sandra L. 2003. "Cohabiting, Dating, and Perceived Costs of Marriage: A Model of Marriage Entry." *Journal of Marriage and Family* 65(1):105–16.

McHale, Susan M., W. T. Bartko, Ann C. Crouter, and M. Perry-Jenkins. 1990. "Children's Housework and Psychological Functioning: The Mediating Effects of Parents' Sex-role Behaviors and Attitudes." *Child Development* 61:1413–26.

McHale, Susan M. and Ann C. Crouter. 1992. "You Can't Always Get What You Want: Incongruence between Sex-role Attitudes and Family Work Roles and Its Implications for Marriage." *Journal of Marriage and Family* 54(3):537–47.

McHugh, Maureen F. 2007. "The Evil Stepmother." Second Wives Café: Online Support for Second Wives and Stepmothers. Retrieved May 2, 2007 (http://secondwivescafe.com).

McLanahan, Sara. 2004. "Diverging Destinies: How Children Are Faring under the Second Demographic Transition." *Demography* 41(4):607–27.

McLanahan, Sara and Marcia J. Carlson. 2002. "Welfare Reform, Fertility, and Father Involvement." *The Future of Children* 12(1):147–65.

McLanahan, Sara, Elizabeth Donahue, and Ron Haskins. 2005. "Introducing the Issue." *The Future of Children* 15(2):3–12.

McLanahan, Sara, Irwin Garfinkel, Nana E. Reichman, and Julien O. Teitler. 2001. "Unwed Parents or Fragile Families? Implications for Welfare and Child Support Policy." Pp. 202–28 in *Out of Wedlock: Causes and Consequences of Nonmarital Fertility,* edited by Lawrence L. Wu and Barbara Wolfe. New York: Russell Sage.

McLanahan, Sara and Gary Sandefur. 1994. *Growing Up with a Single Parent: What Hurts, What Helps?* Cambridge, MA: Harvard University Press.

McLoyd, Vonnie C., Ana Mari Cauce, David Takeuchi, and Leon Wilson. 2000. "Marital Processes and Parental Socialization in Families of Color: A Decade Review of Research." *Journal of Marriage and Family* 62:1070–93.

McMahon, Catherine A., Frances Gibson, Garth Leslie, Jennifer Cohen, and Christopher Tennant. 2003. "Parents of 5-Year-Old In Vitro Fertilization Children: Psychological Adjustment, Parenting Stress, and the Influence of Subsequent In Vitro Fertilization Treatments." *Journal of Family Psychology* 17:361–69.

McMahon, Martha. 1995. *Engendering Motherhood*. New York: Guilford.

McManus, Mike. 2006. "Inside/Out Dads: Helping Prisoners Reenter Society." Retrieved November 17, 2006 (smartmarriages.com).

McManus, Patricia A. and Thomas DiPrete. 2001. "Losers and Winners: The Financial Consequences of Separation and Divorce for Men." *American Sociological Review* 66:246–68.

McNicholas, J. and G. M. Collis. 2004. "Children's Representations of Pets in Their Social Networks." *Child: Care, Health and Development* 27:279–94.

McPherson, Miller and Lynn Smith-Lovin. 2006. "Social Isolation in America: Changes in Core Discussion Networks over Two Decades." *American Sociological Review* 71(June):353–75.

Mead, George Herbert. 1934. *Mind, Self, and Society*. Chicago, IL: University of Chicago Press.

Meadows, Sarah O., Kenneth C. Land, and Vicki L. Lamb. 2005. "Assessing Gilligan vs. Sommers: Gender-specific Trends in Child and Youth Well-being in the United States, 1985–2001." *Social Indicators Research* 70:1–52.

Means-Christensen, Adrienne J., Douglas K. Snyder, and Charles Negy. 2003. "Assessing Nontraditional Couples: Validity of the Marital Satisfaction Inventory—Revised with Gay, Lesbian, and Cohabiting Heterosexual Couples." *Journal of Marital and Family Therapy* 29(1):69–83.

Meckler, Laura. 1999. "Welfare Reform Hurts Poorest." Associated Press, August 22.

Meezan, William, and Jonathan Rauch. 2005. "Gay Marriage, Same-Sex Parenting, and America's Children." *The Future of Children* 15 (2): 157-175.

Mehrota, Meela. 1999. "The Social Construction of Wife Abuse: Experiences of Asian Indian Women in the United States." *Gender and Society* 16:898–920.

Mcilander, Gilbert. 1992. "Christian Approaches: Protestantism." Presented at the Surrogate Motherhood and Reproductive Technologies Symposium, January 13, Creighton University.

Memmott, Mark. 2001. "Sex Trade May Lure 325,000 U.S. Kids." *USA Today*, September 10.

Menjívar, Cecilia and Olivia Salcido. 2002. "Immigrant Women and Domestic Violence: Common Experiences in Different Countries." *Gender and Society* 16:898–920.

Merkle, Erich R. and Rhonda A. Richardson. 2000. "Digital Dating and Virtual Relating: Conceptualizing Computer Mediated Romantic Relationships." *Family Relations* 49(2):187–92.

Messner, Michael A. 1997. *The Politics of Masculinity: Men in Movements*. Thousand Oaks, CA: Sage Publications.

———. 2002. *Taking the Field: Men, Women, and Sports*. Minneapolis, MN: University of Minnesota Press.

Metropolitan Life Insurance Company. 1997. *The Metropolitan Life Survey of the American Teacher, 1997: Examining Gender Issues in the Public Schools*. New York: Metropolitan Life Insurance Company.

Meyer, Daniel R. and Judi Bartfeld. 1996. "Compliance with Child Support Orders in Divorce Cases." *Journal of Marriage and Family* 58(1):201–12.

Meyer, Madonna H. and Marcia L. Bellas. 2001. "U.S. Old-age Policy and the Family." Pp. 191–201 in *Families in Later Life: Connections and Transitions*, edited by Alexis J. Walker, Margaret Manoogian-O'Dell, Lori A. McGraw, and Diana L. G. White. Thousand Oaks, CA: Pine Forge.

Middlemiss, Wendy and William McGuigan. 2005. "Ethnicity and Adolescent Mothers' Benefit from Participation in Home-visitation Services." *Family Relations* 54(2):212–24.

Milardo, Robert M. 2005. "Generative Uncle and Nephew Relationships." *Journal of Marriage and Family* 67(5):1226–36.

Milkie, Melissa A., Marybeth Mattingly, Kei M. Nomaguchi, Suzanne M. Bianchi, and John D. Robinson. 2004. "The Time Squeeze: Parental Statuses and Feelings about Time with Children." *Journal of Marriage and Family* 66:739–61.

Miller, Brent C., Xitao Fan, Mathew Christensen, Harold Grotevant, and Manfred van Dulmen. 2000. "Comparisons of Adopted and Nonadopted Adolescents in a Large, Nationally Representative Sample." *Child Development* 71:1458–73.

Miller, Claudia. 2003. "When It's Good to Go Bananas: Oakland Nonprofit Has Been Helping Families Stay Sane for 30 Years." *San Francisco Chronicle*, October 19.

Miller, Courtney Waite and Michael E. Roloff. 2005. "Gender and Willingness to Confront Hurtful Messages from Romantic Partners." *Communication Quarterly* 53(3):323–38.

Miller, Dawn. 2004. "From the Author. TheStepfamilyLife: A Column from Life in the Blender" (http://www.thestepfamilylife.com).

———. N.d. "Don't Go Nuclear—Negotiate." SelfGrowth.com. Retrieved September 21, 2004 (http://www.selfgrowth.com/articles/Miller).

———. N.d. "Surviving the Blended Family Holiday: Five Tips for the Stressed Out." SelfGrowth.com. Retrieved September 21, 2004 (http://www.selfgrowth.com/articles/Miller).

Miller, Dorothy. 1979. "The Native American Family: The Urban Way." Pp. 441–84 in *Families Today: A Research Sampler on Families and Children*, edited by Eunice Corfman. Washington, DC: U.S. Government Printing Office.

Miller, Elizabeth. 2000. "Religion and Families over the Life Course." Pp. 173–86 in *Families Across Time: A Life Course Perspective*, edited by Sharon J. Price, Patrick C. McKenry, and Megan J. Murphy. Los Angeles, CA: Roxbury.

Miller, Laurie C. 2005a. *Handbook of International Adoptive Medicine*. New York: Oxford University Press.

———. 2005b. "International Adoption, Behavior, and Mental Health." *Journal of the American Medical Association* 293(20):2533–35.

Miller, Timothy. 1999. *The 60s Communes: Hippies and Beyond*. New York: Syracuse University Press.

Mills, C. Wright. 1940. "Situated Actions and Vocabularies of Motive." *American Sociological Review* 5:904–13.

———. [1959] 2000. *The Sociological Imagination*, 40th Anniversary Edition. New York: Oxford University Press.

Mills, Terry L., Melanie A. Wakeman, and Christopher B. Fea. 2001. "Adult Grandchildren's Perceptions of Emotional Closeness and Consensus with Their Maternal and Paternal Grandparents." *Journal of Family Issues* 22(4):427–55.

Mills, Terry L. and Janet M. Wilmoth. 2002. "Intergenerational Differences and Similarities in Life-sustaining Treatment Attitudes and Decision Factors." *Family Relations* 51(1):46–54.

Min, Pyong Gap. 2002. "Korean American Families." Pp. 193–211 in *Minority Families in the United States: A Multicultural Perspective,* 3rd ed., edited by Ronald L. Taylor. Upper Saddle River, NJ: Prentice Hall.

Mincy, Ronald B. 2006. *Black Males Left Behind.* Washington, DC: Urban Institute Press.

Miniño, Arialdi M., Melanie Heron, and Betty L. Smith. 2006. "Deaths: Preliminary Data for 2004." *National Vital Statistics Reports* 54(19). Hyattsville, MD: National Center for Health Statistics. June 28.

Miniño, Arialdi M., Melanie Heron, Sherry L, Murphy, and Kenneth D. Kochanek. 2007. *Deaths: Final Data for 2004.* Health E-Stats. Hyattsville, MD: National Center for Health Statistics. January 11. Retrieved January 29, 2007 (www.cdc.gov/nchs).

Mintz, Steven. 2004. *Huck's Raft: A History of American Childhood.* Cambridge, MA: Harvard University Press.

Mintz, Steven and Susan Kellogg. 1988. *Domestic Revolutions: A Social History of American Family Life.* New York: Free Press.

Molyneux, Guy. 1995. "Losing by the Rules." *Los Angeles Times,* September 3, pp. M1, M3.

Monahan Lang, Molly and Barbara J. Risman. 2007. "A 'Stalled' Revolution or a Still-unfolding One? The Continuing Convergence of Men's and Women's Roles." Discussion Paper, 10th anniversary conference of the Council on Contemporary Families, May 4–5, University of Chicago, Chicago, IL. Retrieved June 4, 2007 (www.contemporaryfamilies.org).

Monestero, Nancy. 1990. Personal communication.

"Monogamy: Is It for Us?" 1998. *The Advocate,* June 23, p. 29.

Monroe, Michael, Richard C. Baker, and Samuel Roll. 1997. "The Relationship of Homophobia to Intimacy in Heterosexual Men." *Journal of Homosexuality* 33(2):23–37.

Monroe, Pamela A. and Vicky V. Tiller. 2001. "Commitment to Work among Welfare-reliant Women." *Journal of Marriage and Family* 63(3):816–28.

Montgomery, Marilyn J. and Gwendolyn T. Sorell. 1997. "Differences in Love Attitudes across Family Life Stages." *Family Relations* 46:55–61.

Moody, Harry R. 2006. *Aging: Concepts and Controversies.* 5th ed. Thousand Oaks, CA: Pine Forge Press.

Moore, David W. 2003. "Family, Health Most Important Aspects of Life." The Gallup Poll. January 3. Retrieved September 13, 2006 (http://poll.gallup.com).

———.2004. "Modest Rebound in Public Acceptance of Homosexuals." May 20 (www.gallup.com).

——— 2005. "Gender Stereotypes Prevail on Working Outside the Home." Washington, DC: Gallup Poll News Service. August 17. Retrieved August 17, 2005 (www.gallup.com/poll).

Moore, Kathleen A., Marita P. McCabe, and Roger B. Brink. 2001. "Are Married Couples Happier in Their Relationships Than Cohabiting Couples? Intimacy and Relationship Factors." *Sexual and Relationship Therapy* 16(1):35–46.

Moore, Teresa. 1993. "Pain of Color-coded Child Rearing." *San Francisco Chronicle,* February 15, p. B3.

Moorman, Sara M., Alan Booth, and Karen L. Fingerman. 2006. "Women's Romantic Relationships after Widowhood." *Journal of Family Issues* 27(9):1281–1304.

Moran, Rachel F. 2001. *Interracial Intimacy: The Regulation of Race and Romance.* Chicago, IL: University of Chicago Press.

"More Binding Marriage Gets a Governor's Participation." 2004. *Omaha World-Herald,* November 14.

"More New Dads Seek Time Off." 2005. *Omaha World-Herald* (*Baltimore Sun*), May 9.

Moretti, Robb. 2002. "The Last Generation to Live on the Edge." *Newsweek,* August 5.

Morford, Mark. 2006. "My Baby Has Rainbow Hair, Gay Parents, Solo Moms, Sperm-swappin' Friends." April 12. Retrieved April 12, 2006 (http://www.sfgate.com).

Morgan, S. Philip. 2003. "Is Low Fertility a 21st Century Demographic Crisis?" *Demography* 40:589–603.

Morgan, S. Philip and R. B. King. 2001. "Why Have Children in the 21st Century? Biological Predispositions, Social Coercion, Rational Choice." *European Journal of Population* 17:3–20.

Morris, A. S., J. S. Silk, L. Steinberg, F. M. Sessa, S. Avenevoli, and M. J. Essex. 2002. "Temperamental Vulnerability and Negative Parenting as Interacting Predictors of Child Adjustment." *Journal of Marriage and Family* 64(2):461–71.

Morris, Frank. 2007. "War Strains Family Life for Military Couples." *Morning Edition.* National Public Radio. February 2.

Morrison, Donna R. and Andrew J. Cherlin. 1995. "The Divorce Process and Young Children's Well-being: A Prospective Analysis." *Journal of Marriage and Family* 57(3):800–12.

Morrison, Donna R. and Amy Ritualo. 2000. "Routes to Children's Economic Recovery after Divorce: Are Cohabitation and Remarriage Equivalent?" *American Sociological Review* 65(4):560–80.

Morrow, Lance. 1992. "Family Values." *Time,* August 31, pp. 22–27.

Mosher, William D., Anjani Chandra, and Jo Jones. 2005. "Sexual Behavior and Selected Health Measures: Men and Women 15–44 Years of Age, United States, 2002." *Advance Data from Vital and Health Statistics,* No. 362. September 15. Hyattsville, MD: U.S. National Center for Health Statistics.

Mott, Mary Ann. 2005. "And to My Dog, I Leave a $10,000 Trust Fund." *New York Times,* May 22.

Mueller, Karla A. and Janice D. Yoder. 1999. "Stigmatization of Non-Normative Family Size Status." *Sex Roles* 41(11/12):901–19.

Mueller, Margaret M. and Glen H. Elder, Jr. 2003. "Family Contingencies across the Generations: Grandparent-Grandchild Relationships in Holistic Perspective." *Journal of Marriage and Family* 65(2):404–17.

Mui, Ada C. 1996. "Depression among Elderly Chinese Immigrants: An Exploratory Study." *Social Work* 41:633–45.

Muller, Chandra. 1995. "Maternal Employment, Parent Involvement, and Mathematics Achievement among Adolescents." *Journal of Marriage and Family* 57(1):85–100.

Mulrine, Anna. 2003. "Love.com." *U.S. News & World Report,* September 29, pp. 52–58.

Mumola, Christopher J. 2000. *Incarcerated Parents and Their Children.* Washington, DC: U.S. Bureau of Justice Statistics.

Munson, Martha and Paul D. Sutton. 2006. "Births, Marriages, Divorces, and Deaths: Provisional Data for 2005." *National Vital Statistics Reports,* 54(20). Hyattsville, MD. July 21.

Murdock, George P. 1949. *Social Structure.* New York: Free Press.

Murkoff, Heidi. 2000. "The Real Parenting Expert Is . . . You." *Newsweek* Special Issue, Fall/Winter, pp. 20–21.

Murphy, Dean E. and Carolyn Marshall. 2005. "Family Feuds over Soldier's Remains." *New York Times,* October 12.

Murphy, Mike, Karen Glaser, and Emily Grundy. 1997. "Marital Status and Long-term Illness in Great Britain." *Journal of Marriage and Family* 59:156–64.

Murray, Bob and Alicia Fortinberry. 2006. *Raising an Optimistic Child: A Proven Plan for Depression-Proofing Young Children—for Life.* New York: McGraw-Hill.

Murray, Christine E. 2004. "The Relative Influence of Client Characteristics on the Process and Outcomes of Premarital Counseling." *Contemporary Family Therapy* 26(4):447–63.

———. 2006. "Professional Responses to Government-endorsed Premarital Counseling." *Marriage and Family Review* 40(1):53–67.

Murray, Christine E. and Thomas L. Murray, Jr. 2004. "Couples' Solution-based Premarital Counseling: Helping Couples Build a Vision for Their Marriage." *Journal of Marital and Family Therapy* 30(3):349–59.

Murray, Sandra L., John G. Holmes, and Dale W. Griffin. 2000. "Self-esteem and the Quest for Felt Security: How Perceived Regard Regulates Attachment Processes." *Journal of Personality and Social Psychology* 78(3):478–98.

Murry, Velma M., P. Adama Brown, Gene H. Brody, Carolyn E. Cutrona, and Ronald L. Simons. 2001. "Racial Discrimination as a Moderator of the Links among Stress, Maternal Psychological Functioning, and Family Relationships." *Journal of Marriage and Family* 63(4):915–26.

Murstein, Bernard I. 1980. "Mate Selection in the 1970s." *Journal of Marriage and Family* 42:777–92.

Musick, Kelly. 2002. "Planned and Unplanned Childbearing among Unmarried Women." *Journal of Marriage and Family* 64(4):915–29.

"Muslim Parents Seek Cooperation from Schools." 2005. CNN.com. September 5. Retrieved September 5, 2005 (http://www.cnn.com).

Mustafa, Nadia and Jeff Chu. 2006. "Between Two Worlds." *Time,* January 8. Retrieved January 14, 2006 (www.time.com).

Mustillo, Sarah, John Wilson, and Scott M. Lynch. 2004. "Legacy Volunteering: A Test of Two Theories of Intergenerational Transmission." *Journal of Marriage and Family* 66(2):530–41.

Myers, David G. 2001. *Social Psychology.* 7th ed. New York: McGraw-Hill.

Myers, David G., and Letha Dawson Scanzoni. 2006. *What God Has Joined Together? A Christian Case for Gay Marriage.* San Francisco, CA: HarperSanFrancisco.

Myers, Jane E., Jayamala Madathil, and Lynne R. Tingle. 2005. "Marriage Satisfaction and Wellness in India and the United States: A Preliminary Comparison of Arranged Marriages and Marriages of Choice." *Journal of Counseling and Development* 83(2):183–90.

Myers, Michael F. 1989. *Men and Divorce.* New York: Guilford.

Myers, Scott M. 2006. "Religious Homogamy and Marital Quality: Historical and Generational Patterns, 1980–1997." *Journal of Marriage and Family* 68(2):292–304.

Myers-Walls, Judith A. 2002. "Talking to Children about Terrorism and Armed Conflict." *The Forum for Family and Consumer Issues* 7(1). Retrieved September 14, 2006 (www.ces.ncsu.edu/depts/fcs/pub/2002w/myers-wall.html).

———. 2005a. "Children as Victims of Hurricane Katrina." Retrieved September 14, 2006 (www.ces.purdue.edu/cfs/topics/HD/ChildrenVictimsHurricaneKatrina.pdf).

———. 2005b. "Talking with Children When the Talking Gets Tough." Retrieved September 14, 2006 (www.ces.purdue.edu/Living_on_Less/Pubs/FF-35.html).

———. 2007. "Purple Wagon." Retrieved July 3, 2007 (www.ces.purdue.edu/purplewagon).

Nachshen, J. S., L. Woodford, and P. Minnes. 2003. "The Family Stress and Coping Interview for Families of Individuals with Developmental Disabilities: A Lifespan Perspective on Family Adjustment." *Journal of Intellectual Disability Research* 47(4–5):285–90.

Nakonezny, P. A., R. D. Shull, and J. L. Rodgers. 1995. "The Effect of No-fault Divorce Law on the Divorce Rate across the 50 States and Its Relation to Income, Education, and Religiosity." *Journal of Marriage and Family* 57(2):477–88.

Nanji, Azim A. 1993. "The Muslim Family in North America." Pp. 229–42 in *Family Ethnicity: Strength in Diversity,* edited by Harriette Pipes McAdoo. Newbury Park, CA: Sage Publications.

Nash, J. Madeleine. 1997. "Special Report: Fertile Minds." *Time,* February 3, pp. 48–56.

National Ag Safety Database. N.d. "From Family Stress to Family Strengths: Stress, Lesson 5" (http://www.cec.gov/niosh/nasd).

National Clearinghouse on Marital and Date Rape. 2005. "State Law Chart." May. Retrieved May 3, 2007 (http://members.aol.com/ncmdr/state_law_chart).

National Organization for Women. 1966. "Statement of Purpose." Washington, DC: N.O.W. Retrieved February 5, 2007 (www.now.org).

National Public Radio (NPR)/Kaiser Family Foundation/Kennedy School of Government. 2004. *Sex Education in America Survey.* Menlo Park, CA: Kaiser Family Foundation. January (www.kff.org).

National Right to Life. 2005. "Abortion's Physical Complications." Washington, DC: National Right to Life Educational Trust Fund. July.

———. 2006. "Abortion's Psycho-Social Consequences." Washington, DC: National Right to Life Educational Trust Fund. December 6. Retrieved March 29, 2007 (www.nrlc.org).

Navarro v. LaMusga. 2004. (Cal. Lexis 6507).

Navarro, Mireya. 2004. "For Younger Latinas, a Shift to Smaller Families." *New York Times,* December 5.

———. 2006a. "Focusing on an Attitude Rather Than a Language." *New York Times,* September 25.

———. 2006b. "Immigration, a Love Story." *New York Times,* December 12.

Nazario, Sonia L. 1990. "Identity Crisis: When White Parents Adopt Black Babies, Race Often Divides." *Wall Street Journal,* September 20.

Neimark, Jill. 2003. "All You Need Is Love: Why It's Crucial to Your Health—and How to Get More in Your Life." *Natural Health* 33(8):109–13.

Nelsen, Jane, Cheryl Erwin, and Roslyn Duffy. 2007. *Positive Discipline for Preschoolers: For Their Early Years, Raising Children Who Are Responsible, Respectful, and Resourceful.* New York: Three Rivers Press.

Nelson, Todd D. 2005. "Ageism: Prejudice against Our Future Self." *Journal of Social Issues* 61(2):207–23.

Neuman, W. Lawrence. 2000. *Social Research Methods.* Boston, MA: Allyn and Bacon.

"NE-UNL Study Finds Wages Benefitted from Immigrants." 2003. *Lincoln Journal Star,* April 17.

Nevius, C. W. 2006. "Kids Flock Back to Parents' Nest." *San Francisco Chronicle,* March 11. Retrieved March 29, 2006 (http://sfgate.com).

Newman, Andrew Adam. 2005. "Smile and Say 'Bone.'" *New York Times,* November 13.

Newman, Louis. 1992. "Jewish Approaches." Presented at the Surrogate Motherhood and Reproductive Technologies Symposium, January 13, Creighton University.

Newport, Frank. 2001. "American Attitudes toward Homosexuality Continue to Become More Tolerant." Poll Analyses. June 4 (http://www.gallup.com).

NICHD Early Child Care Research Network. 1999a. "Child Care and Mother–Child Interaction in the First Three Years of Life." *Developmental Psychology* 35:1399–1413.

———. 1999b. "Child Outcomes When Child Care Center Classes Meet Recommended Standards for Quality." *American Journal of Public Health* 89:1072–77.

———. 2000a. "Characteristics and Quality of Child Care for Toddlers and Preschoolers." *Applied Developmental Science* 4:116–35.

———. 2000b. "The Relation of Child Care to Cognitive and Language Development." *Child Development* 71:960–80.

———. 2003a. "Does the Amount of Time Spent in Child Care Predict Socioemotional Adjustment during the Transition to Kindergarten?" *Child Development* 74:976–1005.

———. 2003b. "Does Quality of Child Care Affect Child Outcomes at Age 4?" *Developmental Psychology* 39:451–69.

Nicholson v. Scopetta. 2004. (N.Y. No. 113).

Nippert-Eng, Christena E. 1996. *Home and Work: Negotiating Boundaries through Everyday Life.* Chicago, IL: University of Chicago Press.

Nock, Steven L. 1995. "A Comparison of Marriages and Cohabiting Relationships." *Journal of Family Issues* 16(1):53–76.

———.1998a. "The Consequences of Premarital Fatherhood." *American Sociological Review* 63:250–63.

———.1998b. *Marriage in Men's Lives.* New York: Oxford University Press.

———. 2001. "The Marriages of Equally Dependent Spouses." *Journal of Family Issues* 22:755–75.

———. 2005. "Marriage as a Public Issue." *The Future of Children* 15(2):13-32.

Nock, Steven L., Laura Sanchez, Julia C. Wilson, and James D. Wright. 2003. "Covenant Marriage Turns Five Years Old." *Michigan Journal of Gender and Law* 10(1): 169-88..

Nolan, David. 1998. "Abortion: Should Men Have a Say?" Pp. 216–31 in *Abortion Law and Politics Today,* edited by Ellie Lee. London, England: Macmillan.

Noland, Virginia J., Karen D. Liller, Robert J. McDermott, Martha Coulter, and Anne E. Seraphine. 2004. "Is Adolescent Sibling Violence a Precursor to Dating Violence?" *American Journal of Health Behavior* 28(Supp. 1): 813–23.

Noller, Patricia and Mary Anne Fitzpatrick. 1991. "Marital Communication in the Eighties." Pp. 42–53 in *Contemporary Families: Looking Forward, Looking Back,* edited by Alan Booth. Minneapolis, MN: National Council on Family Relations.

Nomaguchi, Kei M. and Melissa A. Milkie. 2003. "Costs and Rewards of Children: The Effects of Becoming a Parent on Adults' Lives." *Journal of Marriage and Family* 65:356–74.

Nordwall, Smita P. and Paul Leavitt. 2004. "Court Rules for Battered Women's Rights." *USA Today,* October 24.

"Not in Our House: Oh No?" 2001. *Time,* October 8.

Novak, M. 1997. *Issues in Aging.* New York: Longman.

"Numbers." 2004. *Time,* March 15.

Nyman, C. 1999. "Gender Equality in the Most Equal Country in the World: Money and Marriage in Sweden." *Sociological Review* 47:767–93.

Nystrom, Nancy M. and Teresa C. Jones. 2003. "Community Building with Aging and Old Lesbians." *American Journal of Community Psychology* 31(3-4):293–301.

Oakley, Ann. 1972. *Sex, Gender, and Society.* London, England: Maurice Temple Smith.

Obejas, Achy. 1994. "Women Who Batter Women." *Ms.,* September/October, p. 53.

O'Brien, Karen M. and Kathy P. Zamostny. 2003. "Understanding Adoptive Families: An Integrative Review of Empirical Research and Future Directions for Counseling Psychology." *The Counseling Psychologist* 31(6):679–710.

O'Brien, Marion. 2005. "Studying Individual and Family Development: Linking Theory and Research." *Journal of Marriage and Family* 67:880–90.

———. 2007. "Ambiguous Loss in Families of Children with Autism Spectrum Disorders." *Family Relations* 56(2):135–46.

O'Connor, Anahad. 2003. "H.I.V. Infections on the Rise, Study Says." *New York Times,* November 27.

———. 2005. "The Claim: Hormones in Milk Cause Early Puberty." *New York Times,* March 8.

O'Donoghue, Margaret. 2005. "White Mothers Negotiating Race and Ethnicity in the Mothering of Biracial, Black-White Adolescents." *Journal of Ethnic and Cultural Diversity in Social Work* 14(3/4):125–56.

"The Office Closet Empties Out." 2006. *Business Week,* May 1, p. 16.

Offner, Paul. 2005. "Welfare Reform and Teenage Girls." *Social Science Quarterly* 86(2):306–22.

Ogunwole, Stella U. 2006. *We the People: American Indians and Alaska Natives in the United States.* CENSR 28. Washington, DC: U.S. Census Bureau. February. Retrieved February 28, 2006 (www.census.gov).

O'Hare, William and Mark Mather. 2003. *The Growing Number of Kids in Severely Distressed Neighborhoods: Evidence from the 2000 Census.* Washington, DC: Annie E. Casey Foundation and Population Reference Bureau. September (http://www.kidscount.org; http://www.ameristat.org).

O'Laughlin, E. and L. Bischoff. 2005. "Balancing Parenthood and Academia: Work/Family Stress as Influenced by Gender and Tenure Status." *Journal of Family Issues* 26(1):79–106.

"Old Ways Bring Tears in a New World." 2003. *New York Times,* March 7.

"Older Moms' Birth Risks Called Greater." 1999. *Omaha World-Herald,* January 2.

Olmsted, Maureen E., Judith A. Crowell, and Everett Waters. 2003. "Assortative Mating among Adult Children of Alcoholics and Alcoholics." *Family Relations* 52(1):64–71.

Olson, David H. 1994. *Prepare, Enrich: Counselor's Manual.* Minneapolis, MN: Prepare-Enrich.

Olson, M., C. S. Russell, M. Higgins-Kessler, and R. B. Miller. 2002. "Emotional Processes Following Disclosure of an Extramarital Fidelity." *Journal of Marital and Family Therapy* 28:423–34.

Omaha Public Schools (OPS) Dual Language Research Group. 2006. *Examining the Impact of Parental Involvement in a Dual Language Program: Implications for Children and Schools.* Omaha, NE: Office of Latino and Latin American Studies, University of Nebraska at Omaha.

O'Malley, Jaclyn. 2002. "Abortion Grief Not Etched in Stone." *Omaha World-Herald,* October 16.

"One Hundred Questions and Answers about Arab Americans." N.d. *Detroit Free Press.* Retrieved on April 1, 2004 (http://www.bintjbeil.com/E/news/100q/family.html).

"Online Dating Attracts Older Daters." 2006. *New York Times,* March 15. Retrieved March 16, 2006 (http://www.nytimes.com).

O'Neil, Robin and Ellen Greenberger. 1994. "Patterns of Commitment to Work and Parenting: Implications for Role Strain." *Journal of Marriage and Family* 56(1):101–18.

O'Neill, Nena and George O'Neill. 1974. *Shifting Gears: Finding Security in a Changing World.* New York: M. Evans.

Ontario Consultants on Religious Tolerance. 2006. "Same-sex Parenting." Retrieved October 29, 2006 (http://www.religioustolerance.org).

Ooms, Theodora. 2001. "Policy Responses to Couple Conflict and Domestic Violence: A Framework for Discussion." Pp. 227–39 in *Couples in Conflict,* edited by Alan Booth, Ann C. Crouter, and Mari Clements. Mahwah, NJ: Erlbaum.

———. 2005. *The New Kid on the Block: What Is Marriage Education and Does It Work?* CLASP Policy Brief No. 7. Washington, DC: Center for Law and Social Policy. July. Retrieved September 4, 2005 (www.clasp.org).

Oppenheim, Keith. 2007. "Soldier Fathers Child Two Years after Dying in Iraq." CNN.com. March 20. Retrieved March 20, 2007 (http://cnn.usnews.com).

Oppenheimer, Valerie Kincade. 1997. "Women's Employment and the Gain to Marriage: The Specialization and Trading Model." *Annual Review of Sociology* 23:431–53.

———. 2003. "Cohabiting and Marriage during Young Men's Career Development Process." *Demography* 40(1):127–50.

Orbuch, Terri L. and Lindsay Custer. 1995. "The Social Context of Married Women's Work and Its Impact on Black Husbands and White Husbands." *Journal of Marriage and Family* 57(2):333–45.

Orbuch, Terri L. and Sandra L. Eyster. 1997. "Division of Household Labor among Black Couples and White Couples." *Social Forces* 75:301–32.

Orchard, Ann L. and Kenneth B. Solberg. 2000. "Expectations of the Stepmother's Role." *Journal of Divorce and Remarriage* 31(1/2):107–24.

Orenstein, Peggy. 1994. *School Girls: Young Women, Self-esteem, and the Confidence Gap.* New York: Doubleday.

———. 1998. "Almost Equal." *New York Times Magazine,* April 5, pp. 42–43, 45, 47–48.

Oropesa, R. S. 1996. "Normative Beliefs about Marriage and Cohabitation: A Comparison of Non-Latino Whites, Mexican Americans, and Puerto Ricans." *Journal of Marriage and Family* 58:49–62.

Oropesa, R. S. and Nancy S. Landale. 2004. "The Future of Marriage and Hispanics." *Journal of Marriage and Family* 66(4):901–20.

Oropesa, R. S., Daniel T. Lichter, and Robert N. Anderson. 1994. "Marriage Markets and the Paradox of Mexican American Nuptiality." *Journal of Marriage and Family* 56(4):889–907.

Orthner, Dennis K., Hinckley Jones-Sanpei, and Sabrina Williamson. 2004. "The Resilience and Strengths of Low-income Families." *Family Relations* 53(2):159–67.

Osment, Steven. 2001. *Ancestors: The Loving Family of Old Europe.* Cambridge, MA: Harvard University Press.

Osmond, Marie Withers and Barrie Thorne. 1993. "Feminist Theories: The Social Construction of Gender in Families and Society." Pp. 591–623 in *Sourcebook of Family Theories and Methods,* edited by Pauline G. Boss, William J. Doherty, Ralph LaRossa, Walter R. Schumm, and Suzanne K. Steinmetz. New York: Plenum.

Ostrove, Joan M., Pamela Feldman, and Nancy E. Adler. 1999. "Relations among Socioeconomic Status Indicators and Health for African-Americans and Whites." *Journal of Health Psychology* 4(4):451–63.

Oswald, Ramona F. and Linda S. Culton. 2003. "Under the Rainbow: Rural Gay Life and Its Relevance for Family Providers." *Family Relations* 52(1):72–81.

Otis, Melanie D., Sharon S. Rostosky, Ellen D. B. Riggle, and Rebecca Hamrin. 2006. "Stress and Relationship Quality in Same-sex Couples." *Journal of Social and Personal Relationships* 23(1):81–99.

Ott, Mary A., Susan G. Millstein, Susan Offner, and Bonnie L. Halpern-Felsher. 2006. "Greater Expectations for Adolescents' Positive Motivations for Sex." *Perspectives on Sexual and Reproductive Health* 38(2):84–89.

Owens, Timothy J. 2001. "The Myth of Self-esteem: Finding Happiness and Solving Problems in America." Review of *The Myth of Self-esteem: Finding Happiness and Solving Problems in America,* by John P. Hewitt (St. Martin's, 1998). *Social Forces* 79(3):1203.

Owo, Yvette. 2004. "African-Americans Still Face Discrimination in Schools." *The Daily Texan,* April 30.

"Oxytocin." 1997. *Britannica.* Retrieved August 30, 2006 (http://www.britannica.com).

Ozawa, Martha N. and Yongwoo Lee. 2006. "The Net Worth of Female-headed Households: A Comparison to Other Types of Households." *Family Relations* 55(1):132–34.

Paden, Shelley L. and Cheryl Buehler. 1995. "Coping with Dual-income Lifestyle." *Journal of Marriage and Family* 57(1):101–10.

Page, Jessica R., Heather B. Stevens, and Shelley L. Galvin. 1996. "Relationships between Depression, Self-esteem, and Self-silencing Behavior." *Journal of Social and Clinical Psychology* 15(4):381–90.

Page, Susan and Richard Benedetto. 2004. "Bush Backs Gay-Marriage Ban." *USA Today*, February 24.

Pahl, Jan M. 1989. *Marriage and Money*. Basingstoke, UK: Macmillan.

Painter, Kim. 2006. "Male Life Span Increasing." *USA Today*, June 12.

Papernow, P. 1993. *Becoming a Stepfamily: Patterns of Development in Remarried Families*. San Francisco, CA: Jossey-Bass.

Parcel, Toby L. and Mikaela J. Dufur. 2001. "Capital at Home and at School: Effects on Child School Adjustment." *Journal of Marriage and Family* 63(1):32–47.

"Parents Want More Time with Children and Greater Support." 2005. *Family Focus on . . . Family Strengths and Resilience* FF28: F10, F16. National Council on Family Relations.

Paris, Ruth and Nicole Dubus. 2005. "Staying Connected while Nurturing an Infant: A Challenge of New Motherhood." *Family Relations* 54(1):72–83.

Park, Kristin. 2002. "Stigma Management among the Voluntarily Childless." *Sociological Perspectives* 45:21–45.

———. 2005. "Choosing Childlessness: Weber's Typology of Action and Motives of the Voluntarily Childless." *Sociological Inquiry* 75(3):372–402.

Parke, Mary. 2003. *Are Married Parents Really Better for Children? What Research Says about the Effects of Family Structure on Child Well-Being*. CLASP Policy Brief No. 3. Washington, DC: Center for Law and Social Policy. May.

Parke, R. D. and R. Buriel. 1998. "Socialization in the Family: Ethnic and Ecological Perspectives." Pp. 463–552 in *Handbook of Child Psychology: Social, Emotional, and Personality Development*, edited by N. Eisenberg. New York: Wiley.

Parker, Ashley. 2006. "Looking Out for Pets in the Next Disaster." *New York Times*, June 1.

Parker, Laura. 2005. "When Pets Die at the Vet." *USA Today*, March 15.

Parsons, Talcott. 1943. "The Kinship System of the Contemporary United States." *American Anthropologist* 45:22–38.

Parsons, Talcott and Robert F. Bales. 1955. *Family, Socialization, and Interaction Process*. Glencoe, IL: Free Press.

Paset, Pamela S. and Ronald D. Taylor. 1991. "Black and White Women's Attitudes toward Interracial Marriage." *Psychological Reports* 69:753–54.

Pasley, Kay. 1998a. "Contemplating Stepchild Adoption." *Research Findings*. Stepfamily Association of America (http://www.saafamilies.org).

———. 1998b. "Divorce and Remarriage in Later Adulthood." *Research Findings*. Stepfamily Association of America (http://www.saafamilies.org).

———. 2000. "Does Living in a Stepfamily Increase the Risk of Delinquency in Children?" *Research Findings*. Stepfamily Association of America (http://www.saafamilies.org).

Pasley, Kay, Ted G. Futris, and Martie L. Skinner. 2002. "Effects of Commitment and Psychological Centrality on Fathering." *Journal of Marriage and Family* 64(1):130–38.

Pasley, Kay and Emily Lipe. 1998. "How Does Having a Mutual Child Affect Stepfamily Adjustment?" *Research Findings*. Stepfamily Association of America (http://www.saafamilies.org).

Passno, Diane. 2000. "The Feminist Mistake." *Focus on the Family*, September, pp. 12–13.

Pathman, Donald E., Thomas R. Konrad, and Robert Schwartz. 2001. "The Proximity of Rural African American and Hispanic/Latino Communities to Physicians and Hospital Services." North Carolina Rural Health Research and Policy Analysis Center. Retrieved October 3, 2006 (http://www.schsr.unc.edu).

Patterson, Charlotte. 2000. "Family Relationships of Lesbians and Gay Men." *Journal of Marriage and Family* 62(4):1052–69.

Patterson, Joan M. 2002a. "Family Caregiving for Medically Fragile Children." *Family Focus* (December):F5–F7. National Council on Family Relations.

———. 2002b. "Integrating Family Resilience and Family Stress Theory." *Journal of Marriage and Family* 64(2):349–60.

Pattillo-McCoy, Mary. 1999. *Black Picket Fences: Privilege and Peril among the Black Middle Class*. Chicago, IL: University of Chicago Press.

Paul, Annie Murphy. 2006. "The Real Marriage Penalty." *New York Times*, November 19.

Paul, Pamela. 2001. "Childless by Choice." *American Demographics* (November): 45–50.

———. 2002. *The Starter Marriage and the Future of Matrimony*. New York: Villard.

Peabody, Susan. 2002. "Typical Kinds of Love Addicts." Retrieved August 16, 2006 (http://www.selfgrowth.com/articles/Peabody5.html).

Pearlin, Leonard I. 1975. "Status Inequality and Stress in Marriage." *American Sociological Review* 40:344–57.

Pearson, Jessica and J. Anhalt. 1994. "The Enforcement of Visitation Rights: An Assessment of Five Exemplary Programs." *The Judges Journal* 33(2):2ff.

Pearson, Jessica, Nancy Thoennes, Lanae Davis, Jane C. Venohr, David A. Price, and Tracy Griffith. 2003. *OCSE Responsible Fatherhood Programs: Client Characteristics and Program Outcomes*. Washington, DC: U.S. Office of Child Support Enforcement; Denver, CO: Center for Policy Research and Policy Studies Institute.

Peck, M. Scott. 1978. *The Road Less Traveled: A New Psychology of Love, Traditional Values and Spiritual Growth*. New York: Simon and Schuster.

Peck, M. Scott and Sharon Peck. 2006. *The Top 60 Love Skills You Were Never Taught*. Solana Beach, CA: Lifepath Publishers.

Peck, Peggy. 2001. "Cancer Hard on Marriages." WebMD Medical News Archive (http://my.webmd.com).

Peele, Thomas. 2006. "Court Hears State's Take on Gay Marriage Ban." *Contra Costa Times*, July 10. Retrieved July 11, 2006 (http://www.mercurynews.com).

Peltola, Pia, Melissa A. Milkie, and Stanley Presser. 2004. "The 'Feminist' Mystique: Feminist Identity in Three Generations of Women." *Gender and Society* 18(1):122–44.

Pence, E. and M. Paymar. 1993. *Education Groups for Men Who Batter: The Duluth Model*. New York: Springer.

Pendley, Elisabeth. 2006. *Marriage Works: Before You Say "I Do."* Bellevue, WA: Merril Press.

Penning, M. J. 1990. "Receipt of Assistance by Elderly People: Hierarchical Selection and Task Specificity." *The Gerontologist* 30:220–27.

"*People v. Michael Fortin* [PAS Denied in New York]." 2000. *New York Law Journal*, March 27.

Peplau, Letitia Anne., A. Fingerhut, and K. P. Beals. 2004. "Sexuality in the Relations of Lesbians and Gay Men." Pp. 349–69 in *The Handbook of Sexuality in Close Relationships*, edited by J. H. Harvey, A. Wenzel, and S. Sprecher. Mahwah, NJ: Erlbaum.

Peplau, Letitia Anne, and Adam Fingerhut. 2004. "The Paradox of the Lesbian Worker." *Journal of Social Issues* 60(4):719–35.

Peralta, Robert L. and J. Michael Cruz. 2006. "Conferring Meaning onto Alcohol-related Violence: An Analysis of Alcohol Use and Gender in a Sample of College Youth." *Journal of Men's Studies* 14(1):109–36.

Perez, Lisandro. 2002. "Cuban American Families." Pp. 114–33 in *Minority Families in the United States*, 3rd ed., edited by Ronald L. Taylor. Upper Saddle River, NJ: Prentice Hall.

Perrin, Ellen C. 2002. *Sexual Orientation in Child and Adolescent Health Care.* New York: Kluwer Academic/Plenum.

Perrine, Stephen. 2006. "Keeping Divorced Dads at a Distance." *New York Times,* June 18.

Perry, Andrea and Mary Fromuth. 2005. "Courtship Violence Using Couple Data." *Journal of Interpersonal Violence* 20(9):1078–95.

Personal Responsibility and Work Opportunity Reconciliation Act. 1996. Public Law 104-193. Washington, DC: U.S. Congress.

Pertman, Adam. 2000. *Adoption Nation: How the Adoption Revolution Is Transforming America.* New York: Basic Books.

"Pet Lovers Find Emotional Support from Others Who Share Their Grief." 2002. *Omaha World-Herald,* April 14.

Peters, Arnold and Aart C. Liefbroer. 1997. "Beyond Marital Status: Partner History and Well-being in Old Age." *Journal of Marriage and Family* 59(3):687–99.

Peters, Jeremy W. and David Leonhardt. 2006. "Long a Laggard, Wages Start to Outpace Prices." *New York Times,* December 8.

Peters, Marie F. 2007. "Parenting of Young Children in Black Families." Pp. 203–18 in *Black Families*, 4th ed., edited by Harriette Pipes McAdoo. Thousand Oaks, CA: Sage Publications.

Petersen, Larry R. 1994. "Education, Homogamy, and Religious Commitment." *Journal for the Scientific Study of Religion* 33(2):122–28.

Peterson, Iver. 2005a. "In Suburbs, New Housing Is Unfriendly to Children." *New York Times,* May 30.

———. 2005b. "Princeton Students Who Say 'No' and Mean 'Entirely No.'" *New York Times,* April 18.

Peterson, James L. and Christine Winquist Nord. 1990. "The Regular Receipt of Child Support: A Multistep Process." *Journal of Marriage and Family* 52(2):539–51.

Peterson, Karen S. 2001. "The Good in a Bad Marriage." *USA Today,* June 21.

———. 2002. "'Market Work, Yes; Housework, Hah'" *USA Today,* March 13.

———. 2003. "Adoption Groups Opening Doors to Gays, Report Says." *USA Today,* October 29.

Peterson, Richard R. 1989. *Women, Work, and Divorce.* New York: SUNY Press.

———. 1996. "A Re-evaluation of the Economic Consequences of Divorce." *American Sociological Review* 61:528–36.

Peterson, Richard R. and Kathleen Gerson. 1992. "Determinants of Responsibility for Child Care Arrangements among Dual-earner Couples." *Journal of Marriage and Family* 54(3):527–36.

Pett, Marjorie A., Nancy Lang, and Anita Gander. 1992. "Late-life Divorce: Its Impact on Family Rituals." *Journal of Family Issues* 13:526–53.

Peyser, Marc. 1999. "Home of the Gray." *Newsweek,* March 1, pp. 50–53.

Pew Hispanic Center. 2002. "Hispanic Health: Divergent and Changing." Washington, DC: Pew Hispanic Center. Retrieved February 12, 2007 (www.pewhispanic.org).

———. 2006. "Hispanic Attitudes toward Learning English." Washington, DC: Pew Hispanic Center. Retrieved December 15, 2006 (www.pewhispanic.org).

Pew Research Center. 2005. *Baby Boomers: From the Age of Aquarius to the Age of Responsibility.* Washington, DC: Pew Research Center. December 8. Retrieved January 11, 2007 (www.pewresearch.org).

———. 2006. "Americans Reject Gay Marriage, Back Civil Unions." Angus-Reid Strategies. August 14. Retrieved October 20, 2006 (http://www.angus-reid.com/polls).

———. 2007. *A Portrait of "Generation Next": How Young People View Their Lives, Futures, and Politics.* Washington, DC: Pew Research Center for the People and the Press. January 9. Retrieved January 11, 2007 (www.pewresearch.org).

Pezzin, Liliana E. and Barbara Steinberg Schone. 1999. "Parental Marital Disruption and Intergenerational Transfers: An Analysis of Lone Elderly Parents and Their Children." *Demography* 36(3):287–97.

Deborah and Gina Adams. 2001. "Child Care and Our Youngest Children." *The Future of Children* 11:35–51.

Phillips, Linda R. 1986. "Theoretical Explanations of Elder Abuse: Competing Hypotheses and Unresolved Issues." Pp. 197–217 in *Elder Abuse: Conflict in the Family,* edited by Karl A. Pillemer and Rosalie S. Wolf. Dover, MA: Auburn.

Phillips, Julie A. and Megan M. Sweeney. 2005. "Premarital Cohabitation and Marital Disruption among White, Black, and Mexican American Women." *Journal of Marriage and Family* 67(2):296–314.

Phillips, Roderick. 1997. "Stepfamilies from a Historical Perspective." Pp. 5–18 in *Stepfamilies: History, Research, and Policy,* edited by Irene Levin and Marvin B. Sussman. New York: Haworth.

Picker, Lauren. 2005. "And Now, the Hard Part." *Newsweek*, April 25, pp. 46–51.

Pickhardt, Carl E. 2005. *The Everything Parent's Guide to the Strong-willed Child: An Authoritative Guide to Raising a Respectful, Cooperative, and Positive Child.* Avon, MA: Adams Media.

Pietropinto, Anthony and Jacqueline Simenauer. 1977. *Beyond the Male Myth: What Women Want to Know about Men's Sexuality; A National Survey.* New York: Times Books.

Pillemer, Karl A. 1986. "Risk Factors in Elder Abuse: Results from a Case-control Study." Pp. 239–64 in *Elder Abuse: Conflict in the Family,* edited by Karl A. Pillemer and Rosalie S. Wolf. Dover, MA: Auburn.

Pillemer, Karl and J. Jill Suitor. 2002. "Explaining Mothers' Ambivalence toward Their Adult Children." *Journal of Marriage and Family* 64(3):602–13.

Pines, Maya. 1981. "Only Isn't Lonely (or Spoiled or Selfish)." *Psychology Today* 15:15–19.

Pinker, Steven. 2002. *The Blank Slate: The Modern Denial of Human Nature.* New York: Penguin.

———. 2005. Opening Remarks. "The Science of Gender and Science—Pinker vs. Spelke: A Debate." Cambridge, MA: Harvard University, Mind/Brain/Behavior Initiative. May 16. Retrieved January 1, 2006 (www.edge.org).

Pipher, Mary. 1995. *Reviving Ophelia: Saving the Lives of Adolescent Girls.* New York: Ballantine.

Pirog-Good, Maureen A. and Lydia Amerson. 1997. "The Long Arm of Justice: The Potential for Seizing the Assets of Child Support Obligors." *Family Relations* 46(1):47–54.

Pisano, Marina. 2005. "Young Adults Live in Luxury at Family's Expense." *San Antonio Express.* Retrieved October 29, 2006 (http://www.mysanantonio.com).

Pittman, Joe F., Jennifer L. Kerpelman, and Jennifer M. McFadyen. 2004. "Internal and External Adaptation in Army Families: Lessons from Operations Desert Shield and Desert Storm." *Family Relations* 53(3):249–60.

Pitzer, Ronald L. 1997a. "Change, Crisis, and Loss in Our Lives." University of Minnesota Extension Service (http://www.extension.umn.edu).

———. 1997b. "Perception: A Key Variable in Family Stress Management." University of Minnesota Extension Service (http://www.extension.umn.edu).

Planned Parenthood of Central Missouri v. Danforth. 1976. 428 U.S. 52.

Pleck, Joseph H. 1992. "Prisoners of Manliness." Pp. 98–107 in *Men's Lives,* 2nd ed., edited by Michael S. Kimmel and Michael A. Messner. New York: Macmillan.

Poe, Marshall. 2004. "The Other Gender Gap." *Atlantic Monthly,* February, p. 137.

Poehlmann, Julie. 2005. "Children's Family Environments and Intellectual Outcomes during Maternal Incarceration." *Journal of Marriage and Family* 67(5):1275–85.

Pollack, William. 1998. *Real Boys: Rescuing Our Sons from the Myths of Boyhood.* New York: Random House.

Pollard, Kelvin M. and William P. O'Hare. 1999. "America's Racial and Ethnic Minorities." *Population Bulletin* 54(3). Washington, DC: Population Reference Bureau.

Pollitt, Katha. 2002. "Backlash Babies." *The Nation,* May 13, p. 10.

"Polyamory—An Unconditional Love." 2006. The Love Foundation. Retrieved March 30, 2006 (http://www.thelovefoundation.com).

Polyamory Society. N.d. "Children Education Branch." Retrieved October 4, 2006 (http://www.polyamorysociety.org).

Pomerleau, A., D. Bolduc, G. Malcuit, and L. Cossetts. 1990. "Pink or Blue: Environmental Stereotypes in the First Two Years of Life." *Sex Roles* 22:359–67.

Poniewozik, James. 2002. "The Cost of Starting Families." *Time,* April 15, pp. 56–58.

"Poor People and African Americans Suffer the Most Stress." 2003. *Family Focus* (June):F20–F21. National Council on Family Relations.

Poortman, Anne-Rigt and Judith A. Seltzer. 2007. "Parents' Expectations about Children after Divorce: Does Anticipating Difficulty Deter Divorce?" *Journal of Marriage and Family* 69(1):254–69.

Popenoe, David. 1993. "American Family Decline, 1960–1990: A Review and Appraisal." *Journal of Marriage and Family* 55(3):527–55.

———. 1994. "The Evolution of Marriage and the Problem of Stepfamilies: A Biosocial Perspective." Pp. 3–28 in *Stepfamilies: Who Benefits? Who Does Not?,* edited by Alan Booth and Judy Dunn. Hillsdale, NJ: Erlbaum.

———. 1996. *Life without Father: Compelling New Evidence That Fatherhood and Marriage Are Indispensable for the Good of Children and Society.* New York: Martin Kessler.

———. 1998. "The Decline of Marriage and Fatherhood." Pp. 312–19 in *Seeing Ourselves: Classic, Contemporary, and Cross-cultural Readings in Sociology,* 4th ed., edited by John J. Macionis and Nijole V. Benokraitis. Upper Saddle River, NJ: Prentice Hall.

Popenoe, David and Barbara Dafoe Whitehead. 2000. *The State of Our Unions 2000: The Social Health of Marriage in America.* New Brunswick, NJ: Rutgers University, National Marriage Project.

———. 2005. *The State of Our Unions 2005: The Social Health of Marriage in America.* New Brunswick, NJ: Rutgers University, National Marriage Project. Retrieved August 23, 2006 (http://marriage.rutgers.edu).

Popkin, Michael H. and Elizabeth Einstein. 2006. *Active Parenting: A New Program to Help Create Successful Stepfamilies.* Kennesaw, GA: Active Parenting Publishers.

Population Reference Bureau. 2001. *2001 World Population Data Sheet.* Washington, DC: Population Reference Bureau.

Porter, Eduardo. 2006a. "Cost of Illegal Immigration May Be Less Than Meets the Eye." *New York Times,* April 16.

———. 2006b. "Stretched to Limit, Women Stall March to Work." *New York Times,* March 21.

Porter, Eduardo and Michelle O'Donnell. 2006. "Facing Middle Age with No Degree, and No Wife." *New York Times,* August 6.

Porterfield, Ernest. 1982. "Black-American Intermarriages in the United States." Pp. 17–34 in *Intermarriages in the United States,* edited by Gary Crester and Joseph J. Leon. New York: Haworth.

Porterfield, Shirley L. 2002. "Work Choices of Mothers in Families with Children with Disabilities." *Journal of Marriage and Family* 64(4):972–81.

Portes, Alejandro, Patricia Fernandez-Kelly, and William Haller. 2004. "Segmented Assimilation on the Ground: The New Second Generation in Early Adulthood." CMD Working Paper No. 03-11, Center for Migration and Development, Princeton University, Princeton, NJ. November.

Portes, Alejandro and Rubén Rumbaut. 2000. *Legacies: The Story of the Immigrant Second Generation.* Berkeley: University of California Press.

Postrel, Virginia. 2005. "Yes, Immigration May Lift Wages." *New York Times,* November 3.

———. 2006. "The Work You Do When You're Not at Work." *New York Times,* February 23.

Potoczniak, Michael J., Jon Etienne Mourot, Margaret Crosbie-Burnett, and Daniel A. Potoczniak. 2003. "Legal and Psychological Perspectives on Same-sex Domestic Violence: A Multisystemic Approach." *Journal of Family Psychology* 17:252–59.

"Pow Wow Culture." 2006. *Indian Country Diaries* (TV series). Washington, DC: Public Broadcasting System. Retrieved December 2, 2006 (http://www.pbs.org/indiancountry).

Powell, Brian and Douglas Downey. 1997. "Living in Single-parent Households: An Investigation of the Same-sex Hypothesis." *American Sociological Review* 62:521–39.

Powell, Jean W. 2004. *Older Lesbian Perspectives on Advance Care Planning.* University of Rhode Island.

Power, Kathryn. 2004. "Resilience and Recovery in Family Mental Health Care." *Family Focus* (March):F1–F2. National Council on Family Relations.

Power, Paul W. 1979. "The Chronically Ill Husband and Father: His Role in the Family." *Family Coordinator* 28:616–21.

Press, Julie E. 2004. "Cute Butts and Housework: A Gynocentric Theory of Assortive Mating." *Journal of Marriage and Family* 66(4):1029–33.

Presser, Harriet B. 2000. "Nonstandard Work Schedules and Marital Instability." *Journal of Marriage and Family* 62:93–110.

Preston, Anne E. [2000] 2003. "Sex, Kids, and Commitment to the Workplace: Employers, Employees, and the Mommy Track." Haverford College, Haverford, PA. Unpublished manuscript.

Preston, Julia. 2006a. "Illegal Workers Supplant U.S. Ones, Report Says." *New York Times,* September 22.

———. 2006b. "Immigration and Jobs Link Is Disputed." *New York Times,* August 11.

———. 2006c. "Rules Collide with Reality in the Immigration Debate." *New York Times,* May 29.

———. 2007. "As Pace of Deportation Rises, Illegal Families Are Digging In." *New York Times,* May 1.

Preuschoff, Gisela. 2006. *Raising Girls.* Berkeley, CA: Celestial Press

Preves, Sharon E. 2002. "Sexing the Intersexed: An Analysis of Sociocultural Responses to Intersexuality." *Signs* 27:523–56.

———. 2003. *Intersex and Identity: The Contested Self.* New Brunswick, NJ: Rutgers University Press.

Previti, Denise and Paul R. Amato. 2003. "Why Stay Married? Rewards, Barriers, and Marital Stability." *Journal of Marriage and Family* 65:561–73.

Price, Deb. 2000. "It's Time to Treat Gay Elders with Respect." Partners Task Force for Gay and Lesbian Couples (www.buddybuddy.com/price-2.html).

"Prison Day Camp Extends Family Ties Behind Bars." 2001. *Omaha World-Herald,* August 6.

Proctor, Bernadette D. and Joseph Dalaker. 2003. *Poverty in the United States: 2002.* Current Population Reports P60-222. Washington, DC: U.S. Census Bureau.

"Professor Says Seminary Dismissed Her Over Gender." 2007. *New York Times,* January 27.

Prospero, Moises. 2006. "The Role of Perceptions in Dating Violence among Young Adolescents." *Journal of Interpersonal Violence* 21(4):470–84.

Pruchno, R. A., C. J. Burant, and N. D. Peters. 1997. "Typologies of Caregiving Families: Family Congruence and Individual Well Being." *The Gerontologist* 37:157–67.

"PTSD and Relationships: A National Center for PTSD Fact Sheet." 2006. United States Department of Veterans Affairs National Center for PTSD. Retrieved August 16, 2006 (http://www.ncptsd.va.gov).

Purdy, Matthew. 1995. "A Sexual Revolution for the Elderly: At Nursing Homes, Intimacy Is Becoming a Matter of Policy." *New York Times,* November 6.

Purkayastha, Bandana. 2002. "Rules, Roles, and Realities: Indo-American Families in the United States." Pp. 212–26 in *Minority Families in the United States,* 3rd ed., edited by Ronald L. Taylor. Upper Saddle River, NJ: Prentice Hall.

Purnine, Daniel M. and Michael P. Carey. 1998. "Age and Gender Differences in Sexual Behavior Preferences: A Follow-Up Report." *Journal of Sex & Marital Therapy* 24:93–109.

Pyke, Karen D. 1996. "Class-based Masculinities: The Interdependence of Gender, Class, and Interpersonal Power." *Gender and Society* 10:527–49.

———. 1999. "The Micropolitics of Care in Relationships between Aging Parents and Adult Children: Individualism, Collectivism, and Power." *Journal of Marriage and Family* 61(3):661–72.

———. 2000. "Ideology of 'Family' Shapes Perceptions of Immigrant Children." *Family:* F13–F14. National Council on Family Relations.

———. 2007. "'The Normal American Family' as an Interpretive Structure of Family Life among Grown Children and Vietnamese Immigrants." Pp. 469–90 in *Family in Transition,* 14th ed., edited by Arlene S. Skolnick and Jerome H. Skolnick. Boston, MA: Allyn and Bacon.

Pyke, Karen D. and Vern L. Bengston. 1996. "Caring More or Less: Individualistic and Collectivist Systems of Family Eldercare." *Journal of Marriage and Family* 58(2):379–92.

"The Quest Is On for Male Version of the 'Pill.'" 2004. *Omaha World-Herald* (Associated Press), April 25.

Quindlen, Anna. 2001. "Our Tired, Our Poor, Our Kids." *Newsweek,* March 12, p. 80.

———. 2005. "The Good Enough Mother." *Newsweek,* February 21, pp. 50–51.

Quinn, Jane Bryant. 2006. "As Kids Grow, So Do Risks." *Newsweek,* November 6, p. 49.

Rabin, Roni. 2006. "Health Disparities Persist for Men, and Doctors Ask Why." *New York Times,* November 14.

———. 2007. "It Seems the Fertility Clock Ticks for Men, Too." *New York Times,* February 27.

"Race and Ethnicity in 2001." 2001. Washington, DC: *Washington Post*/Kaiser Family Foundation/Harvard University.

Raley, R. Kelly and Jennifer Bratter. 2004. "Not Even if You Were the Last Person on Earth! How Marital Search Constraints Affect the Likelihood of Marriage." *Journal of Family Issues* 25(2):167–81.

Raley, R. Kelly and Elizabeth Wildsmith. 2004. "Cohabitation and Children's Family Instability." *Journal of Marriage and Family* 66(1):210–19.

Ramirez, Robert R. and G. Patricia de la Cruz. 2003. *The Hispanic Population of the United States: March 2002.* Current Population Reports P-20-545. Washington, DC: U.S. Census Bureau. June.

Rankin, Jane. 2005a. *Parenting Experts? How Their Advice Compares to Research Findings.* Westport, CT: Praeger.

———. 2005b. *Parenting Experts: Their Advice, the Research and Getting It Right.* Westport, CT: Praeger.

Raschick, Michael and Berit Ingersoll-Dayton. 2004. "Costs and Rewards of Caregiving among Aging Spouses and Adult Children." *Family Relations* 53(3):317–25.

Rasmussen Reports. 2006. "78% Willing to Vote for Woman President." CITY: Rasmussen Reports. December 12. Retrieved January 25, 2007 (www.rasmussenreports.com).

Raven, Bertram, Richard Centers, and Arnoldo Rodrigues. 1975. "The Bases of Conjugal Power." Pp. 217–32 in *Power in Families,* edited by Ronald E. Cromwell and David H. Olson. Beverly Hills, CA: Sage Publications.

Real, Terrence. 1997. *I Don't Want to Talk about It: Overcoming the Secret Legacy of Male Depression.* New York: Scribner's.

———. 2002. *How Can I Get Through to You? Reconnecting Men and Women.* New York: Scribner's.

Reardon-Anderson, Jane, Randy Capps, and Michael Fix. 2002. *The Health and Well-being of Children in Immigrant Families,* Series B, No. B-52. Washington, DC: The Urban Institute. November.

Rector, Robert and Kirk A. Johnson. 2005. "Adolescent Virginity Pledges and Risky Sexual Behaviors." Presented at the Eighth Annual National Welfare Research and Evaluation Conference of the Administration for Children and Families, June 15, Washington, DC. Retrieved March 28, 2007 (www.heritage.org).

Rector, Robert E. and Melissa G. Pardue. 2004. *Understanding the President's Healthy Marriage Initiative.* Heritage Foundation (http://www.heritage.org/Research/Family/bg1741.cfm).

Reeves, Terrance J. and Claudette E. Bennett. 2004. *We the People: Asians in the United States.* CDNSR-17. Washington, DC: U.S. Census Bureau. December.

Reich, Robert. 2006. "We've Got More Than Car Trouble." Interview by Kai Ryssdal, National Public Radio. September 20. Retrieved September 20 (http://marketplace.publicradio.org).

Reichert, Dana. 1999. *Broke but Not Deadbeat: Reconnecting Low-income Fathers and Children.* Washington, DC: National Conference of State Legislatures.

Reimann, Renate. 1997. "Does Biology Matter? Lesbian Couples' Transition to Parenthood and Their Division of Labor." *Qualitative Sociology* 20(2):153–85.

Reiss, David, Sandra Gonzalez, and Norman Kramer. 1986. "Family Process, Chronic Illness, and Death: On the Weakness of Strong Bonds." *Archives of General Psychiatry* 43:795–804.

Reiss, Ira L. 1976. *Family Systems in America.* 2nd ed. Hinsdale, IL: Dryden.

———. 1986. *Journey into Sexuality: An Exploratory Voyage.* Englewood Cliffs, NJ: Prentice Hall.

Reiss, Ira L. and G. L. Lee. 1988. *The Family System in America.* 4th ed. New York: Holt, Rinehart & Winston.

Rennison, Callie Marie. 2003. Intimate Partner Violence 1993-2001. BJS Crime Data Brief. Washington DC: U.S. Bureau of Justice Statistics.

Rennison, Callie Marie, and Sarah Welchans. 2000. *Intimate Partner Violence.* Bureau of Justice Statistics Special Report NCJ 178247. May. Washington DC: U.S. Department of Justice.

Renteln, Alison Dundes. 2004. *The Cultural Defense.* New York: Oxford University Press.

Renzetti, Claire M. 1992. *Violent Betrayal: Partner Abuse in Lesbian Relationships.* Newbury Park, CA: Sage Publications.

———. 2001. "Toward a Better Understanding of Lesbian Battering." Pp. 454–66 in *Shifting the Center,* 2nd ed., edited by Susan J. Ferguson. Mountain View, CA: Mayfield.

Reschke, Kathy L. 2003. "Difficult Choices: Low-income Mothers Struggle to Balance Caregiving and Employment." *Family Focus* (June):F8–F10. National Council on Family Relations.

Reynolds v. United States. 1878. 98 U.S. 145, 25 L. Ed. 244.

Rhodes, Angel R. 2002. "Long-distance Relationships in Dual-career Commuter Couples: Review of Counseling Issues." *The Family Journal* 10:398–404.

Richtel, Matt. 2005. "Past Divorce, Compassion at the End." *New York Times,* May 19.

Ridgeway, Cecilia. 2006. "Gender as an Organizing Force in Social Relations: Implications for the Future of Inequality." Pp. 245–64 in *The Declining Significance of Gender?,* edited by Francine D. Blau, Mary C. Brinton, and David B. Grusky. New York: Russell Sage.

Ridgeway, Cecilia L. and Shelley J. Correll. 2004. "Motherhood as a Status Characteristic." *Journal of Social Issues* 60(4):683–700.

Ridgeway, Cecilia and Lynn Smith-Lovin. 1999. "The Gender System and Interaction." *Annual Review of Sociology* 29:191–216.

Riedmann, Agnes and Lynn White. 1996. "Adult Sibling Relationships: Racial and Ethnic Comparisons." Pp. 105–26 in *Sibling Relationships: Their Causes and Consequences,* edited by Gene H. Brody. Norwood, NJ: Ablex.

Riekse, R. J. and H. Holstege. 1996. *Growing Older in America.* New York: McGraw-Hill.

Rigby, Jill M. 2006. *Raising Respectful Children in a Disrespectful World.* New York: Howard Books.

Riger, Stephanie, Susan L. Staggs, and Paul Schewe. 2004. "Intimate Partner Violence as an Obstacle to Employment among Mothers Affected by Welfare Reform." *Journal of Social Issues* 60(4):801–17.

Riley, Glenda. 1991. *Divorce: An American Tradition.* New York: Oxford University Press.

Riley, Matilda W. 1983. "The Family in an Aging Society: A Matrix of Latent Relationships." *Journal of Family Issues* (4):439–54.

Rimer, Sara. 1988a. "Child Care at Home: 2-Women, Complex Roles." *New York Times,* December 26.

Rindfleisch, Nolan. 1999. "Foster Parents More Likely to Continue Role with Encouragement and Support from Social Workers." *Brown University Child and Adolescent Behavior Letter* 15(9):2.

Risch, Gail S., Lisa A. Riley, and Michael G. Lawler. 2004. "Problematic Issues in the Early Years of Marriage: Content for Premarital Education." *Journal of Psychology and Theology* 31(1):253–69.

Risman, Barbara J. 1998. *Gender Vertigo: American Families in Transition.* New Haven, CT: Yale University Press.

Risman, Barbara J. and Danette Johnson-Sumerford. 1998. "Doing It Fairly: A Study of Postgender Marriages." *Journal of Marriage and Family* 60(1):23–40.

Risman, Barbara J. and Pepper Schwartz. 2002. "After the Sexual Revolution: Gender Politics in Teen Dating." *Contexts* (Spring):16–23.

Ritter, Raymond A., Sr., M.D. 1990. *A Healing Life: Memoirs of a Missouri Doctor.* Cape Girardeau, MO: Concord Publishing House.

Roberts, Alison. 2005. "Americans Are Alone Together." *The Sacramento Bee,* November 6, pp. H1, H5.

Roberts, Linda J. 2000. "Fire and Ice in Marital Communication: Hostile and Distancing Behaviors as Predictors of Marital Distress." *Journal of Marriage and Family* 62(3):693–707.

————. 2005. "Alcohol and the Marital Relationship." *Family Focus on . . . Substance Abuse across the Life Span* FF25:F12–F13. Minneapolis, MN: National Council of Family Relations.

Roberts, Nicole A. and Robert W. Levenson. 2001. "The Remains of the Workday: Impact of Job Stress and Exhaustion on Marital Interaction in Police Couples." *Journal of Marriage and Family* 63(4):1052–67.

Roberts, Sam. 2006. "In Queens, Blacks Are the Have-Nots No More." *New York Times*, October 1.

————. 2007a. "51% of Women Are Now Living without Spouse." *New York Times*, January 17.

————. 2007b. "Children's Quality of Life Is on the Rise, Report Finds." *New York Times*, January 11.

Robinson, B. E. and R. L. Barret. 1986. *The Developing Father: Emerging Roles in Contemporary Society*. New York: Guilford.

Robison, Jennifer. 2003. "Young Love, First Love, True Love?" The Gallup Poll. February 11. Retrieved August 28, 2006 (http://www.gallup.com/content).

Rockquemore, Kerry Ann. 2002. "Negotiating the Color Line: The Gendered Process of Racial Identity Construction among Black/White Biracial Women." *Gender and Society* 16(4):485–503.

Rockquemore, Kerry Ann and Tracey A. Laszloffy. 2005. *Raising Biracial Children*. Lanham, MD: AltaMira.

Rodgers, Joseph Lee, Paul A. Nakonezny, and Robert D. Shull. 1997. "The Effect of No-fault Divorce Legislation on Divorce Rates: A Response to a Reconsideration." *Journal of Marriage and Family* 59:1020–30.

Rodgers, Roy H. and James M. White. 1993. "Family Development Theory." Pp. 225–54 in *Sourcebook of Family Theories and Methods: A Contextual Approach*, edited by Pauline G. Boss, William J. Doherty, Ralph LaRossa, Walter R. Schumm, and Suzanne K. Steinmetz. New York: Plenum.

Rodman, Hyman. 1971. *Lower Class Families: The Culture of Poverty in Rural Trinidad*. New York: Oxford University Press.

————. 1972. "Marital Power and the Theory of Resources in Cultural Context." *Journal of Comparative Family Studies* 3:50–69.

Rodrigues, Amy E., Julie H. Hall, and Frank D. Fincham. 2006. "What Predicts Divorce and Relationship Dissolution?" Pp. 85–112 in *Handbook of Divorce and Relationship Dissolution*, edited by Mark A. Fine and John H. Harvey. Mahwah, NJ: Erlbaum.

Rodriguez, Christina M. and Andrea J. Green. 1997. "Parenting Stress and Anger Expression as Predictors of Child Abuse Potential." *Child Abuse & Neglect* 21(4):367–77.

Rodriguez, Gregory. 2003. "Mongrel America." *Atlantic Monthly*, January/February, pp. 95–97.

Roe v. Wade. 1973. 410 U.S. 113.

Rogers, Lesley. 2001. *Sexing the Brain*. New York: Columbia University Press.

Rogers, Michelle L. and Dennis P. Hogan. 2003. "Family Life with Children with Disabilities: The Key Role of Rehabilitation." *Journal of Marriage and Family* 65(4):818–33.

Rogers, Stacy J. 1999. "Wives' Income and Marital Quality: Are There Reciprocal Effects?" *Journal of Marriage and Family* 61:123–32.

Rogers, Stacy J. and Paul R. Amato. 2000. "Have Changes in Gender Relations Affected Marital Quality?" *Social Forces* 79:731–53.

Roisman, Glenn I. and R. Chris Fraley. 2006. "The Limits of Genetic Influence: A Behavior-Genetic Analysis of Infant-Caregiver Relationship Quality and Temperament." *Child Development* 77(6):1656–67.

Romero, Mary. 1992. *Maid in the U.S.A.* New York: Routledge.

Roper, Susanne Olsen and Jeffrey B. Jackson. 2007. "The Ambiguities of Out-of-Home Care: Children with Severe or Profound Disabilities." *Family Relations* 56(2):147–61.

Rosario, Margaret, Eric W. Schrimshaw, Joyce Hunter, and Lisa Braun. 2006. "Sexual Identity Development among Lesbian, Gay, and Bisexual Youths: Consistency and Change over Time." *Journal of Sex Research* 43(1):46–58.

Rose, Stephen J. and Heidi I. Hartmann. 2004. *Still a Man's Labor Market: The Long-term Earnings Gap*. Washington, DC: Institute for Women's Policy Research.

Rosen, Ruth. 2007. "The Care Crisis." *The Nation*, March 12, pp. 11–16.

Rosenberg, Debra. 2001. "A Place of Their Own." *Newsweek*, January 15, pp. 54–55.

————. 2004. "Generation Ambivalent." *Newsweek*, April 26, p. 29.

Rosenblatt, Paul C. and Linda Hammer Burns. 1986. "Long-term Effects of Perinatal Loss." *Journal of Family Issues* 7:237–54.

Rosenbloom, Stephanie. 2005. "Supersize Strollers Ignite Sidewalk Drama." *New York Times*, September 22.

————. 2006. "Here Come the Great-Grandparents." *New York Times*, November 2. Retrieved November 3, 2006 (http://www.nytimes.com).

Rosenbluth, Susan C. 1997. "Is Sexual Orientation a Matter of Choice?" *Psychology of Women Quarterly* 21:595–610.

Rosenbluth, Susan C., Janice M. Steil, and Juliet H. Whitcomb. 1998. "Marital Equality: What Does It Mean?" *Journal of Family Issues* 19(3):227–44.

Roseneil, Sasha and Shelley Budgeon. 2004. "Cultures of Intimacy and Care Beyond 'the Family': Personal Life and Social Change in the Early 21st Century." *Current Sociology* 52(2):135–59.

Rosenfeld, Alvin, and Nicole Wise. 2001. *The Over-Scheduled Child: Avoiding the Hyper-Parenting Trap*. New York: St. Martin's Griffin Press.

Rosenfeld, Jeffrey P. 1997. "Will Contests: Legacies of Aging and Social Change." Pp. 173–91 in *Inheritance and Wealth in America*, edited by Robert K. Miller, Jr. and Stephen J. McNamee. New York: Plenum.

Rosenfeld, Michael J. and Kim Byung-Soo. 2005. "The Independence of Young Adults and the Rise of Interracial and Same-sex Unions." *American Sociological Review* 70(4):541–62.

Ross, Catherine E. 1995. "Reconceptualizing Marital Status as a Continuum of Social Attachment." *Journal of Marriage and Family* 57(1):129–40.

Ross, Mary Ellen Trail and Lu Ann Aday. 2006. "Stress and Coping in African American Grandparents Who Are Raising Their Grandchildren." *Journal of Family Issues* 27(7):912–32.

Rossi, Alice S. 1968. "Transition to Parenthood." *Journal of Marriage and Family* 30:26–39.

————. 1973. *The Feminist Papers*. New York: Bantam.

———. 1984. "Gender and Parenthood." *American Sociological Review* 49:1–19.

Rotenberg, Ken J., George B. Schaut, and Brian O'Connor. 1993. "The Roles of Identity Development and Psychosocial Intimacy in Marital Success." *Journal of Social and Clinical Psychology* 12(2):198–213.

Roth, Benita. 2004. *Separate Roads to Feminism: Black, Chicana, and White Feminist Movements in America's Second Wave.* New York: Cambridge University Press.

Roth, Wendy. 2005. "The End of the One-drop Rule? Labeling of Multiracial Children in Black Intermarriages." *Sociological Forum* 20(1):35–67.

Rothman, Barbara Katz. 1999. "Comment on Harrison: The Commodification of Motherhood." Pp. 435–38 in *American Families: A Multicultural Reader,* edited by Stephanie Coontz. New York: Routledge.

Rovers, Martin W. 2006. *Healing the Wounds That Hurt Relationships.* Peabody, MA: Hendrickson.

Rowden, T., S. Harris, and R. Stahmann. 2006. "Group Premarital Counseling Using a Premarital Assessment Questionnaire." *American Journal of Family Therapy* 34(1):47–61.

Roxburgh, Susan. 1997. "The Effect of Children on the Mental Health of Women in the Paid Labor Force." *Journal of Family Issues* 18(3):270–89.

Roy, Kevin M., Carolyn Y. Tubbs, and Linda M. Burton. 2004. "Don't Have No Time: Daily Rhythms and the Organization of Time for Low-income Families." *Family Relations* 53(2):168–78.

Royster, Deirdre A. 2005. Review of *White Out: The Continuing Significance of Racism,* edited by Ashley W. Doane and Eduardo Bonilla-Silva (Routledge, 2003). *Contemporary Sociology* 35(3):255–56.

Ruane, Michael E. 2006. "Marriages Tested by Scars of War." *Washington Post,* May 27.

Rubin, Lillian B. 1976. *Worlds of Pain: Life in the Working-class Family.* New York: Basic Books.

———. 1997. *The Transcendent Child: Tales of Triumph Over the Past.* New York: Harper Perennial.

———. 2007. "The Approach-Avoidance Dance: Men, Women, and Intimacy." Pp. 319–24 in *Men's Lives,* 7th ed., edited by Michael S. Kimmel and Michael A. Messner. Boston, MA: Pearson.

Rubin, Lisa and Nancy Felipe Russo. 2004. "Abortion and Mental Health: What Therapists Need to Know." *Women and Therapy* 27(3/4):69–90.

Rubin, Roger H. 2001. "Alternative Lifestyles Revisited, or Whatever Happened to Swingers, Group Marriages, and Communes?" *Journal of Family Issues* 22(6):711–26.

Ruefli, Terry, Olivia Yu, and Judy Barton. 1992. "Brief Report: Sexual Risk Taking in Smaller Cities." *Journal of Sex Research* 29(1):95–108.

Rugel, Robert P. and Zoran Martinovich. 1997. "Dealing with the Problem of Low Self-esteem: Common Characteristics and Treatment in Individual, Marital/Family and Group Psychotherapy." *Contemporary Psychotherapy* 42(1):69–76.

Russell, Brenda L. and Debra L. Oswald. 2002. "Sexual Coercion and Victimization by College Men: The Role of Love Styles." *Journal of Interpersonal Violence* 17(3):273–85.

Russell, Diana E. H. 1990. *Rape in Marriage.* 2nd ed. New York: Macmillan.

Russo, Francine. 1997. "Can the Government Prevent Divorce?" *Atlantic Monthly,* October (http.//www .theatlantic.com/issues/97oct/divorce .html).

Russo, Nancy Felipe and Amy J. Dabul. 1997. "The Relationship of Abortion to Well-being: Do Race and Religion Make a Difference?" *Professional Psychology: Research and Practice* 28:23–31.

Russo, Nancy Felipe and Kristin L. Zierk. 1992. "Abortion, Childbearing, and Women's Well-being." *Professional Psychology: Research and Practice* 23:269–80.

Rutter, Michael. 2002. "Nature, Nurture, and Development: From Evangelism through Science toward Policy and Practice." *Child Development* 73(1):1–21.

Ryan, Joan. 2006. "War Without End." *San Francisco Chronicle,* March 26.

Ryan, Kathryn M. and Sharon Mohr. 2005. "Gender Differences in Playful Aggression during Courtship in College Students." *Sex Roles: A Journal of Research* 53(7-8):591–602.

Ryan, Suzanne, Jennifer Manlove, and Kerry Franzetta. 2003. *The First Time: Characteristics of Teens' First Sexual Relationships.* Washington, DC: ChildTrends. August (www.childtrends .org).

Saad, Lydia. 2003. "*Roe v. Wade* Has Positive Public Image." Gallup News Service. January 20 (www.gallup.com/poll).

———. 2004a. "A Nation of Happy People." The Gallup Poll. Retrieved September 18, 2006 (http://poll .gallup.com).

———. 2004b. "No Time for R & R." Gallup Poll Tuesday Briefing. May 11 (www.gallup.com)

———. 2004c. "Where Do Americans Find Personal Contentment?" The Gallup Poll. Retrieved September 18, 2006 (http://poll.gallup.com).

———. 2006a. "Americans at Odds over Gay Rights." The Gallup Poll. May 31. Retrieved July 24, 2006 (http://poll .gallup.com).

———. 2006b. "Americans Have Complex Relationship with Marriage." The Gallup Poll. May 31. Retrieved July 24, 2006 (http://poll.gallup.com).

———. 2006c. "Blacks Committed to the Idea of Marriage." The Gallup Poll. July 14. Retrieved October 10, 2006 (http://poll.gallup.com).

———. 2006d. "One in Four Parents Concerned about Child's Safety at School." The Gallup Poll. Retrieved September 1, 2006 (http://poll .gallup.com).

Saadeh, Wasim, Christopher P. Rizzo, and David G. Roberts. 2002. "This Month's Debate: Spanking." *Clinical Pediatrics* (March):87–91.

Sabatelli, Ronald M. and Constance L. Shehan. 1993. "Exchange and Resources Theories." Pp. 385–411 in *Sourcebook of Family Theories and Methods,* edited by Pauline Boss, William J. Doherty, Ralph La Rossa, Walter R. Schumm, and Suzanne K. Steinmetz. New York: Plenum.

Sachs, Andrea. 1990. "When the Lullaby Ends." *Time,* June 4, p. 82.

———. 2001. "Secrets to a Long and Happy Sex Life." *Time,* May 21.

Sachs, Andrea, Dorian Solot, and Marshall Miller. 2003. "Happily Unmarried." *Time,* March 3.

Sadker, M. and D. Sadker. 1994. *Failing at Fairness: How America's Schools Cheat Girls.* New York: Scribner's.

Safilios-Rothschild, Constantina. 1967. "A Comparison of Power Structure and Marital Satisfaction in Urban Greek and French Families." *Journal of Marriage and Family* 29:345–52.

———. 1970. "The Study of Family Power Structure: A Review 1960–1969." *Journal of Marriage and Family* 32:539–43.

Sage, Alexandria. 2004. "Papers Filed to Fight Ban on Polygamy." Associated Press, January 13.

Saluter, Arlene F. and Terry A. Lugaila. 1998. *Marital Status and Living Arrangements: March 1996.* Current Population Reports P20-496. Washington, DC: U.S. Bureau of the Census.

Samuelson, Robert J. 2005. "The Hard Truth of Immigration." *Newsweek,* June 13, pp. 63–66.

Sanchez, Laura, Steven L. Nock, James D. Wright, and Constance T. Gager. 2002. "Setting the Clock Forward or Back? Covenant Marriage and the 'Divorce Revolution.'" *Journal of Family Issues* 23:91–120.

Sanders, Joshunda. 2004. "Breaking Free from the Tired Old Dating Game: Quirky Singles Forge New Attitudes on Relationships." *San Francisco Chronicle,* February 8.

Sanford, Keith. 2006. "Communication during Marital Conflict: When Couples Alter Their Appraisal, They Change Their Behavior." *Journal of Family Psychology* 20(2):256–66.

Sanghavi, Darshak M. 2006. "Wanting Babies Like Themselves, Some Parents Choose Genetic Defects." *New York Times,* December 5.

Santelli, John S., Laura Duberstein Lindberg, Joyce Abma, Clea Sucoff McNeely, and Michael Resnick. 2000. "Adolescent Sexual Behavior: Estimates and Trends from Four Nationally Representative Surveys." *Family Planning Perspectives* 32:156–65, 194.

Santelli, John S., Laura Duberstein Lindberg, Lawrence B. Finer, and Susheela Singh. 2007. "Explaining Recent Declines in Adolescent Pregnancy in the United States: The Contribution of Abstinence and Improved Contraceptive Use." *American Journal of Public Health* 97(1):150–57.

Santelli, John S., Brian Morrow, John E. Anderson, and Laura Duberstein Lindberg. 2006. "Contraceptive Use and Pregnancy Risk among U.S. High School Students, 1991–2003." *Perspectives on Sexual and Reproductive Health* 38(2):106–11.

Santelli, John S., Roger Rochat, Kendra Hatfield-Timajchy, Brenda Colley

Gilbert, Kathryn Curtis, Rebecca Cabral, Jennifer S. Hirsch, Laura Shieve, and Other Members of the Unintended Pregnancy Working Group. 2003. "The Measurement and Meaning of Unintentional Pregnancy." *Perspectives on Social and Reproductive Health* 35:94–101.

Santos, Fernanda. 2007. "Demand for English Lessons Outstrips Supply." *New York Times,* February 27.

Sapone, Anna I. 2000. "Children as Pawns in Their Parents' Fight for Control: The Failure of the United States to Protect against International Child Abduction." *Women's Rights Law Reporter* 21(2):129–38.

Sarkisian, Natalia, Mariana Gerena, and Naomi Gerstel. 2006. "Extended Family Ties among Mexicans, Puerto Ricans, and Whites: Superintegration or Disintegration?" *Family Relations* 55(3):331–44.

Sarkisian, Natalia and Naomi Gerstel. 2004. "Explaining the Gender Gap in Help to Parents: The Importance of Employment." *Journal of Marriage and Family* 66(2):431–51.

Sassler, Sharon. 2004. "The Process of Entering into Cohabiting Unions." *Journal of Marriage and Family* 66(2):491–505.

Sassler, Sharon and Frances Goldscheider. 2004. "Revisiting Jane Austen's Theory of Marriage Timing: Changes in Union Formation among Men in the Late 20th Century." *Journal of Family Issues* 25(2):139–66.

Satir, Virginia. 1972. *Peoplemaking.* Palo Alto, CA: Science and Behavior Books.

———. 1988. *New Peoplemaking.* Mountain View, CA: Science and Behavior Books.

Sattler, David N. 2006. "Family Resources, Family Strains, and Stress Following the Northridge Earthquake." *Stress, Trauma, and Crisis: An International Journal* 9(3-4).187–202.

Saulny, Susan. 2006. "In Baby Boomlet, Preschool Derby Is the Fiercest Yet." *New York Times,* March 3. Retrieved March 15, 2006 (http://www.nytimes.com).

Savage, Jill. 2003. *Is There Really Sex after Kids?* Grand Rapids, MI: Zondervan Press.

"Save the Date: Relationships Ward Off Disease and Stress." 2004. *Psychology Today* (January/February):32.

Savin-Williams, Ritch. 2006. *The New Gay Teenager.* Cambridge, MA: Harvard University Press.

Sax, Leonard. 2002. "How Common Is Intersex? A Response to Anne Fausto-Sterling." *Journal of Sex Research* 39:174–78.

Sayer, Liana. 2006. "Economic Aspects of Divorce and Relationship Dissolution." Pp. 385–406 in *Handbook of Divorce and Relationship Dissolution,* edited by Mark A. Fine and John H. Harvey. Mahwah, NJ: Erlbaum.

Sayer, Liana and Suzanne M. Bianchi. 2000. "Women's Economic Independence and the Probability of Divorce." *Journal of Family Issues* 21:906–42.

Sayer, Liana C., Philip N. Cohen, and Lynne M. Casper. 2004. *Women, Men, and Work.* New York: Russell Sage.

Sbarra, David A. and Robert E. Emery. 2006. "In the Presence of Grief: The Role of Cognitive-Emotional Adaptation in Contemporary Divorce Mediation." Pp. 553–73 in *Handbook of Divorce and Relationship Dissolution,* edited by Mark A. Fine and John H. Harvey. Mahwah, NJ: Erlbaum.

Scanzoni, John H. 1972. *Sexual Bargaining: Power Politics in the American Marriage.* Englewood Cliffs, NJ: Prentice Hall.

———. 2001a. *The Household in Its Neighborhood and Community. Journal of Family Issues* Special Issue 22(2).

———. 2001b. "Reconnecting Household and Community." *Journal of Family Issues* 22(2):243–64.

Scarf, Maggie. 1995. *Intimate Worlds: Life Inside the Family.* New York: Random House.

Scelfo, Julie. 2004. "Happy Divorce." *Newsweek,* December 6, pp. 42–43.

Schaeffer, Brenda. 1997. *Is It Love or Is It Addiction?* Center City, MN: Hazelden.

Schafer, Alyson. 2006. *Breaking the Good Mom Myth: Every Mom's Modern Guide to Getting Past Perfection, Regaining Sanity, and Raising Great Kids.* Mississauga, ON: J. Wiley & Sons Canada.

Schaie, K. Warner and Glen Elder, eds. 2005. *Historical Influences on Lives and Aging.* New York: Springer.

Scharlach, Andrew, Wei Li, and Tapashi B. Dalvi. 2006. "Family Conflict as a Mediator of Caregiving Strain." *Family Relations* 55(5):625–35.

Schechtman, Morris R. and Arleah Schechtman. 2003. *Love in the Present Tense: How to Have a High Intimacy, Low*

Maintenance Marriage. Boulder, CO: Bull Publishing.

Schieve, Laura, et al. 2002. "Low and Very Low Birth Weight in Infants Conceived with Use of Assisted Reproductive Technology." *New England Journal of Medicine* 346:731–37.

Schmeeckle, Maria. 2007. "Gender Dynamics in Stepfamilies: Adult Stepchildren's Views." *Journal of Marriage and Family* 69(1):174–89.

Schneewind, Klaus A. and Anna-Katharina Gerhard. 2002. "Relationship Personality, Conflict Resolution, and Marital Satisfaction in the First 5 Years of Marriage." *Family Relations* 51(1):63–71.

Schneider, Barbara, Sylvia Martinez, and Ann Owens. 2006. "Barriers to Educational Opportunities for Hispanics in the United States." Pp. 179ff. in *Hispanics and the Future of America,* edited by Marta Tienda and Faith Mitchel. Washington, DC: National Academy Press.

Schneider, J. P., R. R. Irons, and M. D. Corley. 1999. "Disclosure of Extramarital Sexual Activities by Sexually Exploitative and Other Persons with Addictive or Compulsive Sexual Disorders." *Journal of Sex Education and Therapy* 24:277–87.

Schneider, Jodi. 2003. "Living Together." *U.S. News & World Report,* March 24.

Schnittker, Jason. 2007. "Working More and Feeling Better: Women's Health, Employment, and Family Life, 1974–2004." *American Sociological Review* 72(2):221–38.

Schnittker, Jason, Jeremy Freese, and Brian Powell. 2003. "Who Are the Feminists and What Do They Believe? The Role of Generations." *American Sociological Review* 68:607–22.

Schoen, Robert, Nan Marie Astone, Kendra Rothert, Nicola J. Standish, and Young J. Kim. 2002. "Women's Employment, Marital Happiness, and Divorce." *Social Forces* 81:643–62.

Schoen, Robert and Vladimir Canudas-Romo. 2006. "Timing Effects on Divorce: 20th Century Experience in the United States." *Journal of Marriage and Family* 68(3):749–58.

Schoen, Robert and Yen-Hsin Alice Cheng. 2006. "Partner Choice and the Differential Retreat from Marriage." *Journal of Marriage and Family* 68(1):1–10.

Schoen, Robert, Stacy J. Rogers, and Paul R. Amato. 2006. "Wives' Employment and Spouses' Marital Happiness: Assessing the Direction of Influence Using Longitudinal Couple Data." *Journal of Family Issues* 27(4):506–28.

Schoen, Robert and Paula Tufis. 2003. "Precursors of Nonmarital Fertility in the United States." *Journal of Marriage and Family* 65:1030–40.

Schoppe-Sullivan, Sarah J., Sarah C. Mangeisdorf, Geoffrey L. Brown, and Margaret Sokolowski-Szewczyk. 2007. "Goodness-of-fit in Family Context: Infant Temperament, Marital Quality, and Early Coparenting Behavior." *Infant Behavior and Development* 30(1):82–97.

Schor, Juliet B. 1991. *The Overworked American: The Unexpected Decline of Leisure.* New York: Basic Books.

Schott, Ben. 2007. "Who Do You Think We Are?" *New York Times,* February 27.

Schrodt, Paul. 2006. "Development and Validation of the Stepfamily Life Index." *Journal of Social and Personal Relationships* 23(3):427–44.

Schumacher, J. A., S. Feldbau-Kohn, A. Slep, and R. E. Heyman. 2001. "Risk Factors for Male-to-Female Partner Physical Abuse." *Aggression and Violent Behavior* 6:281–352.

Schwartz, Christine R. and Robert D. Mare. 2005. "Trends in Educational Assortative Marriage from 1940 to 2003." *Demography* 42(4):621–46.

Schwartz, Lita Linzer. 2003. "A Nightmare for King Solomon: The New Reproductive Technology." *Journal of Family Psychology* 17:229–37.

Schwartz, Pepper. 1994. *Peer Marriage: How Love between Equals Really Works.* New York: Free Press.

———. 2001. "Peer Marriage: What Does It Take to Create a Truly Egalitarian Relationship?" Pp. 182–89 in *Families in Transition,* 11th ed., edited by Arlene S. Skolnick and Jerome H. Skolnick. Boston, MA: Allyn and Bacon.

———. 2006. *Finding Your Perfect Match.* New York: Penguin Group.

Schwartz, Pepper and Virginia Rutter. 1998. *The Gender of Sexuality.* Thousand Oaks, CA: Pine Forge Press.

Schwartz, Richard D. 1954. "Social Factors in the Development of Legal Control." *Yale Law Journal* 63:471–91.

Schwartz, Seth J. and Gordon E. Finley. 2006. "Father Involvement, Nurturant Fathering, and Young Adult Psychosocial Functioning: Differences among Adoptive, Adoptive Stepfather, and Nonadoptive Stepfamilies." *Journal of Family Issues* 27(5):712–31.

Schweiger, Wendi K. and Marion O'Brien. 2005. "Special Needs Adoption: An Ecological Systems Approach." *Family Relations* 54(4):512–22.

Scott, Ellen K., Andrew S. London, and Nancy A. Meyers. 2002. "Dangerous Dependencies: The Intersection of Welfare Reform and Domestic Violence." *Gender and Society* 16:878–97.

Scott, Janny. 2001. "Rethinking Segregation Beyond Black and White." *New York Times,* July 29.

Scott, Janny and David Leonhardt. 2005. "Class in America: Shadowy Lines That Still Divide." *New York Times,* May 15.

Scott, Lisa. 2006. *Little Did You Know—: 101 Truths about Raising Children from Happy to Sad to Inspirational!* Bloomington, IN: Authorhouse.

Scott, Niki. 1992. "Irate Husband Vents His Side of the Story." *Working Woman,* April 13.

Seaburn, David B. and Giuseppe Erba. 2002. "Sudden Health: The Experience of Families with a Member Who Has Surgery to Correct Epilepsy." *Family Focus* (December):F8–F10. National Council on Family Relations.

Sears, Heather A., E. Sandra Byers, John J. Whelan, and Marcelle Saint-Pierre. 2006. "'If It Hurts You, Then It Is Not a Joke.' Adolescents' Ideas about Girls' and Boys' Use and Experience of Abusive Behavior in Dating Relationships." *Journal of Interpersonal Violence* 21(9):1191–1207.

Seaton, Eleanor K. and Ronald D. Taylor. 2003. "Exploring Familial Processes in Urban, Low-income African American Families." *Journal of Family Issues* 24(5):627–44.

Seccombe, Karen. 2000. "Families in Poverty in the 1990s: Trends, Causes, Consequences, and Lessons Learned." *Journal of Marriage and Family* 62(4):1094–1113.

———. 2007. *Families in Poverty.* New York: Pearson Education.

Seefeldt, Kristin S. and Pamela J. Smock. 2004. "Marriage on the Public Policy Agenda: What Do Policy Makers Need to Know from Research?" Ann Arbor: National Poverty Center, University of Michigan. February 17. Retrieved August 29, 2006 (www.npc.umich.edu).

Seelye, Katherine Q. 1998. "Specialists Report Rise in Adoptions That Fail." *New York Times,* March 24.

Seery, Brenda L. and M. Sue Crowley. 2000. "Women's Emotion Work in the Family: Relationship Management and the Process of Building Father–Child Relationships." *Journal of Family Issues* 21(1):100–27.

Segal, David R. and Mady Wechsler Segal. 2004. "America's Military Population." *Population Bulletin* 59(4):1–40.

Segura, Denise A. and Beatriz M. Pesquera. 1995. "Chicana Feminisms: Their Political Context and Contemporary Expressions." Pp. 617–31 in *Women: A Feminist Perspective,* 5th ed., edited by Jo Freeman. Mountain View, CA: Mayfield.

Seidler, Victor J. 1992. "Rejection, Vulnerability, and Friendship." Pp. 15–34 in *Men's Friendships: Research on Men and Masculinities,* edited by Peter M. Nardi. Newbury Park, CA: Sage Publications.

Seidman, Steven. 2003. *The Social Construction of Sexuality.* New York: W. W. Norton.

Seligman, Katherine. 2006. "I Married Myself." *San Francisco Chronicle Magazine,* February 12, pp. 9–10.

Seltzer, Judith A. 2000. "Families Formed Outside of Marriage." *Journal of Marriage and Family* 62(4):1247–68.

———. 2004. "Cohabitation in the United States and Britain: Demography, Kinship, and the Future." *Journal of Marriage and Family* 66(4):921–28.

Seltzer, Marsha and Tamar Heller, eds. 1997. "Family Caregiving for Persons with Disabilities." *Family Relations* Special Issue 46(4).

"Serious Violent Crime at School Continues to Fall." 2006. Press Release. Washington, DC: Bureau of Justice Statistics. December 3. Retrieved December 4, 2006 (www.ojp.usdog .gov/bjs).

Serovich, Julianne M., Sharon J. Price, and Steven F. Chapman. 1991. "Former In-laws as a Source of Support." *Journal of Divorce and Remarriage* 17(1/2):17–26.

Settersten, Richard A., Jr., Frank F. Furstenberg, Jr., and Rubén G. Rumbaut, eds. 2005. *On the Frontier of Adulthood: Theory, Research, and Public Policy.* Chicago, IL: University of Chicago Press.

Shalit, Wendy. 1999. *A Return to Modesty: Discovering the Lost Virtue.* New York: Free Press.

Shamin, Ishrat and Quamrul Ahsan Chowdhury. 1993. *Homeless and Powerless: Child Victims of Sexual Exploitation.* Dhaka, Bangladesh: University of Dhaka Press.

Shanahan, Michael J. 2000. "Pathways to Adulthood in Changing Societies: Variabilities and Mechanisms in Life Course Perspective." *Annual Review of Sociology* 26:667–97.

Shapiro, Joseph P. 2001a. "The Assisted-living Dilemma." *U.S. News & World Report,* May 21, pp. 64–66.

———. 2001b. "Growing Old in a Good Home." *U.S. News & World Report,* May 21, pp. 57–61.

———. 2006a. "Caregiver Role Brings Purpose—and Risk—to Kids." National Public Radio. March 23. Retrieved March 23, 2006 (http:www.npr.org).

———. 2006b. "Family Ties Source of Strength for Elderly Caregivers." National Public Radio. March 23. Retrieved March 23, 2006 (http:www.npr.org).

Sheehan, Constance L., E. Wilbur Bock, and Gary R. Lee. 1990. "Religious Heterogamy, Religiosity, and Marital Happiness: The Case of Catholics." *Journal of Marriage and Family* 52:73–79.

Shellenbarger, Sue. 1991a. "Companies Team Up to Improve Quality of Their Employees' Child-Care Choices." *Wall Street Journal,* October 17, pp. B1, B4.

———. 1991b. "More Job Seekers Put Family Needs First." *Wall Street Journal,* November 15, pp. B1, B6.

———. 2002. "As Moms Earn More, More Dads Stay Home." *Wall Street Journal,* February 20.

Shellenbarger, Sue and Cindy Trost. 1992. "Partnership of 109 Companies Aims to Improve Care Nationwide for Children and the Elderly." *Wall Street Journal,* September 11, pp. A12.

Shelton, Beth Anne. 1990. "The Distribution of Household Tasks: Does Wife's Employment Status Make a Difference?" *Journal of Family Issues* 11(2):115–35.

Shelton, Beth Anne and Daphne John. 1993. "Ethnicity, Race, and Difference: A Comparison of White, Black, and Hispanic Men's Household Labor Time." Pp. 131–50 in *Men, Work, and Family,*

edited by Jane C. Hood. Newbury Park, CA: Sage Publications.

———. 1996. "The Division of Household Labor." *Annual Review of Sociology* 22:299–322.

Sherif-Trask, Bahira. 2003. "Marriage from a Cross-cultural Perspective." *National Council on Family Relations Report* 48(3):F13–F14.

Sherman, Carey Wexler. 2006. "Remarriage and Stepfamily in Later Life." *Family Focus on . . . Families and the Future* FF32:F8–F9. National Council on Family Relations.

Sherman, Lawrence W. 1992. *Policing Domestic Violence: Experiments and Dilemmas.* New York: Free Press.

Sherman, Lawrence W. and Richard A. Berk. 1984. "Deterrent Effects of Arrest for Domestic Assault." *American Sociological Review* 49:261–72.

Sherman, Paul J. and Janet T. Spence. 1997. "A Comparison of Two Cohorts of College Students in Responses to the Male–Female Relations Questionnaire." *Psychology of Women Quarterly* 21(2):265–78.

Shomaker, Mary Zimmeth. 1994. "From Stepfather to Father." *Liguorian,* June, pp. 54–56.

Shorter, Edward. 1975. *The Making of the Modern Family.* New York: Basic Books.

Shumow, Lee, Deborah Lowe Vandell, and Jill Posner. 1999. "Risk and Resilience in the Urban Neighborhood: Predictors of Academic Performance among Low-income Elementary School Children." *Merrill-Palmer Quarterly* 45:309–331.

Siegel, Bernie S. 2006. *Love, Magic, and Mudpies: Raising Your Kids to Feel Loved, Be Kind, and Make a Difference.* New York: St. Martin's.

Siegel, Judith P. 2000. *What Children Learn from Their Parents' Marriage.* New York: HarperCollins.

Siegel, Mark D. 2004. "To the Editor: Making Decisions about How to Die." *New York Times,* October 3.

Siller, Sidney. 1984. "National Organization for Men." Privately printed pamphlet.

Silvern, Louise, Jane Karyl, Lynn Waelde, William F. Hodges, and Joanna Starek. 1995. "Retrospective Reports of Parental Partner Abuse: Relationships to Depression, Trauma Symptoms and Self-esteem among College Students." *Journal of Family Violence* 10(2):177–86.

Silverstein, Merril. 2000. "The Impact of Acculturation on Intergenerational Relationships in Mexican American Families." *National Council on Family Relations Report* 45(2):F9.

Silverstein, Merril and Vern L. Bengston. 1997. "Intergenerational Solidarity and the Structure of Adult Child–Parent Relationships in American Families." *American Journal of Sociology* 103(2):429–60.

———. 2001. "Intergenerational Solidarity and the Structure of Adult Child–Parent Relationships in American Families." Pp. 53–61 in *Families in Later Life: Connections and Transitions,* edited by Alexis J. Walker, Margaret Manoogian-O'Dell, Lori A. McGraw, and Diana L. G. White. Thousand Oaks, CA: Pine Forge Press.

Silverstein, Merril and Xuan Chen. 1999. "The Impact of Acculturation in Mexican American Families on the Quality of Adult Grandchild–Grandparent Relations." *Journal of Marriage and Family* 61(1):188–98.

Silverstein, Merril and Anne Marenco. 2001. "How Americans Enact the Grandparent Role across the Family Life Course." *Journal of Family Issues* 22(4):493–522.

Simko, Patty. 2006. "Co-Dependency." Retrieved August 16, 2006 (http://www.planetpsych.com/zPsychology_101/codependency.htm).

Simmel, Georg. 1950. *The Sociology of Georg Simmel.* Translated and edited by Kurt H. Wolfe. Glencoe, IL: Free Press.

Simmons, Tavia and Jane Lawler Dye. 2003. *Grandparents Living with Grandchildren: 2000.* Census Bureau Report C2KBR-31. Washington, DC: U.S. Census Bureau.

Simmons, Tavia and Martin O'Connell. 2003. *Married-couple and Unmarried Partner Households: 2000.* Census Special Report CENSR-5 Washington, DC: U.S. Census Bureau.

Simmons, Tavia and Grace O'Neill. 2001. *Households and Families: 2000.* Census 2000 Brief C2KBR/01-8. Washington, DC: U.S. Census Bureau.

Simon, Barbara Levy. 1987. *Never Married Women.* Philadelphia, PA: Temple University Press.

Simon, L. J. 1984. "The Pet Trap: Negative Effects of Pet Ownership on Families and Individuals." Pp. 226–40 in *The Pet Connection,* edited by R. K. Anderson, B.

L. Hart, and L. A. Hart. Minneapolis, MN: Center to Study Animal Relationships and Environments.

Simon, Rita J. 1990. "Transracial Adoptions Can Bring Joy: Letters to the Editor." *Wall Street Journal,* October 17.

Simon, Rita J. and Howard Altstein. 2002. *Adoption, Race, & Identity: From Infancy to Young Adulthood.* New Brunswick, NJ: Transaction Books.

Simon, Robin W. and Leda E. Nath. 2004. "Gender and Emotion in the United States: Do Men and Women Differ in Self-reports of Feelings and Expressive Behavior?" *American Journal of Sociology* 109(5):1137–76.

Simons, Leslie Gordon, Ronald L. Simons, Gene Brody, and Carolyn Cutrona. 2006. "Parenting Practices and Child Adjustment in Different Types of Households: A Study of African American Families." *Journal of Family Issues* 27(6):803–25.

Simoncelli, Tania with Jay Stanley. 2005. *Science under Seige: The Bush Administration's Assault on Academic Freedom and Scientific Inquiry.* New York: American Civil Liberties Union.

Simpson, J. and R. Rholes. 1998. *Attachment Theory and Close Relationships.* New York: Guilford.

Sinclair, Stacey L. and Gerald Monk. 2004. "Couples—Moving Beyond the Blame Game: Toward a Discursive Approach to Negotiating Conflict within Couple Relationships." *Journal of Marital and Family Therapy* 30(3):335–49.

Singer v. Hara. 1974. 11 Wash. App. 247, 522 P2d 1187.

Sirjamaki, John. 1948. "Cultural Configurations in the American Family." *American Journal of Sociology* 53(6):464–70.

Skinner, Denise A. and Julie K. Kohler. 2002. "Parental Rights in Diverse Family Contexts: Current Legal Developments." *Family Relations* 51(4):293–300.

Skinner, Kevin B., Stephen J. Bahr, D. Russell Crane, and Vaughn A. Call. 2002. "Cohabitation, Marriage, and Remarriage: A Comparison of Relationship Quality over Time." *Journal of Family Issues* 23(1):74–90.

Skipp, Catharine and Dan Ephron. 2006. "Trouble at Home." *Newsweek,* October 23, pp. 48–49.

Skloot, Rebecca L. 2003. "The Other Baby Experiment." *New York Times,* February 22.

Skolnick, Arlene S. 1978. *The Intimate Environment: Exploring Marriage and Family.* 2nd ed. Boston, MA: Little, Brown.

———. 1997. "A Response to Glenn: The Battle of the Textbooks; Bringing in the Culture Wars." *Family Relations* 46(3):219–22.

———. 2001. "The Life Course Revolution." Pp. 23–31 in *Families in Transition,* 11th ed., edited by Arlene S. Skolnick and Jerome H. Skolnick. Boston, MA: Allyn and Bacon.

Slade, Eric P. and Lawrence S. Wissow. 2004. "Spanking in Early Childhood and Later Behavior Problems." *Pediatrics* 113(5):1321–30.

Slark, Samantha. 2004. "Are Anti-Polygamy Laws an Unconstitutional Infringement on the Liberty Interests of Consenting Adults?" *Journal of Law and Family Studies* 6(2):451–60.

Slater, Lauren. 2002. "The Trouble with Self-esteem." *New York Times,* February 3, Section 6, p. 44.

———. 2006. "Love: The Chemical Reaction." *National Geographic,* February, pp. 34–49.

Slater, Suzanne. 1995. *The Lesbian Family Life Cycle.* New York: Free Press.

Smalley, Gary. 2000. *Secrets to Lasting Love: Uncovering the Keys to Life-long Intimacy.* New York: Simon and Schuster.

Smerglia, Virginia, Nancy Miller, and Diane Sotnak. 2007. "Social Support and Adjustment to Caring for Elder Family Members: A Multi-study Analysis." *Aging and Mental Health* 11(2):205–17.

Smith, Deborah B. and Phyllis Moen. 1998. "Spousal Influence on Retirement: His, Her, and Their Perceptions." *Journal of Marriage and Family* 60(3):734–44.

———. 2004. "Retirement Satisfaction for Retirees and Their Spouses: Do Gender and the Retirement Decision-making Process Matter?" *Journal of Family Issues* 25(2):262–85.

Smith, Donna. 1990. *Stepmothering.* New York: St. Martin's.

Smith, Peter B. and Michael Harris Bond. 1993. *Social Psychology across Cultures: Analysis and Perspectives.* Boston, MA: Allyn and Bacon.

Smith, Suzanna D. 2006. "Global Families." Pp. 3–24 in *Families in Global and Multicultural Perspective,* 2nd ed., edited by Bron B. Ingoldsby and Suzanna

D. Smith. Thousand Oaks, CA: Sage Publications.

Smith, Tim. 2006. *The Danger of Raising Nice Kids: Preparing Our Children to Change Their World.* Downers Grove, IL: IVP Books.

Smith, Tom W. 1999. *The Emerging 21st Century American Family.* GSS Social Change Report No. 42. Chicago, IL: University of Chicago, National Opinion Research Center.

———. 2003. *Coming of Age in 21st Century America: Public Attitudes towards the Importance and Timing of Transitions to Adulthood.* GSS Topical Report No. 35. Chicago, IL: National Opinion Research Center.

———. 2006. *American Sexual Behavior: Trends, Socio-Demographic Differences, and Risk Behavior.* GSS Topical Report No. 25 updated. Chicago, IL: National Opinion Research Center. March.

Smith, Tovia. 2006. "Technology Lets Parents Track Kids' Every Move." National Public Radio. August 20. Retrieved August 29, 2006 (http://www.npr.org).

Smith-Hefner, Nancy J. 2005. "The New Muslim Romance: Changing Patterns of Courtship and Marriage among Javanese Youth." *Journal of Southeast Asian Studies* 36(3):441–60.

Smits, Jeroen, Wout Ultee, and Jan Lammers. 1998. "Educational Homogamy in 65 Countries: An Explanation of Differences in Openness Using Country-level Explanatory Variables." *American Sociological Review* 63(2):264–75.

Smock, Pamela J. 1993. "The Economic Costs of Marital Disruption for Young Women over the Past Two Decades." *Demography* 30(3):353–71.

Smock, Pamela J. and Sanjiv Gupta. 2002. "Cohabitation in Contemporary North America." Pp. 53–84 in *Just Living Together: Implications of Cohabitation on Families,* edited by Alan Booth and Ann C. Crouter. Mahwah, NJ: Erlbaum.

Smock, Pamela J., Wendy D. Manning, and Sanjiv Gupta. 1999. "The Effect of Marriage and Divorce on Women's Economic Well-being." *American Sociological Review* 64:794–812.

Smolowe, Jill. 1996a. "The Unmarrying Kind." *Time,* April 29, pp. 68–69.

Sniezek, Tamara. 2002. "Getting Married: An Interactional Analysis of Weddings and Transitions into Marriage."

Unpublished dissertation. University of California at Los Angeles.

———. 2007. "When Does a Relationship Lead to Marriage?" Unpublished manuscript.

Snipp, C. Matthew. 2002. *American Indian and Alaska Native Children in the 2000 Census.* Washington, DC: Annie E. Casey Foundation, Population Reference Bureau.

———. 2005. *American Indian and Alaska Native Children: Results from the 2000 Census.* Washington, DC: Population Reference Bureau. August.

Snow, David A. and Cynthia L. Phillips. 1982. "The Changing Self-orientations of College Students: From Institution to Impulse." *Social Science Quarterly* 63(3):462–76.

Sobolewski, Juliana and Paul R. Amato. 2005. "Economic Hardship in the Family of Origin and Children's Psychological Well-being in Adulthood." *Journal of Marriage and Family* 67(1):141–56.

Sobolewski, Juliana and Valarie King. 2005. "The Importance of the Coparental Relationship for Nonresident Fathers' Ties to Children." *Journal of Marriage and Family* 67:1196–1212.

Solis, Dianne and Charlene Oldham. 2001. "Women Break Glass Ceiling by Starting Own Businesses." *Dallas Morning News,* June 18.

Solmonese, Joe. 2006. *The State of the Workplace: For Gay, Lesbian and Transgender Americans 2005 2006.* Washington, DC: Human Rights Campaign Foundation. Retrieved September 8, 2006 (http://www.hrc.org/workplace).

Sommers, Christina Hoff. 2000a. *The War Against Boys.* New York: Simon and Schuster.

———. 2000b. "The War Against Boys." *Atlantic Monthly,* May, pp. 59–75.

Sontag, Susan. 1976. "The Double Standard of Aging." Pp. 350–66 in *Sexuality Today and Tomorrow,* edited by Sol Gordon and Roger W. Libby. North Scituate, MA: Duxbury.

Soukup, Elise. 2006. "Polygamists, Unite!" *Newsweek,* March 20, p. 52.

Sousa, Liliana and Elaine Sorensen. 2006. *The Economic Reality of Nonresident Mothers and Their Children.* Series B, No. B-69. Washington, DC: Urban Institute. May.

South, Scott J., Kyle D. Crowder, and Katherine Trent. 1998. "Children's

Residential Mobility and Neighborhood Environment Following Parental Divorce and Remarriage." *Social Forces* 77:667–93.

Spar, Debora L. 2006. *The Baby Business: How Money, Science, and Politics Drive the Commerce of Conception.* Boston, MA: Harvard Business School Press.

Spelke, Elizabeth S. 2005. Opening Remarks. "The Science of Gender and Science—Pinker vs. Spelke: A Debate." Cambridge, MA: Harvard University, Mind/Brain/Behavior Initiative. May 16. Retrieved January 1, 2006 (www.edge.org)

Spending Patterns by Age. 2000. Issues in Labor Statistics. Summary 00–16. August. Washington, DC: U.S. Department of Labor, Bureau of Labor Statistics.

Spiro, Melford. 1956. *Kibbutz: Venture in Utopia.* New York: Macmillan.

Spitze, G. and J. Logan. 1990. "More Evidence on Women (and Men) in the Middle." *Research on Aging* 12(2):182–96.

Spitze, Glenna, John R. Logan, Glenn Deane, and Suzanne Zerger. 1994. "Adult Children's Divorce and Intergenerational Relationships." *Journal of Marriage and Family* 56(2):279–93.

Spitze, Glenna and Katherine Trent. 2006. "Gender Differences in Adult Sibling Relations in Two-child Families." *Journal of Marriage and Family* 68(4):977–92.

Spragins, Ellyn. 2002. "Full-Time Fathers Are Still Finding Their Way." *New York Times,* May 5.

Spraggins, Renee L. 2005. *We the People: Women and Men in the United States.* CENSR 20. Washington, DC: U.S. Census Bureau.

Sprecher, Susan. 2002. "Sexual Satisfaction in Premarital Relationships: Associations with Satisfaction, Love, Commitment, and Stability." *Journal of Sex Research* 39:190–96.

Sprecher, Susan and P. C. Regan. 1996. "College Virgins: How Men and Women Perceive Their Sexual Status." *Journal of Sex Research* 33:3–15.

Sprecher, Susan, Maria Schmeeckle, and Diane Felmlee. 2006. "The Principle of Least Interest: Inequality in Emotional Involvement in Romantic Relationships." *Journal of Family Issues* 27(9):1255–80.

Sprecher, Susan and Pepper Schwartz. 1994. "Equity and Balance in the Exchange of Contributions in Close Relationships." Pp. 89–116 in *Entitlement and the Affectional Bond: Justice in Close*

Relationships, edited by M. J. Lerner and G. Mikula. New York: Plenum.

Sprecher, Susan and Maura Toro-Morn. 2002. "A Study of Men and Women from Different Sides of Earth to Determine if Men Are from Mars and Women Are from Venus in Their Beliefs about Love and Romantic Relationships." *Sex Roles: A Journal of Research* (March):131–48.

Springen, Karen. 2000a. "Feeling the 50-Year Itch." *Newsweek,* December 4, pp. 56–57.

Springer, S. and G. Deutsch. 1994. *Left Brain/Right Brain,* 4th edition. New York: Freeman.

Srinivasan, Padma and Gary R. Lee. 2004. "The Dowry System in Northern India: Women's Attitudes and Social Change." *Journal of Marriage and Family* 66(5):1108–17.

St. George, Donna. 2006. "Home but Still Haunted." *Washington Post,* August 20.

Stacey, Judith. 1990. *Brave New Families: Stories of Domestic Upheaval in Late Twentieth Century America.* New York: Basic Books.

———. 1993. "Good Riddance to 'The Family': A Response to David Popenoe." *Journal of Marriage and Family* 55(3):545–47.

———. 1996. *In the Name of the Family: Rethinking Family Values in the Postmodern Age.* Boston, MA: Beacon Press.

Stacey, Judith and Timothy J. Biblarz. 2001. "(How) Does the Sexual Orientation of Parents Matter?" *American Sociological Review* 66:159–83.

Stack, Carol B. 1974. *All Our Kin: Strategies for Survival.* New York: Harper and Row.

Stack, Steven and Ira Wasserman. 1993. "Marital Status, Alcohol Consumption, and Suicide: An Analysis of National Data." *Journal of Marriage and Family* 55:1018–24.

Stanley v. Illinois. 1972. 405 U.S. 645, 92 S. Ct. 1208, 31 L.Ed.2d 551.

Stanley, Scott M. 2001. "Making a Case for Premarital Education." *Family Relations* 50:272–80.

Stanley, Scott M., Galena K. Rhoades, and Howard J. Markman. 2006. "Sliding versus Deciding: Inertia and the Premarital Cohabitation Effect." *Family Relations* 55(4):499–509.

Stanton, Glenn T. 2004a. "Why Marriage Matters for Adults." June 21. *Focus on Social Issues: Marriage and Family.* Focus on the Family. Retrieved September 30, 2006 (http://www.family.org/forum).

———. 2004b. "Why Marriage Matters for Children." June 21. *Focus on Social Issues: Marriage and Family.* Focus on the Family. Retrieved September 30, 2006 (http://www.family.org/forum).

Staples, Robert. 1994. *The Black Family: Essays and Studies.* 5th ed. Belmont, CA: Wadsworth.

———. 1999a. *The Black Family: Essays and Studies.* 6th ed. Belmont, CA: Wadsworth.

———. 1999b. "Patterns of Change in the Postindustrial Black Family." Pp. 281–90 in *The Black Family: Essays and Studies,* 6th ed., edited by Robert Staples. Belmont, CA: Wadsworth.

Staples, Robert and Leanor Boulin Johnson. 1993. *Black Families at the Crossroads: Challenges and Prospects.* San Francisco, CA: Jossey-Bass.

"State Court Orders Lesbian Mother to Pay Support." 2005. *South Bend Tribune,* February 19.

Stattin, H. and G. Klackenberg. 1992. "Discordant Family Relations in Intact Families: Developmental Tendencies over 18 Years." *Journal of Marriage and Family* 54:940–56.

Stearns, Peter N. 2003. *Anxious Parents: A History of Modern Childrearing in America.* New York: NYU Press.

Stein, Arlene. 1989. "Three Models of Sexuality: Drives, Identities, and Practices." *Sociological Theory* 7:1–13.

Stein, Ben. 2006. "Out of the Clubhouse and Into the Classroom." *New York Times,* December 10.

Stein, Catherine H., Virginia A. Wemmerus, Marcia Ward, Michelle E. Gaines, Andrew L. Freeberg, and Thomas C. Jewell. 1998. "'Because They're My Parents': An Intergenerational Study of Felt Obligation and Parental Caregiving." *Journal of Marriage and Family* 60(3):611–22.

Stein, Peter J. 2001. Personal communication (Review of seventh edition of this textbook).

Steinhauer, Jennifer. 1995. "Living Together without Marriage or Apologies." *New York Times,* July 6.

———. 2005. "When the Joneses Wear Jeans." *New York Times,* May 29.

———. 2007a. "A Proposal to Ban Spanking Sparks Debate." *New York Times,* January 21.

———. 2007b. "After Bill's Fall, G.O.P. May Pay in Latino Votes." *New York Times,* July 1.

Steinmetz, Suzanne K. 1977. *The Cycle of Violence: Assertive, Aggressive, and Abusive Family Interactions.* New York: Praeger.

"Stepfamily Facts." 2003. Stepfamily Association of America (http://www.saafamily.org/faqs/index.html).

"Stepfamily Stages: A Thumbnail Sketch." N.d. Retrieved July 31, 2007 (http://www.stepfamilytips.com/advice.html).

Stephens, William N. 1963. *The Family in Cross-cultural Perspective.* New York: Holt, Rinehart & Winston.

Stern, Gabriella. 1991. "Young Women Insist on Career Equality, Forcing the Men in Their Lives to Adjust." *Wall Street Journal,* September 16, pp. B1, B3.

Stern, Gary. 2003. "Jewish Intermarriage Still Up, but Rate Slowing." *Journal News,* September 11.

Sternberg, Robert J. 1988a. "Triangulating Love." Pp. 119–38 in *The Psychology of Love,* edited by Robert J. Sternberg and Michael L. Barnes. New Haven, CT: Yale University Press.

———. 1988b. *The Triangle of Love: Intimacy, Passion, Commitment.* New York: Basic Books.

———. 1998. *Love Is a Story: A New Theory of Relationships.* London, England: Oxford University Press.

———. 2006. Robert J. Sternberg's home page. Retrieved August 16, 2006 (http://www.yale.edu/rjsternberg).

Sternberg, Robert J., M. Hojjat, and M. L. Barnes. 2001. "Empirical Tests of Aspects of a Theory of Love as a Story." *European Journal of Personality* 15:199–218.

Stets, Jan E. 1991. "Cohabiting and Marital Aggression: The Role of Social Isolation." *Journal of Marriage and Family* 53(3):669–80.

Stevens, Daphne, Gary Kiger, and Pamela J. Riley. 2001. "Working Hard and Hardly Working: Domestic Labor and Marital Satisfaction in Dual Earner Couples." *Journal of Marriage and Family* 63:514–26.

Stevens, Gillian. 1991. "Propinquity and Educational Homogamy." *Sociological Forum* 6(4):715–26.

Stevenson, Betsey and Justin Wolfers. 2004. *Bargaining in the Shadow of the Law: Divorce Laws and Family Distress.* National Bureau of Economic Research Working

Paper 10175. Cambridge, MA: National Bureau of Economic Research. October 4.

————. 2007. *Marriage and Divorce: Changes and Their Driving Forces.* National Bureau of Economic Research Working Paper 12944. Cambridge, MA: National Bureau of Economic Research. March. Retrieved April 27, 2007 (www.nber.org).

Stewart, Mary White. 1984. "The Surprising Transformation of Incest: From Sin to Sickness." Presented at the annual meeting of the Midwest Sociological Society, April 18, Chicago, IL.

Stewart. Susan D. 1999. "Disneyland Dads, Disneyland Moms?" *Journal of Family Issues* 20:539–56.

————. 2002. "The Effect of Stepchildren on Childbearing Intentions and Births." *Demography* 39:181–97.

————. 2003. "Nonresident Parenting and Adolescent Adjustment." *Journal of Family Issues* 24(2):217–44.

————. 2005a. "Boundary Ambiguity in Stepfamilies." *Journal of Family Issues* 26(7):1002–29.

————. 2005b. "How the Birth of a Child Affects Involvement with Stepchildren." *Journal of Marriage and Family* 67(2):461–73.

————. 2007. *Brave New Stepfamilies: Diverse Paths toward Stepfamily Living.* Thousand Oaks, CA: Sage Publications.

Stinnett, Nick. 1985. *Secrets of Strong Families.* New York: Little, Brown.

————. 1997. *Good Families.* New York: Doubleday.

————. 2003. *Fantastic Families: 6 Proven Steps to Building a Strong Family.* Princeton, NJ: Sound Recording

Stinnett, Nick, Donnie Hilliard, and Nancy Stinnett. 2000. *Magnificent Marriage: 10 Beacons Show the Way to Marriage Happiness.* Montgomery, AL: Pillar Press.

Stinson, Kandi M., Judith N. Lasker, Janet Lohmann, and Lori J. Toedter. 1992. "Parents' Grief Following Pregnancy Loss: A Comparison of Mothers and Fathers." *Family Relations* 41:218–23.

Stock, Robert W. 1997. "When Older Women Contract the AIDS Virus." *New York Times,* July 31, p. B1.

Stoddard, Martha. 2006. "Grandparents Prevail in Visitation Challenge." *Omaha World-Herald,* June 6.

Stolberg, Sheryl Gay. 1997 "For the Infertile: A High Tech Treadmill." *New York Times,* December 14.

Stoll, Michael A. 2004. "African Americans and the Color Line." Washington, DC: Population Reference Bureau. Retrieved December 13, 2006 (www.prb.org).

Stone, Lawrence. 1980. *The Family, Sex, and Marriage in England, 1500–1800.* New York: Harper and Row.

Storey, A. E., C. J. Walsh, R. Quinton, and K. E. Wynne-Edwards. 2000. "Hormonal Correlates of Paternal Responsiveness in New and Expectant Fathers." *Evolution and Human Behavior* 21:79–95.

Storrs, Debbie. 2002. Review of *The Making and Unmaking of Whiteness,* edited by Birgit Brander Rasmussen, Eric Klinenberg, Irene J. Nexica, and Matt Wray (Duke University Press, 2001). *Contemporary Sociology* 31:570–71.

Story, Louise. 2005. "Many Women at Elite Colleges Set Career Path to Motherhood." *New York Times,* September 20. Retrieved September 23, 2005 (http://www.nytimes.com).

Stout, David. 2007. "Supreme Court Upholds Ban on Abortion Procedure." *New York Times,* April 18.

Strand, Erik. 2004. "Out of Touch?" *Psychology Today* (January/February):24.

Stratton, Peter. 2003. "Causal Attributions during Therapy: Responsibility and Blame." *Journal of Family Therapy* 25(2):136–60.

Straus, Murray A. 1993. "Physical Assaults by Wives: A Major Social Problem." Pp. 67–87 in *Current Controversies on Family Violence,* edited by Richard J. Gelles and Donileen R. Loseke. Newbury Park, CA: Sage Publications.

————. 1994. *Beating the Devil Out of Them: Corporal Punishment in American Families.* New York: Lexington Books.

————. 1996. "Presentation: Spanking and the Making of a Violent Society." *Pediatrics* 98:837–49.

————. 1999a. "The Benefits of Avoiding Corporal Punishment: New and More Definitive Evidence." Paper No. CP40–59/CP41B.P. University of New Hampshire: Family Research Laboratory.

————. 1999b. "The Controversy over Domestic Violence by Women: A Methodological, Theoretical, and Sociology of Science Analysis." Pp. 17–44 in *Violence in Intimate Relationships,* edited

by Ximena B. Arriaga and Stuart Oskamp. Thousand Oaks, CA: Sage Publications.

————. 2001. "Communicating the No-spanking Message to Parents." *Journal of Family Communication* 2(1):3–5.

————. 2005. "Women's Violence toward Men Is a Serious Social Problem." Pp. 55–77 in *Current Controversies on Family Violence,* edited by Donileen Loseke, Richard J. Gelles, and Mary M. Cavanaugh. Thousand Oaks, CA: Sage Publications.

————. 2007. "Do We Need a Law to Prohibit Spanking?" *Family Focus on . . . Adolescence* FF34:F7. National Council on Family Relations.

Straus, Murray A. and Denise A. Donnelly. 2001. *Beating the Devil Out of Them: Corporal Punishment in American Families and Its Effect on Children.* 2nd ed. New Brunswick, NJ: Transaction Books.

Straus, Murray A. and Richard J. Gelles. 1986. "Societal Change and Change in Family Violence from 1975 to 1985 as Revealed by Two National Surveys." *Journal of Marriage and Family* 48:465–79.

————. 1988. "How Violent Are American Families? Estimates from The National Family Violence Resurvey and Other Studies." Pp. 14–36 in *Family Abuse and Its Consequences: New Directions in Research,* edited by Gerald T. Hotaling, David Finkelhor, John T. Kirkpatrick, and Murray A. Straus. Newbury Park, CA: Sage Publications.

————. 1995. *Physical Violence in American Families: Risk Factors and Adaptations to Violence in 8,145 Families.* New Brunswick, NJ: Transaction Books.

Straus, Murray A., Richard J. Gelles, and Suzanne K. Steinmetz. 1980. *Behind Closed Doors: Violence in the American Family.* New York: Doubleday.

Straus, Murray A., Sherry L. Hamby, Sue Boney-McCoy, and David B. Sugarman. 1996. "The Revised Conflict Tactics Scales (CTS2): Development and Preliminary Psychometric Data." *Journal of Family Issues* 17:283–316.

Straus, Murray A. and Vera E. Mouradian. 1998. "Impulsive Corporal Punishment by Mothers and Antisocial Behavior and Impulsiveness of Children." *Behavioral Sciences & the Law* 16(3):353–62.

Straus, Murray A. and Carrie L. Yodanis. 1996. "Corporal Punishment in Adolescence and Physical Assaults on Spouses Later in Life: What Accounts for the Link?" *Journal of Marriage and Family* 58(4):825–924.

Strauss, Anselm and Barney Glaser. 1975. *Chronic Illness and the Quality of Life.* St. Louis: Mosby.

Strauss, Robert. 2002. "Dad's 50, Junior's 8. What's the Plan?" *New York Times,* March 12.

Strobe, W. and M. Strobe. 1996. "The Social Psychology of Social Support." Pp. 597–621 in *Social Psychology: Handbook of Basic Principles,* edited by E. T. Higgins and A. Kruglanski. New York: Guilford.

Strömberg, B., G. Dahlquist, A. Ericson, O. Finnström, M. Köster, and K. Stjernquist. 2002. "Neurological Sequaelae in Children Born after In Vitro Fertilization: A Population-based Study." *The Lancet* 395:461–65.

Struening, Karen. 2002. *New Family Values: Liberty, Equality, and Diversity.* Lanham, MD: Rowman and Littlefield.

Stryker, Sheldon. [1980] 2003. *Symbolic Interactionism: A Social Structural Version.* Caldwell, NJ: Blackburn.

"Study: Academic Gains for Women, Stagnation for Men." 2006. CNN. June 2. Retrieved June 4, 2006 (www.cnn.com).

"Study Says White Families' Wealth Advantage Has Grown." 2004. *New York Times,* October 18.

Suchman, Nancy, Marjukka Pajulo, Cindy DeCoste, and Linda Mayes. 2006. "Parenting Interventions for Drug-dependent Mothers and Their Young Children: The Case for an Attachment-based Approach." *Family Relations* 55(2):211–26.

Sullivan, Oriel. 1997. "The Division of Housework among Remarried Couples." *Journal of Family Issues* 18(2):205–23.

Supple, Andres J. and Stephen A. Small. 2006. "The Influence of Parental Support, Knowledge, and Authoritative Parenting on Hmong and European American Adolescent Development." *Journal of Family Issues* 27(9):1214–32.

Suro, Roberto. 1992. "Generational Chasm Leads to Cultural Turmoil for Young Mexicans in U.S." *New York Times,* January 20.

Surra, Catherine A. 1990. "Research and Theory on Mate Selection and Premarital Relationships in the 1980s." *Journal of Marriage and Family* 52:844–65.

Surra, Catherine A. and Debra K. Hughes. 1997. "Commitment Processes in Accounts of the Development of Premarital Relationships." *Journal of Marriage and Family* 59:5–21.

Sussman, L. J. 2006. "A 'Delicate Balance': Interfaith Marriage, Rabbinic Officiation, and Reform Judaism in America, 1870–2005." *CCAR Journal: A Reform Jewish Quarterly* 53(2):38–67.

Sussman, Marvin B., Suzanne K. Steinmetz, and Gary W. Peterson. 1999. *Handbook of Marriage and the Family.* 2nd ed. New York: Plenum.

Suter, Elizabeth, Karla Mason Bergen, Karen Daas, and Wesley Durham. 2006. "Lesbian Couples' Management of Public-Private Dialectical Contradictions." *Journal of Social and Personal Relationships* 23(3):349–65.

Swagger, Paper. 2005. "Self-esteem, Real and Phony." *Harvard Magazine,* September-October. Retrieved August 16, 2006 (http://www.harvardmagazine .com).

Swartz, Susan. 2004. "Singular Lives: SSU Sociologist Kay Trimberger Is Documenting a New Trend of Unmarried Women Who Are Not Only Content, but Happy to Be Single." *Press Democrat,* February 29.

Sweeney, Megan M. and Maria Cancian. 2004. "The Changing Importance of White Women's Economic Prospects for Assortative Mating." *Journal of Marriage and Family* 66(4):1015–28.

Sweeney, Megan M. and Julie A. Phillips. 2004. "Understanding Racial Differences in Marital Disruption: Recent Trends and Explanations." *Journal of Marriage and Family* 66:639–50.

Sweet, James, Larry Bumpass, and Vaughn Call. 1988. "The Design and Content of The National Survey of Families and Households." Working Paper NSFH–1, University of Wisconsin, Center for Demography and Ecology, Madison, WI.

Sweet, Stephen, Raymond Swisher, and Phyllis Moen. 2005. "Selecting and Assessing the Family-friendly Community: Adaptive Strategies of Middle-class Dual-earner Couples." *Family Relations* 54(5):596–606.

Swim, Janet K., K. J. Aikin, W. S. Hall, and B. A. Hunter. 1995. "Sexism and Racism: Old-fashioned and Modern Prejudices." *Journal of Personality and Psychology* 68(2):199–214.

Swinford, Steven P., Alfred DeMaris, Stephen A. Cernkovich, and Peggy
C. Giordano. 2000. "Harsh Physical Discipline in Childhood and Violence in Later Romantic Involvements: The Mediating Role of Problem Behaviors." *Journal of Marriage and Family* 62(2):508–19.

Szabo, Liz. 2004. "American's First 'Test-Tube Baby.'" *USA Today,* May 13.

Szasz, Thomas S. 1976. *Heresies.* New York: Doubleday/Anchor.

Szinovacz, Maximiliane. 1997. "Adult Children Taking Parents into Their Homes: Effects of Childhood Living Arrangements." *Journal of Marriage and Family* 59:700–717.

———. 2000. "Changes in Housework after Retirement: A Panel Analysis." *Journal of Marriage and Family* 62(1):78–92.

Szinovacz, Maximiliane and Anne Schaffer. 2000. "Effects of Retirement on Marital Conflict Tactics." *Journal of Family Issues* 21(3):376–89.

Taffel, Selma. 1987. "Characteristics of American Indian and Alaska Native Births: United States, 1984." *Monthly Vital Statistics Report* 36(3), Supplement. Washington, DC: U.S. National Center for Health Statistics. June 19.

Tafoya, Sonya M., Hans Johnson, and Laura E. Hill. 2004. *Who Chooses to Chose Two? Multiracial Identification and Census 2000.* New York and Washington, DC: Russell Sage Foundation and Population Reference Bureau.

Tak, Young Ran and Marilyn McCubbin. 2002. "Family Stress, Perceived Social Support, and Coping Following the Diagnosis of a Child's Congenital Heart Disease." *Journal of Advanced Nursing* 39(2):190–98.

Takagi, Dana Y. 2002. "Japanese American Families." Pp. 164–80 in *Multicultural Families in the United States,* 3rd ed., edited by Ronald L. Taylor. Upper Saddle River, NJ: Prentice Hall.

Talbot, Kay. 1997. "Mothers Now Childless: Survival after the Death of an Only Child." *Omega* 34(3):177–86.

Talbot, Margaret. 2001. "Open Sperm Donation." *New York Times Magazine,* December 8, p. 88.

Talbott, Maria M. 1998. "Older Widows' Attitudes towards Men and Remarriage." *Journal of Aging Studies* 12(4):429–49.

Tannen, Deborah. 1990. *You Just Don't Understand.* New York: Morrow.

Tanner, Lindsey. 2005. "Study: Children Adopted from Foreign Countries Adjust Surprisingly Well." Associated Press, May 24. Retrieved July 22, 2007 (www.associatedpress.org).

Tarmann, Allison. 2002. "International Adoptions." Pp. 22–23 in *What Drives Population Growth? Population Bulletin* 57(4), by Mary M. Kent and Mark Mather. Washington, DC: Population Reference Bureau. December.

Tashiro, Ty, Patricia Frazier, and Margit Berman. 2006. "Stress-related Growth Following Divorce and Relationship Dissolution." Pp. 361–84 in *Handbook of Divorce and Relationship Dissolution*, edited by Mark A. Fine and John H. Howard. Mahwah, NJ: Erlbaum.

Tatara, Toshio and Lisa Blumerman. 1996. *Summaries of the Statistical Data on Elder Abuse in Domestic Settings: An Exploratory Study of State Statistics for FY 93 and FY 94.* Washington, DC: National Center on Elder Abuse.

Tatara, Toshio and Lisa M. Kuzmeskus with Edward Duckhorn. 1997. *Trends in Elder Abuse in Domestic Settings.* Elder Abuse Information Series No. 2. Washington, DC: National Center on Elder Abuse.

Taylor, Paul, Cary Funk, and Peyton Craighill. 2006. "Are We Happy Yet?" Pew Research Center. Retrieved October 10, 2006 (http://pewresearch.org).

Taylor, Robert J., Linda M. Chatters, M. Belinda Tucker, and Edith Lewis. 1990. "Developments in Research on Black Families: A Decade Review." *Journal of Marriage and Family* 52:993–1014.

Taylor, Robert J., Karen D. Lincoln, and Linda M. Chatters. 2005. "Supportive Relationships with Church Members among African Americans." *Family Relations* 54(4):501–11.

Taylor, Ronald L. 2002a. "Black American Families." Pp. 19–47 in *Minority Families in the United States: A Multicultural Perspective*, 3rd ed., edited by Ronald L. Taylor. Upper Saddle River, NJ: Prentice Hall.

———. 2002b. "Minority Families and Social Change." Pp. 252–300 in *Minority Families in the United States: A Multicultural Perspective*, 3rd ed., edited by Ronald L. Taylor. Upper Saddle River, NJ: Prentice Hall.

———. 2002c. *Minority Families in the United States: A Multicultural Perspective.* 3rd ed. Upper Saddle River, NJ: Prentice Hall.

———. 2007. "Diversity within African American Families." Pp. 398–421 in *Family in Transition*, 14th ed., edited by Arlene S. Skolnick and Jerome H. Skolnick. Boston, MA: Allyn and Bacon.

Taylor, Ronald L., M. Belinda Tucker, and C. Mitchell-Kernan. 1999. "Ethnic Variations in Perceptions of Men's Provider Role." *Psychology of Women Quarterly* 23:741–61.

Teachman, Jay D. 1991. "Who Pays? Receipt of Child Support in the United States." *Journal of Marriage and Family* 53(3):759–72.

———. 2000. "Diversity of Family Structure: Economic and Social Influences." Pp. 32–58 in *Handbook of Family Diversity*, edited by David H. Demo, Katherine R. Allen, and Mark A. Fine. New York: Oxford University Press.

———. 2002a. "Childhood Living Arrangements and the Intergenerational Transmission of Divorce." *Journal of Marriage and Family* 64:717–29.

———. 2002b. "Stability across Cohorts in Divorce Risk Factors." *Demography* 39(2):331–51.

———. 2003. "Premarital Sex, Premarital Cohabitation, and the Risk of Subsequent Marital Dissolution among Women." *Journal of Marriage and Family* 65(2):444–55.

———. 2004. "The Childhood Living Arrangements of Children and the Characteristics of Their Marriages." *Journal of Family Issues* 25(1):86–111.

Teachman, Jay D., Lucky M. Tedrow, and Kyle D. Crowder. 2000. "The Changing Demography of America's Families." *Journal of Marriage and Family* 62(4):1234–46.

Teachman, Jay D., Lucky M. Tedrow, and Matthew Hall. 2006. "The Demographic Future of Divorce and Dissolution." Pp. 59–82 in *Handbook of Divorce and Relationship Dissolution*, edited by Mark A. Fine and John H. Howard. Mahwah, NJ: Erlbaum.

Tennov, Dorothy. [1979] 1999. *Love and Limerence: The Experience of Being in Love.* 2nd ed. New York: Scarborough House.

Tepperman, Lorne and Susannah J. Wilson, eds. 1993. *Next of Kin: An International Reader on Changing Families.* New York: Prentice Hall.

Therborn, Göran. 2004. *Between Sex and Power: Family in the World, 1900–2000.* London, England: Routledge.

"Third of New HIV Cases Acquired Heterosexually." 2004. *Omaha World-Herald*, February 20.

Thoennes, Nancy and Patricia G. Tjaden. 1990. "The Extent, Nature, and Validity of Sexual Abuse Allegations in Custody/Divorce Disputes." *Child Abuse & Neglect* 14:151ff.

Thomas, Adam and Isabel Sawhill. 2005. "For Love *and* Money? The Impact of Family Structure on Family Income." *The Future of Children* 15(2):57–74.

Thomas, Alexander, Stella Chess, and Herbert G. Birch. 1968. *Temperament and Behavior Disorders in Children.* New York: New York University Press.

Thomas, Bernadette and Cindy Dowling. 2006. *A Different Kind of Perfect: Writings by Parents on Raising a Child with Special Needs.* Boston, MA: Trumpeter Press.

Thomason, Deborah J. 2005. "Natural Disasters: Opportunity to Build and Reinforce Family Strengths." *Family Focus on . . . Family Strengths and Resilience* FF28: F11. Minneapolis, MN: National Council on Family Relations.

Thompson, Linda. 1991. "Family Work: Women's Sense of Fairness." *Journal of Family Issues* 12(2):181–96.

Thompson, Linda and Alexis J. Walker. 1991. "Gender in Families." Pp. 76–102 in *Contemporary Families: Looking Forward, Looking Back*, edited by Alan Booth. Minneapolis, MN: National Council on Family Relations.

Thompson, Steven S. 2006. "Was Ancient Rome a Dead Wives Society? What Did the Roman Paterfamilias Get Away With?" *Journal of Family History* 31 (1): 3-27.

Thompson, Tracy. 2006. *The Ghost in the House: Motherhood, Raising Children, and Struggling with Depression.* New York: HarperCollins.

Thomson, Elizabeth and Ugo Colella. 1992. "Cohabitation and Marital Stability: Quality or Commitment?" *Journal of Marriage and Family* 54(2):368–78.

Thomson, Elizabeth, Jane Mosley, Thomas L. Hanson, and Sara S. McLanahan. 2001. "Remarriage, Cohabitation, and Changes in Mothering Behavior." *Journal of Marriage and Family* 63(2):370–80.

Thorne, Barrie. 1992. "Girls and Boys Together . . . But Mostly Apart: Gender Arrangements in Elementary School." Pp. 108–23 in *Men's Lives*, 2nd ed., edited by Michael S. Kimmel and Michael A. Messner. New York: Macmillan.

Thornton, Arland and Deborah Freedman. 1983. "The Changing American Family." *Population Bulletin* 38. Washington, DC: Population Reference Bureau.

Thornton, Arland and Linda Young-DeMarco. 2001. "Four Decades of Trends in Attitudes toward Family Issues in the United States: The 1960s through the 1990s." *Journal of Marriage and Family* 63:1009–37.

"Threats to College-diversity Programs Pose Risks for Boys." 2003. *USA Today,* May 23.

Thurman, Judith. 1982. "The Basics: Chodorow's Theory of Gender." *Ms.,* September, pp. 35–36.

Tichenor, Veronica Jaris. 1999. "Status and Income as Gendered Resources: The Case of Marital Power." *Journal of Marriage and Family* 61:638–50.

———. 2005. *Earning More and Getting Less: Why Successful Wives Can't Buy Equality.* New Brunswick, NJ: Rutgers University Press.

Tiger, Lionel. 1969. *Men in Groups.* New York: Vintage.

Tjaden, Patricia and Nancy Thoennes. 1998. *Prevalence, Incidence, and Consequences of Violence against Women: Findings from The National Violence Against Women Survey.* November. Washington, DC: National Institute of Justice, Centers for Disease Control and Prevention.

———. 2000. "Prevalence and Consequences of Male-to-Female and Female-to-Male Intimate Partner Violence as Measured by The National Violence Against Women Survey." *Violence Against Women* 6:142–61.

Tolan, Patrick H., Jose Szapocznik, and Soledad Sambrano. 2007. *Preventing Youth Substance Abuse.* Washington, DC: American Psychological Association.

Toledo, Sylvie de and Doborah Edler Brown. 1995. *Grandparents as Parents: A Survival Guide for Raising a Second Family.* New York: Guilford.

Tonelli, Bill. 2004. "Thriller Draws on Oppression of Italians in Wartime U.S." *New York Times,* August 2.

Toner, Robin. 2007. "Women Feeling Freer to Suggest 'Vote for Mom.'" *New York Times,* January 29.

Tong, Benson. 2004. *Asian American Children: An Historical Guide.* Westport, CT: Greenwood Press.

Torquati, Julia C. 2002. "Personal and Social Resources as Predictors of Parenting in Homeless Families." *Journal of Family Issues* 23(4):463–85.

Torr, James D. and Karin Swisher. 1999. *Violence Against Women.* San Diego, CA: Greenhaven.

Torres, Zenia. 1997. "Interracial Dating." Unpublished student paper.

Tougas, F., R. Brown, A. M. Beaton, and S. Joly. 1995. "Neosexism: Plus ça change, plus c'est pareil." *Personality and Social Psychology Bulletin* 21:842–49.

"Town's Mayor Tackles Illegal Immigration." MSNBC. Retrieved January 6, 2007 (www.msnbc.com).

Townsend, Aloen L. and Melissa M. Franks. 1997. "Quality of the Relationship between Elderly Spouses: Influence on Spouse Caregivers' Subjective Effectiveness." *Family Relations* 46(1):33–39.

Townsend, Nicholas W. 2002. *The Package Deal: Marriage, Work, and Fatherhood in Men's Lives.* Philadelphia, PA: Temple.

"Tracing Jewish History through Genes." 2003. *Native New Yorker,* May 16.

Trask, Bahira Sherif, Jocelyn D. Taliaferro, Margaret Wilder, and Raheemah Jabbar-Bey. 2005. "Strengthening Low-income Families through Community-based Family Support Initiatives." . . . *Family Strengths and Resilience* FF28. Minneapolis, MN: National Council on Family Relations.

Travis, Carol. 2006. "Letters to the Editor: The New Science of Love." *Atlantic Monthly,* May.

Treas, Judith. 1995. "Older Americans in the 1990s and Beyond." *Population Bulletin* 50(2). Washington, DC: Population Reference Bureau.

Treas, Judith and Deirdre Giesen. 2000. "Sexual Infidelity among Married and Cohabiting Americans." *Journal of Marriage and Family* 62(1):48–60.

Trevathan, Melissa and Sissy Goff. 2007. *Raising Girls.* Grand Rapids, MI: Zondervan.

Trimberger, E. Kay. 2005. *The New Single Woman.* New York: Beacon Press.

Troll, Lillian E. 1985. "The Contingencies of Grandparenting." Pp. 135–50 in *Grandparenthood,* edited by Vern L.

Bengston and Joan F. Robertson. Newbury Park, CA: Sage Publications.

Troll, Lillian E., Sheila J. Miller, and Robert C. Atchley. 1979. *Families in Later Life.* Belmont, CA: Wadsworth.

Trost, Jan. 1997. "Step-family Variations." Pp. 71–84 in *Step-Families: History, Research, and Policy,* edited by Irene Levin and Marvin B. Sussman. New York: Haworth.

Troxel v. Granville. 2000. 530 U.S. 57.

Troy, Adam B., Jamie Lewis-Smith, and Jean-Phillippe Laurenceau. 2006. "Interracial and Intraracial Romantic Relationships: The Search for Differences in Satisfaction, Conflict, and Attachment Style." *Journal of Social and Personal Relationships* 23(1):65–80.

Trudeau, Michelle. 2006. "School, Study, SATs: No Wonder Teens Are Stressed." National Public Radio. October 9. Retrieved October 9, 2006 (http://www.npr.org).

Tsang, Laura Lo Wa, Carol D. H. Harvey, Karen A. Duncan, and Reena Sommer. 2003. "The Effects of Children, Dual Earner Status, Sex Role Traditionalism, and Marital Structure on Marital Happiness over Time." *Journal of Family and Economic Issues* 24:5–26.

Tschann, Jeanne M., Janet R. Johnston, Marsha Kline, and Judith S. Wallerstein. 1989. "Family Process and Children's Functioning during Divorce." *Journal of Marriage and Family* 51(2):431–44.

Tucker, Corinna J., Susan M. McHale, and Ann C. Crouter. 2003. "Conflict Resolution: Links with Adolescents' Family Relationships and Individual Well-being." *Journal of Family Issues* 24(6):715–36.

Tucker, Judith E. ed. 1993. *Arab Women: Old Boundaries, New Frontiers.* Bloomington, IN: Indiana University Press.

Tucker, M. Belinda. 2000. "Marital Values and Expectations in Context: Results from a 21-City Survey." Pp. 166–87 in *The Ties That Bind: Perspectives on Cohabitation and Marriage,* edited by Linda J. Waite. New York: Aldine.

Tuller, David. 2001. "Adoption Medicine Brings New Parents Answers and Advice." *New York Times,* September 4.

Turkat, Ira Daniel. 1997. "Management of Visitation Interference." *The Judges Journal* 36(Spring):17–47. Retrieved May 16, 2007 (www.fact.on.ca).

Turnbull, A. and H. Turnbull. 1997. *Families, Professionals, and Exceptionality: A Special Partnership*. 3rd ed. Upper Saddle River, NJ: Merrill.

Turley, Ruth N. Lopez. 2003. "Are Children of Young Mothers Disadvantaged Because of Their Mother's Age or Family Background?" *Child Development* 74:465–74.

Turner, Ralph H. 1976. "The Real Self: From Institution to Impulse." *American Journal of Sociology* 81:989–1016.

Turrell, Susan C. 2000. "A Descriptive Analysis of Same-sex Relationship Violence for a Diverse Sample." *Journal of Family Violence* 15:281–93.

Twenge, Jean M. 1997a. "Attitudes toward Women, 1970–1995: A Meta-Analysis." *Psychology of Women Quarterly* 21(1):35–51.

———. 1997b. "'Mrs. His Name': Women's Preferences for Married Names." *Psychology of Women Quarterly* 21(3):417–30.

Twenge, Jean M., W. Keith Campbell, and Craig Foster. 2003. "Parenthood and Marital Satisfaction: A Meta-Analytic Review." *Journal of Marriage and Family* 65:574–83.

"Two Brides." 2004. Retrieved March 29, 2004 (http://www.twobrides.com).

Tyre, Peg. 2004. "A New Generation Gap." *Newsweek*, January 19, pp. 68–71.

———. 2006a. "The New First Grade." *Newsweek*, September 11, pp. 34–43.

———. 2006b. "Smart Moms, Hard Choices." *Newsweek*, March 6, p. 55.

Tyre, Peg and Daniel McGinn. 2003. "She Works, He Doesn't." *Newsweek*, May 12, pp. 45–52.

Uchitelle, Louis. 2002. "Job Track or 'Mommy Track'? Some Do Both in Phases." *New York Times*, July 5.

Uchitelle, Louis and David Leonhardt. 2006. "Men Not Working, and Not Wanting Just Any Job." *New York Times*, July 31. Retrieved October 3, 2006 (http://www.nytimes.com).

Udry, J. Richard. 1974. *The Social Context of Marriage*. 3rd ed. Philadelphia, PA: Lippincott.

———. 1994. "The Nature of Gender." *Demography* 31(4):561–73.

———. 2000. "The Biological Limits of Gender Construction." *American Sociological Review* 65:443–57.

"UF Study: Sibling Violence Leads to Battering in College Dating." 2004. *UF News*. Gainesville, FL: University of Florida.

Uhlenberg, Peter. 1996. "Mortality Decline in the Twentieth Century and Supply of Kin over the Life Course." *The Gerontologist* 36:681–85.

Umana-Taylor, Adriana, Ruchi Bhanot, and Nana Shin. 2006. "Ethnic Identity Formation during Adolescence." *Journal of Family Issues* 27(3):390–414.

Umberson, Debra, Kristin Anderson, Jennifer Glick, and Adam Shapiro. 1998. "Domestic Violence, Personal Control, and Gender." *Journal of Marriage and Family* 60(2):442–52.

Umberson, Debra, Meichu D. Chen, James S. House, Kristine Hopkins, and Ellen Slaten. 1996. "The Effect of Social Relationships on Psychological Well-being: Are Men and Women Really So Different?" *American Sociological Review* 61:837–57.

Umminger, April and Frank Pompa. 2005. "Most Think Dogs Count as Company." *USA Today*, November 1.

UNICEF (United Nations Children's Fund). 2005. *Child Poverty in Rich Countries 2005*. Innocenti Research Center Report Card No. 6. Florence, Italy: UNICEF Innocenti Research Center.

———. 2007. *Child Poverty in Perspective: An Overview of Child Well-being in Rich Countries*. Innocenti Research Center Report Card No. 7. Florence, Italy: UNICEF Innocenti Research Center.

"United Nations Drops Gay Civil Rights." 2004. 365Gay.com Newscenter Staff. March 29. Retrieved March 29, 2004 (http://www.sodomylaws.org/world/wonews023.htm).

University of Nebraska. University of Nebraska Medical Center. University of Nebraska-Omaha Institutional Review Board. 2006. "IRB Guidelines." Retrieved January 22, 2007 (www.unmc.edu/irb).

"Urban Parents, Particularly Those Who Are Unmarried, Frequently Have Children by Multiple Partners." 2006. *Perspectives on Sexual and Reproductive Health* 38(4):225–26.

U.S. Administration for Children and Families. African American Healthy Marriage Initiative. N.d. "A Targeted Strategy for Working Effectively with African American Communities." Washington, DC: Administration for Children and Families. Retrieved December 19, 2006 (www.acf.hhs.gov/health marriage).

U.S. Administration on Aging. 2006a. *A Profile of Older Americans: 2006*. Retrieved May 17, 2007 (http://www.aoa.gov).

———. 2006b. *A Statistical Profile of Older Americans Aged 65+*. Retrieved May 10, 2007 (http://www.aoa.gov).

U.S Bureau of Labor Statistics. 2004. *Time Use Survey*. Washington, DC: U.S. Bureau of Labor Statistics.

———. 2005. "Work at Home in 2004." Press Release. September 22. Washington, DC: U.S. Bureau of Labor Statistics.

———. 2006a. "Employment Characteristics of Families in 2005." Press Release, April 27. Washington, DC: U.S. Bureau of Labor Statistics.

———. 2006b. "Highlights of Women's Earnings in 2005." Report 995. Washington, DC: U.S. Bureau of Labor Statistics.

———. 2006c. *A Profile of the Working Poor, 2004*. Report 994. Washington, DC: U.S. Bureau of Labor Statistics. May.

———. 2006d. *Women in the Labor Force: A Databook*. Report 996. Washington, DC: U.S. Bureau of Labor Statistics. September. Retrieved January 18, 2007 (www.bls.gov).

———. 2007. *Usual Weekly Earnings of Wage and Salary Workers: Fourth Quarter 2006*. Washington, DC: U.S. Bureau of Labor Statistics. January 19.

U.S. Census Bureau. 1988. *Households, Families, Marital Status, and Living Arrangements, March 1988: Advance Report*. Current Population Reports, Series P20-432. Washington, DC: U.S. Government Printing Office.

———. 1989. *Statistical Abstract of the United States*. 109th ed. Washington, DC: U.S. Government Printing Office.

———. 1993. *We the Americans: Pacific Islanders*. WE-4. Washington, DC: U.S. Census Bureau. September.

———. 1997. *Statistical Abstract of the United States, 1997*. Washington, DC: U.S. Government Printing Office.

———. 1998. *Statistical Abstract of the United States, 1998*. Washington, DC: U.S. Government Printing Office.

———. 2000. *Statistical Abstract of the United States*. 120th ed. Washington, DC: U.S. Government Printing Office (www.census.gov/stat_abstract).

———. 2003a. *Statistical Abstract of the United States, 2003.* Washington, DC: U.S. Census Bureau.

———. 2003b. "U.S. Census Bureau Guidance on the Presentation and Comparison of Race and Hispanic Origin Data." Washington, DC: U.S. Census Bureau. June 12.

———. 2004. "U.S. Interim Projections by Age, Sex, Race, and Hispanic Origin." Washington, DC: U.S. Census Bureau. March 18. Retrieved December 18, 2006 (www.census.gov).

———. 2005a. "2004 American Community Survey." Washington, DC: U.S. Census Bureau. August 30. Retrieved July 27, 2006 (http://factfinder.census .gov).

———. 2005b. "The Population Profile of the United States: Dynamic Version" (Internet Release). Washington, DC: U.S. Census Bureau. November 8. Retrieved July 27, 2006 (www.census.gov/ population/www/pop-profiledynamic .html

———. 2006a. "2005 American Community Survey." Washington, DC: U.S. Census Bureau. Retrieved August 15, 2006 (http://factfinder.census.gov).

———. 2006b. "America's Families and Living Arrangements: 2005." Washington, DC: U.S. Census Bureau. May 25. Retrieved June 20, 2006 (www.census .gov/population/www/socdemo/ hh-fam/cps2005.html).

———. 2006c. *Statistical Abstract of the United States: 2006.* Washington, DC: U.S. Census Bureau.

———. 2007a. *Statistical Abstract of the United States: 2007.* Washington, DC: U.S. Census Bureau.

———. 2007b. "Women's History Month: March 2007." Press Release CB07-FF.03, January 4. Washington, DC: U.S. Census Bureau. Retrieved May 11, 2007 (www.census.gov).

U.S. Centers for Disease Control and Prevention. 2006a. *2004 Assisted Reproductive Technology Success Rates: National Summary and Fertility Clinic Report.* Atlanta, GA: U.S. Centers for Disease Control and Prevention. December.

———. 2006b. *HIV/AIDS Surveillance Report 2005.* Vol. 17. Atlanta, GA: U.S. Centers for Disease Control and Prevention.

———. 2006c. *Sexually Transmitted Disease Surveillance 2005.* Atlanta, GA:

U.S. Centers for Disease Control and Prevention. November.

———. 2007. "HIV/AIDS among Women." Fact Sheet. Atlanta, GA: U.S. Centers for Disease Control and Prevention. March.

U.S. Children's Bureau. 2000. *Fact Sheet: Child Maltreatment 1999* (www.acf.dhhs .gov/programs/cb/publications/cm99).

U.S. Demographic Internet Staff. 2006. *America's Families and Living Arrangements 2005.* March Current Population Survey. Washington, DC: U.S. Census Bureau. September 21. Retrieved December 26, 2006 (www.census.gov).

U.S. Department of Health and Human Services. Administration for Children and Families. 2004. "Temporary Assistance for Needy Families Information Memorandum." September 30. Retrieved September 14, 2006 (http://www.acf .dhhs.gov/programs).

———. 2005. "Healthy Marriage Matters." Retrieved September 12, 2006 (http://www.acf.dhhs.gov/ healthymarriage/about/factsheets).

———. 2006. "Trends in Foster Care and Adoption: FY 2000–FY 2005." Retrieved February 19, 2007 (http://www.acf.hhs .gov).

U.S. Department of Health and Human Services. Administration on Children, Youth, and Families. 2007. *Child Maltreatment 2005.* Washington, DC: U.S. Government Printing Office. Retrieved April 11, 2007 (www.acf.hhs.gov).

U.S. Department of Health, Education, and Welfare. 1975. *Child Abuse and Neglect. Vol. I, An Overview of the Problem.* Publication (OHD) 75–30073. Washington, DC: U.S. Government Printing Office.

U.S. Department of Health, Education, and Welfare. National Institute of Mental Health. 1978. *Yours, Mine, and Ours: Tips for Stepparents.* Washington, DC: U.S. Government Printing Office.

U.S. Department of Justice. 1998a. *Violence by Intimates: Analysis of Data on Crimes by Current or Former Spouses, Boyfriends, and Girlfriends.* Bureau of Justice Statistics Selected Findings: Domestic Violence, March, NCJ–167237. Washington, DC: U.S. Government Printing Office (www.ojp.usdoj.gov).

———. 1998b. *Stalking and Domestic Violence: The Third Annual Report to Congress under the Violence Against Women*

Act. Washington, DC: Violence Against Women Grants Office.

U.S. Federal Interagency Forum on Child and Family Statistics. 2003. *America's Children: Key National Indicators of Well-being, 2003.* Washington, DC: U.S. Federal Interagency Forum on Child and Family Statistics. February.

———. 2004. *America's Children in Brief 2004: Key National Indicators of Well-Being.* Washington, DC: U.S. Government Printing Office. Retrieved July 7, 2004 (http://childstats.gov).

———. 2005. *America's Children: Key National Indicators of Well-being, 2005.* Washington, DC: U.S. Federal Interagency Forum on Child and Family Statistics.

———. 2006. *America's Children in Brief: Key National Indicators of Well-being, 2006.* Washington, DC: U.S. Federal Interagency Forum on Child and Family Statistics. Retrieved August 13, 2006 (www.childtrends.org).

U.S. Fertility and Family Statistics Branch. 2006. "Parents and Children in Stay-at-Home Family Groups." Washington, DC: U.S. Census Bureau. September 21. Retrieved April 13, 2007 (www.census.gov).

U.S. Food and Drug Administration. 2006. "Mifeprex (mifepristone) Information." Washington, DC: U.S. Food and Drug Administration. April 10. Retrieved March 29, 2007 (www.fda.gov).

U.S. General Accounting Office. 1997. Letter to The Honorable Henry J. Hyde. Office of the General Counsel. January 31 (http://www.frwebgate.access.gpo.gov/ cgi-bin/useftp.cgi/).

———. 2003. *Women's Earnings: Work Patterns Partially Explain Differences between Men's and Women's Earnings.* GAO-04-35. Washington, DC: U.S. General Accounting Office. October.

U.S. House of Representatives Select Committee on Aging. 1992. *Insurmountable Barriers: Lack of Bilingual Services at Social Security Administration Offices.* Washington, DC: U.S. Government Printing Office.

"U.S. Muslims Responding to 9/11." 2004. *Omaha World-Herald,* April 10.

U.S. National Cancer Institute. 2003. "Summary Report: Early Reproductive Events and Breast Cancer Workshop." Bethesda, MD: U.S. National Cancer Institute. March 23.

U.S. National Center for Education Statistics. 2006. *Digest of Education Statistics,*

2005. Washington, DC: U.S. National Center for Education Statistics. June. Retrieved January 31, 2007 (www.nces.ed.gov).

U.S. National Center for Health Statistics. 1990a. "Advance Report of Final Divorce Statistics, 1987." *Monthly Vital Statistics Report* 38(12), Suppl. April 3.

———. 1990b. "Advance Report of Final Marriage Statistics, 1987." *Monthly Vital Statistics Report* 38(12), Suppl. April 3.

———. 1998. "Births, Marriages, Divorces, and Deaths for 1997." *Monthly Vital Statistics Report* 46(12). July 28.

———. 2006. "Births, Marriages, Divorces, and Deaths: Provisional Data for 2005." *National Vital Statistics Reports* 54(20). Hyattsville, MD: U.S. National Center for Health Statistics. July 21.

U.S. National Institute of Child Health and Human Development. 1999. "Only Small Link Found between Hours in Child Care and Mother–Child Interaction." News Release, November 7 (www.nichd .nih.gov/new/release/daycar99).

———. 2002. "The NICHD Study of Early Child Care." Bethesda, MD: U.S. Institute of Health and Human Development.

U.S. Office of Management and Budget. 1999. *Revisions to the Standards for Classification of Federal Data on Race and Ethnicity.* April 1. Washington, DC: U.S. Census Bureau.

"U.S. Scraps Study of Teen-age Sex." 1991. *New York Times,* July 25.

U.S. Senate Special Committee on Aging. 2002. *Long Term Care Report.* Washington DC: U.S. Government Printing Office.

———. 2004. *Findings from Committee Hearings of the 107th Congress.* Washington, DC: U.S. Government Printing Office.

U.S. Social Security Administration. 2007. "Fact Sheet: 2007 Social Security Changes." Retrieved May 7, 2007 (www.ssa .gov.pressoffice/factsheets/colofacts2007).

U.S. Surgeon General. 2001. *The Surgeon General's Call to Action to Promote Sexual Health and Responsible Sexual Behavior.* Hyattsville, MD: U.S. Surgeon General. July 9.

Uttal, Lynet. 1999. "Using Kin for Child Care." *Journal of Marriage and Family* 61:845–57.

———. 2004. "Racial Safety and Cultural Maintenance: The Child Care Concerns of Employed Mothers of Color." Pp. 295–304 in *Race, Class, and Gender,* 5th

ed., edited by Margaret L. Andersen and Patricia Hill Collins. Belmont, CA: Wadsworth.

Utz, Rebecca L., Erin B. Reidy, Deborah Carr, Randolph Nesse, and Camille Wortman. 2004. "The Daily Consequences of Widowhood." *Journal of Family Issues* 25(5):683–712.

Valiente, Carlos, Richard A. Fabes, Nancy Eisenberg, and Tracy L. Spinrad. 2004. "The Relations of Parental Expressivity and Support to Children's Coping with Daily Stress." *Journal of Family Psychology* 18(1):97–107.

Van Biema, David. 2004. "Rising Above the Stained-glass Ceiling." *Time,* June 25, pp. 59–61.

Vandell, Deborah L., Kathleen McCarthy, Margaret T. Owen, Cathryn Booth, and Alison Clarke-Stewart. 2003. "Variations in Child Care by Grandparents during the First Three Years." *Journal of Marriage and Family* 65(2):375–81.

Van den Haag, Ernest. 1974. "Love or Marriage." Pp. 134–42 in *The Family: Its Structures and Functions,* 2nd ed., edited by Rose Laub Coser. New York: St. Martin's.

Vandewater, Elizabeth A. and Jennifer E. Lansford. 2005. "A Family Process Model of Problem Behaviors in Adolescents." *Journal of Marriage and Family* 67(1):100–109.

Vander Ven, Thomas M., Francis T. Cullen, Mark A. Carrozza, and John Paul Wright. 2001. "Home Alone: The Impact of Maternal Employment on Delinquency." *Social Problems* 48: 236–57.

VanDorn, Richard A., Gary L. Bowen, and Judith R. Blau. 2006. "The Impact of Community Diversity and Consolidated Inequality on Dropping Out of High School." *Family Relations* 55(1):105–18.

van Eeden-Moorefield, Brad, Kari Henley, and Kay Pasley. 2005. "Identity Enactment and Verification in Gay and Lesbian Stepfamilies." Pp. 230–33 in *Sourcebook of Family Theory and Research,* edited by Vern L. Bengston, Alan C. Acock, Katherine R. Allen, Peggye Dilworth-Anderson, and David M. Klein. Thousand Oaks, CA Sage Publications.

VanLaningham, Jody, David R. Johnson, and Paul Amato. 2001. "Marital Happiness, Marital Duration, and the U-Shaped Curve: Evidence from a Five-wave Panel Study." *Social Forces* 79:1313–41.

VanLear, C. Arthur. 1992. "Marital Communication across the Generations: Learning and Rebellion, Continuity and

Change." *Journal of Social and Personal Relationships* 9:103–23.

Vannoy, Dana. 1991. "Social Differentiation, Contemporary Marriage, and Human Development." *Journal of Family Issues* 12:251–67.

Van Pelt, Nancy L. 1985. *How to Turn Minuses into Pluses: Tips for Working Moms, Single Parents, and Stepparents.* Washington, DC: Review and Herald, Better Living Series.

Van Yperen, N. W. and Bram P. Buunk 1990. "A Longitudinal Study of Equity and Satisfaction in Intimate Relationships." *European Journal of Social Psychology* 20 (4):287–309.

Vartanian, Thomas P., Wendy Cadge, David Karen, and Page Walker Buck. 2003. "Further Evidence of the Model Minority Myth: A Comparison of Asians and Non-Asians Educational Attainment in the United States." Presented at the annual meeting of the American Sociological Association, August, Atlanta, GA.

Vartanian, Thomas P. and Justine M. McNamara. 2002. "Older Women in Poverty: The Impact of Midlife Factors." *Journal of Marriage and Family* 64(2):532–48.

Vaughan, Diane. 1986. *Uncoupling: Turning Points in Intimate Relationships.* New York: Oxford University Press.

Ventura, Stephanie, Joyce C. Abma, William D. Mosher, and Stanley K. Henshaw. 2006. *Recent Trends in Teenage Pregnancy in the United States, 1990–2002.* Health E-Stats. Hyattsville, MD: U.S. National Center for Health Statistics. December 13. Retrieved January 20, 2007 (www.cdc.gov/nchs).

Ventura, Stephanie J. and Christine A. Bachrach. 2000. "Nonmarital Childbearing in the United States, 1940–99." *National Vital Statistics Reports* 48(16). Hyattsville, MD: U.S. National Center for Health Statistics. October 18.

Ventura, Stephanie J., T. J. Mathews, and Brady E. Hamilton. 2001. "Births to Teenagers in the United States, 1940–2000." *National Vital Statistics Reports* 49(10). Hyattsville, MD: U.S. National Center for Health Statistics. September 25.

Villarosa, Linda. 2001. "Women Now Look Beyond H.I.V. to Children and Grandchildren." *New York Times,* August 7.

———. 2002a. "Once-invisible Sperm Donors Get to Meet the Family." *New York Times,* May 21.

———. 2002b. "Rescued H.I.V. Babies Face New Problems as Teenagers." *New York Times,* March 5.

———. 2003. "Raising Awareness about AIDS and the Aging." *New York Times,* July 8.

Vinciguerra, Thomas. 2007. "He's Not My Grandpa, He's My Dad." *New York Times,* April 12.

Visher, Emily B. and John S. Visher. 1979. *Stepfamilies: A Guide to Working with Stepparents and Stepchildren.* New York: Brunner/Mazel.

———.1996. *Therapy with Stepfamilies.* New York: Brunner/Mazel.

Vogler, Carolyn. 2005. "Cohabiting Couples: Rethinking Money in the Household at the Beginning of the Twenty-First Century." *The Sociological Review* 53(1):1–29.

Voith, V. L. 1985. "Attachment of People to Companion Animals." *Veterinary Clinics of North America* 15:289–95.

Voydanoff, Patricia. 2002. "Linkages between the Work-Family Interface and Work, Family and Individual Outcomes." *Journal of Family Issues* 23(1):138–64.

Waddell, Lynn. 2005. "Gays in Florida Seek Adoption Alternatives." *New York Times,* January 21.

Wadsworth, Martha and Lauren Berger. 2006. "Adolescents Coping with Poverty-related Family Stress: Prospective Predictors of Coping and Psychological Symptoms." *Journal of Youth and Adolescence* 35(1):54–67.

Wagmiller, Robert L., Jr., Mary Clare Lennon, Li Kuang, Philip M. Alberti, and J. Lawrence Aber. 2006. "The Dynamics of Economic Advantage and Children's Life Chances." *American Sociological Review* 71(5):847–66.

Wagner-Raphael, Lynne I., David Wyatt Seal, and Anke A. Ehrhardt. 2001. "Close Emotional Relationships with Women versus Men." *Journal of Men's Studies* 9(2):243–56.

Waite, Linda J. 1995. "Does Marriage Matter?" *Demography* 32(4):483–507.

———. 2001. "The Family as Social Organization: Key Ideas for the Twenty-first Century." *Contemporary Sociology* 29:463–99.

Waite, Linda J., Don Browning, William J. Doherty, Maggie Gallagher, Ye Luo, and Scott M. Stanley. 2002. *Does Divorce Make People Happy? Findings from a Study of Unhappy Marriages.* New York: Institute for American Values.

Waite, Linda J. and Maggie Gallagher. 2000. *The Case for Marriage: Why Married People Are Happier, Healthier, and Better Off Financially.* New York: Doubleday.

Waite, Linda J. and Kara Joyner. 2001. "Emotional and Physical Satisfaction with Sex in Married, Cohabiting, and Dating Sexual Unions: Do Men and Women Differ?" Pp. 239–69 in *Sex, Love, and Health in America,* edited by Edward O. Laumann and Robert T. Michael. Chicago, IL: University of Chicago Press.

Waldfogel, Jane. 2001. "International Policies toward Parental Leave and Child Care." *The Future of Children* 11:99–111.

Walker, Alexis J. 1985. "Reconceptualizing Family Stress." *Journal of Marriage and Family* 47(4):827–37.

Walker, Alexis J., Margaret Manoogian-O'Dell, Lori A. McGraw, and Diana L. G. White, eds. 2001. *Families in Later Life: Connections and Transitions.* Thousand Oaks, CA: Pine Forge Press.

Walker, Karen E. and Frank F. Furstenberg, Jr. 1994. "Neighborhood Settings and Parenting Strategies." Presented at the annual meeting of the American Sociological Association, August, Los Angeles, CA.

Walker, Lenore E. 1988. "The Battered Woman Syndrome." Pp. 139–48 in *Family Abuse and Its Consequences: New Directions in Research,* edited by Gerald T. Hotaling, David Finkelhor, John T. Kirkpatrick, and Murray A. Straus. Newbury Park, CA: Sage Publications.

Walker, Samuel, Cassia Spohn, and Miriam DeLone. 2007. *The Color of Justice: Race, Ethnicity, and Crime in America.* 4th ed. Belmont, CA: Wadsworth.

Wallace, Pamela M. and Ian H. Gotlib. 1990. "Marital Adjustment during the Transition to Parenthood: Stability and Predictors of Change." *Journal of Marriage and Family* 52:21–29.

Waller, Willard. 1951. *The Family: A Dynamic Interpretation* (Revised by Reuben Hill). New York: Dryden.

Wallerstein, Judith S. 2003. "Children of Divorce: A Society in Search of Policy." Pp. 66–96 in *All Our Families: New Policies for a New Century,* 2nd ed., edited by Mary Ann Mason, Arlene Skolnick, and Stephen D. Sugarman. New York: Oxford University Press.

Wallerstein, Judith S. and Sandra Blakeslee. 1989. *Second Chances: Men, Women, and Children a Decade After Divorce.* New York: Ticknor and Fields.

———. 1995. *The Good Marriage: How and Why Love Lasts.* Boston, MA: Houghton Mifflin.

———. 2003. *What About the Kids? Raising Your Children Before, During, and After Divorce.* New York: Hyperion.

Wallerstein, Judith S. and Joan Kelly. 1980. *Surviving the Break-up: How Children Actually Cope with Divorce.* New York: Basic Books.

Wallerstein, Judith S., Julia M. Lewis, and Sandra Blakeslee. 2000. *The Unexpected Legacy of Divorce: A 25 Year Landmark Study.* New York: Hyperion.

Wallis, Claudia. 2004. "The Case for Staying Home." *Time,* March 22, pp. 51–59.

Walsh, David Allen. 2004. *Why Do They Act That Way? A Survival Guide to the Adolescent Brain for You and Your Teen.* New York: Free Press.

———. 2007. *No: Why Kids—of All Ages—Need to Hear It and Ways Parents Can Say It.* New York: Free Press.

Walsh, Froma. 2002a. "A Family Resilience Framework: Innovative Practice Applications." *Family Relations* 51(2):130–37.

———. 2002b. "Bouncing Forward: Resilience in the Aftermath of September 11." *Family Process* 41(1):34–36.

———. 2004. "Family Resilience: A Framework for Clinical Practice." *Family Process* 42(1):1–18.

Walsh, Wendy. 2002. "Spankers and Nonspankers: Where They Get Information on Spanking." *Family Relations* 51(1):81–88.

Walster, Elaine H. and G. William Walster. 1978. *A New Look at Love.* Reading, MA: Addison-Wesley.

Walter, Carolyn Ambler. 1986. *The Timing of Motherhood.* Lexington, MA: Heath.

Wang, Rong, Suzanne M. Bianchi, and Sara B. Raley. 2005. "Teenagers' Internet Use and Family Rules: A Research Note." *Journal of Marriage and Family* 67(5):1249–58.

Ward, J. 1998. "Specialized Foster Care: One Approach to Retaining Good Foster Homes" (http://www.westworld.com/~barbara).

Ward, Margaret. 1997. "Family Paradigms and Older-child Adoption: A Proposal for Matching Parents' Strengths to Children's Needs." *Family Relations* 46(3):257–62.

Wardle, Francis. 2000. "Children of Mixed Race—No Longer Invisible—From Revising School Forms to Reviewing the Curriculum for Inclusiveness, How to Make School More Welcoming to Multicultural Children." *Educational Leadership: Journal of the Department of Supervision and Curriculum Development, N.E.A.* 57(4):68–73.

Wark, Linda and Shilpa Jobalia. 1998. "What Would It Take to Build a Bridge? An Intervention for Stepfamilies." *Journal of Family Psychotherapy* 9(3):69–77.

Warner, Judith. 2005. "The Myth of the Perfect Mother: Why It Drives Real Women Crazy." *Newsweek,* February 21, pp. 42–51.

———. 2006. *Perfect Madness: Motherhood in the Age of Anxiety.* New York: Riverhead Books.

Warren, Chris and Crescy Cannan. 1997. *Social Action with Children and Families: A Community Approach to Child and Family Welfare.* New York: Routledge.

Warren, Gloria. 2003. "A Way Outa' No Way: Grandparents Raising Grandchildren." *Family Focus* (June):F19–F20. Minneapolis, MN: National Council on Family Relations.

Warshak, Richard. 2000. "Remarriage as a Trigger of Parental Alienation Syndrome." *American Journal of Family Therapy* 28(3):229–41.

Waters, Mary C. 1997. "Immigrant Families at Risk: Factors That Undermine Chances of Success." Pp. 79–87 in *Immigration and the Family,* edited by Alan Booth, Ann C. Crouter, and Nancy Landale. Mahwah, NJ: Erlbaum.

———. 2007. "Optional Ethnicities: For Whites Only?" Pp. 198–207 in *Race, Class, and Gender: An Anthology,* edited by Margaret L. Andersen and Patricia Hill Collins. Belmont, CA: Wadsworth.

Watson, Russell. 1984. "Five Steps to Good Day Care." *Newsweek,* September 10, p. 21.

Watt, Toni T. 2002. "Marital and Cohabiting Relationships of Adult Children of Alcoholics." *Journal of Family Issues* 23(2):246–65.

Wax, Naomi. 2001. "Not to Worry: Real Men Can Cry." *New York Times,* October 28.

Weaver, Shannon E., Marilyn Coleman, and Lawrence H. Ganong. 2003.

"The Sibling Relationship in Young Adulthood." *Journal of Family Issues* 24(2):245–63.

Weber, Max. 1948. *The Theory of Social and Economic Organization.* Edited by Talcott Parsons. New York: Free Press.

Weeks, John R. 2002. *Population: An Introduction to Concepts and Issues.* 8th ed. Belmont, CA: Wadsworth.

———. 2007. *Population: An Introduction to Concepts and Issues.* 10th ed. Belmont, CA: Wadsworth.

Weger, H. 2005. "Disconfirming Communication and Self-verification in Marriage: Associations among the Demand/Withdraw Interaction Pattern, Feeling Understood, and Marital Satisfaction." *Journal of Social and Personal Relationships* 22(1):19–31.

Weibel-Orlando, J. 2001. "Grandparenting Styles: Native American Perspectives." Pp. 139–45 in *Families in Later Life: Connections and Transitions,* edited by Alexis J. Walker, Margaret Manoogian-O'Dell, Lori A. McGraw, and Diana L. G. White. Thousand Oaks, CA: Pine Forge Press.

Weigel, Daniel J., Kymberley K. Bennett, and Deborah S. Ballard-Reisch. 2006a. "Influence Strategies in Marriage: Self and Partner Links between Equity, Strategy Use, and Marital Satisfaction and Commitment." *Journal of Family Communication* 6(1):77–95.

Weigel, Daniel J., Kymberley K. Bennett, and Deborah S. Ballard-Reisch. 2006b. "Roles and Influence in Marriages: Both Spouses' Perceptions Contribute to Marital Commitment." *Family and Consumer Science Research Journal* 35(1):74–92.

Weil, Elizabeth. 2006. "What If It's (Sort of) a Boy and (Sort of) a Girl?" *New York Times Magazine,* September 24. Retrieved September 6, 2007 (www.nytimes.com)

Weinberg, Daniel H. 2004. *Evidence from Census 2000 about Earnings by Detailed Occupation for Men and Women.* Census 2000 Special Reports CENSR-15. May.

Weisman, Carol. 2006. *Raising Charitable Children.* St. Louis, MO: F. E. Robbins & Sons.

Weiss, Rick. 1998. "Babies in Limbo: Laws Outpaced by Fertility Advances; Multiple Parties to Conception Muddle Issues of Parentage." *Washington Post,* February 8.

———. 2002. "Multiple Fears about IVF Births: Study; In-Vitro Twins, Triplets Prone to Brain Disorders." *Washington Post,* February 12.

Weitzman, Lenore J. 1985. *The Divorce Revolution: The Unexpected Social and Economic Consequences for Women and Children in America.* New York: Free Press.

Welborn, Vickie. 2006. "Black Students Ordered to Give Up Seats to Whites." *Shreveport Times,* August 24. Retrieved October 2, 2006 (http://www.shreveporttimes.com).

Wells, Brooke E. and Jean M. Twenge. 2005. "Changes in Young People's Sexual Behavior and Attitudes, 1943–1999: A Cross-temporal Meta-Analysis." *Review of General Psychology* 9(3):249–61.

Wells, Karen C., Jeffery Epstein, Stephen Hinshaw, C. Keith Conners, John Klaric, Howard Abikoff, Ann Abramowitz, L. Eugene Arnold, Glenn Elliott, Laurence Greenhill, Lily Hechtman, Betsy Hoza, Peter Jensen, John March, William Pelham, Linda Pfiffner, Joanne Severe, James Swanson, Benedetto Vitiello, and Tim Wigal. 2000. "Parenting and Family Stress Treatment Outcomes in Attention Deficit Hyperactivity Disorder (ADHD): An Empirical Analysis in the MTA Study." *Journal of Abnormal Child Psychology* 28(6):543–59.

Wells, Marolyn, Cheryl Glickauf-Hughes, and Rebecca Jones. 1999. "Codependency: A Grass Roots Construct's Relationship to Shame-proneness, Low Self-esteem, and Childhood Parentification." *American Journal of Family Therapy* 27:63–71.

Wells, Mary S., Mark A. Widmer, and J. Kelly McCoy. 2004. "Grubs and Grasshoppers: Challenge-based Recreation and the Collective Efficacy of Families with At-risk Youth." *Family Relations* 53(3):326–33.

Wells, Robert V. 1985. *Uncle Sam's Family: Issues in and Perspectives on American Demographic History.* Albany, NY: State University of New York Press.

Wentzel, Jo Ann. 2001. "Foster Kids Really Are Ours" (http://www.fosterparents.com).

Werner, Emmy E. 1992. "The Children of Kauai: Resilience and Recovery in Adolescence and Adulthood." *Journal of Adolescent Health* 13:262–68.

Werner, Emmy E. and Ruth S. Smith. 2001. *Journeys from Childhood to Midlife: Risk, Resiliency, and Recovery.* Ithaca, NY: Cornell University Press.

West, Carolyn M. 2003. "'Feminism Is a Black Thing'? Feminist Contributions to Black Family Life." *State of Black America 2003.* Washington, DC: National Urban League.

West, Martha S. and John W. Curtis. 2006. *AAUP Faculty Gender Equity Indicators 2006.* Washington, DC: American Association of University Professors. Retrieved January 31, 2007. (www.aaup.org)

Western, Bruce and Sara McLanahan. 2000. "Fathers Behind Bars: The Impact of Incarceration on Family Formation." Pp. 309–24 in *Families, Crime, and Criminal Justice,* edited by Greer Litton Fox and Michael L. Benson. New York: Elsevier Science.

Wexler, Richard. 2005. "Family Preservation Is the Safest Way to Protect Most Children." Pp. 311–27 in *Current Controversies on Family Violence,* 2nd ed., edited by Donileen R. Loseke, Richard J. Gelles, and Mary M. Cavanaugh. Thousand Oaks, CA: Sage Publications.

"What Happened to the Wedding Bells? Cohabitation Is On the Rise, New Data from Census Reveals." 2003. *Forecast* 23(4):1–4.

"What Is Dignity?" Retrieved March 29, 2004 (http://www.dignityusa.org).

Whealin, Julia and Ilona Pivar. 2006. "Coping when a Family Member Has Been Called to War: A National Center for PTSD Fact Sheet." U.S. Department of Veterans Affairs National Center for PTSD. Retrieved August 16, 2006 (http://www.ncptsd.va.gov).

"When Elder Care Falls to the Young." 2001. National Public Radio. August 29 (http://www.npr .org/programs/morningfeatures).

Whipple, Ellen E. and Cheryl A. Richey. 1997. "Crossing the Line from Physical Discipline to Child Abuse: How Much Is Too Much?" *Child Abuse & Neglect* 21(5):431–44.

Whitchurch, Gail G. and Larry L. Constantine. 1993. "Systems Theory." Pp. 325–52 in *Sourcebook of Family Theories and Methods,* edited by Pauline Boss, William J. Doherty, Ralph La Rossa, Walter R. Schumm, and Suzanne K. Steinmetz. New York: Plenum.

White House Conference on Aging. 2005. *Report to the President and the Congress: The Booming Dynamics of Aging—from Awareness to Action.* Retrieved May 16, 2007 (http://www.whcoa.gov).

"White House Distances Itself from Sex-education Report." 2001. *Omaha World-Herald,* June 29.

White, Jack E. 1993. "Growing Up in Black and White." *Time,* May 17, pp. 48–49.

White, Jacquelyn W., Lex Merrill, and Mary P. Koss. 2001. "Predictors of Premilitary Courtship Violence in a Navy Recruit Sample." *Journal of Interpersonal Violence* 16(9):910–27.

White, James M. and David M. Klein. 2002. *Family Theories: An Introduction.* 2nd ed. Thousand Oaks, CA: Sage Publications.

White, Lynn K. 1990. "Determinants of Divorce: A Review of Research in the Eighties." *Journal of Marriage and Family* 52:904–12.

———. 1994. "Growing Up with Single Parents and Stepparents: Long-term Effects on Family Solidarity." *Journal of Marriage and Family* 56(4):935–48.

———. 1999. "Contagion in Family Affection: Mothers, Fathers, and Young Adult Children." *Journal of Marriage and Family* 61(2):284–94.

White, Lynn K. and Alan Booth. 1985. "The Quality and Stability of Remarriages: The Role of Stepchildren." *American Sociological Review* 50:689–98.

———. 1991. "Divorce Over the Life Course: The Role of Marital Happiness." *Journal of Family Issues* 12:5–21.

White, Lynn K., Alan Booth, and John N. Edwards. 1986. "Children and Marital Happiness." *Journal of Family Issues* 7(2):131–47.

White, Lynn K. and Joan G. Gilbreth. 2001. "When Children Have Two Fathers: Effects of Relationships with Stepfathers and Noncustodial Fathers on Adolescent Outcomes." *Journal of Marriage and Family* 63:155–67.

White, Lynn K. and Bruce Keith. 1990. "The Effect of Shift Work on the Quality and Stability of Marital Relations." *Journal of Marriage and Family* 52:453–62.

White, Lynn K. and Agnes Riedmann. 1992. "When the Brady Bunch Grows Up: Step/Half- and Full-sibling Relationships in Adulthood." *Journal of Marriage and Family* 54(1):197–208.

White, Lynn K. and Stacy J. Rogers. 1997. "Strong Support but Uneasy Relationships: Coresidence and Adult Children's Relationships with Their Parents." *Journal of Marriage and Family* 59(1):62–76.

———. 2000. "Families in Social Locations—Economic Circumstances and Family Outcomes: A Review of the 1990s." *Journal of Marriage and Family* 62(4):1035–52.

Whitehead, Barbara. 1997. *The Divorce Culture.* New York: Random House.

Whitehead, Barbara Dafoe and David Popenoe. 2001. "Who Wants to Marry a Soul Mate?" In *The State of Our Unions 2001: The Social Health of Marriage in America.* Piscataway, NJ: RutgersUniversity, National Marriage Project.

———. 2003. "Did a Family Turnaround Begin in the 1990s?" In *The State of Our Unions 2003: The Social Health of Marriage in America.* Piscataway, NJ: Rutgers University, National Marriage Project. Retrieved September 20, 2006 (http://marriage.rutgers.edu).

———. 2006. *The State of Our Unions 2006: The Social Health of Marriage in America* (includes essay "Life without Children"). Piscataway, NJ: Rutgers University, National Marriage Project. Retrieved July 18, 2006 (http://marriage.rutgers.edu).

Whitman, David. 1997. "Was It Good for Us?" *U.S. News & World Report,* May 19, pp. 56–64.

Whittaker, Terri. 1995. "Violence, Gender and Elder Abuse: Towards a Feminist Analysis and Practice." *Journal of Gender Studies* 4(1):35–45.

"Who Is Homeless?" 2004. National Coalition for the Homeless, Fact Sheet #3 (http://www.nationalhomeless.org/who .html).

"Why Interracial Marriages Are Increasing." 1996. *Jet,* June 3, pp. 12–15.

Whyte, Martin King. 1990. *Dating, Mating, and Marriage.* New York: Aldine.

Wickrama, K. A. S., Frederick O. Lorenz, Rand D. Conger, and Glen H. Elder. 1997. "Marital Quality and Physical Illness: A Latent Growth Curve Analysis." *Journal of Marriage and Family* 59(1):143–55.

"A Widening Gulf in School . . . Leads More and More to a Girls' Club in College." 2003. *Business Week,* May 26, pp. 76–77.

Wiederman, Michael W. and Shannon R. Hurst. 1998. "Body Size, Physical Attractiveness, and Body Image among Young Adult Women: Relationships to Sexual Experience and Sexual Esteem." *Journal of Sex Research* 35(3):272–81.

Wiehe, Vernon R. 1997. *Sibling Abuse: Hidden Physical, Emotional, and Sexual Trauma.* Thousand Oaks, CA: Sage Publications.

Wilcox, W. Bradford. 1998. "Conservative Protestant Childrearing: Authoritarian or

Authoritative?" *American Sociological Review* 63:796–809.

———. 2002. "Religion, Convention, and Paternal Involvement." *American Sociological Review* 64:780–92.

———. 2004. *Soft Patriarchs, New Men: How Christianity Shapes Fathers and Husbands.* Chicago, IL: University of Chicago Press.

Wilcox, W. Bradford and Steven L. Nock. 2006. "What's Love Got to Do with It? Equality, Equity, Commitment and Women's Marital Quality." *Social Forces* 84(3):1321–45.

Wildsmith, Elizabeth and R. Kelley Raley. 2006. "Race-Ethnic Differences in Nonmarital Fertility: A Focus on Mexican American Women." *Journal of Marriage and Family* 68(2):491–508.

Wiley, Angela R., Henriette B. Warren, and Dale S. Montanelli. 2002. "Shelter in a Time of Storm: Parenting in Poor Rural African American Communities." *Family Relations* 51(3):265–73.

Wilkie, Jane Riblett. 1991. "The Decline in Men's Labor Force Participation and Income and the Changing Structure of Family Economic Support." *Journal of Marriage and Family* 53(1):111–22.

Wilkie, Jane Riblett, Myra Marx Ferree, and Kathryn Strother Ratcliff. 1998. "Gender and Fairness: Marital Satisfaction in Two-earner Couples." *Journal of Marriage and Family* 60(3):577–94.

Wilkinson, Doris. 1993. "Family Ethnicity in America." Pp. 15–59 in *Family Ethnicity: Strength in Diversity,* edited by Harriette Pipes McAdoo. Newbury Park, CA: Sage Publications.

———. 2000. "Rethinking the Concept of 'Minority': A Task for Social Scientists and Practitioners." *Journal of Sociology and Social Welfare* 27:115–32.

Willeto, Angela A. A. and Charlotte Goodluck. 2004. "Economic, Social and Demographic Losses and Gains among American Indians." Population Reference Bureau (www.prb.org).

Willetts, Marion C. 2003. "An Exploratory Investigation of Heterosexual Licensed Domestic Partners." *Journal of Marriage and Family* 65(4):939–52.

———. 2006. "Union Quality Comparisons between Long-term Heterosexual Cohabitation and Legal Marriage." *Journal of Family Issues* 27(1):110–27.

Williams, David E. 2006. "More Hurdles as Women Delay Birth." CNN, April 24.

Retrieved May 9, 2006 (http://cnn.worldnews.com).

Williams, David R. and Ruth Williams-Morris. 2000. "Racism and Mental Health: The African American Experience." *Ethnicity and Health* 5(3-4):243–68.

Williams, Joan C. and Holly Cohen Cooper. 2004. "The Public Policy of Motherhood." *Journal of Social Issues* 60(4):849–66.

Williams, Lee M. and Michael G. Lawler. 2003. "Marital Satisfaction and Religious Heterogamy." *Journal of Family Issues* 24(8):1070–92.

Willie, Charles Vert and Richard J. Reddick. 2003. *A New Look at Black Families.* 5th ed. Lanham, MD: Rowman and Littlefield.

Willson, Andrea E., Kim M. Shuey, and Glen H. Elder, Jr. 2003. "Ambivalence in the Relationship of Adult Children to Aging Parents and In-laws." *Journal of Marriage and Family* 65(4):1055–72.

Wilson, James Q. 2001. "Against Homosexual Marriage." Pp. 123–27 in *Debating Points: Marriage and Family Issues,* edited by Henry L. Tischler. Upper Saddle River, NJ: Prentice Hall.

———. 2002. "Why We Don't Marry." *City Journal,* Winter. Retrieved October 2, 2006 (http://www.city-journal.org).

Wilson, William Julius. 1987. *The Truly Disadvantaged: The Inner City, the Underclass, and Public Policy.* Chicago, IL: University of Chicago Press.

Winch, Robert F. 1958. *Mate Selection: A Study of Complementary Needs.* New York: Harper and Row.

Wineberg, Howard. 1996. "The Resolutions of Separation: Are Marital Reconciliations Attempted?" *Population Research and Policy Review* 15:297–310.

Wingett, Yvonne. 2007. "Foster Parents Needed to Help Hispanic Children." *Arizona Republic,* March 5.

Winner, Lauren F. 2006. *Real Sex: The Naked Truth about Chastity.* Grand Rapids, MI: Brazos Press.

Winter, Judy. 2006. *Breakthrough Parenting for Children with Special Needs: Raising the Bar of Expectations.* San Francisco, CA: Jossey-Bass.

Witchel, Alex. 2001. "Voices of the Past: We've Been There, Done That." *New York Times,* October 14.

Wolf, D. A., V. Freedman, and B. J. Soldo. 1997. "The Division of Family Labor: Care

for Elderly Parents." *Journal of Gerontology* 52B:102–9.

Wolf, Marsha E., Uyen Ly, Margaret A. Hobart, and Mary A. Kernic. 2003. "Barriers to Seeking Police Help for Intimate Partner Violence." *Journal of Family Violence* 18:121–29.

Wolf, Rosalie S. 1986. "Major Findings from Three Model Projects on Elderly Abuse." Pp. 218–38 in *Elder Abuse: Conflict in the Family,* edited by Karl A. Pillemer and Rosalie S. Wolf. Dover, MA: Auburn.

———. 1996. "Elder Abuse and Family Violence: Testimony Presented Before the U.S. Senate Special Committee on Aging." *Journal of Elder Abuse & Neglect* 8(1):81–96.

Wolfers, Justin. 2006. "Did Unilateral Divorce Raise Divorce Rates? A Reconciliation and New Results." *American Economic Review* 96(5):1802–20.

Wolfinger, Nicholas H. 1999. "Trends in the Intergenerational Transmission of Divorce." *Demography* 36:415–20.

———. 2005. *Understanding the Divorce Cycle: The Children of Divorce in Their Own Marriages.* New York: Cambridge University Press.

"Women Still Lag White Males in Pay." 2004. CNNMoney, April 20 (http://cnnmoney.com).

Wong, Paul, Chienping Faith Lai, Richard Nagazawa, and Tieming Lin. 1998. "Asian Americans as a Model Minority: Self-perceptions and Perceptions by Other Racial Groups." *Sociological Perspectives* 41(1):95–118.

Wood, Julia T. and Steve Duck. 2006. *Composing Relationships: Communicating in Everyday Life.* Belmont, CA: Thomson/Wadsworth.

Wood, Wendy and Alice H. Eagly. 2002. "A Cross-cultural Analysis of Behavior of Women and Men: Implications for the Origins of Sex Differences." *Psychology Bulletin* 128:699–727.

Woodward, Kenneth L. 2001. "A Mormon Moment." *Newsweek,* September 10, pp. 44–51.

Woolley, Michael E. and Andrew Grogan-Kaylor. 2006. "Protective Family Factors in the Context of Neighborhood: Promoting Positive School Outcomes." *Family Relations* 55(1):93–104.

Working Moms Refuge. 2001. "Factors to Consider When Selecting a Child Care Center" (www.momsrefuge.com/newmoms/tips/childcare_centers.html).

"World's 1st 'Test-tube' Baby Gives Birth." 2007. CNN.com, January 15. Retrieved January 15, 2007 (http://cnn.health .com).

Wright, H. Norman. 2006a. *Be a Great Parent: 12 Secrets to Raising Responsible Children.* Colorado Springs, CO: Life Journey Press.

———. 2006b. *How to Speak Your Spouse's Language: Ten Easy Steps to Great Communication from One of America's Foremost Counselors.* New York: Center Street.

Wright, Paul H. and Katherine D. Wright. 1999. "The Two Faces of Codependent Relating: A Research-based Perspective." *Contemporary Family Therapy* 21(4):527–43.

Wright, Suzanne. 2005. "Willing the World to Listen." *Newsweek,* February 28, p. 47.

Wrigley, Julia and Joanna Dreby. 2005. "Fatalities and the Organization of Child Care in the United States, 1985–2003." *American Sociological Review* 70:729–57.

Wu, Lawrence L. and Barbara Wolfe, eds. 2001. *Causes and Consequences of Nonmarital Fertility.* New York: Russell Sage.

Wulczyn, Fred. 2004. "Family Reunification." *The Future of Children* 14(1):95–113.

Wuthnow, Robert. 2002. *Loose Connections: Joining Together in America's Fragmented Communities.* Cambridge, MA: Harvard University Press.

Xu, Xianohe, Clarke D. Hudspeth, and John P. Bartkowski. 2006. "The Role of Cohabitation in Remarriage." *Journal of Marriage and Family* 68(2):261–74.

Yabroff, Jennie. 2006. "Money Changes Everything." *New York Times,* May 7.

Yalcin, Bektas Murat and Tevfik Fikret Karaban. 2007. "Effects of a Couple Communication Program on Marital Adjustment." *Journal of the American Board of Family Medicine* 20(1):36–44.

Yancey, George and Sherelyn Yancey. 1998. "Interracial Dating." *Journal of Family Issues* 19(3):334–48.

Yellowbird, Michael and C. Matthew Snipp. 2002. "American Indian Families." Pp. 227–49 in *Multicultural Families in the United States,* 3rd ed., edited by Ronald L. Taylor. Upper Saddle River, NJ: Prentice Hall.

Yeung, King-To and John Levi Martin. 2003. "The Looking Glass Self: An Empirical Test and Elaboration." *Social Forces* 81(3):843–79.

Yeung, W. Jean, John Sandberg, Pamela Davis-Kean, and Sandra Hofferth. 2001. "Children's Time with Fathers in Intact Families." *Journal of Marriage and Family* 63(1):136–54.

Yi, Matthew. 2007. "Lawmaker Revises Spanking Proposal." *San Francisco Chronicle,* February 23.

Yin, Sandra. 2007. "New Restrictions Could Limit U.S. Adoptions from Top Two Countries of Origin: China and Guatemala." Washington, DC: Population Reference Bureau. March. Retrieved March 26, 2007 (www.prb.org).

Yorburg, Betty. 2002. *Family Realities: A Global View.* Upper Saddle River, NJ: Prentice Hall.

Yoshioka, Marianne R., Louisa Gilbert, Nabila El-Bassel, and Malahat Baig-Amin. 2003. "Social Support and Disclosure of Abuse: Comparing South Asian, African American, and Hispanic Battered Women." *Journal of Family Violence* 18:171–80.

Youngs, Bettie B., Susan M. Heim, and Jennifer Leigh Youngs. 2006. *Oh Baby! 7 Ways a Baby Will Change Your Life in the First Year.* Charlottesville, VA: Hampton Roads.

Yuan, Anastasia S. Vogt, and Hayley A. Hamilton. 2006. "Stepfather Involvement and Adolescent Well-being." *Journal of Family Issues* 27(9):1191–1213.

Zabin, Laurie Schwab, Rebeca Wong, Robin M. Weinick, and Mark R. Emerson. 1992. "Dependency in Urban Black Families Following the Birth of an Adolescent's Child." *Journal of Marriage and Family* 54(3):496–507.

Zablocki v. Redhail. 1978. 434 U.S. 374, 54 L.Ed.2d 618, 98 S. Ct. 673.

Zak, A. 1998. "Individual Differences in Perception of Fault in Intimate Relationships." *Personality and Individual Differences* 24:131–33.

Zeitz, Joshua M. 2003. "The Big Lie about the Little Pill." *New York Times,* December 27.

Zelizer, Gerald L. 2004. "Time to Break the 'Stained Glass' Ceiling." *USA Today,* September 16.

Zelizer, Viviana K. 1985. *Pricing the Priceless Child: The Changing Social Value of Children.* New York: Basic Books.

———. 1994. *The Social Meaning of Money.* New York: Basic Books.

Zentgraf, Kristine A. 2002. "Immigration and Women's Empowerment:

Salvadorans in Los Angeles." *Gender and Society* 16:625–46.

Zernike, Kate. 2006. "The Bell Tolls for the Future Merry Widow." *New York Times,* April 30. Retrieved April 30, 2007 (http://www.nytimes.com).

Zezima, Katie. 2006. "When Soldiers Go to War, Flat Daddies Hold Their Place at Home." *New York Times,* September 30.

Zhao, Yilu. 2002. "Immersed in 2 Worlds, New and Old." *New York Times,* July 22.

Zill, Nicholas, D. R. Morrison, and M. J. Coiro. 1993. "Long-term Effects of Parental Divorce on Parent–Child Relationships, Adjustment, and Achievement in Young Adulthood." *Journal of Family Psychology* 7:91–103.

Zimmerman, Eilene. 2004. "Bragging Rights: The 'Gifted' Label May Mean Too Much to Parents." *Psychology Today* (January/February):20.

Zimmerman, Jeffrey and Elizabeth Thayer. 2003. *Adult Children of Divorce: How to Overcome the Legacy of Your Parents' Breakup and Enjoy Love, Trust, and Intimacy.* Oakland, CA: New Harbinger Publications.

Zink, Therese, C. Jeff Jacobson, Jr., Stephanie Pabst, Saundra Regan, and Bonnie S. Fisher. 2006. "A Lifetime of Intimate Partner Violence: Coping Strategies of Older Women." *Journal of Interpersonal Violence* 21(5):634–51.

Zoroya, Gregg. 2006. "Families Bear Catastrophic War Wounds." *USA Today,* September 25.

Zsembik, Barbara A. and Zobeida Bonilla. 2000. "Eldercare and the Changing Family in Puerto Rico." *Journal of Family Issues* 21(5):652–74.

Zuang, Yuanting. 2004. "Why Foreign Adoption?" Presented at the annual meeting of the American Sociological Association, August 15, San Francisco, CA.

Zuo, Jiping and Shengming Tang. 2000. "Breadwinner Status and Gender Ideologies of Men and Women Regarding Family Roles." *Social Forces* 43:29–43.

Zurcher, Kristinia E. 2004. "'I Do' or 'I Don't'? Covenant Marriage after Six Years." *Notre Dame Journal of Law, Ethics, and Public Policy* 18:273–92.

Zvonkovic, Anisa M., Kathleen M. Greaves, Cynthia J. Schmiege, and Leslie D. Hall. 1996. "The Marital Construction of Gender through Work and Family Decisions: A Qualitative Analysis." *Journal of Marriage and Family* 58(1):91–100.

Credits

Chapter 1. 10: From *Family Theories: An Introduction,* by David M. Klein and James K. White, p. 22. Copyright © 2002 by Sage Publications, Inc. Reprinted by permission. **12:** Figure adapted from *Shifting Gears,* by Nena O'Neill and George O'Neill, p. 167, 1974. Copyright © 1974 by Nena O'Neill and George O'Neill. Reprinted by permission of the publisher, M. Evans and Company, New York, NY. **15:** David Popenoe and Barbara Dafoe Whitehead. 2005. *The State of Our Unions 2005.* Piscataway, NJ: National Marriage Project, Rutgers, p. 23. Copyright © 2005 David Popenoe and Barbara Dafoe Whitehead. All rights reserved. Reprinted by permission.

Chapter 2. 22: Adapted with permission from "Human Ecology Theory" by Margaret M. Bubolz and M. Suzanne Sontag, p. 419–448 in *Sourcebook of Family Theories and Methods,* ed. by Pauline G. Boss, et al. Copyright © 1993 Springer-Verlag. **32:** © The New Yorker Collection 2000 Mick Stevens from cartoonbank.com. All rights reserved. **36:** © The New Yorker Collection 2003 Michael Shaw from cartoonbank.com. All rights reserved.

Chapter 3. 55: © The New Yorker Collection 2007 Glen Le Lievre from cartoonbank.com. All rights reserved.

Chapter 4. 76–77: From Jodi Kantor, "Nanny Hunt Can Be a 'Slap in the Face' for Blacks," *New York Times,* Dec. 26, 2006. Copyright © 2006 by the New York Times Co. Reprinted by permission. **81:** © The New Yorker Collection 2000 William Haefeli from cartoonbank.com. All rights reserved. **92:** © The New Yorker Collection 1995 Robert Mankoff from cartoonbank.com. All rights reserved. **95:** Excerpt from "The Costs of Being on Top," by Mark E. Kann, *Journal of the National Association for Women Deans, Administrators, and Counselors,* 49 (Summer). Copyright © 1986 by the National Association for Women Deans, Administrators and Counselors. Reprinted by permission. **97.** Reprinted by permission of Anne Gibbons.

Chapter 5. 106: Adapted from "Triangular Love," by Robert J. Sternberg, 1988, fig. 6.1, p. 121. In Robert J. Sternberg and Michael L. Barnes, (eds.) *The Psychology of Love.* Copyright © 1988 Yale University Press. Adapted by permission. **109:** © The New Yorker Collection 1997 Al Ross from cartoonbank.com. All rights reserved. **114:** From *Family Systems in America,* 3E, by I. Reiss © 1980 Wadsworth, a division of Thomson Learning.

Chapter 6. 130: © The New Yorker Collection 1990 Edward Koren from cartoonbank.com. All rights reserved. **134:** © The New Yorker Collection 2003 Michael Maslin from cartoonbank.com. All rights reserved. **139:** © The New Yorker Collection 2005 Michael Maslin from cartoonbank.com. All rights reserved.

Chapter 7. 162: Adapted from "Love and Marriage in Eleven Cultures," by R. Levine, S. Sato, T. Hasimoto and J. Verma, 1995, *Journal of Cross-Cultural Psychology,* 26(5), pp. 554–571. Copyright © 1996 by Sage Publications, Inc. Reprinted by permission.

Chapter 9. 225: © The New Yorker Collection 2003 Liza Donnelly from cartoonbank.com. All rights reserved.

Chapter 10. 255: © The New Yorker Collection 2005 Michael Shaw from cartoonbank.com. All rights reserved.

Chapter 11. 267: Annette Clifford, "Parent: Job Description" from the *Florida Today* newspaper, Melbourne, FL, 1999. Reprinted by permission of the author. **268:** Steve Farkas, Jean Johnson, and Ann Duffett. 2002. *A Lot Easier Said Than Done: Parents Talk about Raising Children in Today's America.* Public Agenda: Report prepared for State Farm Insurance Companies. Reprinted by permission of Public Agenda Foundation, Inc. **275:** Excerpts from Rawson Associates/Scribner, an imprint of Simon & Schuster from *How to Talk So Kids Will Listen and Listen So Kids Will Talk* by Adele Faber and Elaine Mazlish. Copyright © 1980 by Adele Faber and Elaine Mazlish. **280:** © The New Yorker Collection 2002 Tom Cheney from cartoonbank.com. All rights reserved.

Name Index

Abboud, Soo Kim, 282
Abel, Emily K., 499
Abelsohn, David, 430f, 475
Abelson, Reed, 303
Abma, Joyce C., 243, 244, 250, 255
Abraham, Margaret, 372
Achenbaum, W. Andrew, 506
Ackerman, Brian P., 170, 196
Acock, Alan C., 461
Acs, Gregory, 175
Adams, Gina, 317, 321b
Adams, Michele, 88
Adamsons, Kari, 432, 436
Aday, Lu Ann, 285, 395
Adkins, Sue, 267n
Adler, Jerry, 136, 169, 217
Adler, Margot, 496
Adler, Nancy E., 254
Afifi, Tamara D., 273b
Aguirre, Benigno E., 218
Ahmed, Ashraf Uddin, 162
Ahrons, Constance, 432, 435, 437, 439, 443,
    446–447, 447, 447n, 449, 478, 479
Ainslie, Ricardo C., 273b
Ainsworth, Mary D. S., 318n
Aird, Enola G., 266, 272
Akinbami, Lara J., 278
Albrecht, Chris, 170, 196
Albrecht, Stan L., 421
Aldous, Joan, 27, 27n, 28, 155n, 227, 492
Alegria, Margarita, 282
Alexander, C. S., 250
Alexander, Deborah, 4b
Ali, Lorraine, 131
Allen, C. M., 371
Allen, Cheryl, 217, 271b
Allen, Douglas W., 422
Allen, Karen, 4b
Allen, Katherine R., 29, 198, 498b, 505
Allen, M., 8, 197b
Allen, Robert L., 377
Allen, Sarah M., 308
Allen, Walter R., 57, 60
Allgeier, A. R., 138
Alper, Gerald, 102
Alstein, Howard, 259–260
Altman, Irwin, 105
Altman, Lawrence K., 144b, 147
Alvarez, Lizette, 51b, 437
Amatenstein, Sherry, 226b
Amato, Paul R., 17, 158, 176, 177, 178, 194,
    210, 225, 226, 228, 272, 273b, 275, 278,
    312, 352, 358, 359, 360, 414, 414n, 417,
    419, 420, 422, 428, 429, 432, 433, 435,
    441, 442, 443, 445, 468, 471
Ambert, Anne Marie, 284
Amerson, Lydia, 428
Ames, Barbara D., 199, 278
Ames, Elinor W., 260

Amini, Fari, 102, 103, 116, 117
Amsel, Rhonda, 392
Anderlini-D'Onofrio, Serina, 159b
Andersen, J., 470
Andersen, J. D., 471
Andersen, Margaret L., 76, 87, 89
Anderson, Jared R., 280
Anderson, K., 371, 374, 376
Anderson, M., 371, 373
Anderson, Robert N., 156b
Anderson, Stephen A., 222
Andrews, Bernice, 373
Anetzberger, Georgia, 503
Anhalt, J., 436
Ansay, Sylvia J., 51b
Anyiam, Thony, 172b
Apple, Kevin J., 133b
Apter, T. E., 267n
Aquilino, William, 287, 433, 443, 444, 471
Archer, John, 374, 375
Arditti, Joyce A., 407, 408b, 409b, 438, 449
Arendell, Terry, 270, 423, 441, 468, 469
Arenson, Karen W., 84
Ariès, Phillipe, 266
Armour, Stephanie, 304, 306
Armstrong, Elizabeth M., 285
Armstrong, Larry, 103, 105
Arnall, Judy, 268n
Arnett, Jeffrey Jensen, 29, 130, 143, 156b,
    185, 186, 190, 191, 204, 210, 220, 287,
    288, 493
Arnott, Teresa, 93
Aron, Arthur, 116
Aronson, Pamela, 84, 93, 94
Artis, Julie E., 307, 308, 308n, 309
Asada, Jean K., 133b, 220
Aseltine, Robert H., Jr., 420
Ashmun, Joanna M., 111
Astone, Nan M., 27
Atchley, Robert C., 417, 490, 491, 492
Austin, Craig, 503
Avellar, Sarah, 195, 297, 323
Avila, E., 63b
Axinn, William G., 212

Babbie, Earl, 38, 39
Babbitt, Charles E., 166
Babcock, Ginna M., 435
Babcock, Julia, 210
Baca Zinn, Maxine, 55, 57b, 61, 62b, 64, 76,
    93, 96
Bach, George R., 342
Bachrach, Christine A., 248, 258, 259
Badeau, Susan H., 286
Badger, Sarah, 345, 484
Bailey, J. Michael, 125
Baird, Donna D., 245
Bakalar, Nicholas, 254
Baker, Richard C., 203

Bales, Robert F., 31
Ball, Derek, 344
Ballard-Reisch, Deborah S., 331, 352
Ballinger, Bud C. III, 224
Bammer, Cabriele, 382
Bandura, Albert, 87, 88
Banerjee, Neela, 82
Banse, Rainer, 209
Barash, Susan Shapiro, 470, 471, 473, 475
Barbassa, Juliana, 177, 202
Barber, Bonnie L., 432, 433
Barker, Susan, 116
Barnes, M. L., 114
Barnett, Marina, 272
Barnett, Rosalind Chait, 266, 417
Barret, R. L., 438t
Bartfeld, Judi, 428
Barth, Richard P., 260
Bartkowski, John P., 70, 360, 361, 462
Bartlett, Katherine, 193b
Barton, Judy, 130
Barton, Sharon J., 278, 286
Basow, Susan H., 79, 80, 89
Batalova, Jeanne A., 325
Batson, Christie D., 218, 218n
Baum, Angela C., 286
Baumeister, Roy F., 110n, 111
Baumrind, Diana, 274, 380, 382
Baur, Karla, 134, 135, 138
Bausch, Robert S., 258
Bauserman, Robert, 435, 439
Baxter, Janeen, 194
Bay, R. Curtis, 428
Beach, Steven R. H., 227, 242, 338,
    338n, 345
Beals, K. P., 129–130
Beaman, Lori G., 70
Bean, Frank D., 55, 55n, 69, 161
Bearman, Peter S., 147
Beavers, Laura, 62b
Beck, Peggy, 423
Becker, Gay, 254n, 255, 256, 257, 258b, 416
Bedard, Marcia E., 284
Beeghley, Leonard, 325
Beer, William, 464, 470, 475
Begley, Sharon, 111, 147
Belcastro, Philip A., 139, 140
Belicki, Kathy, 380
Belkin, Lisa, 298, 306
Bell, Alan P., 124
Bell, Diane, 380
Bell, M., 198, 199, 200
Bell, R., 269
Bellafante, Ginia, 301
Bellah, Robert N., 102, 110n, 166
Bellas, Marcia L., 488, 488n, 489, 489n, 506
Belluck, Pam, 201, 261, 445
Belsky, Jay, 242, 277, 279, 318b, 319b
Belt, Nancy, 33

Bem, Sandra Lipsitz, 87
Benedetto, Richard, 197*b*
Bengston, Vern L., 14, 16, 48, 161, 204, 285, 288, 399, 402, 486, 493, 493*t*, 494, 496, 500, 504, 505
Benjet, Corina, 276, 277
Bennett, Claudette E., 64
Bennett, Kymberly K., 331, 352
Bennett, Larry W., 378
Bennett, Linda A., 403
Bennetts, Leslie, 427
Benoit, D., 113
Bent-Goodley, Tricia B., 286
Berardo, Felix M., 382
Berg, Barbara, 255
Berg, S. J., 86
Berge, Jerica M., 393
Berger, Brigitte, 102*n*
Berger, Lauren, 395
Berger, Peter L., 32, 102*n*
Berger, R., 464*n*, 465
Berger, Roni, 464*n*, 465, 466*b*
Bergman, Mike, 6*b*, 7*b*, 49, 53, 60, 64, 154, 156*b*, 303
Berk, Richard A., 373, 378, 378*n*
Berk, Sarah Fenstermaker, 307, 373
Berke, Debra L., 305
Berman, Margit, 442
Bernard, Jessie, 300
Berns, Sara B., 336
Bernstein, A., 52, 469, 475
Bernstein, Anne, 463
Bernstein, F., 78*b*
Bernstein, Jeffrey, 343
Bernstein, N., 62*b*, 63*b*, 64, 146
Bernstein, R., 15*b*, 58
Berridge, K., 116
Berry, Marianne, 260
Beutel, Ann M., 80
Bhanot, Ruchi, 284
Bianchi, Suzanne M., 3, 14, 16, 77, 187*t*, 190, 194, 225, 266, 267, 270, 271*f*, 272, 300, 303, 309, 310, 311, 314, 314*f*, 358, 416, 426, 428, 456, 487, 487*n*, 488, 489
Biblarz, Timothy J., 14, 16, 48, 125, 161, 199, 200, 204
Bichler, Joyce, 500
Biddulph, Sharon, 267
Biddulph, Steve, 267
Bierman, Alex, 169
Biernat, Monica, 270
Billingsley, Andrew, 54, 58
Billson, Janet M., 79
Binstock, Georgina, 421
Birch, Herbert G., 270
Bird, Chloe E., 243
Bird, Gloria W., 391
Birditt, Kira S., 501
Bischoff, L., 395
Biskupic, Joan, 193*b*
Black, D. A., 382
Black, Dan, 124, 136*b*, 196
Blackman, Lorraine, 172*b*
Blackwell, Debra L., 216
Blaisure, Karen R., 439
Blake, Nancee, 423
Blakely, Mary Kay, 418
Blakeslee, Sandra, 166, 228, 334, 345, 422, 424, 429, 435, 437, 439, 441
Blalock, Lydia B., 396
Blanchflower, David G., 133
Blankemeyer, Maureen, 497, 502

Blankenhorn, David, 35, 168, 270
Blau, Francine D., 76, 84, 85, 297
Blau, Judith R., 170, 278
Blau, Melinda, 448*b*
Blau, Peter, 363
Blee, Kathleen M., 80
Blieszner, Rosemary, 393
Blinn-Pike, Lynn, 131
Block, J., 343
Block, Sandra, 4*b*, 490
Blood, Robert, 354, 356, 363
Bloom, Barbara, 278
Blow, Adrian J., 133, 134, 135
Bluestone, Cheryl, 280
Blum, Deborah, 86
Blumberg, Rae Lesser, 355, 363, 364, 373
Blumberg, Susan L., 227, 334*b*, 346
Blumer, Herbert, 31*n*
Blumerman, Lisa, 502
Blumstein, Philip, 129, 129*n*, 143, 196, 356–357, 362, 362*b*
Bly, Robert, 96
Bobrow, David, 125
Bock, Jane D., 249
Boden, Joseph M., 254
Bogaert, Anthony F., 124*b*
Bogenschneider, Karen, 12, 25*b*
Bogle, Kathleen A., 132, 132*b*, 133*b*
Bohannan, Paul, 422, 424, 449, 470
Boll, E. S., 32
Bolzendahl, Catherine I., 95
Bond, Michael Harris, 33
Bonilla, Zobeida, 504
Boonstra, Heather D., 252*n*, 253, 254
Booth, Alan, 23, 34, 36, 37, 39, 41, 42, 86, 191, 194, 195, 243, 270, 274, 278, 300, 310, 347, 359, 417, 418, 419, 420, 421, 429, 443, 445, 460, 461, 462, 471, 493
Booth, C., 371
Boraas, Stephanie, 297
Bornstein, Marc H., 277
Borrell, Luisa N., 177, 202
Bosman, Julie, 8*b*
Boss, Pauline G., 22*f*, 34, 390, 391, 392, 393, 394*f*, 397, 398, 403, 405, 465
Bossard, James H., 32
Bosse, Irina, 116
Bost, Kelly K., 270
Bouchard, Emily, 473
Bouchard, Genevieve, 330
Bould, Sally, 26
Boulin Johnson, Leanor, 89
Boumil, Marcia M., 221*b*
Boushey, Heather, 245, 298
Bouton, Katherine, 257
Bowen, Gary L., 170, 278, 406
Bowers, Susan P., 499
Bowlby, John, 209
Bowser, Benjamin P., 139
Boyatzis, Chris J., 274
Bradbury, Thomas N., 208, 227, 242, 331, 338, 338*n*
Bradley, Robert H., 277
Bramlett, Matthew D., 6*b*, 7*b*, 172*b*, 208, 210, 456, 457, 458*b*, 462
Branden, Nathaniel, 110*n*, 111, 334*b*
Brannon, Robert, 79
Brant, Martha, 268
Bratter, Jennifer, 185, 214, 214*n*, 220
Braun, Bonnie, 396, 403
Braver, Sanford, 422, 427, 428, 435, 440, 441

Bray, James H., 459, 469, 470
Brazelton, T. Berry, 267, 273
Breaux, John, 492
Brehm, Sharon S., 33–34, 354, 355
Breitenbecher, Kimberly Hanson, 221*b*
Brennan, Bridget, 228
Brennan, P. A., 395
Brennan, Patricia A., 393
Brennan, Robert, 417
Brenner, N. L., 146
Brewaeys, A., 258*b*
Brewin, Chris R., 373
Brewster, Karin L., 317
Brickley, Margie, 200
Brines, Julie, 307
Brinig, Margaret F., 422
Brink, Roger B., 191
Brinton, Mary C., 76, 85
Brittingham, Angela, 55*n*
Britz, Jennifer Delahunty, 84
Brock, E. Wilbur, 217
Broder, John M., 63*n*
Broderick, Carlfred B., 34, 332, 333, 365*b*, 397
Brodie, Deborah, 422, 440
Brodkin, Adele M., 267*n*
Brody, J., 25*b*, 147
Brodzinsky, Anne B., 29
Brodzinsky, David M., 29
Bronson, Po, 184
Brooke, Jill, 187, 261, 475
Brooks, Clem, 14, 70
Brooks, David, 61, 63*b*, 237*b*
Brooks, Robert, 274, 275, 277
Brooks-Gunn, Jeanne, 250, 278
Broome, Claire V., 414*n*
Brosi, Whitney A., 278
Brotherson, Sean, 228
Broughton, Ross, 104
Brown, D., 258*b*
Brown, Dave, 173
Brown, Deborah Edler, 285
Brown, J., 380, 382
Brown, Louise, 255, 258*b*
Brown, Pamela D., 377
Brown, Patricia Lee, 78*b*, 79, 178, 201
Brown, Susan L., 170, 171, 176, 179, 195, 196, 244
Brownell, Caroline, 305*b*
Brownell, Patricia J., 503
Browning, Christopher R., 278, 380
Browning, James J., 371
Brownridge, Douglas A., 194, 369
Brubaker, Ellie, 501
Brubaker, Timothy H., 492
Bruce, Carol, 268
Brückner, Hannah, 147
Bruess, Clint E., 128, 254*n*
Bruno, Beth, 467*n*
Bryant, A., 403
Bubolz, Margaret M., 22, 23
Buchanan, Christy M., 435
Buchanan, Wyatt, 199, 200
Buckmiller, Nicolle, 393
Budgeon, Shelley, 166
Budig, Michelle, 297
Buehler, Cheryl, 273*b*, 324, 417*n*, 426, 427, 427*n*
Bukhari, Zahid Hussain, 216–217
Bulanda, Ronald E., 272
Bulcroft, Kris, 227, 490
Bulcroft, Richard, 102, 117, 227, 240

Bumpass, Larry, 4, 16*b*, 136*b*, 190, 194, 225
Bunker, Barbara B., 316
Burant, C. J., 501
Burbach, Harold J., 166
Burbach, Mary, 259
Burch, Rebecca, 370
Burchard, Glenice A., 227
Burgess, Ernest, 2, 3, 165
Buriel, R., 269
Burke, Peter J., 227
Burke, Tod W., 198
Burkett, Elinor, 240
Burney, L., 267
Burney, Robert, 112*b*, 112*n*
Burns, A., 89
Burns, Linda Hammer, 392
Burpee, Leslie C., 228
Burr, Jeffrey A., 503
Burr, Wesley R., 405
Burt, Marla S., 470
Burt, Roger B., 470
Burt, Sandra, 267*n*
Burton, L., 500
Burton, Linda M., 396
Burton, Russell, 209, 331
Buscaglia, Leo, 110*n*
Bush, George W., 8, 82, 174
Bushman, Brad, 110*n*, 111
Buss, D. M., 214, 222
Bussey, K., 88
Butler, A., 125
Butler, Judith, 76*n*
Butler, K., 143, 380
Butz, Tim, 201
Buunk, Bram, 33, 161
Buyas, Michael, 391*b*
Buzawa, Carl G., 378
Buzawa, Eve S., 378
Byers, E. S., 125, 138
Byung-Soo, Kim, 216

Cable, Susan, 396, 424, 496
Caffaro, John, 380
Caldera, Yvonne, 89, 269
Caldwell, John, 160
Call, Vaughn, 136*b*, 137*f*, 138, 139
Campbell, Bernadette, 77
Campbell, M., 60
Campbell, Rob, 267*n*
Campbell, S., 211
Campbell, Susan, 96, 475
Campbell, W. Keith, 38, 109, 110*n*, 111, 242, 243
Canary, D. J., 80, 339
Canavan, Margaret M., 380
Cancian, Francesca, 104, 107*b*, 112, 214, 258, 270, 279, 306, 356, 496, 497, 499, 501, 502, 506
Canedy, Dana, 91
Cantor, M. H., 60, 497, 497*n*
Canudas-Romo, Vladimir, 415*n*
Capaldi, Deborah M., 337*b*, 338*n*
Capps, Randy, 63*b*
Caputo, Richard K., 285, 496, 506
Carasso, Adam, 176
Cares, Alison C., 220
Carey, Benedict, 146, 318*b*
Carey, Michael P., 130, 138
Carlson, Darren K., 102
Carlson, Marcia J., 170, 171, 176, 196, 249, 251, 437, 468

Carnochan, Sarah, 468, 470
Carnoy, David, 244
Carnoy, Martin, 244
Carr, Deborah, 493
Carr, Elizabeth, 258*b*
Carroll, Jason S., 345, 393, 484
Carroll, Joseph, 131, 159*b*, 179, 202
Carter, Betty, 29, 90, 390, 403, 403*n*
Carter, Steven, 102, 112
Cartmell, Todd, 267*n*
Carver, Karen, 36, 37, 274
Case, Anne, 36, 469
Casper, Lynne M., 3, 14, 16, 187*t*, 188, 190, 191, 194, 225, 287, 300, 302, 303, 317, 358*f*, 456, 487, 487*n*, 487*t*, 488, 489, 492
Cast, Alicia D., 227
Castro Martin, Teresa, 4, 191*b*
Catalano, Shannan, 369, 369*f*, 370, 370*f*, 371, 380
Cavanaugh, Mary M., 177, 371, 381, 382, 383, 383*n*
Cave, Damien, 78*b*
Ceballo, Rosario, 473
Centers, Richard, 353
Cervantes, N., 378
Chabot, Jennifer M., 199
Chadiha, Letha A., 502
Chadwick, Alex, 201
Chafetz, Janet Saltzman, 323, 363
Chan, Raymond W., 258*b*
Chandra, Anjani, 124, 124*b*, 134, 136*b*, 139, 146, 189, 190, 195, 236, 237*b*, 240, 248, 255, 258
Chang, Lei, 282
Chao, R. K., 282
Chapman, Steven F., 424
Chappell, Crystal Lee Hyun Joo, 261
Chatters, Linda M., 406
Chatzky, Jeann, 501
Cheadle, Jacob, 418
Chen, Xuan, 495, 503
Cheng, Yen-Hsin Alice, 169, 190, 214
Cherlin, Andrew, 7*b*, 14, 17, 154, 158, 164, 165, 166, 169, 170, 174, 175, 176, 177, 178, 179, 185, 190, 415, 415*n*, 432, 433, 465, 474, 495, 496, 505
Chesler, Phyllis, 39
Chess, Stella, 270
Childress, Sarah, 68, 372, 381*n*
Chipungu, Sandra Stukes, 286
Chira, Susan, 317
Chodorow, Nancy, 88
Choi, Heejeong, 501, 502
Choi, Namkee G., 440
Choice, Pamela, 374, 374*f*
Chowdhury, Quamrul Ahsan, 380
Christensen, Andrew, 344
Christensen, Kathleen E., 322, 323
Christiansen, Shawn L., 300
Christopher, F. Scott, 129*n*, 130, 131, 133, 135, 136, 138, 140, 146, 221*b*, 357, 370
Christopherson, Brian, 228, 245
Chu, Jeff, 65
Chung, Grace H., 439
Chung, Juliet, 61
Ciabattari, Teresa, 195
Ciaramigoli, Arthur P., 102, 104, 117
Cicirelli, Victor G., 501
Clark, Margaret S., 308
Clark-Ibanez, Marisol, 216
Clarkberg, Marin, 502

Clarke, L., 461, 484
Clarke, Sally C., 462
Claxton-Oldfield, Stephen, 463, 469
Clayton, Obie, 59, 59*n*
Clements, Mari L., 210, 229, 347
Clemetson, Lynette, 258, 259, 260, 261, 298, 437
Cleveland, Robert W., 489
Clifford, Annette, 267*b*
Clinton, Bill, 177
Clinton, Hillary Rodham, 285
Cloud, Henry, 346
Cloud, John, 279, 280, 346
Coan, James A., 337*b*
Cobb, Nathan P., 208, 211
Coburn, Jennifer, 94
Cochran, Susan D., 140
Cochran, Thad, 285
Coffman, Ginger, 407
Cogan, Rosemary, 224
Cohan, Cathrine L., 37, 225, 226
Cohen, Neil A., 280, 284
Cohen, Patricia, 39, 312
Cohen, Philip N., 188, 287, 325, 358*f*
Cohen, Robin A., 278
Cohen, S., 4*b*
Coiro, M. J., 468
Cole, Harriette, 172*b*
Cole, Thomas, 138
Cole, Wendy, 280
Colella, Ugo, 225
Coleman, Marilyn, 29, 203, 396, 406, 424, 456, 457, 458*b*, 459, 460, 461, 462, 464, 465, 467, 468, 469, 469*n*, 470, 471, 473, 474, 475, 478, 496
Coleman, Marion Tolbert, 355, 363, 364, 373
Coleman, Priscilla, 318*n*
Coleman, Vallerie, 377
Coles, Clifton, 396
Coles, Roberta L., 284
Coll, Cynthia, 284
Collins, Nancy L., 114
Collins, Patricia Hill, 76, 239*b*
Collins, Randall, 355
Collins, Rebecca L., 210
Collins, W., 274
Collis, G. M., 4*b*
Colliver, Victoria, 279
Collymore, Yvette, 381
Colombo, Bernardo, 245
Coltrane, Scott, 80, 88, 243, 300, 307, 308, 308*n*, 325, 352, 355, 356, 357, 358, 360
Colucci, Patricia, 29
Colvin, Jan, 406, 502
Colwell, Malinda, 269
Combs-Orme, Terri, 268
Comerford, Lynn, 423, 424
Condron, Dennis J., 246
Confucius, 282
Conger, Katherine J., 345
Conger, Rand D., 345
Conley, Dalton, 253
Conlin, Michelle, 49, 91, 271*b*
Connell, R. W., 96
Conner, Karen A., 399, 484, 485, 489, 494, 496, 501, 502, 503, 504, 506
Connor, Peggy, 503
Constantine, Larry L., 34
Conte, Jon R., 375*n*
Contreras, Josefina M., 13
Conway-Giustra, Francine, 506
Cooley, Charles Horton, 2, 31, 31*n*, 32, 88

Cooney, Rosemary, 29, 355, 356
Coontz, Stephanie, 14, 16, 30, 155, 158, 158n, 160, 162, 163, 164, 165, 165n, 166, 168, 185, 190, 408, 409, 415, 416, 432, 445
Cooper, Al, 134
Cooper, Holly Cohen, 266
Cooper, Theresa, 503
Cooperman, Alan, 197b
Corley, M. D., 135
Correll, Shelley J., 270
Cose, Ellis, 270, 376, 409b
Cote, D., 397n
Cott, Nancy F., 42, 158n
Cotter, David A., 297
Cotton, Sheila R., 203, 209, 331
Cottrell, Ann Baker, 213
Cottrell, Barbara, 384
Couran, Gaynel, 17b
Couran, George, 17b
Cowan, C. P., 243
Cowan, G., 221b
Cowan, P. A., 243
Cowan, Ruth Schwartz, 307
Coward, Raymond T., 498, 503
Cowley, Geoffrey, 274
Cox, Adam J., 268n
Cox, Martha J., 270
Crabtree, Steve, 133
Craig, Stephen, 90
Craighill, Peyton, 202
Cramer, Duncan, 103, 111
Crary, David, 415
Crase, Kirsten Lee, 286
Crase, Sedahlia Jasper, 286
Cravens, Hamilton, 110n
Crawford, Duane W., 109, 228
Cresswell, Mark, 76n
Crick, Nicki R., 81
Crimmins, Eileen M., 486
Crittenden, Ann, 242
Crooks, Robert, 134, 135, 138
Crosbie-Burnett, Margaret, 59, 471
Crosby, Faye J., 270
Crosby, John F., 103, 110n, 112–114, 333, 336, 342, 345
Crosby, Lynn, 337b, 338n
Crosnoe, Robert, 275
Cross, Peter, 268n
Crouter, Ann C., 23, 34, 191, 195, 270, 274, 278, 300, 325, 347
Crowder, Kyle D., 50b, 219, 432
Crowell, Judith A., 211
Crowley, Ann, 506
Crowley, M. Sue, 272
Crowley, Martha, 171
Crumble, Joseph, 259
Cruz, J. Michael, 221b
Cuber, John, 142, 229
Cue, Kelly L., 221b
Cui, Ming, 339, 346
Cullen, Lisa T., 221
Culton, Linda S., 196
Cummings, E. Mark, 273, 273b, 393
Cunningham, Mick, 194
Cunningham-Burley, Sarah, 495
Curry, Mary, 503
Curtis, John W., 83, 84
Curtis, Kristen Taylor, 217
Custer, Lindsay, 324
Cutler, Neal, 500
Cyr, Mireille, 224

Dabbs, James, 37
Dabul, Amy J., 254
DaCosta, Kimberly McClain, 77b
Dahms, Alan M., 103, 104
Daibo, Ikuo, 107
Dailard, Cynthia, 146, 147
Dalaker, Joseph, 176, 178f
Dalley, Timothy J., 201
Dalphonse, Sherri, 243
Dalvi, Tapashi B., 501
Daly, Martin, 37, 382
Damiano-Teixeira, Karla M., 278
D'Amico, Jean, 62b
Dana, Ophelia, 60
Dance, Theodore, 267n
Dang, Alain, 140
Daniel, John, 500b
Daniels, Roger, 216
D'Antonio, W. V., 216
Danziger, Sandra K., 176, 406
Dao, James, 424
Darlin, Damon, 4
Darroch, Jacqueline E., 251, 252, 252n, 253
Darwin, Charles, 36n
Davey, Adam, 492, 503
Davey, Monica, 67
David, Deborah S., 79
Davidson, J. R., 219
Davies, Curt, 48
Davis, Erin Calhoun, 469
Davis, Fred, 32, 41
Davis, J., 69
Davis, Jessica, 49, 279
Davis, L., 135
Davis, Robert, 219
Davis, W., 435n
Dawkins, Richard, 36, 86, 125
Dawn, Laura, 5
Day, Jennifer Cheesman, 49, 279
Day, Randal D., 276
De-Ath, Erica, 469
de la Cruz, Patricia, 55n, 60, 61
de Santis, Marie, 371
De Vise, Daniel, 188
Dean, Claudia, 69
Dear, Greg E., 110n
DeBoer, Danielle B., 210, 418
DeClaire, Joan, 334b, 336, 340
Dee, Jonathan, 143
Deen, Michelle Radin, 7b
DeFrain, John, 287, 332b
del Pinal, Jorge, 215, 486, 487
Del Vecchio, Tamara, 274
DeLamater, John, 122, 138
DeLeire, Thomas, 169, 170, 190, 196
Dellmann-Jenkins, Mary, 497, 502
DeLone, Miriam, 56
DeMaria, Rita M., 227
DeMaris, Alfred, 111, 194, 223, 225, 352, 357, 360, 371, 462, 470, 474
Demian, 192b, 193b, 196, 197b, 199, 200, 200n
D'Emilio, John, 126, 127–128
Demo, David H., 270, 432, 433, 461
DeNavas-Walt, Carmen, 16b, 52, 52f, 53, 53f, 58, 60, 64, 65, 66, 67, 85f, 489
Denizet-Lewis, Benoit, 132, 132b, 133b, 140
Dentinger, Emma, 502
Depner, Charlene E., 435
Detzner, Daniel F., 63b
Deutsch, G., 86
DeVanas-Walt, Carmen, 52f

DeVaney, Sharon A., 491
Dewan, Shaila K., 261
Dey, Achintya N., 62b
Dicke, Amy, 107–108
Dickinson, Amy, 468, 470
Dickson, Fran C., 217
Diekman, Amanda, 81
Diemer, Matthew A., 113, 332b
Dindia, K., 339
Dinkmeyer, Don, Jr., 274
Dinkmeyer, Don, Sr., 274
Dion, Karen K., 160, 245
Dion, Kenneth L., 160
Dion, M. Robin, 174, 174n
DiPrete, Thomas, 427
DiStefano, Joseph, 172b
Doble, Richard deGaris, 115
Dodson, Jualynne E., 281
Doherty, William J., 164, 168, 280, 440
Doka, Kenneth J., 492
Dolan, Elizabeth M., 396, 403
Dolbin-MacNab, Megan L., 285
Dollahite, David C., 217
Domitrz, Michael J., 221b
Donahoe, Elizabeth, 496
Donahue, Elizabeth, 14, 17
Donnelly, Denise A., 379
Doolittle, Fred, 428
Dore, Margaret K., 435n
Dorman, Clive, 274
Dornbusch, Sanford M., 435
Dornfeld, Maude, 380
Dosani, Sabina, 268n
Dourleijn, Edith, 226
Dowd, James J., 102
Dowling, Cindy, 268
Downey, Douglas, 246, 247, 435
Downey, S., 439
Downs, Barbara, 239b, 250f, 298, 306, 322
Downs, Kimberly J. M., 29
Downs, William R., 380
Doyle, J., 95
Drake, Jennifer, 96
Dreby, Joanna, 317n
Dreifus, Claudia, 257
Driver, Janice L., 330, 334, 347
Drummet, Amy R., 396
Dubus, Nicole, 268
Duck, Steve W., 76, 333
Duenwald, Mary, 124b
Duffett, Ann, 266, 268f
Duffy, Roslyn, 267n
Dufur, Mikaela J., 274
Dugger, Celia W., 212
Dukes, Howard, 273b
Dumka, Larry E., 214
Duncan, Gabriel, 66
Dunleavy, Victoria Orrego, 220
Dunne, John E., 210
Dunnewind, Stephanie, 282
Dunson, David B., 245
Durkheim, Émile, 102, 148
Durose, Matthew R., 367, 369
Dush, Claire M. Kamp, 225, 226
Dutton, Donald G., 224, 371
Duvall, Evelyn M., 27
Dworkin, Shari L., 89
Dwyer, J. W., 502
Dye, Jane Lawler, 7b, 54, 195, 235, 236, 237, 246, 248, 285, 298, 303, 317
Dyk, Patricia H., 391
Dziecj, Billie Wright, 83

Eagly, Alice H., 81, 85, 86, 88
Early, Theresa J., 395
Easterlin, Richard, 236
Eaton, Danice K., 128, 128t, 146, 148
Eaton, Leslie, 439
Ebaugh, Helen Rose, 503
Eckholm, Eric, 26, 59n
Edgell, Penny, 70
Edin, Kathryn, 17, 175, 176, 214, 391
Edmonston, Barry, 4b, 54, 55n, 215, 218, 283
Edwards, Cody S., 133b
Edwards, John N., 42, 243, 380, 461
Edwards, Margie L. K., 406, 407
Eggebeen, David J., 503
Ehrenberg, Marion F., 272
Ehrenreich, Barbara, 278
Ehrensaft, Diane, 255, 272
Ehrhardt, Anke A., 104, 203
Eicher-Catt, Deborah, 435, 436b
Einstein, Elizabeth, 479
Eisenberg, Anne, 4b
Ekerdt, David, 492
El Nasser, Haya, 58, 59
El-Sheikh, Mona, 391
Elder, Glen H., Jr., 24b, 26, 48, 48n, 495, 501
Elfrink, Tim, 51b
Elias, Marilyn, 261, 420
Elicksen, Debbie, 268n
Elkind, David, 280
Ellard, John H., 373
Ellickson, Phyllis L., 210
Ellis, D., 370
Ellis, R. Darin, 499
Ellison, Christopher G., 217
Elrod, Linda D., 439
Emery, Clifton R., 250
Emery, Robert E., 423, 432, 433, 435
Emlen, Stephen T., 86
Emmers-Sommer, Tara M., 80
Emmons, R. A., 335
Enda, Jodi, 94
Engel, Marjorie, 470, 478n
Engels, Friedrich, 35, 417
England, Paula, 84, 132b, 133b, 295, 297
Enos, Sandra, 408b, 409b
Ephron, Dan, 51b
Ephron, Delia, 449
Epstein, Cynthia Fuchs, 81
Erba, Giuseppe, 407
Erera, Pauline, 464n
Erickson, Martha F., 266, 272
Erickson, Nancy S., 383
Erickson, Rebecca J., 435
Eriksen, Shelley, 493, 498
Erne, Diane, 383
Erwin, Cheryl, 267n
Eschbach, Karl, 220
Essex, Elizabeth L., 406, 484
Estenazi, Brenda, 244
Estes, Richard J., 322, 384
Estes, Sarah Beth, 323, 384
Etcheverry, Paul E., 105
Eveld, Edward M., 302
Evenson, Ranae J., 242
Eyster, Sandra L., 80, 308

Faber, Adele, 275b
Facteau, Lorna, 495
Fadiman, Anne, 237b
Fagan, Jay, 272
Fairchild, Emily, 346
Falbo, T., 246

Fancey, Pamela, 501
Fanshel, David, 65, 259
Farkas, Steve, 267, 268f
Fass, Paula S., 24b, 437
Fausto-Sterling, Anne, 78b
Fazio, Elena M., 169
Fea, Christopher B., 496
Feagin, Joe R., 284
Fears, Darryl, 59, 69
Feeney, Brooke C., 114
Fehr, Beverly, 104
Fehring, Richard, 70
Feigelman, W., 260
Feijoo, Ammie N., 146
Fein, Esther B., 405
Feldbau, Shari R., 377
Feldman, Pamela, 169
Feldman, Robert S., 88
Felmlee, Diane, 33, 216, 220
Feng, D., 109
Fennema, Elizabeth, 86
Fenton, Bruce, 192b
Fergusson, David M., 254, 254n
Fernandez-Kelly, Patricia, 60
Ferrante, Joan, 55n, 87
Ferrari, J. R., 335
Ferraro, Kathleen J., 194, 223, 224, 374,
    376, 376n
Ferree, Myra Marx, 325, 355, 366
Few, April L., 224
Fields, Jason, 3, 6b, 7b, 15b, 16, 16b, 61, 169,
    170, 170t, 176, 177, 187, 187t, 191, 194,
    195, 195f, 257, 271b, 285, 287, 298, 301,
    456, 458b, 459, 459f, 487, 487t, 492
Fierstein, Harvey, 143
Fiese, Barbara H., 39
Figley, Charles, 492
Fincham, F. D., 113
Fincham, Frank D., 227, 242, 338, 338n,
    345, 419
Fine, Mark A., 433, 456, 458b, 459, 460, 461,
    462, 463, 464, 468, 470, 474
Finer, Lawrence B., 128, 146, 251, 252, 253
Fingerhut, A., 129–130
Fingerhut, Adam, 199
Fingerman, Karen L., 460, 461, 493, 501
Fink, Paul J., 110n, 111
Finkel, Eli J., 109, 110n, 111
Finkelhor, David, 317n, 370, 380, 381,
    437, 503
Finkenauer, Katrin, 332b
Finley, Gordon E., 260, 474
Finz, Stacy, 193b
Fischer, J., 109
Fisher, Judith, 435
Fisher, Philip A., 469
Fishman, Ann, 58
Fitzpatrick, Mary Anne, 330, 331, 339, 341,
    344, 347
Fitzpatrick, Pamela J., 428
Fix, Michael, 63b
Flaherty, Mary Jean, 495
Flanagan, A. S., 113
Flanagan, Elizabeth, 391
Fleming, Julian, 382
Fletcher, Garth, 102, 113, 209
Flett, Gordon L., 330
Flinn, Mark V., 86, 87
Foley, Lara, 226b
Fomby, Paula, 433
Formichelli, Linda, 269
Formoso, Diana, 272

Fortinberry, Alicia, 267n
Foster, Craig, 38, 109, 110n, 111, 242, 243
Foster, E. Michael, 249
Foster, Joshua D., 111
Foust, Michael, 202
Fowler, Frieda, 275
Fox, Greer Litton, 24b, 268, 371, 391, 435
Fox, James Alan, 367
Fracher, Jeffrey, 125
Fraley, R. Chris, 269
Francis, Meagan, 237b
Franks, Melissa M., 406, 498
Franzetta, Kerry, 128, 251
Fraser, James, 226b
Frazer, Samjen, 140
Frazier, Patricia, 442
Fredriksen, Karen, 464n
Freedman, Deborah, 294
Freedman, Estelle B., 126, 127–128, 247
Freedman, V., 498, 504
Freeman, Jo, 364
Freese, Jeremy, 95
French, J. R. P., 352, 353t
Freud, Sigmund, 85, 123
Frey, Kurt, 107
Frey, William H., 67, 487
Friedan, Betty, 93
Friedman, Joel, 221b
Friedrich, William N., 122, 123f
Friel, Lisa V., 469
Frisco, Michelle, 309–310, 352, 357, 358
Fromby, Paul, 433
Fromm, Erich, 103, 114
Fromuth, Mary, 223
Frost, Jennifer J., 251
Fruhauf, Christine A., 498b
Fry, C. L., 502
Frye, Marilyn, 130
Fu, Xuanning, 218
Fuller, T. L., 113
Funk, Cary, 202
Furman, W., 113
Furstenberg, Frank F., Jr., 4–5, 5, 24b, 26,
    28–29, 146, 158, 160, 176, 178, 186,
    187, 188, 216, 250, 251, 270, 277, 287,
    391, 406, 420, 440, 474, 495, 496
Futris, Ted G., 272

Gable, Shelly, 333
Gaffney, Dennis, 65n
Gager, Constance T., 228
Gagnon, E., 307n
Gagnon, John H., 123, 126
Galinsky, Ellen, 318, 319, 323
Galinsky, M., 464
Gallagher, C., 215n, 216, 218
Gallagher, Maggie, 38, 445
Gallagher, Sally K., 70, 71, 360, 500
Gallo, Eileen, 267n, 268n
Gallo, Jon J., 267n, 268n
Gallup, George H., Jr., 160
Gallup, Gordon G., 370
Galper, J., 4b
Galvin, Shelley L., 111
Gamache, Susan J., 470
Gander, Anita, 492
Gandy, Kim, 83
Gangstad, Jack, 267n
Ganong, Lawrence H., 29, 203, 406, 424,
    456, 457, 458b, 459, 460, 461, 462, 464,
    465, 467, 468, 469, 469n, 470, 471, 473,
    474, 475, 478, 496, 502

Gans, Daphna, 498
Garcia-Beaulieu, Carmen, 295
Gardiner, Karen N., 173, 409b
Gardner, Jonathan, 420
Gardner, Richard, 434n
Gardner, Saundra, 28
Gardyn, Rebecca, 4b
Gareis, Karen, 266, 417
Garey, Anita I., 486
Garfinkel, Irwin, 428n
Garson, David G., 177
Garver, Patricia, 495
Gaston, Marie, 304b
Gaughan, Monica, 185
Gaunt, Ruth, 216
Gavin, Molly R., 496
Geary, David C., 86, 87
Geasler, Margie J., 439
Gecas, Viktor, 31n
Geen, Rob, 285, 286
Gelles, Richard J., 36, 173, 177, 367, 367n,
    370, 371, 375, 375n, 376, 380, 381, 382,
    383, 383n
Genovese, Thomas A., 469, 471, 478
George, William H., 221b
Gerard, Jean M., 273b
Gerena, Mariana, 57b, 67, 160, 161
Gerhard, Anna-Katharina, 346
Geronimus, Arline T., 250
Gerson, Kathleen, 96, 270, 300, 307, 310,
    311, 315, 358
Gerstel, Naomi, 57b, 67, 160, 161, 493, 498,
    499, 500
Ghimire, Dirgha J., 212
Giddens, Anthony, 166, 168, 179, 417
Gidycz, Christine A., 223, 224
Giele, Janet Z., 173
Giesen, Deirdre, 133, 134, 135, 194
Gilbert, C., 397n
Gilbert, Lucia Albino, 130
Gilbert, S., 276
Gilbert, William, 245
Gilbreth, Joan G., 435, 437, 450, 473
Giles-Sims, Jean, 280, 469
Gillespie, Dair, 355
Gillespie, Rosemary, 243
Gillham, Bill, 380
Gilligan, Carol, 92, 92n
Gilman, Lorraine C., 260
Gilmartin, B., 159b
Gilmore, David, 78
Ginott, Alice, 274, 276
Ginott, Haim G., 274, 276
Giordano, Peggy C., 133b, 220, 274
Girtner, Linda K., 437
Glaser, Barney, 405
Glaser, Karen, 169
Glass, Jennifer, 71, 303, 322, 323
Glass, Shirley, 135
Glassner, Barry, 24b
Glendon, Mary Ann, 426
Glenn, Norval, 133b, 208, 227, 243,
    417, 417n
Glick, Jennifer E., 161, 488
Glick, Paul, 187–188, 188, 189f
Glickauf-Hughes, Cheryl, 110n
Glink, Ilyce R., 335
Globerman, Judith, 306
Goddard, Wallace, 274, 276
Goff, Sissy, 268n
Goffman, Erving, 31n, 50b
Gold, J. M., 102

Gold, Steven J., 161
Goldberg, Abbie E., 199
Goldberg, Carey, 91, 92, 378
Goldin, Claudia, 298
Goldner, Virginia, 35
Goldscheider, Calvin, 188
Goldscheider, Frances, 10, 185, 188, 461
Goldstein, Arnold P., 383
Goldstein, Irwin, 124b
Goldstein, Joshua R., 69, 417–418
Goldstein, Sam, 274, 275, 277
Goldstein, Seth, 381n
Goldyn, Cheryl, 409b
Goleman, Daniel, 105, 148, 403
Golish, T., 462
Golombok, Susan, 8, 258b
Gomes, Charlene, 199
Gomes, Peter J., 158n
Gonzales, Nancy A., 281
Gonzalez, Cindy, 55n, 62b, 63b, 384
Gonzalez, Sandra, 34
Goode, Erica, 110n
Goode, William J., 29, 154, 160, 179,
    365–366, 371, 416, 446
Goodluck, Charlotte, 65
Goodman, Brenda, 112b, 112n
Goodman, Emma, 258b
Goodman, Matthew R., 422, 427, 435,
    440, 441
Goodstein, Laurie, 71, 201
Gordon, Jack D., 492
Gordon, Thomas, 289
Gorin, Stephen H., 506
Gorman, Jean Cheng, 284
Gorman, Mary Anne, 501
Gotlib, Ian H., 269
Gottesman, Karen, 268n
Gottlieb, Lori, 114, 116, 392, 406
Gottman, John M., 228, 330, 331, 332, 333,
    334, 334b, 336, 336n, 337b, 338, 338n,
    339b, 340, 341, 343, 344, 345, 347, 356,
    363, 375, 376
Gough, Brendan, 382
Gove, Walter R., 203, 420
Grady, Denise, 256
Graefe, Deborah R., 195
Grall, Timothy S., 428, 435, 440
Granger, Douglas A., 36, 37, 274
Grant, Lorrie, 58
Gratton, B., 487
Gray, Marjory Roberts, 274, 275
Greathouse, Ann N., 317
Greeley, Andrew, 70, 138, 490
Green, Adam Isaiah, 168
Green, Andrea J., 382
Greenberg, Jerrold S., 128, 254n
Greenberg, Susan H., 456
Greenberger, Ellen, 323
Greenblatt, Cathy Stein, 137, 138
Greenfield, Emily A., 287, 288
Greenfield, Patricia M., 276, 282
Greenhouse, Steven, 52
Greenspan, Stanley, 273
Greenstein, G., 193b
Greenwald, John, 497b
Gregoire, Thomas K., 395
Greif, Geoffrey, 435
Grekin, E. R., 395
Griffin, Dale W., 111, 114
Grimm-Thomas, Karen, 300
Grimsley, Kristen Downey, 300
Groat, Theodore, 241

Grogan-Kaylor, Andrew, 278
Gross, Harriet Engel, 316
Gross, Jane, 8, 143, 261, 322, 503, 506
Gross, Michael, 143
Grote, Nancy K., 308
Groze, V., 260
Grundy, Emily, 169
Grusky, David B., 76, 85
Guberman, Nancy, 397b, 502
Gudelunas, David, 196
Gueorguieva, Ralitza V., 250
Guilamo-Ramos, Vincent, 274
Gullickson, Aaron, 220
Gunderson, Amy, 4
Gunnoe, Marjorie, 276
Gupta, Sanjiv, 6b, 9, 445
Gurian, Michael, 90
Guyer, B., 250
Guzzo, Karen Benjamin, 251

Haas, Bruce, 33, 54
Haber, C., 487
Haberman, Clyde, 51b
Hacker, Jacob S., 50b
Hackstaff, Karla B., 166
Haddad, Yvonne Y., 71
Haffner, Debra W., 128, 254n
Hagan, Joseph R., Jr., 25b
Hagedoorn, Mariet, 490
Hagenbaugh, Barbara, 301
Hagestad, G., 306, 391
Hagewen, Kellie J., 236, 237b, 240, 241, 242,
    243, 246
Haines, James, 287
Hakim, Danny, 417n
Hale-Benson, J. E., 89
Hall, Edie Jo, 393
Hall, Elaine J., 94–95
Hall, Julie H., 227, 345, 419
Hall, Matthew, 414, 415, 415n, 417,
    418, 419
Haller, William, 60
Halli, Shiva, 194, 369
Halpern-Felsher, Bonnie L., 148
Halsall, Paul, 158
Hamachek, Don E., 112n
Hamby, Sherry L., 378
Hamer, Jennifer, 59
Hamilton, A., 286
Hamilton, Brady E., 7b, 58, 61, 64, 67, 70,
    83, 154f, 195, 234, 234f, 235, 238b, 238f,
    239b, 244, 247, 248, 248f, 250f
Hamilton, Hayley A., 469
Hamilton, W., 36
Hammack, Philip L., 395
Hammen, C., 395
Hammen, Constance, 393
Hammer, Heather, 437
Hammer, Leslie B., 496, 500
Hammersmith, Sue Kiefer, 124
Hamon, Raeann R., 161, 162, 488, 495
Hanawalt, Barbara, 42
Hanmer, Trudy J., 92
Hans, Jason D., 468, 470, 470n
Hansen, Donald A., 390, 398f, 400
Hansen, Gary L., 135
Hansen, M., 378
Haraway, Donna, 85
Harden, B., 283
Harden, Brenda Jones, 286
Hardesty, Jennifer L., 439
Haring, Michelle, 330

Harknett, Kristen, 69, 202, 251, 406
Harmanci, Reyhan, 216
Harmon, Amy, 256, 425
Harris, B., 499
Harris, C., 134
Harris, J., 89
Harris, Othello, 184
Harris, Philip M., 237b
Harris, Phyllis B., 500
Harris, S., 227
Harrist, Amanda W., 273b
Harroff, Peggy, 142, 229
Hartmann, Heidi, 297, 306
Hartnett, Kelley, 133, 134, 135
Hartocollis, Anemona, 201, 423
Hartog, Henrik, 42
Hartsoe, Steve, 158n, 190n
Harvey, E., 313
Harvey, K., 279
Harway, M., 378
Hasimoto, T., 162f
Haskell, Kari, 285
Haskins, Ron, 14, 17
Hatch, Laurie R., 490
Haub, Carl, 58, 60
Hawke, Sharryl, 246, 247
Hawkins, Alan J., 173, 304, 305, 308
Hawkins, Daniel N., 421
Hay, Elizabeth L., 501
Hayden, D., 307
Hayes, Cheryl D., 250
Hayghe, Howard, 302
Hayne, Dana L., 26
Haynes, Faustina E., 80
Haynie, Dayna L., 279
Hayslip, Bert, 285
Hazen, C., 113
He, Wan, 7b, 488
Heaton, Tim B., 210, 217, 218, 415, 417, 418, 420, 421
Heesink, Jose E. M., 272
Heim, Susan M., 268n, 269
Hein, Holly, 105, 111, 116
Heiss, Jerold, 104
Heller, Tamar, 395
Hench, David, 378
Hendershott, Anne, 316
Henderson, Tammy L., 424, 496
Hendrick, Clyde, 107–108
Hendrick, Susan S., 107–108, 139
Henley, Kari, 458b
Henley, Nancy, 364
Henly, Julia R., 176, 400
Henningson, Ellen, 502
Henretta, J. C., 498
Henshaw, Stanley K., 252, 252n, 253
Herbert, Tracy Bennett, 373
Hermsen, Joan M., 297
Hernandez, Raymond, 380, 384
Heron, Melanie, 49
Herring, Jeff, 160
Hertz, Rosanna, 249, 315, 316–317
Hetherington, E. Mavis, 208, 211, 418, 419, 420, 422, 432, 433, 442, 442b–443b, 443f, 459, 469
Hewitt, Paul L., 330
Hewlett, Sylvia Ann, 240, 245, 445
Heyman, Richard A., 337b, 373, 382
Heywood, Leslie, 96
Hickman, Rachel, 210, 219
Hicks-Patrick, Julie, 285
Hiedemann, Bridget, 420

Hiestand, Michele, 501
Higgs, Deborah C., 380
Hill, Jeffrey E., 304, 305
Hill, Jennifer, 319b
Hill, Laura E., 69
Hill, Nancy E., 214
Hill, Reuben, 28, 390, 398f, 400
Hill, Robert, 59, 270, 281, 286
Hill, Shirley A., 57b, 59, 60
Hilliard, Donnie, 332b, 404, 405
Himes, Christine L., 497, 504
Hines, Melissa, 87
Hinshaw, Stephen P., 407
Hirsch, Jennifer S., 64, 161
Hirschman, Linda, 427
Hitt, Jack, 66, 67
Hochschild, Arlie, 32, 54, 96, 302, 307, 308, 309, 310, 315, 324, 325, 358, 506
Hock, Ellen, 330
Hoelter, Lynette F., 212
Hofferth, Sandra L., 274, 279
Hoffman, Kristin, 380
Hoffman, Lois W., 241
Hoffman, Saul D., 249
Hogan, Dennis P., 27, 391, 393, 401
Hogben, Matthew, 224
Hojjat, Mahzad, 107, 114
Holloway, Lynette, 285
Holm, Kristen E., 393
Holmes, J. G., 344
Holmes, John G., 111, 114
Holmes, S., 254, 314
Holstege, H., 503
Homel, R., 89
Hondagneu-Sotelo, Pierrette, 63b, 64, 76, 80, 93, 96, 305b, 324
Hong, Junkuk, 406, 404
Hook, Misty K., 104
Hopper, Joseph, 422
Hornik, Donna, 462
Horowitz, A., 497
Horowitz, June Andrews, 71
Horwood, L. John, 254, 254n
Hotaling, Gerald, 317n
House, Anthony, 158, 158n
Houseknecht, Sharon K., 189, 243, 445
Houtman, Sally, 285
Houts, Leslie A., 148
Howard, J. A., 132
Howard, Theresa, 4b
Hsieh, K. H., 242
Huber, Joan, 240
Hudgins, Wren, 210
Hudspeth, Clarke D., 462
Huebner, Angela J., 392
Hueveline, Patrick, 190
Hughes, Debra K., 223
Hughes, Diane, 323
Hughes, Mary Elizabeth, 277
Hughes, Michael, 203, 420
Hughes, Mikayla, 133b, 220
Hughes, Patrick C., 217
Hulbert, Ann, 26
Hunt, Ashley N., 337b
Hunt, Gail, 498b
Hunt, Janet G., 315
Hunt, Larry L., 315
Hunter, Andrea G., 93, 94
Hurley, Dan, 414, 414n, 415n, 418
Hurst, Shannon R., 140
Hurwitt, Sam, 186
Huston, A. C., 89

Huston, Ted L., 176, 178, 185, 202, 227, 331, 331f, 332, 355
Hutchinson, Sally, 251
Huyck, M. H., 497
Hwang, Sean-Shong, 218
Hyde, Janet Shibley, 81, 81n, 86
Hymowitz, Kay, 57b

Iacuone, David, 204
Ihinger-Tallman, Marilyn, 461, 468, 479
Ikkink, Karen Klein, 504
Ingersoll-Dayton, Berrit, 496, 498, 499, 500
Ingoldsby, Bron B., 158, 161, 162, 211
Ingrassia, Michele, 259
Inman, Jessica, 268n
Irons, R. R., 135
Irving, Shelley, 414, 414n
Isaacs, Marla Beth, 430f, 475
Isaksen, Lise W., 500
Ishii-Kuntz, Masako, 64, 65, 355
Island, David, 224, 376, 377
Iverson-Gilbert, Judith, 396

Jacklin, Carol Nagy, 86
Jackson, Jeffrey B., 393
Jackson, Pamela Braboy, 27, 29
Jackson, Robert Max, 96–97, 165
Jackson, Shelly, 378
Jacobs, Andres, 189
Jacobs, Jerry A., 310, 311, 315, 358
Jacobson, Cardell K., 220
Jacobson, Neil S., 336, 344, 375–376
Jacoby, Susan, 138, 490
Jaksch, Mary, 102, 103, 116
James, Angela D., 60
Jankowski, Thomas B., 502
Janofsky, Michael, 10
Janus, Alex, 49, 279
Jaret, Charles, 110n, 112b, 112n
Jarrett, Robin L., 396
Jarrott, Shannon E., 498b
Jasinski, Jana L., 370
Jay, David, 124b
Jayakody, R., 277
Jayson, Sharon, 29, 69, 190n
Jefferson, Stephanie M., 396
Jeffries, Vincent, 117
Jenks, R. L., 159b
Jennings, Susan, 287
Jepsen, Christopher A., 191, 214
Jepsen, Lisa K., 191, 214
Jervey, Gay, 268
Jo, Moon H., 63b
Jobalia, Shilpa, 478
Jodl, K. M., 469
Joest, Karen, 409b
Johann, Sara Lee, 371, 373
Johannson, Melanie A., 378
John, Daphne, 307, 308
John, R., 281
Johnson, Bryan R., 220
Johnson, C., 424, 425
Johnson, David R., 36, 42, 309, 359, 417
Johnson, Dirk, 68, 159b, 309
Johnson, Earl S., 428
Johnson, Elizabeth M., 355
Johnson, Hans, 69
Johnson, Jason B., 277, 406
Johnson, Jean, 267, 268f
Johnson, Julia Overturf, 298, 301, 303, 306, 317–318, 322

Johnson, K., 111
Johnson, Kirk A., 148
Johnson, Lyndon, 177, 177*n*
Johnson, Matthew D., 228
Johnson, Michael P., 194, 223, 224, 344, 371, 374, 376, 376*n*
Johnson, P., 308, 324
Johnson, Richard W., 499, 501
Johnson, Robert, 144*b*
Johnson, S., 198
Johnson, Tallese, 54, 317
Johnson, Thomas W., 29
Johnson, Virginia E., 122, 138, 140, 141, 142, 336
Johnson-Sumerford, Danette, 109, 325, 355, 366
Johnston, Janet, 437
Jones, A. J., 464
Jones, B. J., 65
Jones, C., 240
Jones, D., 211, 212
Jones, Damon, 249
Jones, Jeffrey M., 220, 225
Jones, Jo, 124, 124*b*, 134, 136*b*, 139, 146, 255
Jones, Lisa M., 381
Jones, Matthew, 268*n*
Jones, Nicholas A., 54, 68*n*, 69, 237*b*
Jones, Rachel K., 252*n*, 253
Jones, Rebecca, 110*n*
Jones, Teresa C., 505
Jones-Sanpei, Hinckley, 405, 406
Jong-Fast, Molly, 29, 245
Joseph, Elizabeth, 159*b*
Joseph, Nadine, 487*n*
Jourard, Sidney, 229
Joyce, Amy, 84, 129, 237*b*, 306, 322, 323
Joyner, Kara, 139, 218
Juffer, Femmie, 261
Julian, Teresa W., 280
Junn, Ellen Nan, 274

Kader, Samuel, 196*n*
Kahn, Arif Shamim, 217
Kahn, Arnold S., 133*b*
Kahn, Joan P., 426, 428
Kahn, Lawrence M., 84, 85, 297
Kalil, Ariel, 169, 170, 190, 196, 277
Kalish, Susan, 282
Kalmijn, Matthijs, 215, 217, 218
Kamo, Yoshinori, 406, 499
Kan, Marni L., 220
Kane, Emily W., 80, 93
Kanemasa, Yuji, 107
Kann, Mark, 95
Kantor, D., 34
Kantor, Glenda Kaufman, 370
Kantor, Jodi, 76*b*–77*b*
Kantrowitz, Barbara, 274, 280, 287
Kao, Grace, 218
Kaplan, Karen, 125
Kaplan, M., 213
Kaplan-Leiserson, Eva, 500
Karaban, Tevfik Fikret, 346
Karasik, Rona J., 488, 495
Karen, R., 273
Karenga, Ron, 33*b*
Karney, Benjamin R., 208, 227, 331
Katz, Jon, 4*b*
Katz, Lillian, 111
Katz, Lynn F., 273*b*
Katz, Ruth, 310

Kaufman, Gayle, 288, 301, 490, 493, 494
Kaufman, Leslie, 383, 435*n*
Kaufman, Robert L., 59
Kaukinen, Catherine, 370, 371
Kaye, Sarah, 209
Kazdin, Alan E., 276, 277
Keefe, Janice, 501
Kefalas, Maria, 17, 175, 176, 391
Keith, Bruce, 42, 303, 306
Keith, Timothy Z., 438
Keller, Harold, 383
Kellner, Hansfried, 32, 102*n*
Kellogg, Susan, 48*n*
Kelly, Joan, 429, 433, 435, 437, 439
Kelly, John, 210, 422, 432, 433, 442
Kelly, Robert F., 435
Kempe, C. Henry, 367*n*
Kenney, Catherine, 194, 359, 370
Kent, Mary, 62*b*
Kent, Mary M., 55*n*
Kephart, William, 188*n*
Kern, Louis J., 188*n*
Kerpelman, Jennifer L., 393
Kershaw, Sarah, 65, 66, 67, 504
Kessler, Ronald C., 420
Ketcham, Katherine, 102, 104, 117
Keysar, Ariela, 70*n*
Khaleque, Abdul, 273
Kheshgi-Genovese, Zareena, 469, 470, 471, 478
Kibria, Nazli, 63*b*, 284
Kiecolt, K. Jill, 310, 325
Kiernan, Kathleen, 190, 191, 420
Kiger, Gary, 308
Kilbourne, Jean, 90
Killian, Timothy, 502
Kim, Haejeong, 491
Kim, K. Hyoun, 169, 194, 203, 337*b*, 338*n*
Kimmel, Michael S., 86, 88, 92, 95, 96, 125, 374, 375, 376, 439
Kimmel, Tim, 267*n*
Kimura, Doreen, 86
Kindlon, Dan, 89, 90, 92
King, Deborah A., 505
King, R. B., 241
King, Valarie, 189, 190, 194, 195, 437, 494, 495
Kinsey, Alfred, 123, 136*b*
Kirby, Carrie, 222
Kirby, Douglas, 147, 148
Kirmeyer, Sharon, 235, 244
Kirn, Walter, 280
Kitano, Harry, 216
Kitson, Gay C., 419
Kivel, Paul, 377
Klackenberg, G., 242
Kleiman, Carol, 297
Klein, Barbara Schave, 268*n*
Klein, David M., 10*b*
Klein, R. C., 344
Klein, Shirley, 405
Kleinbaum, Stacey, 226
Kleinfield, N. R., 450
Kliman, Jodie, 49
Klohnen, Eva A., 222
Kluger, Jeffrey, 106
Kluwer, Esther S., 272
Knab, Jean, 251, 406
Knapp, Caroline, 4*b*
Knipscheer, Kees, 504
Knobloch, Leanne K., 222
Knoester, Chris, 26, 279, 417, 418, 419

Knox, David, 226*b*, 246, 247
Knox, N., 261
Knudson-Martin, Carmen, 227, 366
Koblinsky, Sally A., 24*b*, 391
Koch, Wendy, 428*n*
Koenig, Larry J., 268*n*
Kohlberg, Lawrence, 87
Kohler, Julie K., 192*b*
Kolata, Gina, 143, 258*b*, 500
Kolodny, Robert C., 142, 336
Komsi, Nina, 269
Komter, A., 356
Konner, Melvin, 130
Konrad, Thomas R., 177
Koop, C. Everett, 146
Koplan, Jeffrey, 267
Kopytoff, Verne, 222
Korbin, Jill, 503
Kosmin, Barry A., 70*n*
Koss, Mary P., 224
Kost, Kathleen A., 270
Kramer, Norman, 34
Krantzler, Mel, 441
Kravets, David, 428
Kreider, Rose M., 7*b*, 15*b*, 16, 16*b*, 169, 170, 170*t*, 176, 177, 195, 257, 258, 414*n*, 415, 419, 456, 458*b*, 459, 459*f*
Krementz, Jill, 430*b*–431*b*, 438
Krishnakumar, Ambika, 273*b*
Krivo, Lauren J., 59
Kroll, Leon, 126*b*
Kroska, Amy, 307
Krotkoff, L. J., 336, 344
Krueger, A., 301
Krueger, Joachim, 112*b*
Krugman, Paul, 52, 63*n*
Kruttschnitt, Candace, 380
Kuchment, Anna, 268, 456
Kuczynski, Alex, 450
Kulczycki, Andrzej, 215
Kurcinka, Mary S., 268*n*
Kurdek, Lawrence, 129*n*, 130, 196–197, 197*b*, 198, 203, 208*n*, 209, 224, 228, 310, 338, 377, 420, 463, 464, 470
Kurtz, Stanley, 159*b*, 201*n*
Kurz, Demie, 24*b*, 26, 375, 376
Kutner, Lawrence, 288, 305
Kvisto, Peter, 344

Lacey, Rachel Saul, 107, 208, 261
Lackey, Chad, 378
Ladner, Joyce A., 282
Lalasz, Robert, 62*b*
Lally, Catherine F., 222
Lamanna, Mary Ann, 241, 259, 353*t*
Lamb, Kathleen A., 170, 194, 196
Lamb, Michael E., 433, 437, 439
Lamb, Vicki L., 92
Lambert, James D., 501, 502
Lambert, Nathaniel M., 217
Lambert, Tracy A., 133*b*
Lambert-Shute, Jennifer, 409*b*
Lamke, Leanne K., 374, 374*f*
Lammers, Jan, 217
Lamon, Susan, 86
Lan, Pei-Chia, 504
Lancaster, Jane B., 36
Land, Kenneth C., 92, 486
Landale, Nancy S., 60, 61, 64, 191*b*
Landry-Meyer, Laura, 285
Lane, Wendy G., 381
Laner, Mary Riege, 76*n*, 78*b*

Lang, Ariella, 392
Lang, Nancy, 492
Langer, Ellen J., 228
Langhinrichsen-Rohling, Jennifer, 226b
Lannon, Richard, 102, 103, 116, 117
Lansford, Jennifer E., 278
Lareau, Annette, 54, 57b, 279, 280
Laris, B. A., 147, 148
LaRossa, Ralph, 32, 355
Larson, Jeffry H., 140, 208, 210, 211, 219
Larzelere, Robert E., 276
Lasch, Christopher, 164, 166
Laslett, Peter, 42
Laszloffy, Tracey A., 282
Lau, Anna S., 282
Laub, G., 131
Laumann, Edward O., 127, 128, 130, 131, 133, 134, 134n, 136, 136b, 139, 380
Laurenceau, Jean-Phillippe, 220
Lauro, Patricia Winters, 8b
Lavee, Yoav, 310
Lavietes, Stuart, 435n
Lavin, Judy, 472b, 479
Lawler, Edward J., 176n
Lawler, Michael G., 217, 228
Lawrance, K., 125
Lawson, Willow, 111, 112n, 116, 333
Le, Benjamin, 105
Leavitt, Paul, 383
LeBlanc, Allen J., 502
LeBlanc, Steve, 196, 199
Lee, Cameron, 396
Lee, Carol E., 247, 247b
Lee, Cheryl Hill, 16b, 52, 52f, 53, 53f, 58, 60, 64, 65, 66, 67, 85f
Lee, Doris, 306b
Lee, Ellie, 254
Lee, Eunju, 161, 499
Lee, F. R., 283
Lee, G. L., 114
Lee, Gary R., 194, 213, 217, 498, 502, 503
Lee, Jennifer, 495
Lee, John Alan, 106–107, 108
Lee, M-Y., 432, 438, 439
Lee, Sharon M., 54, 55n, 64, 215, 216, 218, 283
Lee, Yongwoo, 169, 177, 178
Leff, Lisa, 201
Lehr, William, 34
Leigh, Suzanne, 256
Leinwand, Donna, 24b
Leite, Randall, 393, 436
Leland, John, 66
Leman, Kevin, 268n
LeMasters, E. E., 287, 421
Lento, Jennifer, 223, 224
Leonhardt, David, 51, 52, 54, 84, 176, 420
Lerner, H., 342, 343, 344
Lerner, S., 78b
Letellier, Patrick, 224, 376, 377
Letiecz, Bethany L., 24b
Levenson, Robert W., 228, 330, 331, 332, 333, 336, 338, 338n
Leventhal, Tama, 278
Levin, Irene, 465, 473
Levine, Ann, 428
Levine, Carol, 498b
Levine, James, 435
Levine, Judith A., 250
Levine, Madeline, 57b
Levine, Robert, 162, 162f
Levine, Stephen B., 135, 490

Levinger, George, 419
Levy, D., 203
Lewin, Tamar, 83, 84, 216, 259, 322, 323, 445
Lewis, Catherine C., 319b
Lewis, Edith, 59
Lewis, Julia M., 422, 429
Lewis, Robert, 268n
Lewis, Susan K., 189
Lewis, Thomas, 102, 103, 116, 117
Lewis-Smith, Jamie, 220
Lewontin, Richard, 146
L'Heureux-Dubé, Claire, 429
Li, Wei, 501
Libby, Roger W., 132b
Lichter, Daniel T., 64, 69, 156b, 171, 195, 214, 218, 218n, 225
Lieblich, Julia, 283
Liefbroer, Art C., 226, 492
Lin, Chien, 161
Lin, I-Fen, 36, 469
Lin, Sung-Ling, 187–188, 188
Lincoln, Karen D., 406
Lindberg, Laura Duberstein, 146, 147
Lindsey, Elizabeth, 400b–401b
Lindsey, Eric W., 269, 272
Lino, Mark, 242
Lipe, Emily, 475
Lipman, Joanne, 305b
Lips, Hilary M., 90
Liptak, Adam, 383
Liu, Chien, 134
Liu, William T., 161
Liverman, Catharyn T., 267
Lloyd, Kim M., 191b
Lobiondo-Wood, Geri, 395
Lobo, Arun Peter, 215
Lobo, Susan, 66, 67
Locke, Harvey, 2, 3, 165
Lockhart, Charles, 280
Lofas, Jeannette, 472b
Loftus, Jeni, 129
Logan, John R., 161, 499, 504
Lohr, Steve, 52
London, Andrew S., 373
Long, Edgar C. J., 346
Long, George, 165
Longman, Phillip J., 242
Longmore, Monica A., 111, 133b, 220, 274
Lorenz, Frederick O., 132
Loseke, Donileen R., 375, 389n
Losh-Hesselbart, Susan, 87
Lott, Juanita Tamayo, 64, 65
Love, Jeff, 40
Love, Patricia, 105, 106, 114, 115–116
Lovell, Vicky, 297
Lowenstein, Roger, 63n
Lu, Hsien-Hen, 16b, 161, 194, 225
Lublin, Joann S., 316
Lucas, Jacqueline Wilson, 62b
Luepnitz, Deborah Anne, 435
Lugaila, Terry, 62b, 66, 156b, 184, 195, 415, 416f
Lugo Steidel, Angel G., 13
Luke, Carmen, 282
Lukemeyer, Anna, 278
Luker, Kristin, 240
Lundquist, Jennifer Hickes, 50b, 56
Luschen, Kristen, 308
Luscher, Kurt, 287
Lussier, Gretchen, 424
Lussier, Yvan, 330
Luster, Tom, 33, 54, 278, 380

Lustig, Daniel C., 404
Luthar, Suniya, 27, 54
Luthra, Rohini, 223, 224
Lye, Diane N., 444
Lyman, Rick, 52
Lyman, Stanford M., 31n
Lynch, Jean M., 464n
Lynch, Scott M., 204
Lyons, Linda, 179, 189, 204
Lyons, Nona P., 92

MacCallum, Fiona, 258b
Maccoby, Eleanor, 26, 86–87, 89, 319b, 435, 439
MacDonald, Cameron L., 77b, 305b
MacDonald, William L., 225, 462, 470, 474
MacDorman, Marian F., 58, 61, 64, 66
MacFarquhar, Neil, 211, 213
Machir, John, 497, 502
Macionis, John J., 38
Mackay, Judith, 122, 125, 133, 414
Mackey, Richard A., 113, 332b, 340
Macklin, Eleanor D., 159b
MacQuarrie, Brian, 50b
Madathil, Jayamala, 212
Madden-Derdich, Debra A., 449
Maddock, James W., 222
Madrigal, Luke, 65
Madsen, William, 49
Magdol, Lynn, 194, 368
Magee, Susan, 343
Mahoney, Anne Rankin, 227, 366
Mahoney, Annette, 217
Mahoney, Margaret M., 470
Mahoney, P., 370
Main, M., 209
Mainemer, Henry, 260
Majors, Richard G., 79
Makepeace, James M., 224
Malakh-Pines, Ayala, 222
Malia, Sarah E., 467, 468, 468n, 470n
Maneker, Jerry S., 217
Manis, Jean B., 241
Manlove, Jennifer, 128, 251
Manning, Wendy D., 133b, 170, 171, 176, 179, 189, 190, 191b, 195, 196, 214, 220, 248, 274, 436, 445, 470
Mannis, Valerie S., 249
Mansnerus, Laura, 240
Manton, Kenneth G., 486
Marano, Hara Estroff, 122, 459
Marchand, Jennifer F., 330
Marchione, Marilynn, 256, 258b
Mare, Robert D., 59
Marech, Rona, 211
Marenco, Anne, 494, 495
Margolin, Leslie, 382
Marin, Rick, 302
Marini, Margaret Mooney, 80
Markman, Howard J., 210, 226, 227, 229, 334b, 346
Marks, Nadine F., 287, 288, 501, 502
Marks, S., 27, 331
Markstrom-Adams, Carol, 407
Markway, Barbara, 267n, 268n
Markway, Gregory, 267n, 268n
Marlow, Lenard, 423
Marquardt, Elizabeth, 133b, 159b, 168
Marriott, Michael, 24b
Marschark, Marc, 268n
Marshall, Carolyn, 51b
Marshall, Susan E., 94

Marsiglio, William, 251, 270, 437, 465
Martin, C. L., 89
Martin, Clyde E., 136*b*
Martin, John Levi, 32, 214
Martin, Joyce A., 7*b*, 56*f*, 58, 61, 64, 66, 67, 70, 234*f*, 235, 238*b*, 238*f*, 239*b*, 244, 247, 248, 248*f*, 250, 250*f*
Martin, Philip, 62*b*, 63*b*
Martin, S., 370
Martin, Steven P., 414
Martinez, Gladys M., 235, 242, 243, 244, 249, 255
Martinez, Sylvia, 60
Martino, Steven C., 210
Martinovich, Zoran, 111
Marx, Karl, 35, 417
Masanori, Ishimori, 107
Maslow, Abraham H., 103
Mason, Heather, 133
Mason, Karen A., 409*b*
Mason, Mary Ann, 409, 435, 462, 467, 468, 469, 470
Massinga, Ruth, 286
Masters, Coco, 4*b*
Masters, William H., 122, 138, 140, 141, 142, 336
Masuda, Masahiro, 449
Mather, Mark, 26, 278
Mathews, T. J., 58, 61, 64, 65, 66, 83, 250*f*
Mattessich, Paul, 28
Matthaei, Julie, 93
Matthews, Anne Martin, 255
Matthews, Ralph, 255
Mattingly, Marybeth J., 271*f*, 309
Mauldon, Jane, 250
May, Rollo, 102, 103, 104
Mayer, Egon, 70*n*
Mays, Vickie M., 140
Mazlish, Elaine, 275*b*
McAdoo, Harriette Pipes, 172*b*
McBride-Chang, Catherine, 282
McCabe, Marita P., 191
McClusky, Tom, 201
McCone, David, 50*b*
McCormick, Richard A., 257*n*
McCoy, J. Kelly, 402
McCracken, Coleen, 276
McCubbin, Hamilton I., 390, 397, 400, 402, 404, 405, 406, 407
McCubbin, Marilyn A., 390, 397, 399, 402, 404, 405, 407
McCullough, Lawrence, 78*b*
McDermott, Monica, 68
McDonald, Katrina Bell, 285
McDonald, Merrilyn, 381*n*
McDonald, Thomas P., 395
McDuff, Pierre, 224
McFadyen, Jennifer M., 393
McGhee, Charles, 395
McGinn, Daniel, 210, 301, 306
McGinnis, Sandra L., 186
McGoldrick, Monica, 29, 390, 403, 403*n*
McGuigan, William, 407
McHale, Susan M., 89, 274, 325
McHugh, Maureen, 473
McKay, Gary D., 274
McKelvey, Mary W., 280
McKenry, Patrick C., 169, 194, 203, 280, 436
McLanahan, Sara, 14, 17, 36, 169, 170, 185, 214, 249, 370, 409*b*, 428*n*, 429, 432, 468, 469
McLeod, Jane D., 380

McLoyd, Vonnie C., 59, 61, 80, 276, 281, 282, 283, 284
McMahon, Catherine A., 258*b*
McMahon, Martha, 241
McManus, Mike, 408*b*
McManus, Patricia A., 427
McNamara, Justine M., 489
McNicholas, J., 4*b*
McPherson, Miller, 26
Mead, George Herbert, 31, 31*n*, 88, 89
Meadows, Sarah O., 92
Means-Christensen, Adrienne J., 198
Meckler, Laura, 174
Meezan, William, 199–200
Mehrota, Meela, 372
Meilander, Gilbert, 257*n*
Mellott, Leanna M., 214, 225
Melz, Heidi, 176, 178, 185, 202, 227, 331, 331*f*, 332
Memmott, Mark, 384
Menacker, Fay, 61, 235, 244
Mendelsohn, Gerald A., 222
Menjívar, Cecilia, 372
Merkle, Erich R., 222
Merrill, Lex, 224
Merryman, Ashley, 184
Messner, Michael A., 63*b*, 64, 76, 79, 80, 89, 93, 96, 324
Meyer, Daniel R., 428, 428*n*, 489*n*
Meyer, Madonna H., 488, 488*n*, 489, 506
Meyer, Walter J. III, 380
Meyers, Marcia K., 278
Meyers, Nancy A., 373
Midgley, Elizabeth, 62*b*, 63*b*
Mikach, Sarah, 125
Milardo, Robert M., 161, 406
Milddlemiss, Wendy, 407
Milkie, Melissa A., 77, 94, 169, 242, 266, 270, 271*f*, 272, 309, 310, 311, 314, 314*f*, 358
Miller, Brenda A., 380
Miller, Brent C., 27, 259, 304, 305
Miller, Courtney Waite, 338*n*
Miller, Dawn, 456, 478*n*, 479
Miller, Dorothy, 67
Miller, Elizabeth, 70
Miller, Laurie C., 261
Miller, Marshall, 191
Miller, R. Robin, 184
Miller, Richard B., 478
Miller, Sheila J., 417
Miller, Stephanie Hotta, 392
Miller, Timothy, 189
Mills, C. Wright, 9, 422*n*
Mills, Terry L., 496, 501
Min, Pyong Gap, 371
Mincy, Ronald B., 299
Miniño, Arialdi M., 49
Minnes, P., 393
Mintz, Steven, 48*n*, 266
Mitchell-Kernan, C., 80, 300
Mize, Jacquelyn, 272
Mnookin, Robert, 439
Moen, Phyllis, 279, 491, 492
Mohr, Sharon, 221*b*
Molyneux, Guy, 278
Monahan Lang, Molly, 312
Monestero, Nancy, 142
Money, John, 78*b*
Monk, Gerald, 343
Monk, Peter, 384
Monroe, Michael, 203

Monroe, Pamela A., 278
Montalvo, Braulio, 430*f*, 475
Montanelli, Dale S., 405
Montgomery, Marilyn, 106, 109
Moody, Harry R., 487, 491, 492, 497*b*
Moore, David W., 70, 184, 298
Moore, Henry Spencer, 234*b*
Moore, Joan, 59, 59*n*
Moore, Kathleen A., 191
Moore, T., 284
Moorman, Sara M., 460, 461, 493
Moran, Patricia B., 424
Moran, Rachel F., 220
Moretti, Robb, 24*b*
Morford, Mark, 202*n*
Morgan, S. Philip, 236, 237*b*, 240, 241, 242, 243, 246, 250
Morris, A. S., 274
Morris, Anne, 323
Morris, Frank, 51*b*
Morrison, D. R., 468
Morrison, Donna, 432, 460
Morrison, Kelly, 133*b*, 220
Morrow, Lance, 260
Mortenson, Thor, 91
Mosher, William D., 6*b*, 7*b*, 124, 124*b*, 134, 136*b*, 139, 146, 172*b*, 208, 210, 255, 456, 457, 458*b*, 462
Mott, Mary Ann, 4*b*
Mouradian, Vera E., 276
Mueller, Karla A., 236, 237*b*, 240
Mueller, Margaret M., 495
Mullen, Paul, 382
Muller, Chandra, 303, 313
Mulrine, Anna, 222
Mumola, Christopher J., 408*b*
Munson, Martha, 154*f*
Murdock, George P., 2
Murkoff, Heidi, 268
Murphy, Dean E., 51*b*
Murphy, Jessica C., 396, 403
Murphy, Mike, 169
Murray, Bob, 267*n*
Murray, Christine E., 227
Murray, Kim, 464*n*
Murray, Sandra L., 111, 114, 344
Murray, Thomas L., Jr., 227
Murry, Velma M., 395
Musick, Kelly, 195, 249
Mustafa, Nadia, 65
Mustillo, Sarah, 204
Mutchler, Jan E., 503
Mutsaers, Wim, 461
Myers, Daniel J., 95
Myers, David, 80, 81, 86, 201
Myers, Jane E., 212
Myers, M., 440
Myers, Scott M., 217
Myers-Walls, Judith, 25*b*, 396

Nachshen, J. S., 393
Naiditch, Linda, 498*b*
Nakonezny, P. A., 417*n*
Nash, J. Madeleine, 267
Nath, Leda E., 71, 81
Navarro, Mireya, 61, 63*b*
Naylor, Kristen E., 308
Nazario, Sonia L., 259
Neal, Margaret B., 496, 500
Needle, Richard, 440
Neely, Marjory, 287
Negy, Charles, 198

Neimark, Jill, 109, 111, 112n, 116
Nelsen, Jane, 267n
Nelson, John, 51b
Nelson, Sandi, 175
Nelson, Todd D., 506
Netzer, Julie K., 498
Neuman, W. Lawrence, 337b
Nevius, C. W., 287
Newman, Andrew Adam, 4b
Newman, Barbara M., 285
Newman, Louis, 257n
Newport, Frank, 200
Newton, Phyllis J., 373
Nippert-Eng, Christena E., 32, 308
Nixon, Ron, 259, 260
Nock, Steven L., 17, 79, 97, 173, 179, 243,
    250, 356, 360–361, 362, 444
Nolan, David, 253
Noland, Virginia, 380
Noller, Patricia, 331, 339, 344, 347
Nomaguchi, Kei M., 242
Nord, Christine Winquist, 428
Nordwall, Smita P., 383
Norris, Jeanette, 221b
Norton, Arthur J., 189f
Notarius, Clifford I., 336, 338, 338n
Novak, M., 497
Nyman, C., 359
Nystrom, Nancy M., 505

Oakley, Ann, 76n
Obejas, Achy, 376, 377
O'Brien, Bernard A., 113, 332b, 340
O'Brien, Karen M., 259
O'Brien, Marion, 34, 89, 395, 397
O'Connell, Martin, 6b, 69, 189f, 195f,
    302, 459
O'Connor, Anahad, 122, 144b
O'Connor, Brian, 227, 228
O'Connor, Elizabeth, 198
O'Connor, Michael, 384
O'Donnell, Kathy, 50b
O'Donnell, Michelle, 76, 299, 300
O'Donoghue, Margaret, 282
Offer, Shira, 176, 406
Ogunwole, Stella U., 66, 67
O'Hare, William P., 215, 278
O'Laughlin, E., 395
Oldham, Charlene, 297
O'Leary, K. Daniel, 377
O'Leary, Susan C., 274
Oliker, Stacey J., 270, 279, 306, 496, 497,
    499, 500, 502, 506
Olmsted, Maureen E., 211
Olson, Chad D., 393
Olson, David, 227, 346
Olson, M., 135
O'Malley, Jaclyn, 254
O'Neil, Robin, 323
O'Neill, George, 12f
O'Neill, Grace, 6b
O'Neill, Nena, 12f
Ooms, Theodora, 173, 174, 174n, 227, 373
Oppenheim, Keith, 257
Oppenheimer, Valerie Kincade, 176, 214,
    299, 416
O'Rand, Angela M., 420
Orbuch, Terri L., 80, 308, 324
Orchard, Ann L., 473
Orenstein, Peggy, 90, 297
Oropesa, R. S., 60, 61, 64, 156b, 191b
Orthner, Dennis K., 405, 406

Osment, Steven, 42
Osmond, Marie Withers, 35
Ostrove, Joan M., 169
Oswald, Andrew J., 133, 420
Oswald, Debra L., 108
Oswald, Ramona F., 196
Otis, Melanie D., 198
Ott, Mary A., 148
Overturf, Julia, 62b, 66, 195, 415, 416f
Owen, Stephen S., 198
Owens, Ann, 60
Owens, Timothy J., 110n
Ozawa, Martha N., 169, 177, 178

Pabst, Mary S., 435
Padavic, Irene, 317
Paden, Shelley L., 324
Page, Jessica R., 111
Page, Susan, 197b
Pahl, Jan, 358
Painter, Kim, 83
Palkovitz, Rob, 300
Pallotta, Nicole R., 102
Papernow, P., 478
Parashar, Sangeeta, 414
Parcel, Toby L., 274
Pardue, Melissa E., 174
Paris, Ruth, 268
Park, Kristin, 32, 240, 243
Parke, Mary, 432
Parke, R. D., 269
Parker, A., 4b
Parker, K., 113
Parsons, Talcott, 31, 160–161
Paset, Pamela S., 219
Pasley, Kay, 272, 432, 436, 458b, 460, 461,
    468, 468n, 475, 479
Passno, Diane, 94
Pathman, Donald E., 177
Patterson, Charlotte J., 198, 199, 200,
    258b, 325
Patterson, Joan M., 390, 391, 393, 398, 400,
    402, 402b, 403, 404, 407
Pattillo-McCoy, Mary, 59, 60
Paul, Annie Murphy, 53, 243
Paul, Pamela, 2
Paul, Rhea, 304b
Pavalko, Eliza K., 307, 308, 308n, 309
Payne, Chris, 270
Pearlin, Leonard I., 217
Pearson, Jessica, 428, 436
Peck, P., 404
Peck, Scott M., 102, 105, 114
Peck, Sharon, 105, 114
Pecora, Peter J., 286
Peek, Chuck W., 503
Peele, Thomas, 202
Pelosi, Nancy, 81–82, 82b
Peltola, Pia, 94
Pendley, Elisabeth, 229
Peplau, Letitia A., 129–130, 199
Peralta, Robert L., 221b
Perez, Lisandro, 61
Perkins, Daniel F., 51b
Perlis, Linda, 267n
Perrin, Ellen C., 199, 200
Perrine, Stephen, 436
Perry, Andrea, 223
Perry-Jenkins, Maureen, 300
Pertman, Adam, 259
Pesquera, Beatriz M., 93
Peters, Arnold, 492

Peters, Jeremy W., 51, 52
Peters, Marie F., 281, 284
Peters, N. D., 501
Petersen, Larry R., 216
Peterson, Gary W., 276, 400
Peterson, Iver, 131, 240
Peterson, James L., 428
Peterson, Karen S., 193b, 307, 308, 309,
    421, 426n
Peterson, Richard R., 307
Peterson, Rick, 392
Pett, Marjorie A., 492
Peyser, Marc, 484
Pezzin, Liliana E., 504
Phillips, Cynthia L., 166
Phillips, Deborah, 317, 321b
Phillips, Julie A., 61, 225, 226, 419
Phillips, L., 502
Phillips, R., 462, 478
Pickard, Joseph, 502
Picker, Lauren, 266
Pickhardt, Carl E., 268n
Pietropinto, Anthony, 131
Pillemer, Karl A., 287, 502, 503
Pines, Maya, 246
Pinkard, Odessa, 497, 502
Pinker, Steven, 86
Pipher, Mary, 92
Pirog-Good, Maureen A., 428n
Pisano, Marina, 188, 287
Pittman, Joe F., 393
Pitzer, Ronald, 390, 402
Pivar, Ilona, 392
Place, Elizabeth Latrobe, 267n
Pleck, Joseph H., 89
Poe, Marshall, 91
Poehlmann, Julie, 408b, 409b
Pok, Angela Y. H., 61, 62b, 64
Pollack, Harold, 250
Pollack, William, 88, 89, 90, 92
Pollak, Robert, 33
Pollard, Kelvin M., 215
Pollitt, Katha, 245
Pomerleau, A. D. Bolduc, 88
Pomeroy, Wardell B., 136b
Pompa, Frank, 4b
Poniewozik, James, 245
Poortman, Anne Rigt, 419, 420
Popenoe, David, 2, 7b, 14, 15b, 35, 37, 49,
    168, 173, 186, 187, 226, 241, 469
Popkin, Michael H., 479
Porter, Eduardo, 63n, 76, 298, 299, 300
Porterfield, E., 219
Porterfield, S., 101
Portes, Alejandro, 60, 60n
Posner, Jill, 26
Postrel, Virginia, 63n
Potoczniak, Michael J., 377
Powell, Brian, 95, 435
Powell, Jean W., 504
Power, P., 405, 407
Pratt, Edith L., 217
Press, Julie E., 214
Presser, Stanley, 94, 303
Preston, Anne, 85, 297
Preston, Julia, 62b, 63b, 63n
Preuschoff, Gisela, 268n
Preves, Sharon E., 78b
Previti, Denise, 417, 419, 420
Price, Sharon J., 124, 484
Proctor, Bernadette D., 16b, 52, 52f, 53, 53f,
    58, 60, 64, 65, 66, 67, 85f, 176, 178f

Prospero, Moises, 223
Pruchno, R. A., 501
Purdy, Matthew, 490
Purkayastha, Bandana, 64, 65
Purnine, Daniel M., 130, 138
Pyke, Karen D., 62*b*, 79, 399, 402, 501

Qian, Zhenchao, 64, 69, 171, 214, 218,
    218*n*, 225
Quindlen, Anna, 279
Quinn, Jane Bryant, 287
Quirk, Ann, 435

Rabin, Roni, 83, 244
Raboy, Barbara, 258*b*
Rafferty, Jane, 502
Raley, R. Kelly, 16*b*, 60, 61, 185, 191*b*, 195,
    214, 214*n*
Raley, Sara B., 267
Ramirez, Cynthia, 214
Ramirez, Robert R., 60, 61
Rankin, Jane, 268, 269, 273
Rankin, Robert P., 217
Raschick, Michael, 499, 500
Ratcliff, Kathryn Strother, 325, 355, 366
Rauch, Jonathan, 199–200
Raven, Bertram, 352, 353, 353*t*
Reardon-Anderson, Jane, 63*b*
Reavey, Paula, 382
Rector, Robert, 148, 174
Reddick, Richard J., 59, 139
Reed, Joanna M., 214
Reeves, Terrance J., 64
Reich, Robert, 52
Reichert, Dana, 428
Reimann, Renate, 198
Reiss, David, 34, 403
Reiss, Ira L., 114, 114*f*, 115, 131, 133, 160
Reitzes, Donald C., 32, 110*n*, 112*b*, 112*n*
Rennison, Callie Marie, 367, 376
Renteln, Alison Dundes, 379*n*, 382, 384
Renzetti, Claire M., 377
Reschke, Kathy L., 396
Rhee, Siyon Y., 280, 284
Rhoades, Galena K., 226
Rhoades, Kelly, 33, 54
Rhode, Pam, 192*b*
Rhodes, Angel R., 316
Rholes, R., 209
Rice, Condoleeza, 82
Richardson, Rhonda A., 222
Richey, Cheryl A., 382
Richtel, Matt, 449
Ridder, Elizabeth M., 254
Ridgeway, Cecilia, 78, 81, 96, 270
Riedmann, Agnes, 247, 353*t*, 406, 467
Riekse, R. J., 503
Rigby, Jill M., 266, 267*n*
Riger, Stephanie, 373
Riley, Glenda, 445
Riley, Lisa A., 228
Riley, Matilda W., 505
Riley, Pamela J., 308
Rime, Sara, 305*b*
Rindfleisch, Nolan, 286
Ringgold, Faith, 161*b*
Risch, Gail S., 228
Risman, Barbara J., 29, 109, 146, 312, 325,
    355, 362*b*, 366
Ritter, Raymond A., Sr., 16
Ritualo, Amy, 460

Rivera, Fernando, 272
Rivers, Kerri L., 26
Rizzo, Christopher P., 276
Roberts, A., 184, 186, 203
Roberts, Clare M., 110*n*
Roberts, David G., 276
Roberts, Linda J., 209, 330, 338*n*
Roberts, Nicole A., 228
Roberts, Robert E. L., 14, 16, 48, 161, 204
Roberts, Sam, 54, 184
Robinson, B. E., 438*t*
Robinson, John P., 77, 266, 270, 271*f*, 272,
    309, 310, 311, 314*f*, 358
Robinson, T., 116
Robison, Jennifer, 102
Rockquemore, Kerry Ann, 69, 282
Rodgers, J. L., 417*n*
Rodgers, Roy H., 27, 478
Rodgers, William R. III, 297
Rodman, Hyman, 356
Rodrigues, Amy E., 419
Rodrigues, Arnoldo, 353
Rodriguez, Christina M., 382
Rodriguez, G., 69
Rodriguez, Marnie Salupo, 94–95
Rogers, J. D., 102
Rogers, L., 86, 125
Rogers, Michelle L., 391, 393, 401
Rogers, Stacy J., 177, 228, 288, 312, 359,
    416, 419
Rohner, Ronald P., 273
Roisman, Glenn I., 269
Roll, Samuel, 203
Rolleri, Lori, 147, 148
Roloff, Michael E., 338*n*
Romero, Mary, 305*b*, 315
Roper, Susanne Olsen, 393
Rosario, Margaret, 123, 124
Rose, Stephen J., 297, 306
Rosen, Karen H., 224
Rosen, Ruth, 506
Rosenberg, Debra, 253, 505
Rosenblatt, Paul C., 392
Rosenbloom, Stephanie, 49, 241, 486, 494
Rosenbluth, Susan C., 198, 355
Roseneil, Sasha, 166
Rosenfeld, Alvin, 280
Rosenfeld, Jeffrey P., 460
Rosenfeld, Michael J., 216
Rosenthal, C., 500
Ross, Catherine E., 202, 204, 421*f*, 440, 441
Ross, Mary, 295
Ross, Mary Ellen Trail, 285, 395
Rossi, Alice S., 36, 268, 269
Rotenburg, Ken J., 227–228
Roth, Wendy, 282
Rothman, Barbara Katz, 256
Rovers, Martin W., 345
Rowden, T., 227
Roxburgh, Susan, 323
Roy, Kevin M., 396
Ruane, Michael E., 51*b*
Ruben, Harvey, 450
Rubin, Lillian B., 277, 339
Rubin, Lisa, 254, 254*n*
Rubin, Roger H., 159*b*
Rubin, Tova, 188
Ruefli, Terry, 130
Rugel, Robert P., 111
Rumbaut, Rubén G., 60*n*, 187, 188, 287
Rushing, Beth, 209, 331
Russell, Brenda L., 108

Russell, Diana E. H., 370
Russo, Francine, 227
Russo, Nancy Felipe, 254, 254*n*
Rutter, Michael, 36
Rutter, Virginia, 131
Ryan, Cheryl, 304*b*
Ryan, Joan, 391*b*
Ryan, Kathryn M., 221*b*
Ryan, Suzanne, 128, 251

Saad, Lydia, 6*b*, 59, 129, 154, 172*b*, 179, 200,
    202, 248, 253, 253*t*, 267, 311, 311*t*
Saadeh, Wasim, 276
Sabatelli, Ronald M., 33, 222
Sabourin, Stephane, 330
Sachs, Andrea, 191, 260, 490
Sadker, D., 90
Sadker, M., 90
Saenz, Rogelio, 239*b*
Safilios-Rothschild, Constantina, 354, 355
Sage, Alexandria, 201*n*
Salcido, Olivia, 372
Saluter, Arlene F., 156*b*, 184
Samson, Frank L., 68
Samuelson, Amy, 304*b*, 305*b*
Samuelson, Robert J., 63*n*
Sanchez, Laura, 173, 228
Sandberg, John F., 274, 279
Sandefur, Gary, 170, 429, 432, 468
Sanders, Joshunda, 186
Sanford, Keith, 344
Sanghavi, Darshak M., 122
Santelli, John S., 131, 146, 147, 240*n*
Santos, Fernanda, 62*b*
Sapone, Anna I., 437
Sarfaty, Ruth, 304*b*
Sarkisian, Natalia, 57*b*, 67, 160, 161, 499
Sassler, Sharon, 10, 185, 188, 190, 225, 461
Sastry, Jaya, 445
Satir, Virginia, 103, 111
Sato, S., 162*f*
Sattler, David N., 391
Sauber, S. Richard, 423
Saulny, Susan, 280
Savage, Jill, 269
Savin-Williams, Ritch, 123
Sawhill, Isabel, 177, 179
Sax, Leonard, 78*b*
Sayer, Aline, 199
Sayer, Liana C., 358*f*, 416, 426, 427
Sbarra, David A., 423
Scanzoni, John H., 26, 155
Scanzoni, Letha Dawson, 201
Scarf, Maggie, 229, 331, 345
Scelfo, Julie, 131, 446
Schafer, Alyson, 270
Schaffer, Anne, 490
Schaie, K. Warner, 48*n*
Scharlach, Andrew, 501
Schaut, George B., 227, 228
Schechtman, Arleah, 334
Schechtman, Morris R., 334
Schellenberg, E. Glenn, 77
Schewe, Paul, 373
Schieve, Laura, 258*b*
Schlidt, Andrea Matovina, 70
Schmeeckle, Maria, 33, 461
Schneewind, Klaus A., 346
Schneider, Barbara, 60
Schneider, J. P., 135
Schneider, Jodi, 189*f*
Schnittker, Jason, 95, 312

Schoen, Robert, 169, 190, 214, 228, 241, 312, 415n, 416
Schone, Barbara Steinberg, 504
Schor, Juliet B., 310
Schrodt, Paul, 458
Schumacher, J. A., 176n, 194
Schwartz, Christine R., 53
Schwartz, L., 256
Schwartz, Pepper, 33, 129, 129n, 131, 136, 136b, 137f, 138, 139, 143, 146, 196, 222, 223b, 356–357, 361, 362, 362b, 363
Schwartz, Richard D., 188n
Schwartz, Robert, 177
Schwartz, Seth J., 474
Schweiger, Wendi K., 397
Scott, Ellen K., 373
Scott, Janny, 54, 59
Scott, Lisa, 268n
Scott, Marvin B., 31n
Scott, Mindy E., 189, 190, 194, 195
Scott, N., 96
Seaburn, David B., 407
Seal, David Wyatt, 104, 203
Sears, Heather A., 223
Seaton, Eleanor K., 398
Seccombe, Karen, 177, 278, 279, 284
Sedlak, Andrea, 317n, 437
Seelye, Katherine Q., 260
Seery, Brenda L., 272
Segal, David R., 50b, 51b
Segal, Mady Wechsler, 50b, 51b
Segura, Denise A., 93
Seidler, Victor J., 203
Seidman, Steven, 123, 196, 196n, 200, 201, 202
Seligman, Katherine, 209
Seligman, Martin, 110n–111
Sellers, Sherrill L., 93, 94
Seltzer, Judith A., 186, 189, 194, 225, 226, 419, 420
Seltzer, Marsha, 395
Sengupta, S., 283
Senn, Charlene Y., 77
Serovich, Julianne M., 424
Settersten, Richard A., Jr., 187, 188, 287
Shalit, Wendy, 130
Shamin, Ishrat, 380
Shanahan, Michael J., 28
Shapiro, Jenessa R., 422, 427, 435, 440, 441
Shapiro, Joseph P., 496, 497b
Shapkina, Nadezda, 110n, 112b, 112n
Shaver, P., 113
Sheehan, Constance L., 33, 217
Shellenbarger, Sue, 301, 302, 315, 318, 323
Shelton, Beth Anne, 307, 308
Sherif-Trask, Bahira, 158, 162
Sherman, Carey Wexler, 494, 504
Sherman, Lawrence W., 378, 378n
Sherman, Paul J., 77
Shih, Josephine A., 393
Shin, Nana, 284
Shorofsky, Roanna, 305b
Shorter, Edward, 30
Shrira, Ilan, 111
Shuey, Kim M., 501
Shull, R. D., 417n
Shumow, Lee, 26
Siegel, Bernie S., 267n
Siegel, J., 273b
Siegel, M., 214, 501
Sikes, Melvin P., 284

Sill, Morgan, 138
Siller, Sidney, 95
Silver, Nan, 334b, 344
Silver, Roxane Cohen, 373
Silverstein, Merril, 288, 493, 493t, 494, 495, 498, 503, 505
Simenauer, Jacqueline, 131
Simko, Patty, 110n
Simmons, Tavia, 6b, 69, 189f, 195f, 285, 459
Simon, Barbara, 204
Simon, L., 4b
Simon, Rita, 259–260
Simon, Robin W., 81, 242
Simon, William, 123, 126
Simoncelli, Tanya, 146
Simons, Leslie Gordon, 171, 278
Simpson, J., 209
Sinclair, Stacey L., 343
Singer, Audrey, 215, 486, 487
Singh, Susheela, 146, 147
Sirjamaki, John, 13, 14
Skinner, Denise A., 192b
Skinner, Kevin B., 194, 461
Skinner, Martie L., 272
Skipp, Catharine, 51b
Skloot, Rebecca L., 256
Skolnick, Arlene S., 382, 409, 415, 445
Slade, Eric P., 276
Slark, Samantha, 159b
Slater, Lauren, 111, 112n, 116, 117
Slep, Amy M. Smith, 373, 382
Small, Stephen A., 276, 380
Smalley, Gary, 104–105, 106, 114, 116
Smeeding, Timothy, 278
Smeins, Linda, 227
Smerglia, Virginia, 502
Smith, Amy Symens, 68n
Smith, Betty L., 49
Smith, Christian, 360
Smith, Donna, 473
Smith, Daniel W., 29
Smith, Deborah B., 491, 492
Smith, Herbert L., 50b
Smith, Jane I., 71
Smith, Kristen E., 317
Smith, P., 33
Smith, Ruth S., 277
Smith, Suzanna D., 161, 187, 189
Smith, Tim, 267n, 279
Smith, Tom, 54, 128, 131, 135, 136b, 137, 138, 143
Smith, Tovia, 266
Smith-Hefner, Nancy J., 211
Smith-Lovin, Lynn, 26, 81
Smits, Jeroen, 217
Smock, Pamela J., 6b, 9, 189, 190, 194b, 195, 214, 297, 323, 426, 436, 445, 470
Smolowe, Jill, 201
Sniczek, Tamara, 222, 223
Snipp, C. Matthew, 66, 67
Snow, David A., 166
Snow, Olympia, 285
Snyder, Douglas K., 198
Sobolewski, Juliana, 177, 278, 437
Solberg, Kenneth B., 473
Soldo, B. J., 498, 504
Solis, Dianne, 297
Solmoncse, Joe, 192b
Solomon, Denise H., 222
Solot, Dorian, 191
Sommers, Christina Hoff, 91, 92

Sontag, M. Suzanne, 22, 23
Sontag, Susan, 490
Sorell, Gwendolyn, 106, 109
Sorensen, Elaine, 435
Soukhanov, Anne H., 277
Soukup, Elise, 201n
Sousa, Liliana, 435
South, Scott J., 432
Spar, Debora L., 256, 257
Spector, Robert G., 439
Spelke, Elizabeth S., 86
Spence, Janet T., 77
Spiro, Melford, 188n
Spitze, Glenna, 161, 203, 406, 424, 496, 499, 504
Spock, Benjamin, 289
Spohn, Cassia, 56
Spraggins, Renee L., 83
Spragins, Ellyn, 302
Sprecher, Susan, 33, 104, 129n, 130, 131, 133, 135, 136, 136b, 137f, 138, 139, 140, 146, 214, 221b, 357, 370
Springen, Karen, 274, 492
Springer, S., 86
Srinivasan, Padma, 213
St. George, Donna, 51b
Stacey, Judith, 4, 125, 166, 199, 200, 449
Stack, Carol B., 408b
Stack, Steven, 169
Stafford, Frank, 309
Staggs, Susan L., 373
Stahmann, R., 227
Staines, Graham L., 322, 323
Stanley, Scott M., 210, 226, 227, 229, 334b, 346
Stanton, Glenn T., 168
Staples, Robert, 89, 139, 172b, 219
Starkey, Mary, 305b
Stattin, H., 242
Stearns, Peter, 24b
Steil, Janice M., 355
Stein, A., 126
Stein, B., 52
Stein, C., 498, 503
Stein, Peter J., 204, 318, 319, 323
Steinberg, Laurence, 274, 275
Steinhauer, Jennifer, 54, 63b, 191, 276
Steinmetz, Suzanne K., 345, 367, 376, 380, 400
Stephen, Elizabeth Hervey, 255
Stephens, Crystal M., 279
Stephens, William N., 158n
Stern, G., 316
Stern, Gary, 216
Sternberg, Robert, 105, 106, 106f, 114, 115, 228, 334b
Stets, Jan E., 368, 369
Steuerle, C. Eugene, 176
Stevens, Daphne, 308
Stevens, Gabriella, 216
Stevens, Heather B., 111
Stevenson, Betsey, 414, 417n, 419, 445
Stewart, Mary White, 383
Stewart, Susan D., 34, 250, 251, 435, 456, 457, 462, 465, 467, 469, 470, 475, 479
Stinnett, Nancy, 332b, 404, 405
Stinnett, Nick, 332b, 404, 405
Stinson, Kandi M., 392
Stock, Robert W., 143
Stolberg, Sheryl Gay, 256
Stoll, Michael A., 59
Stone, Brad, 487n

Stone, Lawrence, 30, 162, 164
Story, Louise, 279, 298
Stout, David, 253
Strand, Erik, 272
Stratton, Peter, 102, 399, 404
Straus, Murray A., 276, 277, 367, 367n, 368, 371, 374, 375, 375n, 376, 379, 380, 382
Strauss, Anselm, 405
Strauss, Robert, 245
Strobe, M., 103
Strobe, W., 103
Strömberg, B., 258b
Struening, Karen, 3
Stryker, Sheldon, 31n
Style, Carolyn Briggs, 203, 420
Su, Susan, 440
Subaiya, Lekha, 426, 428
Sugarman, Stephen D., 409
Suggs, Rob, 267n
Suhomlinova, Olga, 420
Suitor, J. Jill, 287
Sullivan, Oriel, 461
Supple, Andres J., 276
Suro, Roberto, 281
Surra, Catherine A., 215, 223
Sussman, L. J., 216, 217
Sussman, Marvin B., 400
Suter, Elizabeth, 196, 198
Sutton, Paul, 7b, 154f, 235, 244
Suzuki, Lalita K., 276, 282
Swagger, Paper, 111
Swartz, Susan, 185
Sweeney, Megan M., 61, 214, 225, 226, 419
Sweet, James, 136b, 190
Sweet, Stephen, 279
Swim, Janet K., 78
Swinford, Steven P., 276, 371
Swisher, Karin, 372, 373
Swisher, Raymond, 279
Sylvester, Kathleen, 323
Szabo, Liz, 258b
Szalacha, Laura A., 284
Szasz, Thomas S., 109
Szinovacz, Maximiliane, 443, 490, 492

Taffel, Selma, 239b
Tafoya, Sonya M., 69
Tak, Young Ran, 404, 406
Takagi, Dana Y., 65
Takeuchi, David T., 282
Talbot, K., 68
Talbot, Margaret, 256n
Talbott, Maria M., 490
Tamis-LeMonda, Catherine S., 280
Tang, Shengming, 324
Taniguchi, Hiromi, 490
Tannen, Deborah, 338
Tanner, Jennifer L., 437
Tanner, Lindsey, 256, 261
Tarmann, Allison, 258
Tashiro, Ty, 442
Tasker, Fiona, 8
Tatara, Toshio, 502
Taylor, Barbara Ewert, 221b
Taylor, Dalmas A., 105
Taylor, Howard F., 89
Taylor, Paul, 202
Taylor, Robert J., 366, 406
Taylor, Ronald D., 219, 398
Taylor, Ronald L., 48, 57b, 59, 60, 61, 65, 80, 300
Taylor, Shelley, 203

Teachman, Jay D., 50b, 59, 170, 194, 196, 225, 240, 414, 415, 415n, 417, 418, 419, 428
Tedrow, Lucky M., 50b, 414, 415, 415n, 417, 418, 419
Templeton, Alan, 54
Tennov, Dorothy, 110n
Tepperman, Lorne, 162, 212
Thayer, Elizabeth, 115, 210
Theiss, Jennifer A., 222
Therborn, Göran, 158
Thivierge, N., 397n
Thoennes, Nancy, 367, 375, 376, 381n
Thomas, Adam, 177, 179
Thomas, Alexander, 270
Thomas, Bernadette, 268
Thomas, Reuben J., 132b, 133b
Thomason, Deborah J., 404, 405
Thompson, Anne I., 397
Thompson, Linda, 270, 272, 307
Thompson, Michael, 89, 90, 92
Thompson, Tracy, 164n, 165, 268
Thomson, Elizabeth, 195, 225
Thorne, Barrie, 35, 89, 90
Thornton, Arland, 16–17, 185, 247, 294, 421, 444
Thurman, Judith, 88
Thye, Shane R., 176n
Tichenor, Veronica Jaris, 307, 355, 357, 358, 359, 360, 362
Tickamyer, Ann R., 80
Tilburg, Theo van, 504
Tiller, Vicky V., 278
Timberlake, Jeffrey M., 190
Tingle, Lynne R., 212
Titone, Vito, 8
Tjaden, Patricia, 367, 375, 376, 381n
Toledo, Sylvie de, 285
Tolnay, Stewart E., 219
Tonelli, Bill, 48
Toner, Robin, 82
Tong, Benson, 282
Toro-Morn, Maura, 104, 214
Torquati, Julia C., 400b, 401b
Torr, James D., 372, 373
Torres, Zenia, 219
Tougas, F., 77
Townsend, Aloen L., 498
Townsend, John Sims, 346
Townsend, Nicholas, 56, 301
Tran, Thanh V., 280, 284
Trask, Bahira Sherif, 407, 408
Travis, Carol, 216
Treas, Judith, 133, 134, 135, 194, 487, 503
Tremblay, M., 397n
Trent, Katherine, 203, 406, 432
Trevathan, Melissa, 268n
Trimberger, E. Kay, 202, 203
Troll, Lillian E., 417, 495
Trost, Cindy, 323
Trost, Jan, 464
Troy, Adam B., 220
Trudeau, Michelle, 280
Tsang, Laura Lo Wa, 243
Tschann, Jeanne M., 434
Tubbs, Carolyn Y., 396
Tucker, Corinna J., 274
Tucker, J., 83
Tucker, M. Belinda, 59, 61, 80, 300
Tufis, Paula, 241
Tuller, David, 261
Turkat, Ira Daniel, 436

Turley, Ruth N. Lopez, 250
Turnbull, A., 404
Turnbull, H., 404
Turner, Ralph H., 166, 243
Turrell, Susan C., 377
Tutty, Leslie M., 378
Twenge, Jean M., 38, 77, 128, 242, 243
Tyler, R. P., 381n
Tyre, Peg, 245, 279, 280, 287, 301

Uchitelle, Louis, 176, 305, 306
Udry, J. Richard, 36, 166
Uhlenberg, Peter, 288, 301, 493, 494, 496
Ultee, Wout, 217
Umana-Taylor, Adriana, 284
Umberson, Debra, 203
Umminger, April, 4b
Uttal, Lynet, 59, 67, 317
Utz, Rebecca L., 492

Valiente, Carlos, 405
Van Biema, David, 82
Van de Vliert, Evert, 272
van Eeden-Moorefield, Brad, 458b
Van Hook, Jennifer, 161, 488
Van Nuys, Heather, 193b
Van Pelt, Nancy L., 472b
van Uzendoorn, Marinus H., 261
Van Yperen, N. W., 33
Vandell, Deborah Lowe, 26, 495
Vander Ven, Thomas M., 313
Vandewater, Elizabeth A., 278
VanDorn, Richard A., 170, 278
VanLaningham, Jody, 417
VanLear, C. Arthur, 345
Vanneman, Reeve, 297
Vannoy, Dana, 103, 104
Vartanian, Thomas P., 64, 489
Vaughan, Diane, 422
Ventura, Stephanie J., 7b, 58, 61, 64, 67, 70, 234, 234f, 235, 238b, 238f, 239b, 244, 247, 248, 248f, 250, 250f
Verma, J., 162f
Villarosa, Linda, 143, 144b, 256n
Vinciguerra, Thomas, 245, 246
Visher, Emily B., 465, 465t, 469, 470, 471
Visher, John S., 465, 465t, 469, 470, 471
Vizenor, Erma J., 95b
Vogler, Carolyn, 359
Voith, V. L., 4b
Voydanoff, Patricia, 391, 396

Waddell, Lynn, 199
Wadsworth, Martha, 395
Wagner-Raphael, Lynne I., 104, 203
Waite, Linda, 25b, 38, 139, 168, 169, 170, 171, 173, 179, 421, 445
Wakeman, Melanie A., 496
Waldfogel, Jane, 322
Walker, Alexis J., 270, 272, 402n
Walker, Karen E., 26
Walker, Lenore E., 373
Walker, Mark, 258b
Walker, Samuel, 56
Wallace, Pamela M., 269
Waller, Willard, 33
Wallerstein, Judith S., 166, 228, 334–335, 345, 422, 423, 424, 429, 432, 433, 435, 437, 438, 439, 441
Wallin, Denise, 419
Wallis, Claudia, 279
Walsh, D., 274

Walsh, Froma, 396, 407
Walsh, W., 279n
Walster, Elaine H., 111
Walster, G. William, 111
Walter, Carolyn Ambler, 245
Walters, Richard H., 87
Wang, Rong, 267
Ward, J., 286
Ward, M., 260
Wardle, Francis, 282
Wark, Linda, 478
Warner, Judith, 270, 272, 280
Warren, G., 395
Warren, Henriette B., 405
Warshak, Richard, 439, 471
Wasserman, Ira, 169
Waterman, Caroline K., 224
Waters, Everett, 211
Waters, Mary C., 63b, 68
Watson, Anne, 318n
Watson, Russell, 321b
Watson, Wendy L., 208, 211
Waugh, Phil, 173
Wax, N., 79
Weaver, Shannon E., 203, 406
Webster, Bruce H., Jr., 489
Weeks, John R., 236, 251
Weger, H., 229, 333, 338n, 339
Weibel-Orlando, J., 495
Weigel, Daniel J., 331, 352
Weil, Elizabeth, 78b
Weinberg, Daniel H., 84, 296
Weinberg, Martin S., 124
Weiner, Neil, 384
Weisman, Carol, 267n
Weiss, Rick, 256, 258b
Weitzman, Lenore J., 423, 426, 426n, 427
Welborn, Vickie, 281
Welchans, Sarah, 367, 376
Wells, Barbara, 55, 57b, 61, 64
Wells, Brooke E., 128
Wells, Marolyn, 110n
Wells, Mary S., 402
Wentzel, Jo Ann, 286
Werner, Emmy E., 277
West, Cornell, 240, 445
West, Martha S., 83, 84, 94
Western, Bruce, 409b
Wexler, Richard, 383, 383n
Whealin, Julia, 392
Whipple, Ellen E., 382
Whitchurch, Gail G., 34
Whitcomb, Juliet H., 355
White, J. E., 284
White, Jacquelyn W., 224
White, James M., 10b, 27
White, Lynn K., 41, 42, 177, 243, 247, 288,
    303, 310, 330, 406, 416, 417, 420, 437,
    443–444, 450, 462, 467, 471, 473
Whitehead, Barbara Dafoe, 2, 7b, 14, 15b, 49,
    168, 173, 226, 241
Whitman, David, 131
Whittaker, Terri, 502

Whyte, Martin King, 227
Wickrama, K. A. S., 169, 203, 420, 490
Widmer, Mark A., 402
Wiederman, Michael W., 140
Wiehe, Vernon R., 380
Wiener, Joshua M., 499, 501
Wilcox, Karen L., 29
Wilcox, W. Bradford, 70, 71, 298, 299, 324,
    356, 358, 361–362, 362
Wildsmith, Elizabeth, 16b, 60, 61, 191b, 195
Wiley, Angela R., 405
Wilkie, Jane Riblett, 300, 325, 355, 366
Wilkinson, Doris, 55n, 161
Willeto, Angela A. A., 65
Willetts, Marion C., 166, 186, 190, 191,
    194, 196
Williams, David E., 244
Williams, David R., 169
Williams, Joan, 322
Williams, Joan C., 266
Williams, John C., 270
Williams, Kirk R., 378
Williams, Kristi, 309–310, 352, 357, 358
Williams, Laurel, 395
Williams, Lee M., 217
Williams, Linda M., 370
Williams, Oliver J., 378
Williams, Sharon Wallace, 503
Williams-Morris, Ruth, 169
Williamson, Sabrina, 405, 406
Willie, Charles Vert, 59, 139
Willson, Andrea E., 501
Wilmoth, Janet M., 501
Wilson, James Q., 172b, 201
Wilson, John, 204
Wilson, Margo I., 37, 382
Wilson, Marie C., 92
Wilson, Susannah J., 162, 212
Wilson, W. J., 59
Winch, Robert, 222
Wineberg, Howard, 421
Winner, Lauren F., 131
Winter, Judy, 268, 268n
Wise, Nicole, 280
Wissow, Lawrence S., 276
Witchel, Alex, 49
Wolf, D. A., 498, 504
Wolf, Marsha E., 371, 372, 379
Wolf, R., 503
Wolfe, Barbara, 249
Wolfe, Donald, 351, 356, 363
Wolfe, Marilyn, 125
Wolfers, Justin, 414, 417, 417n, 419, 445
Wolfinger, Nicholas H., 210, 418
Wolin, Steven J., 403
Wong, Paul, 282
Wood, Julia T., 76, 333
Wood, Wendy, 81, 85, 86, 88
Wooden, Erica M., 273b
Woodford, L., 393
Woods, Tiger, 68
Woodward, Kenneth L., 159b
Woolley, Michael E., 278

Wright, H. Norman, 268n, 346
Wright, John, 224
Wright, Katherine D., 110n
Wright, Paul H., 110n
Wright, Richard G., 502
Wright, S., 409
Wrigley, Julia, 317n
Wu, Lawrence L., 249
Wulczyn, Fred, 286
Wuthnow, Robert, 26
Wyden, Peter, 342
Wynne, Lyman C., 505
Wynne-Edwards, K. E., 86

Xiong, Blong, 63b
Xu, Xianohe, 462

Yabroff, Jennie, 54
Yalcin, Bektas Murat, 346
Yance, Sherelyn, 218
Yancey, George, 218
Yang, Chongming, 345, 484
Yardley, Jim, 261
Yellowbird, Michael, 66, 67
Yeung, King-To, 32
Yeung, W. Jean, 272
Yin, Sandra, 261
Yllo, Kersti, 370
Yodanis, Carrie L., 276
Yoder, Janice D., 236, 237b, 240
Yoon, Jeongkoo, 176n
Yorburg, Betty, 16, 17, 177
Yoshioka, Marianne R., 372
Young-DeMarco, Linda, 16–17, 185, 444
Youngs, Bettie B., 269
Youngs, Jennifer Leigh, 269
Yu, Olivia, 130
Yuan, Anastasia S. Vogt, 469

Zabin, Laurie Schwab, 250
Zak, A., 344
Zamostny, Kathy P., 259
Zawitz, Marianne W., 367
Zeitz, Joshua M., 128, 128n
Zelizer, Viviana K., 42, 82, 241, 359
Zentgraf, Kristine A., 64
Zernike, Kate, 184, 485
Zezima, Katie, 50b
Zhao, Yilu, 261
Zhou, Min, 406, 499
Zierk, Kristin L., 254
Zigler, Edward, 304b
Zill, Nicholas, 468
Zimmerman, E., 280
Zimmerman, Jeffrey, 115, 210
Zink, Therese, 502
Zoroya, Greg, 51b
Zsembik, Barbara A., 504
Zuang, Yuanting, 261
Zuo, Jiping, 324
Zurcher, Kristinia, 444
Zvonkovic, Anisa M., 307

Subject Index

Page numbers followed by *n* refer to footnotes; page numbers followed by *t* refer to tables; page numbers followed by *b* refer to photo captions; and page numbers followed by *f* refer to figures.

AAHMI. *See* African American Healthy
   Marriage Initiative (AAHMI)
AARP, 490
ABC-X model, defined, 400
Abduction, 437
Abortion
  for African Americans, 253*n*
  for American Indians, 253*n*
  approval for, 253*f*
  for Asian Americans, 253*n*
  defined, 252–254
  facts about, 252*n*
  induced, 252
  for Latinos, 61, 253*n*
  men and, 254
  for non-Hispanic whites, 253*n*
  NOW and, 93
  for Pacific Islanders, 253*n*
  parenthood and, 252–254
  partial birth, 253
  politics of, 253
  poverty and, 253*n*
  psychosocial outcomes of, 254
  religion and, 70
  safety of, 253–254
  sexuality and, 146, 147*f*
  spontaneous, 252
  in United States, 250, 252, 253
  women and, 252–254, 252*n*, 253*f*
Abortion rights, 35
Abstinence
  asexuality and, 124*b*
  cybersex and, 126*b*
  defined, 131
  sexual orientation and, 123
"Abstinence only," 147
"Abstinence plus," 147
Abuse. *See also* Violence
  among bisexual couples, 376–377
  among gay males, 376–377
  among lesbians, 376–377
  child (*See* Child abuse)
  child rearing *vs.*, 382
  child-to-parent, 384
  domestic, 166, 173, 502
  elder, 502–503
  emotional, 368, 376, 502
  female-partner, 370
  "normal" child rearing *vs.*, 382
  physical, 368, 376, 381, 502
  psychological, 224
  sexual, 380, 381, 502
  verbal, 223, 224, 368
  wife, 35, 165, 368, 370, 373, 378
Acceptance, love and, 103–104
Accidents, 83
Acculturation, 66, 503, 504
Achievement pressure, 27, 54
ACLU, 193*b*

Acquaintance rape. *See* Date/acquaintance
  rape
Action, in stepfamily development, 478
Active life expectancy, defined, 486
Active Parenting for Stepfamilies
  program, 479
Activism, 93
Adaptability, family crises and, 405–406
Adaptable marriage relationships,
  defined, 229
Adaptation, family crises and, 400–404, 402*b*
Adjustment, family crises and, 400–404, 402*b*
Administration for Children and
  Families, 174*n*
Adolescent births, 66, 249–250
Adolescent sexuality, 146–148
Adolescents
  births to, 249–250
  child-to-parent abuse and, 384
  cohabitation and, 196
  deinstitutionalized marriage and, 170
  depression/substance abuse in, 54
  divorce and, 437
  HIV/AIDS and, 145*b*, 145*f*
  multicultural families and, 69
  raising children and, 287
  stepfamilies and, 468, 469, 471
Adoption and Safe Families Act, 259
Adoptions
  African Americans and, 258, 259, 260
  Alaska Natives and, 258
  American Indians and, 65, 65*n*, 259
  Asian Americans and, 257, 259, 260
  biosocial perspective and, 37
  of children with disabilities, 260
  choices involving, 261
  defined, 257
  disrupted, 260
  dissolved, 260
  diversity and, 259
  education and, 258
  ethnicity and, 259–260
  fathers and, 259
  gay male/men and, 260
  independent, 259
  informal, 258
  in-race, 260
  international, 258, 260–261
  interracial, 259
  Latinos and, 258, 259, 260
  lesbians and, 260
  mothers and, 158, 160
  multicultural families and, 69, 69*b*
  non-Hispanic whites and, 257, 259
  of older children, 260
  Pacific Islanders and, 257
  parenthood and, 257–261
  as parenting option, 257–261
  private, 259

  process for, 259
  public, 259
  of racial/ethnic minority children,
    259–260
  raising children and, 286
  by same-sex couples, 199, 201*b*
  stepchild, 468*n*
  transracial, 259, 260
  women and, 257
Adult Basic Education, 177*n*
Adult children
  aging families and, 493–496
  divorce and, 425, 443–444
  as eldercare providers, 498–499
  parents and, 286–288
  remarriage and, 460
Adult day care, defined, 497*b*
Adult Protective Services, 502
Adultery
  covenant marriage and, 173
  on Internet, 134
  as universal, 133
Adulthood, family development perspective
  and, 28–29
Advertisements, family definitions and, 8*b*
Advertising motifs, family and, 2*b*
Affairs
  emotional, 160
  extramarital, 132–135
Affirmative action, for men, 84
A-frame relationships, defined, 112, 114
African American Healthy Marriage Initiative
  (AAHMI), 174, 196
African Americans/blacks, 48, 52*f*, 53–56,
  55*n*, 57, 58–60, 67, 68, 69
  abortions for, 253*n*
  adoption and, 258, 259, 260
  aging families and, 485–488, 486*f*, 488*n*,
    488*t*, 494, 495, 502, 503
  child abuse and, 381
  child care and, 60, 76*b*–77*b*, 317
  children and, 58, 59, 248, 248*f*, 251,
    280–281
  choosing marriage partner and, 214–215,
    217–218, 218*f*, 218*n*, 220, 225, 226
  cohabitation and, 195
  communication and, 340
  deinstitutionalized marriage and, 169, 171,
    171*b*, 172*b*
  divorce and, 416*f*, 419, 419*t*, 425*f*, 433
  family crises and, 406
  fertility rates among, 238*b*, 238*f*
  gender/gendered identities and, 79–80,
    83, 84, 89–91, 93, 94
  HIV/AIDS and, 144*b*, 145*b*, 145*f*
  intimate partner violence and, 369, 369*f*
  kinship authority and, 160, 161
  labor force and, 295, 298
  marital status of, 156*b*, 157*f*

African Americans/blacks (*cont.*)
  men's market work and, 299
  poverty rate for, 176
  prison and, 408*b*
  raising children and, 270, 276, 278, 280–
    281, 281*b*, 282, 283, 284*b*
  remarriage and, 458*b*
  sexuality and, 128, 128*t*, 139–140
  unmarrieds and, 184, 186, 187*f*
  unpaid family work and, 308
African Methodist Episcopal, gender/
  gendered identities and, 82
Agape
  defined, 108, 108*b*
  martyring *vs.*, 109
Age
  choosing marriage partner and, 214–215,
    216, 219
  gender/gendered identities and, 83
  HIV/AIDS and, 144*b*
  intimate partner violence and, 370
  marital status and, 156*b*, 157*f*
  at marriage, 209–210
  parenthood and, 244
  remarriage and, 460–461, 460*b*
  sex and, 138, 139
  sexual experience and, 128
  unmarrieds and, 203
Age structure, American family and, 49
"Agency," 57
Agentic/instrumental character traits,
  defined, 78
Aging families, 28, 482–508. *See also*
  Eldercare
  aging populations and, 484–487
  caregiving and, 496–504
  divorce/widowhood/remarriage and,
    492–493
  eldercare and, 504–506
  living arrangements and, 487–488
  marriage relationships and, 490–492
  older parents/adult children/
    grandchildren and, 493–496
  in today's economy, 488–490
Aging population, 7*b*, 484–487, 505*b*
Agreement reality, defined, 38
Aid to Families with Dependent Children
  (AFDC), 174*n*
Al-Anon, 405
Alaska Natives, 52*f*, 54, 58, 65*n*, 66, 67, 144*b*,
  145*b*, 145*f*, 238*f*, 239*b*
  adoption and, 258
  aging families and, 486*f*
  children and, 248, 248*f*
  divorce and, 415, 416*f*
Alcohol
  child abuse and, 382
  date/acquaintance rape and, 221*b*
  dating violence and, 224
  family crises and, 405
  intimate partner violence and, 369,
    370, 377
  raising children and, 267, 285, 287
Alcoholics, 211
Alcoholics Anonymous, 405
Alcoholism, 66. *See also* Drinking
Alimony, 427, 427*n*
Allocation of money, marital power
  and, 352
Allocation systems, defined, 358–359
Aloneness, defined, 203
Alternatives to marriage, 190–191, 419–420

Altruistic love, 108, 108*b*
Ambiguity
  boundary, 34, 393, 394*f*, 465, 467
  gender, 78*b*
  role, 470
American Academy of Pediatrics, 25*b*, 200,
  277, 320*b*
AARP, 138
American Business Collaboration,
  312–313
American Civil Liberties Union, 190*n*
American College of Obstretricians and
  Gynecologists, 254
American Indians (Native Americans), 52*f*,
  53, 54, 55, 58, 65–67, 68, 70, 84, 95*b*
  abortions and, 253*n*
  adoption and, 65, 65*n*, 259
  aging families and, 486*f*, 495
  arranged marriages by, 163*b*
  child abuse and, 381
  children and, 65, 65*n*, 66, 67, 248,
    248*f*, 281
  choosing marriage partner and, 215,
    217–218
  cohabitation and, 66
  divorce and, 415, 416*f*
  fertility rates among, 238*f*, 239*b*
  HIV/AIDS and, 144*b*, 145*b*, 145*f*
  intimate partner violence and, 369, 369*f*
  kinship authority and, 161
  raising children and, 280, 281, 282,
    283–284, 284*b*
  unmarrieds and, 184
American Kennel Club study, 4*b*
American Medical Association, 434*n*
American Muslin Women's Association, 71*b*
American Population Association, 168, 171
American Psychiatric Association, 434*n*
American Psychological Association, 81,
  123*n*, 129, 434*n*
American Religious Identification Survey of
  2001, 70*n*
American Society for Reproductive
  Medicine, 256*n*
"Americanized," 65
Americans with Disabilities Act, 404
Amish, 237*b*
Anatomy, gender/gendered identities and,
  76, 85–86
Androgen, 86*n*
Anger
  communication and, 334, 335, 336, 343,
    344, 347
  love and, 109
Anglican churches, gender/gendered
  identities and, 82
Anscombe Society, 131
Anticohabitation laws, 190*n*
Antifeminists, defined, 95
Antinatalism, structural, 240–241
Arab Americans, 215
Arab ancestry, 55*n*
Arab Muslim, 83
Arlington National Cemetery, 68*b*
Arranged marriages, 108, 162, 163*b*, 211–
  213, 212*b*, 213*b*
ART. *See* Assisted reproductive technology
  (ART)
Artificial insemination, same-sex couples
  and, 199, 199*b*
Asexual Visibility and Education Network
  (AVEN), 124*b*

Asexuality, defined, 123, 124*b*
Asexuals, defined, 124*b*
Asian Americans, 52*f*, 53, 54, 55, 57, 58,
  64–69, 64*n*, 68*b*
  abortions for, 253*n*
  adoption and, 257, 259, 260
  aging families and, 486–487, 486*f*, 488,
    488*t*, 499, 503
  arranged marriages by, 163*b*
  child abuse and, 381, 382*n*
  child care and, 317
  children and, 64, 65, 248, 248*f*, 282
  choosing marriage partner and, 215,
    217–218
  divorce and, 415, 416*f*, 419, 419*t*
  family crises and, 406
  fertility rates among, 238*f*, 239*b*
  gender/gendered identities and, 80, 83,
    84, 90–91
  HIV/AIDS and, 144*b*, 145*b*, 145*f*
  intimate partner violence and, 369, 369*f*
  kinship authority and, 161
  labor force and, 295
  marital status of, 156*b*, 157*f*
  men's market work and, 301
  raising children and, 280, 282,
    283–284, 284*b*
  unmarrieds and, 186, 187*f*
Asian Hmong, 237*b*
Asian Indian Americans, raising children
  and, 283
Asian Indians, 213
Assimilation
  American Indians and, 65
  Latinos and, 60*n*
  non-Hispanic white, 68
  segmented, 60
Assisted living, defined, 497*b*
"Assisted marriages," 211. *See also* Arranged
  marriages
Assisted reproductive technology (ART),
  255–256
Association of Black Sociologists, 219
Assortative mating, defined, 214
Asymmetric violence, 374, 375
Athletes, gender/gendered identities
  and, 89
Attachment, defined, 318*n*
Attachment disorder, defined, 260
Attachment style, 113–114, 209, 210, 210*b*
Attachment theory, 113–114, 209
Attitudes
  about children, 240
  about cohabitation, 191*b*, 194
  about employment/family work,
    310–313, 312
  about gender/gendered identities, 76,
    77, 84
  about love, 102, 111
  about policies, 173
  about same-sex couples, 200
  about sexuality, 128, 129, 130
  about Women's Movement, 94
  in choosing marriage partner, 208–211,
    216, 217, 222, 226, 229
  in labor force, 294, 295
  nontraditional, 194
  from religion, 70
  toward marriage, 417
  toward unmarrieds, 185
  of white-collar/blue-collar workers, 54
Authoritarian parenting style, defined, 274

Authoritative coparents, 272*b*
Authoritative parenting, 272–277, 281
Autism Speaks, 409
Autonomy, 104, 113, 185, 187, 203, 331, 352, 356*b*
AVEN. *See* Asexual Visibility and Education Network (AVEN)
Avoidant attachment style, defined, 113, 114
Awareness, in stepfamily development, 478

Babies, 269–270
Baby boom generation, 7*b*, 165*n*, 236, 440
Baby boom/baby boomers, 48, 313, 313*f*, 484, 485*f*, 490
Baby Business, The (Spar), 257
Baird, Eisenstadt v., 128
Bank accounts, unmarrieds and, 192*b*
Bargaining, choosing marriage partner and, 213, 214
Barriers to divorce, 417, 419–420, 420*b*
"Battered child syndrome," 367*n*
Battered husbands, 375*n*
Battered woman syndrome, 373
Battered women, 378, 383
Beauty, aging families and, 490
Behavior
    biosocial perspective and, 36–37
    deinstitutionalized marriage and, 170
    gay male, 129–130
    gender/gendered identities and, 76, 81*b*, 85–86, 87
    labor force and, 295
    lesbian, 129–130
    love and, 102, 103, 111, 115*b*, 116
    permanence/sexual exclusivity and, 158
    raising children and, 273, 273*b*, 274
    religion and, 72
    self-esteem and, 111
    sexual, 123*f*
    sexuality and, 128
Behavioral problems, divorce and, 433
Being realistic, defined, 116
Beliefs, reproductive technology and, 257
Belligerence, 338, 340, 341
Benefits
    of aging families, 488
    of children, 241
    economy/social class and, 50
    friends with, 132, 132*b*–133*b*, 220
    for immigrants, 63*b*, 63*n*
    in military, 51*b*
Bereavement, defined, 492
Between-group variation, 80
Bias, 57
Bicultural families, defined, 67
Bigamy, 201*n*
Binational families, defined, 60, 62*b*
Binuclear family, 446–447, 449, 478
Binuclear Family Study, 446–447, 449, 478
Biology, gender/gendered identities and, 86–87
Biosocial perspective, 23*t*, 36–37, 37*b*, 125, 127
Biracial children, 282. *See also* Multiracial children
Birth control, 70, 127, 128*n*, 138, 147, 147*f*, 149, 251. *See also* Contraception
Birth control pill, 128, 147*f*
Birth rate, 7*b*, 16, 61, 64, 66, 154*f*, 155, 168, 234–237, 244, 247–251, 484, 488. *See also* Fertility; Fertility rates
Bisexual couples, abuse among, 376–377

Bisexuals
    African Americans and, 140
    defined, 123, 124
    sexuality and, 129
Black studies, 67
Blacks. *See* African Americans/blacks
Blended family, 478
Blood transfusions, HIV/AIDS and, 143, 145*n*
Blue-collar families, 53–54, 323
Blue-collar jobs, 295*n*, 299
Blue-collar men, 308
Bonding fights/fighting, defined, 342–345
Borderwork, defined, 89
Boredom, 138–139, 142, 336
Boston University Center for Sexual Medicine, 124*b*
Boundary ambiguity, 34, 393, 394*f*, 465, 467
Bowers v. Hardwick, 128
Boys
    divorce and, 429
    in family, 88–89
    girls *vs.,* 80, 81, 83, 84, 86–92, 92*n*
    raising children and, 269, 273*b*, 276
    sexuality and, 123*f*, 131
Brain, gender/gendered identities and, 86
Brain lateralization, defined, 86
Braschi v. Stahl Associates Company, 8
Brave New Stepfamilies (Stewart), 479
Breaking up
    choosing marriage partner and, 226*b*
    premarital relationship and, 224–225
    unmarrieds and, 193*b*
Bride price, defined, 213
Buddhists, 68*b*, 70, 283, 405
Bullying, 92
Bureau of Justice Statistics, 367, 371
Bush administration, 63*b*

Capital, children as, 241, 241*n*
"Career advancement," 202
Career women, 91
Careers. *See also* Jobs
    dual, 302
    employment/family work and, 315–316
    family, 27*n* (*See also* Family life cycle)
    jobs *vs.,* 302
Caregiver model of elder abuse and neglect, defined, 503
Caregiver stress, 501–502
Caregivers
    child/grandchild, 490*b*
    in home, 317
Caregiving, 496–506
Caregiving trajectory, defined, 501
Carey v. Population Services International, 128
Carhart, Gonzalez v., 253
Caring, love and, 103–104
Case studies, defined, 41
Casual dating, 220–221
Casual sex, 130, 131
Catholicism/Catholics. *See* Roman Catholics
Caucasians, 218, 218*n. See also* Non-Hispanic whites
Celibacy
    asexuality and, 124*b*
    fertility trends and, 236*n*
    HIV/AIDS and, 143
Cell phones, relationships through, 2*f*
Census, 54–55, 66, 68*n*, 69, 196*n*
Census Bureau, 54, 55*n*, 56, 69, 70*n*, 414*n*, 456

Center care
    defined, 317, 317*n*
Center for Economic and Policy Research, 298
Center for Epidemiological Studies Depression Scale (CES-D), 421*f*
Centers for Disease Control and Prevention, 367
CES-D. *See* Center for Epidemiological Studies Depression Scale (CES-D)
Change
    adult developmental, 17–18
    choosing marriage partner and, 229
    communication and, 344, 346, 346*b*
    cultural, 185–186
    demographic, 184–185
    divorce and, 425
    economic, 49–53, 184–185
    family, 14, 16–17
    family crises and, 390, 391*b*
    family systems theory and, 34
    longitudinal studies of, 42
    midlife, 13*b*
    no-power relationship and, 365–366
    personal/family, 96
    raising children and, 285
    social (*See* Social change)
    technological, 184–185, 186
Character traits, 78
Child abduction, 437
Child abuse, 35, 165, 336, 367*n*, 379–384, 379*b*, 434*n*, 469, 469*n*
Child Abuse Prevention and Treatment Act, 379
Child Behavior Checklist, 122
Child care. *See also* Day care
    African Americans and, 60, 76*b*–77*b*, 317
    aging families and, 495, 500
    Asian Americans and, 317
    biosocial perspective and, 36
    center care as, 317
    defined, 316
    diversity and, 304*b*–305*b*
    eldercare and, 506
    employment/family work and, 314*f*
    family, 317
    gender/gendered identities and, 76*b*–77*b*, 80
    labor force and, 297
    market approach to, 317
    mothering approach to, 316–317
    mothers and, 304*b*, 305*b*
    non-Hispanic white, 67, 76*b*–77*b*, 317
    Pacific Islanders and, 317
    parenting approach to, 317
    race/class/gender and, 76*b*–77*b*
    work/family issues and, 316–319, 317*n*, 318*b*–321*b*
Child maltreatment, 379, 381, 382, 384
Child Maltreatment 2005, 381
Child neglect, 379–380
Child population, 58
Child poverty, 14, 16*b*, 24, 24*b*, 53, 58, 66
    deinstitutionalized marriage and, 168, 171
    divorce and, 427
    HMI and, 176–177
    policies for, 173, 177–178, 178*f*
    in United States, 266
Child Protective Services, 378, 383
Child rearing, abuse *vs.,* 382
Child Sexual Behavior Inventory, 122

Child support, 270, 426, 427–428, 428n, 432, 456n
Child Support Amendments, 428n
Child well-being, 445–446
Childcenteredness, 14
Child-free, 240, 240n. *See also* Childlessness
Childhood experiences, intimate partner violence and, 373
Childlessness, 7b, 234, 235, 237b, 240, 243–244, 245, 246
Children
  adoption of (*See* Adoptions)
  adult (*See* Adult children)
  African American, 58, 59, 248, 248f, 251, 280–281
  age structure and, 49
  aging families and, 484, 498b
  Alaska Native, 248, 248f
  American Indian, 65, 65n, 66, 67, 248, 248f, 281
  Asian American, 64, 65, 248, 248f, 282
  biosocial perspective and, 36
  biracial, 282 (*See also* Multiracial children)
  as caregivers, 498b
  choosing marriage partner and, 211, 213, 222, 227, 229
  cohabitation and, 170, 190, 191b, 195–196, 195f
  cost of, 242
  deinstitutionalized marriage and, 165n, 168, 169–171, 170t, 173
  divorce and, 210, 415, 416f, 419–426, 425f, 426b, 428–440, 430b–431b, 445–446
  domestic violence and, 368b
  elderly and, 15b, 16b
  employment/family work and, 313–315, 314f
  ethnicity and, 57
  exchange theory and, 33
  family development perspective and, 29
  family ecology theory and, 24b–25b
  feminist/conflict perspective and, 35
  focus on, 15b–16b, 15f
  gender/gendered identities and, 78b, 87–92, 87b
  happiness and, 242–243
  having, 244–251
  HIV/AIDS and, 143–144, 144b
  HMI and, 174, 174n, 176, 177
  household labor and, 307, 308b
  immigration and, 62b–63b
  interactionist perspective and, 31–32
  isolation of, 27
  joint, 475
  Latino, 60, 61, 248, 248f, 281–282
  love and, 113
  lower-class, 57
  middle-class, 54, 57
  in military, 50b, 51b
  multicultural families and, 69, 69b
  multicultural society and (*See* Multicultural society)
  multiracial, 282–283
  mutual, 475
  non-Hispanic white, 67, 243, 248, 248f, 252f
  permanence/sexual exclusivity and, 158, 159b
  personal/family change and, 96
  pets and, 4b
  preschool, 273–274, 277, 278
  prison and, 408b–409b

  raising (*See* Raising children)
  religious minority, 283
  remarriage and, 458–459, 461
  same-sex partners and, 198–200, 199b
  school-age, 274
  self-esteem and, 110n
  sex education for, 147f
  sexual development of, 122, 123f
  sexual exploitation of, 384
  sexuality and, 126, 140, 142, 149
  shared, 475
  social pressures and, 240
  stepfamilies and, 458–459, 468–469, 468b
  unmarrieds and, 188, 193b, 202
  violence against, 379–384
  websites for, 25b
  white-collar/blue-collar workers and, 54
  working-class, 57
  young adult, 286–288
"Children as Victims of Hurricane Katrina," 25b
Children of Lesbians and Gays Everywhere (COLAGE), 200
Children's allowance, defined, 428
Children's Influence on Family Dynamics: The Neglected Side of Family Relationships (Crouter and Booth), 34
Child-to-parent abuse, 384
Chinese, 283, 504
Chodorow's theory of gender, defined, 88
Choices
  freedom/pressures of, 9–10
  involving adoption, 261
  love and, 102
  making, 10–12
  for marriage partner (*See* Marriage partner)
  men's market work and, 302
  parenthood and, 235, 240, 241, 243, 257
  personal troubles and, 9–10
  reproductive, 93
  reproductive technology, 256, 257
  sexuality and, 148, 149
  societal influences and, 9–10
Choosing by default, defined, 10–11
Choosing knowledgeably
  defined, 11–12
Christians, 70, 71, 131, 173, 283, 299, 405
Chromosomes, gender/gendered identities and, 78b
Church of Jesus Christ of Latter-day Saints. *See* Latter-day Saints (LDS)
Citizenship, 63b
Civil marriage laws, 158n
Civil Rights Act of 1964, 93
Civil Rights Movement, 58, 93
Civil unions
  defined, 201
  divorce and, 423
  same-sex couples and, 197b, 200, 201b
Class
  gender/gendered identities and, 76, 83
  in nanny hunt, 76b–77b
Class position, economy/social class and, 49
Classical perspectives, on marital power, 354–356
Clinton administration, 82
Close-ended questions, 39
Co-dependents, defined, 110n
Coercive power, 353, 353t, 355, 365b, 371, 372f
Cognitive-developmental theory, 87

Cohabitation
  African Americans and, 195
  American Indians and, 66
  births and, 248
  children and, 170, 190, 191b, 195–196, 195f
  choosing marriage partner and, 225–226
  defined, 189
  divorce and, 415, 418, 423
  ethnicity and, 191b
  intimate partner violence and, 369–370
  Latinos and, 60, 61, 191b, 195
  legal side of, 192b–193b
  nonmarital births and, 248
  as nonmarital living arrangement, 186, 189–191, 191b, 192b–193b, 194–196, 194b
  premarital, 190
  remarriage and, 458, 462
  same-sex couples and, 201
  satisfaction and, 194, 203
  stepfamilies and, 456
  unmarried, 190b
  violence and, 368
Cohabiting couples
  children of, 170
  divorce and, 423
  sex and, 136, 139, 169
Cohabiting families, 170, 195–196, 248
Cohabiting households, 175
Cohabiting relationships, nonmarital living arrangements and, 191, 191b, 194–195
Cohabiting stepfamilies, 456
Cohesive families, 332b, 342
Co-housing, 188b
COLAGE. *See* Children of Lesbians and Gays Everywhere (COLAGE)
Collectivism, 16
Collectivist society, 160, 162
College
  gender/gendered identities and, 83
  parenthood and, 236
"Come out," 129
"Coming out," 123
Commitment
  choosing marriage partner and, 211, 216, 220–225, 225
  cohabitation and, 191, 194, 195
  defined, 104, 105, 105b, 106, 106f
  deinstitutionalized marriage and, 170
  in family definition, 8
  marital power and, 352, 357
  men's market work and, 301
  parenthood as, 241, 243
  premarital relationship and, 220–225
  raising children and, 269
  same-sex couples and, 196, 198b
  weddings as, 155f
Commitment to marriage hypothesis, 418
Commitments, xxxii–19
  choice and, 9–12
  exchange theory and, 33
  in family definition, 2–9
  individuality and, 12–18
Committed cohabitors, 191
Committee on Lesbian and Gay Concerns, 123n
Common couple violence, defined, 376
Common residence, in family definition, 8
Communal living. *See* Group/communal living
Communal societies/cultures, 160

Communal values. *See* Familistic (communal) values
Communal/expressive character traits, defined, 78
Communes, defined, 188, 189
Communication, 328–348
  aging families and, 491*b*
  bonding fights and, 342–345
  choosing marriage partner and, 208, 228
  compromise and, 344
  conflict management and, 336, 338–342
  conflict/love and, 334–336
  cooperation and, 141
  deinstitutionalized marriage and, 173
  divorce and, 336, 336*n*, 338, 346, 347, 419
  electronic, 437
  employment/family work and, 315
  family crises and, 405
  HMI and, 174
  individualized marriage and, 166
  love and, 115*b*, 116, 345
  military and, 51*b*
  no-power relationships and, 366
  power politics and, 363–364
  satisfaction and, 330–334, 344
  sex as, 126
  sexuality and, 141, 148, 148*b*, 149
  supportive, 338
  toward better, 345–347
Community, 57, 63*b*, 160
  as family crises resource, 403, 404*b*, 407
  neighborhood and, 26, 27*b*
  raising children and, 289
  religion and, 70, 72
Community divorce, defined, 424–425
Community resources, for eldercare, 497*b*
Commuter marriages, defined, 316
"Companion" animals, 4*b*
Companionate marriage, 104, 165–166, 165*n*, 167*f*, 173
Comparison level, 125
Competent loners, divorce and, 442*b*
Compromise, communication and, 344
Computers, economy/social class and, 49
Conference of Islamic States, 200
"Conferring distinction," 104
Confidence, raising children and, 269*b*
Conflict
  communication and (*See* Communication)
  conflict-free, 347
  denying, 335–336
  interparental, 273*b*
  love and, 334–336
  marital, 273*b*
  raising children and, 273*b*
  work-family, 266
Conflict management, 336–345
Conflict perspective, 23*t*, 35–36, 37*b*
Conflict Tactics Scale (CTS), 367, 368, 375
Conflict-free conflict, 347
Confucian training doctrine, defined, 282
Congregate housing, defined, 497*b*
"Conjugal succession," 2
Connecticut, Griswold v., 128
Consensual marriages, defined, 191*b*
Conservative Christians, 70–71
Consummate love, defined, 105, 106*f*
Contact, in stepfamily development, 478
"Contaminated" leisure, 309
Contempt, 336, 338, 340, 341
Continuing care facility, defined, 497*b*
Continuity, 179

Continuum of social attachment, 203
Contraception, 185, 244, 252. *See also* Birth control
Control group, 40
Conversation, divorce and, 418
Cooperation, communication and, 141
Co-parenting, defined, 478
Co-parents, defined, 439
Costs
  of having children, 242
  housing, 11*b*
  opportunity, 242
  rewards and (*See* Rewards and costs)
  sexuality and, 125
Counseling, 173, 227, 346, 377–378, 407, 444, 445
Counselors
  divorce and, 430*f*
  marriage, 366–367, 421
  remarriage and, 459, 479
Couple connection, 228–229
Couple satisfaction, 330–334
Courtland State University, Oregon, 304*b*
Courtly love, 162–164
Courtship
  defined, 220
  living together as, 190
  remarriage and, 459
Courtship violence, 224
Covenant marriage, defined, 173–174, 444
Covenant marriage laws, 444
Creating a Life (Hewlett), 215
"Creative divorce," 441
Creative Divorce (Krantzler), 441
Credit cards/charge accounts, unmarried and, 192*b*
Creighton University, 228
Criminal justice, 378–379, 383
Criminal justice approach, child abuse and, 383
Crises. *See* Family crises
Crisis nursery, 383
Crisis-related pathway, divorce and, 441
Criticism, defined, 336, 338
Cross-cultural data, defined, 42
Cross-national marriage, defined, 212–213
Cross-sectional data, 42
Crude divorce rate, 414, 414*f*, 414*n*
CTS. *See* Conflict Tactics Scale (CTS)
Cubans, 239*b*
Cultural changes, as reason for increase in unmarrieds, 185–186
Cultural deviant perspective, defined, 57
Cultural equivalent perspective, defined, 57
Cultural heritage, 13
Cultural identity, 55
Cultural images, gender/gendered identities and, 80, 89–90
Cultural scripts, 126–130, 465
Cultural variant perspective, defined, 57
Culture of Fear, The (Glassner), 24*b*
Culture war, defined, 200
Current Population Survey, 310–311, 361, 414*n*
Custodial fathers, 271*b*, 440
Custodial grandparent, defined, 495–496
Custodial mothers, 440
Custodial parent, defined, 427–428
Custody
  aging families and, 496
  divorce and, 427, 434–439, 434*n*
  joint, 438–439, 438*t*

  joint legal/physical, 438
  remarriages and, 479
  shared, 438
Customs, Asian Americans and, 64
Cyberadultery, defined, 134
Cybersex, 126*b*
Cyberspace, choosing marriage partner and, 216

Danforth, Planned Parenthood v., 253
Data
  cross-cultural, 42
  cross-sectional, 42
  on families, 7*n*, 39–42
  on family violence, 367–368
  gender/gendered identities and, 84, 85, 92*n*
  historical, 42
Data collection, methods of, 39–42, 40*b*
Date/acquaintance rape, 220–221, 221*b*
Dating
  casual, 220–221
  defined, 132*b*
Dating violence, 223–224
Day care, 35, 96, 317*n*, 497*b*. *See also* Child care
"Deadbeat dads," 270
Death rates
  individualized marriage and, 168
  for males, 83
  marital status and, 156*b*
"Deceptive differences," 81*b*
Decision making
  about parenthood, 240–241
  exchange theory and, 33
  intimate partner violence and, 374, 374*f*
  power and, 352, 354–355, 359–360, 361
Decline perspective, 173
Dedication, family and, 2
Defense of Marriage Act (DOMA), 197*b*
Defensiveness, 336, 338, 340, 341
"Deficiency needs," 103
Defining the relationship, 222–223
Deinstitutionalization of marriage, defined, 164
Deinstitutionalized marriage, 164–173
  child outcomes/marital status and, 169–171, 173
  companionate marriage and, 165–166, 167*f*
  consequences of, 168–169
  individualized marriage and, 166–168, 167*f*
  institutional marriage and, 164–165, 167*f*
Delayed childbearing, 7*b*
Demand/withdraw interaction pattern, 339
"Demographic avalanche," 484
Demographic change, as reason for increase in unmarrieds, 184–185
Demographics, of white families, 67
Department of Child Protective Services, 285
Department of Defense, child program from, 25*b*
Department of Health and Human Services, 497
Dependence, defined, 111
Dependency, mutual, 115
Dependent family members, 306
Depression
  aging families and, 502
  child abuse and, 380
  communication and, 340
  divorce and, 420, 421*f*
  intimate partner violence and, 369

Depression (*cont.*)
  marital power and, 357
  in parents, 242
  postpartum, 269
  in preteens/adolescents, 54
  raising children and, 287
Developmental tasks, defined, 27
DI. *See* Donor insemination (DI)
Dignity, 196
Dinner Quilt, The (Ringgold), 161*b*
Discipline
  raising children and, 273, 273*b*, 276
  stepparenting and, 474
Discord, marital, 273*b*
Discover, defined, 114
Discovery, love as, 113*b*, 114–117
Discrimination
  Asian Americans and, 55, 64–65
  divorce and, 427*n*
  feminist/conflict perspective and, 35
  gender, 78, 91
  gender/gendered identities and, 85
  labor force and, 297
  minority group and, 55
  Muslim and, 71
  race/ethnicity and 55, 64–66
  raising children and, 281*b*, 282, 283, 284
  same-sex couples and, 197*b*, 198, 202
  sex, 427*n*
Displacement, defined, 336
Disrupted adoptions, 260
Disruption, marital power and, 352
Dissolved adoptions, 260
Diversity
  adoption and, 259
  in Asian Americans, 64
  child care and, 304*b*–305*b*
  ethnicity and, 57
  in families, 4, 184
  family policy and, 25
  family ties/immigration and, 62*b*–63*b*
  family/household, 4
  gender/gendered identities and,
    79–80, 84
  immigration and, 62*b*–63*b*
  in multicultural society, 280–284
  in nanny hunt, 76*b*–77*b*
  neighborhood/community, 26
  in non-Hispanic whites, 68
  parenting and, 280–284
  racial/ethnic, 55, 58, 59
  religious, 70
  same-sex couples and, 198
Division of labor, marital power and, 352
Divorce, 412–452
  age structure and, 49
  aging families and, 490, 492–496, 504
  alternatives to, 419–422
  barriers to, 417, 419–420, 420*b*
  children and, 210, 415, 416*f*, 419–426, 425*f*,
    426*b*, 428–440, 430*b*–431*b*, 445–446
  choosing marriage partner and, 208, 219,
    225, 226
  cohabitation and, 415, 418, 423
  communication and, 336, 336*n*, 338, 346,
    347, 419
  community, 424–425
  companionate marriage and, 166
  covenant marriage and, 173
  custody after, 427, 434–439, 434*n*
  decreased constraints for, 417–418
  economic, 426–427

economic consequences of, 425–428
economic factors for, 416–417
emotional, 422
ethnicity and, 415, 416*f*, 418–419, 419*t*,
    422, 425, 425*f*
extended family and, 424, 424*b*, 433
factors associated with, 418–419
fault, 417*n*, 423
getting the, 422–425
good, 446–447, 449–450
grandparenting and, 424–425, 424*b*,
    495–496
HMI and, 174
intergenerational transmission of,
    210–211, 418
labor force and, 294, 427, 429
legal, 423–424
marital status and, 156*b*, 157*f*
marriage age and, 209–210
marriage expectations and, 416
military and, 50*b*, 51*b*
no-fault, 417, 417*n*, 423, 444, 445
psychic, 449
relatives of, 424
religion and, 70
remarriage and, 462
same-sex couples and, 200*n*, 201
sexuality and, 130, 135
social class and, 416
surviving, 445–450
two-earner marriages and, 303
unilateral, 423 (*See also* No-fault divorce)
unmarrieds and, 184, 203
Divorce divide, defined, 414
Divorce mediation, defined, 423–424
Divorce rate, 2, 7*b*, 7*n*, 16, 48
  African American, 58
  aging families and, 487*n*
  choosing marriage partner and, 220,
    226, 227
  crude, 414, 414*f*, 414*n*
  gender/gendered identities and, 97
  individualized marriage and, 168
  labor force and, 294, 427, 429
  Latinos and, 61
  marital power and, 361
  marital status and, 156*b*
  in military, 50*b*, 51*b*
  refined, 414, 414*f*, 414*n*
  religion and, 71
  same-sex couples and, 202
  in United States, 154*f*, 155, 414–416, 414*f*
  unmarrieds and, 186
Divorce Revolution, The (Weitzman), 426
"Divorce winners," 442*b*
Divorced parents, 443–444
Divorce-extended family, defined, 449–450
Doctor visits, gender/gendered identities
    and, 83
DOMA. *See* Defense of Marriage Act
    (DOMA)
Domestic abuse, 166, 173, 502
Domestic partner
  defined, 191*b*, 192*b*
  same-sex couples and, 196, 198*b*
Domestic partnerships, 197*b*, 200, 201*b*
*Domestic Revolutions: A Social History of
    American Family Life* (Mintz and
    Kellogg), 48*n*
Domestic violence, 35, 71, 165, 174, 176*n*,
    194, 198, 368, 368*b*, 376–377, 378. *See
    also* Intimate partner violence

Domestic violence model, defined, 503
Domestic violence programs, 373–374
Domestic work, labor force and, 297
Donor insemination (DI), 258*b*
Dopamine, defined, 116
Double messages. *See* Mixed/double
    messages
Double remarriages, defined, 462
Double standard of aging
  aging families and, 490
  remarriage and, 461
Dowry, defined, 213
Dramaturgical sociology, 31*n*
Drinking, 83, 209. *See also* Alcoholism
Drug use, HIV/AIDS and, 143
Drugs
  intimate partner violence and, 377
  raising children and, 267, 285, 286
Dual career, 302
Dual-career families/marriage, 3, 315
Dual-centric, 313, 313*b*
Duke University, 25*b*
Duke University Law School, 193*b*
Dunphy v. Gregor, 8
"Dyadic innovation," 168

Early parenthood, 245–246
Earnings. *See also* Income; Wages
  female-to-male, 85*f*
  men/women, 297
Economic advantages, neighborhood/
    community and, 27
Economic change
  inequality and, 49–53
  as reason for increase in unmarrieds,
    184–185
Economic consequences, of divorce,
    425–440
Economic dependence, intimate partner
    violence and, 373
Economic divorce, defined, 426–427
Economic factors, for divorce, 416–417
Economic hardship perspective, defined, 432
Economic insecurity, divorce and, 416
Economic interdependency, in family
    definition, 8
Economic Opportunity Act, 177*n*
Economic resources, economy/social class
    and, 49
Economic support, as family function, 30
Economic value, of children, 241
Economics, of unpaid family work, 307
Economy
  African Americans and, 59
  age structure and, 49
  aging families in, 488–490
  Latinos and, 60*n*
  male dominance in, 84–85
  social class and, 49–54
"Economy of gratitude," 361–362
Economy of scale, 179
Education. *See also* Schools
  adoption and, 258
  age structure and, 49
  aging families and, 485
  of American Indians, 66
  of Asian Americans, 64
  child abuse and, 383–384
  choosing marriage partner and, 214,
    216, 219
  deinstitutionalized marriage and, 169,
    170, 171

gender and, 83–84, 92
HMI and, 174
immigration and, 62b, 63b, 63n
income and, 53
labor force and, 297
of Latinos, 60, 60n
marriage and, 10, 17, 415, 445
multicultural families and, 69
of Pacific Islanders, 65
parent, 439–440
politics and, 146
premarital, 227
raising children and, 266, 279
sex, 146–148, 147f
social class and, 53
women and, 93
Egalitarian marriages, 362b
Egalitarian norm, defined, 356
Egalitarian power, 354
Egalitarian relationships, 80, 360–361
Eisenstadt v. Baird, 128
Elder abuse, defined, 502–503
Elder maltreatment, 502
Elder neglect, defined, 502–503
Elder Wisdom Circle, 496
Eldercare providers, 498–499
Eldercare/elderly care, 306, 319, 322. *See also* Aging families
   changing American family and, 504–506
   child care and, 506
   community resources for, 497b
   defined, 496
   as family process, 501–502
   gender differences in, 499–500
Elderly
   age structure and, 49
   American Indian, 66
   children and, 15b, 16b
   child-to-parent abuse and, 384
   unmarrieds and, 184
Elderly population, 486f
"Electronic communication," divorce and, 437
E-mail
   aging families and, 187n, 499
   extended family and, 266
   military and, 51b
   raising children and, 266
   relationships through, 2n
Embryo screening, 250
Embryo transfer, 258b
Emergency planning, children and, 25b
Emerging adulthood, defined, 28–29
Emotion
   defined, 102b, 103
   love as, 103, 162
Emotional abuse, 368, 376, 502
"Emotional affairs," 160
Emotional child abuse or neglect, defined, 380
Emotional divorce, defined, 422
Emotional interdependence, 111–114
Emotional security, as family function, 30, 31b
Emotional support, 158, 188
Empathy, 103, 104
Empirical evidence, defined, 38
Employment
   aging families and, 489, 500
   children and, 243, 250
   divorce and, 416
   family work and, 310–316, 311t
   gender/gendered identities and, 85

marriage and, 10
men's market work and, 301
part-time, 303
sexuality and, 138
unmarrieds and, 184
women and, 93, 235, 237, 310, 311, 313, 315
Endogamy, defined, 214
"Enduring image of motherhood," 270
Energy, choosing marriage partner and, 223b
Enforced trust, 179
England, Marriage Act in, 158n
Enhancers, divorce and, 442b
ENRICH, 346
Entitlement, defined, 427
Environment
   family ecology perspective and, 22, 24b, 25
   gender/gendered identities and, 86
   human-built, 22, 22f
   natural physical-biological, 22, 22f
   safety/risk in family, 24b
   social-cultural, 22, 22f
   upper-socioeconomic-level, 27
Equal Rights Marriage Fund, 200
Equality
   divorce and, 426
   marital power and, 352, 357, 360
   norms of, 361
   in same-sex couples, 198
   sexuality and, 125
Equilibrium, defined, 34
Equity
   defined, 109
   marital power and, 352, 357, 360
Eros, defined, 107
Estrogen, 86n
Ethics
   of family research, 38–39
   of reproductive technology, 256–257
   of sexual responsibility, 140, 148–149
Ethnic identity, defined, 55
"Ethnic shifting," 66
Ethnicity
   adoption and, 259–260
   aging families and, 485–488, 495, 503–504
   child-to-parent abuse and, 384
   choosing marriage partner and, 216, 217–219
   cohabitation and, 191b
   defined, 55
   discrimination and, 55
   divorce and, 415, 416f, 418–419, 419t, 422, 425, 425f
   eldercare and, 503–504
   extended family and, 57
   fertility rates and, 238b–239b, 238f
   gender/gendered identities and, 79–80, 84
   grandparenting and, 495
   HIV/AIDS and, 145b, 145f
   income by, 52–53, 52f
   intimate partner violence and, 369
   marital status and, 157f
   men's market work and, 301
   parenting and, 280–284
   poverty rate and, 53
   race, 54–69, 55n, 56f
   sexual expression and, 139–140
   sexuality and, 128t
   stepfamilies and, 458b
   studying families and, 57

in United States, 58
unmarrieds and, 184, 186, 187f
unpaid family work and, 308
Euro-American families, defined, 67
Evangelical Christians, 70, 299
Evangelical marriages, 361–362
Event-driven couples, 223
Evolutionary heritage, defined, 36
Evolutionary psychology, 36. *See also* Biosocial perspective
Exchange balance, defined, 33
Exchange perspective, 125
Exchange theory, 23t, 33–34, 37b, 213, 354, 374, 416
Exclusivity, sexual, 133, 158–160, 164, 196
Exogamy, defined, 214
Expectations of permanence, defined, 158
Expectations of sexual exclusivity, defined, 158, 160
Experience hypothesis, defined, 169, 170, 225
Experiential reality, defined, 38
Experiment, defined, 40–41
Experimental group, 40
Expert power, 353, 353t, 355
Exploitation, aging families and, 502
Expressive character traits. *See* Communal/expressive character traits
Expressive sexuality
   defined, 127
   marriage and, 133
   in United States, 148b
Ex-spouses, parent education for, 439–440
Extended family
   African American, 59, 60, 298
   American Indian, 66
   Asian American, 64
   defined, 13, 29, 30b, 160
   divorce and, 424, 424b, 433
   e-mail and, 266
   ethnicity and, 57
   family crises and, 405b, 406
   HMI and, 176
   kinship authority and, 161
   Latino, 61, 64
   permanence/sexual exclusivity and, 158
   same-sex couples and, 199, 200
Extended family households, 16b
Extended kin, 228
Externalizing behavior problems, raising children and, 273b
Extramarital affairs, 132–135
Extramarital sex, 127n, 134, 135, 160
"Extreme poverty," 280
Extrusion, defined, 171

Face-to-face relationships, 2f, 3b
"Facts About Families: American Families Today," 4b
Fairness
   marital power and, 352, 357–358
   unpaid family work and, 309–310
Families and Work Institute, 313, 317
Families Apart: Ten Keys to Successful Co-parenting (Blau), 448b
Familism, defined, 13, 17b
Familistic (communal) values, 13, 14
Family and Community Health Study, 171
Family and Medical Leave Act, 322
Family boundaries, defined, 34
"Family breakdown," 173. *See also* Family decline

Family career, 27n. *See also* Family life cycle
"Family change," 14, 16–17
"Family change" perspective, 177–178
Family child care, defined, 317
Family Circle magazine, 136b
Family cohesion, defined, 330
Family crises, 388–410
    course of, 398–399, 398f
    as disaster or opportunity, 407–410
    HIV/AIDS and, 143
    meeting, 404–407
    theoretical model of, 400–404, 402b
    theoretical perspectives on, 390–391
    what precipitates, 392–398
Family decline, 14, 16–17, 445–446
"Family decline" perspective, defined, 14
Family development perspective, 23t, 27–29, 37b, 390, 391
Family ecology perspective, 22–27, 22f, 23t, 24b, 37b, 266, 391, 391b
Family Energy Project, 23
Family foster care, defined, 286
Family: From Institution to Companionship 1953, The (Burgess and Locke), 2, 165
Family functions, defined, 30
Family Group (Moore), 234b
Family households, 15b
Family instability perspective, defined, 433
Family integrity, 505
Family law, stepfamilies and, 467–468
Family leave, defined, 322
Family life, nonmarital living arrangements and, 189–191, 192b–193b, 194–196
Family life course, 27n, 390
Family life cycle, defined, 27–28, 27n
Family Life 1st, 280
Family myths, 324
Family of orientation, defined, 161
Family of procreation, defined, 161
Family policy, 24–26
Family power, 471
Family preservation, defined, 383
Family Pride Coalition, 200
Family Research Council website, 200
Family Research Laboratory, 367n
Family size, 70, 236, 236b, 237b, 240, 294
Family sponsorship, 62b
Family stress, 388–391, 398, 400–404, 402b
Family structure, defined, 29
Family Support Act, 428n, 436
Family systems theory, 23b, 34, 37b, 391, 391b
Family therapy, 35
Family time, raising children and, 280
Family transitions, defined, 390
Family "turnaround," 173
Family violence, 367–384
Family Violence Research Program, 367n
Family-centric, 313, 313b
Family/families
    aging (*See* Aging families)
    bicultural, 67
    binational, 60, 62b
    binuclear, 446–447, 449, 478
    blended, 478
    blinders of personal experience and, 38
    blue-collar, 53–54, 323
    boys/girls in, 88–89
    choices for (*See* Choices)
    cohabiting, 170, 195–196, 248
    cohesive, 332b, 342
    data and, 7n, 39–42
    defined, 2–9

divorce-extended, 449–450
dual-career, 3, 315
ethics of research on, 38–39
Euro-American, 67
extended (*See* Extended family)
facts about, 6b–7b, 15b–16b
female-headed, 66, 174
fragile, 249, 251
gay, 3, 8b. *See also* Gay male/men and same sex
grandparent, 285
homeless, 278–279, 400b–401b
of individuals, 12–14, 16–18
"instant," 478
interracial/interethnic, 68–69, 69b
lesbian, 3. *See also* Lesbians and same-sex
marginal, 67
married-couple, 5t, 57, 60, 64, 169, 169t, 300, 300f, 425f
married-parent, 175
military, 50b–51b
mother-headed, single-parent, 171b
multiracial/multiethnic, 68–69, 69b
neotraditional, 298–299, 361–362
nuclear (*See* Nuclear family)
one-child, 246–247
of orientation, 161
perspectives on (*See* Perspectives)
pets as, 3, 4b
as place to belong, 13
pluralistic, 168, 184, 196
postmodern, 168
power in (*See* Power)
of procreation, 161
remarried, 456, 464–465 (*See also* Remarriage)
resilient, 398, 404
reversed-role, 3
same sex, 196–202, 376–377
single-father, 64
single-mother, 14, 61, 64, 400b–401b
single-parent (*See* Single-parent families)
in social context (*See* Social context)
as social institution, 158
studying, 37–42, 57
supernormative, 237b
tasks for, 8b
three-generation, 3
traditional, 67
transitional, 67
transnational, 62b, 65
two-parent, 58–59, 61, 62b, 174, 248, 270, 415
violence in (*See* Violence)
vulnerable, 398, 404
white-collar, 52, 53–54
work and (*See* Work)
working-class, 54
Family-friendly workplace policies, defined, 322
Fantasy, in stepfamily development, 478
Father involvement, 171
Fathers
    adoption and, 259
    African American, 59
    aging families and, 494
    biosocial perspective and, 36
    child abuse and, 382
    children and, 241b, 245, 249, 251
    custodial, 271b, 440
    divorce and, 419, 428, 429, 432, 434–437, 435n, 439–441, 443

employment/family work and, 314, 314f
family development perspective and, 29
gender/gendered identities and, 86, 87, 88
Latino, 61
men's market work and, 301, 302
in multicultural society, 270–272
noncustodial, 436–437, 440, 441
personal/family change and, 96
in poverty, 177
as primary parents, 271b
prison and, 408b
race/ethnicity and, 56
raising children and, 266, 268, 269, 269b, 270–272, 272b, 276, 279
religion and, 71
reproductive technology and, 256
social, 277
work/family issues and, 317
Fault divorce, 417n, 423
Fear, intimate partner violence and, 371
"Fear of abandonment," 209
Fecundity, defined, 234n
Federal Bureau of Prisons, 408b
Federal Emergency Management Agency (FEMA), 25b
Federal Office on Violence Against Women, 378
Feelings, love and, 116
FEMA. *See* Federal Emergency Management Agency (FEMA)
Female demand/male-withdraw communication pattern, 337b, 338, 339, 340
Female genital mutilation (FGM), 379, 379n
Female-headed families, 66, 174
Female-headed households, 3, 5t, 53, 169
Female-partner abuse, 370
Females. *See also* Women
    aging families and, 489, 502
    biosocial perspective and, 36
    choosing marriage partner and, 219
    gender inequality and, 81–86, 85f, 86n
    gender/gendered identities and, 76–81, 78b, 80f, 90
    gender/socialization and, 87–92
    life expectancy for, 83
    male dominance and, 81
    unmarrieds and, 184n
Feminine Mystique, The (Friedan), 93
Feminism, 93–95, 93n, 243
Feminist movement, 48, 82–83, 93–95, 131, 166, 173, 174n, 272
Feminist perspective, 23t, 35–36, 37b
Feminist theorist, 102
Feminities, defined, 79. *See also* Women
Fertility, 6b–7b, 14, 70, 234n, 244, 250, 251, 255. *See also* Birth rate
Fertility rates, 17, 67, 236–239. *See also* Birth rate
Fertility trends, 235–239
FGM. *See* Female genital mutilation (FGM)
Fictive kin, 60, 160, 406, 503
Filial responsibility, defined, 498
Filipinos, 218, 218n
Finances
    older women and, 489–490
    unmarrieds and, 192b
Financial resources, divorce and, 419
Financial strains, stepparenting and, 470
First marriages, stepfamilies and, 464–465
"First Wave," of feminism, 93n

First years of marriage, 227–228
Flat Daddies, 50*b*
Flat Mommies, 50*b*
Flexible scheduling, defined, 322
Flextime, defined, 322
Florida Today newspaper, 267*b*
Ford Foundation, 313
Foreign-born blacks, 60
Forgiveness, communication and, 345
Formal kinship care, defined, 286
Fortin, Michael, *People v.*, 434*n*
Fortune 500 companies, 8
Foster care, defined, 285, 286
Foster parents, 285–286
Four Horsemen of the Apocalypse, 336, 338, 340, 341–342
Fragile Families and Child Wellbeing Study, 251
Fragile Families study, 249, 251
Free-choice culture, 212, 212*b*, 213
Frequency, sexual, 135, 136, 137, 137*f*, 138, 139, 140
Friendly parent concept, divorce and, 434*n*
Friends
  divorce and, 425
  HMI and, 176
  as primary group, 3*b*
  self-esteem and, 111
  sexuality and, 132, 132*b*–133*b*
"Friends with benefits," 132, 132*b*–133*b*, 220
Friendships, 203–204, 208, 245
Fulfillment, family, 2
Fun, communication and, 333–334

Gallup poll, 131, 154, 159*b*, 172*b*, 184, 248, 253, 253*f*, 298, 311, 311*t*
Games, 89
GAP. *See* Grandparents as Parents (GAP)
Gay and Lesbian Advocates and Defenders (GLAD), 200
Gay and lesbian (GL) stepfamilies, 458*b*
Gay families, 3, 8*b*
Gay lifestyles, 66
Gay male, lesbian, bisexual, or transgendered (GLBT), 124*b*, 196
Gay male behavior, 129–130
Gay male/men
  abuse among, 376–377
  adoptions and, 260
  children and, 193*b*
  cultural scripts and, 128, 129–130, 129*b*, 129*n*
  defined, 124
  heterosexual expression and, 130*n*
  HIV/AIDS and, 143
  kinship authority and, 160
  men's market work and, 301–302
  race/ethnicity and, 140
  as same-sex couples, 196–202
  same-sex marriages and, 202
  sexual orientation and, 123–124, 123*n*
  sexuality throughout marriage and, 139
  unpaid family work and, 310
Gay partnership, 6*b*
Gender
  aging families and, 499
  divorce and, 419*t*
  intimate partner violence and, 369, 369*f*
  life expectancy and, 484–485
  marital power and, 355, 357, 359, 360
Gender ambiguity, 78*b*
Gender boundaries, 78*b*

Gender differences
  aging families and, 488*n*, 499–500
  biosocial perspective and, 36
  communication and, 337*b*
  in couple communication, 338–342
  gender/gendered identities and, 81, 83, 85, 86, 92, 92*n*
  intimate partner violence and, 376
  in older Americans' living arrangements, 487
  of prisoners, 408*b*
  in providing eldercare, 499–500
  sexuality and, 132, 135
Gender discrimination, 78, 91
Gender expectations, 77–80
Gender inequality, 76, 81–86, 96–97, 165
Gender issues. *See also* Gender/gendered identities
  in feminist/conflict perspectives, 35
  in intimate partner violence, 371–376
Gender model of marriage, defined, 362–363
Gender roles
  African American, 59
  biosocial perspective and, 36
  choosing marriage partner and, 214
  cohabitation and, 194
  counselors and, 366
  defined, 76
  divorce and, 434, 435
  gender/gendered identities and, 78*b*, 87*b*, 89*b*
  Latinos and, 61, 64
  Men's Movements and, 95
  personal/family change and, 96
  religion and, 70
  remarriages/stepfamilies and, 461–462
  structure-functional perspective and, 31
Gender schema theory, defined, 87–88
Gender similarities hypothesis, defined, 81
Gender strategies, for two-earner marriages/relationships, 324
Gendered socialization, intimate partner violence and, 373
Gender/gendered identities, 74–99
  anatomy and, 85–86
  defined, 76, 76*b*, 76*n*
  diversity and, 79–80
  economy and, 84–85
  education and, 83–84
  expectations/cultural messages, 77*b*–81
  future of, 96–97
  health and, 83
  HIV/AIDS and, 145*b*
  inequality and, 81–86
  male dominance and (*See* Male dominance)
  in nanny hunt, 76*b*–77*b*
  politics and, 81–82
  religion and, 82–83
  sexual pleasure and, 141
  sexuality and, 128*t*
  social change and, 92–97
  socialization and, 86–92
  violence and, 223
General Social Survey, 125, 133, 136*b*, 186, 217, 325
Generalized, defined, 39, 88
Generation X, 313, 313*b*
Generation Y, 313, 313*b*
Genes, 36
Genetic history, in family definition, 8

Genetics, aging families and, 485
Genital systems, of males/females, 122
Gentiles, 216
Geographic availability, defined, 214–215
Geographic segregation, 216
Germany, divorce and, 445
Gerontologists, defined, 496
Girls
  boys *vs.*, 80, 81, 83, 84, 86–92, 92*n*
  in family, 88–89
  raising children and, 269, 273*b*
  sexuality and, 123*f*, 131
  stereotypes and, 81*b*
GL stepfamilies. *See* Gay and Lesbian (GL) stepfamilies
GLAD. *See* Gay and Lesbian Advocates and Defenders (GLAD)
GLBT. *See* Gay male, lesbian, bisexual, or transgendered (GLBT)
GlBT, defined, 124*b*
Global interconnections, gender/gendered identities and, 76
Globalization, 23, 48, 51, 162
Goals. *See also* Values
  in choosing marriage partner, 208
  ethnicity and, 57
  gender/gendered identities and, 84
  making choices and, 12, 13, 13*b*
  of Men's Movements, 95
  of NOW, 93
  self-esteem and, 111
  of "welfare reform," 174
Gonzalez v. Carhart, 253
Good dad–bad dad, 270
Good divorce, 446–447, 449–450
Good Divorce, The (Ahrons), 449
Good provider role, defined, 300
Goodenoughs, divorce and, 442*b*
Government
  American Indians and, 65
  child support and, 428
  family policy and, 25–26
  HMI and, 174
  immigrants and, 60*n*
  marital status and, 155*n*
  sexuality and, 128
Grandchildren
  aging families and, 493–496, 498*b*
  as caregivers, 498*b*
  divorce and, 424, 424*b*
Grandparent families, defined, 285
Grandparenthood, 494–496
Grandparents as Parents (GAP), 285
Grandparents/grandparenting
  age structure and, 49
  aging families and, 486
  American Indians and, 66
  custodial, 495–496
  divorce and, 424–425, 424*b*, 495–496
  ethnicity and, 495
  family facts and, 16*b*
  in multicultural society, 285
  noncustodial, 496
  as parents, 285
Granville, Troxel v., 424
Great Depression
  aging families and, 488*n*
  American family and, 48
  labor force and, 294
Great-grandparents
  age structure and, 49
  aging families and, 486

Great-great-grandparents, aging families and, 486
Gregor, Dunphy v., 8
Griswold v. Connecticut, 128
Group homes, defined, 286
Group therapy, 377–378
Group/communal living, as nonmarital living arrangement, 188–189
Gunnysacking, 342, 344
Guttmacher Institute report, 252–253

Habituation
    aging families and, 490
    defined, 138
Habituation hypothesis, defined, 134
Hague Convention on Intercountry Adoption, 260
Hague Convention on International Child Abduction, 437
Handbook of Divorce and Relationship Dissolution (Amato and Irving), 414*n*
Handbook of International Adoptive Medicine (Miller), 261
Happiness
    aging families and, 490
    children and, 242–243
    choosing marriage partner and, 208–209, 219, 227
    courtly love and, 164
    divorce and, 419, 421
    love and, 111
    marital, 330, 338, 419–420, 461
    marital power and, 357, 360
    marriage and, 178–179
    remarriage and, 460*b*, 461–464
    two-earner marriages and, 323
    unpaid family work and, 309–310
Hara, Singer v., 197*b*
Hardwick, Bowers v., 128
Harmonious needs, choosing marriage partner and, 223*b*
Hawaiians. *See* Native Hawaiians
Head Start, 177*n*
"Headship," 70, 82
Health
    aging families and, 490, 499*b*, 502
    children and, 245
    choosing marriage partner and, 229
    deinstitutionalized marriage and, 169, 170
    divorce and, 420
    employment/family work and, 311
    gender and, 83
    unmarrieds and, 184
Health care
    aging families and, 485, 488*n*, 489
    raising children and, 266
    unmarrieds and, 193*b*
Health insurance
    aging families and, 489
    feminist/conflict perspective and, 35
    raising children and, 278, 287
Healthy Marriage Initiative (HMI), 174–177, 174*n*, 175*b*
Hermaphrodites, defined, 78*b*
Heterogamy, 216–220, 219*b*
    defined, 214
    human values and, 220
    interclass marriages and, 217
    interfaith marriages and, 216–217
    interracial/interethnic marriages and, 217–219
    marital stability and, 219–220

Heterosexism, defined, 128–130
Heterosexual cohabiting/married couples, 129–130
Heterosexual expression, 130–135
Heterosexual love, 102
Heterosexual marriage, same-sex couples and, 201
Heterosexuals
    defined, 123
    HIV/AIDS and, 142–143
    majority are, 124*b*
    sexuality and, 128
H-frame relationships, defined, 112, 113
HHMI. *See* Hispanic Healthy Marriage Initiative (HHMI)
Hidden agenda, defined, 474
Hierarchical parenting, defined, 281
Higher-order births, 235, 235*b*
Hindus, 70, 283
Hispanic Healthy Marriage Initiative (HHMI), 174
Hispanics. *See* Latinos (Hispanics)
Historical data, defined, 42
Historical events, American family through, 48–49, 48*n*
Historical Influences on Lives and Aging (Schaie and Elder), 48*n*
Historical research, 42
HIV/AIDS, 129*n*, 130, 135, 142–149, 144*b*–145*b*, 145*n*, 147*f*
    adoptions and, 260
    permanence/exclusivity and, 159*b*
    raising children and, 285
HMI. *See* Healthy Marriage Initiative (HMI)
Hmong, 188, 210, 213, 215*b*
Holiday celebrations, 70, 71
Holistic view of sex, defined, 141–142
Holmes-Rahe Social Readjustment Rating Scale, 401*n*
Home care, defined, 497*b*
"Home of the gray," 484
Home-based work, 303–305
Homeless families, 278–279, 400*b*–401*b*
Homemakers/homemaking, 91, 269, 270, 492
Homogamy, 214–220, 215*b*, 219*b*
    heterogamy and (*See* Heterogamy)
    reasons for, 215–216
    in remarriage, 461
Homophobia, 129, 376
Homosexual love, 102
Homosexual relations, Latinos and, 61
Homosexuality, 70, 123–124, 128–130, 140, 147*f*
Homosexuals
    defined, 123
    as same-sex couples, 196–202
    sexual orientation and, 123*n*
Honoring, 104, 111
"Hook up," 132, 132*b*–133*b*, 220
Horizontal stressors, 403*n*
Hormonal processes, defined, 86
Hormones
    defined, 86*n*
    gender/gendered identities and, 78*b*, 86
Hostility, Asian Americans and, 64
House of Representatives, 81
Household
    aging families and, 487
    children and, 14
    cohabiting, 175
    data for, 7*n*
    defined, 3, 5*t*, 7*n*

extended family, 16*b*
family, 15*b*
female-headed, 3, 5*t*, 53, 169
heterosexual, 195
male-headed, 3, 5*t*, 53, 169
married-couple, 15*b*, 16*b*, 53, 69, 170, 195, 195*f*
multigenerational, 6*b*
nonfamily, 5*t*, 7*n*
one-person, 186
same-sex, 6*b*
same-sex couple, 6*b*, 195*f*
same-sex partner, 6*b*, 195*f*
single parent family, 15*b*
single-father, 15*b*
single-mother, 15*b*, 57, 415
single-parent, 3, 15*b*, 16*b*, 53, 57, 169, 174, 302
single-person, 6*b*
two-parent, 15*b*, 168
types of, 5*t*
unmarried couple, 3, 5*t*, 6*b*, 69
Household income, 52, 52*f*
Household work, 357–358
Househusbands, 96, 301, 302
Housework, 194*b*, 195, 306–310, 358*f*, 416, 461
Housing costs, children/parents and, 11*b*
Huck's Raft: A History of American Childhood (Mintz), 48*n*
Human Rights Campaign, 193*b*
Human sexuality, 125–126
Human-built environment, 22, 22*f*
Hurricane Katrina, 4*b*
"Hurried" child, 279–280
Husbands and Wives: The Dynamics of Married Living (Blood and Wolfe), 354
Hypergamy, defined, 217
Hypogamy, defined, 217
Hypotheses/ideas, 38, 81*n*

I Don't Want to Talk About It (Real), 339–340
IBM, 312
Identity release movement, 256*n*
Identity/identities
    adoption and, 259
    American Indian, 67
    choices and, 13
    cultural, 55
    defined, 31
    ethnic, 55
    gender/gendered (*See* Gender/gendered identities)
    marital power and, 360
    multiracial/multiethnic, 68*n*, 69
    parenthood as, 241
Illegal aliens, 63*b*
Illegal immigrants, 63*n*
Illegitimate needs, defined, 103
Illinois, Stanley v., 193*b*
Illinois Supreme Court, 383
Image of motherhood, 270
Immersion, in stepfamily development, 478
"Immigrant ethos," 63*b*
Immigrant stepfamilies, 466*b*
Immigrants/immigration
    African Americans and, 60
    aging families and, 487–488, 488
    Asian American, 64, 65
    child abuse and, 382, 382*n*, 383–384
    child care and, 304*b*, 307
    choosing marriage partner and, 211, 212, 213, 214, 219*b*

deinstitutionalized marriage and, 165*b*
ethnicity and, 57
family crises and, 406
family ties and, 62*b*–63*b*
fertility rates and, 239*b*
FGM and, 379*n*
gender/gendered identities and, 91
illegal, 63*n*
intimate partner violence and, 372
kinship authority and, 161
Latinos and, 60*n*, 61, 64
legal, 62*b*, 63*b*
marital power and, 355
multicultural families and, 69
non-Hispanic whites and, 68
race/ethnicity and, 54, 55
raising children and, 283*n*
religion and, 68*b*, 70
undocumented, 60, 62*b*, 63*b*
unmarrieds and, 184
Impaired fertility, defined, 255
Impersonal society, 102, 102*n*
In vitro fertilization (IVF), 258*b*
Incarceration, family crises and, 408*b*–409*b*
Incarceration rates, 59, 59*b*, 184
Incest, defined, 380
Inclusive fitness, defined, 36
Income. *See also* Earnings; Wages
adoption and, 258
African American, 58, 59
aging families and, 485, 488, 488*n*, 489, 489*b*, 489*n*
American Indian, 65–66
Asian American, 64
children and, 242, 243, 279
deinstitutionalized marriage and, 169, 169*t*, 170, 171
divorce and, 426, 427
economy/social class and, 49, 52–53, 52*f*
employment/family work and, 313
by ethnicity, 52–53, 52*f*
fertility rates and, 239*b*
HMI and, 176, 176*n*
household, 52, 52*f*
immigration and, 62*b*
labor force and, 298
multicultural families and, 69
non-Hispanic white, 67
Pacific Islander, 65
parenthood and, 236
race/ethnicity and, 55, 56
reproductive technology and, 256
social class and, 53
unmarrieds and, 202, 203
of white-collar/blue-collar workers, 54
Income effect, defined, 416
Income-to-needs ratio, defined, 426, 427
Incomplete institution, defined, 465
Independence, defined, 112
Independence effect, defined, 416
Independent adoptions, 259
Independent adults, parents and, 288
India, arranged marriages in, 211–212, 212*b*
Indian Child Welfare Act of 1978, 65, 259*n*
Individual rights, 13
Individualism, 16, 17*b*, 160, 164
Individualistic (self-fulfillment) values, 13, 14
Individualistic society, defined, 160
Individuality
defined, 13
in family, 12–14, 16–18
in sexual expression, 140

Individualized marriage, 166–168, 167*f*
Induced abortion, defined, 252
Industrial Revolution, 294
Inequality
economic change and, 49–53
economy/social class and, 52, 54
feminist/conflict perspective and, 35
gender, 76, 81–86, 96–97, 165
gender/gendered identities and, 76, 81–86, 93
racial/ethnic. *See* poverty.
reproductive technology and, 256
Infant mortality rates, 235–236, 241
in African Americans, 58
in American Indians, 66
in Asian Americans, 64
defined, 61
in males, 83
in Pacific Islanders, 65
Infants, 269–270, 273
Infatuation, 115, 116
Infertility, 254–257
Infidelity, 133, 135, 160
Inflation, 17, 52, 52*f*, 53
Informal adoption, defined, 258
Informal caregiving, defined, 496
Informational power, 353, 353*t*, 355, 358, 360
Informed consent, defined, 39
In-home caregiver, defined, 317
In-laws, divorce and, 424
In-race adoptions, 260
Insecure/anxious attachment style, 113, 114
"Inside/Out Dad," 408*b*
Instability, 15*b*–16*b*
Instability hypothesis, defined, 433
"Instant families," 478
Instant messaging, relationships through, 2*n*
Institute for American Values, 159*b*
Institute for Research, University of Michigan, 194*b*
Institutional marriage, 164–165, 167*f*
Institutional review board (IRB), 38–39
Instrumental character traits. *See* Agentic/instrumental character traits
Insurance
health (*See* Health insurance)
infertility and, 255–256
unmarrieds and, 192*b*
Interaction, defined, 31
Interaction theory, 125
Interactionist perspective, 29*t*, 31–33, 31*n*, 33*b*, 37*b*, 41, 123, 125–126, 126*b*, 222, 330, 391, 402
Interclass marriages, defined, 217
Interdependence
defined, 112
emotional, 111–114
Interethnic marriages, 217–219. *See also* Intermarriage; Interracial marriage
Interfaith marriage, 71, 216–217
Interference with visitation, defined, 436
Intergenerational relationships, 443–444, 493, 493*t*
Intergenerational transmission of divorce, 210–211, 418
Intermarriage. *See also* Interethnic marriages; Interracial marriage
American Indian, 67
Asian American, 64
choosing marriage partner and, 216, 220
multicultural families and, 69

racial, 10
raising children and, 283
Internal sex structures, gender/gendered identities and, 78*b*
Internalized, defined, 32, 88
Internalizing behavior problems, raising children and, 273*b*
International abduction, 437
International adoptions, 258, 260–261
International Nanny Association, 305*b*
Internet
adultery on, 134
aging families and, 487*n*, 502
American Indians and, 67
choosing marriage partner and, 216, 222
communication and, 346
divorce and, 437
economy/social class and, 49
Men's Movement and, 95
permanence/sexual exclusivity and, 159*b*
raising children and, 266, 267, 271*b*, 279
same-sex couples and, 196, 200*n*
sexual interaction/relationships over, 126
unmarrieds and, 193*b*
Interparental conflict, raising children and, 273*b*
Interparental conflict perspective, defined, 432
Interpersonal exchange model of sexual satisfaction, defined, 125
Interracial adoptions, 259
Interracial marriage, 69*b*, 217–219, 218*f*, 218*n*. *See also* Interethnic marriages; Intermarriage
Interracial/interethnic families. *See* Multicultural families
InterracialMatcher.com, 216
Intersectionality, 93
Intersex Society of North America, 78*b*
Intersexual, defined, 78*b*
Interviews
as data collection, 39
infertility, 255
longitudinal studies and, 41
on marital power, 354
sex surveys and, 136*b*
Intimacy
choosing marriage partner and, 229
communication and, 331
defined, 104, 105*b*, 106
divorce and, 417
family and, 2, 8*b*
love and, 104–106, 105*b*, 106*f*, 111, 113, 116
marital power and, 360
psychic/sexual, 104–105
remarriage and, 460*b*
sex as, 126
sexual, 104
sexuality and, 127, 130, 132, 139, 148, 148*b*
time and, 142
two-earner marriages/relationships and, 324–325
Intimate partner power, defined, 352
Intimate partner violence, 367–376, 376*n*, 377. *See also* Domestic violence
Intimate terrorism, 376*n*
Involuntary infertility, 254–257
IRB. *See* Institutional review board (IRB)
Irish American, raising children and, 282
Iron John (Bly), 96
"Irreconcilable differences," 423, 444

"Irretrievable breakdown," 423, 444
Islam, 71, 71*b*, 82, 131
Isolation of children, 27
I-statements, 274, 342*b*, 343
Italians, 160, 161, 282, 503
Italy, divorce and, 445
IVF. *See* In vitro fertilization (IVF)

Japanese, 218, 218*n*
Jews, 70, 82, 196, 216–217, 283
Job Corps, 177*n*
Job description, parent, 267*b*
Job sharing, defined, 322
Jobs. *See also* Careers
    blue-collar, 295*n*, 299
    careers *vs.*, 302
John Hopkins University, gender/gendered
        identities and, 78*b*
Johnson and Johnson, 312
Joint children, 475
Joint custody, defined, 438–439, 438*t*
Joint legal and physical custody, 438
Joint legal custody, 438
Judaism, 71, 257*n*, 299
Judeo-Christian tradition, 160
Jumping the Broom (Cole), 172*b*
Justice Department, 437

Kin
    defined, 160
    family crises and, 406
    fictive, 60, 160, 406, 503
    virtual, 160
Kin networks, in stepfamilies, 467
"Kin supply," 504
"Kinkeepers," 306
Kinsey reports, 136*b*
Kinship authority, 160–162, 164
Kinship Caregiver Support Act, 285
Kinship groups, 158, 160, 165*b*

Labor force. *See also* Work
    African Americans and, 295, 298
    aging families and, 489, 491, 504
    Asian Americans and, 295
    defined, 294, 294*n*
    divorce and, 294, 427, 429
    leaving, 305–306
    men in, 294–299, 296*f*, 301–302, 307
    reentry into, 305–306
    wives in, 416–417
    women in, 17, 26, 294–299, 294*f*, 295*b*,
        296*f*, 299*b*, 307, 311
Laboratory observation, defined, 40–41
Ladies Home Journal, 420–421
Laissez-faire parenting style
    defined, 274
    Native Americans and, 281
Lambda Legal, 193*b*
LaMusga, Navarro v., 439
Language
    Asian Americans and, 64
    gender/gendered identities and, 91
    immigration and, 62*b*
Laotian, 308
LAS. *See* Love Attitudes Scale (LAS)
Late parenthood, 245–246
Latent kin matrix, defined, 505
Latino studies, 67
Latinos (Hispanics), 52*f*, 53, 55, 55*n*, 56, 56*f*,
    57, 58, 60–61, 60*n*, 61*b*, 62*b*, 64, 67–69
    abortions for, 61, 253*n*

adoption and, 258, 259, 260
aging families and, 486–488, 486*f*, 488*n*,
    488*t*, 503
child abuse and, 381
child care and, 317
children and, 60, 61, 248, 248*f*, 281–282
choosing marriage partner and, 214, 215,
    217–218, 218*f*
cohabitation and, 60, 61, 191*b*, 195
deinstitutionalized marriage and, 169,
    171, 171*b*, 172*b*
divorce and, 415, 416*f*, 419, 419*t*, 425*f*
family crises and, 406
fertility rates among, 238*b*–239*b*, 238*f*
gender/gendered identities and, 80, 83,
    84, 90–91, 93, 94
HIV/AIDS and, 144*b*, 145*b*, 145*f*
intimate partner violence and, 369, 369*f*
kinship authority and, 160, 161
labor force and, 295, 297
marital status of, 156*b*, 157*f*
men's market work and, 301
poverty rate for, 176
prison and, 408*b*
raising children and, 270, 273*b*, 278, 280,
    281–282, 283–284, 284*b*
remarriage and, 458*b*
same-sex couples and, 196
unmarrieds and, 184, 186, 187*f*
unpaid family work and, 308
Latter-day Saints (LDS), 70, 82, 159*b*, 201*n*,
    216, 299
Lawrence et al. v. Texas, 128–129
Legal and physical joint custody, 439
Legal constraints, divorce and, 417–418
Legal divorce, defined, 423–424
Legal immigrants, 62*b*, 63*b*
Legal joint custody, 439
Legal marriage, for same-sex couples, 197*b*,
    200–202, 200*n*, 201*b*
Legal residence, 63*b*
Legitimate needs, defined, 103
Legitimate power, 353, 353*t*, 355, 356*b*, 358,
    359, 360, 361
Leisure gap, defined, 309
Leisure time
    marital power and, 357–358
    two-earner marriages and, 303
Lesbians. *See also* Same-sex
    abuse among, 376–377
    adoptions and, 260
    behavior and, 129–130
    children and, 193*b*
    cultural scripts and, 128, 129–130,
        129*b*, 129*n*
    defined, 124
    families, 3
    heterosexual expression and, 130*n*
    kinship authority and, 160
    lifestyle, 93
    as parents, 198–200, 201
    partnership, 6*b*
    race/ethnicity and, 140
    as same-sex couples, 196–202, 199*b*
    same-sex marriages for, 202
    sexual orientation and, 123–124, 123*n*
    sexuality throughout marriage and, 139
    unpaid family work and, 310
Leveling, defined, 342–343
Levinger's model of divorce decisions,
    defined, 419
Life chances, defined, 49

Life expectancy, 49, 83, 484–486
Life stress perspective, defined, 432
"Lifestyle practitioners," 159*b*. *See also*
    Swinging
Limerence, defined, 110
Listener backchannels, defined, 333
Listening
    communication and, 332–333, 346*b*
    love and, 116
Litigation, divorce mediation *vs.*, 423–424
Living alone
    aging families and, 487, 487*n*
    as nonmarital living arrangement, 184, 187*f*
Living alone together, as nonmarital living
    arrangement, 186–187
Living arrangements
    nonmarital (*See* Nonmarital living
        arrangements)
    of older Americans, 487–488, 487*t*, 488*t*
Living together, 154. *See also* Cohabitation
Living trusts. *See* Wills/living trusts
Living with parents, as nonmarital living
    arrangement, 187–188, 187*t*
Loneliness
    aging families and, 490
    defined, 203
Longevity, 14, 83
Longitudinal research, 33, 41
Longitudinal studies
    data collections methods and, 39
    defined, 41–42
    of "test-tube" babies, 258*b*
Longitudinal Study of Generations, 16, 161
Looking-glass self, defined, 32, 88
Love, 102–109
    altruistic, 108, 108*b*
    caring/acceptance and, 103–104
    choosing marriage partner and,
        211–212
    communication and, 115*b*, 116, 345
    conflict and, 334–336
    consummate, 105, 106*f*
    courtly, 162–164
    defined, 102, 102*b*
    as discovery, 113*b*, 114–117
    as emotion, 103, 162
    finding, 115*b*
    homosexual, 102
    intimacy and, 104–106, 105*b*, 106*b*, 111,
        113, 116
    intimate partner violence and, 356, 373
    keeping, 115–117, 115*b*
    limerence and, 110
    manipulating and, 109–110
    marriage and, 162–164, 417
    martyring and, 109
    misconceptions about, 115–117
    one true, 102
    permanence/sexual exclusivity and, 158
    personal needs and, 103
    pragmatic, 208
    remarriage and, 460*b*
    romantic, 160, 164, 208
    triangular theory of, 105–106, 106*f*, 114
    what is, 102–109, 102*b*
    wheel of, 114–115, 114*f*, 222
"Love at first sight," 102
Love Attitudes Scale (LAS), 107, 108, 109
Love styles, 106–109
Loving ourselves/others, 100–118
    love and (*See* Love)
    self-worth as prerequisite to, 110–114

Loving v. Virginia, 10, 217
Lower-class children, 57
Lower-income marriages, 17
Ludus, defined, 108

"Majority-minority" states, 58
Male dominance
    defined, 81
    in economy, 84–85
    gender/gendered identities and,
        80, 96
    in politics, 81–82
    in religion, 82–83
Male privilege, 96
Male-headed households, 3, 5*t*, 53, 169
Males. *See also* Men
    African American, 59*b*
    aging families and, 489, 502
    Asian American, 65
    biosocial perspective and, 36
    gender inequality and, 81–86, 85*f*, 86*n*
    gender/gendered identities and, 76–81,
        78*b*, 80*f*, 81*b*, 90
    gender/socialization and, 87–92
    immigration and, 63*b*
    life expectancy for, 83
    unmarrieds and, 184*n*
Maltreatment
    child, 379, 381, 382, 384
    elder, 502
MANA. *See* Mexican American Women's
    National Association (MANA)
Mania, defined, 108
Manipulating, defined, 109–110
Marginal families, defined, 67
Marital conflict, raising children
    and, 273*b*
Marital discord, raising children
    and, 273*b*
"Marital dissolution," 423
Marital exchange, 213–214
Marital happiness, 330, 338, 419–420, 461.
    See also Happiness
Marital Instability Over the Life Course
    surveys, 419
Marital power, 352, 353–363, 471. *See also*
    Power
"Marital privacy," 128
Marital quality
    in choosing marriage partner, 225–226
    remarriage and, 462
Marital rape, 95, 370
Marital satisfaction, 226–229, 344, 461
Marital separation, 421
Marital sex, 128
Marital stability, 208–211, 219–220, 338, 461.
    See also Stability
Marital status, 154–155, 156*b*–157*f*, 169–171,
    173, 202
Marital timing, 17
Marital violence, 368
Market approach to child care, defined, 317
Market work
    defined, 295
    men and, 299–302
Marriage as social institution/private
    relationship, 152–181
    defined, 29, 158
    deinstitutionalized marriage and (*See*
        Deinstitutionalized marriage)
    happiness/life satisfaction and, 178–179
    marital status and, 154–155, 156*b*–157*f*

permanence/sexual exclusivity and,
    158–160
policies and, 173–178
"yoke mates" to "soul mates" in,
    160–164
Marriage certificates, 218*n*
Marriage conversation, 222
Marriage counseling, 445
Marriage counselors, 366–367, 421
Marriage disparity, 172*b*
Marriage education programs, 415
Marriage license, 158*n*
Marriage market, 211–214
Marriage partner, 206–231
    cohabitation/marital quality/stability and,
        225–226
    homogamy and (*See* Homogamy)
    marital satisfaction/life choices and,
        226–229
    marriage market for, 211–214
    mate selection/marital stability and,
        208–211
    premarital relationship and (*See*
        Premarital relationship)
Marriage perspective, 171
Marriage premise
    defined, 158
    "yoke mates" to "soul mates" in, 160–164
"Marriage Protection Week," 174
Marriage rate, in United States, 154*f*,
    155, 457*f*
Marriage relationships, aging families and,
    490–492
Marriage-related laws, 158*n*
Marriage(s)
    African American, 58–59
    age structure and, 49
    alternatives to, 190–191, 419–420
    arranged, 108, 162, 163*b*, 211–213,
        212*b*, 213*b*
    attitudes toward, 417
    commuter, 316
    companionate, 104, 165–166, 165*n*,
        167*f*, 173
    consensual, 191*b*
    covenant, 173–174, 444
    cross-national, 212–213
    deinstitutionalized (*See* Deinstitutionalized
        marriage)
    egalitarian, 362*b*
    evangelical, 361–362
    extramarital affairs and, 132–135
    family development perspective and,
        98–29
    feminist/conflict perspective and, 35
    first years of, 227–228
    gender model of, 362–363
    high expectations of, 417
    immigration and, 63*b*
    individualized, 166–168, 167*f*
    institutional, 164–165, 167*f*
    interclass, 217
    interethnic, 217–219
    interfaith, 71, 216–217
    interracial, 69*b*, 217–219, 218*f*, 218*n*
    Latino, 60
    legal, 197*b*, 200–202, 200*n*, 201*b*
    love and, 162–164
    lower-income, 17
    in military, 50*b*
    nonmarital living arrangements and,
        190–191

peer, 361, 362*b*
plural, 10
in post-World War II era, 28
power politics in, 363
preparation for, 227
rewards of, 419–420
same-sex, 8, 10, 61, 66, 197*b*, 200–202,
    200*n*, 201*b*
sexuality throughout, 135–139
social status and, 33
stable unhappy, 421
statistics for, 6*b*
two-career, 302, 315, 316
two-earner, 302–307, 315, 323–325
unhappy, 421
white, 58–59
of white-collar/blue-collar workers, 54
World War II and, 48
Married couples
    deinstitutionalized marriage and, 165*b*
    kinship authority and, 161
    sex and, 136, 139, 140
Married parents, 16*b*
Married-couple families, 5*t*, 57, 60, 64, 169,
    169*t*, 300, 300*f*, 425*f*
Married-couple households, 15*b*, 16*b*, 53, 69,
    170, 195, 195*f*
Married-couple parents, 61
Married-parent families, 175
Marriage education, 445
Martyring
    communication and, 342
    defined, 109
    manipulating and, 110
Marvin v. Marvin, 193*b*
Marxism, 35
Masculinists, defined, 95
Masculinities, defined, 78–79. *See also* Men
Massachusetts, same-sex couples and, 196,
    197*b*, 201–202
Mate selection, 208–211
Mate selection risk, defined, 211
Maternity leave, 96
Meaning, defined, 32
Media
    deinstitutionalized marriage and, 172*b*
    gender/gendered identities and, 81, 87,
        89–90
    permanence/sexual exclusivity and, 159*b*
    raising children and, 267
    sexuality and, 132*b*
    women and, 77, 93, 94
Mediation, divorce, 423–424
Medicaid, 488, 488*n*, 489, 489*n*, 506
Medicare
    age structure and, 49
    aging families and, 488, 488*n*, 489,
        489*b*, 506
MEDS. *See* Mutually economically dependent
    spouses (MEDS)
Men. *See also* Males; Masculinities
    abortion and, 254
    affirmative action for, 84
    African American, 59, 94
    age structure and, 49
    aging families and, 487, 487*t*, 488*n*, 489,
        490, 492, 499
    American Indian, 66
    Asian American, 65
    blue-collar, 308
    child options/circumstances for, 244, 245,
        249, 250

Men (*cont.*)
    childlessness and, 235, 243–244
    choosing marriage partner and, 214,
        214*n*, 219, 222
    cohabitation and, 194*b*, 195
    communication and, 338, 339, 340, 345
    cultural scripts and, 126, 127, 128, 130
    date/acquaintance rape and, 221*b*
    employment/family work and, 310, 311
    exchange perspective and, 125
    feminist movement and, 48
    feminist/conflict perspective and, 35
    gender inequality and, 81–86, 85*f*
    gender/gendered identities and,
        76–81, 88
    gender/social change and, 92–97
    heterosexual expression and, 130, 131,
        132, 133*b*, 134–135
    HIV/AIDS and, 143, 145*f*, 146*b*
    HMI and, 174–176
    income and, 53
    infertility and, 255
    intimate partner violence and, 369, 370,
        371, 373, 374–376, 377, 378
    in labor force, 294–299, 296*f*, 301–302, 307
    life expectancy of, 484
    love/marriage and, 104, 162, 162*f*
    marital power and, 355–361, 358*f*, 362*b*
    market work for, 299–302, 301
    marrage age for, 155*n*, 156*b*
    marriage rate for, 457*f*
    military and, 51*b*
    no-power relationships and, 365–366
    parenthood and, 241, 242
    personal/family change and, 96
    power politics and, 364
    preventing pregnancy and, 251
    in prison, 408*b*
    raising children and, 270, 272, 287
    religion and, 70–71
    remarriage and, 460–461
    reproductive technology and, 257
    same-sex couples and, 196*n*
    sexual develoment/orientation and, 123,
        124, 124*b*, 125
    sexual expression and, 139
    sexual pleasure and, 141
    sexual responsibility and, 149
    sexuality throughout marriage and, 138
    two-earner marriages and, 302, 302*n*, 303,
        324, 325
    unmarrieds as, 184–188, 184*n*, 187*t*,
        203–204
    unpaid family work and, 307, 309, 310
    white-collar, 308
Men's Movement, 92, 95–96
Meta-analysis, defined, 81*n*
Metamessage, 343*n*
Methodism, 70
Metropolitan Community Church, 196
Mexican American Women's National
    Association (MANA), 93
Mexican Americans
    choosing marriage partner and, 225, 226
    cohabitation and, 191*b*
    communication and, 340
    fertility rates among, 238*b*, 239*b*
    gendered identities and, 80
    raising children and, 272, 281
M-frame relationships
    defined, 112, 113, 114
    mutual dependency and, 115

Michigan Office of Services to the
    Aging, 499
Michigan State University, 23
Michigan Women's Employment Survey, 176
Middle age, 138, 184, 189
Middle classes, 60, 216, 280, 281, 281*b*, 337*b*
Middle-class blacks, 59
Middle-class children, 54, 57
Middle-class parents, 54, 57, 279–280
Middle-class whites, 67, 68, 88*n*
Midlife changes, 13*b*
Military
    divorce and, 50*b*, 51*b*
    race/ethnicity and, 56
Military families, 50*b*–51*b*
Miller's typology of urban Native American
    families, defined, 67
Minneapolis experiment, intimate partner
    violence and, 378, 378*n*
Minority, 55, 55*n*, 57, 58, 79, 145*b*, 259–260,
    283, 503
"Minority culture," 57, 60
Minority group, 55, 55*n*, 200
Miscarriage, 252
Misconceptions, about love, 115–117
"Mixed couples," 331
Mixed/double messages, defined, 343
Mobilization, in stepfamily development, 478
"Model minority," 64
Modern sexism, defined, 77–78
Money
    allocation of, 352
    economy/social class and, 49
    exchange theory and, 33
    family crises and, 403
    marital power and, 357, 358–359
Monitoring the Future survey, 2
Monogamous relationship, sexuality
    and, 139
Monogamy, 158, 159*b*, 160
Moral constraints, divorce and, 417–418
Mormons/Mormonism. *See* Latter-day Saints
    (LDS)
Morning on the Cape (Kroll), 126*b*
Mortality rates
    of African American men, 59
    infant (*See* Infant mortality rates)
Mother-headed, single-parent families, 171*b*
Motherhood penalty, defined, 297
Mothering approach to child care, defined,
    316–317
Mothers
    adoption and, 258, 260
    aging families and, 494
    American Indian, 65*n*, 66
    biosocial perspective and, 36
    births to, 249
    child abuse and, 382
    child care and, 304*b*, 305*b*
    child options/circumstances and, 244,
        245, 247–249, 250, 251
    child-to-parent abuse and, 384
    cohabitation and, 195
    custodial, 440
    divorce and, 419, 428, 429, 434–436, 437,
        439, 440–441, 443
    employment/family work and, 313,
        314, 314*f*
    gender/gendered identities and, 77, 87,
        88, 91
    HMI and, 174, 174*n*, 176
    labor force and, 295, 297, 298

of large families, 237*b*
Latino, 61
love and, 113
in multicultural society, 270–272
neighborhood/community and, 26
noncustodial, 435, 436*b*
poverty and, 173, 177
prison and, 408*b*
race/ethnicity and, 56*f*
raising children and, 268, 269, 269*b*, 270–
    272, 271*b*, 271*f*, 276, 278, 279
reproductive technology and, 256
single, 61, 173, 249–250, 314, 314*f*
supplemental, 383
two-earner marriages and, 303, 304, 306
unpaid family work and, 309
unwed, 249
Ms. Foundation for Women, 92
Multicultural families, 68–69, 69*b*
Multicultural society, 264–291
    authoritative parenting in, 272–277
    foster parents in, 285–286
    grandparents in, 285
    mothers/fathers in, 270–272
    parent-child relationships in, 288–289
    parents in, 266–270
    racial/ethnic diversity/parenting in,
        280–284
    social class/parenting and, 277–280
    young adult children/parents in,
        286–288
Multiethnic Placement Act, 259
Multigenerational households, 6*b*
Multipartnered fertility, defined, 250
Multiple birth rate, 235
Multiracial children, 282–283
Multiracial/multiethnic families. *See*
    Multicultural families
Multitasking, 309, 314
Murder victimization, 83
Muslims, 70, 71, 83, 161, 196, 216, 283,
    379, 405
Mutual children, 475
Mutual dependency, defined, 115
Mutual violent control, 376*n*
Mutuality, defined, 115*b*, 116, 141
Mutually economically dependent spouses
    (MEDS), 360–361, 362

Nadir, defined, 399
NAEYC. *See* National Association for the
    Education of Young Children (NAEYC)
Nanny, defined, 302
Nanny hunt, 76*b*–77*b*
Narcissism, 109, 110*n*, 111, 111*n*
National Alliance for Caregiving, 498*b*
National Association for the Education of
    Young Children (NAEYC), 321*b*
National Association of Black Social
    Workers, 259
National Black Justice Coalition, 200
National Cancer Institute, 146, 254
National Child Traumatic Stress
    Network, 25*b*
National Coalition for the Homeless, 278
National Conference on Men and
    Masculinity, 95
National Crime Victimization Survey, 367,
    368–369, 371, 374–375
National Elder Abuse Incidence Study, 502
National Family Violence Surveys, 367–368,
    374, 375, 380

National Fatherhood Institute, 408*b*
National Health and Social Life Survey
 (NHSLS), 124, 125, 134, 136*b*
National Incident-Based Reporting System
 (NIBRS), 367
National Institute of Child Health and
 Human Development (NICHD), 318*b*
National Institute of Justice, 367, 378
National Longitudinal Study of Adolescent
 Health, 69, 147–148, 251
National Longitudinal Survey of Youth
 (NLSY), 51*n*, 170, 433, 460
National Long-Term Care Survey, 497
National Marriage Project, 187
National Opinion Research Center (NORC),
 124, 127, 131, 136, 136*b*, 146, 186,
 217, 325
National Organization for Changing
 Men, 95
National Organization for Men Against
 Sexism (NOMAS), 95
National Organization for Men (NOM), 95
National Organization for Women
 (NOW), 93
National origin, 55*n*
National Right to Life, 253
"National Security Emergencies"
 website, 25*b*
National Study of Black Americans, 406
National Survey of America's Families, 170
National Survey of America's Families and
 Households (NSFH), 241
National Survey of Families and Households
 (NSFH), 136*b*, 137, 194, 250, 276, 287,
 362, 371, 421, 440, 443, 444, 461,
 462, 465
National Survey of Family Growth, 124,
 136*b*, 139, 146
National Urban League report, 94
National Violence Against Women Survey,
 367, 375
Native Americans. *See* American Indians
 (Native Americans)
Native Hawaiians, 52*f*, 53, 54, 55, 58, 64*n*,
 218, 218*n*, 415, 416*f*
Natural physical-biological environment,
 22, 22*f*
Naturalistic observation, defined, 41
"Nature," 36, 37
Navarro v. LaMusga, 439
Near peers, defined, 362*b*
Need, love/power and, 356
"Needs battery," 110
Neglect
 child, 379–380
 elder, 502–503
Neighborhood
 African American, 59, 59*b*
 community and, 26, 27*b*
 Latino, 60
"Neighborhood survival tactics," 24*b*
Neighborhood Watch program, 27*b*
Neighborhood Youth Corps, 177*n*
Neopaganism, 70
Neotraditional families, 298–299, 361–362
Netherlands, civil marriage laws in, 158*n*
Never-married, 156*b*, 157*f*, 184
New Work of Dogs, The (Katz), 4*b*
New Zealand study, 254, 254*n*
Newly established couple stage, 28
NHSLS. *See* National Health and Social Life
 Survey (NHSLS)

NIBRS. *See* National Incident-Based
 Reporting System (NIBRS)
NICHD. *See* National Institute of Child
 Health and Human Development
 (NICHD)
Nicholson v. Scopetta, 383
9/11, 79
NLSY. *See* National Longitudinal Survey of
 Youth (NLSY)
No-fault divorce, 417, 417*n*, 423, 444, 445
NOM. *See* National Organization for Men
 (NOM)
NOMAS. *See* National Organization for Men
 Against Sexism (NOMAS)
Nonbiological parent figures, biosocial
 perspective and, 36
Noncustodial fathers, 436–437, 440, 441
Noncustodial grandparent, defined, 496
Noncustodial mothers, 435, 436*b*
Noncustodial parents, 427, 428, 435*n*, 443
Nonelderly population, 486*f*
Nonfamilial living arrangements, 3
Nonfamily households, 5*t*, 7*n*
Non-Hispanic whites, 52*f*, 53, 55–56, 55*n*,
 57, 58, 60, 61, 64–69, 65*n*. *See also*
 Caucasians
 abortions for, 253*n*
 adoption and, 257, 259
 African Americans and, 58, 59
 aging families and, 485, 486–487, 486*f*,
 488, 488*n*, 488*t*, 494, 495, 503
 child abuse and, 381
 child care and, 67, 76*b*–77*b*, 317
 children and, 67, 243, 248, 248*f*, 252*f*
 choosing marriage partner and, 214–215,
 215*n*, 217–218, 218*f*, 220, 225, 226
 cohabitation and, 191*b*, 195
 communication and, 340
 deinstitutionalized marriage and, 169,
 171*b*, 172*b*
 divorce and, 415, 416*f*, 419, 419*t*,
 425*f*, 433
 fertility rates among, 238*b*, 238*f*, 239*b*
 gender/gendered identities and, 79–80,
 83, 84, 90–91, 93
 HIV/AIDS and, 144*b*, 145*f*
 intimate partner violence and, 369, 369*f*
 kinship authority and, 161
 labor force and, 295
 marital status of, 156*b*, 157*f*
 men's market work and, 301
 middle-class, 67, 68, 88*n*
 poverty rate for, 176*b*
 prison and, 108*b*
 raising children and, 273*b*, 276, 278,
 280, 282
 remarriage and, 458*b*
 sexuality and, 139–140
 two-earner marriages and, 306
 unmarrieds and, 184, 186, 187*f*
 unpaid family work and, 308
Noninitiating partner, 422
Nonmarital birth rate, 7*b*, 61, 247–250
Nonmarital births, 48, 64, 66, 195,
 247–250
Nonmarital childbearing, 16
Nonmarital living arrangements, 182–205
 cohabitation as, 189–191, 192*b*–193*b*,
 194–196
 group/communal living as, 188–189
 living alone as, 186
 living alone together as, 186–187

 living with parents as, 187–188
 same-sex couples as, 196–202
 unmarried/life satisfaction as, 202–204
Nonmarital partnership, 69*b*
Nonmarital pregnancy rates, 16
Nonmarital sex, 127*n*, 128, 131–132, 135,
 147, 185, 187
Nonmarrieds. *See* Unmarrieds/nonmarrieds
Nontraditional attitudes, 194
Nontraditional roles, women in, 77
Nonverbal metamessage, 343*n*
No-power, 363, 365–366
No-power relationships, 363–367
NORC. *See* National Opinion Research
 Center (NORC)
"Normative" family size, 237*b*
Normative order hypothesis, defined, 27
Norms of equality, 361
NOW. *See* National Organization for Women
 (NOW)
NSFH. *See* National Survey of Families and
 Households (NSFH)
Nuclear family
 advertisements and, 8*b*
 defined, 3, 29–30
 divorce and, 424*b*
 ethnicity and, 57
 family development perspective and, 28
 feminist/conflict perspective and, 35–36
 immigration and, 62*b*
 kinship authority and, 161
 non-Hispanic whites and, 67
 stepfamilies and, 468*b*
Nuclear-family model monopoly, 465, 478
Nursing home costs, 489*n*
Nursing homes
 aging families and, 490, 504, 505
 defined, 497*b*
"Nurture," 36

Object relations theory, 88
Objective measures of power, marital power
 and, 352
Objectivity, 38
Observation
 on infertility, 255
 laboratory, 40–41
 naturalistic, 41
Occupation
 gender/gendered identities and, 84–85
 multicultural families and, 69
 social class and, 53
Occupational segregation, 295, 297
Older partners, 138
"One true love," 102
One-child family, 246–247
One-person households, 186
"On-time" transitions, defined, 27
Open sperm donor programs, 256*n*
Open-ended questions, 39
Opportunity costs, defined, 242
Opting out, 298, 306
"Opt-Out Revolution," 298
Oral sex
 statistics on, 146–147
 teenagers and, 148
Orgasm, sexuality and, 126, 127
Origin of Species, The (Darwin), 36*n*
Orthodox Judaism, 299
Outlook, choosing marriage partner
 and, 223*b*
Out-of-wedlock pregnancies, 174

Outsourcing, 51–52
Oxytocin, defined, 116

Pacific Islanders, 52*f*, 53, 54, 55, 58, 64*n*,
    65, 84
    abortions for, 253*n*
    adoptions for, 257
    aging families and, 486*f*
    child abuse and, 381
    child care and, 317
    children and, 248, 248*f*
    choosing marriage partner and, 217–218
    divorce and, 415, 416*f*
    fertility rates among, 237*b*, 238*f*, 239*b*
    HIV/AIDS and, 144*b*, 145*b*, 145*f*
Pack of Two (Knapp), 4*b*
Paid maternity (parental) leave, 322
Para-parent, 277, 289
Parent care, aging families and, 500
Parent education, for co-parenting ex-
    spouses, 439–440
Parent Effectiveness Training (PET), 289
Parental adjustment perspective, defined, 432
Parental alienation syndrome, divorce
    and, 434*n*
Parental Kidnapping Prevention Act, 437
Parental leaves, 35
Parental loss perspective, defined, 432
Parental power, defined, 352
Parent-child relationships, 273*b*, 288–289
Parenthood, 6*b*–7*b*, 232–262
    abortion and, 252–254
    adoption and, 257–261
    decisions about, 140–244
    divorce and, 434
    early/late, 245–246
    family development perspective and, 28–29
    fertility trends and, 235–239
    involuntary infertility and, 254–257
    motivation for, 241–242
    options/circumstances for children and,
        244–251
    postponing, 244–245
    in post-World War II era, 28
    pregnancy prevention and, 251
    raising children and (*See* Raising children)
    reproductive technology and, 254–257
    sharing, 272
    single, 15*b*, 188*b*, 189
    timing of, 244
    transition to, 268–270, 268*b*
Parenting
    authoritative, 272–277
    having children and, 244–251
    hierarchical, 281
    multicultural society and (*See*
        Multicultural society)
    racial/ethnic diversity and, 280–284
    raising children and (*See* Raising children)
    shared, 272
    social class and, 277–280
Parenting alliance, defined, 272, 272*b*
Parenting approach to child care,
    defined, 317
"Parenting plan," 439, 445
Parenting role, 266
Parenting style, defined, 274
Parenting Today's Teen magazine, 286
Parents. *See also* Fathers, Mothers
    adult children and, 286–288
    African American, 280–281
    age structure and, 49

aging families and, 487, 493–496, 494,
    494*b*, 498–499, 501
American Indian, 65*n*, 66
Asian American, 65, 282
child abuse and, 381*n*, 382, 383
child-to-parent abuse and, 384
choosing marriage partner and,
    211–212, 228
custodial, 427–428
deinstitutionalized marriage and, 168,
    169, 170, 171
depression in, 242
divorce and, 210, 422, 425, 432, 437,
    443–444
employment/family work and, 313, 314,
    315–316
ethnicity and, 57
exchange theory and, 33
family development perspective and,
    27, 28
family ecology theory and, 24*b*
foster, 285–286
gender/gendered identities and,
    87–92, 87*b*
grandparents as, 285
Hispanic, 281–282
HIV/AIDS and, 143
HMI and, 176
immigration and, 62*b*–63*b*
independent adults and, 288
intimacy and, 142
job description for, 267*b*
Latino, 60
living with, 187–188
love and, 113, 115
low-income inner-city, 26
married, 16*b*
married-couple, 61
middle-class, 54, 57, 279–280
military and, 50*b*, 51*b*
in modern America, 166–170
multicultural families and, 69
multicultural society and (*See*
    Multicultural society)
multiracial children and, 282–283
Native American, 281
noncustodial, 427, 428, 435*n*, 443
non-Hispanic white, 67
old/new images of, 270
permanence/sexual exclusivity and, 159*b*
in poverty, 173, 177
primary, 272
in prison, 408*b*–409*b*
psychological, 270
raising children and (*See* Raising children)
religious minority, 283
reproductive technology and, 256
same-sex, 198–200, 201
self-esteem and, 110*n*
sex education and, 147, 147*f*
single, 50*b*, 174*n*, 202
unmarrieds and, 186, 187, 188, 193*b*
upper-middle-class, 279–280, 281*b*, 287
upper-socioeconomic-level environment
    and, 27
visiting, 435–437
white-collar/blue-collar workers and, 54
young adult children and, 286–288
Partial birth abortion, 253
Partners
    cohabitation and, 196
    domestic, 191*b*, 192*b*, 196, 198*b*

exchange theory and, 33–34
finding marriage, 162
as individuals/family members, 17–18
military and, 51*b*
older, 138
same-sex, 69, 198–200
Partners Task Force for Gay and Lesbian
    Couples, 200
Part-time employment, 302
Passage through Crisis (Davis), 32
Passion, defined, 105, 106, 106*f*
Passive-aggression, defined, 335
Paterfamilias, 164–165, 164*n*
Paternity leave, 96, 322
Patriarchal authority
    institutional marriage as, 164
    marital power and, 355
Patriarchal power, 356*b*
Patriarchal sexuality, defined, 126–127
Patriarchal system, 354
Patriarchal terrorism, 371, 375–376
Patriarchy
    Asian Americans and, 65
    defined, 35
    ethnicity and, 57
    feminists and, 95
    Latinos and, 80
    Men's Movement and, 95, 96
Peer marriage, defined, 361, 362*b*
Pensions, aging families and, 488, 489
People v. Michael Fortin, 434*n*
Period of family disorganization, defined,
    398–399, 398*f*
Permanence, 158–160, 164, 173, 174,
    179, 186
Permissiveness with affection, defined, 131
Permissiveness without affection, defined,
    131–132
Personal experience, studying families
    and, 38
Personal freedom, 13, 242, 243, 244
Personal needs, love and, 103
Personal power, defined, 352
Personal Responsibility and Work
    Opportunity Reconciliation Act, 174,
    174*n*, 177, 428*n*
Personal troubles, choices and, 9–10
Personality need fulfillment, defined, 115
Perspective(s). *See also* Theoretical
    perspectives
    biosocial, 23*t*, 36–37, 37*b*, 125, 127
    classical, 354–356
    conflict, 23*t*, 35–36, 37*b*
    exchange theory, 23*t*, 33–34, 37*b*, 213,
        354, 374, 416
    family development, 23*t*, 27–29, 37*b*,
        390, 391
    family ecology, 22–27, 22*f*, 23*t*, 24*b*, 37*b*,
        266, 391, 391*b*
    family systems theory, 23*b*, 34, 37*b*,
        391, 391*b*
    feminist, 23*t*, 35–36, 37*b*
    interactionist, 23*t*, 31–33, 31*n*, 33*b*, 37*b*,
        41, 123, 125–126, 126*b*, 222, 330,
        391, 402
    structure-functional, 23*t*, 29–31, 35, 37*b*,
        125, 390
PET. *See* Parent Effectiveness Training (PET)
Pets as family, 3, 4*b*
Physical abuse, 368, 376, 381, 502
Physical attractiveness, 222
Physical pleasure, 127*b*

Physical violence, 223
Physiology, gender/gendered identities and, 76
Pi Kappa Phi fraternity, 221b
Piecework, 303
Pile-up, 397–398, 400–402. See also Stressor overload
Place, communication and, 344
Planned Parenthood v. Danforth, 253
Play, defined, 89
Playboy magazine survey, 136b
Pleasure
    gender and, 141
    physical, 127b
    self-esteem and, 140–141
    sex for, 127–128
    sexual, 131, 140–141, 148
Pleasure bond
    defined, 140
    sex as, 140–142
Pleasuring, defined, 141
Plural marriages, 10
Pluralistic family, 168, 184, 196
Pluralistic society, 266
"Polemical nature of divorce scholarship," 428
Politics
    of abortion, 253
    HIV/AIDS and, 144
    male dominance in, 81–82
    power (See Power politics)
    of sex, 144–148
Polyamory, defined, 159b
Polyamory Society's Children Educational Branch, 159b
Polyandry, defined, 158n
PolyFamily scholarship fund, 159b
Polygamy, 10, 158, 158n, 159b, 201n
Polygyny, 158n, 159b
"PolyKids Zine," 159b
"PolyTeens Zine," 159b
Pool of eligibles, 214–220
Population
    age structure of, 49
    aging, 7b, 484–487, 505b
    American Indian, 66
    Asian American, 64
    child, 58
    elderly, 486f
    gender/gendered identities and, 83
    multiracial identity surveys of, 68n
    nonelderly, 486f
    non-Hispanic white, 67
    Pacific Islander, 65
    in United States, 58, 62b, 70
Population Association of America, 314
Population Reference Bureau, 283
Population Services International, Carey v., 128
Positive affect, defined, 331
Postdivorce pathways, 442b–443b, 443f
Postmodern family, 168
Postpartum depression, 269
Post-traumatic stress disorder, military and, 51b
Poverty
    abortion and, 253n
    African Americans and, 53, 59
    aging families and, 489b
    Asian Americans and, 53, 64
    child (See Child poverty)
    deinstitutionalized marriage and, 169, 171, 171b

divorce and, 416, 425–426, 425f, 427–428, 440
economy/social class and, 53, 53f
extreme, 280
family crises and, 406
fathers in, 177
fertility rates and, 239b
gender/gendered identities and, 91
HMI and, 175, 176–177
immigration and, 62b
neighborhood/community and, 26
Pacific Islanders and, 65
policies for, 173
race/ethnicity and, 53
raising children and, 278–279, 280, 285, 286
in United States, 266
War on, 23, 177, 177n
Poverty rate, 53f, 55, 56, 66, 67, 171b, 176, 485, 488–489
Power, 350–367
    coercive, 353, 353t, 355, 365b, 371, 372f
    communication and, 340
    decision making and, 359–360
    defined, 352–353
    egalitarian, 354
    expert, 353, 353t, 355
    feminist/conflict perspective and, 35
    informational, 353, 353t, 355, 358, 360
    intimate partner, 352
    legitimate, 353, 353t, 355, 356b, 358, 359, 360, 361
    love/need and, 356
    marital, 352, 353 363, 471
    objective measures of, 352
    parental, 352
    patriarchal, 356b
    personal, 352
    referent, 353, 353t, 356, 365b
    resource, 358, 359, 360
    reward, 353, 353t, 371
    sexuality and, 132, 132b
    social, 352, 360
    stepfamilies and, 471
Power bases, 352–353
Power of attorney for finances, unmarrieds and, 192b
Power politics
    alternatives to, 363–366
    defined, 363
    in marriage, 363
    no-power relationships vs., 363–367
Power struggles, disengaging from, 364b
Pragma, defined, 108
Pragmatic love, 208
Predictability, choosing marriage partner and, 223b
Pregnancy
    intimate partner violence and, 370
    out-of-wedlock, 174
    preventing, 251
    risk factors of, 244–245
    as sexual responsibility, 149
    teenage, 249–250
    unintended, 240, 240n
Prejudice
    homosexuals and, 129
    same-sex couples and, 200
Premarital cohabitation, 190
Premarital counseling, 173, 227, 444, 445
Premarital education, 227
Premarital relationship

breaking up and, 224–225
dating violence in, 223–224
defining the relationship in, 222–223
developing, 220–225
physical attractiveness/rapport and, 222
Premarital sex, 127n, 131, 138
PREP. See Prevention and Relationship Enhancement Program (PREP)
Presbyterianism, 70, 82
Preschool children, raising, 273–274, 277, 278
Presidential Commission on the Status of Women, 93
Preteens, depression/substance abuse in, 54
Prevention and Relationship Enhancement Program (PREP), 346
Primary group, defined, 2–3, 2n, 3b
Primary parents, defined, 272
Principle of least interest, defined, 33
Principle of reciprocity, 197b
Prison, family crises and, 408b–409b
Privacy
    marital, 128
    permanence/sexual exclusivity and, 159b
Privacy protection, for homosexuals, 128
Private adoptions, 259
Private face, defined, 505
Private relationship. See Marriage as social institution/private relationship
"Privilege," 67–68
Problem solving
    in choosing marriage partner, 208
    HMI and, 174
Profeminists, defined, 95
"Professional woman," 79
Progesterone, 86n
Pro-life/pro-choice debate, 253, 253b
Pronatalist bias, defined, 240
"Pro-nuptial" family culture, 61
Property
    arranged marriages and, 162
    divorce and, 426
    unmarrieds and, 192b
Property rights, 158
Propinquity/proximity, 215. See also Geographic availability
Protestantism/Protestants, 70, 71, 82, 216–217, 257n, 299
Provider role, 300–301, 324–325
Psychic divorce, defined, 449
Psychic intimacy, defined, 104
Psychological abuse, 224
Psychological parent, 270
Psychology, gender/gendered identities and, 86
Public adoptions, 259
Public Education Network, 91
Public face, defined, 506
Puerto Ricans, 191b, 238b, 503–504
"Putative father registry," 259

Quaranteed child support, defined, 428
Questionnaires
    as data collection, 39
    longitudinal studies and, 41
    raising children and, 273b
    sex surveys and, 136b
Questions
    close-ended, 39
    as data collection, 39
    open-ended, 39
"Quiverfull," 237b

Race
    adoptions and, 259–260
    aging families and, 485, 486–487, 487–
        488, 495, 503–504
    child-to-parent abuse and, 384
    choosing marriage partner and, 214–215,
        216, 217–219
    cohabitation and, 191*b*
    defined, 54
    discrimination and, 55
    divorce and, 415, 416*f*, 418–419, 419*t*, 422,
        425, 425*f*
    eldercare and, 503–504
    ethnicity and, 54–69, 55*n*, 56*f*
    fertility rates and, 238*b*–239*b*, 238*f*
    gender/gendered identities and, 76,
        79–80, 84
    grandparenting and, 495
    HIV/AIDS and, 145*b*, 145*f*
    income by, 52–53, 52*f*
    intimate partner violence and, 369, 369*f*
    marital status and, 157*f*
    in nanny hunt, 76*b*–77*b*
    neighborhood/community and, 26
    parenting and, 280–284
    poverty rate and, 53
    sexual expression and, 139–140
    sexuality and, 128*t*
    stepfamilies and, 458*b*
    in United States, 58
    unmarrieds and, 184, 186, 187*f*
    unpaid family work and, 308
Racial intermarriage, 10
Racism
    deinstitutionalized marriage and, 169
    labor force and, 297
    raising children and, 284
Raising children, 2, 30, 264–291. *See also
        entries* on Fathers, Mothers, Parenting,
        and Parents.
    authoritative parenting and, 272–277
    foster parents and, 285–286
    grandparents and, 285
    mothers/fathers and, 270–272
    parent-child relationships and, 288–289
    parents and, 266–270
    racial/ethnic diversity/parenting and,
        280–284
    social class/parenting and, 277–280
    young adult children/parents and,
        286–288
Random samples, defined, 39
Rape
    date/acquaintance, 220–221, 221*b*
    marital, 35, 370
Rape myths, defined, 221*b*
Rape of the Sabine Woman, The, 221*b*
Rapport, 114, 222
Rapport talk, defined, 338
"Ready Kids," 25*b*
Reality
    agreement, 38
    experiential, 38
Receiver, in communication, 343
Recession, economy/social class and, 53*f*
Rechecking, making choices and, 12, 13*b*
Reconciliation, after marital separation, 421
Recreational sex, 130, 131, 159*b*
Redhail, Zablocki v., 456*n*
Redivorce, defined, 416
Referent power, 353, 353*t*, 356, 365*b*
Refined divorce rate, 414, 414*f*, 414*n*

Reform, intimate partner violence and, 373
Rehabilitative alimony, defined, 427
Reinforcing cycle, defined, 307
"Relational sex," 131
Relationship outcomes, 208*f*
Relationship violence, 377–379
Relationship-driven couples, 223
Relationship(s)
    adaptable marriage, 229
    A-frame, 112, 114
    categories of, 331, 331*f*
    cohabiting, 191, 191*b*, 194–195
    egalitarian, 80, 360–361
    exchange theory and, 33
    face-to-face, 2*f*, 3*b*
    H-frame, 112, 113
    intergenerational, 443–444, 493, 493*t*
    love and (*See* Love)
    marriage, 490–492
    M-frame, 112, 113, 114, 115
    monogamous, 139
    no-power, 363–367
    parent-child, 273*b*, 288–289
    premarital (*See* Premarital relationship)
    private (*See* Marriage as social institution/
        private relationship)
    raising children and, 268, 269
    sex in, 131
    sexual, 125, 130
    sibling, 406
    symbiotic, 110
    through cell phones, 2*f*
    through e-mail, 2*n*
    through instant messaging, 2*n*
    through websites, 2*n*
    two-earner marriages and, 323–325
Relatives of divorce, defined, 424
Relatives of remarriage, defined, 424
Religion
    Asian Americans and, 64
    choosing marriage partner and, 214–215,
        216–217, 219, 227
    community and, 70, 72
    divorce and, 417
    fathers and, 71
    gender roles and, 70
    male dominance in, 82–83
    polygamy and, 201*n*
    premarital counseling and, 173
    raising children and, 283
    remarriage and, 460*b*, 462
    same-sex couples and, 199, 201
    sexuality and, 140
    social context and, 70–72
    unmarrieds and, 186
    violence and, 71
    women and, 70–71, 71*b*
Religious diversity, 70
Religious minority, parents/children and, 283
Remarriage, 454–480
    after divorce, 419, 420
    age and, 460–461
    age structure and, 49
    aging families and, 490, 492–493, 495–496
    children and, 461
    children's living arrangements and,
        458–459, 459*f*
    choosing marriage partner and, 208
    choosing partners for, 459–461
    defined, 456
    divorce and, 424, 444
    double, 462

    facts about, 456–459, 456*n*
    family size and, 237*b*
    grandparenting and, 495–496
    homogamy in, 461
    relatives of, 424
    religion and, 70
    sexuality throughout marriage and, 139
    single, 462
    stepfamilies and, 458*b*
    stepparenting and, 469–475
Remarriage rates, 7*b*
Remarried families. *See also* Remarriage
    defined, 456
    types of, 464–465
Reorganization/recovery, family crises and,
        398*b*, 399
Replacement level of fertility, defined, 7*n*,
        236, 236*n*
Report talk, defined, 338
Representative sample
    defined, 39
    sex surveys and, 136*b*
Reproductive choice, 93
Reproductive issues, feminist/conflict
        perspective and, 35
Reproductive technology, 235, 244, 254–257
Research
    on abortion, 254
    on adoption, 258, 259, 260
    on African Americans, 59, 60
    on aging families, 493, 503, 504
    on American Indians, 67
    on asexuality, 124*b*
    biosocial perspective and, 36, 37
    on child abuse, 384
    on child care, 317, 318*b*–319*b*
    on children, 242, 243, 246–247, 250, 251
    for choosing marriage partner, 208, 209,
        210, 211, 214, 217, 218, 219, 222, 223,
        224, 225, 226, 228, 229
    on cohabitation, 191, 191*b*, 194–195,
        195–196, 196
    communication, 337*b*
    on companionate marriage, 165–166
    on date/acquaintance rape, 221*b*
    on deinstitutionalized marriage,
        168–171, 173
    on economy/social class, 52
    on employment/family work, 316
    ethics of, 38–39
    on ethnicity, 57
    on family crises, 405, 406
    on family development perspective, 29
    on family violence, 367
    on fathers, 270, 272
    on "friends with benefits," 132*b*, 133*b*
    on gender/gendered identities, 80, 81, 83,
        85, 86, 88, 88*n*, 89, 90, 91, 92
    on heterosexual expression, 130, 133,
        134, 135
    historical, 42
    on HMI, 174, 176, 176*n*
    on homeless families, 401*b*
    on "hooking up," 132*b*, 133*b*
    on immigration, 63*b*, 63*n*
    on intimate partner violence, 370, 371,
        373–374, 376–377
    on labor force, 297
    longitudinal, 33, 41
    on love/marriage, 104, 105, 107, 109,
        110*n*, 111, 116, 162, 162*f*
    on marital power, 353–363, 356–360

meta-analysis as, 81*n*
neighborhood/community, 26
on no-power relationships, 366
on parenthood, 241
on permanence/sexual exclusivity, 159*b*
on politics, 146
on race/ethnicity, 56, 139–140
on religion, 70
on same-sex couples, 196, 199, 199*b*
on self-esteem, 110*n*, 111
on sex education, 147
sex surveys for, 136*b*
on sexual development/orientation, 122, 123, 124*b*, 125
on sexual pleasure/self-esteem, 140
on sexuality throughout marriage, 135, 137–138, 139
on stepfamilies, 468, 468*b*
studying families through, 37–38
on two-earner marriages, 303
on unmarrieds, 202, 203
on unpaid family work, 308
Wallerstein, 429, 432
on work/family issues, 322–323
Reservations, American Indians and, 65, 65*n*, 66, 67, 239*b*
Residence-sharing agreements, parent-adult child, 288
Residential stepmothers, 473
Resilience, 388–389
Resilient child, 277
Resilient families, 398, 404
Resolution, in stepfamily development, 478
Resource hypothesis, defined, 354–355
Resource power, 358, 359, 360
Resources
    adoption, 261
    for choosing marriage partner, 213
    community, 497*b*
    in cultural context, 355–356
    defined, 33
    domestic violence and, 368*b*
    economic, 49
    exchange theory and, 33
    family crises and, 403–404, 404*b*, 407
    financial, 419
    marital power and, 354, 355, 356
Responsibility, sexual, 140, 148–149
"Responsible fatherhood" programs, 428
Retirement
    age structure and, 49
    aging families and, 487, 489, 490, 491–492
"Reverse theorizing," 57
Reversed-role families, 3
Reward power, 353, 353*t*, 371
Rewards and costs
    of children, 242
    defined, 33
    sexuality and, 125
Rewards of marriage, 419–420
Reynolds v. United States, 159*b*
Right to Life Movement, 146
Right to move, divorce and, 439
Risk
    of divorce, 419*t*
    extramarital affairs and, 134–135
    in family environment, 24*b*–25*b*
    love and, 117
    mate selection, 211
    in neighborhood/community, 26
    raising children and, 277
    sexuality and, 130

Rituals, 13, 95–96, 403
Roe v. Wade, 253, 253*n*
Role ambiguity, stepparenting and, 470
"Role conceptions," 114
Role sequencing, defined, 27
Role sharing, 417, 491*b*
Role specialization, 417
Role-making, defined, 32, 227
Roles
    defined, 32
    gender (*See* Gender roles)
Role-taking, defined, 32, 88
Roman Catholic Canon Law, 158
Roman Catholics, 70, 71, 82, 173, 196, 199, 216–217, 227, 257*n*, 299, 462
Romantic love, 160, 164, 208
Rome, institutional marriage in, 164–165
Rutgers University, 187

1960's Sexual Revolution, 127–128
Sabotage, defined, 336
Safety
    in family environment, 24*b*
    raising children and, 267
Same-sex couple households, 6*b*, 195*f*
Same-sex couples, 6*b*, 185, 192*b*, 195*f*, 196–202, 196*n*, 198*b*
Same-sex experience, 124
Same-sex marriage, 8, 10, 61, 66, 197*b*, 200–202, 200*n*, 201*b*
Same-sex orientation, 125
Same-sex partners, 6*b*, 69, 195*f*, 198–200
Same-sex sexuality, 124
Sandwich generation, defined, 500–501
Satisfaction
    aging families and, 491
    children and, 241–244
    in choosing marriage partner, 208–209, 212, 217, 220, 223, 226–229
    cohabitation and, 194, 203
    communication and, 330–334, 344
    companionate marriage and, 165
    couple, 330–334
    courtly love and, 164
    divorce and, 416, 419, 421, 422
    employment/family work and, 316
    marital, 226–229, 344, 461
    marital power and, 352, 357
    marriage and, 178–179
    men's market work and, 302
    raising children and, 269*b*
    remarriage and, 461–464
    same-sex couples and, 199, 202
    sexual, 139, 140
    two-earner marriages and, 303, 323, 324
    unmarrieds and, 202–204
"Satisfied single," 79
Savings, aging families and, 488
School-age children, raising, 274
Schools. *See also* Education
    single-sex, 92
    socialization in, 90–91
Science, defined, 38
Scientific investigation, defined, 38, 39
Scientific method, 38
Scientific techniques, application of, 42
Scopetta, Nicholas v., 383
Second shift, defined, 307, 324–325
Second Wave of the Women's Movement, 93
Secondary group, defined, 2*n*
Secure attachment style, defined, 113, 114
Seekers, divorce and, 442*b*

Segmented assimilation, defined, 60
Segregation, 59, 216, 295, 297
Selection, defined, 462
"Selection effect," 319*b*
Selection hypothesis, defined, 169, 226, 433
Self-actualization, 165
Self-care, defined, 317
Self-concept, defined, 13, 31, 32
Self-defense, intimate partner violence and, 375
Self-development
    family development perspective and, 28
    love and, 104
Self-disclosure, 114–115, 127*b*, 139, 222
Self-esteem, 110, 110*n*, 111, 112*b*, 140–141, 284, 373, 380, 440. *See also* Self-worth
Self-fulfilling prophecy, semipermanent marriage as, 417–418
Self-fulfillment values. *See* Individualistic (self-fulfillment) values
Self-identification, 124
Self-identification theory, defined, 87, 88
Self-identity, American Indian, 67
Self-love, 111
Self-revelation, defined, 114–115
Self-sacrifice, 109
Self-worth, 110–114. *See also* Self-esteem
Senate, same-sex couples and, 197*b*
Sender, in communication, 343
Seneca Falls Declaration in 1848, 93*n*
Sense of empowerment, marital power and, 352
Separation
    marital, 421
    as marriage alternative, 420
    religion and, 70
Sept. 11th Victim Compensation Fund, 8
September 11, 2001 attacks, 48–49, 396
"Sequencing moms," defined, 306
Sesame Street, 51*b*
Seven-stage model of stepfamily development, defined, 478
Severe violence, defined, 367
Sex
    age and, 138, 139
    aging families and, 490
    casual, 130, 131
    cohabitation and, 136, 139, 169
    communication and, 335–336
    cultural meanings for, 126
    defined, 76, 76*n*, 126
    deinstitutionalized marriage and, 169
    extramarital, 127*n*, 134, 135, 160
    gender/gendered identities and, 77
    holistic view of, 141–142
    as intimacy, 126
    marital, 128
    marital power and, 357
    nonmarital, 127*n*, 128, 131–132, 135, 147, 185, 187
    oral (*See* Oral sex)
    as pleasure bond, 140–142
    politics of, 144–148
    premarital, 127*n*, 131, 138
    recreational, 130, 131, 159*b*
    relational, 131
    responsibility and, 140, 148–149
    in 1960s, 127–128
    in twentieth century, 127
    unconventional, 139
Sex discrimination, 427*n*
Sex drive, 222

Sex education, 146–148, 147*f*
Sex hormones, 86*n*
Sex ratio, 59, 184, 184*n*, 186
Sex surveys, 136*b*
Sex therapy, 140
Sexism, 77, 297
Sexual abuse, 380, 381, 502
Sexual behavior, 158
Sexual coercion, 221*b*
Sexual development, 122, 123*f*
Sexual dimorphism, defined, 86*n*
Sexual exclusivity, 133, 158–160, 164, 196
Sexual experience, of high school students, 128, 128*t*
Sexual exploitation of children, 384
Sexual expression
    examples of, 122
    family relations and, 142–144
    HIV/AIDS and, 129*n*, 142–144, 144*b*
    race/ethnicity and, 139–140
    sexual orientation and, 123, 132
    sexuality and, 130*n*, 138, 140
    STDs and, 142–144
Sexual frequency, 135, 136, 137, 137*f*, 138, 139, 140
Sexual harassment, 83
Sexual intimacy, defined, 104
Sexual orientation
    asexual as, 124*b*
    defined, 123–125
    gender/gendered identities and, 76
    sexuality and, 147, 147*f*
Sexual pleasure
    gender and, 141
    self-esteem and, 140–141
    sexuality and, 148
Sexual relationships
    exchange perspective and, 125
    gay male/lesbian, 129–130
Sexual responsibility, defined, 140, 148–149
Sexual revolution, 128, 128*n*, 131
Sexual satisfaction, 139, 140
Sexual scripts, 126, 132, 132*b*
Sexual selves. *See* Sexuality
Sexual sharing, 141–142
Sexuality, 120–150
    adolescent, 146–148
    cultural scripts and, 126–130
    expressive (*See* Expressive sexuality)
    heterosexism challenges and, 128–130, 129*n*
    heterosexual expression and (*See* Heterosexual expression)
    human sexuality theoretical perspectives and, 125–126
    intimacy and, 127, 130, 132, 139, 148, 148*b*
    patriarchal, 126–127
    politics of sex and, 144–148
    race/ethnicity and, 139–140
    same-sex, 124
    sex surveys and, 136*b*
    sexual development/orientation and, 122–125
    sexual responsibility and, 148–149
    theoretical perspectives on, 125–126
    throughout marriage, 135–139
    in twenty-first century, 130
Sexually transmitted diseases (STDs), 142, 145*n*, 147*f*, 148, 149
Sexually transmitted infections (STIs), 142*n*
Shared children, 475
Shared custody, 438
Shared parenting, defined, 272

Sharing, 104–106, 141–142, 198
Shelters, intimate partner violence and, 373–374
Shift work, defined, 303
Shifting Gears (O'Neill and O'Neill), 12*f*
Sibling relationships, family crises and, 406
Sibling violence, 380, 381*b*
Siblings
    aging families and, 498, 504, 505
    love and, 103*b*
    one-child family and, 247, 247*b*
Sikh, 283
Silent treatment, 343
Singer v. Hara, 197*b*
Single life, 16
Single mother, 61, 173, 249–250, 314, 314*f*
Single mothers by choice, defined, 249
"Single parent family household," 15*b*
Single parenthood, 51*b*, 188*b*, 189
Single parents, 50*b*, 174*n*, 202
Single remarriages, defined, 462
Single-father families, 64
Single-father households, 15*b*
Singlehood
    nonmarital arrangements and, 188*b*, 189, 190–191
    unattached, 190–191
Single-mother families, 14, 61, 64, 400*b*–401*b*
Single-mother households, 15*b*, 57, 415
Single-parent families, 3, 5*t*, 15*b*, 57, 169, 170, 201, 307, 415, 425–426, 425*f*
Single-parent households, 3, 15*b*, 16*b*, 53, 57, 169, 174, 302
Single-person households, 6*b*
Singles, 156*b*, 184, 185, 188, 202*b*, 203, 204, 204*b*
Single-sex schools, 92
Sleep, raising children and, 268, 269*b*
Smoking, 83
Social advantages, neighborhood/community and, 27
Social capital perspective, defined, 241, 241*n*
Social change
    future of gender and, 96–97
    gender/gendered identities and, 92–97
    men's movement as, 95–96
    personal/family change and, 96
    women's movement as, 93–95
Social class
    choosing marriage partner and, 214, 216
    defined, 53
    divorce and, 416
    economy and, 49–54
    in multicultural society, 277–280
    parenting and, 277–280
    raising children and, 277–280
    sexuality and, 140
Social constraints, divorce and, 417–418
Social context, 46–73
    age structure and, 49
    economy/social class and, 49–54
    historical events and, 48–49
    religion and, 70–72
"Social father," 277
Social influences, choices and, 10
Social institution. *See* Marriage as social institution/private relationship
Social isolation, 54
Social issues, of reproductive technology, 256–257
Social learning theory, defined, 87

Social networks, for unmarrieds, 203–204, 204*b*
Social policy
    divorce and, 445–446
    work/family and, 316–323
Social power, 352, 360
Social pressure
    choosing marriage partner and, 216
    to have children, 240
Social Security
    age structure and, 49
    aging families and, 488, 489, 489*b*, 490, 506
    divorce and, 427
Social Security Act, 428*n*, 488*n*
Social status, sexuality and, 148
Social support
    aging families and, 492
    family crises and, 406
Social welfare approach, child abuse and, 383–384
Social welfare programs, aging families and, 488
Social-cultural environment, 22, 22*f*
Socialization
    defined, 87
    gender and, 86–92
    in schools, 90–91
    settings for, 88–91
    theories of, 87–88
Societal influences, choices and, 9–10
Society for Research in Child Development, 36
Sociobiology, 36. *See also* Biosocial perspective
Sociological Imagination, The (Mills), 9
Sociologists, gender/gendered identities and, 86
Soft Patriarchs (Wilcox), 362
"Soul mate," 168
Sourcebook of Family Theories and Methods, 22*f*
Southern Baptist Convention, gender/gendered identities and, 82
Spanking, 268, 276–277, 280
Spectatoring, defined, 141
"Sperm washing," 143
"Spiraling effect," 330
Spiritual values, family crises and, 405
Spontaneous abortion, 252
Sports, gender/gendered identities and, 89
Spousal support, defined, 427
Spouses
    aging families and, 497, 498
    in middle age, 138
    military and, 51*b*
    young, 137–138
SSI program. *See* Supplemental Security Income (SSI) program
Stability
    in choosing marriage partner, 217, 225–226
    divorce and, 416, 417, 418
    in family definition, 8
    making choices and, 14
    marital, 208–211, 219–220, 338, 461
    remarriage and, 461–464, 471
    of white-collar/blue-collar workers, 54
Stable unhappy marriages, 421
Stahl Associates Company, Braschi v., 8
Stanford Child Custody Project, 432
Stanford Child Custody Study, 439
Stanley v. Illinois, 193*b*

Statistical Abstract of the United States, 70*n*
Status exchange hypothesis, defined, 218
Stay-at-home dads, defined, 301
Stay-at-home moms, 96, 297, 298
STDs. *See* Sexually transmitted diseases (STDs)
STEP. *See* Systematic Training for Effective Parenting (STEP)
Stepchild adoption, 468*n*
Stepchildren
    hostility by, 470–471
    marital stability and, 462
    stepparenting and, 469–471
    well-being of, 468–469, 469*n*
Stepfamilies, 3, 454–480
    ambiguous norms and, 465–469
    biosocial perspective and, 37
    children's living arrangements and, 458–459, 459*f*
    children's well-being in, 468–469, 468*b*
    cohabiting, 456
    creating supportive, 478–577
    divorce and, 444
    family law and, 467–468
    family systems theory and, 34
    first marriages and, 464–465
    gay/lesbian (GL), 458*b*, 464*n*
    HMI and, 176
    immigrant, 466*b*
    kin networks in, 467
    remarriage and, 458*b*
    types of, 464–465
Stepfamily Association of America, 462, 478*n*, 479
Stepfathers, 473–475, 474*b*
Stepliving for Teens: Getting Along with Step-Parents, Parents and Siblings (Block and Bartell), 479
Stepmother trap, defined, 473
Stepmothers, 471, 473, 474, 474*b*
Stepparent, 16*b*, 250–251, 468
Stepparenting, 469–475
Stereotypes
    aging families and, 503
    Asian American, 64
    of childlessness, 240
    choosing marriage partner and, 218
    gender/gendered identities and, 80, 81*b*, 85, 95, 141
    of noncustodial mothers, 435
    of one-child family, 246
    raising children and, 270, 285
    remarriage and, 462–464
    same-sex couples and, 200
    sexual orientation and, 123*n*, 124
Sternberg's triangular theory of love, intimacy, 105–106, 106*f*
STIs. *See* Sexually transmitted infections (STIs)
"Stonewall," 128
Stonewalling, defined, 336, 338, 341–342, 342*b*
Storge, defined, 107–108
Stress. *See also* Worry
    abortion and, 254
    aging families and, 498, 499*b*, 501–502, 501*b*
    caregiver, 501–502
    child abuse and, 382
    children and, 242
    communication and, 336, 338, 339, 340

divorce and, 416, 421–422
employment/family work and, 311
family, 388–391, 398, 400–404, 402*b*
raising children and, 268, 280
same-sex couples and, 198
two-earner marriages and, 303, 324
work/family issues and, 317
Stresses, for children of divorce, 429–440
Stressor overload, 395*b*, 397–398. *See also* Pile-up
Stressor pile-up, 400–402, 400*b*–401*b*
Stressors
    horizontal, 403*n*
    types of, 392–397, 392*f*, 393*b*, 395*b*
    vertical, 403*n*
Stress-related growth, defined, 441–442
Stress-relief pathway, divorce and, 441
Structural antinatalism, defined, 240–241
Structural constraints, defined, 9
Structural interactionism, 31*n*
Structure-functional perspective, 23*t*, 29–31, 35, 37*b*, 125, 390
Students, gender/education and, 83–84
Study of Injured Victims of Violence (SIVV), 369
Subfecundity/secondary infertility, 255
Subjective measure of fairness, marital power and, 352
Substance abuse
    in choosing marriage partner, 209
    raising children and, 281, 287, 289
    in upper-middle/upper-class preteens/adolescents, 54
Suicide, 83, 281
"Super-minority," 282
"Supernormative" families, 237*b*
Supervised visitation, defined, 435*n*
"Superwoman," 79
Supplemental mothers, 383
Supplemental Security Income (SSI) program, 488, 488*n*
Support groups, family crises and, 405
Supportive communication, 338
Supreme Court, 82, 159*b*, 197*b*
Surrogacy, 256
Surveys
    on aging families, 500
    by AARP, 138
    defined, 39
    deinstitutionalized marriage and, 172*b*
    on extramarital affairs, 133
    on family violence, 367, 368, 374
    on gender/gendered identities, 82
    Marital Instability Over the Life Course, 419
    of married people, 154
    multiracial identity, 68*n*
    by Public Education Network, 91
    on religion, 70
    on same-sex couples, 196
    sex, 136*b*
    on sex education, 147
    of women, 93, 94, 94*f*
Survival of the fittest, 36*n*
Sweden, divorce in, 445–446
Swingers, divorce and, 442*b*
Swinging, defined, 159*b*
Symbiotic relationships, defined, 110
Symbolic interaction theory, defined, 88
Symbolic interactionism, 31*n*
Symmetric violence, 374, 375
System, defined, 34

Systematic Training for Effective Parenting (STEP), 289
Systems theory. *See* Family systems theory

"Talking to Children about Terrorism and Armed Conflict," 25*b*
"Talking with Children When the Talking Gets Tough," 25*b*
TANF. *See* Temporary Assistance for Needy Families (TANF)
Taxes
    aging families and, 488*n*
    immigration and, 63*b*
Teachers' practices
    gender/gendered identities and, 90, 91
    self-esteem and, 110*n*
Teams, as primary group, 3*b*
Technological change, as reason for increase in unmarrieds, 184–185, 186
Technology
    adoption and, 261
    economy/social class and, 49, 52
    raising children and, 266
    reproductive, 235, 244, 254–257
    unpaid family work and, 307
Teen birth rates, 16, 64, 234, 244, 249, 250, 250*f*
Teenage pregnancy, 249–250
Teenagers
    birth control and, 251
    cohabitation and, 189
    HIV/AIDS and, 143, 144*b*
    marriage age and, 209–210
    neighborhoods and, 26
    non-Hispanic whites and, 67
    parenthood and, 240
    raising, 274
    sexuality and, 142, 146
Telephone calls, relationships through, 2*n*
Television, American Indians and, 67
Temporary Assistance for Needy Families (TANF), 174, 174*n*, 175, 175*b*, 176, 278
Terrorism
    children and, 25*b*
    intimate, 376*n*
    patriarchal, 371, 375–376
Testosterone levels, 36, 37, 86, 86*n*
"Test-tube" babies, 258*b*
Texas, Lawrence et al. v., 128–129
Text messaging, relationships through, 2*n*
TFR. *See* Total fertility rate (TFR)
Thanksgiving (Lee), 306*b*
"The down low," 140
Themes, family as, 2*b*
Theoretical perspectives. *See also* Perspective(s)
    defined, 22–37
    on family stress/crises, 390–391
    on human sexuality, 125–126
Theory
    attachment, 113–114, 209
    cognitive-developmental, 87
    of complimentary needs, 222
    ethnicity and, 57
    exchange, 23*t*, 33–34, 37*b*, 213, 354, 374, 416
    family systems, 23*b*, 34, 37*b*, 391, 391*b*
    gender schema, 87–88
    interaction, 125
    object relations, 88
    self-identification, 87, 88
    on sexual development, 125

Theory (*cont.*)
  social learning, 87
  studying families through, 37–38
  symbolic interaction, 88
  systems (*See* Family systems theory)
Theory of complementary needs,
  defined, 222
Therapeutic approach, child abuse and, 383
Three-generation families, 3
Time
  communication and, 344
  employment/family work and, 310–313,
    311, 311*t*, 313–314
  family, 280
  intimacy and, 142
  leisure (*See* Leisure time)
  love and, 117
  men's market work and, 301
Title VII, 93
Total fertility rate (TFR), 7*b*, 7*n*, 234, 234*f*,
  238*b*–239*b*, 238*f*
Toys, gender/gendered identities and,
  88–89, 89*b*
Traditional exchange, 213–214
Traditional families, defined, 67
Traditional sexism, defined, 77
Traditionals, defined, 362*b*
Traditions, 13, 162
Trailing spouse, defined, 316
Transgendered, defined, 78*b*
Transition to parenthood, defined,
  268–270, 268*b*
Transitional egalitarian situation,
  defined, 355
Transitional families, defined, 67
Transnational family, defined, 62*b*, 65
"Transnational motherhood," 63*b*
Transracial adoptions, 259, 260
Transsexuals, defined, 78*b*
Treatments, 40
Triangular theory of love, 105–106,
  106*f*, 114
Tribal sovereignty, 65
Triplets, 235, 235*b*
Troxel v. Granville, 424
Twentieth century, sexuality and, 126
Twins, 235, 235*b*
Two-career couples/marriages, 302, 315, 316
Two-caregivers perspective, 171
Two-earner couples/marriages, 302–307,
  315, 323–325
Two-parent families, 58–59, 61, 62*b*, 174,
  248, 270, 415
Two-parent households, 15*b*, 168

UCLA, 25*b*, 253
Unattached singlehood, 190–191
Unattached singles, 203
Uncommitted cohabitors, 190
"Unconventional sex," 139
Underemployment, divorce and, 428
Undocumented immigrants, 60, 62*b*, 63*b*
Unemployment
  divorce and, 428
  Latino, 60
Unhappy marriages, 421
Uniform Child-Custody Jurisdiction and
  Enforcement Act, 437
Uniform Crime Reports of the FBI, 367
Unilateral divorce, 423. *See also* No-fault
  divorce
Unintended pregnancy, 240, 240*n*

Union duration, 134
Unitarian Universalist Association, 196
United Methodist, gender/gendered
  identities and, 82
United Nations Commission on Human
  Rights, 200
United States
  abortion in, 250, 252, 253
  aging population in, 484–487, 489*b*
  birth rate in, 154*f*, 250
  companionate marriage in, 165
  divorce rate in, 154*f*, 155, 414*f*, 445–446
  ethnicity in, 58
  expressive sexuality in, 148*b*
  extramarital sex in, 133
  fertility trends in, 235–239
  as free-choice culture, 212, 212*b*
  immigration in, 62*b*–63*b*
  institutionalized marriage in, 164
  kinship authority in, 160–161
  love/marriage in, 162, 162*f*
  marital power and, 360
  marital status in, 154–155, 156*b*–157*f*
  marriage rate in, 154*f*, 155, 457*f*
  patriarchal authority in, 165
  permanence/sexual exclusivity in, 158,
    159*b*, 160
  population of, 58, 62*b*, 70
  poverty in, 266
  racial/ethnic diversity in, 58
  religion and, 70
  remarriage in, 456–459
  same-sex couples in, 197*b*
  singles in, 184
  structural antinatalism in, 240
  teenage pregnancy in, 250
  TFR in, 234*f*, 234*n*, 238*f*
United States, Reynolds v., 159*b*
University of Chicago, 124, 127, 136*b*
University of Michigan, 194*b*, 307, 309
University of New Hampshire, 367*n*
University of Pennsylvania, 367*n*, 384
University of Wisconsin, 136*b*
Unmarried cohabitation, 190*n*
Unmarried couple households, 3, 5*t*, 6*b*, 69
Unmarried couples, 69
Unmarrieds/nonmarrieds, 156*b*–157*f*,
  169, 184–189, 184*n*, 192*b*–193*b*,
  202–204, 423
Unpaid family work, 306–310, 324
Unpaid leave, 322
Unwed mothers, 249
Upper class, 280
Upper-middle-class parents, 279–280,
  281*b*, 287
Upper-socioeconomic-level environment, 27
U.S. Census Bureau, 2, 5*t*, 15*b*, 217
U.S. Centers for Disease Control and
  Prevention, 124, 128, 133, 136*b*, 146
U.S. Congress, 81
U.S. Constitution, same-sex couples and,
  197*b*, 201
U.S. General Accounting Office, 201, 297
U.S. House of Representatives, same-sex
  couples and, 197*b*
U.S. News & World Report magazine, 131
U.S. Supreme Court, 128, 197*b*, 201*n*, 217
USA Today study, 84
Utah
  fertility in, 70
  polygamy in, 201*n*

Value of children perspective, defined, 241
Values. *See also* Goals
  about children, 240
  African Americans and, 60
  arranged marriages and, 162
  in choosing marriage partner, 208, 211,
    216, 217, 220, 222, 229
  cohabitation and, 191*b*
  employment/family work and, 312
  familistic (communal), 13, 14
  fertility rates and, 239*b*
  fertility trends and, 236, 237
  heterogamy and, 220
  individualistic (self-fulfillment), 13, 14
  making choices and, 11–12, 13*b*
  permanence/sexual exclusivity and, 159*b*
  policies and, 173
  religion and, 70, 72
  reproductive technology and, 257
  sexuality and, 148, 149
  spiritual, 405
  of white-collar/blue-collar workers, 54
Vanishing housework, 309
Vatican, 200
Verbal abuse, 223, 224, 368
Verbal message, 343*n*
Vertical stressors, 403*n*
Vietnam War era, American family and, 48
Vietnamese, 308
Violence. *See also* Abuse
  abortion and, 253
  asymmetric, 374, 375
  against children, 379–384
  cohabitation and, 368
  common couple, 376
  courtship, 224
  dating, 223–224
  domestic, 35, 71, 165, 174, 176*n*, 194,
    198, 368, 368*b*, 376–377, 378 (*See also*
    Intimate partner violence)
  family, 367–384
  feminist/conflict perspective and, 35
  homosexuals and, 129
  intimate partner, 367–376, 376*n*, 377
  marital, 368
  physical, 223
  relationship, 377–379
  religion and, 71
  severe, 367
  sibling, 380, 381*b*
  symmetric, 374, 375
Violent resistance, 376*n*
Virginia Longitudinal Study of Divorce and
  Remarriage, 442, 442*b*, 443*f*
Virginia, Loving v., 10, 217
Virginity pledges, 147–148
"Virtual" kin, 160
"Virtual visits," divorce and, 437
Visitation, 432, 435, 435*n*, 436–437, 496
Visitation Rights Enforcement Act, 436
Visiting parent, 435–437
Vocabularies of motive, defined, 422*n*
Voluntary childlessness, defined, 243
Voting, women and, 93*n*
Vulnerable families, 398, 404

Wade, Roe v., 253, 253*n*
Wage gap, defined, 296
Wages, for men/women, 84–85. *See also*
  Earnings; Income
Wallerstein research, 429, 432
War on Poverty, 23, 177, 177*n*

"War on terror," 48, 49
Washington Post national survey, 69
Wealthy, 53–54
Webcams, military and, 51*b*
Websites
    for children, 25*b*
    choosing marriage partner and, 222
    family policy, 25*n*
    Family Research Council, 200
    military and, 51*b*
    relationships through, 2*n*
"Wedded to life," 203
Weddings, 155, 155*f*, 172*b*, 178
Welfare
    African Americans and, 59
    aging families and, 488*n*
    divorce and, 427
    intimate partner violence and, 373
    Latinos and, 60
    policies for, 173
    raising children and, 278, 279, 285
"Welfare reform," 174, 174*n*
We're Still Family (Ahrons), 449
Wheel of love
    choosing marriage partner and, 222
    defined, 114–115
    Reiss and, 114, 114*f*
White Earth Nation, 95*b*
White-collar families, 52, 53–54
White-collar men, 308
Whiteness studies, 67–68
Whites. *See* Non-Hispanic whites
Wicca, 70
Widowed, 156*b*, 157*f*, 184
Widowerhood, aging families and, 492–493
Widowhood, aging families and, 492–493
Wife abuse, 35, 165, 368, 370, 373, 378
Wills/living trusts, unmarrieds and,
    192*b*–193*b*
Within-group differences, gender/gendered
    identities and, 76
Within-group variation, 80
Women. *See also* Females; Feminities
    abortion and, 252–254, 252*n*, 253*f*
    adoptions and, 257
    African American, 58, 59, 60, 94, 248
    age structure and, 49
    aging families and, 487, 487*t*, 488*n*,
        489–490, 489*n*, 492, 499, 501, 504, 506
    American Indian, 66, 95*b*
    Asian, 65
    battered, 378, 383
    career, 91
    case studies and, 41
    child care and, 304*b*, 305*b*
    child options/circumstances and, 244,
        245, 246, 248, 249, 250

childlessness and, 235, 243–244
choosing marriage partner and, 213, 214,
    214*n*, 219, 222, 223–224, 225
cohabitation and, 189, 190, 191, 191*b*, 194
communication and, 338, 339, 340, 345
companionate marriage and, 165, 165*n*
cultural scripts and, 126, 127, 128,
    129, 130
date/acquaintance rape and, 221*b*
domestic violence and, 368*b*
education and, 93
employment/family work and, 93, 235,
    237, 310, 311, 313, 315
gender inequality and, 81–86, 85*f*
gender/gendered identities and, 76–81,
    79*b*, 88, 91
gender/social change and, 92–97
heterosexual expression and, 130, 131,
    132, 133*b*, 134–135
HIV/AIDS and, 143, 144*b*, 145*b*,
    145*f*, 145*n*
HMI and, 174–176, 175, 176*n*
homemaking and, 91
immigration and, 62*b*, 63*b*
income and, 53
infertility and, 255
intimate partner violence and, 369, 370,
    371, 373, 374, 375, 376, 377, 378, 379
in labor force, 17, 26, 294–299, 294*f*, 295*b*,
    296*f*, 299*b*, 307, 311
Latina, 61, 64
life expectancy of, 484–485
love/marriage and, 104, 162, 162*f*
marital power and, 355–361, 358*f*, 362*b*
marital separation and, 421
marital status for, 155*n*, 156*b*
marriage age and, 209–210
marriage rate for, 457*f*
media and, 77, 93, 94
men's market work and, 299–300, 301
in military, 50*b*, 51*b*, 51*n*
non-Hispanic white, 67
in nontraditional roles, 77
no-power relationships and, 365–366
parenthood and, 234–235, 241, 242, 243
permanence/sexual exclusivity and,
    159*b*, 160
personal/family change and, 96
power politics and, 364
preventing pregnancy and, 251
in prison, 408*b*, 409*b*
raising children and, 270, 287
religion and, 70–71, 71*b*
remarriage and, 457, 458*b*, 460–461
reproductive technology and, 256, 257
role choices of, 26
same-sex couples and, 196*n*

sexual development/orientation and, 123,
    124, 124*b*, 125
sexual expression and, 139
sexual pleasure and, 141
sexual responsibility and, 149
sexuality throughout marriage and, 138
two-earner marriages and, 302, 302*n*, 303,
    324, 325
unmarrieds as, 184–188, 184*n*, 187*t*,
    202–204
unpaid family work and, 306, 307,
    309, 310
voting and, 93*n*
white, 58
Women's Equal Education Act, 91
Women's Movement, 92, 93–95, 94*f*, 96,
    294, 434
Work, 292–327. *See also* Labor force
    employment/family, 310–316
    at home, 303–305
    household, 357–358
    shift, 303
    social policy/family and, 316–323
    two-earner marriages and, 302–306
    two-earner marriages/relationship and,
        323–325
    unpaid family, 306–310, 324
    women/labor force and, 294–299
"Work of attention," 105
Work-centric, 313, 313*b*
Work-family conflicts, 266
Working class, 280
Working poor, 278–279
Working role, 266
Working-class children, 57
Working-class families, 54
Work-marriage-parenthood sequence, 27
World War I, labor force and, 294
World War II
    aging families and, 484
    American family and, 48, 49
    Asian Americans and, 65
    childbearing patterns since, 234
    labor force and, 294
    remarriage after, 456
    self-esteem movement and, 110*n*
    women and, 93
Worry, 267, 268, 268*f*, 272. *See also* Stress

You Just Don't Understand (Tannen), 338
Young adult children, parents and, 286–288
Young spouses, 137–138
Youth Risk Behavior Surveillance System,
    128, 146

Zablocki v. Redhail, 456*n*
Zoroastrian, 283